DR

MEDICAL LAW

MEDICAL LAW

Text, Cases, and Materials

FIFTH EDITION

Emily Jackson

OXFORD
UNIVERSITY PRESS

OXFORD
UNIVERSITY PRESS

Great Clarendon Street, Oxford, OX2 6DP,
United Kingdom

Oxford University Press is a department of the University of Oxford.
It furthers the University's objective of excellence in research, scholarship,
and education by publishing worldwide. Oxford is a registered trade mark of
Oxford University Press in the UK and in certain other countries

First edition 2006
Second edition 2009
Third edition 2013
Fourth edition 2016
Fifth edition 2019

Impression: 1

Public sector information reproduced under Open Government Licence v3.0
(http://www.nationalarchives.gov.uk/doc/open-government-licence/open-government-licence.htm)

Published in the United States of America by Oxford University Press
198 Madison Avenue, New York, NY 10016, United States of America

British Library Cataloguing in Publication Data
Data available

Library of Congress Control Number: 2019934129

ISBN 978–0–19–882584–5

Printed in Great Britain by
Bell & Bain Ltd., Glasgow

To all of my students, past and present

PREFACE

There are a few changes to the organization of the fifth edition of this book. For anyone who is used to using the fourth edition, I thought I should explain what I have done differently this time. First, the chapter on capacity used to cover the medical treatment of both adults who lack capacity and children. Now Chapter 5 just covers adults, and Chapter 6 deals with children. Secondly, because there was always some repetition between Chapter 5 and the second half of Chapter 17 (which covered the withdrawal of life-prolonging treatment from patients who lack capacity), I have incorporated the question of when it is possible to withhold or withdraw life-prolonging treatment from patients who lack capacity into Chapters 5 and 6. Chapter 17 therefore only addresses assisted dying. Thirdly, the chapter that used to deal with embryo and stem cell research now incorporates some discussion of emerging biotechnologies. Fourthly, the freestanding chapter on liability for occurrences before birth has gone, and this is covered, in a slightly shortened form, in Chapter 3 on medical malpractice.

Obviously, I've made these changes because I think they make sense, and avoid repetition, and I hope that readers who are familiar with previous editions don't find them too distracting.

Emily Jackson

NEW TO THIS EDITION

- Coverage of important new cases, including *Bawa-Garba v General Medical Council*; *Great Ormond Street Hospital for Children NHS Foundation Trust v Yates*; *Alder Hey Children's NHS Foundation Trust v Evans*; *Re (Northern Ireland Human Rights Commission's Application for Judicial Review)*; *An NHS Trust v Y*; and *R (on the application of Conway) v Secretary of State for Justice*.

- Coverage of the Independent Review of the Mental Health Act 1983.

- A revised chapter with coverage of some emerging biotechnologies, including artificial intelligence and neurotechnologies.

- Coverage of the implications of genome editing.

- Coverage of the government's proposal to implement an opt-out system for organ donation by 2020.

ACKNOWLEDGEMENTS

We are grateful to the following for permission to reproduce copyright material and commercial documents:

Crown copyright material is reproduced under Class Licence Number C2006010631 with the permission of the Controller of HMSO and the Queen's Printer for Scotland. Parliamentary copyright material is reproduced with the permission of the Controller of Her Majesty's Stationery Office on behalf of Parliament.

BMJ Publishing Group Ltd.: extract from V Larcher, F Craig, K Bhogal, et al on behalf of the Royal College of Paediatrics and Child Health, 'Making decisions to limit treatment in life-limiting and life-threatening conditions in children: a framework for practice', *Archives of Disease in Childhood* 100 (2015).

Cambridge University Press: extract from Bernard Williams, *Making Sense of Humanity and Other Philosophical Papers* (CUP: Cambridge, 1995).

Crown copyright material: extracts from Mental Capacity Act 2005; The Mental Capacity Act 2005 (Independent Mental Capacity Advocates) (General) Regulations 2006; Mental Capacity Act 2005 Code of Practice (TSO: London, 2007); *Guidance on implementing the overseas visitor hospital charging regulations 2015* (DH: London, 2015); *Modernising the Mental Health Act: increasing choice, reducing compulsion* (DHSC, 2018).

Crown Prosecution Service: extract from DPP Policy for Prosecutors in Respect of Cases of Encouraging or Assisting Suicide (CPS, 2010).

England and Wales Court of Appeal: extract from *Re A (Children) (Conjoined Twins: Surgical Separation)* [2000] EWCA Civ 254; *Parkinson v St James and Seacroft University Hospital NHS Trust* [2001] EWCA Civ 530; *Nicklinson v Ministry of Justice* [2013] EWCA Civ 961; *R (on the application of Tracey) v Cambridge NHS Foundation Trust* [2014] EWCA Civ 822; *Great Ormond Street Hospital for Children NHS Foundation Trust v Yates* [2017] EWCA Civ 410; and *Re H (A Child) (Surrogacy Breakdown)* [2017] EWCA Civ 1798.

England and Wales Court of Protection: extract from *M v N* [2015] EWCOP 76; *Wye Valley NHS Trust v B* [2015] EWCOP 60.

General Medical Council: extract from *Confidentiality: good practice in handling patient information* (GMC, 2018).

High Court of Justice of England and Wales (EWHC): extracts from Eleanor King J, *An NHS Trust v DE* [2013] EWHC 2562 (Fam); *Re JA (A Minor) (Medical Treatment: Child Diagnosed with HIV)* [2014] EWHC 1135 (Fam); *W v M (An Adult Patient)* [2011] EWHC 1197 (Fam); *Stone v South East Coast Strategic Health Authority* [2006] EWHC 1668 (Admin); and *Great Ormond Street Hospital for Children NHS Foundation Trust v Yates* [2017] EWHC 1909 (Fam).

House of Lords (UKHL): extracts from *McFarlane v Tayside Health Board* [1999] UKHL 50; *Campbell v MGN (Mirror Group Newspapers)* [2004] UKHL 22; and *Rees v Darlington Memorial Hospital NHS Trust* [2003] UKHL 52.

Incorporated Council of Law Reporting for England and Wales (ICLR): extracts from the Law Reports: Appeal Cases (AC), King's Bench Division (KB), and Queen's Bench Division (QB).

Publications Office of the European Union: extract from Regulation (EU) 2016/679 of the European Parliament and of the Council of 27 April 2016 on the protection of natural persons with regard to the processing of personal data and on the free movement of such data, and repealing Directive 95/46/EC (General Data Protection Regulation); Regulation (EU) No 536/2014 of the European Parliament and of the Council of 16 April 2014 on clinical trials on medicinal products for human use, and repealing Directive 2001/20/EC.

Supreme Court of the United Kingdom: extracts from: *Darnley v Croydon Health Services NHS Trust* [2018] UKSC 50; *Montgomery v Lanarkshire Health Board* [2015] UKSC 11; *Cheshire West and Chester Council v P* [2014] UKSC 19; *Rabone v Pennine Care NHS Foundation Trust* [2012] UKSC 2; *R (Nicklinson and Another) v Ministry of Justice* [2014] UKSC 38; and *Re (Northern Ireland Human Rights Commission's Application for Judicial Review)* [2018] UKSC 27.

Every effort has been made to trace and contact the copyright holders but this has not been possible in all cases. If notified, the publisher will undertake to rectify any errors or omissions at the earliest opportunity.

OUTLINE CONTENTS

CONTENTS

5 | INCAPACITY I: ADULTS   237

6 | INCAPACITY II: CHILDREN   302

7 MENTAL HEALTH LAW 351

8 CONFIDENTIALITY 420

9   GENETIC INFORMATION   470

10   CLINICAL RESEARCH   506

12 | ORGAN TRANSPLANTATION | 625

TABLE OF CASES

TABLE OF LEGISLATION

Page references in **bold** *indicate that the text is reproduced in full.*

UK BILLS

OTHER NATIONAL LEGISLATION

Australia

Belgium

Canada

Ireland

TABLE OF UK STATUTORY INSTRUMENTS

Page references in **bold** *indicate that the text is reproduced in full.*

TABLE OF TREATIES, CONVENTIONS, AND EUROPEAN LEGISLATION

Page references in **bold** *indicate that the text is reproduced in full.*

1

AN INTRODUCTION
TO BIOETHICS

CENTRAL ISSUES

1. Conventional medical ethics focused upon the doctor–patient relationship. Bioethics' remit is much broader, encompassing the dilemmas new technologies may raise for society.

2. Religious approaches to bioethics tend to be less focussed on individual autonomy than secular approaches. Few now believe that modern medicine 'usurps God's will'. Instead, medical progress is, within limits, supported by most religious bioethicists.

3. Utilitarianism is concerned with an action's consequences. Deontological reasoning prioritizes respect for a person's rights. Virtue ethics involves working out what a 'virtuous' person would do in a particular situation.

4. The 'principlist' approach sets out four top-down principles: autonomy,

beneficence, non-maleficence, and justice, which can help to explain what is at stake in medical dilemmas. In contrast, casuistry involves bottom-up reasoning by analogy, using previous cases as a starting point.

5. A feminist ethic of care rejects the individualistic model of patient autonomy, and places more emphasis upon interdependence and relationships.

6. Arguments from 'human dignity' or respect for the 'sanctity of human life' have particular resonance in the medical context, but their meaning is opaque.

7. Slippery slope claims are often empirical claims, to which regulation might be an effective response.

1 INTRODUCTION

The purpose of this chapter is to provide an introduction to bioethical reasoning. The words 'ethics' and 'morality' derive from the Greek (*ethos*) and Latin (*mores*), meaning 'customs'. In their ordinary usage, the words have slightly different connotations. 'Morality' often implies a restrictive code of conduct, setting out the difference between right and wrong. 'Ethics' refers to the systematic analysis of what it means to lead a decent life. Medical ethics is a branch of applied ethics, and it is principally concerned with how we should resolve difficult questions that arise from the practice of medicine.

As we shall see throughout this book, it is impossible to study medical law without confronting complex ethical dilemmas, such as:

- Is it acceptable to withdraw life-prolonging treatment from a patient in a minimally conscious state?
- Should parents be allowed to choose their children's sex?
- What, if anything, would be wrong with paying someone to 'donate' one of their kidneys?
- Should an anorexic teenager be force-fed?
- What limits, if any, should be placed upon women's access to abortion?
- Should euthanasia be legalized?

It would be difficult to work out the appropriate legal response to these questions without also considering their ethical implications.

This opening chapter attempts to summarize various ways in which we might attempt to discuss and resolve ethical dilemmas. We begin by looking at what we might mean by 'medical ethics' and the more recent term 'bioethics'. Next, we consider several different types of ethical reasoning: from religious bioethics to a feminist ethic of care.

When justifying a preference for a particular outcome in the field of medical law and ethics, it is common for people to appeal to the dangers of the 'slippery slope', or to ground their argument in the need to respect 'human dignity' and/or the 'sanctity of human life'. We therefore briefly consider what these claims might involve.

2 BIOETHICS

Medical ethics has a very long history; the Hippocratic oath dates back to the fifth century BC. Conventional medical ethics is concerned with the ethics of good medical practice: that is, with what it means to be a good doctor. Ethical codes of conduct, like the Hippocratic oath, were guidelines that the medical profession imposed upon itself in order to ensure that doctors' behaviour towards their colleagues and their patients met appropriate standards of moral decency. The vantage point was therefore that of the doctor himself: how the doctor should obtain consent; when a doctor can breach his duty of confidentiality; and so on. Until comparatively recently, medical practice was strongly paternalistic: doctors were under a duty to act in their patients' best interests, but it was doctors (as opposed to the patients themselves) who decided what those interests were.

In the next extract Susan Sherwin argues that conventional medical ethics tended to marginalize both the patient's perspective and the broader social causes of ill health.

Susan Sherwin[1]

Until very recently, conscientious physicians were actually trained to act paternalistically toward their patients, to treat patients according to the physician's own judgement about what

[1] 'A Relational Approach to Autonomy in Healthcare' in Susan Sherwin (ed), *The Politics of Women's Health: Exploring Agency and Autonomy* (Temple UP: Philadelphia, 1998) 19–47.

would be best for their patients, with little regard for each patient's own perspectives or preferences. The problem with this arrangement, however, is that health care may involve such intimate and central aspects of a patient's life—including, for example, matters such as health, illness, reproduction, death, dying, bodily integrity, nutrition, lifestyle, self-image, disability, sexuality, and psychological well-being—that it is difficult for anyone other than the patient to make choices that will be compatible with that patient's personal value system ...

A striking feature of most ... discussions about patient autonomy is their exclusive focus on individual patients; this pattern mirrors medicine's consistent tendency to approach illness as primarily a problem of particular patients ... Within the medical tradition, suffering is located and addressed in the individuals who experience it rather than in the social arrangements that may be responsible for causing the problem. Instead of exploring the cultural context that tolerates and even supports practices such as war, pollution, sexual violence, and systemic unemployment—practices that contribute to much of the illness that occupies modern medicine—physicians generally respond to the symptoms troubling particular patients in isolation from the context that produces these conditions.

Heather Draper and Tom Sorrell argue that medical ethics has also ignored the obligations of patients.

Heather Draper and Tom Sorrell[2]

In comparison to what it asks of doctors, mainstream medical ethics makes very few demands of patients, and these usually begin and end with consent. Traditionally medical ethics has asserted that, as autonomous agents, competent patients must be allowed to decide for themselves the course of their medical treatment, and even whether to be treated at all ... Little or nothing is said about what kinds of decisions patients ought to make. Nor is much said about their responsibilities for making good rather than bad decisions. Indeed ... mainstream medical ethics implies that a competent patient's decision is good simply by virtue of having been made by the patient ...

In welfare states, discussion about the use of limited resources extends naturally to a consideration of whether citizens have some sort of moral obligation, other things being equal, to limit their demands on these resources. If the answer is 'Yes', then there may be a civic obligation to follow preventive health measures recommended by one's doctor. If one is advised to stop smoking or over-eating, and one disregards that advice, so that one's condition deteriorates to the point that expensive treatment is required to keep one alive, one may be doing something doubly wrong—breaking obligations to oneself and breaking civic obligations not to use public resources unnecessarily ...

In short, there are duties not to use health services casually ... Someone who indulges their hypochondria by frequent visits to the GP, or who summons an ambulance after getting sunburn; someone who knowingly presents himself at an emergency room with nothing more than severe indigestion; or who calls out a doctor because he needs a prescription that could be filled in office hours next day; all of these patients do something morally wrong, wrong primarily because they have taken away time and resources better spent on more urgent cases.

---

[2] 'Patients' responsibilities in medical ethics' (2002) 16 Bioethics 335–51.

Bioethics is a newer discipline, with a wider remit. The term was first used in the twentieth century, and it is concerned with the life sciences in general, not just with the doctor–patient encounter. Technological progress poses complex dilemmas, particularly at the beginning and end of life, which have implications beyond how an individual doctor should behave towards his patients. For example, once it became possible to (a) perform organ transplants, and (b) keep a patient's heart beating after death, it was necessary to ask whether 'brain-dead' but still breathing patients were a legitimate source of organs for transplantation.

In the next extract, Helga Kuhse and Peter Singer reflect upon the origins and remit of bioethics, suggesting that it was also a response to the rise of patient autonomy, and the decline of medical paternalism.

Helga Kuhse and Peter Singer[3]

Since the 1960s, ethical problems in health care and the biomedical sciences have gripped the public consciousness in unprecedented ways. In part, this is the result of new and sometimes revolutionary developments in the biomedical sciences and in clinical medicine … Another factor has been a growing concern about the power exercised by doctors and scientists, which shows itself in concern to assert 'patients' rights' and the rights of the community as a whole to be involved in decisions that affect them. This has meant greater public awareness of the value-laden nature of medical decision-making, and a critical questioning of the basis on which such decisions are made …

Bioethics, on the other hand, is a more overtly critical and reflective enterprise. Not limited to questioning the ethical dimensions of doctor–patient and doctor–doctor relationships, it goes well beyond the scope of traditional medical ethics in several ways. First, its goal is not the development of, or adherence to, a code or set of precepts, but a better understanding of the issues. Second, it is prepared to ask deep philosophical questions about the nature of ethics, the value of life, what it is to be a person, the significance of being human. Third, it embraces issues of public policy and the direction and control of science.

Ruth Chadwick and Duncan Wilson argue that the emergence of bioethics in the UK can also be traced to increasing political interest in the public accountability of the medical profession.

Ruth Chadwick and Duncan Wilson[4]

We argue that a significant factor in the development of UK bioethics was that politicians in the 1980s and 1990s no longer believed medical researchers should be solely responsible for discussing and resolving ethical questions that arose in the course of their work. From the 1979 election onwards, members of successive conservative and 'New Labour' governments argued that professions should be exposed to outside scrutiny in order to make them publicly accountable. This political shift benefitted individuals who promoted bioethics for different reasons, including the academic lawyer Ian Kennedy, an advocate of civil rights politics who argued it was vital to democratising medicine, and philosophers such as Mary

---

[3] 'What is Bioethics? A Historical Introduction' in Helga Kuhse and Peter Singer (eds), *A Companion to Bioethics* (Blackwell: Oxford, 1998) 3–11.
[4] 'The Emergence and Development of Bioethics in the UK' (2018) 26 Medical Law Review 183–201.

Warnock, among others, who believed engagement with practical issues would make their field relevant . . .

Kennedy discussed these proposals in detail during his 1980 BBC Reith Lectures, broadcast with the provocative title *Unmasking Medicine*. The major thrust of the six lectures was that standards for doctors and medical scientists 'will have to be set by others, and the principle of outside scrutiny, a key feature of consumerism, seems inevitable'.

In the next extract, Daniel Callahan and Bruce Jennings argue that the focus of bioethics is becoming broader still, as it moves away from its initial focus on patient autonomy and high-tech medicine, towards much wider public health considerations.

Daniel Callahan and Bruce Jennings[5]

When the field of bioethics emerged in the late 1960s and early 1970s, it represented a significant broadening of medical ethics. It moved the subject beyond the doctor–patient relationship and medical professionalism into the new territory of, among other things, organ transplants, genetics, reproductive biology, and resource allocation. But little attention was paid by bioethics in its early years to the distinctive ethical problems inherent in public health. That is perhaps not surprising. Bioethics received its initial stimulus from the abuses of human subjects research, the emergence of the patients' rights movement, and the drama of high-technology medicine . . . In early bioethics, the good of the individual, and particularly his or her autonomy, was the dominant theme, not population health . . .

For its part, bioethics has become restless for change, and it is particularly looking for a value orientation that may bring it into closer proximity with public health. There has always been an undercurrent of resistance to the individualistic, autonomy-driven mainstream orientation within bioethics . . . But the obvious need for universal health care, the persistence of racial and ethnic disparities in health status, and the importance of background social and economic factors have caught the eye of many. A shift of direction in the field of bioethics was called for.

3 HOW SHOULD WE MAKE DIFFICULT ETHICAL DECISIONS?

Many people have 'gut feelings' or intuitive reactions to ethical dilemmas. It is very common for people to react to a controversial new technique, such as human cloning, by saying: 'I just think it's wrong.' There are those who believe that what might be called the 'yuck factor' in fact embodies some deep, inner wisdom. This idea is most closely associated with Leon R Kass, whose controversial article 'The Wisdom of Repugnance' admits that '[r]evulsion is not an argument', but goes on to say that,

In crucial cases, however, repugnance is the emotional expression of deep wisdom, beyond reason's power fully to articulate it . . . We are repelled by the prospect of cloning human beings

---

[5] Daniel Callahan and Bruce Jennings, 'Ethics and public health: forging a strong relationship' (2002) 92 American Journal of Public Health 169–76.

not because of the strangeness or novelty of the undertaking, but because we intuit and feel, immediately and without argument, the violation of things that we rightfully hold dear.[6]

Joshua May has attempted to test Kass's assumption that we have a shared response to human reproductive cloning, and he found that disgust was, in fact, a relatively uncommon reaction.

Joshua May[7]

The data indicate a diversity of emotional reactions towards human reproductive cloning . . . The results, however, do not speak much in favour of the basic empirical assumption in the argument from repugnance against human cloning, as the reaction of disgust does not appear to be widespread. Kass and similar theorists are not entirely idiosyncratic in their reactions of disgust, but only a very small portion had this emotion immediately come to mind (11.5%) . . .

Since disgust advocates point to the emotion as a way of arguing for a position on the issue—especially as a way of convincing those who are unsure or 'on the fence'—disgust should presumably show up in many opponents of cloning and in those indifferent to it. Such a premise is required for an argument of the form: take your reaction of repugnance as evidence that there is something wrong with this practice.

John Harris has a more fundamental objection to Kass's reliance upon the wisdom of repugnance.

John Harris[8]

George Orwell once memorably referred to this reliance on intuition as use of 'moral nose'; as if one could simply sniff a situation and detect wickedness. The problem is that nasal reasoning is notoriously unreliable, and olfactory moral philosophy, despite valiant efforts of Kass and others, has done little to refine it or give it a respectable foundation. We should remember that in the recent past, among the many discreditable uses of so-called 'moral feelings', people have been disgusted by the sight of Jews, black people and, indeed, women being treated as equals and mixing on terms of equality with others. In the absence of convincing arguments, we should be suspicious of those who use nasal reasoning as the basis of their moral convictions.

Our gut instincts tend to be immediate, unreasoned responses, and, as Mark Sheehan explains, there is no reason why anyone else should be persuaded by them.

[6] Leon R Kass, 'The wisdom of repugnance' (1997) 216 The New Republic 22.
[7] 'Emotional reactions to human reproductive cloning' (2016) 42 Journal of Medical Ethics 26–30.
[8] John Harris, *Enhancing Evolution: The Ethical Case for Making Better People* (Princeton UP: Princeton, 2007) 130.

Mark Sheehan[9]

> The subjectivity of emotions means that they cannot function in arguments because, unless they are universal, they cannot form the basis of a claim on another person. The reason they cannot form this basis is because that other person may not have that emotion: relying on it means the argument can only apply to those who do. An argument that relies on feeling particular emotions, particularly emotions that we don't all feel in the same way, is weak to that extent and certainly weaker than one that does not.

To convince others, we need to identify coherent reasons or principles that explain or justify our position. In short, we need to find some mechanism for resolving ethical dilemmas that goes beyond an appeal to our 'gut instincts'. As we will see in the following sections, bioethicists are interested in working out what this mechanism should be.

(a) RELIGIOUS BIOETHICS

The comprehensive rejection of medical expertise on religious grounds is now rare; more commonly, someone's religious beliefs may inform their anxiety about modern medicine's power to create and to destroy life. Within a secular and culturally diverse society, religion tends to be regarded as a matter of private faith. As a result, while religious leaders' pronouncements may be important to believers, and will often determine how they approach their own bioethical dilemmas, it is less clear what role they should have in shaping public policy.

In the next extract, Daniel Callahan regrets the 'secularization' of bioethics and suggests that because all religions have a long and rich history of grappling with questions that are of central importance to medical law and ethics—such as the meaning of life and death—religious perspectives might be a particularly useful resource for the comparatively new secular discipline of bioethics.

Daniel Callahan[10]

> The net result of this narrowing of philosophy and the disappearance or denaturing of religion in public discourse is a triple threat. It leaves us, first of all, too heavily dependent upon the law as the working source of morality. The language of the courts and legislatures becomes our only shared means of discourse. That leaves a great number fearful of the law (as seems the case with many physicians) or dependent upon the law to determine the rightness of actions, which it can rarely do since it tells us better what is forbidden or acceptable, than what is commendable or right.
>
> It leaves us, secondly, bereft of the accumulated wisdom and knowledge that are the fruit of long-established religious traditions. I do not have to be a Jew to find it profitable and illuminating to see how the great rabbinical teachers have tried to understand moral problems over the centuries. Nor will Jews find it utterly useless to explore what the popes, or the leading Protestant divines, have had to say about ethics ...

---

[9] 'The role of emotion in ethics and bioethics: dealing with repugnance and disgust' (2016) 42 Journal of Medical Ethics 1–2.

[10] 'Religion and the secularization of bioethics' (1990) 20 Hastings Center Report 2–4.

> It leaves us, thirdly, forced to pretend that we are not creatures both of particular moral communities and the sprawling inchoate general community that we celebrate as an expression of our pluralism. Yet that pluralism becomes a form of oppression if, in its very name, we are told to shut up in public about our private lives and beliefs and talk a form of what Jeffrey Stout has called moral Esperanto.

There are, of course, differences both between and within religions. Within Christianity, for example, views on the moral status of the embryo—and hence the legitimacy of abortion and embryo research—differ markedly. Nevertheless, some similarities between religious approaches to bioethics might be identified. First, religious bioethics tend to emphasize the intrinsic rightness or wrongness of a particular course of action, and be less swayed by pragmatic or consequentialist arguments. In relation to euthanasia, for example, a religious perspective would concentrate upon the legitimacy or otherwise of bringing about another person's death, rather than practical difficulties in setting up an effective regulatory regime.

Secondly, religions tend to share two principal moral concerns: (a) love for one's neighbour (almost every religion contains some version of the Golden Rule: that you should treat your neighbour as you would want to be treated yourself); and (b) a sense of awe and respect for 'God's creation', and especially for the sanctity of human life.

In the next extract, Hazel Markwell and Barry Brown describe how a belief in the sanctity of life informs Roman Catholic responses to a wide variety of bioethical questions.

Hazel Markwell and Barry Brown[11]

> Fundamental to Catholic bioethics is a belief in the sanctity of life: the value of a human life, as a creation of God and a gift in trust, is beyond human evaluation and authority. God maintains dominion over it. In this view, we are stewards, not owners, of our own bodies and are accountable to God for the life that has been given to us.

But while many religions share a belief in the sanctity of life, and hence in the wrongness of killing, what this means in practice can vary dramatically. The Roman Catholic view that a new human person exists from conception has resulted in the prohibition of abortion. In the Episcopal Anglican tradition, there is no consensus, and abortion is a matter of individual conscience. Jewish bioethics does not regard the fetus as having the same status as the pregnant woman, and hence the morality of abortion depends upon whether there is sufficient cause to justify the taking of fetal life. In some schools of Buddhism, the sanctity of life is not confined to human life.

Applied to medicine, however, religious perspectives tend to be less individualistic than secular bioethics, and to place less emphasis on patient autonomy. In Confucianism, for example, as Erika Yu explains, the experience of illness is shared by the patient's family.

---

[11] 'Bioethics for clinicians: Catholic bioethics' (2001) 165 Canadian Medical Association Journal 189–92.

Erika Yu[12]

In the Confucian view, the family has the major responsibility to take good care of its ill member, and healthcare policy in Confucian societies should facilitate the family to fulfill this role. This entails that the family not only should be able to participate in making the patient's medical decisions, but also to learn about the diagnosis and prognosis even prior to the patient ...

For Confucians, illness is not only suffered by the patient, it is a misfortune of the whole family. The Confucian approach to shared decision making is a consensus-building process that not only serves to arrive at a unified and harmonious decision, but also to maintain family integrity. In contrast with the mainstream bioethical principle of informed consent ..., individual autonomy is not presupposed to be of primary importance for Confucians. The patient is not primarily characterized by independence or self-sufficiency.

Thirdly, the idea that life is a gift that is not ours to destroy raises the question of how far man should be allowed to interfere with the natural order. Answers have varied dramatically—from the idea that modern medicine is frustrating God's will, to the more progressive (and much more common) view that the quest for knowledge, and hence medical progress, is itself part of God's creation. Paul Badham explains this shift, from a Christian perspective.

Paul Badham[13]

[M]edical ethics provides the largest number of instances where Christians today almost unanimously accept as good practices which their predecessors in the faith regarded as evil. For many centuries Christians forbade the giving of medicine, deeming it equivalent to the practice of sorcery. The practice of surgery, the study of anatomy and the dissection of corpses for medical research were all at one time firmly forbidden. Later the practices of inoculation and vaccination faced fierce theological opposition. Indeed in 1829 Pope Leo XII declared that whoever decided to be vaccinated was no longer a child of God; smallpox was a judgement of God; vaccination was a challenge to heaven. For similar reasons the initial use of quinine against malaria was denounced by many Christians. The introduction of anaesthesia and, above all, the use of chloroform in childbirth were seen as directly challenging the biblical judgement that, because of their inheritance of the guilt of Eve's original sin, all women must face the penalty that 'in pain you shall bring forth children'. Consequently the use of chloroform in childbirth was vigorously attacked from public pulpits throughout Britain and the United States ...

The root objection to all the medical practices mentioned above was the belief that the duty of human beings was to submit in patience to what God had willed. All innovations in medical practice were initially seen as implying a lack of faith and trust in God's good purposes. Doctors were accused of 'playing God', of being unwilling to accept that God knows what is right for a particular person, of prying into sacred mysteries and areas of God's own prerogative. Yet gradually all mainstream Christian churches have modified their teaching, and the formerly

---

[12] 'Confucianism' in HAMJ ten Have and Bert Gordijn (eds) *Handbook of Global Bioethics* (New York: Springer, 2014) 375–89.
[13] 'Theological Examination of the Case for Euthanasia' in Paul Badham and Paul Ballard, *Facing Death: An Interdisciplinary Approach* (Cardiff University of Wales Press: Cardiff, 1996) 101–16.

criticized activity of the doctor has itself come to be seen as itself a channel of God's love and the vehicle of his providence.

Judaism has a long tradition of accepting medical interventions. The conviction that one's body belongs to God translates into a duty to care for it. Not only is there an emphasis on preventative medicine—such as an interest in hygiene and diet—but also, as Glick explains, within Judaism the treatment of illness is obligatory, on the part of both physicians and their patients.

Shimon Glick[14]

Consonant with the high priority given to life, the Jewish tradition, unlike Anglo-Saxon law, requires the physician to respond to any patient's call for help ... But just as the physician is obligated to render care, so too, the seeking of care by the patient is mandatory. The reason for this obligation is that, in our Jewish tradition, man does not possess title to his life or his body. Man is but the steward of the divine possession which he has been privileged to receive. The terms of that stewardship are not of man's choice, but are determined by God's commands. We forbid suicide and require man to take all reasonable steps to preserve life and health. When beneficence conflicts with autonomy, the former is given precedence by Judaism, a view clearly in conflict with the modern Western consensus ...

In the deliberations as to permissibility of a given act, its being 'natural' or 'unnatural' plays little role. In our tradition, the world is regarded as a deliberately unfinished product placed in the trust of man—himself a finite and imperfect being. Man is expected, indeed commanded ... to engage in completing ... the work of the Creator ...

Healing the ill ... is therefore not only theologically acceptable, but is mandated. This eagerness to modify Nature, together with the great value placed on human life, contributed to the exalted place occupied by the healing profession in Jewish tradition.

Most Muslim theologians agree that technological intervention in nature, so long as its purpose is to improve human welfare, does not contravene the prohibition against altering God's creation. Indeed, it has been argued that scientific research is protected by the *Sharia*, and that medicine is a religious duty in every community. Sahin Aksoy suggests that the duty to help others, if it lies in one's capacity, is so strong that it might encompass an obligation to ensure an adequate supply of organs for transplantation.

Sahin Aksoy[15]

In Islamic law, a person is obliged to act, if the action is in his capacity. It is a crime (that one can be held responsible for) to do something which is forbidden to do, or not to do something which is commanded. If someone dies in a neighbourhood due to hunger or cold, the people of the neighbourhood who are able to take care of him are held responsible and are

---

[14] 'A View from Sinai: A Jewish Perspective on Biomedical Ethics' in Edmund Pellegrino, Patricia Mazzarella, and Pietro Corsi (eds), *Transcultural Dimensions* (University Publishing Group: Frederick, MD, 1992) 73–82.

[15] 'Some principles of Islamic ethics as found in Harrisian philosophy' (2010) 36 Journal of Medical Ethics 226–9.

punished for this 'inaction' or 'non-action'. It is especially important when it is a matter of life and death ...

At the First International Conference on Islamic Medicine, it was agreed that the donation of body parts is a social obligation, of the kind classified in Islamic law as *fard al-kifâya* ... This means the community is under a collective obligation to find the right organs for transplantation in order to preserve the lives and health of its sick members. If a sick person dies while awaiting a transplant, the society as a whole carries some responsibility for that.

Preventative medicine—through the *Sharia*'s rulings on hygiene and self-restraint—is encouraged. The Islamic Code of Medical Ethics, for example, states that:

The natural prophylaxis against some diseases rests in the revival of such religious values as chastity, purity, self-restraint, and refraining from advertently or inadvertently inflicting harm on self or others. To preach these values is preventative medicine and therefore lies within the jurisdiction and obligation of the medical profession.[16]

But while most religions embrace medical interventions that treat disease and relieve suffering, what about interventions that go beyond this? Below, Damian Keown and Lisa Soleymani Lehmann describe Buddhist and then Jewish approaches to enhancement.

Damian Keown[17]

The Buddhist view has always been that the clarity of mind and intellectual lucidity needed to attain nirvana is best achieved through natural methods, and that the primary technique for obtaining clarity of insight is through meditation. Buddhism would, therefore, tend to see artificial enhancement as a temporary 'quick fix' rather than a permanent solution to the underlying problems. Furthermore, while palliation of emotional symptoms may not be harmful in the short term, it can lead to dependency and undermine the achievement of a more permanent solution. Buddhist psychology detects a cyclic pattern in such conditions and observes that unless the causal sequence is permanently reset, the effects will recur indefinitely. What is needed, therefore, is insight into the underlying causes giving rise to these unsatisfactory states of mind, and this insight, it is believed, can be attained only through deep reflexion and analysis of the kind facilitated by meditative practice.

Lisa Soleymani Lehmann[18]

[H]uman beings are mandated to complete God's creation. These sources provide a foundation for Judaism to embrace the use of scientific knowledge and technology to improve the world. From this perspective, Judaism would allow the use of psychopharmaceuticals for

---

[16] Issued by the International Organisation of Islamic Medicine (later called the Islamic Organisation of Medical Sciences) in 1981.

[17] 'Religious perspectives on the use of psychopharmaceuticals as an enhancement technology' (2014) 53 Journal of Religion and Health 1440–55.

[18] Ibid.

the purpose of achieving our full human potential and our God-given task of improving the world. Although most authorities within Judaism generally have a positive view of scientific advancement, the implications of using psychopharmaceuticals for both the individual and society must be considered. The decision to support the use of these drugs for enhancement needs to be weighed against the potential harm to individuals and to society ... The permissibility of using psychopharmaceuticals to enhance ourselves is dependent on a case-by-case analysis of the risks and benefits of using these medications to individuals and to society.

Fourthly, religious bioethics tend to adopt a normative approach to ethical dilemmas. Whereas secular bioethicists might accept that there is no right answer to a controversial ethical question, a person reasoning from a faith perspective would be more likely to decide that a practice either is, or is not acceptable. Fifthly, religious perspectives often consist in the interpretation of past authority, and are always to some extent constrained by the written or oral teachings or texts of the particular tradition.

(b) SECULAR BIOETHICS

If secular bioethics is not looking for the right answers to ethical dilemmas, what is it doing? One possibility might be that reasoned argument and deliberation is the most rational way to resolve difficult questions. In the next extract, Dan Brock argues that the requirement to give reasons, or to justify one's moral views, is an especially important feature of ethical reasoning.

Dan W Brock[19]

[M]oral judgments are unlike some judgments of taste and moral disagreements are unlike some disagreements over matters of taste, because moral judgments must be backed by reasons. If you like vanilla ice cream and I like chocolate, we can just accept this as a difference in taste—there is no correct preference about flavours of ice cream, and if asked why I prefer chocolate, I may be able to repeat only that it tastes better to me. Unlike matters of taste, moral judgments, for example, about whether voluntary euthanasia is wrong, must be backed with reasons ... [T]he very process of having and offering reasons for our moral judgments is the principal feature distinguishing morality from mere expressions of simple taste or preference.

Because the principal role of moral judgments is to guide action ... moral judgments are subject to a special worry. The worry is that they may be no more than a hodgepodge of thinly veiled rationalizations and biases reflecting our own self-interest, prejudices, and arbitrary preferences. General moral principles or theories can help allay this worry by explaining these judgments: they are shown to fit, and to be derivable and made from, a coherent, unified moral conception.

[19] 'Public Moral Discourse' in LW Sumner and Joseph Boyle (eds), *Philosophical Perspectives on Bioethics* (University of Toronto Press: Toronto, 1996) 271–96.

(1) Moral Theories

The question of how we should resolve complex ethical dilemmas has formed the basis of moral philosophy for thousands of years. There is insufficient space here to describe fully the extensive philosophical literature from which medical ethics has borrowed, but three different traditions are worth noting.

First, teleological (from the Greek *telos*: consequences) theories judge the rightness or wrongness of an action in terms of its consequences. To argue that legalizing euthanasia might damage the doctor–patient relationship would be an example of consequentialist or teleological reasoning. Utilitarianism—or the idea that we should act so as to maximize the amount of pleasure or happiness within society—is the most well-known teleological theory.

Secondly, deontological (from the Greek *deontos*: duty) theories, in contrast, insist that the intrinsic rightness or wrongness of an action does not depend upon its consequences, but rather upon whether it is consistent with fundamental moral principles. An example might be basing an argument for the legalization of euthanasia upon the principle of respect for autonomy. The writings of the philosopher Immanuel Kant (1724–1804), and especially his well-known injunction not to treat others solely as a means to an end, are often used as an example of deontological moral theory.[20] In short, as Matti Häyry has pointed out, the utilitarian places the concepts of 'good and bad' before the ideas of 'right and wrong', whereas the Kantian does the opposite.[21]

Thirdly, virtue ethics are derived from Ancient Greek moral philosophy, and in particular the writings of Aristotle, with its emphasis upon human flourishing. Virtue ethics are concerned not only with good outcomes, but also with the character or motivation of the individual: a person acts virtuously if they do the right thing for the right reason.

(a) Utilitarianism

Utilitarianism emerged as a secular alternative to Christian ethics in the late eighteenth and early nineteenth centuries through the work of Jeremy Bentham and later John Stuart Mill. According to utilitarianism, morality lies not in religious obedience, but in the maximization of human welfare. Because the pleasure and wellbeing of each human being matters equally, utilitarianism is essentially egalitarian.

A utilitarian is interested in the consequences of an action, rather than whether it is intrinsically either right or wrong. An example might be the question of whether we should keep our promises. A utilitarian would say that there can be both good and bad consequences from keeping a promise. When the good consequences outweigh the bad consequences, it will be right to keep the promise; when the reverse is true, the promise should be broken. The problem with this is that it ignores the fact that simply having made a promise to another person is, in itself, a good reason to keep it.

A variation on utilitarianism, called 'rule utilitarianism', provides a partial solution. A rule utilitarian would not ask, on a case-by-case basis, which action will maximize welfare, but rather which general rules will, on the whole, lead to the best consequences. When deciding whether doctors should respect patient confidentiality, for example, a strict utilitarian would answer: 'it depends'. Sometimes it will be better to keep patient information secret, but at other times it might not. This case-by-case approach would require doctors to predict the consequences of both revealing and not revealing every single piece of information they hold

---

[20] Immanuel Kant, *Groundwork of the Metaphysics of Morals* (1785).

[21] 'Utilitarianism and Bioethics' in Richard E Ashcroft et al (eds), *Principles of Health Care Ethics*, 2nd edn (Wiley: Chichester, 2007) 57–64.

about each of their patients. This would clearly be an unmanageable task, which would itself have negative consequences because the health service would grind to a halt. So, a rule utilitarian might say that it is sensible to impose a general duty on doctors to respect their patients' confidentiality.

Another problem with strict utilitarianism is its quantitative approach to welfare. It is the total aggregate of wellbeing that matters, not any particular individual's welfare. If killing one healthy person would enable us to transfer her organs into five patients who would otherwise die, might a utilitarian have to conclude that this would be the right thing to do? Again, rule utilitarianism offers a way to avoid this unpalatable conclusion: applying the principle that doctors should 'above all do no harm' will, in general, tend to have better consequences than allowing doctors to kill their patients in order to save other people's lives.

Of course, utilitarianism requires us to work out what counts as 'utility'. While good health is clearly welfare-maximizing, it is not the only thing that matters. Indeed, many of us have dietary and other preferences that may be positively harmful to health. Do we maximize utility by eating vegetables and spending every evening at the gym, or by also eating things we enjoy and going out with friends?

As Kevin Wildes explains, utilitarianism also depends upon a mechanism through which different outcomes can be ranked; otherwise it would be impossible to tell whether consequence A is preferable to consequence B.

Kevin Wildes[22]

> The appeal to the consequences of one's decisions brings no more success [in resolving moral controversies], because it faces the problem of how to assess and evaluate different consequences. For example, some believe that living somewhat longer as a result of chemotherapy is a better consequence, even with the side effects, than dying. Yet for others, living a life unimpaired by treatment is a more important outcome than extending the length of life. To make a judgment among consequences one needs an agreed-upon method by which to rank the outcomes. Therefore a consequentialist must build in some presuppositions about the assessment and ranking of values, both to evaluate possible outcomes of ethical choices and to know which outcomes are more desirable and should be given priority.

(b) Kantianism

The aspect of Kant's philosophy that is most frequently invoked in relation to medical dilemmas is his 'Categorical Imperative'. Kant gives four formulations of the Categorical Imperative, two of which are worth singling out here:[23]

(a) Act only on that maxim whereby you can at the same time will that it should become a universal law.

(b) So act as to treat humanity, whether in your own person or in that of any other, never solely as a means but always also as an end.

---

[22] 'Particularism in Bioethics: Balancing Secular and Religious Concerns' (1994) 53 Maryland Law Review 1220.

[23] Immanuel Kant, Groundwork of the Metaphysics of Morals (1785).

The first imperative requires us to act consistently and justly. The latter (which is more commonly cited by medical ethicists) demands that we do not ever treat another person—or allow ourselves to be treated—purely in order to satisfy another's purposes.

Both are negative tests for actions; that is, they tell us what we must not do: do not act inconsistently, and do not use another person solely for one's own ends. It would also, as John Rawls has pointed out, be 'a serious misconception to think of the Categorical Imperative procedure as an algorithm intended to yield, more or less mechanically, a correct judgement'.[24] Rather, Rawls suggests that the point of the categorical imperative may simply be to inculcate 'a form of moral reflection that could reasonably be used to check the purity of our motives'.[25]

In the next extract, Barbara Secker is concerned that Kantian autonomy, with its emphasis upon independence and rationality, asks too much of patients.

Barbara Secker[26]

This idealistic concept [of autonomy] is of little practical relevance in health contexts where patients, on the whole, bear little resemblance to the Kantian free, independent, exclusively rational individual ... However, patients frequently are in vulnerable positions, are unable to act on their decisions, and require that positive measures be taken on their behalf ...

If we appeal to the Kantian view (based on an ideal of the self as independent and exclusively rational), very few, if any, patients will be regarded as autonomous. Actual patients are likely to be dependent or interdependent, and their decision-making capacity is not always based (exclusively) on reason.

My second concern is that Kantian autonomy appears to place a premium on independence ... [I]f autonomy is morally valuable, and if autonomy is associated with independence, then dependence is regarded as morally inadequate and, consequently, those who are dependent are devalued ... The nature of patienthood, however, is partially characterized by dependency of one kind or another.

Is the ethical practice of medicine principally deontological or utilitarian? The short answer is that it is both: individual doctors must prioritize the needs and rights of their patients, whereas, as Gerard Garbutt and Peter Davies explain, the National Health Service (NHS) must try to do the most good with finite resources.

Gerard Garbutt and Peter Davies[27]

Historically, medicine has described itself, and been described by others, in terms of the interaction of the doctor, the patient and the disease. The transactions between patient and doctor have been private clinical and commercial transactions, and as such have been guarded by

---

[24] John Rawls, *Lectures on the History of Moral Philosophy* (ed Barbara Herman) (Harvard UP: Cambridge, MA, 2000) 166.

[25] Ibid, 148.

[26] 'The appearance of Kant's deontology in contemporary Kantianism: concepts of patient autonomy in bioethics' (1999) 24 Journal of Medicine and Philosophy 43–66.

[27] 'Should the practice of medicine be a deontological or utilitarian enterprise?' (2011) 37 Journal of Medical Ethics 267–70.

privacy and confidentiality. The ethics of such relationships are intrinsically on a deontological footing—they are about how one person should treat another.

This deontological basis of medical care is strongly buttressed by professional codes such as the General Medical Council's good medical practice and its starting premise, 'You must make care of the patient your first concern.' Note the key point here that it is the individual patient who is the focus of attention, and not the wider needs of the healthcare system or the country's economy.

These individual doctor–patient interactions are nestled within a larger payment system that provides the financial and other resources within which these interactions can occur ... In modern complex healthcare systems such as the UK NHS the needs of the system, in terms of its survival as a coherent entity, are rapidly becoming as large as those of the patients in the consulting room. This larger system is unavoidably utilitarian, having to make the best use it can of finite resources ...

[T]here is a tension between the deontology of individual doctor–patient interactions and the utilitarian nature of the NHS as a payment system that exists to enable the delivery of medical services to patients. At root what we see with this question is the old tension between the need to balance overall system resources with the demands of any one individual patient.

(c) Virtue ethics

Recent interest in virtue ethics, which derives from Ancient Greek philosophy, has emerged in reaction to the minimal ethical content of most moral theories. A virtue ethicist is not merely interested in whether an act is permissible, but in whether it would be the right thing to do.

A central feature of virtue ethics is its rejection of the idea that patient autonomy is an absolute or overriding virtue. This means that the fact that an individual wants to do something is not, in itself, a reason for thinking it would be the right thing to do. For example, in relation to euthanasia, Philippa Foot has argued that simply wanting to die is not enough to make death a good thing for a person.[28] Rather, causing a person's death could be virtuous only if her life lacks the most basic human goods.

In Chapter 14, we encounter Rosalind Hursthouse's argument that the morality of abortion depends upon the pregnant woman's reason for terminating a new human life.[29] According to Hursthouse, parenthood is intrinsically good and so a woman who fails to appreciate this, and seeks an abortion for a trivial reason has not reflected with due seriousness, and has therefore not made a virtuous decision. In contrast, a woman who knows that she would be unable to provide her child with a decent life may have acted virtuously in terminating her unwanted pregnancy.

If acting out of self-interest is not virtuous, what is? According to virtue ethicists, virtues are the character traits necessary for human flourishing, such as honesty, compassion, kindness, justice, and courage. While compiling a list of virtues may be comparatively straightforward, this does not necessarily help us to make difficult decisions because different virtues may point in different directions. For example, in deciding which patient should have priority for an available bed, should a non-urgent patient who has already waited for six months be given priority, or should the bed always go to the patient with the most immediately pressing need? The virtues of fairness and compassion are relevant here, but they do not tell us what to do.

---

[28] 'Euthanasia' (1977) 6 Philosophy and Public Affairs 85–112.
[29] 'Virtue theory and abortion' (1991) 20 Philosophy and Public Affairs 223–46.

Or, let us imagine that a doctor is advising a couple on the chance that their second child would have the same inherited condition as their first, when genetic tests have revealed that the husband could not be the first child's father. Does the doctor act virtuously by being honest with the husband? Or would a virtuous person reveal this information only to the wife? Or not at all?

It has also been pointed out that virtuous people will sometimes act wrongly, despite their good intentions. Robert Veatch, for example, is 'concerned about well-intentioned, bungling do-gooders'.[30] A doctor who withholds a diagnosis of terminal cancer from her patient may be acting out of compassion, but this would still be the wrong thing to do.

(2) Principlism and its Critics

Moral philosophy can be a helpful way of framing medical dilemmas, but it will seldom provide clear answers for doctors faced with difficult choices. For example, a doctor might be told that: 'A utilitarian would do X, and a Kantian would do Y', which might be interesting, but is not terribly helpful.

A more practical way to decide medical questions was set out in Tom Beauchamp and James Childress's groundbreaking book *Principles of Biomedical Ethics*, now in its seventh edition. Beauchamp and Childress distilled four basic principles—autonomy, non-maleficence, beneficence, and justice—from 'the most general and basic norms of the common morality'.

- (a) The word *autonomy*—from the Greek *autos* (self) and *nomos* (rule)—initially referred to the self-rule of independent cities. It has since been extended to mean self-governance, and encompasses a cluster of interests such as liberty, privacy, and freedom of choice. Respect for autonomy means that adults who have capacity have the right to make decisions about their medical treatment.

- (b) *Non-maleficence*, or the duty to 'above all do no harm' (*primum non nocere*) has its origins in the Hippocratic oath. This principle captures the idea that doctors should never use their medical training for immoral purposes, such as torture. While it would be difficult to find anyone who thought that it was acceptable for doctors to be involved in torture, in other cases there may be disagreement over what counts as 'harm'. For example, some would argue that it is this principle which prohibits medical participation in euthanasia, whereas others would argue that by bringing an end to a patient's suffering, euthanasia can prevent the greater harm of a protracted and distressing death.

- (c) *Beneficence* refers to the obligation to act for the benefit of others. Since acting to benefit the patient is a primary goal of medicine, beneficence has been seen by some as its foundational value. It is, however, important to distinguish between what one might call the Hippocratic duty of beneficence (that is, the doctor's duty to act in her patient's interests), and 'social' beneficence, which might refer to a wider duty to help others whenever one can. This distinction helps to illuminate the fact that socially beneficent actions may be discretionary: I do not have an obligation to donate one of my healthy kidneys to a stranger. In contrast, Hippocratic duties of beneficence, such as the duty of care healthcare professionals owe their patients, are mandatory.

- (d) *Justice* is often interpreted to mean that we should treat like cases alike. But, of course, this depends upon being able to tell when cases are either 'like' or 'unlike'. When allocating lungs for transplant, do we act justly by making non-smokers a lower priority

---

[30] Robert Veatch, 'The danger of virtue' (1988) 13 Journal of Medicine and Philosophy 13.

than smokers (that is, are these 'unlike' cases?), or should the only relevant criteria be clinical need, in which case the smoker and the non-smoker are 'like' cases? In relation to health care, it is seldom possible to give every patient immediate access to the best medical treatment, so justice instead demands that we ration scarce resources fairly and transparently.

Aside from 'justice', the principles' focus is upon the individual doctor–patient encounter, thus missing the wider implications many bioethical dilemmas have for society as a whole. As a result, Amitai Etzioni has suggested the addition of a fifth principle, that of the 'common good'.

Amitai Etzioni[31]

[I]t is important to note that even the nuanced and enriched set of normative principles developed by Beauchamp and Childress does not include a concept of the common good, above and beyond the concept of justice—for instance, conditions under which individuals have to accept various sacrifices for the good of all. A thicker definition would include common goods that command our moral respect, such as the protection of the environment, basic research, homeland security and public health. These kinds of concerns that Gostin—and communitarians more generally—have about preventing the spread of infectious diseases, responding to bioterrorist attacks, protecting the environment, balancing preventive and acute medical treatments, and determining the extent to which one can foster or force limits on individual choices for the public good, do not find a comfortable home in the most widely followed bioethical texts. Hence, concern for the common good, responsive communitarians would argue, should be added to the already existing core values on which bioethics draws.

These principles are more 'user-friendly' than abstract moral philosophy, but they nevertheless borrow from the traditions we considered earlier. Respect for patient autonomy might be described as a deontological principle because it is regarded as valuable, irrespective of the consequences of the patient's decision. Beneficence and non-maleficence are plainly consequentialist principles, which require us to take into account possible benefits and harms. Virtue ethicists would be principally concerned with the virtues of 'doing good' (beneficence) and acting justly.

While there are those who believe in 'single principle' approaches—a libertarian, for example, believes that actions are right if, and only if, they respect a person's autonomy—most people accept that all of these principles may have a role to play in medical decision-making. Sometimes they will pull in the same direction. For example, in respecting a patient's autonomy, a doctor will often also be doing good: a doctor will act beneficently by telling the patient the truth, respecting her privacy, and facilitating autonomous decision-making.

At other times, the principles may come into conflict with each other. Many of the medical dilemmas we consider in this book could be framed as a clash between two or more of these basic principles. It might even be argued that the reason why some questions are difficult is precisely because they are cases in which principles that most of us accept are in tension with each other. Consider assisted suicide: the principle of autonomy might suggest that a patient's wish to die should be respected. Against this, the principle of non-maleficence might be invoked to say that a doctor must not actively help her patients to die.

---

[31] 'Authoritarian versus responsive communitarian bioethics' (2011) 37 Journal of Medical Ethics 17–23.

Hence, while the principlist approach might enable us to describe a moral dilemma as a conflict between competing principles, and work out what important values are at stake, it will seldom tell us what to do. Rather, when principles conflict there is no escaping the need to decide which factor is more important. One solution might be to rank the principles, but any hierarchy requires justification that cannot be provided by the principles themselves. If, for example, we want to say that autonomy should take priority over beneficence, either in general, or in a particular case, then we need to explain why.

In the next extract, Tom Beauchamp and James Childress explain that the principlist approach requires what they describe as further 'specification' and 'balancing'.

Tom L Beauchamp and James F Childress[32]

Our four clusters of principles do not constitute a general moral theory. They provide only a framework for identifying and reflecting on moral problems. The framework is spare, because prima facie principles do not contain sufficient content to address the nuances of many moral circumstances. We therefore need to examine how to specify and balance these abstract principles ...

Specification is a process of reducing the indeterminateness of abstract norms and providing them with action guiding content. For example, without further specification, 'do no harm' is an all-too-bare starting point for thinking through problems, such as assisted suicide and euthanasia. It will not adequately guide action when norms conflict ...

Principles, rules and rights require balancing no less than specification. We need both methods because each addresses a dimension of moral principles and rules range and scope, in the case of specification, and weight or strength, in the case of balancing. Specification entails a substantive refinement of the range of scope of norms, whereas balancing consists of deliberation and judgment about the relative weights or strength of norms. Balancing is especially important for reaching judgments in individual cases, and specification is especially useful for policy development.

Etzioni suggests that autonomy is frequently likely to come into contact with his additional 'common good' principle, and that the best way to resolve these dilemmas is on a case-by-case basis: if the interference with autonomy is slight and the common good is strong, then the common good should win out. If, on the other hand, the sacrifice of autonomy is substantial and the gains to the common good are marginal, then autonomy should be the trumping principle. But, of course, this does not help us to make a decision when the interference with autonomy and the gains to the common good are equally substantial, or equally slight.

Whether an interference with autonomy is substantial or slight might also be a matter of opinion. For example, when the ban on smoking in public places in the UK was set to be extended to high-security hospitals, some inpatients claimed that the interference with the freedom to smoke in what was effectively their home represented a violation of their human right to a private and family life. The Court of Appeal disagreed: 'Preventing a person smoking does not, at any rate in the culture of the United Kingdom, generally involve such adverse effect upon the person's "physical or moral integrity" ... as would amount to an interference with the right to respect for private or home life within the meaning of Art.8.'[33]

[32] *Principles of Biomedical Ethics*, 7th edn (OUP: Oxford, 2013).
[33] *R (on the application of G) v Nottinghamshire Healthcare NHS Trust* [2008] EWHC 1096 (Admin).

Of course, the Court of Appeal's decision that Article 8 was not engaged was determinative, but the claimants undoubtedly found the interference with their autonomy substantial, going so far as to claim that 'the smoking ban made their lives intolerable'.

While it has been hugely influential, Beauchamp and Childress's approach is not without its critics. In the next extract, K Danner Clouser and Bernard Gert argue that, rather than clarifying difficult questions, principlism can be unsystematic and misleading.

K Danner Clouser and Bernard Gert[34]

We believe that the 'principles of biomedical ethics' approach is mistaken and misleading. Principlism is mistaken about the nature of morality and is misleading as to the foundations of ethics ... Our bottom line, starkly put, is that 'principle', as conceived by the proponents of Principlism, is a misnomer and that 'principles' so conceived cannot function as they are in fact claimed to be functioning by those who purport to employ them. At best, 'principles' operate primarily as checklists naming issues worth remembering when considering a biomedical moral issue. At worst 'principles' obscure and confuse moral reasoning by their failure to be guidelines and by their eclectic and unsystematic use of moral theory ...

Taking what is properly the moral ideal of helping others (and hence not morally required), and lumping it under a 'principle' of beneficence along with genuine duties (which are required), e.g., the duty of health care professionals to help their patients, leads to confusion and misunderstanding. The confusion basically results from treating beneficence as if it were morally required just as noninterference with the freedom of others is morally required.

The appeal of principlism is that it makes use of those features of each ethical theory that seems to have the most support. Thus, in proposing the principle of beneficence, it acknowledges that Mill was right in being concerned with consequences ... In proposing the principle of autonomy, it acknowledges that Kant was right in emphasising the importance of the individual person ... But there is no attempt to see how these different concerns can be blended together as integrated parts of a single adequate theory, rather than disparate concerns derived from several competing theories.

(3) Casuistry

While philosophers and ethicists are accustomed to discussing general and abstract principles, clinicians tend to be more interested in cases. This has contributed to renewed interest in casuistry, or case-based reasoning, a tradition which has its origins in Roman Catholic theology.

In casuistry, instead of starting with broad, abstract principles (a top-down approach), we instead begin with our response to concrete cases and reason by analogy (a bottom-up approach). This is, as John Arras points out, similar to the judiciary's incremental development of the common law.

---

[34] 'A critique of principlism' (1990) 15 Journal of Medicine and Philosophy 219–36.

John D Arras[35]

Developed in the early Middle-Ages as a method of bringing abstract and universal ethico-religious precepts to bear on particular moral situations, casuistry has had a chequered history. In the hands of expert practitioners during its salad days in the sixteenth and seventeenth centuries, casuistry generated a rich and morally sensitive literature devoted to numerous real-life ethical problems, such as truth-telling, usury, and the limits of revenge. By the late seventeenth century, however, casuistical reasoning had degenerated into a notoriously sordid form of logic-chopping in the service of personal expediency. To this day, the very term 'casuistry' conjures up pejorative images of disingenuous argument and moral laxity.

In spite of casuistry's tarnished reputation, some philosophers have claimed that casuistry, shorn of its unfortunate excesses, has much to teach us about the resolution of moral problems in medicine . . .

Contrary to deductivist ethical theories, wherein principles are said to preexist the actual cases to which they apply, the new casuistry contends that ethical principles are 'discovered' in the cases themselves, just as common law legal principles are developed in and through judicial decisions on particular legal cases . . . Rather than stemming originally from some ethical theory, such as Utilitarianism, these principles are said to emerge gradually from reflection upon our responses to particular cases.

In the next extract, Albert Jonsen argues that no moral dilemma is entirely novel, so it makes sense to look at how similar problems have been resolved in the past.

Albert R Jonsen[36]

No ethical problem is completely unprecedented. Regardless how novel, it bears some resemblance to problems that are more familiar. The more familiar ones will often be ones for which resolutions have been offered and sometimes accepted. Thus, one compares the new case with the more familiar one. That comparison almost always involves seeking for the similarities and differences in circumstance . . . In this view, ethical reasoning is primarily reasoning by analogy, seeking to identify cases similar to the one under scrutiny and to discern whether the changed circumstances justify a different judgement in the new case than they did in the former.

Although past experience may be helpful when contemplating a novel dilemma, several problems with casuistry have been identified. First, even if our intuitions will sometimes embody universal moral judgements—an example might be condemnation of Nazi doctors' abuse of research subjects during the Second World War—these are the exception rather than the norm. It is also not clear that our intuitive response to black-and-white cases actually helps us very much when we are faced with more finely balanced moral choices. For example, we can all agree that it would be wrong to kill disabled children. But how does that assist us when we are faced with the more difficult question of whether it could ever be right to withdraw

---

[35] 'Getting down to cases: the revival of casuistry in bioethics' (1991) 16 Journal of Medicine and Philosophy 29–51.
[36] 'Casuistry: an alternative or complement to principles?' (1995) 5 Kennedy Institute of Ethics Journal 237–51.

life-sustaining medical treatment from a permanently and profoundly incapacitated neonate? Some would say that the cases are the same and neither course of action should be permitted, while others would point to relevant differences between the two cases.

Secondly, case-based reasoning will only yield a definite answer if there is some consensus upon what counts as a relevant similarity. Is abortion relevantly similar to murder (the deliberate killing of a person), or is it relevantly similar to contraception (allowing women to control their reproductive capacity)? Without underlying agreement on certain fundamental moral questions, casuistry provides us with little concrete guidance.

Thirdly, the analogy with the common law is imperfect. The common law contains a system of binding precedent, and identifies individuals (ie judges) whose interpretation of previous cases is authoritative. In the field of bioethics, even if we could identify moral 'experts' to adjudicate on competing interpretations of previous authority, there is no reason why anyone else should be bound by their conclusions.

Fourthly, it is not clear how we can be guided by decisions in previous cases unless those decisions are distilled into some sort of general principle. We could, for example, say that depriving someone of their liberty is wrong, but we might also be able to think of exceptional circumstances in which detention might be justified, perhaps because someone is suffering from such a severe mental illness that she would otherwise pose a serious risk of harm to herself. We can therefore derive the general principle that compulsory detention will be legitimate only in order to prevent a serious risk of harm.

Even if casuistry—like principlism—cannot tell us what to do when faced with a difficult dilemma, it is important to recognize the role cases play in modern bioethics. In the previous section, we saw that there will often be a conflict between, say, autonomy and non-maleficence. At a high level of abstraction, it is impossible for us to tell which should take priority. In the context of a real case, however, it may be possible to reason why, in this particular case, there are grounds for thinking that autonomy (or non-maleficence) is more important.

For example, in Chapter 6 we will encounter the case of E, a teenager who wanted to refuse a blood transfusion. Without greater detail than this, it is impossible to tell whether the priority should be to respect E's wishes or to act in his best interests. For example, we need to know more about E's age, and reasoning capacity, and it will be helpful to consider how similar cases were decided in the past. In practice, decision-making in a case like this will be guided not only by principles, but also by careful analysis of the facts in individual cases.

In addition to real cases, bioethicists tend to make extensive use of imagined cases, or thought experiments. Judith Jarvis Thomson's classic essay on abortion (extracted in Chapter 14) asks the reader to imagine that she has woken up to discover that a world-famous violinist has been attached to her body, and that he needs to be wholly dependent upon her for a further nine months.

In the context of the acts/omissions distinction, James Rachels has questioned whether there is a moral difference between Smith, who drowns his cousin, and Jones, who has the same intention, but finds that at the critical moment, the cousin bangs his head and drowns anyway.[37]

Are these hypothetical examples useful? On the one hand, if they are too fantastical, their relevance to real cases may be tenuous, at best. On the other hand, they may offer a fresh lens from which to view a moral problem that has, as Adrian Walsh puts it, 'become stale'.[38] The point of Thomson's violinist analogy is not to claim that an unwanted pregnancy is exactly the

---

[37] James Rachels, 'Active and passive euthanasia' (1975) 292 New England Journal of Medicine 78–80.
[38] Adrian Walsh, 'The Use of Thought Experiments in Health Care Ethics' in Richard E Ashcroft et al (eds), *Principles of Health Care Ethics*, 2nd edn (Wiley: Chichester, 2007) 177–83.

same as waking up attached to a world-famous violinist, rather it prompts us to think about the degree of self-sacrifice involved in carrying a pregnancy to term against one's wishes.

(4) Feminism

There is no single 'feminist' approach to bioethics. At the risk of drastic oversimplification, three different approaches might be identified.

First, liberal feminists' principal focus is on gender inequality. For example, the point of Judith Jarvis Thomson's—at first sight bizarre—analogy between an unwanted pregnancy and finding that one's body is necessary to support the life of a famous violinist, is that the former is an experience which only women can experience, while the latter (hypothetical) experience is gender neutral. If, Thomson reasons, we can agree that it would be unreasonable to expect a person to give up his body for nine months to support the violinist, then we ought to be able to agree that it is unreasonable to expect women to exercise a similar degree of self-sacrifice in relation to an unwanted pregnancy.

Another example of inequality, which we consider in Chapter 10, is women's traditional exclusion from clinical trials, due both to their fluctuating hormonal cycles, and the possibility of pregnancy. Systematic exclusion of women from clinical trials means that medicines are not as safe or as effective when taken by female patients. Liberal feminists are concerned to identify and challenge this sort of inequality in order to promote the fair and equal treatment of both sexes.

A second feminist approach focusses upon oppression. As we see in Chapter 15, feminists were initially among the fiercest critics of reproductive technologies, arguing that (male) scientists and doctors were essentially experimenting on women's bodies, and exploiting women's desire for children by persuading them to consent to dangerously untested new treatments. Now that *in vitro* fertilization (IVF) has become routine, feminist criticism of it is more muted. There has, however, been feminist concern about the potential for the exploitation of women from low-income countries in cross-border commercial surrogacy.

The third feminist approach represents the most direct challenge to bioethics itself. What we might call the 'ethics of care' emerged as a result of some feminists' dissatisfaction with conventional medical ethics. First, traditional medical ethics focused upon the proper conduct of the medical profession, which was, until comparatively recently, heavily male-dominated. Women, on the other hand, are disproportionately represented among patients. Their reproductive capacity, their role as principal carers for children and the elderly, and their greater life expectancy combine to make women more frequent users of medical services than men. Women are also more likely to be employed in health services as carers, either as nurses (whose role used to be confined to carrying out doctors' orders) or as auxiliary staff.

When medical ethicists focus upon the dilemmas facing doctors, they are ignoring the equally important ethical issues that are encountered by carers, nurses, and patients. In the late 1990s, for example, anthropologist Rayna Rapp documented the moral dilemmas pregnant women faced in relation to the decision to use new prenatal testing techniques, such as amniocentesis. These patients were, she argued, 'moral pioneers . . . forced to judge the quality of their own fetuses, making concrete and embodied decisions about the standards for entry into the human community'.[39]

Secondly, drawing on the work of psychologist Carol Gilligan, feminist theorists have argued that abstract moral reasoning, and in particular, an emphasis on individualistic values

---

[39] *Testing Women, Testing the Fetus: The Social Impact of Amniocentesis in America* (Routledge: New York, 1999) 3.

such as autonomy, are distinctively 'male'. Women's existence, according to this analysis, is characterized by connections with others, especially through pregnancy and child-rearing, and this leads them to value relationships more highly than individual autonomy.

Carol Gilligan[40]

The psychology of women that has consistently been described as distinctive in its greater orientation toward relationships and interdependence implies a more contextual mode of judgment and a different moral understanding. Given the differences in women's conceptions of self and morality, women bring to the life cycle a different point of view and order human experience in terms of different priorities.

A third and related point is that the dominant principle of medical ethics, namely patient autonomy, presupposes an independent, largely self-sufficient individual who is able to weigh information in order to reach a rational decision about his medical treatment. Of course, few patients meet this exacting standard, because illness often makes us dependent and vulnerable. More fundamentally, a model of moral reasoning which privileges the rational, self-directed individual relies on a partial and inaccurate understanding of what it is to be human.

All of us were completely dependent on others at the beginning of our lives, and most of us will spend some time unable to function independently before we die. An ethic of care instead takes for granted the inevitability of dependency and the importance of social context. As Wendy Rogers et al explain, none of us is actually invulnerable to ill health or bad luck.

Wendy Rogers, Catriona Mackenzie, and Susan Dodds[41]

We have argued that, rather than vulnerability being a property of only those people who fall into the category 'vulnerable groups' or 'vulnerable populations,' all human life is characterized by vulnerability, and that specific factors exacerbate the vulnerability of specific individuals and groups. A focus on vulnerability highlights our common humanity and offers grounds for solidarity. As biological and social beings, we share much vulnerability—to ill health, to bad luck, to natural and human-generated disasters, and so forth. Although these and other vulnerabilities are not equally distributed, none of us is invulnerable; we all have some experience and understanding of what it is to feel vulnerable . . .

Just as we share much vulnerability, it is also the case that our social practices and institutions can ameliorate vulnerabilities and can help foster resilience. Rather than simply drawing attention to our shared vulnerability to harm, a fuller account of vulnerability can attend to the social practices (such as education, health promotion, access to the range of social services and legal protections) that can promote our well-being and capacities for agency, while reducing vulnerability to need, ill health, or exploitation. Linking vulnerability to vital needs and to flourishing provides an additional and cogent moral reason for action on health inequalities.

---

[40] *In a Different Voice* (Harvard UP: London, MA, 1982).
[41] 'Why bioethics needs a concept of vulnerability' (2012) 5 International Journal of Feminist Approaches to Bioethics 11–38.

In the next extract, Jonathan Herring explains that because caring has traditionally been women's work, it has been systematically undervalued and largely ignored by medical ethicists. This is a mistake, not least because it has been estimated that the social care services provided in the UK by informal and unpaid carers are worth £57 billion per year.[42]

Jonathan Herring[43]

Caring is a gendered activity. It is seen as 'women's work' and as such is ignored in the 'male gaze'. I mentioned earlier the enormous economic value of care and yet it is not given the respect or recognition that other higher profile 'economically productive' activities have. By describing care work as 'voluntary' and 'informal' it is marginalised as unimportant. Hence, the professional doctor–patient relationship is subject to careful and extensive legal regulation and is dealt with at length in the court reports and the wider media. The carer–patient relationship, of greater significance to many patients, is ignored. This all has the impact of care work being unvalued and unnoticed. All of this is convenient to a society in which 'men's' work goes rewarded and valorised, while 'women's' work is invisible and unrecognised. The lack of respect owed to caring has played a significant role in the unequal economic position of women.

Under an ethic of care the practice of caring would be hugely valued within society. Carers would, far from being hidden, come to represent a norm. Social structures and attitudes would need to be set up to encourage and enable caring. This would require adequate remuneration of carers: not the payment of benefits of the kind paid to those 'unable to work', but payment acknowledging the key role they play. Work would need to be done to ensure that the burden of caring did not fall on the few but was shared across the community.

Feminists have also criticized the principle of autonomy for conflating freedom of choice with the 'right to be left alone'. Freedom of choice will be valuable only if a person has a meaningful range of options from which to choose, and this, as Catriona Mackenzie explains, may require the positive provisions of resources, rather than the mere absence of constraints.

Catriona Mackenzie[44]

To exercise autonomy requires both liberty and opportunity. Liberty, or freedom from undue interference, is required because it is difficult for a person to lead a self-governing life if political or personal restrictions prevent her from making choices about matters that are important to her, such as being able to practice her religion, express her political opinions, pursue a career or personal projects, and decide with whom she will have intimate relationships, where she will live, or whether she will have children. However, living an autonomous life or a life of one's own choosing intuitively seems to require more than being free from undue interference by others. It also seems to require access to genuine opportunities, or to a range of significant options, which means access to social goods such as education, health care, housing, and social support; adequate nutrition, sanitation, and personal safety; opportunities for political

---

[42] Office for National Statistics, *Unpaid carers provide social care worth £57 billion* (ONS, 2017).

[43] 'Where are the Carers in Healthcare Law and Ethics?' (2007) 27 Legal Studies 51–73.

[44] 'Autonomy' in John D Arras, Elizabeth Fenton, and Rebecca Kukla (eds) *The Routledge companion to bioethics* (Routledge, 2014).

participation and paid or unpaid employment; and some degree of mobility. These goods require complex social, economic, and political infrastructures. Relational theorists charge that libertarian autonomy places too much emphasis on the importance of negative liberty or freedom from interference, while overlooking the importance for individual autonomy of access to these social goods and the opportunities they make available.

(5) Disability Bioethics

Following on from the acknowledgement that we are all vulnerable to ill-health and dependency, disability bioethics questions conventional bioethics' assumptions about what it means to be impaired or disabled. This represents a significant challenge to conventional bioethics because so many ethical dilemmas depend upon some shared understanding of what makes a life worth living (or not worth living). As Adrienne Asch points out, bioethicists commonly ask 'should this life be saved?', without understanding what it is actually like to live with an impairment.

Adrienne Asch[45]

The dominant bioethics voices have argued that human life had to be respected and valued but not necessarily at any cost or in any state of impairment … Instead of the medical question, 'Can this life be saved?' bioethics invites the question, 'Should this life be saved?' … Bioethics also fails to recognize the extent to which disadvantages experienced by people with disabilities arise through society's lack of accommodation to the different methods of performing valued activities such as learning, communicating, moving, or taking in the world. On the contrary, say disability studies scholars and disability politics. First, life with disability is not the unremitting tragedy portrayed in medical and bioethics literature. Second, the culprit is not biological, psychic, or cognitive equipment but the social, institutional, and physical world in which people with impairments must function – a world designed with the characteristics and needs of the nondisabled majority in mind.

Jackie Leach Scully further points out that the ubiquitous dependencies of able-bodied people are normalised while the less common dependencies of disabled people are pathologized.

Jackie Leach Scully[46]

Societies permit certain dependencies, the ones that (most) people will share, by not seeing them as dependencies at all. Commonly shared dependencies become genuinely invisible. The chief executive officer who boasts of being dependent on no one would be unable to lead the life that she does without a thick network of practical and less tangible supports in the background. They range from the family relationships in which she developed the psychic resources to function as an adult, the social policies that gave her access to schooling, higher education, and health care to the infrastructures and services like rubbish collection that her

---

[45] 'Disability, bioethics and human rights' in Gary L Albrecht, Katherine Seelman, and Michael Bury (eds) *Handbook of disability studies* (Sage, 2001) 297–326.

[46] 'Disability and Vulnerability: On Bodies, Dependence, and Power' in Catriona Mackenzie, Wendy Rogers, and Susan Dodds (eds) *Vulnerability: New Essays in Ethics and Feminist Philosophy* (OUP, 2014).

local community provides, the builders of motorways she uses to drive to work, and the makers of planes and trains that transport her to her meetings. These are dependencies: imagine what would happen to her life if all of these provisions were to disappear overnight.

So permitted dependencies are naturalised and normalised. They are met and supported without question, and in doing so the vocabulary of vulnerability is never used. Other people, and groups, will have needs that fall outside the normative limit. These are nonpermitted dependencies. They are figured as abnormal and classed as rendering those people as especially vulnerable.

Yet a dependency on good roads to commute to work, although more common than a dependency on Braille signage, is still a dependency. The fact that the first is not registered as a dependency at all but as normal while the latter is seen as an exceptional vulnerability is a political choice.

(6) Human Rights

Throughout this book, we will come across attempts to frame individual legal claims—for example, to medical treatment or to privacy—in terms of human rights. Some commentators have argued that the internationalism of human rights, and their moral force, is especially helpful in constructing a global bioethics, capable of addressing issues which, as Sirkku Sellsten explains, inevitably transcend national borders, such as pandemic diseases and environmental hazards.

Sirkku Hellsten[47]

As the globalization of our world continues, the questions of bioethics are more and more clearly recognized to be transnational, issues that can be addressed only with international action. Contagious diseases, genetically modified organisms, changes in biodiversity, the consequences of the use of advanced biotechnology (most notably in biowarfare), the effects of climate change, and other environmental problems do not respect national borders. We also practice medicine, conduct research, and do business (e.g., in pharmaceuticals) across borders. In order to respond rationally to various bioethical challenges, we need to acknowledge our global interdependence and work together despite our cultural, religious, economic, geographical, and political differences.

While they are not the panacea to every ethical problem—for example, medical research on animals raises ethical issues which are not reducible to human rights—Elizabeth Fenton and John Arras suggest that there are good reasons for bioethicists to embrace human rights.

Elizabeth Fenton and John Arras[48]

Individual countries cannot address global health issues, and culturally specific principles are inadequate for addressing global bioethics concerns. We will need a language and moral

---

[47] 'The Role of Philosophy in Global Bioethics: Introducing Four Trends' (2015) 24 Cambridge Quarterly of Healthcare Ethics 185–94.
[48] 'Bioethics and Human Rights: Curb Your Enthusiasm' (2010) 19 Cambridge Quarterly of Healthcare Ethics 127–33.

framework grounded in a foundation of universally shared, transcultural judgments about humankind that will also recognize moral pluralism. The claim has been made that such a foundation already exists in human rights, and that human rights should, therefore, be the new *lingua franca* of bioethics.

There are good reasons for advancing this claim. First, there is a significant overlap between the concerns of public health (which encompasses many global health issues) and the concerns of human rights. Both are interested in the many social conditions that determine health and overall well-being, such as adequate food, water, shelter, and basic healthcare ...

Second, human rights discourse ... 'is already the accepted language of international ethics' ... As such, it serves as the ubiquitous mode of expressing social criticism and is a universally shared framework for addressing social problems.

Third, the human rights movement has both political and legal dimensions that mere moral appeals manifestly lack ... [B]ecause the moral claims of the human rights movement are embedded in legally binding covenants that have been ratified by many state governments, they pack a much more effective punch than standard bioethical exhortations whose only force derives from the cogency of their arguments ...

A general endorsement of human rights does not warrant attempts to shoehorn any and all moral, political, medical, or legal controversies into that linguistic and methodological framework. It bears repeating at this point that human rights constitute only a small, albeit supremely important, subcategory of the larger domain of moral value. Not every ethical or political problem, and not even every problem of justice, implicates legitimate claims of human rights.

(c) COMMON JUSTIFICATORY STRATEGIES

(1) Human Dignity, the Sanctity of Human Life, and Playing God

A common response to novel or controversial medical techniques—such as euthanasia, cloning, and abortion—is to argue that they interfere with human dignity; or that they are at odds with the sanctity of human life; or that they would involve human beings 'playing God'. International agreements on biomedicine have also emphasized the importance of respect for human dignity: the preamble to the Council of Europe's Convention on Human Rights and Biomedicine requires signatories 'to take such measures as are necessary to safeguard human dignity and the fundamental rights and freedoms of the individual with regard to the application of biology and medicine'.

But what do these phrases actually mean? In the next extract, Ruth Chadwick attempts to pin down what might be meant by the expression 'playing God'.

Ruth F Chadwick[49]

[I]t seems clear that the use of the term 'playing God' normally indicates moral disapproval on the part of the speaker, but it is not obvious what is supposed to be bad about taking the decision. Let us consider alternative ways of looking at the question.

---

[49] 'Playing God' (1989) 3 Cogito 186–93.

(a) God's prerogative

From a religious point of view the objection may be that it is for God to give life and for God to take it away. Such a view notoriously has the difficulty however that it seems to imply the rejection of medicine altogether ...

(b) Letting nature take its course

Here the playing-God objection is interpreted as a claim that human beings are interfering with the course of nature, and that this is wrong. As such it can be, and has been, fairly easily answered ... John Stuart Mill points out that it is impossible for humans to let nature take its course because every human action has an impact, however slight, upon nature.

(c) Equality

A third possibility ... is that the objection expresses an intuition about equality ... The suggestion may be that human beings have lives that are of equal value and that it is therefore wrong for one set of people to judge that the lives of others are of less value ...

(d) Omniscience

A further claim about equality may be involved here. The suggestion would be that one thing that human beings have in common is that their knowledge is limited. Those who take decisions about the quality of the lives of others are aspiring to the kind of omniscience that is simply not available to them.

The 'playing God' objection may help to remind us that our actions may have unintended consequences. But it seems doubtful that it can provide a conclusive argument against a course of action.

In a secular society, what might it mean to say that human life is sacred? In the next extract, Ronald Dworkin suggests that there is a universal, and not necessarily religious, sense of awe at the 'miracle' of human creation.

Ronald Dworkin[50]

Any human creature, including the most immature embryo, is a triumph of divine or evolutionary creation, which produces a complex, reasoning being from, as it were, nothing, and also of what we often call the 'miracle' of human reproduction, which makes each new human being both different from and yet a continuation of the human beings who created it ...

The life of a single human organism commands respect and protection, then, no matter in what form or shape, because of the complex creative investment it represents and because of our wonder at the divine or evolutionary processes that produce new lives from old ones, at the processes of nation and community and language through which a human being will come to absorb and continue hundreds of generations of cultures and forms of life and value, and, finally, when mental life has begun and flourishes, at the process of internal personal

[50] *Life's Dominion: An Argument about Abortion and Euthanasia* (HarperCollins: London, 1993).

creation and judgement by which a person will make and remake himself, a mysterious, in-escapable process in which we each participate, and which is therefore the most powerful and inevitable source of empathy and communion we have with every other creature who faces the same frightening challenge. The horror we feel in the wilful destruction of a human life reflects our shared inarticulate sense of the intrinsic importance of each of these dimensions of investment.

On the other hand, Peter Singer argues that the 'sanctity of human life', which he condemns as speciesist, derives from a specifically Christian moral tradition.

Peter Singer[51]

People often say that life is sacred. They almost never mean what they say. They do not mean, as their words seem to imply, that all life is sacred. If they did, killing a pig or even pulling up a cabbage would be as contrary to their doctrine as infanticide. So when in the context of medical ethics people talk of the sanctity of life, it is the sanctity of human life that they really mean ...

[W]hat is the position when we compare severely and irreparably retarded human infants with nonhuman animals like pigs and dogs, monkeys and apes? I think we are forced to con-clude that in at least some cases the human infant does not possess any characteristics or capacities that are not also possessed, to an equal or higher degree, by many nonhuman ani-mals. This is true of such capacities as the capacity to feel pain, to act intentionally, to solve problems, and to communicate with and relate to other beings; and it is also true of such characteristics as self-awareness, a sense of one's own existence over time, concern for other beings, and curiosity ...

So when we decide to treat one being—the severely and irreparably retarded infant—in one way, and the other being—the pig or monkey—in another way, there seems to be no differ-ence between the two that we can appeal to in defense of our discrimination ... The doctrine of the sanctity of human life, as it is commonly understood, has at its core a discrimination on the basis of species and nothing else ...

[T]he intuitions which lie behind [the doctrine of the sanctity of human life] are not insights of self-evident moral truths, but the historically conditioned product of doctrines about immor-tality, original sin and damnation which hardly anyone now accepts; doctrines so obnoxious, in fact, that if anyone did accept them, we should be inclined to discount any other moral views he held. Although advocates of the doctrine of the sanctity of human life now frequently try to give their position some secular justification, there can be no possible justification for making the boundary of sanctity run parallel with the boundary of our own species, unless we invoke some belief about immortal souls.

Human dignity is an especially vague and ambiguous concept. In particular, its scope is poten-tially wider than respect for persons or human rights. We might, for example, be required to treat an embryo or a corpse, neither of which is a person or rights' holder, with dignity, which might mean that we are not entitled to use and dispose of them as if they were things. In the next extract, Charles Foster argues that 'human dignity' captures what is wrong with the use of human body parts without consent or for trivial purposes.

---

[51] Helga Kuhse (ed), *Unsanctifying Human Life: Essays on Ethics* (Blackwell: Oxford, 2002).

Charles Foster[52]

1. *A child's heart, retained for the purposes of medical research*: The child died of a disease being studied at the institute that has retained it. Its heart, which is particularly useful to the researchers, was removed at postmortem without the knowledge of the parents. The rest of the body was returned and buried ...

2. *A human ear ashtray*: Medical students steal an ear from the cadaver they are dissecting. Back at their student squat, they use it as an ashtray. The cadaver was donated for the purposes of medical education, and the donor (the person whose body it is) would have been outraged at this misuse.

3. *A human head football*: Children play football in the street with the head of an unknown person, with no living relatives, dug out by a dog from a mediaeval cemetery ...

What is the best language for describing the wrongness in these examples? Whatever it is, it is not the language of property. The parents in example 1 would be outraged to hear it suggested that the wrong committed by the researchers was morally identical to shoplifting. If the only language available to them was the language of property, they would agree that they had better title to their child's heart than the researchers, but that is hardly an adequate way of expressing their outrage. No doubt the students who stubbed out their cigarettes in the ear are in breach of their obligations as bailors. But there's more to say than that about their conduct. The children who are playing with the head are doing something ethically different from children playing with a stolen football.

Deryck Beyleveld and Roger Brownsword have suggested that human dignity is now invoked chiefly in order to restrict individual's choices, which they refer to as 'human dignity as constraint'. This is commonly done by arguing that a controversial medical practice is 'against human nature'.

Deryck Beyleveld and Roger Brownsword[53]

Many persons feel that a number of scientific interventions are 'unnatural', and cite this as the reason why it is wrong to employ them. This reaction may be linked to the idea that such interventions are contrary to dignity by the following reasoning. Dignity is the property by virtue of which human beings have moral rights or moral standing. All human beings have dignity simply by virtue of being human. Dignity is thus an essential part of human nature. Therefore, to act contrary to human nature is to act contrary to human dignity, and it might, then, be alleged that, for example, assisted reproduction itself is against nature; or 70-year-old women bearing children is against nature; or lesbianism is against nature; or men bearing children is against nature ...

An attempt to explicate respect for human dignity in terms of human nature is not without its problems even if couched within a framework that links having dignity to being human (in a biological sense) ... Suppose that it is held that it is unnatural for a lesbian woman to bear a child, or for a man to bear a child. What is meant by saying that it is unnatural? Clearly, it cannot be meant that it goes against the laws of nature. If something is contrary to the laws of nature

[52] Dignity and the Ownership and Use of Body Parts' (2014) 23 Cambridge Quarterly of Healthcare Ethics 417–30.
[53] *Human Dignity in Bioethics and Biolaw* (OUP: Oxford, 2001).

then it cannot (physically) happen. And, if it is not possible for it to happen then there is no need to prescribe that it ought not to happen or to take steps to prevent it from happening.

Perhaps, then, what is meant is that it cannot happen without human intervention. However, there are so many things that cannot happen without human intervention that this threatens to imply that human action itself is contrary to human nature. Certainly, anyone who adopts such a view must, it seems, hold that all medical intervention without which a person would die is contrary to human nature.

Suzy Killmister suggests another possible meaning for human dignity, namely that it involves the avoidance of humiliation and shame, and ensuring that people's treatment is consistent with standards and values that are, or have been, important to them. To leave a patient in soiled bedsheets, or to expect her to sit in a crowded waiting room in a skimpy hospital gown is to fail to treat her with appropriate dignity.

Suzy Killmister[54]

For most of us, at least part of the trauma of undergoing medical procedures is the shame we experience at having our bodies exposed, the public nature of otherwise deeply private bodily functions, and the childlike dependence to which we are reduced. While such situations are not deliberately inflicted upon the patient, they can nonetheless be experienced as humiliation. This is when the definition of aspirational dignity as the upholding of one's standards becomes crucial. The reason why, for example, being left semi-naked on a hospital trolley is experienced as humiliation, and thus as a violation of dignity, is that the patient has standards of public decency that they strive to maintain in their daily lives, and which they are here being forced to abandon ...

Similarly, insufferable pain and loss of control over bodily functions are seen to compromise the ability of the individual to maintain the standards that they have sought to uphold throughout their life ...

The definition of dignity would thus be as follows: dignity is the inherent capacity for upholding one's principles ... The difference between what autonomy demands and what dignity demands can be drawn out thus: to respect an individual's autonomy requires respect for their self-governance ... To respect an individual's dignity, meanwhile, requires respect for their self-worth.

(2) The Slippery Slope

Another common objection to controversial medical practices is that they might represent the first step on a slippery slope. This is a consequentialist argument in that it does not appeal to the intrinsic wrongness of a particular technique; rather, as Frederick Schauer explains, the fear is that allowing something that may seem fairly innocuous in itself might have unforeseeable, uncontrollable, or dangerous consequences.

---

[54] 'Dignity: not such a useless concept' (2010) 36 Journal of Medical Ethics 160–4.

Frederick Schauer[55]

Sometimes the warning is of 'a foot in the door,' and the British often refer to 'the thin edge of the wedge'. Most commonly we are told to beware of the 'slippery slope'. Yet regardless of the term employed, the phenomenon referred to is the same. The single argumentative claim supported by each of these metaphors, as well as by many others, is that a particular act, seemingly innocuous when taken in isolation, may yet lead to a future host of similar but increasingly pernicious events. But why should this be? What induces people to believe that in some cases neither doctrinal limits nor judicial intervention can prevent the slide down the slippery slope? ...

As a start we can say that a slippery slope argument necessarily contains the implicit concession that the proposed resolution of the instant case is not itself troublesome. By focusing on the consequences for future cases, we implicitly concede that this instance is itself innocuous, or perhaps even desirable. If we felt otherwise, then we would not employ the slippery slope argument, but would rather claim much more simply that this case, in itself, is impermissible. By implicitly conceding that the instant case is, by itself, unobjectionable, the slippery slope argument directs our attention and our fears to the danger case in the future. It is not permitting the instant case that worries us, but rather the possibility that permitting the instant case will lead to the danger case ...

Thus, what can distinguish a slippery slope claim from other warnings about the future is the identification of factors increasing the likelihood not only of slippage, but of slippage in the particular direction that takes us from the instant case to the danger case.

In the next extract, Bernard Williams contrasts two different types of slippery slope claims: the 'horrible result' argument and the 'arbitrary result' argument. He also explains that slippery slope arguments do not necessarily justify banning a practice; rather, a different response might be regulation, which draws a line between acceptable and unacceptable practices.

Bernard Williams[56]

First it is worth distinguishing two types of slippery slope argument. The first type—the horrible result argument—objects, roughly speaking, to what is at the bottom of the slope. The second type objects to the fact that it is a slope: this may be called the arbitrary result argument ...

All of the arguments that I shall be considering use the idea that there is no point at which one can non-arbitrarily get off the slope once one has got onto it—that is what makes the slope slippery. Arguments that belong to the first type that I have distinguished involve, in addition, the further idea that there is a clearly objectionable practice to which the slope leads. The second type of argument, by contrast, relies merely on the point that after one has got on to the slope, subsequent discriminations will be arbitrary ...

The first requirement is that it should be probable in actual social fact that such a process will occur. This requires that there should be some motive for people to move from one step to the next. Suppose it is plausible that there will be a slide, and that there will be, at each stage, pressure to take the next step. What follows from that? The slippery slope argument concludes

[55] 'Slippery Slopes' (1985) 99 Harvard Law Review 361.
[56] *Making Sense of Humanity and Other Philosophical Papers* (CUP: Cambridge, 1995).

that one should not start, and that the first case should not be allowed, on the ground that after the first step there is nowhere to stop …

But there is an obvious alternative. Granted that we are now considering cases in which a definite rule of practice is needed, we have the alternative of drawing a sharp line between cases that are allowed and cases that are not … Is drawing a line in this way reasonable? Can it be effective? The answer to both these questions seems to me evidently to be 'Yes, sometimes' …

[T]he slippery slope argument should be properly understood as in good part an empirical, consequentialist argument … Seen in this light, it seems to me that the slippery-slope style of argument can carry weight, and is to be taken seriously; but that, equally, it need not necessarily carry the day, in the sense of proving that the first step should never be taken. We may, instead, take the path of drawing a line, and that is a perfectly reasonable reaction, in the right circumstances, to the challenge that is indeed posed by the slippery slope considerations.

4 CONCLUSION

In the remainder of this book, we will see that there has been a shift from a paternalistic model of medical decision-making, based upon the idea that 'doctor knows best', towards an autonomy-based model, which assumes that adults with capacity have an almost absolute right to refuse medical treatment. It would, however, be a mistake to regard patient autonomy as the overriding value in all medical decision-making. The right to autonomy is a negative right to prevent unwanted intervention; it does not give patients the right to demand access to whatever medical treatment they might want. Treatment can be denied when resources are scarce; or when treatment would be against the doctors' clinical judgement; or when parliament has decided that the treatment in question is ethically unacceptable and should be legally proscribed (examples include human reproductive cloning and female genital mutilation).

The problem for the law is that there will be very few cases when there is agreement over the legitimacy of controversial medical practices. There will never be a consensus over whether euthanasia should be legalized, for example, or whether it is legitimate to experiment on embryos. In this chapter, we have focused mainly upon how we might go about discussing these questions. We could, for example, look at the consequences of regulating in one way or another. So, in relation to euthanasia, we could ask whether legalization would, on balance, make life better or worse for sick and vulnerable patients. We could also think about what principles might be at stake, and how the tension between autonomy and non-maleficence should be resolved. It might be important to think about what arguments grounded in human dignity or respect for the sanctity of human life mean in this context, and whether there is a slippery slope that either could, or could not, be contained through regulation. None of these considerations can tell us what to do, however, and undoubtedly most of us will also bring our own values and personal experiences to bear on these questions. In relation to euthanasia, for example, someone with strong religious convictions will be influenced by their faith, and someone who has seen a relative die a protracted and painful death may find that that has shaped their judgement. Our 'gut instincts' will inevitably often provide the starting point for our reasoning process, but it is important to remember that, on their own, there is no reason why anyone else should find them persuasive.

FURTHER READING

Ashcroft, Richard E, Dawson, Angus, Draper, Heather, and McMillan, John R (eds), *Principles of Health Care Ethics*, 2nd edn (Wiley: Chichester, 2007) chs 1, 3, 5, 6, 7, 11.

Beauchamp, Tom L and Childress, James F, *Principles of Biomedical Ethics*, 7th edn (OUP: Oxford, 2013).

Caplan, Arthur L and Arp, Robert (eds), *Contemporary Debates in Bioethics* (Wiley Blackwell: Chichester, 2013).

Herring, Jonathan, *Caring and the Law* (Hart Publishing: Oxford, 2013) ch 3.

Leach Scully, Jackie, 'Disability and Vulnerability: On Bodies, Dependence, and Power' in Catriona Mackenzie, Wendy Rogers, and Susan Dodds (eds) *Vulnerability: New Essays in Ethics and Feminist Philosophy* (OUP, 2014).

O'Neill, Onora, *Autonomy and Trust in Bioethics* (CUP: Cambridge, 2002).

Rogers, Wendy, Mackenzie, Catriona, and Dodds, Susan, 'Why bioethics needs a concept of vulnerability' (2012) 5 International Journal of Feminist Approaches to Bioethics 11–38.

2

THE PROVISION OF HEALTHCARE SERVICES: THE NHS, RESOURCE ALLOCATION, AND PUBLIC HEALTH

CENTRAL ISSUES

1. The National Health Service (NHS) was set up in 1948 in order to provide health care for everyone in the UK, free at the point of use and funded from general taxation. Overall responsibility for the delivery of NHS services in England lies with NHS England (health is a devolved matter, so in Wales, Scotland and Northern Ireland responsibility lies with NHS Wales, NHS Scotland and Health and Social Care in Northern Ireland), with most commissioning devolved to Clinical Commissioning Groups (or local health boards in Wales and Scotland, and Health and Social Services Boards in Northern Ireland). Oversight is provided by several bodies including the Care Quality Commission and NHS Improvement.

2. Scarce resources are a fact of life in the NHS, and so one of the most important questions it faces is how to allocate those resources fairly. Should the priority be clinical need or maximizing health gains, for example, and is it ever acceptable to take into account the

patient's responsibility for her ill health, her age, or public opinion?

3. In England and Wales, the National Institute for Health and Care Excellence (NICE) was set up in order to evaluate whether treatments are cost-effective enough to justify NHS provision (in Scotland, a similar task is performed by the Scottish Medicines Consortium).

4. If denied treatment, a patient can make an 'individual funding request' (IFR). Funding decisions are also judicially reviewable. Historically, the judiciary was reluctant to interfere with decisions about the allocation of scarce resources, but more recently, patients have had some success in challenging refusals of IFRs.

5. Patients might wish to seek treatment abroad, and Brexit will affect patients' right to do this within the EU. Non-EU citizens who are receiving care in the UK have attempted to resist deportation on the grounds that depriving them of medical treatment might amount

to inhuman and degrading treatment. These claims have seldom succeeded.

6. Public Health England has responsibility for the promotion of public health. Public health is not confined to the provision of medical treatment, but includes all organized measures to prevent disease, promote health, and prolong life in the population as a whole. It involves the recognition that the public's health is improved not just by medical treatment, but also through effective anti-tobacco and anti-obesity policies, and by tackling the social determinants of health.

1 INTRODUCTION

In this chapter we examine three complex and politically contentious questions. First, we look at how the National Health Service (NHS) is organized; secondly, we consider how resource allocation, or rationing, takes place within the NHS; thirdly, we examine the use of the law to promote public health.

Politicians know that the British public is very attached to the NHS. A former Chancellor of the Exchequer, Nigel Lawson, once said that 'the National Health Service is the closest thing the English have to a religion';[1] and, according to a 2014 Ipsos Mori poll, 52 per cent of the public said that the NHS was what made them most proud to be British (above the royal family at 33 per cent and the BBC at 22 per cent).[2] Successive governments have increased spending on the NHS, but it nevertheless faces a funding crisis. Given an ageing population, and the availability of more and better treatments, the NHS needs substantial increases in spending each year just in order to stand still. In addition, a failure to invest properly in social care increases costs within the NHS, by making it harder to discharge elderly and infirm patients from hospital.[3] Indeed the House of Lords Select Committee on the Long-term Sustainability of the NHS has identified pressures in social care as the NHS's 'greatest external threat':

> The pressures facing social care mean that more people who would otherwise be cared for in the community, in residential homes or in their own home are now presenting in NHS settings, often at GP surgeries or at A&E departments. The adverse impact on the functioning of acute services in hospitals is increasingly serious.[4]

Since the NHS first started treating patients in 1948, demand for healthcare services has outstripped the NHS's capacity to supply them. If 'tragic choices' are unavoidable,[5] it is important to ensure that they are taken fairly and lawfully. We therefore consider how we might distinguish between fair and unfair ways to allocate scarce resources.

---

[1] *The View from Number Eleven* (Doubleday: London, 1992).
[2] Iain Dale, *The NHS: Things that Need to be Said* (Elliott and Thompson: London, 2015), viii.
[3] The King's Fund, *Quarterly Monitoring Report* (October 2015).
[4] HL Paper 151, *The Long-term Sustainability of the NHS and Adult Social Care*, Report of Session 2016–17, para 197.
[5] Guido Calabresi, *Tragic Choices* (WW Norton & Co, 1978).

Finally, it is worth remembering that providing healthcare services is only one way to promote the health of the population as a whole. A focus on the public's health might instead emphasize the importance of preventative measures, such as anti-tobacco policies, and lead to concern about the socioeconomic determinants of health. There is a weight of evidence that poverty and inequality are bad for people's health, so concern for public health might extend far beyond what the NHS can achieve, and look instead at the social and economic drivers of ill health.

2 THE MODERN NHS

After the end of the Second World War, a Labour government was elected under Clement Attlee which promised to expand welfare provision, and in particular to introduce a national health service. The NHS was set up by the National Health Service Act 1946, and it started treating patients two years later. There continues to be strong public support for the idea of a publicly run healthcare system which is free at the point of use, and which provides everyone with good quality care.

As a result of devolution, it no longer makes sense to talk about a UK-wide NHS. Instead, health is a devolved matter, and the Scottish parliament and Welsh and Northern Irish assemblies now take their own decisions about funding and the organization of services. This book will focus on the English NHS, but questions of scarcity and the need for rationing are relevant throughout the UK.

In England, the NHS Constitution sets out patients' rights and responsibilities within the NHS. In its latest version, it affirms the principle of a comprehensive health service, free at the point of use, while also stressing the need to make fair and efficient use of finite resources.

The NHS Constitution for England[6]

Principles

1. The NHS provides a comprehensive service, available to all

It is available to all irrespective of gender, race, disability, age, sexual orientation, religion, belief, gender reassignment, pregnancy and maternity or marital or civil partnership status. The service is designed to improve, prevent, diagnose and treat both physical and mental health problems with equal regard. It has a duty to each and every individual that it serves and must respect their human rights. At the same time, it has a wider social duty to promote equality through the services it provides and to pay particular attention to groups or sections of society where improvements in health and life expectancy are not keeping pace with the rest of the population.

2. Access to NHS services is based on clinical need, not an individual's ability to pay

NHS services are free of charge, except in limited circumstances sanctioned by Parliament
. . .

---

[6] Department of Health and Social Care, 'The NHS Constitution for England' (DHSC: London, 2015).

6. The NHS is committed to providing best value for taxpayers' money

It is committed to providing the most effective, fair and sustainable use of finite resources. Public funds for healthcare will be devoted solely to the benefit of the people that the NHS serves.

(a) SCARCITY

Before the NHS was set up, it had been thought that providing the whole population with free and comprehensive health care, in addition to the other social services which were to be provided through the welfare state, might improve the nation's health, and thus lead to a diminishing demand for healthcare services. As David Hunter explains:

the NHS was founded on a fallacy: that there was a finite amount of ill-health in the population which, once removed, would result in the maintenance of health and the provision of health care becoming cheaper as the need for it dropped off. What has happened is that success in health care has resulted in people living longer potentially to be ill more often and therefore consume more resources.[7]

As soon as the NHS started treating patients, it became obvious that the assumption that the costs of care would fall was hopelessly naïve. Three years after the NHS was set up, prescription charges were introduced, leading to the resignation of Aneurin Bevan, the chief architect of the NHS and the first Secretary of State for Health.

Since 1948, successive governments have increased spending on the NHS at above the rate of inflation. Despite this, for a number of reasons there is likely to be continued pressure on stretched NHS resources.

First, life expectancy has increased dramatically since the 1940s, but our success in extending the average lifespan has not been accompanied by the same level of success in reducing the infirmity and morbidity associated with ageing. Extending the period of old age increases demand for health services. It is also the very elderly sector of the population which is growing most rapidly. In 2018, the Darzi report set out the problem the NHS faces between now and 2030:

The number of people over 65 will increase by 33 per cent – compared to a mere 2 per cent increase in the number of working age adults – while the number of over 85s will nearly double over the same time period. This is a sign of success which should be celebrated, but it will also drive a rising tide of chronic illness – including cancers, mental illness and dementia – which will require a significant shift in the model of care in the NHS and social care system.[8]

Secondly, technological and scientific progress has led to the availability of more sophisticated and expensive treatments for a wide variety of conditions. Not only are more options available, but the numbers of us who qualify as patients has also increased with the emergence of

---

[7] *Desperately Seeking Solutions: Rationing Health Care* (Longman: London, 1997) 20.
[8] Institute for Public Policy Research, *Better health and care for all: A 10-point plan for the 2020s The final report of the Lord Darzi Review of Health and Care* (IPPR, 2018).

treatments for some of the normal consequences of ageing, like the menopause, and for risk factors, such as high cholesterol and high blood pressure. Over the last 10 years, the number of NHS prescription items dispensed in the community has increased by nearly 50 per cent, to 1.1 billion per year.[9]

Thirdly, patients' expectations have risen dramatically. Most of the UK's population has been able to take the NHS's existence, and their right to free, comprehensive health care for granted throughout their lives. We are also becoming less deferential and more demanding. Before seeing a doctor, patients will often have googled their symptoms, and decided what is wrong with them, and what treatment they need.

Fourthly, when a service is provided free of charge, there are fewer constraints on demand than when people have to pay for it 'out of pocket'. With no financial disincentives to seeking medical care, people visit their GP for minor complaints that are overwhelmingly likely to clear up by themselves. Demand for 'free' healthcare services is therefore especially elastic.

Fifthly, as we see in the next chapter, clinical negligence claims represent a significant and increasing drain on NHS funds. In 2017/18, NHS Resolution received 10,673 clinical negligence claims, and paid out almost £2.227 billion in damages and legal fees.[10]

Finally, there is a widespread, although not universally shared, assumption that healthcare resources are inevitably scarce, and hence that rationing is unavoidable. In the next extracts, Alan Maynard adopts this view, and argues that the important task is to ensure that rationing is as fair and transparent as possible, while Ted Schrecker argues that more should be done to interrogate assumptions about scarcity.

Alan Maynard[11]

There are two certainties in life: death and scarcity. A long, good-quality life free of pain, disability and distress from birth to death is the exception rather than the rule. Most people confront morbidity over the life-cycle and demand cures and care which are expensive and often of unproven benefit … The policy issue is therefore not whether, but how, to ration access to health and social care. Society and its political representatives are, however, reluctant to confront this reality … A health service in 'political denial' stunts the development of socially agreed rationing principles, that are openly discussed and accountably applied, and creates a market of special pleading on both the demand (for example, patient advocacy groups) and supply side (for example, the pharmaceutical industry). These are organisations with overlapping goals which result in a single demand: spend more!

Ted Schrecker[12]

The usual axiom in priority-setting using cost-effectiveness analysis is that no matter how high the health budget is, it will never be sufficient to fulfil all demands and therefore priority

---

[9] *Prescriptions Dispensed in the Community, Statistics for England - 2007-2017* (NHS Digital, 2018).

[10] *Annual Report and Accounts 2017-18* (NHS Resolution, 2018).

[11] 'Ethics and health care "underfunding"' (2001) 27 Journal of Medical Ethics 223–7.

[12] 'Priority setting: right answer to a far too narrow question? Comment on "Global developments in priority setting in health"' (2018) 7 International Journal of Health Policy Management 86–8.

setting will always be needed to ensure resources are not wasted on interventions that do not buy much health. The axiom rests on a missing middle premise: that the current budget is the appropriate one. This premise must be interrogated. The presumption that the fiscal constraint imposed by the overall healthcare budget should be taken as given, and subjected neither to ethical nor political analysis, is questionable even under conditions of formal democracy . . .

In setting priorities for their own work [health systems researchers] could do more good, or at least less harm, by 'interrogating scarcity': directing their attention and that of their audiences to the political choices, made domestically and internationally, that mean resources are scarce in some settings, and for some purposes, but not in and for others . . .

A 2015 Nuffield Trust briefing warned flatly that 'the sum of all NICE commissioning guidance for an area would almost certainly be unaffordable'; mainstream academic discussion of the future of the NHS now accepts 'the inevitability of hard choices in healthcare'. Such acceptances come with little scrutiny of the disabling if not homicidal impact of those choices, critique of the political commitments driving them, or acknowledgement that they seldom affect the rich.

In practice, it is important to distinguish between the various different levels at which resource allocation decisions are taken. At the macro level, political choices must be made about how much public money should be spent on the NHS, in the light of competing demands upon the nation's resources. Within the health budget, decisions have to be taken about what treatments the NHS will fund. At a national level, NICE is responsible for determining whether particular treatments are sufficiently cost-effective to justify NHS funding. Clinical commissioning groups operate at the local level to decide which treatments to commission for people in their area.

(b) THE ORGANIZATION OF THE NHS

The NHS has undergone many reorganizations since 1948. In 1991, for example, a purchaser/provider split was introduced in order to give fundholders, such as GPs, a stake in ensuring value for money. Because money would no longer be awarded in block grants, but would instead 'follow the patient', hospitals would effectively have to compete for business. The then Conservative government believed that the injection of competition into the NHS would drive costs down and quality up. Similar motivations were behind the 2012 reforms and the setting up of Clinical Commissioning Groups (CCGs), but, as Lindsay Stirton has explained, in practice it has proved difficult to introduce competition into the health service.

Lindsay Stirton[13]

[S]uccessive reforms of the organisational structure of the NHS have repeatedly aimed towards the same results as earlier ones. For example, the Government's aims in creating NHS Foundation Trusts—including freedom from top-down control, improved responsiveness to patients and local needs, and better management of human resources—were substantially the same as those used to justify the original creation of NHS Trusts. Similarly, the objective of securing GP involvement in commissioning processes has motivated successive rounds of

[13] 'Back to the Future? Lessons on the Pro-Competitive Regulation of Health Services' (2014) 22 Medical Law Review 180–99.

purchasing reform, including the creation of GP fund-holding, their replacement with PCGs/PCTs, the introduction of practice-based commissioning and most recently with the creation of CCGs. Parallels may be drawn with experience in the utilities, where consumers have often shown little interest in 'shopping around' for the best service, and—despite the efforts of regulators to improve standardised provision of information—arguably lack the knowledge to choose between different packages, which are in any case often rapidly changing ... [A] twenty-year perspective shows just how difficult it is to establish workable competition in health services.

The Private Finance Initiative (PFI), first introduced in the early 1990s, did not just apply to hospitals, but its after-effects have been especially significant within the NHS. PFI involved private capital being used to fund large public projects, such as hospitals, with the buildings then being leased back to the NHS, along with contracts for support services, for 25 or 30 years. Politicians' enthusiasm for PFI is easy to understand: new hospitals (with their obvious appeal to voters) could be built without using or borrowing public money. The downside, of course, was that this was not free money and it has saddled the NHS with considerable debts.

The most recent reorganization started in 2010 with the publication of a White Paper, *Equity and Excellence: Liberating the NHS,* by the then Secretary of State for Health, Andrew Lansley. Despite concerted opposition, this resulted in the Health and Social Care Act 2012 and changes that were, according to the then NHS Chief Executive, David Nicholson, 'so big you can see them from space'.[14]

The activities of the NHS can be split into three: commissioning services, providing them, and monitoring their provision. Commissioning is overseen by NHS England. Set up in 2012, it is responsible for allocating resources to all 195 CCGs; overseeing the activities of CCGs; commissioning directly commissioned services; and providing national leadership. The provision of health care throughout the NHS is then monitored by several bodies. The Care Quality Commission inspects services and reports on their quality. NHS Improvement brings together patient safety monitoring systems with financial regulation in order to support providers of NHS care and hold them to account.

One of the dangers of this fragmentation of responsibilities is that it can sometimes be unclear which body is responsible for which service. This happened in relation to pre-exposure prophylaxis (PrEP) for HIV. Although NHS England is responsible for 'services for patients infected with HIV,'[15] PrEP is taken by people who are not infected with HIV in order to minimize the risk of infection in the future. NHS England therefore argued it was not responsible for commissioning, and paying for, the provision of PrEP on the NHS. In *R (on the Application of National Aids Trust) v NHS England and others,*[16] the Court of Appeal rejected this 'altogether too technical and legalistic' interpretation of the rules:

The whole thrust of the Regulations is that local authorities are not to be responsible for HIV patients but rather that NHS England is to be responsible for them. If there is medication that can prevent susceptible persons from becoming infected and it is desirable that such medication be administered to reduce the overall bill for HIV services, NHS England has the power to commission such medication.

---

[14] Quoted in Chris Ham et al, *The NHS under a coalition government—part one: NHS reform* (King's Fund, 2015).

[15] The National Health Service Commissioning Board and Clinical Commissioning Groups (Responsibilities and Standing Rules) Regulations 2012.

[16] [2016] EWCA Civ 1100.

(1) Clinical Commissioning Groups

In 2018–19, CCGs received £75.6 billion of NHS England's total budget of £113 billion. CCGs are responsible for commissioning most healthcare services in their areas, including hospital and community-based health care. All GP practices are members of CCGs. Initially there were 211 CCGs; mergers mean that there are now 195. CCGs are overseen and held to account by NHS England, which also has responsibility for commissioning specialist services that can only be provided efficiently and effectively at national or regional level.

CCGs do not have to use NHS providers, and can instead commission services from 'third sector' (ie charitable) or private providers. Indeed section 75 of the Health and Social Care Act 2012, and Regulations made under it,[17] are specifically intended to prevent anti-competitive practices, so that NHS services do not have 'preferred provider' status. Instead the private sector must be allowed to compete against NHS providers. Although private providers continue to be responsible for a small proportion of NHS services, as John Appleby explains, the rate of growth is significant.

John Appleby[18]

Over the seven years since 2006–7, the proportion of NHS patients treated by non-NHS providers has risen from around 0.5% (73 000) to 2.6% (471 000) of all inpatient episodes ... For outpatient care, the proportion treated by non-NHS providers has risen faster—from 0.2% (123 000) to 5.5% (4.5 million) ... If rates of growth since 2006–7 continue over the next 20 years, non-NHS providers could account for one in five of all outpatient attendances and approaching one in 10 inpatient episodes paid for by the NHS.

It is by no means clear that competition from alternative providers drives up quality. In their study of all providers of primary care services, Felix Greaves et al found that alternative providers in fact provided a worse standard of care on almost all measures.

Felix Greaves et al[19]

Alternative Provider of Medical Services practices performed significantly worse than [traditional GP] practices on 13 of the 17 quality indicators examined in every study year, including all measures of clinical quality ...

The results suggest that alternative providers have not been widely contracted to deliver primary care services, making up only 4% of practices since 2004 ... Practices run by alternative providers supplied consistently worse quality of care than traditional practices—across a broad range of indicators ... [O]ur findings provide little support for the hypothesis that increasing plurality of provision has increased quality of care.

---

[17] National Health Service (Procurement, Patient Choice and Competition) (No 2) Regulations 2013.
[18] 'Paid for by the NHS, treated privately' (2015) 350 British Medical Journal h3109.
[19] 'Performance of new alternative providers of primary care services in England: an observational study' (2015) 108 Journal of the Royal Society of Medicine 171–83.

The 2018 Darzi report was blunt that it is time to end this 'failed experiment' with quasi-markets in healthcare.

Lord Darzi[20]

The health and care system has grown in complexity over the past 70 years, becoming ever more fragmented. This has been greatly exacerbated by the Health and Social Care Act 2012. The 2012 reforms ran counter to international evidence and have not been replicated by any other health system anywhere in the world . . .

At the national level, the 2012 reforms fragmented the leadership functions, with roles split between the Department of Health, NHS England, Health Education England, Public Health England, Monitor and NHS Trust Development Authority (now NHS Improvement), and the Care Quality Commission. By creating a separate institution for each health system function, the 2012 Act has resulted in confusion at individual provider level, with competing priorities and instructions.

In some respects, the 2012 Act was merely the culmination of a 30-year experiment with quasi-markets that began with the 1991 introduction of the internal market . . .

There is some very limited – and highly contested evidence – that the increase in competition between 2000–10 led to a small improvement in quality and efficiency while other studies have found no – or even negative – effects. Likewise, the evidence that the provider commissioner split has driven a new model of more integrated and community focused care is weak: it is exactly because it has failed to do this that we are still trying to reform the health and care service today. Meanwhile, we have significant evidence that the transaction costs of the market are high. Putting services out to tender usually results in NHS providers continuing to provide services; however, the procurement process creates significant direct (for example, the cost of running the process, staffing commissioners) and indirect costs (for example, changeover costs, staff uncertainty, disruption). The reality is that the commissioning arrangements in the NHS appear to subtract value rather than to add value. It is time to end what is very clearly a failed experiment by ending compulsory competitive tendering for services.

The intention behind the Health and Social Care Act 2012 was to delegate more responsibility for rationing decisions to doctors, though it is noteworthy that GPs represented fewer than half of the members of the new CCGs that took on responsibility for commissioning from April 2013.

Nonetheless, GPs undoubtedly have more responsibility over the NHS budget than before. If GPs have financial interests in private providers of care, there may be a risk of perceived or actual conflicts of interest. For example, a CCG might be deciding which hospital should be commissioned to provide routine hip replacement surgery while members of that CCG have a financial interest in a local private provider of hip replacement surgery. The risks of conflicts of interest became even more acute in 2015 when it became possible for CCGs to choose to take on responsibility for commissioning primary care services.

NHS Improvement has the power to ensure that commissioners manage conflicts of interest and that particular interests do not influence their decision-making.[21] Ensuring that

---

[20] *Better health and care for all: A 10-point plan for the 2020s* The final report of the Lord Darzi Review of Health and Care (Institute for Public Policy Research, 2018).

[21] Department of Health, *Securing Best Value for NHS Patients: Requirements for Commissioners to Adhere to Good Procurement Practice and Protect Patient Choice* (DH: London, 2012).

this never happens will be difficult, however, given how common these sorts of financial interests are. In 2015, the National Audit Office investigated conflicts of interests in CCGs, and how they are managed.

National Audit Office[22]

Some 1,300 (41%) of clinical commissioning group (CCG) governing body members in position at the time of our analysis in 2014–15 were also GPs, who may, potentially, have made decisions about local health services and have been paid by their CCG for providing them. Non-GP commissioners may also have potential conflicts of interest, for example where have they have financial or other interests in organisations providing locally commissioned health services …

We could not always assess from publicly available information how CCGs had managed specific conflicts of interest, which limits local transparency. In the 75 instances of potential or actual conflicts we found from our sample of governing body minutes, the level of detail given about the conflict and how it had been managed varied. In 14 cases the information provided was insufficient for us to assess how the CCG managed the conflict … Where CCGs reported information about their controls for managing risks of conflicts of interest, it showed the adequacy of those controls had varied.

A further difficulty that may result from greater GP involvement in commissioning is that doctors are at the sharp end of rationing decisions, unlike politicians or health service managers. It is not easy for a GP to tell her patients that effective treatment is available, but that it will not be provided because the CCG of which she is a member has decided that it is too expensive. Active involvement in rationing, which inevitably means that some patients are denied care because it is too expensive, may also be at odds with the medical profession's primary ethical responsibility to make the health of each patient her first concern; as van Delden et al have put it: 'choosing between patients is not their job'.[23]

On the other hand, it could be argued that the 'gate-keeping' role which has long been played by GPs within the NHS is itself a form of rationing. A person's GP is normally their first point of contact when they feel unwell. If the patient's condition is potentially serious, or requires expert attention, the GP will refer her to an appropriate specialist, usually in a local hospital. Specialist services are therefore only provided to patients whose need for them has been vetted first by their GP, rather than being clogged up by everyone who thinks that they might benefit from seeing a consultant. But, as Barbara McPake et al explain, 'the mechanism works imperfectly, general practitioners have widely varying rates of referral and large numbers of patients directly attend Accident and Emergency departments for minor complaints that could be dealt with by the GP'.[24]

In the UK, doctors have seldom explicitly acknowledged that they are rationing medical treatment, and instead cost–benefit considerations have tended to be absorbed within their clinical discretion. If a patient is suffering from symptoms which are likely to be caused by a minor complaint, but there is a remote chance that there might be something seriously wrong,

---

[22] National Audit Office, *Managing conflicts of interest in NHS clinical commissioning groups* (NAO, 2015).

[23] J JM van Delden, A M Vrakking, A van der Heide, and P J van der Maas, 'Medical decision making in scarcity situations' (2004) 30 Journal of Medical Ethics 207–11.

[24] Barbara McPake, Lilani Kumaranayake, and Charles Normand, *Health Economics: An International Perspective* (Routledge: London, 2002) 202.

doctors will often adopt a 'wait and see' approach: the patient will be asked to return in a week or two if their symptoms have not improved, even though there is a very small chance that they might benefit from undergoing expensive investigative procedures immediately. Few doctors would see this as rationing, but, as Raanan Gillon has explained:

> If one were to take thoroughly to heart the idea that as curative doctors we should never allow concern for cost to others to deflect us from doing whatever we could to benefit our patients, then diagnostic services would be overwhelmed as we tested for rare but possible problems.[25]

(2) Privatization?

In addition to enabling private providers to compete for NHS business, section 165 of the Health and Social Care Act 2012 removed the 'private patient income cap', which had previously limited the proportion of private treatment which could be undertaken by Foundation Trusts to two per cent. Now up to 49 per cent of an NHS Foundation Trust's income can come from treating private patients. This gives some NHS hospitals, especially large specialist hospitals in London, the option of increasing their revenue through expanding their provision of treatment for private patients. The Royal Marsden, for example, earns more than £90 million per year from private patients, 45 per cent of its total revenue.[26] District hospitals do not have the same earning potential. Critics have also been concerned that the expansion of private care within NHS hospitals might mean that NHS patients become second-class citizens within the NHS.[27]

In their review of the reforms effected by the Health and Social Care Act, the King's Fund has concluded that they have not resulted in the privatization of the NHS, as some have argued. Nevertheless, the King's Fund found that their complexity, and the fragmentation of structures that has resulted, have been profoundly damaging to the NHS.

The King's Fund[28]

> Historians will not be kind in their assessment of the coalition government's record on NHS reform ... [T]he reforms have certainly resulted in greater marketisation in the NHS, but claims of mass privatisation were and are exaggerated. Private providers do play a part in providing care to NHS patients, as they have always done, and their share of provision of community and mental health services has somewhat increased. Notwithstanding this, NHS providers continue to deliver the vast majority of care to NHS patients, especially in acute hospital services, and there is little evidence that this will change any time soon ...
>
> Arguments about privatisation distract from the much more important and damaging impacts of the reforms on how the NHS is organised and the ability of its leaders to deal with rapidly

---

[25] Raanan Gillon, 'Ethics, Economics and General Practice' in Gavin Mooney and Alistair McGuire (eds), *Medical Ethics and Economics in Health Care* (OUP: Oxford, 1988) 114–34, 128.

[26] Andrew Gilligan, 'NHS in dash for private cash' Sunday Times, 1 January 2017.

[27] John Lister, 'Breaking the Public Trust' in Jacky Davis and Raymond Tallis (eds), *NHS SOS* (Oneworld: London, 2013) 17–37.

[28] Chris Ham et al, *The NHS under a coalition government—part one: NHS reform* (King's Fund, 2015).

growing financial and service pressures. By taking three years to dismantle the old structures and reassemble them into new ones, the government took scarce time and expertise away from efforts to address these pressures. Although it is not possible to demonstrate a causal relationship with NHS performance, it seems likely that the massive organisational changes that resulted from the reforms contributed to widespread financial distress and failure to hit key targets for patient care.

(3) Brexit

At the time of writing, the terms of the withdrawal deal for exiting the EU are unclear, but it seems likely that Brexit will add to the pressures on the NHS. In particular, there are concerns about the supply of medicines, and, as Tamara Hervey and Sarah McCloskey explain, about the sustainability of the workforce.

Tamara Hervey and Sarah McCloskey[29]

Approximately 200,000 EU27 nationals work in the wider health and care sectors—about 5% of the total workforce. EU27 staff are pivotal to the operation of the NHS, especially in London, the South East of England and Northern Ireland.

The UK has never trained enough doctors for its own needs—some 28,000 doctors are non-UK nationals, around a quarter of the total. NHS England alone depends on some 11,000 doctors from the EU27, which amount to about 10% of all doctors. Add in the further 20,000 NHS England nurses and around 100,000 social care staff from the EU27 and the sheer scale of reliance on EU migrant workers becomes clear.

In anticipation of a 'Brexit effect', the NHS has already invited bids for a £100 million contract to recruit overseas doctors into general practice. And this in a context in which the NHS already has many unfilled posts. Restrictive rules on recruiting non-EU nationals are already causing problems for the NHS, and extending these to EU nationals will aggravate the situation.

The uncertainty posed by the Brexit negotiations to date has already affected staffing levels: the Royal College of Nursing reported a 92% drop in registrations of nurses from the EU27 in England in March 2017, and attributed this, at least in part, to 'the failure of the government to provide EU nationals in the UK with any security about their future'. . . .

[P]otential threats to NHS staffing levels go beyond immediate concerns about immigration. Decisions about future regulatory alignment in services will determine whether the qualifications of medical professionals will continue to be mutually recognised between the UK and the EU27.

3 DIFFERENT RATIONING STRATEGIES

Before we consider the role of the National Institute for Health and Care Excellence in making rationing decisions, we first examine different ways in which rationing might be carried out.

---

[29] 'Staff' in *Brexit and the NHS* (The UK in a Changing Europe, 2018).

(a) FROM IMPLICIT TO EXPLICIT RATIONING

In the NHS's first few decades, patients tended to assume that decisions about their treatment were taken in their best interests, and were unaffected by cost considerations. Rationing was, as Keith Syrett explains, implicit rather than explicit.

Keith Syrett[30]

[F]or many years, rationing in the NHS was not a matter of significant political or public debate. This was in part because lower expectations in the early years of the Service led to acceptance that deficiencies in provision were simply a fact of life. More significantly, most rationing took place under cover of clinical judgment: that is, it was *implicit*, in that 'the reasoning involved [was] not clearly stated to anyone except . . . the person making the decision'. Medical professionals effectively 'converted' political decisions on resource allocation into clinical decisions about treatment by 'internalising' resource limits and providing justification for denial on medical grounds by portraying the decision as optimal or routine in the specific circumstances. Suspicion that such decisions were in reality dictated by resource considerations tended to be minimal because of the existence of high levels of trust between doctors and patients, premised upon the belief that physicians possessed both expertise and access to all medical resources necessary for effective care and that they would act as dedicated patient advocates in attempting to secure these.

Explicit rationing, in contrast, involves being frank with patients that treatment will not be provided because it is too expensive. Because this is likely to make patients upset and angry, there are those who have argued that implicit rationing is 'more conducive to stable social relations and a lower level of conflict'.[31] Implicit rationing works, according to David Mechanic, 'because patients trust that doctors are their agents and have their interests at heart'.[32]

Whatever its downsides, most people now accept that explicit rationing should displace the 'benign deceit' of the past.[33] The existence of an effective treatment which the NHS will not fund is, for many patients, important and relevant information. If you know that potentially effective treatment has been withheld, you might try to pay for it yourself, or seek to challenge the decision.

It could also be argued that the public is now so well informed about the availability of different treatment options, that 'camouflaging' rationing decisions as clinical judgement is no longer an option. As James Sabin has put it: 'personal computers and the internet drive the nails into the coffin of implicit rationing'.[34]

Transparency about rationing facilitates consistency and public accountability,[35] or what Norman Daniels and James Sabin have referred to as 'accountability for reasonableness'.[36]

---

[30] 'Impotence or Importance? Judicial Review in an Era of Explicit NHS Rationing' (2004) 67 Modern Law Review 289–304.

[31] David Mechanic, 'Dilemmas in rationing health care services: the case for implicit rationing' (1995) 310 British Medical Journal 1655–9.

[32] Ibid.   [33] Bill New and Julian LeGrand, *Rationing in the NHS* (King's Fund, 1996) 24.

[34] 'Fairness as a Problem of Love and the Heart: A Clinician's Perspective on Priority Setting' in Angela Coulter and Chris Ham (eds), *The Global Challenge of Healthcare Rationing* (Open UP: Buckingham, 2000) 117–22.

[35] Keith Syrett, *Law, Legitimacy and the Rationing of Health Care* (CUP: Cambridge, 2007) 62–3.

[36] Norman Daniels and James E Sabin, *Setting Limits Fairly—Can We Learn to Share Medical Resources?* (OUP: Oxford, 2000).

According to Daniels and Sabin, there are four requirements for reasonable public decision-making:

- Publicity: decisions, and the grounds for making them, must be transparent and open.
- Relevance: decisions must be based upon relevant criteria.
- Revision and appeals: there must be a process for challenging decisions, and the possibility of their subsequent revision.
- Enforcement: there must be regulation to ensure compliance with these criteria.[37]

The theory is that, if a rationing decision was based on relevant criteria and sound evidence, and if affected patients have a right of challenge, decisions which are always going to be unpopular may nevertheless secure some level of public legitimacy and social acceptability.

Daniels and Sabin's model is not without its critics, however.[38] It could be argued that what counts as a relevant criterion is not just a procedural matter. For example, the decision to take into account a person's responsibility for her own ill health is controversial. Critics have also suggested that Daniels and Sabin should add public participation as a prerequisite of a fair rationing process.[39]

(b) DIFFERENT RATIONING STRATEGIES

The concept of triage (from the French verb *trier*: to sort) emerged on the battlefields of the First World War, when there were insufficient resources to treat every injured soldier. Battlefield triage involves deciding who to treat, based upon both the severity of their injuries and how quickly they might be able to return to active service. If the NHS was overwhelmed with a serious flu pandemic—which might infect more than half of the population—choices akin to battlefield triage might have to be made. Who should have priority for the first doses of the flu vaccine, for example: the nurse who would then be able to care for others, or the sewerage worker who can ensure that the whole population has access to clean water? Although such choices are inevitably difficult, Loren Lomasky points out that decisions taken *in extremis*, when there is little time for reflection, may be less 'dreadful' than the rational, considered choice to treat one patient at the expense of another.

Loren E Lomasky[40]

Two classic examples of triage are the dangerously overloaded lifeboat and the harried medic patching up the wounded on a battlefield. Whatever is done, some salvageable lives will be forfeited. The dreadfulness of these choices though is somewhat softened by the urgency of a crisis: action must be immediate and there is little luxury for reflective deliberation. If called upon to justify his actions, an agent could plead that he was reacting instinctively to the needs of the moment.

Contemporary medical technology is responsible for triage situations of a rather different character. A mechanism is devised that is effective against some previously untreatable condition. Unfortunately, only a small percentage of those afflicted can receive treatment. Who shall

---

[37] Ibid.
[38] Alex Friedman, 'Beyond accountability for reasonableness' (2008) 22 Bioethics 101–12.
[39] Ibid.
[40] 'Medical progress and national health care' (1980) 10 Philosophy and Public Affairs 65–88.

be allowed to live? Here decision-makers are dealing with a series of events predictable well in advance. Not enmeshed in a precipitously developing crisis, they are privileged to assume the role of detached administrator. There is, however, a price to be paid for this relative ease: whatever standards are developed and employed are subject to close scrutiny. Those disfavoured in the selection process are perfectly entitled to ask why . . .

Triage is never unproblematic, but on what basis could a creature of the state adopt any principle of selection? Whoever is excluded can justifiably complain that he is thereby being disadvantaged by the very institution whose special duty is to extend equal protection to all persons.

In the following sections, we examine different criteria that could plausibly be used to ration healthcare services. We might agree that resources should be allocated fairly, but this just begs the question: what do we mean by fair? Do we treat people fairly when we treat them equally? Or should priority always be given to those in the greatest need? Ought we to ensure that resources are allocated where they will do most good, using cost-effectiveness analysis? We could choose to take an individual's responsibility for her own ill health into account; or her social value, or we could opt for a straightforward free market, in which those who can spend the most have access to the best standard of care. In practice, most people would probably advocate a mixed rationing system, in which a number of different factors are taken into account: for example, an approach based upon the cost-effectiveness of treatment might be supplemented by additional criteria, such as the urgency of clinical need.

Before we assess potentially fair rationing criteria, it is worth pointing out that some obviously unfair grounds for distinguishing between patients might nevertheless carry some weight in practice. First, while it would clearly be unethical to take into account the patient's likeability, in practice doctors are human beings capable of feeling compassion for one patient and exasperation with another. It is probably impossible to guarantee that healthcare professionals are never prompted to do more for a patient out of personal sympathy.

Secondly, some patients are simply more demanding and assertive than others. A patient who insists upon a second opinion, or who repeatedly telephones a consultant's secretary, may receivecare that other patients might not have the confidence or the knowledge to seek out. John Butler interviewed healthcare professionals about their attitudes to rationing, and concern was expressed about patients' uneven ability to exert pressure upon healthcare resources.

John Butler[41]

The health visitor was clear about the injustice that could result from rationing by inaccessibility, in which the astute and the persistent were rewarded at the expense of those who lacked the know-how to seek out what they wanted. Those who are put off, she said, will not be the better-educated middle-class families, they will be the poorer families who are under-educated and inarticulate . . .

The surgeon, too, expressed his moral concern at the potential for social bias in the innate responsiveness of the service to the pressure exerted upon it by patients. Those who 'push and shove a bit' will often get the best treatment, but they will not be a cross-section of all those waiting to be seen. He recognized it as wrong (albeit, perhaps, unavoidable) that a class bias will ensue through which cases may not always be seen in the order of their clinical

[41] *The Ethics of Health Care Rationing: Principles and Practices* (Cassell: London, 1999) 230.

urgency. It was the replacement of need by pressure as the determinant of access to secondary care that he saw as wrong.

(1) Equality

As Amy Gutmann explains, equality of access means that everyone with an equivalent health need should have equivalent access to care.

Amy Gutmann[42]

A principle of equal access to health care demands that every person who shares the same type and degree of health need must be given an equally effective chance of receiving appropriate treatment of equal quality so long as that treatment is available to anyone ... The principle requires that if anyone within a society has an opportunity to receive a service or good that satisfies a health need, then everyone who shares the same type and degree of health need must be given an equally effective chance of receiving that service or good.

Equal access also places limits upon the market freedoms of some individuals, especially, but not exclusively, the richest members of society. The principle does not permit the purchase of health care to which other similarly needy people do not have effective access ... Thus, the rigorous implementation of equal access to health care would prevent rich people from spending their extra income for preferred medical services, if those services were not equally accessible to the poor.

In practice, on its own, equality does not tell us very much about how to allocate scarce resources. Instead, it supplements other rationing criteria, such as need or cost-effectiveness, by ensuring that these are employed consistently between patients in order to avoid arbitrary and unfair distribution of resources. As Larry S Temkin explains, because health is so central to our ability to lead a flourishing life, concern for equality might also lead us to give particular priority to the least healthy and/or least well off.

Larry S Temkin[43]

We don't merely recognize the sad but inevitable truth that some people are in poor health or receive little or substandard health care and see the pressing need to address the situation; we rankle at the further fact that there is so much undeserved inequality in the distribution of health states and health care. For many, the situation is not merely unfortunate: it is terribly unfair, and this provides significant additional force to the legitimate claims of many living in poor health ...

Good health isn't *everything*, but it is a *lot*. Freedom from debilitating illness is more than a necessary precondition to a worthwhile human existence. Arguably, good physical and psychological health constitute a large part of what makes a human life worth living.

---

[42] 'For and against equal access to health care' (1981) 59 Milbank Memorial Fund Quarterly/Health and Society 542–60, reprinted in Gregory Pence (ed), *Classic Works in Medical Ethics* (McGraw Hill: Boston, MA, 1998) 367–8.

[43] 'Inequality and Health' in Nir Eyal et al (eds), *Inequalities in Health: Concepts, Measures, and Ethics* (OUP: Oxford, 2013) 13–26.

(2) Need

At first sight, distributing NHS resources according to need might appear attractively fair and simple. Needs, after all, have much greater moral force than wants or desires. But, as Richard Lamm has put it, 'Medical "need" is an infinitely expandable concept. We need what is available, and in a creative and inventive society such as our own, there is no end to what we can do to treat ageing bodies.'[44]

Need could also only operate as a rationing criterion if we were able to construct a hierarchy of needs, so that we could tell whether one patient's need was greater or less than another's. Someone whose life is in danger clearly 'needs' treatment more than someone who will survive without treatment, and so it might be argued that life-saving treatment should always be our first priority. However, this would ignore the question of whether the person could actually benefit from treatment. For example, the life of a patient who is in a permanent vegetative state can be preserved—at enormous cost—for many years. The fact that this sort of treatment will prolong life does not necessarily mean that it should take priority over palliative care, which is not life-extending, but which benefits dying patients by relieving their pain and distress.

Norman Daniels has applied John Rawls's theory of justice to the distribution of health care. Daniels argues that health care is of special importance, and should be regarded as a primary social good, because of its capacity to ensure fair equality of opportunity. Disease and infirmity interfere with a person's range of opportunities. In order to rectify the resulting inequality, priority should be given to those needs which most interfere with 'normal species functioning'. When deciding between competing needs, Daniels argues that we can rank them according to the extent to which normal species function is impaired.

Norman Daniels[45]

> What emerges here is the suggestion that we use impairment of the normal opportunity range as a fairly crude measure of the relative importance of health-care needs at the macro level. In general, it will be more important to prevent, cure, or compensate for those disease conditions which involve a greater curtailment of normal opportunity range.

For example, someone with a broken hip will generally have their normal opportunity range restricted more than someone with a disfiguring scar, and hence we might decide that funding hip replacement operations should be a higher priority than cosmetic surgery.

There are, however, several problems with the attempt to prioritize different health needs by the extent to which they interfere with normal species functioning. First, 'normal species functioning' may sound like an objective criterion, but it is quite difficult to pin down. It is normal for our bodies to degenerate with age, but we would not want to make the treatment of elderly patients a low priority on the grounds that some degree of ill health is 'normal' for them. Moreover, since normal species functioning depends in part upon the availability of healthcare services, there may be a degree of circularity in using 'normal functioning' as a criterion for the distribution of health care.

---

[44] Richard D Lamm, 'Rationing of Health Care: Inevitable and Desirable' (1992) 140 University of Pennsylvania Law Review 1511–32.

[45] 'Health-care needs and distributive justice' (1981) 10 Philosophy and Public Affairs 146–79.

Secondly, in practice it would be extremely difficult to construct an objective, population-wide hierarchy of illnesses and disabilities according to their degree of interference with normal species functioning. For some people, such as surgeons or pilots, losing the sight in one eye could have disastrous consequences, for others its impact might be comparatively slight.

Finally, there would have to be exceptions to Daniels's classification in order to accommodate beneficial treatments that do not attempt to 'restore normal species functioning'. Contraception, for example, does not cure or treat anything; in fact, its purpose is to disrupt normal functioning, yet it is considered such a cost-effective public good that it has always been exempt from the prescription charge.

(3) Maximizing Health Gains

(a) Assessing cost-effectiveness: the QALY

Quality-Adjusted Life Years (QALYs)[46] are an attempt to compare the cost-effectiveness of different treatments objectively so that scarce NHS resources 'do as much good as possible'.[47] The point of QALYs, as Alan Williams explains, is that they not only measure the amount of extra life that a treatment might generate, but also its quality; the assumption being that we should divert resources to treatments which are likely to offer people the longest periods of healthy and active life.

Alan Williams[48]

The essence of a QALY is that it takes a year of healthy life expectancy to be worth 1, but regards a year of unhealthy life expectancy as worth less than 1. Its precise value is lower the worse the quality of life of the unhealthy person (which is what the 'quality adjusted' bit is all about). If being dead is worth zero, it is, in principle, possible for a QALY to be negative, i.e. for the quality of someone's life to be judged worse than being dead.

The general idea is that a beneficial health care activity is one that generates a positive amount of QALYs, and that an efficient health care activity is one where the cost per QALY is as low as it can be. A high priority health care activity is one where the cost-per-QALY is low, and a low priority activity is one where cost-per-QALY is high.

There are a number of stages to the use of QALYs. First, QALYs require us to be able to judge quality of life on a scale ranging from 0 (death) to 1.0 (full health). Next, we multiply patients' life expectancy and quality of life scores, both before and after treatment. The difference between these will be the QALY score. So, for example, let us imagine that, without treatment, a patient with condition A will have two years of life left, and her quality of life is 0.5. Before treatment, the patient's life contains 1 QALY. If treatment X would give her six years with a quality of life of 1.0, post-treatment, her life contains 6 QALYs. The QALY value of treatment

[46] The QALY scale was first developed in the work of Rosser et al in the 1970s. See further R Rosser and VC Watts, 'The measurement of hospital output' (1972) 1 International Journal of Epidemiology 361–8; R Rosser and P Kind, 'A scale of values of states of illness: is there a social consensus?' (1978) 7 International Journal of Epidemiology 347–58.

[47] Alan Williams, 'Economics, QALYs and Medical Ethics: A Health Economist's Perspective' in Souzy Dracopoulou (ed), *Ethics and Values in Health Care Management* (Routledge: London, 1998) 29–37.

[48] 'The value of QALYs' (1985) 94 Health and Social Service Journal 3.

X is therefore 5. The next stage is to calculate the cost per QALY. So let us imagine that treatment X costs £50,000. Since it provides 5 QALYs, the cost per QALY is £10,000. By working out the QALY scores for different treatments, it should be possible to determine which offer the best value for money.

For several reasons, some commentators have challenged the usefulness and fairness of the QALY approach. First, according to the logic of QALYs, the purpose of a health service is to generate the maximum number of quality-adjusted life years at the lowest cost. QALYs therefore assume that society is neutral as to how health benefits are distributed across society, and that it does not matter whether the years of healthy life go to people who are already in good health or to those whose health is poor. In practice most of us would prefer the NHS to fund the treatment of patients with serious conditions, such as cancer and heart disease, in preference to more trivial complaints, such as hay fever or acne, even if these latter treatments are more cost-effective. Our concern is not simply to maximize the aggregate health gain in society at the lowest cost, but rather to ensure that the NHS helps those who are in the greatest need.

Secondly, the emphasis upon maximizing health gains is explicitly utilitarian. QALYs measure units of lifetime, as if they are interchangeable, rather than treating patients as separate individuals who value their own lives, and those of people they love, especially highly. If spending £50,000 on treatment X will enable us to extend patient A's life for five years, while spending £50,000 on treatment Y will only extend patient B's life for one year, it seems clear that treatment X should receive priority over treatment Y. But as John Harris, one of QALYs' most vigorous critics, points out, patient B, who is thereby forced to sacrifice an additional year of life, might not agree.

John Harris[49]

What matters is that the person is not prepared to agree that his interest in continued life is of less value than that of anyone else, nor that that interest necessarily varies with the quality of his life nor with his life expectancy. In short, if a person wants continued existence, then, in my view, his interest in continued existence is entitled to be treated as on a par with that of anyone else.

Simona Giordano explains that while QALYs appear to capture what matters to us—securing the longest life expectancy of the best quality—this is in fact an illusion because 'what matters to people is not "the number of healthy life years the world contains", but the number of healthy years that *they or people they care about* will have'.[50]

Thirdly, it has been suggested that using QALYs to ration treatment will tend to exacerbate existing discrimination against the elderly and the disabled, whose QALY scores are likely to be fairly low because of their reduced life expectancy and/or their lower pre-existing quality of life. People who are unlucky enough to suffer from conditions that are very expensive to treat—and this is usually people with serious illnesses—might fare badly, because the cost per QALY of treating them is likely to be high. This is, in Harris's words, 'a sort of double jeopardy',

[49] 'Double jeopardy and the veil of ignorance—a reply' (1995) 21 Journal of Medical Ethics 151–7, 151.
[50] 'Respect for equality and the treatment of the elderly: declarations of human rights and age-based rationing' (2005) 14 Cambridge Quarterly of Healthcare Ethics 83–92.

whereby people who have already been unlucky enough to be seriously ill or disabled will be further disadvantaged when competing for scarce resources.[51]

John Harris[52]

The ageism of QALY is inescapable, for any calculation of the life-years generated for a particular patient by a particular therapy must be based on the life expectancy of that patient after treatment. The older the patient is when treated, the fewer the life-years that can be achieved by the therapy ... [I]t will usually be more QALY efficient to concentrate on areas of medicine which will inevitably generate more QALYs, neonatal care or paediatrics, for example. And equally, to channel resources away from (or deny them altogether to) areas such as geriatric medicine or terminal care.

This argument has been contested by others, who argue that Harris has overlooked a crucial feature of QALYs, namely, that what is measured is the change in a person's health brought about by an intervention. In order to maximize QALYs, resources should not always be diverted to people whose post-treatment quality of life or life expectancy is greatest, but for whom the QALY gain per pound spent is higher. If I am already fit and healthy, a medical treatment may not alter my QALY score very much, whereas, if my present quality of life is low, my QALY score post-treatment might be much higher. Michael Rawlins and Andrew Dillon—at the time the Chair and CEO of NICE—gave the example of a treatment for osteoporosis, which cost £32,936 per QALY for patients aged 50 years, and £12,191 per QALY for patients aged 70, explaining that 'this occurs because older patients have a greater risk of complications of osteoporosis and thus benefit more'.[53]

Fourthly, the QALY approach may be inconsistent with the principle that people with equal health needs should have equal access to appropriate medical treatment. As Penelope Mullen and Peter Spurgeon explain, if a patient's access to treatment depends upon the costs of treating them, 'systematic discrimination could result against, say, those from ethnic minority groups who require interpreters, those living in poorer housing who might require inpatient stays rather than day surgery and those living in remote, sparsely populated locations'.[54]

Fifthly, when a new treatment is introduced, it may be extremely expensive at first, but its cost may decrease as the technology becomes cheaper, or as the expense of staff training is eliminated. The QALY scale might then discourage innovation in favour of established and currently cheaper treatments, even if there might be cost savings from adopting the new treatment over the longer term.

Sixthly, QALYs assume that it is possible to devise an objective and accurate mechanism for measuring the anticipated length and quality of a person's life. In fact, the medical profession's predictions of life expectancy are unreliable, and speculating about the future quality of a person's life is also inherently uncertain. Treatment outcomes depend upon a wide variety of factors, such as the patient's physical fitness and the quality of aftercare services. Because the

---

[51] 'QALYfying the value of life' (1987) 13 Journal of Medical Ethics 117–23.
[52] 'More and Better Justice' in JM Bell and Susan Mendus (eds), *Philosophy and Medical Welfare* (CUP: Cambridge, 1988) 75–96.
[53] 'NICE discrimination' (2005) 31 Journal of Medical Ethics 683–4.
[54] Penelope Mullen and Peter Spurgeon, *Priority Setting and the Public* (Radcliffe Medical Press: Abingdon, 2000).

QALY calculation is too crude to capture all of the relevant variables, its results will inevitably lack precision.

It could also be argued that it is impossible to reduce such a complex concept as quality of life to a single numerical value between 0 and 1. We would also need to work out who should be charged with making these assessments. Would it be people suffering from the particular illness or disability, or the medical profession, or members of the public? It could be argued that only people who live with a condition know how it affects their quality of life, although if a person has been disabled from birth, it may be difficult for her to judge how life with her disability compares to life without. Doctors and members of the public may be able to speculate about the relative inconvenience or distress caused by a range of disabilities, especially if they have experience of caring for someone with a disabling condition, but they do so from a position of relative ignorance.

Moreover, quality of life judgements are inevitably subjective, whereas QALY scales are supposed to be objective. I might think that depression would be worse than chronic back pain, whereas you might think the opposite. QALY weightings are also arbitrary: they suggest that living for ten years with a quality of life score of 0.9 is equivalent to living for nine years in perfect health. In practice, many of us might prefer a longer life, even if we have to put up with a minor health complaint. At the other extreme, some of us might regard one year of perfect health (1×1), as preferable to spending ten years at death's door (10×0.1), whereas the QALY scale suggests that there is nothing to choose between them.

Using QALYs at the macro level is less problematic, because it would simply involve deciding that treatment X, in general, leads to better patient outcomes, at lower cost, than treatment Y. As John Harris explains, it is at the micro level, when choices have to be made between individual patients, that taking QALYs into account is invidious.

John Harris[55]

There are two ways in which QALYs might be used. One is unexceptionable and useful, and fully in line with the assumptions which give QALYs their plausibility. The other is none of these.

QALYs might be used to determine which of rival therapies to give to a particular patient or which procedure to use to treat a particular condition. Clearly the one generating the most QALYs will be the better bet, both for the patient and for a society with scarce resources ...

But whereas it follows from the fact that given the choice a person would prefer a shorter, healthier life to a longer one of severe discomfort, that the best treatment for that person is the one yielding the most QALYs, it does not follow that treatments yielding more QALYs are preferable to treatments yielding fewer QALYs where different people are to receive the treatments. That is to say, while it follows from the fact (if it is a fact) that I and everyone else would prefer to have, say, one year of healthy life rather than three years of severe discomfort, that we value healthy existence more than uncomfortable existence for ourselves, it does not follow that where the choice is between three years of discomfort for me or immediate death on the one hand, and one year of health for you or immediate death on the other, that I am somehow committed to the judgement that you ought to be saved rather than me.

---

[55] 'QALYfying the value of life' (1987) 13 Journal of Medical Ethics 117–23, 118.

(b) A wide or narrow interpretation of cost-effectiveness?

When health economists engage in cost-effectiveness analysis of medical treatments, they tend to judge 'effectiveness' according to the extent to which a treatment produces a clinical benefit. It would, however, be possible to broaden the scope of these calculations in several ways.

First, it has been estimated that health services affect only about 10 per cent of the principal indices for measuring health (such as infant mortality, absences through sickness, and life expectancy), while 90 per cent are determined by other factors, such as environment, nutrition, and lifestyle.[56] Could it therefore be argued that the cost-effectiveness of new medical technologies should be judged not only against other medical treatments, but also against social measures, which might in fact lead to greater improvements in health at lower cost? Eliminating child poverty, for example, would be likely to have a dramatic—and quite possibly cost-effective—impact upon health; yet raising welfare payments to poor families does not have the same popular appeal as heroic medical interventions to cure the sick.

In order to engage in a cost–benefit calculation, it is also, of course, necessary to work out what counts as a benefit. Are we concerned only with the health benefit to the patient, or might it be legitimate to take into account other benefits from her successful treatment? Enabling employees to return to work has clear social and economic benefits that, if included in the cost–benefit calculation, might lead us to give priority to the treatment of adults of working age, or to those in full-time employment, or even to those who do especially valuable jobs. Should we take into account whether a patient has dependent children who will benefit from her recovery? In deciding what priority substance abuse treatment programmes should receive, is it relevant that successfully treating drug addiction will not only improve the individual addict's life, but also that of her family and the community in which she lives?

Jonathan Glover argues that, while normally judging patients' social value would be invidious, it will sometimes be legitimate to take into account benefits to third parties, such as dependent children, when deciding which patient to treat.

Jonathan Glover[57]

If there are two people whose lives are in question and we have to choose to save only one, the number of people dependent on them should be regarded as very important. If other things are equal, but one has no family and the other is the mother of several young children, the case against deciding between them randomly is a strong one ... Refusal to depart from random choice when knowledge about their dependents is available is to place no value on avoiding the additional misery caused to the children if the mother is not the one saved ...

If we give some weight to the interests of dependents, should we take into account more generalized side effects, such as the relative importance of the contributions to society made by different people? There are good grounds for rejecting this as a general policy. It is a truism that we have no agreed standard by which to measure people's relative contribution to society. How does a mother compare with a doctor or a research scientist or a coal-miner? Any list of jobs ranked in order of social value seems, at least at present, to be arbitrary and debatable. It also seems to introduce the offensive division of people into grades.

---

[56] David J Hunter, *Desperately Seeking Solutions: Rationing Health Care* (Longman: London, 1997) 18.
[57] *Causing Death and Saving Lives* (Penguin: London, 1977) 222–3.

In contrast, John Harris argues that prioritizing those with dependents amounts to offensive discrimination against the childless and friendless.

John Harris[58]

[T]he feeling that it is somehow more important to rescue those with dependents, when elevated to the level of policy, amounts to a systematic preference of those with families over those without ... Dependence ... is not simply dependence on parents, and grief and misery are not confined to family relationships. But even if they were, it is unclear that they would constitute adequate reasons for preferring to save one person rather than another. We should not forget that while the bereaved deserve sympathy, by far the greatest loss is to the deceased, and the misfortune of her friends and relations pales into insignificance besides the tragedy to the individual who must die. It seems as obviously offensive systematically to inflict this loss on the childless, and perhaps the friendless, as it would be to grade people in any other way.

Finally, if systematic family preference became overt public policy, it might begin to seem that a relatively cheap form of insurance against a low-priority rating in the rescue stakes would be the acquisition of a family.

It could further be argued that it would in practice be impossible to calculate the wider benefits of treating an individual. How could doctors be expected to predict accurately their patients' likely contribution to society? It might be simple to find out whether a patient has young children, but not all parents actually support and love their children, and some childless people make a hugely positive contribution to children's lives. Giving priority to patients whose loss might cause tangible harm to other people would involve time-consuming and intrusive investigations.

It is also possible that bias, prejudice, and stereotyping might creep into these judgements. Offering priority to people in high-skilled employment may benefit the country as a whole, but it might also turn out to be indirectly discriminatory. On the other hand, where particular types of care, such as treating people for addiction, are likely to have enormously beneficial effects for society, it seems less obviously unjust to use this as an additional reason for diverting funds to this type of treatment. Taking these broader purposes into account when setting healthcare priorities does not involve claiming that certain people's lives are more valuable than others. Dan Brock therefore argues that taking into account indirect non-health benefits can be legitimate at a macro level, where it does not involve discriminating against particular individuals on account of their relative usefulness.

Dan W Brock[59]

As a rough generalization and all other things being equal, the higher level a macro health care resource allocation or prioritization decision, the more defensible it is to give weight to the indirect non health benefits and costs of alternative resource uses in health care. The closer to micro level choices by health professionals between the needs of their individual patients,

---

[58] *The Value of Life* (Routledge: London, 1985) 104–6.

[59] Dan Brock, 'Separate spheres and indirect benefits' (2003) 1 Cost Effectiveness and Resource Allocation 4.

the stronger the case that these indirect non health benefits and costs should be ignored on grounds of fairness.

While agreeing that social-utilitarian considerations should normally be disregarded, Tom Beauchamp and J Childress argue that in an emergency it may be legitimate to take an individual's social worth into account when rationing treatment.

Tom Beauchamp and James Childress[60]

[J]udgements of comparative social worth are inescapable and acceptable in some situations. For example, in an earthquake when some injured survivors are medical personnel who suffer only minor injuries, they justifiably receive priority of treatment if they are needed to help others. Similarly, in an outbreak of infectious disease, it is justifiable to inoculate physicians and nurses first to enable them to care for others. Under such conditions, a person may receive priority for treatment on grounds of social utility if and only if his or her contribution is indispensable to attaining a major social goal. As in analogous lifeboat cases, we should limit judgements of comparative social value to the specific qualities and skills that are essential to the community's immediate protection without assessing the general social worth of persons. If we limit exceptions based on social utility to emergencies involving necessity, they do not threaten the ordinary moral universe or imply the general acceptability of social-utilitarian calculations in distributing health care.

(4) Age

Is it ever acceptable to take into account a patient's age when rationing treatment? We can quickly dismiss the argument that, because they are more likely to suffer from multiple co-morbidities, treating older people is always less cost-effective. Some elderly individuals are extremely fit and active, while some young people are not. Age may be one variable that affects prognosis, but it is by no means the only or even the most important one. To use sweeping generalizations about a large and diverse section of the population in order to ration services would be arbitrary and unjust.

A more plausible argument in favour of age-based rationing is that an older person is more likely to have had a 'fair innings'. As John Harris explains:

What the fair innings argument needs to do is capture and express in a workable form the truth that while it is always a misfortune to die when one wants to go on living, it is not a tragedy to die in old age; but it is on the other hand, both a tragedy and a misfortune to be cut off prematurely.[61]

But while dying in old age might not be as tragic as premature death, John Harris points out that the 'systematic disvaluing of the old or those with life-threatening illness might have a corrosive effect on social morality and community relations more generally'.[62] There are also several practical arguments against age discrimination in the distribution of healthcare

---

[60] *Principles of Biomedical Ethics*, 6th edn (OUP: Oxford, 2008).
[61] John Harris, *The Value of Life* (Routledge: London, 1985) 93.
[62] 'The age-indifference principle and equality' (2005) 14 Cambridge Quarterly of Healthcare Ethics 93–9.

resources. For example, if treatment enables an older person to live independently for longer, there may be overall cost savings. Moreover, many older people contribute to the care of their relatives, both young and old, once again saving resources that might otherwise have to be spent on childcare or adult social care.[63]

As Tom Walker explains, there might also be times when older people are at greater risk of harm, and hence should be given priority for care, an example might be free flu vaccination for the over-65s.

Tom Walker[64]

Because the risks are higher when older, this means that we should prioritise protection, and preventative measures, for those who are older (along with other high-risk groups). In the case of influenza vaccination, this would mean we should prioritise vaccinations for those who are older over those who are younger. This does not stem from giving the lives of younger adults lower priority. Instead, it stems from the fact that age is associated with increased risk of serious harm.

(5) Individual Responsibility for Ill Health?

Many conditions are caused or exacerbated by a patient's own behaviour. Should this be relevant when allocating scarce resources? If an individual is responsible for creating her own need for healthcare services, should she bear the cost of her treatment, or be a lower priority for NHS care? On the one hand, it might be argued that making access to treatment depend upon whether someone is responsible for her illness could provide a powerful incentive towards healthy behaviour. On the other hand, if the prospect of poor health and premature death does not dissuade someone from engaging in unhealthy activities, it is hardly likely that being a lower priority for NHS care will do so.

Some commentators, such as Robert Blank, have nevertheless suggested that it is fair and just to take individual responsibility into account when rationing scarce resources:

[P]eople who try to take care of themselves are helping underwrite the costs incurred by those who fail to do so. Understandably, there is an increasingly vocal demand to shift the monetary burden to those individuals who knowingly take the health risks ... Considerable initiative for these actions comes from distaste at having to pay for someone else's bad habits.[65]

In practice, however, it would probably be impossible to devise a fair system for attributing responsibility for ill health. First, the obvious examples of smokers, alcoholics, and drug abusers may not attract much public sympathy, but these are not the only sorts of behaviour which may adversely affect one's health. Should we also penalize cyclists whose head injuries were the result of not wearing a helmet; skin cancer sufferers who sunbathed too much when they were young; athletes with sporting injuries; people with type 2 diabetes who used to eat a lot of junk food? The list of people who may have contributed to their own need for healthcare

---

[63] Jana Rogge and Bernhard Kittel, 'Who shall not be treated: Public attitudes on setting health care priorities by person-based criteria in 28 nations' (2016) 6 *PloS one* e0157018.

[64] 'Ageing, justice and resource allocation' (2016) 42 Journal of Medical Ethics 348–52.

[65] Robert Blank, *Rationing Medicine* (Columbia UP: New York, 1988) 199–200.

services is potentially endless, and may include those who have engaged in activities that are positively praiseworthy, such as working long hours under extreme pressure within the NHS.

Secondly, it is questionable whether self-harming unhealthy behaviour is always the result of deliberate choice. Very few people actively choose to become alcoholics or drug addicts. Indeed, alcoholism is increasingly regarded as a disease, which may even be triggered by genetic factors that are outside a person's control.[66]

Thirdly, as we see later, smoking, drug use, and poor diet tend to correlate with socio-economic status, hence penalizing people with unhealthy lifestyles would in practice mean that priority for healthcare services is given to the richest and healthiest sections of society.

Fourthly, at the individual level, it is seldom possible to isolate a single causal factor for ill health. The fact that someone leads a sedentary lifestyle may have contributed to his need for a heart bypass operation, but there are other possible causes. Commonly, genetic predisposition and environmental and lifestyle factors interact with each other to increase someone's susceptibility to a particular disease

While penalizing patients for their poor health might operate unfairly or be impracticable, it could be argued that someone who costs the NHS a great deal of money as a result of her diet or lifestyle, should take responsibility for the fact that her behaviour has an opportunity cost for others. NHS resources are finite and if some people use up more than their fair share—perhaps because they get very drunk every Saturday night and routinely end up in their local accident and emergency department, or because they eat so much junk food that they become morbidly obese—there is less left in the 'pot' for other people.

HM Evans, for example, maintains that a sense of social responsibility should persuade us not to squander public resources and disregard the needs of others.

HM Evans[67]

Public provision of this sort involves mutual benefit and mutual participation: so my own medical treatment is, whatever else it is, liable to be an opportunity cost (however justifiable) in terms of the healthcare needs of others requiring comparable treatment at the time when I am treated. Both in general, and in the specific context of public healthcare provision, I have at least a prima facie moral responsibility to take other people's interests seriously; this implies that I ought not to incur opportunity costs to others avoidably, recklessly or excessively ...

Second, and as a result, the interests of my 'competitor' co-patients produce in me not merely the negative duties of avoiding either uncivil behaviour or needless waste, but also, provocatively, positive duties to promote my own health and, in the case of illness, to recover as quickly as possible.

The NHS Constitution adopts this approach. It does not advocate the denial of care to people who are responsible for their need for treatment; instead it lists taking care of one's health as one of the obligations patients acquire in return for their rights to NHS care: 'Please recognise that you can make a significant contribution to your own, and your family's, good health and wellbeing, and take personal responsibility for it.'[68]

---

[66] DM Dick and LJ Bierut, 'The genetics of alcohol dependency' (2006) 8 Current Psychiatric Reports 151–7.
[67] 'Do patients have duties?' (2007) 33 Journal of Medical Ethics 689–94.
[68] Department of Health and Social Care, 'The NHS Constitution for England' (DHSC: London, 2015).

In addition to individuals taking some responsibility for their health, it is also important, as Jonathan Herring points out, to acknowledge that others may also bear some responsibility, and that the promotion of good health should be a communal endeavour.

Jonathan Herring[69]

There is also a difficulty if patients are held to be responsible for harms to their health but other bodies are not held responsible for their contributions to the health of the public. Politicians whose economic decisions cause ill health, advertisers and sellers of unhealthy products, sellers of alcohol – all these could be seen as responsible for causing ill health but are not held to account directly for that. While there can be limited sanctions in certain situations, such as polluters and producers of unsafe products, prosecutions are rare, the punishments tend to be limited and they are certainly of a different scale to that faced by a patient denied medical treatment.

Health is best understood, I would argue, as a communal, relational thing ... We are all profoundly dependent on others for our physical and psychological well-being. The modern emphasis on self-sufficiency overlooks the many ways we depend on those around us ...

The suggestion that we should deny treatment to patients based on their fault misunderstands the true nature of health. We are a collection of vulnerable people. Few people make all the right choices for their health. Our health is interdependent on those around us, in relationship with us and on our wider environment. Rather than blaming people for their ill health, we would be wiser to spend our efforts promoting healthy communities and relationships.

In practice, it is not uncommon for CCGs to restrict access to elective surgery to smokers and obese patients. Around a third of CCGs have implemented at least one 'clinical threshold policy', which delays access to treatment until after a period of smoking cessation or weight loss. As Virimchi Pillutla et al explain in the next extract, the purpose of such restrictions is ostensibly 'health optimisation', rather than punishment, but the evidence for the most draconian such policies, which have restricted access to all elective surgery on the basis of smoking status and body mass index, is mixed.

Virimchi Pillutla, Hannah Maslen, and Julian Savulescu[70]

The principal justification for proposed rationing measures targeting smokers and obese patients centres on their expected clinical benefits. Mandatory health optimisation processes are expected to positively impact health in two key ways. Firstly, such measures intend to reduce the need for surgical intervention where preoperative health optimisation has sufficient clinical effect. Secondly, that surgical intervention will be more effective due to a reduction in the incidence of perioperative complications associated with smoking and obesity. Importantly, the objective of such rationing measures is not to deny patients access to healthcare services outright or to disadvantage specific patient groups ...

[W]hilst there is a definitive link between smoking cessation and a reduction in perioperative complications, mandatory rationing measures are only justified in virtue of expected clinical

---

[69] 'Rationing by fault' (2018) 121 Theology 112–16.
[70] 'Rationing elective surgery for smokers and obese patients: responsibility or prognosis?' (2018) 19 BMC Medical Ethics 28.

benefits provided that there is not another policy that would alter the smoking behaviour of patients in a more efficient way.

Compared to smoking, the impact of preoperative health optimisation measures for obese patients is less certain; whilst 'moderate weight loss' of 5–10% over a 6 to 12 month period is typically associated with significant clinical benefit, the paucity of empirical evidence evaluating its utility within a perioperative context undermines the clinical justification for mandatory health optimisation measures for obese patients.

Amanda Owen-Smith et al observed consultations in obesity surgery clinics—where losing ten per cent of their bodyweight was a precondition for patients' eligibility for gastric band surgery—and found that this was seldom admitted to have anything to do with rationing, but was instead regarded as a way for patients to ' "earn" the right to surgery'.

Amanda Owen-Smith, Joanna Coast, and Jenny L Donovan[71]

[D]espite a commitment to being open with patients in theory, clinicians experience extreme discomfort in having to explain that there are external constraints on their ability to provide treatment and retreat to more implicit methods in practice. This pattern was clearly demonstrated here, where nearly all clinicians preferred to focus on the perceived clinical benefits of the prioritisation criteria adopted, rather than explaining that there was a shortage in the number of surgery slots available. Of particular, interest was how shared attitudes around personal responsibility for severe obesity seemed to 'pave the way' for such decisions and encouraged patients to collude with implicit rationing . . .

The broader social discourse demanding personal responsibility for health explicitly influenced decision making in clinic, but financial factors were rarely mentioned, meaning that rationing remained largely implicit and non-accountable.

(6) Relevance of Public Opinion

(a) In setting priorities

What role should public opinion play in setting priorities within the NHS? On the one hand, the NHS is funded through taxation, and used by virtually everyone in the country, and so the public, as both taxpayers and service users, has an interest in the distribution of NHS resources. Because depriving citizens of medical treatment on cost grounds is so controversial and potentially divisive, it might also be important to seek public agreement with the principles that inform rationing decisions. Indeed, there is some evidence that when the public are involved in decision-making, this is 'aimed primarily at increasing the credibility of the decision making process and softening public opposition'.[72]

There may be disadvantages in relying too heavily on public opinion, however. Why should the public have any say over whether treatment for schizophrenia is more or less of a priority

---

[71] 'Self-responsibility, rationing and treatment decision making–managing moral narratives alongside fiscal reality in the obesity surgery clinic' (2018) 21 Health Expectations 606–14.

[72] Tom Daniels et al 'Involving citizens in disinvestment decisions: What do health professionals think? Findings from a multi-method study in the English NHS' (2018) 13 Health Economics, Policy and Law 162–88.

than orthopaedic surgery, for example? There is evidence that the public tends to prioritize 'sympathetic' patient groups, such as sick children, and be less keen on funding treatment for drug addicts or people with mental illnesses. 'Rationing by opinion poll' might leave addiction and mental illness inadequately treated, and this would be likely to have negative consequences not only for untreated patients, but also for society as a whole.

In the next extract, Bill New and Julian Le Grand point out that respondents to one-off public opinion surveys are ill-equipped to make complex rationing decisions.

Bill New and Julian Le Grand[73]

[E]ven if perfectly representative samples of the public can be consulted, the legitimacy of their having a direct influence on resource allocation and rationing will still be deeply problematic. The outcome of such exercises will reflect majority opinion and, although it is hard to be sure what that opinion would be, it is likely that the interests of very old, infirm, mentally ill or disabled people will be neglected in favour of the concerns of the majority. High-technology rescue or repair medicine, for example, can easily be conceived as immediately relevant to us all. Furthermore, it is simply naïve to suppose that the lay public have the requisite knowledge to make many decisions which are of a complex, technical nature . . .

Political decision-making—and that is what rationing decisions are—must be open to challenge, scrutiny and debate, and those who make the decisions must bear the responsibility for and deal with the consequences of those decisions . . . Why, for example, should members of the public make considered judgements when they do not face the prospect of being challenged on them, nor of answering for any unfavourable consequences? Accountability would, under these circumstances, be weakened.

(b) The acceptability of incentives

One issue where the question of how much weight we should give to public opinion has been brought into sharp focus is the use of incentives. The problem can be simply stated. If (and this is currently a fairly big 'if') there is clear and compelling evidence that offering financial incentives to people to stop smoking or lose weight would be cost-effective for the NHS, how much weight should we give to the fact that a majority of the public appears to disapprove of this sort of scheme?

In favour of incentives, it is sometimes argued that people would generally prefer not to smoke or be morbidly obese, but the short-term pleasures of smoking and overeating make it difficult for them to give up their unhealthy behaviour. Providing a financial reward then helps to align the unhealthy person's short-term interests with her longer term preferences and best interests. Because smoking, drug use, and obesity impose enormous costs on the NHS, it is possible that modest financial incentives could be a cost-effective use of NHS resources. In the next extract, Marianne Promberger et al consider how we should balance this with evidence that the public believes that paying drug users, smokers, and obese people 'rewards bad behaviour', and is unfair to those who behave healthily without being 'bribed'.

---

[73] *Rationing in the NHS: Principles and Pragmatism* (King's Fund, 1996).

Marianne Promberger et al[74]

There are several possible reasons why people may find financial incentives less acceptable. It may stem from a violation of a cultural norm, namely the use of money in the relationship between a doctor or healthcare provider and a patient ... The perceived unacceptability of financial incentives in the current context may also stem from a marked sense of injustice about offering money, a fungible good, to those who, through their own behaviour, might have avoided this ...

Rejection of incentive schemes by the general public could all too easily be seen by politicians as a reason not to introduce them. This conclusion does not follow from our findings. To answer the question as to whether or not incentive schemes should be introduced would require more evidence on their consequences, intended and unintended, as well as in-depth analysis of the associated ethical issues of using incentives in healthcare ... It may be the case that the results reported here stem from prejudice and illegitimate value judgements, and should thus not be reflected in policy decisions ...

Even if a residual disutility for incentives in health contexts stubbornly persists, benefits may be great enough to justify overriding such concerns. At the other extreme, opposition to 'rewarding bad behaviour' might translate into the very tangible consequence of corroding the goodwill, and eroding the good behaviour, of those not rewarded for their virtue.

In the next extract, Rebecca Brown points out that recipients of incentives for breastfeeding did not believe that they were doing it 'for the money'.

Rebecca C H Brown[75]

Offering incentives to encourage women to breast feed their babies might be seen as an example of the wrong reasons being at work: since breast milk is generally thought to be better for child health, women are advised to breast feed their babies. Those who only breast feed when offered an additional incentive may be criticised for failing to value the health of their child appropriately and caring more about gaining some extra money. A study that interviewed women enrolled on a breastfeeding incentive programme, however, found that many women did not think of themselves as breast feeding 'for the incentives'. In fact, they often said the incentive did not affect whether or not they wanted to breast feed. Instead, the women described the incentive scheme as making them feel valued, boosting their mood and facilitating good relationships with support workers.

(7) Ability to Pay

A free market in health care would replace rationing with market forces. People would be free to purchase health care, either at the point of use or through insurance, and services would be available only if there was consumer demand for them. In their favour, market forces might deter inappropriate use of healthcare services: many of us would make less profligate use of

---

[74] 'Acceptability of financial incentives to improve health outcomes in UK and US samples' (2011) 37 Journal of Medical Ethics 682–7.

[75] 'Social values and the corruption argument against financial incentives for healthy behaviour' (2017) 43 Journal of Medical Ethics 140–4.

GP services if we were charged £100 per visit. Against this, there are many reasons why a free market in medical treatment is an unattractive proposition.

Most importantly, there would always be people who were unable to afford treatment or insurance, and who would therefore experience unnecessary pain, or die preventable deaths, if society was not prepared to cover the costs of their care. Our consumption of healthcare resources is generally concentrated in our last years of life, when we are least able to generate additional income. Even allowing for the pooling of risk via insurance, there is an inverse correlation between socioeconomic status and good health. Insurance premiums are set according to risk rather than wealth, so in a free market the cost of insurance would be lowest for the richest and healthiest, and highest for those who are very ill and/or very poor.

Secondly, although charges might stop people from seeing their GP when there is nothing much wrong with them, people often do not know in advance if their symptoms are trivial or significant. In practice, using charges to discourage the use of services is likely to reduce the likelihood of early diagnosis, which in turn may make treatment more expensive.[76] As Jeremiah Hurley explains, charging people for health care may turn out to be inefficient and costly.

Jeremiah Hurley[77]

Reduced consumption of effective preventive and therapeutic care can cause people to develop wholly preventable conditions or allow mild conditions to become more serious and expensive to treat than they would be if they were caught early. The ultimate costs to the public health care system across the full range of health services can actually increase as a result of user charges. Limiting the magnitude of user charges in an attempt to reduce these adverse effects unfortunately also limits their revenue potential. Further, equity concerns dictate that low-income individuals either be exempt from charges or be liable for a maximum amount of annual out-of-pocket expenditure. Such provisions require costly administrative mechanisms to assess eligibility and to track expenditures against any specified expenditure limits, and the associated administrative costs can substantially reduce the net revenue gain to the public insurer. In the end, when all effects are properly counted, real financial savings to the system often end up far less than promised.

Thirdly, a free market is supposed to work because consumers are able to exercise choice over their spending: they will only buy those goods or services which they want, and they can select providers who best meet their needs. In general patients do not choose medical treatment, in the same way as they might choose to purchase other goods and services. Efficient markets depend upon informed and discerning consumers, but there is a fundamental information imbalance in the doctor–patient relationship, and patients are unable to exercise much control (other than the straightforward right of refusal) over which treatments they receive.

Fourthly, because few people could afford to pay for acute medical treatment as they need it, and no one would want to face the additional stress of trying to borrow money when they are seriously ill, a free market in health care would tend to operate through insurance. And

---

[76] See also, House of Lords Select Committee on the Long-term Sustainability of the NHS, *The Long-term Sustainability of the NHS and Adult Social Care* HL Paper 151, Report of Session 2016–17

[77] 'User charges for health care services: some further thoughts' (2013) 8 Health Economics, Policy and Law 537–41.

there are a number of additional specific problems that arise from using private insurance to cover the costs of health care:

- Some health risks will be uninsurable. Many insurance policies exclude certain conditions, such as self-inflicted injuries, drug abuse, or major epidemics. Very elderly people or those with pre-existing conditions may find it difficult or even impossible to purchase health insurance. There would therefore have to be a state-funded safety net to cover the treatment of risks which private insurance companies choose to exclude from their policies. Thus, the problem of rationing publicly funded care remains.

- When risks are pooled through insurance, low-risk patients will often be charged premiums that appear to be higher than their anticipated benefits, and they may therefore decide not to bother purchasing insurance. As a result, high-risk individuals' premiums will be even higher, and may become unaffordable, thus increasing the proportion of the population that is uninsured and dependent, once again, on the publicly funded safety net.

- Because insurance insulates the patient from the real costs of care, it may encourage people to make more use of medical services than they would in a straightforward free market.

- Insurance schemes also tend to give healthcare providers an incentive to over-treat, and thus waste resources for no additional health gain.

- Finally, the administration costs of a system in which there are multiple private insurers are significantly higher than those of state-run systems. The US spends much more than any other high-income country on health, both in per capita expenditure and as a proportion of GDP, but Americans are not healthier than residents of European countries which spend half as much on their health services. The Commonwealth Fund periodically ranks healthcare systems in high income countries, across a range of measures. In 2010[78] and 2017, the UK was judged to have the most efficient healthcare system, while the US was ranked last:

> Despite having the most expensive health care, the United States ranks last overall among the 11 countries on measures of health system equity, access, administrative efficiency, care delivery, and health care outcomes ... The US spent $9,364 per person on health care in 2016, compared to $4,094 in the UK, which ranked first on performance overall.[79]

Rationing according to the patient's ability to pay might appear to be fundamentally incompatible with the NHS's founding principle that health care should be free at the point of delivery, but it should be noted there are already some health services which are routinely provided in the private sector. Few adults receive free dental or optical care. Most fertility treatment is provided privately. Working adults in England must pay the prescription charge, and people who need long-term social care often have to contribute towards its cost.

An increasing proportion of the services which are provided by the NHS can be purchased privately, and private patients will usually be treated more quickly. Approximately 12 per cent of the UK population is covered by private medical insurance, and people without insurance

---

[78] Karen Davis, Cathy Schoen, and Kristof Stremikis, *How the Performance of the US Health Care System Compares Internationally: 2010 Update* (Commonwealth Fund: New York, 2010).

[79] Eric C Schneider et al, *Mirror, Mirror 2017: International Comparison Reflects Flaws and Opportunities for Better US Health Care* (Commonwealth Fund: New York, 2017).

may choose to pay directly for elective treatment. Although it is by no means the norm, this is clearly rationing according to ability to pay rather than need.

It is also important to remember that a parallel private sector is not a simple 'add-on' to the NHS. Instead, the two interact with each other. The NHS subsidizes the private sector through allowing its employees to carry out private treatment within NHS hospitals, and by permitting NHS consultants to maintain private practices. For some years, NHS trusts have increased capacity by purchasing private sector care for their patients.[80] As we have seen, the Health and Social Care Act 2012 bolsters the private sector's ability to compete for NHS business, and allows NHS Foundation Trusts to increase their income from private patients.

(8) Defining a Package of Care

Another way to ration medical treatment might be to set limits upon which treatments will be funded by the state. A core package of essential services would be provided free of charge, but non-essential services might only be available privately. Rationing policies that exclude particular treatments are open and transparent, and ensure that patients understand the limits of what they can expect from the public health service.

In some countries, there have been explicit attempts to devise packages of healthcare services, but these have not been overwhelmingly successful. In New Zealand, the Core Services Committee could not find any treatment or area of service within the current range of provision that could be completely excluded. So, 'in something of an anti-climax, the Committee recommended that "core" be defined as being what was already being provided prior to the reforms'.[81]

Some health authorities in the UK have specified that they will not fund certain procedures such as tattoo removal and sterilization reversal. The reason for identifying low-priority interventions and excluding them from NHS coverage is not that such treatments are ineffective, or that they are a significant drain on NHS resources. In fact, tattoo removal and sterilization reversal cost very little compared with the maintenance of acute health services. A refusal to fund certain procedures may help to clarify what it is reasonable to expect from the NHS, but it will not solve the funding crisis.

Moreover, blanket exclusions are likely to be unfair and unlawful. Tattoo removal may seem trivial, but what if a person was tattooed while he was a prisoner of war? Fairness demands that a ban on funding for marginal procedures can accommodate exceptional cases.

(9) Rationing by Dilution

Rationing by dilution involves offering less care than is ideal; perhaps by carrying out fewer diagnostic tests, or by spending less time with patients. Rationing by delay means that patients have to wait to be treated, by waiting for an appointment with their GP, or by being put on a waiting list for hospital treatment. Delays in treating patients may reduce demand because some patients will get better while waiting to see a doctor, while others might die. Rationing by deterrence involves the creation, perhaps inadvertently, of barriers that make it difficult for

[80] Christopher Newdick, *Who Should We Treat? Rights, Rationing and Resources in the NHS*, 2nd edn (OUP: Oxford, 2005) 233.

[81] M Cooper, 'Core Services and the New Zealand Health Reforms' in R Maxwell (ed), *Rationing Health Care* (Churchill Livingstone: London, 1995) 799–807, 805.

patients to book appointments: for example, in 2016, 26 per cent of patients had experienced difficulties in getting through to their GP surgery on the telephone, up from 18 per cent in 2012.[82]

As Donald Light explains, health services in the UK continue to be available to everyone, but few get immediate access to the best possible treatment.

Donald Light[83]

The NHS already rations on a massive scale. The NHS rations by delay to get on waiting lists, and then on the waiting lists themselves, and then with the further wait after an appointment has been made. It rations by undersupply of staff, doctors, machines, facilities, etc; by undercapitalisation of run down facilities; by dilution of tests done and services received; by discharge earlier than desirable; and by outright denial to even the chance to wait or be undertreated.

Barbara McPake et al argue that queuing should be regarded as a rationing device, whereby treatment is rationed 'on the basis of the patient's willingness to allocate time in order to receive a service', but it is, they argue, 'an inefficient and inappropriate rationing mechanism' because its true purpose will generally be to maximize 'the efficiency with which health professionals' time is used', rather than to ensure fair distribution of health care.[84] In a similar vein, Alan Williams argues that a narrow focus on the economic costs of health care misses the fact that there are other costs, such as patients' time, which is currently 'used profligately by the system, as any "free" resource would be'.[85] There is a 'cost' incurred when a patient has to wait for four hours in A&E, but this cost is borne by the patient herself and hence is marginalized in debates about the rationing of NHS resources.

(c) Rationing in the NHS: The Role of NICE

The National Institute for Health and Care Excellence (NICE) was set up in 1999,[86] in part to make resource allocation decisions in the NHS more explicit and transparent and to address the problem of the 'postcode lottery'. There are a number of different types of NICE guidance, some of which—like its public health and clinical practice guidance—is not mandatory: an example would be its 2015 guideline on preventing dementia which instructs 'Public Health England, NHS England, relevant national third-sector organisations and health and social care commissioners' that they should: 'Make it clear that some common unhealthy behaviours

---

[82] Ruth Robertson, Lillie Wenzel, James Thompson, and Anna Charles, *Understanding NHS financial pressures: How are they affecting patient care* (Kings Fund, 2017).

[83] Donald W Light, 'The real ethics of rationing' (1997) 315 British Medical Journal 112–15.

[84] Barbara McPake, Lilani Kumaranayake, and Charles Normand, *Health Economics: An International Perspective* (Routledge: London, 2002) 204.

[85] Rudolf Klein and Alan Williams, 'Setting Priorities: What is Holding us Back—Inadequate Information or Inadequate Institutions?' in Angela Coulter and Chris Ham (eds), *The Global Challenge of Healthcare Rationing* (Open UP: Buckingham, 2000) 15–26, 18.

[86] Although the acronym has remained the same, NICE's name has changed twice from the original National Institute for Clinical Excellence: first with the insertion of the word 'health', and then in 2013 'clinical' was changed to 'care' in order to accommodate NICE's role in providing social care guidance.

can increase the risk of dementia and that addressing those behaviours will reduce the likeli-hood of developing dementia and other non-communicable chronic conditions.'[87]

NICE plays a central role in rationing in the UK through its technology appraisals, which assess the clinical and cost-effectiveness of medicines and other treatments in order to deter-mine whether they should be funded by the NHS. CCGs are under an obligation to fund these NICE-approved treatments within three months.

(1) NICE's Cost-Effectiveness Appraisals

NICE's technology appraisals can recommend: (a) the treatment's unrestricted use in the NHS; (b) its restricted or 'optimized' use in a subset of patients only; (c) its use to be confined to clinical trials; or (d) that it should not be used in the NHS. Of the 774 technology appraisals carried out by NICE between 1 March 2000 and 31 May 2018, 56 per cent involved straight-forward approval; 23 per cent of decisions were that the treatment should be available only in certain circumstances; four per cent permitted the use of the treatment but only in research; two per cent recommended that the treatment should be funded by the cancer drugs fund (see below), and in 15 per cent of cases, the guidance was that the treatment should not be provided.[88]

NICE's decision-making process is undoubtedly open and transparent: all of NICE's ap-praisals are available on its website and, before decisions are finalized, there is an opportunity for 'stakeholders'—such as patient groups and the medical profession—to comment upon its draft conclusions. There is also a right of appeal for interested groups, including drugs manufacturers.

NICE has been open about its use of QALYs, although it has also been clear that they are not the only relevant factor. According to NICE, the general threshold for affordability in the NHS is approximately £20,000 per QALY. If treatments costing less than £20,000 are not to be recommended, reasons should be given; perhaps because there are limitations to the evidence of effectiveness. For treatments which cost between £20,000 and £30,000 per QALY, NICE will consider whether there are considerations which justify recommending the technology, such as the particular needs of the patient group. Costs of more than £30,000 per QALY are supposed to be unacceptable, unless there are other compelling factors in favour of its recom-mendation. In practice, however, it seems that £40,000 is the point at which there is a greater than 50 per cent chance of rejection.[89]

Claxton et al evaluated NICE's appraisals and found that the NICE's QALY threshold was significantly greater than that of the majority of non-NICE approved treatments within the NHS, which they calculated to be about £13,000 per QALY.[90] They also found that, in practice, NICE routinely approved treatments which cost significantly more than £30,000 per QALY. As a result of both these findings, as Hawkes explains, Claxton et al's study found that NICE appraisals have considerable opportunity costs for other NHS patients.

---

[87] NICE, *Dementia, disability and frailty in later life—mid-life approaches to delay or prevent onset* (NICE, 2015).

[88] See further 'Summary of decisions' at nice.org.uk.

[89] Nicholas Timmins, Michael Rawlins, and John Appleby, *A Terrible Beauty: A Short History of NICE* (Health Intervention and Technology Assessment Program (HITAP), 2016).

[90] Karl Claxton et al, 'Methods for the estimation of the National Institute for Health and Care Excellence cost-effectiveness threshold' (2015) 19 Health Technology Assessment 14.

Nigel Hawkes[91]

NHS outcomes would be better if it refused to fund any drug that cost more than £13 000 per quality adjusted life year (QALY). NICE says that its threshold is between £20 000 and £30 000 per QALY, but on average, Claxton said, the institute approves drugs that cost £40 000 per QALY and sometimes as high as £50 000.

The York team set out to discover how much a QALY was worth on average across the NHS, by comparing the money spent in 23 different disease areas with the outcomes achieved ... The results ... showed that in the NHS in England as a whole the average cost per QALY was £12 936, a result that showed that the NHS was 'really good value,' Claxton said. This was far below the NICE threshold, meaning that every drug with a cost per QALY greater than that was taking money from other services that could use it more effectively. Outcomes would improve, he said, if all NHS spending on drugs above this level ceased.

For every £10m spent on a new drug that cost £40 000 per QALY, 250 QALYs would be gained, but 773 would be lost because the money spent would not be available for other services. The net harm would be 523 QALYs. The Cancer Drugs Fund [see the following section], which lacks any formal threshold, fares even worse. This year (2014–15) it will spend £280m, which will buy, the York team estimates, 4098 QALYs. But the health lost elsewhere will be 21 645 QALYs—five times as much.

NICE's appraisals are carried out by scientific and clinical experts, but the views of the public are also taken into account via its Citizens Council. This is a representative sample of UK citizens, to whom questions are referred by NICE. The Citizens Council played an important part in the drawing up of *Social Value Judgements*, a document which sets out the social values which NICE adopts when making decisions. In the following extract, NICE sets out its approach to the questions of whether a person's age or their responsibility for their condition should be relevant.

National Institute for Health and Care Excellence[92]

6.3 Age

There is much debate over whether, or how, age should be taken into account when allocating healthcare resources. The Citizens Council considered that health should not be valued more highly in some age groups than in others; and that social roles at different ages should not affect decisions about cost effectiveness. They said, though, that where age is an indicator of benefit or risk, it can be taken into account.

NICE's general principle is that patients should not be denied, or have restricted access to, NHS treatment simply because of their age. The Institute's guidance should refer to age only when one or more of the following apply.

- There is evidence that age is a good indicator for some aspect of patients' health status and/ or the likelihood of adverse effects of the treatment.

- There is no practical way of identifying patients other than by their age (for example, there is no test available to measure their state of health in another way).

---

[91] Nigel Hawkes, 'NICE is too generous in approving drugs, analysis says' (2015) 350 British Medical Journal h955.
[92] *Social Value Judgements*, 2nd edn (July 2008).

- There is good evidence, or good grounds for believing, that because of their age patients will respond differently to the treatment in question.

...

6.6 Behaviour-dependent conditions

The Citizens Council advised that NICE should not take into consideration whether or not a particular condition was self-induced. It was often impossible, in an individual, to decide whether the condition was dependent on their own behaviour or not; and receiving NHS care should not depend on whether people 'deserved' it or not.

NICE should not produce guidance that results in care being denied to patients with conditions that are, or may have been, dependent on their behaviour. However, if the behaviour is likely to continue and can make a treatment less clinically effective or cost effective, then it may be appropriate to take this into account.

(2) Ultra-Orphan and End-of-Life Medicines

In two special cases, NICE modifies its normal QALY range. First, and most recently, NICE has introduced a raised QALY threshold for products that treat very rare health conditions (known as ultra-orphan medicines). A disease is considered 'very rare' if it affects fewer than 1,000 people in the UK. Because of their small market, these medicines are generally very expensive. If they offer substantial health gains to patients, the QALY threshold can be as high as £100,000 to £300,000 per QALY.

Secondly, as cancer drugs become more specialized, and hence target smaller patient groups, drugs that are capable of extending the life of cancer patients for a relatively short period of time are also likely to have a high cost per QALY. As a result, NICE has devised supplementary guidance, to apply to patients with less than two years to live, where the medicine is capable of extending life by at least three months. In such cases, and provided the estimates of life expectancy are robust, the Appraisals Committee is invited to give 'greater weight to QALYs achieved in the later stages of terminal diseases'.

National Institute for Health and Clinical Excellence[93]

2 Criteria for appraisal of end of life treatments

2.1 This supplementary advice should be applied in the following circumstances and when all the criteria referred to below are satisfied:
   2.1.1 The treatment is indicated for patients with a short life expectancy, normally less than 24 months and;
   2.1.2 There is sufficient evidence to indicate that the treatment offers an extension to life, normally of at least an additional 3 months, compared to current NHS treatment, and;
   2.1.3 The treatment is licensed or otherwise indicated, for small patient populations.

Wider access to expensive cancer drugs may appear to be good for patients, but, as James Raftery points out, making exceptions for some patient groups will have an opportunity cost for others.

---

[93] *Appraising Life-Extending, End of Life Treatments* (NICE, 2009).

James Raftery[94]

> The main attraction of the cost per QALY measure is its universal applicability. Making an exception for any group—such as, life-extending treatments for terminally ill patients—limits that universality and sets a precedent for other groups. In addition, setting the threshold higher for some groups within a fixed overall budget results in other patient groups being denied treatment.

In the next extract Anthony Culyer explains why it is important to focus not only on the benefits of prioritising cancer treatment, but also on the health gains that others will lose as a result.

Anthony J Culyer[95]

> Opportunity cost focuses the mind on the fact that cost is not simply money, rather it is the health that could have been bought with that money ... [B]eing right and fair is as much about the rightness and fairness of opportunity costs as it is about the rightness and fairness of the direct health benefits of treatments ...
>
> Giving a greater weight to some patient groups may seem a simple matter, but it can have complex consequences. For example, when evaluating the proposed introduction of a new late-stage cancer medicine, decision-makers may take the view that people near the ends of their lives should receive a greater weight. This makes it more likely that such a new product will pass the threshold test. However, it is highly unlikely that the cancer patients in question are the only patients near the ends of their lives. Many who are already receiving NHS care may also be near death, and their QALYs ought also, on grounds of horizontal justice (in other words, treating people who are alike in like ways), to have a higher weight.

In addition to NICE's special end-of-life criteria, in 2010 the government set up a special Cancer Drugs Fund (CDF). The CDF was intended to make an additional £280 million available each year to cover drugs not (yet) approved by NICE, or where NICE had recommended only restricted access.[96] In 2015, the National Audit Office published an investigation into the CDF's first five years of operation.[97] It found that the Department of Health had not collected data on the outcomes for patients who had received non-NICE approved drugs through the CDF. In addition, the CDF had overspent its allocated budget for the fund by 35 per cent, thus reducing the funds available for other treatments. The National Audit Office found that routine bypassing of NICE evaluations via the CDF had become part of 'mainstream cancer care', and there was universal agreement 'that the Fund is not sustainable in its current form'.[98]

Since 2016, the CDF has become a managed access scheme, through which pharmaceutical companies agree to price reductions in return for early NHS access.

---

[94] 'NICE and the challenge of cancer drugs' (2009) 338 British Medical Journal 67.
[95] 'Health economics and health technology assessment' (2018) *Medicine* (online).
[96] Department of Health, *The Cancer Drugs Fund: Guidance to Support Operation of the Cancer Drugs Fund in 2011–12* (DH: London, 2011) para 4.1.
[97] National Audit Office, *Investigation into the Cancer Drugs Fund* (NAO, 2015).   [98] Ibid.

NHS England[99]

From now on, all new systemic anti-cancer therapy drug indications expected to receive a marketing authorisation will be appraised by NICE following Ministerial referral.

A modified appraisal process for cancer drugs was introduced on 1st April 2016 and now allows NICE to make one of three recommendations:

- Recommended for routine commissioning – 'yes'
- Not recommended for routine commissioning – 'no'
- Recommended for use within the CDF (new)

The new recommendation available to NICE – 'recommended for use within the CDF'– can be used when NICE considers there to be plausible potential for a drug to satisfy the criteria for routine commissioning, but where there is significant remaining clinical uncertainty.

The NICE appraisal process will also start much earlier with the aim of publishing draft guidance prior to a drug receiving its marketing authorisation and then final guidance within 90 days of marketing authorisation wherever possible ...

In order to ensure patients can benefit from new cancer drugs as quickly as possible, pharmaceutical companies will now have the option of accessing interim funding from the point of marketing authorisation for those drugs that have received either a draft recommendation for routine commissioning – 'yes' – or a draft recommendation for use within the CDF. Any pharmaceutical company wishing to take advantage of the new interim funding arrangements will have to agree to the expenditure control mechanism ...

For those drugs that receive a recommendation for use within the CDF, a Managed Access Agreement will need to be agreed between the pharmaceutical company and NHS England ...

The purpose of the 'managed access' period will be to resolve significant remaining clinical uncertainty ... At the end of the managed access period, NICE will re-appraise the drug with a view to deciding whether or not the drug can be recommended for routine commissioning ...

The CDF budget is fixed at £340m.

(3) 'Top-Up' Payments

It used to be the case that a patient could not be an NHS patient and a private patient during the same course of treatment. This meant that if a patient wanted to pay for one aspect of her care privately, such as an expensive cancer drug, she had to opt out altogether, and pay for all of her treatment herself. Some patients might be able to find a few thousand pounds for an expensive new medicine, but very few would be able to pay for all of the costs of caring for them in hospital.

On the one hand, it seems unfair to banish a patient from the NHS just because she wishes to pay for a medicine that the NHS will not fund. On the other hand, permitting NHS patients to buy additional medicines means that the standard of care NHS patients receive may depend upon their ability to pay, which appears to contradict one of the NHS's founding principles. Since 2008, it has been possible for NHS patients to purchase privately funded medicines, although the private treatment should be delivered separately, ideally in a private wing, in order to avoid the NHS cross-subsidizing private treatment.[100]

---

[99] *Appraisal and Funding of Cancer Drugs from July 2016 (including the new Cancer Drugs Fund) A new deal for patients, taxpayers and industry* (NHS England, 2016).

[100] Department of Health, *Guidance on NHS patients who wish to pay for additional private care* (DH, 2009).

(4) NICE and Innovative Medicines

In response to the criticism that it was taking too long for innovative medicines to become available to patients, the government has set up the Accelerated Access Pathway, explained in the next extract. The intention is to speed up approval times for 'transformative' medicines. In return for speedier access to the market, drugs companies are expected to price these products competitively.

Department of Health and Department of Business, Energy and Industrial Strategy[101]

From April 2018, we will introduce an **Accelerated Access Pathway (AAP).** This will be a new route to market that will streamline regulatory and market access decisions; getting those innovations that we believe will be truly transformative to patients more quickly. We will make the process from bench to bedside quicker, cheaper, and easier for innovators and the NHS. The Government's ambition is to bring forward by up to four years patient access to these selected, highly beneficial and affordable, innovations …

Each breakthrough product will benefit from bespoke case management, which will co-ordinate across partners to streamline the journey. In return for these commercial benefits, we expect industry to come forward with a cost proposition that delivers additional value for patients and the NHS beyond that achieved under the current system, and is affordable.

Within NICE itself, the Office of Market Access works with industry in order to speed up the adoption of new medicines, devices, and diagnostics by the NHS. The Early Access to Medicines Scheme (EAMS) was set up in 2014, and it aims to give patients with life-threatening or seriously debilitating conditions access to medicines that do not yet have a marketing authorization when there is a clear unmet medical need. Under the scheme, the Medicines and Healthcare products Regulatory Agency (MHRA) will give a scientific opinion on the benefit/risk balance of the medicine, based on the data available when the EAMS submission was made. If potential benefit is demonstrated to the MHRA's satisfaction, a company will be able to market the product. The first medicine to be approved through this scheme was a novel cancer drug to treat melanoma, pembrolizumab (marketed as Keytruda), which can be provided by the NHS to patients who have not benefited from other therapies, provided that the manufacturer supplies it at an agreed discount.

(5) Evaluating NICE's Effectiveness

Although NICE is widely admired internationally, there have been some criticisms of the way it operates. First, the status of NICE guidance is ambiguous. Any treatments which have been approved by NICE should normally be made available to patients within three months.[102] And the NHS Constitution states that: 'You have the right to drugs and treatments that have been recommended by NICE for use in the NHS, if your doctor says they are clinically appropriate for you'. As this statement makes clear, however, while CCGs may be under a duty to

---

[101] *Making a reality of the Accelerated Access Review: Improving patient access to breakthrough technologies and treatments in a cost-effective model* (DH and DBEIS, 2017).

[102] *Directions to Health Authorities, Primary Care Trusts and NHS Trusts in England* (DH: London, 11 December 2001).

fund NICE-recommended treatments, doctors are not under a duty to prescribe them. The question of what treatment is appropriate for a particular patient remains a matter of clinical discretion, although obviously in fulfilling their duty of care, doctors would be expected to have regard to relevant guidance.

Secondly, despite the quasi-mandatory status of NICE technology appraisals, extra money is not put aside to fund their implementation, and so CCGs must find the resources to pay for NICE-approved technologies and treatments from elsewhere in their budgets. Different CCGs will choose to make savings in different ways, resulting in a new 'postcode lottery', as the cuts necessary to implement NICE's recommendations are made unevenly. Paradoxically, in order to fund NICE recommendations, CCGs might restrict access to treatments which are, in fact, more cost-effective than those recommended by NICE, but which have not been formally appraised.

NICE is not a budget holder and does not have to decide which treatments should be paid for by the NHS. Rather, it looks at different treatments in isolation, and decides whether they meet a threshold level of cost-effectiveness. It therefore cannot tell whether the treatments it recommends are more or less cost-effective than other treatments, which have not had their cost-effectiveness investigated.

Thirdly, implementation of NICE guidance remains variable.[103] There is also some confusion between technology appraisals, which must be implemented and clinical guidelines, which CCGs are supposed to work towards, but which are not mandatory.

House of Commons Health Select Committee[104]

It appears that patients and the public are sometimes not aware that only approved technology appraisals are mandatory and that the NHS is not under any obligation to implement other types of guidance within a specific timeframe. This is partly because of the terminology used by NICE: the term 'guidance' is commonly employed for all types of advice given by the Institute, and does not differentiate between that which is obligatory and that which is not. This has led to confusion about the status of the different types of guidance issued by NICE, and elevated expectations among patients of the type of treatment that they will receive. For example, in vitro fertilisation (IVF) is the subject of a clinical guideline. NICE recommended that PCTs should provide three cycles of IVF to eligible patients. Many patients therefore believe that the NICE guideline means that they should have access to three cycles of IVF through the NHS.

The Committee questioned the logic of this differential status of guidelines and appraisals: 'it seems illogical that technology appraisals must be implemented while eminently sensible elements of clinical guidelines are not obligatory'.[105]

Fourthly, NICE's 'topic selection' process is not random, but rather is intended to ensure that NICE issues guidance on novel or expensive treatments in a rolling programme of appraisals, decided upon in collaboration with the Horizon Scanning Research and Intelligence Centre at the University of Birmingham. While it is sensible for NICE to concentrate its

---

[103] Trevor A Sheldon et al, 'What's the evidence that NICE guidance has been implemented? Results from a national evaluation using time series analysis, audit of patients' notes, and interviews' (2004) 329 British Medical Journal 999.

[104] *National Institute for Health and Clinical Excellence*, First Report of Session 2006–07, paras 289–90.

[105] Ibid, para 292.

resources on evaluating the cost-effectiveness of expensive new treatments, when coupled with the duty to fund NICE recommendations, the result of this prioritized review may be that only certain patient groups benefit from the requirement to fund NICE-approved treatments. This skews funding towards new and expensive medicines for acute illness, and away from low-tech interventions and preventative and primary care. It also means that NICE has spent more time evaluating new medicines, at the expense, perhaps, of promoting disinvestment from cost-ineffective existing medicines.

Leila Rooshenas et al observed CCG meetings and found multiple barriers to disinvestment, not least because so much of the CCGs' time was taken up with implementing NICE recommendations.

Leila Rooshenas et al[106]

Discussions of new opportunities for disinvestment were largely absent from observed commissioning group meetings, which largely focused on new investments. Interviews and observed meetings revealed practical and ideological barriers to disinvestment, including an absence of guidance and capacity to engage in disinvestment, difficulties in collaboration, reluctance to engage in explicit rationing, and a perceived lack of central/political support …

[W]e found little evidence of tools to support disinvestment decision-making. Our study showed the direct and indirect consequences of not having a clear disinvestment process—both in terms of identifying worthwhile opportunities for disinvestment, and implementing proposals as policy …

Despite general consensus that disinvestment is a cornerstone to sustaining some health systems, disinvestment in practice is imbued with difficulties. A lack of guidelines and capacity make it difficult to engage in disinvestment. Furthermore, 'disinvestment' is a poorly demarcated term that sparks a range of different understandings. First steps towards advancing the disinvestment agenda should consider providing a clear definition of the term, and developing specific tools and guidelines to support decision-makers.

In response to the concern that it should do more to promote disinvestment, NICE has set up a 'do not do' database, which contains a long list, extracted from its guidance and appraisals, of treatments that should not be prescribed within the NHS. Examples include pharmacological interventions to aid sleep, unless sleep problems persist after the patient has followed a sleep plan; antidepressants for patients suffering from mild depression; and antibiotics in a range of specific cases.

NHS England has also tried to reduce low-value prescribing, issuing guidance on 18 products that are not cost-effective or are deemed to be a low priority, including some painkillers, herbal treatments, dietary supplements and antidepressants, on which the NHS spends around £141 million a year,[107] with some products like homeopathy being completely blacklisted.

Fifthly, giving 'interested parties'—such as the pharmaceutical industry and patient advocacy groups (which are often funded by the industry) —a right to make representations and a right of appeal has led to the criticism that NICE might be too easily swayed by powerful lobbying interests.

---

[106] "'I won't call it rationing …'": an ethnographic study of healthcare disinvestment in theory and practice' (2015) 128 Social Science & Medicine 273–81.

[107] *Items which should not routinely be prescribed in primary care: Guidance for CCGs* (NHS England, 2017).

Finally, in the next extract Michael Calnan et al draw on their study of NICE appraisal committees to suggest that there is more uncertainty and 'muddle' involved than is sometimes assumed.

Michael Calnan, Ferhana Hashem, and Patrick Brown[108]

The interpersonal uncertainty associated with a lack of trust in the drug manufacturers' competencies and motives led to several stances, strategies, or tactics. One was a general skepticism adopted by the committee toward the drug manufacturers' submissions requiring them to prove that their case was a genuine one ...

A similarly critical or ambivalent stance was adopted by the committees toward the testimonies of the patient and clinical experts, as there was concern about the latter's conflicts of interest and possibilities of being 'captured' by the drug industry, or having too narrow an experiential focus rather than being concerned with what was best for the NHS patient population as a whole. The ambivalence or caution expressed about the opinions of these experts led to their evidence being used as supplementary or supportive information to the overall decision of the committee ...

The stereotype of NICE as a procedurally rational, evidence-based regulatory institution contrasts with the messy process of committee decision making above; [David] Mechanic's description of muddling through elegantly is apposite here. This was exemplified by the informal strategies used by individual committee members for dealing with residual uncertainty and aspects of complexity, particularly in relation to the technicality and sheer volume of information provided. These strategies included developing rules of thumb, using 'gut reactions' based on intuitive/tacit knowledge, and other ways of simplifying highly complex material ...

Potential solutions to some of the problems raised by this study might include giving the committee a further decision outcome, such as 'intolerable uncertainty' or insufficient data, which would assist in placing an onus on manufacturers to make their submissions as clear and transparent as possible.

4 CHALLENGING RATIONING DECISIONS

(a) JUDICIAL REVIEW

As we saw earlier, one requirement of Daniels and Sabin's 'accountability for reasonableness' is that rationing decisions should be open to challenge. Judicial review is available to scrutinize the legality but not the merits of decisions taken by public authorities, such as CCGs or NICE.

A patient who believes that a CCG has wrongly deprived her of treatment can apply for judicial review on the grounds that the CCG acted illegally, unfairly, or irrationally. A patient could also apply for judicial review of a decision on the grounds that it infringed her rights under the Human Rights Act 1998.

It is noteworthy that there were no challenges to NHS funding decisions in the first 30 years of the NHS's existence. As we saw earlier, implicit rationing meant that in the past patients

---

[108] 'Still elegantly muddling through? NICE and uncertainty in decision making about the rationing of expensive medicines in England' (2017) 47 International Journal of Health Services 571–94.

were seldom aware that treatment was rationed. In addition to being better informed, patients' expectations are now higher, and they are more willing to complain.

One of the first judicial review cases to attract media attention was the 'Child B' case, or *R v Cambridge Health Authority, ex parte B*.[109] Jaymee Bowen, who was ten years old, had developed acute myeloid leukaemia. Consultants at Addenbrooke's Hospital in Cambridge, and at the Royal Marsden Hospital in London, agreed that the only possible treatment (intensive chemotherapy and a second bone marrow transplant) would be unlikely to succeed, and was not in her best interests. Her father sought second opinions from other doctors in the UK and in the US. Treatment in the US would have been prohibitively expensive, but he did find one doctor at the Hammersmith Hospital in London who was prepared to treat his daughter privately, and he sought an extra-contractual referral from Cambridge and Huntingdon Health Authority to pay for the £75,000 treatment. His request was refused, not because the treatment was too expensive but because her doctors believed that it would be ineffective and inappropriate. Jaymee's father then applied for judicial review of this decision.

At first instance, Laws J called upon the health authority to justify its decision by explaining the priorities which had led it to refuse to fund Child B's treatment. Later the same day, the Court of Appeal overturned his judgment on the grounds that the health authority had acted rationally and fairly, and that court intervention in such a case would be misguided.

R v Cambridge Health Authority, ex parte B[110]

Sir Thomas Bingham MR

I have no doubt that in a perfect world any treatment which a patient, or a patient's family, sought would be provided if doctors were willing to give it, no matter how much it cost, particularly when a life was potentially at stake. It would however, in my view, be shutting one's eyes to the real world if the court were to proceed on the basis that we do live in such a world. It is common knowledge that health authorities of all kinds are constantly pressed to make ends meet. They cannot pay their nurses as much as they would like; they cannot provide all the treatments they would like; they cannot purchase all the extremely expensive medical equipment they would like; they cannot carry out all the research they would like; they cannot build all the hospitals and specialist units they would like. Difficult and agonising judgments have to be made as to how a limited budget is best allocated to the maximum advantage of the maximum number of patients. That is not a judgment which the court can make.

As a result of media coverage of this case—*The Sun*'s headline was 'Condemned by Bank Balance'—an anonymous private benefactor came forward to pay for Jaymee Bowen's treatment. The consultant who had agreed to treat Jaymee privately decided against a second bone marrow transplant, and instead gave her an experimental donor lymphocyte infusion. Jaymee survived for a few more months and died the following year.

One of the reasons for the courts' reluctance to interfere with funding decisions is that they are not in a position to know about the other—possibly more compelling—claims upon the NHS's scarce resources. If funds are diverted to patient A, there may not be enough to pay for the treatment of patients B, C, or D, none of whom has been represented before the court. This point was emphasized by Lord Donaldson MR in *Re J (A Minor)*:[111]

---

[109] [1995] 1 WLR 898.   [110] [1995] 1 WLR 898.   [111] [1992] 4 All ER 614.

> I would stress the absolute undesirability of the court making an order which may have the effect of compelling a doctor or health authority to make available scarce resources (both human and material) to a particular child, without knowing whether or not there are other patients to whom those resources might more advantageously be devoted.

More recently, there have been a number of cases in which the courts have found that health authorities have acted unlawfully when deciding not to fund particular treatments. In *R v North West Lancashire Health Authority, ex parte A*,[112] Auld LJ agreed that health authorities were entitled to make lists of treatments which were not a priority, and he agreed that it would 'make sense' to give gender reassignment surgery a lower priority than treatment for cancer, heart disease, or kidney failure. But he found that the health authority's policy did not make adequate provision for an individual's exceptional circumstances to be taken into account, and that the policy should therefore be reformulated in order to (a) acknowledge properly that transsexualism is an illness, and (b) make effective provision for exceptions in individual cases. In practice, it is possible that the health authority could still refuse to fund these applicants' gender reassignment surgery, as long as it offered them reasons for its decision.

Of course, the reasons given for refusing treatment must be defensible. In *R (on the application of Rose) v Thanet Clinical Commissioning Group*, a CCG had refused to fund oocyte preservation for a woman with Crohn's disease who was about to undergo treatment that would leave her infertile. One of the reasons it gave was that it disagreed with NICE's updated guideline on the effectiveness of oocyte preservation. Jay J found that Thanet CCG was not obliged to follow the NICE guideline, but that it could not legitimately disagree with NICE's evaluation of the scientific evidence.

R (on the application of Rose) v Thanet Clinical Commissioning Group [113]

Jay J

The extent of the public law obligation is to have regard to the relevant NICE guideline and to provide clear reasons for any general policy that does not follow it . . .

The Defendant has no compliance obligation as such, but the issue in the instant case is whether CCGs may legitimately disagree with NICE on matters concerning the current state of medical science. NICE's view is that the evidence base supports the effectiveness of oocyte cryopreservation, and the CCG's sole basis for not following the NICE recommendation is that it disagrees. No basis or reasoning on grounds of exceptionality has been put forward. In my judgment the Defendant could have found other reasons for not following the NICE recommendation, but not this one. It follows that the new ART policy is unlawful.

R v North and East Devon Health Authority, ex parte Coughlan[114] is an exceptional case in which the applicant was entitled to more than defensible reasons for a rationing decision. Following a road traffic accident in 1971, Miss Coughlan was tetraplegic and required constant care. In 1993, she and seven other seriously disabled patients were moved to Mardon House, a purpose-built unit, which they were assured would be their 'home for life'. In 1996, the health authority recommended that Mardon House should be closed, and alternative arrangements made for her care.

---

[112] [2000] 1 WLR 977.   [113] [2014] EWHC 1182 (Admin).   [114] [2001] QB 213.

Miss Coughlan applied for judicial review of this decision. The Court of Appeal found that the patients had a legitimate expectation not only to be treated fairly by the health authority, but also to the substantive benefit of a home for life in Mardon House. Frustrating that legitimate expectation would be so unfair that it would amount to an abuse of power. Lord Woolf suggested that a failure to honour the substantive promise made to the applicant was 'equivalent to a breach of contract in private law'.

It is important to remember that one of the reasons for treating public law differently from private law is that public authorities have a duty to balance competing claims upon their resources. The health authority's evidence to the Court of Appeal stated that Mardon House had become 'a prohibitively expensive white elephant' which 'left fewer resources available for other services'. Of course, keeping one's promises is important, but if maintaining Mardon House might jeopardize the health authority's ability to offer services to other patients, whose interests were not represented in this case, could it be argued that the Court of Appeal strayed into judging the merits, as opposed to the legality, of the decision?

Against this, Paul Craig and Søren Schønberg have suggested that the Court of Appeal in *Coughlan* rightly separated two different exercises of power by the health authority: the promise to Miss Coughlan and the policy decision to close Mardon House. Craig and Schønberg agree that the policy change was not irrational in the *Wednesbury* sense,[115] but instead the breach of promise amounted to an abuse of power.[116]

More recently, there have been several cases in which patients have challenged refusals to fund expensive cancer drugs. In the first of these, *R (Ann Marie Rogers) v Swindon Primary Care Trust and the Secretary of State*, Ms Rogers suffered from stage 1 breast cancer. She had had a mastectomy, and, as a result of her son's research on the internet, she asked to be tested for HER2 breast cancer, which could apparently be treated with a new drug, Herceptin, which was unlicensed for use in patients like Ms Rogers and had not yet been appraised by NICE.

Ms Rogers tested positive for HER2. Her consultant, Dr Cole, asked Swindon PCT if Ms Rogers could pay for Herceptin, while remaining an NHS patient. Its response was that she could not. Ms Rogers paid for two doses of Herceptin herself, but she was unable to pay for the whole course of treatment. The PCT's policy was not to fund the 'off-licence' prescription of drugs, unless the patient's case was exceptional. It therefore conducted an 'exceptional case review' of Ms Rogers' circumstances, and decided that, because she was in the same position as other sufferers of stage 1 breast cancer, her case could not be considered exceptional.

Ms Rogers sought judicial review of this decision on the grounds that it was arbitrary and hence irrational. The Court of Appeal found that the PCT had acted irrationally. Because all women with stage 1 breast cancer were in the same situation as Ms Rogers, the PCT's 'exceptionality' review procedure was meaningless.

R (Ann Marie Rogers) v Swindon Primary Care Trust and the Secretary of State[117]

Sir Anthony Clarke MR (giving the judgment of the Court)

The essential question is whether the policy was rational; and, in deciding whether it is rational or not, the court must consider whether there are any relevant exceptional circumstances

---

[115] Following the decision in *Associated Provincial Picture Houses Ltd. v Wednesbury Corporation* [1948] 1 KB 223, a decision is said to be *Wednesbury* unreasonable if it is so unreasonable that no reasonable public authority would make the same decision.

[116] 'Substantive Legitimate Expectations after *Coughlan*' (2000) Public Law 684–701.

[117] [2006] EWCA Civ 392.

which could justify the PCT refusing treatment to one woman within the eligible group but granting it to another. And to anticipate, the difficulty that the PCT encounters in the present case is that while the policy is stated to be one of exceptionality, no persuasive grounds can be identified, at least in clinical terms, for treating one patient who fulfils the clinical requirements for Herceptin treatment differently from others in that cohort ...

If that policy had involved a balance of financial considerations against a general policy not to fund off-licence drugs not approved by NICE and the healthcare needs of the particular patient in an exceptional case, we do not think that such a policy would have been irrational ...

The non-medical personal situation of a particular patient cannot in these circumstances be relevant to the question whether Herceptin prescribed by the patient's clinician should be funded for the benefit of the patient. Where the clinical needs are equal, and resources are not an issue, discrimination between patients in the same eligible group cannot be justified on the basis of personal characteristics not based on healthcare.

For these reasons we have reached the conclusion that the policy of the PCT is irrational.

Note that Sir Anthony Clarke specifically ruled out using 'non-medical' or personal circumstances as a reason to distinguish between different patients. In deciding whether a woman's case was 'exceptional', non-clinical considerations—the example he gave was a patient who had to care for a disabled child—had to be treated as irrelevant. Swindon PCT had said that its decision was not based upon cost. This was because the then Secretary of State for Health, Patricia Hewitt, had stated publicly that PCTs should not refuse to fund Herceptin on cost grounds. If the PCT had cited cost as a reason not to fund Herceptin for Ms Rogers, ironically the Court of Appeal admitted that they would have been on stronger ground.

In R (on the application of Otley) v Barking and Dagenham NHS Primary Care Trust,[118] the health authority's 'exceptionality policy' was held to be lawful. What was not lawful, however, was its application to Ms Otley, who was suffering from metastatic colorectal cancer, and tumours in her liver. Ms Otley had responded poorly to chemotherapy. Her sister discovered the existence of a new drug, Avastin, on the internet. Avastin was licensed in the US and in many European countries, but not in England and Wales. It cost between £1,000 and £1,500 per cycle.

Ms Otley paid for five cycles of Avastin, which she took in combination with other drugs. Her response was excellent: there were minimal side effects; she felt much better; and the tumours appeared to have shrunk. Ms Otley's doctor applied to her local PCT to fund a further five prescriptions of Avastin. The application was refused and Ms Otley applied for judicial review of that decision.

Mitting J found that while 'the policy is entirely rational and sensible', its application to Ms Otley's case was irrational. The panel had failed to take into account the fact that there were no other options available to Ms Otley. Ms Otley was young and fit; she could not tolerate other drugs; she appeared to have benefited from Avastin and had suffered no side effects. Resource considerations could not be a decisive factor in Ms Otley's case because the anticipated outlay—of another five cycles of Avastin—would be relatively modest and certainly would not jeopardize the trust's capacity to provide care for other patients. According to Mitting J, 'on any fair minded view of the exceptionality criteria identified in the critical analysis document, her case was exceptional'.

[118] [2007] EWHC 1927 (Admin).

In *R (Murphy) v Salford Primary Care Trust*, another case in which a patient challenged the refusal to pay for an expensive new cancer drug, this time for the treatment of renal cancer, Burnett J set out the principles to be applied in these cases.

R (Murphy) v Salford Primary Care Trust[119]

Burnett J

The legal principles that are in play are not controversial:

a. When an NHS body makes a decision about whether to fund a treatment in an individual patient's case it is entitled to take into account the financial restraints on its budget as well as the patient's circumstances.

b. Decisions about how to allocate scarce resources between patients are ones with which the Courts will not usually intervene absent irrationality on the part of the decision-maker. There are severe limits on the ability of the Court to intervene.

c. The Court's role is not to express opinions as to the effectiveness of medical treatment or the merits of medical judgment.

d. It is lawful for an NHS body to decide to decline to fund treatment save in exceptional circumstances, provided that it is possible to envisage such circumstances.

Seven grounds were put forward as to why Ms Murphy's case should be treated as exceptional, such as the fact that she also suffered from breast cancer, which excluded her from a clinical trial of this new drug, and that she had had mental health problems. The panel considered each of these factors individually, and none was judged sufficient to mark Ms Murphy out as an exceptional case. Burnett J decided that, in addition to their individual consideration, the panel should also have looked at Ms Murphy's case 'in the round':

As a matter of general principle when considering a series of factors which might inform the overall decision, it is of course necessary to look at them individually ... But having looked at all factors individually, it seems to me that it is necessary to consider them in the round.

Burnett J therefore quashed the original decision and remitted it back to the Commissioning Panel, which could, of course, come to the same decision again, provided that before doing so it considered Ms Murphy's circumstances 'in the round'.

In *R (on the application of Ross) v West Sussex Primary Care Trust*,[120] the judge found that the PCT's exceptionality review process was unlawful because it had required Mr Ross to prove that his case was unique. As Judge Grenfell explained: 'the Review and Appeal Panels [fell] into error simply on the ground that they clearly thought that, because other patients could find themselves in the Claimant's position, therefore, he did not come within the exceptionality [policy]'.

But while there have been successful applications for judicial review of funding decisions, it continues to be difficult to prove that an exceptionality review policy and the way it is implemented is irrational, especially given the cost constraints under which the NHS must operate.

---

[119] [2008] EWHC 1908 (Admin).   [120] [2008] EWHC 2252 (Admin).

In *R (on the application of C) v Berkshire West Primary Care Trust*, the Court of Appeal was adamant that neither the trust's policy of treating breast augmentation surgery as a 'non-core' treatment for gender identity disorder, nor its decision that C was not an exceptional case, was irrational.

R (on the application of C) v Berkshire West Primary Care Trust[121]

Hooper LJ

The appellant in this case was seeking NHS funding for a surgical operation where the PCT had reasonably concluded (as the judge found and was, in my view, entitled to find) that there was an absence of evidence that it was likely to be clinically effective to improve the appellant's health ... I understand why the appellant feels aggrieved that the respondent funds the core gender reassignment procedures outlined in the Policy, notwithstanding the absence of evidence of limited clinical effectiveness, but does not also fund breast augmentation surgery for persons like the appellant ... But the answer in law to that feeling is that the respondent, in exercising its statutory responsibilities, has to make very difficult choices as to what procedures to fund and not to fund and the choice made in this case is not irrational.

In addition, it is worth reiterating that a finding that a funding refusal was unlawful does not mean that funding will be made available.[122] In *R (on the application of SB) v NHS England*, for example, Andrews J was clear that the individual funding request panel's decision to refuse to fund Kuvan for a severely autistic seven-year-old child, whose phenylalanine levels could not be controlled adequately through dietary management, was irrational, but she warned that a decision grounded in a proper interpretation of exceptionality and clinical effectiveness might still be to refuse to fund Kuvan for S.

R (on the application of SB) v NHS England[123]

Andrews J

[O]nce it is accepted that the incidence and severity of S's autism is such that, compared with the other children of a similar age with PKU (even those who also have less severe autism) his behaviour precludes his phenylalanine blood levels from being satisfactorily managed within target levels on the standard treatment of diet and supplements alone, it is difficult to see how the panel could reach any other rational conclusion than that he was likely to gain significantly more clinical benefit from taking Kuvan than other children with PKU whose condition could be managed by the conventional treatment alone ...

If 'clinical effectiveness' is properly interpreted, the evidence that Kuvan is clinically effective is overwhelming. In my judgment, there is no room for a rational conclusion that Kuvan is not clinically effective or that the evidence of its clinical effectiveness (for the precise purposes for which it is sought to be used here) is insufficient. Given that the supposed absence of

---

[121] [2011] EWCA Civ 247.
[122] See, for example, the comments of Ouseley J in *R (on the application of Gordon) v Bromley NHS Primary Care Trust* [2006] EWHC 2462 (Admin).
[123] [2017] EWHC 2000 (Admin).

evidence of clinical effectiveness was the specific reason given ... for turning down the application, that is such a material error that it suffices in and of itself to warrant quashing the decision and sending it back for reconsideration ...

Whilst this judgment is bound to give rise to a degree of optimism, I must caution against raising hopes too high. The fact that this claim for judicial review has succeeded does not mean that there will necessarily be a favourable outcome to this IFR application. However much one might hope that on the next occasion the panel will decide that the net additional expenditure of treating S with Kuvan would be justified having regard to the likely clinical benefit of keeping his blood phenylalanine levels consistently within the range that would avoid his suffering any additional neurological impairment, thereby potentially enabling him to realise his maximum functioning potential, they could still lawfully decide to refuse funding. It is their decision, and their decision alone; and provided it is taken on the basis of the correct interpretation of the IFR policy, and a proper understanding of the case put before the panel and the supporting evidence, it will not be open to challenge.

R (on the application of S (A Child)) v NHS England was therefore a most unusual case in which Collins J not only held that it was 'impossible' not to categorise the claimant as exceptional, but also ordered that sodium oxybate should be provided for three months, on a trial basis, to a teenager with severe narcolepsy.

R (on the application of S (A Child)) v NHS England [124]

Collins J

Her condition is rare, and her failure to respond to the usual treatment is also rare. But she is in a very rare situation in that she suffers from a particularly rare form of the condition ... Since exceptional cannot mean unique, it is in my view difficult if not impossible to see that the claimant should not be considered to meet the exceptionality test. If she is not exceptional, who is? I should add that in her case there is clear evidence that her mental and physical health is suffering and will get worse. Thus she will benefit from the treatment with sodium oxybate to a greater extent than others who are not receptive to the usual treatment ...

Normally in cases such as this ... the remedy would be to quash the decision and to require reconsideration in accordance with the judgment given. But I am satisfied that this case is indeed exceptional to the extent that a decision to refuse the treatment could not be supportable. Accordingly, I took the unusual step of making an interim order that the defendant should fund the provision of sodium oxybate to the claimant for a three month trial period.

(b) INDIVIDUAL FUNDING REQUESTS (IFRS)

Since the *North West Lancashire* case, it has been clear that it is unlawful for health authorities not to provide a route through which an individual patient can claim that their circumstances are exceptional, and, as is clear from the cases described above, patients who challenge funding decisions are almost always challenging refusals of these individual funding requests

---

[124] [2016] EWHC 1395 (Admin).

(IFRs). It is increasingly common for patients to make IFRs: 68,051 were processed in 2016–17, an increase of 47 per cent over the previous four years. While 52 per cent of these were approved, up from 43 per cent four years ago, there is, as Gareth Iacobucci points out, considerable regional variation in how IFRs are handled, leading to concerns about a post-code lottery in discretionary funding.

Gareth Iacobucci[125]

[T]he sharp increase in the overall number of requests means that thousands more patients are being turned down for funding each year, while many others are forced to wait for their treatment while their request is considered.

Again, there is much variation in how many requests are approved. Southern Derbyshire CCG received just 14 requests last year for procedures such as cataract surgery but approved none. In contrast, Stafford and Surrounds CCG processed 2123 requests, including 764 for skin excision, 232 for cataracts, and 163 for hip or knee replacement, but approved them all. Doctors' leaders told The BMJ that the increase in the requests and the wide variation in access was discriminating against patients in some parts of the country.

While it might be clear that a patient's situation does not have to be unique in order for her to be judged exceptional, Amy Ford has argued that exceptionality 'has been far too broadly and loosely defined': if a patient might be more likely to benefit from treatment, that could be relevant, but not decisive; her social circumstances should not normally be relevant; and her prognosis might or might not be a factor.

Amy Ford[126]

If we take the five cancer patients who sought judicial review of the funding decisions made by their respective PCTs, Ann Rogers, Linda Gordon, Victoria Otley, Jean Murphy, and Colin Ross, and apply the criteria outlined above to them, using the information available to us in the court reports about their circumstances, the manifest lack of objectivity in the concepts that emerges, aside from the suggestion that social circumstances can be disregarded, means that each individual could be determined to be both exceptional and unexceptional, depending on how the criteria are interpreted . . .

In the absence of clear legal criteria on the determination of exceptionality, reaching decisions which are robust enough to withstand judicial review is challenging and PCTs are exposed to the risk of costly legal action. Furthermore, the money and time spent by PCTs on defensive legal action cannot be invested in improving clinical care. Clinicians are left bewildered as to why some seemingly very similar patients are deemed exceptional, when others are not. The process of applying for funding on the basis of exceptional circumstances creates unrealistic expectations for patients, fuelled by media hype and indirect marketing by pharmaceutical companies. In addition, seeking recourse in the courts is not an option easily accessible to all, further increasing inequities between patients.

---

[125] 'Pressure on NHS finances drives new wave of postcode rationing' (2017) 358 British Medical Journal j3190.
[126] 'The Concept of Exceptionality: A Legal Farce?' (2012) 20 Medical Law Review 304–36.

(c) THE HUMAN RIGHTS ACT 1998

If a patient is denied treatment which might save her life, would it be possible to argue that her right to life, protected under Article 2, has been violated? Article 2 not only obliges public bodies to refrain from deliberately taking its citizens' lives, but it can also sometimes require them to take adequate measures to protect life.[127] While patients will not generally be able to use Article 2 to force health authorities to fund expensive medicines, in exceptional circumstances, it might be possible to challenge a refusal to provide potentially life-saving measures on human rights grounds.

One such exceptional case was *Savage v South Essex Partnership NHS Foundation Trust*,[128] in which the House of Lords found that, where a mentally ill patient was a known suicide risk, there was an obligation, under Article 2, to do all that could reasonably be expected in order to prevent that risk materializing. The duty to provide services under Article 2 was triggered, according to Lady Hale, by 'a "real and immediate risk to life" about which the authorities knew or ought to have known at the time'.

If sufficiently serious, could a denial of medical treatment also amount to 'inhuman or degrading treatment', prohibited under Article 3? At first instance in *R (on the application of Watts) v Bedford Primary Care Trust*, Munby J rejected the patient's claim that having to wait a year for a hip replacement operation might amount to a breach of Article 3.

R (on the application of Watts) v Bedford Primary Care Trust[129]

Munby J

Article 3 is not engaged unless the 'ill-treatment' in question attains a minimum level of severity and involves actual bodily injury or intense physical or mental suffering. However that is not this case. Making every allowance for the constant pain and suffering that the claimant was having to endure—and I do not seek in any way to minimise it—the simple fact in my judgment is that nothing she had to endure was so severe or so humiliating as to engage Article 3.

In contrast, in *Price v United Kingdom*, the prison authority's inadequate treatment of a four-limb-deficient thalidomide victim with numerous health problems amounted to a violation of Article 3.

Price v United Kingdom[130]

Judgment of the European Court of Human Rights (ECtHR)

There is no evidence in this case of any positive intention to humiliate or debase the applicant. However, the Court considers that to detain a severely disabled person in conditions where she is dangerously cold, risks developing sores because her bed is too hard or unreachable, and is unable to go to the toilet or keep clean without the greatest of difficulty, constitutes degrading treatment contrary to Article 3.

---

[127] ECtHR, Guide on Article 2 of the European Convention on Human Rights: Right to life (ECtHR, 2019).
[128] [2008] UKHL 74.　　[129] [2003] EWHC 2228 (Admin).　　[130] (2001) 34 EHRR 1285.

There have also been attempts to argue that a refusal to fund treatment might amount to unlawful interference with a patient's private and family life, and hence breach Article 8. In *R (on the application of Condliff) v North Staffordshire Primary Care Trust*,[131] Mr Condliff's PCT had a policy only to fund gastric band operations for patients whose body mass index (BMI) was greater than 50. Mr Condliff was morbidly obese and suffered from a range of associated health problems, but because his BMI was 43, he did not fit within the PCT's policy. He made an individual funding request (IFR) on the grounds that his was an exceptional case. The PCT's individual funding request policy specified that the patient's case could only be considered exceptional for clinical reasons. Social factors, such as the patient's family circumstances, were irrelevant. An appendix to the policy explained why:

> If, for example, treatment were provided which had the effect of keeping someone in paid work, this would tend to discriminate in favour of those of working age and against the retired. If a treatment were provided differentially to patients who were carers this would tend to favour treatment for women over men. If treatment were provided in part on the basis that a medical condition had affected a person at a younger age than that at which the condition normally presents, this would constitute direct age discrimination.

Mr Condliff argued that the failure to fund his gastric band operation was having a devastating effect on his private and family life—his wife had to deal with the consequences of his incontinence throughout the night, for example—and that this should have been taken into account. At first instance, and on appeal to the Court of Appeal in *R (on the application of Condliff) v North Staffordshire Primary Care Trust*, Mr Condliff's claim was refused.

R (on the application of Condliff) v North Staffordshire Primary Care Trust[132]

Toulson LJ

The PCT has grappled with the difficult ethical and practical questions involved in setting its IFR policy. In arriving at that policy the PCT has struck what it considers to be a fair balance between the interests of individuals and the community (for example, whether patients who are carers should have priority over others) and a fair balance between different patients with similar health conditions ...

Nothing in the authorities therefore leads me to conclude that the policy of the PCT, properly understood, is to be regarded as showing a lack of respect for Mr Condliff's private and family life, so as to bring article 8 into play. If, however, article 8 is applicable, there were legitimate equality reasons for the PCT to adopt the policy that it did and its decision was well within the area of discretion or margin of appreciation properly open to it ... The sad fact remains that the PCT on proper medical advice does not consider his condition to be exceptional for someone with his diabetes, obesity and co-morbidities.

Mr Condliff subsequently submitted a successful IFR request, this time presenting fresh evidence that his clinical circumstances were exceptional, on the grounds that he would benefit more from this operation than other comparable patients.

---

[131] [2011] EWCA Civ 910.   [132] Ibid.

Regardless of the usefulness or otherwise of Convention rights to patients who wish to challenge rationing decisions, the Human Rights Act 1998 has undoubtedly led to a greater emphasis upon the proportionality of decisions to restrict access to medical treatment. Keith Syrett has argued that because proportionality 'requires a court to assess the balance struck between competing interests by the decision-maker and the relevant weight accorded to interests and considerations', it represents a much more searching standard of scrutiny than *Wednesbury* unreasonableness.[133]

(d) JUDICIAL REVIEW CLAIMS AGAINST NICE

As a public body, NICE's decisions can be subject to judicial review, but given the expertise of those who carry out its technology appraisals; the openness and transparency of its processes, and its active involvement of stakeholders, it would be hard to establish procedural impropriety. Nevertheless, there have been a handful of applications for judicial review of NICE decisions, most of which have come from the pharmaceutical industry, and most of which have involved technical issues about the use of data and access to modelling assumptions.[134]

In *Eisai Ltd v National Institute for Health and Clinical Excellence*, the manufacturer of donepezil (brand name Aricept) challenged the decision of NICE's appeal panel, and NICE's subsequent guidance—that Aricept should not be funded for patients in the earlier stages of Alzheimer's disease (AD)—on the grounds of procedural unfairness, discriminatory effects, and irrationality. At first instance, Eisai succeeded only on the discrimination aspect of their claim. Mini mental-state examinations, used to judge AD's severity, produced inaccurate results in non-native English speakers and people with learning difficulties, and hence breached NICE's obligations under equality law.

Eisai then appealed successfully to the Court of Appeal on the grounds of procedural fairness. Their claim was that, by giving them access to 'read only' versions of NICE's economic modelling formulae, it was impossible for them to check or comment upon the reliability of NICE's calculations. In *Eisai Ltd v National Institute for Health and Clinical Excellence*,[135] the Court of Appeal held that 'procedural fairness does require release of the fully executable version of the model'.

Giving Eisai access to the functional version of the modelling tool did not alter the judgement that Aricept's cost per QALY for patients with mild AD was too great to justify NHS provision. In August 2009, after the Court of Appeal's decision, NICE reiterated that for people with mild AD, Aricept's cost per QALY ranged from £56,000 to £72,000, and this was still too high to make Aricept cost-effective.[136] The following year NICE changed its mind on Aricept and two similar drugs, however, citing new evidence of the drugs' effectiveness. There had not been a new landmark study, and NICE itself had described the evidence base as 'disappointing'. Nevertheless, by adjusting its calculations to give more weight to the costs of caring for someone with AD, the cost per QALY was reduced to £30,000 and NHS provision was judged acceptable.[137]

---

[133] *Law, Legitimacy and the Rationing of Health Care* (CUP: Cambridge, 2007) 166–7.

[134] See, eg, *R (on the application of Bristol-Myers Squibb) v National Institute for Health and Clinical Excellence* [2009] EWHC 2722 (Admin) and *Servier Laboratories v National Institute for Health and Clinical Excellence* [2010] EWCA Civ 346.

[135] [2008] EWCA Civ 438.

[136] Zosia Kmietowicz, 'NICE decision on dementia drugs was based on "common sense" not evidence, expert says' (2010) 341 British Medical Journal 5642.

[137] Ibid.

There has been one case in which patients have sought to challenge a NICE patient care guideline. In *R (on the application of Fraser) v National Institute for Health and Clinical Excellence*,[138] two patients who had been diagnosed with Myalgic Encephalomyelitis (ME) claimed that NICE had acted irrationally by giving too little consideration to pharmaceutical treatments for ME, and had prioritized instead psycho-social treatments, such as cognitive behavioural therapy and graded exercise therapy. They advanced a number of grounds for this claim, many alleging bias or conflict of interest on the part of NICE's expert advisers. All were rejected, and the court also noted that legal proceedings of this type might serve as a disincentive to healthcare professionals from involving themselves in NICE's decision-making processes in the future.

(e) BREACH OF STATUTORY DUTY

The National Health Service Act creates a duty on the part of the Secretary of State, which is now shared with NHS England, and with CCGs.

National Health Service Act 2006 sections 1 and 3, as amended

1 Secretary of State's duty to promote health service

(1) The Secretary of State must continue the promotion in England of a comprehensive health service designed to secure improvement—

(a) in the physical and mental health of the people of England, and

(b) in the prevention, diagnosis and treatment of illness ...

(4) The services so provided must be free of charge except in so far as the making and recovery of charges is expressly provided for by or under any enactment, whenever passed ...

1H The National Health Service Commissioning Board and its general functions ...

(2) The [National Health Service Commissioning] Board is subject to the duty under section 1(1) concurrently with the Secretary of State [except in relation to that part of the health service which is provided in pursuance of the public health functions of the Secretary of State or local authorities ...

3(1) Duties of clinical commissioning groups as to commissioning certain health services. A clinical commissioning group must arrange for the provision of the following to such extent as it considers necessary to meet the reasonable requirements of the persons for whom it has responsibility:

(a) hospital accommodation,

(b) other accommodation for the purpose of any service provided under this Act,

(c) medical, dental, ophthalmic, nursing and ambulance services,

(d) such other services or facilities for the care of pregnant women, women who are breastfeeding and young children as the group considers are appropriate as part of the health service,

---

[138] [2009] EWHC 452 (Admin).

> (e) such other services or facilities for the prevention of illness, the care of persons suffering from illness and the after-care of persons who have suffered from illness as the group considers are appropriate as part of the health service,
>
> (f) such other services or facilities as are required for the diagnosis and treatment of illness.

Notice that the statutory duty under the National Health Service Act is to *promote* rather than to *provide* a comprehensive health service. As Lord Woolf made clear in *R v North and East Devon Health Authority, ex parte Coughlan*,[139] 'a comprehensive health service may never, for human, financial and other resource reasons, be achievable'.

Under the National Health Service Act there is no penalty or remedy prescribed for breach of the duties imposed upon the Secretary of State. And in the context of other social services, the House of Lords has confirmed that the purpose of legislation is to benefit society as a whole, rather than to offer private remedies to individual citizens.[140]

In contrast to the National Health Service Act, a rather more specific obligation is imposed on health authorities by section 17(2) of the Mental Health Act 1983: 'It shall be the duty of the district health authority ... to provide ... after-care services for any person to whom this section applies.' This is a duty to provide, rather than to promote aftercare. Nevertheless, the courts have been reluctant to find health authorities liable to individual patients for failing to make appropriate provision. In *Clunis v Camden and Islington Health Authority*, the Court of Appeal rejected Clunis's claim that the health authority might be liable for breach of its statutory duty to provide him with appropriate aftercare services.

Clunis v Camden and Islington Health Authority [141]

Beldam LJ

The primary method of enforcement of the obligations under section 117 is by complaint to the Secretary of State. No doubt, too, a decision by the district health authority or the local social services authority under the section is liable to judicial review at the instance of a patient ... [But] the wording of the section is not apposite to create a private law cause of action for failure to carry out the duties under the statute.

(f) SEEKING TREATMENT ABROAD

Could a patient who has been denied treatment in the UK, or who wants to avoid UK waiting lists, seek reimbursement for treatment abroad? Brexit will almost certainly affect UK citizens' rights to obtain medical treatment in other EU countries, so readers should be advised to check the latest available information on the NHS Confederation's website.[142]

---

[139] [2001] QB 213.
[140] See, eg, the comments of Lord Browne-Wilkinson in *X v Bedfordshire County Council* [1995] 3 All ER 353.
[141] *Clunis v Camden and Islington Health Authority* [1998] QB 978.
[142] <https://www.nhsconfed.org/regions-and-eu/nhs-european-office/>

An EU Directive on access to cross-border healthcare provision within Europe came into force in 2013,[143] and was implemented in the UK by amendments to the National Health Service Act 2006. Member States are entitled to require prior authorization in order to manage the potential outflow of patients. Prior authorization can be refused on safety grounds, or, under section 6BB(5)(d) of the National Health Service Act 2006, if the treatment could be provided in the UK 'within a period of time that is medically justifiable, taking into account the patient's state of health at the time ... and the probable course of [his] medical condition'. At the time of writing, it seems likely that UK patients will lose the right to obtain medical treatment in EU countries.

(g) THE RIGHTS OF NON-RESIDENTS

Under section 175 of the National Health Service Act 2006, only those who are 'ordinarily resident' in the UK have the right to free health care. Whether or not someone has a British passport is irrelevant. The question of whether a failed asylum seeker could be 'ordinarily resident' in the UK came before the court in *R (on the application of YA) v West Middlesex University Hospital NHS Trust*. The Court of Appeal relied upon *obiter* comments in an earlier immigration case to establish, first, 'if [the person's] presence in the country is unlawful, for example in breach of the immigration laws, he cannot rely on his unlawful residence as constituting ordinary residence', and, secondly, that there is a 'principle of public policy that the *propositus* [person immediately affected] cannot profit from his unlawful act'.

R (on the application of YA) v West Middlesex University Hospital NHS Trust[144]

Ward LJ

[T]he Secretary of State's duty ... is to continue the promotion in England of a comprehensive health service designed to secure improvement in the health 'of the people of England'. Note that it is the people *of* England, not the people *in* England, which suggests that the beneficiaries of this free health service are to be those with some link to England so as to be part and parcel of the fabric of the place. It connotes a legitimate connection with the country ... This strongly suggests that, as a rule, the benefits were not intended by Parliament to be bestowed on those who ought not to be here ...

Failed asylum seekers ought not to be here. They should never have come here in the first place and after their claims have finally been dismissed they are only here until arrangements can be made to secure their return, even if, in some cases, like the unfortunate YA, that return may be a long way off.

The National Health Service (Charges to Overseas Visitors) Regulations 2015, as amended by the National Health Service (Charges to Overseas Visitors) (Amendment) Regulations 2017, set out when overseas visitors should and should not be charged for NHS services. Regulation 3 specifies that the NHS should charge payments upfront, and withhold services until the

---

[143] Directive of the European Parliament and the Council on the application of patients' rights in cross-border healthcare (2011/24/EU).
[144] [2009] EWCA Civ 225.

estimated cost is paid in full, unless doing so would prevent or delay immediately necessary or urgent services.

Unless the person has travelled to the UK for the purpose of seeking that treatment, regulation 9 provides that no charges are made for accident and emergency services (but only before someone becomes an inpatient); family planning services (which do not include termination of pregnancy); treatment for sexually transmitted diseases; treatment provided for a condition caused by torture; female genital mutilation; domestic violence; or sexual violence, and treatment for a list of specified diseases where treatment will protect public health, including TB, leprosy, rabies, malaria, and HIV (HIV was added to this list as a result of evidence that antiretroviral medication substantially reduced the risk of onward transmission).

The Department of Health has issued guidance on the Regulations which spells out when treatment should be given without first seeking payment, but which also specifies that attempts should be made to recover the costs of that treatment.

Department of Health[145]

8.2. Relevant bodies must also ensure that treatment which clinicians consider to be immediately necessary or urgent is provided to any patient, even if they have not paid in advance. Failure to provide immediately necessary treatment may be unlawful under the Human Rights Act 1998. Urgent treatment should also always be provided to any person, even if deposits have not been secured. Non-urgent treatment must not be provided unless the estimated full charge is received in advance of treatment . . .

8.4. Immediately necessary treatment is that which a patient needs promptly:

- to save their life; or
- to prevent a condition from becoming immediately life-threatening; or
- to prevent permanent serious damage from occurring.

8.5. Relevant bodies must always provide treatment which is classed as immediately necessary by the treating clinician irrespective of whether or not the patient has been informed of, or agreed to pay, charges, and it must not be delayed or withheld to establish the patient's chargeable status or seek payment. It must be provided even when the patient has indicated that they cannot afford to pay.

8.6. Due to the severe health risks associated with conditions such as eclampsia and preeclampsia, and in order to protect the lives of both mother and unborn baby, all maternity services must be treated as being immediately necessary . . .

8.7. Urgent treatment is that which clinicians do not consider immediately necessary, but which nevertheless cannot wait until the person can be reasonably expected to leave the UK. Clinicians may base their decision on a range of factors, including the pain or disability a particular condition is causing, the risk that delay might mean a more involved or expensive medical intervention being required, or the likelihood of a substantial and potentially life-threatening deterioration occurring in the patient's condition if treatment is delayed until they return to their own country.

8.8. For urgent treatment, relevant bodies are strongly advised to make every effort, taking account of the individual's circumstances, to secure payment in the time before treatment is scheduled. However, if that proves unsuccessful, the treatment should not be delayed or withheld for the purposes of securing payment.

---

[145] *Guidance on Implementing the Overseas Visitors Hospital Charging Regulations* (DH: London, 2015).

8.9. Treatment is not made free of charge by virtue of being provided on an immediately necessary or urgent basis. Charges found to apply cannot be waived and if payment is not obtained before treatment then every effort must be made to recover it after treatment has been provided.

8.10. Non-urgent treatment is routine elective treatment that can wait until the patient leaves the UK. Relevant bodies must not provide non-urgent treatment until the estimated full cost of treatment has been received.

A different issue arises when a failed asylum seeker or other illegal immigrant is desperately ill and facing deportation to a country where she will not receive the care that she needs. On a number of occasions, the courts have been asked to consider whether deportation in such cases could amount to inhuman and degrading treatment, and hence be a violation of Article 3.

In *D v United Kingdom*,[146] D, who was due to be deported to St Kitts after his release from prison, was suffering from HIV/AIDS. His illness was at a very advanced stage, and death was imminent. Deportation to St Kitts would mean that D would not have access to treatment, including palliative care, and his death was likely to be painful and distressing. The ECtHR decided that 'in the very exceptional circumstances of this case and given the compelling humanitarian considerations at stake, it must be concluded that the implementation of the decision to remove the applicant would be a violation of Article 3'.

Subsequent cases have fleshed out when a patient's circumstances will be sufficiently 'exceptional' to make deportation a breach of Article 3. The bar is a very high one, as we can see from *N v United Kingdom*. N was a Ugandan citizen whose application for asylum had been refused. N had been diagnosed with advanced HIV/AIDS, and as a result of the treatment she had received in the UK, her condition had stabilized. N had a good chance of surviving for decades if treatment continued; without treatment, N would be unlikely to live for more than two years. N claimed that forcing her to return to Uganda would amount to inhuman and degrading treatment. The House of Lords dismissed her appeal on the grounds that her case was not sufficiently exceptional.[147]

N then took her case to the ECtHR. In *N v United Kingdom*, a majority in the ECtHR agreed with the House of Lords that N's case did not meet the high exceptionality threshold set by *D v United Kingdom*.

N v United Kingdom[148]

Judgment of the ECtHR

The decision to remove an alien who is suffering from a serious mental or physical illness to a country where the facilities for the treatment of that illness are inferior to those available in the Contracting State may raise an issue under Article 3, but only in a very exceptional case, where the humanitarian grounds against the removal are compelling. In the *D* case the very exceptional circumstances were that the applicant was critically ill and appeared to be close to death, could not be guaranteed any nursing or medical care in his country of origin and had

---

[146] (1997) 24 EHRR 423.   [147] *N v Secretary of State for the Home Department* [2005] UKHL 31.
[148] Application no 26565/05 (2008).

no family there willing or able to care for him or provide him with even a basic level of food, shelter or social support.

The Court does not exclude that there may be other very exceptional cases where the humanitarian considerations are equally compelling. However, it considers that it should maintain the high threshold set in *D v the United Kingdom* ...

Advances in medical science, together with social and economic differences between countries, entail that the level of treatment available in the Contracting State and the country of origin may vary considerably. While it is necessary, given the fundamental importance of Article 3 in the Convention system, for the Court to retain a degree of flexibility to prevent expulsion in very exceptional cases, Article 3 does not place an obligation on the Contracting State to alleviate such disparities through the provision of free and unlimited health care to all aliens without a right to stay within its jurisdiction. A finding to the contrary would place too great a burden on the Contracting States.

D v United Kingdom is treated as the paradigm example of an 'exceptional' case, and yet treatment options for HIV have improved dramatically since D's case was decided.[149] If the critical factor which marked D's case out was his imminent death, the existence of antiretroviral drugs which enable HIV sufferers to lead longer and healthier lives makes it virtually impossible for someone currently receiving effective treatment to fit within the *D v United Kingdom* exception.

In *GS (India) v Secretary of State for the Home Department*, six claimants were seeking to challenge their deportation on the grounds that they would be at risk of an early death if deported. Five of the claimants were suffering from end-stage kidney disease; the sixth was at an advanced stage of HIV/AIDS. None of their claims succeeded under Article 3. It was not enough to show that a claimant would suffer gravely if deported, it also had to be shown, as Laws LJ, put it in his judgment, 'that the impugned state should be held responsible for his plight'.

GS (India) v Secretary of State for the Home Department[150]

Underhill LJ

The starting point as regards this part of the claim must be that, as the European Court of Human Rights has repeatedly affirmed, article 3 does not confer on a person who is liable to removal the right to remain in the territory of a contracting state in order to benefit from medical treatment which would not be available to him in the state to which he is returned. To put it another way, the returning state cannot be regarded as having responsibility for the inadequacy of the healthcare system in the country of return or, therefore, for the suffering which the person who is returned may undergo as a result of that inadequacy ... [T]hat principle applies even where the life of the person removed would be 'significantly shortened' by the inability to access treatment.

---

[149] Stephanie Palmer, 'AIDS, Expulsion and Article 3 of the European Convention on Human Rights' (2005) 5 European Human Rights Law Review 533–40.
[150] [2015] EWCA Civ 40.

In this case, the claimants had additionally attempted to resist deportation through Article 8. Such claims are also usually unsuccessful.[151] In *R (on the application of Razgar) v Secretary of State for the Home Department (No 2)*,[152] for example, R was an Iraqi of Kurdish origin who had been refused asylum in Germany. R resisted removal from the UK on the ground that it would violate his human rights under Article 8, because he was receiving psychiatric treatment for depression and post-traumatic stress disorder. The House of Lords found that it would be possible to rely on Article 8 to resist removal if it would damage a person's mental health, but that the threshold was again very high, amounting, according to Lord Bingham, to 'something very much more extreme than relative disadvantage'. Indeed, Lady Hale's judgment started with the observation that 'it is not easy to think of a foreign healthcare case which would fail under article 3 but succeed under article 8'.

Unsurprisingly, therefore, in *GS (India) v Secretary of State for the Home Department*, five of the six claimants' Article 8 claims were also dismissed (in the sixth case, the Secretary of State had accepted that it is arguable that the Upper Tribunal had failed adequately to consider GM's Article 8 claim, and the case was remitted back by consent for redetermination).

GS (India) v Secretary of State for the Home Department[153]

Underhill LJ

First, the absence or inadequacy of medical treatment, even life-preserving treatment, in the country of return, cannot be relied on at all as a factor engaging article 8: if that is all there is, the claim must fail. Secondly, where article 8 is engaged by other factors, the fact that the claimant is receiving medical treatment in this country which may not be available in the country of return may be a factor in the proportionality exercise; but that factor cannot be treated as by itself giving rise to a breach since that would contravene the 'no obligation to treat' principle.

5 PUBLIC HEALTH

(a) WHAT IS PUBLIC HEALTH LAW?

Public health law is concerned not with the medical treatment of individual patients, but instead with measures to benefit the health of the public as a whole. This involves monitoring the public's health, and designing interventions in order to reduce the overall burden of disease, disability, and premature mortality within the population. A wide variety of interventions might help to improve the health of the public, including vaccination programmes; sex education; needle-exchange programmes; fluoridation of tap water; low emissions zones; safe cycle lanes; and encouraging people to stop smoking, drink less alcohol, and reduce their sugar intake.

Public health interventions might or might not benefit a particular individual. A good example is the mandatory wearing of seat belts, a policy that has significantly reduced deaths

---

[151] See also *Bensaid v United Kingdom* (2001) 33 EHRR 10.   [152] [2004] UKHL 27.
[153] [2015] EWCA Civ 40.

from road traffic accidents. I might never be involved in a crash in which wearing a seat belt saves my life; indeed, I might be involved in a crash in which wearing a seat belt fails to save my life. But regardless of whether or not I will ever benefit from wearing a seat belt, it is very clearly in the interests of the population as a whole that everyone wears a seat belt when driving.

Public health interventions thus save 'statistical lives', rather than heroically rescuing specific individuals. As Ronald Bayer et al explain: 'This creates a political problem because public health officials cannot claim credit for rescuing identifiable persons—credit that has a powerful appeal in a culture of individualism.'[154] Geoffrey Rose further points out that because even the most effective public health measures may offer little in the short term for a particular person, it can be hard to motivate the individual subject: 'Mostly people act for substantial and immediate rewards, and the medical motivation for health education is inherently weak. Their health next year is not likely to be much better if they accept our advice or if they reject it.'[155]

A public health approach to cancer would focus not on funding expensive cancer drugs, but on the fact that 35 per cent of all cancers are attributable to 'modifiable risk factors',[156] including 'tobacco use; alcohol consumption; unhealthy diets and physical inactivity; infections; occupational exposures, such as asbestos; and environmental factors, such as radiation and chemical pollution'.[157]

In relation to smoking, for example, hardly anyone starts smoking in adulthood. Unless teenagers continue to start to smoke, the tobacco industry's consumers will eventually die out. As a result, the industry is dependent upon persuading teenagers to smoke, while public health policies are intended to make starting smoking seem expensive, inconvenient, and unattractive. To this end, the World Health Organization's *Framework Convention on Tobacco Control* sets out a range of regulatory measures, from higher taxes to plain packaging, that states should implement in order to discourage young people from taking up smoking.

Responsibility for public health was delegated to local government in 2013, with support from Public Health England (PHE), an Executive Agency of the Department of Health and Social Care. PHE is charged with bringing together evidence on public health and supporting local government, via its Health and Wellbeing Boards, to protect the public's health. It also has a role in preparing for public health emergencies, such as flu pandemics. PHE has set out its seven priorities: tackling obesity, reducing smoking, reducing harmful drinking, ensuring that every child has the best start in life, reducing dementia risk, tackling antimicrobial resistance, and reducing tuberculosis.[158]

PHE publishes extraordinarily detailed annual health profiles for each region in the country. These describe health inequalities both within each area, and across the UK, and, as a result, they make for sobering reading. For example, in the London Borough of Camden: 'Life expectancy is 10.0 years lower for men and 7.5 years lower for women in the most deprived areas of Camden than in the least deprived areas.'[159] In Blackpool: 'Life expectancy is 13.6 years lower for men and 9.6 years lower for women in the most deprived areas of Blackpool than in

---

[154] 'Introduction' in Ronald Bayer et al (eds), *Public Health Ethics* (OUP: Oxford, 2007) 27–31.

[155] Geoffrey Rose, 'Sick Individuals and Sick Populations' in Ronald Bayer et al (eds), *Public Health Ethics* (OUP: Oxford, 2007) 33–43.

[156] Otis W Brawley, 'Avoidable cancer deaths globally' (2011) 61 CA: A Cancer Journal for Clinicians 67–8.

[157] Robert Beaglehole, Ruth Bonita, and Roger Magnusson, 'Global cancer prevention: an important pathway to global health and development' (2011) 125 Public Health 821–31.

[158] Public Health England, *From evidence into action: opportunities to protect and improve the nation's health* (PHE, 2014); *Strategic plan for the next four years: better outcomes by 2020* (PHE, 2016).

[159] Public Health England, *Local Authority Health Profiles* (PHE, 2018).

the least deprived areas'.[160] PHE also regularly publishes *Health Matters*, each edition of which 'focuses on a specific public health topic, setting out the scale of the problem and the evidence for cost-effective interventions' .[161]

Since health interventions are not the only way to improve the public's health, both the National Audit Office and the King's Fund have argued that, to be more effective, PHE needs to have a greater cross-departmental role.[162]

The King's Fund[163]

Public Health England needs to urgently offer its expertise to other government departments—for free if necessary—to ensure that the impacts of wider government actions adequately take into account impacts on inequalities in health. More broadly, a mechanism such as the sub-committee on public health needs to be brought back into the centre of government to adequately assess and hold to account wider government actions on inequalities in health, as policies are developed ...

The persistence of low life expectancy in some areas means that the state, centrally and locally, has not tackled inequalities in health adequately. Inequalities in health are not self-correcting, and the role of wider determinants, lifestyles and services need to be addressed together rather than in isolation from—or in opposition to—each other.

The Darzi report spelled out some of the costs of not intervening.

Lord Darzi[164]

There is also a compelling economic and fiscal case for investing in early intervention. Smoking costs our economy in excess of £11 billion per year, of which around £2.5 billion falls on the NHS. Obesity is even more expensive, totaling £5.1 billion to the NHS every year, with the wider costs to society estimated to be over five times that amount. And, finally, alcohol consumption, which costs society as a whole £52 billion per year, around £3 billion of which is to the NHS.

(b) PUBLIC HEALTH INTERVENTIONS

If some of the biggest gains to the public's health might come from lifestyle changes, what is the role of the state in enabling and/or persuading people to lead healthier lives? If changes in behaviour can prevent ill health and premature death, are paternalistic measures justifiable, or

---

[160] Public Health England, *Local Authority Health Profiles* (PHE, 2018).

[161] See, for example, Public Health England, *Health matters: obesity and the food environment* (2017); *Health matters: stopping smoking - what works?* (2018).

[162] National Audit Office, *Public Health England's grant to local authorities* (NAO, 2014).

[163] David Buck and David Maguire, *Inequalities in life expectancy: changes over time and implications for policy* (King's Fund, 2015).

[164] *Better health and care for all: A 10-point plan for the 2020s* The final report of the Lord Darzi Review of Health and Care (Institute for Public Policy Research, 2018).

should we be wary of the 'nanny state' telling us how to lead our lives? Public health advocates would argue that this way of framing the issue is misconceived, and that unhealthy behaviour may not be the result of autonomous choice. Nevertheless, resistance to top-down legislative interventions had led to interest into whether it might be preferable to 'nudge' people into healthier behaviour.

Of course, some unhealthy activities, such as illegal drug use, are against the law. Using the criminal law to prohibit practices that are bad for people's health might seem like an especially tough and uncompromising way to influence behaviour. In reality, however, illegality tends to make drug taking even more risky; it is, for example, not uncommon for illicit drugs to be 'bulked out' or cut with poisonous substances. A 'harm reduction' approach would accept that people are likely to take drugs anyway, and focus instead on ways to make drug use safer, perhaps by providing access to clean needles.

Finally, and most radically, if the most accurate predictors of future ill health and low life expectancy are absolute poverty and relative inequality, might economic redistribution be justifiable on health grounds?

(1) Paternalism?

Some public health measures, such as minimum unit alcohol pricing and bans on smoking in public places, are intended to restrict people's 'freedom' to harm themselves. At first sight, this might appear to be contrary to John Stuart Mill's harm principle.

John Stuart Mill[165]

That the only purpose for which power can be rightfully exercised over any member of a civilized community, against his will, is to prevent harm to others. His own good, either physical or moral, is not a sufficient warrant. He cannot rightfully be compelled to do or forbear because it will be better for him to do so, because it will make him happier, because, in the opinion of others, to do so would be wise, or even right ... The only part of the conduct of anyone, for which he is amenable to society, is that which concerns others. In the part which merely concerns himself, his independence is, of right, absolute. Over himself, over his own body and mind, the individual is sovereign.

Matti Häyry is concerned not only with the paternalism of public health interventions, but also with the surveillance of the population that would be a necessary part of measuring their success.

Matti Häyry[166]

The emphasis on longer lives can be counterproductive if the extended length of lives is treated as a goal in itself, as opposed to being a means to happiness, responsibility or flourishing ... The emphasis on 'fewer diseases' can have similar effects, as people may

---

[165] *On Liberty* (John W Parker and Son: London, 1859) 21–2.
[166] 'Public health and human values' (2006) 32 Journal of Medical Ethics 519–21.

value their self-made lifestyle choices more than disease prevention, when these conflict with each other . . .

When public health is promoted by studying the conditions of longer and healthier lives, individuals, groups and communities will be placed under a magnifying glass for extended durations. This means constant surveillance, probable intrusions into people's private lives and possible leaks of sensitive information . . .

Furthermore, when public health is promoted by 'implementing policies and measures', this is often carried out without consulting the people and communities. The upshot of this is that, at best, benevolent paternalistic control is imposed on people's lives, without their consent or against their will, or that, at worst, detrimental procedures are launched in the name of the common good or public interest.

It is also not uncommon for those who are against public health measures to make the sort of slippery slope claim described in the next extract.

David Resnik[167]

I argue that while trans fat bans may help to improve public health, they represent a worrisome policy trend, because they open the door to further restrictions on food. Though few people will mourn the loss of artificial trans fats from restaurant food, the issue here is much larger than that. At stake is a freedom that most of us exercise every day but often take for granted: the freedom to choose what we eat ... Today, trans fats; tomorrow, hot dogs ... Emboldened by victories against trans fats, health advocates could go after red meats, processed meats, sugared drinks, and other unhealthy foods.

Richard Epstein makes another slippery slope claim by contrasting the 'old' public health—such as clean air legislation—with the new public health, which, he argues, wrongly categorizes obesity and smoking as 'epidemics' in order to justify intrusive state action.

Richard Epstein[168]

The old public health established the principle that epidemics offer strong reason for decisive public intervention, whether by quarantine, vaccination, or the creation of public sewers and waste disposal systems. Today, the new public health uses the term 'epidemic' to justify state regulation to limit tobacco consumption or control obesity, even though these activities do not pose risks of communicable disease or any other form of recognizable externalities (*pace* secondhand smoke) to other individuals ...

[T]he designation of obesity as a public health epidemic is designed to signal that state coercion is appropriate, and it is just that connection that is missing. Education and persuasion, yes—but these can be supplied by private institutions and foundations without government coercion or participation ...

---

[167] 'Trans fat bans and human freedom' (2010) 10 American Journal of Bioethics 27–32.
[168] 'Let the shoemaker stick to his last: a defense of the "old" public health' (2013) 46 Perspectives in Biology and Medicine S138–S159.

One fashionable proposal is to think of a 'fat tax' that might be levied on certain foods. But taxes of this sort are highly problematic because of the imperfect fit between the incidence of the tax and its social objectives. Thus, a tax on certain kinds of goods strikes all consumers of that product no matter what their individual health profiles. The person who counts calories and exercises faithfully is now penalized because she chooses to eat a cream pie as part of a sound overall diet.

The 'nanny state' is an especially powerful metaphor commonly invoked in order to criticize public health interventions. As Roger Magnusson explains, it is effective not just against freedom-limiting measures, but has even been used to criticize 'talking down' to people by giving them more information.

Roger Magnusson[169]

The metaphor has force because it associates government action with a fussing, over-bearing nanny who intrudes into the private lives of citizens and treats them as infants who cannot be trusted to make their own decisions . . .

Nanny state theorists have become experts in framing health interventions as insults to the dignity and intelligence of ordinary people. This helps to explain why the nanny state critique applies not only to interventions that truly restrict the freedom of individuals (e.g. smoke-free laws), but to non-coercive, information-based interventions—like health warnings, and clearer nutrition labelling—that are aligned with the values of consumerism: informed choices and personal responsibility . . .

No one wants to be told that the government believes they are too stupid to decide what food to buy, or that they are 'helpless automatons manipulated into consuming whatever big corporations choose to produce'. Ironically, it is this same, treasured sense of self-sufficiency that makes nanny state name-calling a powerful ally as the tobacco, alcohol and processed food industries seek to maintain market share and their influence over consumer purchasing patterns.

Critics of public health policies, like Christopher Snowdon, tend to characterize the sorts of behaviour that pose a risk to health as entirely self-regarding actions.

Christopher Snowdon[170]

Matters that are routinely described as 'public health issues'—most notably, drinking, smoking and eating—are matters of private, not public, behaviour. Aside from instances of excessive alcohol consumption leading to public disorder, these personal habits should barely feature on the radar of a liberal democracy . . .

Is a greater risk of diabetes a price worth paying for enjoying an excess of high-calorie food? Is a greater risk of liver disease a price worth paying for years of beer-guzzling? Is a greater mortality risk a price worth paying for a lifetime's smoking? Who is to draw the line? The mandarins of 'public health' would draw it as near to zero as is politically feasible, but in an enlightened

---

[169] 'Case studies in nanny state name-calling: what can we learn?' (2015) 129 Public Health 1074–82.
[170] 'The Disease of Public Health', Spiked, 28 October 2013.

society the judgement can only be made by the one person who bears all the risk and enjoys all the benefits: the individual.

On the other hand, it could be argued that someone who becomes seriously ill as a result of exercising his freedom to smoke, drink, and live on junk food does not do so in isolation from those who will bear the burdens and the costs of his care. As Mary Ann Glendon has put it: 'the independent individualist, helmetless and free on the open road, becomes the most dependent of individuals in the spinal injury ward'.[171] People who are exercising their freedom to drive dangerously pose a risk to the health of others, that can be controlled only through government action.

James Wilson[172]

Government policies such as adequate speed restrictions, mandatory motorcycle helmets and car seat belts, enforcement of proper seating restraints for children and enforcement of blood-alcohol concentration limits make a very significant difference to the risks citizens are exposed to. Individuals cannot adequately control these risk factors for themselves: I may be able to reduce some risks by wearing a seat belt and not speeding, but I cannot prevent other drivers from speeding or drunk-driving. These risks from others' driving behaviours are potentially catastrophic for my health, and can practically be reduced by government action. Thus, through my morally important interest in my own health, I also have a morally important interest in risk factors being removed from the social environment.

Framing restrictions upon what can be sold to consumers as an interference with their freedom to choose also misses the point that large corporations already restrict our choices. As Nicholas Freudenberg and Sandro Galea put it: 'no consumer ever entered a restaurant demanding a portion of trans fats. Rather, food companies constrain consumer options through decisions made primarily to increase profits.'[173] Christopher Newdick suggests that if we are concerned about the paternalism of public health interventions, we should be 'equally concerned to engage with the private, *commercial* forces nudging us towards ill health.'

Christopher Newdick[174]

Accepting behavioural psychologists' findings that we are constantly nudged from all directions, the question is not simply how governments should behave, it is which 'nanny' do we prefer – publicly accountable government or self-interested private corporations? Yet, by permitting the 'nanny industry' to dominate the debate, we impose vast personal and social cost on the community.

---

[171] Mary Ann Glendon, *Rights Talk: The Impoverishment of Political Discourse* (The Free Press: New York, 1991).

[172] 'The right to public health' (2016) 42 Journal of Medical Ethics 367–75.

[173] Nicholas Freudenberg and Sandro Galea, 'The impact of corporate practices on health: implications for health policy' (2008) 29 Journal of Public Health Policy 86–104.

[174] 'Health equality, social justice and the poverty of autonomy' (2017) 12 Health Economics, Policy and Law 411–33.

Smoking is addictive. It is clearly not impossible to stop smoking, but people often find it difficult. For many smokers, buying a packet of cigarettes is not an autonomy-enhancing expression of free will, but rather a burden of habit and addiction. Of course, that is not true of the first cigarettes that someone smokes, but this will usually have been when they were 'in their early to middle teens', when Goodin argues that they 'were incapable of meaningfully consenting to the risks in the first instance'.[175] In the next extract, Kalle Grill and Kristin Voigt argue in favour of a ban on smoking, in order to protect future smokers.

Kalle Grill and Kristin Voigt[176]

The degree to which smokers value the freedom to smoke is likely to vary. Indeed, about a third would favour a ban, which indicates that they do not value the opportunity to smoke very highly, or at least that this value is outweighed by other considerations. Furthermore, it seems that the majority of smokers plan to quit and wish they had never started. Therefore, the freedom to smoke may be unimportant for many—possibly the majority of—smokers ...

Consider now all those potential *future* people who have not yet faced the choice of whether or not to smoke. With an effective ban, these people will not be tempted by the presence of cigarettes. They will not encounter social settings where smoking is advantageous. They may simply regard smoking a historical curiosity. While their freedom is restricted by a ban, it seems likely that the lost option will be quite insignificant to most of them.

Of course, as we know from the consumption of illegal drugs, a ban is not necessarily an effective way to stop people from doing something.

Nevertheless, it could be argued that freedom of choice is autonomy-enhancing only if a person is choosing from a menu of decent options. The freedom to choose to work in a dangerous workplace, when the other option is destitution, is not an example of an individual being sovereign over himself. In the next extract, Lawrence Gostin suggests that it makes no sense to reify individual freedom of choice.

Lawrence O Gostin[177]

It is false to believe that a small limit on unfettered choice matters more to individuals, families, and communities than the crushing burdens of disease, suffering, and early death. When we recognize that the disproportionate burdens of diabetes and cardiovascular disease rest on society's poorest and most vulnerable people, a *failure* to act has deep moral dimensions.

The life choices of the disadvantaged are already severely constrained by their physical environments and socioeconomic status. To ignore the burdens of suffering from ill health, and fail to take known effective action, is far more morally culpable than a miniscule limit on their 'choice' to eat an artificial, palpably harmful additive ingredient.

---

[175] 'No Smoking: The Ethical Issues' in Ronald Bayer et al (eds), *Public Health Ethics* (OUP: Oxford, 2007) 117–26.

[176] 'The case for banning cigarettes' (2016) 42 Journal of Medical Ethics 293–301.

[177] 'Trans fat bans and the human freedom: a refutation' (2010) 10 American Journal of Bioethics 33–4.

Gostin and Gostin further argue that 'hard' paternalism, in the form of effective public health laws, is sometimes justifiable, in part in order to increase someone's range of choices in the future.

Lawrence O Gostin and Kieran G Gostin[178]

If the collective benefits are high and the individual burdens are low, the rhetorical assertion that a policy is paternalistic should not operate as a political trump. Public health paternalism that markedly improves health and well-being within the population offers a 'broader freedom'. This term is used advisedly to mean that when people have better opportunities for health and longevity, and live in more vibrant, productive communities, they have enhanced prospects for life and a wider range of choices for now and into the future . . .

When a person becomes seriously ill or disabled, the adverse effects on his or her autonomy, let alone full enjoyment of life, are palpable. This does not even take into account the losses that accrue to society when countless people develop preventable injuries and diseases due to their own activities.

It is also clear that not all choices are equally central to one's ability to be the author of one's own life plan. Interfering with someone's freedom to marry or start a family is rather different from reducing the salt content of junk food. As James Wilson explains, 'if a government passed a law on avowedly paternalistic grounds mandating that prepackaged meals could not contain more than a certain percentage of salt, few people would be worried they had thereby been deprived of the ability to author their own life, given the ready availability of salt cellars'.[179]

A further consequence of the neo-liberal emphasis upon freedom of choice is, as Alasdair Waldrope explain, individuals have no one but themselves to blame for their poor choices.

Alistair Wardrope[180]

By emphasizing the causal connection between individual behaviours and health outcomes, individual responsibility for health is rendered most salient; illness then comes to be seen as 'self-inflicted' and thus worthy of blame. If individual behaviour is emphasized as causally explanatory of health problems, then such health problems may be treated as evidence of irresponsible, weak-willed, lazy or otherwise deviant behaviour; these characteristics then stereotype individuals suffering from such health problems, with resulting stigmatization.

Given that, on average, the poorest in society lead the unhealthiest lives, stigmatizing people who have 'chosen' to smoke or eat unhealthily in practice means further castigating the most disadvantaged in society. In the next extract, the final report of the Lord Darzi review of health and care emphasizes the importance of collective action.

---

[178] 'A broader liberty: JS Mill, paternalism and the public's health' (2009) 123 Public Health 214–21.

[179] James Wilson, 'Why it's time to stop worrying about paternalism in health policy' (2011) 4 Public Health Ethics 269–79.

[180] 'Relational autonomy and the ethics of health promotion' (2015) 8 Public Health Ethics 50–62.

Lord Darzi[181]

The narrative of personal responsibility and willpower is counter-productive. It disables necessary action and it runs counter to the evidence. Most people want to be in better health – tapping into this desire and helping and supporting them is likely to be a more effective route than scolding and shaming them. Moreover, choices are driven by range of factors including people's upbringing, financial situation and education, as well as external influences such as affordability, availability and advertising ...

Technology is driving us towards ever more sedentary lifestyles. It is now easier than ever to be entertained while being inactive. Inactivity is bad for both our mental and our physical health. It is vital that we make a determined effort to reverse this trend ...

We therefore need to promote healthy towns and cities. This could include measures such as outdoor gyms in public spaces, more pedestrianised streets, new cycle routes, restrictions on fast food outlets and so on ...

Progress on smoking can be maintained by extending smoke free areas onto our highstreets and parks alongside other public places. England should also step up action to address alcohol consumption by following Scotland's lead and introducing a minimum price on alcohol. Analysis shows that a 50p minimum unit price could reduce alcohol-related deaths by over a 1,000 and save £1.1 billion in costs over a five-year period. We must also step up our response to the obesity crisis. The sugar tax is a step in the right direction, but England should learn from Australia, Finland and Norway by extending it to include milk drinks, cakes, biscuits and confectionary.

In its 2007 report on public health, the Nuffield Council on Bioethics (NCOB) attempted to steer a middle course between the liberal 'harm principle' and the recognition that restrictions upon freedom in order to protect public health can sometimes be justifiable. The NCOB set out a 'stewardship' model, with what they described as an 'intervention ladder'. On this model, public health interventions require justification, and the greater the interference with a person's freedom, the stronger the justification would have to be.

Nuffield Council on Bioethics[182]

Our proposed 'intervention ladder' suggests a way of thinking about the acceptability and justification of different public health policies. The least intrusive step is generally 'to do nothing', or at most monitor the situation. The most intrusive is to legislate in such a way as to restrict the liberties of individuals, the population as a whole, or specific industries. In general, the higher the rung on the ladder at which the policy maker intervenes, the stronger the justification has to be. A more intrusive policy initiative is likely to be publicly acceptable only if there is a clear indication that it will produce the desired effect, and that this can be weighed favourably against any loss of liberty that may result.

1. Do nothing or simply monitor the current situation.

2. Provide information. Inform and educate the public, for example as part of campaigns to encourage people to walk more or eat five portions of fruit and vegetables per day.

---

[181] *Better health and care for all: A 10-point plan for the 2020s* The final report of the Lord Darzi Review of Health and Care (Institute for Public Policy Research, 2018).
[182] *Public health: ethical issues* (NCOB, 2007).

3. Enable choice. Enable individuals to change their behaviours, for example by offering participation in an NHS 'stop smoking' programme, building cycle lanes, or providing free fruit in schools.

4. Guide choices through changing the default policy. For example, in a restaurant, instead of providing chips as a standard side dish (with healthier options available), menus could be changed to provide a more healthy option as standard (with chips as an option available).

5. Guide choices through incentives. Regulations can be offered that guide choices by fiscal and other incentives, for example offering tax-breaks for the purchase of bicycles that are used as a means of travelling to work.

6. Guide choice through disincentives. Fiscal and other disincentives can be put in place to influence people not to pursue certain activities, for example through taxes on cigarettes, or by discouraging the use of cars in inner cities through charging schemes or limitations of parking spaces.

7. Restrict choice. Regulate in such a way as to restrict the options available to people with the aim of protecting them, for example removing unhealthy ingredients from foods, or unhealthy foods from shops or restaurants.

8. Eliminate choice. Regulate in such a way as to entirely eliminate choice, for example through compulsory isolation of patients with infectious diseases.

While the NCOB intervention ladder assumes that the provision of information is a neutral activity, the way in which information is presented matters. For example, public health campaigns which are intended to persuade more women to breastfeed for longer, by presenting it as the natural and best option, may 'exacerbate the pressure that women feel to breastfeed and the anxiety, guilt and shame that some women feel when they do not breastfeed'.[183]

In the next extract, Ronald Bayer and Amy Fairchild draw attention to interesting differences in the use of fear-based public health campaigns. These have been outlawed in the case of HIV/AIDS, on the grounds of their stigmatizing effects, while public health messaging around drink-driving and tobacco use has long relied upon the use of shocking and frightening imagery.

Ronald Bayer and Amy L Fairchild[184]

In the mid-1980s, in the face of an Australian campaign (The Grim Reaper) to arouse fear to motivate behaviour change to combat the emerging HIV epidemic, the first generation of AIDS activists responded with indignation. Fear is a bad motivator for change became a claim that was both empirical and moral. Fear did not work and, in fact, would backfire. Fear was also harmful because it imposed unfair psychological and social burdens ...

While a virtual moratorium on the use of fear in the case of HIV/AIDS was, for a time, observed ..., public health more generally continued to rely on stirring emotion. Fear, for example, had long been a theme of efforts to prevent drunk driving. Antismoking campaigns became particularly hard-hitting after the 1990s and globally, graphic images of death and disfigurement have covered one side of cigarette packages in many nations ...

---

[183] Jessica Martucci and Anne Barnhill 'Examining the use of "natural" in breastfeeding promotion: ethical and practical concerns' (2018) 44 Journal of Medical Ethics 615–20.

[184] 'Means, ends and the ethics of fear-based public health campaigns' (2016) 42 Journal of Medical Ethics 391–6.

The literature on HIV prevention has, in consistently raising the spectre of stigma, remained almost entirely hostile to the use of fear. In sharp contrast, increasingly graphic, sometimes deliberately stigmatising, emotional warnings have been consistently credited with declines in the incidence of smoking since the mid-1950s.

(2) 'Nudge'

Cass Sunstein and Richard Thaler's influential book *Nudge* adopts a non-paternalistic approach,[185] which is four rungs up the Nuffield Council's intervention ladder. They have called their approach 'libertarian paternalism', while others have described it as the 'psychological state'.[186] Instead of direct regulatory interventions—such as placing limits on the sugar content of food—the 'nudge' approach instead relies upon designing 'choice architecture' in order to prompt people to make healthier choices for themselves. As Sunstein and Thaler put it: 'To count as a mere nudge, the intervention must be easy and cheap to avoid. Nudges are not mandates. Putting the fruit at eye level counts as a nudge. Banning junk food does not.'[187]

Nudge theory recognizes that we do not always make considered choices, and it exploits our tendency to make decisions quickly and intuitively. When we order a large portion of chips, if this is the default option, it is not because we have weighed up carefully the pros and cons of eating a large portion of chips, it is *because* it is the default option.

Cass Sunstein and Richard Thaler[188]

Our emphasis is on the fact that in many domains, people lack clear, stable or well ordered preferences. What they choose is strongly influenced by the details of the context in which they make their choices, for example, default rules, framing effects (that is the wording of possible options), and starting points ...

Libertarian paternalism is a relatively weak and non-intrusive type of paternalism, because choices are not blocked or fenced off. In its most cautious forms, libertarian paternalism imposes trivial costs on those who seek to depart from the planner's preferred option. But the approach we recommend nonetheless counts as paternalistic, because private and public planners are not trying to track people's anticipated choices, but are self-consciously attempting to move people in welfare promoting directions.

In the UK, the government has shown considerable interest in nudge theory and the possibility of using 'non-regulatory' ways to effect behavioural change. In 2010, the coalition government set up the Behavioural Insights Team, known as the 'nudge unit', which first operated within the Cabinet Office, and which is now a 'social purpose company' owned partly by the UK government. Drawing on 'ideas from the behaviour science literature', one of its purposes is to enable people to make better choices for themselves. It evaluates different interventions in order to find out what works and what does not work. For example, including the costs of a

---

[185] *Nudge: Improving Decisions About Health, Wealth, and Happiness* (Penguin: London, 2009).

[186] Rhys Jones, Jessica Pykett, and Mark Whitehead, *Changing Behaviours: On the Rise of the Psychological State* (Edward Elgar: Cheltenham, 2013).

[187] *Nudge: Improving Decisions About Health, Wealth and Happiness* (Penguin: New York, 2008) 6.

[188] 'Libertarian Paternalism is not an Oxymoron' (2003) 70 University of Chicago Law Review 1159–202.

missed appointment in an appointment reminder text message reduced the number of missed appointments by 3 per cent.[189]

The obesity epidemic is unlikely to be solved by putting fruit at eye level, and some would argue that instead of tweaking individual's choices, it might be more effective to target the food industry, and place legal restrictions upon what they are allowed to sell, and where. Of course, these sorts of restrictions are unpopular with large corporations, and it is therefore unsurprising that the food industry has been a strong supporter of the government's interest in non-regulatory measures to tackle obesity.

The House of Lords Select Committee on Science and Technology evaluated non-regulatory ways to change behaviour, and concluded that, in isolation, such measures were unlikely to be effective. For example, it pointed out that the campaign to nudge people into fastening their seat belts every time they get into their cars (with the catchphrase 'clunk click every trip'), was accompanied by making seat-belt wearing compulsory, and that without legislation it is unlikely that this 'nudge' would have been effective.

House of Lords Science and Technology Select Committee[190]

In general, the evidence supports the conclusion that non-regulatory or regulatory measures used in isolation are often not likely to be effective and that usually the most effective means of changing behaviour at a population level is to use a range of policy tools, both regulatory and non-regulatory. Given that many factors may influence behaviour, this conclusion is perhaps unsurprising . . .

We therefore urge ministers to ensure that policy makers are made aware of the evidence that non-regulatory measures are often not likely to be effective if used in isolation and that evidence regarding the whole range of policy interventions should be considered before they commit to using non-regulatory measures alone.

More specifically, Kirk Allen et al evaluated the difference between regulatory and non-regulatory measures to reduce consumption of trans fats, and found, unsurprisingly, that a total ban would be much more effective than either better labelling or a partial ban (in restaurants and fast-food outlets).

Kirk Allen et al[191]

A total ban on trans fatty acids in processed foods might prevent or postpone about 7200 deaths (2.6%) from coronary heart disease from 2015–20 and reduce inequality in mortality from coronary heart disease by about 3000 deaths (15%). Policies to improve labelling or simply remove trans fatty acids from restaurants/fast food could save between 1800 (0.7%) and 3500 (1.3%) deaths from coronary heart disease and reduce inequalities by 600 (3%) to 1500 (7%) deaths, thus making them at best half as effective . . . The sum of all savings for

---

[189] Michael Hallsworth et al, 'Stating appointment costs in SMS reminders reduces missed hospital appointments: findings from two randomised controlled trials' (2015) 10 PLoS ONE e0137306.

[190] *Behaviour Change*, 2nd Report of Session 2010–12.

[191] 'Potential of trans fats policies to reduce socioeconomic inequalities in mortality from coronary heart disease in England: cost effectiveness modelling study' (2015) 351 British Medical Journal h4583.

the total ban would be about £297m . . . , while for other policies the best estimates would lie in the range of £80–147m.

Of course, the state does not have a monopoly on nudging people into making particular decisions, and the imperceptible manipulation of choice is not always motivated by concern for public health. As Meredith Stark and Joseph Fins point out, computer algorithms use the data we put into search engines and social media in order to produce targeted advertising, which may unwittingly steer us towards particular health choices.

Meredith Stark and Joseph J Fins[192]

Imagine an individual searches for information on a painful arthritic knee. Having typed keywords into a search engine, browsed various websites, and joined the arthritis group of a social networking site, the individual begins to see, on the margins of various web pages, advertisements for a specific brand of pain reliever. Perhaps the ads even tout the suitability of that brand for arthritic pain. Soon ads are displayed for a nearby orthopedic practice and associated surgical center, the leading regional provider of knee replacements . . .

From other ads now displayed, the patient even knows the brand name of a leading type of artificial joint and why that brand is best . . . In discussions with the surgeon at the center, the patient conveys her choice, and the physician incorporates these strong patient preferences into his treatment recommendation, as this is clearly an informed patient who has researched and thought comprehensively about all of the various options. Or has she? . . .

Intrusion in and appropriation of the space afforded patients to be more active participants in healthcare decisions are perhaps all the more paradoxical, as the availability of these online tools ostensibly should function to increase autonomy, allowing individuals more access to information and more input into health decisions. Instead, owing to intricate means of behavioral targeting, these strategies may be lulling individuals into a sense of informed decisionmaking while actually directing them toward specified outcomes, in a manner that thwarts voluntariness, engineers choice, and surreptitiously exploits decisional vulnerabilities.

(3) Harm Reduction

Although its potential remit is much wider, a harm reduction approach to public health came to prominence as a result of the HIV/AIDS pandemic. The spread of HIV/AIDS can be prevented by condom use and clean needles. In countries where prostitution and heroin use are illegal, providing condoms and sexual health advice to sex workers, and clean needles and/or methadone to heroin users, involves the recognition that the criminalization of these practices is not going to prevent them, and that it is preferable instead to reduce the risk of harm they pose to individuals.

Harm reduction programmes are accepted as best practice by the World Health Organization and UNAIDS, and there is now a weight of evidence that they work.[193] They do, however, face resistance from those who believe that distributing syringes, or providing safe places for the

---

[192] 'Engineering medical decisions' (2013) 22 Cambridge Quarterly of Healthcare Ethics 373–81.
[193] See, eg, Cecile M Denis et al, 'Impact of 20 years harm reduction policy on HIV and HCV among opioid users not in treatment' (2015) 146 Drug & Alcohol Dependence e261.

injection of drugs, enables illegal drug use. In the next extract, Bela Fishbeyn uses Russia as an example of the ideological rejection of a harm reduction approach to heroin addiction.

Bela Fishbeyn[194]

Many countries have, at one point or another, enacted drug policies that are influenced by ideology instead of evidence, including the depiction of drug use as a character flaw or moral weakness ... Policies grounded in ideology that focus on eradication as the goal often lead to the misapplication of criminal law, arbitrary health policies, and, as a result, can negatively impact the health of not only that specific population but that of society as well ...

The success of substitution therapy, primarily in the form of methadone, has been widely studied in a variety of countries and exhaustive empirical data supports its multi-faceted success ... Despite these positive results, methadone—and indeed every other form of substitution therapy—is illegal or unavailable in some countries, including Russia.

This resistance to a proven successful and inexpensive health policy has left Russia with one of the fastest growing epidemics in the world, with injecting drug use accounting for close to 70% of new HIV infections. Russia also happens to be one of the world's top consumers of heroin, with ... over 2.5 million injecting opiate users, totaling about 2.29 per cent of the country's population—more than any other country in the world. Yet the implementation of harm reduction measures continues to be controversial in Russia and almost all treatment options for Russia's injecting drug users are abstinence-oriented. Russian physicians themselves were amongst the strongest agents behind the resistance to substitution therapy, arguing that offering methadone is merely 'substituting one drug for another'.

A harm reduction approach might also be used to challenge laws which exacerbate risks to health. For example, the illegality of homosexual sex in 72 countries makes HIV transmission in those countries more, rather than less, likely.

Jorge Saavedra, Jose Antonio Izazola-Licea, and Chris Beyrer[195]

Most obviously, where same-sex behavior is criminalized, [men who have sex with men] remain hidden, they will be very cautious or refuse to get an HIV test, even if they feel they need it, and those seeking to reach them with services, from condoms and lubricants to education and treatment outreach, can be harassed for supporting illegal activities. A recent example is from Nepal, where police have beaten peer outreach workers for attempting to distribute condoms.

In countries where homosexuality is legal, commentators have sought to challenge the criminalization of HIV transmission on similar grounds, namely that it will discourage testing and hence make transmission more, rather than less, likely.

---

[194] 'When ideology trumps: a case for evidence-based health policies' (2015) 15 The American Journal of Bioethics 1–2.

[195] 'Sex between men in the context of HIV: the AIDS 2008 Jonathan Mann Memorial Lecture in health and human rights' (2008) 11 Journal of the International AIDS Society 9.

Matthew Weait[196]

It is also the case that HIV epidemics are driven largely by undiagnosed infection, not by people who are diagnosed positive—and criminal law generally only addresses those who know their status because it is concerned not only with agents' actions and their consequences, but with those who may reasonably be treated as having acted in a sufficiently blameworthy way ... [C]riminalisation may lead people to believe that new partners will explicitly disclose their HIV positive status to avoid liability, leading to a false sense of security and heightened risk-taking ... [T]here is evidence that criminalisation complicates in an unhelpful way the relationship between patients and health-care workers. Finally, criminal cases more often than not lead to lurid, inaccurate and sensationalist reporting in the popular media—more often than not, these days, the only kind of reporting there is about HIV—and give the impression that people living with the virus are 'monsters', 'murderers' and 'assassins' bent on harming and killing others. Nothing, of course, could be further from the truth but these stories reinforce the stigma and fear surrounding HIV. This does absolutely nothing to encourage people to test regularly and to know their status—a precondition for accessing treatment, and so guaranteeing their own health and reducing the risk of onward transmission to others.

A harm reduction approach to public health is not limited to preventing HIV transmission. For example, as the following extracts explain, there is currently considerable debate over whether e-cigarettes, which are increasingly marketed by the tobacco industry, are an effective harm reduction technique.

Lawrence O Gostin and Aliza Y Glasner[197]

Public health advocates have debated whether e-cigarettes are effective harm reduction tools or offer a pathway to smoking. By delivering nicotine and mimicking oral inhalation, e-cigarettes could reduce dependency on combustible cigarettes and prevent relapse. Alternatively, e-cigarettes could become a gateway to smoking by exposing young people to the world of nicotine and relegitimizing tobacco use in society. Probably both scenarios are true: e-cigarettes can help older, entrenched smokers to quit smoking, whereas younger nonsmokers could transition from electronic to combustible cigarettes once they are addicted to nicotine.

Yvette van der Eijk[198]

The public health community, which is usually united in its goal to minimise or eliminate tobacco-related harm, is now experiencing significant divisions on the ENDS [electronic nicotine delivery system] issue. Most arguments 'for' or 'against' an ENDS market are

---

[196] 'Unsafe law: health, rights and the legal response to HIV' (2013) 9 International Journal of Law in Context 535–64.

[197] 'E-cigarettes, vaping, and youth' (2014) 312 Journal of the American Medical Association 595–6.

[198] 'Ethics of tobacco harm reduction from a liberal perspective' (2016) 42 Journal of Medical Ethics 273–7.

consequentialist: that ENDS will improve or worsen public health. However, the mixed nature of current evidence, as well as the unavailability of long-term evidence, means that neither argument can be ascertained (for now). As it stands, there is little agreement on whether public health advocates should cooperate with the TI [tobacco industry] in reducing the public health impact of smoking, how children should be protected from experimenting with ENDS, or how smokers should be supported in their cessation or harm reduction efforts.

(4) The Social Determinants of Health

Life expectancy varies dramatically both between and within countries. Average life expectancy in Nigeria is 55 years; in Japan it is 84 years. Women in the UK live to 82, on average;[199] unless they are homeless, when average female life expectancy is 43.[200] People who suffer from mental illness die 15–20 years earlier than those who do not.[201] Importantly, however, it is not just that poverty and disadvantage are associated with ill health. As Michael Marmot has explained:

the social gradient in health is not confined to those in poverty. It runs from top to bottom of society, with less good standards of health at every step down the social hierarchy. Even comfortably off people somewhere in the middle tend to have poorer health than those above them.[202]

In the 1960s, Michael Marmot and colleagues carried out a study that has become known as Whitehall I, in which they tracked the mortality rates of 18,000 male British civil servants.[203] The men were put into one of four categories, depending upon their occupational status: senior administrators (that is, people at the top of the civil service such as permanent secretaries); professionals and executives; clerical (that is, people who dealt with paperwork); and 'other' (which included messengers and porters).

Across all causes of death, those with higher occupational status had lower percentages of deaths. Even amongst affluent individuals, higher social status was associated with better health outcomes. For example, in Whitehall I, the percentage in each group dying of heart disease between 1967 and 1977 was: senior administrator = 2.16 per cent; professional/executive = 3.58 per cent; clerical = 4.90 per cent; other = 6.59 per cent. For lung cancer, the respective percentages were: 0.35, 0.73, 1.47, and 2.33.

A second Whitehall II study included women and the results were the same.[204] Multiple studies since, including Sir Douglas Black's 1980 report *Inequalities in Health* (known as the Black Report) and its 1987 update, Margaret Whitehead's *The Health Divide*, have established unequivocally that 'the risk of death is greater for lower socio-economic groups at all stages of the life course and for all causes of death'.[205]

---

[199] Office for National Statistics, *National life tables, UK: 2015 to 2017* (ONS, 2018).

[200] Crisis, *Homelessness: a silent killer* (Crisis, 2011).

[201] Public Health England, *From evidence into action: opportunities to protect and improve the nation's health* (PHE, 2014).

[202] 'Introduction' in Michael Marmot and Richard Wilkinson, *Social Determinants of Health*, 2nd edn (OUP: Oxford, 2005).

[203] M G Marmot et al, 'Employment grade and coronary heart disease in British civil servants' (1978) 32 Journal of Epidemiology and Community Health 244–9.

[204] M G Marmot et al, 'Health Inequalities among British civil servants: the Whitehall II study' (1991) 337 The Lancet 1387–93.

[205] Michael P Kelly, 'The Development of an Evidence-Based Approach to Tackling Health Inequalities in Britain' in Amanda Killoran, Catherine Swann, and Michael P Kelly (eds), *Public Health Evidence: Tackling Health Inequalities* (OUP: Oxford, 2006) 41–62.

The evidence suggests that there are three drivers of this social gradient in health: social status, social affiliations, and stress in early life.

Richard Wilkinson[206]

Social status is linked to health not simply through the direct physical effects of exposure to better or worse material conditions. It is also a matter of position in the social hierarchy, people's experience of superior and dominant status versus inferior and subordinate status, coupled with processes of stigmatization and exclusion of those nearer the bottom of the hierarchy ...

The second group of psychosocial risk factors are those connected with social affiliations and involvement ... [S]ocial affiliations of almost any kind are protective of health. Close 'confiding' relationships, social support, friendship networks, and involvement in wider community life, all seem beneficial. Apparently confirming these connections, hostility and 'negative' relationships have been shown to be harmful to health ...

The third important category of psychosocial influences on health were those occurring in early life ... People who were smaller as babies are, for instance, more likely to suffer from heart disease, diabetes, and stroke in later life. Although low birth weight was initially thought to reflect poor nutrition in pregnancy, it now looks as if it is more likely—at least in the rich countries—to reflect the effect of maternal stress ... in the developing foetus ... [T]here is also good evidence that stress and lack of stimulation in early childhood compromises future health.

Jonathan Wolff fleshes out some of the reasons why a supportive social network might lead to better health outcomes.

Jonathan Wolff[207]

One possibility is simply that having people around you helps you talk through your problems and seek solutions. Another is that regular contact with others reduces stress. But here is another possibility. A supportive social network helps you rest. This could be important. Very often someone in recovery from an illness will need to take some rest to allow the body's natural healing processes to come into effect. But to a mother with young children and no family around her to help, what does it mean to be ordered to rest? Or a self-employed small business person? Or someone on a low wage with no sick pay and an unsympathetic employer? Rest could be impossible, or lead to even more serious problems.

In 2008, Sir Michael Marmot was asked by the then Secretary of State for Health to propose evidence-based strategies for addressing health inequalities in England. In the 2010 Marmot Review, he pointed out that the social gradient in health has an economic as well as a human cost.

---

[206] Richard Wilkinson, 'Ourselves and Others—For Better or Worse: Social Vulnerability and Inequality' in Michael Marmot and Richard Wilkinson, *Social Determinants of Health* (OUP: Oxford, 2005).

[207] 'How should governments respond to the social determinants of health?' (2011) 53 Preventive Medicine 253–5.

The Marmot Review[208]

The benefits of reducing health inequalities are economic as well as social. The cost of health inequalities can be measured in human terms, years of life lost and years of active life lost; and in economic terms, by the cost to the economy of additional illness. If everyone in England had the same death rates as the most advantaged, people who are currently dying prematurely as a result of health inequalities would, in total, have enjoyed between 1.3 and 2.5 million extra years of life. They would, in addition, have had a further 2.8 million years free of limiting illness or disability. It is estimated that inequality in illness accounts for productivity losses of £31–33 billion per year, lost taxes and higher welfare payments in the range of £20–32 billion per year, and additional NHS healthcare costs associated with inequality are well in excess of £5.5 billion per year. If no action is taken, the cost of treating the various illnesses that result from inequalities in the level of obesity alone will rise from £2 billion per year to nearly £5 billion per year in 2025.

It is not just absolute poverty that is associated with worse health outcomes, but relative inequality. On this point, Kate Pickett and Danny Dorling suggest that the Marmot Report did not go far enough.

Kate E Pickett and Danny Dorling[209]

We suggest that a major (but significant) problem with the UK Marmot Review is that it fails to deal with the need to reduce inequality by focusing on the top end of the social hierarchy, as well as the bottom. Although the Review calls for the establishment of a 'minimum income for healthy living', there is no suggestion that a maximum income or a constraint on the ratio of top-to-bottom incomes in institutions would also help reduce inequalities, and so improve the health and well-being of the population as a whole ... We suspect that more radical policy measures were not proposed because the political climate in Britain across the mainstream party spectrum, whilst accepting the rhetoric of 'fairness', is actually diffident in its support for the policies needed to create more equality.

There is a great deal of evidence that improving people's environment and life chances, and reducing inequality, have measurable effects on their health. The World Health Organization has suggested that action is needed under three broad headings:

World Health Organization[210]

- Improve the conditions of daily life—the circumstances in which people are born, grow, live, work, and age.
- Tackle the inequitable distribution of power, money, and resources—the structural drivers of those conditions of daily life—globally, nationally, and locally.

---

[208] *Fair Society, Healthy Lives* (Institute of Health Equity, 2010).

[209] 'Against the organization of misery? The Marmot Review of health inequalities' (2010) 71 Social Science & Medicine 1231–3.

[210] *Closing the gap in a generation: health equity through action on the social determinants of health* (WHO: Geneva, 2008).

- Measure the problem, evaluate action, expand the knowledge base, develop a workforce that is trained in the social determinants of health, and raise public awareness about the social determinants of health.

Tackling the social determinants of health is difficult, however, because they are so diffuse and varied. Action is needed across almost all central and local government departments: employment, education, transport, and urban planning, as well as health and welfare. Even if the evidence is overwhelming, Gemma Carey and Brad Crammond found that politicians may nevertheless need to be persuaded that any policy intervention will result in an immediate gain that will play well with voters. In their interviews with policy-makers, one explained that:

[Just because] something might be printed in the New England Journal of Medicine, or the Lancet or the BMJ ... it wouldn't get the time of day unless it was accompanied by market research that showed what the impact of that would be in marginal seats.[211]

In the next extract, Jonathan Wolff proposes a policy that might have a positive impact upon one of the social determinants of health, and which might even be cost-effective, but which is unlikely to play well with politicians.

Jonathan Wolff [212]

If it is true that chronic stress is detrimental to health, then it is incumbent on us to think who in UK society is under the greatest chronic stress and to consider what could be done about it ... I conjecture that one very vulnerable group in this respect are people commonly known as 'benefit cheats'. I am not here referring to those involved in significant fraud, but rather those in receipt of benefit who also do a relatively small amount of cash in hand work in order to do such things as have a night out once a week or to buy birthday or Christmas presents for their children. For people who would much rather simply have a decently paying job, the stress of being on the wrong side of the law must be significant. And it may well contribute to stress related disorders and hence the social gradient of health. An enlightened policy would be to allow those in receipt of benefits to earn some money without needing to declare it for tax or benefit assessment purposes. Now it may be that this would not actually cost the Treasury anything, and might even reduce the need for some categories of bureaucrats, but if it does cost money a bid could be made to the Department of Health, under its social determinants support budget.

In contrast, Mark A Rothstein is concerned about the potential reach of public health policy, once all of the social, political, economic, and cultural determinants of health are taken into account.

---

[211] Gemma Carey and Brad Crammond, 'Action on the social determinants of health: views from inside the policy process' (2015) 128 Social Science & Medicine 134–41.
[212] 'How should governments respond to the social determinants of health?' (2011) 53 Preventive Medicine 253–5.

Mark A Rothstein[213]

Just because war, crime, hunger, poverty, illiteracy, homelessness, and human rights abuses interfere with the health of individuals and populations does not mean that eliminating these conditions is part of the mission of public health ... It is incongruous to embrace the broadest meaning of public health at the same time that our legal system and public health infrastructure are based on a narrow definition of public health jurisdiction, authority, and remedies ... The broad power of government to protect public health includes the authority to supersede individual liberty and property interests in the name of preserving the greater public good. It is an awesome responsibility, and therefore it cannot and must not be used indiscriminately.

As we saw earlier, commentators who accuse public health interventions of being unduly paternalistic often individualize the problem of health inequalities, by maintaining that the solution is for individuals to improve their own health, rather than for the state to attempt to improve their material conditions. So, for example, rates of smoking in lower socioeconomic groups are much higher than in more affluent groups. Should we therefore blame poor individuals for not taking better care of their own health, or should we try to understand the reasons why, as Amanda Killoran et al explain, 'smokers living with multiple disadvantage are an extremely hard target group for smoking cessation activities'?

Amanda Killoran, Lesley Owen, and Linda Bauld[214]

Such communities are characterized by a lack of social mobility and a fatalistic attitude: 'an overwhelming lack of self-belief, self esteem and hope'. There is no culture of quitting, and smoking is perceived to be the norm. Although the risks of smoking are known, these seem minor compared with other difficulties such as low income and debt, low educational achievement and lack of job opportunities, and physical and mental health problems. Most postpone quitting until a point when life is more under control, but have little confidence that this point will ever be reached. The findings indicate that most low-income smokers require a dramatic and sustained upturn in personal circumstances for smoking cessation to be a viable option.

Ironically, health education campaigns tend to be most successful among groups who are already comparatively healthy. As Koonal Shah et al point out, this may lead to a tension between maximizing public health, which can be achieved at relatively low cost by improving the health of the most advantaged, and reducing health inequalities, which will require greater expenditure for less overall gain.

---

[213] Mark A Rothstein, 'Rethinking the meaning of public health' (2002) 30 Journal of Law, Medicine and Ethics 144–9.
[214] 'Smoking Cessation: An Evidence-Based Approach to Tackling Health Inequalities' in Amanda Killoran, Catherine Swann, and Michael P Kelly (eds), *Public Health Evidence: Tackling Health Inequalities* (OUP: Oxford, 2006) 341–6.

Koonal K Shah et al[215]

[P]ublic health interventions that produce overall health improvement often exacerbate relative health differences between the most and least advantaged groups in society ...

It is often the case that public health programmes tend to benefit individuals who are already quite healthy, and therefore result in increased health inequalities. This is true of smoking cessation services, for example, which in the past have been found to be least likely to attract people from sectors of the population where smoking rates are high ... For example, suppose the targeted programme has a cost per QALY gained of £15,000, but spending the same amount of money on a universal version of the programme (which mainly benefits more advantaged individuals) would be associated with a cost per QALY gained of £10,000. In this case, it would be possible to increase population health by approving a universal version of the programme rather than the targeted version. The decision to spend money on the targeted intervention is then an *implicit* decision to depart from 'a QALY is a QALY is a QALY' and to give greater weight to the health gains for the disadvantaged population.

While eradicating social disadvantage might be the only way to eliminate relative health inequalities, targeting spending on health care in the most disadvantaged areas appears to be effective in reducing absolute inequalities. Between 2001 and 2011, a health inequalities component was incorporated into the NHS allocation formula in order to allocate more resources to deprived areas. Ben Barr et al found that it reduced mortality rates, and that the return from every pound spent in a deprived area was greater than in more affluent areas.

Ben Barr, Clare Bambra, and Margaret Whitehead[216]

The policy of allocating greater NHS resources to more deprived areas led to a reduction in absolute health inequalities in mortality amenable to healthcare. Investment of NHS resources in more deprived areas was associated with a greater improvement in outcomes than investment in more affluent areas. Our study suggests that any change in resource allocation policy that reduces the proportion of funding allocated to deprived areas may reverse this trend and widen geographical inequalities in mortality from these causes.

NHS England has continued to use a funding formula which allocates additional funding to deprived areas, and indeed there is now a statutory obligation to have regard to the need to reduce health inequalities.

Health and Social Care Act 2012 section 1C

In exercising functions in relation to the health service, the Secretary of State must have regard to the need to reduce inequalities between the people of England with respect to the benefits that they can obtain from the health service.

---

[215] 'NICE's social value judgements about equity in health and health care' (2013) 8 Health Economics, Policy and Law 145–65.
[216] 'The impact of NHS resource allocation policy on health inequalities in England 2001–11: longitudinal ecological study' (2014) 348 British Medical Journal g3231.

Of course, while this might look progressive, 'having regard to the need to reduce inequalities' does not require specific action or set a specific target for the reduction or elimination of health inequalities. The scope of section 1C is also limited; it refers only to inequalities in access to *health services*. As we have seen, the social determinants of health inequalities go far beyond differential access to NHS services. As Alex Scott-Samuel and Katherine Elizabeth Smith point out, political action on health inequalities has tended to focus on 'downstream' solutions, despite a lack of evidence that they will work, while failing to address the 'upstream' causes of inequality.

Alex Scott-Samuel and Katherine Elizabeth Smith[217]

While it can be politically expedient for governments to make commitments to reducing health inequalities, they cannot, within current political, social and economic norms, realistically propose actions which evidence suggests will substantially reduce them—such as tackling power inequalities, social status and connections, or class inequality. In this context, policy actors and researchers working in the United Kingdom have devised a parallel fantasy world in which proximal, downstream, easily tackled exposures are posited as potential solutions to health inequalities. This is, we argue, a 'utopian' exercise in the sense that this word is traditionally understood; an impossible dream in which the long-established social gradient in health is gradually flattened via a series of downstream interventions and policies which, for the most part, focus on trying to change behaviours that affect health outcomes, particularly in poorer communities, rather than trying to change the social and economic environments which inform people's circumstances and decision-making.

6 CONCLUSION

In the UK, we are, as our politicians realize, very attached to the principle of universal access to free health care. At the same time, few of us are willing to pay much higher rates of income tax. Given an ageing population, there will never be sufficient funds to eliminate the need to make tough choices about the allocation of scarce resources. It is also important to recognize that there are limits to what the NHS can achieve, given the extent to which our health is affected by our environment, lifestyle, income, and social status.

In the coming years, it will be vitally important to find a way to adequately fund social care, so that NHS hospitals do not collapse under the weight of providing inpatient care to people who could be cared for in the community, if a comprehensive and well-funded social care system were in place. It will also be important to find a way to address the NHS's significant staff shortages, which are set to be exacerbated by Brexit and other restrictions on immigration. In the final extracts in this chapter, Rudolf Klein suggests that the NHS's survival in something resembling its original form could be said to be remarkable, while Tim Doran is concerned about the implications for staff and patients of a system that is constantly at breaking point.

---

[217] 'Fantasy paradigms of health inequalities: utopian thinking?' (2015) 13 Social Theory & Health 418–36.

Rudolf Klein[218]

Perhaps the most remarkable aspect of the National Health Service as it celebrates its 70th birthday, is its survival in an institutional form that would still be recognised by its original architect, Nye Bevan. Cushioned in overwhelming public support, with the medical profession long since transformed from being its most hostile critics into its most committed defenders, it has survived successive waves of reorganisation and periods of fiscal austerity ...

[T]he NHS scores strongly on the equity criterion in international comparisons. So, for example, the 2017 Commonwealth Fund study of 11 rich country care systems put the United Kingdom first on this criterion, using a survey that compared the experience of higher and lower income groups in their access to, and experience of, care. And the NHS has proved a powerful instrument of income redistribution ...

Where the NHS differs [from other tax funded public services] is in its degree of political visibility. This cuts both ways. On the one hand, it encourages often premature warnings about impending doom. In particular the medical profession has a long record of advertising its grievances by talking up the shortcomings of the NHS. On the other hand, public affection for the NHS means it gets special treatment: so while other public services have seen their budgets cut, the NHS has (in relative terms) been protected. Thus the increasing visibility of longer waiting times, cancelled operations and missed targets persuaded an otherwise grudging Chancellor of the Exchequer to give the NHS an extra £6.3 billion over three years as an eve of 70th birthday present – utterly inadequate in the view of those working in it but large enough to make other government services envious.

Tim Doran

[T]here are objective signs of chronic and mounting distress across the NHS, with the underlying problem of ever more patients being admitted into ever fewer beds ...

It is not necessary to be committed to the NHS's ideals in order to work for it, but many do and it certainly helps. But righteousness should not be the reason why people come to work and policymakers should not rely on it. A pleasant and supportive environment should be a minimum expectation, with sufficient resources – including adequate time – to deal with patients appropriately. When these expectations are not met, not only are there adverse consequences for individual staff and their patients, but the whole fabric of the NHS is unpicked, as collegiality breaks down into factionalism and compassion sours into indifference and cruelty. Of all the NHS's challenges in the coming years – technical, organisational and professional – maintaining kindness towards both staff and patients is perhaps the greatest.

FURTHER READING

Calnan, Michael, Hashem, Ferhana, and Brown, Patrick, 'Still elegantly muddling through? NICE and uncertainty in decision making about the rationing of expensive medicines in England' (2017) 47 International Journal of Health Services 571–94.

---

[218] 'The National Health Service (NHS) at 70: Bevan's double-edged legacy' (2018) 13 Health Economics, Policy and Law 1–10.

Eyal, Nir et al (eds), *Inequalities in Health: Concepts, Measures, and Ethics* (OUP: Oxford, 2013).

Ford, Amy, 'The Concept of Exceptionality: A Legal Farce?' (2012) 20 Medical Law Review 304–36.

Herring, Jonathan, 'Rationing by fault' (2018) 121 Theology 112–16.

Klein, Rudolf, The National Health Service (NHS) at 70: Bevan's double-edged legacy' (2018) 13 Health Economics, Policy and Law 1–10.

Magnusson, Roger, 'Case studies in nanny state name-calling: what can we learn?' (2015) 129 Public Health 1074–82.

Newdick, Christopher, Health equality, social justice and the poverty of autonomy' (2017) 12 Health Economics, Policy and Law 411–33.

Stirton, Lindsay, 'Back to the Future? Lessons on the Pro-Competitive Regulation of Health Services' (2014) 22 Medical Law Review 180–99.

Syrett, Keith, 'Health technology appraisal and the courts: accountability for reasonableness and the judicial model of procedural justice' (2011) 6 Health Economics, Policy and Law 469–88.

Wilson, James, 'The right to public health' (2016) 42 Journal of Medical Ethics 367–75.

3

MEDICAL MALPRACTICE

CENTRAL ISSUES

1. In a clinical negligence action, establishing that a doctor owes her patient a duty of care is straightforward. More complex issues arise when the claim is that a doctor's negligence resulted in injury to someone else.

2. According to the *Bolam* test, as modified by *Bolitho*, a doctor will not be found to have acted negligently if she acted in accordance with a practice accepted as proper by a responsible body of medical opinion, provided that that opinion is capable of withstanding logical analysis.

3. Having established that the doctor has breached her duty of care, the claimant must prove that this breach caused her injuries. This may be difficult in clinical negligence cases because the patient is usually already ill.

4. Particularly complex issues arise in cases where the 'damage' caused by the defendant's negligence is the birth of a child.

5. There is a great deal wrong with the clinical negligence system: it is costly and inefficient; few claimants succeed and it could be said to foster a 'blame culture', which may make learning from mistakes less likely.

6. Other ways to deal with poor medical practice exist. In rare cases, doctors might face prosecution for gross negligence manslaughter. More commonly, a doctor's 'fitness to practise' might be challenged by the General Medical Council. It is also possible for patients to complain about their care via the NHS complaints system.

1 INTRODUCTION

In this chapter, we consider the law's response to medical treatment that has gone wrong. It has tended to be assumed that people who have been injured as a result of poor medical treatment will want financial compensation. In practice, evidence suggests that an explanation, an apology, and reassurance that the incident will not be repeated are more important to patients.[1]

---

[1] *Making Amends: A Consultation Paper Setting Out Proposals for Reforming the Approach to Clinical Negligence in the NHS* (DH: London, 2003) 75.

The tort of negligence also has a rather narrow focus upon personal injury. An action in negligence is possible only if the patient has suffered physical injury or a recognized psychiatric illness (pure economic loss is unlikely to be caused by clinical negligence). The tort of negligence is therefore ill equipped to deal with some of the poor care and suffering that was identified in Robert Francis QC's report into failings at Mid-Staffordshire NHS Foundation Trust,[2] such as leaving patients unwashed, with inadequate access to food, drink, toilet facilities, and clean sheets.

We begin this chapter by looking briefly at the possibility of an action for breach of contract, before exploring the different stages involved in a clinical negligence claim. In recent years, there has been a great deal of criticism of the way in which medical mishaps are handled. Despite its limited scope and its failure to offer patients their preferred remedies, the volume of clinical negligence cases, and their costs, have increased dramatically: in the past ten years, the number of cases has doubled and their costs have quadrupled.[3] In 2017-18, the clinical negligence system cost the NHS £2.2 billion.

Negligence is not the only way to address inadequate care, and so we also consider the NHS complaints system; the possibility of disciplinary action by the General Medical Council (GMC); and the circumstances in which a doctor might be prosecuted for gross negligence manslaughter.

In this chapter, our focus is mainly upon doctors' mistakes, rather than those of other healthcare workers. This is partly because doctors are principally responsible for patient care, and hence responsible when something goes wrong, and partly because the bulk of litigation has been against the medical profession.

It should also be noted that one 'special case' in the tort of negligence, namely the question of liability for failing to provide sufficient information to patients, is covered in the next chapter, when we consider informed consent.

2 BREACH OF CONTRACT

If health care is provided in the private sector, the patient will have a contract with her doctor and/or with the clinic or hospital where she receives treatment. The nature of these contracts varies. For example, a patient may make an agreement directly with a doctor, who will arrange for the patient's admission. Alternatively the patient's agreement might be with a hospital, which then employs a doctor to provide the necessary services. The terms of contracts for private health care will also differ: for example, some may contain a term that specifies the identity of the treating doctor.

Contracts for private health care include terms that are implied by statute: under sections 4 and 9 of the Supply of Goods and Services Act 1982, medical devices must be of satisfactory quality and fit for their purpose. Statutory limits on the use of exclusion clauses also apply; for example, it is not possible to exclude or restrict liability for death or personal injury caused by negligence.[4]

It is possible, if unlikely, that a contract could contain an express term guaranteeing the outcome of the procedure. Few doctors would ever choose to give such a warranty, however, and

---

[2] The Mid Staffordshire NHS Foundation Trust Public Inquiry (DH: London, 2013).

[3] House of Commons Committee of Public Accounts, *Managing the costs of clinical negligence in hospital trusts*, Fifth Report of Session 2017–19.

[4] Unfair Contract Terms Act 1977, s 2(1).

the courts would be very unlikely to imply such a term into a contract for healthcare services. In *Thake v Maurice*, a failed sterilization case, Neill LJ stated:

> I do not consider that a reasonable person would have expected a responsible medical man to be intending to give a guarantee. Medicine, though a highly skilled profession, is not, and is not generally regarded as being, an exact science. The reasonable man would have expected the defendant to exercise all the proper skill and care of a surgeon in that speciality; he would not in my view have expected the defendant to give a guarantee of 100% success.[5]

In this case, the Court of Appeal did accept that there might be some circumstances in which a guarantee of success might reasonably be inferred. Nourse LJ gave the example of an operation to amputate a limb. A patient who goes into hospital to have her right leg amputated could reasonably expect that the operation will remove her right, rather than her left leg. Such cases are likely to be rare, and more commonly, a reasonable person would not expect a doctor to guarantee a successful outcome.

In *Thake v Maurice*, the Court of Appeal held that the patient's contract contained an implied term that the doctor would exercise reasonable care and skill. In practice, this is indistinguishable from the duty to take reasonable care in the tort of negligence, owed by all doctors to their patients. Because the vast majority of malpractice claims are brought in negligence, it is within our discussion of clinical negligence actions that we flesh out what is meant by 'reasonable care and skill'.

3 NEGLIGENCE

In order to succeed in an action in negligence, the claimant must establish that:

(a) she is owed a duty of care by the defendant (this will usually be the treating doctor, and her employer will be vicariously liable. GPs are a special case, and are sued personally, though they will be insured by a medical defence union); and

(b) the defendant breached that duty by failing to exercise reasonable care; and

(c) the breach of duty caused the claimant's injuries, and that those injuries are not too remote.

There are then a number of defences which may be available to the defendant. In the following sections, we go through these stages in turn.

(a) THE EXISTENCE OF A DUTY OF CARE

It is well established that doctors (and other healthcare professionals) owe a duty of care to their patients. The duty is to exercise reasonable care and skill in diagnosis, advice, and treatment. Provided that the doctor committed the tort in the course of her employment, her employer will be vicariously liable for her negligence.

In three situations, the existence of a duty of care is more complicated.

---

[5] *Thake v Maurice* [1986] QB 644.

(1) When Does the Doctor–Patient Relationship Come into Being?

Because a doctor is under no legal obligation to treat a 'stranger', it is important to know when the transition from 'stranger' to 'patient' takes place. The common law position is that a duty of care is imposed upon the doctor once she has assumed responsibility for the patient's care.

In hospitals, the duty may arise as soon as the patient presents herself for treatment, before she is actually seen by a doctor. This was the case in *Barnett v Chelsea and Kensington Hospital Management Committee*. After drinking tea later discovered to have contained arsenic, three men had started vomiting and attended the casualty department of the defendant's hospital. The nurse telephoned Dr Banerjee, who was on duty at the time. He told her to tell the men to go home and call their own doctors. The men died hours later from arsenic poisoning. One of the men's widows brought an action in negligence. Nield J held that Dr Banerjee had owed the men a duty of care, which he had breached by failing to examine them himself. (Later in this chapter we will see that this action failed on the question of causation.)

Barnett v Chelsea and Kensington Hospital Management Committee [6]

Nield J

I have no doubt that Nurse Corbett and Dr Banerjee were under a duty to the deceased to exercise that skill and care which is to be expected of persons in such positions acting reasonably . . . Without doubt Dr Banerjee should have seen and examined the deceased. His failure to do either cannot be described as an excusable error as has been submitted, it was negligence. It is unfortunate that Dr Banerjee was himself at the time a tired and unwell doctor, but there was no-one else to do that which it was his duty to do.

The doctor's duty of care will arise only when she knows of the patient's need for medical services. For some patients, such as those over the age of 75, who must be offered an annual consultation, a GP's duty of care might extend to seeking out the patient, but normally it is only when the patient requests the doctor's assistance that the duty of care comes into being.

(2) Who Else Might Owe Duties of Care to Patients?

In addition to being vicariously liable for its employees' negligence, might an NHS body owe a primary duty of care to patients to ensure that they receive adequate treatment? In *Wilsher v Essex AHA*,[7] for example, the Court of Appeal was of the view that the health authority owed patients a duty of care to provide qualified medical staff. As Sir Nicolas Browne-Wilkinson V-C explained, 'a health authority which so conducts its hospital that it fails to provide doctors of sufficient skill and experience to give the treatment offered at the hospital may be directly liable in negligence to the patient'.

An obvious problem in relation to this sort of primary duty is that scarce resources are the norm within the NHS. Courts may be prepared to find that a hospital was negligent if it failed to provide a minimally adequate standard of care—as was the case in *Bull v Devon AHA*,[8] when a woman in labour with twins had to wait an hour for a registrar to arrive—but they are reluctant to interfere with policy decisions about the allocation of limited resources. Rather

---

[6] [1969] 1 QB 428.   [7] [1987] QB 730.   [8] [1993] 4 Med LR 117 (CA).

than relying upon a hospital's primary duty to provide adequate treatment, it will almost always be more straightforward for an injured patient to bring an action in negligence against an individual employee, whose employer will be vicariously liable.

An interesting issue arose in *Darnley v Croydon Health Services NHS Trust*. After being assaulted, and suffering a blow to his head, the appellant attended the trust's A&E department on a busy night. The receptionist told him that he would be seen within four or five hours, but she failed to tell him that he would be seen by a triage nurse within 30 minutes, who would have been likely to decide that a patient with a head injury should be seen more quickly. After waiting for 19 minutes, the appellant went home, where his condition deteriorated. By the time he underwent neurosurgery to remove a haematoma, he had suffered partial paralysis and was left with long-term disabilities, which would have been avoided if he had received prompt treatment. He claimed that the question was whether the receptionist, or the trust acting through the receptionist, had been negligent in not giving him accurate information about waiting times. Although Mr Darnley lost in the High Court and the Court of Appeal—on the grounds that it would not be fair, just, and reasonable to impose a duty of care on the Trust to provide accurate information about waiting times—the UK Supreme Court unanimously allowed his appeal. Lord Lloyd-Jones explained that, in reality, this was not a case where the existence of a duty of care could be in any doubt. The trust owed Mr Darnley a duty to provide accurate information about waiting times, that duty had been breached and had caused Mr Darnley's brain damage.

Darnley v Croydon Health Services NHS Trust[9]

Lord Lloyd-Jones (with whom Lady Hale and Lords Reed, Kerr, and Hodge agreed)

In the specific context of this case, where misleading information was provided as to the time within which medical attention might be available, it is not appropriate to distinguish between medically qualified professionals and administrative staff in determining whether there was a duty of care. That distinction may well be highly relevant in deciding whether there was a negligent breach of duty; there the degree of skill which can reasonably be expected of a person will be likely to depend on the responsibility with which he or she is charged. In the present circumstances, however, questions as to the existence and scope of a duty of care owed by the trust should not depend on whether the misleading information was provided by a person who was or was not medically qualified. The respondent had charged its non-medically qualified staff with the role of being the first point of contact with persons seeking medical assistance and, as a result, with the responsibility for providing accurate information as to its availability . . .

While it is not the function of reception staff to give wider advice or information in general to patients, it is the duty of the NHS Trust to take care not to provide misinformation to patients and that duty is not avoided by the misinformation having been provided by reception staff as opposed to medical staff . . .

A receptionist in an A & E department cannot, of course, be expected to give medical advice or information but he or she can be expected to take reasonable care not to provide misleading advice as to the availability of medical assistance. The standard required is that of an averagely competent and well-informed person performing the function of a receptionist at a department providing emergency medical care . . .

[9] [2018] UKSC 50.

It is not unreasonable to require that patients in the position of the appellant should be provided on arrival, whether orally by a receptionist, by leaflet or prominent notice, with accurate information that they would normally be seen by a triage nurse within 30 minutes ...

The trial judge made the critical finding that it was reasonably foreseeable that a person who believes that it may be four or five hours before he will be seen by a doctor may decide to leave. In the light of that finding I have no doubt that the provision of such misleading information by a receptionist as to the time within which medical assistance might be available was negligent ...

Far from constituting a break in the chain of causation, the appellant's decision to leave was reasonably foreseeable and was made, at least in part, on the basis of the misleading information that he would have to wait for up to four or five hours before being seen by a doctor.

(3) Could Healthcare Workers Ever Owe Non-Patients a Duty of Care?

Usually, the only person likely to be injured by a doctor's mistake is the patient herself. In the next sections, we consider four scenarios in which a third party might claim that they were owed a duty of care by a healthcare professional:

- wrongful pregnancy;
- psychiatric injury;
- failure to prevent the patient from causing harm;
- medical examinations.

(a) 'Wrongful pregnancy'

Where a sterilization operation has been carried out negligently, or a patient has been given negligent advice about its success, it is, as we see later, possible to recover damages for the pain and discomfort associated with pregnancy and childbirth. These are suffered only by women. If a man's sterilization has failed, the 'damage' is therefore suffered not by the patient himself, but by a third party. She will generally only be able to recover damages if she was within the doctor's contemplation at the time of the operation, because she was the patient's wife or partner.

In *McFarlane v Tayside Health Board*,[10] the male patient was married and his wife was in a sufficiently proximate relationship with her husband's doctors. In contrast, in *Goodwill v BPAS*,[11] in which the woman who became pregnant met the patient, Mr MacKinlay, only after he had had his vasectomy, the court decided that a doctor carrying out a vasectomy does not owe a duty to all of his patient's future sexual partners. Peter Gibson LJ explained that the plaintiff was 'like any other woman in the world, a potential future sexual partner of his, that is to say a member of an indeterminately large class of females who might have sexual relations with Mr MacKinlay during his lifetime'.

(b) Psychiatric injury

It is possible that someone close to the patient might suffer psychiatric injury as a result of witnessing her negligent medical treatment. In such cases, the third party is described as a secondary victim, and the limiting principles developed in *Alcock v Chief Constable of South Yorkshire*[12]

---

[10] [1999] UKHL 50.   [11] [1996] 1 WLR 1397.   [12] [1992] 1 AC 310.

and *White v Chief Constable of South Yorkshire*[13] apply. In short, (a) the claimant must have a close relationship with the primary victim; (b) she must be close in time and space to the incident and she must witness it, or its immediate aftermath, with her unaided senses; (c) she must suffer a recognizable psychiatric illness, such as post-traumatic stress disorder (PTSD) as a result; and (d) the psychiatric illness must be caused by a sudden shocking or horrifying event.

There have been cases in which relatives have recovered for psychiatric injury caused by witnessing a loved one's negligent medical treatment. In *North Glamorgan NHS Trust v Walters*,[14] a mother whose newborn baby's death was the result of the defendant's negligence, and who witnessed his distressing final 36 hours, was said to have suffered the requisite 'shock'. And in *RE v Calderdale & Huddersfield NHS Foundation Trust*,[15] RE's mother and grandmother suffered PTSD after witnessing his negligent and traumatic delivery. RE's mother could recover under *Page v Smith*[16] as a primary victim, because RE was still part of her body at the time. RE's grandmother had been present at his birth, and believed that he had died, and Goss J held that this event had been 'sufficiently sudden, shocking and objectively horrifying'.

Where the claimant is a primary victim, and suffers psychiatric injury, there is no need for it to be caused by a sudden, shocking event. In *YAH v Medway NHS Foundation Trust*, the hospital had admitted liability for XAS's cerebral palsy, caused by 'a culpable delay in delivering XAS after clear signs of distress were evident on the CTG trace'. XAS's mother sought damages for 'psychiatric injuries associated with XAS's birth'. Whipple J found that she could recover, because XAS had been part of her body when his injuries occurred, but that if she had instead been a secondary victim, his delivery was not 'shocking' in the *Alcock* sense.

YAH v Medway NHS Foundation Trust [17]

Whipple J

There is no requirement for a primary victim who brings a claim for 'pure' psychiatric injury to show that the injury was caused by shock. To return to Lord Ackner's axiom, old-fashioned though it is, a primary victim can in principle claim for psychiatric injury which has been caused not by shock, but by 'the accumulation over a period of time of more gradual assaults on the nervous system', which have given rise to a recognised psychiatric condition ...

Although the Claimant's experiences during the delivery of XAS and afterwards were shocking and traumatic, using those terms in the ordinary way, they do not constitute 'shock' in an *Alcock* sense. Thus, the Claimant would not, if she was a secondary victim, have been entitled to recover damages.

In practice, the *Alcock* and *White* standard limiting criteria are often problematic in clinical negligence cases. In *Liverpool Women's Hospital NHS Foundation Trust v Ronayne*, Mr Ronayne had suffered an adjustment disorder as a result of witnessing a rapid deterioration in his wife's condition, after she was readmitted to hospital following a negligently performed hysterectomy. The Court of Appeal unanimously held, first, that there was not the necessary

[13] [1999] 2 AC 455. Both *Alcock* and *White* arose out of the Hillsborough stadium disaster in 1989, and involved claims brought by friends or relatives (*Alcock*) and policemen (*White*).

[14] [2002] EWCA Civ 1792. [15] [2017] EWHC 824 (QB). [16] [1996] AC 155.

[17] [2018] EWHC 2964 (QB).

element of suddenness, and, secondly, that what the claimant had seen was not sufficiently horrifying.

Liverpool Women's Hospital NHS Foundation Trust v Ronayne [18]

Tomlinson LJ (with whom Sullivan and Beatson LJJ agreed)

Having been told of the severity of his wife's condition and that she was being administered a cocktail of antibiotics, it cannot in my judgment be said that what thereafter occurred had the necessary element of suddenness.

Furthermore what the Claimant saw on these two occasions was not in my judgment horrifying by objective standards. Both on the first occasion and on the second the appearance of the Claimant's wife was as would ordinarily be expected of a person in hospital in the circumstances in which she found herself. What is required in order to found liability is something which is exceptional in nature. On the first occasion she was connected to monitors and drips. The reaction of most people of ordinary robustness to that sight, given the circumstances in which she had been taken into the A&E Department, and the knowledge that abnormalities had been found, including a shadow over the lung, necessitating immediate exploratory surgery, would surely be one of relief that the matter was in the hands of the medical professionals, with perhaps a grateful nod to the ready availability of modern medical equipment. The same is more or less true of her swollen appearance on the second occasion ...

I can readily accept that the appearance of Mrs Ronayne on this occasion must have been both alarming and distressing to the Claimant, but it was not in context exceptional and it was not I think horrifying in the sense in which that word has been used in the authorities. Certainly however it did not lead to a sudden violent agitation of the mind, because the Claimant was prepared to witness a person in a desperate condition and was moreover already extremely angry.

In the next extract, Andrew and John Burrows draw on this case in order to argue that the 'sudden shocking event' requirement makes no sense.

Andrew S Burrows and John H Burrows[19]

Even if one accepts that, over and above the need to prove non-remote negligently caused psychiatric illness, there should be control mechanisms for secondary victims so as to prevent opening the floodgates of litigation, those controls should not be arbitrary. Yet the need to show a sudden and shocking event appears to be just that. If a person has suffered a psychiatric illness, why should it make any difference whether that illness was induced by a sudden shocking event or by a sequence of unpleasant events over a period of time? The effect on the claimant is ultimately the same in the sense that that person has suffered a psychiatric illness. It is true that the type of psychiatric illness in question may differ. Indeed, on the facts of this case the county court judge precisely found that the claimant was not suffering from PTSD but from an adjustment disorder. But it has never been suggested that

[18] [2015] EWCA Civ 588.
[19] 'A Shocking Requirement in the Law on Negligence Liability for Psychiatric Illness: *Liverpool Women's Hospital NHS Foundation Trust v Ronayne* [2015] EWCA Civ 588' (2016) 24 Medical Law Review 278.

the only type of recognised psychiatric illness falling within the tort of negligence is PTSD. To allow recovery for an adjustment disorder but then to say that the illness must be caused by a sudden shocking event is incoherent.

Jyoti Ahuja further argues that the *Alcock* limiting criteria are at odds with evidence of what is especially traumatic for bereaved relatives. In fact, coming upon the immediate aftermath and seeing it with one's unaided senses may mean that someone is *less* likely to suffer serious psychological harm.

Jyoti Ahuja[20]

The proximity requirement views trauma as resulting primarily from the sight of the mutilated body of the loved one, and assumes that the pain is less when the body is not witnessed. This is, however, contrary to research evidence. Studies suggest that bereaved relatives who are denied the choice to view the body of their loved one may suffer more than those who were given the opportunity . . . Recovery has been found to be especially hard when the body of the loved one is never found . . .

The law, paradoxically, might deny recovery to those who possibly suffer the greatest distress . . .

Imagined images may often be worse than reality. . . Contrary to judicial assumptions, it does not appear that those who hear about the death from another source are spared much of the emotional pain that those who see it themselves have to endure.

Rachael Mulheron has also pointed out that the need for the claimant to have suffered a 'recognizable psychiatric illness' is problematic, because these diagnostic categories are designed in order to plan treatment, rather than to allocate blame.

Rachael Mulheron[21]

The diagnostic classifications were not intended or approved for legal (forensic) use, but were designed for research and clinical diagnostic purposes, as DSM-IV itself points out: 'When the DSM-IV categories, criteria, and textual descriptions are employed for forensic purposes, there are significant risks that diagnostic information will be misused or misunderstood. These dangers arise because of the imperfect fit between the questions of ultimate concern to the law and the information contained in a clinical diagnosis' . . .

For one thing, clinically speaking, an accurate diagnosis (say, whether a patient has a depressive episode or a mixed anxiety and depressive disorder) is important when planning *treatment*; but from a litigious point of view, the emphasis is different, because the court is seeking to ascertain whether the claimant has suffered any *compensable damage*.

---

[20] 'Liability for Psychological and Psychiatric Harm: The Road to Recovery' (2015) 23 Medical Law Review 27–52.
[21] 'Rewriting the Requirement for a "Recognized Psychiatric Injury" in Negligence Claims' (2012) 32 Oxford Journal of Legal Studies 77–112.

(c) Failure to prevent the patient from causing harm

There are a number of ways in which patients who are not offered proper advice or treatment might pose a risk to others. First, if a doctor realizes that her patient is unfit to drive, she is under a duty to tell her not to drive, and to inform the Driver and Vehicle Licensing Agency. If she instead does nothing, it is foreseeable that a third party might be injured as a result. Secondly, patients with infectious diseases pose a risk to third parties, so a doctor's negligent failure to diagnose her patient's condition, or to offer her appropriate advice or treatment, might put others at risk. Thirdly, if a doctor does not 'section' a psychiatric patient whom she believes to be likely to harm someone else (see further Chapter 7), it is foreseeable that someone might be hurt. In these situations, could a doctor owe these foreseeably injured third parties a duty of care?

It is important to remember that in such cases the doctor has not directly caused the claimant's injury; rather, she would be being sued for an omission, or a failure to prevent harm from occurring. As a result, a three-stage test applies: (1) the claimant's injury must be foreseeable; (2) there must be a proximate relationship between the claimant and the doctor; and (3) the imposition of a duty must be fair, just, and reasonable.[22] While it might be relatively straightforward to establish foreseeability, proving that there is a sufficient relationship of proximity, and that imposing a duty of care would be fair, just, and reasonable, will often be much more problematic.

The question of whether doctors might be under a duty to protect a member of the public from a dangerous psychiatric patient arose in *Palmer v Tees Health Authority*.[23] A man who had a long history of psychiatric problems abducted, sexually assaulted, and murdered a four-year-old girl, Rosie Palmer. Rosie's mother claimed that the defendant health authority's medical staff had failed to diagnose that there was a real, substantial, and foreseeable risk that this man would commit serious sexual offences against children, and that the defendants should therefore be liable for her daughter's death, and for her own PTSD and pathological grief reaction.

It was not disputed that the injuries to Rosie and her mother might have been foreseeable; but the judge held that there was not a relationship of sufficient proximity between the health authority and Rosie Palmer,[24] and that it was not fair, just, and reasonable to impose a duty of care upon the defendants. Mrs Palmer's appeal to the Court of Appeal was dismissed, Stuart Smith LJ pointing out that where a future victim was not identifiable, it would in practice be impossible to protect them from harm:

> An additional reason why in my judgment in this case it is at least necessary for the victim to be identifiable (though as I have indicated it may not be sufficient) to establish proximity, is that it seems to me that the most effective way of providing protection would be to give warning to the victim, his or her parents or social services so that some protective measure can be made.

There have been no cases in which claimants have sued medical professionals or their employers for failure to prevent a patient from causing injuries through dangerous driving or infectious disease. It is, however, likely that the courts would find that injuring other road

---

[22] *Caparo v Dickman* [1990] 2 AC 605.   [23] [1999] Lloyd's Rep Med 351 (CA).

[24] This case could therefore be distinguished from *Robinson v Chief Constable of West Yorkshire Police* [2018] UKSC 4, because Mrs Robinson was in the immediate vicinity when the officers attempted to arrest Williams, and hence it was foreseeable that she might be injured in the course of him attempting to escape.

users or infecting close contacts were foreseeable consequences of the failure to provide reasonable care to the patient, but that it would be much more difficult to establish the requisite proximity.

In the case of infectious disease, unless both the claimant's existence and her risk of infection were known to the doctor, it would be difficult to argue that there was a sufficiently proximate relationship. Even if the claimant was identifiable in advance as someone likely to be infected by the patient, perhaps because the doctor knew about their sexual relationship, other considerations, such as the duty to protect patient confidentiality (considered in Chapter 8), might mean that it would not be fair, just, or reasonable to impose a duty to protect the claimant from infection.

(d) Genetic testing

In two recent cases, the question has arisen whether the doctor of a patient with a genetic disease might owe a duty of care to the patient's relatives. Both cases involved the possible creation of a novel duty of care. Because *ABC v St George's Healthcare NHS Foundation Trust* is directly concerned with the circumstances in which a doctor might be under a duty to breach her duty of confidentiality,[25] we deal with it in Chapter 8.

In *Smith v University of Leicester NHS Trust*,[26] the claimants' case was that there had been a negligent failure accurately to diagnose that their second cousin, Mr Caven, was suffering from a serious genetic condition (adrenomyeloneuropathy). Mr Caven had consulted a neurologist who had ordered testing that would have identified his condition, but it was not carried out. If it had been, the risk to Mr Caven's relatives would have been known, and genetic testing would have been advised. The fact that his cousins also had this condition would have been likely to have been detected sooner, and the outcomes for them would have been significantly better (by this time, one cousin had died). Their claim was, however, rejected on the grounds that 'a third party cannot recover damages for a personal injury suffered because of an omission in the treatment of another'. His Honour Judge McKenna found that 'to extend the duty of care to a patient's second cousins (even though on the particular facts of the case there was the potential for them to be affected by an omission in the treatment of that patient) is to go well beyond the existing law and fails therefore the test of what is "fair just and reasonable"'.

(b) BREACH

(1) What is the Standard of Care?

Having established (usually straightforwardly) that she was owed a duty of care, the next stage for a claimant in a negligence action is to prove that the doctor breached her duty of care. In order to work out whether there has been a breach, it is necessary to establish what standard of care could reasonably have been expected. In ordinary tort actions, defendants are judged by what is known as the 'reasonable man' test. This does not mean that the doctor is judged by what it would be reasonable to expect from the 'man on the Clapham omnibus'. Rather, the doctor must meet the standard of care that can be expected from a doctor 'skilled in that particular art':[27] a GP must act as a reasonable GP; a neurosurgeon as a reasonable neurosurgeon, and so on. If a GP were to attempt a specialist procedure, such as anaesthesia, she would be

---

[25] [2017] EWCA Civ 336.   [26] [2016] EWHC 817 (QB).
[27] *Bolam v Friern Hospital Management Committee* [1957] 1 WLR 582.

judged by the standard of a reasonable anaesthetist. If the GP is unable to meet this standard, she might be found negligent for undertaking treatment beyond her competence.

The standard of care will be judged at the time when the alleged negligence occurred. If the claimant was injured during childbirth 20 years ago but only now brings an action for her injuries, the obstetrician will be judged by the standards of reasonable and responsible obstetric care 20 years ago. In *Roe v Minister of Health*,[28] heard in 1954, the defendants had administered contaminated anaesthetic to the claimant in 1947, but the particular risk of contamination only became known in 1951. The Court of Appeal found that there had been no negligence, Denning LJ famously saying, 'We must not look at the 1947 accident with 1954 spectacles.'

The central problem in judging the standard of care is that reasonable doctors within the same area of expertise may disagree. If differences of medical opinion are inevitable, how should the court decide which view should be preferred? As many law students will recall, the answer to this question has been dominated by the *Bolam* test, qualified by the *Bolitho* gloss.

(a) The Bolam *test*

In *Bolam v Friern Hospital Management Committee*, John Bolam, who was suffering from depression, was advised by a consultant at the defendants' hospital to undergo electroconvulsive therapy (ECT). He was not warned that ECT carried a small risk of fracture, nor was he physically restrained or given relaxant drugs. As a result, Mr Bolam sustained a fractured hip. At the time, medical opinion varied, both as to the desirability of warning patients of the risk of fracture associated with ECT, and as to whether it was appropriate to use relaxant drugs and physical restraint.

Bolam v Friern Hospital Management Committee[29]

McNair J (in his direction to the jury)

A doctor is not guilty of negligence if he has acted in accordance with a practice accepted as proper by a responsible body of medical men skilled in that particular art . . . Putting it the other way round, a doctor is not negligent, if he is acting in accordance with such a practice, merely because there is a body of opinion that takes a contrary view. At the same time, that does not mean that a medical man can obstinately and pig-headedly carry on with some old technique if it has been proved to be contrary to what is really substantially the whole of informed medical opinion. Otherwise you might get men today saying: 'I don't believe in anaesthetics. I don't believe in antiseptics. I am going to continue to do my surgery in the way it was done in the eighteenth century.' That clearly would be wrong.

The *Bolam* test appears to treat medical negligence differently from most other negligence actions. When deciding whether an employer or a driver has been negligent, the standard of care is set by the court, using the device of the reasonable man. When the defendant is a doctor, however, the standard of care has historically been set by other doctors, via the *Bolam* test. This judicial deference to medical opinion may have been partly due to the complexity of

---

[28] [1954] 2 QB 66.   [29] [1957] 1 WLR 582.

medical evidence, but might also be explained by a sense of professional solidarity, and by the high regard in which the medical profession has conventionally been held.

(b) Bolam + Bolitho: *a less deferential approach?*

In 1997, in *Bolitho v City and Hackney Health Authority*, the House of Lords adopted a more robust, and potentially less deferential, version of the *Bolam* test. Patrick Bolitho, who was two years old, had been admitted to hospital suffering from breathing difficulties. His condition deteriorated, and he suffered a cardiac arrest, leading to brain damage and subsequently to his death. The on-duty paediatric registrar did not see him, but even if she had, she said that she would not have intubated him. Intubation was the only procedure that could have prevented respiratory failure, but it was not without risks.

The expert witnesses for each side expressed diametrically opposed views about whether a failure to intubate was reasonable. On the facts, the House of Lords held that the registrar had not breached her duty of care, but the case is important for Lord Browne-Wilkinson's comments on the circumstances in which the court would be likely to decide that there had been negligence, despite the evidence of expert witnesses who agreed with the defendant's course of action.

Bolitho v City and Hackney Health Authority[30]

Lord Browne-Wilkinson

In the vast majority of cases the fact that distinguished experts in the field are of a particular opinion will demonstrate the reasonableness of that opinion. In particular, where there are questions of assessment of the relative risks and benefits of adopting a particular medical practice, a reasonable view necessarily presupposes that the relative risks and benefits have been weighed by the experts in forming their opinions. But if, in a rare case, it can be demonstrated that the professional opinion is not capable of withstanding logical analysis, the judge is entitled to hold that the body of opinion is not reasonable or responsible.

I emphasise that, in my view, it will very seldom be right for a judge to reach the conclusion that views genuinely held by a competent medical expert are unreasonable. The assessment of medical risks and benefits is a matter of clinical judgment which a judge would not normally be able to make without expert evidence . . . It is only where a judge can be satisfied that the body of expert opinion cannot be logically supported at all that such opinion will not provide the bench mark by reference to which the defendant's conduct falls to be assessed.

I turn to consider whether this is one of those rare cases. Like the Court of Appeal, in my judgment it plainly is not.

Essentially, the *Bolam + Bolitho* test for the standard of care in negligence is now a two-stage one. First, the court must ask whether the doctor acted in accordance with responsible medical opinion. If she did not, her conduct would be judged negligent according to the traditional *Bolam* test. An example of straightforward *Bolam* negligence is *Fallon v Wilson*. This was a case in which a mother took her premature baby, Alice Fallon, who had only just been discharged from hospital, to see her GP. While in Dr Wilson's consulting room, Alice's condition markedly deteriorated. Despite this, Dr Wilson advised Alice's mother to take her home and

---

[30] [1998] AC 232.

keep her warm. Although there was some dispute over what actually happened in the GP surgery, expert evidence was that—if Alice's mother's account was correct—the right response would have been to refer Alice to hospital immediately. Soon after Alice was taken home, she stopped breathing and she was then taken straight to hospital. Had Dr Wilson's failure to refer her to hospital immediately amounted to a breach of his duty of care? Once Eady J had established that, on certain matters of fact, Alice's mother's account was correct, he found that Dr Wilson had not acted as a reasonable GP.

Fallon v Wilson [31]

Eady J

On 15 January 1997, however, at some point between 17.00 and 17.30, he was called upon to make a judgment in a busy surgery on limited information and in the light of his long experience. I regret to say, however, that in making that judgment he fell short of the standard to be expected of a competent practitioner in the situation that confronted him. It was an inadequate response to advise merely that Alice should be kept warm.

I find in the light of the evidence that she should have been referred to hospital straight away and that, accordingly, there was a breach of duty on the Defendant's part . . . There would be a low threshold for referral in the case of a premature baby—and, in particular, a baby who had been born at 27 weeks and had still by the time of the consultation not reached the equivalent of full term.

If, however, the doctor did act in accordance with a body of responsible medical opinion, that is not the end of the matter, and the claimant has a second opportunity to prove that the doctor was negligent if she can establish that this body of medical opinion is 'not capable of withstanding logical analysis'.

What does this mean in practice? Most obviously, it will be relatively straightforward for the court to determine that expert evidence 'does not withstand logical analysis' if the doctor failed to do something—such as take a simple precaution or examine the patient—in circumstances when it would be obvious to a lay person that they should have done so. For example, in *Marriott v West Midlands RHA*,[32] Mr Marriott had suffered a head injury and had been unconscious for 20–30 minutes. When he subsequently suffered from lethargy, headaches, and loss of appetite, his GP did not refer him to hospital. Since it would seem obvious that doctors should be concerned about such symptoms reported by someone who has recently suffered a head injury, the Court of Appeal decided that the evidence given by the expert witness who defended the doctor's conduct could not be logically supported.

In *Muller v King's College Hospital NHS Foundation Trust*, Kerr J drew a distinction between cases in which the patient's condition was unknown and the alleged negligence was the doctor's failure to diagnose her condition, and cases in which the patient's condition was known and the doctor was alleged to have treated her negligently. In a 'pure diagnosis' case, there cannot be two right answers to the question of how a patient should be treated, as might be the case in a 'negligent treatment' case. Rather the diagnosis is simply wrong, and an expert witness who claims that a pathologist would have acted competently by missing obvious signs of melanoma was not expressing a defensible opinion.

---

[31] [2010] EWHC 2978 (QB).   [32] [1999] Lloyd's Rep Med 23.

Muller v King's College Hospital NHS Foundation Trust[33]

Kerr J

In a case involving advice, treatment or both, opposed expert opinions may in a sense both be 'right', in that each represents a respectable body of professional opinion. The same is not true of a pure diagnosis case such as the present, where there is no weighing of risks and benefits, only misreporting which may or may not be negligent. The experts expressing opposing views on that issue cannot both be right . . .

The signs of malignant melanoma were plain to see on the slides. Dr Foria's view that failing to see them at the time was not negligent, was a view formed in good faith, honestly and sincerely. He is, in my judgment, right to say that a pathologist who is, in general, competent, might have missed the malignant melanoma; but he is not right to say that a normally competent pathologist would be acting competently on this particular occasion, if she missed it.

(c) The role of guidelines

Doctors and other healthcare professionals have access to best practice guidance, issued by professional bodies such as the Royal Colleges, or treatment protocols published by the National Institute for Health and Care Excellence. Professional guidance will also be available to help the court determine the standard of reasonable care. As Margaret Brazier and José Miola explain, the 'judge confronted by individual experts who disagree about good practice will in certain cases be able to refer to something approaching a "gold standard"'.[34]

This does not mean that any healthcare professional who deviates from clinical guidance will be found to have been negligent if something goes wrong, however. Guidelines are, by definition, not mandatory. Nevertheless, as we can see from the following case, they will often form a useful starting point. In *C v North Cumbria University Hospitals NHS Trust*, a midwife was found not to have been negligent in delivering a second dose of a drug used to stimulate contractions during a difficult delivery.

C v North Cumbria University Hospitals NHS Trust[35]

Green J

[The guidelines] are not merely informal documents produced by manufacturers. They are intended to be relied upon and should accordingly carry considerable weight in favour of a midwife who acts consistently with them. In particular the guidance represents a balancing of risks and benefits such that if the guidelines are adhered to then that is inherently likely to reflect a properly balanced (reasonable) decision . . .

In conclusion my view is that *prima facie* a midwife who acts in accordance with the guidelines should be safe from a charge of negligence. However, in the present case since it is common ground that in some regards the guidelines are not satisfactory I do not decide this case upon the basis that adhering to guidelines is sufficient. I consider that the fact that

---

[33] [2017] EWHC 128 (QB).

[34] 'Bye-Bye *Bolam*: A Medical Litigation Revolution?' (2000) 8 Medical Law Review 85–114.

[35] [2014] EWHC 61 (QB).

Midwife Bragg acted in accordance with the guidelines is a factor militating against negligence but I also assess Midwife Bragg's conduct against the benchmark of the other surrounding facts and circumstances.

(2) Is the Standard of Care Fixed?

Many law students will recall the case of *Nettleship v Weston*,[36] in which a learner driver was found to have been negligent for failing to meet the standard of care that would be expected of a reasonably experienced driver. Does this mean that the standard of care in medical negligence is fixed and objectively determined, or might it vary according to the circumstances? In the next sections, we briefly consider whether it would be reasonable to expect a lower standard of care in four different situations:

- if resources are scarce;
- if the doctor is treating the patient in an emergency;
- if the doctor is inexperienced;
- if the doctor is practising alternative medicine.

(a) Scarce resources

As we saw in chapter 2, the NHS often cannot provide an optimum standard of care. This political reality makes judging the standard of care in negligence difficult: if less than perfect care is inevitable, how do courts tell when treatment has failed to meet an acceptable standard? Let us take the common example of having to wait to be treated in an overstretched accident and emergency department. It would not be negligent to expect someone with a sprained ankle to wait for a few hours, but a similar failure to attend to someone who had had a heart attack would fail to meet this basic minimum standard of care.

In *Mulholland v Medway NHS Foundation Trust*, Anthony Mulholland claimed that there had been a negligent failure to refer him for tests that would have led to earlier diagnosis of his brain tumour. Green J held that the practitioners in a busy A&E department did not have the luxury of time, and that, in the circumstances, it had not been negligent to rely upon the conclusions of Mr Mulholland's GP and the stroke team.

Mulholland v Medway NHS Foundation Trust[37]

Green J

In forming a conclusion about the conduct of a practitioner working within triage within an A&E Department context cannot be ignored. The assessment of breach of duty is not an abstract exercise but one formed within a context—which here is that of a busy A&E where the task of the triaging nurse is to make a quick judgment call as to where next to send the patient. The A&E department was busy seeing up to 200 patients per day. There is no opportunity for a triage nurse to devote a great deal of time to the taking of a detailed history or the performance of an extensive diagnosis ... The reasonable nurse is one who operates in a

---

[36] [1971] 2 QB 691.   [37] [2015] EWHC 268 (QB).

busy A&E which has a procedure which the nurse will follow for streaming and which does not contemplate an exhaustive diagnosis being formed ...

[D]octors in A&E do not have the luxury of long and mature consideration. They take decisions at short notice in a pressurised environment. They cannot (ordinarily) consult the country's leading experts at the drop of a hat having given those experts months or even years to prepare their expert opinions. If Dr Chong had been given the week off in order to research Mr Mulholland's case she might, just possibly, have listed a Jacksonian seizure on her list of possible causes. But in my judgment the standard of care owed by an A&E doctor must be calibrated in a manner reflecting reality. It was not, in the circumstances confronting her, negligent of Dr Chong to omit this sort of specialised neurological condition from her assessment.

(b) Emergencies

In an emergency, it might be difficult for doctors to provide the same standard of care as might normally be expected. Following a major disaster, such as a bomb blast, hospitals may be overwhelmed with casualties. Off-duty doctors in the UK are not under a legal duty to offer assistance if they come upon a medical emergency, but a failure to assist in an emergency might prompt disciplinary action by the General Medical Council. GMC guidance on the duties of a doctor states that: 'You must offer help if emergencies arise in clinical settings or in the community, taking account of your own safety, your competence and the availability of other options for care'.[38] If a doctor does stop at the scene of an accident, the lack of equipment will inevitably compromise the standard of care that she can provide. In such circumstances, would it be reasonable to expect a lower standard of care than normal?

Once a doctor has undertaken to offer care to an injured person, she undoubtedly assumes a duty of care towards her. But since what is expected of doctors is reasonable care, it is appropriate to take into account the surrounding circumstances. It would clearly not be reasonable to expect a doctor who is treating patients at the scene of an accident to provide the level of care that would be available in a well-equipped intensive care unit.

(c) Inexperience

Should a doctor's inexperience affect the standard of care that can reasonably be expected of her? On the one hand, doctors have to learn by experience, and it would seem harsh for junior doctors to be liable in negligence for their inability to reach the standard of care that would be expected from an experienced doctor. But, on the other hand, if the standard of care were to fluctuate according to the doctor's experience, patients would be well advised to refuse to be treated by anyone who is inexperienced, and the system through which junior doctors learn 'on the job' would break down.

In 1987, in *Wilsher v Essex AHA*,[39] Glidewell LJ held that 'the law requires the trainee or learner to be judged by the same standard as his more experienced colleagues'. More recently, in *FB v Princess Alexandra NHS Trust*, FB's mother had called the out-of-hours service during the night because FB, who was 12 months old, had a high temperature, erratic breathing, and was rolling her eyes. The triage nurse called an ambulance and when she arrived at hospital, FB was seen by Dr Rushd, who diagnosed an upper respiratory tract infection and discharged her. FB's condition deteriorated and she was eventually diagnosed with pneumococcal meningitis and multiple brain infarcts, as a result of which she suffered permanent brain damage. At

---

[38] *Good Medical Practice* (GMC: London, 2013) para 26. [39] [1987] 1 QB 730.

first instance, Jay J held that it would have been negligent if an experienced doctor had failed to elicit the relevant facts (such as FB's eye rolling) from her mother, but that such a failure by an inexperienced Senior House Officer (SHO) in the A&E department did not amount to negligence. The Court of Appeal allowed FB's appeal and found that Dr Rushd had been negligent. It is, however, worth noting Jackson LJ's words of sympathy for the plight of junior doctors.

FB v Princess Alexandra NHS Trust[40]

Jackson LJ

Whether doctors are performing their normal role or 'acting up', they are judged by reference to the post which they are fulfilling at the material time. The health authority or health trust is liable if the doctor whom it puts into a particular position does not possess (and therefore does not exercise) the requisite degree of skill for the task in hand.

Thus in professional negligence, as in the general law of negligence, the standard of care which the law requires is an imperfect compromise. It achieves a balance between the interests of society and fairness to the individual practitioner ...

The conduct of Dr Rushd in the present case must be judged by the standard of a reasonably competent SHO in an accident and emergency department. The fact that Dr Rushd was aged 25 and 'relatively inexperienced' does not diminish the required standard of skill and care. On the other hand, the fact that she had spent six months in a paediatric department does not elevate the required standard. Other SHOs in A&E departments will have different backgrounds and experience, but they are all judged by the same standard ...

Before parting with this case, I must acknowledge that junior hospital doctors work long hours under considerable pressure. They are often involved in life and death decisions. The pressures can be even greater when they are working all night, as Dr Rushd was here. If mistakes are made, it is devastating for the patient and it is expensive for the NHS trust. Doctors, however, are human. Even good and conscientious doctors may, from time to time, fall short. That is not a reason to lose heart or (even worse) to abandon medical practice. Those who have learnt from past mistakes often have even more to offer.

(d) Complementary and alternative medicine

How should the courts determine the standard of care that can reasonably be expected of a practitioner of complementary or alternative medicine? Should a Chinese herbalist be judged against the reasonable practitioner of Chinese herbal medicine, or should he be expected to meet the same standard of care as an orthodox clinician? Interestingly, there have been virtually no cases brought by patients who claim that they have been injured as a result of alternative therapies. This is not necessarily because such treatments are safe; rather, it is possible that patients who believe that they have been left worse off after using alternative medical treatments are less likely to complain, and may be reluctant to consult a conventional doctor about their symptoms.

The issue has arisen only once in the UK. In *Shakoor v Situ*, Mr Situ, a practitioner of traditional Chinese herbal medicine, had been consulted by Abdul Shakoor about a skin condition for which the only orthodox medical treatment was surgery. After taking nine doses of the

---

[40] [2017] EWCA Civ 334.

herbal remedy, Mr Shakoor suffered acute liver failure and died. It had been established that, on the balance of probabilities, his death was probably caused by the remedy, but Bernard Livesey QC rejected his widow's claim that Mr Situ had been negligent.

Shakoor v Situ [41]

Bernard Livesey QC

The Chinese herbalist . . . does not hold himself out as a practitioner of orthodox medicine. More particularly, the patient has usually had the choice of going to an orthodox practitioner but has rejected him in favour of the alternative practitioner for reasons personal and best known to himself and almost certainly at some personal financial cost . . . The decision of the patient may be enlightened and informed or based on ignorance and superstition. Whatever the basis of his decision, it seems to me that the fact that the patient has chosen to reject the orthodox and prefer the alternative practitioner is something important which must be taken into account. Why should he later be able to complain that the alternative practitioner has not provided him with skill and care in accordance with the standards of those orthodox practitioners whom he has rejected?

On the other hand, it is of course obviously true to say that the alternative practitioner has chosen to practice in this country alongside a system of orthodox medicine and must abide by the laws and standards prevailing in this country . . .

Accordingly, a claimant may succeed in an action against an alternative practitioner for negligently prescribing a remedy either by calling an expert in the speciality in question to assert and prove that the defendant has failed to exercise the skill and care appropriate to that art . . . Alternatively, the claimant may prove that the prevailing standard of skill and care 'in that art' is deficient in this country having regard to risks which were not and should have been taken into account.

In short, there are two ways in which a claimant might establish negligence on the part of an alternative medical practitioner. First, she could prove that the defendant did not meet the standard of care of a reasonable practitioner of that particular 'art'. Secondly, even if the defendant did act as a reasonable alternative practitioner, it would still be open to the claimant to establish that the prevailing standard of care in that 'art' is itself deficient, on the grounds that it fails to take account of published evidence of toxicity.

(3) Proof of Breach

It is for the claimant to prove on the balance of probabilities that the defendant has breached her duty of care. The maxim *res ipsa loquitur* ('the thing speaks for itself') allows the courts, in certain circumstances, to draw an inference that the defendant was negligent. An example might be if a surgical instrument is left inside the patient's body after surgery. It would be difficult to think of circumstances in which this had occurred, but no one had breached their duty of care. Similarly, if a patient went into hospital in order to have her cancerous right kidney removed, and her healthy left kidney was removed instead, again the inference might reasonably be drawn that the surgeon had been negligent.

[41] [2001] 1 WLR 410.

Essentially, then, *res ipsa loquitur* is just an elaborate way of saying that there will occasionally be circumstances in which a judge would be entitled to find that the defendant had been negligent without the need for expert witnesses to establish that the defendant's actions fell below the appropriate standard of care. It does not reverse the burden of proof, such that it is for the defendant to prove that she was not negligent, rather it applies in simple and unusual cases where negligence can be inferred by a lay person, from the facts themselves.

Hobhouse LJ's judgment in *Ratcliffe v Plymouth and Torbay Health Authority* offers a helpful explanation of the limited application *res ipsa loquitur* is likely to have in actions against doctors. Mr Ratcliffe had undergone an operation on his ankle, and had been given a spinal anaesthetic to relieve post-operative pain. The operation itself was a success, but Mr Ratcliffe was left with a serious neurological defect, causing severe pain, a total loss of sensation in his leg and penile numbness. He contended that this raised an inference that the spinal anaesthetic had been given negligently. His claim was dismissed, and the Court of Appeal dismissed his appeal.

Ratcliffe v Plymouth and Torbay Health Authority[42]

Hobhouse LJ

Res ipsa loquitur is no more than a convenient Latin phrase used to describe the proof of facts which are sufficient to support an inference that a defendant was negligent and therefore to establish a prima facie case against him . . . The burden of proving the negligence of the defendant remains throughout upon the plaintiff. The burden is on the plaintiff at the start of the trial and, absent an admission by the defendant, is still upon the plaintiff at the conclusion of the trial . . . The plaintiff may or may not have needed to call evidence to establish a prima facie case. The admitted facts may suffice for that purpose . . . In practice, save in the most extreme cases of blatant negligence, the plaintiff will have to adduce at least some expert evidence to get his case upon its feet . . .

Res ipsa loquitur is not a principle of law: it does not relate to, or raise, any presumption. It is merely a guide to help to identify when a prima facie case is being made out.

In *Zahir v Vadodaria*,[43] a case in which a patient was unhappy with the appearance of her nose following a rhinoplasty operation, it was once again confirmed that the principle of *res ipsa loquitor* 'is applicable in only the most unusual of clinical negligence actions'. As Garnham J explained, there are:

no guaranteed outcomes in plastic surgery and the need for revision surgery is not in itself an indicator of negligence. In a discipline which is dependent on resecting millimetres of human tissue and predicting its precise manner of repair, it cannot be said that, because an undesirable outcome is the result, there must necessarily have been negligence in the performance of the surgeon.

---

[42] [1998] Lloyd's Rep Med 168.   [43] [2016] EWHC 1215 (QB).

(c) CAUSATION

Once a claimant has established that the doctor has breached her duty of care, she still has to prove that it was this breach of duty that caused her injuries. In practice, causation poses particular difficulties in medical negligence actions because there may be at least two possible causes of the patient's injury: the doctor's actions and the patient's pre-existing condition. Where there are multiple possible causes, proving causation on the balance of probabilities is problematic. The patient's health may have deteriorated even if the care she received was non-negligent, which means that often what has been lost is the *chance* of being restored to full health. The courts are then forced to speculate about what might have happened if the doctor had not breached her duty of care.

(1) The 'But For' Test

The standard test for causation is often referred to as the 'but for' test: but for the defendant's negligence, would the claimant have suffered this injury? This means that the claimant must show that their injury was caused by the doctor's negligence, rather than something that would have happened anyway. It is not enough to show both that the doctor breached her duty of care, and that the claimant's health has got worse; rather, there must be a causal link between the two.

The application of the 'but for' test was straightforward in *Barnett v Chelsea and Kensington Hospital Management Committee*, the case we considered earlier involving a man who had died from arsenic poisoning, after being sent home from the hospital's casualty department.

Barnett v Chelsea and Kensington Hospital Management Committee[44]

Nield J

There has been put before me a timetable which, I think, is of much importance. The deceased attended at the casualty department at 8.05 or 8.10am. If Dr Banerjee had got up and dressed and come to see the three men and examined them and decided to admit them, the deceased could not have been in bed in a ward before 11am. I accept Dr Goulding's evidence that an intravenous drip would not have been set up before 12 noon . . .

If the principal condition is one of enzyme disturbance—as I am of the view that it was here—then the only method of treatment which is likely to succeed is the use of the specific or antidote which is commonly called BAL [dimercaprol]. Dr Goulding said this in the course of his evidence: 'The only way to deal with this is to use the specific BAL. I see no reasonable prospect of the deceased being given BAL before the time at which he died' . . .

I regard that evidence as very moderate, and that it might be a true assessment of the situation to say that there was no chance of BAL being administered before the death of the deceased.

The simplicity of the application of the 'but for' test in *Barnett* is the exception rather than the rule, however, and proving causation is often much more difficult. Not only may there be more

---

[44] [1969] 1 QB 428.

than one possible cause of the patient's injuries, but also it is not always possible to be certain what the outcome would have been if the patient had been properly treated.

In *Wilsher v Essex AHA*,[45] there were five possible causes of Martin Wilsher's near blindness, one of which was the fact that he had negligently been given excess oxygen on two occasions. The House of Lords found that he had failed to prove that it was the excess oxygen that caused his injuries. According to Lord Bridge, 'whether we like it or not, the law, which only Parliament can change, requires proof of fault causing damage as the basis of liability in tort'.

In what are called 'loss of a chance' cases, the doctor's breach of duty has deprived the patient of the opportunity of recovery. In *Hotson v East Berkshire AHA*, Stephen Hotson, then 13 years old, had injured his hip in a fall. He was taken to hospital, where his injury was not correctly diagnosed, and he was sent home. After five days of severe pain, Stephen was taken back to hospital, where a proper diagnosis was made and he was given emergency treatment. He was, however, left permanently disabled.

At trial, the judge found that even if Stephen's injury had been diagnosed and treated immediately, there was still a 75 per cent risk of his disability developing, but that the breach of duty had turned that risk into an inevitability, thus denying him a 25 per cent chance of a good recovery. The judge awarded him 25 per cent of the full value of the damages awardable for the claimant's disability, and this was upheld by the Court of Appeal. The health authority appealed successfully to the House of Lords.

Hotson v East Berkshire AHA[46]

Lord Ackner

I have sought to stress that this case was a relatively simple case concerned with the proof of causation, on which the plaintiff failed, because he was unable to prove, on the balance of probabilities, that his deformed hip was caused by the authority's breach of duty in delaying over a period of five days a proper diagnosis and treatment. Where causation is in issue, the judge decides that issue on the balance of the probabilities . . .

Once liability is established, on the balance of probabilities, the loss which the plaintiff has sustained is payable in full. It is not discounted by reducing his claim by the extent to which he has failed to prove his case with 100% certainty.

According to *Hotson*, the court must be satisfied that it is *more likely than not* that the claimant's injuries would have been avoided if the doctor had not been negligent. If there is a 55 per cent chance that the patient would have made a complete recovery if she had received non-negligent treatment, she can recover in full, whereas if there is a 45 per cent chance of recovery, her claim fails because she has not proved on the balance of probabilities that her injuries were caused by the defendant's negligence.

The problem with framing the issue in this way is that the courts are engaged in an inevitably hypothetical inquiry about what *might have happened* if the doctor had not acted as she did, and this sort of speculation is not well suited to precise quantification in percentage terms.

In *Hutchinson v Epsom and St Helier NHS Trust*,[47] the question for the judge was whether a heavy drinker would have stopped drinking if he had been told he had end-stage liver disease.

---

[45] [1988] 1 AC 1074.   [46] [1987] 1 AC 750.   [47] [2002] EWHC 2363 (QB).

On the evidence of his wife, the judge found that he would have done. For obvious reasons, it is impossible to judge the truth or falsity of this finding.

In the non-medical case of *Fairchild v Glenhaven Funeral Services*,[48] the House of Lords adopted a rather more flexible approach to causation, and compensated employees for the lost chance of not contracting mesothelioma from exposure to asbestos. At the same time, the House of Lords suggested that clinical negligence cases were different, and should be governed by the more restrictive approach to causation in *Wilsher*. As Lord Hoffmann explained:

> [T]he political and economic arguments involved in the massive increase in the liability of the National Health Service . . . are far more complicated than the reasons . . . for imposing liability upon an employer who has failed to take simple precautions.

Certainly in *Gregg v Scott*, a case in which a GP's failure to diagnose a lymphoma (a type of cancer) and refer Malcolm Gregg to a specialist, reduced his chance of survival from 42 to 25 per cent, a majority of the House of Lords confirmed that *Fairchild* did not affect the requirement that the claimant must prove causation on the balance of probabilities.

Gregg v Scott[49]

Lord Hoffmann

In effect, the Appellant submits that the exceptional rule in *Fairchild* should be generalised and damages awarded in all cases in which the defendant may have caused an injury and has increased the likelihood of the injury being suffered . . .

It should first be noted that adopting such a rule would involve abandoning a good deal of authority . . . Furthermore, the House would be dismantling all the qualifications and restrictions with which it so recently hedged the *Fairchild* exception. There seem to me to be no new arguments or change of circumstances which could justify such a radical departure from precedent . . .

[A] wholesale adoption of possible rather than probable causation as the criterion of liability would be so radical a change in our law as to amount to a legislative act. It would have enormous consequences for insurance companies and the National Health Service . . . I think that any such change should be left to Parliament.

Lord Nicholls (dissenting)

The loss of a 45% prospect of recovery is just as much a real loss for a patient as the loss of a 55% prospect of recovery. In both cases the doctor was in breach of his duty to his patient. In both cases the patient was worse off. He lost something of importance and value. But, it is said, in one case the patient has a remedy, in the other he does not . . . This is rough justice indeed.

In *Bailey v Ministry of Defence*, the claimant, Grannia Bailey had inhaled her own vomit and suffered a cardiac arrest after an operation to remove a gallstone. Her claim was that this only happened because her negligent post-operative care had left her too ill and weak to prevent

---

[48] [2002] UKHL 22, applied in *Barker v Corus* [2006] UKHL 20.   [49] [2005] UKHL 2.

herself from reacting normally when she vomited. The Court of Appeal held that in cases of cumulative causes, it was sufficient to establish that the first defendant's lack of care had made a material contribution to the weakness of her condition, which led to her cardiac arrest and subsequent brain damage.

Bailey v Ministry of Defence[50]

Waller LJ

In my view one cannot draw a distinction between medical negligence cases and others. I would summarise the position in relation to cumulative cause cases as follows. If the evidence demonstrates on a balance of probabilities that the injury would have occurred as a result of the non-tortious cause or causes in any event, the claimant will have failed to establish that the tortious cause contributed. Hotson's case exemplifies such a situation . . . In a case where medical science cannot establish the probability that 'but for' an act of negligence the injury would not have happened but can establish that the contribution of the negligent cause was more than negligible, the 'but for' test is modified, and the claimant will succeed.

The instant case involved cumulative causes acting so as to create a weakness and thus the judge in my view applied the right test, and was entitled to reach the conclusion he did.

Bailey is a complex case, but it is different from *Hotson* and *Gregg*. In those cases, the patient had a pre-existing condition or illness that was not adequately treated. In both cases, medical experts agreed that, on the balance of probabilities, the damage was not caused by the inadequate treatment. In *Bailey*, Ms Bailey's weakness, which made her unable to react normally to vomiting, had two causes, one tortious (her inadequate treatment) and one non-tortious (pancreatitis). The difficulty was that it was impossible to determine the exact contribution of both causes.

If medical experts could have been certain, on the balance of probabilities, that Ms Bailey's pancreatitis would *on its own* have caused her to be so weak that she was likely to inhale her own vomit, then her inadequate treatment would not have caused her weakened state. Since that was not possible, and it was clear that her inadequate treatment had materially contributed to her weakened state, it also materially contributed to her inability to react normally to vomiting, and therefore was a cause of her injuries.[51]

As Janet Smith, writing extra-judicially, explains, this benefits claimants (and disadvantages defendants) where there is evidential uncertainty:

This passage [from Waller LJ's judgment] draws attention to the disadvantage which defendants face where the claimant's medical condition is not well understood... In *Bailey*, the claimant succeeded in full because the doctors could not assess the contributions. So the 'but for' rule was modified.[52]

The case of *Gouldsmith v Mid Staffordshire General Hospitals NHS Trust* raises a different sort of 'loss of a chance' question. At first instance, the judge found that it had been negligent not to refer the patient, who suffered from lesions on her left hand, to a specialist hospital. Mrs

---

[50] [2008] EWCA Civ 883.   [51] See also *Williams v The Bermuda Hospital Board* [2016] UKPC 4.
[52] 'Causation—The Search for Principle' (2009) 2 Journal of Personal Injury Law 101–13.

Gouldsmith had established that most but not all specialists would be likely to have operated on her hand, and that operating would have avoided the subsequent amputation of her fingers. At first instance, the judge found that she had not proved, on the balance of probabilities, that if she had been referred to a specialist hospital, she would have had this operation.

By a majority, the Court of Appeal disagreed. They found that having established that most specialists would have operated prima facie justified the conclusion that the specialist to whom the respondents should have referred her would be likely to have done so. It was not necessary for the claimant to prove that the specialist would have, in fact, operated, but just that it was more likely than not that she would have done.

Gouldsmith v Mid Staffordshire General Hospitals NHS Trust[53]

Pill LJ

[H]er establishment of the fact shifted the evidential burden of proof on to the respondents. It was open to them to have countered, had they had the material with which to do so, with evidence that the reference would be likely to have been to a particular specialist who would not have operated on the appellant. In the absence of credible evidence of that character the answer to the first question proffered on behalf of the appellant should have secured judgment for her.

An even more complex issue arose in *Wright v Cambridge Medical Group*. The defendant GP practice admitted negligence in failing to see a baby, who was in fact suffering from an undiagnosed super-infection, and refer her to hospital, following the mother's description of her symptoms on the telephone. They claimed, however, that the negligent failure to refer Clarice Wright to hospital immediately did not cause her injury because, even if she had been promptly referred, she would, in any event, not have been treated properly at the hospital, and therefore would still have suffered the permanent damage to her hip which was caused by her inadequately treated infection. When Clarice was eventually admitted to hospital two days after the telephone call, a catalogue of errors meant that she was not immediately treated with appropriate antibiotics. At first instance, Mackay J had held that it was therefore for the claimant to prove that she would have been treated non-negligently if she had been admitted to hospital on 15 April, but the Court of Appeal found that he had misdirected himself, and that a claimant did not have to prove that an earlier referral would have led her to have been competently treated.

Wright v Cambridge Medical Group[54]

Lord Neuberger MR

[I]t seems to me that, in a case where a doctor has negligently failed to refer his patient to a hospital, and, as a consequence, she has lost the opportunity to be treated as she should have been by a hospital, the doctor cannot escape liability by establishing that the hospital would have negligently failed to treat the patient appropriately, even if he had promptly referred

---

[53] [2007] EWCA Civ 397.   [54] [2011] EWCA Civ 669.

> her. Even if the doctor established this, it would not enable him to escape liability, because, by negligently failing to refer the patient promptly, he deprived her of the opportunity to be treated properly by the hospital.

A key problem for the Court of Appeal was that this action was brought only against the GP practice, rather than—as would have been more sensible—joining the hospital as defendants. This was a case in which there were two successive instances of negligence—the late referral and the subsequent inadequate treatment in hospital. If Clarice had sued both tortfeasors, they might have been left to fight out or agree their respective contribution to her loss between themselves.

(2) Remoteness

There is another hurdle to overcome once a claimant has succeeded in proving factual causation: it is also necessary to establish that the type of damage is not too remote, that is, the type of damage must be foreseeable, although its extent, and the manner in which it occurred, need not be.[55] Normally in clinical negligence cases the type of damage will be some sort of physical injury, which is obviously a foreseeable consequence of negligent medical care. As a result, there are hardly any medical cases where remoteness has been an issue.

One exception is *R v Croydon Health Authority*.[56] The claimant had undergone a pre-employment chest X-ray, and the radiographer failed to alert her to an abnormality (primary pulmonary hypertension or PPH), which would be exacerbated by pregnancy. She argued that if she had known that she had PPH, she would not have become pregnant. The Court of Appeal dismissed her claim for the costs arising from the birth of her child. Kennedy LJ held that the 'damage was, as is sometimes said, too remote'. While the radiographer might have been responsible for failing to observe an abnormality which affected her fitness to work, 'her domestic circumstances were not his affair'.

A further dimension to remoteness is the question of whether a new intervening act (a *novus actus interveniens*) has broken the chain of causation. If a psychiatric patient who was known to be at risk of taking her own life succeeds in committing suicide as a result of a negligent failure to keep her under appropriate surveillance, has the chain of causation been broken by the patient's own action? In *Kirkham v Chief Constable of Greater Manchester*,[57] the court rejected the claim that the deceased's suicide had been a *novus actus* on the grounds that it was the very act that the defendants had been under a duty to prevent. If there was no prior indication that a patient was at risk of committing suicide, her action would be more likely to break the chain of causation.[58]

(d) DEFENCES

There are several possible defences to a claim in negligence. A partial defence would exist if the patient had been contributorily negligent. Under section 1 of the Law Reform (Contributory Negligence) Act 1945, damages can be reduced in proportion to the extent of the claimant's responsibility for her injuries. Contributory negligence usually has little role to play in clinical

---

[55] The *Wagon Mound* [1961] AC 388.   [56] (1997) 40 BMLR 40.   [57] [1990] 2 QB 283.
[58] *Hyde v Tameside AHA*, The Times, 15 April 1981.

negligence cases, however. Doctors' responsibility for medical treatment means that, if something goes wrong, it is unlikely to be regarded as the patient's fault.

Where the patient was wholly responsible for her injuries, this may simply lead to a finding that the doctor had not been negligent at all. In *Venner v North East Essex Health Authority and Another,*[59] a woman who was about to undergo a sterilization operation was advised to stop taking the contraceptive pill, and to take other contraceptive precautions prior to the operation. Before the operation she was asked whether there was any chance that she could be pregnant, to which she answered 'no', despite the fact that she had had unprotected sexual intercourse. She was in fact pregnant when the operation took place, and subsequently gave birth to a healthy child. Tucker J found that there had been no negligence, and the patient herself—a mature woman who understood the likelihood of conception—was responsible for her pregnancy.

The defence of *volenti non fit injuria*[60] is extremely unlikely to affect clinical negligence claims. It is difficult to imagine a case in which the patient could be said to have voluntarily assumed the risk of being injured by her doctor's negligence.

There have been cases where the defence of illegality (or *ex turpi causa non oritur actio*[61]) has been raised. In *Clunis v Camden and Islington Health Authority*, a man with mental health problems, who had killed a passenger on the London Underground, argued that the health authority had failed to treat him with reasonable care and skill, and that if they had, he would have been sectioned and would not have killed Jonathan Zito. The Court of Appeal applied the defence of illegality to reject his claim.

Clunis v Camden and Islington Health Authority[62]

Beldam LJ

In the present case the plaintiff has been convicted of a serious criminal offence. In such a case, public policy would in our judgment preclude the court from entertaining the plaintiff's claim unless it could be said that he did not know the nature and quality of his act, or that what he was doing was wrong . . . The court ought not to allow itself to be made an instrument to enforce obligations alleged to arise out of the plaintiff's own criminal act and we would therefore allow the appeal on this ground.

(e) LIMITATION PERIODS

Most personal injury cases must be brought within three years either of the date when the injury occurred, or the date when the patient realized, or should have realized, that she might be able to sue.[63] If the patient dies as a result of her injuries, her relatives have three years from the date of death, or from the date when they realize, or should have realized, that an action

---

[59] The Times, 21 February 1987.

[60] This translates as 'to a willing person, no injury is done', and means that there is no liability when an injured person 'volunteered' to run the risk.

[61] This translates as 'from a dishonourable cause an action does not arise', and means that actions can be barred by the claimant's illegal behaviour.

[62] [1988] QB 978 (CA). [63] Limitation Act 1980, ss 11(4) and 14(1).

could be brought.[64] Section 14 of the Limitation Act sets out when this three-year period starts to run:

Limitation Act 1980 section 14

14 (1) . . . references to a person's date of knowledge are references to the date on which he first had knowledge of the following facts—

(a) that the injury in question was significant; and

(b) that the injury was attributable in whole or in part to the act or omission which is alleged to constitute negligence . . . ; and

(c) the identity of the defendant; and

(d) if it is alleged that the act or omission was that of a person other than the defendant, the identity of that person and the additional facts supporting the bringing of an action against the defendant . . .

(2) For the purposes of this section an injury is significant if the person whose date of knowledge is in question would reasonably have considered it sufficiently serious to justify his instituting proceedings for damages.

One of the problems section 14 presents in medical cases is that it may be particularly difficult for an individual to determine whether their injury was 'attributable in whole or in part to the act or omission which is alleged to constitute negligence'. Medical treatment is not always successful, and so an individual may have just been unlucky. It is not necessary for the claimant to be sure that their injuries are due to negligence; rather, time starts to run when they could be said to have constructive knowledge of the possibility of litigation.

In *Forbes v Wandsworth Health Authority*, Mr Forbes had had an unsuccessful operation on his left leg in October 1982. As a result, he had to have his leg amputated. In June 1991 he consulted a solicitor. Advice from a vascular surgeon obtained in October 1992 suggested that the amputation could have been avoided. In December 1992, Mr Forbes issued proceedings against the defendant health authority. At first instance, the judge held that his action was not time-barred because he had no reason to suspect or think that the removal of his leg was due to the act or omission of the defendant. Before the health authority's appeal was heard by the Court of Appeal, Mr Forbes died. By a majority, its appeal was allowed.

Forbes v Wandsworth Health Authority[65]

Stuart-Smith LJ

It seems to me that where, as here, the plaintiff expected or at least hoped that the operation would be successful and it manifestly was not, with the result that he sustained a major injury, a reasonable man of moderate intelligence, such as the deceased, if he thought about the matter, would say that the lack of success was 'either just one of those things, a risk of the operation or something may have gone wrong and there may have been a want of care; I do not know which, but if I am ever to make a claim, I must find out'.

---

[64] Ibid.   [65] [1997] QB 402 (CA).

In my judgment, any other construction would make the 1980 Act unworkable since a plain-tiff could delay indefinitely before seeking expert advice and say, as the deceased did in this case, I had no occasion to seek it earlier. He would therefore be able, as of right, to bring the action, no matter how many years had elapsed. This is contrary to the whole purpose of the 1980 Act which is to prevent defendants being vexed by stale claims which it is no longer possible to contest.

In *Whiston v London Strategic Health Authority*, the claimant suffered from cerebral palsy as a result of oxygen deprivation during childbirth. Until early adulthood, he was relatively unimpaired by his condition, obtaining a PhD and regular employment. His condition then worsened and by 2005, when he was 31, the deterioration had become significant. At that point, he discussed with his mother, a trained nurse, the circumstances of his birth—in which a junior doctor had persisted for too long with a forceps delivery with the wrong type of forceps—and in 2006, 32 years after his birth, he brought an action alleging that his injuries were caused by his negligent delivery.

The Court of Appeal found that his claim was statute-barred. The claimant had known for most of his life that his disabilities were the result of his birth, and the Court of Appeal found that a reasonable person would have asked his mother about the circumstances of his birth, and discovered that the junior doctor might have been at fault.

Whiston v London Strategic Health Authority[66]

Dyson LJ

I take into account the fact that a person who suffers from a disability at birth is more likely to be accepting of his disability (because he has never known anything different) than a person who suffers an injury during adult life. But where the disability becomes more serious as he becomes an adult and he knows that the disability is in some way related to the circumstances of his delivery (rather than, say, the result of some genetic disorder), it seems to me that there comes a time when a reasonable person would want to know about the circumstances of his birth which have given rise to the problem. There comes a time when the reasonable person in the circumstances of the claimant would ask his mother, particularly since she is a nurse and a trained midwife.

A finding that a claim is statute-barred is not the end of the matter, however. Section 33 of the Limitation Act 1980 gives the court discretion to extend the limitation period where it would be equitable to do so. In deciding whether to exercise this discretion, the court has to balance the degree to which the statutory limitation period prejudices the claimant, with the degree to which an extension of that period would prejudice the defendant. The court will have regard to a number of factors, such as the reasons for the delay and the conduct of both parties. In *Forbes v Wandsworth Health Authority*,[67] the court declined to exercise its discretion, in part because Mr Forbes was now dead, which meant that 'the potential damages recoverable

---

[66] [2010] EWCA Civ 195.   [67] [1997] QB 402 (CA).

for the benefit of the estate of the deceased are significantly less than they would have been if the deceased were still alive', and in part because there was only a 'modest' chance of his case succeeding.

In contrast, in *Whiston* the court balanced the disadvantage to the defendant hospital in trying to defend a stale claim, by which time some relevant notes would have been destroyed, with the disadvantage to the now very seriously disabled claimant. Because his disabilities were such that damages would be likely to be 'substantial', Dyson LJ explained that 'if he is not permitted to pursue this claim, he will therefore lose all prospect of his future needs being properly provided for 'and all prospect of recovering compensation for the loss of the substantial earnings that, but for his disability, he is likely to have achieved'. It was therefore 'equitable to allow this claim to proceed'.

For children and adults who lack capacity, the limitation period does not begin to run until or unless they gain capacity.[68] In such cases, it will be possible to bring an action many years after the alleged negligent act, when evidence as to the precise circumstances which led to the claimant's injuries may no longer be reliable.

4 LIABILITY FOR THE BIRTH OF A CHILD

Usually clinical negligence actions arise when a doctor negligently causes harm to a patient. Complicated issues arise when the 'harm' that results from the doctor's negligence is the birth of a child, or a child's disability. Four scenarios can be distinguished. First, and most straightforwardly, negligence during pregnancy could result in a fetus suffering injuries that mean it is born disabled. Here the complicating issue is that the fetus was not a legal person when it was injured, and hence was not owed a duty of care when the injuries were sustained.

More complicated still are cases where the 'damage' is the conception or birth of a child. This can arise where the child claims that, but for the defendant's negligence, she would not have been born. Alternatively, the parents might claim that the child's conception should have been prevented, or the mother might claim that she should have been given the option of termination. In all these cases, the courts have grappled with a tension between ordinary tort principles—in which damages should put the claimant in the position she would have been in if the tort had not been committed—and a reluctance to regard a child's life as compensatable damage.

(a) PRENATAL INJURY

At common law, a fetus is not a legal person, which means that it cannot be owed a duty of care. On the other hand, it is plainly foreseeable that negligent conduct might cause injuries to a fetus, and result in a child being born disabled.[69] At common law, the courts' solution was to say that the child only suffers damage when she is born, and acquires legal personality, at which point the duty of care 'crystallizes'.[70] This is also the solution adopted by the Congenital Disabilities (Civil Liability) Act 1976.

---

[68] Limitation Act 1980, section 28.   [69] *Donoghue v Stevenson* [1932] AC 562.
[70] *Burton v Islington Health Authority* [1993] QB 204.

Congenital Disabilities (Civil Liability) Act 1976 sections 1 and 4

1(1) If a child is born disabled as the result of such an occurrence before its birth as is mentioned in subsection (2) below, and a person (other than the child's own mother) is under this section answerable to the child in respect of the occurrence, the child's disabilities are to be regarded as damage resulting from the wrongful act of that person and actionable accordingly at the suit of the child.

(2) An occurrence to which this section applies is one which—

  (a) affected either parent of the child in his or her ability to have a normal, healthy child; or

  (b) affected the mother during her pregnancy, or affected her or the child in the course of its birth, so that the child is born with disabilities which would not otherwise have been present.

(3) Subject to the following subsections, a person (here referred to as 'the defendant') is answerable to the child if he was liable in tort to the parent or would, if sued in due time, have been so; and it is no answer that there could not have been such liability because the parent suffered no actionable injury, if there was a breach of legal duty which, accompanied by injury, would have given rise to the liability.

(4) In the case of an occurrence preceding the time of conception, the defendant is not answerable to the child if at that time either or both of the parents knew the risk of their child being born disabled (that is to say, the particular risk created by the occurrence); but should it be the child's father who is the defendant, this subsection does not apply if he knew of the risk and the mother did not . . .

(7) If in the child's action under this section it is shown that the parent affected shared the responsibility for the child being born disabled, the damages are to be reduced to such extent as the court thinks just and equitable having regard to the extent of the parent's responsibility . . .

4(3) Liability to a child under section 1 [1A] or 2 of this Act is to be regarded . . . as liability for personal injuries sustained by the child immediately after its birth.

Under section 1(3) the duty owed to a child under the Act is a derivative one, and exists only when a duty is owed to the child's mother or father. The child's parent does not actually have to have suffered actionable damage, but the defendant must have been in breach of a duty of care owed to one of the child's parents.

This has a number of consequences. First, where the child suffers injuries because of a decision taken by the pregnant woman, for example to refuse caesarean delivery, the child could have no claim. Secondly, the defences of *volenti non fit injuria* and contributory negligence apply.[71] Where the parent's claim would have been defeated by the defence of *volenti*, the child can have no action for her injuries. If the child's injuries are partly attributable to the defendant's fault, and partly attributable to her parent's behaviour, then under section 1(7) any damages must be reduced according to the extent to which the parent is responsible for the child being born disabled.

Thirdly, the Act confines liability to cases where the child is disabled as a result of an 'occurrence'. In *Multiple Claimants v Sanifo-Synthelabo*[72] the claimants had suffered injuries as a result of the epilepsy medication their mothers had taken during pregnancy.

---

[71] See further Chapter 3.   [72] [2007] EWHC 1860 (QB).

The court was asked to determine certain preliminary issues, one of which was whether there could have been an 'occurrence' for the purposes of the 1976 Act. The problem was, as Andrew Smith J pointed out, that the wording of the Act 'does not allow for the possibility that the occurrence was by way of an accumulation of the drug within the mother'. Expert evidence would be needed, he concluded, to determine whether the alleged 'transplacental spread' could properly be described as an 'occurrence'. Legal aid was withdrawn in this case before it reached the courtroom, and so this issue remains unresolved.

The 1976 Act was amended in 1990 by the Human Fertilisation and Embryology Act, which added section 1A and section 4(4)(A) in order to include liability to the child for damage caused during fertility treatment. The application of the 1976 Act to cases where the child is born disabled as a result of the negligent selection of embryos raises the interesting question of whether this might amount to a 'wrongful life' claim (see below). In these cases, the negligent embryo selection did not cause the child's disabilities. Rather, the negligent selection caused this child to exist. The child's claim must therefore be that if the doctors had exercised proper care and skill, she would not have existed. It is not clear that parliament intended to create a statutory wrongful life action for children born following negligent embryo selection, and yet it appears to have done so. As yet, there have been no cases.

Under section 1(1) of the Congenital Disabilities (Civil Liability) Act 1976, liability is confined to people 'other than the child's own mother', so a child cannot bring an action against her mother for injuries sustained *in utero*. (Fathers are not exempt, perhaps because the most common scenario in which a father might injure a fetus would be an assault on the mother.) Allowing a child to sue her mother would, the Law Commission had argued, create additional stress within the family.[73] Since a mother is normally already responsible for her child's care, any damages she might be ordered to pay would in practice usually be paid to herself.

An exception is, however, created in section 2 if the child's injuries were caused by her mother's negligent driving. The reason for this exception is compulsory road traffic insurance, which means that the damages will be paid by the mother's insurance company.

(b) 'WRONGFUL LIFE'

In a wrongful life claim, 'but for' the defendant's negligence, the child would not have been born and the damage she has suffered—that is, her wrongful life—would have been avoided. It is not claimed that the defendant's action caused the child's disability, but rather that her parents were negligently deprived of the option not to give birth to this child.

The issue has arisen in only one English case—*McKay v Essex AHA*—in which the Court of Appeal rejected the possibility that life itself could be compensatable damage. Mrs McKay had come into contact with rubella when she was in the early stages of pregnancy. She sought medical advice, but her blood samples were mislaid, and she was wrongly informed that she had not been affected by rubella, and that she need not consider a termination. Mary McKay was born seriously disabled as a result of rubella infection during pregnancy.

---

[73] *Report on Injuries to Unborn Children* (Law Com Report No 60, Cmnd 5709, 1974).

McKay v Essex AHA[74]

Ackner LJ

What then are her injuries, which the doctor's negligence has caused? The answer must be that there are none in any accepted sense. Her complaint is that she was allowed to be born at all, given the existence of her pre-natal injuries. How then are her damages to be assessed? Not by awarding compensation for her pain, suffering and loss of amenities attributable to the disabilities, since these were already in existence before the doctor was consulted. She cannot say that, but for his negligence, she would have been born without her disabilities. What the doctor is blamed for is causing or permitting her to be born at all. Thus, the compensation must be based on a comparison between the value of non-existence (the doctor's alleged negligence having deprived her of this) and the value of her existence in a disabled state.

But how can a court begin to evaluate non-existence, 'the undiscovered country from whose bourn no traveller returns?' No comparison is possible and therefore no damage can be established which a court could recognise.

There are some tensions in this reasoning. On the one hand, the Court of Appeal was anxious to stress that being born could not constitute damage because the law always treats life as beneficial. But, on the other hand, all three judges claimed that it is impossible to compare existence and non-existence. Surely we can only reach the first conclusion if we have compared the two outcomes, and decided that life is generally better than 'non-life'?[75] The child in a wrongful life action is not necessarily claiming that she would have been better off if she had never existed. It is perfectly possible for the benefit of a disabled child's life to coexist with the financial expense of adjustments to help the child live with her disability.

In any event, is it true that the law is incapable of comparing existence and non-existence? As we see in Chapters 5 and 6, when decisions are taken about withholding and withdrawing life-prolonging treatment, there are times when the courts have decided that measures that would prolong a patient's life are not in her best interests.

In jurisdictions where wrongful life actions have had more success, the courts have concentrated on the fact that the claimant's disabled existence is attributable to the defendant's negligence, and have downplayed the existential problem that dominated the judgments in *McKay*, namely that the child's claim is that they should not have been born. In 2005, for example, the Dutch Supreme Court awarded damages to both the parents and the child, after a midwife decided no further investigation was necessary when told that two members of the father's family suffered from a serious chromosomal abnormality.[76] Kelly Molenaar was born suffering from severe mental and physical disabilities. The Hoge Raad considered whether awarding damages would violate the principle of 'the dignity of human life', but decided that it would, in fact, support that dignity by enabling Kelly to lead a more bearable life.

---

[74] [1982] QB 1166.

[75] Harvey Teff, 'The Action for "Wrongful Life" in England and the United States' (1985) 34 International & Comparative Law Quarterly 423–41.

[76] *Leids Universitair Medisch Centrum v Kelly Molenaar*, no C03/206, RvdW 2005, 42 (18 March 2005).

(c) WRONGFUL PREGNANCY

If a woman becomes pregnant following a negligently performed sterilization operation, or is given negligent advice about her or her partner's sterility, there are three possible outcomes. First, she might miscarry or the baby might be stillborn, in which case an action for her pain and suffering would be uncontroversial. Secondly, she could decide to terminate the pregnancy. Again, a claim for the costs of an abortion, and any associated pain and suffering or loss of income, would be straightforward.

The third possibility is that the woman carries the pregnancy to term and gives birth to a live baby. In this third scenario, if the patient can establish that the sterilization operation was negligently performed, or that she and/or her partner were given negligent pre- or post-operative advice, the claim will be for damages to compensate them for the costs associated with giving birth to a child that they did not want.

In wrongful pregnancy cases, the costs of the child's upbringing are undoubtedly foreseeable losses, but should they be recoverable in tort? This question was first considered by the House of Lords in *McFarlane v Tayside Health Board*. Six months after Mr McFarlane had undergone a vasectomy operation, the surgeon negligently informed him that his sperm counts were negative, and that he and Mrs McFarlane no longer needed to use contraception. Eighteen months later, Mrs McFarlane became pregnant and gave birth to their fifth child. A majority of the House of Lords (Lord Millett dissenting) found that Mrs McFarlane was entitled to general damages for the pain, suffering, and inconvenience of pregnancy and childbirth, but the Lords were unanimous that the McFarlanes were not entitled to be compensated for the costs associated with Catherine's upbringing.

McFarlane v Tayside Health Board[77]

Lord Steyn

It is possible to view the case simply from the perspective of corrective justice. It requires somebody who has harmed another without justification to indemnify the other. On this approach the parents' claim for the cost of bringing up Catherine must succeed. But one may also approach the case from the vantage point of distributive justice. It requires a focus on the just distribution of burdens and losses among members of a society. If the matter is approached in this way, it may become relevant to ask commuters on the Underground the following question: Should the parents of an unwanted but healthy child be able to sue the doctor or hospital for compensation equivalent to the cost of bringing up the child for the years of his or her minority, i.e. until about 18 years? My Lords, I am firmly of the view that an overwhelming number of ordinary men and women would answer the question with an emphatic 'No'. And the reason for such a response would be an inarticulate premise as to what is morally acceptable and what is not . . . Instinctively, the traveller on the Underground would consider that the law of tort has no business to provide legal remedies consequent upon the birth of a healthy child, which all of us regard as a valuable and good thing.

---

[77] [1999] UKHL 50.

Lord Hope

It is not difficult to see that in such cases a very substantial award of damages might have to be made for the child's upbringing ... It might well be thought that the extent of the liability was disproportionate to the duties which were undertaken and, consequently, to the extent of the negligence . . .

There are benefits in this arrangement as well as costs. In the short term there is the pleasure which a child gives in return for the love and care which she receives during infancy. In the longer term there is the mutual relationship of support and affection which will continue well beyond the ending of the period of her childhood.

In my opinion it would not be fair, just or reasonable, in any assessment of the loss caused by the birth of the child, to leave these benefits out of account. Otherwise the pursuers would be paid far too much. They would be relieved of the cost of rearing the child. They would not be giving anything back to the wrongdoer for the benefits. But the value which is to be attached to these benefits is incalculable. The costs can be calculated but the benefits, which in fairness must be set against them, cannot. The logical conclusion, as a matter of law, is that the costs to the pursuers of meeting their obligations to the child during her childhood are not recoverable as damages.

Lord Millett

There is something distasteful, if not morally offensive, in treating the birth of a normal, healthy child as a matter for compensation . . . In my opinion the law must take the birth of a normal, healthy baby to be a blessing, not a detriment. In truth it is a mixed blessing. It brings joy and sorrow, blessing and responsibility. The advantages and the disadvantages are inseparable. Individuals may choose to regard the balance as unfavourable and take steps to forgo the pleasures as well as the responsibilities of parenthood. They are entitled to decide for themselves where their own interests lie. But society itself must regard the balance as beneficial. It would be repugnant to its own sense of values to do otherwise. It is morally offensive to regard a normal, healthy baby as more trouble and expense than it is worth . . .

It does not, however, follow that Mr and Mrs McFarlane should be sent away empty handed . . . They have suffered both injury and loss. They have lost the freedom to limit the size of their family. They have been denied an important aspect of their personal autonomy. Their decision to have no more children is one the law should respect and protect. They are entitled to general damages to reflect the true nature of the wrong done to them. This should be a conventional sum which should be left to the trial judge to assess, but which I would not expect to exceed £5000 in a straightforward case like the present.

The costs of Catherine McFarlane's upbringing were, according to the majority, pure economic loss. (Lord Millett dissented on this point.) For cases involving pure economic loss, a three-stage test applies:[78]

(a) The loss should be foreseeable;

(b) There must be a relationship of sufficient proximity between the doctor and their patient;

(c) It should be fair, just, and reasonable to impose a duty of care in these circumstances.

---

[78] *Caparo v Dickman* [1990] 2 AC 651.

The House of Lords accepted that the birth of a child, and the costs of her upbringing, were foreseeable consequences of negligently advising Mr and Mrs McFarlane that sterility had been achieved. There was also a relationship of sufficient proximity between the doctor who gave this advice and Mrs McFarlane. The House of Lords rejected the McFarlanes' claim on the grounds that imposing liability on the health authority for the costs of their healthy child's upbringing would not be fair, just, and reasonable.

Three different reasons were given for this conclusion. First, some of the Law Lords suggested that it would be unfair to compensate the parents for the costs of rearing a child, unless these could be reduced in order to take into account the pleasure that the child would bring to her parents. However, they refused to embark upon this sort of offset exercise on the grounds that it would be impossible and/or unseemly.

Is it really true that damages would have to be reduced in order to reflect the benefits the child brings to her parents? Lord Clyde acknowledged that when parents bring an action for the death of their child, their damages are not reduced in order to reflect the money that they will save by not having to pay for the child's upkeep. The House of Lords also assumed that damages for the *economic costs* of bringing up a child would have to be reduced in order to take account of the *emotional benefits* of the child's companionship. A trade-off between incommensurate goods is unusual. We would not normally say that an injured employee's damages for being unable to work should be reduced in order to reflect the pleasure of having more time to spend with his family. Lord Clyde gave the example of a mineworker rendered unfit for work underground: if he claims damages for loss of earnings, the defendant is not entitled to offset 'the pleasure and benefit which he may enjoy in the air of a public park'.

Even if it were accepted that an offset calculation is necessary, it might also be argued that the question of whether an unplanned child's existence represents a net gain for a family is a question of fact. It may be true that most people, most of the time, consider that the advantages of having a child, even if she was initially unwanted, outweigh the disadvantages. But this will not always be the case. For some families, the birth of another child might be a disaster.

In his dissenting judgment in the Court of Appeal in *Rees v Darlington Memorial Hospital NHS Trust*,[79] discussed below, Waller LJ gave the example of an impoverished single mother with four children, who believes that having a fifth child will lead to her mental breakdown, and who has no support from her family. If the birth of an unwanted child provokes the mother's physical or mental collapse, and results in all of her children being taken into care, she may be able to prove that the advantages of having another child have not, in fact, outweighed the disadvantages. Yet the law will not allow her to bring forward such evidence, because it has already decided that, in Lord Millett's words, 'society itself must regard the balance as beneficial'.

Given that the claimants in wrongful pregnancy cases have undergone invasive surgery in order permanently to prevent the possibility of conception, it is plain that, at the time of the operation at least, they believed that the disadvantages of having another baby outweighed any joy that an additional child might bring. People are sterilized precisely in order to avoid the 'benefits' of conceiving a child. It is perhaps odd that the law insists that such people should regard the failure of their surgery as a 'blessing' and an occasion for joy. If the benefits of parenthood always outweigh its disadvantages, it is unclear why anyone would want to be sterilized in the first place.

---

[79] [2002] EWCA Civ 88.

Secondly, Lord Hope and Lord Clyde were concerned that the size of any claim in damages for a child's upbringing would be disproportionate to the degree of fault. Moreover, not only would compensating parents for the costs of private education for the whole of a child's life lead to some extremely high awards, but it would also result in invidious distinctions between claimants, since wealthy parents would receive much more money for their unwanted children than poor parents.

Lord Millett objected to this argument on the grounds that damages in tort are not intended to correspond to the gravity of fault, but rather to put the claimant in the position they would have been if the negligent act had not occurred. A minor and common lapse of judgement while driving—such as momentarily taking one's eyes off the road in order to admire the view—might have catastrophic consequences, and it would not be open to the driver to argue that the level of damages would be disproportionate to the degree of fault.

Thirdly, Lord Steyn based his judgment upon considerations of distributive justice, admitting that his was a moral judgment. In the next extract, Laura Hoyano suggests that an appeal to commuters on the London Underground represents an abdication of judicial responsibility for producing coherent principled decisions.

Laura Hoyano[80]

The transmogrification of the man on the Clapham omnibus is not limited to a change of public transport, as he is no longer just a convenient measure for the standard of care expected on non-experts, but also the gatekeeper for negligence law itself . . . How much time is there between stops on the London Underground, to allow those passengers to assimilate the evidence, weigh up all the factors, and look down the track to future implications of their decision—as is the duty of the judiciary? Not only might London commuters not represent public opinion in the country as a whole, but they might not produce a clear majority, particularly in a complex case. With the utmost respect to Lord Steyn, it is not satisfactory for tort law to be based upon an 'inarticulate premise as to what is morally acceptable and what is not' . . .

Distributive justice . . . permits the judiciary to abdicate its responsibility to identify and explain intellectually rigorous and coherent principles as the basis for decisions, in favour of an empirically untested appeal to public opinion, yielding unpredictable results which invite reversal at every level of appeal, depending on each judge's subjective and avowedly instinctive notions of what justice requires. Thus distributive justice is no more illuminating—and arguably less—than the public policy which the Law Lords were anxious to eschew.

A final underlying reason for the Lords' rejection of the McFarlane's claim may have been the concern that scarce NHS resources should not be diverted to the parents of healthy children. But while it is undoubtedly true that Tayside Health Board has more pressing demands upon its budget than Catherine McFarlane's upkeep, it is not normally open to a court to deny a claimant damages because the defendant could deploy the money more usefully elsewhere.

In *McFarlane*, Lord Millett made an interesting suggestion, which was not taken up by any of the other judges, namely that the McFarlanes should be entitled to a 'conventional sum' of £5,000 to compensate them for the wrongful interference with their freedom to limit the size of their family.

---

[80] 'Misconceptions about Wrongful Conception' (2002) 65 Modern Law Review 883–906.

It was inevitable that issues that were not directly dealt with by the judgments in *McFarlane* would be raised in subsequent litigation, and it was not long before the question of whether *McFarlane* applied to disabled children came before the courts in *Parkinson v St James and Seacroft University Hospital NHS Trust*.

Angela Parkinson already had four children and did not think she could cope with a fifth. She was sterilized, but the operation was performed negligently, and she subsequently became pregnant. Her son Scott was born suffering from a serious behavioural disorder. At first instance, Longmore J held that Mrs Parkinson could recover the additional costs associated with Scott's special needs, and his judgment was upheld by the Court of Appeal.

Parkinson v St James and Seacroft University Hospital NHS Trust [81]

Brooke LJ

The birth of a child with congenital abnormalities was a foreseeable consequence of the surgeon's careless failure to clip a fallopian tube effectively . . .

[I]f principles of distributive justice are called in aid, I believe that ordinary people would consider that it would be fair for the law to make an award in such a case, provided that it is limited to the extra expenses associated with the child's disability.

Hale LJ

From the moment a woman conceives, profound physical changes take place in her body and continue to take place not only for the duration of the pregnancy but for some time thereafter . . . Along with these physical and psychological consequences goes a severe curtailment of personal autonomy. Literally, one's life is no longer just one's own but also someone else's . . .

The process of giving birth is rightly termed 'labour'. It is hard work, often painful and sometimes dangerous. It brings the pregnancy to an end but it does not bring to an end the changes brought about by the pregnancy. It takes some time for the body to return to its pre-pregnancy state, if it ever does, especially if the child is breast-fed. There are well known psychiatric illnesses associated with childbirth and the baby blues are very common . . .

Quite clearly, however, the invasion of the mother's personal autonomy does not stop once her body and mind have returned to their pre-pregnancy state . . . Parental responsibility is not simply or even primarily a financial responsibility . . . The primary responsibility is to care for the child. The labour does not stop when the child is born. Bringing up children is hard work . . . The obligation to provide or make acceptable and safe arrangements for the child's care and supervision lasts for 24 hours a day, seven days a week, all year round, until the child becomes old enough to take care of himself . . .

A disabled child needs extra care and extra expenditure. He is deemed, on this analysis, to bring as much pleasure and as many advantages as does a normal healthy child. Frankly, in many cases, of which this may be one, this is much less likely. The additional stresses and strains can have seriously adverse effects upon the whole family, and not infrequently lead, as here, to the break-up of the parents' relationship and detriment to the other children. But we all know of cases where the whole family has been enriched by the presence of a disabled

---

[81] [2001] EWCA Civ 530.

member and would not have things any other way. This analysis treats a disabled child as having exactly the same worth as a non-disabled child. It affords him the same dignity and status. It simply acknowledges that he costs more.

It is important to remember that in *Parkinson*, the defendant's negligence did not cause Scott's behavioural disorder; rather, it caused Scott, who just happened to be disabled, to be conceived. Because there is always a small risk—in *Parkinson* it was put at between one in 200 and one in 400—that a child might be born suffering from a congenital abnormality, the birth of a disabled child is a foreseeable consequence of any negligent sterilization operation.

It should, however, be noted that the maintenance costs of a healthy child are more foreseeable than the statistically less likely possibility that a child will be born disabled.[82] It is also true that the costs of bringing up a disabled child are likely to be higher than those of a healthy child, and so the concern expressed by Lords Clyde and Hope in *McFarlane* about the level of damages being disproportionate to the degree of fault might be more compelling on the facts in *Parkinson*.

In *Parkinson*, the Court of Appeal appeared less than enthusiastic about the implications of *McFarlane*. In particular, Hale LJ's impassioned description of the physical and psychological invasions of pregnancy and motherhood was not specifically directed to the burdens of being a mother of a disabled child, but applies to motherhood in general. Nevertheless, *McFarlane* was binding upon them, and so the important question was whether Scott's disabilities meant that Angela Parkinson's case could be distinguished. The Court of Appeal decided that the cases were different, and the extra costs incurred as a result of the child's disability were recoverable.

What if it is not the child but the parent who is disabled? *Rees v Darlington Memorial Hospital NHS Trust* involved a woman who was sterilized because she was concerned that her blindness would make it difficult for her to look after a child. The operation was carried out negligently and, two years later, Karina Rees gave birth to a healthy child. She claimed damages not only for the pain and discomfort of pregnancy and childbirth, but also for the additional costs incurred as a result of her disability.

In *Rees v Darlington Memorial Hospital NHS Trust*,[83] the Law Lords unanimously declined to revisit its judgment in *McFarlane*. Only four years had elapsed and it would, in Lord Bingham's words, 'reflect no credit on the administration of the law if a line of English authority were to be disapproved in 1999 and reinstated in 2003 with no reason for the change beyond a change in the balance of legal opinion'. While JK Mason acknowledges that 'see-saw lawmaking' is undesirable, he argues that 'the man in the street might well think that, if something is wrong, the sooner it is put right, the better'.[84]

Having upheld the decision in *McFarlane*, the Lords next had to consider whether an exception should be made where the mother was disabled. On this question, the House of Lords was divided. By a 4:3 majority it held that *Rees* could not be distinguished: the child was healthy so *McFarlane* applied. There could therefore be no recovery for any of the costs associated with the child's upbringing. In contrast, the dissenting judges would have allowed Karina Rees to recover for the extra costs associated with her disability. It should, however, be noted that the majority added a significant 'gloss'.

---

[82] Laura CH Hoyano, 'Misconceptions about Wrongful Conception' (2002) 65 Modern Law Review 883–906.
[83] [2003] UKHL 52.
[84] *The Troubled Pregnancy: Legal Rights and Wrongs in Reproduction* (CUP: Cambridge, 2007).

Rees v Darlington Memorial Hospital NHS Trust [85]

Lord Bingham

The policy considerations underpinning the judgments of the House [in *McFarlane*] were, as I read them, an unwillingness to regard a child (even if unwanted) as a financial liability and nothing else, a recognition that the rewards which parenthood (even if involuntary) may or may not bring cannot be quantified and a sense that to award potentially very large sums of damages to the parents of a normal and healthy child against a National Health Service always in need of funds to meet pressing demands would rightly offend the community's sense of how public resources should be allocated . . .

Subject to one gloss, therefore, which I regard as important, I would affirm and adhere to the decision in *McFarlane*.

My concern is this. Even accepting that an unwanted child cannot be regarded as a financial liability and nothing else and that any attempt to weigh the costs of bringing up a child against the intangible rewards of parenthood is unacceptably speculative, the fact remains that the parent of a child born following a negligently performed vasectomy or sterilisation, or negligent advice on the effect of such a procedure, is the victim of a legal wrong . . .

I can accept and support a rule of legal policy which precludes recovery of the full cost of bringing up a child in the situation postulated, but I question the fairness of a rule which denies the victim of a legal wrong any recompense at all beyond an award immediately related to the unwanted pregnancy and birth . . .

To speak of losing the freedom to limit the size of one's family is to mask the real loss suffered in a situation of this kind. This is that a parent, particularly (even today) the mother, has been denied, through the negligence of another, the opportunity to live her life in the way that she wished and planned. I do not think that an award immediately relating to the unwanted pregnancy and birth gives adequate recognition of or does justice to that loss. I would accordingly support the suggestion favoured by Lord Millett in *McFarlane* that in all cases such as these there be a conventional award to mark the injury and loss, although I would favour a greater figure than the £5,000 he suggested (I have in mind a conventional figure of £15,000) and I would add this to the award for the pregnancy and birth . . . The conventional award would not be, and would not be intended to be, compensatory. It would not be the product of calculation. But it would not be a nominal, let alone a derisory, award. It would afford some measure of recognition of the wrong done.

Lord Steyn (dissenting)

In the present case the idea of a conventional award was not raised at first instance or in the Court of Appeal. For my part it is a great disadvantage for the House to consider such a point without the benefit of the views of the Court of Appeal. And the disadvantage cannot be removed by calling the new rule a 'gloss'. It is a radical and most important development which should only be embarked on after rigorous examination of competing arguments . . .

No United Kingdom authority is cited for the proposition that judges have the power to create a remedy of awarding a conventional sum in cases such as the present. There is none. It is also noteworthy that in none of the decisions from many foreign jurisdictions, with varying results, is there any support for such a solution. This underlines the heterodox nature of the solution adopted.

Like Lord Hope I regard the idea of a conventional award in the present case as contrary to principle. It is a novel procedure for judges to create such a remedy. There are limits to

[85] [2003] UKHL 52.

permissible creativity for judges. In my view the majority have strayed into forbidden territory. It is also a backdoor evasion of the legal policy enunciated in *McFarlane*. If such a rule is to be created it must be done by Parliament. The fact is, however, that it would be a hugely controversial legislative measure. It may well be that the Law Commissions and Parliament ought in any event, to consider the impact of the creation of a power to make a conventional award in the cases under consideration for the coherence of the tort system.

In the next extract, Samantha Singer suggests that, in *Rees*, considerations of distributive justice would in fact point in favour of recovery.

Samantha Singer[86]

The House of Lords' decision that the entire financial costs of raising children like Ms Rees' son should lie with the individual, disabled parent is wholly shortsighted . . . By denying disabled parents damages for negligence—whether for the full expenses of bringing up the child or the additional costs—the risks that children in Ms Rees' son's situation will face being placed in care must increase. In turn, the fear of having their children removed often breeds reluctance in disabled parents to seek help in caring for their children. If this devastating end is avoided, the children of disabled parents often find themselves acting as carers for their parents. Indeed, Lord Millett used this fact as a reason for Ms Rees to be grateful for her surgeon's negligence:

> Once the child is able to go to school alone and be of some help around the house, his or her presence will to a greater or lesser extent help to alleviate the disadvantages of the parent's disability. And once the child has grown to adulthood, he or she can provide immeasurable help to an ageing and disabled parent.

It is surprising that such a naïve and unhelpful passage found its way into a speech in the House of Lords. What parent would wish this existence upon their child? Certainly not Karina Rees—this was part of her reason for being sterilised.

The gloss added by the majority in *Rees* is grounded in the recognition that, while full compensation for the birth of a healthy baby might be inappropriate and unaffordable, the parents in these cases have undoubtedly been wronged: they have been deprived of their freedom to control the size of their family. In short, the majority in *Rees* decided that it did not want to compensate Karina Rees according to ordinary negligence principles because this would give her too much money. Instead, it preferred to compensate her according to its own novel scheme—the modest 'conventional award'—which would acknowledge that she had been wronged, without giving her exorbitant damages.

As JK Mason puts it, 'it is hard to find a commentator who does not, at this point, start to scratch his or her head'.[87] One possible explanation is that the majority in *Rees* was attempting to find a judicial solution to some of the problems clinical negligence poses for the NHS. Patients who are treated negligently deserve some recognition that they received inadequate care, which may have caused them harm, inconvenience, discomfort, or financial loss. But, at

---

[86] 'Casenote: *Rees v Darlington*' (2004) 26 Journal of Social Welfare and Family Law 403–15.
[87] *The Troubled Pregnancy: Legal Rights and Wrongs in Reproduction* (CUP: Cambridge, 2007) 176.

the same time, giving them full compensation for all of their losses has an opportunity cost, insofar as it reduces the resources the NHS has to spend on providing treatment to the rest of the population. In these circumstances, it could be argued that it would be more sensible for patients who are the victims of inadequate treatment to receive a standard notional award, which recognizes that a wrong has been done to them, but does not attempt to provide full compensation.

But while a standardized compensation scheme within the NHS might have merits, it is not clear that a decision of a narrow majority in the House of Lords is the right way to bring about such a system. The purpose of the 'conventional award' is also opaque. It is there to compensate for 'a wrong comprised of an affront to autonomy',[88] which would be a novel head of damages. However, in a case in which the baby was stillborn, *Less v Hussain*,[89] His Honour Judge Cotter QC found that the conventional award could apply only where the parents 'suffer real as opposed to theoretical losses': 'in the present case there are no such losses. Absent such losses I do not believe that an award should be made'.

The conventional award is not meant to be derisory, and yet, while better than nothing, it comes nowhere near the amount that would be payable according to normal tort law principles. In the end, JK Mason may be right that it looks rather like 'a form of conscience money or as a charity designed to offset the sense of injustice left by the original *McFarlane* decision'.[90]

Would it make any difference if the sterilization operation had been carried out privately, and the patient had a contract with the hospital? The answer appears to be 'no'. In *ARB v IVF Hammersmith*, ARB brought an action in contract against a fertility clinic for the costs of an unwanted child's birth. ARB and R had had one child together through IVF, and had several embryos in storage. After the couple split up, R forged ARB's signature on a 'consent to thaw' form, and underwent embryo transfer without ARB's knowledge, leading to the birth of a second child, E. Although Jay J held that the clinic had breached an express contractual obligation to ARB, not to thaw and transfer an embryo to R without his written consent, his claim for substantial damages, including the cost of E's future wedding, was rejected on policy grounds, and his appeal to the Court of Appeal was unsuccessful.

ARB v IVF Hammersmith [91]

Nicola Davies LJ

If it is impossible for a court to calculate the value to be attributed to the benefit of a child, so as to set off such value against the financial cost of the child's upbringing as a matter of legal policy in tort, how is the task possible for a court if such loss results from a breach of contract? Added to this is the sense, reflected in the judgments in *Rees* and *McFarlane*, that it is morally unacceptable to regard a child as a financial liability . . .

Mr Halpern QC, on behalf of the appellant, sought to distinguish the facts of this case upon the basis that ARB had paid for the services which he received pursuant to the contract ... Taken through to its conclusion, such an argument would permit a person who has the means to pay for such private services to sue in contract and, if the appellant's submission were to succeed, recover damages for such loss, whereas the individual who does not have

---

[88] Ibid, 179.   [89] [2012] EWHC 3513 (QB).
[90] *The Troubled Pregnancy: Legal Rights and Wrongs in Reproduction* (CUP: Cambridge, 2007) 178.
[91] [2018] EWCA Civ 2803.

the means to pay for private treatment would have to bring a claim in tort, which would be ir-recoverable following *Rees* and *McFarlane*. The fundamental unfairness resulting from such a factual position serves to underpin the reasoning behind the legal policy and the need for the same in contract and tort.

(d) 'WRONGFUL BIRTH'

In a wrongful birth action, the parents' claim is that the defendant's negligence led to their child's birth, usually because negligent prenatal screening deprived the woman of the option to terminate the pregnancy. The 'damage' in these cases is the birth of a disabled child, and, according to ordinary tort law principles, damages should attempt to put the mother in the position she would have been if the tort had not been committed.

Two important issues arise. First, the child's mother must establish that, if she had known that her child was likely to be born disabled, she would have taken steps to avoid its birth; that is, that she would have had an abortion. This will be difficult because the woman is necessarily speculating about how she would have reacted to the diagnosis, with the benefit of hindsight, and with the knowledge that her claim for damages depends upon her claiming that she would have terminated the pregnancy.

In *Deriche v Ealing Hospital NHS Trust*,[92] for example, Mrs Deriche had contracted chicken pox during pregnancy. Because her reaction to having been told of the possibility of a 'congenital malformation' was not to investigate the possibility of a termination, Buckley J was not persuaded by her assertion that she would have terminated the pregnancy if the fetal anomaly scan had identified her son's disabilities: 'her assertion that any problem would have caused her to have a termination is, I am afraid, a product of the tragedy that subsequently occurred and I cannot accept it as an accurate statement of her state of mind in 1996'.

In addition to the factual difficulty of proving that, if she had known about the fetus's disability, the claimant would have terminated the pregnancy, it might also be argued that this puts a child's mother in an invidious position. By the time the case reaches court, the child is likely to be a much loved member of the family. The only way a mother can seek damages to help her to cope with her child's special needs is to prove that, if she had known about her child's disabilities, she would have prevented her birth by having an abortion.

Secondly, what would it mean to put the mother in the position she would have been in if the tort had not been committed? Should damages cover all of the costs of the child's up-bringing, or only those associated with the disability? On the one hand, the defendant's negligence caused this child to be born, and if the child had not been born, then none of the costs associated with her upbringing would have been incurred. On the other hand, if the child had been healthy, the pregnancy would not have been terminated, and the parents would, in any event, have incurred the costs of caring for a healthy child. It might therefore be argued that it is only the additional costs associated with the disability that were caused by the defendant's negligence. This was the approach taken by Toulson J in *Lee v Taunton and Somerset NHS Trust*:[93] 'If, following a termination of her pregnancy with George, she had continued with her attempts and had been successful, she would have incurred the costs of bringing up a healthy child in any event.'

---

[92] [2003] EWHC 3104 (QB).   [93] [2001] 1 FLR 419.

In *Khan v MNX*, the respondent's nephew was diagnosed with haemophilia. Because she was anxious not to have a child with haemophilia, the respondent consulted her GP in order to find out whether she was a carrier of the haemophilia gene. The GP arranged a blood test which revealed only that she was not herself a haemophiliac. In order to find out whether she was a carrier, she should have been referred for genetic testing, which would have revealed that she was. The respondent was simply told that her results were normal.

It was accepted that if the testing had been carried out non-negligently, the respondent would have known that she was a carrier. She would have undergone prenatal testing for haemophilia, and when she found out that her fetus was affected, she would have terminated the pregnancy. Liability for the costs associated with her son FGN's haemophilia was therefore accepted. The question for the court was whether she could also recover for the costs associated with his autism.

At first instance, Yip J found that she could: 'but for' the GP's negligence, FGN would not have been born and the costs associated with his autism would have been avoided. The Court of Appeal allowed the GP's appeal, applying the 'scope of duty' limits imposed by *South Australian Asset Management Corporation v York Montague Ltd* (SAAMCO).[94] These required the courts to ask three questions:

1. What was the purpose of the procedure/information/advice which is alleged to have been negligent?

2. What was the appropriate apportionment of risk between the doctor and the patient, taking account of the nature of the advice, procedure, information?

3. What losses would in any event have occurred if the defendant's advice/information was correct or the procedure had been performed?

In a decision that may have wider resonance in clinical negligence cases, the Court of Appeal found that Dr Khan had not been under a duty to protect the respondent from all the risks associated with pregnancy, only to protect her against the risk of haemophilia.

Khan v MNX[95]

Nicola Davies LJ

As to what risks the respondent would consider were still hers to bear at the time of and following the consultation and which risks had been shifted to the appellant, the respondent would have accepted prior to and during any pregnancy that she remained willing to accept the risk of having a child born with autism but would not have accepted that she still had a risk of having a child born with haemophilia as this had been addressed by the appellant . . .

The scope of the appellant's duty was not to protect the respondent from all the risks associated with becoming pregnant and continuing with the pregnancy. The appellant had no duty to prevent the birth of FGN, this was a decision that could only be made by the respondent taking into account matters such as her ethical views on abortion, her willingness to accept the risks associated with any pregnancy and was outwith the limits of the advice/treatment which had been sought from the appellant. It has not been any part of the respondent's case that the appellant had a duty to advise more generally in relation to the risks of any future pregnancy. The risk of a child born with autism was not increased by the appellant's advice, the purpose and scope of her duty was to advise and investigate in relation to haemophilia in order to provide the respondent with an opportunity to avoid the risk of a child being born with haemophilia.

5 PROBLEMS WITH CLINICAL NEGLIGENCE

(a) COSTS TO THE NHS

In 2017/18, NHS Resolution received 10,673 clinical negligence claims, up from 6,652 in 2009/10. The amount paid out also increased, from £787 million to almost £2.227 billion, of which a significant proportion (27 per cent) is spent on legal costs.[96]

Regardless of how deserving individual claimants' cases might be, diverting scarce NHS funds to the payment of damages and lawyers' fees reduces the amount of money available for patient care. As Alan Merry and Alexander McCall Smith explain:

If damages become payable, then that means that there is a correspondingly reduced amount available for the maintenance of wards and equipment, the purchase of drugs or the provision of treatment. A medium-sized award, therefore, may be crudely translated into ten fewer hip replacements.[97]

In the following extract, John Harris suggests that victims of medical negligence should compete for scarce NHS funds according to ordinary rationing criteria, in the same way as patients, rather than being given absolute priority.

John Harris[98]

In most healthcare systems the need to prioritise patients for care and to ration the resources available is now well recognised . . . However, one group of claimants for healthcare resources have been guaranteed top priority for receipt of funds available for health care—victims of medical accidents. This fact has been scarcely noted and its justice seldom questioned . . .

If people who need treatment to save their life can be told that scarcity of resources does not allow them to be treated, why, equally, should not people who need legal redress and compensation (out of the same limited pot of money) be told that the resources necessary to fund the professional help and compensation that they need are either exhausted or committed to those with a greater need? . . .

If public resources available for patient care are to be cash limited and patients forced to compete for priority within those limits, why should not the same be true of access to litigation and compensation? Why, in short, are some victims of medical accidents given priority over the victims of all other types of accidents, injuries, and illnesses? . . .

I think it plausible to insist that the health related needs of victims of medical accidents or negligence compete on at least an equal footing with other such needs rather than having automatic and absolute priority.

[96] *Annual Report and Accounts 2017/8* (NHS Resolution, 2018).
[97] *Errors, Medicine and the Law* (CUP: Cambridge, 2001) 212.
[98] 'The injustice of compensation for victims of medical accidents' (1997) 314 British Medical Journal 1821.

(b) FAILURE TO PROVIDE REMEDIES TO INJURED PATIENTS

Most patients who have suffered injury as a result of their medical treatment never even consider litigation. Only four per cent of people who experience a harmful incident will make a claim.[99] Interestingly, according to the National Audit Office 'the profile of patients who make claims differs significantly from those who suffer adverse events. For example, at a national level, older people (aged 65 and over) experience 53% of harmful incidents reported, but they only make 23% of all claims'.[100]

Some patients may not realize that they are eligible to bring a claim. Others, as Linda Mulcahy explains, may decide that the difficulties of pursuing a legal action outweigh the small chance of receiving compensation:

> Patients may also *choose* not to make a complaint or clinical negligence claim . . . for some, avoiding disputes is a positive and rational choice. Asked why they had not voiced their dissatisfaction, this subset said they had other priorities, wished to put negative experiences behind them or avoid confrontation.[101]

Of the 16,338 claims resolved by NHS Resolution in 2017/18, 70 per cent were resolved without any formal legal proceedings, usually through some sort of negotiation or mediation; litigation was abandoned or cases were settled in 30 per cent of cases, and only 0.8 per cent went to a full trial (with judgment for the NHS in the majority of cases).[102]

For the majority of claimants, stressful and expensive litigation ends in disappointment. Even when claimants are awarded damages, many are still dissatisfied because they have not been given an explanation, an apology, or reassurance that the same thing will not happen again.[103]

The fear that doctors might not apologize to patients in case this might be used against them in court has been addressed by the introduction of a statutory duty of candour, via regulation 20 of the Health and Social Care Act 2008 (Regulated Activities) Regulations 2014. Failure to apologise, defined as 'an expression of sorrow or regret',[104] is now a criminal offence, punishable by a fine of up to £2500.

Health and Social Care Act 2008 (Regulated Activities) Regulations 2014 regulation 20

1. Registered persons must act in an open and transparent way with relevant persons in relation to care and treatment provided to service users in carrying on a regulated activity.

2. As soon as reasonably practicable after becoming aware that a notifiable safety incident has occurred a registered person must—

   (a) notify the relevant person that the incident has occurred in accordance with paragraph (3), and

---

[99] National Audit Office, *Managing the costs of clinical negligence in trusts* (NAO, 2017).
[100] Ibid.
[101] Linda Mulcahy, *Disputing Doctors: The Socio-Legal Dynamics of Complaints about Medical Care* (Open UP: Maidenhead, 2003) 64–6.
[102] *Annual Report and Accounts 2017/8* (NHS Resolution, 2018).
[103] Linda Mulcahy, *Disputing Doctors: The Socio-Legal Dynamics of Complaints about Medical Care* (Open UP: Maidenhead, 2003) 96.
[104] Regulation 20(7).

(b) provide reasonable support to the relevant person in relation to the incident, including when giving such notification.

3. The notification to be given under paragraph (2)(a) must—

   (a) be given in person by one or more representatives of the registered person,

   (b) provide an account, which to the best of the registered person's knowledge is true, of all the facts the registered person knows about the incident as at the date of the notification,

   (c) advise the relevant person what further enquiries into the incident the registered person believes are appropriate,

   (d) include an apology, and

   (e) be recorded in a written record which is kept securely by the registered person.

4. The notification given under paragraph (2)(a) must be followed by a written notification given or sent to the relevant person containing—

   (a) the information provided under paragraph (3)(b),

   (b) details of any enquiries to be undertaken in accordance with paragraph (3)(c),

   (c) the results of any further enquiries into the incident, and

   (d) an apology ...

5. In relation to a health service body, 'notifiable safety incident' means any unintended or unexpected incident that occurred in respect of a service user during the provision of a regulated activity that, in the reasonable opinion of a health care professional, could result in, or appears to have resulted in—

   (a) the death of the service user, where the death relates directly to the incident rather than to the natural course of the service user's illness or underlying condition, or

   (b) severe harm, moderate harm or prolonged psychological harm to the service user.

In 2015, the General Medical Council and the Nursing and Midwifery Council issued a joint statement on the Professional Duty of Candour. This sets out in considerable detail what is expected of healthcare professionals, for example by giving guidance on how to say 'sorry' to patients.

General Medical Council and Nursing and Midwifery Council[105]

16. We do not want to encourage a formulaic approach to apologising since an apology has value only if it is genuine. However, when apologising to a patient, you should consider each of the following points.

(a) You must give patients the information they want or need to know in a way that they can understand.

(b) You should speak to patients in a place and at a time when they are best able to understand and retain information.

(c) You should give information that the patient may find distressing in a considerate way, respecting their right to privacy and dignity.

(d) Patients are likely to find it more meaningful if you offer a personalized apology—for example 'I am sorry ... '—rather than a general expression of regret about the incident on the

[105] *Openness and honesty when things go wrong: the professional duty of candour* (GMC and NMC, 2015).

organisation's behalf. This doesn't mean that we expect you to take personal responsibility for system failures or other people's mistakes.

(e) You should make sure the patient knows who to contact in the healthcare team to ask any further questions or raise concerns. You should also give patients information about independent advocacy, counselling or other support services that can give them practical advice and emotional support.

Notice that this guidance states that apologies are meaningful only if genuine. Is a forced apology 'a mere perfunctory gesture', as claimed by Yinchu Wang in the following extract, or is Gijs van Dijck right that forced apologies might nevertheless serve other useful purposes?

Yinchu Wang[106]

We have all become adept at recognising and discounting enforced emotions. No one really believes that the person serving us coffee genuinely regards us as a friend or that the smiles lavished on us on an airline is because we are in some ways special. We have come to expect it but at the same time disregard it as a mere perfunctory gesture. In doing the same to healthcare workers, we risk generating the same kind of expectation as well as cynicism . . .

Any rule concocted to demand compassion from the healthcare professional is unlikely to yield results. At most, it will generate service that is better in *form*, but not *content*. Even this has limits: as the content deteriorates, it grows apart from the form and makes it ultimately inadequate. At worst, it damages the healthcare workers, generates cynicism in the service users. Most importantly, it distracts us from the issues which are far more important to patient care, for example, adequate staffing and training, hospital beds, etc.

Gijs van Dijck[107]

Of course, ordered apologies are not always appreciated . . . However, some receivers feel that compelled apologies can help them move on, provide personal vindication or public validation, for example by sending a powerful message to society about the wrong or harm, particularly in situations of corporate defendants.

The pattern that emerges from empirical studies conducted in legal and non-legal settings is that sincere apologies are preferred, but are not necessarily required in order for them to be beneficial to victims . . .

The exchange of humiliation on the side of the wrongdoer and power on the side of the victim to accept, reject or successfully claim an apology has been said to be the clearest explanation of how apologies can restore dignity and self-respect. The humiliation element further explains why sincerity is not the sole predictor of an effective apology, as humiliation may take place either with or without the apology being sincere.

Furthermore, apologies can enhance psychological healing because they provide acknowledgement, validation and/or closure.

---

[106] 'Smiling through clenched teeth: why compassion cannot be written into the rules' (2016) 42 Journal of Medical Ethics' 7–9.

[107] 'The Ordered Apology' (2017) 37 Oxford Journal of Legal Studies 562–87.

It remains to be seen whether, as Christopher Mellor suggests, one practical result of clinicians having to admit to patients, or relatives, that something has gone seriously wrong with their treatment might be an increase in clinical negligence claims.

Christopher Mellor[108]

[T]he practical effect in many cases will be that healthcare providers will be required to tell patients/patients' families, that they believe they have caused serious injury or death. Whilst it is recommended that such notification should not amount to an admission of liability, it will obviously have an influence on subsequent negligence claims. Furthermore, the fact that the duty will arise in the absence of any complaint being made, or any litigation being commenced, adds further to its novelty. It could effectively amount to a statutory duty that requires a potential defendant to inform a potential claimant that they may have a claim: that very notion obviously seems entirely anomalous in an adversarial system of law.

(c) A COMPENSATION CULTURE?

Despite the low chance of success and dissatisfaction with available remedies, patients have been increasingly willing to sue when their medical treatment goes wrong, leading to fears of a US-style 'compensation culture'. This is thought to have two negative consequences for the NHS. First, it means that money that could be used to improve patient care is spent instead on legal fees. Secondly, it is feared that the threat of litigation may lead doctors to practise 'defensive medicine', in which they opt for treatment which is legally safest, rather than that which is in the best interests of their patients. An example might be the high caesarean delivery rates in the US, prompted by obstetricians' understandable fear of litigation if something goes wrong during a natural delivery (obstetricians in the US are, on average, sued three times in their careers, and their insurance premiums are very high indeed).

It is not, however, clear that doctors are primarily motivated by a desire to avoid litigation. As Lady Hale said in *Gregg v Scott*:[109] 'of course doctors and other healthcare professionals are not solely, or even mainly, motivated by the fear of adverse legal consequences. They are motivated by their natural desire and their professional duty to do their best for their patients.'

Furthermore, as Philip Havers and Jessica Elliott point out in the next extract, the claim that the fear of being sued might prompt doctors to practise defensive medicine is difficult to evaluate, because it is not clear that there is anything necessarily wrong with taking a cautious approach, and indeed it will sometimes be the right thing to do.

Philip Havers and Jessica Elliott[110]

The increase in medical malpractice litigation over recent years has been accompanied by claims that, in response to the threat of litigation, doctors now practise defensively. This involves undertaking procedures which are not medically justified but are designed to protect the doctor from a claim for negligence. The most commonly cited examples are unnecessary

---

[108] 'A duty of candour: a change in approach' (2014) 20 Clinical Risk 36–46.   [109] [2005] UKHL 2.
[110] 'Breach of Duty' in Judith Laing and Jean McHale (eds), *Principles of Medical Law*, 4th edn (OUP: Oxford, 2017) 163–235.

diagnostic tests, such as X-rays, and unnecessary Caesarean section deliveries. However, applying the *Bolam* test, a reasonable doctor would not undertake an *unnecessary* procedure and so a doctor could not avoid a finding of negligence by performing one. In fact, to the extent that the procedure carries some inherent risk, a practitioner acting in this way may increase his chances of being sued. Moreover, there is little clear understanding within the medical profession of what the term 'defensive medicine' means. 'Defensive' may mean simply treating patients conservatively or even 'more carefully', and this begs the question whether that treatment option is medically justified in the patient's interests. Nonetheless, the courts have apparently acknowledged the existence of the phenomenon of defensive medicine, despite the fact that there is virtually no empirical, as opposed to anecdotal, evidence of such practices in this country.

The so-called 'compensation culture' has also been blamed for the emergence of Claims Management Companies (CMCs). These are organizations which encourage people to bring personal injury claims, through high-pressure sales techniques, like cold-calling and unsolicited text messages. The Compensation Act 2006 attempted to regulate CMCs by controlling advertising and setting up a mandatory authorization scheme for CMCs, administered by the Claims Management Regulator, within the Ministry of Justice. Since 2013, it has been an offence for CMCs to pay or receive payment for referrals of personal injury cases.[111] As a result, there are now fewer CMCs—1,238 in 2017/18, compared with 2,693 in 2012/13.

(d) WHAT ABOUT OTHER PEOPLE WITH DISABILITIES?

Finally, it is worth remembering that most people who live with serious illness and disability will not receive any damages at all. Only those who can prove that another's negligence caused their ill health will receive generous financial assistance with the costs of their care. To illustrate this, compare the results in two cases in which babies suffered cerebral palsy as a result of oxygen deprivation during birth. In *Whiten v St George's Healthcare NHS Trust*, where negligence was successfully established, the child received £5,685,507.79 in damages to compensate him for his cerebral palsy.[112] In contrast, in *Jones v North West Strategic Health Authority*, failure to prove that the oxygen deprivation that caused another child's cerebral palsy was the result of negligence meant that he received nothing at all.[113]

The needs of brain-damaged children do not depend upon whether or not their disabilities were caused by negligence. It is often said that tort law serves two purposes, compensation and deterrence. If we are principally concerned with compensating the victims of medical accidents, a social security system, or welfare state, which allocates resources according to need might then be fairer than the tort of negligence. Of course, such a system would not deter negligent behaviour, but at the same time, is it really plausible to argue that what motivates obstetricians to deliver babies safely is the fear that NHS Resolution might settle a large claim on their behalf?

In 1970, with the first publication of *Accidents, Compensation and the Law*, Patrick Atiyah drew attention to the unfairness of drawing a distinction between individuals with identical needs in this way.

---

[111] Legal Aid, Sentencing and Punishment of Offenders Act 2012, s 56.
[112] *Whiten v St George's Healthcare NHS Trust* [2011] EWHC 2066 (QB).
[113] *Jones v North West Strategic Health Authority* [2010] EWHC 178 (QB).

Patrick Atiyah[114]

> It has been suggested that the view that brain-damaged babies deserve more generous compensation than the congenitally disabled is rooted in the desire for accountability, not compensation. More generally, it might be argued that compensating victims of human causes at a higher level than victims of natural causes is a way of giving effect to notions of personal responsibility: a person should be required to pay compensation for injuries if, but only if, that person was in some sense responsible for the disabilities . . .
>
> Nevertheless, if compensation for disabilities was paid by individuals, the argument based on personal responsibility might have some force. However, we have seen that most tort compensation is not paid by individuals, but by insurers, corporations and the government, and in this light it is less clear why tort-type benefits should only be available to those injured by human action. On the whole, those disabled people who can recover tort damages . . . are much better provided for than those disabled people who must rely on social security benefits alone. Can this be justified in the light of the fact that the tort system and the social security system are, in effect, both financed by the public at large?

It is not just the expense, inconvenience, and unfairness of negligence claims that has come under attack. Even more importantly, as we see in the next section, it is increasingly recognized that the clinical negligence system may work against ensuring that mistakes are learned from.

5 LEARNING FROM MISTAKES

The tort system is not an effective way to ensure that mistakes are not repeated. When damages are not paid by the individual who was at fault, the deterrent effect of tort law is fairly weak. Even if doctors fear being sued because of the damage it might do to their reputation, paradoxically the most egregious examples of negligence will be settled quickly and quietly by the doctor's employer.

More significantly, as Alan Merry and Alexander McCall Smith put it: 'A point which is often misunderstood is that human error, being by definition unintentional, is not easily deterred'.[115] For example, most doctors will have prescribed or administered the wrong drug, or the wrong dose of a drug, to a patient at some point. Medication errors are common: there are thought to be about 237 million medication errors in England each year, 72 per cent of which have little or no potential for harm.[116]

If, however, the patient dies or is injured as a result of a medication error, the doctor (or in practice, her employer) might be sued for negligence. Alan Merry and Alexander McCall Smith describe this as 'outcome bias', whereby culpability depends on the consequences of an action, rather than upon its blameworthiness.[117] A system of deterrence built upon such haphazard foundations is unlikely to work. Instead, a more effective way to prevent human error is to anticipate likely mistakes, and to design systems intended to minimize the risk

---

[114] Peter Cane, *Atiyah's Accidents, Compensation and the Law*, 8th edn (Butterworths: London, 1993) 331–2.

[115] *Errors, Medicine and the Law* (CUP: Cambridge, 2001) 2.

[116] Rachel A Elliott et al, *Prevalence and Economic Burden of Medication Errors in The NHS in England. Rapid evidence synthesis and economic analysis of the prevalence and burden of medication error in the UK* (Policy Research Unit in Economic Evaluation of Health and Care Interventions, 2018).

[117] *Errors, Medicine and the Law* (CUP: Cambridge, 2001), 46–7.

materializing. For example, a systems approach to medication errors might involve ensuring that different drugs do not have confusingly similar packaging, or that drugs with similar names are not stored together.

Historically, there was a difference between the practice of medicine and other high-risk activities, such as the aviation industry,[118] where human error is anticipated, and non-punitive reporting systems are in place in order to ensure that learning from mistakes is the norm. Over the past two decades, the NHS has moved some considerable way towards more open reporting. This began with the Department of Health Expert Group's report, *An Organisation with A Memory*.

Department of Health Expert Group[119]

- Human error may sometimes be the factor that immediately precipitates a serious failure, but there are usually deeper, systemic factors at work which if addressed would have prevented the error or acted as a safety-net to mitigate its consequences . . .

- There is evidence that 'safety cultures', where open reporting and balanced analysis are encouraged in principle and by example, can have a positive and quantifiable impact on the performance of organisations. 'Blame cultures' on the other hand can encourage people to cover up errors for fear of retribution and act against the identification of the true causes of failure . . .

- Human error is commonly blamed for failures because it is often the most readily identifiable factor operating in the period just prior to an adverse event. Yet two important facts about human error are often overlooked. First, the best people can make the worst mistakes. Second, far from being random, errors fall into recurrent patterns. The same set of circumstances can provoke similar mistakes, regardless of the people involved. Any attempt at risk management that focuses primarily upon the supposed mental processes underlying error (forgetfulness, inattention, carelessness, negligence, and the like) and does not seek out and remove these situational 'error traps' is sure to fail.

A further recommendation from the Expert Group related to the importance of reporting not only adverse events themselves, but also near misses. If data is only gathered when serious harm has resulted, this risks 'skewing learning towards a very small cross-section of accidents'.[120] In the aviation industry, pilots are under a duty to report near misses since these are likely to yield information that could help to ensure that a similar mistake, which might on another occasion cause a serious accident, is not repeated.

The crucial point is that instead of expecting medical staff to be infallible, it is more realistic to assume that mistakes are inevitable, and to try to build protections into the system to anticipate them and minimize their impact. To take a mundane example, the designers of word-processing packages take it for granted that users are likely to close documents without remembering to save their work. As a result, prompting mechanisms are built into computer

---

[118] Although compared with the NHS, the aviation industry is relatively low risk. The then Chief Medical Officer, Sir Liam Donaldson, estimated that the odds of dying as a result of hospital treatment are 33,000 times that of dying in an air crash: Vivienne Harpwood, *Medicine, Malpractice and Misapprehensions* (Routledge-Cavendish: Abingdon, 2007) 38.

[119] *An Organisation with a Memory* (DH: London, 2000) viii–ix, 21.   [120] Ibid, 39.

software to remind users that they might want to save documents before closing them, and back-up documents are generated automatically.

In recent years, there has been considerable progress towards the open reporting of 'all patient safety' incidents, including 'those that caused no harm or minimal harm to patients' and 'near misses'. NHS Improvement, previously the National Patient Safety Agency, runs the National Reporting and Learning System (NRLS). In addition to extracting information from existing local risk management systems, NHS employees are also able to report patient safety incidents anonymously and directly through an online form. When reporting began in 2004, the number of adverse incidents reported in England and Wales in the NRLS's first three months of operation was 158. The total number of incidents reported in its first decade of operation was 10,809,052, and between January and March 2018 alone, 486,986 incidents were reported.[121] Superficially, this might look disastrous—as though there has been an exponential rise in adverse events—but, in reality, it suggests that non-punitive reporting is working, and that the NHS is in a much better position to learn from errors than it was 15 years ago. Having gathered information about incidents—an example might be a patient identification error resulting from two patients having the same hospital number—NHS Improvement issues alerts to ensure that all other NHS bodies are able to learn from them.

Serious incidents are defined as 'adverse events, where the consequences to patients, families and carers, staff or organisations are so significant or the potential for learning is so great, that a heightened level of response is justified'.[122] They must be reported within two working days, and investigated in order to prevent recurrence. NHS England is clear that '[t]he occurrence of a serious incident demonstrates weaknesses in a system or process that need to be addressed to prevent future incidents'.

The NHS maintains a list of serious incidents which it categorises as 'never events', that is mistakes that should never happen, such as wrong site surgery. There were 209 never events in the most recently reported quarter (from April to August 2018), of which 83 involved wrong site surgery and 48 involved a foreign object being left in the patient's body after a procedure.

NHS Improvement[123]

Never Events are patient safety incidents that are wholly preventable where guidance or safety recommendations that provide strong systemic protective barriers are available at a national level and have been implemented by healthcare providers . . .

Failure to report a Never Event is unacceptable and can signal cultural and safety failings in an organisation. The reporting and investigation of Never Events may be an indicator of the organisation's attitude to patient safety and openness. As noted by Sir Liam Donaldson: 'to err is human, to cover up is unforgivable, and to fail to learn is inexcusable'.

Openness about mistakes is also important for patients who have been the victims of medical mishaps, who, as we have seen, are often more interested in an explanation and an apology than they are in financial compensation. Indeed, litigation appears to be more likely where patients believe that there has been a cover-up, or that a mistake has gone unacknowledged. Vincent et al's study of the motivations of litigants found that the decision to take legal action

---

[121] *NRLS national patient safety incident reports: commentary* (NHS Improvement, 2018).
[122] *Serious Incident Framework: Supporting learning to prevent recurrence* (NHS England, 2015).
[123] *Never Events policy and framework* (NHS Improvement, 2018).

was determined not only by the original injury, but also by insensitive handling and poor communication afterwards.[124]

While there is now broad support for adopting a 'systems' approach to error, in the next extract Oliver Quick argues that eliminating blame and individual accountability is not without risks.

Oliver Quick[125]

The focus on systems also risks diluting the notion of individual professional responsibility that has been central to medical autonomy and accountability . . .

In the medical context, if blaming the system becomes the default response, to what extent will this shelter the incompetent or poor performer? Sir Donald Irvine, president of the GMC during the turbulent times of the Bristol affair, warned against this over-emphasis on the system which may mask individual failings. A recent example of this followed a surgeon's conviction for manslaughter with the judge remarking that:

> It was not your fault that you were allowed to go on operating, subject to restrictions, for another two years. Much of the evidence of these events was known at the time and the balance of the evidence was easily discoverable had it occurred to anyone making elementary inquiries.

As comments such as this become a more common reaction to error, it is worth questioning whether this drift towards blaming others and organisations risks underplaying the ethics of individual conscience.

6 REFORMING CLINICAL NEGLIGENCE

There have been a number of attempts to improve the functioning of the clinical negligence system. Since 1995, NHS Resolution (previously the NHS Litigation Authority), has encouraged the earlier admission of liability, and the provision of explanations and apologies. New cases now take, on average, 426 days to resolve, compared with 5.5 years in 1999/2000.[126]

Reforms to the civil justice system mean that parties are given incentives to settle actions quickly. Where a case does go to court, pre-trial agreements to determine what the court will be asked to decide are now encouraged, and the court has a more proactive role in case management. Civil Procedure Rules emphasize that expert witnesses' primary duty is to assist the court to determine the truth, and not to offer partisan evidence to support one party's point of view, and in straightforward cases, the judge can appoint a single expert. Where more experts are used, they may be invited to submit a joint report.

The Clinical Negligence Scheme for Trusts (CNST), administered by NHS Resolution, was set up in 1995 in order to help NHS trusts fund litigation by pooling resources, so that

---

[124] C Vincent, 'Why do people sue doctors? A study of patients and relatives taking legal action' (1994) 343 The Lancet 1609–13.

[125] 'Outing Medical Errors: Questions of Trust and Responsibility' (2006) 14 Medical Law Review 22, 41–2.

[126] National Audit Office, *Managing the costs of clinical negligence in trusts* (NAO, 2017).

one high-value case does not bankrupt an NHS provider. As a condition for discounted premiums, it requires the development of clinical incident reporting systems and compliance with its risk management standards.

As we see later, the NHS complaints system has also been reformed. Unfortunately, however, the complaints and the claims systems still largely operate independently of each other, with patients having to choose whether to lodge a complaint or to pursue a claim. It would perhaps make more sense to have a single-track system, providing all patients with an explanation, apology, and assurance that steps have been taken to avoid repetition.

One possible reform that has not found favour in England is moving towards a no-fault compensation scheme. Although removing the need to prove fault would simplify and speed up the process of compensation, the problem of establishing causation remains, and in medical cases, this is a significant obstacle. It also means that arbitrary lines continue to be drawn between patients who are eligible for compensation because they can prove that their injuries were caused by a medical mishap, and those who cannot. As we have seen, the needs of a brain-damaged baby are the same, regardless of whether her injuries were caused by asphyxia at birth or a congenital disability. A no-fault compensation scheme would continue to distinguish between patients on grounds other than need.

Indeed, precisely because 'no fault' schemes must distinguish between medical mishaps and injuries that happen in the ordinary course of things, it is, as Joanna Manning points out in the context of New Zealand's no-fault compensation scheme, difficult to eliminate considerations of negligence.

Joanna M Manning[127]

Lapsing into negligence thinking seems to arise particularly in respect of omissions and failures in the treatment process, such as misdiagnoses or delayed diagnoses, failures to give treatment or timely treatment, failure to refer to a specialist or hospital or to give the proper information to enable informed consent to be given. The theory is that ACC [Accident Compensation Corporation] no longer makes a positive finding of fault on behalf of a health professional or organization. But, in order to assess and determine whether there has been such a failure, the focus, including in the expert clinical advice, remains fixed on what a practitioner or service should have done in the relevant circumstances according to current guidelines and standards of accepted practice . . .

What was not anticipated at the time of the reform was how difficult it is to actually achieve the elimination of fault. Even though the courts and ACC are no longer making formal findings of individual and organizational fault in resolving treatment injury claims, they are continuing to make findings of negligence as part of the reasoning process in certain kinds of treatment injury claim.

No-fault schemes may be cheaper to administer, but they are also likely to attract higher numbers of claims. In New Zealand, for example, the proportion of the population making claims each year is more than double that in England.

---

[127] 'Plus ça change, plus c'est la même chose: negligence and treatment injury in New Zealand's accident compensation scheme' (2014) 14 Medical Law International 22–51.

Despite this, in Scotland, the No Fault Compensation Review Group, chaired by Sheila McLean, recommended that the Scottish government should implement a no-fault system of compensation.

No Fault Compensation Review Group[128]

The potential benefits of a no fault approach would be that:

• More people would obtain compensation, because of the removal of the requirement to prove fault;

• Compensation could be awarded much more quickly, because:

  ○ There is no need to prove fault;

  ○ Care needs could be met by a guarantee of ongoing care provision by the state;

  ○ The award could be made by administrative means or tribunal, rather than following an adversarial process;

  ○ Money currently leaving the NHS would be retained in the system, thus improving NHS resources overall;

  ○ There may be a considerable saving in legal fees.

Following a consultation process, in which significant concerns were raised about the overall costs of such a scheme, the Scottish Government nevertheless decided to 'proceed with caution'.

The Scottish Government[129]

6.10.10 Given the complexity of the issues and the potential costs we will proceed with caution to:

• Explore the scope, shape and development of a no-fault compensation in Scotland for injuries resulting from clinical treatment and the subsequent introduction of such a scheme. This will involve further detailed work especially in relation to projected cost and eligibility criteria; and

• consider how the scheme could more effectively contribute to patient safety, learning, improvement and how it links with and supports safe disclosure of adverse events and aligns with the complaints and claims procedure.

In Wales, the National Health Service (Concerns, Complaints and Redress Arrangements) (Wales) Regulations 2011 implemented a fast track redress system. If there is 'qualifying liability in tort', the responsible body may offer compensation (up to a limit of £25,000); a contract for care and treatment; an apology; an explanation; and a report on action taken to prevent recurrence of the event. If the offer is accepted, the complainant waives the right to bring civil legal proceedings.

---

[128] *Reports and Recommendations*, vol 1 (Scottish Government, 2011).
[129] Consultation Report—Consultation on recommendations for no-fault compensation in Scotland for injuries resulting from clinical treatment (Scottish Government, 2014).

The Welsh scheme retains the need to establish clinical negligence, and delegates this complex task to NHS staff. From the patient's point of view, however, there is now a unified system for reporting incidents, complaints, and claims, which reduces complexity, and may additionally mean that what starts as a 'complaint' actually leads to the payment of compensation. As Vivienne Harpwood points out, the amount paid out in compensation has increased, but costs have been reduced.

Vivienne Harpwood[130]

An increase of up to 60 per cent in the number of complaints about healthcare throughout Wales was reported soon after the scheme was introduced ... Anecdotal evidence suggests that the duty on Health Boards to offer compensation when it is determined that a qualifying liability exists, has already resulted in a rise in compensation payments to claimants ... However, there is evidence that costs have been substantially reduced in respect of lower value clinical negligence claims, a factor which might balance out the rise in compensation payments to some extent.

The NHS Redress Act, which would have implemented a similar system throughout England and Wales, received Royal Assent in 2006 but it was never implemented in England. In his report into reform of the funding of the civil justice system, Lord Justice Jackson argued in favour of the resurrection of the NHS Redress Scheme,[131] but at the time of writing, it looks very unlikely that an NHS Redress Scheme will be set up in England.

The Department of Health had predicted that the increase in the number of cases might be as high as 43 per cent, although it also envisaged that opportunistic claims would be rejected quickly, and in the longer term, it expected to see substantial savings in legal costs.[132] Nevertheless, Department of Health economists estimated that, even with a payout cap of £20,000, the financial effect of the scheme would be likely to range from a saving of £7 million to a cost of £48 million.[133]

Concerns about the affordability of a redress scheme may mean, as Emma Cave points out, that English patients have access to a weaker form of redress than their counterparts in Wales and Scotland.

Emma Cave[134]

The necessity to ensure that redress is 'joined-up' is receiving inadequate attention. In this time of austerity measures, the focus is naturally on cutting costs, but losing sight of adequate access to justice will itself prove costly. Advances made in relation to the complaints process and professional regulation are limited by the adverse effects clinical negligence has

---

[130] 'Clinical Negligence and Poor Quality Care: Is Wales "Putting Things Right"?' in Pamela Ferguson and Graeme Laurie (eds), *Inspiring a Medico-Legal Revolution: Essays in Honour of Sheila McLean* (Ashgate: Aldershot, 2015) 139–53.
[131] The Rt Hon Lord Justice Jackson, *Review of Civil Litigation Costs, Final Report* (TSO: London, 2010) ch 23, paras 7 and 8.
[132] Ibid, ch 23, paras 7 and 8.   [133] Ibid.
[134] Emma Cave, 'Redress in the NHS' (2011) 27 Journal of Professional Negligence 138–57.

on the doctor patient relationship. Where financial compensation is barred by virtue of limitations on legal aid and civil law reform, more pressure will be placed on the complaints system and professional regulation to deliver appropriate sanction, communication and correction. If Scotland adopts a no fault system and the redress scheme in Wales proves effective, the dichotomy in access to justice will be sorely felt in England.

Instead, in England, the government has consulted on two new schemes to try to reduce clinical negligence costs: fixed recoverable legal costs for low-value cases, and a voluntary alternative scheme for birth injury cases. Obstetric claims represent 10 per cent of claims, but 48 per cent of all damages awarded. Moreover, the average length of time between the incident and the award for compensation in these cases is 11.5 years.[135] NHS Resolution has already introduced an early notification scheme for all obstetric incidents that might result in severe brain injury. In 2017/8, NHS Resolution received 416 notifications, and explained the benefits of early notification:

Early involvement means that for these cases we have been able to provide families with a written apology, offer financial support and practical advice on how to access support in caring for their child and provide support for the staff involved. In all of these cases, liability was admitted outside of a formal litigation process, avoiding the associated stress to families and staff, costs and impact on Court resources.[136]

7 THE NHS COMPLAINTS SYSTEM

A patient who is dissatisfied with her medical treatment, who is unable or unwilling to bring an action in negligence, may nevertheless want to complain about the care that she, or someone she cares about, has received. The Patient Advice and Liaison Service (PALS) was set up in order to listen to patients' concerns, and to offer information and support. PALS officers are available in all hospitals and they will liaise with others in order to try to resolve problems before a formal complaint is made.

If informal resolution does not succeed, there is then a two-stage process for formal complaints. Local resolution is the first and usually the only stage—only two per cent of complaints progress beyond the local resolution stage. Complaints can be resolved locally through a report which sets out how the complaint was considered, the conclusions reached, and, if relevant, a remedial action plan. An Independent Complaints Advocacy Service exists to ensure that complainants have access to support in articulating their concerns and in navigating the complaints system.

In 2017/18 a total of 208,626 written complaints were received, up from 131,022 in 2007/8.[137] But, as the Health Select Committee has explained, most dissatisfied patients do not complain.

[135] A Rapid Resolution and Redress Scheme for Severe Avoidable Birth Injury: Government Summary Consultation Response (DH, 2017).

[136] *Annual Report and Accounts 2017/8* (NHS Resolution, 2018).

[137] NHS Digital, *Data on Written Complaints in the NHS 2017-18* (HSCIC, 2018).

House of Commons Health Select Committee[138]

The 'toxic cocktail' of service users reluctant to complain and providers reluctant to listen must be avoided at all costs, as it inevitably leads to a spiral of decline in service quality. Patients must be empowered to give constructive feedback on services which they believe are substandard. Anna Bradley, Chair of Healthwatch England, told us that:

> One in three [patients and carers] says that they have had personal experience, or know someone who has had personal experience, of a really quite serious incident, but only half of them have done anything about it ... One in four of them says they did not do anything about it because they did not think anyone would be interested. Three in five said they did not know how to do anything about it. One in two said no one would do anything about it anyway and they did not trust that they would get a decent response. As we also know, very many people ... just feel too vulnerable.

As this shows, the complaints process is seen as complex and difficult to navigate, and can prove off-putting.

If someone is not satisfied with the way in which the local NHS body has dealt with her complaint, the next stage is to complain to the Parliamentary and Health Service Ombudsman. A complaint to the Ombudsman has to be made within a year of when the patient became aware of the events that are the subject of the complaint, and the patient must show that she has suffered some hardship or injustice.

In practice, the vast majority of complaints that the Ombudsman receives are not fully investigated, often because local resolution has not been exhausted. It is not usually possible to obtain damages, although in rare cases, where there is proof of financial loss, the Ombudsman may order some financial payment.

In 2017-18, the Ombudsman received 24,644 complaints about the NHS and completed 2,355 investigations. This should be put into the context of the volume of NHS activity: on average the Ombudsman investigates 6.2 complaints for every 100,000 clinical episodes in each acute trust. Just over a third (36 per cent) of complaints against NHS bodies are upheld or partially upheld.[139]

Some of the most commonly cited reasons for complaints are receiving an inadequate apology (34 per cent), poor communication (31 per cent), and that the response to the original complaint was wrong or incomplete (24 per cent). Staff attitude was a factor in 21 per cent of cases. The Ombudsman has also found that the number of complaints varies considerably between different trusts. This should not be taken as a measure of hospital performance, however, partly because of the different work undertaken by different hospitals, and partly because 'some NHS organisations have better information for patients about making a complaint and encourage learning from complaints'.[140] A high number of complaints may indicate that the hospital has a proactive attitude towards learning from mistakes.

Following Robert Francis QC's report into failings at Mid-Staffordshire hospital (see below), the government asked Ann Clwyd MP and Professor Tricia Hart to conduct a detailed review of complaints handling in the NHS and make recommendations for improvement.

---

[138] Health Select Committee, *Complaints and Raising Concerns*, Fourth Report of Session 2014–15.
[139] Parliamentary and Health Service Ombudsman, *Complaints about the NHS in England: Quarter One* (PHSO, 2018).
[140] Parliamentary and Health Service Ombudsman, *Complaints about acute trusts 2016* (PHSO, 2016).

They found that patients and their relatives found it difficult to complain and that, far from valuing complaints, some NHS hospitals appeared to want them to 'go away'.[141]

In response, the Department of Health set up a Complaints Programme Board (CPB) in order to improve complaints handling in the NHS, and one outcome has been that, since 2014, how an organization handles complaints has been a mandatory key line of inquiry in Care Quality Commission (CQC) inspections. Indeed, the CQC has said that how an NHS body responds to complaints is a proxy for whether it is a well-run organization:

> Complaints handling is an excellent proxy for an open, transparent and learning culture that we would expect to see in well-led organisations ... A service that is safe, responsive and well-led will treat every concern as an opportunity to improve. It will encourage its staff to raise concerns without fear of reprisal. It will respond to complaints openly and honestly.[142]

8 PROFESSIONAL REGULATION

The GMC is the medical profession's regulatory body (the Nursing and Midwifery Council fulfils a similar role in relation to nurses). Doctors can only practise medicine in the UK if they are registered with the GMC. In cases of seriously poor practice, a patient (or another healthcare professional) might report a doctor to the GMC. The GMC can investigate if a doctor's fitness to practise is impaired, as a result of misconduct, deficient performance, criminal conviction, ill health, or the decision of another healthcare regulator (an example might be a decision of the Human Fertilisation and Embryology Authority that a clinician has failed to fulfil her obligations under the Human Fertilisation and Embryology Act 1990).

As John Chamberlain notes, over the two decades, there has been a dramatic increase in the number of enquiries received by the GMC.

John Martyn Chamberlain[143]

> Aside from 2006, when the number of enquiries reduced sharply, the figures reveal that the number of enquiries received by the GMC has increased by 640% over the last 17 years, from 1503 in 1995 to 9624 in 2014. The total of 9624 enquiries represents 4% of all medical practitioners on the GMC register in 2014 ...
>
> In the last two decades, there has been an increase in the questioning of medical authority, with the result that individuals are more likely to complain about their doctor and/or the treatment that they have received ... ·
>
> However, it is equally important to bear in mind that complainants are often motivated by strong emotions, such as anger, frustration, and the grief of losing a loved one, and research suggests that as a result they often act out of an altruistic sense of social justice, seeing it as their personal duty to ensure that the poor care that they feel that they or their relatives have

---

[141] *A Review of the NHS Hospitals Complaints System Putting Patients Back in the Picture* (DH: London, 2013).
[142] Care Quality Commission, *Complaints Matter* (CQC, 2014).
[143] 'Malpractice, Criminality, and Medical Regulation: Reforming the Role of the GMC in Fitness to Practise Panels' (2017) 25 Medical Law Review 1–22.

experienced does not happen to other people in future. As a result, the fact that the majority of complaints the GMC receives are not taken forward (75% in 2014) raises questions surrounding its gatekeeper role when it comes to ensuring patients can seek satisfactory non-financial altruistic forms of redress.

Fitness to practise and interim order panel hearings are now conducted independently of the GMC by the Medical Practitioners Tribunal Service (MPTS). If a doctor's fitness to practise is found to be impaired, she can be erased ('struck off') or suspended from the medical register, or conditions may be imposed upon her practice, such as a requirement that she refrains from carrying out a particular procedure. In 2017, there were 195 fitness to practise hearings, in which 62 doctors were erased from the register; 76 were suspended; conditions were imposed in 13 cases; warnings given in 13; and 27 cases resulted in a finding of no impairment.[144]

'Seriously deficient performance' is defined as 'a departure from good professional practice, whether or not it is covered by specific GMC guidance, sufficiently serious to call into question a doctor's registration'. This definition is rather circular and question-begging: performance is seriously deficient when it is a departure from good practice serious enough to call into question a doctor's registration. It is, however, clear that it is not necessary to prove that a patient has been harmed by the doctor's 'seriously deficient performance'.

Since 2003, appeals against Fitness to Practise Panel decisions have been to the High Court. The Court of Appeal in *Fatnani v General Medical Council*[145] was clear that such appeals should not be an occasion for re-sentencing: that is, it is not for the court to substitute its view as to the appropriate punishment for a doctor whose practice amounted to serious professional misconduct.

As part of a raft of reforms instituted in response to the perceived failings of the regulation of the medical profession highlighted by the case of Harold Shipman,[146] section 29 of the National Health Service Reform and Health Care Professions Act 2002 gives the Council for Healthcare Regulatory Excellence the power to appeal against the decisions of fitness to practise panels on the grounds of 'undue leniency'. Because fitness to practise panels are concerned with preserving public confidence in the medical profession, as well as with patient safety, a punishment might be judged unduly lenient if it focused only upon whether the doctor continued to pose a risk to patients, and did not give sufficient attention to public interest considerations.

A similar provision exists in relation to nurses' registration, and in *Council for Healthcare Regulatory Excellence v Nursing and Midwifery Council*,[147] the Court of Appeal held that the fitness to practise panel of the Nursing and Midwifery Council had given too much weight to a nurse's remorse and insight into her failings, and insufficient weight to the need to uphold public confidence in the nursing profession. Nurse Grant had acted insensitively and in a bullying way towards patients and colleagues over a prolonged period of time—including being rude and insensitive to a woman who had had to deliver her baby after its death *in utero*. Unlike a case in which the healthcare professional's performance was clinically deficient, where remedial action may mean that their fitness to practise is no longer impaired by

---

[144] General Medical Council, *Annual Report 2017* (GMC, 2018).   [145] [2007] EWCA Civ 46.
[146] Dr Shipman was found guilty of 15 murders in 2000, but it is believed that he almost certainly murdered more than 250 of his patients.
[147] [2011] EWHC 927 (Admin).

the time of the hearing, in cases of egregious conduct towards patients, the need to preserve confidence in the profession may result in finding that their fitness to practise is impaired, regardless of any remedial action taken in the meantime.[148]

Also in response to the case of Harold Shipman, when the GMC had been alerted to a police investigation but had said that it had no powers to alter Dr Shipman's registration unless or until he was convicted, section 41A of the Medical Act 1983 provides for the making of interim orders to suspend registration or make it subject to conditions 'for the protection of the public' or where this would be 'otherwise in the public interest'. These interim orders can be made initially for up to 18 months, but with court approval they are renewable indefinitely.

Paula Case's analysis of all interim orders made in a nine-month period in 2009 found that in 44 per cent of cases, the interim sanction was more draconian than the final one, suggesting that sometimes the pre-trial process is effectively part of the punishment.[149] She also drew attention to a tension within section 41A, which is thus far unresolved in the case law. On the one hand, if the justification for making an interim order is the need to protect the public, the bar might be set quite high, with orders only being made if the healthcare professional poses a risk to patients. Yet, on the other hand, if the justification is that the order is 'otherwise in the public interest', reputational risk to the profession might be sufficient, and the bar might be set much lower.

In *Yeong v General Medical Council*—a case in which a doctor had had a sexual relationship with a patient, and tried to argue that the fact that the Interim Order Panel had not ordered full suspension cast doubt upon the decision of the fitness to practise panel (FTPP) to do so— Sales J took the former approach, emphasizing that interim orders should principally be used in order to deal with an immediate risk to patients.

Yeong v General Medical Council[150]

Sales J

[T]he role of the Interim Orders Panel at the interim hearing stage is very different from the role of the FTPP at the final hearing. It will not typically be appropriate for the Interim Orders Panel at the interim stage (ie before a full hearing on the merits) to impose sanctions on grounds based simply on the importance in the public interest of maintaining clear standards of behaviour, as distinct from dealing with an immediate risk posed by a practitioner in relation to his treatment of patients . . . Therefore, the absence of sanction imposed by the Interim Orders Panel does not indicate that the FTPP was wrong to impose the sanction of suspension after the full hearing at the end of the disciplinary process.

Conversely, in relation to two doctors who had been involved in the case of Baby P, a toddler who had died after suffering horrifying neglect and abuse, lengthy interim orders were made, Case suggests, solely in order to promote public confidence. The orders were made

---

[148] See further Paula Case, 'The public interest in a finding of impairment' (2011) 27 Journal of Professional Negligence 177–80.

[149] Paula Case, 'Putting Public Confidence First: Doctors, Precautionary Suspension, and the General Medical Council' (2011) 19 Medical Law Review 339–71.

[150] [2009] EWHC 1923 (Admin).

'under the watchful eye of the media', but there was no suggestion of 'dishonesty, criminal offences, or of posing a risk to patients which could not be addressed by imposing conditions on their registration'.

In the following extract, Case argues that there is a further danger that 'protecting the public interest' may elide into promoting public confidence in the regulator itself. Given the profound consequences interim suspension has for individual doctors, it is questionable whether these should ever be made in order to promote confidence in the muscularity of professional regulation.

Paula Case[151]

A construction of interim suspension powers which envisage their use as a tool for protecting public confidence has serious implications for the doctor concerned . . . [T]here is something instinctively problematic about applying an *interim* sanction on the grounds of protecting the profession's reputation . . .

The danger which accompanies the assumption that confidence in the profession and in its regulator are co-extensive, is that self-preservation strategies of the regulator can masquerade as attempts to build confidence in the profession . . . What is . . . questionable is whether the 'public interest' should include bolstering the reputation of *the regulator* at significant expense.

Since 2005, in order to retain their licence to practise, doctors have to 'revalidate', by demonstrating that they remain up to date and fit to practise. Doctors must prove that their own practice over the previous five years has been in line with the principles set out in the GMC's guide to the duties of a doctor, *Good Medical Practice*. This means collecting and keeping data and information drawn from their day-to-day medical practice. The GMC also demands evidence of participation in an internal appraisal scheme.

In addition to professional regulation, the National Clinical Assessment Service (NCAS), now part of NHS Resolution, was set up in 2001 to support the NHS in dealing with doctors and dentists whose performance gives cause for concern. The NCAS provides advice about the local handling of cases, and can carry out clinical performance assessments of individual practitioners. Where the assessment reveals that the practitioner's performance could be improved, the NCAS will put in place an action plan. In the most serious cases, practitioners can be suspended or excluded from work.

9 WHISTLEBLOWING

Healthcare workers will often be better placed than patients to spot a colleague's poor performance. The GMC's guide to good medical practice states that doctors must take steps to protect patients where they suspect a colleague may be unfit to practise (a similar duty is placed on nurses by the Nursing and Midwifery Council[152]).

---

[151] Paula Case, 'Putting Public Confidence First: Doctors, Precautionary Suspension, and the General Medical Council' (2011) 19 Medical Law Review 339–71.

[152] *Raising and Escalating Concerns: Guidance to Nurses and Midwives* (NMC, 2015).

General Medical Council[153]

> 25c If you have concerns that a colleague may not be fit to practise and may be putting pa-
> tients at risk, you must ask for advice from a colleague, your defence body or us. If you are
> still concerned you must report this, in line with our guidance and your workplace policy, and
> make a record of the steps you have taken.

In practice, however, it is often difficult for doctors and nurses to raise concerns about colleagues' poor performance. The Public Interest Disclosure Act 1998 is supposed to protect
employees who have disclosed information in the public interest from dismissal and vic-
timization, and NHS trusts are under a duty to investigate staff concerns, and to guarantee
that staff who raise concerns responsibly and reasonably will be protected against victimiza-
tion. Despite this, there continue to be powerful cultural and institutional barriers to open
reporting.

Zosia Kmietowicz[154]

> Nearly a third of respondents (31%) admitted to having witnessed incidents of poor care of
> patients that they did not report but that they now wished they had. When asked why they
> had not reported the incident, 67% said that they were worried they would not be supported
> by their trust's management, 48% were worried they would not be supported by their col-
> leagues, and 49% feared the effect that raising concerns might have on their career.

In his inquiry into poor patient care at Mid-Staffordshire Hospital—thought to have led to between 400–1,200 unnecessary patient deaths[155]—Robert Francis QC expressed concern that
healthcare professionals who had tried to raise concerns about practices within the hospital
had been discouraged from doing so.

Robert Francis QC[156]

> A study of the experiences of those involved in these three episodes arising out of raising
> serious concerns is not encouraging. It must not be forgotten what pressures can be applied
> to deter staff from coming forward, and how little it can take to dissuade nervous individuals
> from pursuing matters. Any failure to go the extra mile to protect and respect those who raise
> genuine concerns has to be seen against a national background, in which there are frequent
> reports of injustices being perpetrated against whistle-blowers. How many such reports are
> correct is not in point: staff locally will see in every failure to take the appropriate and ex-
> pected steps internally as reinforcement of what they read happening elsewhere.

---

[153] *Good Medical Practice* (GMC: London, 2013).
[154] 'Half of English hospital doctors fear raising concerns, finds survey' (2013) 347 British Medical
Journal f7053.
[155] Tony Delamothe, 'Repeat after me "Mid-Staffordshire"' (2010) 340 British Medical Journal 132.
[156] *Robert Francis Inquiry report into Mid-Staffordshire NHS Foundation Trust* (DH: London, 2011) para 193.

In their report on Complaints and Raising Concerns, the House of Commons Health Select Committee recommended that efforts should be made to identify and apologize to NHS staff who have suffered as a result of raising concerns.

Health Select Committee[157]

114. The failure to deal appropriately with the consequences of cases where staff have sought protection as whistleblowers has caused people to suffer detriment, such as losing their job and in some cases being unable to find similar employment. This has undermined trust in the system's ability to treat whistleblowers with fairness. This lack of confidence about the consequences of raising concerns has implications for patient safety.

115. We expect the NHS to respond in a timely, honest and open manner to patients, and we must expect the same for staff. We recommend that there should be a programme to identify whistleblowers who have suffered serious harm and whose actions are proven to have been vindicated, and provide them with an apology and practical redress.

10 THE CRIMINAL LAW

In extreme cases, if a patient's death is caused by a doctor's gross negligence, a conviction for manslaughter is possible, although, as Hannah Quirk points out, these cases are not straightforward.

Hannah Quirk[158]

White-collar crime, committed by 'a person of respectability and high social status in the course of his occupation' has long presented difficulties for the police. 'White-coat' suspects present even greater challenges—not only do they possess professional status and specialist expertise in the subject under investigation, but they usually have no malicious intention, have not acted for personal gain and often arouse sympathy. Prosecutors are aware that 'judges and juries do not like having these cases (particularly involving doctors) in front of them'... Another challenge in bringing medical manslaughter charges is that 'prosecutors, judges and juries all struggle with the ill defined concept of gross negligence.'

As Quirk indicates, it is not easy to work out when negligence should be considered gross. In *R v Adomako*, the defendant had been the anaesthetist during an eye operation, and had failed to notice that the tube from the ventilator had become disconnected. The patient suffered a cardiac arrest and died. The House of Lords held that negligence is 'gross' when it is so bad that it should be criminal.

---

[157] Health Select Committee, *Complaints and Raising Concerns*, Fourth Report of Session 2014–15.
[158] 'Sentencing White Coat Crime: The Need for Guidance in Medical Manslaughter Cases' (2013) 11 Criminal Law Review 871–88.

R v Adomako [159]

Lord Mackay

The jury will have to consider whether the extent to which the defendant's conduct departed from the proper standard of care incumbent upon him, involving as it must have done a risk of death to the patient, was such that it should be judged criminal.

It is true that to a certain extent this involves an element of circularity, but in this branch of the law I do not believe that is fatal to its being correct as a test of how far conduct must depart from accepted standards to be characterised as criminal. This is necessarily a question of degree and an attempt to specify that degree more closely is I think likely to achieve only a spurious precision. The essence of the matter, which is supremely a jury question, is whether, having regard to the risk of death involved, the conduct of the defendant was so bad in all the circumstances as to amount in their judgment to a criminal act or omission.

In *R v Sellu*,[160] the Court of Appeal held that the judge's direction to the jury—namely that they simply had to consider whether Mr Sellu's conduct 'fell below the standard "in a way that was gross or severe"'—was insufficient. According to Sir Brian Leveson P, the jury had to be 'assisted sufficiently to understand how to approach their task of identifying the line that separates even serious or very serious mistakes or lapses, from conduct which...was "truly exceptionally bad and was such a departure from that standard that it consequently amounted to being criminal"'.

To be convicted of gross negligence manslaughter, the doctor must be aware at the time that the breach of duty gives rise to 'a serious and obvious risk of death'. This question arose recently in *R v Rose*,[161] a case in which an optometrist had failed to notice abnormalities behind a child's eye which, if they had been identified would be likely to have led to earlier diagnosis of the acute hydrocephalus which was the cause of his sudden death five months later. The images which the optometrist had looked at were normal, and not, in fact, those of Vincent's eyes. At the time of breach, therefore, there was not a 'serious and obvious risk of death'.

R v Rose [162]

Sir Brian Leveson P

[W]e conclude that, in assessing reasonable foreseeability of serious and obvious risk of death in cases of gross negligence manslaughter, it is not appropriate to take into account what the defendant would have known but for his or her breach of duty. Were the answer otherwise, this would fundamentally undermine the established legal test of foreseeability in gross negligence manslaughter which requires proof of a 'serious and obvious risk of death' at the time of breach. The implications for medical and other professions would be serious because people would be guilty of gross negligence manslaughter by reason of negligent omissions to carry out routine eye, blood and other tests which in fact would have revealed fatal conditions notwithstanding that the circumstances were such that it was not reasonably foreseeable that failure to carry out such tests would carry an obvious and serious risk of death. For these reasons, this appeal is allowed and the conviction is quashed.

---

[159] [1995] 1 AC 1.   [160] [2016] EWCA Crim 1716.
[161] [2017] EWCA Crim 1168.   [162] Ibid.

> We add that this decision does not, in any sense, condone the negligence that the jury must have found to have been established at a high level in relation to the way that Ms Rose examined Vincent and failed to identify the defect which ultimately led to his death. That serious breach of duty is a matter for her regulator; in the context of this case, however, it does not constitute the crime of gross negligence manslaughter.

In the next extracts, Karl Laird and Alexandra Mullock are critical of this decision. Laird argues that it serves to excuse cases of negligent ignorance, while Mullock suggests that it makes the test for gross negligence manslaughter closer to that of subjective recklessness.

Karl Laird[163]

> It is submitted that the Court of Appeal seems to have underappreciated the fact that the practical impact of its judgment is that the more egregious the breach of the duty of care, the less likely it is that the defendant will be found guilty. This is because the defendant may have been so negligent that he or she was not in a position to appreciate the risk of death. This, with respect, is a surprising state of affairs ...
>
> There is no principled distinction between the case of the optometrist who conducts an internal investigation negligently and the optometrist who is so negligent that he or she does not even attempt an internal investigation. If anything, the latter seems more culpable than the former. For this reason, it is irrational that he or she is at less risk of being held criminally liable.

Alexandra Mullock[164]

> A further interesting dimension of the court's rationale in *Rose* relates to their concern over possible policy implications; that if the conviction in *Rose* was upheld, a failure to undertake a significant range of medical tests could incur widespread liability for GNM [gross negligence manslaughter]. Respectfully, however, this potential might have been over-estimated and we might also question whether weakening the obligation to undertake important, potentially life-saving tests is conducive to greater patient safety ... Essentially *Rose* has shifted the test from an objectively assessed standard of gross negligence to a threshold that requires the defendant to knowingly take a risk with the victim's life. This approach is more akin to subjective recklessness than gross negligence.

It has been suggested that the vagueness, circularity, and possible subjectivity of the need to establish that what the defendant did was 'so bad as to be criminal', or 'truly exceptionally bad', has the potential to operate unfairly. Moreover, because there can only be a prosecution if the patient dies as a result of the gross negligence, it will fail to capture a doctor who has behaved 'truly exceptionally badly', but where fortuitously, or as a result of the skill and dedication of

---

[163] '*R v Rose*' (2018) Criminal Law Review 76–81.
[164] 'Gross Negligence (Medical) Manslaughter and the Puzzling Implications of Negligent Ignorance: *Rose v R* [2017] EWCA Crim 1168' (2018) 26 Medical Law Review 346–56.

other doctors,[165] the patient did not die. Given that a truly exceptionally bad doctor has to also be unlucky in order to face prosecution, this may weaken any deterrent effect of the threat of criminal sanctions. As Margaret Brazier and Amel Aghrani put it: 'Any deterrent effect of the criminal law would be much greater if it embraced gross negligence causing serious injury and not only fatal errors'.[166]

In the next extract, Oliver Quick draws upon his interviews with Crown Prosecutors to argue not that gross negligence should be extended, but rather that gross negligence manslaughter should be abolished.

Oliver Quick[167]

[S]everal reasons for principle and practice point to its abolition. First, the offence is too broad for prosecutorial judgment to be consistently applied, and this translates into particular harshness for those operating in error-ridden activities who are exposed to risk of prosecution by virtue of their socially vital work, and often at the mercy of moral luck. An analysis of the interview responses suggests that no meaningful hierarchy of seriousness is adopted in relation to classifying errors as gross. Respondents struggled to pin down their understanding of the term gross, often initially relying on gut instinct . . .

The statistics show that a disproportionate number of non-white practitioners figure in medical manslaughter prosecutions. This is a troubling finding and one that may be understood with reference to a number of sociological explanations, such as the training and language skills of overseas-trained practitioners, as well as their ability to gain employment and superior supervision in better performing hospitals. The high number may also be related to racist attitudes that creep into the decisions to complain about and consider investigating individuals in the first place.

More recently, Quick has advocated replacing gross negligence manslaughter with an offence based on subjective recklessness: 'where a doctor has special knowledge that certain procedures carry with them certain risks, and fails to investigate those risks without justification, criminal responsibility can be properly attributed on the basis of recklessness'.[168]

Gross negligence manslaughter cases are unusual. Since 2013, 15 healthcare professionals have been prosecuted in relation to the deaths of nine patients, resulting in six convictions. More doctors face investigation over allegations of gross negligence manslaughter: over the same period, the CPS was involved in 151 cases of suspected gross negligence manslaughter. As well as causing anxiety among doctors, these cases are also distressing for bereaved relatives, because the police investigation will often delay the internal investigation into the circumstances of a patient's death.

The most high-profile conviction for gross negligence manslaughter in recent years has been the *Bawa-Garba* case, and its aftermath, in which the General Medical Council appealed against the decision of the Medical Practitioners Tribunal that Dr Bawa-Garba, whose fitness

---

[165] *Kay v Ayrshire and Arran Health Board* [1987] 2 All ER 888.

[166] Margaret Brazier and Amel Alghrani, 'Fatal medical malpractice and criminal liability' (2009) 25 Journal of Professional Negligence 51–67.

[167] 'Prosecuting "Gross" Medical Negligence: Manslaughter, Discretion and the Crown Prosecution Service' (2006) 33 Journal of Law and Society 421–50, 449.

[168] 'Medicine, Mistakes and Manslaughter: A Criminal Combination?' (2010) 69 Cambridge Law Journal 186–203.

to practise had been found to be impaired on the grounds of her conviction for gross negligence manslaughter, should be suspended from practice for one year, rather than erased from the register.

The reason this case attracted attention was that Dr Bawa-Garba had worked for 13 hours without a break. The Tribunal had taken these systemic failings into account, as well as evidence that Dr Bawa-Garba had otherwise been an excellent doctor, who did not pose a risk to patients. Although the High Court agreed with the GMC that the only appropriate sanction following a conviction for gross negligence manslaughter was erasure from the register, the Court of Appeal overturned this decision and restored the Tribunal's decision.

Bawa-Garba v General Medical Council[169]

Lord Burnett, Sir Terence Etherton MR and Rafferty LJ

The task of the jury was to decide on the guilt or absence of guilt of Dr Bawa-Garba having regard to her past conduct. The task of the Tribunal, looking to the future, was to decide what sanction would most appropriately meet the statutory objective of protecting the public pursuant to the over-arching objectives in section 1(1A) and 1(B) of the Medical Act 1983, namely to protect, promote and maintain the health, safety and well-being of the public, to promote and maintain public confidence in the medical profession, and to promote and maintain proper professional standards and conduct for members of the profession …

[D]ifferent degrees of culpability are capable of satisfying the requirements of gross negligence manslaughter, some failings being more serious or even substantially more serious than others, even though they all constitute severe or gross negligence. That is reflected in the different sentences available for a conviction for the offence of gross negligence manslaughter. In the present case the sentence passed by Nicol J of two years imprisonment suspended for two years was a conspicuously light sentence …

The Tribunal was just as much entitled to take into account, in determining the appropriate sanction, systemic failings on the part of the Trust, as part of the context for Jack's tragic death and Dr Bawa-Garba's role in it, as well as matters of personal mitigation, as Nicol J was entitled to do in determining the appropriate sentence for her crime …

Undoubtedly, there are some cases where the facts are such that the most severe sanction, erasure, is the only proper and reasonable sanction. This is not one of them. Once it is understood that it was permissible for the Tribunal to take into account the full context of Jack's death, including the range of persons bearing responsibility for that tragedy and the systemic failings of the Trust … , and that the Tribunal plainly had in mind its overriding obligation to protect the public for the future … , it is impossible to say that the suspension sanction imposed by the Tribunal was not one properly open to it and that the only sanction properly and reasonably available was erasure.

Following considerable disquiet among the medical profession about the *Bawa-Garba* case, the Department of Health commissioned a panel chaired by Sir Norman Williams to carry out a rapid policy review of gross negligence manslaughter. It recommended that 'a working group should be set up to set out a clear explanatory statement of the law on gross negligence manslaughter', and that the GMC should no longer have the right to appeal against MPTS sanction decisions.

[169] [2018] EWCA CIV 1879.

Gross negligence manslaughter in healthcare: The report of a rapid policy review[170]

6.4 Healthcare professionals who meet the high threshold set for gross negligence manslaughter should be investigated and prosecuted. It is equally important that cases where there is no realistic prospect of the test being met are resolved at the earliest opportunity. This would allow bereaved families to understand as soon as possible the circumstances of their relative's death, because a police investigation can lead to the suspension of any internal investigation. It would also remove the threat to individual professionals of prosecution and allow them to continue to provide healthcare. The delays caused by drawn out investigations and failed prosecutions have a detrimental effect on patient confidence and expectations, as well as on healthcare professionals and the health service . . .

7.2. A common understanding of the law and the high level at which the bar for gross negligence manslaughter is set should provide reassurance to healthcare professionals that the offence only arises in the most serious cases of 'truly exceptionally bad' breaches of a duty of care that result in death . . .

7.3. The panel believes that a shared understanding of gross negligence manslaughter would result in only those cases where there is a realistic prospect of prosecution being reported to the CPS. It would also help families to understand why a prosecution might, or might not, be appropriate in specific cases . . .

11.16. It is the view of the panel that the decision to give the GMC an appeal right has had significant unwelcome and unintended consequences. The panel was concerned about the level of fear and mistrust that the medical community reported about the GMC. This is heightened by the right of appeal against MPTS decisions, which has undermined doctors' trust in the GMC and has had a significant impact on their ability and willingness to engage with the regulator. This is deterring reflection and learning from errors to the detriment of patient safety.

At the same time, the GMC announced that it would conduct a review of how it handles cases involving gross negligence manslaughter, including 'Whether sufficient regard is taken into all the circumstances in which the medical practitioner found themselves at the time of the fatality, such as system pressures, errors or failures'. This review will be published in 2019.

Concerns have been expressed that 'it is easier to convict an individual doctor for gross negligence manslaughter than it is to effect similar accountability on an organisation'.[171] So while it is now possible to prosecute NHS bodies for their failings under the Corporate Manslaughter and Homicide Act 2007, there have been no convictions. The first unsuccessful prosecution took place in 2015, following the death of Frances Cappuccini due to complications after a successful caesarean section. In addition to prosecuting one of the anaesthetists involved in her care for gross negligence manslaughter (the other anaesthetist had since left the country), the Trust was also prosecuted for the failures of senior management in the appointment, appraisal and supervision of the anaesthetists.[172] Coulson J found that there was no case to answer and ordered the jury to acquit both defendants.

Invoking the cases of Dr Ubani, who was exhausted, stressed, and working as a locum on his first shift in England, and who accidentally administered ten times the recommended dose of diamorphine to a patient, and Dr Ramnath who, 'in the pressure cooker' atmosphere of a busy intensive care unit, had injected her patient with a lethal injection of adrenalin, Margaret

[170] DHSC, 2018.
[171] Ash Samanta and Jo Samanta, 'Gross negligence manslaughter and doctors: ethical concerns following the case of Dr Bawa-Garba' (2019) 45 Journal of Medical Ethics, 10–14.
[172] *R v Cornish and another* [2015] EWHC 2967 (QB).

Brazier and Amel Alghrani suggest that corporate manslaughter might sometimes be more appropriate than prosecution of the incompetent doctor.

Margaret Brazier and Amel Alghrani[173]

There is no evidence that either Dr Ubani or Dr Ramnath, or the many other doctors and nurses convicted of manslaughter, acted with any intent to cause harm. These two high pro-file cases help us by their very facts. At first sight both errors were crass. Establishing liability in tort for clinical negligence would be simple, and the degree of negligence is high on any scale of poor practice. Yet other factors played a key part in the events that ended with a patient's death and criminal convictions for the doctors. Any 'system' that permitted an ex-hausted doctor with poor English and a lack of familiarity with medical practice in the UK to treat patients looks defective. A hospital that failed to notice the stress affecting Dr Ramnath, failed in its duty to her and the patient. And so many would ask should it be the relevant NHS Trusts that face prosecution for corporate manslaughter?

Although corporate manslaughter has not so far been used successfully against the NHS, there have been convictions under the Health and Safety at Work Act 1974. In *R v Southampton University Hospital Trust*,[174] the Trust pleaded guilty to failing to discharge the duty imposed on it by the Health and Safety at Work Act to people other than employees. This case followed the successful prosecution of two junior doctors in *R v Misra*.[175] In addition to the doctors' own gross negligence, there had also been serious failures in their supervision. Initially, the Trust was fined £100,000, but this was reduced on appeal to £40,000, in part to reflect the fact that rapid steps had been taken to put proper systems in place after these failures had been identified.

Existing criminal offences were of little use in tackling some of the scandalously poor care Robert Francis QC had found at Mid-Staffordshire NHS Foundation Trust.

Robert Francis QC[176]

The first inquiry heard harrowing personal stories from patients and patients' families about the appalling care received at the Trust. On many occasions, the accounts received related to basic elements of care and the quality of the patient experience. These included cases where:

- Patients were left in excrement in soiled bed clothes for lengthy periods.
- Assistance was not provided with feeding for patients who could not eat without help.
- Water was left out of reach.
- In spite of persistent requests for help, patients were not assisted in their toileting.
- Wards and toilet facilities were left in a filthy condition.
- Privacy and dignity, even in death, were denied.
- Triage in A&E was undertaken by untrained staff.
- Staff treated patients and those close to them with what appeared to be callous indifference.

---

[173] Margaret Brazier and Amel Alghrani, 'Fatal medical malpractice and criminal liability' (2009) 25 Journal of Professional Negligence 51–67.
[174] [2006] EWCA Crim 2971.   [175] [2004] EWCA Crim 2375.
[176] *Robert Francis Inquiry report into Mid-Staffordshire NHS Foundation Trust* (DH: London, 2013).

Amel Alghrani et al explain why an offence of wilful neglect might be of more practical use than gross negligence.

Amel Alghrani et al[177]

Wilful neglect is a conduct crime rather than a result crime (meaning that it need not be shown that tangible injury was caused). The chance element that arises with gross negligence manslaughter, where liability depends on there being a provable death, is absent. It would mean that there would not be the current discrepancy whereby a doctor who finds himself in a difficult situation makes a badly negligent error may find himself facing a manslaughter charge, yet a professional who persistently neglects a patient with no justification or excuse need not fear the criminal law.

A criminal offence of wilful neglect by care workers (which includes anyone who provides health care) and care providers was introduced by the Criminal Justice and Courts Act 2015.

Criminal Justice and Courts Act 2015 sections 20 and 21

20 Ill-treatment or wilful neglect: care worker offence

(1) It is an offence for an individual who has the care of another individual by virtue of being a care worker to ill-treat or wilfully to neglect that individual.

(2) An individual guilty of an offence under this section is liable—

(a) on conviction on indictment, to imprisonment for a term not exceeding 5 years or a fine (or both);

(b) on summary conviction, to imprisonment for a term not exceeding 12 months or a fine (or both).

21 Ill-treatment or wilful neglect: care provider offence

(1) A care provider commits an offence if—

(a) an individual who has the care of another individual by virtue of being part of the care provider's arrangements ill-treats or wilfully neglects that individual,

(b) the care provider's activities are managed or organised in a way which amounts to a gross breach of a relevant duty of care owed by the care provider to the individual who is ill-treated or neglected, and

(c) in the absence of the breach, the ill-treatment or wilful neglect would not have occurred or would have been less likely to occur.

As Karen Yeung and Jeremy Horder explain, the point of creating a criminal offence of wilful neglect is not principally to regulate the practice of medicine, but rather to send a strong message that the mistreatment of vulnerable patients is unacceptable.

---

[177] 'Healthcare scandals in the NHS: crime and punishment' (2011) 37 Journal of Medical Ethics 230–2.

Karen Yeung and Jeremy Horder[178]

[T]he criminal law's role in this context is not to play a frontline part in deterring and coercing people into complying with proper standards of behaviour. Rather, its central function applies only to the worst kinds of unacceptable ill-treatment. When it is used against such serious wrongdoers, the criminal law carries a uniquely symbolic and expressive significance that is lacking when less draconian regulatory instruments, or civil liability, are used. A criminal conviction amounts to a public proclamation that the conduct in question is seriously wrongful and worthy of condemnation and punishment, whether or not it leads directly to a substantial improvement in healthcare quality. In light of the appalling failures of care evidenced by the Francis Report, there is no doubt that the criminal law could properly have been invoked, not primarily because it will deter such failures of care in the future, but because it is the most powerful and important social institution through which we hold to account, and express public censure of, those who have mistreated others in a wholly unacceptable and highly culpable way.

11 CONCLUSION

It is commonly said that tort law serves two purposes: compensation and deterrence. In the context of medical negligence, we have seen, first, that it does not offer an efficient compensation scheme for patients who suffer injury or damage as a result of negligent treatment and, secondly, that it does not effectively deter poor practices or encourage good ones. Worse still, not only is tort law costly and inefficient, but it may actually contribute towards poor care by inhibiting the open reporting of errors, which is the best way to ensure that they are learned from, rather than repeated.

There are also reasons to believe that the situation is likely to get worse. The financial pressure on the NHS may mean that more claims for delayed diagnosis and treatment are brought into the system, while at the same time, understaffing may make it harder for trusts to resolve complaints effectively when they are first made. As the House of Commons Public Accounts Committee explains, this has the potential to operate as a vicious circle, in which more clinical negligence actions place further pressure on scarce NHS resources, which may in turn affect the standard of care available to patients and increase further the number of claims against the NHS.

House of Commons Committee of Public Accounts[179]

Increasing financial pressures on the NHS have started to affect waiting times and the quality of care, which risks leading to even more clinical negligence claims and in turn even greater cost. Almost 40% of clinical negligence claims against trusts are related to a failure or delay to

---

[178] 'How can the criminal law support the provision of quality in healthcare?' (2014) 23 British Medical Journal Quality & Safety 519–24.

[179] House of Commons Committee of Public Accounts, *Managing the costs of clinical negligence in hospital trusts*, Fifth Report of Session 2017–19.

diagnose or treat a patient. Many trusts face financial challenges and ever-rising demand, including delivering stretching efficiency savings. The Care Quality Commission, in its 2016–17 State of Care Report, highlighted that future quality of care is precarious as the system struggles with complex demand, access and cost pressures. The increasing financial pressure on trusts, has already started affecting standards of care. In particular, more and more patients are waiting longer for their treatments, which could increase the risk of future clinical negligence claims. NHS staff are working under huge pressure which may also affect trusts' ability to deal effectively with complaints. Spending on clinical negligence is forecast to increase from 1.8% of trusts income in 2015–16 to 4% by 2020–21, further reducing the amount of money available for patient care …

The government has been slow and complacent in its response to the rising costs of clinical negligence. This Committee has raised concerns about the rising costs of clinical negligence claims on numerous occasions, going back to at least 2002, but costs have continued to rise. Annual spending is expected to double by 2020–21 to £3.2 billion compared with £1.6 billion in 2016–17, and current action proposed is unlikely to stop this growth.

FURTHER READING

Ahuja, Jyoti, 'Liability for Psychological and Psychiatric Harm: The Road to Recovery' (2015) 23 Medical Law Review 27–52.

Alghrani, Amel et al, 'Healthcare scandals in the NHS: crime and punishment' (2011) 37 Journal of Medical Ethics 230–2.

Burrows, Andrew S and Burrows, John H, 'A Shocking Requirement in the Law on Negligence Liability for Psychiatric Illness: *Liverpool Women's Hospital NHS Foundation Trust v Ronayne* [2015] EWCA Civ 588' (2016) 24 Medical Law Review 278.

Chamberlain, John Martyn, 'Malpractice, Criminality, and Medical Regulation: Reforming the Role of the GMC in Fitness to Practise Panels' (2017) 25 Medical Law Review 1–22.

Mullock, Alexandra, 'Gross Negligence (Medical) Manslaughter and the Puzzling Implications of Negligent Ignorance: *Rose v R* [2017] EWCA Crim 1168' (2018) 26 Medical Law Review 346–56.

Quick, Oliver, 'Medicine, Mistakes and Manslaughter: A Criminal Combination?' (2010) 69 Cambridge Law Journal 186–203.

Yeung, Karen and Horder, Jeremy, 'How can the criminal law support the provision of quality in healthcare?' (2014) 23 British Medical Journal Quality & Safety 519–24.

4

INFORMED CONSENT

CENTRAL ISSUES

1. Before providing medical treatment to an adult with capacity, a doctor should obtain her informed consent.

2. A failure to inform the patient 'in broad terms' about the medical treatment she is about to receive could lead to an action in battery.

3. More commonly, if a patient wants to argue that she was not properly informed, she might bring an action in negligence, and claim that the doctor had breached her duty of care.

4. The doctor's duty is to inform patients about material risks, and since the UK Supreme Court judgment in *Montgomery v Lanarkshire,* the test for materiality is whether a reasonable person in the patient's position would be likely to attach significance to the risk, or the doctor should reasonably be aware that the particular patient would be likely to attach significance to it.

5. Causation raises particular difficulties in 'informed consent' cases. This is because the patient has to prove that, if she had been told about the risk which has now materialized, she would have refused to undergo the treatment which caused her injury. This is a speculative inquiry, in which the patient has the benefit of hindsight.

1 INTRODUCTION

One of the first principles of medical law is that patients with capacity must give consent to their medical treatment. Touching a person without her consent—however benevolently—is prima facie unlawful. For consent to be valid, it must be given voluntarily, by someone who has the capacity to consent, and who understands what the treatment involves. We deal with capacity and voluntariness in the next chapter. Here we are concerned with the question of how much information must be provided to patients before they consent to medical treatment.

First, we consider the ethical justifications for informing patients about their medical treatment. Next we look at how the law protects patients' interests in information disclosure, through the torts of battery and negligence, before exploring alternatives to the law of tort.

2 WHY INFORM PATIENTS?

In the past, doctors were under no duty at all to provide patients with information about their prognosis, or the advantages and disadvantages of different treatments. On the contrary, the assumption was that a doctor would exercise his customary care and skill in deciding what treatment was best for his patient. The Hippocratic oath assumes that treatment decisions are for the doctor alone:

> I swear by Apollo and Aesculapius that I will follow that system of regimen which according to my ability and judgment I consider for the benefit of my patients.[1]

Indeed, Hippocrates even enjoined physicians to take positive steps to conceal information from their patients:

> Perform [your duties] calmly and adroitly, concealing most things from the patient while you are attending to him ... turning his attention away from what is being done to him; ... revealing nothing of the patient's future or present condition.[2]

Until relatively recently, it was thought that informing patients about a poor prognosis, worrying side effects, or the availability of alternative treatments would be likely to cause distress and confusion. Keeping patients in ignorance, and maintaining their trust and hope was especially important given that most treatments were ineffective, and any improvements resulted largely from the placebo effect. Silence and deception were intended to benefit patients by maintaining their belief in the possibility of a cure.

Occasionally providing information was judged to be in a patient's best interests: when surgical procedures were carried out without anaesthesia, for example, it was important for patients to prepare themselves for the infliction of excruciating pain. In the 1767 case *Slater v Baker and Stapleton*,[3] a surgeon had, without the patient's consent, refractured his leg and placed it in an experimental apparatus to stretch and strengthen it during healing. The failure to seek consent before refracturing a patient's leg amounted to professional misconduct, in part because 'It is reasonable that a patient should be told what is about to be done to him, that he may take courage and put himself in such a situation as to enable him to undergo the operation.'

It was not until the twentieth century that patients were thought to be in need of information in order to exercise control over their treatment. In part, this was a result of the growing importance of the principle of patient autonomy. It was also thought, as Michael Jones explains, that giving patients information might help to redress the imbalance of knowledge and power within the doctor–patient relationship.

Michael Jones[4]

> It is a trite observation that the doctor–patient relationship involves a major imbalance of power, some of which stems from social norms—patients expect to be at a disadvantage,

---

[1] Hippocrates, 'Oath of Hippocrates' in *1 Hippocrates* 299–301 (trans WHS Jones) (Heinemann: London, 1962).
[2] Hippocrates, *Decorum* (trans W Jones) (Harvard UP: Cambridge, MA, 1967) 267.
[3] 2 Wils KB 359, 95 ER 850 (1767).
[4] 'Informed Consent and Other Fairy Stories' (1999) 7 Medical Law Review 103–34.

because of their lack of knowledge, their lack of training, and sometimes because we want to believe desperately that the doctor is all knowing and all powerful and therefore will definitely make the correct diagnosis and provide a complete cure. Although some of this disparity is inherent in most professional–client relationships those relationships are not generally conducted when the client is ill (and on occasion when the client is at the disadvantage of being naked, apart from a flimsy robe). Part of the imbalance between doctor and patient is due to the patient's lack of information, and, on one view, it is the function of the law to redress the imbalance by providing patients with the 'right' to be given that information, or perhaps more accurately imposing a duty on doctors to provide it.

While it is true that there is an information imbalance in the doctor–patient relationship, doctors are not always omniscient and all-powerful. In addition to the problem of false positives and false negatives, and the inevitability of human error, medical knowledge itself is often uncertain and tentative. Telling patients the truth may sometimes involve the doctor explaining what is not known, and what is uncertain.

There may be more than one treatment option, and since few treatments have no risks or side effects, it will often be necessary to weigh the advantages and disadvantages of different interventions, and of doing nothing. Doctors' special skill may enable them to diagnose a patient's condition and to carry out medical procedures, but it does not enable them to decide which treatment best accommodates the patient's own priorities. On the contrary, the patient is the expert when the question is how tolerable she would find a particular side effect. Following a diagnosis of breast cancer, for example, if there is a choice between chemotherapy and mastectomy, this is best made by the patient, in the light of her doctor's advice about success rates and adverse consequences.

Harry Lesser[5]

[T]here is not always a medically best course of action, for two reasons. One is that medicine has at least three aims—to prolong life, to remove obstacles to a person's physical and mental functioning and to relieve suffering. Very often these three all come together ... But this is not always so; if, for example, the choice is to relieve pain at the cost of leaving patients feeling 'woozy' and confused, or to help them to be mentally alert at the cost of appreciable physical pain, then there is no 'better' course of action, even medically, except in terms of the individual patient's preference, whichever it may be: it is honourable to choose alertness and the price of physical suffering, but in no way dishonourable to choose the reverse ...

[D]octors' expertise enables them to know the possible consequences of various alternatives and to have some idea of their likelihood; but there is still no right answer to the question which alternative is best, which risks are worth taking and which are not, except in terms of what the patient chooses.

The Hippocratic principle that the doctor decides which treatment the patient receives has thus been replaced by a *partnership* model of decision-making, in which both the doctor and the patient have specialist knowledge which must be shared in order that the patient can make

---

[5] 'The Patient's Right to Information' in Margaret Brazier and Mary Lobjoit (eds), *Protecting the Vulnerable: Autonomy and Consent in Health Care* (Routledge: London, 1991) 150–60.

the best possible decision *for herself*. The doctor is a source of information and expert advice, but the ultimate decision is for the patient.

Applying some of the concepts explored in Chapter 1, there are both deontological and consequentialist justifications for the twin elements of informed consent: (a) to seek the patient's consent prior to treatment; and (b) to ensure that the patient has sufficient information about the proposed treatment. The deontological justification is respect for patient self-determination and bodily autonomy: the patient has the right to decide what is done to her body, and in order to do so, she needs information about the proposed treatment.

The consequentialist justification for informed consent would instead emphasize the beneficial consequences that flow from involving patients in decisions about their care. For example, there might be better outcomes from treatment regimes which patients have chosen, and with which they are more likely to comply.

While giving patients information is important, several criticisms might be made of the concept of 'informed consent'. First, the expression 'informed consent' is both ambiguous and misleading. It is not entirely clear whether the word 'informed' refers to the doctor's conduct (has she informed the patient?) or the patient's state of mind (is the patient informed?). Has consent been 'informed' if information has been provided, regardless of whether the patient has in fact read, listened to, or understood anything? Or must the consent itself have been 'informed' by the patient's consideration of all relevant information?

The rather confusing implication of the phrase 'informed consent' is that consent is either informed or uninformed, when in fact this is not a binary question, and instead the important issue is working out *how much* information patients need in order to be adequately—though probably not fully—informed. PDG Skegg has suggested that:

> It is regrettable, although entirely understandable, that it was not the expression 'sufficiently informed consent' which became so common. This would have alerted users to the fact that there is an issue of how informed it is necessary to be, in the context and for the purpose in question.[6]

In short, to say that consent should be 'informed' does not tell us how much information should be provided.

Presenting patients with lengthy and complex consent forms may inhibit rather than promote genuine communication between doctors and their patients. There is, for example, some evidence that patients' understanding of consent forms is inversely related to their length. To take a mundane example, we all know that the longer the 'terms and conditions' on a website, the more likely we are to click that we have read them when we have not. Information overload could also prompt patients to attach disproportionate importance to a very remote risk, and, as a result, refuse treatment that is overwhelmingly likely to be both safe and successful.

Giving patients detailed information about every risk associated with a treatment, and ensuring that they have understood it, would take time, and therefore cost money. If doctors had to disclose everything, scarce NHS resources might be diverted to unnecessarily lengthy and alarming consent procedures.

In practice, the process of obtaining patient consent for invasive treatments and diagnostic procedures is commonly limited to one or two encounters before the procedure takes place,

---

[6] 'English Medical Law and "Informed Consent": An Antipodean Assessment and Alternative' (1999) 7 Medical Law Review 135–65.

when the doctor offers the patient information about its risks and benefits, before asking the patient to sign a consent form. This model of decision-making may be unsatisfactory for two reasons.

First, it sits uneasily with the reality of medical treatment, which will rarely involve one single decision, but rather a series of decisions taken as more information becomes available. Consent forms exacerbate the false perception that consent is a one-off event, rather than a process that takes place over time. A doctor's duty to communicate effectively with her patients may be especially important *during* treatment, and should not be confined to some brief bureaucratic ritual when the patient is first admitted to hospital. In their interviews with healthcare professionals, Rob Heywood et al found that many of them perceived the consent form to have been driven by lawyers, and believed that it hampered rather than enhanced informed decision-making.

Rob Heywood et al[7]

[T]he medical practitioners within the study seem to suggest the process has become too formalised and bureaucratic. They perceive the most important basis for consent as being an ethical imperative grounded in the wishes and needs of the patient, which is about more than obtaining a signature on a form. They suggest there is a danger that lengthy and elaborate forms detract from the consent process itself, a process which should discuss the treatment, its risks and benefits.

Concerns were raised over problems with bureaucracy and 'red-tape' in the consent process. The feeling was that this is driven by 'the law'. The contention is grounded in the fact that both doctors and patients involved in the consent process may be happy to proceed with treatment based on the fact that there is a signature on a form. A signature is certainly not conclusive evidence that any discussion whatsoever has taken place between the doctor and the patient about the proposed procedure.

Secondly, although patients are free to withdraw their consent at any point, some may wrongly believe that signing a consent form binds them to its contents. In fact, there is no need for consent to medical treatment to be in writing (aside from specific statutory exceptions, contained in the Mental Health Act 1983 and the Human Fertilisation and Embryology Act 1990). As the Department of Health's guidance makes clear:

The validity of consent does not depend on the form in which it is given. Written consent merely serves as evidence of consent: if the elements of voluntariness, appropriate information and capacity have not been satisfied, a signature on a form will not make the consent valid.[8]

In other contexts, a person who signs a document will usually have made a binding commitment to fulfil their side of the bargain, so it is unsurprising that many patients do not understand that their right to refuse treatment persists throughout their care.

---

[7] Rob Heywood et al, 'Informed Consent in Hospital Practice: Health Professionals' Perspectives & Legal Reflections' (2010) 18 Medical Law Review 152–84.

[8] Department of Health, *Reference Guide to Consent for Examination or Treatment* 2nd edition (DH: London, 2009).

In their small empirical study of patients' perceptions of the consent process, Rob Heywood et al discovered that patients valued openness and good communication, and thought that this helped people to cope with bad news and to prepare themselves for treatment and its aftermath. They did not think this had anything to do with the consent process, however, which they instead regarded as a non-optional precondition for access to medical treatment.

Rob Heywood, Ann Macaskill, and Kevin Williams[9]

Few patients mentioned or even implied that consent was about their right to self-determination. Instead it seems to be viewed as a means to an end; something that is *necessary* and that they have to do in order to get to the next stage, treatment . . .

Despite patients looking favourably on openness and disclosure, there is evidence to suggest that any information provided is not used in the decision-making process and that patients make their decision long before they reach the 'consenting stage'. In other words, the patients in this study failed to make the link between the actual signing of the consent form and the information that was given to them in order that they could make an informed choice. The legal rules governing consent and information disclosure attempt to protect patient autonomy and redress the imbalance of power in the doctor–patient relationship. However, the patients in this study were not predominantly concerned with these factors, or at least they did not perceive them as the most important basis for disclosure. They failed to make the link between *information disclosure* and the *consent process* and did not relate consent to any notions of self-determination. Instead the importance they attached to pre-operative information was the way in which it enhanced coping mechanisms and the recovery process.

In their survey of 732 patients who had undergone obstetric surgery within the previous month, Andrea Akkad et al found similar levels of confusion about the purpose of the consent forms that they had signed.

Andrea Akkad et al[10]

[M]ost participants (646, 88%) believed it was a legal requisite to sign a consent form before surgery. A fifth (20%) did not know whether they could change their mind after they had signed the form, and 118 (16%) incorrectly thought that signing a consent form removed their right to compensation . . . One in 10 patients reported that they did not know what they agreed to when they signed the consent form . . . Almost half of all participants (46%) believed that the main function of signing the consent form was to protect the hospital from litigation, and two thirds (68%) thought it gave doctors control over what happened . . .

Many patients did not see written consent as functioning primarily in their interests nor as a way of making their wishes known. As suggested in previous work, many thought the primary function of the form was to protect the hospital.

[9] 'Patient perceptions of the consent process: qualitative inquiry and legal reflection' (2008) 24 Journal of Professional Negligence 104–21.

[10] 'Patients' perceptions of written consent: questionnaire study' (2006) 333 British Medical Journal 528.

Misunderstandings about the consent process are especially common in preventative screening programmes. When invited to participate in screening—such as triennial cervical smear tests or annual mammograms for women over the age of 50—many people think that they have been 'called in' for testing, rather than being asked if they wish to be screened. It is often assumed that screening is self-evidently beneficial, and that there is no need to weigh up its risks and benefits. While people appreciate being offered a leaflet that explains what is going to happen, they may not understand that its purpose is to enable them to decide whether they wish to be screened.[11]

This may be exacerbated by the way in which information is provided. In their analysis of the leaflets sent to UK patients invited to take part in routine breast screening Gøtzsche et al found that they overemphasized the benefits of screening and downplayed the existence of significant risks.

Peter C Gøtzsche et al[12]

No mention is made of the major harm of screening—that is, unnecessary treatment of harmless lesions that would not have been identified without screening … It is in violation of guidelines and laws for informed consent not to mention this common harm, especially when screening is aimed at healthy people … Another harm is false positive diagnoses… We now know that the psychosocial strain of a false alarm can be severe and may continue after women are declared free from cancer … A third harm is caused by radiotherapy of overdiagnosed women.

If 2000 women are screened regularly for 10 years, one will benefit from the screening, as she will avoid dying from breast cancer. At the same time, 10 healthy women will, as a consequence, become cancer patients and will be treated unnecessarily. These women will have either a part of their breast or the whole breast removed, and they will often receive radiotherapy and sometimes chemotherapy. Furthermore, about 200 healthy women will experience a false alarm. The psychological strain until one knows whether it was cancer, and even afterwards, can be severe.

It is certainly true that simply providing patients with information does not ensure that they have understood it. Not only is risk inherently difficult to understand, but, as Onora O'Neill points out, illness may undermine an individual's capacity to digest information.

Onora O'Neill[13]

A person who is ill or injured is highly vulnerable to others, and highly dependent on their action and competence. Robust conceptions of autonomy may seem a burden and even unachievable for patients; mere choosing may be hard enough. And, in fact, the choices that patients are required to make are typically quite limited. It is not as if doctors offer patients a smorgasbord of possible treatments and interventions, a variegated menu of care and cure. Typically a diagnosis is followed with an indication of prognosis and suggestions for treatment to be undertaken. Patients are typically asked to choose from a smallish menu—often a menu

---

[11] Wenche Osterlie et al, 'Challenges of informed choice in organised screening' (2008) 34 Journal of Medical Ethics e5.

[12] 'Breast screening: the facts—or maybe not' (2009) 338 British Medical Journal b86.

[13] *Autonomy and Trust in Bioethics* (CUP: Cambridge, 2002) 38–9.

of one item—that others have composed and described in simplified terms. This may suit us well when ill, but it is a far cry from any demanding exercise of individual autonomy.

Arthur Caplan goes further and suggests that we need robust assistance in order to make good decisions for ourselves, especially when we are ill and tired.

Arthur L Caplan[14]

Autonomy often does not work in healthcare. Our brains are not designed to let us act upon it ... [W]e bring too much affect and magical thinking along with us as subject or patient; and our basic memory and perceptual skills fail us when the topic is who is going to stick a needle in our arm or give us a brand new pill in our life-and-death fight against cancer ...

There is nothing wrong with healthcare providers strongly suggesting a course of care, raising their voice so that you hear their message about health promoting activities, or telling you what they would do if it was their mother in that bed.

Strongly suggesting a course of prevention, care or palliation in the face of a patient's expression of a different choice may be paternalistic but it is a projection of what is good based not upon the doctor's values but upon expertise and experience.

3 LEGAL PROTECTION FOR PATIENTS' INTERESTS IN INFORMATION DISCLOSURE

We now turn to consider what legal claim is appropriate when consent has not been properly informed. Does a lack of adequate information vitiate the patient's consent altogether, in which case the claim would be for unlawful touching or battery? Or is the provision of information part of the doctor's ordinary duty of care, meaning that a failure to offer adequate information might ground an action in negligence? In English law, the duty to obtain the patient's consent prior to treatment is protected by the tort of battery, while the duty to ensure that the patient has been given enough information (whatever that might mean) is treated as an aspect of the doctor's ordinary duty of care.

An action in battery will be successful only if the patient did not consent to the medical treatment that she received. Given that obtaining consent prior to treatment is routine, it would be most unusual for a patient not to be told what is going to happen to her, and actions in battery are rare. The courts have been reluctant to find that a failure to give the patient information about risks or alternatives invalidates the patient's consent, which means that most cases involving allegations of inadequate disclosure are brought in negligence.

For an action in negligence to be possible, damage must have been caused by the doctor's breach of duty. Patients who have been inadequately informed prior to treatment can bring an action in negligence only if they happen to have suffered injury as a result of the doctor's failure to disclose a piece of information. As we see later, this means that tort law covers a small subset of cases of inadequate disclosure.

---

[14] 'Why autonomy needs help' (2014) 40 Journal of Medical Ethics 301–2.

(a) BATTERY

Trespass to the person can be both a tort (battery) and a crime (assault). The patient's consent will absolve a medical practitioner from liability in battery for unlawful touching as long as the consent is 'real'; and to be real, the patient must have been told what the doctor is planning to do. If a patient consented to a completely different procedure, an action in battery is possible. If, for example, a patient consented to the removal of her appendix, but the doctor removed her womb as well, then because she did not consent to a hysterectomy, she could bring an action in battery, as well as in negligence.

Trespass to the person can also be a criminal offence. In *R v Tabassum*,[15] T—who had no medical qualifications at all—was convicted of indecent assault after he persuaded several women to consent to him showing them how to carry out breast self-examination. Each complainant said they had consented only because they thought that T was medically qualified. The Court of Appeal upheld his conviction on the grounds that 'consent was given because they mistakenly believed that the defendant was medically qualified … and that, in consequence, the touching was for a medical purpose. As this was not so, there was no true consent'.

In contrast, in *R v Richardson*,[16] a dentist continued to treat her patients after her registration had been suspended. Her patients were not mistaken as to her identity, because she had treated them before, but they wrongly assumed she was entitled to practise dentistry. According to the Court of Appeal, 'either there is consent to actions on the part of a person in the mistaken belief that he or they are other than they truly are, in which case it is assault or, short of this, there is no assault'. Because 'the complainants were fully aware of the identity of the appellant', the Court of Appeal quashed her conviction.

The advantage of an action in battery is that it is not necessary to establish that any physical harm has been caused by the inadequate disclosure. As we see later, causation represents an obstacle to many claimants' actions in negligence because of the need to prove that proper disclosure would have prompted the patient to reject the treatment. Instead, following a successful action in battery, a patient can be compensated for the dignitary harm of being treated without valid consent.

Patients who are inadequately informed about an alternative treatment option will be able to recover in negligence only if the treatment that they received goes wrong and they suffer physical injury as a result. Yet the patient's right to make an informed choice about which therapeutic option is best for them may have been infringed even if their treatment does not cause them physical injury.

It is no defence to a charge of battery that the doctor was acting in the best interests of her patient, or that she exercised all reasonable care and skill. Evidence of accepted medical practice is also irrelevant: if the failure to provide information to a patient vitiates her consent, the fact that the defendant can point to other doctors who would have acted in the same way will not absolve her of responsibility. There could also be no 'therapeutic exception' (discussed later) if the cause of action is battery rather than negligence. If certain information is necessary for consent to be real, the doctor cannot claim exemption from the need to disclose it because disclosure might cause the patient serious distress or anxiety.

There has been little enthusiasm on the part of the judiciary for using the tort of battery in order to protect patients' interests in information disclosure, however. Provided that the patient agreed to the procedure that was in fact carried out, her consent will be effective and there could be no action in battery. The leading case is *Chatterton v Gerson*, in which Bristow

---

[15] [2000] 2 Cr App R 328 (CA).   [16] (1998) 43 BMLR 21 (CA).

J held that consent would be real as long as the patient had been informed 'in broad terms' about the nature of the procedure.

In order to treat Miss Chatterton's chronic pain, the defendant doctor operated to block a sensory nerve. His and Miss Chatterton's accounts of what information was provided differed. Dr Gerson said his normal practice was to explain to patients before the operation that it would result in numbness, and that it might involve temporary loss of muscle power. Miss Chatterton claimed not to have been so warned. She lost sensation in her right leg, and claimed that her consent to the operation was vitiated by Dr Gerson's failure to tell her about this risk.

Chatterton v Gerson [17]

Bristow J

In my judgment once the patient is informed in broad terms of the nature of the procedure which is intended, and gives her consent, that consent is real, and the cause of the action on which to base a claim for failure to go into risks and implications is negligence, not trespass. Of course if information is withheld in bad faith, the consent will be vitiated by fraud. Of course if by some accident, as in a case in the 1940s in the Salford Hundred Court where a boy was admitted to hospital for tonsillectomy and due to administrative error was circumcised instead, trespass would be the appropriate cause of action against the doctor, though he was as much the victim of the error as the boy. But in my judgment it would be very much against the interests of justice if actions which are really based on a failure by the doctor to perform his duty adequately to inform were pleaded in trespass.

In *The Creutzfeldt-Jakob Disease Litigation*,[18] the claimants had been treated with Human Growth Hormone (HGH), which had been extracted from pituitary glands that had been unlawfully harvested from dead bodies. They argued that they gave consent on the understanding that the drug had been prepared lawfully, and that this consent was vitiated by the fact that the pituitaries had been harvested unlawfully. May J dismissed their claim, arguing that 'a person may succeed in a claim for failure to inform or warn only if the failure alleged amounts to negligence. To frame such a claim in battery is not only deplorable but insupportable in law.'

Judicial hostility to the use of battery in medical cases may be due to the connotations of a charge of battery. A doctor who fails to tell a patient about a small risk inherent in a proposed treatment does not intend to injure her. Because a battery will also often be an assault, judges have been reluctant to criminalize by association well-meaning but misguided decisions to withhold information from patients.

In addition, battery has its limitations. Medical treatment can amount to battery only if there has been some physical contact between doctor and patient, and there are many medical decisions which do not involve touching. The prescription of medicines, for example, does not involve any physical contact, and so a patient who is inadequately informed about a drug's side effects could not bring an action in battery.

There have been a handful of successful cases, however. In *Appleton v Garrett*, a dentist had deliberately carried out extensive and wholly unnecessary dental treatment for personal

---

[17] [1981] QB 432 (QBD).   [18] [1995] 54 BMLR 1 (QBD).

financial gain, and had been struck off as a result. His intentional and fraudulent wrongdoing may have helped to persuade the court to find him liable for battery rather than negligence.

Appleton v Garrett[19]

Dyson J

The evidence undoubtedly establishes that none of these eight plaintiffs was given any information on which to base a suitably informed consent. None was told why Mr Garrett was of the view that massive restorative treatment was required, often on perfect teeth. Typically, the plaintiff went for a normal routine check-up, and was subjected to the course of treatment without any explanation at all . . .

I am quite satisfied that the failure to inform in these eight cases was not mere negligence and that Mr Garrett withheld information deliberately and in bad faith. The scale of the unnecessary treatment was so great that it must have been obvious to him that it was indeed unnecessary. The radiographs that he took before he embarked on the treatment showed in many cases that the teeth in these young plaintiffs were free from caries and were in what has been described as 'virgin condition'. Much of the treatment on these teeth was considerable in its scope and extent . . .

I conclude therefore that Mr Garrett deliberately embarked on large-scale treatment of these plaintiffs which he knew was unnecessary and that he deliberately withheld from them the information that the treatment was unnecessary because he knew that they would not have consented had they known the true position. . . I find, therefore, that none of the plaintiffs consented, at any rate to the treatment of those teeth that required no treatment, and that, at least in relation to those teeth, the tort of trespass to the person has been made out.

(b) NEGLIGENCE

Before we come to the standard 'failure to warn' negligence action, it is worth mentioning that it is possible that the failure to obtain consent at all could also amount to negligence. *Border v Lewisham and Greenwich NHS Trust*[20] was an unusual case in which, at first instance, the judge had accepted the claimant's evidence that the doctor did not discuss whether to insert a cannula (an intravenous tube) into her left arm. As she had put it: 'he just went, "I don't have any choice", bang, in it went without me having any more to say'.

Immediately before inserting the cannula, the claimant had told Dr Prenter that she had recently undergone a procedure which made it risky to cut her left arm. Despite finding that she had not given consent to its insertion, the judge went on to consider whether inserting the cannula had been the right thing to do. Perhaps oddly, the claim had not been framed as one of trespass to the person at trial. Such a finding was therefore not open to the Court of Appeal, because it would be an injustice to the defendant, who 'would have been permitted to adduce additional evidence on the issue', with the result that 'different findings of fact might have emerged if the claim [of trespass] had been included at the outset'. Instead, the Court of Appeal was clear that a finding that the doctor had inserted a cannula without the patient's consent amounted to a breach of his duty of care: 'A finding of absence of consent to the

---

[19] (1995) 34 BMLR 23 (QBD).   [20] [2015] EWCA Civ 8.

insertion of the cannula leads inexorably in this case to a finding of breach of duty in inserting it'.[21] The case was remitted back to the trial judge on the question of causation.

More usually in negligence actions, the patient's consent will have been sufficiently informed to avoid a charge of battery, but the patient might instead claim that the doctor's failure to disclose information about a risk associated with treatment amounted to negligence. As we saw in the previous chapter, there are three stages to an action in negligence. First, the defendant must owe the claimant a duty of care; secondly, she must breach that duty; and, thirdly, the breach must have caused the claimant's damage.

(1) The Duty of Care

At the outset it is worth noting that liability for the failure to disclose information amounts to a duty to act positively, rather than to refrain from causing harm. Although such duties tend to be exceptional in English law, it is accepted that one aspect of a doctor's duty of care to her patients is to provide them with information. The chief problem has then been working out when the doctor has breached this duty; that is, how much information is required in order to fulfil the doctor's duty of care?

(2) The Standard of Care: From *Sidaway* to *Montgomery*

Now of largely historical interest, the first House of Lords case to consider the question of how much information patients should be given before consenting to medical treatment was *Sidaway v Board of Governors of the Bethlem Royal Hospital and the Maudsley Hospital*.[22]

Mrs Sidaway had complained that she had not been told about an operation's small risk— estimated to be between 1 and 2 per cent—of damage to her spinal column. She claimed that if she had been warned, she would not have had the operation. This risk had in fact materialized, and Mrs Sidaway was now seriously disabled. The House of Lords unanimously rejected Mrs Sidaway's claim that the failure to warn her of this risk had been negligent. They were also agreed that the duty to disclose information is part of the doctor's ordinary duty of care. There were, however, marked differences in their approaches to determining the relevant standard of care.

According to Lord Diplock, the *Bolam* test applied to all aspects of a doctor's duty of care, and he saw no reason to treat advice differently from diagnosis and treatment: the doctor's disclosure should therefore be judged by its conformity with responsible medical practice. At the other extreme, Lord Scarman argued that the doctor's duty of disclosure arose from the patient's 'basic human right' to make her own medical decisions. The test should therefore be what the prudent patient, in this patient's position, would want to know.

Falling somewhere in between were the judgments of Lord Bridge, with whom Lord Keith agreed, and Lord Templeman, all of whom supported a modified *Bolam* test. Disclosure was 'primarily a matter of clinical judgment', but in certain circumstances, the judge might conclude that a risk ought to have been disclosed even if there was a body of responsible medical opinion that would not have warned the patient of it.

Thirteen years later, in *Pearce v United Bristol Healthcare NHS Trust*,[23] the Court of Appeal moved closer to the 'reasonable patient' test in determining whether the 0.1–0.2 per cent risk of stillbirth associated with waiting for a natural birth should have been disclosed to a pregnant woman whose baby's birth was two weeks overdue, and who had begged to have her labour induced or to undergo a caesarean section. According to Lord Woolf MR, 'if there is a

---

[21] Per Richards LJ.   [22] [1985] AC 871.   [23] (1998) 48 BMLR 118 (CA).

significant risk which would affect the judgment of a reasonable patient, then in the normal course it is the responsibility of a doctor to inform the patient of that significant risk'. In this case, however, Lord Woolf MR also held that 'The doctors called on behalf of the defendants did not regard that risk as significant; nor do I'. Lord Woolf thus appeared to rely upon the doctors', rather than the patient's assessment of whether a small risk of stillbirth was 'significant'.

In his judgment in the House of Lords in *Chester v Afshar*, a case we discuss in detail later, Lord Steyn nevertheless quoted with approval Lord Woolf's approach in *Pearce*, and said that patients have the 'right' to be informed of 'small but well-established' risks of serious injury, though once again, he does not specify whether seriousness is judged from the patient's or the doctor's perspective.

Chester v Afshar[24]

Lord Steyn

A surgeon owes a legal duty to a patient to warn him or her in general terms of possible serious risks involved in the procedure … In modern law medical paternalism no longer rules and a patient has a prima facie right to be informed by a surgeon of a small, but well established, risk of serious injury as a result of surgery.

The move away from *Sidaway* towards a more patient-centred test for the standard of care was continued in the case of *Birch v University College London Hospital NHS Foundation Trust*.[25] Mrs Birch had been warned about the one per cent risk of stroke associated with catheter angiography, but she was not told that that she could have had a slightly less accurate MRI scan, with no risk of stroke. Mrs Birch then suffered a stroke, and Cranston J held that the doctor had breached his duty of care by failing to tell her about the comparative risks of angiography versus MRI: 'in my judgment there will be circumstances where consistently with Lord Woolf MR's statement of the law in *Pearce v United Bristol Healthcare NHS Trust* the duty to inform a patient of the significant risks will not be discharged unless she is made aware that fewer, or no risks, are associated with another procedure'.

(a) Montgomery v Lanarkshire

In the years following *Sidaway*, English law had been gradually moving towards a more patient-centred test for disclosure. This journey was completed in 2015, when *Sidaway* was overruled by the case of *Montgomery v Lanarkshire Health Board*.[26]

Nadine Montgomery brought an action for damages following the birth of her severely disabled son. Mrs Montgomery suffered from diabetes, and, as a result, was likely to have a larger than normal baby. Shoulder dystocia, where the baby's shoulders are too wide to pass through the mother's pelvis without medical intervention, is a particular concern in diabetic pregnancies. Mrs Montgomery had been told that she was having a larger than usual baby, but she was not told about the risk of shoulder dystocia, which was agreed to be 9–10 per cent. The consultant obstetrician and gynaecologist, Dr McLellan, accepted that this was a significant risk, but her practice was not to spend time discussing the risks of shoulder dystocia, in part

---

[24] [2004] UKHL 41.   [25] [2008] EWHC 2237 (QB).   [26] [2015] UKSC 11.

because the risk of serious damage to the baby was small and in part because patients would then ask for caesarean delivery, which would not be in their interests.

Dr McLellan accepted that Mrs Montgomery had expressed concern about the size of the baby and the risk that it might be too big to be delivered vaginally, but she had not asked 'specifically about exact risks'. In the event, mechanical efforts to deal with Mrs Montgomery's baby's shoulder dystocia led to him suffering profound disabilities, including cerebral palsy.

The UK Supreme Court unanimously held that Dr McLellan's failure to be frank with Mrs Montgomery amounted to a breach of her duty of care. Its judgment is notable for its wholesale rejection of the reasonable doctor test and its adoption instead of the partnership model of medical decision-making embodied in General Medical Council (GMC) guidance.

Montgomery v Lanarkshire Health Board[27]

Lords Kerr and Reid (with whom Lords Neuberger, Clarke, Wilson, and Hodge and Lady Hale[28] agreed)

Since *Sidaway's* case, however, it has become increasingly clear that the paradigm of the doctor–patient relationship implicit in the speeches in that case has ceased to reflect the reality and complexity of the way in which healthcare services are provided, or the way in which the providers and recipients of such services view their relationship. One development which is particularly significant in the present context is that patients are now widely regarded as persons holding rights, rather than as the passive recipients of the care of the medical profession. They are also widely treated as consumers exercising choices . . .

Other changes in society, and in the provision of healthcare services, should also be borne in mind. One which is particularly relevant in the present context is that it has become far easier, and far more common, for members of the public to obtain information about symptoms, investigations, treatment options, risks and side-effects via such media as the internet (where, although the information available is of variable quality, reliable sources of information can readily be found), patient support groups, and leaflets issued by healthcare institutions . . . It would therefore be a mistake to view patients as uninformed, incapable of understanding medical matters, or wholly dependent on a flow of information from doctors . . .

The social and legal developments which we have mentioned point away from a model of the relationship between the doctor and the patient based on medical paternalism. They also point away from a model based on a view of the patient as being entirely dependent on information provided by the doctor. What they point towards is an approach to the law which, instead of treating patients as placing themselves in the hands of their doctors (and then being prone to sue their doctors in the event of a disappointing outcome), treats them so far as possible as adults who are capable of understanding that medical treatment is uncertain of success and may involve risks, accepting responsibility for the taking of risks affecting their own lives, and living with the consequences of their choices . . .

The correct position, in relation to the risks of injury involved in treatment, can now be seen to be substantially that adopted in *Sidaway* by Lord Scarman . . . An adult person of sound mind is entitled to decide which, if any, of the available forms of treatment to undergo, and her consent must be obtained before treatment interfering with her bodily integrity is undertaken. The doctor is therefore under a duty to take reasonable care to ensure that the patient is aware of any material risks involved in any recommended treatment, and of any reasonable alternative or

---

[27] [2015] UKSC 11.

[28] Lady Hale added some observations on pregnancy and childbirth, but also said that she 'entirely agreed' with the majority.

variant treatments. The test of materiality is whether, in the circumstances of the particular case, a reasonable person in the patient's position would be likely to attach significance to the risk, or the doctor is or should reasonably be aware that the particular patient would be likely to attach significance to it.

The doctor is however entitled to withhold from the patient information as to a risk if he reasonably considers that its disclosure would be seriously detrimental to the patient's health. The doctor is also excused from conferring with the patient in circumstances of necessity, as for example where the patient requires treatment urgently but is unconscious or otherwise unable to make a decision . . .

Three further points should be made. First, it follows from this approach that the assessment of whether a risk is material cannot be reduced to percentages. The significance of a given risk is likely to reflect a variety of factors besides its magnitude: for example, the nature of the risk, the effect which its occurrence would have on the life of the patient, the importance to the patient of the benefits sought to be achieved by the treatment, the alternatives available, and the risks involved in those alternatives. The assessment is therefore fact-sensitive, and sensitive also to the characteristics of the patient.

Secondly, the doctor's advisory role involves dialogue, the aim of which is to ensure that the patient understands the seriousness of her condition, and the anticipated benefits and risks of the proposed treatment and any reasonable alternatives, so that she is then in a position to make an informed decision. This role will only be performed effectively if the information provided is comprehensible. The doctor's duty is not therefore fulfilled by bombarding the patient with technical information which she cannot reasonably be expected to grasp, let alone by routinely demanding her signature on a consent form.

Thirdly, it is important that the therapeutic exception should not be abused. It is a limited exception to the general principle that the patient should make the decision whether to undergo a proposed course of treatment: it is not intended to subvert that principle by enabling the doctor to prevent the patient from making an informed choice where she is liable to make a choice which the doctor considers to be contrary to her best interests . . .

Approaching the present case on this basis, there can be no doubt that it was incumbent on Dr McLellan to advise Mrs Montgomery of the risk of shoulder dystocia if she were to have her baby by vaginal delivery, and to discuss with her the alternative of delivery by caesarean section.

Significantly, the Supreme Court in *Montgomery* went beyond the 'prudent patient test', according to which the doctor should give each patient that information which the reasonable person in the patient's position would want to know. The prudent (or reasonable) patient test, while an improvement on *Bolam*, might still fail to protect individual patients' interests in information. People have different priorities, beliefs, and family histories, all of which affect the relative importance they attach to the risks and benefits of medical treatment. Giving every patient the information which the abstract reasonable patient would consider material might be preferable to the *Bolam* standard, but it would still result in some patients being deprived of information which might be especially important to them.

Instead the Supreme Court in *Montgomery* acknowledged that people have variable information needs, and it imposed a duty upon doctors to tailor their disclosures according to the individual patient's priorities and concerns:

The test of materiality is whether, in the circumstances of the particular case, a reasonable person in the patient's position would be likely to attach significance to the risk, *or the doctor is or should reasonably be aware that the particular patient would be likely to attach significance to it.* [My emphasis]

Of course, within the modern and increasingly impersonal health care system, doctors cannot be expected to know in advance what matters to an individual patient. Indeed, under the *Montgomery* test for materiality, doctors are only under a duty to inform the patient about a risk if they know or should know that it matters to the individual patient. Michael Dunn et al therefore argue that this is not strictly an autonomy-focussed test, because that would require doctors proactively to *find out* about what matters to the patient.

Michael Dunn et al[29]

Risk should be disclosed, not when the particular patient accords significance to the risk, but only when the doctor is (or should reasonably be) aware of this fact. This qualification suggests a requirement on the patient to be active in disclosing relevant information about her values, or at the very least to signpost to the doctor that she has concerns of a particular kind that are relevant to the risk disclosure question and that the doctor needs to follow up on. Yet, an autonomy-focused approach would be one that required the doctor to strive herself to obtain a robust understanding of her patient's values in order to ensure that these values were respected in the treatment decisions to be made.

Certainly, GMC guidance requires doctors to attempt to discover the patient's particular concerns or priorities through appropriate questioning (NB at the time of writing, the GMC is consulting on new consent guidance, which should be finalized in 2019. There is, however, no doubt that it will continue to require doctors to tailor their information provision to the needs of the individual patient[30]).

General Medical Council[31]

28. The amount of information about risk that you should share with patients will depend on the individual patient and what they want or need to know. Your discussions with patients should focus on their individual situation and the risk to them . . .

31. You should do your best to understand the patient's views and preferences about any proposed investigation or treatment, and the adverse outcomes they are most concerned about. You must not make assumptions about a patient's understanding of risk or the importance they attach to different outcomes.

The decision in *Montgomery* has been broadly welcomed by most legal commentators.[32] And, since it largely mirrors GMC guidance, Anne Maree Farrell and Margaret Brazier have argued that it will make little difference in practice.

---

[29] 'Between the reasonable and the particular: Deflating autonomy in the legal regulation of informed consent to medical treatment' (2018) Health Care Analysis 1–18.

[30] The draft guidance is called *Decision making and consent: Supporting patient choices about health and care.* The final version will be available at <www.gmc-uk.org/>.

[31] GMC, *Consent: Patients and Doctors Making Decisions Together* (2008).

[32] Rob Heywood, 'RIP *Sidaway*: patient-oriented disclosure—a standard worth waiting for?' (2015) 23 Medical Law Review 455–66.

Anne Maree Farrell and Margaret Brazier[33]

The reality is that *Montgomery* will make little difference to healthcare practice and consent in the UK, which for over 10 years has focused principally on a reasonable patient test. The Supreme Court endorsed a view of consent most lawyers, and doctors thought already prevailed, and largely reflects UK General Medical Council (GMC) guidance on the issue. In short, there is little cause for doctors to panic that the 'litigation floodgates' have opened in relation to consent and information non-disclosure claims ...

The Supreme Court's decision in *Montgomery* confirms a patient-centred test for disclosing risk and obtaining consent in medical treatment, which had in any case prevailed for many years with the blessing of the GMC. For many, this legal affirmation is long overdue and largely uncontroversial, and so should not cause doctors any anxiety or concern ...

Given recent healthcare scandals in the NHS, the Court's legal recognition of the importance of recognising patient autonomy in disclosing risks about medical treatment and care must surely be a welcome development.

Against this, Rob Heywood and José Miola suggest that it was, in fact, a good thing for the ethical standards demanded of doctors by the GMC to exceed the standard of care required by law.

Rob Heywood and José Miola[34]

[W]e believe that the gap between the legal standard and the ethical standard was a positive development and one that should have remained. In short, in our view it should be possible for a doctor to be acting *unethically* and thus face sanction by the GMC, but not *unlawfully*. The latter, we feel, should be limited to serious breaches of patient autonomy. The 'heavy boots' of the law are not required in *every* case, but only those where professional regulation is insufficient. Moreover, aligning the law with the professional obligations leaves one at the mercy of the other. On the one hand, if the Supreme Court's intention is to follow the ethical standard, then the law will rely on that standard remaining high and prioritising patient autonomy. On the other, if the purpose is to force the GMC to maintain its current requirements at least—as they cannot be relaxed without the professional standard then being *less* demanding than the law, which would not be reasonable—then the law will have essentially performed a takeover of the professional ethical standard.

There have also been some substantive criticisms of the decision in *Montgomery*. As Jonathan and Elsa Montgomery explain, the Supreme Court appeared to misunderstand that there are, in fact, significant risks to women from caesarean delivery, and that giving all women the option of a caesarean section would be contrary to good practice guidance.

---

[33] 'Not so new directions in the law of consent? Examining *Montgomery v Lanarkshire Health Board*' (2016) 42 Journal of Medical Ethics 85–8.
[34] 'The changing face of pre-operative medical disclosure: placing the patient at the heart of the matter' (2017) 133 Law Quarterly Review 296–321.

Jonathan Montgomery and Elsa Montgomery[35]

The Supreme Court's decision on liability turned on the fact that the claimant should have been offered a caesarean section in circumstances in which the collective wisdom of the clinical community, as enshrined in RCOG [Royal College of Obstetricians and Gynaecologists] and NICE guidelines, did not suggest it was indicated. A clinician seeking to avoid legal liability can therefore no longer regard compliance with professional guidelines as a protection but must consider which aspects will be accepted by the judiciary and which not ...

According to the Supreme Court, 'the risk involved in an elective caesarean section, for the mother (is) extremely small and for the baby virtually non-existent' and this was in stark contrast to those involved in vaginal delivery. However, this is not consistent with the conclusions reached by NICE, which draws attention to a number of respects in which the relative risks to women involved in caesarean section are greater than those for vaginal delivery and which it advises should be drawn to the attention of women. These include the fact that it is almost five times as likely that a woman who has a CS, rather than a vaginal birth, will suffer a cardiac arrest and over twice as likely that she will need a hysterectomy due to postpartum haemorrhage ...

[The Supreme Court] took upon itself to determine that a treatment was a 'reasonable alternative' in a way that is inherently unpredictable. It departed from established guidelines and disregarded their evidential basis. As a result it seems to require professionals to advise on treatments that they do not regard as clinically appropriate, in a manner that is not wholly unprecedented, but is nevertheless in tension with the basic principle of medical law ... that choice of whether a treatment was clinically indicated should be for medical judgement, not patient or judicial determination. This seems a fundamental shift in approach, although it is not entirely clear that this was intentional.

Jonathan Montgomery is furthermore disappointed in the justices' rewriting of the facts in order to present Nadine Montgomery as a stereotypical intimidated and infantilized patient.

Jonathan Montgomery[36]

In non-medical contexts, it is part of being a modern consumer that we take responsibility for choosing how informed our consent will be. This seemed to be what lay behind the analysis in the Courts of Sessions of Nadine Montgomery's discussions with her doctor. However, this was cast aside by the Supreme Court in favour of a much more traditional model of the patient in which 'the social and psychological realities or the relationship between patient and her doctor' mean that 'few patients do not feel intimidated or inhibited to some degree'. While the Courts of Session sought to assess Nadine Montgomery's capacity as an individual, the Supreme Court developed a set of rules based on a stereotypical patient ...

Women using maternity services are quite capable of taking responsibility for their own care, and Nadine Montgomery seemed to the judges in the two Courts of Sessions to have done so. The Supreme Court thought differently. In my view, it is to be regretted that the law continues to infantalize such women, and patients in general, by operating on the basis that they will only know things if professionals tell them, and only understand them if professionals explain them. Taking patients as citizens seriously means recognizing their right to control information flows and accepting the decisions that they make.

---

[35] 'Montgomery on informed consent: an inexpert decision?' (2016) 42 Journal of Medical Ethics 89–94.
[36] 'Patient No Longer? What Next in Healthcare Law?' (2017) 70 Current Legal Problems 73–109.

In addition to the question of how *Montgomery* has been applied in subsequent cases, three further specific issues remain post-*Montgomery*. First, the case is clear that there must now be a 'dialogue' between doctors and their patients, but what does this, in fact, require? Secondly, is the 'therapeutic exception', left open by the Supreme Court, in tension with its patient-centred test for materiality? Thirdly, how might the Supreme Court's suggestion that a patient can decide that she does not wish to be informed of risks of injury work in practice?

(i) *A subjective test for materiality in practice?*

Of course, a doctor is only under a duty to warn about risks that she knew about, or should have known about, and, unlike the question of whether a risk is material, the question of whether it is known 'is a matter falling within the expertise of medical professionals'.[37] In *Duce v Worcestershire Acute Hospitals NHS Trust*,[38] the Court of Appeal found that the claimant's case did not get as far as the question of whether she would have wanted to know about the risk of chronic post-operative pain, because her claim had 'failed at the first hurdle':

> In 2008 there was insufficient understanding among gynaecologists of the existence of a risk of 'chronic pain, or of neuropathic (or nerve) pain, whether that was long term or short term' to justify the imposition of a duty to warn of such a risk. That reasoning is consistent with the *Montgomery* approach – a clinician is not required to warn of a risk of which he cannot reasonably be taken to be aware.

Since *Montgomery*, there have been some cases where the legacy of the *Bolam* test is still detectable. In *A v East Kent Hospitals University NHS Foundation Trust*,[39] for example, despite saying that, 'It is … clear from Montgomery that what is a material risk cannot be reduced to percentages, is fact sensitive and sensitive to the characteristics of the patient', Dingemans J appeared to rely upon percentages (ie that the risk was 1 in 1000, rather than 3 per cent) in order to decide that the risk that Mrs A's fetus suffered from a chromosomal abnormality was 'theoretical, negligible or background':

> In my judgment the decision in Montgomery affirms the importance of patient autonomy, and the proper practice set out in the GMC Guidance and the proper approach set out in *Pearce* and *Wyatt*. It is not authority for the proposition that medical practitioners need to warn about risks which are theoretical and not material.

And what of the duty, post-*Montgomery*, to disclose information that the doctor ought reasonably to know matters to this patient? In *Grimstone v Epsom and St Helier University Hospitals NHS Trust*,[40] the claimant who led an active life and was very concerned about her mobility after a hip replacement operation, had not been informed about the success rates with a new type of replacement hip. McGowan J appeared to be persuaded that there was no duty to give this information to the patient because *other doctors* would not have done so:

> The 'concern' expressed by the Claimant's expert, Mr Charnley, that the data or lack of it was not explained to the patient cannot outweigh the view of the equally expert witness called by the Defendant, Mr Hamer, that a reasonable body of doctors in the same position would not have given such information to a patient … All the clinicians accepted it was an appropriate device to have used in this case.

---

[37] Per Hamblen LJ in *Duce v Worcestershire Acute Hospitals NHS Trust* [2018] EWCA Civ 1307.
[38] [2018] EWCA Civ 1307.　　[39] [2015] EWHC 1038 (QB).　　[40] [2015] EWHC 3756 (QB).

(ii) Dialogue?

The Supreme Court stressed the importance of 'dialogue' in order that a doctor can find out what matters to the patient. In practice, however, dialogue can be time-consuming, and resource intensive, and, as Angelikar Reichstein points out, it will not always be easy for a doctor to establish how much information an individual patient wants.

Angelikar Reichstein[41]

While the judges in *Montgomery* highlighted the GMC's guidelines that require doctors to engage in conversation with their patients and determine how much and which information is wished for and needed, the question remains how realistic this requirement is. Due to time constraints, there will not always be the time for a doctor to get to know her patient to a degree that lets her find out how much information is required by the patient and what kind of decisions the doctor should take on her behalf. While the guidelines by the GMC state that '[y]ou must listen to patients, take account of their views, and respond honestly to their questions', this does not seem to take into account the time pressure doctors are facing.

Under the National Health Service (NHS), appointments tend to be around 10 min long … As a further complication, in NHS clinics it is not given that a patient will always be seen by the same doctor. How then is a doctor supposed to know how much information is the right amount for a specific patient? … [T]his is easier to judge in hindsight than it probably is for a physician at the time of treatment.

A further practical difficulty, highlighted by Roderick Bagshaw, is how far doctors need to engage in dialogue when their recommendation is to 'wait and see' if the patient's symptoms persist. As we saw in Chapter 2, because patients often see their GPs for complaints that are likely to clear up on their own, doctors will often suggest that the patient returns if they do not feel better within a week or so. Does *Montgomery* alter how much information doctors should disclose during such conversations?

Roderick Bagshaw[42]

Perhaps the most controversial question relating to the scope of the new rule, however, may be how far it should be applied to recommendations of 'non-treatment', that is situations where a professional recommends waiting to see if a problem resolves itself without intervention. In such circumstances, must a doctor now identify the further tests or treatments that *could* be commenced immediately, and any significant risks that may be associated with a delay? The practical problem here may be that 'non-treatment' is frequently recommended where there is considerable uncertainty about the cause of a patient's problems, the severity of any underlying illness, and hence the prognosis, which makes it very difficult to catalogue and discuss all the possibilities and how, if at all, delay may impinge on their treatment. Moreover, in some cases further difficulties may flow from the fact that the 'costs' of immediate, in all probability unnecessary, tests or treatment, may primarily involve the dissipation of resources available to others rather than some disadvantage to the patient.

[41] 'Case Comment—*Webster v Burton Hospital NHS Foundation Trust*' (2017) 25 Medical Law Review 654–61.
[42] 'Modernising the doctor's duty to disclose risks of treatment' (2016) 132 Law Quarterly Review 182–6.

(iii) The therapeutic exception

The Supreme Court in *Montgomery* accepted that, in exceptional circumstances, there could be a 'therapeutic exception' to the duty of disclosure: if a doctor believes that a particular piece of information would cause serious harm to the patient, then that information may reasonably be withheld. In order that the therapeutic exception does not introduce, by the backdoor, a paternalistic 'doctor knows best' approach to information disclosure, 'serious harm' must be physical or mental harm to the patient *other than that which the doctor believes would be caused by her decision to refuse to have the treatment in question*. This is enshrined in the GMC's guidance to doctors:

> 16. You should not withhold information necessary for making decisions for any other reason, including when a relative, partner, friend or carer asks you to, unless you believe that giving it would cause the patient serious harm. In this context 'serious harm' means more than that the patient might become upset or decide to refuse treatment.[43]

Even with this caveat, the therapeutic exception is, as Emma Cave explains, anomalous and confusing.

Emma Cave[44]

> In law ..., commitment to the TE [therapeutic exception] is problematic for a number of reasons. The TE does not apply to other professions. Barristers cannot avoid telling their clients of the risk that the case will be lost although it will cause emotional breakdown, just as well-meaning professors cannot withhold catastrophic marks from their students for fear that the news will exacerbate an underlying medical condition. Furthermore, the privilege has potential to result in an overly complicated legal approach. Lords Kerr and Reed recognized that the new test for disclosure may result in less certainty and more litigation. Clinicians will find it harder to predict whether the Court will consider their decision not to disclose a risk unreasonable ...
>
> Insofar as the TE puts in the hands of clinicians the power to decide what is detrimental enough to warrant non-disclosure of material information that the courts have found necessary in order to equip patients to make an informed choice, the TE forms a potential contradiction to commitment to patient choice ...
>
> In England and Wales, the existence of the TE raises the potential for the *Bolam* test to remain relevant to information disclosure cases. In the context of risk disclosure, it is unnecessary and anomalous. It sacrifices coherence and clarity and will constitute a source of confusion for practitioners.

In practice, as Anne Maree Farrell and Margaret Brazier put it: 'If a patient has capacity, then on what basis can you judge she is not fit to deal with information? More guidance may be needed both from professional bodies and the courts in order to provide greater clarity for doctors on this point'.[45]

---

[43] GMC, *Consent: Patients and Doctors Making Decisions Together* (GMC, 2008).

[44] 'The ill-informed: Consent to medical treatment and the therapeutic exception' (2017) 46 Common Law World Review 140–68.

[45] 'Not so new directions in the law of consent? Examining *Montgomery v Lanarkshire Health Board*' (2016) 42 Journal of Medical Ethics 85–8.

(iv) Delegating the need for information

In addition to the therapeutic exception, Lords Kerr and Reid recognised another possible exception to the duty of disclosure, namely if the patient makes it clear that she does not want to discuss the risks of treatment:

> A person can of course decide that she does not wish to be informed of risks of injury (just as a person may choose to ignore the information leaflet enclosed with her medicine); and a doctor is not obliged to discuss the risks inherent in treatment with a person who makes it clear that she would prefer not to discuss the matter. Deciding whether a person is so disinclined may involve the doctor making a judgment; but it is not a judgment which is dependent on medical expertise.

In some ways, this is sensible. People have different ways of coping with illness: some will become experts in their condition and its treatment, while others would prefer not to think about it. When we are ill and in pain, we may not feel able to digest and weigh complex information: it is in practice not uncommon for patients to ask their doctors what they would do if they were in the patients' shoes.

Where a patient has a high level of trust and confidence in her doctor, could it be argued that she exercises her own autonomous choice by expressing a preference for the doctor to make the decision for her? Indeed, Nana Kongsholm and Klemnes Kappel point out that in other contexts we often make decisions grounded in trust rather than information, and that it is possible to 'trust intelligently'.

Nana CH Kongsholm and Klemnes Kappel[46]

> Suppose a good friend of mine has taken me to dinner at his favourite restaurant, where I have not dined before. Upon being seated we are presented with an extensive and detailed menu, but before I start to consider my options, my friend suggests that he orders us both his preferred dish. Knowing that he usually has good taste and trusting that he would not order me something that I would not enjoy, I promptly close my menu and acquiesce. In this case, all relevant information about my options is readily available, but I ground the decision about my course of action in the trust that I hold in my friend regarding said course of action. Or, to take an example from the medical realm: suppose, having a nasty infection, I go to see my family doctor, who has been treating me since I was a child (and my parents before me). He has compassion for my suffering, pulls out a powerful antibiotic from his medicine cabinet that he happens to have on hand, and recommends that I start taking it immediately to combat my infection. Feeling confident that he a) has the necessary expertise to know that the antibiotic will work against my infection, b) knows my medical history enough to safely assume that I will not have an unfortunate allergic reaction or the like, c) given our long personal relationship has a genuine interest in my well-being, and d) that he, all the previous points aside, is under certain professional obligations and will be met with repercussions should he engage in malpractice, I feel grateful for his care and without asking further questions promptly start my antibiotic regimen.
>
> These common decision-making scenarios show that we often base decisions about our actions – even ones that may affect our well-being – on our *trust* in the agents proposing

---

[46] 'Is Consent Based on Trust Morally Inferior to Consent Based on Information?' (2017) 31 Bioethics 432–42.

them, and less on *information* about what they entail. This type of decision-making is not typically considered to be imprudent or irresponsible on behalf of the agent (under proper circumstances), and it would not be unreasonable for the agent to generally expect good consequences as a result of this type of decision-making.

Ulrik Kihlbom agrees and argues that if a patient chooses to let her doctor decide upon her treatment, based upon well founded trust, she is in fact exercising autonomy:

if I, as the patient, choose to let you, as the physician, determine my treatment, and I have well founded beliefs that you will choose the treatment that best promote my values, and that the risks of the treatment you will choose, is in accordance with my attitudes towards different kinds of risks, I will exercise my autonomy, not waive my right to exercise it.[47]

In such circumstances, even if a patient wants to let her doctor choose for her, Neil Manson nevertheless suggests that she might value the provision of information, because frank and open communication is a sign of respect and trustworthiness.

Neil C Manson[48]

Human beings have a deeply entrenched interest in being respected ... The *fact* that a clinician is willing to inform a patient about treatment options may be viewed as indicative of respect (provided it is done so in respectful manner). The clinician treats the patient as someone who is capable of being informed, and who has an interest in being informed. A patient can have an interest in being respected without thereby wanting to make decisions herself ...

The fact that the clinician is willing to engage in communication may help to inspire confidence in the clinician as a trustworthy agent ... The fact that the clinician is willing to talk in detail about the intervention may be taken to be a reasonable, but not infallible, basis for judging that the clinician is honest, open, has 'nothing to hide' and is likely to be trustworthy in other respects. In contrast, evasive speech or trying to steer the patient's questions away from details, may be taken as evidence that the clinician does not give a strong consideration to the patient's interests ...

Suppose a patient ... wants to entirely defer her decision making to a clinician. It is not irrational or irrelevant to seek assurances that the decision will be made in a reasonable way, and the disclosure of information can provide this kind of assurance. That is, a patient can want to be assured that a good decision *will be made* (by someone else) without wanting to make that decision herself.

But even if it makes sense to say that a patient might exercise choice by delegating decision-making to her trusted doctor, what happens if she seeks subsequently to claim that, if she had been informed about a particular risk, she would not have consented to treatment? Of course, as Kihlbom points out, a doctor should record on the consent form that the patient declined information, but a consent form is not a binding contract, and a future court would

---

[47] 'Autonomy and negatively informed consent' (2008) 34 Journal of Medical Ethics 146–9.
[48] 'Why do patients want information if not to take part in decision making?' (2010) 36 Journal of Medical Ethics 834–7.

not be bound by the patient's apparent waiver of her right to information. Doctors might therefore find themselves in the uncomfortable position of not knowing exactly when they are entitled to rely upon a patient's uninformed decision not to receive information about their care.

(b) When and how should information be provided?

The Supreme Court in *Montgomery* was also clear that giving patients information, without trying to ensure that it is comprehensible, is plainly not sufficient. Healthcare professionals must present information in a way that patients will be able to understand. If the patient cannot understand English, access to translated information, or to an interpreter, might be necessary. It might be unsatisfactory to delegate the task of informing patients to junior doctors, who may have limited experience of communicating with patients, and who may not be able to answer all of the patients' questions.

The context in which information is disclosed is also important. However comprehensive the disclosure, giving a patient information about the risks associated with surgery immediately before or after an operation might nevertheless be negligent. In *Lybert v Warrington Health Authority*[49] the surgeon discussed the irreversibility of sterilization, and the risks of failing to achieve sterility immediately after the patient had undergone the operation. The court concluded that the surgeon had been negligent because the warning was not sufficiently emphatic and clear, and because the timing and the conditions in which it was given were inappropriate.

Jones v Royal Devon and Exeter NHS Foundation Trust was an unusual case in which David Blunt QC, sitting as a recorder, awarded damages for spinal damage caused during an operation when the patient had been informed that a different surgeon would be performing the operation just before she went into theatre.[50] Because there was evidence that the identity of the surgeon mattered to the patient, who had postponed her operation until a particular surgeon, with a national reputation, was available, the judge held that the Trust was in breach of its duty to her by informing her that a less experienced surgeon would be operating on her immediately before she was wheeled into the operating theatre. The judge held that that was too late a stage to provide her with that information. If she had been informed appropriately about the change of surgeon, the judge held that she would not have had the operation then, and would therefore not have suffered the damage to her spine.

The central problem is that it is difficult to communicate effectively with patients. Research indicates that patients are seldom able to recall information that has been disclosed to them about their condition and its treatment. It is common for patients to sign consent forms without reading them. Perfect patient comprehension is an unrealistic goal. Again GMC guidance suggests that doctors should actively try to ensure that patients have actually understood the information that has been provided.

General Medical Council[51]

21. You should check whether the patient needs any additional support to understand information, to communicate their wishes, or to make a decision. You should bear in mind

---

[49] [1996] 7 Med LR 71.   [50] 22 September 2015 (unreported).
[51] GMC, *Consent: Patients and Doctors Making Decisions Together* (2008). NB new GMC consent guidance will be published in 2019.

that some barriers to understanding and communication may not be obvious; for example, a patient may have unspoken anxieties, or may be affected by pain or other underlying problems. You must make sure, wherever practical, that arrangements are made to give the patient any necessary support. This might include, for example: using an advocate or interpreter; asking those close to the patient about the patient's communication needs; or giving the patient a written or audio record of the discussion and any decisions that were made . . .

34. You must use clear, simple and consistent language when discussing risks with patients. You should be aware that patients may understand information about risk differently from you. You should check that the patient understands the terms that you use, particularly when describing the seriousness, frequency and likelihood of an adverse outcome. You should use simple and accurate written information or visual or other aids to explain risk, if they will help the patient to understand.

(c) What was said?

A further practical problem lies in establishing what information was, in fact, disclosed to the patient. Patients are unlikely to have made notes at the time, and many years later may not be able to recall accurately what they were told. Doctors' notes may not record every detail of the conversations they have had with patients, and it is often difficult for doctors to remember exactly what was discussed, particularly if the consultation happened several years ago. The courts will therefore often be faced with two honest but contradictory accounts of what was, and was not, said.

Evidence of a doctor's usual practice will be relevant, though in many cases the judge will simply have to decide who is the more credible witness. In *Chatterton v Gerson*, for example, Bristow J believed the doctor's account of the pre-operation discussions:

> I have come to the conclusion that on the balance of probability Dr Gerson did give his usual explanation about the intrathecal phenol solution nerve block and its implications of numbness instead of pain plus a possibility of slight muscle weakness, and that the plaintiff's recollection is wrong; and on the evidence before me I so find.[52]

In contrast, in the first instance decision in *Chester v Afshar*, the trial judge had preferred the claimant's account on the grounds that it had the 'ring of truth and [was] most unlikely to be the result of either invention or reconstruction.'[53]

In a post-*Montgomery* case, Dingemans J relied upon the need for dialogue in order to clear up contradictory evidence from the doctor and the patient. In *Hassell v Hillingdon Hospitals NHS Foundation Trust*, Mrs Hassell complained that the surgeon who carried out the operation on her spine, which had left her paralysed, had not warned her of this risk, or discussed with her more conservative treatment options. Although the surgeon, Mr Ridgeway, claimed to have done this, Dingemans J found that he had not done so, because if he had engaged in a dialogue with her, she would have corrected his misunderstanding that she had previously had physiotherapy for her neck problems.

---

[52] *Chatterton v Gerson* [1981] QB 432.   [53] [2002] EWCA Civ 724.

Hassell v Hillingdon Hospitals NHS Foundation Trust [54]

Dingemans J

Although this misunderstanding was understandable because Mrs Hassell had been having physiotherapy for other complaints, he could not have had this misunderstanding if he had discussed other treatment options with Mrs Hassell. This is because his misunderstanding would have been corrected by Mrs Hassell who was articulate and would have pointed out that she had not had physiotherapy. *Montgomery* makes it clear that there must be a dialogue and if there had been a dialogue Mr Ridgeway would have known that Mrs Hassell had not yet had physiotherapy for the neck and upper arm problems.

(d)   A duty to answer questions

The Supreme Court in *Montgomery* was critical of Lord Diplock's suggestion in *Sidaway* that an educated and inquiring patient (the example he used was a judge) would receive personalized information because 'the doctor would tell him whatever it was the patient wanted to know'. As Margaret Brazier has pointed out, this would mean that educated, middle-class patients, who are not intimidated by a consultant's expertise, would have access to more and better information frightened, inarticulate patients.

Margaret Brazier[55]

The less articulate, the apprehensive, those who feel socially ill at ease with the consultant, or whose doctors are hard-pressed in inner city clinics, will be hesitant to initiate discussions. Not 'bothering' the doctor is a deeply entrenched tradition in many parts of Britain. It implies that the patient doubts the doctor's skill, raises fears of offending those who are going to care for you, and may just seem plain rude. It does not follow though that the tradition of patient silence implies lack of interest or desire to participate in decision-making if that opportunity is offered by the doctor.

Montgomery places the final nail in the coffin of Lord Diplock's distinction: patients do not have to be able to ask the right questions in order to obtain personalized information. Rather, the doctor may be under a duty to probe the patient's values and preferences in order to find out what matters to her.

Montgomery v Lanarkshire Health Board [56]

Lords Kerr and Reid

The significance attached in *Sidaway* to a patient's failure to question the doctor is however profoundly unsatisfactory ... It is indeed a reversal of logic: the more a patient knows about

---

[54] [2018] EWHC 164 (QB).
[55] 'Patient Autonomy and Consent to Treatment: The Role of the Law?' (1987) 7 Legal Studies 169–93.
[56] [2015] UKSC 11.

the risks she faces, the easier it is for her to ask specific questions about those risks, so as to impose on her doctor a duty to provide information; but it is those who lack such knowledge, and who are in consequence unable to pose such questions and instead express their anxiety in more general terms, who are in the greatest need of information. Ironically, the ignorance which such patients seek to have dispelled disqualifies them from obtaining the information they desire. Secondly, this approach leads to the drawing of excessively fine distinctions between questioning, on the one hand, and expressions of concern falling short of questioning, on the other hand: a problem illustrated by the present case. Thirdly, an approach which requires the patient to question the doctor disregards the social and psychological realities of the relationship between a patient and her doctor, whether in the time-pressured setting of a GP's surgery, or in the setting of a hospital. Few patients do not feel intimidated or inhibited to some degree.

(3) Causation

In order to succeed in an action in negligence, the claimant must not only prove that the doctor owed her a duty of care which has been breached, but also that the negligent non-disclosure caused the claimant to suffer injury or loss. The claimant who has managed to establish that her doctor was in breach of her duty to give her sufficient information—itself by no means an easy task—therefore has three further obstacles to a successful claim. She must prove that:

(a) she has suffered an injury that has made her worse off than she would have been if the procedure had not been performed; and

(b) her injury is the materialization of the negligently undisclosed risk; and

(c) if she had been informed of this risk, she (or a reasonable patient) would not have consented to the procedure, and so the injury would not have occurred.

(a) Causation in practice

Applying the 'but for' test to disclosure cases means that causation will be established if the claimant can prove that proper disclosure would have led her to refuse the treatment that has resulted in her injury. But this is a speculative inquiry about what the patient might have done in different circumstances, and, in addition, the claimant now has the benefit of hindsight. She now *knows* that the particular risk *has* materialized. From her perspective, the 0.1 per cent risk of a bad outcome has ceased to be a remote hypothetical possibility, and has become a 100 per cent certainty. It is therefore likely that her assertions of what she would have done had she known about this risk will be coloured by her knowledge that she is among the unlucky 0.1 per cent of patients.

The 'but for' test would ordinarily require us to ask whether this patient would have refused to be treated if she had been properly informed. If she would have had the treatment anyway, the doctor's breach of duty did not cause her loss. If, on the other hand, she would have declined the treatment, and hence avoided exposing herself to the risk that has now materialized, causation is established. Causation is thus normally judged subjectively.

In disclosure cases, concerns about relying too heavily on the patient's hindsight-influenced testimony has led some judges to adopt a hybrid subjective/objective test, such as that employed in *Smith v Barking, Havering and Brentwood Health Authority*,[57] in

---

[57] (1988) reported [1994] 5 Med LR 285.

which Hutchison J suggested that an objective test should be used to 'test' the truth of the patient's assertion from the witness box that she would have refused to have treatment if she had known about the undisclosed risk. If a reasonable patient would have agreed to the proposed treatment even if she had been told about this risk, then the onus would be on the patient to produce some evidence to back up her claim that she would have refused to be treated:

> If everything points to the fact that a reasonable patient, properly informed, would have assented to the operation, the assertion from the witness box, made after the adverse outcome is known, in a wholly artificial situation and in the knowledge that the outcome of the case depends upon the assertion being maintained, does not carry great weight unless there are extraneous or additional factors to substantiate it.

While a patient with unusual religious beliefs might be able to demonstrate that she would not have acted in the same way as a reasonable patient, it will often be difficult for a claimant to produce evidence to support her assertion that she would have responded idiosyncratically to information about a remote risk. Furthermore, adopting an objective test for establishing causation will enable the doctor to rely on evidence that patients who know about the risk do generally consent to treatment, and this sort of solid, empirical evidence may seem more persuasive than the claimant's after-the-fact assertion that she would not have consented if she had known about this risk.

However, adopting an objective approach to causation confuses the question of the credibility of the claimant's evidence with its objective reasonableness. A patient is under no duty to make the same decision as a reasonably prudent patient. On the contrary, as we see in the next chapter: 'A mentally competent patient has an absolute right to refuse to consent to medical treatment for any reason, rational or irrational, or for no reason at all, even where that decision may lead to his or her own death.'[58]

In the next extract, Alexander Capron argues that testing a claimant's evidence against what a hypothetical reasonable person in her situation would have done significantly undermines the patient's right to make foolish or eccentric choices. The credibility of evidence from a patient with peculiar priorities should be assessed in the ordinary way—does the judge believe her account?—rather than against a standard of objective reasonableness.

Alexander Morgan Capron[59]

> [T]he patient owes no one a duty to decide prudently or to require for his decision only the facts that an ordinary person would want... An 'individualized test of causation is indicated because informed consent seeks to assure patients the right to make even irrational decisions'. To deny recovery because ... a reasonable person would not have cared about a certain factor (although ... the factor did matter to the particular patient-plaintiff) undermines the fundamental purpose of the informed consent rule, the promotion of individual autonomy.

[58] *Re MB* (1997) 38 BMLR 175, per Butler-Sloss LJ.
[59] 'Informed Consent in Catastrophic Disease Research and Treatment' (1974) 123 University of Pennsylvania Law Review 340.

More recent cases in the UK have appeared to adopt a more straightforwardly subjective test for causation, tempered only by the judge's assessment of the witness's credibility.[60] In *Birch v University College London Hospital NHS Foundation Trust*, Cranston J accepted Mrs Birch's evidence that she would have opted for an MRI scan if she had been properly informed about the risk of stroke from catheter angiography.

Birch v University College London Hospital NHS Foundation Trust[61]

Cranston J

To establish liability on the defendant's part, Mrs Birch needs also to demonstrate, on the balance of probabilities, that had she been so informed she would have declined catheter angiography ... In her evidence Mrs Birch said explicitly that if the comparative risks had been explained to her she would have chosen an MRI. I accept that evidence. Mrs Birch struck me as an intelligent and sensible individual, well able to have made that decision ... It is clear to me that had she been given a fair and balanced account in the way I have held was necessary she would have rejected catheter angiography in favour of MRI. In other words, properly informed she would have declined the procedure leading to her stroke.

In a post-*Montgomery* case, *FM v Ipswich Hospital NHS Trust*, where the issue was again whether a woman would have opted for a caesarean section if she had been given proper information about shoulder dystocia, His Honour Judge McKenna acknowledged that he had to be cautious about evidence given with the benefit of hindsight, but he nevertheless believed that Mrs M would have sought a caesarean section, despite the doctor's assertion that most patients in her situation would have agreed to vaginal delivery.

FM v Ipswich Hospital NHS Trust[62]

His Honour Judge McKenna

I must however be cautious about placing too much reliance on Mrs M's evidence that she would have opted for a caesarean section. As counsel for the Defendant submitted, she now knows that the alternative of a vaginal birth was in fact what led to F being significantly disabled and it is unrealistic to expect her to be able to set aside that knowledge ...

Mrs M plainly wanted to avoid another traumatic birth like J's at any cost ... It was of course the evidence of Mr Tuffnell that he was able to persuade most of his patients not to elect for caesarean sections in such cases and that therefore his experience was that most patients did not ... [C]rucially in any event, what this court is concerned with is what these particular parents would have done in the particular circumstances of this case.

On the balance of probabilities therefore I conclude that Mrs M, in discussions with the obstetrician following the ultrasound scan, would not have been influenced by statistics but would have put the wellbeing of her baby ahead of herself and elected, and if necessary pushed, for caesarean section.

---

[60] See, eg, *O'Keefe v Harvey-Kemble* (1999) 45 BMLR 74 (CA) and *Gowton v Wolverhampton Health Authority* [1994] 5 Med LR 432.
[61] [2008] EWHC 2237 (QB).   [62] [2015] EWHC 775 (QB).

What if the patient can establish that she would not have consented to have this particular treatment at this time if she had been properly informed, but she cannot prove that she would never have undergone the procedure in the future? Here the question of causation becomes especially complicated. Applying the 'but for' test, it could be argued that the patient can establish that the doctor's inadequate disclosure caused her injury: she would not have undergone the operation when she did, and therefore the risk would not have materialized on this occasion. But, on the other hand, she might have undergone the same operation—and exposed herself knowingly to an identical risk—at a later date.

This issue first came before the English courts in *Chester v Afshar*,[63] a case in which Mr Afshar, a neurosurgeon, did not warn Miss Chester, who was reluctant to undergo surgery to treat her chronic back pain, that there was a 0.9–2 per cent risk that the operation would cause cauda equine syndrome (a serious condition involving pain, loss of sensation, and bowel and bladder dysfunction). Miss Chester's evidence was that, if she had been warned of this risk, she would not have agreed to have the operation when she did, but would have sought a second opinion, advice on alternatives, and taken more time to think it over. She admitted that she might, nevertheless, have consented to go ahead with the operation at a later date.

By a 3:2 majority the House of Lords applied the reasoning adopted in an earlier, though factually different, Australian case, *Chappel v Hart*,[64] and found that it was not necessary for a patient to prove that she would have refused the operation for the rest of her life if she had been properly advised. Instead, the fact that 'but for' the defendant's negligence, she might nevertheless have been exposed to an identical risk at a later date would only be relevant when quantifying her loss. Normally, of course, the chance that the particular risk would materialize if she had the operation on another occasion would be very small and so any reduction in damages would be likely to be nominal. An exception to this would be if the claimant was especially susceptible to the risk, so that the chance of the same risk materializing in the future would, in fact, be high.

Chester v Afshar[65]

Lord Steyn

[I]t is a distinctive feature of the present case that but for the surgeon's negligent failure to warn the claimant of the small risk of serious injury the actual injury would not have occurred when it did and the chance of it occurring on a subsequent occasion was very small. It could therefore be said that the breach of the surgeon resulted in the very injury about which the claimant was entitled to be warned ...

I have come to the conclusion that, as a result of the surgeon's failure to warn the patient, she cannot be said to have given informed consent to the surgery in the full legal sense. Her right of autonomy and dignity can and ought to be vindicated by a narrow and modest departure from traditional causation principles.

Lord Hope

For some [patients] the choice may be easy—simply to agree to or to decline the operation. But for many the choice will be a difficult one, requiring time to think, to take advice and to weigh up the alternatives. The duty is owed as much to the patient who, if warned, would find

---

[63] [2004] UKHL 41.   [64] (1998) 72 AJLR 1344.   [65] [2004] UKHL 41.

the decision difficult as to the patient who would find it simple and could give a clear answer to the doctor one way or the other immediately.

To leave the patient who would find the decision difficult without a remedy, as the normal approach to causation would indicate, would render the duty useless in the cases where it may be needed most. This would discriminate against those who cannot honestly say that they would have declined the operation once and for all if they had been warned. I would find that result unacceptable.

The majority in *Chester* admitted to departing from traditional causation principles, in order to ensure that 'due respect is given to the autonomy and dignity of each patient' (per Lord Steyn). The defendant's failure to give Miss Chester information about the risks associated with this operation had deprived her of the opportunity to make a fully informed choice. In a sense, then, it could be argued that the majority found for the claimant not because she had proved that the lack of proper information caused her to be exposed to a risk to which she would not have been exposed if she had been properly informed, but rather because she had been deprived of the right to weigh up the risks in order to make an informed choice.

Underlying the judgments of the majority of the House of Lords was a reluctance to penalize Miss Chester for her honesty in admitting that she could not be certain that she would not have undergone the operation at some point in the future, even if properly warned.

In contrast, in their vigorous dissenting judgments, Lords Bingham and Hoffmann followed the dissenting judgment of McHugh J in *Chappel v Hart*,[66] and argued that Miss Chester had in fact failed the 'but for' test, since the timing of the operation did not affect the risk of injury.

Lord Bingham (dissenting)

Miss Chester has not established that but for the failure to warn she would not have undergone surgery. She has shown that but for the failure to warn she would not have consented to surgery on Monday 21 November 1994. But the timing of the operation is irrelevant to the injury she suffered, for which she claims to be compensated. That injury would have been as liable to occur whenever the surgery was performed and whoever performed it.

Lord Hoffmann (dissenting)

The claimant argued that as a matter of law it was sufficient that she would not have had the operation at that time or by that surgeon, even though the evidence was that the risk could have been precisely the same if she had it at another time or by another surgeon.

In my opinion this argument is about as logical as saying that if one had been told, on entering a casino, that the odds on no 7 coming up at roulette were only 1 in 37, one would have gone away and come back next week or gone to a different casino. The question is whether one would have taken the opportunity to avoid or reduce the risk, not whether one would have changed the scenario in some irrelevant detail. The judge found as a fact that the risk would have been precisely the same whether it was done then or later or by that competent surgeon or by another.

---

[66] [2004] UKHL 41.

It follows that the claimant failed to prove that the defendant's breach of duty caused her loss. On ordinary principles of tort law, the defendant is not liable. The remaining question is whether a special rule should be created by which doctors who fail to warn patients of risks should be made insurers against those risks ...

I can see that there might be a case for a modest solatium in such cases. But the risks which may eventuate will vary greatly in severity and I think there would be great difficulty in fixing a suitable figure. In any case, the cost of litigation over such cases would make the law of torts an unsuitable vehicle for distributing the modest compensation which might be payable.

It could be argued that the majority in *Chester* did not bend the normal rules of causation. As Jane Stapleton explains:

had she been warned Miss Chester would have had the operation, if at all, at a different time. The *a priori* estimate of the risk she would then have faced is 1-2 per cent, so it would have been more likely than not that, but for the breach, she would not have suffered the syndrome.[67]

In contrast, Charles Foster agrees with the dissenting judges, and argues that the majority effectively abolished the need for claimants to prove causation.

Charles Foster[68]

This is Alice in Wonderland stuff. Causation is not established but, since it should be, it will be deemed to be. Where a duty exists for some reason that can be described in terms of human rights (and what duty cannot be?) a breach will entitle the claimant to damages on policy grounds, even if causation cannot be proved. The House of Lords has stretched the rules of causation before—notably in *Fairchild v Glenhaven Funeral Services*. But *Chester* goes much further: it abolishes the requirement for causation in any meaningful sense ...

The reasoning was, basically: a human right has been breached. That is a bad thing because human rights are important. Therefore, although causation is not really established, we will say that it is. The claimant is therefore entitled, presumably, to damages identical to those that she would have received had she been able to prove that a proper warning would have led her to decline the operation. Surely a more logical thing to do would be to award her the fairly notional damages that she would have got under the European Convention on Human Rights for the article 8 breach she had suffered. Indeed, Lord Hoffmann conceded that 'there might be a case for a modest solatium'.

Causation in consent cases of the *Chester* type has always been difficult to prove. Now it will be easy. Claimants' witness statements will in future, no doubt, say: 'If I had been properly warned, I would have gone off and pondered.' That will be difficult to gainsay.

Kumaralingam Amirthalingam further argues that the decision in *Chester* reflects an increasing tendency to view causation as a matter of moral accountability rather than factual cause.

---

[67] 'Occam's Razor Reveals an Orthodox Basis for *Chester v Afshar*' (2006) 122 Law Quarterly Review 426–48.
[68] 'It Should Be, Therefore It Is' (2004) 154 New Law Journal 7151.

Kumaralingam Amirthalingam[69]

Recently, causation has transcended its role in attributing causal responsibility and has been used instead to fix liability on a party who, in the court's eyes, ought to have been held accountable even if there were no evidence that that party actually caused the injury. The current mantra is that causation must be seen in the context of the purpose of the law and should not be separated from questions of liability. Effectively, this means that courts may find a defendant causally responsible if at the end of the day, despite the absence of actual evidence of a causal link, it is fair, just and reasonable that the defendant, rather than the plaintiff, should bear the loss. This confuses causation with the broader question of liability, more properly addressed at the duty or remoteness stage.

If Miss Chester's loss is better described as the loss of the right to make an informed choice, rather than exposure to a risk to which she would not have been subjected with proper information, it could be argued that damages should be awarded for this deprivation of autonomy, rather than for the physical injury she suffered.

It is interesting that the majority in *Chester* did not consider the possibility of making a 'conventional award', as the majority of the House of Lords had done in *Rees v Darlington Memorial NHS Trust*[70] (see Chapter 3), in order to recognize that she had 'been denied, through the negligence of another, the opportunity to live her life in the way that she wished and planned'. The majority awarded Miss Chester full damages for physical injury, despite the fact that their judgments describe the real loss in this case as the deprivation of the right to make an informed choice. As JK Mason and Douglas Brodie point out, this may mean that Miss Chester was overcompensated.

JK Mason and Douglas Brodie[71]

However, the measure of damages allowed does not, in truth, reflect the loss suffered because, at the end of the day, the loss lay in an invasion of autonomy per se, and an award of full damages can be said to over-compensate. What is, in some ways, surprising is that the solution adopted in *Rees v Darlington Memorial NHS Trust* was not applied here. There, the requirements of distributive justice meant that damages should not be awarded to compensate the plaintiff for the loss that had arisen as the result of a failed sterilisation operation ... The solution adopted was to award a 'modest' conventional sum by way of general damages to acknowledge the infringement of the plaintiff's autonomy by the fault of the defendant.

The possibility of a conventional award was mentioned by Lord Hoffmann, however, in his dissenting judgment in *Chester*: 'I can see that there might be a case for a modest solatium.' In the end, however, he rejects this solution for two reasons: it would be difficult to settle on an appropriate amount, and, it would not be cost-effective to use litigation in order to pursue what would always be a modest award.

---

[69] 'Medical Non-Disclosure, Causation and Autonomy' (2002) 118 Law Quarterly Review 540–4, 542.
[70] [2003] UKHL 52.
[71] 'Bolam, Bolam—Wherefore Are Thou *Bolam*?' (2005) 9 Edinburgh Law Review 298–305.

In the next extract, Tamsyn Clark and Donal Nolan explain that the tensions in *Chester* derive precisely from trying to squeeze what is essentially a fairly modest interference with autonomy—namely, being deprived of more time for reflection—into a personal injury tort.

Tamsyn Clark and Donal Nolan[72]

These tensions arise because of a basic lack of fit between a 'duty to disclose' based on a patient's 'right to choose' and a medical negligence framework built around compensation for physical injury. The result is that the 'duty of disclosure' is (in the words of Izhak England) 'double-faced':

> Janus-like one face is looking into the direction of patient autonomy; the other face stares into the direction of medical injuries seeking compensation. The result is a strange disharmony in the real world: patient autonomy is sanctioned if a medical accident has happened, and compensation for medical accidents is granted where an infringement of patient autonomy has occurred.

This 'strange disharmony' was all too apparent in *Chester*. The felt need to protect patient autonomy drove the House of Lords to depart from well-established principles that stood in the way of recovery for the claimant's physical injury. However, the result was an award of damages that was both unjust, since the claimant was over-compensated, and incoherent, because it was contrary to a central tenet of negligence doctrine. In our view, *Chester* demonstrates that there is only one way in which the tensions in the law of non-disclosure can be resolved, and harmony restored. This is to break the connection with physical injury, and to give redress for the autonomy violation in its own right.

More recently, in *Shaw v Kovac*, the Court of Appeal rejected the suggestion that interference with autonomy could be a separate head of loss. The patient, Mr Ewan, had died following an operation to insert a transaortic valve implant. His daughter, Mrs Shaw, brought an action in negligence, claiming that neither he nor his family had been given proper information about the risks of surgery. Liability was eventually conceded and damages assessed, but on appeal, it was argued, unsuccessfully, that the judge should have also awarded a sum for 'the unlawful invasion of the personal rights' for Mr Ewan and his 'loss of personal autonomy', and it was suggested that £50,000 would be an appropriate figure.

Shaw v Kovac [73]

Davis LJ

[S]uch an argument is not available to the claimant. Indeed it would bristle with difficulties.

(1) First, and in itself fatal, such a cause of action has never been pleaded. It cannot be raised now. The judge below was perhaps benevolent in permitting heads of loss to be argued in a way not previously pleaded. But such benevolence cannot – even leaving aside any

---

[72] 'A critique of *Chester v Afshar*' (2014) 34 Oxford Journal of Legal Studies 659–92.
[73] [2017] EWCA Civ 1028.

> potential limitation points – be extended to formulating a new cause of action. That of itself disposes of the point.
>
> (2) In any event, the failure to give proper advice so as to obtain informed consent to what would otherwise be an unauthorised invasion of Mr Ewan's body is properly formulated – as here it was – as an action in negligence/breach of duty. That is quite clear on the authorities …
>
> A claim in negligence of this kind requires proof of damage as a necessary part of the cause of action: it is not one of those torts which is actionable per se. In the present case, damage has been pleaded and proved and an award of substantial damages made. In those circumstances I can see no room for a further award of nominal damages, as such, at all.

One of the conceptual difficulties with recognising lost autonomy as actionable damage is, as Craig Purshouse points out, interferences with autonomy may not leave a claimant *objectively* worse off.

Craig Purshouse[74]

> For damage to be actionable in negligence a claimant must show that they are objectively, and more than minimally, worse off. However, 'most interferences with autonomy would fall far short of this standard'. There are many interferences with autonomy that make people objectively better off, have only a minimal effect on an individual and, if the liberal individualistic definition is adopted, autonomy is an inherently subjective concept. As such, it is not consistent with the law's definition of actionable damage.

(b) Additional problems with causation

There are further reasons why causation raises particular difficulties in actions for negligent non-disclosure of information. First, a successful claim in negligence for failure to disclose a material risk is in practice synonymous with strict liability for medical mishaps. Informed consent therefore becomes a route for patients to seek financial compensation for unfortunate but blameless outcomes. Doctors who exercised all reasonable care and skill might be found liable for the consequences of a risk which they could have done nothing to prevent, just because their pre-operation disclosures were inadequate.

As Peter Cane explains, 'whatever the ideological basis of the duty to warn (or, in other words, the interest which it protects), its importance in practice lies in providing a basis for imposing liability for physical injury not caused by negligence'.[75] Gerald Robertson further suggests that this expansion of liability might be a deliberate response to the limits of a fault-based compensation system.

Gerald Robertson[76]

> It is beyond doubt that one effect of the recognition of the doctrine of informed consent is to expand the liability of the medical profession. The explanation for this is quite simple. Courts, particularly in this country, constantly stress the truism that things can go wrong in

---

[74] 'Autonomy, Affinity, and the Assessment of Damages: *ACB v Thomson Medical Pte Ltd* [2017] SGCA 20 and *Shaw v Kovak* [2017] EWCA Civ 1028' (2018) Medical Law Review online first.

[75] 'A Warning about Causation' (1999) 115 Law Quarterly Review 21–7, 23.

[76] 'Informed Consent to Medical Treatment' (1981) 97 Law Quarterly Review 102–26.

the course of medical treatment without that treatment having necessarily been performed negligently ... This means that a large number of patients who suffer injury in the course of medical treatment will, under a fault-based system of compensation such as our own, go without compensation because they are the victims, not of negligent performance of the treatment, but rather of the risks incident thereto. One way in which to remedy this situation, within the present fault-based framework, is to expand liability by making the doctor answerable in damages for failing to warn the patient of these risks prior to undergoing treatment. In this way a greater number of medical accident victims receive compensation, by means of extending the liability of the medical profession beyond the bounds of actual negligent performance of treatment.

Secondly, because the claimant must prove that the inadequate disclosure caused her injury, cases generally only come before the courts where the patient has not been informed about the risk of an adverse outcome, which has then materialized.[77] Adequate information is not, however, confined to disclosure of risks. In order to exercise meaningful choice, it is important that patients are told about alternatives to the proposed treatment. As Marjorie Maguire Shultz explains, negligently depriving the patient of choices will seldom result in the sort of damage or injury which is recognized in tort law.

Marjorie Maguire Shultz[78]

Thus, a patient not told about a method of sterilization that is more reversible than the one performed may have difficulty convincing a court that nonreversibility is a cognizable physical injury. A patient who alleges that, properly informed, she would have chosen a lumpectomy rather than a radical mastectomy might find it hard, under existing negligence rules, to characterize the successful operation that removed her breast and eradicated her cancer as having 'injured' her. Similarly, the patient with a desire to go home or to a hospice to die, who is instead maintained alive by hospital machinery, might have difficulty establishing 'injury' under definitions of an interest in physical well-being rather than choice.

Some patients might want to know if animal products were used in the preparation of a pharmaceutical product or device. For example, meshes used in surgery may be of animal origin—usually from pigs or cows—and for some patients this is undoubtedly 'material information'.[79] If the procedure in which an animal-derived product was used was successful, it would only be possible to bring an action in negligence for non-disclosure if the patient could establish that she had suffered a recognizable psychiatric injury as a result of discovering that an animal product had been left in her body. A vegan patient might consider that her right to make an informed choice had been compromised by non-disclosure of this sort of

---

[77] Although note the unusual facts in the case mentioned earlier, *Jones v Royal Devon and Exeter NHS Foundation Trust* 22 September 2015 (unreported), in which the claimant recovered on the grounds that the Trust had been negligent in informing the claimant about the fact that a less experienced surgeon would be carrying out her surgery just before she went into the operating theatre.

[78] 'From Informed Consent to Patient Choice: A New Protected Interest' (1985) 95 Yale Law Journal 219.

[79] Muhammad Hanif Shiwani, 'Surgical meshes containing animal products should be labelled' (2011) 343 British Medical Journal 261.

information, but, unless she had suffered a psychiatric injury, tort law would offer no protection of her interest in this information.

Patients might also want to know if their doctor is going to benefit financially from their decision to opt for a particular course of treatment. They might want to know how much experience a surgeon has, and her success rates. In practice, as Caitriona Cox and Zoe Fritz point out, it is unusual for doctors to be honest about their lack of experience.

Caitriona L Cox and Zoe Fritz[80]

Medical students and trainees—particularly surgical—are rarely encouraged to be totally honest about lack of experience. Yet studies have shown that patients want to know if it is the clinician's first time performing a procedure and about their physician's level of training more generally. There thus exists a tension between what patients want to be informed of and what tends to be disclosed in practice.

In the following extract, Frances Miller discusses another sort of information which might be increasingly important for patients, but which is marginalized by the tort of negligence. As we saw in Chapter 2, rationing of scarce medical resources has become inevitable, and it will not always be possible to provide every patient with the best available treatment. If treatment is withheld on the grounds of cost, are patients entitled to be told that a treatment exists which will not be available to them unless they pay for it privately?

Frances Miller[81]

If physicians withhold the information that potentially beneficial treatment is being denied their patients for economic reasons, they not only usurp the possibility of patient choice or self-help on the matter, but they assume a staggering moral burden. The traditional justification for silence under such circumstances is that it would be cruel and inhumane to tell patients that therapy might help them, but that they have no access to it. One can construct a powerful argument, however, that silence under such circumstances often is not only equally cruel and inhumane, but also morally unacceptable.

Physicians truly are 'playing God' in such circumstances, but they may not have all the facts. Some patients may have their own resources for obtaining medical care about which their doctors are unaware. Others may choose to invest their energies in trying to change rationing policies that affect them detrimentally, rather than passively accepting denial of care as their lot.

Amanda Owen-Smith et al's empirical research found that while most patients did want to know if their care had been rationed, where the withheld treatment was life-saving and unaffordable, this sort of information could be extremely distressing.

---

[80] 'Should non-disclosures be considered as morally equivalent to lies within the doctor–patient relationship?' (2016) 42 Journal of Medical Ethics 632–5.
[81] 'Denial of Health Care and Informed Consent in English and American Law' (1992) 18 American Journal of Law and Medicine 37.

Amanda Owen-Smith, Joanna Coast, and Jenny Donovan[82]

Nearly all patients said they wanted to know how financial factors affected their access to healthcare, and this was normally because they wanted to be granted the autonomy to decide whether to contest decision-making or to access care in the private sector . . .

However, nearly all also acknowledged that it would be very distressing to know about rationing if you were unable to access care through another route, and one patient in this situation regretted having been told. Half of informants felt that explicitness was not the right approach for all patients, and four identified situations where they would not want to know (such as if the treatment was likely to be life-saving, or they were unable to afford treatment in the private sector).

> Knowing what it's like when you're at that point, to be told there is this treatment and be told that we won't get funding for it . . . I think that would probably have made me suicidal. (Pa9)

> If it's 20 or 30 thousand a year, no one could keep that up for very long . . . and I think myself I'd rather not know that. (Pa20)

Thirdly, 'causation' appears to have acquired a rather special meaning in failure to warn cases. As Peter Cane has explained, the doctors in these cases rarely 'caused' the injury in question 'in the central sense of the word "cause" as it is used outside the law', because 'failure to warn of a risk does not "cause" the materialization of the risk'.[83] Rather, the injury has usually been caused by an unfortunate and inherently unlikely combination of circumstances, and the doctor simply '*create[d] the situation* in which an extraordinary sequence of events could occur' (emphasis in original).[84]

(c) MOVING AWAY FROM BATTERY AND NEGLIGENCE

Both battery and negligence are imperfect mechanisms for protecting a patient's right to information about her treatment. Battery will only be relevant where the treatment involves unlawful touching, and in any event the courts have been reluctant to use it in non-disclosure cases. Regardless of the patient-centred approach adopted by the Supreme Court in *Montgomery*, negligence continues to require proof that the inadequate information caused physical harm. What alternatives might there be?

(1) The New Zealand Code

In the next extract, Joanna Manning describes the system which exists in New Zealand. If a patient wishes to obtain compensation for a doctor's failure to warn her of a particular risk, under the no-fault compensation scheme, it will still be necessary to establish a causal link between the failure to warn and physical injury. However, in addition a Code of Rights offers additional protection to patients' interests in information disclosure, since it is a breach of the Code not to disclose information which the reasonable patient would consider material.

---

[82] 'Are patients receiving enough information about healthcare rationing? A qualitative study' (2010) 36 Journal of Medical Ethics 88–92.

[83] 'A Warning about Causation' (1999) 115 Law Quarterly Review 21–7.   [84] Ibid.

While the Code does not provide financial compensation to patients who have been inadequately informed—which is instead the function of the compensation scheme—it nevertheless places doctors under a robust duty to give patients sufficient information to enable them to make informed choices.

Joanna Manning[85]

One of the advantages of the Code is its recognition that a consumer is likely to want a wider range of information than about risks in making decisions about treatment. Right 6, in referring to 'the information that a reasonable consumer, in that consumer's circumstances, would expect to receive', recognises that the information patients might need is not confined to information about risks, but extends to other types of information that may be needed to enable them to make an informed decision about their care ...

It is not necessary to show that the patient suffered harm as a result of a failure to be sufficiently informed. So, it is strictly irrelevant to whether there has been a breach of Right 6 that the Commissioner finds it probable that, even if the health provider had explained the risks of the procedure, the patient would have gone ahead with it in any event. The patient is entitled to appropriate information irrespective of whether it would have been a determinative factor in the decision to proceed ... This properly reflects the paramount interest that the duty of disclosure and the concept of informed consent is designed to secure—the individual's autonomy and right to decide in an informed manner, not just the interest in bodily safety.

(2) A Fiduciary Relationship?

If the doctor–patient relationship could be said to be fiduciary in nature, we might have an alternative basis for imposing an obligation on doctors to disclose material information. Since equitable duties of disclosure arise in relationships where one party is unusually vulnerable to the other's ability to exercise some discretion or power over her interests, they might seem a promising basis for a more patient-orientated approach to informed consent.

It is uncontroversial that the doctor–patient relationship is one of trust and confidence, and, in other contexts, the courts have recognized that it might be fiduciary in character. A presumption of the invalidity of gifts and bequests from patient to doctor, for example, was established in the nineteenth century.[86] There are obligations which doctors owe to their patients—most obviously, the duty of confidentiality—which are equitable in nature, and which arise because equity has acknowledged the special dependency which exists within the doctor–patient relationship. Conceding that fiduciary relationships normally arise only when property interests are at stake, Margaret Brazier has nevertheless argued that 'in a sense the patient does entrust his most precious property, his body and health to the doctor'.[87]

In other countries, there have been times when the courts have categorized the doctor's duty of disclosure as a fiduciary obligation,[88] but there has been little support for this approach among the English judiciary. In *Sidaway* in the Court of Appeal,[89] Dunn LJ said that the fiduciary relationship 'has been confined to cases involving the disposition of property, and has

---

[85] 'Informed Consent to Medical Treatment: The Common Law and New Zealand's Code of Patients' Rights' (2004) 12 Medical Law Review 181.
[86] *Rhodes v Bate* (1866) 1 Ch App 252.
[87] 'Patient Autonomy and Consent to Treatment: The Role of the Law?' (1987) 7 Legal Studies 169–93, 191.
[88] *Miller v Kennedy* 522 P 2d 852 (1974).   [89] [1984] QB 491.

never been applied to the nature of the duty which lies upon a doctor in the performance of his professional treatment of his patient'. In the House of Lords,[90] Lord Scarman was the only Law Lord to consider the possibility of a fiduciary relationship between doctor and patient, and he was similarly dismissive:

> there is no comparison to be made between the relationship of doctor and patient with that of solicitor and client, trustee and *cestui qui trust* or the other relationships treated in equity as of a fiduciary character.

4 GOOD MEDICAL PRACTICE

Until *Montgomery v Lanarkshire*, there appeared to be a gap between tort law's fairly minimal requirements and the codes of practice and the patient-specific standard of disclosure contained in good practice guidance.[91]

General Medical Council[92]

2. Whatever the context in which medical decisions are made, you must work in partnership with your patients to ensure good care. In so doing, you must:
   (a) listen to patients and respect their views about their health
   (b) discuss with patients what their diagnosis, prognosis, treatment and care involve
   (c) share with patients the information they want or need in order to make decisions
   (d) maximise patients' opportunities, and their ability, to make decisions for themselves
   (e) respect patients' decisions.

3. For a relationship between doctor and patient to be effective, it should be a partnership based on openness, trust and good communication . . .

7. The exchange of information between doctor and patient is central to good decision-making. How much information you share with patients will vary, depending on their individual circumstances. You should tailor your approach to discussions with patients according to:
   (a) their needs, wishes and priorities
   (b) their level of knowledge about, and understanding of, their condition, prognosis and the treatment options
   (c) the nature of their condition
   (d) the complexity of the treatment, and
   (e) the nature and level of risk associated with the investigation or treatment.

---

[90] [1985] AC 871 at 884.

[91] See, for example, Department of Health, *Reference Guide to Consent for Examination or Treatment* 2nd edition (DH: London, 2009).

[92] GMC, *Consent: Patients and Doctors Making Decisions Together* (GMC, 2008). NB new GMC consent guidance will be published in 2019.

8. You should not make assumptions about:

    (a) the information a patient might want or need

    (b) the clinical or other factors a patient might consider significant, or

    (c) a patient's level of knowledge or understanding of what is proposed.

Of course, doctors who fail to follow GMC guidance are not immediately struck off the medical register, but the latest version of *Good Medical Practice* robustly states that 'Serious or persistent failure to follow this guidance will put your registration at risk.'[93]

A defect of both tort law and professional guidance is that the 'informed consent' process involves only the healthcare professional and her patient: a clinician provides information and the patient makes a decision for herself, on her own. In practice, however, we commonly involve those close to us in our medical decisions, and take account of their views. Indeed, Roy Gilbar suggests that in the majority of cases, relatives' involvement enhances patients' capacity to make informed choices.

Roy Gilbar[94]

In the majority of cases, the involvement of the relatives in the decision-making process helped the patient be more autonomous when she/he had to make a decision. It enabled the patient to be more informed and to consider the various implications of the available options diligently in a focused manner. In the majority of cases, it helped the patient feel more confident and in control of the situation . . .

In as much as [the patients in this study] quite naturally reacted emotionally to the information they received, they could not absorb the information properly. For them the relatives' presence in the consultation room was essential. Without it, serious legal questions about their ability to make informed decisions might have been raised . . .

Overall, the patients needed their relatives to help them make the decisions and therefore voluntarily involved them in the decision-making process, allowing them to have an impact on it . . .

The current case law and guidelines request clinicians to pay attention to family pressure which can amount to undue influence . . . However, the default legal position should not be confrontational, namely in treating the family as the enemy of the doctor and the patient. On the contrary, it should assume that relatives help the patient make better decisions by considering the various ramifications of each decision together and by reaching decisions that suit the patient's personal and familial circumstances.

5 CONCLUSION

The importance of the decision in *Montgomery v Lanarkshire* cannot be overstated. It aligns the standard of care in tort law with professional guidance on consent, and it is now clear

---

[93] (GMC, 2014), para 6.

[94] 'Family involvement, independence, and patient autonomy in practice' (2011) 19 Medical Law Review 192–234.

that a doctor is under a duty to provide whatever information she should be aware matters to the individual patient. The doctor no longer 'knows best', instead, patients are rights-holders who cannot be assumed to be reliant entirely upon their doctor for medical information. Rupert Jackson, writing extra-judicially, has suggested that this 'onslaught on *Bolam*' will not stop here.

Rupert Jackson[95]

In the latter part of the twentieth century many claimants had their guns trained on *Bolam*. . . Finally, just a month ago, the invaders captured the citadel. In *Montgomery v Lanarkshire Health Board* the Supreme Court held that the majority in *Sidaway* was wrong. The *Bolam* test did not determine the extent of a doctor's duty to advise … Now that the invaders have broken through the castle walls, they will not stop there. I predict that over the coming years there will be continuous onslaught on *Bolam*. The argument will be that the ordinary principles of tortious liability should apply to the professions in the same way that they apply to everybody else. There is no reason for the courts to accord special protection to the professions. Whether any of those attacks will succeed I do not know and it would be wrong for me, as a judge, to predict.

FURTHER READING

Bagshaw, Roderick, 'Modernising the doctor's duty to disclose risks of treatment' (2016) 132 Law Quarterly Review 182–6.

Cave, Emma, 'The ill-informed: Consent to medical treatment and the therapeutic exception' (2017) 46 Common Law World Review 140–68.

Clark, Tamsyn and Nolan, Donal, 'A critique of *Chester v Afshar*' (2014) 34 Oxford Journal of Legal Studies 659–92.

Heywood, Rob and Miola, José, 'The changing face of pre-operative medical disclosure: placing the patient at the heart of the matter' (2017) 133 Law Quarterly Review 296–321.

Manson, Neil, 'Why do patients want information if not to take part in decision making?' (2010) 36 Journal of Medical Ethics 834–7.

Montgomery, Jonathan, 'Patient No Longer? What Next in Healthcare Law?' (2017) 70 Current Legal Problems 73–109.

Reichstein, Angelikar 'Case Comment—*Webster v Burton Hospital NHS Foundation Trust*' (2017) 25 Medical Law Review 654–61.

---

[95] 'The Professions: Power, Privilege and Legal Liability', Peter Taylor Memorial Lecture to the Professional Negligence Bar Association, 21 April 2015, paras 4. 11 and 4. 12.

5

INCAPACITY I: ADULTS

CENTRAL ISSUES

1. The principle of patient autonomy means that, if an adult has capacity, she has the right to refuse medical treatment, even if her refusal will result in her death.

2. Under the Mental Capacity Act 2005, adults who lack capacity should be treated in their best interests.

3. Most medical decisions for patients who lack capacity are taken by their doctors. The courts are involved only when there is a dispute, or doubt about

what treatment is in the patient's best interests.

4. 'Best interests' has a much wider meaning than just clinical best interests, and in recent years, the courts have placed considerable weight upon the patient's own values and beliefs.

5. The inherent jurisdiction was not abolished by the Mental Capacity Act, and it has been used by the courts in order to protect capacitous but vulnerable adults.

---

1 INTRODUCTION

One of the first principles of medical law is that a competent adult patient must first give consent to medical treatment. As Cardozo J famously said in the US case, *Schloendorff v New York Hospital*:[1] 'Every human being of adult years and sound mind has a right to determine what shall be done with his own body.'

For consent to be valid: first, the patient must have the capacity to consent; secondly, her consent must be given voluntarily; and thirdly, she must understand, in broad terms, the nature of the treatment to which she has consented. The question of how much information should be provided to patients was dealt with in the previous chapter. Here we are concerned with how decisions are made when adult patients lack the capacity to consent. We cover decision-making for children in the next chapter.

---

[1] 105 NE 92 (1914).

2 THE CONSENT REQUIREMENT

(a) CRIMINAL LAW

It is commonly believed that it is the patient's consent to medical treatment that prevents it from being both a civil wrong and a criminal assault. This is only true for treatment that does not involve cutting the patient's body. For non-invasive medical procedures, like taking a patient's blood pressure, consent offers a defence to what might otherwise be unlawful touching. But because consent cannot offer a defence to the infliction of actual or grievous bodily harm, something other than consent must explain the legality of surgery.

In *Attorney General's Reference (No 6 of 1980)*,[2] the Court of Appeal referred to the accepted legality of, among other things, 'reasonable surgical interference . . . as needed in the public interest'. In *R v Brown*, a case in which the House of Lords decided that causing actual bodily harm through consensual sadomasochistic practices was an offence, the Lords agreed that 'proper' medical treatment does not constitute a criminal offence, but as Lord Mustill explains, the patient's consent could not, on its own, explain this exception.

R v Brown[3]

Lord Mustill

Many of the acts done by surgeons would be very serious crimes if done by anyone else, and yet the surgeons incur no liability. Actual consent, or the substitute for consent deemed by the law to exist where an emergency creates a need for action, is an essential element in this immunity; but it cannot be a direct explanation for it, since much of the bodily invasion involved in surgery lies well above any point at which consent could even arguably be regarded as furnishing a defence. Why is this so? The answer must in my opinion be that proper medical treatment, for which actual or deemed consent is a prerequisite, is in a category of its own.

At common law, therefore, for public interest reasons, rather than because the patient gave consent, 'reasonable' and 'proper' medical treatment stands completely outside the criminal law.

Of course, the use of qualifying words like 'reasonable' and 'proper' means that not every surgical intervention will fall within this public interest exception. Female circumcision is specifically proscribed by the Female Genital Mutilation Act 2003, but if it is judged not to be 'reasonable surgical interference', it might also amount to a criminal offence at common law.

Amputating a person's healthy limbs in order to increase her income from begging would not be 'proper' medical treatment. More complicated is the question of whether it could ever be legitimate to amputate a person's healthy limb when its presence is causing her distress. In 2000 it was revealed that a surgeon in Scotland had performed elective single-leg amputations on two physically healthy individuals who suffered from a rare sort of body dysmorphic disorder, in which the patient wishes to be an amputee.[4] The surgeon involved said that 'at follow up, both patients remain delighted with their new state'.[5]

---

[2] *Attorney General's Reference (No 6 of 1980)* [1981] QB 715.   [3] [1994] 1 AC 212.
[4] Sarah Ramsay, 'Controversy over UK surgeon who amputated healthy limbs' (2000) 355 The Lancet 476.
[5] Ibid.

On the one hand, operating in order to transform a non-disabled individual into a disabled one self-evidently causes grievous bodily harm, and seems manifestly 'unreasonable'. Yet, on the other hand, we now accept as 'reasonable' both gender reassignment surgery and cosmetic surgery, and, in each case, the operation alters the patient's physical body so that it better fits her own, or her preferred body image. In the next extract, Tracey Elliott questions whether a sharp distinction can be drawn between procedures that are generally assumed to be 'proper medical treatment'—such as cosmetic surgery, live organ donation, and gender reassignment surgery—and healthy limb amputation.

Tracey Elliott[6]

As in the case of healthy limb amputation, both live organ donation and gender reassignment surgery invariably involve the removal of healthy body parts... In addition, while it has been argued by some commentators that proper medical treatment 'must serve some therapeutic purpose', live organ donation offers no therapeutic benefits for the donor, and in the case of cosmetic surgery, any therapeutic purpose may be difficult, if not impossible to find... It is perhaps difficult to see how an operation upon a young woman to enlarge her breasts to enormous proportions so that she may become a glamour model or television game show contestant might be said to be in the public interest...

Given that the removal of healthy body parts in gender reassignment surgery in order to treat a severe psychological condition is lawful; might not healthy limb amputation be regarded as being justified upon a similar basis? ... Cosmetic surgery is lawful in spite of the fact that procedures are frequently undertaken merely to satisfy personal vanity or increase earning potential: aesthetic surgery has become part of a burgeoning 'beauty' industry, in which 'customers' are encouraged to take active steps to modify their bodies to attain or maintain their ideal physical image. If the criminal law has no place in controlling cosmetic surgery performed by qualified surgeons upon competent adults with their consent, why should it have any place in controlling other forms of surgery performed in similar circumstances?

(b) THE FORM CONSENT SHOULD TAKE

Consent to medical treatment does not need to be in writing. There are a few procedures, such as fertility treatment, where there is a statutory requirement to obtain written consent,[7] but this is exceptional.

For most routine medical treatment the patient's consent can be inferred from her behaviour. If I put out my arm to have a blood sample taken, it can be assumed that I am consenting to having a needle pierce my skin. In most encounters with healthcare professionals, formal consent procedures are non-existent. Rather, by seeking treatment and complying with instructions, the patient indicates her willingness to be treated.

Where the treatment involves surgery, it is good medical practice, albeit not a legal requirement, to obtain the patient's consent in writing, through her signature on a standard consent

[6] 'Body Dysmorphic Disorder, Radical Surgery and the Limits of Consent' (2009) 17 Medical Law Review 149–82.
[7] See further Chapter 15.

form. It is, however, important to remember that the consent form is not a contract between the doctor and her patient. Rather, the patient's consent must be ongoing throughout her treatment, and she is free to refuse treatment at any time.

(c) THE PRINCIPLE OF AUTONOMY

The principle that an adult with capacity must not be treated without her consent protects both her autonomy and her bodily integrity. As we can see from these statements from the House of Lords' judgment in *Airedale NHS Trust v Bland*, it is clear that, if an adult patient has capacity, she has the right to refuse medical treatment, even if this is not in her best interests.

Airedale NHS Trust v Bland [8]

Lord Mustill

If the patient is capable of making a decision on whether to permit treatment, . . . his choice must be obeyed even if on any objective view it is contrary to his best interests.

Lord Goff

[T]he principle of self-determination requires that respect must be given to the wishes of the patient, so that if an adult patient of sound mind refuses, however unreasonably, to consent to treatment or care by which his life would or might be prolonged, the doctors responsible for his care must give effect to his wishes, even though they do not consider it to be in his best interests to do.

Indeed, the patient's right of refusal exists regardless of whether her reasons are bizarre, irrational, or non-existent, and even if she might die as a result.

Re T (Adult: Refusal of Treatment) [9]

Lord Donaldson MR

This right of choice is not limited to decisions which others might regard as sensible. It exists notwithstanding that the reasons for making the choice are rational, irrational, unknown or even non-existent.

Staughton LJ

An adult whose mental capacity is unimpaired has the right to decide for herself whether she will or will not receive medical or surgical treatment, even in circumstances where she is likely or even certain to die in the absence of treatment.

[8] [1993] AC 789.   [9] [1993] Fam 95.

In addition to the common law's robust protection of autonomy, the patient's right to make her own medical decisions is protected by her Article 8 right to respect for her private and family life, which undoubtedly incorporates a right to make decisions about what happens to one's body.

It is therefore settled law that adults with capacity have the right to make irrational and life-threatening decisions to refuse medical treatment. In Chapter 1, we saw that some commentators have criticized the priority given to autonomy on the grounds that it is an excessively individualistic value. Respecting a patient's right to reject life-saving medical treatment ignores the impact that this might have upon other people, such as her dependent children. At times, then, there may be a tension between a patient's legal right to refuse treatment, and her moral obligations to others.

It is also important to note that the right patients have is to *refuse* treatment, not to insist upon it. Doctors cannot be forced to give treatment which they do not consider to be clinically indicated, regardless of how much a patient wants it.

In the next extract, Paddy McQueen draws attention to the fact that doctors commonly to refuse to sterilize young women (but not young men). It is, however, hard to see how sterilization could be said to be *clinically* inappropriate for a woman who is adamant that she never wants to have children, unless a doctor is assuming, paternalistically, that she is likely to change her mind.

Paddy McQueen[10]

There is evidence that many women, especially those without children and under the age of 30, have great difficulty in being sterilised. A commonly reported reason for this is the concern that they will later regret their decision. However, empirical research does not show high levels of poststerilisation regret, even for women with no children. Furthermore, even though poststerilisation regret is possible, I have argued that it does not carry much normative weight. If an individual is capable of making autonomous choices and has good reasons for requesting sterilisation, then it should be offered to them. The possibility that they may later regret is a risk that they ought to be allowed to take. There also appears to be a worrying gender asymmetry with regard to approved sterilisation requests. Concerns about voluntary sterilisation might be grounded in questionable gender discourses that essentialise women in terms of childbearing and parenthood. If this is the case, then it should be challenged. One's gender is irrelevant to whether a sterilisation request should be approved, and there is no reason to think that women are less capable of autonomous decision-making when it comes to choices about reproduction.

(d) PREGNANT WOMEN'S AUTONOMY?

In two cases, the Court of Appeal confirmed that pregnancy does not affect a patient's right to refuse unwanted medical intervention. In *Re MB (An Adult: Medical Treatment)*, although

---

[10] 'Autonomy, age and sterilisation requests' (2017) 43 Journal of Medical Ethics 310–13.

MB was judged to lack capacity temporarily as a result of her needle phobia, Butler-Sloss LJ was emphatic that:

> A competent woman who has the capacity to decide may, for religious reasons, other reasons, for rational or irrational reasons or for no reason at all, choose not to have medical intervention, even though the consequence may be the death or serious handicap of the child she bears, or her own death.[11]

A year later, in *St George's NHS Trust v S*, the emergency caesarean section that had been performed upon S against her wishes was held to have been unlawful. Judge LJ defended the pregnant woman's right to refuse treatment that could save her fetus's life, even if her decision might appear to be 'morally repugnant'.

St George's NHS Trust v S[12]

Judge LJ

In our judgment while pregnancy increases the personal responsibilities of a woman it does not diminish her entitlement to decide whether or not to undergo medical treatment. Although human, and protected by the law in a number of different ways . . . , an unborn child is not a separate person from its mother. Its need for medical assistance does not prevail over her rights. She is entitled not to be forced to submit to an invasion of her body against her will, whether her own life or that of her unborn child depends on it. Her right is not reduced or diminished merely because her decision to exercise it may appear morally repugnant.

While the Court of Appeal's judgment in *St George's NHS Trust v S* robustly asserts the primacy of patient autonomy, Matthew Thorpe, writing extra-judicially, has suggested that, in practice, this decision is easier for an appellate court than it was for the judge who had to make the decision in the 'heat of the moment', when two lives were in immediate danger.

Matthew Thorpe[13]

It is, perhaps, easier for an appellate court to discern principle than it is for a trial court to apply it in the face of judicial instinct, training, and emotion . . . It is simply unrealistic to suppose that the preservation of each life will not be a matter of equal concern to the Family Division judge surveying the medical dilemma. Whatever emphasis legal principle may place upon adult autonomy with the consequent right to choose between treatments, at some level the judicial outcome will be influenced by the expert evidence as to which treatment affords the best chance of the happy announcement that both mother and baby are doing well.

---

[11] *Re MB (An Adult: Medical Treatment)* [1997] 2 FLR 426.   [12] [1999] Fam 26.
[13] 'The Caesarean Section Debate' (1997) 27 Family Law 663–4.

3 WHAT IS INCAPACITY?

If a patient has capacity, then, unless she has been sectioned under the Mental Health Act 1983 (see Chapter 7), her refusal of medical treatment is decisive. In contrast, if a patient lacks capacity, she can be treated without consent, in her best interests. It is therefore vitally important to be able to tell whether or not a patient has capacity.

There are two possible approaches to the assessment of capacity: one based upon status and the other upon function:

- According to the *status* approach, some categories of patients lack capacity because of their status (an example would be being under the age of 18), regardless of their actual decision-making ability.

- The *functional* approach instead focuses on the individual's capabilities. On this approach, a child's capacity to make a particular decision would have to be individually assessed. A sensible and mature 14-year-old might be judged to have capacity, whereas a less mature 15-year-old might not.

The status approach is the simplest—it is more straightforward to find out a child's age than it is to judge her reasoning skills—but it is the functional approach which best promotes patient autonomy.

English law adopts a combination of the status and the functional approaches to capacity: all adults are presumed to have capacity, and all children under the age of 16 are presumed to lack capacity. Although these presumptions are status-based, they are just starting points that can be rebutted by evidence of the person's actual decision-making capacity. The difference between adults and children is therefore a shift in the burden of proof: evidence must be brought forward to establish that an adult does not have capacity; conversely, it would be for a 15-year-old to establish that she does, in fact, have the capacity to make a particular decision.

There appears to be one exception to this hybrid approach. As we see in Chapter 6, when children want to take certain life-threatening decisions—most commonly to refuse a blood transfusion on religious grounds—it is virtually impossible for them to establish that they have capacity, and instead their 'status' as minors appears, in practice, to be decisive.

In reality, of course, capacity is a question of degree. Although patients at either end of the spectrum are easily identified—a permanently comatose patient clearly lacks capacity, whereas it may be obvious that an intelligent university student is able to make his or her own decisions—towards the middle, it may be harder to tell whether someone is able to make decisions for herself.

Questioning a patient's decision-making capacity only tends to happen in two situations. First, if the patient belongs to a group whose members often or normally lack capacity, healthcare professionals may be alerted to the possibility that she may not be able to consent to treatment. A person suffering from Alzheimer's disease may or may not still have capacity, but the presence of a degenerative brain disorder might lead doctors to question her ability to make decisions. People suffering from certain disorders are therefore more likely to have their capacity assessed, and, as a result, are more likely to be found to lack capacity.

Secondly, if a patient's doctors believe that her decision is seriously misguided or irrational, they may be more likely to question her capacity. The irrationality of a patient's choice does not justify a finding of incapacity. On the contrary, if a patient has capacity, then her decision must be respected regardless of how foolish or irrational it seems to others. But it is probably inevitable that doctors are more likely to question a patient's capacity when she refuses treatment, than they are when she agrees with her doctors' recommendation.

Of course, if healthcare professionals are unlikely to question a patient's decision-making capacity when she has consented to a proposed treatment, the pool of patients who are judged to lack capacity will be smaller than it would be if all patients' decision-making capacity was scrutinized.

Vanessa Raymont et al assessed the decision-making capacity of acutely ill medical inpatients, and found that almost half of them lacked capacity, but since none of them had refused treatment, the treating doctors had treated their acquiescence as if it were a valid consent.

Vanessa Raymont et al[14]

If we accept that a high proportion of acutely ill medical inpatients do not have mental capacity to make decisions about current treatment, our findings have implications for clinical practice, legislation, and the doctor–patient relationship. The current position is to assume capacity unless there is strong evidence to the contrary. We suspect that a substantial proportion of patients with decisional difficulties place their trust in doctors, and passively acquiesce with treatment plans. Thus, incapacity is frequently overlooked ...

However, to accept the passive acquiescence of such patients as evidence of true consent would be dangerous when important and irreversible decisions need to be made. Before making such decisions, the clinician should have considered the possibility that the patient is unable to give valid consent.

(a) MENTAL CAPACITY ACT 2005

At the beginning of the twenty-first century, there were several reasons for introducing statutory reform of the law relating to the treatment of adults who lack capacity. The common law framework was believed to be unclear, leaving medical professionals and carers uncertain how to act. In an ageing population, the number of people who will become incapacitated is also increasing. In the UK, there are 850,000 people living with dementia, and this is expected to increase to one million by 2025, and two million by 2051.

Although we focus only on medical decisions, it is worth noting that the Mental Capacity Act (MCA) 2005 covers more than just the medical treatment of people who lack capacity, and extends to the management of their financial affairs, and decisions about where they should live.

(1) The 'Principles'

Section 1 of the MCA sets out five statutory principles which capture the most basic and important assumptions underpinning the statutory scheme.

Mental Capacity Act 2005 section 1

1(1) The following principles apply for the purposes of this Act.

(2) A person must be assumed to have capacity unless it is established that he lacks capacity.

---

[14] 'Prevalence of mental incapacity in medical inpatients and associated risk factors: cross-sectional study' (2004) 364 The Lancet 1421–7.

(3) A person is not to be treated as unable to make a decision unless all practicable steps to help him to do so have been taken without success.

(4) A person is not to be treated as unable to make a decision merely because he makes an unwise decision.

(5) An act done, or decision made, under this Act for or on behalf of a person who lacks capacity must be done, or made, in his best interests.

(6) Before the act is done, or the decision is made, regard must be had to whether the purpose for which it is needed can be as effectively achieved in a way that is less restrictive of the person's rights and freedom of action.

The Act's Code of Practice, updated most recently in 2014, sets out how these principles, and the legislative provisions described later, should apply in practice.

The Act applies to people over the age of 16. Young people aged 16 and 17 are in a slightly curious position. If they lack capacity, they can be treated under the MCA, and, as we see in Chapter 6, the presumption of capacity that applies to them is slightly different from the more robust presumption which applies to over-18s.

(2) Definition of Incapacity

(a) What is incapacity?

The first principle in section 1 of the Act is there is a presumption of capacity, which can be rebutted only if the patient fails the Act's two-stage test for capacity. The first stage is that the person must be suffering from 'an impairment of, or a disturbance in the functioning of, the mind or brain'.

Mental Capacity Act 2005 section 2

2 People who lack capacity

(1) For the purposes of this Act, a person lacks capacity in relation to a matter if at the material time he is unable to make a decision for himself in relation to the matter because of an impairment of, or a disturbance in the functioning of, the mind or brain.

(2) It does not matter whether the impairment or disturbance is permanent or temporary.

This 'diagnostic threshold' means that someone will not fall within the provisions of the Act unless they are suffering from some sort of mental impairment, which can be either temporary or permanent. The Code of Practice suggests that a wide variety of conditions will be covered.

Mental Capacity Act Code of Practice

4.12 Examples of an impairment or disturbance in the functioning of the mind or brain may include the following:

• conditions associated with some forms of mental illness

- dementia
- significant learning disabilities
- the long-term effects of brain damage
- physical or medical conditions that cause confusion, drowsiness or loss of consciousness
- delirium
- concussion following a head injury, and
- the symptoms of alcohol or drug use.

The Code of Practice also attempts to address the problem, described previously, of the under-diagnosis of incapacity (a) in patients suffering from chronic physical illness, and (b) among patients who agree with a doctor's proposed treatment plan:

Mental Capacity Act Code of Practice

4.26 ... Temporary factors may also affect someone's ability to make decisions. Examples include acute illness, severe pain, the effect of medication, or distress after a death or shock ...

4.45 ... Be aware that the fact that a person agrees with you or assents to what is proposed does not necessarily mean that they have capacity to make the decision.

Once this diagnostic requirement has been satisfied, the second stage is to work out whether the person is able to make a decision for himself. Section 3(1) sets out what is meant by being 'unable to make a decision'.

Mental Capacity Act 2005 section 3

3 Inability to make decisions

(1) For the purposes of section 2, a person is unable to make a decision for himself if he is unable—

(a) to understand the information relevant to the decision,

(b) to retain that information,

(c) to use or weigh that information as part of the process of making the decision, or

(d) to communicate his decision (whether by talking, using sign language or any other means).

(2) A person is not to be regarded as unable to understand the information relevant to a decision if he is able to understand an explanation of it given to him in a way that is appropriate to his circumstances (using simple language, visual aids or any other means).

(3) The fact that a person is able to retain the information relevant to a decision for a short period only does not prevent him from being regarded as able to make the decision.

The test for capacity is decision-specific: the question is whether the person has the capacity to make a particular decision. A person might therefore have capacity in relation to some decisions, and lack it in relation to others. In theory, this means that someone's capacity ought to be assessed in relation to every decision that arises about their treatment.

The test for capacity is whether the person can understand the information that is relevant to the particular decision, retain it, and use it in order to make a choice. It is sufficient if the person can retain information temporarily. Section 3(3) of the Act specifies that someone who can retain information only for short periods of time should nevertheless be entitled to make her own decisions. This might be particularly important for patients suffering from progressive memory loss: they could be judged to have capacity to make a decision even if they are likely to have forgotten what they have been told a few days later.

Moreover, the Code of Practice suggests that efforts should be made to help people to retain information:

> If they have difficulty understanding, it might be useful to present information in a different way (for example, different forms of words, pictures or diagrams). Written information, audio-tapes, videos and posters can help people remember important facts.[15]

The fourth limb of section 3(1)—namely that P is not able to communicate his decision—applies only to patients, such as those who are in a coma or suffering from locked-in syndrome, who cannot express a view by even the most minimal means, such as squeezing an arm or blinking an eyelid.[16]

What is meant by 'information relevant to the decision'? Does a person have to be able to understand, retain, and use complex clinical information, or is it enough that they have a very basic understanding of what is proposed? In *Heart of England NHS Foundation Trust v JB*, Peter Jackson J found that all that was necessary was that JB had a 'broad, general understanding' of the benefits and risks of amputation, rather than a more detailed understanding of the relative risks of different types of amputation.

Heart of England NHS Foundation Trust v JB[17]

Peter Jackson J

[W]hat is in my view required is that she should understand the nature, purpose and effects of the proposed treatment, the last of these entailing an understanding of the benefits and risks of deciding to have or not to have one or other of the various kinds of amputation, or of not making a decision at all.

What is required here is a broad, general understanding of the kind that is expected from the population at large. JB is not required to understand every last piece of information about her situation and her options ... [W]hat is required is an understanding of the nature, purpose and effects of the proposed treatment. In this sense 'the proposed treatment' is surgical treatment for a potentially gangrenous limb, and is not limited to one of the possible operations. Treating each type of amputation as different is an impractical and unnecessary distinction that would diminish the scope of JB's capacity.

---

[15] Mental Capacity Act 2005 Code of Practice, para 4.18.   [16] Ibid, para 4.23.
[17] [2014] EWHC 342 (COP).

In order to protect their autonomy, it is important that patients are not disqualified from making decisions because they cannot understand all of the possible ramifications of a relatively simple decision. For example, in the case of contraception, it should be enough, as Bodey J explained in *A Local Authority v A*,[18] that a woman understands what a contraceptive injection will involve, rather than needing to have a full understanding of what it would be like for her to have a baby: 'in my judgment, the test for capacity should be so applied as to ascertain the woman's ability to understand and weigh up the immediate medical issues surrounding contraceptive treatment'.

(b) Common law incapacity: the inherent jurisdiction

If someone with borderline capacity does not satisfy the diagnostic threshold, and hence does not lack capacity within the terms of the MCA, that is not necessarily the end of the matter. In a number of cases, the courts have invoked the inherent jurisdiction, which predated the MCA, in order to protect vulnerable but capacitous adults.[19] In *DL v A Local Authority*, for example, the Court of Appeal held that the inherent jurisdiction still existed for vulnerable adults who, while not suffering from mental incapacity within the definition of the Act, were incapacitated from making decisions as a result of 'constraint, coercion, undue influence or other vitiating factors'.

DL v A Local Authority[20]

McFarlane LJ

My conclusion that the inherent jurisdiction remains available for use in cases to which it may apply that fall outside the MCA 2005 is not merely arrived at on the negative basis that the words of the statute are self-limiting and there is no reference within it to the inherent jurisdiction. There is, in my view, a sound and strong public policy justification for this to be so. The existence of 'elder abuse', as described by Professor Williams, is sadly all too easy to contemplate. Indeed the use of the term 'elder' in that label may inadvertently limit it to a particular age group whereas, as the cases demonstrate, the will of a vulnerable adult of any age may, in certain circumstances, be overborne. Where the facts justify it, such individuals require and deserve the protection of the authorities and the law so that they may regain the very autonomy that the appellant rightly prizes ...

Where, on a strict mental health appraisal, such an individual does not lack capacity in the terms of the MCA 2005 and therefore falls outside the statutory scheme, but other factors, for example coercion and undue influence, may combine with his borderline capacity to remove his autonomy to make an important decision, why, one may ask, should that individual not be able to access the protection now afforded to adults whose mental capacity puts them on the other side of that borderline?

The development by the courts of the inherent jurisdiction, as a way to protect vulnerable but capacitous adults, has been welcomed by some commentators, and criticized by others.

---

[18] [2010] EWHC 1549 (Fam).

[19] *Re G (An Adult)* [2004] EWHC 2222 (Fam); *Re SA (Vulnerable Adult with Capacity: Marriage)* [2006] 1 FLR 867 and *Re SK* [2005] 2 FLR 230.

[20] [2012] EWCA Civ 253.

Jonathan Herring argues that it is protective of autonomy and human rights, and welcomes its acknowledgement that incapacity is not synonymous with mental disorder,[21] whereas Michael Dunn et al worry about the negative consequences of ignoring the vulnerable adult's perspective.

Jonathan Herring[22]

The use of the inherent jurisdiction challenges the binary divide between those who have capacity and those who do not, set up in the Mental Capacity Act 2005. It does this by offering the potential for legal intervention when a person has capacity, but only just . . .

Yet one final advantage to the use of the vulnerable adult jurisdiction is that the law is brought close in line to the ideals in the United Nations Convention on the Rights of Persons with Disabilities. The ability to intervene and make decisions will discriminate less on the grounds of whether a person has a mental disorder and enable the law to provide a set of protective mechanisms for those who lack autonomy . . .

[The inherent jurisdiction] is a helpful acknowledgement that a person may have legal capacity for the purposes of the MCA, yet not be able to make a properly autonomous decision. In such a case it can hardly be said to be respectful of autonomy to grant legal weight to their decision. The jurisdiction is also a recognition that autonomy is not an all-or-nothing concept, but should be understood as scalar. A richly autonomous decision deserves more respect than a weakly autonomous one. The inherent jurisdiction enables a more subtle approach to be taken to autonomy.

Michael C Dunn, Isabel CH Clare, and Anthony J Holland[23]

[W]e note that all cases where protective interventions have been justified for 'vulnerable adults' who are deemed situationally vulnerable, are characterised by the presence of a 'villain'. This 'villain' is usually considered to be difficult to engage with, to be acting in his/her own interests against the objective 'best interests' of the 'vulnerable adult', and/or unlikely to change his/her behaviour. In the cases examined, this person has always been a close family member, but this need not be so . . .

If G recognised the malign influence of her father, but valued his role in her life above and beyond this, could she really be described as 'vulnerable', and thus in need of court intervention? If SA valued her cultural heritage, and wished for her mother and father to have an active role in arranging her marriage, surely more attention should have been focused on attempts to work with them as a family to resolve the issue facing the court? Rather than viewing her parents as hostile, inflexible, and lacking in insight and understanding, intervention would then have prioritised the maintenance of close relationships between family members. If this is not the approach taken, inadvertent negative consequences might arise. When an individual has restrictions placed on his/her contact with family members in order to protect him/her, but has

---

[21] See also Kirsty Keywood, 'The vulnerable adult experiment: Situating vulnerability in adult safeguarding law and policy' (2017) 53 International Journal of Law and Psychiatry 88–96.

[22] *Vulnerable Adults and the Law* (Oxford University Press, 2016).

[23] 'To Empower or To Protect? Constructing the 'vulnerable adult' in English Law and Public Policy' (2008) 28 Legal Studies 234–53.

always lived in the parental home with little or no contact with any other persons, a protective intervention might safeguard that individual's welfare in the short-term, but result in a general deleterious effect on that person's quality of life in the long-term.

In the next extract, Emma Cave links the inherent jurisdiction to other developments in the law, namely moves towards adult safeguarding and mandatory reporting, and suggests that doctors may need be concerned about whether to respect apparently autonomous refusals of treatment.

Emma Cave[24]

A more paternalistic emphasis permeates recent legal developments that could require professionals to report abuse or neglect, even in light of an individual's objection ... There is a growing faction in support of broader mandatory reporting laws that aim, in part, to save victims from what might be considered involuntary decisions to reject intervention ...

Doctors must now have in mind the potential not only for mental incapacity under the 2005 Act, but also for common law incapacity borne of involuntariness ... It is possible that a doctor who accepted a refusal of treatment from a patient who lacked capacity at common law due to involuntariness might be found guilty of wilful neglect if it could be shown that the doctor acted recklessly. Let us imagine that a patient refuses a recommended round of chemotherapy under pressure from a relative; or refuses treatment for fractured ribs by command of an abusive partner. Even if the abuse does not operate as an 'impairment of the mind or brain' sufficient to satisfy the diagnostic threshold in section 2(1) of the 2005 Act, an argument might be made that conforming with the expressed will of these patients constitutes neglect if the doctor ought reasonably to have approached the High Court to exercise its inherent jurisdiction in order to facilitate a voluntary decision.

(c) The right to take unwise or irrational decisions?

While section 1(4) of the Act is clear that a 'person is not to be treated as unable to make a decision merely because he makes an unwise decision', there is an ambiguity here. On the one hand, if a patient satisfies the test for capacity, it does not matter if the decision she wants to take is irrational or eccentric. On the other hand, it is sometimes difficult to distinguish between a person's bizarre wishes, which must nevertheless be respected, and a person's inability to use and weigh information, which may mean that she fails section 3(1)(c) of the test for capacity.

In practice, Paula Case points out a worrying tendency for psychiatrists asked to assess a person's capacity to point in their evidence to P's lack of 'insight'. Insight is a term commonly used in psychiatry to indicate that a person accepts her diagnosis (and conversely, someone who lacks insight may not think that there is anything wrong with them). 'Insight' does not appear in the Act, however, and the danger is that a someone who wants to make an unwise decision is pathologized as lacking insight.

---

[24] 'Protecting Patients from their Bad Decisions: Rebalancing Rights, Relationships, and Risk' (2017) 25 Medical Law Review 527–53.

Paula Case[25]

Where P's refusal or non-cooperation are pathologised through the medical device of insight, this can also be said to undermine P's right to make unwise decisions (protected by section 1(4) of the MCA) and is at odds with the statutory principle that aspects of P's behaviour should not be equated with incapacity (section 2(3)(b)). It also threatens to displace the ethos of the statutory framework which is to assess the *procedure* by which P is making decisions rather than the *content* of those decisions (section 1(4) and section 2(3) (b) taken together) ...

[T]he fact of refusal in and of itself can too readily be treated by professionals dealing with the Act as giving rise to cause for concerns about capacity. Where this approach is adopted, refusals of care are in effect pathologised, a practice which is at odds with the philosophy underpinning the MCA of appraising people's decision-making *processes* rather than the *content* of their decisions ...

[A]n absence of insight is identified in cases where there is merely a failure to internalise the medical or professional viewpoint of P's best interests. Where this occurs, the rejection of treatment/services can too easily be construed as a manifestation of a 'lack of insight' which in turn indicates disorder or incapacity. In short, a lack of cooperation is potentially pathologised.

Interestingly, the 2018 NICE guideline on decision-making and mental incapacity now spells out that lacking insight and lacking capacity are not the same thing.

National Institute for Health and Care Excellence[26]

Practitioners should be aware that a person may have decision-making capacity even if they are described as lacking 'insight' into their condition. Capacity and insight are two distinct concepts. If a practitioner believes a person's insight/lack of insight is relevant to their assessment of the person's capacity, they must clearly record what they mean by insight/lack of insight in this context and how they believe it affects/does not affect the person's capacity.

When assessing capacity, the critical question should be whether someone can make *a* decision, not whether she can make a sensible or a responsible decision. In *The Mental Health Trust v DD*, one of several Court of Protection decisions concerning DD, a pregnant woman with a complex obstetric history, learning difficulties, and an autistic spectrum disorder, Cobb J explained that he had to 'review with particular care whether DD's decision making is simply "unwise" rather than evidence of her incapacity'. If her decision-making were merely 'unwise', he would 'have no right under the Mental Capacity Act 2005 to intervene'.

---

[25] 'Dangerous Liaisons? Psychiatry and Law in the Court of Protection—Expert Discourses of 'Insight' (and 'Compliance')' (2016) 24 Medical Law Review 360–78,
[26] *Decision-making and Mental Capacity* (NICE, 2018).

The Mental Health Trust v DD [27]

Cobb J

Her decision-making is undoubtedly 'unwise', but it is not, in my judgment, just 'unwise'; it lacks the essential characteristic of discrimination which only comes when the relevant information is evaluated, and weighed. I am satisfied that in relation to each of the matters under consideration her impairment of mind (essentially attributable to her autistic spectrum disorder, overlaid with her learning disability) prevents her from weighing the information relevant to each decision.

In contrast, in *Re SB (A Patient) (Capacity to Consent to Termination)*, Holman J disagreed with the view of the treating psychiatrist, that a pregnant woman with bipolar disorder did not have capacity. She had paranoid and persecutory beliefs, and counsel for the NHS Trust had said that she was 'not thinking straight'. Holman J found that even if her reasoning was skewed by paranoia, she was able to make the decision to terminate her pregnancy.

Re SB (A Patient) (Capacity to Consent to Termination) [28]

Holman J

It seems to me ... that even if aspects of the decision making are influenced by paranoid thoughts in relation to her husband and her mother, she is nevertheless able to describe, and genuinely holds, a range of rational reasons for her decision. When I say rational, I do not necessarily say they are good reasons, nor do I indicate whether I agree with her decision, for section 1(4) of the Act expressly provides that someone is not to be treated as unable to make a decision simply because it is an unwise decision. It seems to me that this lady has made, and has maintained for an appreciable period of time, a decision. It may be that aspects of her reasons may be skewed by paranoia. There are other reasons which she has and which she has expressed. My own opinion is that it would be a total affront to the autonomy of this patient to conclude that she lacks capacity to the level required to make this decision.

King's College NHS Foundation Trust v C was another case in which the judge found that a patient had capacity, despite psychiatrists' evidence that she did not. MacDonald J explained that C had sought to live life:

entirely and unapologetically on her own terms; that life revolving largely around her looks, men, material possessions and 'living the high life'. In particular, it is clear that during her life C has placed a significant premium on youth and beauty and on living a life that, in C's words, 'sparkles'.

After taking an overdose of paracetamol, C had suffered kidney failure and wished to refuse dialysis. With dialysis, C would have a good prognosis; without it, she would die. Two experts thought C was unable to weigh information about her prognosis in order to make a choice,

---

[27] [2014] EWCOP 11.   [28] [2013] EWHC 1417 (COP).

but MacDonald J disagreed. He found that C did understand and believe her prognosis, it was just that she chose to give it no weight 'within the context of her own values and outlook'. As C had capacity, she had the right to refuse dialysis. C died two weeks later.

Kings College NHS Foundation Trust v C[29]

MacDonald J

[T]he rationale expressed by C for refusing treatment was that she believed she may need dialysis for the rest of her life, saw a bleak future if she could not have a life of socialising, drinking and partying with friends, that getting old scared her both in terms of illness and appearance . . .

The decision C has reached to refuse dialysis can be characterised as an unwise one. That C considers that the prospect of growing old, the fear of living with fewer material possessions and the fear that she has lost, and will not regain, 'her sparkle' outweighs a prognosis that signals continued life will alarm and possibly horrify many, although I am satisfied that the ongoing discomfort of treatment, the fear of chronic illness and the fear of lifelong treatment and lifelong disability are factors that also weigh heavily in the balance for C. C's decision is certainly one that does not accord with the expectations of many in society. Indeed, others in society may consider C's decision to be unreasonable, illogical or even immoral within the context of the sanctity accorded to life by society in general. None of this however is evidence of a lack of capacity. The court being satisfied that, in accordance with the provisions of the Mental Capacity Act 2005, C has capacity to decide whether or not to accept treatment C is entitled to make her own decision on that question based on the things that are important to her, in keeping with her own personality and system of values and without conforming to society's expectation of what constitutes the 'normal' decision in this situation (if such a thing exists). As a capacitous individual C is, in respect of her own body and mind, sovereign.

Does this mean that an anorexic patient, who has 'chosen to attach no weight' to information about her need for food, might nevertheless have capacity? In practice, anorexia has been treated as a rather special case, because the condition itself interferes with the patients' ability to use or weigh information.

Mental Capacity Act Code of Practice

4.21 . . . Sometimes people can understand information but an impairment or disturbance stops them using it . . .

4.22 For example, a person with the eating disorder anorexia nervosa may understand information about the consequences of not eating. But their compulsion not to eat might be too strong for them to ignore.

For example, *A Local Authority v E* involved a 32-year-old woman with anorexia whose death was imminent. E was adamant that she did not want to eat or be fed. Despite describing E as

---

[29] [2015] EWCOP 80.

being 'fully aware of her situation' and 'intelligent and charming', Peter Jackson J found that she lacked capacity, and that feeding her against her wishes was in her best interests.

A Local Authority v E [30]

Peter Jackson J

There is no doubt that E has an impairment of, or a disturbance in the functioning of, the mind or brain in the form of her anorexia. Equally it is clear that in terms of MCA s. 3(1) she can understand and retain the information relevant to the treatment decision and can communicate her decision.

However, there is strong evidence that E's obsessive fear of weight gain makes her incapable of weighing the advantages and disadvantages of eating in any meaningful way. For E, the compulsion to prevent calories entering her system has become the card that trumps all others. The need not to gain weight overpowers all other thoughts.

A particularly clear illustration of the fact that anorexia destroys someone's capacity to weigh information about their need for food comes from the fact that sufferers might have capacity in relation to other medical decisions, and lack capacity only in relation to their anorexia. This was the case in *An NHS Trust v X*. Ms X lacked capacity in relation to the treatment of anorexia, but she retained the ability to weigh information about her alcohol dependence disorder.

An NHS Trust v X [31]

Cobb J

Because Ms X is body dysmorphic she believes she is larger than she is and is unlikely therefore to understand how ill she in fact is. In any event, [Dr Glover] was firmly of the view that Ms X was unable to weigh the relevant information: '... *her ability to weigh the decision in the balance is significantly disturbed by her fear of weight gain. This disturbance is sufficient to render [Ms X] incapacitous with respect to these decisions.*' ... On the evidence which I have heard, I am entirely satisfied that Ms X lacks capacity to litigate and to make decisions about her eating disorder.

Both Dr A and Dr Glover were clear in drawing a distinction between Ms X's capacity to make decisions around her eating disorder (anorexia) and her use of alcohol. They both considered that Ms X was able to understand, retain, and crucially weigh up, the decision around drinking; they felt that her drinking was responsive to events—she appeared to be making choices about when to drink, when to drink more, and when to drink less. In particular, Dr Glover was of the view that Ms X was able to weigh information such as the calorific content of alcohol, and appeared to be aware of the consequences for her liver functioning of continued abusive drinking, including the prospect that it could kill her; Dr Glover considered that she may limit her alcohol consumption on occasion for this reason. In short, both doctors considered that she had capacity to make decisions about alcohol and I accept these opinions.

---

[30] [2012] EWHC 1639 (Fam).   [31] [2014] EWCOP 35.

It follows that my jurisdiction is limited to making best interests decisions only in relation to the treatment of anorexia nervosa and not in relation to the management or treatment of her alcohol dependence disorder.

In the next extract, John Coggon highlights two issues that flow from the decision-specific test for capacity evident in *An NHS Trust v X*. First, it might be difficult to untangle the application of an 'advance decision' if P only had capacity in relation to one of her disorders when she made the advance decision, and, secondly, it illustrates that it may not make sense to refer to the 'competent patient'.

John Coggon[32]

Cobb J, having affirmed her capacity, necessarily finds the advance decision to be valid, notwithstanding that it would have no contemporary application. However, his judgment highlights the complication that although Ms X had capacity in relation to alcohol, she lacked it in relation to her anorexia and conditions arising because of that. A practical difficulty would arise if it were impossible to establish definitively the cause of a particular health problem. Thus, the precise extent to which the advance decision might be binding is to be doubted; we have a situation where the scope of the patient's competence seems quite unclear . . .

This case provides a clear illustration of how and why 'the competent patient' does not, in truth, exist as a free-standing concept in English mental capacity law. A patient can only be competent in reference to a specific issue. Decision-specific capacity is ignored when universal claims are asserted through the idea of 'the competent patient'.

Jillian Craigie and Ailsa Davies make the interesting suggestion that the ease with which anorexia is said to impair capacity, as compared to alcohol dependency, derives from the background assumption that anorexic patients are blameless, and unable to help themselves, whereas alcoholic patients are perceived to be more blameworthy, and hence in control of their decision to drink.

Jillian Craigie and Ailsa Davies[33]

Like those who are alcohol dependent, people with anorexia play a significant part in the development of their condition, when they pursue diet and exercise regimes that at some point get out of control. In this way, anorexia looks much more like substance dependency than pneumonia or appendicitis.

On the other hand, what strongly distinguishes substance dependency from anorexia is that anorexia develops in the pursuit of things that our society values. Thinness and exercise are considered virtuous, along with traits associated with anorexia such as perfectionism and resistance against bodily desires . . .

---

[32] 'Alcohol Dependence and Anorexia Nervosa: Individual Autonomy and the Jurisdiction of the Court of Protection' (2015) 23 Medical Law Review 659–67.

[33] 'Problems of control: Alcohol dependence, anorexia nervosa, and the flexible interpretation of mental incapacity tests' (2018) 26 Medical Law Review online first.

> The mental picture of a person with anorexia is likely to be a well-mannered young woman; while the mental picture associated with alcohol dependency is likely to be a disheveled older man … Perhaps negative associations with alcohol dependency evoke feelings of anger and antipathy, and these connect to seeing the person as blameworthy … On the other hand, perhaps the positive associations with anorexia evoke feelings of sadness and sympathy, which connect to seeing the person as an innocent victim. This seems likely to foreground the impact of the impairment on decisions, making a wide interpretation of the MCA's test seem appropriate to apply—enabling a finding of incapacity …
>
> When control is the central issue, questions of the capacity to refuse treatment for anorexia are discussed using language referring to distorted, biased, and overpowered thought. This makes it clearer that the question is not a binary matter about whether the person has any control at all, but one about the difficulties the person faces in relation to control. This more subtle language, however, was not used in the judgments concerning alcohol dependency, with significance in the case of *Ms X* instead given to the idea that she was always making a choice to drink.

It is important to note that a finding that a patient with anorexia lacks capacity does not automatically mean that force-feeding will be authorized. As we can see from the next case involving a 46-year-old woman with severe and chronic anorexia, there are times when judges have agreed with medical opinion that it may be in the patient's best interests to receive no further treatment.

Cheshire and Wirral Partnership NHS Foundation Trust v Z [34]

Hayden J

> Thus, it is hoped, and, in my judgement, it can be no more than that, that an indication to her that the hospital, the Trust and the doctors will withdraw from her life, to respect her wishes and her autonomy, may lead to a sense of emotional wellbeing which may at least enable her to cooperate and in some way, perhaps, to prolong life … It is almost certainly a pious hope that Z will, if left broadly to her own devices, manage effectively to confront this terrible illness, which has darkened her life since she was 15. I am aware that her parents express a belief that she can manage this and I have no difficulty in understanding why they might cling to that hope. I however must be more objective in my analysis and reasoning. Although it will be a terribly painful for Z and her parents to hear it expressed in these terms, I have come to the clear conclusion that I am choosing between 3 palliative care options.

Heather Draper has pointed out an interesting distinction between chronic undereating usually caused by psychological problems, where a finding of incapacity appears to be almost automatic, and chronic overeating, which might similarly be prompted by psychological problems such as low self-esteem, and which can be similarly life-threatening, but where a diagnosis of incapacity would be unlikely. [35]

---

[34] [2016] EWCOP 56.

[35] 'Anorexia nervosa and respecting a refusal of life-prolonging therapy: a limited justification' (2000) 14 Bioethics 120–33.

Of course, one explanation for this difference is that anorexia is classified as a mental illness in the International Classification of Diseases (ICD-10), whereas extreme overeating is not.[36] Heather Draper has also contrasted an anorexic's refusal of food with a woman's rejection of radical mastectomy.

Heather Draper[37]

Let us take a step back from the emotionally charged issue of anorexia and consider a parallel case—that of a woman who knows that with a radical mastectomy and chemotherapy she has a good chance of recovering from breast cancer but who refuses to have the operation because, in her opinion, living with only one breast or no breasts at all will be intolerable. She is *also* making a decision based on her perception of her body image and we might think that this is an irrational perception. Nevertheless, operating without her consent is unthinkable.

(d) Equal treatment

Buttressing the presumption of capacity, the Act spells out certain factors which must not be used to ground a finding of incapacity.

Mental Capacity Act 2005 section 2

2(3) A lack of capacity cannot be established merely by reference to—

(a) a person's age or appearance, or

(b) a condition of his, or an aspect of his behaviour, which might lead others to make unjustified assumptions about his capacity.

The intention of this section is clear: to remind healthcare professionals that they should not rely on stereotypes and assumptions when judging capacity. The use of the word 'merely' is, however, rather odd, since the implication is that a lack of capacity could be established based upon a person's age or appearance, provided that there are other factors which also justify this finding. It could be argued that 'unjustified assumptions about his capacity' should not be relevant at all, rather than being potentially relevant if backed up by other factors.

This unfortunate wording is repeated in section 4 when deciding what treatment to offer. The insertion of the word 'merely' implies that someone's appearance or behaviour could be relevant to the decision as to what is in their best interests, as long as it is not the only factor.

Mental Capacity Act 2005 section 4

4(1) In determining for the purposes of this Act what is in a person's best interests, the person making the determination must not make it merely on the basis of—

(a) the person's age or appearance, or

---

[36] For discussion, see further Rebecca Dresser, 'Feeding the Hunger Artists: Legal Issues in Treating Anorexia Nervosa' (1984) 2 Wisconsin Law Review 297.

[37] "Treating anorexics without consent: some reservations' (1998) 24 Journal of Medical Ethics 5–7.

(b) a condition of his, or an aspect of his behaviour, which might lead others to make unjustified assumptions about what might be in his best interests.

(3) Assisted Decision-Making

The second statutory principle, in section 1(3), provides that 'a person is not to be treated as unable to make a decision unless all practicable steps to help him to do so have been taken without success'. This is bolstered by section 3(2).

Mental Capacity Act 2005

3(2) A person is not to be regarded as unable to understand the information relevant to a decision if he is able to understand an explanation of it given to him in a way that is appropriate to his circumstances (using simple language, visual aids or any other means).

The Code of Practice goes into considerable detail about the support which people might need, and offers guidance on how to maximize their decision-making ability.

Mental Capacity Act Code of Practice

2.7 The kind of support people might need to help them make a decision varies. It depends on personal circumstances, the kind of decision that has to be made and the time available to make the decision. It might include:

- using a different form of communication (for example, non-verbal communication)
- providing information in a more accessible form (for example, photographs, drawings, or tapes)
- treating a medical condition which may be affecting the person's capacity or
- having a structured programme to improve a person's capacity to make particular decisions (for example, helping a person with learning disabilities to learn new skills) . . .

3.10 To help someone make a decision for themselves, all possible and appropriate means of communication should be tried.

- Ask people who know the person well about the best form of communication (try speaking to family members, carers, day centre staff or support workers). They may also know somebody the person can communicate with easily, or the time when it is best to communicate with them.
- Use simple language. Where appropriate, use pictures, objects or illustrations to demonstrate ideas.
- Speak at the right volume and speed, with appropriate words and sentence structure. It may be helpful to pause to check understanding or show that a choice is available.
- Break down difficult information into smaller points that are easy to understand. Allow the person time to consider and understand each point before continuing.

- It may be necessary to repeat information or go back over a point several times.
- Is help available from people the person trusts (relatives, friends, GP, social worker, religious or community leaders)? If so, make sure the person's right to confidentiality is respected.
- Be aware of cultural, ethnic or religious factors that shape a person's way of thinking, behaviour or communication . . .
- If necessary, consider using a professional language interpreter . . .
- Would an advocate (someone who can support and represent the person) improve communication in the current situation? . . .

3.13 . . . Where possible, choose a location where the person feels most at ease. For example, people are usually more comfortable in their own home than at a doctor's surgery.

3.14 . . . Try to choose the time of day when the person is most alert—some people are better in the mornings, others are more lively in the afternoon or early evening. It may be necessary to try several times before a decision can be made.

In an emergency, extensive steps to support the person to make their own decision may not be practicable. The Code suggests that when an urgent decision is required, and 'treatment cannot be delayed while a person gets support to make a decision . . . the only practical and appropriate steps might be to keep a person informed of what is happening and why'.[38]

When it considered reforms to the law on capacity, as part of its review of the Deprivation of Liberty Safeguards (which we consider in Chapter 7), the Law Commission proposed that there should be a scheme through which people could appoint 'supporters' to help them make decisions for themselves.

Law Commission[39]

14.51 We remain of the view that the establishment of a supported decision-making scheme would offer clear benefits. In particular, it would bolster the second principle of the Mental Capacity Act which requires that all practicable steps must be taken to help a person to make a decision before they are treated as lacking capacity to make that decision; the evidence from consultation suggested that compliance with the principle is patchy and inconsistent, which was consistent with the findings of the House of Lords Select Committee on the Mental Capacity Act. Service users and patients also welcomed the opportunity of being able to appoint someone they knew and trusted to help them make important decisions and felt this would lead to improved outcomes.

Although the Law Commission advocated a regulation-making power to allow the Secretary of State to establish a supported decision-making scheme, this proposal was not taken forward by the government.

---

[38] Para 2.9.   [39] *Mental Capacity and Deprivation of Liberty*, Law Com no 372 (2017).

(4) How Should People Who Lack Capacity be Treated?

(a) The least restrictive alternative

When deciding between possible courses of action, there should always be a presumption in favour of the least intrusive one, and consideration should be given as to whether it is necessary to act at all. So, for example, if a woman who lacks capacity cannot cope with her heavy periods, hysterectomy must be an option of last resort, and less intrusive ways to control her menstrual cycle, such as contraceptive injections or implants, should be tried first.

A Local Authority v K was the first post-MCA non-therapeutic sterilization case.[40] K was a 21-year-old woman with Down's syndrome and mild to moderate learning difficulties. Her parents were concerned that as she grew older, they would be able to exercise less control over her behaviour, thus increasing the risk that she might engage in wanted or unwanted sexual activity. A hormonal contraceptive implant had been tried, but K had experienced adverse side-effects, and had found its insertion traumatic.

K's parents believed that sterilization would be in her best interests, and they had considered taking her abroad if it was not possible to sterilize K in the UK. Cobb J found that K lacked capacity, but that sterilization would not be in her best interests because it was not the least restrictive alternative: 'there are less restrictive methods of achieving the purpose of contraception than sterilisation, and that in the event of a need for contraception, these ought to be attempted'.

(b) The best interests test

People who lack capacity must be treated in their best interests, and section 4 sets out a non-exhaustive list of relevant factors.

Mental Capacity Act 2005 section 4

4(2) The person making the determination must consider all the relevant circumstances and, in particular, take the following steps.

(3) He must consider—

(a) whether it is likely that the person will at some time have capacity in relation to the matter in question, and

(b) if it appears likely that he will, when that is likely to be.

(4) He must, so far as reasonably practicable, permit and encourage the person to participate, or to improve his ability to participate, as fully as possible in any act done for him and any decision affecting him . . .

(6) He must consider, so far as is reasonably ascertainable—

(a) the person's past and present wishes and feelings (and, in particular, any relevant written statement made by him when he had capacity),

(b) the beliefs and values that would be likely to influence his decision if he had capacity, and

(c) the other factors that he would be likely to consider if he were able to do so.

(7) He must take into account, if it is practicable and appropriate to consult them, the views of—

(a) anyone named by the person as someone to be consulted on the matter in question or on matters of that kind,

---

[40] [2013] EWHC 242 (COP).

(b) anyone engaged in caring for the person or interested in his welfare,

(c) any donee of a lasting power of attorney granted by the person, and

(d) any deputy appointed for the person by the court,

as to what would be in the person's best interests and, in particular, as to the matters mentioned in subsection (6).

(i) Temporary incapacity

The 'best interests' test applies to all patients who lack capacity, and this is clearly not an homogenous group. Someone who is unconscious when they arrive at A&E after an accident, or a patient in surgery who has been anaesthetized, is in a very different position from a permanently comatose patient. If a patient temporarily lacks capacity, under section 4(3), regard must be had to whether and when she might be expected to regain capacity. This means that if the person's incapacity is likely to be short-lived, decisions should be taken only if it would not be possible to wait until she regains capacity. So, for example, life-saving surgery would be in the best interests of a person who is unconscious after a road traffic accident, but sterilization would not.

Section 4(3) does not just apply to emergency treatment, and is also intended to capture the idea that, if capacity might be regained, consideration must be given to the possibility of delaying treatment so that the patient can take the decision for herself. For example, a bipolar patient might lack capacity during a manic episode, but be expected to regain it once her condition stabilizes; section 4(3) means that only immediately necessary medical decisions should be taken while she is unwell.

(ii) Not just medical best interests

It is evident that the best interests test accommodates factors other than the patient's immediate clinical needs, and can also take account of their emotional and welfare interests. In *B v D*, for example, Baker J decided that it would be in the best interests of a 27-year-old ex-soldier, who had suffered a traumatic brain injury after being assaulted in a bar by a colleague, to be allowed to spend some of his compensation payment on travelling to Belgrade to receive experimental stem cell treatment. This was in his best interests not because it was likely to do him any good, but because it was what he wanted.

B v D [41]

Baker J

The key factor amongst the advantages of allowing D to undergo stem cell treatment, and the disadvantages of refusing, is that it accords with D's wishes. I accept that D has a significantly limited understanding of what the treatment entails and of the prospect of success and of the possible risks. But I am satisfied that he wants the treatment and that he wants it very much . . .

The key factors on the other side of the argument – the disadvantages of allowing treatment and the advantages of refusing it – are that it is unsupported by any or at least any significant

---

[41] [2017] EWCOP 15.

body of research, that it has not been subjected to clinical trials, and that the evidence that it is, or might be, an effective treatment for traumatic brain injury is almost entirely anecdotal …

In this case, I think it almost certain that D will be much more than miserable if he is denied the opportunity to have stem cell treatment. I do not accept that his reaction will be confined to mere 'disappointment'. It is highly likely that he will demonstrate an adverse reaction in his behaviour which may significantly impede and delay his rehabilitation. In saying that, I do not deny the possibility that D may also be distressed, and suffer an adverse reaction, if the treatment does not go well, or if he suffers side-effects or contracts an illness as a result of the treatment … Thus, as identified in the balance sheet above, regardless of treatment outcome there may be psychological benefit to D arising from his having his wishes respected and knowing that what he sees as a potential treatment avenue has at least been tried.

Could an intervention which is intended to benefit *someone else* ever be in P's best interests? This is possible, but only where there could be said to be some benefit to P as well. The Code of Practice gives an example of taking a blood sample when investigating a familial genetic predisposition to cancer.[42]

When the Mental Capacity Bill was debated in Parliament, the British Medical Association had raised the question of HIV testing after a healthcare professional has suffered a needlestick injury. If a blood test reveals that the patient is HIV positive, the healthcare professional could receive post-exposure prophylaxis treatment in order to prevent infection. Testing the incapacitated patient will also usually be in her best interests, because it will enable her to receive effective treatment. If, however, the patient is not going to recover, a blood sample taken for the purposes of HIV testing would not be in her best interests. Instead it might be justified by the claim that the patient herself, if she had capacity, would have been likely to agree to have a blood sample taken in order to protect the health of those treating her.

Perhaps the clearest example of a non-clinical best interests decision was *An NHS Trust v DE*, in which it was held to be in DE's best interests to undergo a vasectomy. Not only was DE clear that he did not want to have any more children, but also a vasectomy would enable DE to re-establish the independence he had achieved before his girlfriend PQ had become pregnant three years previously. Eleanor King also found that DE would benefit from the relief a vasectomy would bring to his parents, FG and JK, whose anxiety DE found distressing.

An NHS Trust v DE[43]

Eleanor King J

Section 4(6)(c) requires the court to take into account other factors which DE would be likely to consider if he were able to do so; the so called 'substituted judgment' test although it is but one factor with 'best interests' the final test. In this context the court must take into account the Mental Capacity Act Code of Practice para 5.48 which allow actions that benefit other people, as long as they are in the best interests of the person who lacks capacity. DE is very close to his parents; he loves and relies upon them. If they are upset he is upset. The court can take into account the benefits to FG and JK of DE having a vasectomy if it is a factor DE would consider if he had capacity. It is likely that DE would consider the benefit to his parents

---

[42] Para 5.48.   [43] [2013] EWHC 2562 (Fam).

of relieving them of the anxiety and strain that they have been suffering and of which he has been very conscious . . .

Such a benefit to the parents would be of significant benefit to DE, not only because he would benefit from them being happier and less anxious, but also because relieved of the anxiety of a second pregnancy, I am satisfied that JK would feel able significantly to relax the level of supervision she felt to be necessary and that, despite her general misgivings about PQ, would once again promote and support the relationship as she did prior to the pregnancy . . .

PQ's pregnancy followed by the interim declaration that DE did not have the capacity to consent to sexual relations has had very serious consequences for DE, resulting in his losing, for a period, all autonomy and his being supervised at all times. Whilst there has been some easing of supervision, his life is still very different from his life before XY was born and he is still never alone with PQ . . .

It is simply stating the obvious to observe that DE's quality of life is incomparably better when he can go and have a coffee in town with PQ or go to the local gym with his friend . . .

In my judgment DE's hard earned achievements, whether learning to swim by imitation as he can't process spoken instruction, or getting a bus on his own must be treasured, valued and measured in the same terms as the winning of an Iron Man or completing the Paris to Peking rally would be for a person without his disabilities.

In a pre-Mental Capacity Act case, *Re Y (Mental Patient: Bone Marrow Donation)*,[44] acting as a bone marrow donor to her desperately ill sister was held to be in the best interests of a severely cognitively impaired adult. There could be no possible clinical benefit to Y from undergoing an uncomfortable procedure in order to donate bone marrow to her sister. Rather, the donation would be of immeasurable benefit to Y's mother (who was already in poor health), as well as to her sister, who might otherwise die. Because it would help to maintain her relationships with her mother and sister, the operation was said to be for Y's 'emotional, psychological and social benefit'. Connell J explicitly stated that it was doubtful 'that this case would act as a useful precedent in cases where the surgery involved is more intrusive', such as organ donation.

Where the proposed procedure would benefit someone else, it is, as the Code of Practice makes clear, especially important to be clear that the purpose of seeking the views of family members is to find out what the person herself would have wanted.

Mental Capacity Act Code of Practice

4.49 . . . Family members and close friends may be able to provide valuable background information . . . But their personal views and wishes about what *they* would want for the person must not influence the assessment.

Against this, Jonathan Herring and Charles Foster contest whether it is either possible or desirable to try to isolate the interests of the person who lacks capacity from those of her family members. Because acting altruistically is fundamentally good, they question whether Connell J needed to establish that donating bone marrow would benefit Y. Rather, they argue that

---

[44] [1996] 2 FLR 787.

acting altruistically towards people with whom one has relationships is inherently, and not merely instrumentally, part of a person's best interests.

Jonathan Herring and Charles Foster[45]

> If a patient has context—has relationships—she necessarily has obligations to those to whom she relates ... Thus acting morally towards others is a central part of ensuring her own best interests ...
>
> It is morally right to be altruistic, and it is in the best interests of the donor to do the morally right thing ... Doing the right thing is an important part of living as a properly oriented human being: it is an important part of human thriving. A judge's job in determining best interests can more accurately be described as maximising the flourishing of the human in question. Flourishing people are altruistic people.

(iii) Consulting others

Aside from formally appointing someone with a lasting power of attorney (discussed below), under section 4(7) carers and family members must be consulted in order to elicit information about the patient's values and beliefs. A doctor should only proceed without consultation if it would not be 'practicable and appropriate'. In *Winspear v City Hospitals Sunderland NHS Foundation Trust*, a DNACPR (do not attempt cardio-pulmonary resuscitation) notice had been placed upon Carl Winspear's notes at 3am. It was cancelled when his mother became aware of it, and had no impact on Carl's death later that day, but the failure to consult his mother failed to meet the requirements of section 4(7), and, since it was not in accordance with the law, amounted to a breach of Article 8.

Winspear v City Hospitals Sunderland NHS Foundation Trust[46]

Blake J

> If ... it is both practicable and appropriate to consult then in the absence of some other compelling reason against consultation, the decision to file the DNACPR notice on the patient's medical records would be procedurally flawed. It would not meet the requirements of s4(7) MCA; it would accordingly not be in accordance with the law. It would be an interference that is not justified under Article 8(2) for two reasons:
>
> (i) a decision that is not taken 'in accordance with law' cannot justify an interference with the right to respect afforded under Article 8(1);
>
> (ii) if consultation was appropriate and practicable there is no convincing reason to depart from it as an important part of the procedural obligations inherent in Article 8.
>
> I can see every reason why a telephone call at 3.00am may be less than convenient or desirable than a meeting in working hours, but that is not the same as whether it is practicable.

There may, of course, be a tension between the duty to consult others and the principle of patient confidentiality, considered in more detail in Chapter 8. The Code of Practice makes

---

[45] 'Welfare means Relationality, Virtue and Altruism' (2012) 32 Legal Studies 480–98.
[46] [2015] EWHC 3250 (QB).

it clear that section 4(7) does not suspend the incapacitated person's right to confidentiality, but rather that healthcare professionals need to balance the duty to consult with the duty to respect confidentiality.

Mental Capacity Act Code of Practice

> 5.56 Decision-makers must balance the duty to consult other people with the right to confidentiality of the person who lacks capacity. So if confidential information is to be discussed, they should only seek the views of people who it is appropriate to consult, where their views are relevant to the decision to be made and the particular circumstances.

Mary Donnelly has argued that care must be taken to ensure that reports of a person's previously expressed views in fact represent their wishes. Elderly patients, for example, may have made vague and ambiguous statements about not wanting to be a burden, but these may have been prompted by a wish for comfort and reassurance, rather than representing a considered view about their future medical treatment.

Mary Donnelly[47]

> While the consultative model is a good one, it is important to remember that even close friends or family members cannot always know the past preferences or the relevant beliefs and values of the person lacking capacity. Statements such as 'I would rather die than be dependent' may reflect a desire for reassurance, or may be a result of temporary depression or fear, and may not represent the person's considered views on future care should they lose capacity.

For patients who do not have close friends or family, sections 35 to 37 provide for the appointment of an Independent Mental Capacity Advocate (IMCA) to support and represent them. Under section 37(3), an IMCA must be appointed before a person is given 'serious medical treatment', if no close family member or friend is available to consult about his wishes or feelings. The Mental Capacity Act 2005 (Independent Mental Capacity Advocate) (General) Regulations 2006 set out in detail how and when IMCAs should be appointed, their functions, and their role in challenging decisions. They also define 'serious medical treatment'.

Mental Capacity Act 2005 (Independent Mental Capacity Advocate) (General) Regulations 2006 regulation 4

> 4(2) Serious medical treatment is treatment which involves providing, withdrawing or withholding treatment in circumstances where—
>
> (a) in a case where a single treatment is being proposed, there is a fine balance between its benefits to the patient and the burdens and risks it is likely to entail for him,

---

[47] 'Best Interests, Patient Participation and the Mental Capacity Act 2005' (2009) 17 Medical Law Review 1–29.

> (b) in a case where there is a choice of treatments, a decision as to which one to use is finely balanced, or
>
> (c) what is proposed would be likely to involve serious consequences for the patient.

The Code of Practice gives some examples of serious medical treatment, including treatment for cancer, electroconvulsive therapy, major surgery, termination of pregnancy, and withholding clinically assisted nutrition and hydration (CANH). If the treatment is needed urgently in an emergency, an IMCA need not be appointed, although this should be done for any follow-up serious treatment.

The IMCA is specifically charged with trying to elicit the person's wishes and values, and with ensuring that they have been given all the support they need to be involved in decision-making.

Mental Capacity Act 2005 (Independent Mental Capacity Advocate) (General) Regulations 2006 regulation 6

> 6(5) The IMCA must evaluate all the information he has obtained for the purpose of—
>
> (a) ascertaining the extent of the support provided to P to enable him to participate in making any decision about the matter in relation to which the IMCA has been instructed;
>
> (b) ascertaining what P's wishes and feelings would be likely to be, and the beliefs and values that would be likely to influence P, if he had capacity in relation to the proposed act or decision;
>
> (c) ascertaining what alternative courses of action are available in relation to P;
>
> (d) where medical treatment is proposed for P, ascertaining whether he would be likely to benefit from a further medical opinion.

(iv) Relevance of the patient's views

The best interests checklist instructs decision-makers to consider the patient's own views and beliefs, both past and present. If a patient has never been able to express an opinion, her values may be unknown or non-existent. But where there is any evidence of the factors that do or did matter to the patient herself, then her 'best interests' are not to be judged purely objectively, according to what the doctor believes to be clinically indicated. Rather, the patient's views and values are important when deciding what is best for her.

The Act does not specify what weight should be given to the patient's wishes: they are important, but not decisive. As Helen Taylor explains, 'The MCA has drawn attention to the need for decision makers to consider a range of issues wider than the patient's clinical interests, yet provides insufficient guidance on how the statutory principles should be applied in practice'.[48] Nor does the Act distinguish between P's present wishes and her preferences before she lost capacity; both are relevant, though Lucy Series suggests that, in practice, the courts are more likely to overrule the wishes of never-competent patients.

---

[48] Helen J Taylor, 'What are "best interests"? A critical evaluation of "best interests" decision-making in clinical practice' (2016) 24 Medical Law Review 176–205.

Lucy Series[49]

Interestingly, the cases where the Court of Protection does authorise interventions that conflict with a person's wishes and feelings often involve people with learning disabilities. It would be useful to explore whether less weight is placed on the wishes and feelings of certain populations than others – this may relate to perceptions that their values and feelings are less 'authentic' because they were not formulated in the past at a time when the person had 'capacity', or greater difficulty directly engaging with the wishes and feelings of individuals with communication impairments.

Despite the fact that section 4 does not give the patient's wishes any particular priority, Mary Donnelly has suggested that a decision to go against the preference of the person who lacks capacity now requires rigorous justification.

Mary Donnelly[50]

At a practical level, the participation requirement should, at a minimum, necessitate the acknowledgement, if this is the case, that the person lacking capacity has an alternative preference. This in turn should lead to a rigorous scrutiny of the evidence presented in favour of the argument that the decision-maker should act against this preference. It cannot be enough for a decision-maker simply to acknowledge the views of the person lacking capacity before reaching a decision which takes no account of these views.

Of course, each decision in the Court of Protection is fact-specific, so comparing one decision in which a person's wishes were disregarded with a decision, in a different case, in which another person's wishes were decisive does not necessarily establish anything other than that the patients' situations were different.

Nevertheless, since the UK Supreme Court's 2013 judgment in *Aintree University Hospitals Foundation Trust v James*,[51] the patient's wishes and feelings have carried considerable weight when determining what is in her best interests.

David James was 68 years old and suffered from multiple co-morbidities. His condition fluctuated and he had been receiving treatment for stroke, cardiac arrest, recurring infections, and multiple organ failure. The trust where he was being treated had sought declarations that Mr James lacked capacity (which was uncontentious), and that it would be lawful to discontinue or withhold CPR, renal replacement therapy, and invasive therapy for low blood pressure. Mr James's family wanted treatment to continue.

By the time the case was heard by the Court of Appeal, Mr James's condition had deteriorated, the declarations were granted and Mr James died. Because of a difference between the way in which Peter Jackson J and the Court of Appeal had applied the best interests test, Mr James's widow was given leave to appeal to the Supreme Court.

---

[49] 'The Place of Wishes and Feelings in Best Interests Decisions: Wye Valley NHS Trust v Mr B' (2016) 79 Modern Law Review 1101–15.

[50] 'Best Interests, Patient Participation and the Mental Capacity Act 2005' (2009) 17 Medical Law Review 1–29.

[51] [2013] UKSC 67.

In *Aintree University Hospitals Foundation Trust v James*, the Supreme Court unani-mously decided that Peter Jackson J's approach had been the right one (the Court of Appeal had suggested that the patient's wishes could be overridden by what was judged objectively to be in his best medical interests). Best interests must be judged subjectively, with treat-ment only being futile if *this patient* would consider continued existence to be futile. Given the change of facts when it heard the case, however, the Court of Appeal had been right to grant the declarations sought, albeit not for the reasons it had given.

Aintree University Hospitals Foundation Trust v James [52]

Lady Hale (with whom the other Justices agreed)

The most that can be said, therefore, is that in considering the best interests of this particular patient at this particular time, decision-makers must look at his welfare in the widest sense, not just medical but social and psychological; they must consider the nature of the medical treatment in question, what it involves and its prospects of success; they must consider what the outcome of that treatment for the patient is likely to be; they must try and put themselves in the place of the individual patient and ask what his atti-tude to the treatment is or would be likely to be; and they must consult others who are looking after him or interested in his welfare, in particular for their view of what his attitude would be ...

The purpose of the best interests test is to consider matters from the patient's point of view. That is not to say that his wishes must prevail, any more than those of a fully capable patient must prevail. We cannot always have what we want. Nor will it always be possible to ascertain what an incapable patient's wishes are. Even if it is possible to determine what his views were in the past, they might well have changed in the light of the stresses and strains of his current predicament. In this case, the highest it could be put was, as counsel had agreed, that 'It was likely that Mr James would want treatment up to the point where it became hopeless'. But in so far as it is possible to ascertain the patient's wishes and feelings, his beliefs and values or the things which were important to him, it is those which should be taken into account because they are a component in making the choice which is right for him as an individual human being.

Two years after *Aintree*, in *Wye Valley NHS Trust v B*, Peter Jackson J declared that it would not be in the best interests of a man who lacked capacity to amputate his foot against his wishes, despite the fact that, without amputation, it was thought that Mr B would be likely to die within a few days. Peter Jackson J had visited Mr B in hospital, where he had been adamant that he did not want the operation: 'I don't want it. I'm not afraid of death. I don't want interference. Even if I'm going to die, I don't want the operation.' Peter Jackson J explained why it was important not to discount the beliefs and values of someone who lacked capacity. (It is worth noting that, despite the doctors' predictions, Mr B survived for 18 months without having had his foot amputated).

---

[52] [2013] UKSC 67.

Wye Valley NHS Trust v B[53]

Peter Jackson J

Where a patient lacks capacity it is accordingly of great importance to give proper weight to his wishes and feelings and to his beliefs and values. On behalf of the Trust in this case, Mr Sachdeva QC submitted that the views expressed by a person lacking capacity were in principle entitled to less weight than those of a person with capacity. This is in my view true only to the limited extent that the views of a capacitous person are by definition decisive in relation to any treatment that is being offered to him so that the question of best interests does not arise. However, once incapacity is established so that a best interests decision must be made, there is no theoretical limit to the weight or lack of weight that should be given to the person's wishes and feelings, beliefs and values ...

This is not an academic issue, but a necessary protection for the rights of people with disabilities. As the Act and the European Convention make clear, a conclusion that a person lacks decision-making capacity is not an '*off-switch*' for his rights and freedoms. To state the obvious, the wishes and feelings, beliefs and values of people with a mental disability are as important to them as they are to anyone else, and may even be more important. It would therefore be wrong in principle to apply any automatic discount to their point of view ...

Mr B has had a hard life. Through no fault of his own, he has suffered in his mental health for half a century. He is a sociable man who has experienced repeated losses so that he has become isolated. He has no next of kin. No one has ever visited him in hospital and no one ever will. Yet he is a proud man who sees no reason to prefer the views of others to his own. His religious beliefs are deeply meaningful to him and do not deserve to be described as delusions: they are his faith and they are an intrinsic part of who he is. I would not define Mr B by reference to his mental illness or his religious beliefs. Rather, his core quality is his '*fierce independence*', and it is this that is now, as he sees it, under attack ...

I am quite sure that it would not be in Mr B's best interests to take away his little remaining independence and dignity in order to replace it with a future for which he understandably has no appetite and which could only be achieved after a traumatic and uncertain struggle that he and no one else would have to endure. There is a difference between fighting on someone's behalf and just fighting them. Enforcing treatment in this case would surely be the latter.

A few months later, Mostyn J also decided to visit the patient who lacked capacity before making his decision. In *A Hospital NHS Trust v CD*, he explained why it had been an enlightening experience.

A Hospital NHS Trust v CD[54]

Mostyn J

I took the view that it would be right if I were to meet CD face to face and I did so at the mental hospital on the first day of the hearing. It was an enlightening experience and one which I would recommend to any judge hearing a similar case. Mr Justice Jackson met Mr B and it is obvious from his judgment that the encounter was critically valuable. The reason it was enlightening for me was that the person I met was different in many respects to the

---

[53] [2015] EWCOP 60.   [54] [2015] EWCOP 74.

> person described in the papers. CD was engaging and polite. She was articulate. She was amusing. She listened carefully to questions and answered them equally carefully. True, there were comments that suggested powerful delusional forces; and Dr FH explained that she was heavily medicated. But even so, the person I met was a world away from the violent sociopath described in the papers.

Of course, sometimes it will be impossible to hear directly from P herself, and the judge will instead rely on evidence gathered from those close to P as to what she would have wanted. For example, in *St George's Healthcare NHS Trust v P*, Newton J attached considerable weight to the views of Mr P's family that he would have found his current existence worthwhile.

St George's Healthcare NHS Trust v P[55]

Newton J

Mr Moore pointed to the most undignified existence that a patient must necessarily have when nursed in ICU [intensive care unit] and suggested that that was not an existence that most people would tolerate, let alone welcome, when there is so little prospect of functional recovery.

In looking at those aspects and as to whether or not P would assess his life as being regarded as worthwhile I attach far more weight to the relevant expressions of his articulate and well informed family members and friends who have direct knowledge of P's pre-injury knowledge, understanding and philosophy, in particular those who know about his beliefs and values.

In the light of his previously expressed strong views, coupled with his strong religious beliefs, the weight of the evidence all falls heavily to one side which is that the preservation of any life would be considered by P to be of significant value. His present circumstances are a life which P would find worthwhile, even though I entirely accept many others would not adopt the same position.

Although members of P's family are usually well-placed to be able to give an accurate account of P's wishes, this is not always the case. In *Abertawe Bro Morgannwg University Local Health Board v RY*, for example, the patient's daughter's evidence was found to be unreliable. RY was 81 years old and had been unconscious since he had suffered a cardiac arrest. There was evidence that he experienced pain from the deep suctioning that was necessary to clear his tracheostomy tube. With no prospect of improvement, RY's treating team believed that it would be in his best interests to withdraw him from the ventilator, leading inevitably to his death. His daughter CP said that her father 'would want everything done' in order to preserve his life, because, as a result of his religious beliefs, he was of the view that 'any life is better than no life'. In reality, Hayden J found that these were her beliefs, rather than her father's.

Interestingly, while Hayden J considered that he had sufficient evidence to come to a clear conclusion that continued treatment was no longer in RY's best interests, he declined to make an order immediately, on the grounds that 'it is appropriate to allow a short period for all the professionals and the family involved to reflect on my judgment'. In particular, he hoped that CP would reflect upon the information that deep suctioning caused her father pain, because it was 'very much in RY's best interests if his daughter and the experts can ultimately agree and therefore plan

---

[55] [2015] EWCOP 42.

together the circumstances in which he should live whatever time remains to him'. It seems likely that this is what happened, because in a postscript to the judgment, Hayden J stated that RY died peacefully in hospital shortly after his judgment was delivered to the parties.

Abertawe Bro Morgannwg University Local Health Board v RY[56]

Hayden J

In this case RY's 'voice' has remained resistantly silent … There was no reference to his having contemplated what he would wish to happen in such circumstances as he now finds himself …

I have felt unable to rely on CP's account of her father's wishes for a number of reasons. I do not doubt that she loves him dearly, even though I suspect that their relationship has not always been equable. I also consider that she has a strong faith. She told me that her wishes were indistinguishable from those she has advanced as her father's i.e. even a wholly compromised life, punctuated by pain, would be better than no life …

There are however some unfortunate aspects of the evidence which undermine CP's credibility as a witness.

CP has behaved in a manner on the ward which has been alarming to both patients and staff, she has been voluble and offensive in her criticisms of medical staff and she has, now by her own admission, told lies. She has given an account of her family life which has not always been consistent, indeed it has been, at times, contradictory. She has also asserted that her family would say to this Court *'whatever she told them to'* …

Thus I am in the position here of evaluating RY's best interest with no evidence of sufficient quality to indicate to me what his wishes would be, were he in a position to communicate them. It would be both wrong to speculate and, in my judgement, flawed to assume that in the absence of clear and reliable evidence as to RY's views, the emphasis on the 'sanctity of life' becomes in someway greater. This powerful and important consideration will always weigh heavily in the balance but it must not be permitted to quash all other considerations.

Two points follow from this case. First, it is clear that cogent evidence of the patient's previously expressed wishes is not the only consideration that can outweigh sanctity of life considerations. Rather, where the patient's view is unknown, the question turns to whether the treatment in question is overly burdensome. Secondly, as Mary Donnelly explains, this case also points to the importance of testing family members' evidence earlier in the process, so that a patient is not subjected to months of invasive treatment which is later found not to have been in her best interests.

Mary Donnelly[57]

7 months elapsed between the time RY's children were advised that ongoing ventilation would not be in RY's best interests and the Court of Protection hearing discussed in this commentary. During this time, RY suffered pain and indignity, especially in the 2 months following the tracheostomy and move from ITU [intensive care unit]. For 5 months, too, ITU resources were diverted to provide treatment which, at the outset had been regarded by medical professionals

---

[56] [2017] EWCOP 2.
[57] 'Decisions at The end of Life: "The Inimitable Hallmark of the Lawyer"?' (2018) 26 Medical Law Review 531–40.

as inappropriate. We do not know whether other patients died or suffered impaired health as a result of not being able to access ITU treatment during this period, but it would seem reasonable to assume that the long-term absence of an ITU bed had a negative impact on patient care. For all of this time, it appears that everyone, including the Court in its initial engagement with the case, operated on the basis that RY's wishes and feelings were accurately represented by CP. It seems remarkable that there was (apparently) no mechanism to raise questions about (not to mind evaluate) CP's statements, which very quickly fell apart on closer inspection.

Post-*Aintree*, persuasive evidence of a patient's preference for no treatment has tended to be decisive, even when it is not set out in a binding advance decision (see below). In *Sheffield Teaching Hospitals NHS Foundation Trust v TH*, a heavy drinker had been very clear with his ex-wife and his friends that he did not want to receive any more treatment in hospital. Hayden J bluntly summed up his situation.

Sheffield Teaching Hospitals NHS Foundation Trust v TH[58]

Hayden J

He declined all support. He wished for no intervention from outside services. He was frustrated and angry with his disabilities. As he was never going to improve, he would rather die young and drink to the end he said. He expressed it uncompromisingly. 'My brain is fucked, I am fucked and I want to drink as it's the only thing I enjoy.' …

I have no doubt that he would wish to leave the hospital and go to the home of his ex-wife and his mate's Spud and end his days quietly there and with dignity as he sees it. Privacy, personal autonomy and dignity have not only been features of TH's life, they have been the creed by which he has lived it. He may not have prepared a document that complies with the criteria of section 24, giving advance directions to refuse treatment but he has in so many oblique and tangential ways over so many years communicated his views so uncompromisingly and indeed bluntly that none of his friends are left in any doubt what he would want in his present situation.

(v) *The Law Commission's proposed reform to section 4*

When the Law Commission was charged with considering reform to the Deprivation of Liberty Safeguards, considered in Chapter 7, it also recommended a modest change to section 4 of the Mental Capacity Act, in order to spell out that P's wishes and values should have to be 'ascertained' rather than simply considered, and that they should be given 'particular weight' when deciding what is in a patient's best interests.

Law Commission[59]

14.7 … Family carers reported that best interests decisions by health and social care professionals were often made without reference to their loved one's wishes and feelings, and that

---

[58] [2014] EWCOP 4.   [59] *Mental Capacity and Deprivation of Liberty*, Law Com no 372 (2017).

professionals often 'pick and choose' which factors on the check-list to prioritise to suit their own preferred outcomes. Consultees suggested that the concept of best interests was often interpreted in a medical and paternalistic sense ...

14.16 ... we have concluded that the better approach is to make clearer that steps need to be taken to identify a person's wishes and feelings and to bolster the weight to be given to ascertainable wishes and feelings in the best interests determination. Further 'teeth' would be given to this approach by placing additional requirements on professionals to explain their decisions not to follow a person's ascertainable wishes and feelings. Currently, section 4(6) requires the decision-maker to 'consider, so far as is reasonably ascertainable' the person's wishes and feelings. We think that this passive formulation is too weak, and the draft Bill amends this to establish that the decision-maker must 'ascertain, so far as is reasonably practicable' the person's wishes and feelings ...

14.17 The draft Bill then requires that, in making the best interests determination, the decisionmaker 'must give particular weight to any wishes or feelings ascertained'. Whilst the meaning of 'particular weight' is too case specific to be capable of being defined precisely, it would evidently give ascertained wishes and feelings a higher status than all the other factors which a decision-maker is required to consider under section 4(6).

When the Mental Capacity Amendment Bill was published in 2018, it did not contain any amendments to section 4. The government's Impact Assessment simply stated that 'the Law Commission also proposed making some wider amendments to the Mental Capacity Act which we have decide not to legislate for at this point, as we think there are other effective levers to deliver improvement in these areas'.[60]

It is not clear whether the publication in 2018 of a NICE guideline on decision-making and mental capacity is one of those 'other levers'. The NICE guideline is specifically addressed to service providers, commissioners and practitioners, and it suggests that the best interests decision should reflect P's wishes and feelings 'unless it is not possible or appropriate to do so'.

National Institute for Health and Care Excellence[61]

1.5.13 Carers and practitioners must, wherever possible, find out the person's wishes and feelings in order to ensure any best interests decision made reflects those wishes and feelings unless it is not possible/appropriate to do so. Where the best interests decision ultimately made does not accord with the person's wishes and feelings, the reasons for this should be clearly documented and an explanation given. The documentation of the assessment should also make clear what steps have been taken to ascertain the person's wishes and feelings and where it has not been possible to do this, the reasons for this should be explained.

While the NICE guideline now instructs decision-makers to place considerable emphasis upon P's wishes and feelings, it does not offer any further guidance on the circumstances in which it would be impossible or inappropriate to respect P's wishes. In addition, the NICE guideline is arguably inconsistent with the wording of section 4(6) of the Mental Capacity Act, according to which the patient's wishes are just one relevant factor among many. Instead

---

[60] Department of Health and Social Care, Mental Capacity Amendment Bill Impact Assessment (DHSC, 2018).
[61] *Decision-making and Mental Capacity* (NICE, 2018).

of clarifying the weight to be given to P's wishes, the creation of a gap between the statutory wording and NICE guidance may add to healthcare professionals' confusion.

I have argued elsewhere that the Law Commission's proposal did not go far enough, and that in order to provide clearer guidance to healthcare professionals, and to ensure greater consistency of decision-making, the statute should instead be amended to include a presumption that, in certain circumstances, P's wishes should be decisive.

Emily Jackson[62]

> First, if respecting her refusal would not be likely to result in any significant harm to her, overruling her wishes would not serve an important medical purpose. The psychological and emotional harm, and the erosion of trust, that might be likely to result from imposing treatment upon her against her wishes would not be outweighed by significant health benefits . . .
>
> Secondly, if respecting the person's wishes might result in significant harm to her, but those wishes nevertheless reflect her deeply and profoundly held values (rather than resulting from a phobia or delusion, for example), then Article 8 could require us to refrain from treating her against her wishes, despite this risk of harm. Once again, the psychological harm that is done to someone by imposing treatment upon her, where to do so goes against beliefs that are profoundly important to her, should be put in the balance with the physical harm that might be caused if she does not receive the treatment in question . . .
>
> [B]usy and non-legally trained healthcare professionals are unlikely to consult the law reports regularly, and need clearer prospective guidance than the Act and its Code of Practice currently provides that an incapacitated patient's refusal of medical treatment should be taken seriously, and should be overruled only if the risk to which she would thereby be exposed meets a threshold level of seriousness, *and* her refusal is not grounded in values or beliefs that are of profound importance to her.

(vi) Compliance with the UN Convention on the Rights of Persons with Disabilities

The United Nations' Convention on the Rights of Persons with Disabilities (CRPD) poses a direct challenge to the very existence of a special regime to cover the treatment of people suffering from cognitive impairments. Because Article 12(4) of the UN CRPD specifies that 'measures relating to the exercise of legal capacity respect the rights, will and preferences of the person', it has been suggested, notably by the UN Committee on the Rights of Persons with Disabilities, that this 'requires both the abolition of substitute decision-making regimes and the development of supported decision-making alternatives'.

The UN Committee's interpretation is controversial and by no means universally agreed, but its implications are dramatic, suggesting that any 'best interests' decision-making by others is incompatible with the Convention. In all cases, the person's 'will and preferences' must take priority. Of course, there are people who cannot communicate, or who have never had any discernible will or preferences, and the Committee suggests that, in such cases, 'where it is not practicable to determine the will and preferences of an individual, the "best interpretation of will and preferences" must replace the "best interests" determinations'.[63]

---

[62] 'From 'Doctor Knows Best' to Dignity: Placing Adults Who Lack Capacity at the Centre of Decisions About Their Medical Treatment' (2018) 81 Modern Law Review 247–81.

[63] UN Committee on the Rights of Persons with Disabilities, *General comment No. 1 (2014) Article 12: Equal recognition before the law* Eleventh session 31 March–11 April 2014, para 21.

In the next extract, Mary Donnelly points out that 'best interpretation of will and preferences' misleadingly assumes that we are always able to tell what someone else would want.

Mary Donnelly[64]

Even presuming that the person who is interpreting will and preferences fits (insofar as humans can) within Eva Kittay's ideal of the 'transparent caregiver', who separates his or her own needs from those of a cared-for person, there are evident risks in constructing a narrative about another person. Most immediately, we may get the interpretation wrong. An example provided by Kittay relates how both she, as a loving mother, and Peggy, as a long-time, devoted, professional carer, struggle to discern the needs of her daughter, who has profound capacity impairments: 'When Sesha is ill, we don't know what bothers her, what hurts her, what the pain feels like. We are deprived of a vital avenue for diagnosis. This makes her so vulnerable, and makes us crazy.'

The problem is that the best interpretation standard refuses to acknowledge that there are things that we do not, and cannot, know . . .

[R]eplacing the shorthand of best interests with the shorthand of will and preferences would be overly simplistic and misleading. A more suitable alternative could draw on the terminology of rights, i.e. all actions must respect the rights of the person. Although this terminology is in many ways as indeterminate as that of best interests, its adoption could help realign decision-making frameworks to afford greater recognition to a person's will and preferences while also recognising the more complex interplay of factors at play.

(c) Withdrawing Life-Prolonging Treatment

(i) Section 4(5)

When the Mental Capacity Act 2005 was debated in parliament, there was concern that, by placing advance refusals of life-prolonging treatment on a statutory footing, the Act would introduce 'euthanasia by the back door'. This concern was misplaced because the Act did not change the law relating to refusing life-prolonging treatment, and in fact introduced additional safeguards. Nevertheless, the government's response to this anxiety was a curious amendment to section 4:

4(5) Where the determination relates to life-sustaining treatment he must not, in considering whether the treatment is in the best interests of the person concerned, be motivated by a desire to bring about his death.

The use of the word 'desire' is odd, but the intention of this section is clear: although the decision to withhold or withdraw life-sustaining treatment can be in a person's best interests, ending the patient's life must never be the doctor's sole intention.

Normally, of course, the preservation of life will be in a patient's best interests, but the Mental Capacity Act Code of Practice makes clear that this is not always the case. Where life-prolonging treatment would be futile, overly burdensome, or where there is no prospect of recovery, it may be withdrawn or withheld.

---

[64] 'Best Interests in the Mental Capacity Act: Time to say Goodbye?' (2016) 24 Medical Law Review 318–32.

Mental Capacity Act Code of Practice[65]

> 5.31 All reasonable steps which are in the person's best interests should be taken to pro-
> long their life. There will be a limited number of cases where treatment is futile, overly burden-
> some to the patient or where there is no prospect of recovery. In circumstances such as these,
> it may be that an assessment of best interests leads to the conclusion that it would be in the
> best interests of the patient to withdraw or withhold life-sustaining treatment, even if this
> may result in the person's death. The decision-maker must make a decision based on the best
> interests of the person who lacks capacity. They must not be motivated by a desire to bring
> about the person's death for whatever reason, even if this is from a sense of compassion . . .
>
> 5.33 Importantly, section 4(5) cannot be interpreted to mean that doctors are under an ob-
> ligation to provide, or to continue to provide, life-sustaining treatment where that treatment
> is not in the best interests of the person, even where the person's death is foreseen. Doctors
> must apply the best interests' checklist and use their professional skills to decide whether life-
> sustaining treatment is in the person's best interests. If the doctor's assessment is disputed,
> and there is no other way of resolving the dispute, ultimately the Court of Protection may be
> asked to decide what is in the person's best interests.

(ii) Withdrawing CANH from patients in prolonged disorders of consciousness

The first case to consider whether artificial feeding (now known as clinically assisted nutrition and hydration (CANH)) could be withdrawn from a patient who lacked capacity predated the MCA by more than a decade. Tony Bland had suffered serious brain damage in
the Hillsborough football stadium disaster in 1989 and had been in a permanent vegetative
state (PVS) for three years. (The term PVS is still in common usage, but the word 'vegetative'
is upsetting for families; it is to be hoped that it will soon be replaced in common usage by
a more neutral term such as 'extreme prolonged disorder of consciousness' or 'unresponsive
wakefulness syndrome'[66]).

With the agreement of his family, in *Airedale NHS Trust v Bland* the trust responsible for
the hospital where Tony Bland was being treated sought declarations that they could lawfully
discontinue all life-sustaining treatment and medical support measures designed to keep him
alive, including the termination of ventilation, nutrition, and hydration by artificial means.

The *Bland* case raised several new legal and ethical questions, including whether withholding CANH might satisfy both the *actus reus* and *mens rea* of the crime of murder. In
Airedale NHS Trust v Bland, the House of Lords unanimously rejected the Official Solicitor's
appeal, and confirmed that Airedale NHS Trust was entitled to the declarations sought.

Airedale NHS Trust v Bland[67]

Lord Browne-Wilkinson

As to the guilty act, or *actus reus*, the criminal law draws a distinction between the commission of a positive act which causes death and the omission to do an act which would have

[65] (DH, 2007).
[66] Steven Laureys, 'Unresponsive wakefulness syndrome: a new name for the vegetative state or apallic syndrome' (2010) 8 BMC Medicine 68.
[67] [1993] AC 789 (HL).

prevented death ... Apart from the act of removing the nasogastric tube, the mere failure to continue to do what you have previously done is not, in any ordinary sense, to do anything positive: on the contrary it is by definition an omission to do what you have previously done. The positive act of removing the nasogastric tube presents more difficulty. It is undoubtedly a positive act, similar to switching off a ventilator in the case of a patient whose life is being sustained by artificial ventilation. But in my judgment in neither case should the act be classified as positive, since to do so would be to introduce intolerably fine distinctions. If, instead of removing the nasogastric tube, it was left in place but no further nutrients were provided for the tube to convey to the patient's stomach, that would not be an act of commission.

In short, the *Bland* case established several important propositions. First, the Lords were unanimous that the principle of the sanctity of life, while important, was not absolute. Secondly, CANH was agreed to be medical treatment and not basic care. Thirdly, withdrawing CANH was, in law, an omission rather than an action.

Now, the withdrawal of CANH from patients is not uncommon and it will be accompanied by palliative care in order to ensure that the patient's death is pain-free and peaceful. However, the withdrawal of CANH can be extremely distressing for relatives: the deliberate decision to starve someone to death may be inconsistent with our most basic need to care for those we love.

Celia Kitzinger and Jenny Kitzinger[68]

Failing to feed (or to provide water) to a loved one via whatever route (orally or by tube)—even because of the conviction that they would prefer to be dead—is a highly emotive issue with deep cultural resonance ... Interviewees were often concerned that, even with a confirmed VS [vegetative state] diagnosis, it was possible that their relative would experience pain and suffering and there was a widespread perception that lethal injections would be more humane, compassionate and dignified than 'death from neglect' as a result of treatment withdrawal ... If you've made that decision, you might as well do it as humanely as you possibly can ... To starve somebody to death seems a particularly cruel thing to do.

Even when families were told by clinicians that the person would receive palliative care, they still found ANH withdrawal unacceptable—if not for the patient, then for the rest of the family. One mother says:

We hated it. They reassured us that, you know, 'oh he would be sedated, he wouldn't feel any pain.' But we would have to sit there for up to three weeks to, basically, watch him die ... Many interviewees had thought about killing the patient themselves—with varying levels of seriousness ... Although, in the end, each of these interviewees had decided that carrying out a 'mercy killing' was not the answer, they were angry that the current system had, they felt, forced them into the position where they were contemplating it, and some felt guilty at their failure to carry through.

If the diagnosis of PVS is correct, it is now accepted that keeping a person alive will not be in her best interests. As Ryder J explained in *A Primary Care Trust v CW*:[69]

[68] 'Withdrawing artificial nutrition and hydration from minimally conscious and vegetative patients: family perspectives' (2015) 41 Journal of Medical Ethics 157–60.
[69] [2010] EWHC 3448 (Fam).

whether or not the withdrawal of life-sustaining treatment measures is in CW's best interests will depend upon whether or not his diagnosis of PVS is correct. If it is correct, in other words if he has no awareness of self or environment and no prospect of recovery, then the provision of any treatment is futile and cannot be in his best interests.

More complex issues have arisen in the last decade, when the courts have been faced with the question of whether it could be lawful to withdraw life support from someone in a minimally conscious state (MCS). 'Minimal consciousness', in which a person has some awareness of her environment but lacks full consciousness, covers a wider spectrum of patients than PVS. It can be the result of sudden trauma, but it might also describe someone's lack of capacity towards the end of a degenerative illness.

The first MCS case to come before the courts was *Re M (Adult Patient) (Minimally Conscious State: Withdrawal of Treatment)*.[70] M had been about to go on a skiing holiday when she became drowsy and confused and lapsed into a coma, leaving her with extensive and irreparable brain damage. It was initially thought that M was in a PVS, but investigations revealed that her condition was instead one of minimal consciousness.

M could experience some pain and discomfort: she made a loud noise when her incontinence pads needed changing, for example. It might be thought that the fact that M had negative sensory experiences and that she might have some limited insight into her condition, would be worse than being in a PVS, in which someone is completely unaware of what has happened to them. L Syd M Johnson, for example, has said that 'many persons prospectively considering the possibility of living in a MCS—of being permanently and profoundly disabled, unable to interact meaningfully, but consciously aware—might view it as a fate worse than the vegetative state, and indeed, a fate worse than death'.[71]

Nevertheless, in his pre-*Aintree* judgment, Baker J decided that, because her professional carers believed that M could experience comfort and even small pleasures, such as turning her face towards the sun, the principle of the preservation of life took priority. A DNACPR order was to remain in force, but the positive withdrawal of life support was held not to be in M's best interests.

Baker J's judgment was noteworthy for the comparative lack of weight he attached to the evidence from M's family about her wishes and beliefs (M's partner of 30 years said she would have been 'horrified' by the thought of living in her present condition): 'We have no way of knowing how she now feels about her current life. In those circumstances, the court must be particularly cautious about attaching significant weight to statements she made before her collapse'.

Although each case is fact-specific, in the MCS cases that have been decided post-*Aintree*, the judiciary has tended to place much more emphasis upon evidence from the patient's family about what she would have wanted.[72]

In *M v N*, Mrs N was 68, and profoundly incapacitated by multiple sclerosis. She was minimally conscious, although one of the experts believed that she satisfied the criteria for a diagnosis of PVS. When her own parents had dementia and had had to go into a home, she could not bear to visit them, and had said to her children: 'if I ever get like that shoot me!'

The Official Solicitor had originally opposed the application for a declaration that it would be lawful to discontinue CANH, on the grounds that 'the strong presumption in favour of

---

[70] [2011] EWHC 2443 (Fam).

[71] 'The right to die in the minimally conscious state' (2011) 37 Journal of Medical Ethics 175–8.

[72] See, for example, *United Lincolnshire Hospitals NHS Trust v N* [2014] EWCOP 16.

the benefit of the continuance of life had not been displaced'. After hearing the family's evidence, and following consultation with counsel, he changed his mind, and decided it would be wrong for him to continue to oppose the application. Given the importance of the case, Hayden J nevertheless delivered a judgment setting out why CANH was no longer in Mrs N's best interests.

M v N[73]

Hayden J

For one who has set such store by outward appearance and who has been so attentive to the impression she created on others, her decline, in the way I have outlined, is particularly poignant. Some might well have endured all that Mrs N has with phlegmatism and fortitude. Mrs N is simply not such a person. I am satisfied, as the family say, that some considerable time ago now she had simply had enough and that, as they see it, to force nutrition and hydration upon her is to fail to respect the person she is and the code by which she has lived her life . . .

As is clear from the above analysis this case is not concerned with a right to die. No such right exists. What is in focus here is Mrs N's right to live her life at the end of her days in the way that she would have wished. I am required to evaluate the 'inviolability of life' as an ethical concept and to weigh that against an individual's right to self determination or personal autonomy. Not only do these principles conflict, they are of a fundamentally different complexion. The former is an ideological imperative found in most civilised societies and in all major religions, the latter requires an intense scrutiny of an individual's circumstances, views and attitudes. The exercise is almost a balance of opposites: the philosophical as against the personal. For this reason, as I have already indicated, I consider that a formulaic 'balance sheet' approach to Mrs N's best interests is artificial.

As I have already set out and at some length, I am entirely satisfied that Mrs N's views find real and authoritative expression through her family in this courtroom. I start with the assumption that an instinct for life beats strongly in all human beings. However, I am entirely satisfied that Mrs N would have found her circumstances to be profoundly humiliating and that *she* would have been acutely alert to the distress caused to her family, which *she* would very much have wanted to avoid. LR told me that Mrs N would not have wanted to have been a burden; that I also believe to be entirely reliable.

There is an innate dignity in the life of a human being who is being cared for well, and who is free from pain. There will undoubtedly be people who for religious or cultural reasons or merely because it accords with the behavioural code by which they have lived their life prefer to, or think it morally right to, hold fast to life no matter how poor its quality or vestigial its nature. Their choice must be respected. But choice where rational, informed and un-coerced is the essence of autonomy. It follows that those who would not wish to live in this way must have their views respected too.

I am entirely satisfied that there is no prospect of her achieving a life that *she* would consider to be meaningful, worthwhile or dignified . . . Quite simply, I have come to the conclusion that it would be disrespectful to Mrs N to preserve her further in a manner I think *she* would regard as grotesque.

[73] [2015] EWCOP 76.

The patient's wishes appeared to be given much more weight in *M v N* than they were in *Re M*, and this might be explained by the fact that *M v N* is a post-*Aintree* decision, and thus reflects the emphasis placed on the patient's point of view by the Supreme Court. In the next extract, Richard Huxtable suggests that there might be other factors at play.

Richard Huxtable[74]

There are four features of this case which could dampen the reception anticipated from autonomy's enthusiasts and which also help to explain why M and N had such different fates.

First, it cannot have harmed the case for withdrawing CANH from N that the declaration sought was unopposed ... Opinions appeared more divided in M's case. Perhaps, then, the degree of consensus in N's situation exerted some influence over the final decision.

Secondly, despite the dominance of autonomy in his decision, N's wishes were not the only factors for which Hayden J had regard. Note how he also cited 'the intrusive nature of the treatment and its minimal potential to achieve any medical objective'... As such, the judge was mindful of other conceptions of best interests, since he judged there to be little chance of improving N's quality of life (and thus her mental state) or significantly extending her life (and thus promoting an objective good). Contrast N's situation with M's, who was thought to have a life expectancy of 10 years, and for whom the court felt there were options available for enhancing her quality of life.

Thirdly, even the injection of autonomy might not be all that it appeared ... Perhaps not just 'any reason' will make the grade: what is needed is a well evidenced, durable, and consistent package of wishes and values ... Although they do not (or cannot) say so outright, perhaps the judges require compelling evidence of the durability and consistency of the patient's wishes before the sanctity of life will be ousted.

Finally, a darker reading might be possible. N's case was decided days before MacDonald J confirmed that C, a 50-year-old woman, had the capacity to refuse life-saving dialysis ... Whilst they evidently differ, N and C both appear to have been strong-willed and independent, but also 'shallow' and somewhat 'difficult' individuals. Might such characteristics incline the court away from enforced treatment?

In *Briggs v Briggs*, Mr Briggs had sustained serious brain injuries in a road traffic accident. His treating team thought that he should be transferred to a rehabilitation unit, but Charles J was clear that 'if the decision that P would have made, and so their wishes on such an intensely personal issue can be ascertained with sufficient certainty it should generally prevail over the very strong presumption in favour of preserving life'. Charles J was of the view that Baker J's suggestion in *Re M* that the court should be 'particularly cautious about attaching significant weight' to M's previously expressed wishes 'runs counter to the holistic approach that the Supreme Court confirms is to be taken to enabling P to do what he would have wanted if of full capacity'.

[74] 'From Twilight to Breaking Dawn? Best Interests, Autonomy, and Minimally Conscious Patients: *M v N* [2015] EWCOP 76 (Fam)' (2016) 24 Medical Law Review 622–32.

Briggs v Briggs[75]

Charles J

Members of the family told me that in their view Mr Briggs would regard his present situation as horrible and one that he would not wish to continue. Included within the reasons given are that a life in which he did not have the ability to communicate with his wife and child is not one that he would be willing to have. In her second statement his wife says in her view even if Mr Briggs was peaceful, if he was experiencing anything at all, she can imagine Mr Briggs asking 'why are you torturing me?'

Mr Briggs' wife and family are convinced that if he was able to express it his view would be 'enough is enough' because his view on his best case scenario would be that for him this was not a life that was worth living. So they are convinced that he would refuse consent to the continuation of his treatment by CANH. In line with that his police colleague said she just knows that Mr Briggs would not have wanted to be kept alive like this.

I have concluded that as I am sure that if Mr Briggs had been sitting in my chair and heard all the evidence and argument he would, in exercise of his right of self-determination, not have consented to further CANH treatment that his best interests are best promoted by the court not giving that consent on his behalf.

This means that the court is doing on behalf of Mr Briggs what he would have wanted and done for himself in what he thought was his own best interests if he was able to do so.

Giles Birchley has suggested that appeals to 'what the patient would have wanted' may serve a purpose other than simply enhancing P's autonomy. Rather, it could also provide reassurance to the family and lessen the burden of life and death decision-making.

Giles Birchley[76]

We might explain the discussion of character in these judgments as a simple reassurance to families. By suggesting that the outcome is 'what the patient would have wanted', we address the burden of responsibility or distress that families may otherwise carry . . .

Making decisions on behalf of others is morally burdensome. It may be more than a family, clinician, or judge can bear to make an extremely weighty decision without some sense it would be agreed to by the patient.

Although it could not be relevant to an individual best interests decision, on a macro level, Derick Wade suggests that it might be worth considering whether the continued provision of CANH to patients in prolonged disorders of consciousness is a cost effective use of NHS resources. Given that the extended life it provides is likely to be of minimal or no quality, its cost per quality-adjusted life year (see Chapter 2) might be likely to be high.

---

[75] [2016] EWCOP 53.
[76] '" . . . What God and the Angels Know of us?" Character, Autonomy, and Best Interests in Minimally Conscious State' (2018) 26 Medical Law Review 392–420.

Derick T Wade[77]

The cost of caring for someone left minimally conscious or totally unaware is between £90 000 and £120 000 each year. Given an average life expectancy, the total cost for one person after the first year will be about £1.0 million … The cost consequences of individual healthcare decisions of this magnitude (£1.0 million) for so little benefit (remaining unchanged) should not be ignored …

To put it bluntly, the consequences of deciding to continue treatment of one unconscious person for 10 years are that

- Each year 10 people with severe hip pain cannot have a total hip arthroplasty and remain with a poor quality of life (NHS cost = £5500 each, private cost £11 000 each).
- Each year two people with Band 6 Cystic fibrosis will not get treatment (£40 000 NHS tariff cost).
- Over 10 years, five other people will die who would not have and 23 people will lose a year of their life.

There needs to be some societal discussion about the resources devoted to continuing treatment of people who gain little or no benefit. The numbers may be large, including people who have sustained an acute brain injury, and people in the end stages of progressive disorders such as multiple sclerosis or Alzheimer's disease.

(5) Court Involvement

A new specialist court was set up to administer the MCA. Section 15 sets out the powers the Court of Protection has to make declarations.

Mental Capacity Act 2005 section 15

15 Power to make declarations

(1) The court may make declarations as to—

  (a) whether a person has or lacks capacity to make a decision specified in the declaration;

  (b) whether a person has or lacks capacity to make decisions on such matters as are described in the declaration;

  (c) the lawfulness or otherwise of any act done, or yet to be done, in relation to that person.

(2) 'Act' includes an omission and a course of conduct.

Where there is a dispute or uncertainty, an application to the Court of Protection should normally be made by the NHS trust, or other body responsible for the patient's care. If there is a dispute between family members, one of them may wish to apply to the court. Any person who is alleged to lack capacity will also be able to make an application, though more usually

---

[77] Using best interests meetings for people in a prolonged disorder of consciousness to improve clinical and ethical management' (2018) 44 Journal of Medical Ethics 336–42.

she will be made a party to the proceedings, and the Official Solicitor will be appointed to protect her interests.

It is worth noting a peculiarity in the Official Solicitor's role in these cases. He (or she) is not appointed to represent P's views, but to protect her interests. These are not necessarily the same thing. As a result, as Alexander Ruck Keene et al explain, there may be cases where there is no one to speak on P's behalf.

Alexander Ruck Keene, Peter Bartlett, and Neil Allen[78]

There are, in consequence, a number of cases in which it is clear that P's litigation friend (most often, but not exclusively, the Official Solicitor) has either not positively advanced or indeed conceded matters where it is clear that, where P represented in the conventional sense, their representative would have taken a very different case. The consequence has been that no-one before the court has argued P's corner for them.

In practice, therefore, P faces two judges—one determining what substantive decisions to make on their behalf, and one deciding whether or not even to advance any arguments on their behalf as to those decisions ...

[Amendments to the Court of Protection Rules and/or the accompanying Practice Direction should] make clear that the primary duty of a litigation friend acting on behalf of P should— where P's wishes and feelings can reliably be identified—be to proceed on the basis that the case that they put to the court is derived from those wishes and feelings. In other words, the task of the litigation friend acting for P is to *represent* P, not their conception of P's interests or best interests.

Court involvement in decisions about the medical treatment of people who lack capacity is unusual, and in the vast majority of cases, decisions are taken by doctors, in consultation with the patient's relatives. According to the Code of Practice, some especially controversial decisions must be brought to the court, including live organ donation and non-therapeutic sterilisation.

In *Airedale NHS Trust v Bland*,[79] the House of Lords had suggested that, until a body of experience and practice had built up, it was good practice to seek court approval for decisions to withdraw CANH from patients in a PVS. This requirement was restated in the Code of Practice and the Court of Protection Rules. Following first instance decisions in which judges had questioned the need for court approval, there was some confusion over whether it was legally necessary to seek court approval for the withdrawal of CANH from patients in an MCS or PVS, collectively referred to as prolonged disorders of consciousness (PDOC).

Then, in *An NHS Trust v Y*, a case in which the family and treating team of Mr Y, a man in an MCS, agreed that CANH was no longer in his best interests, the NHS Trust responsible for his care sought a declaration from the High Court that it did not need to seek endorsement from the Court of Protection. After O'Farrell J held that, as a matter of law, court approval was not required, the Official Solicitor obtained leave to take the case straight to the UK Supreme Court for this question to be resolved. As a result of the Supreme Court's judgment, it is now clear that, as with other medical treatments, applications to the court should be made only

---

[78] 'Litigation Friends or Foes? Representation of "P" before the Court of Protection' (2016) 24 Medical Law Review 333–59.
[79] [1993] AC 789.

where there is disagreement or a lack of clarity over whether withdrawal of CANH is in the best interests of a patient in a PDOC.

An NHS Trust v Y[80]

Lady Black

I have difficulty in accepting that there are readily apparent and watertight categories of patient, with PDOC patients clearly differentiated from, say, patients with a degenerative neurological condition or critically ill patients, in such a way as to justify judicial involvement being required for the PDOC patients but not for the others . . .

[Q]uite apart from the pressure that court cases place on the overstretched resources of NHS trusts, they add greatly to the strain on families facing acutely distressing decisions. In a case where all the proper procedures have been observed and there is no doubt about what is in the best interests of the patient, there is much to be said for enabling the family and the patient to spend their last days together without the burden and distraction, and possibly expense, of court proceedings . . .

The documentation supplied to us shows that the difficulty that there is in assessing the patient and in evaluating his or her best interests is well recognised. The process is the subject of proper professional guidance, covering vitally important matters such as the involvement in the decision-making process of a doctor with specialist knowledge of prolonged disorders of consciousness, and the obtaining of a second opinion from a senior independent clinician with no prior involvement in the patient's care.

If, at the end of the medical process, it is apparent that the way forward is finely balanced, or there is a difference of medical opinion, or a lack of agreement to a proposed course of action from those with an interest in the patient's welfare, a court application can and should be made . . .

If the provisions of the MCA 2005 are followed and the relevant guidance observed, and if there is agreement upon what is in the best interests of the patient, the patient may be treated in accordance with that agreement without application to the court.

In the next extract, Simon Halliday et al suggest that court approval in these cases had both benefits and burdens.

Simon Halliday, Adam Formby, and Richard Cookson[81]

First, we can see that the declaratory relief judgments often operate as memorials of the living dead that anticipate the funerals that will follow in due course. The judgment of the court performs a function of ceremonially moving the family on from a state of limbo. Second, it also offers the family a formal affirmation of the extreme difficulty of their situation and the reality of their suffering . . . There is evidence of the comfort and reassurance that these judgments can give . . . [T]he judgments often stress the appropriateness of letting the patient die. Research shows that family members often do not want to seek withdrawal of CANH

---

[80] [2018] UKSC 46.
[81] 'An Assessment of the Court's Role in the Withdrawal of Clinically Assisted Nutrition and Hydration from Patients in the Permanent Vegetative State' (2015) 23 Medical Law Review 556–87.

[clinically assisted nutrition and hydration] ... For such relatives, the jurisdiction of the court can help them not to feel responsible for the patient's death ...

Interview data certainly confirm that the declaratory relief process carries potential emotional burdens for families. First, for some relatives, the prospect of declaratory relief may be distressing because they feel that the court is an illegitimate forum for such decisions to be made. For some relatives, the requirement to go to court is an unwelcome legal intrusion into the family domain ... Second, some relatives, like many lay people who face the prospect of involvement in court procedure, feel some anxiety about the formalities of the process ... Finally, the delay to the ending of the patient's life caused by the court process can be very upsetting for some families.

If there is agreement that CANH is not in the patient's best interests, one of the difficult issues that arose from the need to seek court approval was that, pending the hearing, the doctors would have to continue to give treatment that they did not consider to be in the patient's best interests, and hence breach their obligation under section 1(5) of the Mental Capacity Act. Because of delays in bringing these cases to court, some patients were therefore treated against their best interests for many years.

Drawing upon the case of 'G', who had suffered a brain injury in 1994, but who only had CANH, which the judge described as 'overwhelmingly' not in his best interests, removed in 2017, Jenny and Celia Kitzinger argue that the removal of the need to go to court may help, but that it is not a complete solution.

Jenny Kitzinger and Celia Kitzinger[82]

Overall, what we see in this case is that instead of treatments being decided by reference to G's best interests, an entire infrastructure and reams of official documentation supported treatment-by-default. This was implemented in the complete absence of any evidence that it was in his best interests, and in the face of ample evidence that it was futile and possibly unlawful – and long after his parents had come to believe he would not have wanted his life prolonged ...

Families, and staff too, feel trapped in a system of 'care delivery' which seems to have its own logic and momentum. It seems that some of the healthcare workers involved in G's care had been deeply troubled by the situation but did not know there were options, or did not feel they had the skills to challenge what was happening, or felt it was not their place to raise the question of whether or not continued life-prolonging treatment was right ... Even once the parents initiated the discussion and the Health Board started proceedings there was still an additional delay before the case reached court. As a result of all these factors G's human right not to receive futile and unwanted treatment was breached for decades ...

Although removal of the perceived need to go to court will be an important step towards getting rid of one source of delay, it is clear that this will not completely resolve the problem of treatment-by-default for patients in permanent vegetative states – or indeed in other prolonged disorders of consciousness.

---

[82] 'Why futile and unwanted life-prolonging treatment continues for some patients in permanent vegetative states (and what to do about it): Case study, context and policy recommendations' (2017) 24 International Journal of Mental Health and Capacity Law 129–43.

(6) Advance Decisions

There is an exception to the application of the best interests test if the patient had made a valid and applicable advance decision (AD) to refuse treatment. If a decision is both valid and applicable, then under section 26(1) 'the decision has effect as if he had made it, and had had capacity to make it, at the time when the question arises whether the treatment should be carried out or continued': that is, it is like a contemporaneous refusal. As with a contemporaneous refusal, P is entitled to make an unwise decision, which is not in her best interests. The Code of Practice spells this out.

Mental Capacity Act Code of Practice

> 9.36 Where an advance decision is being followed, the best interests principle does not apply. This is because an advance decision reflects the decision of an adult with capacity who has made the decision for themselves. Healthcare professionals must follow a valid and applicable advance decision, even if they think it goes against a person's best interests.

ADs are defined in section 24.

Mental Capacity Act 2005 section 24

> 24(1) 'Advance decision' is a decision made by a person ('P'), after he has reached 18 and when he has capacity to do so, that if—
>
> (a) at a later time and in such circumstances as he may specify, a specified treatment is proposed to be carried out or continued by a person providing health care for him, and
>
> (b) at that time he lacks capacity to consent to the carrying out or continuation of the treatment, the specified treatment is not to be carried out or continued.

Section 24(1) specifies that ADs must have been made when an adult had capacity, and must specify which treatment should not be carried out or continued when P lacks capacity. It is only advance refusals of treatment that are decisive; an advance request for treatment might be relevant under section 4(6)(a) when deciding what is in a person's best interests, but it could not be binding on anyone.

In line with the MCA's first statutory principle, the assumption should be that the person had capacity when she made the advance decision.

Mental Capacity Act Code of Practice para 9.8

> 9.8 In line with principle 1 of the Act, that 'a person must be assumed to have capacity unless it is established that he lacks capacity', healthcare professionals should always start from the assumption that a person who has made an advance decision had capacity to make it, unless they are aware of reasonable grounds to doubt the person had the capacity to make the advance decision at the time they made it.

In practice, however, if someone suffers from a condition that might have affected her capacity when she made her AD, doubt may be cast on whether or not she had capacity at the time.

In *A Local Authority v E*,[83] for example, E had attempted to execute an AD refusing force-feeding but, despite her psychiatrist's view that she had capacity at the time, Peter Jackson J held that she did not, and hence it was not a binding AD for the purposes of the Act. In E's case, given her long history of anorexia, the presumption of capacity appeared to have been converted into a presumption of incapacity, which could have been rebutted only if there had been a thorough capacity assessment when she signed her AD. According to Peter Jackson J, 'a full, reasoned and contemporaneous assessment evidencing mental capacity to make such a momentous decision would in my view be necessary'.

Someone who suffers from a condition which might affect her capacity would therefore be well advised to undergo a capacity assessment at the same time as making her AD. The Act's failure to require patients to do so leaves many ADs open to subsequent challenge.

Rob Heywood[84]

Amid the range of formalities that were included in the Mental Capacity Act 2005, what mechanisms are in place within the legislation to ensure that a patient is competent at the time they actually draft their advance decision? The answer is, quite simply, none . . .

The law may have also resisted requiring a formal assessment of capacity for a number of other reasons. First, it would be in direct conflict with the golden thread that runs through the Mental Capacity Act 2005, the presumption of capacity. Requiring an assessment of a patient's capacity by a witness as a prerequisite to validating the advance decision reverses this and works from the starting position that patients are incapable of exercising their right of choice before someone else confirms they are capable of doing so . . .

[I]t would certainly add a further and perhaps unwelcome layer of complexity to insist that the witness must be a trained professional with expertise in assessing capacity. It stands to reason that this would inhibit access by making the process of creating an advance decision more costly, time-consuming, and bureaucratic. Yet, as the law stands, we are still left with a situation in which the central feature of the advance decision, the feature which gives it teeth, is left untested and this will always render it vulnerable to attack.

Cressida Auckland agrees and recommends further formalising the process of creating ADs.

Cressida Auckland[85]

As a doctor later called upon to implement a directive has no opportunity to assess whether the person would have had capacity, it would not therefore seem such a significant step to require clear evidence of a contemporaneous capacity assessment at the time of drafting the decision . . .

---

[83] [2012] EWHC 1639 (Fam).
[84] 'Revisiting Advance Decision Making Under the Mental Capacity Act 2005: A Tale of Mixed Messages' (2015) 23 Medical Law Review 81–102.
[85] 'Protecting me from my Directive: Ensuring Appropriate Safeguards for Advance Directives in Dementia' (2018) 26 Medical Law Review 73–97.

A proforma should be designed . . . , and should be easily accessible both online (for example on the NHS and Gov.uk websites), and in GP surgeries. Once completed, the doctor may then assess the person's understanding of the things included within the directive and their capacity, and, based on a discussion with them about the reasoning behind the directive, suggest changes or other things to include or exclude from its remit. The doctor may also make suggestions on measures to improve the specificity and interpretation of it, if deemed necessary . . .

Like drafting a will, a person can, if they prefer, choose to do it themselves, without either legal advice or a proforma, and this may be effective. However, if the person wants to ensure there are no complications in the implementation of it, they are advised to follow legal advice. Adopting this method would help to ensure that the advance directive was competent and informed, as well as enhancing the specificity and applicability of the directive.

(a) Validity

Section 25(2) sets out when an AD will not be valid.

Mental Capacity Act 2005 section 25

25(2) An advance decision is not valid if P—

(a) has withdrawn the decision at a time when he had capacity to do so,

(b) has, under a lasting power of attorney created after the advance decision was made, conferred authority on the donee (or, if more than one, any of them) to give or refuse consent to the treatment to which the advance decision relates, or

(c) has done anything else clearly inconsistent with the advance decision remaining his fixed decision.

Under section 25(2)(c) the decision is not valid if the P has acted in a way which is 'clearly inconsistent' with the decision. What does this mean? One obvious example might be if someone has explicitly renounced the religious beliefs upon which her previous refusal was based.

In practice, it may be difficult to tell whether a person's subsequent actions are 'clearly inconsistent' with her AD. The Act does not specify whether the actions that invalidate the AD under section 25(2)(c) must have taken place while P still had capacity. On the one hand, the failure to specify when the 'clearly inconsistent' actions should take place would seem to lead to the conclusion that any inconsistent conduct should invalidate the decision, regardless of whether P had by that time lost capacity. Yet, on the other hand, section 24(3) specifies that P may withdraw or alter an AD only 'when he has capacity to do so', so it would be odd if someone who lacks capacity could nevertheless invalidate her previous AD simply by acting inconsistently with it.

The Code of Practice recommends that patients should be advised to regularly review and update their ADs because a recently reviewed decision is more likely to be valid than one made several years ago.

(b) Applicability

Section 25(3)–(6) specifies when an advance decision will not be applicable.

Mental Capacity Act 2005 section 25

25(3) An advance decision is not applicable to the treatment in question if at the material time P has capacity to give or refuse consent to it.

   (4) An advance decision is not applicable to the treatment in question if—

      (a) that treatment is not the treatment specified in the advance decision,

      (b) any circumstances specified in the advance decision are absent, or

      (c) there are reasonable grounds for believing that circumstances exist which P did not anticipate at the time of the advance decision and which would have affected his decision had he anticipated them.

An AD will therefore lapse if the person regains capacity. It is also necessary that the AD precisely covers the situation in which the P now finds himself, and that there has not been a change of circumstances which casts doubt upon whether the AD reflects P's views. An example might be where a patient executes an advance refusal of a particular medication because she finds its side effects intolerable. If, in the meantime, a new version has been developed which does not have those side effects, there may be reasonable grounds for believing that this would have affected the patient's decision.

When deciding whether an AD is applicable, the Code of Practice recommends that healthcare professionals consider a number of factors.

Mental Capacity Act Code of Practice

9.43 So when deciding whether an advance decision applies to the proposed treatment, healthcare professionals must consider:

- how long ago the advance decision was made, and

- whether there have been changes in the patient's personal life (for example, the person is pregnant, and this was not anticipated when they made the advance decision) that might affect the validity of the advance decision, and

- whether there have been developments in medical treatment that the person did not foresee (for example, new medications, treatment or therapies).

The Code of Practice recommends that, when drawing up an AD, it is important to try to anticipate as many eventualities as possible, in order to avoid doubt about whether it applies in the circumstances that have arisen.

Mental Capacity Act Code of Practice

9.16 It is a good idea to try to include possible future circumstances in the advance decision. For example, a woman may want to state in the advance decision whether or not it should still apply if she later becomes pregnant. If the document does not anticipate a change in circumstance, healthcare professionals may decide that it is not applicable if those particular circumstances arise.

Again, it is advisable for people to regularly update their ADs, in order to minimize the chance that it will have been invalidated by changes in circumstances.

Mental Capacity Act Code of Practice

9.29 . . . Decisions made a long time in advance are not automatically invalid or inapplicable, but they may raise doubts when deciding whether they are valid and applicable. A written decision that is regularly reviewed is more likely to be valid and applicable to current circumstances—particularly for progressive illnesses. This is because it is more likely to have taken on board changes that have occurred in a person's life since they made their decision.

It is unclear whether section 25(4)(c) could apply to a scenario in which a now demented individual appears to be contented and does not want to die, despite having issued an otherwise binding AD refusing life-sustaining treatment. Is the fact that P appears to be happy living with dementia a circumstance 'which P did not anticipate at the time of the advance decision and which would have affected his decision'? If interpreted in this way, the scope of section 25(4)(c) is potentially extremely broad since it would almost always be possible to argue that P made her AD in a state of relative ignorance about what it would actually be like to be incapacitated.

Indeed, some commentators have gone so far as to suggest that profound incapacity may sever the 'psychological continuity' between the competent individual who issued the AD, and the person who now lacks capacity and requires life support, meaning that the incapacitated person should not necessarily be bound by her previous self's wishes. As Rebecca Dresser puts it:

If little or no psychological connectedness and continuity exist between the individual at the two points in time, then there is no particular reason why the past person, as opposed to any other person, should determine the present person's fate.[86]

Allen Buchanan[87]

[The] very process that renders the individual incompetent and brings the advance directive into play can—and indeed often does—destroy the conditions necessary for her personal identity and thereby undercuts entirely the moral authority of the directive . . .

So long as the degree of psychological continuity which we take to be necessary for the preservation of personal identity is present, the advance directive has full moral authority . . . [But] presumably a point is eventually reached at which the degree of psychological continuity between the author of the advance directive and the incompetent individual is so small that the advance directive of the former has no authority at all over the latter.

---

[86] Rebecca Dresser, 'Life, Death, and Incompetent Patients: Conceptual Infirmities and Hidden Values in the Law' (1986) 28 Arizona Law Review 380–1, 373.

[87] 'Advance directives and the personal identity problem' (1988) Philosophy and Public Affairs 131–54.

The idea that the adult who lacks capacity should not be bound by their capacitous self's AD is a controversial one, however. Laura Pritchard-Jones is concerned that it misrepresents dementia, which does not result in a complete loss of identity, but rather in 'a gradual change in cognitive functioning, with fluctuations and lucid periods during their illness':

> A key problem with this literature, however, is that it dichotomises the dementia patient, and frequently presents them at two extremes: the 'un-demented', and the 'entirely demented' person. This approach masks the spectrum of symptoms that a person with dementia in fact experiences.[88]

Others have argued that the whole purpose of writing an AD is to bind our future selves. Ronald Dworkin, for example, has said that ADs express values that we should continue to respect because the person who lacks capacity is not just a collection of current interests, but rather is a person with a past.[89] Similarly, Nancy Rhoden has argued that the 'notion that a person is one person, and one person only, from birth through old age' is 'deeply embedded in our culture'.

Nancy K Rhoden[90]

> If we are to make decisions about them as persons, we must view them not only as they are in the present, but also as the persons they were—persons who had strong opinions about how their body, even when insensate, should be treated . . . We must see the person as she, when competent, would have imagined herself after incompetency, rather than viewing her from the outside and as she is now . . .
>
> [A]n entirely present-oriented view is a bad way to view even persons who left no living will; it is unlikely that they would want to be viewed just as a body that can experience only physical sensations . . . Considering the patient only in the immediate present divides the patient from her past, her history, her values, and her relationships—from all those things that make her human.

In the next extract, Inez de Beaufort explains why she would want her previously competent wishes to take priority.

Inez de Beaufort[91]

> For me, the thought of my children spending their precious time visiting me when I do not recognize them is very painful, as is the idea that I know that they would suffer from that situation. Their suffering would, in my view, not be compensated by any interest I have in continuing my life. They will be sad because they knew me as the person I was, and feel powerless in not being able to save me from this fate. The fact that I consider this, and take

---

[88] Laura Pritchard-Jones, '"This Man with Dementia"— "Othering" the Person with Dementia in the Court of Protection' (2016) 24 Medical Law Review 518–43.
[89] Ronald Dworkin, 'Autonomy and the demented self' (1986) 64 Milbank Quarterly 4, 14 (Supp II).
[90] 'Litigating Life and Death' (1988) 102 Harvard Law Review 375, 414.
[91] 'The view from before' (2007) 7 American Journal of Bioethics 57–8.

> their future feelings at heart in viewing my possible future is an essential part of me, of who I am and what I value.
>
> When I am demented, I may enjoy the visit of my 'mother' or whomever I think is visiting me, and I may be genuinely pleased about that. But the purpose and point of my AED [advance euthanasia directive] is precisely that I do not want to end up in the situation of someone who cannot be there for her loved ones anymore . . . The argument that you will be another you, and you will experience things differently when you are demented, does not convince me. To the contrary, because what I want to prevent is precisely this fact that I will experience things differently. I do not want to become someone who does not recognize her children anymore even if the demented-me would not suffer from not recognizing them anymore.

If all ADs were subjected to a 'present best interests' review, whereby the AD is not binding if it conflicts with what appears to be in the person's best interests now, there would, as Sabine Michalowski points out, be little point in making an AD, since exactly the same decision would be taken in its absence. People make ADs precisely because they worry about what decisions will be taken on their behalf in the future.

Sabine Michalowski[92]

> To disregard the decision made by the competent patient because it violates the general (or one person's) perception of the patient's present interests would mean that the validity of an advance directive is subjected to a 'present best interests' assessment exercised by a third party at the time a treatment decision needs to be made. Advance directives would then no longer be a means by which a patient can ensure that his/her own subjective values govern his/her medical treatment towards the end of life.

(c) Advance refusals of life-saving treatment

Section 25(5) and (6) set out additional requirements for advance refusals of life-sustaining treatment. The P must specifically acknowledge that he intends to refuse treatment even if this puts his life at risk; the decision must be in writing and signed by P, or a representative in P's presence, and the signature must be witnessed.

These requirements are important in practice because it is precisely this sort of treatment that people making what are often called 'living wills' want to refuse. Few people will execute ADs in order to refuse mundane or trivial treatments. Rather, a person might want prospectively to refuse all blood products on religious grounds; or she might want to set out when she would not want to receive CPR or CANH. In such cases, ADs must be in writing, signed, and witnessed.

Without legal advice, then, it is likely that many advance refusals will be invalid, as was the case in *An NHS v D*,[93] in which D, who was now in a PVS, had tried to refuse life-prolonging treatment in a signed written letter, but his signature had not been witnessed (in practice, this did not make any difference because the court decided that life-prolonging treatment was not in his best interests).

---

[92] 'Advance Refusals of Life Sustaining Treatment' (2005) 68 Modern Law Review 958.
[93] [2012] EWHC 885 (COP).

(d) Effects of advance decisions

Where there is doubt about the validity or applicability of an advance decision, under section 26(4) an application can be made to the court for a declaration. If the AD is valid and applicable, the court has no power to overrule it. While the court's advice is being sought, under section 26(5) nothing in the AD should prevent the provision of life-sustaining treatment or steps to prevent a deterioration in the P's condition.

An advance decision that is not valid or applicable is not completely irrelevant, however. In the absence of a binding AD, the doctor will decide what treatment is in the patient's best interests, and if the AD expresses the person's wishes or feelings, it will be relevant under section 4(6)(a). The Code of Practice reiterates that a finding that an AD does not apply does not therefore mean that doctors are entitled to provide the treatment it attempted to refuse.

Mental Capacity Act Code of Practice

9.45 If an advance decision is not valid or applicable to current circumstances:

- healthcare professionals must consider the advance decision as part of their assessment of the person's best interests if they have reasonable grounds to think it is a true expression of the person's wishes, and

- they must not assume that because an advance decision is either invalid or not applicable, they should always provide the specified treatment (including life-sustaining treatment)—they must base this decision on what is in the person's best interests.

As we saw earlier, in *Sheffield Teaching Hospitals NHS Foundation Trust v TH*,[94] TH's preference to have no further treatment was respected even though Hayden J found that 'the stringent requirements of Section 24 are not met', and there was 'no advance decision to refuse treatment here'.

Although only advance refusals of treatment can be binding, it is increasingly common for dying patients to be encouraged to express their preferences about what should happen to them in their final days and weeks. This sort of advance care planning might include making a formal advance decision to refuse resuscitation, but it could also incorporate positive preferences about what treatment the patient would like to receive, and where she would like to die. As Carolyn Johnston explains, advance care planning can be beneficial for patients and their families.

Carolyn Johnston[95]

With appropriate training, ACP [advance care planning] is a valuable process for promoting patient-centred care for future treatment. It can be of benefit to the patient, his or her loved ones, and health and care providers. A qualitative study found that patients with end stage renal disease perceived the process of ACP a means of providing hope through provision of information, empowerment and enhancing relationships with staff and loved ones. Patients identify ACP as an important element in a trusting doctor–patient relationship, and evidence shows that ACP and end of life discussions reduce stress, anxiety and depression in surviving relatives. In a

---

[94] [2014] EWCOP 4.
[95] 'Advance Decision Making—Rhetoric or Reality?' (2014) 34 Legal Studies 497–514.

study investigating the impact of ACP on end of life care in elderly patients, family members were more likely to be satisfied with the quality of the patient's death from both their own perspective and the perceived perspective of the patient where ACP was used. ACP is associated with fewer hospital admissions from residential care and when undertaken in a hospital environment improves treatment in accordance with patient prior wishes. ACP has broader goals than the creation of [advance decisions to refuse treatment] and the discussion with healthcare/trained professionals enables provision of information about realistic healthcare choices.

(7) Avoiding Liability

Normally it will be a doctor (rather than a judge) who decides whether a person lacks capacity and what treatment would be in her best interests. It is, of course, possible that the doctor might get one or both of these decisions wrong. If it turns out that the patient did, in fact, have capacity, has a doctor who mistakenly treated her without consent committed an assault or battery?

According to section 5 of the Act, in order to be protected from a charge of battery or assault, a doctor needs: (a) to take 'reasonable steps' to establish whether the P has capacity; (b) have a 'reasonable belief' that the person lacks capacity; and (c) 'reasonably believe' that the treatment is in P's best interests.

Mental Capacity Act 2005 section 5

5 Acts in connection with care or treatment

(1) If a person ('D') does an act in connection with the care or treatment of another person ('P'), the act is one to which this section applies if—

    (a) before doing the act, D takes reasonable steps to establish whether P lacks capacity in relation to the matter in question, and

    (b) when doing the act, D reasonably believes—
      (i) that P lacks capacity in relation to the matter, and
      (ii) that it will be in P's best interests for the act to be done.

(2) D does not incur any liability in relation to the act that he would not have incurred if P—

    (a) had had capacity to consent in relation to the matter, and

    (b) had consented to D's doing the act.

The MCA Code of Practice makes clear that when judging the reasonableness of a decision-maker's beliefs, healthcare professionals will be assumed to be more skilled in assessing capacity than informal carers—that is, it will be harder for them to establish that they acted reasonably by wrongly deciding the person lacked capacity. It also specifies that detailed records should be kept.[96]

In the next extract, Mary Donnelly points out that the Act does not contain any formal mechanism to hold assessors of capacity to account. Of course, a disgruntled patient could challenge the decision that she lacked capacity by bringing an action in battery. But not only does the Act contain protections for doctors who have acted reasonably, it is also important to

---

[96] Para 6.33.

remember that, given the circumstances of many people with borderline capacity, this sort of 'privatized' enforcement is unlikely to be ineffective.

Mary Donnelly[97]

The framework includes no mechanisms to monitor the performance of assessors. Thus, monitoring is essentially a private matter, dependent on people either challenging the results of assessments in the Court of Protection or taking tort actions . . . There are two problems with reliance on this kind of private monitoring. First, it requires the person him or herself, or someone acting on his or her behalf, to initiate the legal process. For a person of borderline capacity, this may represent a considerable burden. Secondly, legal actions of this kind are less effective at changing underlying patterns of behaviour than at developing ways to prove compliance with strict legal norms. Thus, the requirement to take practical steps to help the person make the decision could be addressed by a bland recitation of formal steps taken which would do nothing to enhance the actual communication between the parties . . . The MCA tells assessors what to do but is much more reticent in actually ensuring that they do this.

As we see later, the House of Lords post-legislative scrutiny committee echoed Donnelly's criticisms of the Act's lack of 'teeth'.

A doctor might also make a mistake in relation to an advance decision. Because a valid and applicable advance refusal of treatment has exactly the same effect as a contemporaneous one, if a doctor wrongly relies on an invalid AD, or wrongly treats in the face of a valid AD, she could be liable in negligence or battery. Section 26(2) and (3) provide for exemption from liability in certain circumstances.

Mental Capacity Act 2005 section 26

26(2) A person does not incur liability for carrying out or continuing the treatment unless, at the time, he is satisfied that an advance decision exists which is valid and applicable to the treatment.

(3) A person does not incur liability for the consequences of withholding or withdrawing a treatment from P if, at the time, he reasonably believes that an advance decision exists which is valid and applicable to the treatment.

There is a significant difference between the test for avoiding liability depending upon whether the doctor has wrongly treated despite the existence of a valid AD, or not treated because she was relying on an invalid AD.

If the doctor wrongly fails to comply with a valid AD—that is, she gives treatment that the patient has refused—the doctor will not be liable unless at the time she was 'satisfied' that there was a valid AD in existence. This means doctors will only face liability if they blatantly disregard what they know (or are 'satisfied') to be a valid AD. Hence, if a doctor has doubts about an AD's validity, it will be relatively straightforward to establish that she was not 'satisfied' that

---

[97] 'Capacity Assessment under the Mental Capacity Act 2005: Delivering on the Functional Approach?' (2009) 29 Legal Studies 464–91.

a valid AD existed, and she can therefore ignore it. It is not necessary for those doubts to be objectively reasonable: if the doctor is not 'satisfied' that it is binding on her, she is not bound.

In contrast, under section 26(3), if a doctor refrains from treating a patient because she wrongly believes that her AD is valid, she will avoid liability for any harm caused by her failure to treat provided that she reasonably believed that the AD was valid. Taken together, these provisions suggest that doctors should be wary of complying with ADs where they have any doubts at all about their validity. A doctor could be liable for withholding treatment if her belief in the AD's validity is later judged not to have been reasonable, whereas she will be liable for ignoring a valid AD only if she knowingly disregarded it.

In the next extract, Alasdair Maclean argues that giving this protection to doctors who treat a patient despite the existence of a valid AD shows that the MCA's protection of patients' 'precedent autonomy' is trumped by its protection of clinical discretion.

Alasdair Maclean[98]

The statute tries to balance four things: respect for the patient's self-determination, facilitation of healthcare provision, protection of the incompetent adult's welfare and protection of the treating physician. In trying to achieve this balance, the Government has arguably tipped the scale towards protection and facilitation and away from individual autonomy. If the provisions were intended to protect the competent patient's precedent autonomy, then the Act is open to criticism for the resulting vulnerability of advance directives. The Act is arguably most successful in facilitating the provision of healthcare by supporting clinical discretion and protecting the physician who acts in good faith. Thus, the Act provides patients with a trump that only works when healthcare professionals and/or the courts are comfortable with the patient's decision.

(8) The Use of Restraint

In exceptional circumstances, it can be legitimate to use force or restraint in order to ensure someone receives medical treatment. Restraining P will not attract liability provided the conditions in section 6(2) and (3) are met:

Mental Capacity Act 2005 section 6

6(2) The first condition is that D reasonably believes that it is necessary to do the act in order to prevent harm to P.

(3) The second is that the act is a proportionate response to—

(a) the likelihood of P's suffering harm, and

(b) the seriousness of that harm.

The Code of Practice makes clear that the onus will be on D to prove that restraint is necessary, and not just convenient.

---

[98] 'Advance Directives and the Rocky Waters of Anticipatory Decision-Making' (2008) 16 Medical Law Review 1–22.

Mental Capacity Act Code of Practice para 6.44

6.44 Anybody considering using restraint must have objective reasons to justify that restraint is necessary. They must be able to show that the person being cared for is likely to suffer harm unless proportionate restraint is used. A carer or professional must not use restraint just so that they can do something more easily. If restraint is necessary to prevent harm to the person who lacks capacity, it must be the minimum amount of force for the shortest time possible.

In *DH v NHS Foundation Trust*,[99] Sir Nicholas Wall P was impressed with the care that had been taken over the treatment of PS, who needed to undergo treatment for cancer which she was resisting because of her needle and hospital phobia. PS was likely to refuse to attend hospital so the trust had arranged for a consultant anaesthetist to travel with an ambulance crew to PS's home in order to give her a sedative in a soft drink. If 'persuasion fails', Sir Nicholas Wall P authorized the use of 'force if necessary to sedate her and convey her to hospital'.

The 'least restrictive alternative' principle in section 1(6) is relevant here. In authorizing the use of physical restraint in a further case involving DD, a woman for whom pregnancy was extremely risky, Cobb J stressed that it should be used only after less restrictive alternatives had failed.[100]

Mental Health Trust v DD

Cobb J

The issue of forced entry to her home and restrictions on her freedom of movement arise again today as they have arisen on previous occasions. Again, not without considerable reservation, I do nonetheless consider it in DD's best interests that I give authorisation to the Applicant to exercise physical restraint for the purposes of giving DD the relevant contraception injection, by professionals who have received training in the relevant techniques and only as a last resort, where less restrictive alternatives have failed; it is important that at all times the professionals should maintain DD's dignity.

The use of force or restraint also must not interfere with the patient's right, under Article 3 of the Human Rights Act 1998, to be free from inhuman and degrading treatment.[101]

(9) Proxy Decision-Making

The Mental Capacity Act introduced, for the first time, the option of proxy medical decision-making for incapacitated adults. This involves P nominating one or more people, referred to as 'donees', with lasting power of attorney (LPA) who, under section 9(1)(a), will have the authority to make decisions about 'P's personal welfare, or specified matters concerning his personal welfare'. A donee is permitted to take decisions about life-sustaining

---

[99] [2010] EWHC 1217 (Fam).   [100] *Mental Health Trust v DD* [2014] EWCOP 44.
[101] As we see in Chapter 8, in *Herczegfalvy v Austria* (Application No 10533/83) 24 September 1992, the European Court of Human Rights held that 'a measure which is a therapeutic necessity cannot be regarded as inhuman or degrading. The Court must nevertheless satisfy itself that the medical necessity has been convincingly shown to exist'.

treatment only if P has included a clear statement to this effect. Donees cannot take decisions if P regains capacity, or if she has made a binding advance decision to refuse a particular treatment.

If more than one donee is appointed, the donor can specify, under section 10(4), whether they should act 'jointly' or 'severally' in relation to different decisions. If they are to act jointly, all the donees must agree on every decision; if they can act 'severally', the decision of one donee is sufficient. An LPA could also specify that the donees must agree where a serious medical decision has to be made, but that they could act independently in relation to more trivial decisions. If the LPA does not specify this, and more than one donee is appointed, they will have to act jointly in relation to all decisions.

The power of the donee of an LPA is, under section 9(4), subject to the provisions of the Act. Donees are therefore bound by the requirement to take decisions in P's best interests, guided by the section 4 checklist. If someone has not nominated a 'donee', her close friends or relatives should be consulted under section 4(7)(e) when assessing her best interests, although their views will be advisory rather than determinative.

There are two potential problems with proxy consent under the MCA, highlighted in the next extract. First, empirical studies suggest that we are not very good at predicting what others would decide, even when we know them very well indeed. Secondly, because a donee does not have the same freedom as the patient to take decisions which conflict with her best interests, they are an imperfect proxy.

Anthony Wrigley[102]

There is evidence to indicate that we are simply not very good at making substituted judgements for other people, not even for close relatives . . . This empirical evidence suggests that as a practical means of extending the autonomous wishes and desires of a patient who now lacks capacity, substituted judgement is an extremely poor method, as it is likely to be unrepresentative and could lead to errors . . .

The MCA places fairly obvious restrictions on what a proxy can and can't consent to . . . Upon analysis, the MCA has created a situation where lip service is paid to the notion of a proxy consenter, but when the matter is pursued, the ethical and, ultimately, legal status of such a proxy seems diminished to that of an advisor. This should not be taken in a negative light, however, because this role of advisor to a professional medical team is the most useful and morally authoritative role a proxy can take . . . Ultimately, 'proxy consent' should not be seen as consent at all, but rather 'assistance' to those best placed to judge the patient's best interests.

(10) The Mental Capacity Act in Practice

The Mental Capacity Act 2005 is framed in strikingly patient-friendly terms, especially when contrasted with the mental health legislation that we consider in Chapter 7. Through various measures, such as the principle of assisted decision-making and the priority given to the patient's wishes, the MCA expands the group of people able to make decisions for themselves, or have a meaningful say over decisions involving their care. Although it described the Act as

---

[102] 'Proxy consent: moral authority misconceived' (2007) 33 Journal of Medical Ethics 527–31.

'visionary',[103] the House of Lords Select Committee's post-legislative scrutiny of the Mental Capacity Act found that it was not well understood, and that implementation was patchy.

House of Lords Select Committee on the Mental Capacity Act 2005[104]

The empowering ethos of the Act has not been widely implemented. Our evidence suggests that capacity is not always assumed when it should be. Capacity assessments are not often carried out; when they are, the quality is often poor. Supported decision-making, and the adjustments required to enable it, are not well embedded. The concept of unwise decision-making faces institutional obstruction due to prevailing cultures of risk-aversion and paternalism. Best interests decision-making is often not undertaken in the way set out in the Act: the wishes, thoughts and feelings of P are not routinely prioritised. Instead, clinical judgments or resource-led decision-making predominate. The least restrictive option is not routinely or adequately considered ...

The presumption of capacity, in particular, is widely misunderstood by those involved in care ... The general lack of awareness of the provisions of the Act has allowed prevailing professional practices to continue unchallenged, and allowed decision-making to be dominated by professionals, without the required input from families and carers about P's wishes and feelings.

A fundamental change of attitudes among professionals is needed in order to move from protection and paternalism to enablement and empowerment. Professionals need to be aware of their responsibilities under the Act, just as families need to be aware of their rights under it.

The Committee recommended that there should be a single oversight body whose role would be to ensure that the Act's empowering ethos is, in practice, translated into more empowering care for those who lack capacity.[105] In 2015, the government established a National Mental Capacity Forum, chaired by Baroness Ilora Finlay, to bring together stakeholders in order to better promote effective understanding and implementation of the Act. It has also set up an online MCA Directory, in order to provide convenient access to a range of MCA tools and guidance,[106] and, as we have seen, in 2018, decision-making and mental capacity was the subject of a NICE guideline.[107]

4 CONCLUSION

It is clear that a great deal turns on whether a patient has capacity. For patients with capacity, the principle of autonomy dominates, and the patient is entitled to refuse treatment, including life-saving treatment, for irrational reasons or even for no reason at all. If, on the other hand, the patient lacks capacity, doctors are entitled to act paternalistically and treat the patient in her best interests. Since the consequences of lacking capacity are that one's wishes can be

---

[103] House of Lords Select Committee on the Mental Capacity Act 2005, Report of Session 2013–14, *Mental Capacity Act 2005: Post-Legislative Scrutiny*.

[104] Ibid.   [105] Ibid.

[106] See further <www.scie.org.uk/mca-directory/keygovernmentdocuments.asp>.

[107] *Decision-making and Mental Capacity* (NICE, 2018).

overridden, it is important that a clear definition of incapacity exists, and that it is applied objectively and consistently.

For some patients, such as those in PVS, it will be self-evident that they lack the capacity to make decisions about their medical treatment. But while the law insists upon a binary 'either/or' categorization of patients as either having or lacking capacity, the reality is that decision-making capacity exists on a spectrum. Towards either end of the spectrum, it may be obvious that the patient has, or does not have capacity. In the middle, decisions will be more difficult.

Since the capacity/incapacity line is so critical, it is also important to consider who should be charged with making this assessment. While independent review by the courts is possible, usually the decision is made by the patient's doctors. Two important points follow from this. First, doctors are undoubtedly much less likely to question a patient's decision-making capacity when she has agreed to a proposed treatment. This means that uncooperative patients are more likely to be judged to lack capacity, and to be treated against their wishes.

Secondly, once the doctor has determined that a patient lacks capacity, then, in the absence of a binding AD, she is entitled to treat the patient according to her assessment of the patient's best interests, as structured by the section 4 checklist. In most cases, then, doctors are responsible for applying both the test for incapacity and the best interests test.

Of course, cases can and are brought before the courts, and in the case of especially controversial treatments such as non-therapeutic sterilization, court involvement should be routine. But in the ordinary run of things, it is important to acknowledge that it is not judges, but rather doctors, who must interpret and apply both the test for capacity and the best interests test. In the light of this, it is concerning that in 2017, the Law Commission confirmed the House of Lords' Select Committee's earlier finding that the Mental Capacity Act continues to be poorly understood by healthcare professionals.[108] It is also disappointing that the government decided not to take the opportunity offered by reforming the Deprivation of Liberty safeguards (discussed in Chapter 8) to update the Mental Capacity Act.

Law Commission[109]

14.25 We frequently heard of 'blanket' assessments of capacity being undertaken, which were based on a person's diagnosis alone and excluded family members, and the assumption of capacity being used by professionals in order to justify not providing assessments or assistance to people. Family members reported that hospital and care home workers were often too ready to use restrictive forms of intervention (such as restraint and sedation). One consultee described the Mental Capacity Act as a 'tool' used by professionals to 'bully' and 'side line' vulnerable people and their families.

14.26 We also received general comments from health and social care professionals. Many were concerned that poor knowledge of the Mental Capacity Act was widespread; many pointed to NHS staff and doctors as falling short in this respect. Stuart Turner (social worker) stated that 'one of the greatest failings in how the Mental Capacity Act has been implemented is that the majority of health and social care staff just did not understand it'.

---

[108] House of Lords Select Committee on the Mental Capacity Act 2005, Report of Session 2013–14, *Mental Capacity Act 2005: Post-Legislative Scrutiny*.
[109] *Mental Capacity and Deprivation of Liberty*, Law Com no 372 (2017).

FURTHER READING

Auckland, Cressida, 'Protecting me from my Directive: Ensuring Appropriate Safeguards for Advance Directives in Dementia' (2018) 26 Medical Law Review 73–97.

Case, Paula, 'Dangerous Liaisons? Psychiatry and Law in the Court of Protection—Expert Discourses of 'Insight' (and 'Compliance')' (2016) 24 Medical Law Review 360–78.

Cave, Emma, 'Protecting Patients from their Bad Decisions: Rebalancing Rights, Relationships, and Risk' (2017) 25 Medical Law Review 527–53.

Donnelly, Mary, 'Best Interests in the Mental Capacity Act: Time to say Goodbye?' (2016) 24 Medical Law Review 318–32.

Herring, Jonathan, *Vulnerable Adults and the Law* (Oxford University Press, 2016).

Jackson, Emily, 'From 'Doctor Knows Best' to Dignity: Placing Adults Who Lack Capacity at the Centre of Decisions About Their Medical Treatment' (2018) 81 Modern Law Review 247–81.

Johnston, Carolyn, 'Advance Decision Making—Rhetoric or Reality?' (2014) 34 Legal Studies 497–514.

Taylor, Helen J, 'What are "best interests"? A critical evaluation of "best interests" decision-making in clinical practice' (2016) 24 Medical Law Review 176–205.

6

INCAPACITY II: CHILDREN

CENTRAL ISSUES

1. Parents normally give consent to their children's medical treatment.

2. The parents' decision can be overruled by a court, if the decision the parents wish to take is not in the child's best interests.

3. The court may also become involved if the parents cannot agree with each other, or if the treatment is particularly controversial.

4. Mature minors can acquire the right to consent to treatment, when they have sufficient understanding or when they reach the age of 16, but they do not necessarily have the same right to refuse treatment.

1 INTRODUCTION

Medical decisions for babies and young children are almost always taken by their parents. The courts will become involved only where the parents cannot agree with each other about certain treatments, or where the treatment is especially controversial, or where the doctors believe that the decision the parents wish to take is not in the child's best interests. While the law which applies to medical decisions involving children is clear and simple—the child's best interests are the paramount consideration—these cases can nevertheless be distressing and emotionally charged.

Although childhood lasts from birth until the age of 18, in practice, children acquire some rights and responsibilities before they reach the age of majority. At what age can a child consent to medical treatment? As we see below, this will depend upon the child's age and the nature of the medical treatment, as well as the individual child's decision-making capacity.

2 PARENTAL CONSENT

Anyone with parental responsibility for a child can give consent to her medical treatment. If they are married, both parents automatically have parental responsibility. If they are unmarried, the father will have parental responsibility if he is registered on the child's birth certificate, or if he has made a parental responsibility agreement with the mother, or if he has obtained a parental responsibility order from the court. Non-parents may also have parental responsibility (perhaps because the child is living with them, and they have a child arrangements order), in which case they too would be able to give a valid consent to medical treatment. Non-parents who have temporary care of the child—such as teachers and childminders—are entitled to do what is reasonable in all the circumstances to safeguard or promote the child's welfare.[1]

Provided that both parents have parental responsibility, each would normally be able to give a valid consent to their child's medical treatment without consulting the other. As Dame Elizabeth Butler-Sloss P explains in *Re J (Specific Issue Orders: Child's Religious Upbringing and Circumcision)*, the consent of both parents is only necessary for certain treatments, such as non-therapeutic circumcision.

Re J (Specific Issue Orders: Child's Religious Upbringing and Circumcision)[2]

Dame Elizabeth Butler-Sloss P

There is, in my view, a small group of important decisions made on behalf of a child which, in the absence of agreement of those with parental responsibility, ought not to be carried out or arranged by one parent carer although she has parental responsibility under s 2(7) of the Children Act 1989. Such a decision ought not to be made without the specific approval of the court ... The issue of circumcision has not, to my knowledge, previously been considered by this court, but in my view it comes within that group. The decision to circumcise a child on grounds other than medical necessity is a very important one; the operation is irreversible, and should only be carried out where the parents together approve of it or, in the absence of parental agreement, where a court decides that the operation is in the best interests of the child.

It is worth noting that not everyone agrees that that parents should be able to consent jointly to non-therapeutic male circumcision. Rather, there are those who believe that it is anomalous to tolerate the cutting of boys' genitals, when cutting girls' genitals is a criminal offence.[3] Brian Earp, for example, argues that the decision should wait until the child can make a decision for himself:

Children of whatever sex or gender should not have healthy parts of their most intimate sexual organs removed, before such a time as they can understand what is at stake in such a surgery and agree to it themselves.[4]

Interestingly, in *Re B and G (children) (care proceedings)*, Sir James Munby P appeared to agree that, just like FGM, non-therapeutic male circumcision causes 'significant harm'; but it is harm that society is 'prepared to tolerate'.

Re B and G (children) (care proceedings)[5]

Sir James Munby P

In my judgment, if FGM Type IV amounts to significant harm, as in my judgment it does, then the same must be so of male circumcision ...

---

[1] Children Act 1989, s 3(5)(b).   [2] [2000] 1 FLR 571.
[3] Female Genital Mutilation Act 2003.
[4] 'In defence of genital autonomy for children' (2016) 42 Journal of Medical Ethics 158–63.
[5] [2015] EWFC 3.

Whereas it can never be reasonable parenting to inflict *any* form of FGM on a child, the position is quite different with male circumcision. Society and the law, including family law, are prepared to tolerate non-therapeutic male circumcision performed for religious or even for purely cultural or conventional reasons, while no longer being willing to tolerate FGM in any of its forms. There are, after all, at least two important distinctions between the two. FGM has no basis in any religion; male circumcision is often performed for religious reasons. FGM has no medical justification and confers no health benefits; male circumcision is seen by some (although opinions are divided) as providing hygienic or prophylactic benefits. Be that as it may, 'reasonable' parenting is treated as permitting male circumcision.

In the next extract, Brian Earp et al set out some possible reasons why FGC (female genital cutting) and MGC (male genital cutting) are treated differently by the law. They also argue that it is unsatisfactory that boys' interest in being able to make this decision for themselves is protected only if their parents happen to disagree about circumcision.

Brian D Earp, Jennifer Hendry, and Michael Thomson[6]

There are a number of solutions to this puzzle, with cultural familiarity being among the most significant. Put simply, the Western world's familiarity with Jewish circumcision since antiquity has contrasted with its long-standing 'ignorance of female circumcision ... the discovery [of which] during the eighteenth century was met with a combination of incredulity, fascination, and horror' ...

When FGC is raised in public conversation, it is usually the most severe forms in the least sanitary conditions that are emphasised (the young girl in a remote African village being cut and infibulated by a village elder), with limited mention of the more 'mild' forms of FGC, such as ritual nicking of the clitoral prepuce as is carried out by health professionals in some Muslim-majority countries including Malaysia. However, when male circumcision is the focus of public discourse, it is most often described in its least invasive forms, and in sanitary conditions such as a hospital setting ..., with limited awareness of the more extreme and unsanitary forms of MGC that are carried out in other contexts (e.g. ritual circumcision among the Xhosa of South Africa, where more than 400 boys died between 2008 and 2014 due to complications associated with their initiations). Such thinking both stems from, and perpetuates, a gendered opposition that does not reflect the full reality ...

[T]here is authority for stating that in post-separation families where there is disagreement about the cutting of a male child's genitals, the decision is likely to be deferred until the boy is old enough to make this decision for himself. This deferral recognises the harm, pain and risks involved, as well as the child's right to make decisions regarding his own body and permanent marks of religious affiliation. The paradox here is that the law only recognises the child as having these rights when the parents disagree. Where the parents agree, these rights are not protected.

Marie Fox and Michael Thomson further argue that the 'current vogue for relational approaches' may not be helpful in relation to MGC:

---

[6] 'Reason and Paradox in Medical and Family Law: Shaping Children's Bodies' (2017) 25 Medical Law Review 604–27.

Our concern with such approaches is that thin understandings of relationality can collapse into little more than an acknowledgment of the importance of family relationships. In so doing, they risk continuing to prioritise family integrity over the child's interests and rights, thus reinforcing the parental power which has allowed parents to literally shape their children's bodies.[7]

In *Re C (Welfare of Child: Immunisation)*,[8] a case in which the mother and the father disagreed over whether their child should receive the MMR vaccine, Thorpe LJ said that: 'In my opinion this appeal demonstrates that hotly contested issues of immunization are to be added to that "small group of important decisions".'

Hence, where the parents agree with each other, consent to circumcision and vaccination lies within a zone of parental discretion, and the court will not impose its own view of whether the procedure is in the child's best interests. Where those with parental responsibility cannot agree, or where the child is in care and her parent refuses to consent to vaccination,[9] the court will make the decision according to its assessment of the child's best interests. In the case of routine childhood vaccinations, because they are supported by responsible medical opinion, vaccination is overwhelmingly likely to be found to be in a child's best interests.[10]

Vaccination decisions are usually made on behalf of very young children who are not capable of expressing a view, but what if the children are older and do not want to be vaccinated? This was the case in *F v F (MMR Vaccine)*. L and M were now aged 15 and 11, and agreed with their mother that they did not want to be vaccinated. When L and M were young, the parents had agreed not to have them vaccinated, but their father had since changed his mind. Theis J found that neither child was *Gillick*-competent (see below), and that vaccination was in both children's best interests.

F v F (MMR Vaccine)[11]

Theis J

Whilst I am acutely aware of both L and M's wishes and feelings in relation to this issue, ... I consider their views have inevitably been influenced by a number of factors which affects the weight that should be attached to those wishes and feelings. First, from their perspective the parents were initially united in their decision for them not to be vaccinated and they can't understand why their father has changed his mind ... This perhaps displays a lack of maturity and an appreciation that views can change for a variety of reasons. Second, they have become focussed on the issue of the ingredients of the vaccine without being able to consider and balance the wider picture, and the consequences or actions of them not having it, including medication (and its contents) that would be required in the event of them becoming ill from one of the vaccine preventing diseases. Third, it is not surprising that they are likely to have become influenced by their mother's views. Those views are clearly strongly held and will inevitably have influenced both children ...

It is unfortunate the parents were not able to reach a consensus on this issue; that would have been best for both the children. In the absence of that the responsibility falls on the court to exercise that parental responsibility for the parents having regard to the welfare interests of each child.

---

[7] Marie Fox and Michael Thomson, 'Bodily Integrity, Embodiment, and the Regulation of Parental Choice' (2017) 44 Journal of Law and Society 501–31.

[8] [2003] EWCA Civ 1148.   [9] *Barnett London Borough Council v AL* [2017] EWHC 125 (Fam).

[10] See also *LCC v A, B, C & D* [2011] EWHC 4033 (Fam).   [11] [2013] EWHC 2683 (Fam).

In the next extract, Emma Cave is concerned about the consequences of ordering older children to be vaccinated against their wishes.

Emma Cave[12]

L and M might refuse to cooperate, in which case the first difficulty will be to find a doctor willing to carry out the procedure. The doctor would be protected from a claim in battery by virtue of the court's decision, but this is unlikely to remove the ethical concerns many doctors will have about non-consensual inoculation of older minors. The second problem is that a coercive medical procedure is one of the most serious invasions of bodily autonomy sanctionable in a democratic society.

In an emergency, if no one with parental responsibility is available to give consent, doctors are entitled to treat the child in her best interests. If treatment could reasonably be delayed until the parents can be found, or a court order obtained, doctors should not proceed with treatment.

Gillick v West Norfolk and Wisbech AHA[13]

Lord Templeman

I accept that if there is no time to obtain a decision from the court, a doctor may safely carry out treatment in an emergency if the doctor believes the treatment to be vital to the survival or health of an infant and notwithstanding the opposition of a parent or the impossibility of alerting the parent before the treatment is carried out.

Parents can consent to their child's medical treatment, but do they also have the right to refuse? Parental authority exists for the benefit of the child, so it does not give parents the right to make harmful decisions. Hence, if one or both of the parents refuse to consent to treatment that the doctors believe would be in the child's best interests, approval can be sought from another source, namely the courts.

3   COURT INVOLVEMENT

The court has the power to authorize the medical treatment of children through wardship, its inherent jurisdiction, and more recently through statute. Wardship differs slightly from the inherent jurisdiction—if a child is a ward of court, the court must make all important decisions about her upbringing, whereas the inherent jurisdiction can apply to a one-off decision. In practice, however, the two processes are largely indistinguishable. Both derive from the Crown's prerogative power as *parens patriae*, exercised by judges of the High

---

[12] 'Adolescent Refusal of MMR Inoculation *F (mother) v F (Father)*' (2014) 77 Modern Law Review 630–40.
[13] [1984] QB 581.

Court, and both give the courts more sweeping powers than are possessed by parents and mature minors.

As with adults, the court can declare that treatment would be lawful, in a child's best interests, but it will not force a doctor to act contrary to her clinical judgement. As Lord Donaldson MR explained in *Re J (A Minor) (Wardship: Medical Treatment):*[14]

> I have to say that I cannot at present conceive of any circumstances in which this would be other than an abuse of power as directly or indirectly requiring the practitioner to act contrary to the fundamental duty which he owes to his patient. This, subject to obtaining any necessary consent, is to treat the patient in accordance with his own best clinical judgment.

Hence, when the court becomes involved in disputes over a child's medical treatment, it can declare that a particular treatment would be lawful, and it can overrule both a parent's and a child's refusal, but it cannot compel doctors to do something which is contrary to their clinical judgement.

If a child's parents refuse to consent to treatment that the doctors believe to be in her best interests, the NHS Trust where the child is being treated can apply to the court for a declaration that treatment would be lawful. It is also possible that another concerned individual might apply if, for example, the doctors and the parents were intending to do something that was not in the child's best interests. This happened in the 1970s in *Re D (A Minor) (Wardship: Sterilisation),*[15] in which an educational psychologist succeeded in her application to have an 11-year-old girl made a ward of court, in order to prevent her from being sterilized at her parents' request.

In addition, under the Children Act 1989, the court can issue a specific issue order or a prohibited steps order to determine what treatment a child should receive.[16] In *Re C (Welfare of Child: Immunisation),*[17] the fathers of two children who were living with their mothers sought specific issue orders to enable their children, who had received none of the recommended childhood vaccines, to be immunized. The judge ordered each mother to have her child immunized, and the Court of Appeal upheld his decision.

Under section 1 of the Children Act, in any question affecting a child's upbringing, her welfare must be the 'paramount consideration'.[18] What does this mean in practice? It is clear from the General Medical Council (GMC) guidance on the treatment of under-18s, that, as with adults, best interests is not confined to the child's clinical best interests. If the child is able to express her own wishes, these are relevant, regardless of whether she is *Gillick*-competent (discussed later). The GMC guidance also embodies the 'least restrictive alternative' principle.

General Medical Council[19]

> 12. An assessment of best interests will include what is clinically indicated in a particular case. You should also consider:
>
>   a. the views of the child or young person, so far as they can express them, including any previously expressed preferences

---

[14] [1991] 2 WLR 140.   [15] [1976] 2 WLR 279.   [16] Section 8(1).
[17] [2003] EWCA Civ 1148.   [18] Section 1(1).
[19] *0–18 Years: Guidance for all Doctors* (GMC, 2018).

b. the views of parents

c. the views of others close to the child or young person

d. the cultural, religious or other beliefs and values of the child or parents

e. the views of other healthcare professionals involved in providing care to the child or young person, and of any other professionals who have an interest in their welfare

f. which choice, if there is more than one, will least restrict the child or young person's future options.

(a) CONTROVERSIAL MEDICAL TREATMENTS

There are times when it may not be obvious whether a particular medical procedure is in a child's best interests. Blood tests for the purposes of establishing paternity have been held to be in the child's best interests: taking blood causes only mild discomfort, and the child is likely to benefit from knowing the truth about her origins.[20] Bone marrow, blood, or organ donation (see further Chapter 12) are not in a child's best clinical interests, although just like in *Re Y (Mental Patient: Bone Marrow Donation)*,[21] discussed in Chapter 5, it could be argued that saving a sibling's life by donating bone marrow is likely to be in a child's emotional best interests. As yet, there have been no cases in the UK where the court has considered an application for a child to become a solid organ donor, although it could be predicted that it would be more difficult to establish that this would be in her best interests.

There have also been no cases in which the courts have had to determine whether aesthetic as opposed to reconstructive cosmetic surgery would be in a child's best interests. We therefore do not know what a court would decide if faced with a case in which parents want their child with Down's syndrome to have facial reconstructive surgery in order to look more 'normal', so that she will be less likely to be teased and/or discriminated against.[22]

Sterilization carried out in order to avoid pregnancy, rather than as treatment for a medical disorder, has been treated as a 'drastic step',[23] for which court approval is required. Improvements in contraceptive techniques mean that requests to perform sterilization operations on girls should now be rare. Because long-acting contraceptives, such as injections or implants, can achieve the same effect, an irreversible operation under general anaesthetic would seldom be the 'least restrictive alternative'.

Could surgical and other interventions ever be appropriate where the purpose is not to avoid pregnancy, but instead to stop a disabled child growing up? This issue first arose in the US in 2007, when the parents of a nine-year-old girl called Ashley published a blog explaining their decision to stunt her growth through chemical and surgical means. Unsurprisingly, there was an explosion of media interest in what her parents described as 'the Ashley treatment'.

Ashley X was nine years old, and very severely brain damaged. She suffered from static encephalopathy, which meant that she was unable to move around, or sit up unaided. Her

---

[20] *Re F (A Minor) (Blood Tests: Parental Rights)* [1993] 3 All ER 596; *Re H (A Minor) (Blood Tests: Parental Rights)* [1996] 4 All ER 28.

[21] [1996] 2 FLR 787.

[22] See further RB Jones, 'Parental consent to cosmetic facial surgery in Down's syndrome' (2000) 26 Journal of Medical Ethics 101–2.

[23] *Re B (A Minor)* [1988] AC 199, per Lord Templeman.

parents' fear was that, as Ashley got bigger, they would cease to be able to care for her on their own. They believed that Ashley's quality of life would be better if she remained small enough to be cuddled and carried easily by her parents.

When Ashley began to display the early signs of puberty, her parents asked doctors to remove her uterus, appendix, and breast buds, and to give her oestrogen. Before going ahead, the doctors obtained approval from the hospital's clinical ethics committee, which had agreed that this treatment was in Ashley's best interests.

A year later, there were reports that a British mother was seeking a hysterectomy for her daughter, Katie Thorpe, in order to avoid the pain and discomfort of menstruation.[24] The hospital refused to agree to the operation, and the case did not come before a court.

If a doctor in the UK had agreed to perform a hysterectomy on a girl like Katie Thorpe, or to carry out the full 'Ashley treatment', there is no doubt that the case would have to come before the court for a declaration as to whether or not it would be lawful, and in making that decision, the court would apply the best interests test.

A child's best interests undoubtedly encompasses her emotional and psychological well-being. On the one hand, if radical surgery would dramatically improve a child's quality of life, perhaps by enabling her to be carried by her parents, rather than by the sort of hoist used to transport industrial pallets, might this be in her best interests? On the other hand, the 'least restrictive alternative' principle would mean that long-acting contraceptives should be preferred to a hysterectomy, and, perhaps more importantly, better equipment and access to professional carers and other resources might be a less invasive way than surgery and growth restriction to ensure that a disabled child could continue to be cared for at home.

N Tan and Iain Brassington[25]

[W]e would do well to remind ourselves that the direct benefits to Ashley of this invasive treatment were minimal. The treatment was not palliative: it did not address any existing symptoms. Nor did it purport to modify the prognosis of the underlying condition in any way . . . Strikingly, Ashley's doctors' reason for their intervention was that

. . . [T]he primary benefit offered by growth attenuation is the *potential to make caring for the child less burdensome and therefore more accessible*. A smaller person is not as difficult to move and transfer from place to place.

What is notable about the statement is the manner in which it seems to shift the moral focus from Ashley and her needs towards her carers and theirs. It is not clear, though, whether this reason suffices to justify intervention ... Increased movement and stimulation could feasibly be achieved, for example, by non-invasive environmental adjustments such as harnesses, hoists and the provision of carers. In a sense, the wider Ashley treatment—taking into account that it also involved a hysterectomy, appendicectomy and breast bud removal to protect against problems of as yet unknown severity that might not appear anyway—might represent less of an attempt to meet the challenges of Ashley's condition than an attempt not to *have* to meet them.

---

[24] Owen Bowcott, 'Hospital refuses plea for hysterectomy on cerebral palsy girl', The Guardian 19 January 2008; 'Katie Thorpe's mother to renew hysterectomy bid', BBC News 29 October 2013.

[25] 'Agency, duties and the "Ashley treatment" ' (2009) 35 Journal of Medical Ethics 658–61.

In the next extract, Nicola Kerruish and John McMillan provide an account of how a New Zealand couple who had chosen growth attenuation (GA) treatment for their daughter explained their decision.

Nicola Kerruish and John R McMillan[26]

This case study provides important insights into how one set of parents reasoned about GA therapy for their child. The key findings relate to how Anna's parents weighed up the harms and benefits of treatment and considered this to be the type of decision they should be able to make. Their reasoning is based on the belief that attenuating Anna's growth would maximise her quality of life, by permitting them to maintain a parent-to-newborn-like relationship ...

No one can be certain about treatment outcomes, particularly for children such as Anna whose interests are ultimately 'unknowable' (as the very nature of severe intellectual disability prevents us from accessing the experience of those affected). What we can say is that these parents clearly describe how basic discomforts and pleasures may be magnified for Anna in a way that may be difficult for anyone not directly and intimately involved in caring for such a child to fully comprehend.

In 2016, Peter Jackson J was faced with an entirely novel decision. JS was 14 years old, and dying from cancer. She wanted her body to be taken to the US for cryonic preservation. This would require special measures to be taken immediately after her death, which the hospital trust was prepared to allow in the hope that this would reduce JS's distress about her impending death. JS's mother supported her decision, but her father did not, and because she was a minor, JS was unable to make a will appointing her mother as her executor. Peter Jackson J used a specific issue order to enable JS's mother to make decisions about her body after death. His judgment contains an important postscript, added after JS's death.

Re JS (Disposal of Body)[27]

Peter Jackson J

[B]oth as to preservation of the body and as to the question of who should be permitted to view it, I conclude that the mother is best placed to manage this unusual and difficult situation. I will therefore make orders placing responsibility in her hands and prevent the father from intervening ...

The making of a specific issue order is governed by the welfare principle. In this case the predominant features are JS's wishes and feelings and her acute emotional needs. These are best met by an order granting the mother the right to make arrangements during JS's lifetime for the preservation of her body after death. In making this order, the court is not approving the choice of arrangements, but it is giving JS and her mother the opportunity to make that choice.

---

[26] 'Parental reasoning about growth attenuation therapy: report of a single-case study' (2015) 41 Journal of Medical Ethics 745–9.
[27] [2016] EWHC 2859 (Fam).

Postscript

On 8 November, I received a detailed note from the solicitors for the hospital trust in which the events surrounding JS's death are described from the point of view of the hospital. It records that JS died peacefully in the knowledge that her body would be preserved in the way she wished.

However, the note makes unhappy reading in other ways. The Trust expresses very real misgivings about what occurred on the day of JS's death. In brief and understated summary:

(1) On JS's last day, her mother is said to have been preoccupied with the post-mortem arrangements at the expense of being fully available to JS.

(2) The voluntary organisation is said to have been under-equipped and disorganised, resulting in pressure being placed on the hospital to allow procedures that had not been agreed. Although the preparation of JS's body for cryogenic preservation was completed, the way in which the process was handled caused real concern to the medical and mortuary staff . . .

It may be thought that the events in this case suggest the need for proper regulation of cryonic preservation in this country if it is to happen in future.

(b) DISAGREEMENTS BETWEEN PARENTS AND DOCTORS

Most of the cases in which the courts have had to make decisions about a child's medical treatment have involved parents (or, as we see later, the child herself) disagreeing with doctors about what treatment should, or should not, be provided. The difficult question that arises is whether parents can ever legitimately take a different view from doctors about what is in their child's best interests. The answer to this question has usually been 'no': the courts will override parental refusals, and as we see later, refusals by the child too, in order to protect the child's best interests.

In *Re C (A Child) (HIV Test)*, the mother, who was HIV-positive, rejected conventional medical thinking on the causes and treatment of HIV/AIDS, and refused to allow her child to be tested. At first instance, Wilson J overruled her objections on the grounds that it was overwhelmingly in the child's best interests to be tested for HIV, and the Court of Appeal refused permission to appeal.

Re C (A Child) (HIV Test) [28]

Butler-Sloss LJ

In my view, the child is clearly at risk if there is ignorance of the child's medical condition. The degree of intrusion into the child of a medical test is slight . . . It does not matter whether the parents are responsible or irresponsible. It matters whether the welfare of the child demands that such a course should be taken . . . This child has the right to have

[28] [1999] 2 FLR 1004.

sensible and responsible people find out whether she is or is not HIV positive . . . What seems to me to be crucial is that someone should find out so that one knows how she should be looked after.

More recently, in *An NHS Trust v SR*, the court overruled his mother's refusal to consent and ordered that a seven-year-old boy should receive radiotherapy to treat his brain tumour. N's mother was concerned that radiotherapy might leave her son infertile, or damage his IQ. Given that, without it, N's life was in danger, the court's conclusion that her judgement had 'gone awry' was unsurprising. As Bodey J put it: 'one cannot enjoy even a diminished quality of life if one is not alive'. Bodey J explained that the court would only prefer a complementary alternative to conventional medical treatment where an experienced clinician advocated that treatment, and was willing to carry it out.

An NHS Trust v SR[29]

Bodey J

I have to keep firmly in mind what is required for there to be any realistic prospect of the court's preferring some complementary alternative to the standard mainstream treatment for N's condition. It is not just a question of demonstrating that there is research and experimentation going on out there; nor that there are ideas and possibilities being floated, nor even that there are reported success stories of cures occurring without the use of radiotherapy and/or chemotherapy. What is required is the identification of a clinician experienced in treating children aged about 7 having this kind of brain cancer; a clinician with the access to the necessary equipment and infrastructure to put the suggested treatment into effect and able and willing to take over the medical care of and responsibility for N.

Similarly, in *Re JM (A Child)*,[30] in which the parents of a ten-year-old child with a rare and aggressive form of cancer wished to treat it with Chinese medicine, rather than surgery, Mostyn J's conclusion that surgery would be in his best interests was unsurprising:

It is a strong thing for me, a stranger, to disagree with and override the wishes of J and his parents. But I have absolutely no doubt that J must be given the chance, a very good chance, of a long and fulfilling life rather than suffering, quite soon, a ghastly, agonising, death.

There has been one exceptional, and now rather old case in which the court refused to authorize a liver transplant against the parents' wishes, despite the likelihood that the child would be likely to die without a transplant. In *Re T (A Minor) (Wardship: Medical Treatment)*,[31] the Court of Appeal found that the parents' refusal to consent to their son's transplant was not prompted by 'scruple or dogma', and that there was 'genuine scope for a difference of view between parent and judge'. *Re T* is, however, probably best regarded as an idiosyncratic and anomalous judgment. Commenting upon it in *Re C (Welfare of Child: Immunisation)*,[32] for

---

[29] [2012] EWHC 3842 (Fam). [30] [2015] EWHC 2832 (Fam). [31] [1997] 1 WLR 242.
[32] [2003] EWCA Civ 1148.

example, Thorpe LJ said 'the outcome of that appeal, denying a child life-prolonging surgery, is unique in our jurisprudence and is explained by the trial judge's erroneous focus on the reasonableness of the mother's rejection of medical opinion'.

In *The NHS Trust v A (A Child)*, Holman J was impressed by the reasonableness of A's parents and the decision that they had made. They had refused to consent to a bone marrow transplant (BMT), in part because of the suffering it would cause A, and because it was not guaranteed to succeed. But since the BMT would give A, who would otherwise die, a 50 per cent chance of a normal life, Holman J decided that it would be in her best interests.

The NHS Trust v A (A Child)[33]

Holman J

My mind has wavered during the course of the hearing. I have been deeply impressed by the parents…They are in intimate and constant contact with A. They witnessed her suffering during the ordeal. They know her happiness and contentment at home now. But by the end of the hearing, and in agreement with the guardian, I have become convinced that it is in the overall best interests of A to undergo a BMT …

If a BMT could only prolong by a relatively short period her life; or if it would leave her alive but probably seriously impaired (e.g. significantly brain damaged) then I would or might take a different view. But in my view a 50 per cent prospect of a full, normal life (even though infertile) when set against the certainty of death before the age of one or one and a half, does in this case outweigh all other considerations and disadvantages.

Re King (A Child) was an unusual case, which had been played out dramatically in the media. Ashya King was five years old and suffering from brain cancer. Dissatisfied with the treatment available in the UK, his parents had taken him abroad. At first, it looked as though a desperately sick child's health was in danger as a result, and European arrest warrants were issued. Ashya was made a ward of court, but by the time the case reached the court, the picture had changed and his 'parents had put forward a treatment plan that was coherent and reasonable'. Baker J therefore authorized his removal to Prague for innovative proton treatment.

Re King (A Child)[34]

Baker J

Having considered the evidence, I concluded that there was no reason to stand in the way of the parents' proposal. In some cases, this court is faced with a dispute between medical authorities and parents who are insisting on a wholly unreasonable course of treatment, or withholding consent to an essential therapy for their child—for example, a blood transfusion. This is manifestly not such a case. The course of treatment proposed by Mr and Mrs King

---

[33] [2007] EWHC 1696 (Fam).   [34] [2014] EWHC 2964 (Fam).

is entirely reasonable. Ashya has a serious medical condition. Any parents in the position of Mr and Mrs King would do whatever they could to explore all options. Some parents would follow the advice of the local doctors to use conventional radiotherapy, others would prefer the relatively untested option of proton therapy (assuming the funds can be made available to meet the cost of transport and treatment) in the hope that the toxic effects of radiation will be reduced. Both courses are reasonable and it is the parents who bear the heavy responsibility of making the decision. It is no business of this court, or any other public authority, to interfere with their decision.

In the next extract, Jo Bridgeman is critical of Baker J's reliance upon the reasonableness of Mr and Mrs King's decision to take their son to Prague for unproven therapy.

Jo Bridgeman[35]

His Lordship approved the 'reasonable' course of action proposed by Ashya's parents but neglected to provide a reasoned and principled analysis of the best interests of a child whose parents were refusing consent to conventional post-operative treatment because of a preference for innovative and as yet unproven therapy only available, privately funded, abroad . . .

However, Baker J, approving the agreed treatment plan to secure the post-operative treatment Ashya urgently required, gave no further consideration to either his welfare or his rights. Baker J expressed the view that the 'course of treatment proposed by Mr and Mrs King is entirely reasonable'. . . This view, that is, the reasonable choice of parents cannot be challenged by public authorities or re-considered by the court, does not reflect established law and thus creates potential for uncertainty about respective responsibilities in future disputes.

(c) END-OF-LIFE DECISION-MAKING

It would be a mistake to imagine that all decisions about withholding or withdrawing life-prolonging treatment come before the courts. On the contrary, in neonatal intensive care units (NICUs), decisions to withdraw life-prolonging measures are common: it has been estimated that up to 70 per cent of deaths in NICUs are preceded by discussions about limiting or withholding treatment.[36] In paediatric intensive care units (PICUs) between 43 per cent and 72 per cent of deaths result from decisions about treatment withdrawal.[37]

The Royal College of Paediatrics and Child Health has issued guidance about the circumstances in which it may be appropriate to consider withholding or withdrawing life-sustaining treatment (LST) from children.

---

[35] 'Misunderstandings, Threats and Fear of the Law in Conflicts over Children's Healthcare' (2015) 23 Medical Law Review 477–89.
[36] Making decisions to limit treatment in life-limiting and life-threatening conditions in children: a framework for practice 3rd edn (Royal College of Paediatrics and Child Health, 2015).
[37] Ibid.

Royal College of Paediatrics and Child Health[38]

Situations in which it is appropriate to limit treatment

The underlying ethical justification for all decisions to withhold or withdraw LST is that such treatment is not in the child's best interests. There are three sets of circumstances where it may be appropriate to consider limitation of treatment.

Limited quantity of life

If treatment is unable or unlikely to prolong life significantly, it may not be in the child's best interests to provide it.

A. Brain death

B. Imminent death

C. Inevitable demise

In some situations death is not imminent (within minutes or hours) but will occur within a matter of days or weeks. It may be possible to extend life by treatment but this may provide little or no overall benefit for the child. In this case, a shift in focus of care from life prolongation per se to palliation is appropriate.

Limited quality of life: where there is no overall qualitative benefit

A. Burdens of treatments

... If a child's life can only be sustained at the cost of significant pain and distress it may not be in their best interests to receive such treatments, for example, use of invasive ventilation in severe irreversible neuromuscular disease ...

B. Burdens of illness and/or underlying condition

... Some children have such severe degrees of illness associated with pain, discomfort and distress that life is judged by them (or on their behalf if they are unable to express their wishes and views) to be intolerable. All appropriate measures to treat and relieve the child's pain and distress should be taken. If, despite these measures, it is genuinely believed that there is no overall benefit in continued life, further LST should not be provided ...

C. Lack of ability to derive benefit

In other children the nature and severity of the child's underlying condition may make it difficult or impossible for them to enjoy the benefits that continued life brings. Examples include children in Persistent Vegetative State (PVS), Minimally Conscious State, or those with such severe cognitive impairment that they lack demonstrable or recorded awareness of themselves or their surroundings and have no meaningful interaction with them, as determined by rigorous and prolonged observations. Even in the absence of demonstrable pain or suffering, continuation of LST may not be in their best interests because it cannot provide overall benefit to them ...

Informed, competent, supported refusal of treatment

... In some circumstances the child or young person, who often has extensive experience of illness, clearly and repeatedly refuses treatment that professionals may regard as being in their best interests. In practice these refusals are likely to occur in situations where the young

[38] Ibid.

> person's life is limited in quantity or quality or both (as outlined in 'Limited quantity of life and Limited quality of life: where there is no overall qualitative benefit') and where limitation of treatment may have already been considered as a possible option. Examples might include a child who requires cardiac transplantation for cardiomyopathy induced by therapy for leukaemia, or lung transplantation for complications of cystic fibrosis.
>
> ... If the child/young person does understand the nature and consequences of their decision, is assessed as having capacity to make the decision and is supported by their parents, the provision of further LST may no longer be ethically justifiable even if it has the potential to provide some limited clinical benefit.

Re A (A Child) was a very unusual case involving treatment withdrawal from a brain dead child. A was 19 months old when he choked on the stalk of a satsuma. He lost consciousness, leading to cardiac arrest and profound and irreversible brain injury. Brain stem tests, carried out four days later, revealed that A had died. He was, however, still attached to a ventilator and his parents were unable to contemplate removing him from it. They wanted to take A, while still being ventilated, back to Saudi Arabia where life support could not be withdrawn. A had been dead for 48 hours when the hospital applied for declarations that it would be lawful for him to be withdrawn from the ventilator. Hayden J granted the declarations sought.

Re A (A Child)[39]

Hayden J

Whilst expressing profound respect for the father's views, the time has now come to permit the ventilator to be turned off and to allow Child A, who died on 10th February, dignity in death. For those reasons, I propose to make the declarations sought by the Trust, with the indicated amendments, confident that this hospital will do everything they can to make this inevitably painful process as dignified as possible for all concerned.

More commonly, the cases that come before the courts tend to involve the RCPCH's second category—'limited quality of life: where there is no overall qualitative benefit'—and generally the courts only become involved in cases where the doctors and the parents disagree about treatment withdrawal.

The most common sort of dispute arises when the doctors believe that life support should be withdrawn, while the parents want treatment to continue, sometimes as a result of their religious faith. In *King's College Hospital NHS Foundation Trust v T*, for example, Z was 17 months old and gravely ill. He had suffered a catastrophic irreversible hypoxic-ischemic injury, which had destroyed most of his brain tissue. There was no prospect of meaningful movement, vision, communication, engagement with others, or feeding, and indeed Z's condition was so poor that tests had been carried out in order to discover if he met the criteria for brain-stem death. Z was being kept alive on a mechanical ventilator, which the doctors now wished to withdraw, with the result that Z would die within an hour. As committed and devout Christians, Z's parents believed that they did not have the right to agree to life-sustaining treatment being withdrawn. They also believed that, given time, God might work a miracle and Z might recover enough to participate more fully in life. Russell J granted permission for Z to be removed from the ventilator.

---

[39] [2015] EWHC 443 (Fam).

King's College Hospital NHS Foundation Trust v T[40]

Russell J

On balance I am driven to conclude that the mechanical ventilation is only just sustaining life with no other benefit. When I consider his best interests holistically, the life support confers little benefit as it prolongs all the likely discomfort and possible pain and increases the probability of further infection leading to further invasive treatment and complications which will itself contribute to further physical deterioration without any real hope of restoring his health. His brain injuries are so profound, so catastrophic and the likelihood of further deterioration to his brain from hydrocephalus and the probability of lung infection and injury with continued ventilation all add to the conclusion that on balance not only is there no benefit, but in fact there is a strong probability of further pain, suffering and deterioration. Very sadly and with great reluctance I grant permission to withdraw the mechanically assisted ventilation.

When faced with an application for a declaration of the lawfulness of treatment withdrawal, as with all other medical decisions, the child's best interests are the court's paramount concern.[41] In applying the best interests test, medical evidence is crucial but that does not mean that the court will simply rubber stamp the doctors' point of view, as we can see from *An NHS Trust v B*.

MB suffered from Type 1 spinal muscular atrophy (SMA). He could barely move, could not breathe unaided, could not swallow, and suffered from epilepsy. The doctors treating him considered that MB's quality of life had become so poor and the burdens of treatment so great that it would be unethical to continue artificially to keep him alive. They sought a declaration that it would be lawful to withdraw his endotracheal tube, which would lead to his death within a few minutes. His parents disagreed, and wanted treatment to continue.

Holman J recognized that there were some treatments, such as cardiopulmonary resuscitation, which went beyond maintaining ventilation and which required the positive infliction of pain. If they became necessary, Holman J thought this would mean that MB had moved naturally towards his death, and that it would then be in MB's best interests to withhold those treatments.

In applying the best interests test, in *An NHS Trust v B*, Holman J drew up a 'balance sheet' with the benefits or advantages of treatment on one side, and the burdens or disadvantages on the other side. On the benefits side were MB's capacity to gain pleasure from DVDs, CDs, and stories and, more importantly, from his relationship with his parents and family. The burdens were the discomfort, distress, or pain which accompanied the procedures to which he was subject, coupled with his inability to communicate his suffering. Holman J concluded that because MB's life did still contain benefits, treatment should continue.

An NHS Trust v B[42]

Holman J

I fully accept all the burdens of discomfort, distress and some pain to which M is daily subjected, but from which I would now specifically exclude, if the need arises, CPR and the other treatments I have just described. Even excluding these, I accept that there is almost relentless

---

[40] [2014] EWHC 3315 (Fam).   [41] Children Act 1989, s 1.   [42] [2006] EWHC 507 (Fam).

discomfort, periods of distress and relatively short episodes of pain (deep suctioning). It is indeed a helpless and sad life.

But that life does in my view include within it the benefits that I have tried to describe and will not repeat. Within those benefits, and central to them, is my view that on the available evidence I must proceed on the basis that M has age appropriate cognition, and does continue to have a relationship of value to him with his family, and does continue to gain other pleasures from touch, sight and sound . . .

It is impossible to put a mathematical or any other value on the benefits. But they are precious and real and they are the benefits, and only benefits, that M was destined to gain from his life. I do not consider that from one day to the next all the routine discomfort, distress and pain that the doctors describe (but not the ones I have now excluded) outweigh those benefits so that I can say that it is in his best interests that those benefits, and life itself, should immediately end. On the contrary, I positively consider that as his life does still have benefits, and is his life, it should be enabled to continue, subject to excluding the treatment I have identified.

A year later, in *Re K (A Minor)*, Sir Mark Potter P distinguished K's situation from that of MB. She could gain no pleasure from life and, as a result, it would be in her best interests to cease to provide artificial feeding (known as total parenteral nutrition or TPN).

Re K (A Minor)[43]

Sir Mark Potter P

In this case K is less than 6 months old and has a developmental age of only 3 months. She has no accumulation of experiences and cognition comparable with that of MB. She is not, and with her short expectation of life is never likely to be, in a position to derive pleasure from DVDs or CDs and the only indication of real feelings of pleasure in her limited developmental state is enjoyment of a bath. On the evidence before me there is no realistic sense in which one can assign to her the simple pleasure of being alive or having other than a life dominated by regular pain, distress and discomfort and unrelieved by the pleasures of eating . . .

She has no prospect of relief from this pitiful existence before an end which is regarded as virtually certain by the age of one year and likely to be appreciably less . . . In these circumstances, I have no doubt that it would not only be a mercy, but it is in her best interests, to cease to provide TPN while she is still clinically stable, so that she may die in peace and over a comparatively short space of time, relieved by the palliative treatment contemplated, which will cause her neither pain nor discomfort and will enable her to live out her short life in relative peace in the close care of her parents who love her.

Taken together, these two cases suggest that if the child has some meaningful cognitive development and awareness, the court may favour life-prolonging measures, even where these cause some discomfort. But where that discomfort coexists with an inability to gain any pleasure from everyday life, life-prolonging treatment is less likely to be in a child's best interests.

In most of these cases, the courts are concerned to weigh up the burdens and the benefits of treatment. But if the child is unconscious, she may not experience any benefits or burdens.

---

[43] [2006] EWHC 1007 (Fam).

Invasive treatment will not be burdensome for her, but nor does her life contain any meaningful benefits (unless simply being alive, despite being wholly unaware of that fact, is regarded as a benefit). In such cases, the question is instead whether the treatment is futile.

An example of such a case is *NHS Trust v Baby X*, in which the question for the court was whether baby X—who had suffered profound and irreversible brain damage—should be removed from a mechanical ventilator, with the expectation that he would die within minutes or hours. The staff in the children's hospital where X was being treated had concluded that it was no longer in X's best interests to remain on artificial ventilation: there was no prospect of any improvement and so continuing treatment would be futile. X's parents, on the other hand, wanted the treatment to continue. In part this was because they still believed that improvement was possible, but also their religious faith prevented them from consenting to a course of action which would result in X's death.

Hedley J accepted that treatment was not, in fact, burdensome for X because he had no awareness and could not experience pain. But since no improvement was possible, treatment would be futile, and Hedley J declared that it would be lawful to withdraw X from the ventilator.

NHS Trust v Baby X[44]

Hedley J

In the end I have to conclude that X's welfare requires his removal from ventilation on to palliative care ... The essence of the reasoning which supports this conclusion is as follows. First, I recognise the desire to preserve life as the proper starting point to which I add that X is very probably unaware of any burden in his continued existence. Against that, secondly, I have set both his unconsciousness or unawareness of self, others or surroundings and the evidence that any discernible improvement is an unrealistic aspiration. Thirdly, I have acknowledged his ability to continue for some time yet on ventilation but have balanced that with the risk of infection or other deterioration and the desire to avoid death in isolation from human contact. Fourthly, having accepted that treatment serves no purpose in terms of improvement and has no chance of effecting it, I have taken into account its persistent, intense and invasive nature. Fifthly, I have noted the treating consultant's view that X shows no desire to live or capacity to struggle to survive which are the conventional marks of a sick child; although I think that observation as such is correct, I would not want that to have significant let alone decisive weight in this balance.

Essentially for those reasons and on that balance I reach the conclusion that X should in future be treated on the basis of palliative care. This is, of course, not an order of the court. It is a declaration that so to treat would be lawful as being in X's best interests.

(d) CHARLIE GARD AND ALFIE EVANS

In 2017, the world was gripped by the sad case of Charlie Gard, a baby suffering from infantile-onset mitochondrial DNA depletion syndrome (MDDS). Charlie's parents wanted to take him to the US in order to receive an experimental treatment called nucleoside therapy, and they

[44] [2012] EWHC 2188 (Fam).

had raised the money to do so through a crowd-funding campaign. There had been no clinical trials of nucleoside therapy in patients with Charlie's condition, and the US doctor who was willing to give it to Charlie had not examined him. The doctors treating Charlie at Great Ormond Street Hospital (GOSH) considered that it would not be in Charlie's best interests to travel to receive therapy which medical experts in the UK believed had no chance of working. At first instance, Francis J agreed.

On appeal, lawyers for Charlie Gard's parents tried to rely upon Baker J's judgment in *Re King* in order to argue that there are now two categories of disputes between parents and doctors. In category 1 cases, where the parents are not proposing a viable alternative form of treatment, decisions should be decided on the basis of the court's view of the child's best interests. But they argued that Charlie Gard's case fell into a new category 2, along with *Re King*; namely, that where the parents are proposing a viable alternative treatment, the court should not interfere with the parents' choice, unless it would be likely to cause the child significant harm. The Court of Appeal rejected this argument (we return to the question of whether this *should* be the test below).

Great Ormond Street Hospital for Children NHS Foundation Trust v Yates[45]

McFarlane LJ

To postpone the withdrawal of treatment, which is otherwise accepted to be the better course for this young child, to go to America to receive treatment which has 'zero' prospect of improving his condition, would only prolong his existence in a manner which all, most sadly, agree can no longer be justified as being in his best interests ...

Where ... as in this case, the judge has made clear findings that going to America for treatment would be futile, would have no benefit and would simply prolong the awful existence that he found was the current state of young Charlie's life, he was fully entitled, on the basis of those findings to conclude as he did. The consequence of that conclusion is that the proposal for nucleoside therapy was not a viable option before the court ...

My primary conclusion, therefore, on looking at *Re King*, is that Mr Justice Baker's words provide no basis for saying that he was holding that any test based on significant harm is to be applied to cases relating to the medical treatment of children ... If, contrary to my primary reading, Mr Justice Baker did intend to state, where a parent puts forward a viable option for treatment, that the High Court only has jurisdiction to interfere with a parent's choice of that medical treatment if the child is likely to suffer significant harm as a result, then, in my view, such a statement has no foundation as a matter of law, is contrary to established authority and is therefore plainly in error ...

It goes without saying that in many cases, all other things being equal, the views of the parents will be respected and are likely to be determinative. Very many cases involving children with these tragic conditions never come to court because a way forward is agreed as a result of mutual respect between the family members and the hospital, but it is well recognised that parents in the appalling position that these and other parents can find themselves may lose their objectivity and be willing to 'try anything', even if, when viewed objectively, their preferred option is not in a child's best interests. As the authorities to which I have already made reference underline again and again, the sole principle is that the best interests of the child must prevail and that must apply even to cases where parents, for the best of motives, hold on to some alternative view.

---

[45] [2017] EWCA Civ 410.

In social media campaigns, on Twitter and Facebook, the Charlie Gard case was caricatured as the state interfering with parents' rights to make decisions about their children. Incendiary and alarmist posts represented GOSH, and the judge involved in the case, as Charlie's 'executioners'. In his final judgment in the case, Francis J condemned the abuse of medical staff at GOSH and suggested that greater use should be made in these cases of mediation.

Great Ormond Street Hospital for Children NHS Foundation Trust v Yates [46]

Francis J

The parents have had to face the reality, almost impossible to contemplate; that Charlie is beyond any help even from experimental treatment and that it is in his best interests for him to be allowed to die. Given the consensus that now exists between parents, the treating doctors and even Dr Hirano, it is my very sad duty to confirm the declarations that I made in April this year, and I now formally do so. I do not make a mandatory order.

I remind myself, and others listening to this judgment, that the nucleoside therapy for which the parents had been contending has not even been tried on mice with the same strain of mitochondrial disease from which Charlie suffers, let alone humans ...

It has sadly come in to the public domain recently that some of the staff at that hospital have been subjected to serious threats and abuse. I made it clear before, and make it clear now, that I am completely satisfied that these fine parents have nothing whatever to do with those threats. Each and every man and woman working at Great Ormond Street Hospital is dedicated to the treatment of sick, very often desperately sick, children. These surgeons, physicians, doctors, nurses, ancillary staff, technicians and all others working there are dedicated to the pursuit of excellence in the treatment of sick children and it is in my judgment a disgrace that they should have been subjected to any form of abuse whatsoever and it is to be condemned ...

In this country children have rights independent of their parents. Almost all of the time parents make decisions about what is in the best interests of their children and so it should be. Just occasionally, however, there will be circumstances such as here where a hospital and parents are unable to decide what is in the best interests of a child who is a patient at that hospital ...

[I]t is my clear view that mediation should be attempted in all cases such as this one even if all that it does is achieve a greater understanding by the parties of each other's positions. Few users of the court system will be in a greater state of turmoil and grief than parents in the position that these parents have been in and anything which helps them to understand the process and the viewpoint of the other side, even if they profoundly disagree with it, would in my judgment be of benefit and I hope that some lessons can therefore be taken from this tragic case which it has been my duty to oversee.

The Charlie Gard case was followed just months later by that of Alfie Evans, a toddler with a catastrophic neurodegenerative condition that had destroyed almost all of his brain. The doctors at Alder Hey hospital believed that further treatment would be both futile and inhumane, but Alfie's parents wanted to fly him to Bambino Gesu Hospital in Rome, in the hope of prolonging his life. Hayden J found that it would be in Alfie Evans' best interests for treatment to be withdrawn.

---

[46] [2017] EWHC 1909 (Fam).

Alder Hey Children's NHS Foundation Trust v Evans[47]

Hayden J

Properly analysed, Alfie's need now is for good quality palliative care. By this I mean care which will keep him as comfortable as possible at the last stage of his life. He requires peace, quiet and privacy in order that he may conclude his life, as he has lived it, with dignity.

The plans to take him to Italy have to be evaluated against this analysis of his needs. There are obvious challenges. Away from the intensive care provided by Alder Hey PICU, Alfie is inevitably more vulnerable, not least to infection. The maintenance of his anticonvulsant regime, which is, in itself, of limited effect, risks being compromised in travel. The journey, self-evidently will be burdensome. Nobody would wish Alfie to die in transit.

All of this might be worth risking if there were any prospect of treatment, there is none. For this reason the alternative advanced by the father is irreconcilable with Alfie's best interests.

Before the Court of Appeal, lawyers for Alfie's parents attempted unsuccessfully to mount a novel legal claim, this time claiming that the hospital was unlawfully detaining Alfie. Once again, there was huge media interest in the case, including incendiary posts on social media, and demonstrations at the hospital, and the Court of Appeal was also concerned about the impact upon other patients and their parents.

Alder Hey Children's NHS Foundation Trust v Evans[48]

Davis, King and Moylan LJJ

The application of a different legal label, namely habeas corpus, does not change the fact that the court has already determined the issues which the parents now seek, again, to advance. Their views, their rights do not take precedence and do not give them an 'unfettered right' to make choices and exercise rights on behalf of Alfie. As the Supreme Court said in this case the rights of the child will, if inconsistent with the rights of the parents, prevail over them. The 'gold standard' for determining the rights of a child, including decisions about medical treatment, is by an objective assessment of and decision as to what is in his best interests. There has been a thorough, rigorous assessment leading to a decision which has been upheld by the Court of Appeal and the Supreme Court. There is no scope for the same issues to be re-litigated through a different legal label . . .

It is not surprising that Alfie's tragic situation should cause emotions to run high. But, we cannot conclude this judgment without recording our dismay and concern at what we have been told have been the consequences of what has taken place at the hospital in recent days. These matters have not been the subject of any court determination. However, if true they are alarming. We were told that some members of the hospital staff could not get to the hospital because of road blockages; that staff, patients and family members were upset and frightened by what was taking place; that a group supporting the parents went into the Paediatric Intensive Care Unit to the concern of staff. If these events have taken place it is not difficult to see how they would impact negatively on the treatment being provided to patients at the hospital. Hospitals must be places which provide peace and calm. What we have been told has occurred is the very opposite.

---

[47] [2018] EWHC 308 (Fam).   [48] [2018] EWCA Civ 805.

In the next extract, Ranjana Das describes how the online communities set up in the wake of these cases have mobilised anti-expert populist rhetoric.[49]

Ranjana Das[50]

I have argued that the Charlie's Army online community has attempted to intervene in a complicated legal battle between state healthcare services and private individuals by producing and maintaining populist discourse ... I have argued that this was achieved through the creation of moral and ethical distinctions between an evil outgroup (state healthcare and the judiciary) and a wronged in-group (private individuals and parents of ill children) and a rejection of professional expertise with 'common sense'. These distinctions were maintained I pointed out, through blame attribution using emotive language and descriptors of violence (for instance, describing healthcare providers as 'murderers' and 'scum'), all of which served to maintain us-versus-them boundaries which associate ordinariness with vulnerability ...

It is important to note that the group has been reaching out to the parents of other very ill, often terminally ill children with complex and rare medical conditions, and similar groups are emerging on social media, each arguing against medical expertise and each mobilizing a moral distinction between private parents who are presented as having been purposefully wronged on the one hand, and intentionally harmful and misguided public services on the other, with these polarised conversations punctuated by interventions from populist figures such as preachers, pro-life pastors and activists and psychic mediums.

(e) SHOULD 'BEST INTERESTS' BE REPLACED BY 'SIGNIFICANT HARM'?

As we have seen, in the Charlie Gard case, the courts rejected the parents' claim that the test for interference with parental autonomy should not be the best interests of the child, but whether the parents' decision places the child at risk of significant harm. This argument was advanced some years ago by Douglas Diekema.

Douglas Diekema[51]

There are several good reasons for this presumption to respect parental autonomy and family privacy. First, because most parents care about their children, they will usually be better situated than others to understand the unique needs of their children, desire what's best for their children, and make decisions that are beneficial to their children. Second, the interests of family members may sometimes conflict, and some family members may be subject to harms as a consequence of certain decisions. Parents are often better situated than others

---

[49] See also Udo Schuklenk, 'Bioethics culture wars–2018 edition: Alfie Evans' (2018) 32 Bioethics 270–1; Iain Brassington, 'Alfie Evans: Please, just stop' Journal of Medical Ethics Blog April 2018: http://blogs.bmj.com. gate3.library.lse.ac.uk/medical-ethics/2018/04/24/alfie-evans-please-just-stop/.

[50] 'Populist discourse on a British social media patient-support community: The case of the Charlie Gard support campaign on Facebook' (2018) 24 Discourse, Context & Media 76–84.

[51] 'Parental refusals of medical treatment: the harm principle as threshold for state intervention' (2004) 24 Theoretical Medicine and Bioethics 243–64.

outside of the family to weigh the competing interests of family members in making a final decision. Third, parents should be permitted to raise their children according to their own chosen standards and values and to transmit those to their children. Finally, in order for family relationships to flourish, the family must have sufficient space and freedom from intrusion by others. Without some decision-making autonomy, families would not flourish, and the important function served by families in society would suffer . . .

The real question is not so much about identifying which medical alternative represents the best interest of the child, but rather about identifying a harm threshold below which parental decisions will not be tolerated . . .

For the medical professional facing a parent refusing to consent to a suggested course of treatment, the proper question is not, 'Is this intervention in the child's best interest?' but rather 'Does the decision made by the parents significantly increase the likelihood of serious harm as compared to other options?' Parental decisions that do not significantly increase the likelihood of serious harm as compared to other options should be tolerated.

In recent years, in response to the Charlie Gard case, some commentators have revived Diekema's argument.

Dominic Wilkinson and Tara Nair[52]

Parents make suboptimal decisions about their children all the time. For example, they make decisions about what to feed their child, what type of car to drive and which school to enrol their child in. They might choose to install the latest safety equipment to protect their child from accidents around the home or they may not. They may enrol the child in classes to learn a sport, or musical instrument or second language, or not. In all of these domains, and in many more, parents make decisions that are not in the best interests of their children. Yet, we do not think that the state should be in the business of interfering with these everyday decisions. Rather, in those other areas of life parents are given a degree of freedom. We accept that it is important to allow parents to make decisions, good and bad, for themselves and their children. Only if their decision-making risks serious harm to the child will the state step in to intervene.

The significant harm threshold proposed by Diekema and others is a familiar one to family lawyers; it is the est which governs whether a child should be removed from her parent(s) and taken into the care of the local authority.[53] One of the dangers of importing it into decisions about a child's medical treatment is that, if a court were to decide that the parents' refusal to consent to a particular course of action put the child at risk of significant harm, the necessary implication is that the criteria for removing the child from the parents' care would also be met.[54]

The reality is that courts do not overrule parental decisions about their children's medical treatment which fall within a zone of reasonableness. On the contrary, they start from the

---

[52] 'Harm isn't all you need: parental discretion and medical decisions for a child' (2016) 42 Journal of Medical Ethics 116–18.

[53] Children Act 1989, section 31(2)(a). The risk of significant harm must also be attributable to the care provided by the parent, or to the child being beyond parental control (section 31(2)(b)).

[54] Jo Bridgeman, 'A threshold of significant harm (f)or a viable alternative therapeutic option?' (2018) 44 Journal of Medical Ethics 466–70.

assumption that parents are normally best placed to make medical decisions for their children. In *In the matter of E (A Child) (Medical Treatment)*,[55] for example, Sir James Munby P was faced with a non-urgent medical decision for a child who was yet to be placed for adoption, and he explained why the decision should be postponed until it could be made by E's new adoptive parents:

> Judges do not necessarily know best. Usually a child's long-term carers, whether parents, adoptive parents or long-term foster carers are much better placed than a judge to decide what should happen to their child.

In addition, it could be argued that under the best interests test itself, any harm that the child is likely to suffer is directly relevant. Section 1(3)(e) of the Children Act 1989 directs the court to consider 'any harm which he has suffered or is at risk of suffering'. The courts are also specifically directed to consider not making an order at all. Section 1(5) specifies that:

> Where a court is considering whether or not to make one or more orders under this Act with respect to a child, it shall not make the order or any of the orders unless it considers that doing so would be better for the child than making no order at all.

As Jo Bridgeman explains, this means that court orders should always be a last resort.

Jo Bridgeman[56]

> Doctors are under a 'responsibility to work in partnership with parents' through a process of discussion and negotiation, to agree a treatment plan reflecting their parental and professional judgment of the best interests of the child accommodating parental wishes as far as 'professional judgment and conscience' allows ...
>
> When professionals disagree with parental decisions about what is best for the child, they should first seek to ensure that the parents understand the facts and that they understand the reasons for the parental view. Where there is disagreement, fulfilment of professional duties may require doctors to engage in further discussion, secure second opinions, involve support and advocacy services, or ethical and religious advisors in the attempt to reach agreement on the best interests of the child ...
>
> The principles of the Children Act place the Trust under a duty to support the partnership of care, seek to defuse the situation, and to attempt to resolve the disagreement in the interests of the child whose treatment is at issue. This could be by facilitating further communication between parents and professionals, directing parents to reliable sources of independent advice, or to counselling services, or ensuring they get support from the Patient Advice and Liaison Service (PALS), ethical, or religious advisors. It may secure a second opinion, and explore whether consideration by the Clinical Ethics Committee, mediation, or other alternative dispute resolution may resolve the disagreement. Working together in the interests of the welfare of the child, parents, professionals, and the Trust have an interest in agreeing the way forward seeking to avoid the need to refer the question of the best treatment for a child to the court in potentially divisive, stressful, legal proceedings.

---

[55] [2016] EWHC 2267 (Fam).
[56] 'The Provision of Healthcare to Young and Dependent Children: The Principles, Concepts, and Utility of the Children Act 1989' (2017) 25 Medical Law Review 363–96.

Cressida Auckland and Imogen Goold suggest that there would also be practical difficulties in applying a significant harm test for intervention.

Cressida Auckland and Imogen Goold[57]

The introduction of a 'significant harm' threshold of the kind proposed would have been problematic. While arguably the court's power to intervene ought to be limited ... , the threshold proposed was understandably rejected. The effect would have been to leave it to the court to determine whether the actions of the parents would cause 'significant harm'. This would often be subjective, influenced by the person's culture, religious beliefs, and social matrix and would be difficult to apply in medical cases ... The likely effect of adopting this threshold would therefore be that the inquiry would descend into a discussion of what is meant by 'harm' and how much of it is necessary to be 'significant' in a medical context. While the same considerations apply in the context of a 'best interests' assessment, the latter provides a well-established analytical framework which has developed over decades and allows harm to be considered within a wider context of other considerations.

Re-framing the analysis to include a presumption of parental authority unless rebutted by serious harm would also result in the parent's authority being subjected to direct evaluation by the court, which would be called upon to scrutinise their reasoning before overtly overriding it, if it is not accepted. This would arguably challenge the authority of the parents more directly than under the 'best interests' approach, where although parents' views are given considerable weight, they remain just one of many important factors that must be taken into account when determining a child's interests.

(f) MEDIATION

In the Charlie Gard and Alfie Evans cases, the relationships between the parents and healthcare professionals had broken down, and the adversarial court setting only made things worse.[58] While social media may have aggravated the tensions between these parents and the treating doctors, this is by no means a new phenomenon.[59] Litigation can also be extremely expensive: the NHS spent £470,000 on legal fees in the Charlie Gard and Alfie Evans cases.

Although it did not work in the Charlie Gard case, perhaps because the relationship between the parents and the doctors was already beyond repair, there has been increased interest in whether mediation or greater use of specialist ethics support services might represent a better way to resolve these disputes.[60] As Jo Bridgeman points out, in addition to being stressful for all involved, protracted litigation in the *Gard* and *Evans* cases meant

---

[57] 'Defining the Limits of Parental Authority: Charlie Gard, Best Interests and the Significant Risk of Harm Threshold' (2018) 134 Law Quarterly Review 37–42.

[58] See also *Kings College Hospital NHS Foundation Trust v Thomas* [2018] EWHC 127 (Fam).

[59] See, for example, *Glass v United Kingdom* Application no 61827/00 (2004); *Portsmouth NHS Trust v Wyatt* [2004] EWHC 2247 (Fam); [2005] EWHC 117 (Fam); [2005] EWHC 693 (Fam); [2005] EWCA Civ 1181; [2006] EWHC 319 (Fam); [2006] EWCA Civ 529.

[60] Richard Huxtable, 'Clinic, courtroom or (specialist) committee: in the best interests of the critically ill child?' (2018) 44 Journal of Medical Ethics 471–5.

that these children received treatment that was not in their best interests for long periods of time.

Jo Bridgeman[61]

The process of trying to convince Charlie's parents of the futility of their hope was prolonged by the legal process as their hopes were raised by each appeal but then dashed as the view of the treating clinicians agreed by the judge continued to prevail ...

The protracted legal process was traumatic for Charlie's parents, stressful for Charlie's clinicians and nurses and, Lady Hale said, put the judiciary in the position of being 'complicit in directing a course of action which is contrary to Charlie's best interests'. Decisions were made by the judge about Charlie's life-sustaining treatment, the experimental therapy and his end of life care but the legal process did not resolve the sincerely and strongly held differences of opinion between his parents and clinicians over what was best for him.

In addition, as Dominic Wilkinson and Julian Savulescu point out, treating Charlie at GOSH while litigation continued will have had an opportunity cost for other children.

Dominic Wilkinson and Julian Savulescu[62]

Continued intensive care in this case, in the face of a very low probability of improvement and high costs of treatment, represents an unreasonable and unfair use of limited healthcare resources. However, in an effort to adjudicate the difficult ethical question of the benefits and burdens of treatment for Charlie, treatment was prolonged at public expense for months. In that time, it is virtually certain that some children were denied transfer to the highly specialised intensive care unit at Great Ormond Street Hospital because of lack of capacity. It is virtually certain that in that time some elective (but vital) surgery was delayed. Because of concern for the well-being of other children needing the vital resource of the intensive care unit, it may have been better to allow the parents to take Charlie overseas months ago. Indeed, even if we accept that that would have been contrary to Charlie's best interests, it may have been a lesser harm overall.

The Nuffield Council on Bioethics has advocated the greater use of Clinical Ethics Committees (CECs) and mediation.

Nuffield Council on Bioethics[63]

CECs could be charged to review all decisions made in relation to withdrawal of intensive care, whether such decisions are made by agreement between parents and professionals

---

[61] 'Gard and Yates v GOSH, the guardian and the United Kingdom: reflections on the legal process and the legal principles' (2017) 17 Medical Law International 285–302.

[62] 'Hard lessons: learning from the Charlie Gard case' (2018) 44 Journal of Medical Ethics 438–42.

[63] *Critical Care Decisions in Fetal and Neonatal Medicine: Ethical Issues* (NCOB, 2006).

or not. Such a review would ensure an external and independent evaluation of a baby's inter-ests . . . Rapid advice would sometimes be required and mechanisms would be needed to achieve this. Such provision may well not be possible in all circumstances, for example with regard to decisions about resuscitation; however, one basis for such a mechanism would be for some members of existing CECs, or other facilitators, to be available on call to hospital staff . . .

When disagreements arise about the care of a very ill baby, there is rarely a 'right' answer and therefore the potential benefits of mediation merit examination. In the UK, mediation is increasingly used to assist parties in disputes that might otherwise be adjudicated in the courts. Mediation empowers the parties to a dispute to seek to resolve their disagreement themselves.

In practice, where the parents and the medical team disagree, considerable effort is already put into trying to reach a consensus, before an application is made to the court. Brierley et al's study of all deaths in the Great Ormond Street PICU revealed that informal me-diation, sometimes with religious leaders, was commonly attempted when parents and doctors could not agree. Where the religious belief which prompted the parents' refusal to accept medical advice was fundamentalist in origin—and based upon a belief in mir-acles—Brierley et al suggest that mediation is less likely to work and there should be fast-track access to the courts.

Joe Brierley, Jim Linthicum, and Andy Petros[64]

During the 3-year period 203 children had withdrawal or limitation of invasive care recom-mended by the medical team and in 186 cases families agreed that this was in the child's best interests. However, in the remaining 17 cases agreement could not be achieved with the families. We reviewed the case notes and found a predominant theme of expression of strong religious belief influencing the family's response to the critical illness of their child. Of these 17 initial cases, 6 were resolved by considering the best interest of the child, further time for the families and ongoing multidisciplinary discussions. However, 11 (65%) involved challenging protracted discussions, largely based upon the belief in the sanctity of life as a result of the parents' religious convictions . . .

For some religious groups with more fundamentalist beliefs, expectation of a miracle cure . . . is commonplace. Traditional mechanisms for resolution of end-of-life disagreements based upon local cultural, secular or religious values were not infrequently unsuccessful. Protracted dialogue was often unable to resolve these differences, while the child was subject to pain and discomfort from invasive ventilation, suctioning and multiple injections. We suggest it is time to reconsider current ethical and legal structures and facilitate rapid default access to courts in such situations when the best interests of the child are compromised in expectation of the miraculous.

[64] 'Should religious beliefs be allowed to stonewall a secular approach to withdrawing and withholding treat-ment in children?' (2013) 29 Journal of Medical Ethics 574–7.

4 THE CONJOINED TWINS CASE: *RE A*

(A) *RE A (CHILDREN) (CONJOINED TWINS: SURGICAL SEPARATION)*

When the courts were first asked to authorize the separation of conjoined twins, a new problem arose. In *Re A (Children) (Conjoined Twins: Surgical Separation)* the facts were that the weaker twin (known as Mary) would die if she was separated from the stronger twin (known as Jodie). If the twins were separated, Jodie would have a good chance of leading a normal life. Without an operation to separate the twins, Jodie's heart would be likely to fail within a few months, leading to the deaths of both babies. The parents, who were devout Roman Catholics from the Mediterranean island of Gozo, refused to consent to an operation that would kill one of their daughters. The hospital then applied for a declaration that it could lawfully carry out separation surgery.

At first instance, Johnson J attempted to justify the operation by describing it as an omission, because the operation would withdraw the supply of blood which Mary was receiving from Jodie. This explanation was rejected by the Court of Appeal. Invasive surgery is unquestionably an action, and this meant that the doctors carrying out the operation would be guilty of murdering Mary, unless a defence was available.

Each of the four judges who heard the case started from the utilitarian presumption that saving one life must be preferable to losing two lives. The problem, of course, was that Jodie's life could only be saved by doing something that would kill Mary. So the judgments in *Re A (Children) (Conjoined Twins: Surgical Separation)* can be read as attempts to justify a course of action which, on the face of it, is impermissible in order to achieve 'the lesser of two evils', that is, the death of one child rather than two.

Re A (Children) (Conjoined Twins: Surgical Separation)[65]

Ward LJ

Just as the parents hold firm views worthy of respect, so every instinct of the medical team has been to save life where it can be saved. Despite such a professional judgment it would, nevertheless, have been a perfectly acceptable response for the hospital to bow to the weight of the parental wish however fundamentally the medical team disagreed with it. Other medical teams may well have accepted the parents' decision. Had St Mary's done so, there could not have been the slightest criticism of them for letting nature take its course in accordance with the parents' wishes. Nor should there be any criticism of the hospital for not bowing to the parents' choice.

Family Law

The question is whether this proposed operation is in Mary's best interests. It cannot be. It will bring her life to an end before it has run its natural span. It denies her inherent right to life. There is no countervailing advantage for her at all. It is contrary to her best interests. Looking at her position in isolation and ignoring, therefore, the benefit to Jodie, the court should not sanction the operation on her . . .

---

[65] [2000] EWCA Civ 254.

If the duty of the court is to make a decision which puts Jodie's interests paramount and that decision would be contrary to the paramount interests of Mary, then, for my part, . . . [g]iven the conflict of duty, I can see no other way of dealing with it than by choosing the lesser of the two evils and so finding the least detrimental alternative . . .

Mary may have a right to life, but she has little right to be alive. She is alive because and only because, to put it bluntly, but nonetheless accurately, she sucks the lifeblood of Jodie and she sucks the lifeblood out of Jodie. She will survive only so long as Jodie survives. Jodie will not survive long because constitutionally she will not be able to cope. Mary's parasitic living will be the cause of Jodie's ceasing to live. If Jodie could speak, she would surely protest, 'Stop it, Mary, you're killing me.' Mary would have no answer to that. Into my scales of fairness and justice between the children goes the fact that nobody but the doctors can help Jodie. Mary is beyond help.

Hence I am in no doubt at all that the scales come down heavily in Jodie's favour.

Criminal Law

I have to ask myself whether I am satisfied that the doctors recognise that death or serious harm will be virtually certain (barring some unforeseen intervention) to result from carrying out this operation. If so, the doctors intend to kill or to do that serious harm even though they may not have any desire to achieve that result. It is common ground that they appreciate that death to Mary would result from the severance of the common aorta. Unpalatable though it may be . . . to stigmatise the doctors with 'murderous intent', that is what in law they will have if they perform the operation and Mary dies as a result . . .

The reality here—harsh as it is to state it, and unnatural as it is that it should be happening— is that Mary is killing Jodie. . . Mary uses Jodie's heart and lungs to receive and use Jodie's oxygenated blood. This will cause Jodie's heart to fail and cause Jodie's death as surely as a slow drip of poison. How can it be just that Jodie should be required to tolerate that state of affairs? . . . I can see no difference in essence between . . . resort to legitimate self-defence and the doctors coming to Jodie's defence and removing the threat of fatal harm to her presented by Mary's draining her life-blood. The availability of such a plea of quasi self-defence, modified to meet the quite exceptional circumstances nature has inflicted on the twins, makes intervention by the doctors lawful.

Robert Walker LJ

The surgery would plainly be in Jodie's best interests, and in my judgment it would be in the best interests of Mary also, since for the twins to remain alive and conjoined in the way they are would be to deprive them of the bodily integrity and human dignity which is the right of each of them . . .

The operation would give her, even in death, bodily integrity as a human being. She would die, not because she was intentionally killed, but because her own body cannot sustain her life . . . The proposed operation would not be unlawful. It would involve the positive act of invasive surgery and Mary's death would be foreseen as an inevitable consequence of an operation which is intended, and is necessary, to save Jodie's life. But Mary's death would not be the purpose or intention of the surgery, and she would die because tragically her body, on its own, is not and never has been viable.

In deciding whether the separation operation should take place despite the parents' objections, the court's paramount consideration was the children's best interests. But here there were two children whose best interests could not be reconciled. The operation was clearly in Jodie's best interests, because it was the only way in which she could survive. But—according to Ward and Brooke LJJ—it was equally clearly not in Mary's best interests, because it would kill her. Robert Walker LJ tried to argue that the operation would in fact be in Mary's best interests as well, because it would restore her bodily integrity, and allow her to die with the dignity of a separated body.

What should the court do when faced with two children whose interests are diametrically opposed? Ward and Brooke LJJ agreed that Jodie's interests should take priority because Mary was 'destined for death'. But the problem that it might nevertheless be murder remained. Ward LJ's solution was to say that Mary was effectively killing Jodie, by 'draining her lifeblood', and that the operation could be justified as quasi self-defence. Brooke LJ, on the other hand, invoked the defence of necessity: here, he said, the doctors were entitled to operate because it was the lesser of two evils. Robert Walker LJ appeared to justify the operation through the doctrine of double effect: Mary's death is a foreseen but unintended consequence of saving Jodie's life.

Following the Court of Appeal's judgment, an appeal to the House of Lords was anticipated, and seven Law Lords were convened to hear the appeal. The parents had, however, had enough, and decided to accept the Court of Appeal's decision. The operation went ahead, leading to Mary's death and Jodie's survival. Jodie—whose real name is Gracie—returned to Gozo with her parents the following year where she was able to lead a healthy and active life.

(b) COMMENTARY ON *RE A*

Unsurprisingly *Re A* generated considerable academic controversy. In the next extract, John Harris rejects the Court of Appeal's reasoning and instead argues that the operation could be justified because Mary was not yet, and never would be, a 'person', and death would therefore not deprive her of a life that she would be capable of valuing.

John Harris[66]

If we say that Mary is going to 'die anyway' we may not be concentrating on the *duration* of the life expectancy but on some other feature of that life expectancy. I believe that there is something about Mary's life expectancy that makes plausible the decision in *Re A* . . . It is that the life expectancy of Mary between the time when the operation would take place and her inevitable death, would not have been expectancy of what might be called 'biographical life', not the life of a person. Indeed neither Mary nor Jodie had started living biographical lives, neither were persons properly so called at the time of the operation. On this analysis, the life Mary would lose by the performance of the operation which would kill her, would not have been life from which she could benefit significantly, not life that could ethically be distinguished from her life *in utero*.

It is interesting to contemplate whether the Court of Appeal would have made the same decision in a scenario with identical facts aside from the children's ages. Let us imagine that Jodie

---

[66] 'Human Beings, Persons and Conjoined Twins: An Ethical Analysis of the Judgment in *Re A*' (2001) 9 Medical Law Review 221–36.

and Mary were in fact 10-year-old conjoined twins, with separate personalities, who had lived quite happily together, but whose health had suddenly deteriorated because their one heart could no longer support two bodies. In those circumstances, is it possible that the court might have given more weight to the parents' refusal to sign the consent form for an operation that would kill one of their daughters?

If, instead, the conjoined twins whose heart had started to fail had been adults who expressed a clear wish not to be separated, it is unimaginable that the defence of necessity would have been invoked to sanction the killing of one twin in order to save the other.

Even in the case of newborn babies, Raanan Gillon argues that the parents' view that it would be wrong to kill one daughter in order to save the other was not eccentric and should have been accorded greater respect.

Raanan Gillon[67]

The parents were neither incompetent nor negligent—the standard justifications for depriving parents of such authority—and their reasoning was not eccentric or *merely* religious, but was widely acceptable moral reasoning—as was the contrary moral reasoning justifying an operation. The court should thus have declined to deprive the parents of their normal responsibilities and rights in order to impose its own preferred resolution of the moral dilemma, and should have allowed the parents to refuse medical intervention—while still ruling as it did, that such separation would not have been unlawful had the parents consented.

The Court of Appeal's preference for separation—articulated most strongly in Robert Walker LJ's suggestion that an intact, albeit dead, body might be in Mary's best interests—is questioned from a different perspective in the next extract. Drawing upon evidence that suggests that conjoined twins who live long enough to express an opinion do not necessarily want to be separated, Bratton and Chetwynd question the Court of Appeal's assumption that separation is always in conjoined twins' best interests.

MQ Bratton and SB Chetwynd[68]

The ethical and legal thinking that treats conjoined twins as if they were physically separate entities who have unfortunately become entangled and need to have their separate existence restored, seems to have things the wrong way round. Conjoined twins are not separate and never have been. If we separate them, we should at the very least recognise that we are creating two new separate entities from two who were one, and that in doing so we are removing from each of them part of themselves. It may, of course, be a decision that we need to make for the benefit of both twins, but we should be wary of assuming that a physically separate existence is automatically in their best interests. If we are more comfortable faced by singletons, if they conform better to the hidden assumptions of our ethical, legal,

---

[67] 'Imposed separation of conjoined twins—moral hubris by the English courts?' (2001) 27 Journal of Medical Ethics 3–4.

[68] 'One into two will not go: conceptualising conjoined twins' (2004) 30 Journal of Medical Ethics 279–85.

and medical notions of what is normal and acceptable, that does not mean these are good enough reasons to change conjoined twins to fit.

Finally, Barbara Hewson draws attention to Ward LJ's observation that it would have been equally legitimate for the doctors to comply with the parents' wishes and let both children die. This comment may have been prompted by media interviews with paediatric surgeons from Great Ormond Street Hospital in London, who said that if the twins had been born there, the parents' wishes would have been respected.

Barbara Hewson[69]

Thus the whole case turned on a contingency: the fact that the twins happened to be in Manchester, rather than London. On any view, this is arbitrary, and cannot but undermine the application of a doctrine of necessity. By definition, necessity cannot properly apply to a course of action which is entirely optional and which only comes into play if one happens to live in town A rather than in town B.

Another striking aspect of Ward LJ's judgment is his use of pejorative language, both about Mary and her parents. Initially, he cites a consultant's evidence that 'Mary does very little and her twin does all the work'. Subliminally, this description creates an impression of unworthiness . . . Ward LJ seizes on these medical metaphors: 'She lives on borrowed time, all of which is borrowed from Jodie. It is a debt she can never repay.' This makes Mary seem positively culpable, in terms of conventional legal morality. By the end, in a logical leap, he portrays Mary as a killer: 'she sucks the lifeblood out of Jodie'. . . Mary emerges from this forensic denunciation as akin to Dracula: not only monstrous, but also evil. Buoyed up by his disturbing metaphors, Ward LJ readily concludes that Mary 'has little right to be alive' . . .

Anatomically, Ward LJ's description was inaccurate: Mary was not sucking anything from Jodie. Rather the reverse: Jodie's heart was responsible for circulating blood around both of them. This was not Mary's fault.

5 CHILDREN'S RIGHT TO MAKE THEIR OWN MEDICAL DECISIONS

(a) A RIGHT TO PARTICIPATE

Even if parents have the legal right, subject to oversight by the courts, to consent to the medical treatment of children who are not yet *Gillick*-competent (see later), such children should still be consulted about their treatment. Depending upon the treatment in question, the views of a minor who lacks capacity might nevertheless carry very considerable weight. For example, in *Re X (A Child) (Capacity to Consent to Termination)*, X was 13 years old and lacked capacity in relation to the decision to terminate her pregnancy. Sir James Munby P was nevertheless clear that such an operation should go ahead only if she was 'accepting'.

---

[69] 'Killing Off Mary: Was the Court of Appeal Right?' (2001) 9 Medical Law Review 281–98.

Re X (A Child) (Capacity to Consent to Termination)[70]

Sir James Munby P

Only the most compelling arguments could possibly justify compelling a mother [sic] who wished to carry her child to term to submit to an unwanted termination. It would be unwise to be too prescriptive, for every case must be judged on its own unique facts, but I find it hard to conceive of any case where such a drastic form of order—such an immensely invasive procedure—could be appropriate in the case of a mother who does not want a termination, unless there was powerful evidence that allowing the pregnancy to continue would put the mother's life or long-term health at very grave risk. Conversely, it would be a very strong thing indeed, if the mother wants a termination, to require her to continue with an unwanted pregnancy ...

A child or incapacitated adult may, in strict law, lack autonomy. But the court must surely attach very considerable weight indeed to the albeit qualified autonomy of a mother who in relation to a matter as personal, intimate and sensitive as pregnancy is expressing clear wishes and feelings, whichever way, as to whether or not she wants a termination ...

'Consent', of course, is not the appropriate word, for by definition a child of X's age who, like X, lacks Gillick capacity, cannot in law give a valid consent. But something of the nature of consent or agreement, using those words in the colloquial sense, is required. The Consultant's word 'accepting' in my judgment captures the nuance very well ... Given that X's expressed wishes at the end of the hearing thus accorded with my assessment of her best interests, it was clearly appropriate for me to supply the necessary consent to enable the termination to proceed.

(b) GILLICK COMPETENCE

Until the case of *Gillick v West Norfolk and Wisbech AHA* in 1986, it was not clear whether doctors could lawfully treat a minor without her parent's consent. Victoria Gillick had challenged a Memorandum of Guidance, from the Department of Health and Social Security (DHSS), as it then was, which stated that in exceptional cases, a doctor could decide whether contraceptive advice or treatment should be provided to under-16s without parental consent. Mrs Gillick, who was the mother of five girls, wrote to her local health authority seeking an assurance from them that no contraceptive advice or treatment would be given to any of her children while they were under the age of 16, without her knowledge and consent. The health authority refused, and Mrs Gillick sought a declaration that the Memorandum was unlawful. In the Court of Appeal, she succeeded, but by a 3:2 majority, the House of Lords allowed the DHSS's appeal.

Gillick v West Norfolk and Wisbech AHA[71]

Lord Fraser

Nobody doubts, certainly I do not doubt, that in the overwhelming majority of cases the best judges of a child's welfare are his or her parents. Nor do I doubt that any important medical treatment of a child under 16 would normally only be carried out with the parents' approval.

---

[70] [2014] EWHC 1871 (Fam).   [71] [1984] QB 581.

That is why it would and should be 'most unusual' for a doctor to advise a child without the knowledge and consent of the parents on contraceptive matters . . .

There may well be other cases where the doctor feels that because the girl is under the influence of her sexual partner or for some other reason there is no realistic prospect of her abstaining from intercourse. If that is right it points strongly to the desirability of the doctor being entitled in some cases, in the girl's best interest, to give her contraceptive advice and treatment if necessary without the consent or even the knowledge of her parents. The only practicable course is to entrust the doctor with a discretion to act in accordance with his view of what is best in the interests of the girl who is his patient . . .

But there may well be cases, and I think there will be some cases, where the girl refuses either to tell the parents herself or to permit the doctor to do so and in such cases, the doctor will, in my opinion, be justified in proceeding without the parents' consent or even knowledge provided he is satisfied on the following matters: (1) that the girl (although under 16 years of age) will understand his advice; (2) that he cannot persuade her to inform her parents or to allow him to inform the parents that she is seeking contraceptive advice; (3) that she is very likely to begin or to continue having sexual intercourse with or without contraceptive treatment; (4) that unless she receives contraceptive advice or treatment her physical or mental health or both are likely to suffer; (5) that her best interests require him to give her contraceptive advice, treatment or both without the parental consent.

Lord Scarman

I would hold that as a matter of law the parental right to determine whether or not their minor child below the age of 16 will have medical treatment terminates if and when the child achieves a sufficient understanding and intelligence to enable him or her to understand fully what is proposed. It will be a question of fact whether a child seeking advice has sufficient understanding of what is involved to give a consent valid in law.

Lord Fraser recognized that, in certain circumstances, doctors might judge that giving advice about contraception without the parents' consent might be in a child's best interests. His judgment does not give children the right to treatment without parental consent, but instead gives doctors discretion to act in their patient's best interests. This is not especially radical.

In contrast, Lord Scarman's judgment is potentially more far-reaching. He suggests that when the child achieves sufficient maturity and understanding, her parents' right to consent to her medical treatment terminates, and is replaced by the minor's right to make her own decisions. Lord Scarman did not go so far as to say that the *Gillick*-competent child had the right to take decisions against her own best interests, however. Instead he suggested, more modestly, that the *Gillick*-competent child would be able 'to exercise a *wise* choice in his or her own interests' (my emphasis).

Twenty years later, in *R (on the application of Axon) v Secretary of State for Health*, in deciding that a *Gillick*-competent child under the age of 16 could give a valid consent to abortion, Silber J held that the parental right to make decisions terminated once the child acquired *Gillick* competence. Like Lord Fraser, however, he framed this in terms of doctors being able to treat under-16s without parental knowledge or consent when they considered this to be appropriate. Silber J rejected Mrs Axon's application for judicial review of Department of Health guidance which had made it clear that people under the age of 16 could expect confidentiality when seeking advice about contraception and abortion.

R (on the application of Axon) v Secretary of State for Health[72]

Silber J

[T]he reasoning of the majority [in *Gillick*] was that the parental right to determine whether a young person will have medical treatment terminates if and when the young person achieves a sufficient understanding and intelligence to understand fully what is proposed, with the result that the doctor was entitled in cases in which it was appropriate to do so, to provide advice and treatment to a young person on sexual matters without parental knowledge.

Silber J was 'fortified' in coming to this conclusion by the fact that young women would be deterred from seeking advice and treatment on sexual matters without the assurance of confidentiality, and that this would have 'very undesirable and far-reaching consequences'.

More recently, in *An NHS Trust v A*, a case involving a girl who was pregnant and only just over the age of 13, Mostyn J did appear to spell out the potentially radical implications of a finding of *Gillick* competence. If A was *Gillick*-competent, and Mostyn J found that she was, then that was 'the end of the matter', and the decision to have or not have an abortion was for her alone.

An NHS Trust v A[73]

Mostyn J

[I]f I am to determine that A does have sufficient understanding and intelligence to know what a termination would involve, then that is the end of the matter . . .

It is implicit in that decision [*Gillick*] that provided the child, under the age of 16, has sufficient understanding and intelligence, she can then be lawfully prescribed with contraception even if the result of that would lead her to take steps which are wholly contrary to her best interests. So, the question of best interests does not really inform the primary decision I have to make which is whether she has the necessary capacity . . .

I am completely satisfied that A has sufficient understanding and intelligence within Lord Fraser's definition and I accordingly make a declaration to that effect. It will now be for A to decide what she wishes to do.

In the next extract, Kirsty Moreton suggests that it may have been easier for Mostyn J to take an apparently radical stance on childhood autonomy, given that A's wishes, in fact, coincided with the professionals' view as to what would be in her best interests. She also suggests that it is revealing that A was thought to need help with coping with her decision, although she was apparently able to make that decision entirely autonomously.

---

[72] [2006] EWHC 37 (Admin).   [73] [2014] EWHC 1445 (Fam).

Kirsty L Moreton[74]

> [A] more cynical interpretation is that *ABC* is really a best interests decision, dressed up in autonomy language . . .
>
> [T]here is an irony within *ABC* summed up in Mostyn J's statement that if A continued with the pregnancy, then 'her family and, indeed, Social Services will need to give her considerable support and assistance' while in the event of a termination 'her family will need to be at her side and to assist her and support her'. It is inconsistent that the law rejects collaboration in the decision-making process only to call upon it to deal with the consequences of that decision . . .
>
> Furthermore, reaching the outcome that it did may have been simpler for the court as the case involved the question of consent rather than refusal.
>
> But it has to be queried whether the fact that A's wishes appeared to have concurred with the opinions of the doctors and the Court that a termination was in her best interests, may have fostered a situation of 'dependent compliance', and thereby facilitated a finding of competence.

(c) LIFE-THREATENING DECISIONS

In the cases that followed *Gillick*, the courts' respect for mature minors' autonomy has not extended to giving them exactly the same right as adults with capacity to make foolish or irrational decisions, especially when those choices might be life-threatening. This has happened in two ways.

First, it has proved relatively easy to establish that children who are gravely ill are not *Gillick*-competent. In part, this is because capacity has to be judged in the context of the particular decision: the more complicated the decision, the greater the capacity needed to make it. So a child might be able to consent to having her broken leg put in a plaster cast, but might not be capable of refusing life-saving surgery.

In *Re S (A Minor) (Consent to Medical Treatment)*,[75] Johnson J found that a 15-year-old girl suffering from thalassaemia who no longer wanted to undergo monthly blood transfusions, was not competent to make this decision:

> It does not seem to me that her capacity is commensurate with the gravity of the decision which she has made. It seems to me that an understanding that she will die is not enough. For her decision to carry weight she should have a greater understanding of the manner of the death and pain and the distress.

Indeed, it sometimes seems that the test for capacity when the child wishes to make a life-or-death decision, especially if it is religiously inspired, is set so high that no child could ever be judged *Gillick*-competent.

In *Re E (A Minor) (Wardship: Medical Treatment)*, a 15-year-old boy, A, who was suffering from leukaemia, wished to refuse a blood transfusion because of his Jehovah's Witness beliefs. Ward J found that to be *Gillick*-competent it was not enough that A, who was 'obviously

---

[74] '*Gillick* Reinstated: Judging Mid-Childhood Competence in Healthcare Law' (2015) 23 Medical Law Review 303–14.
[75] [1994] 2 FLR 1065.

intelligent', knew that he would die, but also that he would have to understand the manner of his death and the extent of his and his family's suffering.

Re E (A Minor) (Wardship: Medical Treatment)[76]

Ward J

I find that A is a boy of sufficient intelligence to be able to take decisions about his own well-being, but I also find that there is a range of decisions of which some are outside his ability fully to grasp their implications. Impressed though I was by his obvious intelligence, by his calm discussion of the implications, by his assertion even that he would refuse well knowing that he may die as a result, in my judgment A does not have a full understanding of the whole implication of what the refusal of that treatment involves . . .

I am quite satisfied that A does not have any sufficient comprehension of the pain he has yet to suffer, of the fear that he will be undergoing, of the distress not only occasioned by that fear but also—and importantly—the distress he will inevitably suffer as he, a loving son, helplessly watches his parents' and his family's distress. They are a close family, and they are a brave family, but I find that he has no realisation of the full implications which lie before him as to the process of dying. He may have some concept of the fact that he will die, but as to the manner of his death and to the extent of his and his family's suffering I find he has not the ability to turn his mind to it nor the will to do so . . .

One has to admire—indeed one is almost baffled by—the courage of the conviction that he expresses. He is, he says, prepared to die for his faith. That makes him a martyr by itself. But I regret that I find it essential for his well-being to protect him from himself and his parents, and so I override his and his parents' decision.

Of course, most adults do not fully understand what it is like to die, and it could therefore be argued that children like A are being held to an excessively demanding test for capacity. The durability of A's beliefs was confirmed when he continued to refuse blood after his 18th birthday, and died as a result. This was not because he had suddenly acquired an understanding of what it would be like to die, rather he had simply achieved the status of adulthood.

In *Re L (Medical Treatment: Gillick Competency)*,[77] Sir Stephen Brown P found that a 14-year-old girl who wanted to refuse a life-saving blood transfusion on religious grounds was not *Gillick*-competent. In part this was because she lacked vital information about the likely nature of her death because it had been deliberately withheld from her. This seems, with respect, to be a misreading of the *Gillick* test for competence, which is supposed to judge whether the child is capable of understanding information, not whether she has been given sufficient information to enable her to make an informed choice. Since the patient's doctors will largely control her access to information, as Andrew Grubb points out, it would be regrettable if an absence of information automatically led to a finding of incompetence:

The fact that L was ignorant of the detail that the court required her to understand was hardly her fault. Of itself, this did not render her incompetent; rather, it left her uninformed. It cannot be right that a doctor may manipulate a patient's capacity to make a decision by failing to provide relevant information.[78]

[76] [1993] 1 FLR 386.   [77] [1998] 2 FLR 810.
[78] 'Commentary on *Re L (Medical Treatment: Gillick-Competency)*' (1999) 7 Medical Law Review 58–61.

In all these cases, the standard of competence demanded of children who wanted to refuse treatment was extremely high, and perhaps even unattainable. It is also interesting to consider whether these cases would have been brought before the courts, and findings of incapacity made, if these children had instead *consented* to blood transfusions.

Cases in which minors have sought to refuse a relatively straightforward life-saving procedure, such as a blood transfusion, for religious reasons, can perhaps be distinguished from cases in which a terminally ill child wishes to refuse extremely burdensome treatment. A decade ago, Herefordshire Primary Care Trust sought a court declaration that a heart transplant could be performed on a 13-year-old girl against her wishes, but they dropped the case after a child protection officer found that she was adamant that she did not want the operation.[79] She changed her mind the following year, and a heart transplant was performed.

No cases involving a child's refusal of chemotherapy have reached the courts, but this does not mean that it never happens. On the contrary, it can be assumed that there have been cases in which doctors have respected teenagers' refusals of burdensome treatment, like chemotherapy, where a dying child might reasonably conclude that they have had enough. Certainly, as we saw earlier, the Royal College of Paediatrics and Child Health are clear that there may be times when it is appropriate to respect a *Gillick*-competent child's refusal of life-sustaining treatment, usually 'in situations where the young person's life is limited in quantity or quality or both'.

A slightly different issue arose in *An NHS Trust v SK*.[80] SK was an 11-year-old boy who was dying of cancer. His mother refused to believe that he was dying, and therefore refused to consent to a palliative treatment programme. SK was not *Gillick*-competent, and Macdonald J decided, straightforwardly, that it would be in SK's best interests to receive palliative chemotherapy in order to relieve his pain. Nevertheless, Macdonald J was also clear that it would not be in SK's best interests to compel him to receive treatment against his wishes:

An NHS Trust v SK[81]

Macdonald J

Overall, whilst I am satisfied that palliative chemotherapy should be declared to be in SK's best interests such that he can be administered the same notwithstanding his parent's lack of consent if he agrees to this, I am further satisfied that the Children's Guardian is entirely correct when he advises the court that seeking to *compel* SK to accept treatment during the final weeks of his life in a manner that will place him in opposition to his mother, from whom he will draw valuable emotional support during that period, and in circumstances where the prospect of success of such treatment are by no means certain, cannot be said to be in his best interests.

As we saw in the previous chapter, the Mental Capacity Act Code of Practice is clear that capacity can fluctuate, and that someone could have the capacity to make a decision one day, and lack it on another. In contrast, in *Re R (A Minor) (Wardship: Consent to Treatment)*, a case we consider later, Lord Donaldson appeared to hold that *Gillick*-competence cannot fluctuate, but instead is a 'developmental stage'.

---

[79] BBC News, 'Girl wins right to refuse heart', 11 November 2008. [80] [2016] EWHC 2680 (Fam).
[81] [2016] EWHC 2680 (Fam).

Re R (A Minor) (Wardship: Consent to Treatment)[82]

Lord Donaldson MR

[E]ven if [R] was capable on a good day of a sufficient degree of understanding to meet the Gillick criteria, her mental disability, to the cure or amelioration of which the proposed treatment was directed, was such that on other days she was not only 'Gillick incompetent', but actually sectionable. No child in that situation can be regarded as 'Gillick competent' . . . 'Gillick competence' is a developmental concept and will not be lost or acquired on a day to day or week to week basis.

More recently, in *Re JA (A Minor) (Medical Treatment: Child Diagnosed with HIV)*, a 14-year-old boy, J, was found to be *Gillick*-competent in relation to some decisions, but not others. J had been diagnosed as HIV positive. His parents were both HIV positive, but they disputed their diagnoses and rejected conventional antiretroviral treatment (ART). J did not want to take ART, and the question for the court was whether he was *Gillick*-competent in relation to that decision.

Re JA (A Minor) (Medical Treatment: Child Diagnosed with HIV)[83]

Baker J

It is plain that J is an intelligent, thoughtful and articulate teenager. He has received a very considerable amount of information about HIV and AIDS from a variety of sources . . .

On the other hand, in what I regard as the key exchange with the court during his informal oral evidence, J stated that he did not think the diagnosis of HIV given to him was true because he did not have the proof. He did not feel a piece of paper was enough. If he does not accept the diagnosis, it must follow, in my judgment, that he does not fully understand the implication of not receiving the treatment. He therefore lacks the understanding necessary to weigh up the information and arrive at a decision. Applying the test laid down by the House of Lords, this points to a conclusion that he is not *Gillick* competent.

To an extent, however, there is an element of unreality about this analysis. It could be argued, that if J were to give his consent, his parents having indicated that they would not oppose the treatment, the Trust would in reality provide the treatment without delay. In those circumstances, it could be argued that J falls into the category of patients identified in *Re W* [discussed in the next section], namely someone capable of giving consent but whose refusal to give consent is capable of being overridden by the court . . .

I conclude that, as J does not accept his diagnosis, he does lack the understanding of the consequences of not taking ART medication and therefore the understanding needed to weigh up the pros and cons before making a decision as to whether to take the medication. On balance, at this precise point in time, he is therefore not *Gillick* competent to make a decision as to whether or not to take ART.

As set out above, the test for *Gillick* competence is decision-specific. A person who is not *Gillick* competent in respect of some treatments may be *Gillick* competent in respect of others. The decision to take ART is a complex decision which turns in part on J's acceptance of the

---

[82] [1992] Fam 11 (CA).   [83] [2014] EWHC 1135 (Fam).

diagnosis. The decision to undergo monitoring, blood tests and chest x-rays is less complex, and in any event in this case J has agreed to these measures. Equally, the decision to accept psychotherapy and peer support is less complex . . . In all the circumstances, I conclude that he is *Gillick* competent in respect of decisions whether to undergo monitoring, and receive psychotherapy and peer support.

Baker J also mentions the second and more controversial way in which the courts have ignored teenagers' decisions, namely by drawing a distinction between consent to treatment and refusal. *Gillick*, on this view, endows mature minors with the right to consent, but does not give them a corresponding right to refuse. Baker J admits that there is an 'element of unreality' in an analysis that decides that J lacks *Gillick* competence to refuse ART, when, if he had agreed to treatment, it is likely that his consent would have been regarded as effective.

It was Lord Donaldson MR in *Re R* (and *Re W*, discussed in the following section), who first proposed this distinction between consent and refusal. In *Re R (A Minor) (Wardship: Consent to Treatment)*, R, who was 15, had been admitted to an adolescent psychiatric unit. In a lucid interval, R indicated that she would refuse compulsory administration of anti-psychotic medication. The local authority began wardship proceedings, requesting court approval for the administration of the proposed medication without R's consent.

Re R (A Minor) (Wardship: Consent to Treatment)[84]

Lord Donaldson MR

In a case in which the '*Gillick* competent' child refuses treatment, but the parents consent, that consent enables treatment to be undertaken lawfully, but in no way determines that the child shall be so treated. In a case in which the positions are reversed, it is the child's consent which is the enabling factor and again the parents' refusal of consent is not determinative. If Lord Scarman intended to go further than this and to say that in the case of a '*Gillick* competent' child, a parent has no right either to consent or to refuse consent, his remarks were obiter, because the only question in issue was Mrs. Gillick's alleged right of veto. Furthermore I consider that they would have been wrong

The . . . refusal of the '*Gillick* competent' child is a very important factor in the doctor's decision whether or not to treat, but does not prevent the necessary consent being obtained from another competent source.

Because of the similarities between the decision in *Re R* and that in *Re W* (where the Family Law Reform Act 1969 applied), we examine the implications of Lord Donaldson's distinction between consent and refusal after mention has been made of the statute which applies to children aged 16 and 17.

---

[84] [1992] Fam 11 (CA).

(d) THE FAMILY LAW REFORM ACT 1969

The Mental Capacity Act 2005 (MCA) applies to anyone over the age of 16. If a 16- or 17-year-old lacks capacity under the MCA, she could be treated in her best interests. More usually, teenagers of 16 and 17 are likely to be *Gillick* competent but, in addition, section 8 of the Family Law Reform Act 1969 provides that their consent to medical treatment shall be as effective as it would be if they were an adult.

Family Law Reform Act 1969 section 8

8(1) The consent of a minor who has attained the age of sixteen years to any surgical, medical or dental treatment which, in the absence of consent, would constitute a trespass to his person, shall be as effective as it would be if he were of full age; and where a minor has by virtue of this section given an effective consent to any treatment it shall not be necessary to obtain any consent for it from his parent or guardian ...

(6) In this section 'surgical, medical or dental treatment' includes any procedure undertaken for the purposes of diagnosis, and this section applies to any procedure (including, in particular, the administration of an anaesthetic) which is ancillary to any treatment as it applies to that treatment.

(7) Nothing in this section shall be construed as making ineffective any consent which would have been effective if this section had not been enacted.

It is worth noting that section 8 only applies to diagnosis and treatment. Bone marrow or organ donation, and non-therapeutic research, are not covered, and the validity of a 16- or 17-year-old's consent to such procedures would be governed by the common law: that is, by whether the child is *Gillick* competent.

It is also important to remember that section 8 only creates a presumption in favour of capacity, which can be rebutted in the same way as the presumption of capacity in adulthood, namely by evidence that the child is not, in fact, able to understand, retain, and weigh information in order to make a choice, and if this is the case, the MCA applies.

The most controversial question raised by section 8 is whether it applies only to consent, or whether it also gives 16- and 17-year-olds the right to refuse medical treatment. On the one hand, it might be argued that the right to refuse must complement the right to consent, otherwise this becomes the rather thin 'right' to agree with the doctor. A right to agree, unless accompanied by a parallel right to disagree, could hardly be said to protect patient autonomy.

On the other hand, the section itself refers only to the minor's 'consent' being effective, and states that it displaces the 'need' to obtain parental consent. Not only is it silent as to refusal, but also section 8(3) specifically states that although the 16- or 17-year-old has become capable of giving an effective consent, this does not render ineffective any consent (such as that of the parents), which existed before. It might then be argued that this section's principal purpose was simply to protect doctors, by enabling them to act lawfully when a 16- or 17-year-old gives consent, rather than to remove the parental right to consent.

Certainly this was the preferred interpretation of the Court of Appeal in *Re W (A Minor) (Medical Treatment: Court's Jurisdiction)*. W, a 16-year-old girl suffering from anorexia, wanted to refuse treatment for her anorexia, and claimed, unsuccessfully, that section 8 conferred on her the same right as an adult to refuse medical treatment.

Re W (A Minor) (Medical Treatment: Court's Jurisdiction)[85]

Lord Donaldson MR

On reflection I regret my use in *In Re R (A Minor) (Wardship: Consent to Treatment)* of the keyholder analogy because keys can lock as well as unlock. I now prefer the analogy of the legal 'flak jacket' which protects the doctor from claims by the litigious whether he acquires it from his patient who may be a minor over the age of 16, or a '*Gillick* competent' child under that age or from another person having parental responsibilities which include a right to consent to treatment of the minor. Anyone who gives him a flak jacket (that is, consent) may take it back, but the doctor only needs one and so long as he continues to have one he has the legal right to proceed . . .

There is ample authority for the proposition that the inherent powers of the court under its parens patriae jurisdiction are theoretically limitless and that they certainly extend beyond the powers of a natural parent. There can therefore be no doubt that it has power to override the refusal of a minor, whether over the age of 16 or under that age but '*Gillick* competent'. It does not do so by ordering the doctors to treat which, even if within the court's powers, would be an abuse of them or by ordering the minor to accept treatment, but by authorising the doctors to treat the minor in accordance with their clinical judgment, subject to any restrictions which the court may impose.

(e) A CHILD'S RIGHT TO REFUSE TREATMENT

The reasoning adopted by Lord Donaldson in both *Re R* and *Re W* can be simply stated. Doctors must have an effective consent before they can lawfully provide medical treatment. *Gillick* competence and the Family Law Reform Act 1969 endow older children with the right to give a valid consent to medical treatment, and hence allow doctors to proceed without seeking an additional consent from a parent. But the parental right to consent is not thereby extinguished; rather, it coexists both with the child's right to consent, and with the court's even broader right to authorize medical treatment.

Because a doctor needs only one effective consent, once a child is *Gillick* competent (or 16 or 17 years old), there are three possible sources of this consent: the parents, the courts, and the mature minor. Consent from any one of these three sources will protect the doctor from prosecution or liability in tort. That means that the parents' or the court's consent will be effective, even if the mature minor refuses to give her consent. The mature minor therefore has no right to have her refusal respected. As Thorpe J explained in *Re K, W and H (Minors) (Medical Treatment)*:[86]

The decision of the Court of Appeal in *Re R* made it plain that a child with *Gillick* competence can consent to treatment, but that if he or she declines to do so, consent can be given by someone else who has parental rights or responsibilities.

---

[85] [1993] Fam 64 (CA).   [86] [1993] 1 FLR 854.

In *Re W*, Lord Donaldson MR did not qualify the courts' right to overrule the mature minor, but both Balcombe and Nolan LJJ attempted to confine the courts' and parents' power to overrule the mature minor's refusal to cases in which the treatment is necessary to prevent death or severe permanent injury.

This was also the approach adopted in the more recent case of *Re P (A Child)*, in which Baker J declared that, despite his finding that she did not lack capacity under the Mental Capacity Act, it would be lawful to give antidote treatment to a 17-year-old who had taken an overdose of paracetamol and was refusing to agree to be treated with an antidote.

Re P (A Child)[87]

Baker J

In exercising its inherent jurisdiction, the court must have the child's welfare as its paramount consideration. The wishes and feelings of the child, in particular those of a 17-year-old young person who is almost an adult, are an important component of the analysis of her welfare. They are not, however, decisive. In addition, the court must consider other factors and in particular in this situation any harm she has suffered or is at risk of suffering. In this case, the risk of harm is clearly at a high level. If she does not receive treatment to counteract the effects of the overdose of paracetamol, she will undoubtedly suffer serious damage to her liver and in probability will die ...

In this case, balancing the competing factors, I have no hesitation in concluding that the balance comes down firmly in favour of overriding P's wishes. I recognise that this is not to be taken lightly. The wishes of a young person aged seventeen and a half are important. They are, of course, entitled to be taken into account as part of her Article 8 rights under ECHR. On the other hand, those rights are not absolute. Here, they are outweighed by her rights under Article 2—everyone's right to life shall be protected by law. The court is under a positive or operational duty arising from Article 2 to take preventative measures to protect an individual whose life is at risk ...

In those circumstances, this court is under a heavy duty to take what steps it can to protect P's life which is manifestly in danger tonight. Accordingly, I have made an order including a declaration that it is lawful and in P's best interests for the medical practitioners having responsibility for her care and treatment to treat her for the effects of her overdose notwithstanding the fact that she is refusing treatment.

Until a child reaches the age of 18, her wishes are therefore important, but can be trumped by the need to do whatever is necessary to save her life. As Ward J has put it in *Re E (A Minor) (Wardship: Medical Treatment)*,[88] the court 'should be very slow to allow an infant to martyr himself'.

Certainly for religiously inspired refusals of blood products, the right to make life-ending decisions appears to be governed by a *status-based* test for competence. Caroline Bridge and Andrew Grubb argue that it would be better if the courts were explicit about this.

---

[87] [2014] EWHC 1650 (Fam).   [88] [1993] 1 FLR 386.

Caroline Bridge[89]

[J]udges should not go through the pretence of applying a functional test of capacity when the outcome of the young person's decision is not one that they, or probably society, would countenance. The law should openly declare that welfare reigns when grave decisions with momentous outcomes are considered and recognise that adolescent autonomy is, inevitably, circumscribed.

Andrew Grubb[90]

Clearly, the court is striving to act on its 'hunch' that society should not let children make a decision to die. In truth, it comes down to no more than the court (as society's instrument) acknowledging that at some point citizens must be allowed to make their own decisions, even ones which others might perceive as harmful to them. That point is the age of majority, which for us is 18 . . . Once that point is reached, the state does not have a compelling interest to prevent rational citizens from reaching (most) decisions. Until that point, however, the protective duty of society permits intervention. If this is the public policy of this country, it would be far better for the courts . . . simply to say so rather than to obfuscate matters by distorting the legal concept of competence.

As we have seen, *Re E (A Minor) (Wardship: Medical Treatment)*[91] is a clear illustration of the application of a status test for capacity, because A lacked capacity the day before his 18th birthday, but he gained it the next day, at which point he became entitled to, and subsequently did, refuse a blood transfusion.

Most academic commentators have been critical of Lord Donaldson's distinction between consent and refusal. John Eekelaar, for example, has argued that Lord Donaldson is concerned only with consent's narrow legal function as a defence to a charge of assault. In contrast, if consent is viewed as a way of respecting autonomy, children should have the right to say 'no' as well as 'yes' to treatment.

John Eekelaar[92]

Lord Donaldson said that there were two reasons for requiring that a patient consents to medical treatment. The 'clinical' reason was that it made treatment easier. The 'legal' reason was 'to provide those concerned in the treatment with a defence to a criminal charge of assault or battery or a civil claim for damages for trespass to the person'. This is an astonishingly narrow view of the requirement, which . . . is surely rooted in the fundamental civil rights of all citizens that their personal integrity should not be infringed without their consent or lawful justification. Lord Donaldson is not unaware of this, for in a later case involving an adult, he

---

[89] 'Religious Beliefs and Teenage Refusal of Medical Treatment' (1999) 62 Modern Law Review 585–94, 594.
[90] 'Commentary on *Re L (Medical Treatment: Gillick Competency)*' (1999) 7 Medical Law Review 58–61.
[91] [1993] 1 FLR 386.
[92] 'White Coats or Flak Jackets? Children and the Courts Again' (1993) 109 Law Quarterly Review 182–7.

relates it to the right 'to choose whether to consent to medical treatment, to refuse it or to choose one rather than another of the treatments being offered . . . '.

Lord Donaldson seems to be reluctant to accept that the law should protect minors, even if competent, in the same manner. Rather, his primary concern is to fashion the law so as to minimise the risk of legal action against doctors.

In the next extract, John Harris argues that if a child understands enough to give consent to a particular treatment, then she also understands enough to refuse it.

John Harris[93]

The idea that a child (or anyone) might competently consent to a treatment but not be competent to refuse it is a palpable nonsense, the reasons for which are revealed by a moment's reflection on what a competent consent involves. To give an informed consent you need to understand the nature of the course of action to which you are consenting, which, in medical contexts, will include its probable and possible consequences and side effects and the nature of any alternative measures which might be taken and the consequences of doing nothing.

So, to understand a proposed treatment well enough to consent to it is to understand the consequences of a refusal. And if the consequences of a refusal are understood well enough to consent to the alternative then the refusal must also be competent.

Similarly, Sarah Elliston suggests that Lord Donaldson's 'gloss' means that children's medical decisions will be respected only if 'they know what is good for them'.

Sarah Elliston[94]

The situation we are faced with now is that the most that a competent child can expect is that their consent to medical intervention will be determinative. Therefore it may be seriously doubted whether any real question of autonomous decision making by them arises. Their consent is a mere acceptance or endorsement of a procedure that may be authorised to be carried out anyway . . .

At present, the law in England permits those under 18 to have their medical decisions respected if, but only if, they know what is good for them and accept the treatment that is proposed. Such a situation is both illogical and unjust and may have wider implications for the way in which children are viewed in our society, in that it suggests that children are in some way less entitled to full respect as members of our society by virtue of their status.

It could even be argued that a right to refuse unwanted medical treatment might be *more* important than the right to consent to it. Jane Fortin draws attention to the practical consequences of ordering a fully grown adolescent to have treatment that he does not want:

---

[93] 'Consent and end of life decisions' (2003) 29 Journal of Medical Ethics 10–15.
[94] 'If You Know What's Good for You: Refusal of Consent to Medical Treatment by Children' in Sheila McLean (ed), *Contemporary Issues in Law, Medicine and Ethics* (Ashgate: Dartmouth, 1996) 29–55.

the case-law is surprisingly reticent over the practical details. Indeed, the courts have barely mentioned that the implication of authorizing treatment against the wishes of a fully grown adolescent is that he may have to be held down physically to undergo it.[95]

Indeed, the logical consequence of Lord Donaldson's consent/refusal distinction would be that, even if a pregnant 16-year-old girl is *Gillick*-competent, both her parents and the courts would retain the right to consent to a termination of pregnancy, which could be performed lawfully despite her competent refusal. Of course, this would not happen in practice, as Balcombe LJ explained in *Re W (A Minor) (Medical Treatment: Court's Jurisdiction)*.

Re W (A Minor) (Medical Treatment: Court's Jurisdiction)[96]

Balcombe LJ

In the course of the arguments before us it was suggested that a construction of section 8 of the Act of 1969 which denies a 16- or 17-year-old girl an absolute right to refuse medical treatment, but leaves it open to her parents to consent to such treatment, could in theory lead to a case where a pregnant 16-year-old refuses an abortion, but her parents' consent to her pregnancy being terminated. So it could in theory, but I cannot conceive of a case where a doctor, faced with the refusal of a mentally competent 16-year-old to having an abortion, would terminate the pregnancy merely upon the consent of the girl's parents... I find it equally difficult to conceive of a case where the court, faced with this problem and applying the approach I have indicated above, would authorise an abortion against the wishes of a mentally competent 16-year-old. The dilemma is therefore more apparent than real.

In the next extract, Charles Foster and José Miola are critical of the courts' willingness to leave a lacuna in the law to be filled by 'medical ethics', suggesting that abortion should instead be treated as a special case.

Charles Foster and José Miola[97]

Lord Donaldson is recognising that the law does not fulfil what he implies is its desired function, but at the same time he expresses such confidence in medical ethics as a regulatory tool that he is happy to delegate the issue to it . . .

Thus his Lordship assumed that 'medical ethics' would effectively police the medical profession's conduct. However, . . . not only do the GMC and BMA guidelines relating to this issue contain no specific prohibition of such a procedure, but doctors are repeatedly encouraged to seek legal advice in order to decide what they should do . . .

The result is that the law delegates responsibility to decision-making to professional medical ethics, while professional medical ethics in turn abrogates responsibility back to the law . . .

---

[95] 'Children's Rights and the Use of Physical Force' (2001) 13 Child and Family Law Quarterly 243.
[96] [1993] Fam 64 (CA).
[97] 'Who's in Charge? The Relationship between Medical Law, Medical Ethics and Medical Morality?' (2015) 23 Medical Law Review 505–30.

There was no need for Lord Donaldson's unhappy formulation in *Re W*. Should the unwilling 17 year old be forced by her parents to have an abortion? No. But that is really because abortion is a rather special type of 'treatment'. It cannot simply be lumped together with appendectomies.

In recent years, Neil Manson and Faye Tucker have mounted an interesting new defence of Lord Donaldson's consent/refusal distinction. Adolescence, they have argued, is a time of 'transitional paternalism', in which a teenager is learning to make decisions for herself, but—in the same way as when we learn to drive in a car with dual controls car—someone else can step in if her decision would jeopardize her wellbeing.

Neil C Manson[98]

Rather than moving in a 'single step' from no power to unshared power, there is a transition period in which she has a shared power. This shared power is akin to the parental normative power in that, for many actions the adolescent has the final word about whether or not her treatment is to be permissible. But in *some* cases, where a refusal poses serious risk of severe harm, other parties have the power to permit the treatment . . .

[A]dolescence is a period where there is a gradual expansion of autonomy, more and more options become open, actions become permissible, new powers are acquired, but the paternalistic protection of minors is only gradually diminished until, at majority, full adult rights and responsibilities are acquired.

Faye Tucker[99]

As children become adolescents, they get closer to being self-governing agents and, therefore, paternalism ought to be *gradually* rolled back . . . Adults can promote children's distinctive interest in becoming self-governing in the long run, in part by providing them with experience of making decisions . . .

Cultivation of a young person's capacity for self-governance provides the best justification of transitional paternalism in general, and explains why normative powers are shared during this transitional period . . .

Consider the dual controls in a driving instructor's car. In this situation, the learner driver is given some autonomy in her inexperienced driving decisions, but there is a second set of controls that can be used by the instructor should the learner need assistance. The sharing of power in *this* case provides a space where the learner is able to experience a limited amount of autonomy in which to learn to drive, without assuming complete responsibility for her decisions. In this way the learner is protected from making bad mistakes, and she is also acquiring the skills she needs to drive unaided in the future.

In the clinical context, adolescents are able to make decisions for themselves insofar as their decisions do as good a job as adults' decisions in protecting and promoting their own interests . . . When refusal of a clinical action puts an adolescent's welfare at risk, others hold the power to consent on her behalf.

[98] 'Transitional Paternalism' (2015) 29 Bioethics 66–73.
[99] 'Developing Autonomy and Transitional Paternalism' (2016) 30 Bioethics 759–66.

6 THE USE OF FORCE

The inherent jurisdiction gives courts the power to authorize the use of reasonable force in order to ensure that the child receives the treatment in question. As with adults, force should be used only when it is a 'therapeutic necessity', otherwise it might breach the child's Article 3 right not to be subject to inhuman and degrading treatment.

The use of force might also be challenged under Article 5 (the right to liberty and security). The detention of persons of 'unsound mind' can be justified under Article 5(1)(e), but Jane Fortin suggests that some of the adolescents whose refusals of life-saving treatment have been overridden in the cases described above were certainly not of 'unsound mind'. Fortin therefore argues that the use of force could only be justified if Article 2 (the right to life) is allowed to trump Article 5.

Jane Fortin[100]

How then is the court to gain its authority to force such a patient to undergo medical treatment without itself infringing Article 5? In such circumstances, it might survive an Article 5 challenge by turning to Article 2 for a solution, when confronted by a teenager refusing life-saving treatment. It might argue that since a minor's rights under the Convention sometimes inevitably conflict, notably his rights under Articles 2 and 5, it must find an appropriate balance between those rights. Although a minor patient is entitled to freedom from restraint under Article 5, this right may be outweighed by the patient's right to life itself, particularly if he lacks the capacity to comprehend the implications of refusing life-saving treatment. Furthermore, Article 2 imposes a positive obligation on all public authorities, including the courts, to take all reasonable steps to preserve life. A court, when exercising its inherent jurisdiction, might therefore argue that it cannot ignore its duty to save the life of a desperately ill adolescent.

7 CONCLUSION

There is nothing conceptually difficult about the law which governs the medical treatment of young children. Parents make almost all decisions on behalf of their children, and in the rare cases in which the courts become involved, as McFarlane LJ put it in the Charlie Gard case, 'the sole principle is that the best interests of the child must prevail'. But while the law might be simple and clear, that does not mean that these cases are easy. On the contrary, disputes between doctors and parents over the medical treatment of their children could not be more heart-wrenching. Although it is normal for cases involving children to take place in private, and for the child's identity to be disguised, parents sometimes choose to waive this anonymity in order to publicize their plight. Once this sort of dispute becomes the subject of debate on social media, it can be picked up and discussed by people around the world, including the President of the United States and the Pope, unfettered by their lack of knowledge or understanding of the facts of the case.

---

[100] 'Children's Rights and the Use of Physical Force' (2001) 13 Child and Family Law Quarterly 243.

Although the Charlie Gard and Alfie Evans cases did not raise any new legal issues, the social media storms that surrounded them were new, and in some respects profoundly disturbing. Parents' desire to do anything to keep their child alive is, of course, understandable, but the abuse that was directed towards healthcare professionals, the judiciary and the NHS from people who knew virtually nothing about the cases was, as Bernadette Richards explains, troubling.

Bernadette Richards[101]

The names of these children become a call to arms and instead of permitting a dignified consideration of what is in their best interests, their names and faces are splashed across the internet and news feeds along with assertions of parental rights, lying doctors, and uncaring healthcare systems. The question to be asked then is how can this possibly be in anyone's best interests? It cannot be helping the terminally ill child and neither can it truly be helping the parents through this most difficult time. We also lose sight of the reality of the human faces behind the much maligned health and legal system that are trying to focus on the needs of the child and come to a decision that serves the interests of that child ...

High profile cases have always been subject to the court of public opinion but, thanks to the technological developments of recent years, it now has increasing reach and increasing power ...

Medical disputes present complex legal and ethical questions that cannot be solved by shouting (in person or online) and raising 'armies' and it is crucial that political leaders, both inside of the relevant jurisdiction and outside of it, exercise restraint and respect the judicial process. Questions and disputes such as these need to be resolved quietly and with dignity protecting the child, the parents, and the healthcare providers. As Hayden J pointed out, to deny this is disrespectful to the judicial process, the parties to the dispute and, most importantly, the sick child whose interests must, at all times, remain paramount.

FURTHER READING

Bridgeman, Jo, 'The Provision of Healthcare to Young and Dependent Children: The Principles, Concepts, and Utility of the Children Act 1989' (2017) 25 Medical Law Review 363–96.

Huxtable, Richard, 'Clinic, courtroom or (specialist) committee: in the best interests of the critically ill child?' (2018) 44 Journal of Medical Ethics 471–5.

Manson, Neil C, 'Transitional Paternalism' (2015) 29 Bioethics 66–73.

Moreton, Kirsty L, 'Gillick Reinstated: Judging Mid-Childhood Competence in Healthcare Law' (2015) 23 Medical Law Review 303–14.

Richards, Bernadette, 'Social Media: The Unnamed Plaintiff' (2018) 15 Journal of Bioethical Inquiry 309–12.

Tucker, Faye, 'Developing Autonomy and Transitional Paternalism' (2016) 30 Bioethics 759–66.

Wilkinson, Dominic and Nair, Tara, 'Harm isn't all you need: parental discretion and medical decisions for a child' (2016) 42 Journal of Medical Ethics 116–18.

---

[101] 'Social Media: The Unnamed Plaintiff' (2018) 15 Journal of Bioethical Inquiry 309–12.

7

MENTAL HEALTH LAW

CENTRAL ISSUES

1. In a significant exception to the principle of patient autonomy, it can be lawful to detain and treat a mentally disordered patient, even if she has capacity and is refusing treatment. To be lawful, compulsory treatment must be treatment for her mental disorder, and must not amount to 'inhuman and degrading treatment'.

2. Most mentally ill patients are not, however, subject to compulsory powers. Among hospital inpatients, a minority has been 'sectioned'. Most are admitted informally.

3. The 'Deprivation of Liberty Safeguards' were supposed to offer safeguards to patients who have not been subject to compulsory powers, but who are not, in practice, free to leave. They were overly complicated, and overinclusive, and are due to be replaced.

4. Detaining people on the grounds of their mental illness, or interfering with their bodily integrity, both of which are permissible under the Mental Health Act, would appear to be contrary to the UN Convention on the Rights of Persons with Disabilities.

5. In 2017, the government announced an independent review of Mental Health Law, which issued its final report at the end of 2018. The review panel was charged with understanding the rising rates of detention, and the over-representation of people from black and minority ethnic groups. Its final report made a series of recommendations for reform, including giving patients more choice and control over their treatment.

1 INTRODUCTION

In this chapter we attempt a broad overview of mental health law in the UK. We begin with a short history of mental health policy. Next we consider the various stages involved in the treatment of mental illness, starting with a definition of mental disorder and a description of how patients are admitted to the mental health system.

We looked at the law which covers adults who lack mental capacity in Chapter 5, and at the outset it is important to remember that mentally ill people are not necessarily incapable of making medical decisions. If they have capacity, mentally ill patients have the same right to refuse medical treatment as other capacitous adults, but the Mental Health Act 1983 creates important exceptions to this. Finally, we explore discharge from the mental health system, and we look at how ex-patients can be kept on a 'long leash', through the use of community treatment orders.

The fundamental legal difference between mental health law and other areas of medical law is that it authorizes the detention and compulsory treatment of people suffering from mental illness. Detention and treatment without consent are radically out of line with the principle of patient autonomy which now dominates medical law. What justification could there be for treating people with mental health problems differently?

(a) It might enable a patient to access medical treatment. If a mentally ill patient is incapable of giving consent to treatment, the only way for her to receive treatment is for her to be treated without consent. This obviously only applies to mentally ill patients who *also* lack capacity. For mentally ill patients with capacity, further justification is required.

(b) It could be argued that detention and treatment without consent are sometimes necessary to protect the patient from herself. Someone who is depressed and suicidal, for example, might subsequently be glad that she was prevented from taking her own life.

(c) Finally, it has been argued that detention and compulsory treatment may be necessary to protect the public from dangerous mentally ill patients.

The idea that the public needs protection from people with mental health problems was the driver behind the 2007 reforms to the Mental Health Act 1983. It is problematic, however, because it was invoked in order to justify what is essentially *preventative detention*: that is, detaining someone not because they have been found guilty of a criminal offence, but because there is perceived to be a *risk* that they *might* cause harm to others. Not only does this create an exception to some basic principles of criminal justice, but it also rests upon the mistaken assumption that a diagnosis of mental illness is an accurate predictor of future violent behaviour. We do not detain men who regularly binge drink on the grounds that there is a chance that they might, in the future, get involved in a pub brawl or hit their partner. Rather, detention is possible only after they have broken the law.

There is considerable media interest whenever mentally ill people commit serious offences. If a person who has previously had contact with mental health services commits a crime, it is often suggested that there must have been a failure on the part of those services. Even if it is not possible to predict in advance that someone is going to break the law, there seems to be an assumption that mental health services should be able to prevent mentally ill people from harming others.

Nancy Wolff [1]

If the public remains committed to the perfectability expectation, each violent act committed by a person with a mental illness will be interpreted as potentially avoidable, which could motivate the public to rightfully (a) demand that the government allocate more money to reduce future events through more secure care and supervision of high-risk individuals or (b) support legal reforms that constrain the civil liberties of persons with mental illness.

[1] 'Risk, response and mental health policy: learning from the experience of the United Kingdom' (2002) 27 Journal of Health Politics, Policy and Law 801–32.

Although fear of mentally ill people has by no means disappeared, it is noteworthy that the tone of more recent debates about reforms to mental health law is markedly different, emphasizing instead patient rights and the importance of 'parity of esteem' between mental and physical illness.

At the outset, it should be noted that the very existence of mental illness is doubted by what is referred to as the 'anti-psychiatry' movement. These critics, including Thomas Szasz and Erving Goffman, have argued that psychiatry is not concerned with treating the sick, but instead with controlling strange or inconvenient behaviour. And, of course, as Szasz explains in the next extract, if there is no such thing as mental illness, a special set of laws governing the treatment of the mentally ill would also be unnecessary.

Thomas Szasz[2]

If 'mental illness' is a bona fide illness—as official medical, psychiatric, and mental health organizations, such as the World Health Organization, the American and British Medical Associations, and the American Psychiatric Association, maintain—then it follows, logically and linguistically, that it must be treated like any other illness. Hence, mental hygiene laws must be repealed. There are no special laws for patients with a peptic ulcer or pneumonia; why, then, should there be special laws for patients with depression or schizophrenia?

If, on the other hand, 'mental illness' is, as I contend, a myth, then, also, it follows that mental hygiene laws should be repealed ... When I assert that mental illness is a myth, I am not saying that personal unhappiness and socially deviant behaviour do not exist; but I am saying that we categorize them as diseases at our peril.

The expression 'mental illness' is a metaphor which we have come to mistake for a fact. We call people physically ill when their body-functioning violates certain anatomical and physiological norms; similarly, we call people mentally ill when their personal conduct violates certain ethical, political, and social norms ...

We should guard against ... the discomfort that the mental patient's behaviour may cause us. Labeling conduct as sick merely because it differs from our own may be nothing more than discrimination disguised as medical judgment.

2 A SHORT HISTORY OF MENTAL HEALTH LAW AND POLICY

There is a long history of subjecting people who have been classified as 'mad' to special treatment. Compulsory detention has been possible for hundreds of years, although it used to be the preserve of poor law officers and Justices of the Peace, rather than doctors. While private asylums existed, most 'lunatics' were paupers, and kept in poorhouses. Conditions were appalling. Beatings, whippings, and rape were common, and prolonged restraint was the norm. A Select Committee established in 1877 proposed a number of reforms, such as the provision of a system of asylums at public expense; a requirement that two medical certificates accompany an application to detain an individual; and a system of independent inspection

---

[2] *Law, Liberty and Psychiatry: An Inquiry into the Social Uses of Mental Health Practices* (Routledge & Kegan Paul: London, 1974).

of asylums. From the Lunacy Act 1890 onwards, a series of statutes brought such a system into being.

The Mental Treatment Act 1930 was intended to reduce the stigma associated with mental illness. Prompted by sympathy for the plight of 'shell-shocked' soldiers returning from the First World War, there was a shift towards 'medicalism'; that is, the idea that the mentally ill are patients who need treatment, rather than disruptive individuals who need to be removed from society.

The Percy Commission was set up to consider further reform in the 1950s, and its report culminated in the passage of the Mental Health Act 1959. This emphasized voluntary rather than compulsory admission to hospital, and short-term rather than permanent detention. Although based upon the 1959 Act, the Mental Health Act 1983 attempted to offer more legal safeguards, in order to protect the rights of mentally ill patients. A 2007 amending statute made a number of significant changes, but the 1983 Act's basic structure remains intact.

At the time of writing, the Independent Review of the Mental Health Act 1983 has made a series of recommendations for further reform.[3] The government committed immediately to implementing two of them—namely allowing people to make 'advance choice documents' and to nominate a person to be involved in decisions about their care—in a new Mental Health Bill—and it is due to respond in full to the Review's recommendations after this book has gone to press.

Many commentators have analysed mental health law as if it were a pendulum swinging between legalism (with an emphasis upon legal protection) and medicalism (where the medical profession determines how patients should be treated). In addition, as Jennifer Brown explains, new legalism emphasizes positive rights to services, as well as due process safeguards.

Jennifer Brown[4]

For medicalism, the purpose of mental health law is to provide for the care and treatment of persons with psycho-social disabilities. Mental health laws that are consistent with medicalism can be said to be based on paternalistic considerations, or the 'best interests' of the person. As such, open textured law that is enabling and permits maximum medical discretion within a loose framework of rules is preferable . . .

Mental health laws that are consistent with legalism prescribe due process safeguards, including the restriction of the statutory definition of mental disorder, strict statutory criteria for detention, recognition of the right to refuse treatment and a judicial review of the decision to detain. These safeguards along with statutory minimum standards should guide and restrict the discretion of those involved in the detention and treatment of persons with psycho-social disabilities . . .

The purpose of mental health laws that are consistent with new legalism, is to provide due process safeguards in addition to adequate care and treatment in the least restrictive setting and therefore persons with psycho-social disabilities are seen as those who have the right to a certain level of care, treatment and independent living.

---

[3] The Independent Review of the Mental Health Act 1983, *Modernising the Mental Health Act, Increasing choice, reducing compulsion* (DHSC, 2018).

[4] 'The changing purpose of mental health law: From medialism to legalism to new legalism' (2016) 47 International Journal of Law and Psychiatry 1–9.

Nicola Glover-Thomas points out that legal constraints not only protect patients' rights, but also help to legitimate psychiatric practice.

Nicola Glover-Thomas[5]

Clearly, the law acts as a mechanism of control because it establishes a framework in which care decisions are made and incorporates legal safeguards surrounding detention, treatment and other coercive aspects of the legislation. The formation of these safeguards protects both the patient and those working within the psychiatric field. They legitimate psychiatric practices because they ensure the decisions are made in a procedurally sound way ... The existence of a formal legal framework allows the public to accept decisions which overtly remove rights from individuals. The need for psychiatrists to seek second medical opinions and to obtain opinions from other professionals allows psychiatric practice to be seen as accountable and legitimate.

Before we look at the law in detail, it is worth highlighting three trends in mental health policy.

(a) DECARCERATION

The twentieth century saw two dramatic shifts in attitudes towards institutionalizing people with mental illnesses. In 1850, there were 7,140 inpatients; by 1954 there were 148,000. Asylums were believed to offer humane and decent surroundings for some of the most marginal members of society. They also undoubtedly facilitated greater social control and surveillance of the insane.[6]

Then, in the second half of the twentieth century, the asylums were closed down. Patients who receive inpatient care—at any one time, this will be around 21,000 patients[7]—now do so on psychiatric wards in general hospitals or, increasingly, in privately run care homes.

Several reasons are commonly given for this move towards decarceration. First, community care was (misguidedly) assumed to be cheaper than keeping a patient in an institution. Secondly, the discovery of widespread abuse within institutions meant that asylums were no longer seen as places of safety. Thirdly, the development of drugs, such as anti-psychotics, contributed to a medical model of mental disorders: that is, that they are illnesses that can be effectively managed, if not cured. Finally, the discovery that mental illness is in fact much more common than had been previously realized contributed to the view that a diagnosis of mental disorder did not necessarily justify locking someone up.

A growing emphasis on community care is evident in mental health policy from the 1960s onwards, but while the number of hospital beds declined, other services were not put in place to replace inpatient care. It had been assumed that mentally ill people would be cared for at home, and readily reintegrated into the community. This assumption proved to be hopelessly over-optimistic. It has not been easy for people with mental illnesses to find jobs and accommodation, and their families are not always able or willing to look after them.

---

[5] *Reconstructing Mental Health Law and Policy* (Butterworths: London, 2002).

[6] See further, Michel Foucault, *The Birth of the Clinic: An Archaeology of Clinical Perception* (Penguin: London, 1973).

[7] *Mental Health Act Statistics: Annual Figures England 2017-18* (NHS Digital, 2018).

High-quality community care is expensive, perhaps even more so than treatment provided in a hospital setting, where patients can be guaranteed to stay put. The principal failing of community care is not that decarceration is a bad idea. No one would want to return to the days when people with mental disorders were kept in vast asylums, effectively 'out of sight and out of mind'. Rather, the mistake has been to underestimate the cost of providing high-quality care and other services—such as housing and help with finding employment—which people with mental disorders may need in order to live functioning lives in the community.

Jill Stavert suggests that we have tended to think about mental health patients' rights as the right to be free from unwarranted detention. In the community, socio-economic rights to services and resources may be of much greater importance.

Jill Stavert[8]

Over the last two decades we have come some way in Europe towards recognising that those suffering from mental illness require enforceable rights so that they are not subjected to abuse and neglect. These rights are, however, mainly civil rights which are applicable to the patient–institution relationship. If care takes place outside institutions, a far greater emphasis on socio-economic rights is required. This will enable those with mental illness to access and receive those services and that support which is necessary for them to function as effectively as possible within the communities in which they live.

(b) DETENTION FOR DANGEROUSNESS

In the debates leading up to the 2007 amending statute, the then Labour government focused on a small number of patients suffering from what it described as dangerous and severe personality disorders (DSPD). The government was concerned that the 1983 legislation placed obstacles in the way of the detention of DSPD patients, in part because it is not clear that personality disorders are treatable. In the next extract, Eric Matthews argues that this is because personality disorders are not really illnesses.

Eric Matthews[9]

[T]here are some conditions classified as mental disorders ... in which the harm caused by the disorder is not, or at least not primarily, to the disordered person, but to others. The various sorts of sexual deviation called 'paraphilias', such as paedophilia, represent good examples. These disorders seem to have no parallel among physical illnesses: someone who is physically ill suffers him- or herself, and any harm caused to others (e.g. through infection) is contingent. But a paedophile does not himself suffer from his paedophilia (except indirectly, in that he suffers social disapproval): those who suffer are the children he abuses ...

---

[8] 'Mental health, community care and human rights in Europe: still an incomplete picture?' (2007) Journal of Mental Health Law 182.

[9] 'Mental and Physical Illness—An Unsustainable Separation?' in Nigel Eastman and Jill Peay (eds), *Law Without Enforcement: Integrating Mental Health and Justice* (Hart Publishing: Oxford, 1999) 47–58.

Paedophiles are often said to be 'untreatable': but that is rather misleading. They do not *require* treatment in the medical sense, since their condition is not an illness, not something which causes them suffering contrary to their own wishes. It is their personality itself, and the wishes which emanate from it, which are said to be disordered. The treatment which they require is that which would prevent this disordered personality causing harm to others ...

This suggests that what is legally required to deal with such cases is, again, not a 'Mental Health Act', which among other things has the unfortunate effect of reinforcing popular prejudices about the allegedly violent and dangerous character of all mentally ill people ... Rather we need to address the difficult issues involved in the containment of people who behave in anti-social ways.

Matthews' view is not shared by the World Health Organization's *International Statistical Classification of Diseases and Related Health Problems*, eleventh revision (known as ICD-11), which contains definitions of 'disruptive behaviour and dissocial disorders'.[10] The Diagnostic and Statistical Manual (known as DSM-V), published by the American Psychiatric Association, sets out diagnostic criteria for all recognized mental disorders, including a wide range of personality disorders, such as antisocial personality disorder and narcissistic personality disorder. While their inclusion in the DSM might appear to be evidence that personality disorders are mental illnesses, these diagnostic manuals are themselves controversial: for example, homosexuality was only deleted from the DSM's list of mental disorders in 1974.[11]

Regardless of whether personality disorders are mental illnesses or not, the then government's emphasis upon detaining dangerous people was heavily criticized. Psychiatrists, for example, feared that they would be forced to detain people where there is no clinical reason for keeping them in hospital, thus undermining their role as doctors, whose first priority is the care of their patients.

There are two further practical problems with the assumption that mental health law can reduce the risk posed by dangerous individuals. First, it presupposes that it is, in fact, possible accurately to predict which patients pose a risk to others, whereas the evidence points in the opposite direction: in practice, it is extremely difficult accurately to predict dangerousness.[12]

Secondly, this 'public safety' approach to mental disorder presupposes that there is, in fact, a correlation between mental illness and dangerousness. Again, the evidence does not bear this out. It is also perhaps interesting that other factors that are implicated in the homicide statistics, such as alcohol use, do not tend to lead to the same levels of public anxiety and desire for surveillance and control. In commenting on an earlier draft Bill, the Royal College of Psychiatrists pointed out that not only was the emphasis on risk misguided, but that, by deterring potentially violent individuals from seeking help, this approach might actually increase the danger they pose to the public.

---

[10] WHO, International Classification of Diseases 11th Revision ICD-11.

[11] See further Roy Porter, 'Is Mental Illness Inevitably Stigmatizing?' in A Crisp (ed), *Every Family in the Land: Understanding Prejudice and Discrimination against People with Mental Illness* (Royal Society of Medicine Press: London, 2004) 3–13.

[12] John Monahan et al, *Rethinking Risk Assessment: The MacArthur Study of Mental Disorder and Violence* (OUP: Oxford, 2001).

Royal College of Psychiatrists[13]

Every death is a tragedy, for the victim, perpetrator, their family and friends and any profes-sionals involved. The percentage of homicides committed each year by the mentally ill, as a percentage of the total is falling. The following figures are not intended to minimize the im-portance of each death but may help to put the matter into perspective.

For each citizen killed by a mentally ill person:

- 10 are killed by corporate manslaughter
- 20 by people who are not mentally ill
- 25 by passive smoking
- 125 by NHS hospital acquired infection.

The proposed legislation is extremely unlikely to have any impact on suicide or homicide rates. With reference to suicide, recent research demonstrated that even within the high-risk group of in-patients there would need to be 100 patients detained unnecessarily in order to prevent one suicide. With regard to homicide, [Crawford] has shown that with a predictive test with a sensi-tivity and specificity of 0.8 (far better than anything available currently) 5000 people would need to be detained to prevent one homicide. Szmukler has shown that if the predictive test became even better (0.9) this would still require the detention of 2000 people to prevent each homicide. This emphasises that prevention of homicide and suicide can only ever arise as a secondary benefit from improved mental health care for a population and never via prediction per se of such events.

The starting point in risk reduction is encouraging patients to seek help and talk about their thoughts and feelings ... It is hard to believe that potential patients will not be deterred from the services if they know that psychiatrists will have a duty to enforce treatment on them, not only in hospital but also in the community, even when they are perfectly able to make deci-sions for themselves. Patient avoidance will certainly limit effective intervention.

In the next extract, Angela Sweeney et al describe how the emphasis on risk can itself have a negative effect on service users' mental wellbeing.

Angela Sweeney et al[14]

In the context of the community, public fear of service users has consistently been described as a key cause of discrimination, and evidence suggests that it is a barrier to seeking support from mental health services. Our participants sometimes feared community rejection: many had lost friends, and described loneliness as their biggest problem. Similarly, an international literature review concluded, 'rejection and avoidance of people with mental illness appear to be a universal phenomena'. This can be so severe that it causes mental distress, and in our study occasionally resulted in people needing additional support from services ...

Mental health policy has responded to perceptions of dangerousness by facing in two dir-ections at once. There is a focus on risk management and public order, leading to policies of control and compulsion such as the Mental Health Act 2007. Yet policy is also shaped by the human rights agenda and social inclusion, leading to a focus on choice and anti-discrimination. This has meant that service users are encouraged to enact choices whilst fearing compulsion

[13] *Evidence Submitted to the Joint Committee on the Draft Mental Health Bill* (RCP: London, 2004) 31–4.
[14] 'The role of fear in mental health service users' experiences: a qualitative exploration' (2015) 50 Social Psychiatry and Psychiatric Epidemiology 1079–87.

if they do not make the choices that are sanctioned by powerful mental health professionals. Those who choose not to engage with mental health services can be labelled resistant.

(c) NON-DISCRIMINATION

It is noteworthy that the tone of more recent government discussion of mental illness has been less focused on risk-avoidance, and more concerned with reducing stigma. The Independent Review of the Mental Health Act, set up in 2017, was charged with reviewing mental health legislation in order to make recommendations 'in relation to rising detention rates, racial disparities in detention, and concerns that the Act is out of step with a modern mental health system'. This is in line with the UN Convention on the Rights of Persons with Disabilities, the purpose of which is 'to promote, protect and ensure the full and equal enjoyment of all human rights and fundamental freedoms by all persons with disabilities, and to promote respect for their inherent dignity'.[15]

In 2013, NHS England launched a 'parity of esteem' campaign, in order to ensure that mental illness is diagnosed and treated on a par with physical illness.[16] The Mental Health Taskforce's Five Year Forward View for Mental Health advocated increased funding on the grounds that it is 'a point of basic parity between physical and mental health that types of care and therapies shown to lead to improved mental health outcomes and found to be cost-effective should be made available to people with mental health problems'.[17]

While an emphasis on parity of esteem and a commitment to increased funding is to be welcomed, funding for mental health services has not yet kept pace with these good intentions. As we see later, more patients are detained each year, while the number of inpatient beds has decreased. A 2015 briefing from the King's Fund set out the problem.

The King's Fund[18]

While increased political support and a stronger policy focus is welcome, parity of esteem for mental health remains a long way off.

Funding for mental health services has been cut in recent years. Our analysis shows that around 40 per cent of mental health trusts experienced reductions in income in 2013/14 and 2014/15. There is widespread evidence of poor-quality care. Only 14 per cent of patients say that they received appropriate care in a crisis, and there has been an increase in the number of patients who report a poor experience of community mental health care.

Bed occupancy in inpatient facilities is frequently well above recommended levels, with community services, in particular crisis resolution and home treatment teams, often unable to provide sufficient levels of support to compensate for reductions in beds. This is having a negative impact on safety and quality of care …

A Royal College of Psychiatry report described wards as overcrowded and understaffed, with 15 per cent of wards lacking segregated sleeping accommodation and fewer than 60 per

---

[15] Article 1.
[16] See further, Martin McShane and Geraldine Strathdee, *Valuing mental and physical health together equally* (NHS England, 2013).
[17] Mental Health Taskforce to the NHS in England, *The Five Year Forward View for Mental Health* (DH, 2016).
[18] *Mental Health Under Pressure* (King's Fund, 2015).

> cent having separate lounges for men and women. Patients and carers report that many acute wards are not always safe, therapeutic or conducive to recovery and in some cases could have a negative effect on an inpatient's wellbeing and mental health.

Stephen Allison et al are concerned that the priority should be on increasing the number of available beds, rather than on changing the law.

Stephen Allison, Tarun Bastiampillai and Doris A Fuller[19]

> Successive UK governments have been responsible for the rapid decline in the number of available psychiatric beds, which ... has decreased from 93 public hospital-based psychiatric beds per 100 000 population in 1998 to 46 beds per 100 000 population in 2014—a figure that is considerably lower than that of the 2015 OECD average (71 beds per 100 000 population). The UK has substantially fewer beds than the leading countries of the European Union, such as France (87 beds per 100 000 population) and Germany (127 beds per 100 000 population) ...
>
> In England, psychiatric bed closures between 1988 and 2008 were associated with additional detentions, and this inverse relationship appears to be continuing.
>
> During the 2017 general election campaign, a Conservative party publication about mental health highlighted the fact that 'vulnerable people are being subjected to detention, including in police cells, unnecessarily'. In contrast to the Care Quality Commission, the Conservative Party did not attribute the unnecessary detentions to decreased bed numbers and reduced community services. Instead, [it] blamed 'discrimination and the overuse of detention' by mental health professionals. The Conservative Party proposed replacing the Mental Health Act; however, we are concerned that Mental Health Act reforms will make it more difficult to detain patients. This approach could be dangerous for people with severe mental illness, if it lowers the numbers who receive treatment ...
>
> Funding more psychiatric beds would reduce the detention rates by allowing timely voluntary admission to a local acute psychiatric bed at an earlier stage of illness.

The Care Quality Commission's report on the increased use of detention found that the delivery of mental health services is becoming more complex.

Care Quality Commission[20]

> Staff in some areas believed that rising inequality, particularly in areas of relative deprivation, is a factor in the rise in detentions. They flagged issues with loneliness, poor housing options or homelessness, unemployment, poor physical health and family breakdown. The people we spoke with reported that the delivery of mental health care is becoming more complex overall, especially in responding to the needs of people who are homeless, rough sleepers, asylum seekers, immigrants, or those experiencing modern slavery. As well as it being more likely that people from these population groups will need mental health care, because of their

---

[19] 'Should the Government change the Mental Health Act or fund more psychiatric beds?' (2017) 4 The Lancet Psychiatry 585–6.
[20] *Mental Health Act: The rise in the use of the MHA to detain people in England* (CQC, 2018).

transient state it is likely they may be unknown to local services and often difficult for health and social services to provide them with support before, during or after admission to prevent readmission through individualised management and personal care plans. This may increase the likelihood of them relapsing and being re-detained.

Finally, as Peter Bartlett explains, the problems faced by people with mental health problems cannot be solved by mental health services alone.

Peter Bartlett[21]

It is impossible to look at the current system regarding mental disability without profound dismay. It is not at all clear that we have successfully integrated people with mental disabilities into our communities. A brief glance at the employment statistics serves as a stark reminder of how far we have to come: in the country as a whole, 72.5% of working-age adults are employed; for people with any disability, this drops to 47.5%; for people with a mental illness, this plummets to 13.5%; for people receiving secondary mental health services, the figure drops to 3.4%. This is notwithstanding that between 86% and 90% of people with mental disorders who are unemployed in fact want to work. The domestic law remains mired in a world of detention and compulsory treatment on terms that have little theoretical basis to support them and which reinforce stigma. While the status quo cannot be viewed as an option, therefore, it is difficult to see how we progress.

3   WHAT IS MENTAL ILLNESS?

Mental health problems are common: one in every four adults will experiences at least one diagnosable mental health problem each year.[22] Some mental disorders are relatively easy to live with; others can be fatal. Mental illness is often more difficult to diagnose than physical illness. Unlike the X-rays, blood tests, and scans which are used to diagnose broken bones, HIV, and cancer, it can be much harder to establish precisely what is wrong with a person's mental health. But while diagnosis might be difficult, it is also particularly important, given that mental health law can sanction involuntary detention and compulsory treatment. Some people believe that brain-imaging techniques will lead to more accurate and objective diagnoses, but at present, psychiatrists continue to diagnose mental disorders by listening to the patient's description of her symptoms and observing her behaviour.

In order to define mental illness it might first be necessary to have some idea of what we consider to be normal mental functioning. But, for obvious reasons, this is incredibly difficult to pin down. Feeling sad from time to time is normal, and is certainly not evidence of mental illness. On the other hand, major depression is an extremely debilitating condition which is as capable of interfering with a person's ability to lead a normal life as serious physical illness.

---

[21] 'Identity, law, policy and *Communicating Mental Health*' (2017) 43 Medical Humanities 130–3;
[22] *Mental Health Taskforce to the NHS in England, The Five Year Forward View for Mental Health* (DH, 2016).

(a) DEFINING MENTAL DISORDER

Under the 1983 Act, as amended, the statutory definition of mental disorder is contained in section 1(2).

Mental Health Act 1983 section 1

1(2) In this Act—

'mental disorder' means any disorder or disability of the mind;

(2A) But a person with learning disability shall not be considered by reason of that disability to be—

(a) suffering from mental disorder . . .

(b) requiring treatment in hospital for mental disorder . . .

unless that disability is associated with abnormally aggressive or seriously irresponsible conduct on his part.

(3) Dependence on alcohol or drugs is not considered to be a disorder or disability of the mind for the purposes of subsection (2) above.

(4) In subsection (2A) above, 'learning disability' means a state of arrested or incomplete development of the mind which includes significant impairment of intelligence and social functioning.

Before it was amended in 2007, the Act specifically stated that no one should be treated as mentally disordered by reason only of 'promiscuity or other immoral conduct' or 'sexual deviancy'. This was in order to rule out the previously common practice of confining to asylums people who did not conform to accepted moral standards. At the start of the twentieth century, becoming pregnant outside marriage was believed to be evidence of moral depravity and mental defectiveness. Towards the end of the twentieth century, when the large asylums were closed down, it was clear that they contained many elderly women who had been perfectly sane when they were committed as unmarried pregnant women, but who had since become institutionalized and incapable of living independently.

In 2007 this provision was removed, because the government believed it placed an obstacle in the way of detaining sex offenders with personality disorders, since the implication was that someone should not be treated as mentally disordered where the principal manifestation of their personality disorder was their sexual deviancy. In short, it was thought that mental health legislation should facilitate, rather than obstruct, the detention of paedophiles.

It is important to remember that simply being defined as mentally disordered does not necessarily mean that someone will be subject to formal powers: it is a necessary but certainly not a sufficient condition. The other necessary conditions are described in the next section.

4 ADMISSION TO THE MENTAL HEALTH SYSTEM

The increasing use of private providers, and reporting difficulties, means that the latest statistics on the number of detentions in 2017–18 are known to be incomplete. The reported figure of 49,551 is therefore an underestimate, and NHS Digital in fact believe that the number of detentions increased by 2.4 per cent since the previous year.[23] During 2017–18, 2,510,745 people were in contact with mental health, autism and learning disability services, and 103,952 of these spent time in hospital.[24] Even though the proportion of those who have been compulsorily detained or 'sectioned' has increased in recent years, it continues to be a tiny minority of those suffering from mental illness. Interestingly, then, 'mental health law' has little application to the vast majority of people living with mental disorders.

There are three routes to admission to the mental health system: informal admission; detention under the Mental Capacity Act's 'deprivation of liberty' procedure; and formal detention.

(a) VOLUNTARY ADMISSION UNDER THE 1983 ACT

Under section 131 of the 1983 Act, anyone who 'requires treatment for mental disorder' may be admitted informally.

Mental Health Act 1983 section 131

131(1) Nothing in this Act shall be construed as preventing a patient who requires treatment for mental disorder from being admitted to any hospital or registered establishment in pursuance of arrangements made in that behalf and without any application, order or direction rendering him liable to be detained under this Act, or from remaining in any hospital or registered establishment in pursuance of such arrangements after he has ceased to be so liable to be detained.

If the patient is willingly seeking inpatient treatment, there are clear advantages in avoiding the use of compulsory powers. Restricting a patient's liberty may reduce patient trust, and if a patient has chosen to admit herself to hospital, she may be more likely to cooperate with treatment, and find the experience less distressing.

Of course, it is possible that the patient will come under pressure, perhaps from her family, to agree to informal admission, and, in practice, she may not have anywhere else to go. It is also possible for an informally admitted patient subsequently to be formally detained under section 5 of the 1983 Act. Once in hospital, as Phil Fennell explains in the next extract, informally admitted patients are not necessarily free to leave.

Phil Fennell[25]

Even if there were an unlimited right for informal patients to leave hospital, to speak of mentally incapacitated patients having it makes little sense. There may be nowhere else capable of providing the care which the patient needs, he may have no home to go to and be too dependent to survive in sheltered accommodation. Any hospital or nursing home accepting responsibility for looking after mentally incapacitated informal patients thereby assumes a duty of care towards them. That duty of care extends to preventing them from leaving when to do so would put them at risk. Not being detained does not make an informal patient 'freer'.

---

[23] *Mental Health Act Statistics: Annual Figures England 2017-18* (NHS Digital, 2018).
[24] *Mental Health Bulletin, Annual Report—2017-18* (NHS Digital, 2018).
[25] 'Doctor Knows Best? Therapeutic Detention under Common Law, the Mental Health Act and the European Convention' (1998) 6 Medical Law Review 322–53.

In the next extract, Michael Cavadino draws upon his interviews with patients at an unidentified NHS psychiatric hospital, which he refers to as Fardale, in order to examine whether informal patients' stays in hospital are genuinely voluntary.

Michael Cavadino[26]

On the question of whether they would like to leave hospital, a substantial minority of the informal patients (38 per cent) said that they would ... So why were so many patients still in hospital informally who would rather leave? ... Of the informal patients who expressed a desire to leave, 14 per cent did indeed believe that they were not free to leave hospital ... But in most cases, patients perceived other constraints as being more important. Foremost among these other constraints was lack of accommodation, or suitable accommodation, outside the hospital ...

It seems, then, that although there are indeed *some* informal patients who stay in hospital because they feel coerced to do so, factors such as lack of accommodation are of much greater importance than the fear of legal or extra-legal force—certainly in the eyes of the patients themselves.

There are also times when patients are informally admitted because they are too incapacitated to express a preference. Notice that section 131 states that nothing in the Act prevents a patient from '*being* admitted' to hospital, implying that there is no need for informal patients actively to admit themselves.

Informal admission in such circumstances potentially leaves the patient without the formal protections which are in place to protect compulsorily detained patients. This was the issue that arose in the *Bournewood* case, which led to the introduction of the Deprivation of Liberty Safeguards.

In *R v Bournewood Community and Mental Health NHS Trust, ex parte L*,[27] HL was a 48-year-old man, who was autistic and profoundly mentally incapacitated. He had been living with paid carers for a number of years, but on a visit to a day centre he had become agitated and was admitted informally to Bournewood hospital. His carers were denied access to him, on the grounds that if he saw them, he might want to leave. If HL had tried to leave, the trust admitted that he would have been compulsorily detained, but it also argued that, so long as HL was not trying to leave, he could continue to be kept in hospital informally under section 131. A majority in the House of Lords agreed.

In *HL v United Kingdom* the European Court of Human Rights (ECtHR) took a different view and found that HL had been detained, and that the lack of protections in place for people in his position did not satisfy the requirements of Article 5(4), the right to liberty and security: 'Everyone who is deprived of his liberty by arrest or detention shall be entitled to take proceedings by which the lawfulness of his detention shall be decided speedily by a court and his release ordered if the detention is not lawful'.

---

[26] *Mental Health Law in Context* (Dartmouth: Aldershot, 1989).
[27] *R v Bournewood Community and Mental Health NHS Trust, ex parte L* [1998] 3 WLR 107.

HL v United Kingdom[28]

Judgment of the ECtHR

[T]he concrete situation was that the applicant was under continuous supervision and control and was not free to leave. Any suggestion to the contrary was, in the Court's view, fairly described by Lord Steyn [dissenting] as 'stretching credulity to breaking point' and as a 'fairy tale'... The Court therefore concludes that the applicant was 'deprived of his liberty' within the meaning of Article 5 § 1 of the Convention...

[T]he Court finds striking the lack of any fixed procedural rules by which the admission and detention of compliant incapacitated persons is conducted. The contrast between this dearth of regulation and the extensive network of safeguards applicable to psychiatric committals covered by the 1983 Act is, in the Court's view, significant ...

The Court therefore finds that this absence of procedural safeguards fails to protect against arbitrary deprivations of liberty on grounds of necessity and, consequently, to comply with the essential purpose of Article 5 § 1 of the Convention. On this basis, the Court finds that there has been a violation of Article 5 § 1 of the Convention.

As a result of this decision, the government had to put in place measures to plug what had become known as the '*Bournewood* gap': namely, the lack of any mechanism to authorize and challenge the de facto detention of patients like HL who are compliant and incapacitated. The Deprivation of Liberty Safeguards (DoLS)—which are contained in the Mental Capacity Act—came into force in 2008. They have not been a success and are due to be replaced, probably by 2020.

(b) MCA 'DEPRIVATION OF LIBERTY' SAFEGUARDS

(1) What is a 'Deprivation of Liberty'?

The Deprivation of Liberty Safeguards apply only when someone is actually deprived of her liberty, as opposed to having her freedom restricted. The distinction between restriction and deprivation of liberty is therefore important, but it may be a fine one and a question of degree.

The central question is (as it was in the *Bournewood* case) whether the person who lacks capacity is free to leave. If she is, then she has not been deprived of her liberty. If, however, she would be stopped from leaving were she to attempt to do so, then she is being deprived of her liberty, and a DoLS authorization is necessary. Whether or not the incapacitated person wishes to leave, or is able to do so, is irrelevant. Instead the focus is on how those caring for him would react were she to try to leave.

Is a patient deprived of her liberty when caring for her inevitably involves a degree of restraint? This was the question that arose in the UK Supreme Court decision in *Cheshire West and Chester Council v P*.[29] In the first case two sisters, P and Q, had learning disabilities and did not have the capacity to give a valid consent to any arrangements for their care. The Court of Appeal had held that although neither sister was free to leave their accommodation, the 'relative normality' of their living arrangements, which were no more intrusive than was necessary for their own protection, meant that neither P nor Q was deprived of her liberty.

---

[28] Application no 45508/99 (5 October 2004).   [29] [2014] UKSC 19.

In the second case, P was a 39-year-old man, with cerebral palsy and Down's syndrome, who lacked the mental capacity to make decisions about his care. His occasionally aggressive behaviour, and his habit of putting his incontinence pads in his mouth, necessitated some physical restraint. Once again, the Court of Appeal held that the restraints to which P was subject were 'normal' for someone with his capabilities, and therefore did not amount to a deprivation of liberty.

By a majority, in *Cheshire West and Chester Council v P*, the Supreme Court decided that even where the restraints to which individuals were subject were a necessary consequence of their learning disabilities, that nevertheless amounted to a deprivation of liberty, for which a DoLS authorization was required.

Cheshire West and Chester Council v P[30]

Lady Hale

[A]s it seems to me, what it means to be deprived of liberty must be the same for everyone, whether or not they have physical or mental disabilities. If it would be a deprivation of my liberty to be obliged to live in a particular place, subject to constant monitoring and control, only allowed out with close supervision, and unable to move away without permission even if such an opportunity became available, then it must also be a deprivation of the liberty of a disabled person. The fact that my living arrangements are comfortable, and indeed make my life as enjoyable as it could possibly be, should make no difference. A gilded cage is still a cage . . .

So is there an acid test for the deprivation of liberty in these cases? . . . The answer, as it seems to me, lies in those features which have consistently been regarded as 'key' in the jurisprudence which started with *HL v United Kingdom*: that the person concerned 'was under continuous supervision and control and was not free to leave' . . .

It is very easy to focus on the positive features of these placements for all three of the appellants. The local authorities who are responsible for them have no doubt done the best they could to make their lives as happy and fulfilled, as well as safe, as they possibly could be. But the purpose of article 5 is to ensure that people are not deprived of their liberty without proper safeguards, safeguards which will secure that the legal justifications for the constraints which they are under are made out: in these cases, the law requires that they do indeed lack the capacity to decide for themselves where they should live and that the arrangements made for them are in their best interests. It is to set the cart before the horse to decide that because they do indeed lack capacity and the best possible arrangements have been made, they are not in need of those safeguards.

Lord Carnwath and Lord Hodge (dissenting on *P* and *Q*)

We are concerned that nobody using ordinary language would describe people living happily in a domestic setting as being deprived of their liberty . . . No doubt P and Q can be said to have had their liberty restricted, by comparison with a person with unimpaired health and capacity. But that is not the same as a deprivation of liberty. Parker J summarised their position in this way:

[30] [2014] UKSC 19.

> The 'concrete situation' is that each lives exactly the kind of life that she would be capable of living in the home of her own family or a relative: their respective lives being dictated by their own cognitive limitations.

Essentially, then, there is a two-pronged 'acid test' to determine whether someone is being deprived of their liberty: are they under continuous supervision and control, and are they free to leave?

Of course, many patients who are seriously ill in hospital are under continuous supervision and not free to leave, but it does not make much sense to say that a hospital must apply for a DoLS authorization for every patient in an Intensive Care Unit. This question was resolved by the Court of Appeal in *R (Ferreira) v HM Senior Coroner for Inner South London*.

R (Ferreira) v HM Senior Coroner for Inner South London [31]

Arden LJ

In the case of a patient in intensive care, the true cause of their not being free to leave is their underlying illness, which was the reason why they were taken into intensive care. The person may have been rendered unresponsive by reason of treatment they have received, such as sedation, but, while that treatment is an immediate cause, it is not the real cause. The real cause is their illness, a matter for which (in the absence of special circumstances) the state is not responsible. It is quite different in the case of living arrangements for a person of unsound mind. If she is prevented from leaving her placement it is because of steps taken to prevent her because of her mental disorder. *Cheshire West* is a long way from this case on its facts and that, in my judgment, indicates that it is distinguishable from the situation of a patient in intensive care.

(2) What are the 'Deprivation of Liberty Safeguards'?

Schedule 1A to the Mental Capacity Act 2005, as amended, fleshes out six requirements, all of which must be met before a deprivation of liberty may be authorized.

Mental Capacity Act 2005 Schedule 1A Part 3

(a) the age requirement: the patient must be at least 18 years old.

(b) the mental health requirement: the patient must be suffering from a mental disorder within the meaning of the MHA.

(c) the mental capacity requirement: the patient must lack capacity.

(d) the best interests requirement;

- it is in the best interests of the relevant person to be deprived of liberty

---

[31] [2017] EWCA Civ 31.

- it is necessary for them to be deprived of liberty in order to prevent harm to themselves, and

- deprivation of liberty is a proportionate response to the likelihood of the relevant person suffering harm and the seriousness of that harm.

(e) the eligibility requirement: they must not be detained under the Act or subject to restrictions on their freedom in the community.

(f) the no refusals requirement: there must not be a valid and applicable advance refusal of the treatment for which the deprivation of liberty authorization of liberty is sought.

Deprivation of liberty thus has to be (a) necessary to protect P from harm, (b) proportionate, and (c) in P's best interests. Consistent with the MCA's section 4 checklist (see Chapter 5), best interests is not confined to the patient's *clinical* best interests. In *A London Local Authority v JH*,[32] Eldergill J was presented with evidence that there were some health risks in JH continuing to be cared for by her husband at home. Because this was her preferred option, she could only be taken to and kept in a nursing home—which would have been clinically preferable—if she was deprived of her liberty. Taking into account the strength of JH's preference to continue to live with her husband, the deprivation of her liberty was not in her best interests and no order was made.

As part of the DoLS procedure, a representative, who must be someone that the P knows and trusts, must be appointed. If there is no one available to act as their representative, an Independent Mental Capacity Advocate (IMCA) must be appointed to represent and support the person.

A deprivation of liberty can be authorized by 'the supervisory' body, which will be the local authority. Applications for authorizations are made by the person responsible for running the hospital or care home in which the patient is being treated or cared for and, if granted, the authorization will last for 12 months. Under section 21A of the Mental Capacity Act, the authorization can be subject to review by the Court of Protection, which may vary or terminate it. It is also possible for applications to be made to the Court of Protection by the patient or someone acting on her behalf.

Indeed, there may be circumstances when the local authority is under a duty to facilitate the authorization's review by the court. This was the case in *Hillingdon v Neary*,[33] in which Peter Jackson J found that the local authority had to do more than simply point out that the patient had the right to challenge the DoLS authorization. At his father's request, the London Borough of Hillingdon had taken Steven Neary, who suffered from autism and a severe learning disability, into respite care for a few days. Steven stayed there for a year, against both his own and his father's wishes. The local authority maintained that it had Steven's father's consent for the first four months, and thereafter was entitled to rely upon DoLS authorizations that it had effectively granted to itself. Peter Jackson J found that Steven had been deprived of his liberty throughout. Because the local authority had granted authorizations 'on the basis of perfunctory scrutiny of superficial best interests assessments', the DoLS authorizations had been unlawful.

---

[32] [2011] EWHC 2420 (COP).   [33] [2011] EWHC 1377 (COP).

(3) The Relationship Between DoLS and Compulsory Admission Under the Mental Health Act 1983

In addition to DoLS, incapacitated patients can also be detained under the Mental Health Act 1983, as described in the next section. Under Schedule 1A, para 5, if the incapacitated person meets the criteria for detention and objects to being detained in the hospital, or to some or all of the proposed treatment, he is ineligible for detention under DoLS, and the Mental Health Act must be used.

The existence of this provision was one factor behind Charles J's decision in *GJ v Foundation Trust*, that the Mental Health Act (MHA) should have primacy over the Mental Capacity Act (MCA), and that practitioners are not free to 'pick and choose' between the two procedures when depriving someone of their liberty.

GJ v Foundation Trust[34]

Charles J

In my judgment, the MHA 1983 has primacy in the sense that the relevant decision makers under both the MHA 1983 and the MCA should approach the questions they have to answer relating to the application of the MHA 1983 on the basis of an assumption that an alternative solution is not available under the MCA . . .

[I]n my view this does not mean that the two regimes are necessarily always mutually exclusive. But it does mean . . . that it is not lawful for the medical practitioners referred to in ss 2 and 3 of the MHA 1983, decision makers under the MCA, treating doctors, social workers or anyone else to proceed on the basis that they can pick and choose between the two statutory regimes as they think fit having regard to general considerations (e.g. the preservation or promotion of a therapeutic relationship with P) that they consider render one regime preferable to the other in the circumstances of the given case.

My reasons for this conclusion are:

(a) It is in line with the underlying purpose of the amendments to the MCA 2005, to fill a gap namely the '*Bournewood Gap*'. This shows that the purpose was not to provide alternative regimes but to leave the existing regime under the MHA 1983 in place with primacy and to fill a gap left by it and the common law.

(b) The regime under the MHA 1983 has been in place for some time and includes a number of checks and balances suitable to its subject matter that are not replicated under the MCA.

Because DoLS apply only to patients who lack capacity, to rule out the use of DoLS, the patient's objection to detention or treatment will not be a competent one. It need not even be verbal; rather, as Matthew McKillop et al explain, objection can be inferred from a person's behaviour.

Matthew McKillop, John Dawson, and George Szmukler[35]

Capacity to object is irrelevant . . . It is clear too than an effective objection need not be a verbal one. In determining whether a person has objected, eligibility assessors are required to take

---

[34] [2009] EWHC 2972 (Fam).
[35] 'The concept of objection under the DOLS regime' (2011) Journal of Mental Health Law 61.

into account the person's behaviour, as well as their wishes, feelings, beliefs and values. These latter views will normally require communication through language, either verbally or otherwise, but the concept of behaviour clearly encompasses all the responses of a person to their deprivation of liberty, including physical responses ...

An inability to communicate feelings verbally, combined with an inability to make controlled movements indicative of a desire to leave a place, would make objection very difficult. Some individuals may be so profoundly disabled that there is no feasible way for them to object to a deprivation of liberty.

(4) What is Wrong with DoLS?

The short answer is 'a great deal'. In addition to the weight of academic criticism they have attracted, they have been criticized by the judiciary, by the House of Lords Select Committee on the Mental Capacity Act 2005, and by the Law Commission. First, as Brenda Hale, writing extra-judicially, points out, they are unnecessarily complicated.

Brenda Hale[36]

The Schedules [to the Mental Capacity Act 2005] consist of a total of 205 paragraphs, and there are then a further 40 regulations, and all this to define a single, simple power. It is not just the length of the Schedules which makes them so impenetrable, but their obscure language, their relentless over-specification of detail, and their convoluted structure which makes it impossible to find the answer to any question in any one place.

In his evidence to the House of Lords post-legislative scrutiny Select Committee, Charles J, Vice-President of the Court of Protection, described the experience of writing a judgment on DoLS 'as if you have been in a washing machine and spin dryer',[37] and in *Cheshire West*, Lady Hale said that 'the safeguards have the appearance of bewildering complexity'.

Secondly, there have been criticisms of the way in which DoLS have been drafted. The draconian language is at odds with the rest of the Mental Capacity Act, and in its initial consultation paper, the Law Commission pointed out that carers find it baffling and upsetting.

Law Commission[38]

Terms such as 'standard authorisations', 'managing authority' and 'supervisory body' have been described variously as cumbersome, Orwellian, and failing to reflect modern health and social care functions. Particular criticism has been directed at the label 'Deprivation of Liberty Safeguards'. It is suggested that care providers are put off by the label, and do not want to acknowledge that they are depriving people of their liberty because they see themselves as

---

[36] 'Taking stock' (2009) Journal of Mental Health Law 111–27.
[37] House of Lords Select Committee on the Mental Capacity Act 2005, Report of Session 2013–14, *Mental Capacity Act 2005: Post-Legislative Scrutiny* (TSO: London, 2014) para 271.
[38] *Mental Capacity and Deprivation of Liberty: A Consultation Paper* (Law Commission, 2015) para 2.37.

helping and protecting people. Carers have described to us the distress caused when informed that their loved one needs to be made subject to the 'Deprivation of Liberty Safeguards'— especially where nobody is dissatisfied with the care and support arrangements.

As Alex Ruck Keene pointed out in evidence to the Joint Committee on Human Rights, under DoLS, 'an individual in an adult foster placement with a devoted carer is in the same legal situation as an individual detained in a high-end psychiatric institution objecting to treatment'.[39] In the next extract, Ruth Cairns et al agree that the term 'deprivation of liberty' is counterintuitive where a care relationship is working well. They also highlight the sheer numbers of patients affected by *Cheshire West*.

Ruth Cairns, Matthew Hotopf, and Gareth S Owen[40]

Around 200 000 people with dementia live in care homes, and some 40 000 people with learning disabilities live in residential and nursing homes. If the acid test is applied, many will require deprivation of liberty safeguards. On general medical wards, 40% of patients lack capacity to make decisions about care, with higher proportions on elderly care wards and intensive treatment units. Are these patients free to leave? In a large number of cases the answer is no. Are they under the complete supervision and control of those caring for them? The answer, for many inpatients, is probably yes.

If care homes and acute hospitals are looked at through this legal lens, deprivations of liberty are widespread. Yet a healthcare worker's lens is different. The understanding of individual patients' disabilities and their acceptance of offers of care are regarded as important indications of whether a care relationship is working. If it is thought to be working, then identifying a deprivation of liberty is likely to be a foreign instinct.

Thirdly, most compliant, incapacitated patients are not in hospital, but instead live in care homes and supported living facilities. There are 20,000 care homes in the UK, many of them small and privately run, where knowledge and understanding of DoLS is likely to be poor or non-existent. The responsibility for applying for a DoLS authorization rests with the care home's proprietor, but comparatively few owners of care homes understand the need to do this. It is therefore by no means clear that DoLS have plugged the *Bournewood* gap for most patients to whom they should apply.

In addition, because DoLS only apply to hospitals and care homes, they do not offer any safeguards for incapacitated people living in supported living facilities, who may be especially vulnerable because such places are not subject to inspection by the Care Quality Commission.

Fourthly, some of the protections that exist for patients under the Mental Health Act—the need for second opinions in relation to some controversial medical treatments, for example— are not replicated for patients deprived of their liberty under the DoLS process. Instead medical treatment must simply be appropriate and in their best interests. The requirement that continued detention be subject to review by the tribunal is also absent, and there is no requirement to fund aftercare, once someone ceases to be deprived of their liberty. It is therefore

[39] House of Commons and House of Lords **Joint Committee on Human Rights**, *The Right to Freedom and Safety: Reform of the Deprivation of Liberty Safeguards inquiry* (2018) para 35.
[40] 'Deprivation of liberty in healthcare' (2014) 348 British Medical Journal g3390.

at least arguable that DoLS continue to leave compliant, non-objecting patients with fewer protections and rights than their objecting, detained counterparts.

Fifthly, it could be argued that there are potential conflicts of interest for local authorities, which commission and pay for social care services, while also authorizing deprivations of liberty within those services. How likely is it that a local authority will decline to authorize living arrangements for which it is also ultimately responsible?

Sixthly, DoLS are directed towards ensuring that hospitals and care homes do not inadvertently breach incapacitated persons' Article 5 rights. Although important legally, whether or not their living arrangements have been authorized via DoLS may make little practical difference to compliant, incapacitated patients. Of more practical importance, but irrelevant under DoLS, are such individuals' Article 8 rights: for HL himself, being prevented from seeing his carers may have made much more difference to his quality of life than whether he was, in fact, free to leave.

Seventhly, the decision in *Cheshire West* has revealed the scale of the problems inherent in DoLS. In 2017–18, there were 227,400 DoLS applications,[41] compared with 7,157 in their first year of operation. A further consequence of the dramatic increase in the number of affected patients after *Cheshire West*, is a dramatic increase in the number of people who become entitled, as a result of Article 5, to have the lawfulness of their detention reviewed speedily by a court. As a result, the Court of Protection was immediately faced with a huge increase in its caseload.

In *A Hospital NHS Trust v CD*, for example, Mostyn J found it counter-intuitive to have to authorize a Deprivation of Liberty in order that a woman, who desperately wanted the operation to go ahead, could undergo surgery to remove large ovarian masses.

A Hospital NHS Trust v CD[42]

Mostyn J

But for we hoplites who have to administer it at first instance the scope and ramifications of the test are, with respect, extremely confusing … I do not accept the criticism that my approach to these cases is 'distorted' by my 'passionate' and 'tenacious' belief that *Cheshire West* is wrong. Rather, it is a loyal approach which tries to apply literally and purposively the Supreme Court's test while at the same time pointing out how confusing and curious it is, to say nothing of the cost it causes to the public purse …

[CD] actively and fervently wishes to undergo the operation to remove the surgical masses. How can it be said that in taking her to the hospital and having the operation performed there under general anaesthetic amounts to her being deprived of her liberty? …

She says she will go freely to the hospital but, as explained above, that is not a decision she can make. The decision I make on her behalf is intrinsically coercive even if she is enthusiastically compliant. If she changes her mind she will be taken to the hospital and operated on nonetheless. Although counterintuitive this state of affairs is to my mind clearly within the Supreme Court's test and it is therefore necessary to authorise her deprivation of liberty under Article 5.

---

[41] *Mental Capacity Act 2005: Deprivation of Liberty Safeguards England 2017-18* (NHS Digital, 2018).
[42] [2015] EWCOP 74.

Finally, it is not clear that DoLS have solved the problem of de facto detention. In their study of admissions to inpatient adult mental health services in Coventry and Warwickshire, Benjamin Perry et al found that de facto detention was still common. In part, this may have been because doctors did not want to saddle patients with the stigma of having been sectioned, but it deprives these 'voluntary' patients of the safeguards of the MHA and DoLS.

Benjamin Ian Perry, Swaran Preet Singh, and David Hedley White[43]

It is vital that all patients admitted to inpatient mental health services as voluntary patients make a free decision to be admitted, and are deemed capacitous to make the decision. They must be provided with enough information for the decision to be considered informed. Without this there is a risk of coercion and extra-legal deprivation of liberty ... Our findings suggest that currently, these standards are not being adhered to.

The stigma faced by patients with mental illness is real, and may well be amplified by a history of detention under the MHA. This may weigh heavy on the minds of those professionals tasked with decisions surrounding legal frameworks in the admission of acutely unwell psychiatric patients. Whilst our findings highlight the possibility of coercion and extralegal deprivation of liberty in voluntary patients, it is likely that the professionals involved believed they were acting in the patient's best interests ...

The MHA exists to protect patients and has safeguards to empower them. Without these safeguards in place, patients are disempowered, unprotected and arguably more stigmatized.

(5) Reform of DoLS

In 2014, the House of Lords Select Committee on the Mental Capacity Act declared that DoLS were not fit for purpose and recommended their replacement. The Law Commission then undertook a review, and its proposals formed the basis of the Mental Capacity (Amendment) Bill, which is at the time of writing before Parliament.[44]

The new Liberty Protection Safeguards will apply not only to hospitals and care homes, but extend to supported living arrangements and treatment provided in a domestic setting. They will provide legal authorization for specific arrangements that deprive a person who lacks capacity of her liberty, in her best interests, rather than authorizing the deprivation of liberty in general.

Under Schedule AA1, a responsible body (the hospital manager, CCG or local authority) will be able to authorize arrangements which give rise to a deprivation of liberty if it has consulted the 'cared-for person' herself, and others close to her in order to ascertain her wishes or feelings, and is satisfied that three conditions are met:

1. the person who is the subject of the arrangements lacks the capacity to consent to the arrangements;

2. the person is of unsound mind (the meaning is the same as under Article 5); and

3. the deprivation of liberty is necessary and proportionate.

---

[43] 'Capacity assessment and information provision for voluntary psychiatric patients: a service evaluation in a UK NHS Trust' (2017) 22 International Journal of Mental Health and Capacity Law 107–18.

[44] The final text of the Act will be available on the parliament website. Readers seeking commentary on the final Act might be advised to look for further information here: <http://www.mentalcapacitylawandpolicy.org.uk/>.

Someone who is not involved in the day-to-day care of, or in providing treatment to, the person must carry out a pre-authorization review to determine whether it is reasonable for the responsible body to conclude that the authorization conditions are met. If the non-capacitous person is objecting to the proposed arrangements, an Approved Mental Capacity Professional must carry out the pre-authorization review and determine whether the authorization conditions are met.

John Fanning[45]

How will decision-makers determine whether a patient, who lacks capacity, is objecting? Should they interpret 'objection' narrowly so that it applies only to plainly articulated refusals? If so, what about patients whose refusals may be fleeting or unpredictable? What about patients who lack the faculties of speech or movement? Alternatively, should decision-makers view anything less than passive acquiescence as an objection? If so, would there be any meaningful distinction between the absence of capacity and objection?

There should be regular review of the authorization by the responsible body or care home, and there is a right to challenge the authorization before the Court of Protection. The responsible body should also appoint an Independent Mental Capacity Advocate (IMCA) or an appropriate person to represent and support the person when an authorization is being proposed and while an authorization is in place.

If someone is detained under the MHA, then an authorization under this route is not available. Authorizations will lapse after 12 months, if not renewed, and can be made for shorter periods. Renewal is possible for one more year, in the first instance and thereafter for three year periods.

(c) INVOLUNTARY ADMISSION UNDER THE 1983 ACT

Before we flesh out the most common routes through which patients are compulsorily detained under the Mental Health Act, it is worth noting that there are other ways into the mental health system. In an emergency, a patient can be admitted under section 4 on the basis of one medical recommendation that 'it is of urgent necessity for the patient to be admitted and detained under section 2'.

Under section 136, if a police officer finds 'a person who appears to him to be suffering from mental disorder and to be in immediate need of care or control' in a public place, he can be removed to a place of safety for 72 hours 'for the purpose of enabling him to be examined by a registered medical practitioner and to be interviewed by an Approved Mental Health Professional (AMHP) and of making any necessary arrangements for his treatment or care'.

If the person's behaviour poses 'an unmanageably high risk to other patients, staff or users of a healthcare setting', a police station may be used as a place of safety,[46] but this should be exceptional. The Crisis Care Concordat was launched in 2014 in order to try to reduce the use of police custody for those in need of mental health crisis care, and in part as a result of the roll-out of street triage schemes, the use of police custody as a place of safety dropped by 56

---

[45] 'Continuities of Risk in the Era of the Mental Capacity Act' (2016) 24 Medical Law Review 415–33.
[46] Mental Health Act Code of Practice 2015, para 16.38.

per cent the following year.[47] Under the Mental Health Act 1983 (Places of Safety) Regulations 2017 police cells can now be used as places of safety only where the person's behaviour 'poses an imminent risk of serious injury or death'; no other suitable place of safety is available, and a healthcare professional is available throughout the period of detention. The Independent Review of the Mental Health Act 1983 has recommended that the law should go further still, and that 'police cells should be removed altogether as a place of safety in the Act by 2023/24'.[48]

Finally, under section 5 a voluntarily admitted patient can be compulsorily detained for up to 72 hours in order to prevent him from leaving hospital, after which continued detention is possible only if the formal powers in section 3 are invoked.

(1) The Process of Applying for Formal Powers

The 1983 Act provides for the compulsory admission of patients for assessment under section 2, and for treatment under section 3.

Mental Health Act 1983 sections 2 and 3

2(2) An application for admission for assessment may be made in respect of a patient on the grounds that—

(a) he is suffering from mental disorder of a nature or degree which warrants the detention of the patient in a hospital for assessment (or for assessment followed by medical treatment) for at least a limited period; and

(b) he ought to be so detained in the interests of his own health or safety or with a view to the protection of other persons.

(3) An application for admission for assessment shall be founded on the written recommendations in the prescribed form of two registered medical practitioners, including in each case a statement that in the opinion of the practitioner the conditions set out in subsection (2) above are complied with.

(4) ... [A] patient admitted to hospital in pursuance of an application for admission for assessment may be detained for a period not exceeding 28 days beginning with the day on which he is admitted, but shall not be detained after the expiration of that period unless before it has expired he has become liable to be detained by virtue of a subsequent application, order or direction under the following provisions of this Act...

3(2) An application for admission for treatment may be made in respect of a patient on the grounds that—

(a) he is suffering from mental disorder of a nature or degree which makes it appropriate for him to receive medical treatment in a hospital; and

(b) it is necessary for the health or safety of the patient or for the protection of other persons that he should receive such treatment and it cannot be provided unless he is detained under this section; and

(c) appropriate medical treatment is available for him.

(3) An application for admission for treatment shall be founded on the written recommendations in the prescribed form of two registered medical practitioners, including in each case

---

[47] Care Quality Commission, *The state of care in mental health services 2014 to 2017* (CQC, 2018).

[48] Final report of the Independent Review of the Mental Health Act 1983, *Modernising the Mental Health Act, Increasing choice, reducing compulsion* (DHSC, 2018).

a statement that in the opinion of the practitioner the conditions set out in subsection (2) above are complied with ...

(4) In this Act, references to appropriate medical treatment, in relation to a person suffering from mental disorder, are references to medical treatment which is appropriate in his case, taking into account the nature and degree of the mental disorder and all other circumstances of his case.

Applications for section 2 and 3 orders can be made by the patient's nearest relative, but most are made by an Approved Mental Health Professional (AMHP), usually a social worker, and the application must be supported by two medical practitioners, one of whom must be approved under section 12(2) of the Act, 'as having special experience in the diagnosis or treatment of mental disorder', and one of whom must have 'previous acquaintance with the patient'.

Under section 2, an individual can be detained for assessment for up to 28 days, after which the patient must either be: (a) discharged; (b) admitted as an informal patient; or (c) detained under section 3. Because a bed must be provided to someone who is detained for assessment under section 2, it is possible that the recent increase in detentions is driven by the shortage of beds.

Nicola Glover-Thomas[49]

There are several reasons for the increased use of Section 2. The provision is thought to assist with access to mental health services. The availability of beds has decreased and bed shortages are resulting in delayed admission. With bed occupancy rates in inpatient facilities being well above recommended levels, use of voluntary admission as a preferred method of entering the mental health system is being hampered by scarce resources. Where a patient is deemed in need of care in hospital, resort to civil commitment may be the quickest means of opening up services.

Under section 3, individuals can be admitted for treatment, initially for up to six months, and this can be renewed for a further six months. Thereafter, the individual can be detained for a year, with annual renewal for long-term inpatients.

The justifications for compulsory detention under the Act are a combination of preventing the individual from harming herself and/or others, and enabling her to receive treatment. For example, under sections 2 and 3, the person must be suffering from a mental disorder of, 'a nature or degree which warrants admission to hospital' (section 2), or, 'which makes it appropriate for him to receive medical treatment in a hospital' (section 3), both of which have a therapeutic intent. But under section 2, detention is permissible if the patient 'ought to be detained' to protect the health or safety of the patient, or to protect other persons, or under section 3, detention must be 'necessary for the health or safety of the patient or for the protection of other persons'.

These powers are available only when the patient needs to receive assessment or treatment in hospital, that is, to become an inpatient. It would not be possible to use section 3 where the intention is immediately to discharge the patient under a Community Treatment Order (discussed later). It is also necessary to prove that the treatment cannot be provided unless

---

[49] 'Decision-Making Behaviour under the Mental Health Act 1983 and Its Impact on Mental Health Tribunals: An English Perspective' (2018) 7 Laws 12.

the patient is detained, so where it would be possible to provide treatment in the community, section 3 is not satisfied. This is sometimes referred to as the 'least restrictive alternative' principle: treatment in hospital must be necessary, not just convenient.

It should, however, be noted that the use of the word 'or' may run counter to the 'least restrictive alternative' principle. This is because, in theory at least, a patient might be detained because she is suffering from a disorder whose *nature* warrants detention in hospital, but to a *degree* which does not. We return to this point again later in the context of discharge from hospital.

In the next extract, Jill Peay further suggests that the patient's 'need' to be in hospital may arise not because of the nature of her illness, but as a result of her attitude towards treatment.

Jill Peay[50]

Curiously, in clinical terms, 'the need to be in hospital' may not arise. This is not because the illness *can only* be treated in hospital, but because the patient will not *accept* treatment where he is (in the community). Since the only route by which *compulsory* treatment can be legally achieved is via the Act, and since the Act only allows compulsory treatment *in hospital*, such treatment can only be achieved via admission to hospital. Hence, the person is perceived as needing to be in hospital because of his/her attitude to treatment, which may or may not be determined by the illness itself.

The statute takes for granted that it will be possible to tell when a patient poses a risk sufficient to justify detention. In practice, as Nicola Glover-Thomas's empirical research suggests, those charged with making decisions under the Act take a range of different factors into account. Interestingly, too, Glover-Thomas's research suggested that, in practice, people living in deprived areas may be more likely to satisfy the risk threshold.

Nicola Glover-Thomas[51]

It is perhaps telling that without a clear definitional guide under the 2007 Act, there was a significant variation in the meanings attributed to risk by decision-makers in the research sample ...

The overwhelming view of the research sample was that 'past behaviour' is regarded as the 'main predictor' of a patient's current risk profile. In addition, decision-makers must be aware of contextual factors, such as the effects of illicit substances and alcohol, particularly in relation to how these affect the patient's mental state. These factors, which feature in a patient's psychiatric background, are then fed into the overall risk assessment process ...

[T]he suggestion that a patient's socio-economic background could become a dominant feature in a Mental Health Act risk assessment was categorically refuted by the interviewees: 'it's not about socio-economic status, it's about support networks, it's about alternatives to admission'. In spite of this, it was acknowledged that where an individual is living in a deprived area where there are limited support services, the risk of harm to self or others is deemed higher than for someone living in an affluent area with family and friends rallying round ...

---

[50] *Decisions and Dilemmas: Working with Mental Health Law* (Hart Publishing: Oxford, 2003).
[51] 'The Age of Risk: Risk Perception and Determination Following the Mental Health Act 2007' (2011) 19 Medical Law Review 581–605.

Gut instinct has a significant role to play and this stems largely from professional experience and the context of decision-making—whether decision-makers are working in an in-patient or community environment. Decision-makers certainly do identify relevant factors, as discussed above, but they then filter these by using 'personal intuition' in order to generate an outcome.

(2) The 'Treatability' Requirement

The, at first sight, innocuous condition for detention in section 3(d), namely that 'appropriate medical treatment is available' in fact represented one of the most contested aspects of the 2007 reforms. Under the original Act, detention was only possible if treatment was 'likely to alleviate or prevent a deterioration of his condition'. This was known as the 'treatability' requirement, and the then government wanted to remove it because it is not clear that personality disorders are, in fact, treatable. If it is not lawful to detain untreatable patients, it might be difficult to justify the detention of personality-disordered individuals.

Since making it easier to detain people with 'dangerous and severe personality disorders' was one of the government's primary goals, this meant abandoning or modifying the treatability requirement. The reason this matters is that detaining people who cannot be treated, just in order to protect others, amounts to preventative detention. Psychiatrists, in particular, argued that their role was to treat patients who are unwell, rather than to lock up antisocial individuals.

The government did not succeed in removing the treatability requirement altogether, but they were able to amend it. The Act now provides that appropriate medical treatment has to be available; it no longer needs to be likely to work. Medical treatment receives a further definition in section 145(4).

Mental Health Act 1983 section 145

145(4) Any reference in this Act to medical treatment, in relation to mental disorder, shall be construed as a reference to medical treatment the purpose of which is to alleviate, or prevent a worsening of, the disorder or one or more of its symptoms or manifestations.

The Code of Practice gives more detailed guidance on what appropriate treatment means. It specifically spells out that locking someone up is not appropriate medical treatment, but it also indicates that the test will be satisfied if treatment is available, even if the patient refuses to engage with it. 'Talking cures', almost by definition, will not work without the patient's co-operation, and so the 'availability of treatment' criterion for detention may be satisfied, even if the patient is not actually receiving any treatment at all.

Mental Health Act Code of Practice 2015

23.18 Simply detaining someone, even in a hospital, does not constitute medical treatment.
23.19 A patient's attitude towards the proposed treatment may be relevant in determining whether the appropriate medical treatment test is met. An indication of unwillingness to co-operate with treatment generally, or with a specific aspect of treatment, does not make such treatment inappropriate.

23.20 In particular, psychological therapies and other forms of medical treatments which, to be effective, require the patient's co-operation are not automatically inappropriate simply because a patient does not currently wish to engage with them. Such treatments can potentially remain appropriate and available as long as it continues to be clinically suitable to offer them and they would be provided if the patient agreed to engage.

The Independent Review of the Mental Health Act 1983 has recommended that it should be more difficult to satisfy the criteria for detention; that appropriate treatment should not just be 'available', but must be likely to benefit the patient, and that clinicians should become less risk averse.

The Independent Review of the Mental Health Act 1983[52]

Under the current legislation, a person can be detained where it is 'necessary for' or 'justified in the interests of' the patient's health or safety or for the protection of others'. We think this sets the bar too low. Because 'health' encompasses 'mental health', a person can be detained under the Act to avoid any deterioration in their mental health or relapse even if there is no other risk. This may have allowed professionals to become increasingly risk averse; to become too quick to use 'risk' as a catch-all justification when they are afraid of consequences that may never happen, indeed probably won't happen. This has not been helped by a lack of provision of community alternatives that could mitigate harm. A major concern for service users is that consideration of risk has become the only way patients are understood and treated; that they are seen: 'primarily as risk entities, rather than as human beings who are in need of compassionate care and treatment'.

We want to reverse this trend; to use new detention criteria to give professionals the backing they need to take more risks with risk. We believe the Act needs to be more explicit about how serious the harm has to be to justify detention and/or treatment, or how likely it is that the harm will occur. We are recommending that there must be a substantial likelihood of significant harm to the health, safety or welfare of the person, or the safety of any other person. But our recommendations will not work if they are seen as 'stand-alone'. If the Government agrees, tackling the problem of risk aversion must happen across the board. There is little point in mental health professionals deciding to accept a greater perceived risk if the courts, regulators, media and others do the opposite.

The current criteria allows for any vague notion of risk to be put forwards as grounds; our proposed criteria require that the likelihood of harm is substantial, and that this is backed up by evidence. This will make it harder to detain people in a way that is more aligned with the gravity of the removal of their liberty. Requiring that the potential harm is significant will mean detention will only be permitted in the most serious of cases. We are also proposing that, when making an application for detention under the MHA, the AMHP must clearly state on the application form what specific harm they have identified, and how detention will reduce this, including why alternatives are not available or suitable ...

We are recommending tightening the current criteria so that not only must appropriate treatment be available that cannot be delivered unless the person is detained, but also that the treatment would benefit the patient. 'Benefit', for the great majority of patients, would include contributing to the patient's discharge, and not solely to public safety (although we certainly do

---

[52] Final report of the Independent Review of the Mental Health Act 1983, *Modernising the Mental Health Act, Increasing choice, reducing compulsion* (DHSC, 2018).

not under estimate the importance of this). Consideration must be given to community alternatives, and it must be clear that the person cannot be treated in the community. This should support a greater shift towards treatment in the community, wherever possible.

(3) The Use of Compulsory Powers in Practice

As we saw earlier, the proportion of patients who are admitted compulsorily is increasing, and it is also increasingly common for NHS patients to be admitted to private care facilities. The Care Quality Commission monitors patients who are deprived of their liberty and issues annual reports on its findings. In 2018, it published a special report on the increased use of the Mental Health Act to detain people.

Care Quality Commission[53]

Between 2005/06 and 2015/16, the reported number of uses of the Mental Health Act (MHA) increased by 40%. It is well established that people from Black and minority ethnic groups are much more likely to be detained than those in White British groups …

- There is no single cause for the rise in rates of detention this decade. It is highly likely that a range of factors are at play both nationally and locally.

- The rise in part suggests a system under considerable pressure. Staff in some areas have limited access to community services that can act as true alternatives to admission. At the same time, these services may have no bed available for an admission when it is needed. This creates a dilemma for both patient and staff, and reduces the likelihood that detention can be avoided – either by providing a less restrictive community alternative or by an informal admission to prevent further deterioration. In some places, this might amount to a vicious cycle where pressure on beds leads to clinical practices that increase the likelihood of patients being detained, which itself increases the pressure on beds.

- We found no evidence that professionals are using the Mental Health Act to admit people who do not meet the criteria for detention, for example to 'game' the system to obtain a bed for the patient.

- We think it is unlikely that reform of mental health legislation on its own will reduce the rate of detention. There must also be action to address the underlying problems that almost certainly contribute to the rise this decade.

As the CQC indicates, a consistent feature of admissions under the Mental Health Act has been the over-representation of people from Black, Asian, and minority ethnic (BAME) groups, both in terms of all admissions, and in the use of compulsory powers.[54] In 2017–18, detention rates for people who identify as 'Black or Black British' (288.7 detentions per 100,000 population) were the highest, over four times those of people who identify as White (71.8 per 100,000 population).[55]

---

[53] *Mental Health Act: The rise in the use of the MHA to detain people in England* (CQC, 2018).
[54] Bernard Audini and Paul Lelliott, 'Age, gender and ethnicity of those detained under Part II of the Mental Health Act 1983' (2002) 180 British Journal of Psychiatry 222.
[55] *Mental Health Act Statistics: Annual Figures England 2017-18* (NHS Digital, 2018).

There is considerable debate over whether the reasons for this are patient-related or service-related. Patient-related explanations would point to a higher incidence of mental health problems within BAME groups, as a result of the pressures faced by people who are discriminated against, and who may be more likely to experience poverty and deprivation. Service-related explanations suggest these statistics represent institutional racism, perhaps because unwarranted assumptions about people from minority ethnic groups are made within the mental health system.

In 2002, the Sainsbury Centre conducted a review of the relationship between mental health services and African and Caribbean communities, and concluded that there was a vicious circle at play, as a result of what they described as 'circles of fear'. Partly as a result of poor and discriminatory service provision, and partly due to the particular stigma attached to mental illness in some communities, black people were less likely to access treatment services in the early stages of mental illness. They were therefore more likely to reach a crisis point, when detention might be needed, or where their first contact with mental health services is via the police, rather than their GP.[56] This would then reinforce the perception of mental health services as coercive, thus deterring early access to treatment.

The Sainsbury Centre for Mental Health[57]

There is a profound paradox at the centre of black people's experience of mental health services in England. Young black men, in particular, are heavily over-represented in the most restrictive parts of the service, including secure services. And black people generally have an overwhelmingly negative experience of mental health services. Yet these same communities are not accessing the primary care, mental health promotion and specialist community services which might prevent or lessen their mental health problems. They are getting the mental health services they don't want but not the ones they do or might want …

Black people with potential mental health problems are not engaging with services at an early point in the cycle when they could receive less coercive and more appropriate services. Instead they tend only to come to services in crisis when they face a range of risks including over- and mis-diagnosis, police intervention and use of the Mental Health Act. In order to break this cycle, it is necessary to address the issue both from the perspective of services—by making primary care and other services more welcoming, accessible and relevant—and from the perspective of the black community—by increasing understanding and knowledge and reducing the stigma associated with mental illness.

As we saw earlier, the Independent Review of the Mental Health Act 1983 was specifically charged with considering how to tackle the disproportionate use of compulsory powers for people from minority ethnic groups, and it made a number of recommendations, including the provision of culturally appropriate advocacy and making sure the psychiatric profession is more representative of the communities it serves.

---

[56] Ruchika Gajwani et al, 'Ethnicity and detention: are Black and minority ethnic (BME) groups disproportionately detained under the Mental Health Act 2007?' (2016) 51 Social Psychiatry and Psychiatric Epidemiology 703–11.

[57] *Breaking the Circles of Fear: A Review of the Relationship Between Mental Health Services and African and Caribbean Communities* (SCMH, 2002).

The Independent Review of the Mental Health Act 1983[58]

In line with the Organisational Competence Framework (OCF), our wider recommendations include:

- Ensuring the provision of culturally-appropriate advocacy services (including Independent Mental Health Advocates) for people of ethnic minority backgrounds, in doing so responding appropriately to the diverse needs of individuals from diverse communities.

- Raising the bar for individuals to be detained under the Mental Health Act, as well as any subsequent use of Community Treatment Orders.

- Providing the opportunity for people to have more of a say in the care they receive, ensuring that people from ethnic minority backgrounds are involved in the care and treatment plans developed for them and thus increasing the likelihood that they are more acceptable.

- Increasing the opportunities available to challenge decisions about the care offered and received in a more meaningful way.

- Addressing endemic structural factors through the piloting and evaluation of behavioural interventions to combat implicit bias in decision-making.

- Reducing the use of coercion and restrictive practices within inpatient settings, including in relation to religious or spiritual practices.

- Seeking greater representation of people from ethnic minority backgrounds, especially those of black African and Caribbean heritage in key health and care professions.

- Endorsing ongoing work to explore how the use of restraint by police is reduced, encouraging police services to support people experiencing mental distress or ill health as a core part of day-to-day business.

- Extending the powers of the Mental Health Units (Use of Force) Act [see below]... to seclusion.

- Improving the quality and consistency of data and research on ethnicity and use of the Mental Health Act across public services, including criminal justice system organisations and Mental Health Tribunals.

- Giving individuals the ability to choose which individuals from their community are involved with, and receive information about, their care.

(d) RESTRICTED PATIENTS AND THE CRIMINAL JUSTICE SYSTEM

It is possible for people who are convicted in the criminal courts to be diverted to the mental health system if they suffer from a mental disorder. Under section 37 of the Mental Health Act 1983, a court can make a hospital order where someone has been found guilty of an offence punishable by imprisonment. Before making such an order, the court has to be satisfied that the section 3 grounds for admission are satisfied, and, under section 27(2)(b), the court must be 'of the opinion, having regard to all the circumstances including the nature of the offence and the character and antecedents of the offender, and to the other available methods of dealing with him, that the most suitable method of disposing of the case is by means of an order under this section'. The effect of a hospital order is that the person will be detained in one

---

[58] *Modernising the Mental Health Act. Increasing choice, reducing compulsion, Final report of the Independent Review of the Mental Health Act 1983* (DHSC, 2018).

of the three high security special hospitals (Ashworth, Broadmoor, and Rampton) or, where appropriate, in a medium secure ward.

It should, however, be remembered that a significant proportion of the ordinary prison population suffers from mental health problems. Although reliable data on the incidence of mental health disorders in prisons are not collected, on arrival in prison, 23 per cent of prisoners report that they have had prior contact with mental health services, and more may develop mental health problems while in prison.[59]

In *Jean-Luc Rivière v France*,[60] the ECtHR found that containing mentally disordered offenders in prison could constitute a breach of Article 3. Detaining a seriously mentally disordered person, without medical supervision appropriate to his condition, 'entailed particularly acute hardship and caused him distress or adversity of an intensity exceeding the unavoidable level of suffering inherent in detention'. It would clearly not be feasible to empty UK prisons of all prisoners with mental health problems, but in order not to breach their human rights, appropriate medical services should nevertheless be available to them.

In addition to being detained at the outset in a special hospital, there is also some movement between the prison system and the mental health system. This is especially marked when prisoners are nearing the end of their sentences, but are perceived to pose a continuing risk to the public. Detention under section 3 of the Mental Health Act has been used to prevent the release of people who have completed their sentences and hence can no longer be detained within the criminal justice system.

5 TREATMENT OF THE MENTALLY ILL

At the outset, it is important to remember that the normal rules which cover consent to medical treatment apply to people with mental disorders. Adults with capacity have the right to refuse medical treatment, regardless of whether they are suffering from a mental disorder, and those who lack capacity may be treated in their best interests, under the Mental Capacity Act. There are, however, some important exceptions that apply only to those who have been formally admitted to the mental health system. Some of these create special protections for compulsorily detained individuals, while others permit the treatment without consent of patients who have capacity.

(a) TREATMENT UNDER SECTION 57 OF THE MENTAL HEALTH ACT 1983

Under section 57 of the Act, certain types of treatment cannot be given without both the patient's consent *and* the agreement of a doctor appointed to give a second opinion (known as a SOAD). The SOAD must consult two other people who have been involved in the patient's medical treatment, at least one of whom must be a nurse.

The treatments to which section 57 applies are psychosurgery ('any surgical operation for destroying brain tissue or for destroying the functioning of brain tissue') and chemical castration ('the surgical implantation of hormones for the purpose of reducing male sex drive').

---

[59] National Audit Office, *Mental Health in Prisons* (NAO, 2017).
[60] Application no 33834/03 (2006).

Under section 57, these treatments cannot be given without the patient's consent, so it would not be lawful to carry out psychosurgery or chemical castration on patients who lack capacity, unless such treatment could fit within the emergency exception in section 62 (discussed below).

Section 57 is seldom used. The surgical implantation of hormones would be unusual: most treatments to suppress a male patient's sex drive take the form of pills or injections, neither of which are covered by this section. Such drugs can therefore be given under section 63 (discussed below) for up to three months, after which they would fall within section 58, and require the patient's consent or a second opinion.

(b) TREATMENT UNDER SECTION 58 OF THE MENTAL HEALTH ACT 1983

Under section 58, the administration of psychiatric medicines for periods longer than three months requires the informed consent of a competent patient *or* a second opinion from an independent doctor that *either* the patient is not capable of consenting *or* the patient is capable and has not consented, but it is nevertheless appropriate for them to receive the treatment.

Mental Health Act 1983 section 58

58(3) Subject to section 62 below, a patient shall not be given any form of treatment to which this section applies unless—

(a) he has consented to that treatment and either the approved clinician in charge of it or a registered medical practitioner appointed for the purposes of this Part of this Act by the Secretary of State has certified in writing that the patient is capable of understanding its nature, purpose and likely effects and has consented to it; or

(b) a registered medical practitioner appointed as aforesaid (not being the responsible clinician or the approved clinician in charge of the treatment in question) has certified in writing that the patient is not capable of understanding the nature, purpose and likely effects of that treatment or being so capable has not consented to it but that it is appropriate for the treatment to be given.

There is no need for a second opinion if medication is given for less than three months (this will fall within section 63, discussed below). Patients who are discharged within this three-month period will therefore not have their medication regime reviewed. There have been calls for this three-month period to be shortened, since three months is quite a long time for someone to be subject to unwanted, compulsory medication. Under section 58(2), the Secretary of State has the power to reduce this period, but he has not chosen to exercise it.

Electro-convulsive therapy (ECT) used to be subject to the same provision, and hence could be given without consent to a capacitous, refusing patient provided that it was authorized by a SOAD. Following pressure from service users, among others, it is now dealt with separately in section 58A, and cannot be given without consent, unless section 62 applies in an emergency (see below). Under section 58A, ECT can be given only if the patient has consented or, if the patient lacks capacity, it is appropriate for it to be given and the patient did not refuse it in an advance directive.

It is important to note that if a patient who lacks capacity is detained under the Mental Health Act, the Mental Capacity Act does not apply to treatments which are covered by sections 57, 58, and 58A. This has two principal consequences. First, it means that long-term medication for mental disorder or ECT is not governed by the 'best interests' checklist,[61] with its emphasis upon the wishes and feelings of the incapacitated adult. Instead, a much lower threshold applies, namely whether the doctor believes that such treatment is 'appropriate'. Secondly, it is not possible to rely only upon the best interests test in order to justify carrying out psychosurgery or chemical castration on patients who lack capacity, rather the criteria in section 57 must be satisfied.

The need for a second opinion under sections 57 and 58 was intended to protect the interests of detained patients. Peter Bartlett has, however, suggested that the presence of a second opinion may, in practice, make it difficult for psychiatric patients to challenge treatment through tort law:

> As for medication, the very protections provided by section 58 make a negligence action effectively impossible. How can a claim be made that the psychiatrist is negligent under *Bolam* when an SOAD, an officially selected and trained expert in the field, has signed off the treatment?[62]

In the past, there was undoubtedly a tendency for the SOAD to rubber stamp the first clinician's judgement. In the 1990s, for example, Phil Fennell found that SOADs approved treatment plans in 96 per cent of cases.[63] In *R (Wilkinson) v Broadmoor Special Hospital Authority*, the Court of Appeal was critical of the tendency to regard the SOAD's role as one of review, rather than independent assessment, and argued that a less deferential approach was necessary.

R (Wilkinson) v Broadmoor Special Hospital Authority[64]

Simon Brown LJ

Whilst, of course, it is proper for the SOAD to pay regard to the views of the RMO [responsible medical officer] who has, after all, the most intimate knowledge of the patient's case, that does not relieve him of the responsibility of forming his own independent judgment as to whether or not 'the treatment should be given'. And certainly, if the SOAD's certificate and evidence is to carry any real weight in cases where, as here, the treatment plan is challenged, it will be necessary to demonstrate a less deferential approach than appears to be the norm.

SOADs are now under a duty to provide reasons for their decisions. In *R (Wooder) v Feggetter*, the claimant's clinician decided that he should receive anti-psychotic medication, despite his refusal to consent. The SOAD had provided the necessary certificate under section 58(3)(b), but the claimant, who wanted his delusional condition to be treated without drugs, argued that the SOAD should provide reasons. The Court of Appeal agreed.

---

[61] Mental Capacity Act 2005 section 4.
[62] 'Psychiatric Treatment in the Absence of Law?' (2006) 14 Medical Law Review 124–31.
[63] Phil Fennell, *Treatment without Consent* (Routledge: London, 1996) 211.
[64] [2001] EWCA Civ 1545.

R (Wooder) v Feggetter[65]

Brooke LJ

With the coming into force of the Human Rights Act 1998 the time has come, in my judgment, for this court to declare that fairness requires that a decision by a SOAD which sanctions the violation of the autonomy of a competent adult patient should also be accompanied by reasons … I would be disposed to grant a declaration that fairness demands that a SOAD should give in writing the reasons for his opinion when certifying under section 58 of the Mental Health Act 1983 that a detained patient should be given medication against his will, and that these reasons should be disclosed to the patient unless the SOAD or the RMO considers that such disclosure would be likely to cause serious harm to the physical or mental health of the patient or any other person.

(c) TREATMENT UNDER SECTION 62 OF THE MENTAL HEALTH ACT 1983

An exception to sections 57 and 58 is created by section 62:

Mental Health Act 1983 section 62

62(1) Sections 57 and 58 above shall not apply to any treatment—

    (a) which is immediately necessary to save the patient's life; or

    (b) which (not being irreversible) is immediately necessary to prevent a serious deterioration of his condition; or

    (c) which (not being irreversible or hazardous) is immediately necessary to alleviate serious suffering by the patient; or

    (d) which (not being irreversible or hazardous) is immediately necessary and represents the minimum interference necessary to prevent the patient from behaving violently or being a danger to himself or to others …

  (3) For the purposes of this section treatment is irreversible if it has unfavourable irreversible physical or psychological consequences and hazardous if it entails significant physical hazard.

This means that, in an emergency, all treatments covered by sections 57 and 58 can be given without a second opinion or the patient's consent. Given that the treatments covered by section 57 are rarely used, and are unlikely to be 'immediately necessary', section 62's suspension of the protection contained in section 57 is of little practical importance. Instead, section 62 is mainly used to suspend the second opinion requirements in sections 58 and 58A, in relation to medication and ECT.[66] Although used comparatively infrequently, the principal

---

[65] [2002] EWCA Civ 554.

[66] Phil Fennell, *Treatment Without Consent: Law, Psychiatry and the Treatment of Mentally Disordered People since 1845* (Routledge: London, 1996) 199; Andy Bickle et al, 'Audit of statutory urgent treatment at a high security hospital' (2007) Journal of Mental Health Law 66.

effect of section 62's suspension of section 58 is that emergency ECT can be administered to a capacitous, refusing patient without her consent.

(d) TREATMENT UNDER SECTION 63 OF THE MENTAL HEALTH ACT 1983

Of more practical importance is section 63, which permits medical treatment for mental disorder to be provided without consent.

Mental Health Act 1983 section 63

The consent of a patient shall not be required for any medical treatment given to him for the mental disorder from which he is suffering, not being a form of treatment to which section 57, 58 or 58A above applies, if the treatment is given by or under the direction of the approved clinician in charge of the treatment.

Mental Health Act 1983 section 145(4)

Any reference in this Act to medical treatment, in relation to mental disorder, shall be construed as a reference to medical treatment the purpose of which is to alleviate, or prevent a worsening of, the disorder or one or more of its symptoms or manifestations.

Although the statute does not specify this, it has been taken for granted that it is also permissible to use force to administer treatment authorized under section 63. In *R v Broadmoor Special Hospital Authority, ex parte S, H and D*, Auld LJ suggested that the power to detain and treat without consent was, by implication, accompanied by 'the necessary incidents of control'.

R v Broadmoor Special Hospital Authority, ex parte S and others[67]

Auld LJ

Sections 3 and 37 of the 1983 Act provide for detention, not just for its own sake, but for treatment. Detention for treatment necessarily implies control for that purpose ... Both statutes leave unspoken many of the necessary incidents of control flowing from a power of detention for treatment, including: the power to restrain patients, to keep them in seclusion ... , to deprive them of their personal possessions for their own safety and to regulate the frequency and manner of visits to them.

---

[67] The Times, 17 February 1998.

The Mental Health Units (Use of Force) Act 2018 requires mental health units to publish data on how and when force is used. Force is defined in section 1(6)(a) and (b) as 'the use of physical, mechanical or chemical restraint on a patient' or 'the isolation of a patient'. The Act requires all mental health units to improve training and oversight, and to appoint a person to be accountable for its policies and for a reduction in the use of force.

It is important to remember that section 63 applies to adults with capacity. If a patient consents to treatment, there would be no need to resort to the power contained in section 63. In practice, then, this section enables treatment for mental disorder to be given to a capacitous adult, against her wishes, without the need for a second opinion. As a result, section 63 is radically out of step with the principle of patient autonomy.

Genevra Richardson[68]

At present the law in England and Wales is unusually inconsistent and discriminatory in the way it deals with questions of competence and patient autonomy with regard to mental disorder. The Mental Health Act 1983 permits a person suffering from a mental disorder of the necessary degree to be detained in hospital and treated for that disorder against her competent wishes ... Thus, while the common law grants patient autonomy a central role in relation to both physical and mental disorder, in relation to treatment of mental disorder of sufficient severity statute requires patient autonomy to cede to the values of paternalism and social protection. It was suggested above that the paternalist justification for this statutory approach originated in the now contested belief that mental disorder equates to loss of judgment. It is therefore interesting to note that the statutory powers of compulsion are limited to treatment for mental disorder; compulsory patients can still refuse treatment for physical disorder: judgment, it seems, is lost in relation to treatment for *mental* disorder only ...

Much, therefore, turns on the meaning given to mental disorder and if it is interpreted too generously there is a danger that a competent patient could be forced to accept treatment for a condition which has little or no bearing on his or her mental state.

As Genevra Richardson points out, much turns on the breadth or narrowness of the interpretation of the words 'treatment for the mental disorder from which he is suffering'. In the past, section 63 was used in order to justify a wide range of treatments, including caesarean delivery,[69] and the force-feeding of anorexic patients.

Re KB (Adult) (Mental Patient: Medical Treatment)[70]

Ewbank J

[A]norexia nervosa ... is an eating disorder and relieving symptoms is just as much a part of treatment as relieving the underlying cause. If the symptoms are exacerbated by the patient's refusal to eat and drink, the mental disorder becomes progressively more and more difficult to treat and so the treatment by nasogastric tube is an integral part of the treatment of the

---

[68] 'Autonomy, Guardianship and Mental Disorder: One Problem, Two Solutions' (2002) 65 Modern Law Review 702–23.
[69] *Tameside & Glossop Acute Services Unit v CH (a patient)* [1996] 1 FLR 762.
[70] [1994] 2 FCR 1051.

mental disorder itself. It is also said that the treatment is necessary in order to make psychiatric treatment of the underlying cause possible at all ... feeding by nasogastric tube in the circumstances of this type of case is treatment envisaged under s 63 and does not require the consent of the patient.

It is, of course, clear that force-feeding does not cure anorexia, and, as Penney Lewis explains in the next extract, repeated episodes of force-feeding can make recovery less likely.

Penney Lewis[71]

The anorexic's holy grail is control ... Force-feeding crushes the patient's will, destroying who the patient is. This is the antithesis of what a successful, therapeutic treatment must be ... The patient may be force-fed up to a more healthy weight and then discharged from hospital, free to return to her previous eating pattern and to lose the weight she has been forced to gain. As her trust has been violated, she may be less likely to seek medical help for her anorexia or for any other medical problem. The gain has been short-term, rather than long-term. The immediate crisis has been averted, but long-term damage has been done. Forcing treatment upon a young sufferer of anorexia merely reinforces her lack of self-confidence by taking this decision out of her control, and denies her the capacity for self-directed action which must be developed if she is to recover from this illness. Anorexics who have been force-fed may turn to the more life-threatening behaviour associated with bulimia, including vomiting and laxative abuse. They may be more likely to commit suicide, or to become entrenched in their refusal to eat and thereby become chronic sufferers.

Kirsty Keywood points out that the courts appeared surprisingly disinterested in whether force-feeding is an effective 'treatment' for anorexia.

Kirsty Keywood[72]

A number of clinicians perceive involuntary treatment as being necessary in a small number of cases in order to preserve life, restore weight, and restore patients' cognitive abilities to a sufficient degree that they may engage meaningfully in psychotherapy, without necessarily damaging the therapeutic alliance between doctor and patient. Others observe that compulsory treatment, with its higher mortality rate at follow up, may well compromise the relationship between doctor and patient and erode further the patient's self-esteem. Indeed, the courts' assessment of the appropriateness of involuntary treatment pays little regard to the consequences of overriding the expressed wishes of the patient diagnosed with anorexia nervosa. Notwithstanding the paucity of evidence that involuntary treatment of anorexia nervosa yields significant benefits to the patient in the long term, it is perhaps surprising that the courts have not given greater consideration to the appropriateness of interventions such as non-consensual nasogastric feeding ... The courts have traditionally premised their

---

[71] 'Feeding Anorexic Patients Who Refuse Food' (1999) 7 Medical Law Review 21–37.
[72] 'Rethinking the anorexic body: how English law and psychiatry "think"' (2003) 26 International Journal of Law and Psychiatry 599–616.

> judgments on a set of assumptions about the appropriateness of involuntary intervention in
> the treatment of anorexia nervosa which find (as yet) no firm empirical support within the do-
> mains of evidence-based medicine.

In *R v Collins, ex parte Brady*,[73] Ian Brady, one of the Moors murderers who was detained under the Mental Health Act 1983, had gone on hunger strike in order to protest against his perceived ill-treatment. Maurice Kay J held that force-feeding was justified under section 63 as treatment for the mental disorder from which he was suffering, because 'the hunger strike is a manifestation or symptom of the personality disorder'.

Using section 63 to compel refusing patients to undergo force-feeding sits rather oddly with the special protections given to other sorts of treatment in sections 58 and 58A of the Act. Neither ECT nor long-term medication can be given to a refusing patient without the approval of a SOAD. Forcibly inserting a nasogastric tube, against a patient's wishes, is arguably as intrusive as ECT or long-term medication, and yet it is not subject to the same restrictions.

More recently, in *Nottinghamshire Healthcare NHS Trust v RC*, it was acknowledged that while it might be possible to invoke section 63 in order to carry out a blood transfusion upon a man whose personality disorder resulted in serious self-harming behaviour, it would be 'an abuse of power' to impose a blood transfusion on him.

Nottinghamshire Healthcare Trust v RC[74]

> **Mostyn J**
>
> It cannot be disputed that the act of self harming, the slashing open of the brachial artery, is a symptom or manifestation of the underlying personality disorder. Therefore to treat the wound in any way is to treat the manifestation or symptom of the underlying disorder. So, indisputably, to suture the wound would be squarely within section 63. As would be the administration of a course of antibiotics to prevent infection. A consequence of bleeding from the wound is that haemoglobin levels are lowered. While it is strictly true, as Dr Latham says, that 'low haemo-globin is not wholly a manifestation or symptom of personality disorder', it is my view that to treat the low haemoglobin by a blood transfusion is just as much a treatment of a symptom or manifestation of the disorder as is to stitch up the wound or to administer antibiotics ...
>
> In my judgment it would be an abuse of power in such circumstances even to think about imposing a blood transfusion on RC having regard to my findings that he presently has capacity to refuse blood products and, were such capacity to disappear for any reason, the advance decision would be operative. To impose a blood transfusion would be a denial of a most basic freedom. I therefore declare that the decision of Dr S is lawful and that it is lawful for those responsible for the medical care of RC to withhold all and any treatment which is transfusion into him of blood or primary blood components (red cells, white cells, plasma or platelets) notwithstanding the existence of powers under section 63 MHA.

A more restrictive interpretation of section 63 was also evident in *An NHS Trust v A*, a case involving an Iranian doctor who was, like Ian Brady, on hunger strike, but where his physical need for nutrition was not said to be a manifestation of his mental disorder.

---

[73] [2000] Lloyd's Rep Med 355.   [74] [2014] EWCOP 1317.

An NHS Trust v A[75]

Baker J

I have found the views articulated by the treating clinicians, and in particular Dr WJ, persuasive. She does not consider that the administration of artificial nutrition and hydration to Dr A in the circumstances of this case to be a medical treatment for his mental disorder, but rather for a physical disorder that arises from his decision to refuse food. That decision is, of course, flawed in part because his mental disorder deprives him of the capacity to use and weigh information relevant to the decision. The physical disorder is thus in part a consequence of his mental disorder, but, in my judgment, it is not obviously either a manifestation or a symptom of the mental disorder.

In *R (on the application of B) v Ashworth Hospital Authority*, a slightly different question arose. The House of Lords had to consider whether section 63 only applied to treatment for the particular mental disorder that initially justified the patient's detention. B had been detained on the grounds that he was suffering from schizophrenia, but while he was in hospital he was diagnosed with a psychopathic disorder. B argued that the decision to transfer him to a ward for patients with psychopathic disorders, in order that he could be given treatment under section 63, was unlawful, because this was not the type of mental disorder that had justified his detention. The House of Lords rejected this argument.

R (on the application of B) v Ashworth Hospital Authority[76]

Lady Hale

I conclude that the words of section 63 mean what they say. They authorise a patient to be treated for any mental disorder from which he is suffering, irrespective of whether this falls within the form of disorder from which he is classified as suffering in the application, order or direction justifying his detention.

As I said earlier, compulsory patients are a vulnerable group who deserve protection from being forced to accept inappropriate treatment. But restricting their treatment to that which is designed for their 'classified' disorder is so haphazard as to be scarcely any protection at all ... [P]sychiatry is not an exact science. Diagnosis is not easy or clear cut. As this and many other cases show, a number of different diagnoses may be reached by the same or different clinicians over the years. As this case also shows, co-morbidity is very common ...

Once the state has taken away a person's liberty and detained him in a hospital with a view to medical treatment, the state should be able (some would say obliged) to provide him with the treatment which he needs. It would be absurd if a patient could be detained in hospital but had to be denied the treatment which his doctor thought he needed for an indefinite period while some largely irrelevant classification was rectified.

There has been some criticism of Lady Hale's conflation of detention and forcible treatment. Peter Bartlett has argued that forcibly injecting someone with medication may be more

---

[75] [2013] EWHC 2442 (COP).   [76] [2005] UKHL 20.

intrusive than the deprivation of liberty, and hence should require further justification.[77] Kris Gledhill further points out that a consequence of the Lords' decision in *B* is 'that a person can be detained for treatment in relation to one form of disorder but also treated for a form of disorder, which would not have justified his or her detention in the first place'.[78]

The Independent Review of the Mental Health Act 1983 has recommended that it should become more difficult to impose treatment on a patient without her consent.

The Independent Review of the Mental Health Act 1983[79]

- Shared decision-making between clinicians and patients should be used to develop care and treatment plans and all treatment decisions as far as is practicable.

- It should be harder for treatment refusals to be overridden, and any overrides should be recorded, justified and subject to scrutiny.

- Statutory advance choice documents (ACDs) should be created that enable people to make a range of choices and statements about their inpatient care and treatment. These should be piloted to identify the detail needed to inform/impact practice.

- Decisions about medication should, wherever possible, be in line with the patient's choice and patients should have a right to challenge treatments that do not reflect that choice.

- Patients should be able to request a SOAD review from once their care and treatment plan has been finalised or 14 days after their admission whichever is the sooner; and again, following any significant changes to treatment.

- Patients should be able to appeal treatment decisions at the Mental Health Tribunal following a SOAD review.

(e) THE IMPACT OF THE HUMAN RIGHTS ACT ON TREATMENT OF PEOPLE WITH MENTAL DISORDERS

Since the Human Rights Act 1998 came into force in 2001, the courts have had to consider whether treatment without consent might violate a patient's Convention rights.

(1) Article 3

According to Article 3 'no one shall be subjected to torture or to inhuman or degrading treatment or punishment'. This is supposed to be an absolute right, with no qualification, but the ECtHR's judgment in *Herczegfalvy v Austria* appears to create an exception to this absolute prohibition, provided that the inhuman or degrading treatment could be said to be medically necessary treatment for the patient's mental disorder.

---

[77] 'A Matter of Necessity? Enforced Treatment under the Mental Health Act' (2007) 15 Medical Law Review 86–98.

[78] 'The House of Lords and the unimportance of classification: a retrograde step' (2005) Journal of Mental Health Law 174.

[79] Final report of the Independent Review of the Mental Health Act 1983, *Modernising the Mental Health Act, Increasing choice, reducing compulsion* (DHSC, 2018).

Herczegfalvy v Austria[80]

Judgment of the ECtHR

While it is for the medical authorities to decide, on the basis of recognised rules of medical science, on the therapeutic methods to be used, if necessary by force, to preserve the physical and mental health of patients who are entirely incapable of deciding for themselves and for whom they are therefore responsible, such patients nevertheless remain under the protection of art 3, the requirements of which permit of no derogation.

The established principles of medicine are admittedly in principle decisive in such cases; as a general rule, a measure which is a therapeutic necessity cannot be regarded as inhuman or degrading. The court must nevertheless satisfy itself that the medical necessity has been convincingly shown to exist.

Herczegfalvy concerned a detained patient who was handcuffed and strapped to his bed, and these measures were said to be a therapeutic necessity:

In this case, according to the psychiatric principles generally accepted at that time, medical necessity justified the treatment in issue, including forcibly administered food and neuroleptics, isolation, and attaching handcuffs to a security bed. Thus, there was no violation of Article 3.

In *R (on the application of Munjaz) v Ashworth Hospital Authority*,[81] by a majority, the House of Lords held that a hospital authority's policy on seclusion, which provided for more infrequent review than that set out in the Mental Health Act Code of Practice, did not amount to inhuman or degrading treatment. The Lords took the view that the risk of ill-treatment was, in practice, very low and it would be disproportionate to require the hospital to change its policy. Stephanie Palmer has argued that this reasoning is problematic insofar as it introduces a proportionality balancing exercise into an unqualified Convention right: 'The unconditional wording of Article 3 renders the motivation for the alleged treatment irrelevant: the ends can never justify the means.'[82]

The introduction of qualifications to the Article 3 prohibition is contrary to the absolute approach advocated by the Committee for the Prevention of Torture, Inhuman or Degrading Treatment or Punishment.

Committee for the Prevention of Torture, Inhuman or Degrading Treatment or Punishment[83]

The admission of a person to a psychiatric establishment on an involuntary basis should not be construed as authorising treatment without his consent. It follows that every competent patient, whether voluntary or involuntary, should be given the opportunity to

---

[80] (1992) 15 EHRR 437.   [81] [2005] UKHL 58.

[82] Stephanie Palmer, 'A Wrong Turning: Article 3 ECHR and Proportionality' (2006) 65 Cambridge Law Journal 438–52.

[83] Council of Europe, *Report of the Committee for the Prevention of Torture, Inhuman or Degrading Treatment or Punishment* (Council of Europe, 2000) para 41.

refuse treatment or other medical intervention. Any derogation from this fundamental principle should be based upon law and only relate to clearly and strictly defined exceptional circumstances.

Peter Bartlett suggests that the courts' interpretation of section 63 does not meet this standard, because 'it allows unfettered treatment of any mental disorder with which the confined patient is affected without the patient's consent, no matter how small or great and whether or not the patient has capacity to consent to it'.[84]

To avoid being categorized as inhuman or degrading treatment, the medical necessity must be 'convincingly shown to exist'. What does this mean in practice, and how high is the standard of proof? These questions arose in *R (on the application of N) v M and Others*, a case in which a patient wanted to refuse anti-psychotic medication. Because she had obtained an independent opinion that she should not be given anti-psychotic medication, she argued, unsuccessfully, that it could not have been 'convincingly shown' that a medical necessity existed.

R (on the application of N) v M and Others[85]

Dyson LJ

In the light of [*Herczegfalvy v Austria*], it is common ground that the standard of proof required is that the court should be satisfied that medical necessity has been 'convincingly' shown … The phrase 'convincingly shown' is easily understood. The standard is a high one. But it does not need elaboration or further explanation …

Mr Kelly's submission on analysis involves the proposition that, in a case where there is a responsible body of opinion that a patient is not suffering from a treatable condition, then it cannot be convincingly shown that the treatment proposed is medically necessary. We reject this submission … In our judgment, the fact that there is a responsible body of opinion against the proposed treatment is relevant to the question whether it is in the patient's best interests or medically necessary, but it is no more than that.

In *R (on the application of JB) v Haddock (Responsible Medical Officer)*, the Court of Appeal decided that it was not necessary to show that the treatment, which was found to be a medical necessity, would actually work. While the Court of Appeal resisted expressing the burden of proof in forensic terms, they suggested that it probably amounted to no more than that there was a likelihood of therapeutic benefit.

R (on the application of JB) v Haddock (Responsible Medical Officer)[86]

Auld LJ

The s 58(3) power to treat a patient capable of consent against his will or a patient incapable of consent is potentially a violation of his Art 3 right not to be subjected to degrading treatment

---

[84] 'Psychiatric Treatment in the Absence of Law?' (2006) 14 Medical Law Review 124–31.
[85] [2002] EWCA Civ 1789.   [86] [2006] EWCA Civ 961.

and/or his Art 8 right to respect for his private life. However, it is common ground that, while the risk of infringement of those rights may be greater when the patient is capable of giving or refusing consent, it is not necessarily an infringement to treat him against his will where such treatment can be convincingly shown to be medically or therapeutically necessary ...

To require of psychiatrists a state of mind of precision and sureness in matters of diagnosis akin to that required of a jury in a criminal case, even in this fraught context of forcible treatment potentially violating detained patients' human rights, is not sensible or feasible ... And, as to whether the treatment will do any good, it is unreal to require psychiatrists, under the umbrella of a requirement of medical or therapeutic necessity, to demonstrate sureness or near sureness of success, especially when the Act itself, in s 58(3)(b) hinges the SOAD's certificate on his conclusion as to 'the likelihood' of it benefiting him.

Accordingly I do not consider that the requirement on a court to be convinced, in this context, of medical necessity in the light of the medical evidence and other evidence, is capable of being expressed in terms of a standard of evidential proof. It is rather a value judgement as to the future—a forecast—to be made by a court in reliance on medical evidence according to a standard of persuasion. If it is to be expressed in forensic terms at all, it is doubtful whether it amounts to more than satisfaction of medical necessity on a balance of probabilities, or as a 'likelihood' of therapeutic benefit.

Peter Bartlett is critical of the decision in *Haddock*, suggesting that it invokes professional uncertainty as grounds for weakening, rather than strengthening, the protection of patients' human rights.

Peter Bartlett[87]

This is an odd argument from a human rights standpoint, as it suggests that the fact that an area is fraught with uncertainty is a justification for restricting human rights protection within that area. If we are serious that treatment without consent constitutes an 'invasion', to use Auld LJ's word, it would instead seem that enforced interventions in such uncertain circumstances ought to be approached with particular caution ...

B's expert witness had called into question the appropriateness of treatment with antipsychotic medication for personality disorder. He acknowledged that such treatment was used by some clinicians, but stated that the evidence base for its efficacy was weak. Evidence-based practice is not a new concept in medicine; it seems not unreasonable to insist that practitioners wishing to treat persons without consent should at the very least be able to demonstrate a solid and objective foundation for their belief that the treatment would be beneficial to the patient ...

The outcome of the *Haddock* case would appear to be that any rights under Articles 3 or 8 of the ECHR to be free from involuntary treatment are to be subject to the professional practice of the psychiatric profession: that is not to be subject to significant scrutiny.

While section 63 can be used to justify the compulsory treatment of capacitous patients, the protection that is superimposed upon it by the Human Rights Act applies equally to patients who lack capacity. Hence, if a patient who lacks capacity does not want to be treated, treating

---

[87] 'A Matter of Necessity? Enforced Treatment under the Mental Health Act' (2007) 15 Medical Law Review 86–98.

her against her wishes could amount to inhuman or degrading treatment, and thus would be acceptable only if it could be convincingly shown to be a therapeutic necessity. In *Keenan v United Kingdom*, the solitary confinement of an incapacitated patient, who hanged himself shortly after he was placed in solitary confinement, was held to have amounted to a violation of Article 3.

Keenan v United Kingdom[88]

Judgment of the ECtHR

The lack of effective monitoring of Mark Keenan's condition and the lack of informed psychiatric input into his assessment and treatment disclose significant defects in the medical care provided to a mentally ill person known to be a suicide risk. The belated imposition on him in those circumstances of a serious disciplinary punishment—seven days' segregation in the punishment block and an additional twenty-eight days to his sentence imposed two weeks after the event and only nine days before his expected date of release—which may well have threatened his physical and moral resistance, is not compatible with the standard of treatment required in respect of a mentally ill person. It must be regarded as constituting inhuman and degrading treatment and punishment within the meaning of Article 3 of the Convention.

Accordingly, the Court finds a violation of this provision.

(2) Article 2

In *Keenan* the ECtHR also considered whether the failure to protect Mark Keenan might amount to a breach of the state's positive obligations under Article 2, to protect his right to life. The Court asked itself 'whether the authorities knew or ought to have known that Mark Keenan posed a real and immediate risk of suicide and, if so, whether they did all that reasonably could have been expected of them to prevent that risk?' It held that while the risk was real, the authorities' response to the risk of suicide was sufficient to discharge their duties under Article 2.

More recently, in *Savage v South Essex Partnership NHS Foundation Trust*, the House of Lords found that hospital authorities are under a general obligation to try to prevent suicides in detained patients, but that also—where there is a real and immediate risk of a particular patient committing suicide—there is a more specific 'operational' obligation under Article 2 to do all that can reasonably be expected to prevent her from committing suicide.

Savage v South Essex Partnership NHS Foundation Trust[89]

Lord Rodger

The hospital authorities are ... responsible for the health and wellbeing of their detained patients. Their obligations under article 2 include an obligation to protect those patients from self-harm and suicide. Indeed ... the very fact that patients are detained carries with it a risk of suicide against which the hospital authorities must take general precautions.

---

[88] Application no 27229/95 (2001) 10 BHRC 319.   [89] [2008] UKHL 74.

I am accordingly satisfied that, as a public authority, the trust was under a general obligation, by virtue of article 2, to take precautions to prevent suicides among detained patients in Runwell Hospital ...

The hospital's systems of work—and, doubtless, also its plant and equipment—had to take account of the risk that detained patients might try to commit suicide. When deciding on the most appropriate treatment and therapeutic environment for detained patients, medical staff would have to take proper account of the risk of suicide. But the risk would not be the same for all patients. Those who presented a comparatively low risk could be treated in a more open environment, without the need for a high degree of supervision. Those who presented a greater risk would need to be supervised to an appropriate extent, while those presenting the highest risk would have to be supervised in a locked ward. The level of risk for any particular patient could be expected to vary with fluctuations in his or her medical condition. In deciding what precautions were appropriate for any given patient at any given moment, the doctors would take account of both the potentially adverse effect of too much supervision on the patient's condition and the possible positive benefits to be expected from a more open environment. Such decisions involve clinical judgment ...

[A]rticle 2 imposes a further 'operational' obligation on health authorities and their hospital staff. This obligation is distinct from, and additional to, the authorities' more general obligations. The operational obligation arises only if members of staff know or ought to know that a particular patient presents a 'real and immediate' risk of suicide. In these circumstances article 2 requires them to do all that can reasonably be expected to prevent the patient from committing suicide. If they fail to do this, not only will they and the health authorities be liable in negligence, but there will also be a violation of the operational obligation under article 2 to protect the patient's life.

The House of Lords decided that the question of whether there had, in this case, been a breach of Carol Savage's rights, should be allowed to go to trial. Two years later, in *Savage v South Essex Partnership NHS Foundation Trust*,[90] Mackay J held that the trust had not done all that could reasonably have been expected of them to prevent Carol Savage's suicide. He awarded her daughter £10,000 in damages, not to compensate for her mother's death but as 'a symbolic acknowledgement' of her loss.

Four years after the House of Lords' decision in *Savage*, the UK Supreme Court extended the operational duty to prevent a patient from committing suicide to a patient who had not been formally detained. Following a number of suicide attempts, Melanie Rabone had been admitted to hospital as an informal patient in April 2005. The risk of further attempts at suicide was judged to be moderate to high. At the time of her admission, it was noted that, if she tried to leave, she should be assessed for detention under the Mental Health Act. On 19 April, Melanie requested home leave, which was granted; the following day she committed suicide. Her parents brought both a civil negligence claim and a claim for damages for breach of a positive duty to protect Melanie's right to life under Article 2 against the Pennine Care NHS Foundation Trust.

The trust admitted that the decision to allow home leave was negligent and it settled that claim on behalf of Melanie's estate for £7,500. Her parents' Article 2 claim for damages was unsuccessful in the High Court and in the Court of Appeal, but in *Rabone v Pennine Care NHS Foundation Trust*, the Supreme Court allowed their appeal. It held that informally admitted patients might be just as vulnerable and just as much under the control of the

---

[90] [2010] EWHC 865 (QB).

state as detained patients. In reality, Melanie should not have been free to leave. In these circumstances, the operational duty under Article 2 could be owed if there was a 'real and immediate risk' to life. Because preventing Melanie from attempting suicide was the reason why she had been admitted to hospital, it was clear that the risk in this case was real and immediate.

Rabone v Pennine Care NHS Foundation Trust[91]

Lord Dyson

When finding that the article 2 operational duty has been breached, the ECtHR has repeatedly emphasised the vulnerability of the victim as a relevant consideration. In circumstances of sufficient vulnerability, the ECtHR has been prepared to find a breach of the operational duty even where there has been no assumption of control by the state . . .

The jurisprudence of the operational duty is young. Its boundaries are still being explored by the ECtHR as new circumstances are presented to it for consideration. But it seems to me that the court has been tending to expand the categories of circumstances in which the operational duty will be found to exist . . .

As regards the differences between an informal psychiatric patient and one who is detained under the MHA, these are in many ways more apparent than real . . . She had been admitted to hospital because she was a real suicide risk. By reason of her mental state, she was extremely vulnerable. The trust assumed responsibility for her. She was under its control. Although she was not a detained patient, it is clear that, if she had insisted on leaving the hospital, the authorities could and should have exercised their powers under the MHA to prevent her from doing so . . . In reality, the difference between her position and that of a hypothetical detained psychiatric patient, who (apart from the fact of being detained) was in circumstances similar to those of Melanie, would have been one of form, not substance.

Lady Hale

There is a difficult balance to be struck between the right of the individual patient to freedom and self-determination and her right to be prevented from taking her own life. She wanted to go home and her doctor thought that it would be good for her to begin to take responsibility for herself. He was obviously wrong about that, but was he so wrong that the hospital is to be held in breach of her human rights for failing to protect her?

[I]in this case it also appears that there was no proper assessment of the risks before she was given leave and no proper planning for her care during the leave . . . There is every indication that had she remained in hospital she would not have succeeded in killing herself. The question was whether she should have been allowed to go home for a whole weekend. Having regard to the nature and degree of the risk to her life, and the comparative ease of protecting her from it, I agree that her right to life was violated.

In the next extract, Nicola Glover-Thomas points out that the practical consequence of the *Rabone* and *Savage* decisions may be increased use of compulsory powers.

---

[91] [2012] UKSC 2.

Nicola Glover-Thomas[92]

The practical impact of these cases is noteworthy … The recognition of the operational duty to protect the life of a specific individual in cases of suicide risk where it is known or should have been known that there was a 'real and immediate risk of suicide' has reinforced the obligation placed upon health care professionals. Given the acknowledged difficulty surrounding accurate risk assessment, an issue that was highlighted in *Rabone*, both *Savage* and *Rabone* present significant implications for public bodies who assume responsibility of vulnerable people.

The effect of *Cheshire West*, *Savage* and *Rabone* has led to greater sensitivity to risk and the potential repercussions should something go wrong. When there is doubt or uncertainty, it is now more likely the civil commitment provisions in the MHA 1983 will be seen as the best option and use of informal hospitalisation will be less attractive.

(3) Article 8

The right to be free from non-consensual medical treatment might also be protected by Article 8, the right to respect for private and family life. In *X v Austria*,[93] for example, the European Commission explicitly stated that 'compulsory medical intervention, even if it is of minor importance, must be considered an interference with this right'. In practice, however, the protection offered by Article 8 is qualified if the interference can be shown to be 'necessary in a democratic society' for, among other things, 'the protection of health'. This, as the Court of Appeal explained in *R (on the application of N) v M and Others*,[94] means that if the treatment has been convincingly shown to be medically necessary, neither Article 3 nor Article 8 will have been violated, since the interference with the right to respect for private life would be proportionate, and justified within the terms of Article 8(2).

Article 8 has also been invoked in order to challenge other sorts of restrictions on mental health patients' freedom, such as, in *R (on the application of G) v Nottinghamshire Healthcare NHS Trust*,[95] the smoking ban in Rampton hospital. The Administrative Court rejected the inpatients' claim that Article 8 created a 'right to smoke' in what was effectively one's home.

(f) THE UNITED NATIONS CONVENTION ON THE RIGHTS OF PERSONS WITH DISABILITIES

The UK has signed and ratified the United Nations Convention on the Rights of Persons with Disabilities (CRPD). It is, however, arguable that the provisions in the Mental Health Act that permit compulsory treatment and detention are non-compliant.

Articles 14 and 17 of the Convention specifically address the liberty and bodily integrity of people with mental disabilities.

UN Convention on the Rights of Persons with Disabilities

Article 14

1. States Parties shall ensure that persons with disabilities, on an equal basis with others:

   a. Enjoy the right to liberty and security of person;

---

[92] 'Decision-Making Behaviour under the Mental Health Act 1983 and Its Impact on Mental Health Tribunals: An English Perspective' (2018) 7 Laws 12.
[93] (1980) 18 DR 154 at 156.   [94] [2002] EWCA Civ 1789.   [95] [2008] EWHC 1096 (Admin).

b. Are not deprived of their liberty unlawfully or arbitrarily, and that any deprivation of liberty is in conformity with the law, and that the existence of a disability shall in no case justify a deprivation of liberty ...

Article 17

Every person with disabilities has a right to respect for his or her physical and mental integrity on an equal basis with others.

Unlike the European Convention, with its 'unsound mind' exception to the right to liberty, the UN CRPD states explicitly that mental disability does not justify the deprivation of liberty or interference with someone's physical or mental integrity. As Peter Bartlett explains, this is extraordinarily significant.

Peter Bartlett [96]

For people with mental disabilities, the CRPD represents an additional and highly significant change. Previously, international regulation had assumed that control of this group was in some circumstances justified; the issue was determining the bounds of permitted compulsion. The CRPD takes no such starting point. Indeed, as will be discussed below, the CRPD appears to proceed on the basis that disability cannot be used as a factor in determining whether compulsion may be imposed. For people with mental disabilities, this would be an extraordinary change ... The UN High Commissioner for Human Rights has stated that the CRPD requires the abolition of laws that allow for detention, for the removal of legal capacity, or for criminal defences, when those laws rely in whole or in part on mental disability. Insofar as this is correct, it is difficult to see that UK mental health legislation is remotely compliant. The terms of the CRPD also raise profound questions about the compliance of UK legislation governing mental capacity. The government would appear to be in denial about this, taking the view that UK legislation is in fact in compliance with the CRPD.

George Szmukler agrees that by singling out people with disabilities for special treatment, mental health legislation is almost inevitably non-compliant.

George Szmukler[97]

What is clear ... is that any law that allows an interference with the rights of a person that is restricted to persons with a disability is discriminatory. Mental health legislation, virtually everywhere, transgresses this injunction. 'Mental disorder' in one form or another appears on the face of the legislation. No matter how many other criteria are specified – whether the law additionally only permits the person's detention or involuntary treatment in the interests of the

---

[96] 'The United Nations Convention on the Rights of Persons with Disabilities and Mental Health Law' (2012) 75 Modern Law Review 752–78.

[97] 'The UN Convention on the Rights of Persons with Disabilities: "Rights, will and preferences" in relation to mental health disabilities' (2017) International Journal of Law and Psychiatry 90–7.

person or to protect others – in thus singling out a particular group of people with a disability for special interference, such legislation in the view of the Committee breaches the Convention.

Of course, as John Dawson points out, completely expunging any reference to mental impairment from the law might itself cause difficulties.

John Dawson[98]

It is not discrimination to say that a blind person can be denied the right to drive, under the relevant legislation, when they cannot see. Nor is it discrimination to say that a person's firearms license can be suspended when acute paranoid delusions about their neighbours affect their ability to use a weapon responsibly—even when that decision does involve treating that person differently to others, and does rely on aspects of their mental functioning, that may be associated with a disability, when applying the legal test … [O]nly an impoverished legal system would consider it wholly irrelevant to a person's ability to make a will, or take full responsibility for hitting someone, or serve on a jury or as a judge, or continue as a company director, that they currently suffer significant cognitive impairment as a consequence of Alzheimer's disease.

Dawson advocates a 'conservative' interpretation of the Convention, which would not completely rule out substitute decision-making. But this would appear to be at odds with the General Comment, issued by the UN's Committee on the Rights of Persons with Disabilities in 2014,[99] which gave the words in the Convention a literal interpretation. According to the Committee's General Comment, the CRPD prohibits compulsory treatment, involuntary admission, and substitute decision-making. In their 2017 report into the UK's compliance with the CRPD, the Committee's conclusion was blunt and uncompromising:

The Committee recommends that the State party [the UK]: Repeal legislation and practices that authorize non-consensual involuntary, compulsory treatment and detention of persons with disabilities on the basis of actual or perceived impairment.[100]

In the next extract, Melvyn Freeman et al are critical of the Committee's interpretation, suggesting that, in practice, it might interfere with individuals' right to health, and increase stigma.

Melvyn Freeman et al[101]

[I]f a person having a severe exacerbation of affective or psychotic illness is not provided proven, effective treatment, can he or she be said to be receiving the highest attainable

---

[98] 'A realistic approach to assessing mental health laws' compliance with the UNCRPD' (2015) 40 International Journal of Law and Psychiatry 70–9.

[99] Committee on the Rights of Persons with Disabilities, General Comment No. 1, *Article 12: Equal Recognition Before the Law*, 11th session, 31 March–11 April 2014.

[100] United Nations Committee on the Rights of Persons with Disabilities, *Concluding observations on the initial report of the United Kingdom of Great Britain and Northern Ireland* (3 October 2017, CRPD/C/GBR/CO/1), para 35.

[101] 'Reversing hard won victories in the name of human rights: a critique of the General Comment on Article 12 of the UN Convention on the Rights of Persons with Disabilities' (2015) 2 The Lancet Psychiatry 844–50.

standard of health? Best evidence so far on psychiatric disorders tells us that some severe psychotic illnesses can impair decision-making capacity ... That is, decision-making might be by definition impaired and hence merely supporting decisions when a person is in a state of severe psychosis, including treatment decisions, could seriously undermine that person's right to health care ...

Importantly, the likelihood of a person making a recovery to the point of regaining capacity and therefore being able to give informed consent is often diminished without treatment. In the example of psychosis, we might be undermining the right to health to allow a person to stay in a psychotic state and never allow them to get to a point of refusing or accepting treatment in an informed manner.

One might imagine that a consequence of the General Comment's interpretation is that there might end up being more persons with severe mental illness untreated in the community, which might exacerbate ignorance, fear, and stigma surrounding mental disorders. An unintended consequence of the General Comment might be more public calls for the locking up of people with mental disabilities or human rights violations of untreated persons with severe mental illness in the community.

More optimistically, Genevra Richardson considers whether the Convention might help to ensure that service users are routinely involved in decisions about their care.

Genevra Richardson[102]

There are, however, grounds for optimism. At the heart of supported decision-making lies the need to encourage and enhance the participation of service users at all stages of their care. This can only improve services and, even in the absence of large-scale legislative reform, it can be emphasized and encouraged across the sector in relation to both intellectual impairments and psychosocial disorders ...

The importance of participative decision-making is certainly now recognized officially, but a major culture shift may be required if we are to achieve a fundamental move away from the imposition of substitute decisions, in favour of finding ways of encouraging the participation of service users in practice, and of supporting them to make their own decisions. Perhaps the UN Convention can provide the necessary spur ...

There is now a small but growing literature discussing the possible measures of support that might be developed, such as the Swedish system of mentors and personal assistants ... 'Social connectedness' interventions have also been trialled in the simple form of sending a series of reassuring postcards to patients who had been admitted after self-harm ...

If we are to achieve a significant cultural shift from substitute, to participative and supported decision-making, across the entire sector much, much more work is needed. That, in my view, would be a significant paradigm shift to aim for right now while we await the political will to tinker once again with the law.

Although it is Articles 14 and 17 which have received most attention in the context of mental health law, it is worth noting that other parts of the Convention might also be significant. In particular, the Convention not only protects negative rights to be free from forced treatment

---

[102] 'Mental Disabilities and the Law: From Substitute to Supported Decision-Making?' (2012) 65 Current Legal Problems 333–54.

and detention, but, as Jill Stavert and Rebecca McGregor explain, it also contains positive social and economic rights to services. An example is Article 26.

Article 26

1. States parties shall take effective and appropriate measures, including through peer support, to enable persons with disabilities to attain and maintain maximum independence, full physical, mental, social and vocational ability, and full inclusion and participation in all aspects of life. To that end, States Parties shall organize, strengthen and extend comprehensive habilitation and rehabilitation services and programmes, particularly in the areas of health, employment, education and social services, in such a way that these services and programmes:

    (a) Begin at the earliest possible stage, and are based on the multidisciplinary assessment of individual needs and strengths;

    (b) Support participation and inclusion in the community and all aspects of society, are voluntary, and are available to persons with disabilities as close as possible to their own communities, including in rural areas.

Jill Stavert and Rebecca McGregor[103]

The positive duties [articles 25 and 26] impose on states to provide services specifically related to a person's disability considerably open up the right to health for individuals with mental disorder both to prevent such disorder and to minimise its impact …

Article 25 of the CRPD recognises the 'right to the enjoyment of the highest attainable standard of health', and does this by linking this right with the provision of services… Article 26(1), in identifying the right to habilitation and rehabilitation, contains extensive requirements for full inclusion and participation in society.

6 DISCHARGE

Once a patient has been detained, it is important that her detention continues to be justified by her condition. If she no longer needs to be detained, she should be discharged. As the ECtHR explained in *Winterwerp v The Netherlands*,[104] in order to fall within the 'unsound mind' exception to the right to liberty in Article 5(1)(e), 'the mental disorder must be of a kind or degree warranting compulsory confinement. What is more, the validity of continued confinement depends upon the persistence of such a disorder.'

The responsible clinician (RC) has an ongoing duty to consider whether the conditions that justified the patient's original detention continue to exist. Because the extent to which a patient is affected by their mental disorder may fluctuate, Article 5(4) requires that there is a formal mechanism to review or challenge the lawfulness of continued detention at reasonable intervals.

---

[103] 'Domestic legislation and international human rights standards: the case of mental health and incapacity' (2018) 22 The International Journal of Human Rights 70–89.

[104] Application no 6301/73, ECHR series A, vol 33 (1979).

(a) REVIEW OF DETENTION

Detentions under section 2 will automatically lapse after 28 days, and unless the patient is formally detained under section 3, the patient must be discharged. For patients detained under section 3, section 68 provides that hospital managers have a duty to refer their case to the First-Tier Tribunal (Mental Health) after six months, and thereafter every three years.

Under section 66 of the 1983 Act, a patient who has been admitted to hospital compulsorily under section 2 or 3 of the Act has a right to request that the Tribunal considers whether they should be discharged. In practice, orders for the discharge of patients are comparatively rare. In 2016/17, there were 30,079 applications to the tribunal, with 17,744 hearings; in 73 per cent of hearings, detention was upheld as justified in whole or in part and in the interests of the patient.[105]

Tribunal hearings take place on hospital premises. This has practical advantages, but, as Nicola Glover-Thomas has pointed out, it can also present problems. First, there is a risk that 'hearings may not be seen to be acting as an independent judicial mechanism because they convene within the same space as the detention process'.[106] Secondly, given that hearings take place 'up and down the country', it is difficult to ensure consistency between different tribunals' decision-making.

Of course, not all patients have the capacity to exercise their right to challenge their detention, and in the case of *MH v United Kingdom*, the question arose whether, for such patients, automatic referral to a court was necessary in order that the lawfulness of their detention could be reviewed speedily by a court, as required by Article 5. MH was a woman in her thirties with Down's syndrome, who had been admitted under section 2. She lacked the capacity to appeal to the Tribunal herself, but the House of Lords unanimously held that the failure to refer her case for judicial review of her detention did not amount to a breach of Article 5(4).[107] MH then appealed to the European Court of Human Rights, which eight years later held that the UK must have 'special safeguards' in place to protect the rights of those who lack the capacity to challenge the lawfulness of their detention.

MH v United Kingdom[108]

Judgment of the ECtHR

As the right set forth in Article 5 § 4 of the Convention is guaranteed to everyone, it is clear that special safeguards are called for in the case of detained mental patients who lack legal capacity to institute proceedings before judicial bodies ...

Neither the applicant nor her mother acting as her nearest relative was able in practice to avail themselves of the normal remedy granted by the 1983 Act to patients detained under section 2 for assessment. That being so, in relation to the initial measure taken by social services depriving her of her liberty, the applicant did not, at the relevant time, before the elucidation of the legal framework by the House of Lords in her case, have the benefit of effective access to a mechanism enabling her to 'take proceedings' of the kind guaranteed to her by Article 5 § 4 of the Convention ...

---

[105] Care Quality Commission, *Monitoring the Mental Health Act in 2016-17* (CQC, 2018).

[106] Nicola Glover-Thomas, 'Decision-Making Behaviour under the Mental Health Act 1983 and Its Impact on Mental Health Tribunals: An English Perspective' (2018) 7 Laws 12.

[107] *R (on the application of H) v Secretary of State for Health* [2005] UKHL 60.

[108] Application no 11577/06 (22 October 2013).

> Therefore, in the particular circumstances of the present case there was a violation of Article 5 § 4 of the Convention in relation to the applicant's initial detention by administrative order for the purposes of medical assessment in hospital.

The government's response was that changes introduced by the 2007 Act, and an amendment to the Code of Practice, have cured this defect.[109] A local authority now has a duty to make independent mental health advocates (IMHAs) available to help detained patients,[110] including taking such steps as are practicable to enable them to understand their right to access the courts and to representation.[111] In addition, the Code of Practice now provides that 'If a patient lacks capacity to decide whether to seek a review of detention or a CTO, an IMHA should be introduced to the patient so that the IMHA can explain what help they can offer.'[112]

(b) CRITERIA FOR REVIEW

Tribunals do not judge whether the initial decision to detain was right or wrong. Rather, as Collins J explained in *R (on the application of Care Principles Ltd) v Mental Health Review Tribunal*, tribunals assess whether, on the balance of probabilities, grounds for detention exist at the time of the hearing.

R (on the application of Care Principles Ltd) v Mental Health Review Tribunal[113]

Collins J

[T]he Tribunal is concerned with the condition of the patient when the Tribunal considers the matter. Whether or not he was properly taken into hospital is not material for that consideration ... The question before the Tribunal is: is the detention proper now? The burden is upon the hospital, or those who seek his continued detention, to establish that that detention is necessary and within the terms of the Act.

It is always necessary for any such detention to be justified. The standard required is the balance of probabilities. The Tribunal has to be persuaded that it is more probable than not that the detention is needed.

Section 72 sets out the criteria for discharge.

Mental Health Act 1983 section 72

72(1) ...

    (a) the tribunal shall direct the discharge of a patient liable to be detained under section 2 above if [it is] not satisfied—

        (i) that he is then suffering from mental disorder of a nature or degree which

---

[109] Ministry of Justice, *Responding to human rights judgments: Report to the Joint Committee on Human Rights on the Government response to human rights judgments 2013–14* (MoJ, 2014).

[110] Section 130A.   [111] Section 130D.

[112] Mental Health Act 1983 Code of Practice, para 4.23.   [113] [2006] EWHC 3194 (Admin).

warrants his detention in a hospital for assessment (or for assessment followed by medical treatment) for at least a limited period; or

(ii) that his detention as aforesaid is justified in the interests of his own health or safety or with a view to the protection of other persons;

(b) the tribunal shall direct the discharge of a patient liable to be detained otherwise than under section 2 above if [it is] not satisfied—

(i) that he is then suffering from mental disorder of a nature or degree which makes it appropriate for him to be liable to be detained in a hospital for medical treatment; or

(ii) that it is necessary for the health or safety of the patient or for the protection of other persons that he should receive such treatment; or

(iia) that appropriate medical treatment is available for him; or

(iii) in the case of an application by virtue of paragraph (g) of section 66(1) above, that the patient, if released, would be likely to act in a manner dangerous to other persons or to himself.

Notice that, as with detention under sections 2 and 3, for continued detention to be justified, the patient has to be suffering from a mental disorder of a nature *or* degree which warrants detention in hospital. In *R v Mental Health Review Tribunal for the South Thames Region, ex parte Smith*,[114] the court held that this means that someone might be detained on the grounds that the condition from which they are suffering generally justifies detention, even if at the time of the application, they are not affected to a 'degree' which warrants detention in hospital. Peter Bartlett and Ralph Sandland are critical of this wording.

Peter Bartlett and Ralph Sandland[115]

[T]he requirement in *Winterwerp* is for unsound mind sufficient to 'justify' detention, and we would want to argue, as has not been done to date before the European Court, that a test which allows nature 'or' degree permits detention when a person's disorder is of a nature but *not* of a degree to justify compulsory hospitalisation, which is outside of the spirit of the Convention. In our, perhaps optimistic, view, the preferable and Convention-compliant wording must be that the mental disorder in question is of both a nature *and* a degree to warrant detention.

If the Tribunal decides that the criteria for detention are not made out, it must order the patient's discharge. Discharge can, however, be deferred, if arrangements have to be made for the patient's accommodation and/or care.

The Tribunal must give reasons for its decision. Where there is conflicting evidence, the Tribunal must explain, in language that can be understood by the patient, why one witness's evidence was preferred. In *R v Ashworth Hospital Authority, ex parte H*,[116] the Tribunal ordered the immediate discharge of a patient, despite the fact that five out of six medical reports had been against discharge. The Court of Appeal found that this decision was *Wednesbury*[117]

---

[114] The Times, 9 December 1998.
[115] *Mental Health Law: Policy and Practice*, 3rd edn (OUP: Oxford, 2007) 403.
[116] [2002] EWCA Civ 923.
[117] *Associated Provincial Picture Houses v Wednesbury Corporation* [1948] 1 KB 223.

unreasonable, since no reasonable tribunal could have come to this decision in the light of the evidence before it, and furthermore that the Tribunal's reasons—namely that it simply preferred the evidence of the one doctor who believed discharge to be appropriate—were insufficient.

(c) THE NEED FOR SPEEDY REVIEW

The question of how 'speedy' the legal challenge must be to satisfy Article 5(4) arose in *R (on the application of C) v Mental Health Review Tribunal*.[118] C had been detained in hospital under section 3 of the Mental Health Act 1983 and immediately applied to the Tribunal for discharge. At the time, it was the practice of the Tribunal to list hearings of applications for discharge eight weeks after the application had been made. C submitted that the practice was arbitrary and insufficiently 'speedy', and the Court of Appeal agreed:

> I do not consider lawful a practice which makes no effort to see that the individual application is heard as soon as reasonably practicable, having regard to the relevant circumstances of the case. Such a practice will inevitably result in some applications not leading to the speedy decision required by article 5(4).[119]

Similarly, in *R v Mental Health Review Tribunal, ex parte KB*,[120] a conjoined application was brought by a number of patients who had waited between four and 27 weeks for a hearing. The reasons for the delays included difficulties in preparing reports and in timetabling tribunal hearings. Stanley Burton J found that lack of resources did not offer a defence to the breach of Article 5(4), and it was 'irrelevant to the question whether there has been an infringement of Article 5(4) which government department or other public authority was at fault'.

(d) STATUS OF THE TRIBUNAL DECISION

If the responsible clinician (RC) disagrees with the Tribunal's decision to order a patient's discharge, is there anything to stop her simply readmitting the patient under section 3? Of course, if circumstances have changed significantly between the time of the hearing and the time of readmission, this might be legitimate. But where there has not been a substantial change of circumstances, RCs should not attempt to override the Tribunal's decision through a new admission.

In *R v East London and the City Mental Health NHS Trust, ex parte Von Brandenburg*,[121] the patient's discharge had been ordered by the Tribunal, but had been deferred for seven days so that suitable accommodation could be found. Six days later, the patient's clinician arranged for his readmission under section 3 of the Mental Health Act 1983. The patient sought judicial review of the decision to readmit him.

The House of Lords found that it would not be lawful to readmit a patient despite the Tribunal's decision to discharge her, unless the Approved Mental Health Practitioner (AMHP) 'has formed the reasonable and bona fide opinion that he has information not known to the Tribunal which puts a significantly different complexion on the case as compared with that which was before the Tribunal'.[122] Re-sectioning is therefore only appropriate where new

---

[118] [2001] EWCA Civ 1110.   [119] Per Lord Phillips MR.   [120] [2002] EWHC 639 (Admin).
[121] [2003] UKHL 58.   [122] Per Lord Bingham.

material facts have come to light, and must not be used to override Tribunal decisions with which the RC disagrees.

7 COMMUNITY CARE

There are two types of community care: first, primary care services are supposed to ensure that mentally disordered individuals living in the community have access to appropriate treatment. Secondly, as we see below, community treatment orders enable a degree of control and supervision to be exercised over people who are not ill enough to be detained in hospital.

Compulsory treatment in the community is not possible, however. In *R (on the application of H) v Mental Health Review Tribunal*, a patient who had been discharged from hospital was subject to a condition that he should receive fortnightly injections. Holman J reiterated that the Mental Health Act 1983 could not be used to force a patient to submit to treatment in the community.

R (on the application of H) v Mental Health Review Tribunal[123]

Holman J

The law with regard to consent to treatment is clear ... An adult of full capacity has an absolute right to choose whether to consent to medical treatment ... Thus in this case, on each occasion that SH attends, or should attend, for his fortnightly depot injection he has an absolute right to choose whether to consent to it or not. The treating doctor or nurse must, on each occasion, satisfy himself that the apparent consent is a real consent and that the independence of the patient's decision or his will has not been overborne.

(a) AFTERCARE SERVICES

Section 117 of the Mental Health Act 1983 requires clinical commissioning groups and local social services, in cooperation with voluntary agencies, to provide aftercare services to those who have been discharged from detention under the Act. Usually, aftercare services involve medical treatment, help with accommodation, and assistance with education and training. Services must be provided free of charge,[124] and where the Tribunal has ordered a conditional discharge, the health authority must ensure that the appropriate arrangements are in place.[125]

But what if a health authority cannot find health care professionals who are prepared to take responsibility for a patient's treatment after discharge? This issue arose in *Camden and Islington Health Authority, ex parte K*, where it proved impossible to find a psychiatrist willing to supervise the applicant's care in the community. The House of Lords held that section 117 should not be taken to impose an absolute and unworkable obligation on health authorities.

---

[123] [2007] EWHC 884 (Admin).

[124] *R v Manchester City Council, ex parte Stennett* [2002] UKHL 34.

[125] *R v Ealing District Health Authority, ex parte Fox* [1993] 1 WLR 373.

Camden and Islington Health Authority, ex parte K[126]

Lord Phillips

[S]ection 117 imposes on health authorities a duty to provide aftercare facilities for the benefit of patients who are discharged from mental hospitals. The nature and extent of those facilities must, to a degree, fall within the discretion of the health authority, which must have regard to other demands on its budget . . .

I can see no justification for interpreting section 117 so as to impose on health authorities an absolute obligation to satisfy any conditions that a Tribunal may specify as prerequisites to the discharge of a patient . . . An interpretation of section 117 which imposed on health authorities absolute duties which they would not necessarily be able to perform would be manifestly unreasonable . . .

If a health authority is unable, despite the exercise of all reasonable endeavours, to procure for a patient the level of care and treatment in the community that a Tribunal considers to be a prerequisite to the discharge of the patient from hospital, I do not consider that the continued detention of the patient in hospital will violate the right to liberty conferred by article 5.

K then appealed to the ECtHR, which confirmed that there had been no violation of Article 5(1)(e).[127]

Kolanis v United Kingdom[128]

Judgment of the ECtHR

As events in the present case showed, the treatment considered necessary for such conditional discharge may not prove available, in which circumstances there can be no question of interpreting Article 5 § 1(e) as requiring the applicant's discharge without the conditions necessary for protecting herself and the public or as imposing an absolute obligation on the authorities to ensure that the conditions are fulfilled.

A different issue arose in *Secretary of State for Justice v MM*, in which MM, a mentally disordered offender, applied for conditional discharge. MM had a diagnosis of learning disability, autistic spectrum disorder, and pathological fire setting, and on conviction for arson, he had been subject to a hospital order under section 37 of the Mental Health Act, and a restriction order under section 41. MM was anxious to leave hospital, and was willing to consent to a very restrictive regime in the community. The level of restriction, supervision and monitoring under which he could safely be released would amount to a deprivation of liberty within the meaning of article 5: that is, he would be required to live at a particular place, which he would not be free to leave, and he would not be allowed out without an escort.

Although it was agreed that MM had the capacity to consent, the Tribunal did not consider that it had the power to impose conditions that amounted to a deprivation of liberty, and, by a four to one majority (Lord Hughes dissenting), the UK Supreme Court agreed. In short, if

---

[126] [2001] EWCA Civ 240.

[127] See also *R v Secretary of State for the Home Department, ex parte IH* [2003] UKHL 59.

[128] [2005] ECHR 411.

parliament had intended to allow restricted patients to consent to the deprivation of their liberty in the community, it would have said so explicitly.

Secretary of State for Justice v MM [129]

Lady Hale (with whom Lord Kerrs and Lloyd-Jones and Lady Black agreed)

The first reason is one of high principle: the power to deprive a person of his liberty is by definition an interference with his fundamental right to liberty of the person. This engages the rule of statutory construction known as the principle of legality, as explained in the well-known words of Lord Hoffmann in *R v Secretary of State for the Home Department, Ex p Simm*

> '... the principle of legality means that Parliament must squarely confront what it is doing and accept the political cost. Fundamental rights cannot be overridden by general or ambiguous words. This is because there is too great a risk that the full implications of their unqualified meaning may have passed unnoticed in the democratic process. In the absence of express language or necessary implication to the contrary, the courts therefore presume that even the most general words were intended to be subject to the basic rights of the individual.'

The words of sections 42(2) and 73(2) are about as general as it is possible to be ...

The second reason is one of practicality. The patient's continued co-operation is crucial to the success of any rehabilitation plan. There is, as the FtT [First tier Tribunal] found in this case, always a concern that the patient's willingness to comply is motivated more by his desire to get out of hospital than by a desire to stay in whatever community setting he is placed ... The patient could withdraw his consent to the deprivation at any time and demand to be released ...

This leads to the third and perhaps most compelling set of reasons against such a power: it would be contrary to the whole scheme of the MHA ... There is no ... express power to convey a conditionally discharged restricted patient to the place where he is required to live or to detain him there. If the MHA had contemplated that such a patient could be detained, it is inconceivable that ... provision would not have been made for that purpose ...

For all those reasons, I conclude that the MHA does not permit either the FtT or the Secretary of State to impose conditions amounting to detention or a deprivation of liberty upon a conditionally discharged restricted patient.

Interestingly, shortly after the Supreme Court's decision, in *Hertfordshire County Council v AB*, and admitting that her decision might 'inevitably [be] of short life', Knowles J invoked the inherent jurisdiction of the High Court (see Chapter 5) in order to authorize a care plan for AB which amounted to a deprivation of liberty. AB, who had capacity despite his mild learning disability, had committed serious sexual offences against children. He was convicted and the criminal court imposed a Hospital Order. Eight years later, AB was discharged, subject to conditions which included a requirement to comply with his care and risk management plan. AB was supervised at all times, and it was clear that his care plan amounted to a deprivation of liberty.

[129] [2018] UKSC 60.

Hertfordshire County Council v AB [130]

Knowles J

AB is presently subject to a care and risk management plan, which on the basis of the Court of Appeal's decision in *MM* and upheld by the Supreme Court, is unlawful.

In circumstances where AB is subject to a plan which has been very carefully designed for his particular benefit and also to protect members of the public, the choice for him if that plan is ruled unlawful is stark; indeed, that choice amounts to either consenting to his return to confinement in hospital or indeed a consent to a relaxation of the restrictions in that care plan so that they would no longer amount to a deprivation of his liberty. That would, in my view, place AB in an invidious position. He would not receive the support which he clearly needs and which all the professionals involved in his care consider that he needs which would keep him safe and, indeed, importantly, keep members of the general public safe from his behaviour.

In those circumstances, where the Court of Appeal has said that AB's consent to a deprivation of liberty is not lawful, the applicant invited me, both in AB's interests and in the interests of the general public as a whole, to authorise the extension of the inherent jurisdiction so as to regularise that care plan and to do so (a) by declaring that it involved a deprivation of liberty and (b) by providing for a regular court review of that plan.

It seems to me that, in these particular circumstances this is precisely the use to which the inherent jurisdiction should be put, exercised cautiously ...

I do so in this particular case for reasons which I have already averted to and I do so only to fill the legislative void created by the Court of Appeal's decision in *MM*.

(b) COMMUNITY TREATMENT ORDERS

One of the most significant changes introduced by the 2007 Act is the community treatment order (CTO). CTOs are intended to ensure that patients receive treatment in the least restrictive environment. They are also supposed to address what is known as the 'revolving door' problem: a patient is admitted to hospital, her condition is stabilized, and she is discharged into the community, only to stop taking her medication, resulting in her deterioration and readmission to hospital, where the pattern repeats itself.

Under section 17A, in order to make a community treatment order, the responsible clinician (RC) must have the written agreement of an Approved Mental Health Professional (AMHP), and the criteria in section 17A(5) must be satisfied.

Mental Health Act 1983 section 17A

17A(5) ...
  (a) the patient is suffering from mental disorder of a nature or degree which makes it appropriate for him to receive medical treatment;
  (b) it is necessary for his health or safety or for the protection of other persons that he should receive such treatment;
  (c) subject to his being liable to be recalled as mentioned in paragraph (d) below, such treatment can be provided without his continuing to be detained in a hospital;

---

[130] [2018] EWHC 3103 (Fam).

(d) it is necessary that the responsible clinician should be able to exercise the power under section 17E(1) below to recall the patient to hospital; and

(e) appropriate medical treatment is available for him.

Essentially, while CTOs do not permit treatment with compulsion in the community, they provide for immediate recall, under section 17E, if the patient becomes in need of compulsory treatment.

Mental Health Act 1983 section 17E

17E(1) The responsible clinician may recall a community patient to hospital if in his opinion—

    (a) the patient requires medical treatment in hospital for his mental disorder; and

    (b) there would be a risk of harm to the health or safety of the patient or to other persons if the patient were not recalled to hospital for that purpose.

If a patient is recalled, she can be detained for up to 72 hours, after which time she may be discharged, and continue to be subject to the CTO; or, if she refuses to comply with a condition in the CTO or continues to refuse treatment, the CTO can be revoked and she will become a detained patient once again.

Treatment without consent can be given as soon as the patient is recalled, so it is clearly possible that the power of recall could be used temporarily in order to force treatment upon the patient, who is then released until her need for compulsory medication arises again. It is therefore possible that a patient could 'yo-yo' between recall (and compulsory depot injections[131]) and living in the community under a CTO.

In addition to giving the power of recall to hospital, a CTO can be used to impose conditions—such as that the patient make himself available for treatment or desist from certain behaviour—if those conditions are necessary *or* appropriate for one of three purposes, set out in section 17B(2):

(a) ensuring that the patient receives medical treatment;

(b) preventing risk of harm to the patient's health or safety;

(c) protecting other persons.

The statute does not specify what sort of conditions might be imposed: rather, the RC has a wide discretion, subject only to the need for the condition to be 'necessary or appropriate' for one of these three rather broad purposes. Once again, the use of the word 'or' makes this criterion especially loose—or 'lax indeed', according to Phil Fennell.[132] Necessary *and* appropriate would have forced the RC to consider whether the condition was necessary to fulfil a purpose *and* appropriate in these particular circumstances. 'Necessary *or* appropriate' instead suggests that a condition could be attached because it was thought appropriate, even if it is not, in fact, necessary.

---

[131] A depot injection is a slow-release and slow-acting injection, through which one dose of anti-psychotic medication can last for several weeks. It must be given by a healthcare professional.

[132] Phil Fennell, *Mental Health: The New Law* (Jordan: Bristol, 2007) 212.

While the Code of Practice does state that the conditions should be kept to a minimum and restrict freedom as little as possible, CTOs undoubtedly have the potential to interfere with a person's private life. An RC might decide that a patient should not be allowed to associate with certain individuals, for example, if seeing them might make it more likely that the patient will resume her drug habit.

Mental Health Act Code of Practice 2015

29.31 The conditions must not deprive the patient of their liberty and should:

- be kept to a minimum number consistent with achieving their purpose
- restrict the patient's liberty as little as possible while being consistent with their care plan and recovery goal
- have a clear rationale, linked to one or more of the [statutory] purposes
- be clearly and precisely expressed, so that the patient can readily understand what is expected.

29.32 The nature of the conditions will depend on the patient's individual circumstances. They should be stated clearly having regard to the least restriction principle. Subject to paragraph 29.31, they might cover matters such as:

- where and when the patient is to receive treatment in the community
- where the patient is to live, and
- avoidance of known risk factors or high-risk situations relevant to the patient's mental disorder.

In addition to the conditions that may be attached to CTOs, sections 64A to 64K authorize the giving of 'relevant treatment' to community patients. 'Relevant treatment' is defined as medicines for mental disorder and ECT, and can be provided to capacitous patients in the community only if they consent and there is, within a month of the CTO being issued, a certificate from a SOAD authorizing treatment. For patients who lack capacity, treatment in the community can be given under section 64D.

Patients have the right to apply to the Tribunal if one of more of the conditions for making a CTO are not satisfied, and the Tribunal must order discharge if, for example, the power of recall to hospital is no longer necessary.

CTOs have been subject to several criticisms. First, as Tania Gergel and George Szmukler explain, they represent a significant increase in the use of coercive powers.

Tania Gergel and George Szmukler[133]

If we extend [the risk-based criterion] to an individual subject to an ongoing CTO, but now sufficiently stable to live outside of a controlled inpatient environment, we are not simply allowing coercion based on risk of some kind of harm in the near future. We are, effectively, extending this to a judgement that, should a stable individual decide to discontinue treatment, the risk

---

[133] 'The ethics of coercion in community mental health care' in Andrew Molodynski, Jorun Rugkåsa, and Tom Burns (eds), *Coercion in Community Mental Health Care: International Perspectives* (OUP: Oxford, 2016) 55.

from discontinuation is sufficiently high to over-ride their right to make treatment decisions. Given the moral imperative to limit coercion and respect the right to self-determination wherever possible, we need to think very carefully about whether such an extension is justifiable ...

Furthermore, given that community coercion is not constrained by a 'ceiling effect' which limits numbers of involuntary patients to available hospital beds, it may be opening the floodgates for subjecting increasing numbers to such measures ...

Living in the community while subject to such an order might contribute to feelings of social isolation in a number of ways, such as increased feelings of stigmatisation; altering dynamics in relationships with non-clinicians, such as carers or hostel workers, who play the part of assessing adherence; increasing fear of further coercion which may discourage an individual from seeking help. CTOs have been unpopular with many patients, both in terms of increasing coercion and also in decreasing legitimate debate about the problems associated with certain medications.

Drawing on the study of the views of people subject to CTOs, Deborah Corring et al found that they disproportionately emphasize the administration of medication, at the expense of other services, such as psychotherapy, and help with housing and employment, which may be equally or perhaps more important in helping patients to function in the community.

Deborah Corring, Richard O'Reilly, and Christina Sommerdyk[134]

Treatment plans associated with CTOs primarily require patients to attend clinical appointments and to take prescribed medication. Thus, it is not surprising that subjects of CTOs report that it is 'all about taking medication.' One approach to 'attenuate' the negativity of this perception is to ensure that patients on CTOs are offered additional needed services. It is clear from this review ... that access to intensive services is valued by subjects on CTOs.

In practice, CTOs are used increasingly frequently. In 2017–18, it was reported that there were 4784 new CTOs issued (though this is an underestimate as a result of incomplete reporting).[135] Once again, there is evidence of the over-representation of patients from minority ethnic groups. In 2017–18, CTO use was highest for 'Black or Black British' people (56 uses per 100,000 population), over eight times the rate for White people (6.5 uses per 100,000 population).[136]

Despite their increasing use, there is little evidence for the effectiveness of CTOs. Indeed, Rugkåsa et al go so far as to suggest that there is no evidence of patient benefit.

Jorun Rugkåsa, John Dawson, and Tom Burns[137]

It is hard to dismiss the consistent conclusions from three RCTs [randomized controlled trials] and three reviews. It is not our intention to sweep aside the methodological limitations with the existing RCTs; no study is perfect. We believe, however, that the lack of evidence for

---

[134] 'A systematic review of the views and experiences of subjects of community treatment orders' (2017) 52 International Journal of Law and Psychiatry 74–80.

[135] *Mental Health Act Statistics: Annual Figures England 2017-18* (NHS Digital, 2018).

[136] Ibid.

[137] 'CTOs: what is the state of the evidence?' (2014) 49 Social Psychiatry and Psychiatric Epidemiology 1861–71.

patient benefit, particularly when combined with restrictions to personal liberty, is striking and needs to be taken seriously. Clinicians have a duty to provide their patients with treatment in the least restrictive environment. The paucity of rigorous experimental research evidence for such an invasive intervention ... is quite remarkable. It raises a question of whether this would have been accepted in other branches of medicine. Surely major, intrusive interventions in community psychiatry should be expected to conform to the highest standards of evidence.

The rationales for introducing CTOs are usually to reduce repeated relapses and to provide a less restrictive alternative to hospital ... The weight of empirical evidence, however, is against them. CTOs do neither appear to reduce relapse and readmission nor, overall, to reduce coercion.

Despite evidence that they do not work, Ritz DeRidder et al suggest that clinicians are likely to continue to use CTOs, in part because of pressure on beds.

Ritz DeRidder et al[138]

A number [of clinicians] commented also that a general pressure on beds may lead to inappropriate use of CTOs to facilitate early discharge or to make readmission 'easier' if needed. Clearly these raise ethical concerns if compulsory powers are being commonly used as a practical measure to access services that should be available regardless of legal status. It has also been reported anecdotally that clinicians feel pressurised to use CTOs in case there is a negative outcome such as suicide or aggression and they are criticised for not having done so.

The Independent Review of the Mental Health Act 1983 considered that CTOS are significantly overused, but it did not (yet) recommend their complete abolition.

The Independent Review of the Mental Health Act 1983[139]

During the course of the Review we have become convinced that there are some service users for whom, despite our doubts, the CTO does play a constructive role. For these reasons we do not propose their abolition at this stage.

However, we think CTOs are significantly overused. We want to see a dramatic reduction in the number of CTOs, and for them to be used in a much more targeted way. We propose a tightening of criteria (and requiring both community and inpatient clinicians agree a CTO is necessary), an extension of the powers of the Tribunal to include dealing with conditions of a CTO, and making it particularly difficult to extend beyond two years without a compelling reason. We further propose that research is commissioned, which must report within five

---

[138] 'Community treatment orders in the UK 5 years on: a repeat national survey of psychiatrists' (2016) 40 British Journal of Psychiatry Bulletin 119–23.
[139] *Modernising the Mental Health Act, Increasing choice, reducing compulsion Final report of the Independent Review of the Mental Health Act 1983* (DHSC, 2018).

years, to see if these aims have been met. If the situation has not improved, then the argument for abolition would be difficult to resist. Expressed in the vernacular, CTOs are in the
last chance saloon.

8 THE INDEPENDENT REVIEW OF MENTAL HEALTH LAW

As we have seen, in 2017, the government appointed a panel, chaired by Sir Simon Wesseley, to review mental health law in the UK, and to make recommendation for improvement in relation to rising detention rates, racial disparities in detention, and concerns that the Act is out of step with a modern mental health system. An interim report was produced in May 2018, and a final report in December 2018. At the time of writing, the government has welcomed its report, committed immediately to allowing patients to make advance choice documents and to nominate an individual to be involved in decisions about their care, and has said that it will issue a full response in 2019. A key recommendation of the Review was that there should be four new principles on the face of the Act.

The Independent Review of the Mental Health Act 1983[140]

We are recommending that the new principles should become an introduction to the MHA, sitting 'on the face' of the Act (within, and at the front of, the body of the Act itself), and governing everything within it. They would provide the statutory basis for all actions taken under the Act, setting standards for services, and providing patients with clear expectations for their care and treatment. Our intention is that everyone, including patients and mental health professionals, should have easy access to these principles, and that they should be used to hold services to account and to guide organisations' approaches to a revised Act . . .

We are therefore recommending the following purpose and principles:

1. The purpose of this Act is to confer and authorise the powers (including coercive powers) necessary for the treatment of mental disorder and to safeguard the dignity and rights of those who are made subject to the exercise of such powers and for related purposes.

2. In exercising any powers under this Act, a person must have regard to the following principles –

   (a) Choice and Autonomy: all practicable steps must be taken to:
       (i) support a person subject to this Act to express their will and preferences;
       (ii) have particular regard to the person's will and preferences, even where an intervention in the absence of consent is expressly authorised by this Act;
       (iii) promote the person's dignity, and accord them due respect, including respecting their social and caring relationships; and iv. take steps to ensure that the person understands their rights and entitlements whilst they are subject to the Act.

   (b) Least Restriction: The exercise of any power under this Act shall be done in the least restrictive and least invasive manner consistent with the purpose and principles of this Act.

[140] *Modernising the Mental Health Act, Increasing choice, reducing compulsion Final report of the Independentsection 63 Review of the Mental Health Act 1983* (DHSC, 2018).

> (c) Therapeutic Benefit: care and treatment must be designed to meet the person's needs in a timely manner within a supportive, healing environment with a view to ending the need to be subject to coercive powers under this Act.
>
> (d) The person as an Individual: care and treatment must be provided and commissioned in a manner that:
>
> > (i) respects and acknowledges the person's qualities, strengths, abilities, knowledge and past experience; and
> >
> > (ii) In particular, respects and acknowledges person's individual diversity including any protected characteristics under the Equality Act.

9 CONCLUSION

In recent years, there has been increasing interest in the possibility of a 'fusion law', whereby incapacity is the only justification for treatment without consent. In Scotland, under the Mental Health (Care and Treatment) (Scotland) Act 2003 compulsory powers can be used only where the patient is suffering from 'significantly impaired ability to make decisions' about treatment. The Scottish Code of Practice spells out that 'impaired decision-making is not simply disagreeing with the doctors'.

In Northern Ireland, following the Bamford Review's recommendations,[141] the Mental Capacity Act (Northern Ireland) 2016 permits compulsory detention and/or treatment only when a person (a) lacks capacity, and (b) it would be in their best interests. The law comes into force in 2018, so at the time of writing it is too early to judge how it will work in practice, but clearly capacity assessments will become even more significant, if they can be used to justify detention, and complicated questions will arise for people with fluctuating capacity.

When the Law Commission produced its recommendations on reform of the Deprivation of Liberty safeguards, it expressed the view that 'the introduction of fusion law in Northern Ireland provides a unique opportunity to review mental health law in England and Wales with a view to the introduction of mental capacity-based care and treatment for mental disorders', and it 'strongly urge[d] the UK Government and the Welsh Government to take this opportunity'.[142]

In the next extracts, George Szmukler and Scott Weich disagree over whether fusion law is the solution to endemic discrimination against the mentally ill.

George Szmukler[143]

> We have accepted such discrimination for so long because of deeply rooted, stigmatising stereotypes of people with mental illness—that is, that they are incapable of exercising judgment and that dangerousness is intrinsic to mental illness. Mental health law is shaped by both assumptions.

---

[141] Maura McCallion and Ursula O'Hare, 'A new legislative framework for mental capacity and mental health legislation in Northern Ireland: an analysis of the current proposals' (2010) Journal of Mental Health Law 84–90.

[142] *Mental Capacity and Deprivation of Liberty* (Law Commission, 2015).

[143] 'Has the Mental Health Act had its day? Yes' (2017) 359 British Medical Journal j5248.

Can we create a legal framework that is non-discriminatory? Indeed we can. Such a framework is based on decision making ability and best interests but also incorporates the regulation of detention and involuntary treatment with strong human rights protections. Robust assessments, with high agreement between assessors, can be made. A key point is that the law must be generic: namely, that it applies to everyone who has a problem with decision making, whether the diagnosis is physical or psychiatric, and in any setting—medical, surgical, psychiatric, or in the community. A specific 'mental health' law is not necessary: the law should be formulated so as to apply throughout all medical specialties, from psychiatry to orthopaedics.

Scott Weich[144]

Instead of tackling the parlous state of mental health services we're about to embark on further protracted legalistic debate. What, then, of 'fusion' legislation, which argues for compulsory treatment only when decision making capacity is impaired, irrespective of cause? Sadly, it's not CRPD-compliant ...

The law is not the problem. Only properly resourced mental health services can reduce rates of compulsion and assure decent, humane outcomes for patients and their families. Because UK services are so thinly stretched, abandoning the MHA would discriminate against people with mental illness by denying them care ...

Unless services are properly resourced, changing the law won't make things better for patients, and it might make them very much worse.

Although the changes proposed by the Independent Review of the Mental Health Act 1983 would make it harder to justify detention and compulsory treatment, and require more attention to be paid to the patient's wishes, it also recognizes that compulsion should still be possible as a last resort. John Fanning has argued that if unless civil commitment to protect mentally disordered patients from the risk of harm they may pose to themselves and/or others is abolished completely, it is impossible to eliminate differential treatment on the ground of mental disorder.

John Fanning[145]

[I]t surely cannot be right that a person suffering from a serious mental illness whose effects may lead him to harm himself or others should go without the care and treatment that will help him. For all its faults as a legal apparatus, it cannot be denied that the MHA serves a very practical – and even compassionate – function in seeking to prevent the devastating consequences of some mental illnesses ...

Ultimately, it comes down to an inescapably binary distinction: either civil commitment is abolished as an historical anachronism, or it remains as a flawed and often difficult-to-justify exception to the general principles which underpin the liberal legal order ...

---

[144] 'Has the Mental Health Act had its day? No' (2017) 359 British Medical Journal j5248.
[145] *New Medicalism and the Mental Health Act* (Hart Publishing, 2018) 259, 267.

Even the Mental Health Alliance has published evidence which shows that the majority of service users and their carers, family and friends regard the power to 'section' patients as a necessary expedient. Rightly or wrongly, civil commitment continues to be regarded as an important practical component of mental health law in England ... If we ask what it is that we would like the law to achieve, the answer is likely to be much the same as it does already.

FURTHER READING

Allison, Stephen, Bastiampillai, Tarun, and Fuller, Doris A, 'Should the Government change the Mental Health Act or fund more psychiatric beds?' (2017) 4 The Lancet Psychiatry 585–6.

Bartlett, Peter, 'The United Nations Convention on the Rights of Persons with Disabilities and Mental Health Law (2012) 75 Modern Law Review 752–78.

Brown, Jennifer, 'The changing purpose of mental health law: From medialism to legalism to new legalism' (2016) 47 International Journal of Law and Psychiatry 1–9.

Fanning, John, *New Medicalism and the Mental Health Act* (Hart Publishing, 2018).

Glover-Thomas, Nicola, 'Decision-Making Behaviour under the Mental Health Act 1983 and Its Impact on Mental Health Tribunals: An English Perspective' (2018) 7 Laws 12.

Perry, Benjamin Ian, Singh, Swaran Preet, and White, David Hedley, 'Capacity assessment and information provision for voluntary psychiatric patients: a service evaluation in a UK NHS Trust' (2017) 22 International Journal of Mental Health and Capacity Law 107–18.

Richardson, Genevra, 'Mental Disabilities and the Law: From Substitute to Supported Decision-Making?' (2012) 65 Current Legal Problems 333–54.

8

CONFIDENTIALITY

CENTRAL ISSUES

1. There are both deontological and utilitarian justifications for the doctor's duty to respect patient confidentiality: (a) information about a person's health is private, and she should have the right to control who has access to it; and (b) without an assurance of confidentiality, a patient might withhold information that is necessary in order to diagnose and treat her properly.

2. There are several sources for the legal duty of confidentiality. It is protected at common law; through Article 8 of the European Convention on Human Rights, and through the Data Protection Act 2018 and the EU's General Data Protection Regulation,

which will be incorporated into UK law by the European Union (Withdrawal) Act 2018.

3. The legal duty of confidentiality is not absolute. The reality of modern medical treatment is that patient information will be shared among a team of healthcare professionals. Information can also be disclosed where the public interest in disclosure outweighs the public interest in respecting confidentiality, perhaps because there is a risk of serious harm to others.

4. Genetic information raises particularly complex issues in relation to confidentiality, and these are dealt with in Chapter 9.

1 INTRODUCTION

Unlike patient autonomy, which is a relatively recent preoccupation of medical law and ethics, a doctor's duty to respect her patients' confidentiality has its origins in the first codes of medical ethics. The Hippocratic oath, for example, states that:

> whatsoever things I see or hear concerning the life of men, in my attendance on the sick or even apart therefrom, which ought not to be noised abroad, I will keep silence thereon, counting such things to be as sacred secrets.

Patient confidentiality receives unqualified protection in the modern version of the Oath, the Declaration of Geneva:

> I will respect the secrets which are confided in me, even after the patient has died.

In this chapter, we begin by considering the ethical justifications for protecting patient confidentiality. We then examine the legal sources of the duty of confidence. Next, we flesh out exceptions to the duty of confidence, and the remedies available for its breach. Finally, we look briefly at patients' rights to gain access to their medical records.

2 WHY RESPECT CONFIDENTIALITY?

Both deontological (duty-based) and teleological (consequentialist) reasoning (see Chapter 1) can be used to justify the existence of a duty of confidence between a doctor and her patients. Deontological arguments would emphasize the patient's right to privacy, and her interest in controlling access to what will often be sensitive and personal information. The consequentialist argument for respecting patient confidentiality is, as Raanan Gillon explains, that good medical care depends upon patients being honest with their doctors.

Raanan Gillon[1]

> [I]n order to do a good job for their patients doctors often need to have information of a sort that people generally regard as private, even secret . . . Doctors routinely ask a series of questions about bodily functions that people would not dream of discussing with anyone else. When a patient's medical problems may relate to genitourinary functions a doctor may need to know about that patient's sexual activities, sometimes in detail. When a patient's problems are psychological a doctor may need to know in great detail about the patient's experiences, ideas and feelings, relationships past and present, even in some contexts about the person's imaginings and fantasies . . .
>
> Such intrusive medical inquiries are based not on prurience or mere inquisitiveness but on the pursuit of information that is of potential assistance to the doctor in treating and helping the patient. Nonetheless many patients are unlikely to pass on this information unless they have some assurances of confidentiality . . .
>
> In the context of transmissible diseases, especially sexually transmissible diseases, so long as the patient continues to trust his or her doctor the doctor is left in a position of being able to educate and influence the patient in ways that can reduce the likelihood of the disease being passed on. As soon as confidentiality is broken the trusting relationship is likely to be undermined and the opportunity to help reduce the spread of disease is lost.

Although important, confidentiality is not an absolute obligation. The Hippocratic oath only instructs doctors to keep secret that 'which ought not to be noised abroad', the implication being that there are circumstances in which information should be 'noised abroad'.

---

[1] 'Confidentiality' in Helga Kuhse and Peter Singer (eds), *A Companion to Bioethics* (Blackwell: Oxford, 1998) 425–31.

Most obviously, an absolute duty of confidentiality would be incompatible with the reality of medical treatment, where information has to be shared with other healthcare professionals. In hospitals, for example, treatment is provided by teams of doctors and nurses. Patients may be referred to specialist consultants, or for diagnostic procedures, such as blood tests, X-rays, and scans. If information about the patient's condition could never be shared with anyone else, the provision of health care would grind to a halt.

While the belief that what one tells one's doctor 'will go no further' has probably always been an illusion, Lawrence Gostin points out that new technologies facilitate the wide sharing of information.

Lawrence Gostin[2]

Only a few generations ago, physicians kept minimal written records about their patients. Physicians usually knew their patients and did not see a need to maintain extensive written reminders of patients' clinical histories. Today, the quantity of health records and the nature of the data they contain have increased substantially. The health records of patients, therefore, contain significant amounts of sensitive information that are available for inspection by many others . . .

The combination of emerging computer and genetic technologies poses particularly compelling privacy concerns. Science has the capacity to store a million fragments of DNA on a silicon microchip . . . This technology can markedly facilitate research, screening, and treatment of genetic conditions. But it may also permit a significant reduction in privacy through its capacity to inexpensively store and decipher unimaginable quantities of highly sensitive data.

Aside from sharing information within the health service, other exceptions to the duty of confidentiality exist, usually justified by the 'public interest'. Because the principal justification for respecting patient confidentiality is also the public interest, working out whether disclosure is justified in a particular case will often involve a complex balancing exercise.

If a patient confides in his doctor that he has committed a very serious crime, such as child abuse, should the doctor inform the police? What if the offence is recreational drug use? On the one hand, there is a clear public interest in the prevention and detection of crime but, on the other, it is also in the public interest for paedophiles and drug users to come forward to seek help and treatment.

Given the number of variables to be taken into account, it is difficult for doctors to know exactly when their primary duty of confidentiality will be trumped by competing considerations. To make an already confusing situation worse, the law in this area is especially difficult to understand. This is largely because there are several possible sources of the legal duty of confidentiality.

A legal duty of confidence exists in vastly different situations, from duties under the Official Secrets Act 1989 to the protection of commercially sensitive information. The Data Protection Act 2018 clearly applies to medical records, but because its remit is much wider than this (covering, for example, a right to be forgotten on social media), its application to the doctor–patient relationship can be confusing.

---

[2] 'Health Informational Privacy' (1995) 80 Cornell Law Review 451.

At the outset, it should be remembered that not all patient information is equally sensitive. A patient might be anxious to keep her HIV status private, but be much less concerned about whether a consultant has used an X-ray of her broken foot in a lecture to junior doctors.

Furthermore, it could be argued that the priority given to patient confidentiality rests upon an unrealistically individualistic model of medical decision-making. In practice, most patients do not want to keep information about their health secret from the whole world. Rather, while people might not want their employers or insurers, or the media, to have access to their medical records, they often want to discuss their health issues with people who are close to them. Patients facing difficult medical choices, or the diagnosis of serious illness, may want a partner, family member, or friend to be present during discussions with their doctors. In the next extract, Roy Gilbar argues that, in the context of familial relationships, the strict rule of confidentiality should be reconsidered.

Roy Gilbar[3]

While the relationship between patients and employers or insurers is primarily confrontational, with patients anxious to protect their rights and not be discriminated against, the relationship with family members is generally based on care, commitment and mutual responsibility . . .

[P]atients often consider the interests of their relatives and the implications of their decision on their familial relationship, while doctors are willing to involve family members more than the law currently permits to help the patient cope with the bad news. In other words, doctors and patients value the patient's familial relationship as a separate and significant component in this area. Thus, the strict legal rule of medical confidentiality, which is adopted by many lawyers and policy-makers, should be reconsidered . . .

Doctors in various areas of medicine have learned to accept that the support and comfort that family members provide to the patient during all the stages of his/her illness is important, and that the family rather than the individual patient, should be considered as the unit of medical care. This, in many cases, leads to the conclusion that adhering to a strict rule of confidentiality may compromise the interests of the patient instead of promoting them.

It may be true that most people are happy to discuss their health with close friends and relatives, but disclosure should still lie within the patient's control. Not all intimate and familial relationships are harmonious and supportive, and there will be times when a patient might have good reasons for wanting to keep information about her health from her partner or her relatives.

3 A DUTY OF CONFIDENTIALITY

In the following sections we examine a number of different sources of the legal duty of confidence.

---

[3] 'Medical Confidentiality Within the Family: The Doctor's Duty Reconsidered' (2004) 18 International Journal of Law, Policy and the Family 195–213.

(a) AT COMMON LAW

The origins of the legal duty of confidence lie in the equitable jurisdiction of the Chancery Division to grant injunctions in order to prevent the infringement of legal and equitable rights. In *Attorney General v Guardian Newspapers (No 2)*, a case in which the government sought to restrain a retired secret service employee from publishing his memoirs, Lord Goff explained when a duty of confidence arises.

Attorney General v Guardian Newspapers (No 2)[4]

Lord Goff

[A] duty of confidence arises when confidential information comes to the knowledge of a person (the confidant) in circumstances where he has notice, or is held to have agreed, that the information is confidential, with the effect that it would be just in all the circumstances that he should be precluded from disclosing the information to others.

Lord Goff went on to suggest three limiting principles: first, that the information must itself be confidential, and not already in the public domain; secondly, there is no duty of confidentiality in relation to useless information or trivia; and, thirdly, the duty to respect confidentiality is not an absolute one, and can sometimes be trumped where there is a weightier public interest in disclosure.

The factors that give rise to a duty of confidentiality are thus vague and question-begging: effectively a duty of confidence arises when someone knows, or ought to know, that the information she has acquired is confidential. It is both the nature of the information and the circumstances in which it was disclosed that create a duty of confidentiality.

For our purposes, however, the position is relatively clear. Medical information is exactly the sort of information which is treated as confidential, and the doctor–patient relationship is plainly one in which a duty of confidence arises. As Boreham J stated in *Hunter v Mann*:[5] 'in common with other professional men, for instance a priest and there are of course others, the doctor is under a duty not to disclose, without the consent of his patient, information which he, the doctor, has gained in his professional capacity, save . . . in very exceptional circumstances'.

In *W v Egdell*, a case which we consider in more detail later, the existence of a duty of confidence between Dr Egdell and W was not in doubt.

W v Egdell[6]

Bingham LJ

It has never been doubted that the circumstances here were such as to impose on Dr Egdell a duty of confidence owed to W. He could not lawfully sell the contents of his report to a newspaper, as the judge held. Nor could he, without a breach of the law as well as professional etiquette, discuss the case in a learned article or in his memoirs or in gossiping with friends, unless he took appropriate steps to conceal the identity of W. It is not in issue here that a duty of confidence existed.

---

[4] [1990] AC 109.   [5] [1974] QB 767.   [6] [1990] Ch 359.

An alternative basis for the existence of a common law duty of confidentiality would be that it is an aspect of the doctor's duty of care. A doctor who discloses information that she should have been kept private will not have acted as a reasonable doctor. The patient might therefore be able to bring an action in negligence, but only if she has suffered damage or loss as a result of the negligent disclosure: an example might be being turned down for insurance coverage. More commonly, the 'harm' that results from a breach of confidentiality will be less tangible, and an action in tort less promising.

It is usually assumed that the duty of confidentiality is owed to the patient, rather than to those treating her. However, health providers might also have an interest in ensuring the confidentiality of their patient records. In *Ashworth Hospital Authority v Mirror Group Newspapers (MGN)*, the *Mirror* newspaper had published information about the medical treatment of Ian Brady, one of the Moors murderers. Ian Brady had been keen to publicize what he perceived to be his ill treatment, and he had attempted to put information about his treatment into the public domain. The hospital obtained an order requiring the newspaper to identify the employee who had leaked Brady's medical notes. On appeal, the House of Lords decided that the security of medical records was of such overriding importance that it was essential that the person who had disclosed them to the newspaper was identified and punished, even if the patient himself did not object to the disclosure.

Ashworth Hospital Authority v Mirror Group Newspapers (MGN)[7]

Lord Woolf

[W]hile Ian Brady's conduct in putting similar information into the public domain could well mean that he would not be in a position to complain about the publication, this did not destroy the authority's independent interest in retaining the confidentiality of the medical records contained in Ashworth's files . . . The care of patients at Ashworth is fraught with difficulty and danger. The disclosure of the patients' records increases that difficulty and danger and to deter the same or similar wrongdoing in the future it was essential that the source should be identified and punished. This was what made the orders to disclose necessary and proportionate and justified. The fact that Ian Brady had himself disclosed his medical history did not detract from the need to prevent staff from revealing medical records of patients . . . The source's disclosure was wholly inconsistent with the security of the records and the disclosure was made worse because it was purchased by a cash payment.

The decision in *Ashworth* was not the end of the story, however. Instead of disclosing the name of the staff member who had leaked Brady's records, MGN only disclosed the name of the investigative journalist, Mr Ackroyd. Ashworth Hospital had by this time been subsumed within the Mersey Care NHS Trust, which then brought an action against Ackroyd, requiring him to reveal his sources (he had admitted there was more than one). By this time, more facts had emerged about the circumstances of the leak: first, the motivation had not, in fact, been financial greed, as had previously been assumed; secondly, only part of Brady's notes had been disclosed; and, thirdly, it was not clear that the source had been a member of the hospital's staff.

---

[7] [2002] 1 WLR 2033.

In *Mersey Care NHS Trust v Ackroyd (No 2)* the Court of Appeal dismissed an appeal against Tugendhat J's first instance decision that Mr Ackroyd did not have to disclose his sources.

Mersey Care NHS Trust v Ackroyd (No 2) [8]

Sir Anthony Clarke MR

[T]he question for the judge was whether he was persuaded by the hospital that it was necessary and proportionate to order Mr Ackroyd to disclose his source. That involved a balancing of considerations that could properly be urged on one side and the other. As explained above, the carrying out of that balance was essentially a matter for the judge ... It can be seen from the above discussion of the findings of the judge on the facts, and his conclusions based on them, that he took into account the key considerations on either side of the argument. In these circumstances we do not think that there is any basis on which we could properly interfere with the balance he struck.

In short, the confidentiality of medical records often has to be balanced, on a case-by-case basis, with other important interests, such as press freedom, and it is often difficult to tell in advance of this fact-specific balancing exercise, which will take priority.

(b) THE HUMAN RIGHTS ACT 1998

A patient's interest in confidentiality also receives protection from Article 8 of the European Convention on Human Rights: the 'right to respect for private and family life'. Article 8 is not an absolute right, and is qualified by Article 8(2):

(1) Everyone has the right to respect for his private and family life, his home and his correspondence.

(2) There shall be no interference by a public authority with the exercise of this right except such as is in accordance with the law and is necessary in a democratic society in the interests of national security, public safety or the economic well-being of the country, for the prevention of disorder or crime, for the protection of health or morals, or for the protection of the rights and freedoms of others.

In relation to medical information, it will generally be straightforward to establish that the disclosure of medical information constitutes a prima facie violation of Article 8.

An unusual case in which Article 8 was held not to have been engaged was *Department of Health v Information Commissioner*, in which Cranston J found that where individuals were very unlikely to be identifiable, there was no interference with Article 8(1). The Department of Health had sought to resist a Freedom of Information Act request from a pro-life pressure group to publish statistical data about the conditions that had justified late terminations of pregnancy, on the grounds of fetal abnormality. Cranston J held that the chance of identifying individual women was 'remote'—but note, not non-existent—and that Article 8 therefore did

---

[8] [2007] EWCA Civ 101.

not apply. Given the potentially devastating consequences of identifying women who had undergone late abortions, it is interesting that a remote risk of identification was not thought to engage their human rights.

Department of Health v Information Commissioner[9]

Cranston J

The Department of Health had never suggested that identification was probable. Rather its case had been that if there was some meaningful possibility of identification the disputed information should not be released, given that the circumstances were of an unparalleled sensitivity and the consequences ghastly . . . [T]he Tribunal accepted the devastating consequences of identification. While it placed great weight on them, it concluded that these consequences were all dependent upon a patient being identified. The Tribunal was satisfied that this was extremely remote . . .

In my view, the Tribunal was not flawed in concluding that the risk of individual identification is so remote that the right under Article 8.1 was not engaged.

In relation to medical information, more usually Article 8 will be engaged, and the principal obstacle to a successful claim will be the possibility that disclosure was justifiable under Article 8(2).

In *Z v Finland*, for example, Z was married to a man who had been charged with a number of sexual offences. He was HIV positive, and in order to find out when he became aware of his HIV status, the police sought and gained access to Z's medical records. The European Court of Human Rights (ECtHR) held that seizing Z's medical records, and ordering her doctors to give evidence, was justifiable under Article 8(2): a legitimate aim was being pursued and the measures taken were not disproportionate.

Z v Finland[10]

Judgment of the ECtHR

In view of the highly intimate and sensitive nature of information concerning a person's HIV status, any state measures compelling communication or disclosure of such information without the consent of the patient call for the most careful scrutiny on the part of the court, as do the safeguards designed to secure an effective protection . . .

At the same time, the court accepts that the interests of a patient and the community as a whole in protecting the confidentiality of medical data may be outweighed by the interest in investigation and prosecution of crime and in the publicity of court proceedings, where such interests are shown to be of even greater importance.

Disclosure without consent was also justified under Article 8(2) in *Stone v South East Coast Strategic Health Authority*. The convicted murderer Michael Stone sought to suppress publication of a homicide inquiry, which contained considerable detail about his medical treatment.

---

[9] [2011] EWHC 1430 (Admin). [10] (1997) 25 EHRR 371.

Davis J acknowledged his right to privacy, and the argument that publication might deter patients from being frank with their doctors and with homicide inquiry panels. However, this was outweighed by the public interest in knowing more about the treatment that Mr Stone had, and perhaps more importantly had not, received. Also relevant was the fact that the need for this inquiry arose from Mr Stone's own criminal acts, and that a great deal of information about his treatment was already in the public domain. Davis J further decided that a redacted (where personal information is blacked-out) or summarized version of the report would be useless, and 'might be viewed with scepticism by the public, who might even suspect a cover-up'.

Stone v South East Coast Strategic Health Authority[11]

Davis J

So far as Mr Stone is concerned, much the most weighty point in his favour, as it seems to me, is his very entitlement to claim a right of privacy: in respect moreover of an aspect of private information (medical information) which—as the jurisprudence from Europe shows—is regarded as a vital and central element of that which should be protected under Article 8. Further, that is reinforced by other and wider considerations of the public interest: first, that persons may talk freely with their doctors, probation officers and other such persons without being deterred by risk of subsequent disclosure . . . ; second, that such persons may give access to such information for the purposes of an inquiry without being deterred from doing so through fear of such matters later being released into the public domain.

But it seems to me that the force of those points is significantly outweighed by a number of other considerations . . .

[T]here is a true public interest in the public at large knowing of the actual care and treatment supplied (or, as the case may be, not supplied) to Mr Stone: and knowing, and being able to reach an informed assessment of, the failures identified and steps that may be recommended to be taken to address identified deficiencies . . .

[I]t is, I think, of importance as a justification for restricting Mr Stone's right to privacy in this context that this inquiry, and all this publicity, have arisen out of Mr Stone's own acts—acts found to have been criminal. He has, as it were, put himself in the public domain by reason of those criminal acts, which inevitably created great publicity . . .

I also think it a point of considerable importance as a justification for restricting Mr Stone's right to privacy in this context that a great deal of information relating to the background, treatment and mental health of Mr Stone has already been put in the public domain, and at a significant level of detail.

In addition to Article 8(2)'s qualification of the right to privacy, Article 8 has to be put into the balance with Article 10, the right to freedom of expression, and section 12 of the Human Rights Act, which specifies that, 'The court must have particular regard to the importance of the Convention right to freedom of expression.' There is no presumptive priority for either right; rather, the competing interests have to be balanced according to the facts of the individual case. In *Campbell v Mirror Group Newspapers*, for example, the House of Lords determined that the model Naomi Campbell's right to privacy took priority over the press's freedom to publish information about her attendance at Narcotics Anonymous (NA), and accompanying photographs.

---

[11] [2006] EWHC 1668 (Admin).

Campbell v Mirror Group Newspapers[12]

Lady Hale

The political and social life of the community, and the intellectual, artistic or personal development of individuals, are not obviously assisted by poring over the intimate details of a fashion model's private life . . .

The weight to be attached to these various considerations is a matter of fact and degree. Not every statement about a person's health will carry the badge of confidentiality or risk doing harm to that person's physical or moral integrity. The privacy interest in the fact that a public figure has a cold or a broken leg is unlikely to be strong enough to justify restricting the press's freedom to report it. What harm could it possibly do? Sometimes there will be other justifications for publishing, especially where the information is relevant to the capacity of a public figure to do the job. But that is not this case and in this case there was, as the judge found, a risk that publication would do harm. The risk of harm is what matters at this stage, rather than the proof that actual harm has occurred. People trying to recover from drug addiction need considerable dedication and commitment, along with constant reinforcement from those around them. That is why organisations like NA were set up and why they can do so much good. Blundering in when matters are acknowledged to be at a 'fragile' stage may do great harm.

In *W v M (An Adult Patient)*, the Court of Protection was about to hear an application (considered in Chapter 5) in which it would decide, for the first time, the legality of withholding artificial nutrition and hydration from a patient in a minimally conscious state. It was an issue of public importance, which militated in favour of a public hearing, but this had to be balanced with the Article 8 rights of the patient herself (M), and those of her mother, sister, and partner (W, B, and S). Also relevant were their Article 6 rights (the right to a fair trial), since all three of them had stated that press intrusion would be likely to lead them to drop the case.

W v M (An Adult Patient)[13]

Baker J

It is axiomatic that the freedom to report proceedings in open court is in the public interest. The court has determined that the issues in this case are sufficiently important to justify public hearing, and the press must be allowed to report the proceedings as far as possible . . .

The evidence manifestly demonstrates that M's right to respect for family and private life would be infringed by any publication that identified her, or any attempt by the media to communicate with or photograph her.

In my judgment, the article 8 rights engaged in this case are not only those of M, but also those of W, B and S. On the evidence filed in this case, any publication of the identity of W, B and S, or any attempt by the media to communicate with, or take a photograph of, those three individuals would not only infringe their own article 8 rights, but also the article 8 rights of M, since, on the evidence of B and S, it would be likely to reduce the frequency of their visits to the care home.

I also take into account the statements by B and S that the risk of press intrusion might lead them to abandon these proceedings altogether. It is therefore arguable that, if it failed to restrain the press from identifying, communicating with or photographing the family members,

[12] [2004] UKHL 22.　　[13] [2011] EWHC 1197 (Fam).

> the court would be infringing the article 6 rights of B, S and M. Given the importance of the issues at stake in these proceedings, such an infringement would be extremely serious . . .
>
> In my judgment, the balance manifestly falls in this case in favour of granting the orders sought by the applicant and the Official Solicitor. The terms of the order will ensure that the article 8 rights of family members are properly protected. The freedom of expression enjoyed by the press will be restricted, but the extent of that restriction will, in my judgment, not prevent the press from reporting the issues, evidence (including expert evidence) and arguments at the hearing.

In contrast, in *R (on the application of T) v HM Senior Coroner for West Yorkshire*, the Court of Appeal found in favour of press freedom when it carried out a similar balancing exercise in a case in which a teenager had concealed the body of her baby, after its birth or stillbirth.

R (on the application of T) v HM Senior Coroner for West Yorkshire[14]

Lord Thomas CJ

> One very important aspect of the principle of open justice is the naming of those before the court . . . Any restriction on the principle of open justice, including the making of an order for anonymity, requires cogent justification . . .
>
> The Coroner rightly accepted that the claimant's article 8 rights were engaged. An order for anonymity would prevent her name being reported and might well reduce the risk of her exposure to humiliation and abuse . . . To be balanced against those considerations was first the right of the press freely to report her name . . . Secondly, the facts of this particular case give rise to a significant public interest. The conduct of the claimant was not in any sense a private matter . . . She had concealed a baby's body for six days and failed to report the birth or still-birth. If the baby was born alive, there would be the further public interest in ascertaining the cause of death. In addition she had made a false allegation of rape against some innocent man . . . In our view, there is a significant public interest in such issues being a subject for public discussion and debate on as fully informed a basis as is possible.

In *R (on the application of B) v Stafford Combined Court*, there was a conflict between two competing interests: the need for a fair trial and a patient's right to confidentiality. B was a 14-year-old girl who was the main prosecution witness in the trial of a defendant, W, who was convicted subsequently of sexually abusing her. His legal team had sought access to her psychiatric records, on the grounds that they were relevant to her credibility as a witness. At first instance, the judge had held that W's interest in a fair trial was more important than B's interests in the confidentiality of her medical records, and ordered disclosure. The judge had then invited B to attend court. There was no arrangement or opportunity for her to be represented, and in court she agreed reluctantly to disclosure, because she could not face the prospect of the trial being delayed.

B applied successfully for judicial review of the Crown Court decision ordering disclosure of her medical records. In *R (on the application of B) v Stafford Combined Court*, May LJ was critical of the judge's conduct, and found that the court itself had breached B's Article 8 rights.

---

[14] [2017] EWCA Civ 318.

R (on the application of B) v Stafford Combined Court [15]

May LJ

I strongly deprecate what happened on 6 December 2005. It seems to me to be quite un-acceptable for a vulnerable 14-year-old school girl known to have attempted suicide, the victim of alleged sexual abuse and a prosecution witness in the impending trial, to be brought to court at short notice, without representation or support, to be faced personally with an apparent choice between agreeing to the disclosure of her psychiatric records or delaying a trial which was bound to cause her concern and stress.

In my judgment, procedural fairness in the light of article 8 undoubtedly required in the present case that B should have been given notice of the application for the witness summons, and given the opportunity to make representations before the order was made. Since the rules did not re-quire this of the person applying for the summons, the requirement was on the court as a public au-thority, not on W, the defendant. B was not given due notice or that opportunity, so the interference with her rights was not capable of being necessary within article 8(2). Her rights were infringed and the court acted unlawfully in a way which was incompatible with her Convention rights.

(c) THE DATA PROTECTION ACT 2018 AND THE GENERAL DATA PROTECTION REGULATION

The General Data Protection Regulation (GDPR) came into force throughout the EU in 2018. Because member states were given some discretion over how to implement some aspects of the new Regulation—for example, there are some exemptions to the need for specific consent for the use of data in clinical research—a new Data Protection Act which supports and supplements the GDPR became law at the same time. The GDPR will remain in force after Brexit, and its provi-sions will be transposed into UK law as a result of the European Union (Withdrawal) Act 2018.

The GDPR is intended to give individuals more control over their personal data and to simplify the regulatory environment for business. The main reason for reform was the need to keep pace with the 'new digital environment' in which Europe's 250 million internet users are uploading more and more personal data online. It makes provision, for example, for a 'right to be forgotten' in relation to online information, and a right to obtain a portable electronic copy of one's personal data. Data Protection Authorities are to be given greater investigative powers and the power to issue fines of up to €20 million.

The GDPR is not directed specifically at medical information, and so a set of rules which are intended to protect individuals' interests in their data in the world of social media and on-line shopping may not necessarily be a good fit with health records. For example, a right to be forgotten makes sense in the context of social media, but it might be problematic within the NHS, when there are very good reasons to retain patient records.

Personal data is defined very broadly. Under Article 4 it is 'any information relating to an identified or identifiable natural person', known as a data subject. Processing is also broadly defined, and includes anything done with or to personal data, including collection, storage and destruction. Like its predecessor, the GDPR contains a set of principles, set out in Article 5. Health information counts as a 'special category' of personal information, to which Articles 9 and 89 apply.

---

[15] [2006] EWHC 1645 (Admin).

General Data Protection Regulation

Article 5

Personal data shall be:

a. processed lawfully, fairly and in a transparent manner in relation to the data subject

b. collected for specified, explicit and legitimate purposes and not further processed in a manner that is incompatible with those purposes ...

c. adequate, relevant and limited to what is necessary in relation to the purposes for which they are processed ('data minimisation');

d. accurate and, where necessary, kept up to date ...

e. kept in a form which permits identification of data subjects for no longer than is necessary for the purposes for which the personal data are processed ...

f. processed in a manner that ensures appropriate security of the personal data, including protection against unauthorised or unlawful processing and against accidental loss, destruction or damage, using appropriate technical or organisational measures ('integrity and confidentiality').

Article 9

1. Processing of personal data revealing racial or ethnic origin, political opinions, religious or philosophical beliefs, or trade union membership, and the processing of genetic data, biometric data for the purpose of uniquely identifying a natural person, data concerning health or data concerning a natural person's sex life or sexual orientation shall be prohibited.

2. Paragraph 1 shall not apply if one of the following applies:

   a. the data subject has given explicit consent to the processing of those personal data for one or more specified purposes ...

   c. processing is necessary to protect the vital interests of the data subject or of another natural person where the data subject is physically or legally incapable of giving consent ...

   e. processing relates to personal data which are manifestly made public by the data subject ...

   f. processing is necessary for reasons of substantial public interest, on the basis of Union or Member State law which shall be proportionate to the aim pursued, respect the essence of the right to data protection and provide for suitable and specific measures to safeguard the fundamental rights and the interests of the data subject;

   g. processing is necessary for the purposes of preventive or occupational medicine, for the assessment of the working capacity of the employee, medical diagnosis, the provision of health or social care or treatment or the management of health or social care systems and services on the basis of Union or Member State law or pursuant to contract with a health professional and subject to the conditions and safeguards referred to in paragraph 3;

   h. processing is necessary for reasons of public interest in the area of public health, such as protecting against serious cross-border threats to health or ensuring high standards of quality and safety of health care and of medicinal products or medical devices, on the basis of Union or Member State law which provides for suitable and specific measures to safeguard the rights and freedoms of the data subject, in particular professional secrecy;

> i.   processing is necessary for archiving purposes in the public interest, scientific or histor-ical research purposes or statistical purposes in accordance with Article 89(1) based on Union or Member State law which shall be proportionate to the aim pursued, respect the essence of the right to data protection and provide for suitable and specific meas-ures to safeguard the fundamental rights and the interests of the data subject.
>
> 3. Personal data referred to in paragraph 1 may be processed for the purposes referred to in point (h) of paragraph 2 when those data are processed by or under the responsibility of a professional subject to the obligation of professional secrecy under Union or Member State law or rules established by national competent bodies or by another person also subject to an obligation of secrecy under Union or Member State law or rules established by national competent bodies.
>
> 4. Member States may maintain or introduce further conditions, including limitations, with regard to the processing of genetic data, biometric data or data concerning health.

Article 89 allows member states to make derogations to data subjects' rights (to access, rectifi-cation, restriction of processing and the right to object) for 'scientific research purposes', pro-vided that appropriate safeguards are in place, such as pseudonymisation, and provided that 'such rights are likely to render impossible or seriously impair the achievement of the specific purposes, and such derogations are necessary for the fulfilment of those purposes'.

(d)   OTHER STATUTORY PROVISIONS

In certain situations, additional obligations to respect confidentiality are created by statute. For example, section 33 of the Human Fertilisation and Embryology Act 1990 imposes re-strictions upon the disclosure of information held in confidence by the Human Fertilisation and Embryology Authority and by people working in licensed centres. Under the Abortion Regulations 1991, there is a duty to report each termination of pregnancy to the appropriate Chief Medical Officer, but there are also restrictions upon any further disclosure of this information.

(e)   GOOD MEDICAL PRACTICE

The General Medical Council (GMC)'s latest good practice guidance *Confidentiality: good practice in handling patient information* is supplemented by more specific guidance on, for example, disclosing information for education and training purposes; reporting gunshot and knife wounds; and disclosing information about serious communicable diseases.

General Medical Council[16]

> 1.   Trust is an essential part of the doctor-patient relationship and confidentiality is central to this. Patients may avoid seeking medical help, or may under-report symptoms, if they think their personal information will be disclosed by doctors without consent, or without the chance to have some control over the timing or amount of information shared.

---

[16]   *Confidentiality: good practice in handling patient information* (GMC, 2018).

2. Doctors are under both ethical and legal duties to protect patients' personal information from improper disclosure. But appropriate information sharing is an essential part of the provision of safe and effective care. Patients may be put at risk if those who are providing their care do not have access to relevant, accurate and up-to-date information about them ...

9. Confidentiality is an important ethical and legal duty but it is not absolute. You may disclose personal information without breaching duties of confidentiality when any of the following circumstances applies.

   (a) The patient consents, whether implicitly or explicitly, for the sake of their own care or for local clinical audit.

   (b) The patient has given their explicit consent to disclosure for other purposes.

   (c) The disclosure is of overall benefit to a patient who lacks the capacity to consent.

   (d) The disclosure is required by law or the disclosure is permitted or has been approved under a statutory process that sets aside the common law duty of confidentiality

   (e) The disclosure can be justified in the public interest.

Although GMC good practice guidance does not have the status of law, it is certainly not without teeth. As we have seen, the legal sources of the duty of confidentiality are complex and confusing, so in practice GMC guidance is more useful to doctors faced with a dilemma about whether to breach patient confidentiality. In addition, failure to comply with GMC guidance may lead to disciplinary proceedings, and if found guilty of serious professional misconduct, the doctor can be struck off the medical register. The Nursing and Midwifery Council's *Code of Professional Conduct* sets out similar duties and penalties for nurses, midwives, and health visitors.

In addition, any failure to follow GMC guidance might offer evidence that a doctor had not acted as a reasonable medical practitioner and was therefore in breach of his duty of care. Proving that a doctor has been negligent might be relatively straightforward where there has been a clear breach of GMC guidance, but as noted earlier, the patient will only be able to bring an action in negligence if damage was caused by the breach of confidence.

In 1997, a review of the use of patient-identifiable information in the NHS, chaired by Fiona Caldicott, set out six guiding principles, which were updated in 2013.

The Caldicott Principles[17]

1. Justify the purpose(s)

Every proposed use or transfer of personal confidential data within or from an organisation should be clearly defined, scrutinised and documented, with continuing uses regularly reviewed, by an appropriate guardian.

2. Don't use personal confidential data unless it is absolutely necessary

Personal confidential data items should not be included unless it is essential for the specified purpose(s) of that flow. The need for patients to be identified should be considered at each stage of satisfying the purpose(s).

---

[17] *Information: to share or not to share? The Information Governance Review* (DH: London, 2013).

3. Use the minimum necessary personal confidential data

Where use of personal confidential data is considered to be essential, the inclusion of each individual item of data should be considered and justified so that the minimum amount of personal confidential data is transferred or accessible as is necessary for a given function to be carried out.

4. Access to personal confidential data should be on a strict need-to-know basis

Only those individuals who need access to personal confidential data should have access to it, and they should only have access to the data items that they need to see. This may mean introducing access controls or splitting data flows where one data flow is used for several purposes.

5. Everyone with access to personal confidential data should be aware of their responsibilities

Action should be taken to ensure that those handling personal confidential data—both clinical and non-clinical staff—are made fully aware of their responsibilities and obligations to respect patient confidentiality.

6. Comply with the law

Every use of personal confidential data must be lawful. Someone in each organisation handling personal confidential data should be responsible for ensuring that the organisation complies with legal requirements.

7. The duty to share information can be as important as the duty to protect patient confidentiality

Health and social care professionals should have the confidence to share information in the best interests of their patients within the framework set out by these principles. They should be supported by the policies of their employers, regulators and professional bodies.

The Department of Health's *Confidentiality: NHS Code of Practice* lays out detailed guidance on the use of identifiable patient information,[18] supplemented in 2010 by more specific guidance on public interest disclosures. In 2016, NHS England updated its *Confidentiality Policy*, which sets out 'the requirements placed on all staff when sharing information within the NHS and between NHS and non-NHS organisations', one of which is compliance with the *NHS Code of Practice*.

4 PATIENTS WHO LACK CAPACITY

On the one hand, it is clear that the doctor's duty to respect patient confidentiality is universal. Medical records self-evidently contain confidential information, and if the duty of confidentiality arises from the nature of the information itself, then it must apply equally to the records

---

[18] (DH: London, 2003).

of patients who lack capacity. In *Venables v News Group Newspapers*,[19] for example, Dame Elizabeth Butler-Sloss P explained that 'Children, like adults, are entitled to confidentiality in respect of certain areas of information. Medical records are the obvious example.'

On the other hand, it will sometimes be necessary to involve others in decisions about the treatment of children and adults who lack capacity. Obviously, a baby or young child's right to confidentiality does not involve keeping information from her parents. On the contrary, a young child's parents are under a duty to take decisions about her medical treatment, and they can only do this if they are properly informed. The doctor's duty of confidentiality is therefore owed to the parent(s) and the child, rather than just to the child herself.

The House of Lords decision in the *Gillick* case (considered in Chapter 6) established that children who have reached an age of sufficient maturity will, in certain circumstances, have the right to keep information about their medical treatment from their parents. Following *Gillick*, in *R (on the application of Axon) v Secretary of State for Health*, Silber J confirmed that 2004 Department of Health guidance, which stated that children had a right to confidentiality in relation to treatment for abortion, was lawful.

R (on the application of Axon) v Secretary of State for Health[20]

Silber J

This application raises a tension between two important principles of which the first is that a competent young person under sixteen years of age (who is able to understand all aspects of any advice, including its consequences) is an autonomous person, who first should be allowed to make decisions about his or her own health and second is entitled to confidentiality about such decisions even vis-à-vis his or her parents. The second principle is that a parent of a young person has a responsibility for that young person's health and moral welfare with the consequence that he or she should be informed if a medical professional is considering providing advice and treatment on sexual matters to that young person so that the parent could then advise and assist the young person. There is also a significant public policy dimension because there is evidence that without the guarantee of confidentiality, some of these young people might not seek advice or treatment from medical professionals on sexual matters with potentially disturbing consequences . . .

[I]n the period between the decision of the Court of Appeal in *Gillick* and that of the House of Lords during which medical professionals were required to pass on information to children's parents, the number of young women aged under 16 who sought advice on contraception fell from 1.7 per resident thousand to 1.2 per resident thousand, which was a striking and disturbing reduction of just under one-third . . . These statistics provide clear and powerful evidence of what happens when young people are not assured of confidentiality when they are considering obtaining advice and treatment on sexual matters.

Interestingly, the 2004 guidance which was challenged in *Axon* did not confine a child's right of confidentiality to children who are *Gillick*-competent:

The duty of confidentiality owed to a person under 16, in any setting, is the same as that owed to any other person. This is enshrined in professional codes. All services providing advice and treatment on contraception, sexual and reproductive health should produce an explicit

---

[19] [2001] 2 WLR 1038.   [20] [2006] EWHC 37 (Admin).

confidentiality policy which reflects this guidance and makes clear that young people under 16 have the same right to confidentiality as adults.[21]

If only *Gillick*-competent children can consent to treatment without parental knowledge, then, in practice, the right to keep information from their parents will arise only for children who are competent to give consent. Under-16s who are not *Gillick*-competent are therefore in a rather curious position. They are owed a duty of confidentiality, which may not arise in practice because their inability to give consent means that their parents will usually have to be involved in decisions about their medical treatment.

Adults who lack capacity are undoubtedly also owed a duty of confidentiality but, as we saw in Chapter 5, under section 4(7) of the Mental Capacity Act 2005 people who are involved in their care should be consulted about the patient's wishes and beliefs. The Mental Capacity Act Code of Practice insists that the duty of confidence still applies, and that discussions with carers must be necessary and proportionate.

Mental Capacity Act 2005 Code of Practice

5.56 Decision-makers must balance the duty to consult other people with the right to confidentiality of the person who lacks capacity. So if confidential information is to be discussed, they should only seek the views of people who it is appropriate to consult, where their views are relevant to the decision to be made and the particular circumstances.

5.57 There may be occasions where it is in the person's best interests for personal information (for example, about their medical condition, if the decision concerns the provision of medical treatment) to be revealed to the people consulted as part of the process of working out their best interests. Healthcare and social care staff who are trying to determine a person's best interests must follow their professional guidance, as well as other relevant guidance, about confidentiality.

The GMC's confidentiality guidance further suggests that doctors should seek the agreement of the adult who lacks capacity to sharing information with others.

General Medical Council[22]

44. You may disclose personal information if it is of overall benefit to a patient who lacks the capacity to consent. When making the decision about whether to disclose information about a patient who lacks capacity to consent, you must:

    (a) make the care of the patient your first concern

    (b) respect the patient's dignity and privacy

    (c) support and encourage the patient to be involved, as far as they want and are able, in decisions about disclosure of their personal information …

---

[21] Department of Health, *Best Practice Guidance for Doctors and other Health Professionals on the Provision of Advice and Treatment to Young People under 16 on Contraception, Sexual and Reproductive Health* (DH: London, 2004).

[22] *Confidentiality: good practice in handling patient information* (GMC, 2018).

46. You might need to share personal information with a patient's relatives, friends or carers to enable you to assess the overall benefit to the patient. But that does not mean they have a general right of access to the patient's records or to be given irrelevant information about, for example, the patient's past healthcare ...

48. If a patient asks you not to disclose personal information about their condition or treatment, and you believe they lack capacity to make that decision, you should try to persuade them to allow an appropriate person to be given relevant information about their care. In some cases, disclosing information will be required or necessary, for example under the provisions of mental health and mental capacity laws.

49. If the patient still does not want you to disclose information, but you consider that it would be of overall benefit to the patient and you believe they lack capacity to make that decision, you may disclose relevant information to an appropriate person or authority. In such cases, you should tell the patient before disclosing the information and, if appropriate, seek and carefully consider the views of an advocate or carer. You must document in the patient's records your discussions and the reasons for deciding to disclose the information.

Degenerative brain diseases, such as Alzheimer's and other types of dementia, raise particularly difficult questions in relation to patient confidentiality. Depending on the stage the patient has reached when her dementia is diagnosed, her partner or relatives may have to be involved in the diagnostic process, and in decisions about her care. Indeed, Pucci et al's research indicated that most relatives of patients suffering from Alzheimer's disease believed that the patient should not be told about the diagnosis, for fear of provoking or aggravating depressive symptoms.[23]

As the Nuffield Council on Bioethics has pointed out, carers of people with dementia need both support and information in order to fulfil their caring role.

Nuffield Council on Bioethics[24]

3.22 Whilst the principle of patient confidentiality is an important one in the doctor–patient relationship, a diagnosis of dementia has implications not only for the person with dementia, but also for close family members who are likely to take on a significant caring role and need appropriate information and support to do so . . .

7.26 When a person with dementia lacks capacity to make a particular decision about their health or welfare, it is clearly in their best interests that those involved in making the decision on their behalf have access to the necessary information and are appropriately supported. Professionals should be made aware of the legitimate reasons why carers may ask for medical or other confidential information, and ordinarily start from the assumption that if a carer is involved in making a decision on behalf of the person with dementia, then they will need the same level of information as any other member of the care team. In short, carers should be provided with any information that it is necessary for them to know in order to carry out their caring role.

[23] E Pucci et al, 'Relatives' attitudes towards informing patients about the diagnosis of Alzheimer's disease' (2003) 29 Journal of Medical Ethics 51–4.
[24] *Dementia: Ethical Issues* (NCOB, 2009).

5 DECEASED PATIENTS

The Department of Health's Code of Practice[25] and GMC Guidance are both clear that the duty to respect patient confidentiality continues to exist after the patient has died.

General Medical Council[26]

134. Your duty of confidentiality continues after a patient has died.

136. In other circumstances, whether and what personal information may be disclosed after a patient's death will depend on the facts of the case. If the patient had asked for information to remain confidential, you should usually abide by their wishes. If you are unaware of any instructions from the patient, when you are considering requests for information you should take into account:

(a) whether disclosing information is likely to cause distress to, or be of benefit to, the patient's partner or family

(b) whether the disclosure will also disclose information about the patient's family or anyone else

(c) whether the information is already public knowledge or can be anonymised or de-identified

(d) the purpose of the disclosure.

Although it has always been the case that there was an ethical duty to respect confidentiality after death, until relatively recently, it was unclear whether the legal duty of confidence applied after a patient's death. In *Lewis v Secretary of State for Health*, a doctor had been reluctant to disclose patient records, after the patients' deaths, to the Redfern Inquiry, which was investigating the removal and retention of tissue samples from individuals who had worked at the Sellafield nuclear plant. The first question for Foskett J was whether it was at least arguable that the duty of confidentiality applied after these patients' deaths. Having concluded that it was, he decided that disclosure could nevertheless be justified in the public interest.

Lewis v Secretary of State for Health[27]

Foskett J

There is no doubt that it is the view of those who administer the medical profession, both in the United Kingdom and worldwide, that the professional obligation of the doctor is to maintain the medical confidences of the patient after the patient's death. The Hippocratic oath, the Declaration of Geneva and guidance given by the General Medical Council all point to this professional obligation. The content of an obligation imposed upon a professional by his profession is not, of course, necessarily coterminous with the obligation imposed by law in similar circumstances although it may be a useful indicator of the perceived values by which the relationship of the professional to his client (in this case, patient) are to be judged.

---

[25] *Confidentiality: NHS Code of Practice* (DH: London, 2003) para 12.
[26] *Confidentiality: good practice in handling patient information* (GMC, 2018).
[27] [2008] EWHC 2196 (QB).

In the course of argument, I ventured the proposition that if anyone is asked whether they thought that something said in confidence to their doctor would remain confidential after their death, the answer would almost certainly be 'yes'. That seems to me to accord with contemporary notions of what is accepted practice and indeed it might even reflect notions of what the law, not merely professional ethics, may require . . .

I have not the slightest doubt that this is an appropriate case in which to hold that the public interest in disclosure of the material sought outweighs the other public interest, namely, that of maintaining the confidentiality of medical records and information, provided, of course, proper safeguards are put in place to ensure that no inappropriate information becomes public.

This was followed by *Press Association v Newcastle Hospitals Foundation Trust*, in which the Press Association sought to discharge a reporting restriction order which had prevented them from naming a woman who had since died. Peter Jackson J had declared that it would be lawful for LM's doctors to withhold the blood transfusion to which she had refused to consent. LM was a Jehovah's Witness with no relatives or close friends. The Press Association had submitted that anonymity was no longer necessary because LM had died. Peter Jackson J held that the court did have the power to preserve anonymity after death, but that, in the present case, that power should not be exercised and LM's identity could be disclosed.

Press Association v Newcastle Hospitals Foundation Trust [28]

Peter Jackson J

It is not in dispute between the parties that the court has the power to make an order preventing the reporting of the deceased's name in order to uphold the rights of others, such as medical or care staff or family members . . . What is in dispute is the existence of any independent right to protection for the deceased person herself. This comes into sharp focus in LM's case, because she had no known family or friends. In consequence, she cannot be kept anonymous for the sake of others . . .

None of the information given in the judgment or referred to during the hearing is of particular sensitivity or confidentiality, nor does it reflect any discredit on LM. The physical, mental and spiritual challenges that she faced could confront anyone. Also, her way of life, whether better described as independent or isolated, makes it unlikely that any wider harm will come from linking her name with her story.

There is a proper interest in the name of a person who dies being a matter of public record, whether or not there is to be an inquest. The right to privacy is only likely to outweigh this consideration in very special circumstances . . .

I take account of the fact that LM was a private person who would not have wanted her private information to be made public. I also have regard to her medical confidentiality. In this instance, that has not been extensively breached. The fact that she suffered from mental illness would have been apparent to those who knew her and little detail is given of her physical illness. Nor can it be said that to reveal her name would deter applications in similar situations when the degree of scrutiny given to this case is considered.

All things considered, I find that the balance in this case falls in favour of discharging that part of the order that confers anonymity on LM. But there is a balance to be struck, and in other cases the conclusion might be different.

---

[28] [2014] EWCOP 6.

Towards the end of 2015, there was considerable, and in the case of some newspapers, lurid press interest in the Court of Protection's decision in *King's College NHS Foundation Trust v C*,[29] that a 50-year-old woman, who was said to have lost her 'sparkle', had capacity and was therefore entitled to refuse dialysis. Pixelated photographs of C and her daughters had been published and a *Sun* headline had read: 'Socialite who chose to die at 50 rather than grow old was a "man eater obsessed with sex, money and cars"'. In *Re C (Deceased)*, Charles J continued the reporting restrictions indefinitely, in order to protect the interests of C's daughters.

Re C (Deceased)[30]

Charles J

It only takes a moment to realise how personal and emotionally difficult it was for them to give or support the giving of evidence concerning their lives and that of their mother which could found the view that their mother had the capacity to make a decision effectively to end her life that they thought was unwise and they did not want her to make. The giving of that evidence took courage and I suggest shows a recognition by C's children of the importance of their mother's wishes, feelings and beliefs being made known to the COP [Court of Protection] and thus of their devotion and responsibility. Much of the evidence is extremely personal and goes to the core of the private mother and child relationship which clearly does not end when the child attains the age of majority.

In contrast, in *M v Press Association*, reporting restrictions in *M v N*,[31] a case involving the withdrawal of life-sustaining treatment from a woman in a minimally conscious state, which had attracted little press interest and certainly no upsetting headlines, were lifted after Mrs N's death.

M v Press Association[32]

Hayden J

Though there is of course no guarantee against press intrusion, there is no evidence at all of any having occurred in the last few months ... Nor does a dispassionate analysis of the facts point to any significant intrusion in the future ...

I have no doubt that those closest to M and her family, those who matter to the family the most, will have identified Mrs N from the facts of the case. For those beyond that circle, the name of the individual serves only to make her story more real and the issues it raises more acute. Therein lies the public interest. By contrast the introduction of both Mrs N's and M's name into the public domain has relatively limited impact on M's privacy or Article 8 rights more generally. Certainly there is no real evidence to that effect ...

I am acutely conscious of M's deep seated wish to preserve her mother's anonymity in this case, as well of course, as her own. For the reasons I have analysed above I have come to the firm conclusion that the balance here weighs more heavily in favour of freedom of expression.

While the right to confidentiality can survive a person's death, it may be easier to establish that it is outweighed by other considerations after a person has died. In the next extract, Mary

---

[29] [2015] EWCOP 80.   [30] [2016] EWCOP 21.
[31] [2015] EWCOP 76.   [32] [2016] EWCOP 34.

Donnelly and Maeve McDonagh explain why the living have an interest in the maintenance of confidentiality after a patient's death.

Mary Donnelly and Maeve McDonagh[33]

In light of the conceptual challenges faced by accounts of posthumous harm, it may be more helpful to focus on a less ambitious case in favour of protecting the 'interests' of the dead. This argument is not that the dead are harmed by posthumous events but that the living may be harmed by the prospect of posthumous events … Thus, the interests of the living person may be harmed, not by the attribution of posthumous harm … , but by the prospect that posthumous harm will occur. If a living person cannot be confident that, for example, a degree of respect will be shown to his or her dead body or that his or her wishes will be respected after death, then he or she may experience harm in the sense of considerable anxiety and unhappiness while alive. The same might be said in respect of a person's broader reputation or place in his or her family's affections. The thought that this would be threatened after his or her death would no doubt be a source of considerable concern to a (living) person. Thus, one might reasonably argue that failure to accord a certain degree of protection to the dead could significantly harm the interests of the living.

Insofar as one of the reasons to respect confidentiality after death is the distress disclosure could cause to surviving relatives, the duty of confidentiality owed to the dead will weaken with the passage of time.

General Medical Council[34]

138. Archived records relating to deceased patients remain subject to a duty of confidentiality, although the potential for disclosing information about, or causing distress to, surviving relatives or damaging the public's trust will diminish over time.

We can see a particularly clear example of this in the case of *Éditions Plon v France*. Ten days after the death of ex-French President François Mitterrand, his doctor sought to publish a book which revealed that Mitterrand had been suffering from cancer for the whole of his presidency. Mitterrand's widow and children sought, and were granted, a temporary injunction to prevent publication. According to the judge who granted the injunction:

By their very nature, they constitute a particularly serious intrusion into the intimate sphere of President François Mitterrand's private family life and that of his wife and children. The resulting interference is especially intolerable in that it has occurred within a few days of President Mitterrand's death and burial.

The decision of a court ten months later to continue these injunctions was overturned by the ECtHR. In *Éditions Plon v France*,[35] the ECtHR found that ten months after Mitterrand's

---

[33] 'Keeping the Secrets of the Dead? An Evaluation of the Statutory Framework for Access to Information About Deceased Persons' (2011) 31 Legal Studies 42–70.
[34] *Confidentiality: good practice in handling patient information* (GMC, 2018).
[35] (2006) 42 EHRR 36.

death, the balance had shifted and the public interest in free expression now outweighed the duty to respect the medical secrets of the dead:

> the more time that elapsed, the more the public interest in discussion of the history of President Mitterrand's two terms of office prevailed over the requirements of protecting the President's rights with regard to medical confidentiality.

6 EXCEPTIONS TO THE DUTY OF CONFIDENTIALITY

Before we consider exceptions to the duty of confidentiality, it is worth noting that breaches of confidentiality do not always involve deliberate decisions to share information. Rather, inadvertent breaches of confidentiality are almost certainly more common.

David Oliver[36]

> Patients' names, preferred names, instructions about moving and handling, and diet are often above the bed, with drug charts and other charts in folders nearby . . .
>
> The welcome move to unrestricted visiting and involvement of carers means a greater risk of confidentiality breaches. We don't have the time to clear visitors from every area or take them to private rooms for a chat when they are already at the bedside. Moreover, bedside conversations can greatly benefit care and communication, but closed curtains aren't sound-proof. Then there is email. Patients' relatives are increasingly emailing doctors for updates and answers to questions. NHS internet servers are not secure enough for sending confidential communication. But is replying over a potentially insecure communication channel worse than leaving families without prompt reassurance or information?

Patient data might also be inadvertently shared through breaches of IT security. Sophisticated encryption systems can be used to protect electronic patient records, but they cannot eliminate simple human errors, like leaving information on a computer screen visible to other people. NHS England's *Confidentiality Policy* reminds staff of the importance of avoiding carelessness.

NHS England[37]

4.4 Carelessness

4.4.1 All staff have a legal duty of confidence to keep person-identifiable or confidential information private and not to divulge information accidentally. Staff may be held personally liable for a breach of confidence and must not:

- Talk about person-identifiable or confidential information in public places or where they can be overheard.

---

[36] 'Confidentiality on the Wards – Regulations and Reality' (2017) 356 British Medical Journal j1253.
[37] *Confidentiality Policy* (NHS England, 2014).

- Leave any person-identifiable or confidential information lying around unattended, this includes telephone messages, computer printouts, faxes and other documents, and
- Leave a computer terminal logged on to a system where person-identifiable or confidential information can be accessed, unattended.

(a) CONSENT

If the patient explicitly consents to the disclosure of information, the doctor is no longer under a duty keep it secret. This is not strictly speaking an exception to the duty of confidence: rather, the patient's agreement to disclosure means that no duty of confidence exists.

More complicated is the question of whether a patient could ever be said to have given their implied consent to disclosure. In order to establish that there was implied consent to disclosure, as the GMC's guidance to doctors and the Department of Health's Code of Practice make clear,[38] the patient must be aware of the practice of disclosure and have been given an opportunity to object to it.

General Medical Council[39]

28. You may rely on implied consent to access relevant information about the patient or to share it with those who provide (or support the provision of) direct care to the patient if all of the following are met.

(a) You are accessing the information to provide or support the individual patient's direct care, or are satisfied that the person you are sharing the information with is accessing or receiving it for this purpose.

(b) Information is readily available to patients, explaining how their information will be used and that they have the right to object. This can be provided in leaflets and posters, on websites, and face to face. It should be tailored to patients' identified communication requirements as far as practicable.

(c) You have no reason to believe the patient has objected.

(d) You are satisfied that anyone you disclose personal information to understands that you are giving it to them in confidence, which they must respect.

Catherine Stanton points out that the new GMC guidance is more explicit than its predecessor about the potential risks to the patient from *not* sharing data for patient care.

Catherine Stanton[40]

Whereas the previous guidance referred solely to the positive benefit for information sharing, the new guidance highlights that patients may be put at risk if those caring for them do not

---

[38] *Confidentiality: NHS Code of Practice* (DH: London, 2003) para 14.
[39] *Confidentiality: good practice in handling patient information* (GMC, 2017).
[40] 'Patient Information: To Share or Not to Share?' (2018) 26 Medical Law Review 328–45.

have access to such information. The onus is now very clearly on the professional to share relevant information for a patient's direct care, unless the patient has objected. The guidance highlights in particular the context of multi-agency and multidisciplinary care where information sharing is so important for providing effective care.

Paragraph 29 of the latest GMC guidance sets out a new 'surprise test': 'If you suspect a patient would be surprised to learn about how you are accessing or disclosing their personal information, you should ask for explicit consent unless it is not practicable to do so.'

In the next extract, Victoria Chico and Mark Taylor suggest that evidence of the public acceptability of the uses of health data might be useful in determining how much information needs to be provided in order to establish that there was broad consent to its use. For example, relatively little information may be necessary to establish consent to the sharing of data within the NHS, whereas much more detail may need to be provided for there to be implied consent to data sharing with commercial organisations.

Victoria Chico and Mark J Taylor[41]

Although there is general support for the use of health data to provide public health benefits, there are nuances within that support, and different uses of patient health data by different organisations enjoy different levels of acceptance. For example, work done by Wellcome has found that it is more acceptable to disclose health data to universities and charities than to commercial organisations. Further acceptability declined sharply where the intended disclosee was a private provider either inside or outside the health sector ...

The growing evidence concerning people's views on the acceptability of the use of their health data could be an important indicator of where specific information ought to be provided. Where the conditions of who can use the data and why are deliberately constructed to conform with those more likely to be readily accepted—being less likely to be surprising or contentious—then consent may be 'real' even on the basis of little fine-grained information. However, where data is to be used by organisations, or for purposes, that are less widely expected or supported (e.g. shared outside the NHS or the medical research context), then it will be important to provide significantly more information about these uses, and in more detail, before persons feel that they are 'broadly aware' of the nature of the potential uses such that they can be considered to have accepted them.

In *R (on the application of W, X, Y and Z) v The Secretary of State for Health v The Secretary of State for the Home Department*, W, X, Y, and Z were likely to be affected by a change in the Immigration Rules which would mean that anyone not resident in the UK could be refused entry or leave to remain if they had unpaid NHS debts of more than £1,000, incurred for treatment other than A&E services, family planning, or treatment with public health implications. They challenged this change on the grounds that the relevant bodies had no power to disclose confidential information about the date and cost of their medical treatment without their consent. At first instance, it had been held that the information was not confidential. On appeal, in *R (on the application of W, X, Y and Z) v The Secretary of State for Health v The Secretary of*

---

[41] 'Using and Disclosing Confidential Patient Information and the English Common Law: What are the Information Requirements of a Valid Consent?' (2018) 26 Medical Law Review 51–72.

State for the Home Department, the Court of Appeal decided that the information was private, but that there could be no expectation of privacy with respect to the Secretary of State and the Home Office.

R (on the application of W, X, Y and Z) v The Secretary of State for Health and The Secretary of State for the Home Department[42]

Lord Dyson MR

We do not see how overseas visitors who, before they are treated in an NHS hospital, are made aware of the fact that, if they incur charges in excess of £1,000 and do not pay them within 3 months, the Information may be passed to the Secretary of State for onward transmission to the Home Office for the stated immigration purpose can have any, still less any reasonable, expectation that the Information will not be transmitted in precisely that way. They will, however, have a reasonable expectation of privacy in relation to the Information vis-à-vis anyone else ... It follows that, even if the claimants had a right to privacy and confidentiality in the Information, it was not infringed by the disclosure.

(b) PUBLIC INTEREST

As we have seen, there is an exception to the duty of confidentiality where the public interest in disclosure of information outweighs the public interest in protecting patient confidentiality. In *Attorney General v Guardian Newspapers*,[43] Lord Goff explained that:

although the basis of the law's protection of confidence is that there is a public interest that confidences should be preserved and protected by the law, nevertheless that public interest may be outweighed by some other countervailing public interest which favours disclosure.

Because there is a strong public interest in protecting confidentiality, only weighty countervailing public interest factors will override the doctor's prima facie duty of confidence, and disclosures should always be justified and kept to a minimum. In the following sections we consider several overlapping public interest justifications for the disclosure of confidential information.

(1) Preventing Harm to Others

Where the possibility of harm to others is used to justify disclosure, there should be a real risk of serious harm.

General Medical Council[44]

63. Confidential medical care is recognised in law as being in the public interest. The fact that people are encouraged to seek advice and treatment benefits society as a whole as well

---

[42] [2015] EWCA Civ 1034.   [43] [1988] 3 WLR 776.
[44] *Confidentiality: good practice in handling patient information* (GMC, 2018).

as the individual. But there can be a public interest in disclosing information to protect individuals or society from risks of serious harm, such as from serious communicable diseases or serious crime.

64. If it is not practicable or appropriate to seek consent, and in exceptional cases where a patient has refused consent, disclosing personal information may be justified in the public interest if failure to do so may expose others to a risk of death or serious harm. The benefits to an individual or to society of the disclosure must outweigh both the patient's and the public interest in keeping the information confidential.

65. Such a situation might arise, for example, if a disclosure would be likely to be necessary for the prevention, detection or prosecution of serious crime, especially crimes against the person . . .

66. Other examples of situations in which failure to disclose information may expose others to a risk of death or serious harm include when a patient is not fit to drive, or has been diagnosed with a serious communicable disease, or poses a serious risk to others through being unfit for work.

If a doctor believes that a patient's condition affects her fitness to drive, she should advise the patient not to drive, and explain that she has a legal duty to inform the Driver and Vehicle Licensing Agency. The GMC has produced specific guidance on this issue,[45] which advises doctors that, if they are unable to persuade the patient to stop driving, and they believe that there is a risk of death or serious harm as a result, they should contact the DVLA 'promptly and disclose any relevant medical information, in confidence, to the medical adviser'.[46]

W v Egdell is a relatively straightforward example of the public interest in disclosure trumping the public interest in protecting confidentiality. W had killed five people and wounded two others, and had been detained in a secure hospital. His application for release was turned down. His solicitors commissioned an independent psychiatrist's report from Dr Egdell, which indicated that W continued to pose a risk to the public. Dr Egdell disclosed this information both to the hospital and to the Secretary of State. W applied unsuccessfully for an injunction to stop them from using the report, and for damages for breach of confidence.

W v Egdell[47]

Bingham LJ

There is one consideration which in my judgment, as in that of the judge, weighs the balance of public interest decisively in favour of disclosure. It may be shortly put. Where a man has committed multiple killings under the disability of serious mental illness, decisions which may lead directly or indirectly to his release from hospital should not be made unless a responsible authority is properly able to make an informed judgment that the risk of repetition is so small as to be acceptable. A consultant psychiatrist who becomes aware, even in the course of a confidential relationship, of information which leads him, in the exercise of what the court considers a sound professional judgment, to fear that such decisions may be made on the basis of inadequate information and with a real risk of consequent danger to the public is entitled to take such steps as are reasonable in all the circumstances to communicate the grounds of his concern to the responsible authorities.

---

[45] *Confidentiality: patients' fitness to drive and reporting concerns to the DVLA or DVA* (GMC, 2017).
[46] Para 9.   [47] [1990] Ch 359.

While the balancing exercise in *W v Egdell* was relatively straightforward, other situations may be less clear-cut. What if the patient has never actually harmed anyone, but has violent thoughts or fantasies?

In the well-known US case *Tarasoff v Regents of the University of California*, the patient, Poddar, had confided in a university psychotherapist, Dr Moore, that he intended to harm T, a fellow student who had rejected his advances. The therapist informed the university police, but did not inform T herself, whom the patient subsequently murdered. The California Supreme Court held that the university's employee was under a duty to protect T by disclosing these threats to her.

Tarasoff v Regents of the University of California[48]

Justice Tobriner

When a therapist determines, or pursuant to the standards of his profession should determine, that his patient presents a serious danger of violence to another, he incurs an obligation to use reasonable care to protect the intended victim against such danger . . . We conclude that the public policy favoring protection of the confidential character of patient–psychotherapist communications must yield to the extent to which disclosure is essential to avert danger to others. The protective privilege ends where the public peril begins.

Commenting on the likely response to a *Tarasoff*-type case in the UK, Sheila McLean and JK Mason have suggested that 'the probability is that there would be no legal obligation to warn the person at risk but that, should the doctor do so, the breach of confidentiality would be regarded as justified'.[49] In short, both warning and not warning would be within the bounds of acceptable conduct. Doctors are therefore in the difficult position of having to make a judgement about whether the circumstances justify the disclosure of information acquired in confidence.

While there is plainly a public interest in preventing a patient from harming someone else, routine disclosure in such circumstances might make patients reluctant to share information about their fantasies with their psychotherapists, which in turn might make it more likely that their underlying problems will remain untreated. Paradoxically, then, routinely breaching the confidentiality of potentially dangerous patients might increase the risks such patients pose to others. This point was made forcefully in Justice Clark's dissenting judgment in *Tarasoff*.

Justice Clark

Assurance of confidentiality is important for three reasons. First, without substantial assurance of confidentiality, those requiring treatment will be deterred from seeking assistance. . . Second, the guarantee of confidentiality is essential in eliciting the full disclosure necessary for effective treatment . . . Third, even if the patient fully discloses his thoughts, assurance that the confidential relationship will not be breached is necessary to maintain his trust in his psychiatrist—the very means by which treatment is effected . . .

By imposing a duty to warn, the majority contributes to the danger to society of violence by the mentally ill and greatly increases the risk of civil commitment—the total deprivation of liberty—of

---

[48] 551 P 2d 334 (Cal 1976).
[49] *Legal and Ethical Aspects of Healthcare* (Greenwich Medical Media: London, 2003) 42.

those who should not be confined. Although . . . only a relatively few receiving treatment will ever present a risk of violence, the number making threats is huge, and it is the latter group—not just the former—whose treatment will be impaired and whose risk of commitment will be increased.

Similar difficulties arise in relation to communicable diseases. If a doctor knows that an HIV-positive individual has not informed his sexual partner of his HIV status, does the public interest in disclosure trump the public interest in protecting confidentiality? Although it might at first sight seem that alerting his sexual partner may enable that person to take steps to avoid infection, there are two reasons why confidentiality should prevail. First, there is a strong public interest in encouraging people to come forward for HIV testing and treatment, by promising them confidentiality in relation to their test results. Secondly, now that it is clear that someone whose viral load is being controlled effectively by antiretroviral medication is highly unlikely to pass on the disease, treating the patient is a more effective way to prevent onward transmission than breaching his confidentiality.

What if the HIV-positive person is also a healthcare worker? The risk of HIV transmission by healthcare workers is negligible: there have only ever been three reported cases worldwide.[50] Nevertheless, guidance from Public Health England is clear that HIV-positive healthcare workers should be cleared to perform exposure-prone procedures only if their viral load is below a certain level.[51] Regular retesting is required. If a healthcare worker refuses to be tested, she will not be cleared to perform exposure-prone procedures. Where there has been a risk that a patient has been exposed to a healthcare worker's blood, the patient should be informed, and post-exposure prophylaxis offered, if a new blood test reveals that the healthcare worker's viral load is above the specified level.

Before viral load testing made it possible to tell whether an HIV-positive healthcare worker was at risk of passing on the virus, and before regular HIV testing became mandatory for workers carrying out exposure-prone procedures, there were cases in which the courts had to balance the confidentiality of HIV-positive healthcare workers with other considerations, such as press freedom. In *H (A Healthcare Worker) v Associated Newspapers Ltd*, for example, H was a health care worker, who had been diagnosed as HIV-positive. The *Mail on Sunday* wanted to publish a story about H's legal challenge to his employer's decision to carry out a 'lookback' exercise and inform his patients.

H obtained an injunction restraining the soliciting or publication of any information which might directly or indirectly lead to the disclosure of his identity, or his whereabouts, or his speciality. The Court of Appeal stressed the importance of maintaining patient confidentiality, and granted orders restraining the publication of information of H's and N's identity. It refused to order that his speciality too should be kept secret. The risk that this would reveal H's identity was too small to justify inhibiting debate 'on what is a matter of public interest'.

H (A Healthcare Worker) v Associated Newspapers Ltd[52]

Lord Phillips MR

The consequences to H if his identity were to be disclosed would be likely to be distressing on a personal level. More than this, there is an obvious public interest in preserving the

---

[50] Public Health England, *The management of HIV infected healthcare workers who perform exposure prone procedures: updated guidance* (PHE, 2014).
[51] Ibid.   [52] [2002] EWCA Civ 195.

confidentiality of victims of the AIDS epidemic and, in particular, of healthcare workers who report the fact that they are HIV positive. Where a lookback exercise follows, it may prove impossible to preserve the identification of the worker but, if healthcare workers are not to be discouraged from reporting that they are HIV positive, it is essential that all possible steps are taken to preserve the confidentiality of such reports.

There is clearly a difference between disclosing information about a healthcare professional's health status to the press and disclosing it to an employer or to the GMC. Where a healthcare worker might be putting patients or colleagues at risk because of her failure to disclose relevant information about her health, disclosing this to an appropriate person will not be a breach of confidentiality, whereas publicly broadcasting the same information might be. This was the issue in *Saha v General Medical Council*, in which Stephen Morris QC, sitting as a High Court Judge, explained that informing the GMC about a doctor's Hepatitis B status did not amount to a breach of his confidentiality.

Saha v General Medical Council[53]

Stephen Morris QC

Medical confidentiality is not an absolute right, but necessarily involves a balancing of competing public interests. The public interest in patient safety and welfare is an extremely important consideration. A further highly relevant consideration is the persons to whom the disclosure has taken place or is envisaged; disclosure to a person who is aware of the confidentiality and who has a role in its consideration or evaluation (such as a health care worker) is to be distinguished from general disclosure or publication . . .

In my judgment, the disclosure by the three doctors of the Appellant's records, ultimately, to the GMC was justified by reference to the concerns that each of them had at the relevant time, and indeed each was under a duty to do so.

(2) Preventing or Detecting Crime

Both GMC guidance and the Department of Health Code of Practice specifically mention that disclosure of confidential information may be justified where it would assist in the prevention or detection of a serious crime.

Department of Health[54]

30. Under common law, staff are permitted to disclose personal information in order to prevent and support detection, investigation and punishment of serious crime and/or to prevent abuse or serious harm to others where they judge, on a case by case basis, that the public good that would be achieved by disclosure outweighs both the obligation of confidentiality to the individual patient concerned and the broader public interest in the provision of a confidential service.

---

[53] [2009] EWHC 1907 (Admin).   [54] *Confidentiality: NHS Code of Practice* (DH: London, 2003).

Section 11 of the Police and Criminal Evidence Act 1984 classifies medical records as 'excluded material' to which the police will not usually be allowed access. An exception exists if the police are investigating a 'serious arrestable offence'.[55] In such cases, the police may obtain a special procedure warrant that will require the disclosure of medical records. During a trial, the judge has discretion to excuse a witness from answering a question when it would involve a breach of confidence, but equally he can order that confidential information is disclosed if it is necessary in the interests of justice.

Under section 172 of the Road Traffic Act 1988, a person can be required to give information which may lead to the identification of a driver who is alleged to have committed certain offences. In *Hunter v Mann*, a doctor had treated two people who had been involved in a car crash on the same day as a hit-and-run accident had occurred. A police officer asked the doctor to disclose the names and addresses of the two people he had treated, but he refused on the grounds that he would be breaching his duty of confidentiality. He was convicted under the Road Traffic Act 1972 (which preceded the 1988 Act), and his conviction was upheld on appeal.

Hunter v Mann[56]

Boreham J

May I say, before leaving this case, that I appreciate the concern of a responsible medical practitioner who feels that he is faced with a conflict of duty. That the appellant in this case was conscious of a conflict and realised his duty both to society and to his patient is clear from the finding of the justices, but he may find comfort, although the decision goes against him, from the following. First that he has only to disclose information which may lead to identification and not other confidential matters.

Often, of course, disclosure justified by the need to prevent serious crime could often also be justified by the 'harm to others' exception we have just considered. But the two are not necessarily synonymous. There is a public interest in the detection of crime even when there is no immediate risk of reoffending, and even when the crime itself did not involve physical injury, though obviously, the less serious the criminal offence, the less likely that the public interest in protecting confidentiality will be trumped by the public interest in facilitating the prevention and detection of crime.

Complex issues arise if the patient refuses to consent to the disclosure of a suspected crime where she is the only victim, and no one else is at risk. Under the Serious Crimes Act 2015, healthcare professionals are under a duty to notify the police if they discover a case of female genital mutilation carried out on a girl/young woman under the age of 18.[57] But what if a healthcare worker suspects that an adult patient is a victim of domestic abuse, and she is refusing to consent to the sharing of information with the police or other agencies?

The GMC guidance states that 'You should ... usually abide by the patient's refusal to consent to disclosure, even if their decision leaves them (but no one else) at risk of death or serious harm'.[58] 'Usually' suggests that there might be an exception to this, and, in a footnote, the GMC explains that 'this is an uncertain area of law, and, if practicable, you should seek

---

[55] Schedule 1.   [56] [1974] QB 767.   [57] Section 74.
[58] *Confidentiality: good practice in handling patient information* (GMC, 2018) para 59.

independent legal advice before making such a disclosure without consent'.[59] The same foot-note suggests that 'in very exceptional circumstances', 'where there is clear evidence of an imminent risk of serious harm to the individual, and where there are no alternative (and less intrusive) methods of preventing that harm', disclosure without consent might be justifiable.

In the next extract, Emma Cave suggests that this may be a scenario in which the courts should invoke the inherent jurisdiction of the High Court to protect vulnerable adults.

Emma Cave[60]

Where an individual withholds consent to allow the doctor to disclose evidence of harmful abuse or neglect, a number of issues arise. On one hand, the patient's rights and interests in keeping the information confidential and public policy considerations around the need to ensure that people who suffer abuse feel able to talk frankly to healthcare professionals militate against disclosure. On the other hand, the desire to bring the perpetrators to justice and the uncertainty regarding the validity of the abused person's refusal to consent to disclosure may provide reasons to overrule the patient . . .

Scotland and Wales have enacted legislation – the Social Services and Well-being (Wales) Act 2014 and the Adult Support and Protection (Scotland) Act 200753 – to require doctors and other agencies to notify local authorities where an adult is at risk of abuse. In England, the route is significantly less clear . . .

We now know that the Mental Capacity Act test is not exhaustive. Those who cannot decide by reason of coercion, undue influence or other factors may lack capacity at common law . . . if the patient retains capacity but lacks the ability to make a voluntary consent or refusal then, as the law stands, the doctor should apply to the High Court to exercise its inherent jurisdiction.

In 2010, the Department of Health issued supplementary guidance on public interest disclosures which explains that although some crimes are clearly 'serious', and would justify breaching confidentiality, there are also grey areas where judgements have to be made.

Department of Health[61]

12. . . . 'Serious crime' is not clearly defined in law but will include crimes that cause serious physical or psychological harm to individuals. This will certainly include murder, manslaughter, rape, treason, kidnapping, and child abuse or neglect causing significant harm and will likely include other crimes which carry a five-year minimum prison sentence but may also include other acts that have a high impact on the victim.

13. On the other hand, theft, fraud or damage to property where loss or damage is not substantial are less likely to constitute a serious crime and as such may not warrant breach of confidential information, though proportionality is important here. It may, for example, be possible to disclose some information about an individual's involvement in crime without disclosing any clinical information.

[59] Footnote 19.

[60] 'Disclosure of Confidential Information to Protect the Patient: The Role of Legal Capacity in the Evolution of Professional Guidance' (2015) 3 Journal of Medical Law and Ethics 7–23.

[61] *Confidentiality: NHS Code of Practice Supplementary Guidance: Public Interest Disclosures* (DH: London, 2010).

14. In the grey area between these two extremes a judgement is required to assess whether the crime is sufficiently serious to warrant disclosure. The wider context is particularly important here. Sometimes crime may be considered as serious where there is a prolonged period of incidents even though none of them might be serious on its own (e.g. as sometimes occurs with child neglect). Serious fraud or theft involving significant NHS resources would be likely to harm individuals waiting for treatment. A comparatively minor prescription fraud might be serious if prescriptions for controlled drugs are being forged.

The GMC has issued specific guidance on what doctors should do where they suspect that a patient has been a victim of gun or knife crime. The police should be informed quickly whenever a person arrives at hospital with a gunshot wound or an injury from an attack with a knife, blade, or other sharp instrument. At this initial stage, personal information should not be disclosed, but, if the police seek further information, doctors may disclose this without the patient's consent if they believe that someone else may be at risk, or in order to assist in the detection of what is clearly a serious crime. Of course, the potential downside to routine disclosure in such cases is that if an injured person fears either retribution or their own arrest, it might act as a disincentive to seeking medical attention for what might be very serious injuries.

General Medical Council[62]

5. ... the police should usually be informed whenever a person presents with a gunshot wound. Even accidental shootings involving lawfully held guns raise serious issues for the police about, for example, firearms licensing. The police should also usually be informed when a person presents with a wound from an attack with a knife, blade or other sharp instrument ...

12. If it is probable that a crime has been committed, the police will ask for more information. If practicable or appropriate, you should ask for the patient's consent before disclosing personal information unless, for example, doing so:
    - may put you or others at risk of serious harm
    - would be likely to undermine the purpose of the disclosure, by prejudicing the prevention, detection or prosecution of a serious crime ...

13. If the patient refuses consent or cannot give it (e.g. because they are unconscious), you can still disclose information if it is required by law or if you believe disclosure is justified in the public interest.

14. Disclosures in the public interest may be justified when:
    - failure to disclose information may put someone other than the patient at risk of death or serious harm ...
    - disclosure is likely to help in the prevention, detection or prosecution of a serious crime.

It is worth noting that disclosure has also been justified in non-criminal proceedings. In *A Health Authority v X*,[63] a complex case involving disciplinary procedures for medical malpractice, the Court of Appeal held that disclosure, subject to conditions, would be justified on

---

[62] *Confidentiality: Reporting gunshot and knife wounds* (GMC, 2018).
[63] [2001] EWCA Civ 2014.

the grounds that the administration of disciplinary proceedings was analogous to the administration of criminal justice. According to Thorpe LJ:

> There is obviously a high public interest, analogous to the public interest in the due administration of criminal justice, in the proper administration of professional disciplinary hearings, particularly in the field of medicine.

Similarly, in *Woolgar v Chief Constable of the Sussex Police*,[64] the Court of Appeal held that the police were entitled to disclose information to a professional regulatory body on public interest grounds. Following the death of a patient in her care, and allegations of the over-administration of diamorphine, W, a registered nurse, had been arrested and interviewed by the police. No criminal charges were brought, but the regulatory body for nursing and midwifery sought access to those interviews. W, and the Royal College of Nursing on her behalf, resisted this on the grounds that a person who is interviewed by the police has a reasonable expectation that what they say will go no further. The Court of Appeal accepted that there was an expectation of confidentiality, but that this was outweighed by a stronger public interest in disclosure. As Kennedy LJ explained:

> Even if there is no request from the regulatory body, it seems to me that if the police come into possession of confidential information which, in their reasonable view, in the interests of public health or safety, should be considered by a professional or regulatory body, then the police are free to pass that information to the relevant regulatory body for its consideration.

(3) Teaching, Research, and Audit

Without access to patient information, it would be impossible to train medical staff, conduct clinical research, and carry out audits of patient care. Usually, of course, the patient's consent to the use of her medical notes should be sought. But in certain circumstances, disclosure without consent may be legitimate. Initially, fitting this within the 'harm to others' exception that we considered earlier might seem unpromising, since the benefits to patients from well-trained staff, properly tested treatments, and regulated services, although substantial, are not sufficiently direct or immediate to establish that any particular instance of disclosure will avert an immediate risk of death or serious injury.

Remember, however, that the balancing exercise does not just involve looking at the harm that might be prevented by disclosure, but also involves taking into account the importance of respecting patient confidentiality in the particular case. Where the disclosure involves the use of medical records in an epidemiological study, with no intention to disclose the patient's identity, or to feed any information back to her, the public interest in protecting secrecy may be more easily outweighed by the public interest in improved health care provision.

For research purposes, it may be possible to anonymize data, and in *R v Department of Health, ex parte Source Informatics*, the Court of Appeal decided that disclosing anonymized information cannot amount to a breach of confidence. The applicants had paid GPs and pharmacists for anonymized information from prescription forms, which they then sold to pharmaceutical companies. The Department of Health had issued advice that anonymization

---

[64] [1999] 3 All ER 604.

did not remove the duty of confidence, and that general practitioners and pharmacists should not participate in the scheme. The applicants applied for judicial review, seeking a declaration that the Department of Health's policy guidance was wrong. Latham J dismissed their application, and they appealed successfully to the Court of Appeal.

R v Department of Health, ex parte Source Informatics[65]

Simon Brown LJ

To my mind the one clear and consistent theme emerging from all these authorities is this: the confidant is placed under a duty of good faith to the confider and the touchstone by which to judge the scope of his duty and whether or not it has been fulfilled or breached is his own conscience, no more and no less. One asks, therefore, on the facts of this case: would a reasonable pharmacist's conscience be troubled by the proposed use to be made of patients' prescriptions? Would he think that by entering Source's scheme he was breaking his customers' confidence, making unconscientious use of the information they provide? . . .

In my judgment the answer is plain. The concern of the law here is to protect the confider's personal privacy. That and that alone is the right at issue in this case. The patient has no proprietorial claim to the prescription form or to the information it contains . . .

If, as I conclude, his only legitimate interest is in the protection of his privacy and, if that is safeguarded, I fail to see how his will could be thought thwarted or his personal integrity undermined. . . [I]n a case involving personal confidences I would hold . . . that the confidence is not breached where the confider's identity is protected . . .

I would . . . hold simply that pharmacists' consciences ought not reasonably to be troubled by co-operation with Source's proposed scheme. The patient's privacy will have been safeguarded, not invaded. The pharmacist's duty of confidence will not have been breached.

As we can see in the following extracts, the idea that anonymization solves the problem of patient confidentiality has been called into question in recent years.

Effy Vayena and Alessandro Blasimme[66]

Anonymization as a means of control, however, suffers from two limitations. The first is conceptual: anonymous use of data does not necessarily enable control over uses for specific purposes. For example, a person might not wish their data to be contributing to a particular kind of research due to social, cultural, religious, or other reasons. But individual control over the purpose of use cannot be exercised if the data have been anonymized. In this respect, anonymization may in fact hinder autonomy . . . The second limitation is pragmatic: there is mounting evidence pointing to the actual weaknesses of anonymization technologies, through increasing capabilities in data analytics. Hence, thinking about anonymization as if it were absolutely reliable creates a false sense of security and ultimately a false sense of control.

---

[65] [2001] QB 424.
[66] 'Biomedical big data: new models of control over access, use and governance' (2017) 14 Journal of Bioethical Inquiry 501–13.

Bonnie Kaplan[67]

[T]he foundation of much privacy regulation is the idea that if there is no personally identifiable information, there is no privacy harm ... Relying on de-identification assumes that patients mainly are concerned not to have their names attached to data about them. However, this is not always how they see it ... Patients who think it wrong that they themselves have no commercial interest in data about themselves, but that others do, may be distressed by practices they consider unethical by data aggregators, pharmaceutical companies, or individuals who sell patient data and so may not wish to contribute to these endeavors' profits. Also at issue is who determines if data are identifiable. Whether an official, such as a data controller in the EU, can identify an individual is not the same as whether a marketer, newspaper reporter, neighbor, or other party could.

While completely anonymized data which is incapable of identifying an individual may not be 'personal data' for the purposes of the GDPR, it will often be difficult to ensure that there is no possibility of linking the individual and their information. If linkage is possible, then the GDPR applies to the processing of that information. Even if the disclosure of anonymized records is not a breach of confidence, the process of anonymization itself undoubtedly involves the 'processing' of personal data, and will therefore be subject to the GDPR.

Under Article 6 of the GDPR, the processing of personal data is lawful only if one of several conditions are satisfied, the first being that 'the data subject has given consent to the processing of his or her personal data for one or more specific purposes'. Without the data subject's consent, processing will be lawful only if it is 'necessary', for example, 'in order to protect the vital interests of the data subject or of another natural person', or 'for the purposes of the legitimate interests pursued by the controller or by a third party'.

In the *Source Informatics* case, patient information was obtained for the purposes of treatment, and then used for commercial purposes by Source Informatics. This would appear to breach the previous Data Protection legislation, and Article 5 of the GDPR, that information should be 'collected for specified, explicit and legitimate purposes and not further processed in a manner that is incompatible with those purposes'. Although the GDPR specifies that 'further processing for ... scientific ... research purposes' shall 'not be considered to be incompatible with the initial purposes', Source Informatics were not intending to carrying out research, but to exploit the data for commercial gain.

In order to trace the progression of disease, it is sometimes necessary to use coded (or pseudonymized) data, where the patient is not identified, but where it would be possible to trace the information back to the patient. If information had to be completely anonymized (and hence usable without consent), it would be impossible to validate and update data, and eliminate the duplication of records. If patient consent to the use of records is necessary when data has been pseudonymized rather than anonymized, this would be a significant obstacle to the generation of useful data. Cancer registries, for example, hold an enormous amount of information about past patients, and if these historical records could not be used without tracing every patient and retrospectively asking for consent, invaluable epidemiological research into the causes of cancer would be impossible.

---

[67] 'Selling Health Data: De-Identification, Privacy, and Speech' (2015) 24 Cambridge Quarterly of Healthcare Ethics 256–71.

Moreover, as Michael Ferriter and Martin Butwell explain in the next extract, there would also be a danger of 'consent bias' since some people (perhaps those suffering from diseases which attract stigma) might be less likely than others to give consent, and the data would therefore no longer be representative of the population as a whole. Patients who have died or lost capacity would also be excluded, once again skewing the results. Seeking consent could also cause unnecessary alarm to patients who might worry that a request to re-examine their medical records is prompted by concern about their health.

Michael Ferriter and Martin Butwell[68]

There are whole areas of observational research—epidemiological research using case notes, case registers and disease registers—which do not require direct contact with the patient and where gaining consent may be impractical, impossible or undesirable: impractical because of dealing with such large numbers; impossible because of tracing all the participants; undesirable because in seeking consent the sample may be biased; or in gaining consent, needless anxiety may be caused to participants . . .

[C]onsent can fundamentally damage research by introducing bias. On a technical level, one of the strengths of carrying out research where hitherto consent has not been needed is its freedom from many such biases. It is acknowledged that certain groups of people are more likely to consent to take part in research than others. For whatever reasons, younger patients, men and members of ethnic minorities are all less likely to consent to participate in health research. This leads to a consequent bias in research carried out, problems in generalisation to the wider population as a whole and, ultimately, to the disadvantage of people in less compliant groups . . .

The crucial question that needs to be asked is: Has anyone ever been harmed by the use of their healthcare data in a case or disease register?

Identifiable data can be used without consent if it meets the criteria in Article 9(2) of the GDPR. Unchanged by the GDPR, section 251 of the National Health Service Act 2006 makes special provision for the use of data without patient consent.

National Health Service Act 2006 section 251

251 Control of patient information

(1) The Secretary of State may by regulations make such provision for and in connection with requiring or regulating the processing of prescribed patient information for medical purposes as he considers necessary or expedient—

(a) in the interests of improving patient care, or

(b) in the public interest . . .

(4) Regulations under subsection (1) may not make provision requiring the processing of confidential patient information for any purpose if it would be reasonably practicable to achieve that purpose otherwise than pursuant to such regulations, having regard to the cost of and the technology available for achieving that purpose.

---

[68] 'Confidentiality and Research in Mental Health' in Christopher Cordess (ed), *Confidentiality and Mental Health* (Jessica Kingsley Publishers: London, 2001) 159–69.

Section 251 allows the Secretary of State to make regulations which authorize the disclosure of confidential patient information without consent where it is needed to support essential NHS activity. Under regulation 5 of the Health Service (Control of Patient Information) Regulations 2002, this does not mean that regulations must be laid before parliament on each occasion, rather the Secretary of State can essentially give what is known as 'section 251' support to applications to use patient-identifiable data for specified purposes, such as contacting patients in order to invite them to participate in medical research.

Section 251 can only be used to support medical purposes that are, first, in the interests of patients or the wider public; secondly, where consent is not a practicable alternative; and, thirdly, where anonymized information will not suffice. It was originally intended to be a transitional arrangement, while the NHS developed mechanisms to seek and record consent, and more sophisticated anonymization techniques, but it is now acknowledged that section 251 powers are necessary in the longer term.

Responsibility for advising on section 251 applications lies with the Confidentiality Advisory Group within the Health Research Authority (HRA). The HRA itself can approve research applications and, for non-research applications, it advises the Secretary of State for Health on whether to give approval. If the application fits within an established precedent—for example, applications to identify a cohort of patients and subsequently seek their consent or time-limited access to undertake record linkage/validation or to anonymize the data—applicants can use the 'precedent set pathway' and receive approval from a sub-committee of the CAG more quickly.

Detailed information about all the projects which have received section 251 support is publicly available. For each project, there is a summary explaining why the use of identifiable information is necessary. For example, the research project summarized below needed section 251 approval in order to access GP records to assess the frequency of prescribing errors:

> This research application from the University of Nottingham set out the purpose of a research study to assess error rates in prescribing by GP registrars … A recommendation … was requested to cover access by a CCG-employed pharmacist to notes of 1,000 GP patients in the East Midlands, in order to assess the appropriateness of the most recent 100 prescriptions issued by each of 10 GP registrars recruited to the study. Access was requested to patient records on GP practice sites in order to extract anonymised data.[69]

In the next extract, Ian Brown et al argue that it has become too easy to use identifiable data without consent. Instead they argue that this should only be possible where the research is necessary to protect the public against very serious diseases.

Ian Brown, Lindsey Brown, and Douwe Korff [70]

> Medical research using patient records is rarely required to meet a serious and immediate threat of harm to particular people, although it can of course result in longer-term benefits to the general public, such as improved health …
>
> In our opinion, this means that the law … should not just allow the use of patient data without the latter's consent for certain generally-defined types of research. Rather, such use of

[69] 'April 2013 onward: Approved Research Applications', available at <www.hra.nhs.uk>.
[70] 'Using NHS patient data for research without consent' (2010) 2 Law, Innovation and Technology 219–58.

such data can only ever be allowed on a case-by-case basis, and only if the particular research that is proposed serves a particularly important public interest. This allows, for instance, the compulsory reporting of certain very serious infectious diseases in order to protect the general public, and use of this reporting data for statistical purposes and for research into measures to counter such a disease. It will not allow the use of patient data without consent for research into less serious diseases.

Any authorisation for use of patient data for secondary research purposes (without consent) must also be strictly 'necessary' for such a purpose—that is, there must really not be any other measures available that impinge less on the patients' privacy and autonomy. This has two implications. Under the law, it should only be possible to authorise disclosure without consent for very important research (as defined above), but even then only if it is really impossible or prohibitively difficult to obtain the consent of the data subject.

Do patients in fact mind if their records are used in research and audit? In the next extract, Martin PM Richards et al explain that patients in a breast cancer study seemed unconcerned about the use of their medical notes for the purposes of research.

MPM Richards et al[71]

None of those we interviewed had any concerns about confidentiality in relation to the ABC study. We asked if they knew how they had been selected for the study. None did; most simply assumed the researchers would have been told by their GPs or the cancer clinic of their breast cancer. Such possible passing on of information did not cause any concerns. In fact, the sample had been identified through the regional cancer registry but this was not stated in the information given at recruitment. The existence of such a registry was unknown to all but one of the interviewees ...

Women were asked how they would feel if their blood sample was passed to other medical researchers for work on other diseases 'such as heart disease or mental illness'. All said they would be quite happy for this to be done. They were further asked what they would feel about their samples going to a commercial company or a drug company for research. Most were also content with this though a couple were a little hesitant. One had concerns over patenting and said she would only agree if it was for a drug that would be available to everyone. She said she thought that cancer research should be done by the government, not private companies ...

Our interviews suggest that those who have had breast cancer are pleased to take part in genetic epidemiological research and do not perceive any particular issues related to confidentiality. Furthermore, participants said they were content for their blood samples to be used for other medical research. Most, but not all women, included commercial or drug company research in this.

On the other hand, in their study of public attitudes towards biomedical research, the Wellcome Trust found that while people generally did not mind their NHS records being used for research purposes, they appreciated being asked first. The view was consistently expressed that 'grounded in social conventions of courtesy: it is polite to ask. Not being

---

[71] 'Issues of consent and feedback in a genetic epidemiological study of women with breast cancer' (2003) 29 Journal of Medical Ethics 93–6.

asked is impolite and signals disrespect and being taken for granted. Implicit consent is no consent at all.'[72]

We can see a stark illustration of this finding in the response to the care.data programme. Led by NHS England and the Health and Social Care Information Centre, the intention behind care.data was to use the data held by the NHS in order to improve patient care, by, for example, understanding trends in public health and being able to plan the provision of NHS services more effectively. Powers to do this had been created under the Health and Social Care Act 2012, which had established the Health and Social Care Information Centre and empowered it to obtain identifiable patient information from GP practices, unless patients had specifically opted out. The NHS Constitution had also been amended to include an expectation that patients would be willing to share their information for planning and research purposes.

A public information campaign was launched, but not very successfully—the leaflet that was supposed to be sent to all households often failed to arrive, or was discarded as junk mail—and the programme had to be put on hold.

In the next extract, Pam Carter et al warn of the dangers of assuming that public support for the use of their data in specific research projects will translate into support for unspecified future uses.

Pam Carter, Graeme T Laurie, and Mary Dixon-Woods[73]

[M]ost of what is known about patients' support for research is based on quite particular examples of research participation—often those where patients already have an interest in a medical condition and where they are asked for quite specific consent to a project or programme... The extent to which the findings of this body of research about participation in specific, relatively well-bounded studies or cohorts by defined, consenting patients can be generalised to the broader conception of NHS citizenship implicit in the new policy direction is not clear.

There are many reasons to doubt that *care.data* could *reasonably* assume that the public would automatically confer upon it the same legitimacy and endorsement as that enjoyed by research where individual informed consent is sought and clear information about study aims is provided. For instance, the mobility of electronic data and the practical difficulties of specifying in advance the research questions for which data might be used or the populations to be studied mean that *care.data* was in many ways quite distinct from conventional research projects . . .

If *care.data* is to succeed, patients need to have the confidence that their medical records will be held securely, anonymised appropriately, and that secondary use of this personal data is in the public interest: the conditions of the social licence need to be respected in ways that go beyond compliance laid down in a legal framework.

(4) Statutory Exceptions

Under the Health Protection (Notification) Regulations 2010, registered medical practitioners (RMPs) are under a duty to notify a proper officer at their local authority Health Protection Team (HPT) if they have 'reasonable grounds for suspecting' that the patient:

- has a notifiable disease as listed in Schedule 1 to the Notification Regulations; or
- has an infection not included in Schedule 1 which in the view of the RMP presents, or could present, significant harm to human health (eg emerging or new infections); or

---

[72] Wellcome Trust, *Public Perspectives on the Governance of Biomedical Research: A Qualitative Study in a Deliberative Context* (Wellcome Trust: London, 2007) 87.

[73] 'The social licence for research: why care.data ran into trouble' (2015) 41 Journal of Medical Ethics 404–9.

- is contaminated (eg with chemicals or radiation) in a manner which, in the view of the doctor presents, or could present, significant harm to human health; or

- has died with, but not necessarily because of, a notifiable disease, or other infectious disease or contamination that presents or could present, or that presented or could have presented, significant harm to human health.

Schedule 1 contains a long list of notifiable diseases, including measles, mumps, rubella, food poisoning, TB, and whooping cough. Notification must include a set of prescribed information about the patient, including, but not limited to, her name and address; occupation (this might be important if the patient could have infected others at work, for example if her job involves handling food); overseas travel history, and information about the onset of her symptoms. The proper officer is then under a duty to pass this information to Public Health England within strict time limits.

The Health Protection (Local Authority Powers) Regulations 2010 and the Health Protection (Part 2A Orders) Regulations 2010 permit various powers to be exercised over people who are unwilling to cooperate with voluntary measures: for example, a child can be required to stay away from school. Local authorities can also apply to a lay magistrate for a Part 2A Order, and these can be more draconian. If necessary to protect public health, a Part 2A Order can require a person to undergo medical examination (but crucially, it cannot require them to receive treatment or vaccination); be taken to hospital; be kept in isolation or quarantine; answer questions about their health or other circumstances or have their health monitored and the results reported. Such powers should be used only if it is not possible to secure voluntary cooperation in order to avert a health risk, and their use must be proportionate in order not to represent a breach of Articles 5 and 8 of the European Convention on Human Rights.

The Health Service (Control of Patient Information) Regulations 2002 further allow for the common law duty of confidence to be set aside in certain circumstances in order to protect public health. Under regulation 3, confidential information may be processed in order to diagnose, control, and monitor communicable diseases, and, as we saw earlier, regulation 5 allows confidential information to be processed, with the approval of the Health Research Authority or the Secretary of State for Health, for other medical purposes, including research.

7 REMEDIES

If a patient discovers an impending breach of confidence, she can apply for an injunction to prevent disclosure. But what if the disclosure has already taken place? If an action in negligence is possible because the breach of confidence also amounted to a breach of the doctor's ordinary duty of care, then it might be possible to recover damages for harm caused as a result. But what if the patient has not suffered injury or economic loss, and the only 'harm' is the patient's distress?

Usually, it is not possible to recover damages for injury to feelings or reputation, but there are exceptions, such as damages for defamation. It is not entirely clear whether the courts would be willing to award damages for the injured feelings caused by a breach of confidentiality. At first instance in *W v Egdell*, Scott J stated that he thought this was 'open to question', and the point was not considered when the case reached the Court of Appeal:

I think [it] open to question whether shock and distress caused by the unauthorised disclosure of confidential information can . . . properly be reflected in an award of damages . . . In my

> judgment, W would not, even if I had found Dr Egdell to be liable, have been entitled to damages. He would have had to be content with a declaration and an injunction.[74]

In *Cornelius v De Taranto*, a psychiatric report, which contained certain potentially defamatory statements, had been circulated without the subject's consent. At first instance, Morland J awarded the claimant £3,750 damages, which included £3,000 'for the injury to the claimant's feelings caused by the unauthorized disclosure of the confidential information'.

Cornelius v De Taranto[75]

Morland J

Under art 8 of the Convention for the Protection of Human Rights and Fundamental Freedoms 1950 'everyone has the right to respect for his private and family life' . . . In my judgment, it would be a hollow protection of that right if in a particular case in breach of confidence without consent details of the confider's private and family life were disclosed by the confidant to others and the only remedy that the law of England allowed was nominal damages. In this case an injunction or order for delivery up of all copies of the medico-legal report against the defendant will be of little use to the claimant. The damage has been done . . .

In the present case, in my judgment, recovery of damages for mental distress caused by breach of confidence, when no other substantial remedy is available, would not be inimical to 'considerations of policy' but indeed to refuse such recovery would illustrate that something was wrong with the law . . .

My conclusion is that I am entitled to award damages for injury to feelings caused by breach of confidence. Although it is a novel instance of such a remedy, it is in accord with the movement of current legal thinking.

On appeal, the Court of Appeal did not specifically address the question of compensation for breach of confidence, but it left the damages award intact.

One of the purposes of the GDPR was to increase the penalties for misuse of data, and it sets maximum administrative fines of up to €20 million, or 4 per cent of annual global turnover, whichever is higher. The Information Commissioner's Office (ICO) can also issue warnings and reprimands; impose a temporary or permanent ban on data processing and order the rectification, restriction or erasure of data. In addition, Article 82 of the GDPR gives individuals the right to compensation for damages resulting from a breach of the GDPR: 'Any person who has suffered material or non-material damage as a result of an infringement of this Regulation shall have the right to receive compensation from the controller or processor for the damage suffered'.

8 ACCESS TO MEDICAL RECORDS

Under Article 15 of the GDPR, patients have a right of access to personal data, which includes their health records. In addition to access to the records themselves, patients have the right

---

[74] *W v Egdell* [1989] 2 WLR 689.   [75] (2001) 68 BMLR 62.

to know for what purposes their data has been processed, and to whom it has been, or will be disclosed.

The Freedom of Information Act 2000 provides another route for access to information held by public bodies. Personal information is, however, exempt from the Freedom of Information Act's provisions both in relation to the patient's own access to her health records and to third parties seeking access to them. It is only non-personal health information, such as health policy decisions, which might be subject to requests under the Freedom of Information Act.

Clearly, a patient might want access to her medical records is if she is contemplating an action in negligence. Under section 33 of the Senior Courts Act 1981, she can apply for a court order which will require the relevant doctor or hospital to disclose her records or notes. There must be a real prospect of litigation before disclosure will be ordered, however. A patient cannot use section 33 in order to engage in a 'fishing expedition' in the hope that some evidence of negligence might emerge. In addition, limitations can be imposed upon disclosure, for example the court might decide to restrict disclosure to the patient's legal and/or medical advisers.

9 ELECTRONIC PATIENT RECORDS

Most people probably assume that the NHS holds one central electronic patient record of their medical history. In fact, each patient—unless they object—has two electronic patient records. The summary care record will contain details about a patient's allergies and any medication they are taking. This is available nationally, so that if a person is taken to hospital in an emergency, the doctors treating her can have ready access to important information, without having to track down and make contact with her GP's surgery. The detailed record is only available locally.

In the next extracts, Ross Anderson is concerned about increased electronic sharing of information, while Mark Walport maintains that effective use of electronic patient records is the best way to improve patient care.

Ross Anderson[76]

> The summary care record was marketed to the public as a way for accident and emergency staff to check up on unconscious patients. According to Tony Blair, if you ended up in hospital in Bradford, doctors could look up your records with your general practitioner in Guildford. But this is nonsense. Very few patients have conditions that must be made known to emergency staff; for those that do, the properly engineered solution is MedicAlert. Unconscious patients often can't be reliably identified, so a database is less robust than a tag or card; the record doesn't have everything accident and emergency staff might want to see; and it is not even available in Scotland (let alone on a beach in Turkey) . . .
>
> Furthermore, the summary care record's consent procedures are completely unsatisfactory; sharing medical data requires informed consent, yet large numbers of patients are unaware that the record even exists. Expecting patients to be aware of it, and to opt out every time they interact with health care, is ridiculous . . . [T]his is not just a matter of law but goes

---

[76] 'Do summary care records have the potential to do more harm than good? Yes' (2010) 340 British Medical Journal 3020.

to the heart of the relationship between patients and doctors. The summary care record and the national information technology plan will make even highly sensitive information such as mental health records available by default to hundreds of thousands of people—and not just in the core NHS but in Whitehall, local authorities, and research laboratories. This is totally at odds with the expectations of patients, with safe systems engineering, and with prudent clinical practice, as well as with human rights law.

Mark Walport[77]

There is another huge potential benefit of a nationwide electronic patient record system, to improve treatment through research. Research provides the evidence that medical treatments work or, equally importantly, that they don't. It is an integral part of the best health systems . . . I do not believe that Connecting for Health has been marketed well to either patients or the medical profession. There has been much too much about its use as a management tool and too little about its primary aim, which should be to improve care . . . But one thing is certain—the best care requires the best medical records. A world class NHS demands a world class infrastructure. The future for medical records is digital.

Perhaps they are both right. Information sharing for research purposes is undoubtedly the best way to understand the causes of disease and improve health outcomes. At the same time, the IT systems that facilitate the sharing of data as sensitive as a patient's medical records need to be exceptionally robust.

It should, however, be noted that the greatest threat to patient confidentiality is probably human error, rather than data sharing for health and research purposes. In 2015, for example, it was revealed that a London clinic had sent a newsletter to 780 HIV-positive patients without taking steps to hide the distribution list, thus revealing every other patient's name and email address. In response, the Secretary of State for Health asked the Care Quality Commission to review data security measures within the NHS, and to incorporate checks on data security into its inspection regimes. While more robust data security measures may be able to minimize the risk of inadvertent disclosure, it is impossible to eliminate human frailty.

10   BIG DATA AND MHEALTH

New challenges to patient confidentiality are posed by the uses of 'big data' and the gathering of health-relevant information on mobile devices, known as mHealth. Big data refers to the ability to store and use vast quantities of data electronically. This could be used for research purposes, but also for treatment and diagnostic purposes. 'Machine learning' will enable a computer to be able to tell more effectively than a human being whether a scan shows early signs of malignancy, for example. But in order to do this, algorithms will need access to large databases of sensitive medical information.

---

[77] 'Do summary care records have the potential to do more harm than good? No' (2010) 340 British Medical Journal 3022.

Importantly, if machine learning is based upon skewed data sets, its results may be similarly skewed. As Philipp Kellmeyer explains:

> If an ANN [artificial neural network] for skin cancer detection, for example, was mostly trained on images from light-skinned individuals, it might perform better in screening light-skinned than dark-skinned individuals, which would effectively introduce an ethnic bias into the diagnostic procedure.[78]

According to Ziad Obermeyer and Ezekiel Emanuel, there may be also dangers in believing that an algorithm-identified correlation establishes causation:

> Algorithms may be good at predicting outcomes, but predictors are not causes. The usual common-sense caveats about confusing correlation with causation apply; indeed, they become even more important as researchers begin including millions of variables in statistical models.[79]

Nevertheless, Obermeyer and Emanuel go on to explain how machine learning has the potential to improve outcomes.

Ziad Obermeyer and Ezekiel J Emanuel[80]

> First, machine learning will dramatically improve prognosis. Current prognostic models ... are restricted to only a handful of variables, because humans must enter and tally the scores. But data could instead be drawn directly from EHRs [electronic health records] ... , allowing models to use thousands of rich predictor variables ...
>
> Second, machine learning will displace much of the work of radiologists and anatomical pathologists. These physicians focus largely on interpreting digitized images, which can easily be fed directly to algorithms instead. Massive imaging data sets, combined with recent advances in computer vision, will drive rapid improvements in performance, and machine accuracy will soon exceed that of humans. Indeed, radiology is already part-way there: algorithms can replace a second radiologist reading mammograms and will soon exceed human accuracy. The patient-safety movement will increasingly advocate use of algorithms over humans — after all, algorithms need no sleep, and their vigilance is the same at 2 am as at 9 am ...
>
> Third, machine learning will improve diagnostic accuracy. A recent Institute of Medicine report drew attention to the alarming frequency of diagnostic errors and the lack of interventions to reduce them. Algorithms will soon generate differential diagnoses, suggest high-value tests, and reduce overuse of testing.

MHealth, explained in the following extract, involves the increasingly common use of 'wellness apps' to gather health-specific, and hence sensitive data about an individual, which is then transmitted, stored and processed by commercial companies.

---

[78] 'Big Brain Data: On the Responsible Use of Brain Data from Clinical and Consumer-Directed Neurotechnological Devices' (2018) Neuroethics 1–18.

[79] 'Predicting the future—big data, machine learning, and clinical medicine' (2016) 375 New England Journal of Medicine 1216.

[80] Ibid.

Federica Lucivero and Karin R Jongsma[81]

The expectation of a 'mobile revolution' in healthcare is based on the fact that mobile phones are always in our pockets, portable and increasingly cheap. According to these narratives, the portability of mHealth systems and the ubiquity of the mobile network allow patients to freely move around while being checked remotely by healthcare providers and monitoring themselves outside the spaces traditionally dedicated to healthcare ...

Take for example an app that uses smartphone cameras to check moles for skin cancer risk: the user holds the device over a spot on her skin and takes a picture, and the app's algorithm immediately analyses the spot and recommends an action to take (e.g., whether the user should go to a specialist) or provides relevant information on skin cancer. This system allows users to archive their skin pictures, keep track of changes over time and share them with their doctor. These types of apps claim to prevent risks of skin cancer by offering a cheap tool for early self-assessment ...

However, despite the hype around mHealth, there are still many uncertainties around the safety, reliability and accuracy of mHealth systems. Risks include security issues and harms that may derive from potential disclosure of sensitive information to third parties or identity theft, and risks of false results. For example, a skin screening app may not be accurate and might fail to recognise an early-stage melanoma, falsely reassuring rather than alerting the user ...

Data collected and processed by wearable sensors and apps may contain sensitive information that is made accessible to several actors, as once such data are obtained they can be reproduced and used endlessly. For example, data may be analysed by the manufacturers for improving the app performance or sold to third parties for research or marketing. Users of such wearables and apps often have limited control over who has access to their data.

Similar issues arise in relation to self-testing kits, including for serious conditions such as HIV. On the one hand, the privacy of being able to test oneself at home is attractive to many, but this may increase the risk of user error, and both false positives and false negatives have serious consequences. There is also no guarantee that a person will seek appropriate health care and advice in the light of a positive result. Moreover, as Jonathan Youngs and Carwyn Hooper point out, a person might use a self-testing kit to test *someone else*, which raises obvious questions about the validity of the consent and protection of confidentiality.

Jonathan Youngs and Carwyn Hooper[82]

Consider: *Jennifer* meets Steve at a club. After a few drinks she invites him back to her place. They go to the bedroom. Jennifer turns to Steve and remarks, 'Oh by the way, before we have sex, I'm going to need you to take this HIV test'.

Perhaps there is nothing wrong here? Steve does not have to take the test. Doing so will be his choice. He may also derive a benefit from it; one study analysed the use of HIV self-testing kits in this manner among high-risk MSM [men who have sex with men], and concluded that it reduced HIV transmission ... We concede, however, that there are far better ways of learning

---

[81] 'A mobile revolution for healthcare? Setting the agenda for bioethics' (2018) Journal of Medical Ethics 685–9.

[82] 'Ethical implications of HIV self-testing' (2015) 41 Journal of Medical Ethics 809–13.

about an HIV diagnosis and that there are concerns here about coercion. A negative self-test might also be used as an excuse not to use barrier protection.

What of more worrying scenarios such as an abusive spouse forcing his/her partner to be tested? Reactive self-test results might well act as catalysts for blame and domestic violence within abusive relationships, separated from the support or protection of the health services. These tests could also be carried out on children or adults who lack capacity or even used coercively by employers or insurance companies?

In 2016, Google DeepMind and the Royal Free London NHS Foundation Trust announced that they were going to be working together to produce a smartphone app to help manage acute kidney injury. This involved the Royal Free giving Google access to 1.6 million patients' personal data over the course of several years. The Information Commissioner's Office subsequently ruled that the Royal Free had breached the previous Data Protection Act by not adequately informing patients that their data would be used in order to test the app, and thereby not giving them the option to opt out.

In the next extract Julia Powles and Hal Hodson explain some of the implications of this sort of arrangement between large tech companies and the NHS.

Julia Powles and Hal Hodson[83]

It is worth noting that in digesting our medical records and histories, machine learning systems have the potential to uncover new hypotheses and trends about us, as a population, that are difficult to adapt to and deal with. It may turn out, for instance, that certain kinds of people are particularly susceptible to requiring an expensive medical intervention over the course of their lives ... It is essential that society is prepared for these newfound patterns, and able to protect those people who find themselves newly categorized and potentially disadvantaged ...

The value embodied in these NHS datasets does not belong exclusively to the clinicians and specialists who have made deals with DeepMind. It also belongs to the public who generated it in the course of treatment. There is a pressing need for the NHS to consult broadly on the value-for-data aspects of these transfers, to ensure that the British public gets the best possible value out of any future deal. This value might take the form of an NHS stake in any products that DeepMind, a for-profit company, develop and sell using NHS data. It could be as simple as a binding agreement to share any future products with the entire NHS at a discount, or for free.

A further way in which the internet may be affecting the uses of patient data is through patients themselves placing information about their treatment, or that of their children, online. Sometimes this can be done in order to criticise the doctors involved in their care. In such circumstances, however frustrating it may be for doctors, they are bound by their duty of confidentiality, and are therefore unable to respond in anything other than very general terms. In *Re C (A Child) (Care Proceedings: Disclosure of Documents)*, Sir James Munby P gave short shrift to a doctor's claim that he should be able to defend himself by putting information about his patient into the public domain.

---

[83] 'Google DeepMind and healthcare in an age of algorithms' (2017) Health and Technology 1–17.

Re C (A Child) (Care Proceedings: Disclosure of Documents)[84]

Sir James Munby P

Accepting, as I am prepared to for the purposes of argument, that Dr X has been traduced and defamed by the mother, his former patient, that does not, of itself, as I have explained, liberate him from his continuing duties of confidentiality ... Here the remedy being sought by Dr X – permission to put the mother's medical records and related documents into the public domain, at a time and in circumstances of his own choosing and without any of the safeguards usually imposed – is wholly disproportionate to anything which he can legitimately or reasonably demand.

The GMC has issued specific guidance to doctors on responding to criticism in the media.

General Medical Council[85]

You must not put information you have learned in confidence about a patient in the public domain without that patient's explicit consent. You should usually limit your public response to an explanation of your legal and professional duty of confidentiality ... If you deny allegations that appear in public media, you must be careful not to reveal, directly or by omission or inference, any more personal information about the patient than a simple denial demands.

11 CONCLUSION

Doctors are unquestionably under a duty to respect their patients' confidentiality, but the duty is not an absolute one. On the contrary, in a wide range of situations, the duty to respect confidentiality is suspended or modified. For example, patient notes will be shared among healthcare professionals; information can be disclosed where there is a serious risk of harm to others; patient records can be used for epidemiological research and clinical audit. Most exceptions to the duty of confidentiality could be justified on 'public interest' grounds, but the 'public interest' exception to the duty of confidence does not offer very clear guidance to doctors about when the disclosure of patient information will be justifiable. Essentially, the public interest exception requires the merits of disclosure in a particular case to be weighed against the general public interest in the maintenance of patient confidentiality.

Finally, it is worth bearing in mind that discussion about the use of data without consent has taken place against the backdrop of the revelations, by Edward Snowden, of the extent of state surveillance of electronic communications. As Mark Taylor points out, this makes it even more important to be able to clearly explain and justify the use of data in the public interest.

---

[84] [2015] EWFC 79.   [85] *Confidentiality: responding to criticism in the media* (GMC, 2017).

Mark Taylor[86]

To put it simply, without a clearer determination of what is meant by 'the public interest', there is understandable concern that any given individual's interests might be sacrificed 'for the greater good' with that 'good' being defined and enjoyed by others …

We need to do this better. There are classic examples of how gathering and linking data has enabled important insights—e.g. smoking and lung cancer—and of times when an inability to make the links quickly enough has had tragic consequences—e.g. thalidomide. The idea of the public interest needs to be developed to make clear that the reasons for such use must be accessible to members of the public … The public interest should only be called upon to defend interferences that individual members of the public can be given reason to accept. If people have confidence that data will *only* be used in ways that they have reason to accept, even when any legal requirement for individual informed consent may be formally overridden by the demands of 'the public interest', then the social legitimacy of the systems will be promoted.

FURTHER READING

Carter, Pam, Laurie, Graeme T, and Dixon-Woods, Mary, 'The social licence for research: why *care.data* ran into trouble' (2015) 41 Journal of Medical Ethics 404–9.

Chico, Victoria and Taylor, Mark J, 'Using and Disclosing Confidential Patient Information and the English Common Law: What are the Information Requirements of a Valid Consent?' (2018) 26 Medical Law Review 51–72.

Donnelly, Mary and McDonagh, Maeve, 'Keeping the Secrets of the Dead? An Evaluation of the Statutory Framework for Access to Information About Deceased Persons' (2011) 31 Legal Studies 42–70.

Kaplan, Bonnie, 'Selling Health Data: De-Identification, Privacy, and Speech' (2015) 24 Cambridge Quarterly of Healthcare Ethics 256–71.

Lucivero, Federica and Jongsma, Karin R, 'A mobile revolution for healthcare? Setting the agenda for bioethics' (2018) Journal of Medical Ethics 685–9.

Obermeyer, Ziad and Emanuel, Ezekiel J, 'Predicting the future—big data, machine learning, and clinical medicine' (2016) 375 New England Journal of Medicine 1216.

Powles, Julia and Hodson, Hal 'Google DeepMind and healthcare in an age of algorithms' (2017) Health and Technology 1–17.

Stanton, Catherine, 'Patient Information: To Share or Not to Share?' (2018) 26 Medical Law Review 328–45.

---

[86] 'Information governance as a force for good? Lessons to be learnt from care.data' (2014) 11 SCRIPTed 1.

9

GENETIC INFORMATION

CENTRAL ISSUES

1. Genetic information raises some complex issues in relation to confidentiality:

   (a) The inherently shared nature of genetic information poses challenges for an individualistic model of confidentiality.

   (b) Genetic tests are often predictive rather than diagnostic. Results may provide information about a healthy person's risk of future ill health, which might be of interest to third parties, such as employers and insurers.

2. In some countries—but not in the UK—genetic discrimination is specifically prohibited by law.

3. In the UK, most genetic testing takes place within the NHS. Direct-to-consumer genetic testing is commonly used by the 'worried well' in order to find out about their susceptibility to an increasing number of conditions.

4. In the future, pharmacogenetics may transform the way in which medicines are prescribed, by enabling doctors to know in advance whether a drug is likely to be safe and effective for a particular patient.

---

1 INTRODUCTION: WHAT IS GENETIC INFORMATION?

Progress in the field of genetics has been especially rapid since the mapping of the human genome in 2003. The sequence of most of our 20–25,000 genes is identical (99.9 per cent), and we share a surprising proportion of our DNA with chimpanzees (96 per cent), and, even more surprisingly, with fruit flies (60 per cent).

In this chapter, we are principally concerned with questions about the regulation of access to genetic information. One reason why this is important is that faulty genes, or mutations, can increase someone's chance of developing disease(s) in the future. Genetic test results can therefore reveal predictive information about a person's future health prospects.

There are several different sorts of genetic disease. Single gene disorders are conditions that are caused by a particular genetic mutation, and they can be further divided into two groups. First, if the gene is dominant, a single gene inherited from either parent will cause the disease. An example is Huntington's disease, an incurable neurological degenerative disease, which people usually develop between the ages of 30 and 50, and which causes progressive deterioration of bodily functions and cognitive abilities. If someone with the Huntington's mutation reproduces, there is a 50 per cent chance that their child will inherit the disease. The penetrance of the mutation is also high: if a person has inherited it, then, provided she does not die first from another cause, she can be certain that she will develop Huntington's disease.

Secondly, if a single gene disorder is recessive, a person will develop the disease only if she inherits the relevant gene from both parents. People who have one copy of the gene are carriers. They will not develop the disease themselves, but if they reproduce with another carrier, there is a one-in-four chance that their child will receive a double dose of the relevant gene, and hence will suffer from the disease. As Figure 9.1 shows, there is also a one-in-four chance that their child will be unaffected and not carry the gene at all, and a one-in-two chance that their child will also be a carrier.

Examples of recessive genetic conditions are cystic fibrosis (a chronic lung disease), and sickle cell disease (a serious blood disorder). Within some population groups, being a carrier for one of these conditions is fairly common. Among people of European descent, one in 25 are carriers of the cystic fibrosis gene. Sickle-cell trait (being a carrier of the sickle-cell gene) is more common among people of African, Eastern Mediterranean, Asian, and Middle-Eastern descent. Families are often unaware that they are passing on this gene until a family member has a baby with another carrier.

A third group of genetic diseases are X-linked disorders, which are triggered by a mutation on the X chromosome. Women have two X chromosomes, and so they normally have a second normal X chromosome to compensate for the defective one. As a result, women are usually carriers of these diseases, which they pass on to their male offspring. Men have an X and a Y chromosome, and so if they inherit a mutation on their X chromosome from their mothers, they will develop the disease. Examples of X-linked disorders are Duchenne Muscular Dystrophy and haemophilia.

Chromosomal disorders arise when a person has an abnormality in their chromosomes, perhaps because they have too many copies of a particular chromosome. Examples are Down's syndrome and Turner syndrome.

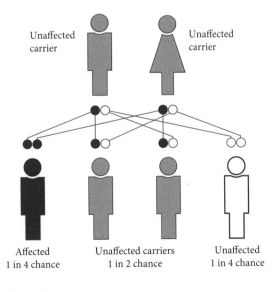

Figure 9.1

Single gene disorders are unusual. Most illnesses are complex and multifactorial; that is, they may result from the interaction of several genes, and from the interaction between a person's genes and the environment. Some people have genes that predispose them to heart disease, for example, but whether or not they develop heart disease, and at what age, will also be determined by lifestyle factors, such as diet, exercise, alcohol consumption, and smoking.

In recent years, there has been particularly rapid progress in identifying susceptibility genes: that is, genes which increase a person's risk of developing a condition, but where there is no guarantee that they will do so. This means that their penetrance (unlike Huntington's) is less than 100 per cent. Certain types of cancer can be triggered by genetic mutations. Approximately five per cent of breast cancers are the result of faulty BRCA1 and BRCA2 genes, which increase the lifetime risk of developing breast cancer to 60–80 per cent, and the lifetime risk of ovarian cancer to around 60 per cent.

Finding out that someone has a particular genetic mutation raises several specific issues. First, our capacity to identify genetic disorders outstrips our capacity to treat them. It has been possible to test for the Huntington's mutation for many years, but there is still no cure. This means that the decision to be tested is often different from being tested for conditions like cancer or HIV, where a positive test result will lead to discussions about appropriate treatment.

A positive test for Huntington's instead involves the discovery that one will develop an incurable and fatal condition. Suicide rates in people who receive positive Huntington's test results are higher than normal,[1] and it is not surprising that many people who know they are at risk choose not to be tested (we return to this point later).

The only way in which 'something can be done' when one knows that an untreatable genetic condition runs in one's family, is to undergo prenatal or preimplantation genetic diagnosis (see further Chapters 14 and 15), or to reproduce with donor gametes (sperm or eggs), or not to reproduce at all.

A second important difference is that genetic test results are often predictive, rather than diagnostic. If I discover that I have the BRCA1 mutation, I may be healthy now and for decades to come. Indeed, it is possible that I will never develop breast or ovarian cancer. But I have found out that I am much more likely than most women to develop both cancers, and at a younger age than normal. Given that this may affect my future health and life expectancy, insurance companies have an obvious interest in this sort of information.

Genetic information is also shared, so if I find out that I have the BRCA1 mutation, I must have inherited it from one of my parents. Discovering this information about myself means that I also know that other family members may be at risk. As Lori Andrews explains in the next extract, this means that genetic test results raise particularly interesting questions about confidentiality. The problem is obviously most acute for identical twins, who share the same DNA. If one twin is diagnosed with a genetic disorder, she cannot avoid knowing that her twin sister has the same genetic mutation. For other relatives, the implications of a relative's positive diagnosis are less certain, but nonetheless significant.

Lori B Andrews[2]

A parent and a child have half their genes in common, as do siblings. Cousins share one-quarter of their genes, as do grandparents and grandchildren. The acquisition and disclosure

---

[1] Thomas D Bird, 'Outrageous fortune: the risk of suicide in genetic testing for Huntington's disease' (1999) 64 American Journal of Human Genetics 1289–92.

[2] 'A Conceptual Framework for Genetic Policy: Comparing the Medical, Public Health and Fundamental Rights Models' (2001) 79 Washington University Law Quarterly 221.

of genetic information raise new and profound questions of 'gen-etiquette', questions about the moral obligations owed to relatives. If a woman learns she has a genetic mutation predisposing her to breast cancer, does she have a moral or even a legal duty to share that information with her sister? What about an estranged cousin? ...

Genetic information influences people's relationships with third parties, such as insurers and employers. While individuals might want to know their own genetic makeup in order to make important life decisions, such information can also be used against them ... The chilling irony of genetic testing is that, even in rare cases where a treatment exists, people may be afraid to get tested for the disorder because their insurer might drop them entirely or an employer may refuse to hire them based on their test results.

DNA samples might also be useful to the police by enabling them to create a DNA database that could be searched rapidly whenever biological traces are found at a crime scene. The public interest in the identification and prosecution of criminals is clearly substantial, but difficult questions arise about whose DNA should be placed on this sort of forensic database, and how long it should be kept. DNA databases and biobanks might also be useful for research purposes, and to assist the management and planning of health care provision.

One of the most important issues that arises in relation to genetic test information is therefore confidentiality, and we begin this chapter with a discussion of various third parties' interests in genetic test results and DNA profiles, and the extent to which genetic privacy is protected by the law.

The second important issue raised by genetic information is the possibility of discrimination against those found to have genetic disorders. Adam Moore recounts an extreme example of genetic discrimination in Orchemenos, Greece, where sickle-cell anaemia is common.[3] Researchers tested everyone in the village so that carriers could ensure they did not marry each other. It was assumed that carriers would choose to marry non-carriers, in order to avoid having children with sickle-cell disease. The problem was that the non-carriers refused to co-operate. Carriers became a stigmatized subclass, and were forced to marry among themselves, which of course meant that there were even more babies born with the condition than before.

The potential for genetic discrimination may be exacerbated by the fact that some genetic traits are particularly associated with particular ethnic groups. Ashkenazi Jews, for example, are disproportionately likely to inherit the BRCA1 or BRCA2 mutations, and to carry the gene associated with Tay-Sachs disease.

In 2008, the US passed the Genetic Information Nondiscrimination Act, which prevents discrimination by employers and health insurers. In contrast in the UK, the government explicitly decided against including 'genetic discrimination' within the categories of unlawful discrimination which were brought together in the Equality Act 2010.

The third issue is the expansion of genetic testing, and in particular the growth of direct-to-consumer testing. For some years, there has been a market in paternity testing 'kits', which enable suspicious men to test their children's DNA in order to confirm or rebut paternity. Now there are many companies which supply genetic screening kits to the genetically curious and the 'worried well'. For £149, 23andMe will ship a 'health and ancestry' testing kit direct to a consumer. After returning a tube containing her saliva, the customer will receive information about her inherited traits, risk factors, and ancestral origins.

---

[3] 'Owning genetic information and gene enhancement techniques: why privacy and property rights may undermine social control of the human genome' (2000) 14 Bioethics 97–119.

Several difficult practical and legal issues arise from direct-to-consumer testing. If I return a tube containing someone else's saliva, could I find out information about them that is none of my business? Is it a good idea to receive complicated and potentially alarming news by email, rather than in the course of a consultation with a trained professional?

Finally, we consider the implications of pharmacogenetics, and the possibility that a genetic test could reveal whether a medicine is likely to work for a patient, and whether that patient is likely to suffer adverse side effects. If our genetic make-up affects the way in which we metabolize medicines, pharmacogenetics could reduce the 'trial and error' approach to prescribing, and lead to more accurate, personalized medication regimes.

2   GENETIC PRIVACY

Let us first turn to consider in more detail the various third parties who might have an interest in acquiring a patient's genetic test results.

(a)   INSURERS

In the UK, a minority of the population purchases health insurance, but other sorts of insurance—such as life insurance for the purposes of obtaining a mortgage or to ensure that one's dependants do not suffer financially as a result of one's death—are common. The Association of British Insurers estimates that private health insurance covers about 4 million people in the UK, while 25.7 million people are covered by life insurance, or income protection, or critical illness insurance policies.

On the one hand, it instinctively seems unfair if a genetic test result, which is plainly not within her control, prevents someone from obtaining insurance, or means that she faces hugely increased premiums. On the other hand, insurance contracts rely on the duty of 'utmost good faith' (*uberrimae fides*) in the disclosure of risk. Insurance companies already take into account a person's health status, family history, and lifestyle risks, such as smoking, when setting premiums. Someone who has just been diagnosed with cancer, for example, would be under a duty to disclose that fact when seeking health insurance.

Preventing insurance companies from taking genetic information into account might have adverse consequences. If individuals discover that they are very likely to suffer from a serious disease, they might purchase a great deal of insurance, whereas other people with no elevated risk of future ill health might not bother buying insurance at all. This phenomenon is known as adverse selection. Plainly, it would be very difficult to maintain a functioning market in insurance if only people who are 'bad' risks choose to insure themselves.

In 2001, insurance companies in the UK agreed to impose a voluntary moratorium on the use of positive genetic test results to set insurance premiums. This moratorium was extended several times and in 2018 was replaced by the *Code on Genetic Testing and Insurance,* a voluntary code of practice agreed between HM Government and the Association of British Insurers.[4] The Code sets out a strictly limited exception to the ban on the use of genetic test results in setting premiums. For income protection insurance of more than £30,000 per year; life insurance cover greater than £500,000, and health insurance (critical illness, income protection, or long-term care insurance) cover greater than £300,000, positive genetic test results

---

[4] HM Government and ABI, *Code on Genetic Testing and Insurance* (2018).

may be used provided that the government has approved the test in question. Ninety-seven per cent of insurance policies are below these limits. For policies above these amounts, the only test approved so far is for Huntington's disease for life insurance worth more than £500,000.

The Code also spells out that insurers will not ask an applicant to disclose the results of a predictive genetic test taken after insurance cover has started. Nor will they ask about the genetic test results of blood relatives or results obtained in the context of scientific research.

The Code only rules out the use by insurers of positive results. Negative test results can be disclosed voluntarily. So a person with a family history of Huntington's disease, who has been tested and knows that she has not inherited the mutation, can ask an insurer to take this fact into account, rather than basing her premiums on her family history.

It is impossible to know the extent of adverse selection as a result of this ban on the use by insurers of positive genetic test results in almost all circumstances. Cathleen Zick et al studied the insurance-purchasing behaviour of people following testing for a variation on the ApoE gene, which appears to correlate with an increased risk of late onset Alzheimer's disease. They found that those who received a positive test result were nearly six times more likely to have altered their long-term care insurance arrangements than those whose results were negative.[5]

With the growth in direct-to-consumer genetic screening, more individuals may find out that they are at increased risk of developing a wide range of conditions, such as Parkinson's disease or dementia, and be prompted to take out critical illness cover that they might not otherwise have purchased.

(b) EMPLOYERS

For several reasons, as Alexander Capron explains, employers might find genetic test results useful when planning recruitment and promotion.

Alexander Capron[6]

First, an employee who is prone to get sick will generate expenses: medical treatment costs, sick days, and potentially even disability benefits. Second, if the problem might be described as job-related, then the genetic condition could lead directly to workers' compensation payments—for instance, a genetic predisposition to a bad back in an employee who has to do a lot of lifting. Finally, employers generally want to avoid hiring persons who are going to be sick a great deal because such persons cannot be relied upon to be present when needed and the expense of training them may thus be wasted if they become totally disabled.

Employers might also want to know about the risk an employer might pose to others: for example, an airline would want to know whether its pilots were at increased risk of epilepsy or narcolepsy.

Genetic test results might reveal that a person is particularly susceptible to a workplace hazard, such as chemicals used in industrial processes. Excluding potential employees with a genetic predisposition to work-related injuries may seem sensible, both in order to protect the

---

[5] Cathleen D Zick et al, 'Genetic testing for Alzheimer's disease and its impact on insurance purchasing behavior' (2005) 24 Health Affairs 483–90.

[6] 'Which Ills to Bear? Reevaluating the "Threat" of Modern Genetics' (1990) 39 Emory Law Journal 665.

employee's health and to avoid having to pay compensation. But it could be argued that this looks at the problem of workplace hazards from the wrong direction. Employing individuals who are more resistant to dangerous workplaces assumes that the environment could not be made any safer. Rather than excluding people who are particularly susceptible to toxic substances, it might be preferable to make the working environment safer for everyone.

It could also be argued that this apparently benevolent concern for employees' health is unduly paternalistic. An individual might rationally choose to engage in work that poses a small risk to her health in preference to unemployment, which itself may have an adverse effect on her physical and mental health, and that of her children. Few people now have jobs for life, and it seems disingenuous for employers to rely upon possible future ill health as a reason not to employ someone on a short-term contract.

In the US, employers' interest in their employees' health status is magnified by the fact that health insurance is often provided by employers. Not only might a high-risk employee have a shorter or less productive working life, but also their insurance premiums are likely to be higher, making them more costly to employ even while they are healthy.

In the next extract, Richard Epstein argues that full disclosure should be the norm where there are informational asymmetries between people who know that they will develop Huntington's disease and their employers or insurers. Epstein would extend this duty of disclosure to potential spouses who, he argues, have a right to know that the person they are marrying will develop a terminal degenerative disease in middle age.

Richard A Epstein[7]

I think that in the case of Huntington's disease it is immoral for a person to marry (or even take a job) and conceal the condition from the potential spouse or employer. This conclusion is valid in commercial settings as well as in marital ones so long as it results in selective knowledge to one side that is denied to the other. When an individual has knowledge that he is at risk of incapacitation, perhaps from family history, then full disclosure should be the norm ...

At this point it is critical to note that the plea for privacy is often a plea for the right to misrepresent one's self to the rest of the world ... No doubt the individual who engages in this type of deception has much to gain. But equally there can be no doubt that this gain exists in all garden variety cases of fraud as well. To show the advantage of the fraud to the party who commits it is hardly to excuse or to justify it, for the same can be said of all cases of successful wrongs. On the other side of the transaction, there is a pronounced loss from not knowing the information when key decisions have to be made. For example, a woman may choose the wrong husband; an employer may pass up a good employee with a strong medical record and a clear upward path in favor of a worker who will, in the end, be the source of enormous personal and financial costs.

(c) FAMILY MEMBERS

Genetic disease is transmitted through procreation, and so the results of genetic tests will often reveal information (albeit sometimes imprecise and uncertain) about other family members.

[7] 'The Legal Regulation of Genetic Discrimination: Old Responses to New Technology' (1994) 74 Boston University Law Review 1.

If a person finds out that she has a particular genetic condition, she knows that one or both of her parents passed on the relevant gene(s), and that her siblings are also at increased risk.

Indeed, the reason for undergoing genetic testing in the first place will often be a shared family history of a particular condition. One of the first diagnostic tools is usually to construct a family tree showing which other members of the family had, or might have had, the disease in question.

There is an inevitable tension between an individualistic model of confidentiality, in which a person's health information is regarded as paradigmatically private, and the inherently shared nature of genetic information. As a result, there are those who have argued that genetic information is, in some sense, 'communal'. As Alastair Kent points out, this tends to be the view of members of families who are at risk of genetic disease:

> Among those living in families where there is a diagnosis of a substantial risk of genetic disease, there is a strongly held view that such information should not be seen as the private property of the individual. Rather it should be seen as family information held in common by all those to whom it applies.[8]

Although genetic counselling is non-directive, genetic counsellors will usually encourage disclosure,[9] and there is no doubt that sharing genetic information within families is the norm. Drawing upon their interviews with 33 patients who had been seen for hereditary cancers and cardiac conditions in NHS genetics centres, Sandi Dheensa et al explain that most people with genetic diagnoses believe that there is a duty to disclose to at risk relatives.

Sandi Dheensa, Angela Fenwick and Anneke Lucassen[10]

> Almost all participants saw genetic information as essentially familial, with several saying something akin to 'this isn't my information, I don't own the gene'. Participants perceived relatives as having a right to know about their potential risk and themselves as having a 'duty' to help them by sharing.
>
> Participants said their views would be unchanged even if they were estranged from their at-risk relatives. Several said a patient's refusal to share information would be selfish, with another saying it would be irresponsible and another 'a betrayal' ...
>
> [P]articipants found it generally acceptable for HCPs [healthcare professionals] to share information without the tested person's explicit consent. Participants thought that this would indeed constitute a breach of patient confidence, but that this harm was trivial compared with the benefit of knowing about risk ...
>
> Notably, a small minority of participants laid more emphasis on the importance of HCPs encouraging patients to share information themselves. Their main reasons were that receiving unexpected information from HCPs could distress relatives and disclosure could erode trust and make people reluctant to reveal information ...
>
> Crucially, none thought that HCPs should respect patients' refusals on the basis that the information was private and personal to them.

[8] 'Consent and confidentiality in genetics: whose information is it anyway?' (2003) 29 Journal of Medical Ethics 16–18.

[9] Laura E Forrest et al, 'Communicating genetic information in families—a review of guidelines and position papers' (2007) 15 European Journal of Human Genetics 612–18.

[10] '"Is this knowledge mine and nobody else's? I don't feel that." Patient views about consent, confidentiality and information-sharing in genetic medicine' (2016) 42 Journal of Medical Ethics 174–9.

Although it is not common in practice—one study found that clinicians were concerned about patients' non-disclosure to relatives in fewer than one per cent of cases[11]—what should a clinician do if the person who has received a positive genetic test result refuses to tell her relatives? Could disclosure without her consent ever be justifiable? In the next extract, Meaghann Weaver suggests that a blanket rule is inappropriate, and that clinicians should adopt an 'ethic of care' case-by-case approach to disclosure without consent.

Meaghann Weaver[12]

[W]hat if a woman diagnosed with BRCA1 mutation chooses to disclose genetic findings to her two sisters but not her third sister because of that sister's severe depression and fragile psychological state but the healthcare provider feels compelled to discloses genetic findings to that sister and the sister subsequently attempts to harm herself? A blind standard of physician disclosure should not be seen as best practice. Instead, relationally-informed and patient-empowered disclosure should be seen as the best approach . . .

The ethic of care focuses on the particularities of the situation because it recognizes the dangers of applying general rules (such as a mandate to disclose to genetic relatives) without regard for the affected individuals and their specific needs: the relationships in which she is involved or not involved, how disclosure will impact those persons and those relationships, and the social values of her family and culture.

Alissa Brownrigg suggests that five factors should be taken into account when deciding whether to disclose a person's positive genetic test result to other family members:

(1) the severity of the disease identified by testing;

(2) the availability of preventive or curative options for that disease;

(3) the accuracy and reliability of the test performed;

(4) the ability of the physician or health care provider to interpret and address issues relevant to the test performed; and lastly,

(5) the protections afforded to the tested individual against discrimination.[13]

In the next extract, Allen Buchanan cautions against treating all genetic tests in the same way. There are some genetic conditions, such as hereditary haemochromatosis, which are serious, but for which a safe, relatively non-invasive, cheap, and effective treatment exists. Here the potential to avert harm by disclosure is strong. In contrast, hereditary Alzheimer's disease is untreatable. Buchanan argues that genetic conditions thus exist upon a spectrum, with conditions like haemochromatosis at one end and Alzheimer's at the other.

---

[11] Roy Gilbar and Charles Foster, 'It's arrived! Relational Autonomy Comes to Court: *ABC v ST George's Healthcare NHS Trust* [2017] EWCA 336' (2018) 26 Medical Law Review 125–33.

[12] 'The Double Helix: Applying an Ethic of Care to the Duty to Warn Genetic Relatives of Genetic Information' (2016) 30 Bioethics 181–7.

[13] Alissa Brownrigg, 'Mother Still Knows Best: Cancer-Related Gene Mutations, Familial Privacy and a Physician's Duty to Warn' (1999) 26 Fordham Urban Law Journal 247.

Where a condition lies on this spectrum is also subject to change as more genetic diseases become treatable.

Allen Buchanan[14]

At present, with a few exceptions, diagnosis for genetic diseases outstrips treatment. This is especially true for the genetic tests that currently receive the most extensive media coverage and public discussion, including tests for the BRCA1 and BRCA2 genes, the APO E4 Alzheimer's gene test, and the test for the Huntington's gene. In each of these cases, the medical benefit of testing is very dubious at present because there is no effective treatment for the condition ...

The situation is quite different if there is an effective treatment for a potentially lethal disease that can be detected by a genetic test. In this case, the clinician will reasonably believe that there is a single right course of action, and that the ethical responsibilities of the patient are clear from the perspective of widely accepted and easily defended values.

At present there are few such conditions. Perhaps the clearest case of a lethal late-onset disease that meets this description is hereditary hemochromatosis. If detected early enough, hereditary hemochromatosis has a simple, inexpensive, virtually riskless, and fully effective treatment; yet this disease has devastating effects on the liver, heart, and endocrine system if left untreated ... It is reasonable to expect that in the future there will be more cases where those who test positive for a serious genetic condition will have the option of a successful treatment.

Could a doctor's duty of care extend to a duty to inform family members about a relative's genetic diagnosis? In *ABC v St George's Healthcare NHS Foundation Trust*, the claimant sought to argue that her father's doctors owed her a duty of care to inform her about her father's diagnosis with Huntington's disease.

The claimant had been pregnant when her father was diagnosed. At the time, she was known to the medical team caring for her father, because he was in a secure hospital, having murdered her mother, and she had been engaging in family therapy at the hospital. Her father had been asked to consent to disclosure to her at the time, but he refused. She subsequently found out accidentally about her father's diagnosis, and tests revealed that she had inherited the condition from him. The claimant maintained that she would have terminated the pregnancy if she had been informed that she was at risk of the disease, and of passing it on to her children.

In the first legal claim of its kind, the claimant argued that her father's doctors had breached the duty of care they owed to her, by failing to inform her about her risk of inheriting Huntington's, claiming that she had suffered psychological harm as a result. She also claimed that the failure to inform her of her genetic risk breached her Article 8 rights. In the event that her daughter, who had not been tested, had inherited the disease, she also claimed for any extra expense this entailed.

It is worth noting that, in line with the wrongful pregnancy cases we considered in Chapter 3, there would be multiple difficulties in claiming for the costs associated with her daughter's upbringing. In addition, it would be unethical to test the daughter for Huntington's disease, because she should be able to decide for herself whether to be tested, once she is old enough to make that decision. Given that, even if her daughter

---

[14] 'Ethical responsibilities of patients and clinical geneticists' (1998) 1 Journal of Health Care Law and Policy 391.

had inherited the Huntington's mutation, she would not suffer any symptoms until she is middle-aged, it would be hard for the claimant to argue that she faced increased costs during her daughter's childhood.[15]

At first instance, Nicol J struck out her claim, but on appeal, the Court of Appeal decided that there was a potentially arguable claim and the case was remitted for trial. At the time of writing, that trial has not yet taken place. Of course, it is possible that this case might be settled and, if it is, the question of whether a duty could be owed in these circumstances will remain undecided but 'arguable', leaving healthcare professionals in an unsatisfactory legal limbo.

ABC v St George's Healthcare NHS Foundation Trust [16]

Irwin LJ

The real concern is a 'floodgates' argument. In written submissions to us, the Defendants submit that such problems as these may arise in a variety of medical scenarios aside from those involving genetic conditions. The examples given include a patient suffering from a sexually transmitted disease who refuses to tell his or her previous sexual partners; a patient whose vasectomy has failed but who refuses to tell his sexual partner; a patient who is suffering from a contagious disease who refuses to tell family or friends; a patient dying from a long, distressing illness and who does not wish his family to be told for fear of psychiatric harm; and a terminally ill patient who refuses to allow his pregnant partner to be told, for fear she might choose to terminate the pregnancy . . .

To my way of thinking there is at least one important distinction between the situation of a geneticist and all the other examples given. However problematic, and whatever the implications for 'third parties', the clinician usually only has knowledge of medical facts about the existing patient. It is only in the field of genetics that the clinician acquires definite, reliable and critical medical information about a third party, often meaning that the third party should become a patient . . .

Moreover, in many of the other scenarios envisaged, the practicalities of addressing the implications preclude effective remedy. Some former sexual partners may be known, but they do not constitute a closed class of individuals whose risk is defined by the genetic link to the patient, and who, for the most part, will be contactable.

I accept the difficulty presented by the 'floodgates' concern. This argument would have to be considered very carefully, particularly given the principle that the common law of negligence should advance by incremental steps. It may be that the distinction I have tentatively suggested as applying to genetic cases might on close consideration be thought insufficiently robust to sequestrate genetic cases from a broad range of other situations. However, it does not seem to me unarguably so, and therefore it does not seem to me the Defendants' submission justifies a strikeout of the action.

In the next extract, Roy Gilbar and Charles Foster celebrate what they describe as the Court of Appeal's relational approach to autonomy.

---

[15] Victoria Chico, 'Non-disclosure of genetic risks' (2016) 16 Medical Law International 3–26.
[16] [2017] EWCA Civ 336.

Roy Gilbar and Charles Foster[17]

> The Court of Appeal in *ABC* plainly endorsed this relational construction of the principle of autonomy, because it acknowledged that any decision made by one individual has implications for her significant others. The court recognised that the personal decision of the patient to undergo genetic testing had implications for her family as a unit and for the interests of individual relatives in making informed decisions. They implied that dealing with inherited diseases is not a task the patient faces alone: it is a familial challenge. They declared that if a patient refuses disclosure, clinicians as the agents of society might have a responsibility to help relatives put at risk by that refusal.
>
> We welcome the arrival of relational autonomy into the English courts. While the court suggested that the widening of the ambit of the duty of care should be restricted to genetic medicine, there are no good grounds for such a restriction. *ABC* entails a redefinition of the ambit not only of the duty of care, but of the nature and ambit of humans. Humans are quintessentially relational entities. They cannot rationally be quintessentially relational entities for the purpose of genetic counselling but not for the purpose of obstetrics or orthopaedics.

A different sort of claim was also struck out in *Smith v University of Leicester NHS Trust*.[18] Here the patient's second cousins argued that the negligent failure to diagnose the patient's genetic disease delayed their access to treatment. It is easy to see why the claim did not proceed: it would not be fair, just and reasonable for a doctor's duty of care to her patient to extend to a duty to ensure the prompt diagnosis of her second cousins.

In *Spencer v Spencer*,[19] the confidentiality issues raised by disclosure were rather different because the patient had died, and the claimant, who thought that he might be his son, was seeking access to a DNA sample taken when the deceased was being treated for bowel cancer. The dead patient's putative son claimed that he needed access to this sample in order to resolve the question of his paternity, and to establish whether he also faced an elevated risk of bowel cancer. The argument against allowing post-mortem DNA testing in the absence of consent was that it might 'discourage patients from providing DNA during medical treatment'. Peter Jackson J held that this was outweighed by the arguments in favour of providing the sample to the claimant:

> Mr Spencer's interest in knowing his biological parentage, the questions raised by the medical history, and the marked advantages of scientific testing as a means of resolving both issues, collectively carry more weight in the particular circumstances of this case than the counter-indicators to testing that undoubtedly exist.

It is also important to recognize that disclosure to relatives might jeopardize their right *not to know* about their predisposition to genetic disease. Where a condition is incurable, a positive test result could cause depression and anxiety. While there is currently a ban on the use of genetic test results by insurers in almost all circumstances, this will not necessarily last forever, so individuals might also worry about their ability to purchase insurance in the future. In short, there may be good reasons for preferring to remain in ignorance. As a result, it should not be surprising that comparatively few family members who know that there is a risk that they have

---

[17] 'It's arrived! Relational Autonomy Comes to Court: *ABC v ST George's Healthcare NHS Trust* [2017] EWCA 336' (2018) 26 Medical Law Review 125–33.
[18] [2016] EWHC 817.   [19] [2016] EWHC 851 (Fam).

inherited the Huntington's mutation choose to be tested: one study found that fewer than 15 per cent of at-risk individuals had opted to take the test.[20]

There is also evidence that both positive and negative test results may be difficult to come to terms with within families at risk of Huntington's. Marcela Gargiulo et al's study found that 58 per cent of asymptomatic carriers and 24 per cent of non-carriers were depressed in the months after being tested.[21] Tibben et al report that some of those who tested negative for the gene found themselves rejected by their families, once it became apparent that they no longer shared a bond which had previously brought the family closer.[22]

It is also important to note that it is not only direct disclosure that might threaten the right 'not to know'. Simply alerting relatives to the existence of information, and asking them whether they wish to receive it, reveals that there is something to worry about.

The right 'not to know' is enshrined in a number of international documents, for example Article 5c of the UNESCO Declaration on the Human Genome provides that:

> The right of every individual to decide whether or not to be informed of the results of genetic examination and the resulting consequences should be respected.

Is a right to ignorance in tension with the duty of doctors to be honest and frank with their patients? Graeme Laurie thinks not, and argues instead that our right to control information about ourselves encompasses a right not to know that information.

Graeme Laurie[23]

> To disclose genetic information to someone who has not expressed a desire to know can be disrespectful in two ways.
>
> First, furnishing an individual with information that she has actually said she does not want to receive disrespects her wishes and is an affront to her as an autonomous person. The pivotal ethical principle of respect for autonomy surely requires that we respect her wishes.
>
> Second, even if no wish has been expressed, we cannot ignore the spatial privacy interests which are also compromised ... Control of information about ourselves must be an essential part of any concept of ourselves as autonomous persons, but 'control' should not be limited merely to control of who has access to that information. It should also include the facility not to accept the information *ab initio* ...
>
> The precise content of the 'right' not to know will be context specific. For example, in the familial milieu, it might include a right not to be given information about a relative's diagnosis or a right not to be required to take part in linkage studies in order to build up an overall family profile. In the context of insurers and employers, it would certainly include a right not to be required to undergo testing and would probably also include a right to resist disclosure of test results if these were required simply to further the interests of third parties ...

---

[20] PJ Morrison, S Harding-Lester, and A Bradley, 'Uptake of Huntington disease predictive testing in a complete population' (2011) 80 Clinical Genetics 281–6.

[21] Marcela Gargiulo et al, 'Long-term outcome of presymptomatic testing in Huntington disease' (2009) 17 European Journal of Human Genetics 165–71.

[22] A Tibben et al, 'Testing for Huntington's disease with support for all parties' (1990) 335 The Lancet 553.

[23] 'In Defence of Ignorance: Genetic Information and the Right Not to Know' (1999) 6 European Journal of Health Law 119–32.

> Yet irrespective of context—and in each case—the kernel of the right not to know is the concept of respect for an individual privacy interest in not being subjected to unwarranted information about themselves.

The need to protect the right 'not to know' is one reason why parents can generally only consent to the genetic testing of their children if this will enable the child to receive treatment; that is, the testing must be done for therapeutic reasons, rather than in order to find out information about future risk.

In addition to ensuring the child herself can exercise her right not to know, there has been concern over the motives of parents seeking to test their children, although as PJ Malpas points out, parents are likely to have their child's best interests at heart when making decisions about genetic testing.

PJ Malpas[24]

> A parent may comment that they would not save for their affected child's college education, intending instead to use that money to ensure that the child had a very positive and memorable childhood. One can imagine the parents who, knowing the child may only live until his or her early adulthood, devote their energies and resources into supporting and enabling the child's self esteem and confidence, and providing the child with opportunities they may otherwise not have had. For instance, travelling the world, regularly spending more time with older extended family members, actively pursuing a child's passions and hobbies, deciding not to send the child to boarding school, doing more together as a family, or simply spending more time with the child by limiting work hours.

JA Anderson et al interviewed parents whose children had undergone whole genome sequencing, and found that most of them felt that they had no choice but to receive as much information as possible, including results about conditions other than the one for which testing was carried out (known as secondary variants (SVs)).

JA Anderson et al[25]

> Despite support for WGS [whole genome sequencing] as a diagnostic test, many parents (16/23; 70%) also expressed ambivalence about this new test. Ambivalence stemmed from the required balancing between perceived benefits and risks associated with SVs as well as from a sense that they would be remiss as parents to *not* know what is knowable.
>
> Participants characterised SVs as potentially concerning in four ways: the potential for psychological distress (18/23; 78%), the potential for insurance discrimination (14/23; 61%), making sense of ambiguous findings (8/23; 35%), and managing the 'weight' of inflicted insight (8/23; 35%) …

[24] 'Predictive genetic testing of children for adult-onset diseases and psychological harm' (2008) 34 Journal of Medical Ethics 275–8.
[25] 'Parents' perspectives on whole genome sequencing for their children: qualified enthusiasm?' (2017) 43 Journal of Medical Ethics 535–9.

> Despite their misgivings regarding SVs, most parents said yes to the receipt of all or some of them. However, our data suggest that some parents' choices about SVs were driven by a perceived moral obligation to learn, to the extent possible, the full range of current and future risks for their children, no matter how unpleasant. Faced with this opportunity parents felt they had no choice.

Commenting on the same study, Ainsley Newson has said that 'it is worrying that in this study even those parents who expressed reservation about receiving adult-onset SVs still obtained them', noting that simply offering a test to parents 'may not be neutral. If a particular suite of information is being offered, that offer may be interpreted as implicit encouragement to accept it'.[26]

It is possible to imagine a scenario in which one person's right to know comes into direct conflict with her family member's right not to know. In the next extract, Zornitza Stark et al discuss how their clinical genetics team made a decision in a case in which a man who was planning to have children wished to undergo testing for a familial neurodegenerative condition. He and his partner planned to use preimplantation genetic diagnosis if he tested positive. A positive result would not just reveal that he had the condition, but would also confirm that his at-risk parent did as well. The at-risk parent was adamant that they did not want to know, and had said they would commit suicide if they found out.

Zornitza Stark et al[27]

> It was clear that opposite testing preferences were strongly held by both parties, and that a compromise that completely avoided the possibility of distress to one or other party was not possible. The treating team had to make an ethical choice, and therefore undertook an analysis of the likelihood as well as the severity of harm to each party. A decision to deny or further postpone predictive testing in the young man would be harmful to him and his partner and his relationship with his parents, as well as impinge on his right to autonomy, and on his and his partner's right to reproductive autonomy.
>
> On the other hand, a decision to offer predictive testing only had a chance of resulting in an adverse outcome. The clinical team considered this chance to be quite low since for an adverse outcome to occur, the young man who had testing would need to test positive for the genetic mutation (25% chance) and this information would need to become known by the at-risk parent, and then the at-risk parent would need to actually suffer harm, either by carrying through with their stated intention to [commit] suicide or by experiencing significant irresolvable psychological distress. This is a long string of events of low probability.
>
> Even in the event that the test returned a positive result, given the commitment from both parties to non-disclosure within the family, the chance that the result would be disclosed to the at-risk parent, and that they would indeed [commit] suicide would be substantially lower (estimated by the team to be a few per cent overall risk). On balance, testing of the young man

---

[26] Ainsley J Newson, 'Whole genome sequencing in children: ethics, choice and deliberation' (2017) 43 Journal of Medical Ethics 540–2.

[27] 'Predictive genetic testing for neurodegenerative conditions: how should conflicting interests within families be managed?' (2016) 42 Journal of Medical Ethics 640–2.

was judged to have a high chance of producing an outcome that respected the wishes and protected the rights of all involved. Had the son stated that he would reveal his result to his at-risk parent, we would not have offered testing as the risk of harm to the parent would have approached 25% and this would be too high a risk in our view.

(d) THE POLICE

Unlike most other biobanks, as Annemie Patyn and Kris Dierickx point out, the justification for storing a person's DNA in a forensic database cannot be that they have given their informed consent.

Annemie Patyn and Kris Dierickx[28]

While medical biobanks can rely on the principle of 'informed consent', forensic DNA databases cannot. After all, individuals do not benefit from having their own data stored in such a database: the inclusion of a DNA profile is favourable only for other persons, not for the tested persons themselves. Consequently, these databases are controlled by the government or police services, who can force someone's data to be included in the database.

Consent to store data in a forensic DNA database thus can hardly be given at the level of the individual, but, rather, is a societal choice ... While forensic DNA databases (probably) increase security, at the same time they restrict the liberty of citizens. A society thus has to determine what importance it attaches to these different values.

If the DNA of every citizen were recorded and stored on a central police database, the identification of criminals from biological traces left at a crime scene would be more straightforward. But while the police might benefit from a population-wide genetic database, it would be impractical and ethically dubious. Universal testing would be expensive, and the database would be useful only if non-volunteers could be forced to give samples. If there is no reason to suspect someone of committing a crime, what justification could there be for taking a sample without her consent?

More plausible are databases of DNA profiles extracted from samples taken from people who have been arrested or convicted of offences. Samples will have been taken anyway, and the costs of retaining DNA profiles and/or samples would be relatively low. But should a distinction be drawn between those who have been convicted, and those who have been acquitted or released without charge? Should we also distinguish between serious and trivial offences?

Until the end of 2008, section 64(1A) of the Police and Criminal Evidence Act 1984 allowed DNA samples to be retained from all suspects—that is, anyone who had ever been arrested—regardless of whether they were subsequently convicted of an offence, provided that the samples were used only for the prevention and detection of crime. Samples taken

---

[28] 'Forensic DNA databases: genetic testing as a societal choice' (2010) 36 Journal of Medical Ethics 319–20.

from volunteers, who supplied them in order to eliminate themselves from suspicion, were also routinely retained.

Unsurprisingly, given the number of people whose profiles could be retained, the UK's National DNA Database (NDNAD) became one of the largest in the world, containing the DNA profiles of approximately six per cent of the population. For some minority ethnic groups, the proportion was much higher: over-representation of people from particular groups in police arrest practices automatically translated into their over-representation on the database. In London, for example, 55 per cent of the unconvicted people on the database were Black or Asian.[29]

In 2008, the European Court of Human Rights (ECtHR) unanimously held that retaining samples and DNA profiles from people who had been acquitted or never charged was an interference with their Article 8 rights, and that, while it served a legitimate aim, namely the detection of crime, it was disproportionate and could not be regarded as necessary in a democratic society.

Marper v United Kingdom[30]

Judgment of the ECtHR

[T]he Court is struck by the blanket and indiscriminate nature of the power of retention in England and Wales. The material may be retained irrespective of the nature or gravity of the offence with which the individual was originally suspected or of the age of the suspected offender; fingerprints and samples may be taken—and retained—from a person of any age, arrested in connection with a recordable offence, which includes minor or non-imprisonable offences. The retention is not time-limited; the material is retained indefinitely whatever the nature or seriousness of the offence of which the person was suspected.

In conclusion, the Court finds that the blanket and indiscriminate nature of the powers of retention of the fingerprints, cellular samples and DNA profiles of persons suspected but not convicted of offences, as applied in the case of the present applicants, fails to strike a fair balance between the competing public and private interests and that the respondent State has overstepped any acceptable margin of appreciation in this regard.

Four years after this judgment, the Protection of Freedoms Act 2012 amended the Police and Criminal Evidence Act 1984 in order to eliminate indefinite and indiscriminate retention of samples. The retention of all DNA samples is now prohibited after six months. In this time, the sample can be analysed and a DNA profile produced for inclusion in the database. In exceptional circumstances, such as complex court cases, a court order can permit longer retention of the DNA sample.

DNA profiles, which are essentially just a string of 20 numbers, and two letters to indicate gender, can be retained according to the rather complicated scheme shown in the following table (NB qualifying offences are serious violent or sexual offences, terrorism offences, and burglary offences).

---

[29] Nuffield Council on Bioethics, *The Forensic Use of Bioinformation: Ethical Issues* (NCOB, 2008).
[30] Application nos 30562/04 and 30566/04 (2008).

CATEGORY	RETENTION
CONVICTION Adult	Indefinite
CONVICTION Under-18 qualifying offence	Indefinite
CONVICTION Under-18 conviction minor offence	First conviction: five years (plus length of any custodial sentence), or indefinite if the custodial sentence is five years or more
	Second conviction: indefinite
NON-CONVICTION Qualifying offence: charge	Three years plus possible two-year extension by court
NON-CONVICTION Qualifying offence: arrested	Possible three years on application to Biometrics Commissioner (or indefinite retention if they hold a previous conviction for a recordable offence) plus two-year extension possible
NON-CONVICTION Minor offence: penalty notice	Two years
NON-CONVICTION Minor offence: arrested or charged	No retention-but speculatively searched to check if they match to any crime on the database
NATIONAL SECURITY	Indefinite

While the new scheme does not adopt a one-size-fits-all approach to retention, it continues to be problematic. It permits the indefinite retention of the DNA profiles of every adult who has been convicted, and of every child who has been convicted of more than one offence.

More significantly, the scheme retains the dubious assumption that some suspicion continues to attach to people who have been arrested but not convicted of certain offences. The reason for this is that people who have been arrested but not convicted of serious offences are statistically more likely to commit crime than those who have never been arrested. But while it might be useful, as the campaigning organization Liberty has argued, it undermines the presumption of innocence.

Liberty[31]

> 11. We are also concerned about the potential for retention to be extended by Court order. While initially the application procedure looks attractive, in as much as there is judicial oversight, we believe it is seriously flawed. The proposed model allows a Court to formally state that while a person has not been proven guilty of any offence, doubts remain about them which justify the retention of their biometric material after the blanket three year period. Those for whom such an application was successfully granted would be made to feel that there was greater suspicion over them than others against whom an application had been unsuccessful. To introduce an application procedure whereby a Court adjudicates on whether there is enough evidence against an accused to raise some doubt, but not enough evidence to prove guilt beyond a reasonable doubt, is a major, and we submit a dangerous, step ...
>
> 13. Another significant concern on the face of the Bill is provisions permitting the indefinite retention of any biometric information which a chief officer concludes should be retained in the interests of national security, subject only to the reviewing function of the newly appointed Commissioner. There is nothing in the Bill to prevent a high proportion of DNA and fingerprints being retained on undefined notions of national security.

[31] *Liberty's Second Reading Briefing on the Protection of Freedoms Bill in the House of Commons* (Liberty, 2011).

In the next extract, Stephen Sedley, writing extra-judicially, advocated a different solution to the inequity of storing samples from people who have come into contact with the police, but who have not been convicted.

Stephen Sedley[32]

My argument is that the case is growing for a national database holding the DNA profile of everyone living in or entering the country. The present system, sanctioned by legislation, is that the police may take and keep a DNA sample from everyone they arrest, whether or not the person is charged or convicted. This has the unfortunate effect of putting the innocent on a par with the guilty. It draws a not very logical line between innocent people who have and have not passed through the hands of the police. But it does not follow that the law should be moved back to what it once was, so as to require the police to destroy their DNA records of everyone not eventually convicted. What follows no less logically is that the taking and retention of an individual's DNA profile should not depend at all on whether he or she happens to have come into the hands of the police ... It can be, in fact, something rather worse than a fortuity. We know that there is an ethnic imbalance in arrests for certain types of offence, as well as in the use of stop and search powers. This ... has the unacceptable consequence that members of some ethnic minorities face a disproportionately high chance of getting on to the police DNA database without being convicted of anything. A universal and uniform database will at least resolve this problem.

In 2007, several years after the National DNA Database (NDNAD) was established, an Ethics Group was set up to monitor its operation and uses (in 2017, this was replaced by the Biometrics and Forensics Ethics Group). In its first annual report, the Ethics Group considered, and rejected, the possibility of a population-wide database.

NDNAD Ethics Group[33]

- A database containing the DNA profiles of all the supposed inhabitants of the United Kingdom at any one time would in fact never absolutely do so in practical terms. There would for example, be those who would avoid profiling (by illegal means or on the grounds of human rights), temporary visitors, migrant workers, and the deliberate submission of false identities.

- Despite the existing legislative controls, there are unknown and unpredictable social consequences of being potentially able to identify the parentage and sibling status of all individuals. The ramifications extend beyond the discovery of unexpected birth relationships to inheritance rights and the penetration of genetic traits.

- Consequently, it is inappropriate without public debate and fraught with ethical and social problems and questions of personal freedom, to allow a criminal intelligence database to convert into a national repository of the nation's DNA characteristics. Arguing that the database should be expanded to include all the population, (the majority of whom will never commit a crime), to prevent inequality and discrimination is, on balance, unsustainable when issues of proportionality and personal privacy are taken into account.

---

[32] An extract from a lecture, ' "Rarely Pure and Never Simple": The Law and the Truth', delivered in 2004 at Leicester University, and published under the title 'Short cuts' (2005) 27 London Review of Books.
[33] 1st Annual Report (Home Office: London, 2008).

It is often assumed that forensic databases, which rely upon compulsion, have little in common with biobanks for which samples are provided voluntarily. In the next extract, Helena Machado and Susana Silva suggest question this assumption.

Helena Machado and Susana Silva[34]

First, the dichotomy of voluntary and compulsory participation fails to consider certain concrete situations which do not fall clearly into one category or the other (e.g., volunteers or victims of crime who provide DNA samples for criminal genetic databases, as well as disease registries and investigations into public health emergencies when data have been collected without the need for individual informed consent). Second, this contraposition between DNA samples collected by compulsion (associated with criminal genetic databases) and the voluntary provision of human biological material (linked to medical databases) is based on an individualistic approach to ethics which focuses mainly on the potential restriction of individual civil rights, while failing to consider collective and political concerns, such as institutional oversight, public trust, and transparency in the governance of genetic databases. Third, the emphasis on 'free choice' on the part of those contributing to biobanks has been extensively criticised, and several commentators have shown that the concept of 'voluntary participation' is ambiguous and unclear. In the forensic criminal field, refusal to be a volunteer might be the basis for being added to the list of 'suspects'. The so-called practice of 'DNA dragnets' in criminal investigation consists of asking hundreds, even thousands, of people for their blood or saliva, in the hope of finding the one person whose DNA matches DNA left at a crime scene ...

Although all Western criminal jurisdictions ban the speculative automated exchange of information between forensic and medical contexts, in exceptional circumstances (for instance, for identification of victims of mass disasters and catastrophes) forensic use of medical biobanks is allowed.

A further issue that arises in relation to the forensic use of genetic information is its use in the courtroom, where a match between the DNA profile of an individual and samples found at a crime scene is often assumed to offer irrefutable, objective evidence of guilt. This may be misleading, however, for several reasons. First, the fact that DNA evidence proves that person X was in a location where a crime was committed does not establish that person X committed that crime; merely that person X has been there at some point in the past. Secondly, there is always the possibility of human error or contamination or degradation of samples: crime scenes, almost by definition, are the antithesis of ideal laboratory conditions.

Thirdly, let us imagine that there is a match between the DNA of an individual suspect and that of the person who committed the crime, and that the chance of this happening randomly is put at one in a million. While that sounds like fairly conclusive evidence of guilt, in a country with a population of 66 million, there might be 65 other individuals whose DNA might have been left at the crime scene. If one takes into account people from other countries who might also be a match, there may be many hundreds of people worldwide who could be 'identified' by this sample. Of course, there may be other evidence that points to the defendant being the perpetrator, but DNA evidence alone does not establish their guilt.

---

[34] 'Public participation in genetic databases: crossing the boundaries between biobanks and forensic DNA databases through the principle of solidarity' (2015) 41 Journal of Medical Ethics 820–4.

(e) OTHER DNA DATABASES

There are now a wide variety of collections of DNA samples and profiles, often described as biobanks. Most exist for the purposes of research, but they vary hugely in size and scope. Some collections are small disease-specific registries, whereas others are large-scale epidemiological resources. In the next extract, Susan Gibbons suggests that small and large biobanks may result in different sorts of risks to the interests of participants whose samples or sensitive information is stored.

Susan MC Gibbons[35]

Regulators may wish to expect more detailed and demanding standards, procedures, and protocols from 'bigger' biobanks (however defined).

But 'size' can cut both ways ... A good example here is oversight and governance. Greater scrutiny may be thought necessary for 'bigger' databases—commensurate, say, with the potentially greater risks to participants' privacy, confidentiality, and consent (insofar as relevant) posed by widespread data set interlinking, having multiple collaborators or end-users, international transfers of materials (especially to jurisdictions lacking equivalent legal protections), or the amassing of much more detailed and revealing phenotypic and genotypic material. Yet, 'smaller' biobanks may well be less visible, and so less amenable to external scrutiny. Unlike 'bigger' biobanks, they are also highly unlikely to have their own bespoke, internal oversight committees, or governance systems. Following the REC [research ethics committee] approval stage, they may not be subject to any formal ongoing monitoring at all. Here too, then, arguably a greater potential danger to significant rights and interests arises.

UK Biobank is a research initiative which is tracking the health of a representative sample of the population from the time at which they signed up until their deaths.[36] Between 2006 and 2010, UK Biobank recruited half a million volunteers aged between 40 and 69. Recruits gave a blood sample, answered questions about their lifestyle and medical history, and perhaps most significantly, granted full access to their past and future medical records. Participants in the project gave generic consent at the outset to their data's use in research, and to being contacted in the future by UK Biobank or other researchers. Since 2012, researchers have been able to apply for access to UK Biobank's samples and data, and several hundred projects are currently underway. In the next extract, its Ethics and Governance Council explains a recent access decision.

UK Biobank Ethics and Governance Council[37]

In March 2017 UK Biobank announced a significant new initiative between two pharmaceutical companies, the UK-based GSK and US-based Regeneron. The companies received approval through the standard access process to use UK Biobank samples to sequence the

---

[35] 'Regulating Biobanks: A Twelve-Point Typological Tool' (2009) 17 Medical Law Review 313–46.
[36] Jean V McHale, 'Regulating Genetic Databases: Some Legal and Ethical Issues' (2004) 12 Medical Law Review 70–96.
[37] *Annual Review 2016/2017* (UK Biobank, 2017).

participants' exomes, that is, the 1-2% of the genome that contains the protein-coding genes that scientists believe to have most relevance for drug discovery . . .

It is clear to us that the value of data obtained from whole exome sequencing would be significant and that the proposal is a major investment in the resource by these companies – about $150 million if all 500,000 participants are sequenced . . . Use by commercial companies was explicitly mentioned in the initial participant information materials and so we consider that this type of research is not outside the consent of the participants if used to further medical research. However, we recommended that UK Biobank ensures that clear and transparent information about this development is made available for participants and the public. UK Biobank agreed to email its participants to update them on this development.

People are free to withdraw from UK Biobank, and there are three different levels of withdrawal: no further contact (UK Biobank would no longer contact the person but would be able to continue to use their information, including their future health records, and stored samples); no further access (UK Biobank would no longer contact the person or obtain additional information from their health records, but would still have permission to use the information and samples provided previously), and most drastic, 'no further use' (there would be no use of any information and their samples would be destroyed).[38]

Unlike the NDNAD, from the outset UK Biobank has had to operate within an ethics and governance framework. In 2018, its Ethics and Governance Council was replaced by the UK Biobank Ethics Advisory Committee (an advisory committee of the UK Biobank Board) with the following remit:

to provide advice to the Board on ethical issues that arise during the maintenance, development and use of the UK Biobank resource, including:

- identifying, defining and examining relevant ethical issues:
- providing advice, guidance and recommendations on relevant ethical issues; and
- reviewing and advising on policies which have an ethical dimension that is relevant to UK Biobank.

In order to maximize a biobank's usefulness, participants' consent should be as general or generic as possible. In the next extract, Margaret Otlowski argues that obtaining 'broad' consent is not only convenient for researchers, but may also be better for participants.

Margaret FA Otlowski[39]

[R]epeated consent may be seen not only as impracticable but also as intrusive from the research participant's perspective, and may in fact operate as a deterrent. From other research, there is some indication of consent 'fatigue' and of people not wanting extensive

---

[38] UK Biobank, *Ethics and Governance Framework version 3.0* (UK Biobank, 2007). Version 4.0 is in preparation at the time of writing.
[39] 'Tackling Legal Challenges Posed By Population Biobanks: Reconceptualising Consent Requirements' (2012) 20 Medical Law Review 191–226.

information . . . There is also accumulating evidence that patients who consent to donate their tissue are keen to see that the maximum benefit will be obtained from its use, and just want researchers to get on with their work . . .

If we reflect on what subjects would normally be expected to be informed about when their specific consent is sought (aims/objectives, methods, demands, risks and harms, inconvenience and discomfort, possible outcomes including commercialisation potential, right to withdraw etc), much of this can be dealt with in advance in more generic terms . . .

Further, there are a number of strategies that can be taken to help promote ongoing active consent: after the initial collection of samples and information, it is essential that open lines of communication be maintained so that subjects can be kept informed of research directions and possible planned uses of samples and information in the future.

It is also important that participants understand that complete anonymization of a DNA sample—which by its very nature identifies the person whose sample it is—is impossible.

Harald Schmidt and Shawneequa Callier[40]

Provided that the biological or genetic material is of suitable quality and quantity, samples that contain DNA always, by their very nature, retain a link to the person from whom they came: 'DNA is itself uniquely identifiable.' Reidentification may require a great deal of effort, time and expense, as illustrated by the processes employed to identify victims of a natural disaster or terrorism (such as the Tsunami in the Indian Ocean in 2004 or the attacks on the World Trade Center in 2001). But it is wrong to suggest that such reidentification is impossible. As a number of recent scientific developments have demonstrated, it is increasingly easier to establish such matches. This trend looks set to continue, and the growing interconnectivity of increasingly larger and numerous genetic and non-genetic databases are of particular relevance, as are different ways in which people engaging in consumer-driven genomics might themselves initiate matching.

Michelle Bayefsky has pointed out that a 'focus on the personal character of the genome has had a skewing impact on the policy dialogue surrounding genetics and genomics', and she advocates instead a 'common heritage' approach to the human genome.

Michelle J Bayefsky[41]

If the genome is our common heritage, there should be fair access to genomic data. The genome should not be monopolized by a few – whether by commercial entities, research programs or privileged nations . . .

Global sharing of genomic data can also be justified using utilitarian reasoning, since larger pools of genomic information will result in greater research opportunities and public benefits. However, beyond consequentialist logic, the notion that genomic information ought to

[40] 'How anonymous is "anonymous"? Some suggestions towards a coherent universal coding system for genetic samples' (2012) 38 Journal of Medical Ethics 304–9.

[41] 'The human genome as public: Justifications and implications' (2017) 31 Bioethics 209–19.

be shared because the human genome is the common heritage of humankind provides a powerful reason for international data-sharing . . .

To date, nearly all participation in national biobanking efforts has been voluntary, with individuals providing informed (and usually broad) consent to contribute their DNA given certain parameters on privacy, identifiability and the research that will be conducted. However, based on the CR [common resource] framework, an argument can be made for stronger public action aimed at recruiting participants to genomic databases, with the ultimate goal of harnessing population-wide genomic data to improve public health.

One such action would be to create a national biobank for genomic information without obtaining the explicit informed consent of participants . . .

It is important to remember, however, that the success of public health measures often depends on maintaining the public trust. If large portions of the population oppose conducting genomics research on stored samples, it would be counterproductive to forge ahead, potentially causing long-term damage to the public's trust in public health agencies.

3 GENETIC DISCRIMINATION

Should genetic discrimination in the workplace or in the supply of goods and services be outlawed in the same way as other sorts of discrimination? It is unlawful to discriminate on the grounds of disability, so where someone has a genetic condition 'which has a substantial and long-term adverse effect on his ability to carry out normal day-to-day activities',[42] unjustified discrimination is already against the law. For obvious reasons, this does not cover pre-symptomatic individuals.

In the next extract, Lawrence Gostin advocates the specific prohibition of genetic discrimination.

Lawrence O Gostin[43]

Discrimination based upon actual or perceived genetic characteristics denies an individual equal opportunity because of a status over which she has no control. Discrimination based on genetic factors can be as unjust as that based on race, gender or disability. In each case, people are treated inequitably, not because of their inherent abilities, but solely because of pre-determined characteristics. The right to be treated equally and according to one's abilities in all the diverse aspects of human endeavor is a core social value.

Genetic discrimination is harmful not merely because it violates core social values, but also because it thwarts the creativity and productivity of human beings, perhaps more than the disability itself. By excluding qualified individuals from education, employment, government service or insurance, the marketplace is robbed of skills, energy and imagination. Such exclusion promotes physical and economic dependency, draining rather than enriching social institutions.

---

[42] Equality Act 2010, s 6(1)(b).
[43] 'Genetic Discrimination: The Use of Genetically Based Diagnostic and Prognostic Tests by Employers and Insurers' (1991) 17 American Journal of Law and Medicine 109.

In the US, the Genetic Information Nondiscrimination Act 2008 (GINA) prohibits providers of health insurance and employers from discriminating against individuals on the basis of genetic test results, and forbids them from requesting or demanding that a person undergoes a genetic test. Certain sorts of insurance are not covered: an insurer is allowed to ask for genetic test results before providing life insurance, disability insurance, and long-term care insurance. This means that, despite the existence of GINA, people may continue to be deterred from undergoing genetic testing in case it increases their insurance premiums for these excluded types of insurance.

Furthermore, GINA does not protect people who are symptomatic, and hence once the genetic condition manifests itself, discrimination is not prohibited under the Act. While discrimination on the grounds of disability is outlawed, there may be a legal limbo in the period after a person first experiences symptoms, but before she becomes sufficiently disabled to be covered by disability discrimination legislation.

In addition, the Harvard Law Review's commentary on GINA criticizes its 'genetic exceptionalism'. The consequence of GINA is that people with other sorts of knowledge about their likelihood of future ill health are treated less favourably than those whose predictive diagnoses happen to be genetic.

Harvard Law Review[44]

Although superficially appealing, GINA suffers from significant flaws. It implies and promotes genetic exceptionalism—the idea that genetic information needs special treatment—despite lacking a sound basis for separating genetic conditions from nongenetic ones that people did not knowingly cause and cannot change ...

Though instinctively accepted by most people outside the bioethics community, genetic exceptionalism produces unsettling results. Consider three women who have the same increased probability of breast cancer: one who carries the BRCA1 gene, a second who has unknown environmental hazards in her neighborhood, and a third who was exposed to diethylstilbestrol as a fetus. None of these women deserves blame for her predisposition to cancer, but under GINA an insurer could deny coverage or raise premiums based on the exposure-based conditions but not the genetic one ... The blamelessness of all three women makes it difficult to support giving benefits to the first woman but denying them to the others. The apparent equivalence of this genetic and nongenetic information makes separate genetic antidiscrimination legislation questionable—why should we care less about those with nongenetic health risks? ... Passing antidiscrimination legislation for genes, but not for uncontrollable nongenetic factors, seems at best an unfinished job.

James Mittra agrees, and asks why genetic information should receive special protection, when other sorts of diagnoses—a positive HIV test, for example—must be disclosed.

James Mittra[45]

The practice of fair discrimination, as an underlying commercial philosophy, dictates that individuals pay a premium for life assurance that is commensurate with the risks they bring

---

[44] (2009) 122 Harvard Law Review 1038.

[45] 'Predictive genetic information and access to life assurance: the poverty of "genetic exceptionalism"' (2007) 2 BioSocieties 349–73.

to the insurance pool. If a genetic test with demonstrable predictive efficacy predisposes an individual to a particular disease that is actuarially relevant, fairness demands that they are charged a higher premium for commercial insurance or are denied coverage. Those who argue that we should privilege such individuals, and bestow on them a specific right of non-disclosure, appear to permit inequity within the market. The implicit logic of their argument is that those individuals whose risk status has been discovered through a specific genetic test are more deserving of protection, and therefore have a greater moral claim to access a particular insurance product, than those individuals denied cover because an uninsurable risk has been identified by a clinical test not deemed sufficiently novel or problematic to justify unique treatment.

Ine Hoyweghen et al contrast faulty genes with lifestyle factors, such as smoking and being overweight, which, just like genetic tests, tell us something about a person's risk of future health. They argue that treating genetic risk factors differently from lifestyle risk factors reflects a normative judgement about whether a person deserves the solidarity of mutual insurance.

Ine Hoyweghen, Klasien Horstman, and Rita Schepers[46]

The legal prohibition of genetics in insurance then seems to introduce a kind of fault-based labelling in insurance ... Although both lifestyle and family history can be identified as asymptomatic risks and as predictors for an individual's future health status, lifestyle has gained ascendancy in the risk calculation process. Both sections of the group share the fact that the illness is not yet developed, and will possibly never do so, but the legal and moral evaluation of these risks in insurance is completely different ... Risk selection is neither a purely technical procedure nor simply the application of insurance principles—but much more of a social and normative undertaking. In the selection of risks, insurance expresses normative claims ... of who does or who does not deserve solidarity.

In bringing equality legislation together into the single Equality Act 2010, and against the advice of the Human Genetics Commission, the government chose not to specifically prohibit genetic discrimination.

Department for Communities and Local Government[47]

8.29 At present, there is little, if any, evidence of discrimination against those who have a genetic predisposition, or that genetic testing is being used in a way which would give rise to such discrimination in the UK. We therefore do not believe there is currently a need to legislate to prohibit discrimination on grounds of genetic predisposition.

8.30 However, we wholeheartedly endorse the Human Genetics Commission's view that no-one should be unfairly discriminated against on the basis of their genetic characteristics

---

[46] 'Genetic "risk carriers" and lifestyle "risk takers": which risks deserve our legal protection in insurance?' (2007) 15 Health Care Analysis 179.

[47] *Discrimination Law Review: A Framework for Fairness: Proposals for a Single Equality Bill for Great Britain* (DCLG, 2007).

and we are committed to the continued monitoring of the use of genetic testing in the UK. There is a need to ensure that individuals are able to take medically recommended genetic tests secure in the knowledge that the results will not be used unfairly, while recognising the needs of employers to protect the public and their workforce and the need of insurers to be able to assess risk.

In the next extract, Aisling de Paor and Charles O'Mahony argue that employers may, in fact, be under a duty not to discriminate on the grounds of genetics as a result of the more broadly drafted UN Convention on the Rights of Persons with Disabilities.

Aisling de Paor and Charles O'Mahony[48]

Employers also have general obligations to the public regarding health and safety and may be held liable for harm caused by their employees to members of the public. In certain industries or with certain positions, for example pilots, train drivers or bus drivers, where the public are vulnerable to harm, employers may argue that (genetic) testing for predisposition to mental illness should be permitted. This argument has recently come to the fore in the aftermath of the Germanwings case [in which a plane was deliberately crashed by its co-pilot] and may enhance an employer's desire to use genetic technologies in certain circumstances and in certain industries . . .

The CRPD is drafted broadly to promote inclusion of all individuals with disabilities, including those with putative disabilities and genetic predisposition to disability (including predisposition to mental illness) . . .

The broad approach taken in the CRPD in prohibiting the discriminatory behaviour of third parties is reflected particularly in Article 5, which provides specifically for the principles of equality and non-discrimination. It requires, inter alia, the prohibition of discrimination 'on the basis of disability' and guarantees to persons with disabilities equal legal protection against discrimination . . .

The CRPD specifically addresses disability in the field of employment in Article 27, which recognises the right of persons with disabilities to work on an equal basis with others and prohibits discrimination on the basis of disability.

4 DIRECT-TO-CONSUMER GENETIC TESTING

Until relatively recently, only 'at risk' individuals were plausible candidates for genetic testing. But whole genome testing is becoming cheaper and more accessible, and there has been rapid progress in identifying markers associated with an increasingly wide range of common diseases. This sort of information does not have the predictive accuracy of the test for Huntington's disease: rather, it may show that a person is slightly more at risk than the rest of the population of developing one condition, and slightly less at risk of developing another.

---

[48] 'The need to protect employees with genetic predisposition to mental illness? The UN Convention on the Rights of Persons with Disabilities and the case for regulation' (2016) 45 Industrial Law Journal 525–55.

It is therefore now possible to offer genetic screening to healthy, asymptomatic individuals with no family history of genetic disease. Personal genome analysis is usually performed by looking at as many as a million genetic variations known as single nucleotide polymorphisms (SNPs). As Peter Donnelly explains, genome-wide analysis is likely to show that each of us is in a high-risk group for one or more conditions.

Peter Donnelly[49]

For a particular disease, most individuals will have inherited some sequence variants that confer risk and some variants that provide protection, and they will therefore have an overall risk around the average ... Across 50 diseases, making the simplifying assumption that susceptibility to each disease is independent of susceptibility to every other disease, almost everyone will be in the top 5% of risk for at least one disease, and nearly half of all people will be in the top 1% for at least one disease. So, for example, I will be at particularly high risk of developing some diseases because of common variants that I inherited. At present, it is unclear which diseases these are, but with the advent of personal genomics, I can find out.

In practice, is it useful to find out that one faces a slight increase in risk compared with the population as a whole?[50] Gert van Ommen and Martina Cornel explain what predictive genetic tests in relation to type 2 diabetes might reveal: 'Although the average inhabitant of the Netherlands now has a lifetime risk of developing type II diabetes of 13%, for some people this might be 10 or 17% after testing'.[51] It is hard to see how one would benefit from the knowledge that one's risk of diabetes is 17 per cent, rather than 13 per cent.

Indeed, it is possible that the results of genetic tests with a low predictive value might be positively harmful, as Bertrand Jordan and Daniel Fu Chang Tsai explain in relation to autism.

Bertrand R Jordan and Daniel Fu Chang Tsai[52]

So far, whole-genome association studies for autism can predict only a higher risk of disease susceptibility: an increase of the incidence from 0.7% (1/150) to 10%. That is, only 1 in 10 children who test positive are expected to actually have an autistic syndrome. This is of low predictive value, and the high false positive rate will inevitably have strong psychosocial impact on the individual and family involved ...

Extra burden may be generated by the pressure of seeking for more psychiatric evaluations and diagnosis, methods for prevention, and various types of therapeutic intervention including alternative treatment. The children may be stigmatised by being regarded as sick, abnormal, or different from other siblings or classmates, and consequently subjected to different management or even discrimination. If the test result is in fact a false positive, all these hardships would be totally unnecessary and in effect counterproductive.

---

[49] 'Progress and challenges in genome-wide association studies in humans' (2008) 456 Nature 728–31.
[50] A Cecile JW Janssens et al, 'A critical appraisal of the scientific basis of commercial genomic profiles used to assess health risks and personalize health interventions' (2008) 82 American Journal of Human Genetics 593–9.
[51] 'Recreational genomics? Dreams and fears on genetic susceptibility screening' (2008) 16 European Journal of Human Genetics 403–4.
[52] 'Whole-genome association studies for multigenic diseases: ethical dilemmas arising from commercialization—the case of genetic testing for autism' (2010) 36 Journal of Medical Ethics 440–4.

When evaluating genetic test results, it is also important not to confuse absolute and relative risk. If the risk of developing stomach cancer in the population as a whole is one per cent, and a predictive test suggests that my risk is double that of the general population, that sounds serious, and as though it is something that I should be concerned about. In fact it means that I now have a two per cent chance of developing stomach cancer, and a 98 per cent chance of being free from stomach cancer. Without specialist genetic counselling to help people make sense of complex predictive information, people who are at very low risk of developing conditions may become unnecessarily anxious.

Although it has had a chequered history with the US Food and Drug Administration (FDA), 23andMe is one of the most well established providers of direct-to-consumer genetic testing. For £149, consumers can receive reports on their genetic risk factors, inherited conditions, traits, and drug responses, as well as ancestry information. Part of the sales pitch for direct-to-consumer genetic testing has been that information about elevated risk enables people to take steps to reduce their lifetime risk, by making changes to their lifestyle. Of course, it could be argued that we all already know what lifestyle changes are likely to reduce our risk of developing common conditions, such as cancer. Someone who is worried about his risk of heart disease does not need a genetic test result in order to learn that he ought to exercise more, eat less sugar, drink less alcohol, and stop smoking.

One possible danger of these new tests is that people who receive results that tell them that they are not at increased risk of, say, heart disease will wrongly believe that it is less important for them to give up smoking or do more exercise. It is also possible that people's reactions to learning that they face an elevated risk of ill health—particularly where it suggests that addiction to smoking or alcoholism[53] may be 'in their genes'—could be fatalism rather than behavioural modification.

In practice, as Gareth Hollands et al explain, the evidence suggests that people do not alter their behaviour very much as a result of receiving information about their genetic risks.

Gareth J Hollands et al[54]

The evidence in this review suggests that communicating DNA based disease risk estimates has little or no effect on health related behaviour . . .

We outlined three possible competing hypotheses on the possible behavioural impact of DNA based disease risk information evident in the literature—that it strongly motivates risk-reducing behaviour change, that it demotivates risk-reducing behaviour change, and, finally that, at best, it has only a small effect on risk-reducing behaviour. Our results do not support the first two hypotheses, but are consistent with the third, suggesting that high expectations of the potency of such communications to change behaviour are unfounded. This is consistent with the results of a recent cohort study reporting no impact on diet or physical activity of direct-to-consumer genome-wide testing . . .

The available evidence does not provide support for the expectations raised by researchers and proponents of personalised medicine as well as direct-to-consumer testing companies that the receipt of results from DNA based tests for gene variants that confer increased risk of

[53] Christian Hopfer, 'Alcoholism: study boosts evidence on linkage regions associated with alcoholism' (2006) 14 European Journal of Human Genetics 1231–2.

[54] 'The impact of communicating genetic risks of disease on risk-reducing health behaviour: systematic review with meta-analysis' (2016) 352 British Medical Journal i1102.

common complex diseases motivates behaviour change. Concerns that communicating DNA based disease risk estimates may demotivate behaviour change are also unsupported by the results of this review.

In relation to certain psychiatric conditions, there is also a danger, as Lisa Bortolotti and Heather Widdows point out, that the communication of an elevated risk becomes a self-fulfilling prophesy: 'A general worry is that people may become more prone to depressions as a result of being told that they are at risk of developing depression'.[55] And, as David Melzer et al explain, the risks from both false negatives and false positives may be considerable.

David Melzer et al[56]

Onlookers may view most of this activity as genetic astrology, producing entertaining horoscopes. Unfortunately, ... misleading results could trigger erroneous treatment and involve major hazards. Recent reports that false negative ... testing in breast cancer led to women being denied specific treatment indicates the high stakes involved. On the other hand, direct marketing of the BRCA1 and 2 familial breast cancer tests to women at low risk (for whom evidence of utility is lacking) was criticised for risking unfounded anxiety and unnecessary prophylactic surgery. False reassurance from tests for common diseases could result in effective prevention measures, such as controlling weight and exercising, being ignored.

One of the most important issues raised by direct-to-consumer genetic testing is the question of consent. There are two potential problems here. First, if a sample is obtained at home, there is no guarantee that the person whose DNA is sent for analysis is, in fact, the person who purchased the test. If I could persuade you to let me have some of your saliva, could I then find out extremely personal information about you, without your knowledge? Could parents send in their children's saliva in order to obtain information about their child's risk of future ill health?

Section 45 of the Human Tissue Act 2004 attempts to address the possibility of 'DNA theft' by making it an offence to analyse someone's DNA without consent:

45 (1) A person commits an offence if—

(a) he has any bodily material intending—

(i) that any human DNA in the material be analysed without qualifying consent, and

(ii) that the results of the analysis be used otherwise than for an excepted purpose.

Qualifying consent means the person's own consent, or, in the case of a child who is not *Gillick*-competent, consent from someone with parental responsibility. Under Schedule 4, excepted purposes include 'the medical diagnosis or treatment of the person whose body manufactured the DNA.' That means that a parent could use a child's sample for diagnostic purposes,

---

[55] 'The right not to know: the case of psychiatric disorder' (2011) 37 Journal of Medical Ethics 673–6.
[56] 'Genetic tests for common diseases: new insights, old concerns' (2008) 336 British Medical Journal 590–3.

but predictive genetic testing would not be permissible. In practice, however, it is difficult to prevent parents from sending their children's samples for testing.

In their study of Canadian users of direct-to-consumer genetic testing websites, Emily Christofides and Kieran O'Doherty found that a significant proportion had sent someone else's sample for analysis.

Emily Christofides and Kieran O'Doherty[57]

While most of the participants had provided their own biological sample for testing ($n = 133$), 30 had provided their child's sample, 26 had provided their partner's, and 16 provided another family members' biological sample. Additionally, four had provided a sample from their partner's child, three from a past partner, three from a potential parent/child and three from some other individual (note that participants may have provided more than one person's sample).

When asked if they had obtained permission to provide another person's sample, 62% of the 60 participants who had submitted someone else's sample for testing reported that they had received permission to do so and 38% reported that they had not. Indeed, 13 of the company sites we examined specifically advertised the ability to test using 'discreet' samples (eg gum, toothbrush).

The second concern is whether consent to this sort of testing could be said to be properly informed. The only information people receive about these tests is from the companies' websites, the principal purpose of which is to persuade potential customers to buy their kits, rather than to offer unbiased, objective information about the value, or otherwise, of predictive testing. In addition, before sending their sample for testing, people should be told what will happen to their genetic information and to the sample itself, but a minority of websites in fact provides this sort of information.[58]

In 2010, the since disbanded Human Genetics Commission laid out the principles which ought to apply to direct-to-consumer testing, and these stressed the importance of information provision.

Human Genetics Commission[59]

2.2 Promotional and technical claims for genetic tests should accurately describe both the characteristics and the limitations of the tests offered, and the test provider should not overstate the utility of a genetic test ...

5.1 Where the test is a genetic test in the context of inherited or heritable disorders, that test should only be provided to consumers who are given a suitable opportunity to receive pre- and post-test counselling ...

6.2 A genetic test should be carried out only after the person concerned has given free and informed consent. Informed consent can only be provided when a consumer has received

---

[57] 'Company disclosure and consumer perceptions of the privacy implications of direct-to-consumer genetic testing' (2016) 35 New Genetics and Society 101–23.

[58] Ibid.

[59] *A Common Framework of Principles for Direct-to-Consumer Genetic Testing Services* (HGC, 2010).

sufficient relevant information about the genetic test to enable them to understand the risks, benefits, limitations and implications (including the implications for purchasing insurance) of the genetic test.

6.3 The test provider should take reasonable steps to assure themselves that a biological specimen provided for testing was obtained from the person identified as the sample provider …

6.9 … Genetic tests in respect of children when, according to applicable law, that child does not have capacity to consent should normally be deferred until the attainment of such capacity, unless other factors indicate that testing during childhood is clinically indicated.

Inevitably the safeguards in place when someone purchases a genetic test online are in sharp contrast with the non-directive counselling which the NHS provides in order to help individuals to decide whether or not to be tested. As Angus Clarke and Carina Wallgren-Pettersson point out, non-directive counselling does not mean simply providing information and leaving patients to make decisions on their own; rather, non-directive counselling involves asking patients:

to consider a number of 'what if …?' scenarios, so that they do not undertake a genetic test without considering the full range of options in front of them (including a decision not to have the test) and the full range of potential outcomes of testing (including an unclear result or an important but unanticipated finding).[60]

Following genetic counselling, an individual may decide that they would rather not be tested. In contrast, it is less likely that someone will decide not to go ahead with testing once they have purchased a testing kit, for which they will have had to pay up front.

In addition to the range of practical problems raised by purchasing genetic test results online, rather than receiving expert advice from a clinical geneticist, Nikolas Rose situates the growth of genome-wide association studies within broader social trends towards the individualization both of risk and of responsibility for ill health.

Nikolas Rose[61]

This growing empire of risk management tries to bring our medical future into the present, making it calculable and obliging us to act in the light of such calculations in the name of a new kind of biological prudence. Such risk assessments partake of the apparently unquestionable logic of preventive medicine. This is not so much 'discipline and punish' as 'screen and intervene'—to identify risks before they become apparent in frank illness, and intervene early and preventively by a combination of therapeutic measures and lifestyle changes. It is in this context that we can locate the growing use of screening tests—whether from genomics or neuroscience—and the belief that these novel medical technologies can make the invisible seeds of future health or illness visible. And the promise of these tests is to move from risks assessed epidemiologically to susceptibilities assessed individually—that is to say, to the individualization of risk.

---

[60] 'Ethics in genetic counselling' (2018) Journal of Community Genetics 1–31.
[61] 'Race, risk and medicine in the age of "your own personal genome"' (2008) 3 Biosocieties 423–39.

5 PHARMACOGENETICS

Pharmacogenetics has the potential to transform the way in which medicines are designed and used. Most drugs are developed and prescribed for the whole population, even though we know that patients respond to drugs in different ways: a medicine which is effective for some patients may not work for others. Treatments for conditions such as diabetes, depression, and asthma may be effective in only 60 per cent of patients, and for some treatments for cancer, the figure is as low as 25 per cent.[62]

In addition, some patients suffer adverse reactions to medicines, and others will need a higher or lower dose than normal. Doctors therefore often engage in a 'trial-and-error' prescribing process. The delays this may cause are particularly significant for antidepressants, which often have to be taken for six weeks before any therapeutic effect is noticeable. Obviously, if it were possible for a doctor to know in advance whether or not a medicine would be likely to suit a particular patient, it would be possible to ensure that she receives effective medication immediately, and does not undergo useless or dangerous treatment.

Genetic differences between patients are responsible for some of these differences in the way in which drugs are absorbed and metabolized. Pharmacogenetics would involve carrying out a genetic test before a medicine is prescribed in order to find out whether it would be likely to work, what dose would be appropriate, and whether the patient would be likely to suffer any adverse reactions. In practice, pharmacogenetics would be likely to identify genotype groups for whom a particular medicine would be effective, or for whom it poses an unacceptable risk of adverse side effects.

A good example of how pharmacogenetics works comes from trastuzumab (brand name Herceptin). Trastuzumab is effective only for the 25–30 per cent of patients with breast cancer in whom the oncogene, HER2, is present at abnormally high levels. It is therefore only prescribed to this subset of breast cancer patients, and prescription is always preceded by a test to identify the patient's HER2-status.

A pharmacogenetic algorithm can also be used to predict the correct dose of Warfarin, an anticoagulant drug used in patients who are at risk of stroke or heart attack. Some patients need as much as ten times the standard dose, while others can only tolerate lower levels.[63]

Pharmacogenetic medicine could involve the Medicines and Healthcare products Regulatory Agency (which licenses medicines in the UK) requiring the use of a pharmacogenetic test as a condition of issuing a licence for a medicine's use. It might also be possible for drugs which have been withdrawn from circulation because of adverse reactions to be reinstated for use only in population subgroups in whom they do not pose a risk of unacceptable side effects.

As well as improving patient care, reducing prescribing errors has the potential to save NHS resources, by eliminating the prescription of drugs that do not work, and by reducing the number of GP appointments a patient needs before she is prescribed a drug that suits her. Clinical trials could also be designed so that the drug is only tested on subgroups in whom it is likely to be safe and effective.

---

[62] *Pharmacogenetics: Ethical Issues* (NCOB, 2003).

[63] The International Warfarin Pharmacogenetics Consortium, 'Estimation of the Warfarin dose with clinical and pharmacogenetic data' (2009) 360 New England Journal of Medicine 753–64.

Despite these obvious benefits, pharmacogenetics raises a number of important questions. First, if clinical trials were redesigned so that a drug was only tested on a genetically selected subgroup, there could be no guarantee that it would be safe for a patient with a different genotype, thus potentially increasing the risk of prescription errors.

Secondly, although genes undoubtedly affect the metabolism of medicines, other factors—such as the patient's age, sex, diet, or exposure to other drugs—will also have an impact. Genetic tests alone cannot establish exactly what medicine will work effectively, in what dose, and with what side effects.

Thirdly, genetic test results will rarely come in the form of a 'yes/no' answer, but rather are more likely to suggest the probability of success and safety. This means it will be necessary to decide what probability of effectiveness justifies treatment. If a genetic test reveals that the only available treatment for a patient's condition has a 30 per cent chance of working, does this justify prescribing it? And should the choice lie with the patient or the doctor? From the point of view of those in charge of NHS resources, a 30 per cent chance of efficacy looks poor, but if this is the only available treatment, the patient might nevertheless be keen to try it.

Fourthly, pharmacogenetics will involve a massive expansion of genetic testing, which raises all of the issues we considered earlier in this chapter, namely confidentiality, discrimination, and the patient's right 'not to know' information which may be inadvertently discovered during testing.

Fifthly, the ability to target drugs more effectively will not necessarily reduce NHS expenditure on drugs. Rather, if there is a dramatic reduction in the quantity of drugs prescribed, pharmaceutical companies will face a corresponding reduction in their profits, unless, as seems likely, they respond by increasing their prices. Prescribing itself will also become more expensive, since it will no longer just take a couple of minutes for a doctor to write a prescription, but instead samples will have be taken and sent for testing, and the results interpreted. It is therefore by no means clear that there would be an overall reduction in costs as a result of pharmacogenetic testing; indeed, it is possible that costs may rise.

Sixthly, drug companies are likely to concentrate their research and development budgets on drugs which will work for the majority of patients, leaving others with unusual diseases, or unusual genetic reactions, with no effective treatment. It is also possible that population differences in metabolizing medicines may be drawn along racial lines. If this is the case—and there seems to be some evidence that it might be—it suggests that race might have significance at the molecular level, while being an irrelevant difference at the level of social policy. This has led some US commentators to resist what they have described as a move towards 'race-based medicine'.[64]

Finally, as Johannes Van Delden et al point out in the next extract, there is, of course, the danger that genetic tests might reveal that there is no effective treatment for a particular patient. As well as being extremely upsetting, being identified as hard, or even impossible, to treat could have negative practical consequences for an individual in the future, such as difficulties in obtaining insurance. This in turn might prompt people to refuse genetic testing, with the result that the doctor cannot know whether the patient is in the subgroup for whom a medicine is unsuitable or dangerous.

[64] Dorothy E Roberts, 'Is race-based medicine good for us? African American approaches to race, biomedicine and equality' (2008) 36 Journal of Law, Medicine and Ethics 537.

Johannes Van Delden et al[65]

The first problem that might occur in genotyping is that by testing the patient it might be revealed that the patient is a non-responder for all available drug options. The patient turns out to be an 'orphan' for whom genotyping provided no advantage, but only the knowledge that he probably cannot be treated . . . [S]omeone might turn out to be a non-responder for multiple drugs, which might give him the label 'hard to treat'. Therefore, some patients might not want to be tested for pharmacogenetic profiles, as they do not want to gain knowledge that might put them in a disadvantageous position.

This leads to the question of what a physician should do if a patient refuses to be genotyped. He could give the patient the 'bulk drug', but by doing so he in fact gives the patient a suboptimal treatment. Besides, he knowingly increases the risk of potentially dangerous side-effects by not testing the patient. If such side-effects emerge, who can then be considered to be responsible for them, the physician or the patient?

The Nuffield Council on Bioethics considered this problem, and argued that the way in which pharmacogenetics are presented to the public will inevitably affect people's willingness to undergo pre-treatment genetic testing.

Nuffield Council on Bioethics[66]

A question arises regarding whether patients will have the option to receive treatment without taking an associated test. It cannot be assumed that patients will be keen to take a pharmacogenetic test, even if it will improve the likelihood of their receiving a safe and effective treatment. Such an aversion may be irrational, but may be based on a legitimate fear that information produced by the test could make it difficult to obtain insurance, or that it might indirectly reveal information about a medical condition which cannot be effectively treated . . .

Patients might not be given the most beneficial medicines if these may only be prescribed with a genetic test they refuse to take. Even more serious is the possibility that a medicine may be administered without an associated pharmacogenetic test, and result in a serious, predictable and avoidable adverse reaction. We think it likely that the acceptance of pharmacogenetics will depend not only on which tests are introduced and for which purposes they are used, but also on the way they are presented to the public at large and to individual patients.

6 CONCLUSION

In the past, genetic testing was relevant only to the relatively small proportion of the population who knew that they were at risk of passing on an inherited condition. Now we know that all of us will have a number of faulty genes, some of which might mean that we are at higher than average chance of developing a range of conditions in later life. As it becomes easier to find out this information, questions of genetic privacy and discrimination become relevant to

---

[65] 'Tailor-made pharmacotherapy: future developments and ethical challenges in the field of pharmacogenomics' (2004) 18 Bioethics 303–21.

[66] *Pharmacogenetics: Ethical Issues* (NCOB, 2003), xxii, 7.

an increasing proportion of the population. If the prescription of a growing number of medicines must be preceded by a genetic test, again, issues of confidentiality and discrimination have much wider significance than has previously been the case.

While new developments in genetics are fast-moving and undeniably exciting, it is also important to bear in mind that there are other fairly accurate predictors of future ill health which we should not ignore just because they seem more prosaic. We know, for example, that child poverty has a dramatic impact upon a child's health prospects in later life. Having an unhealthy diet—which often correlates with relative poverty—increases one's chance of developing heart disease and cancer. It is easy to be seduced into imagining that my 'personal genome analysis' holds the key to my future life chances when, in fact, how much I exercise, and what I eat and drink, not to mention my socio-economic status, may be at least as important.

FURTHER READING

Bayefsky, Michelle J, 'The human genome as public: Justifications and implications' (2017) 31 Bioethics 209–19.

Christofides, Emily and O'Doherty, Kieran, 'Company disclosure and consumer perceptions of the privacy implications of direct-to-consumer genetic testing' (2016) 35 New Genetics and Society 101–23.

Gilbar, Roy and Foster, Charles, 'It's arrived! Relational Autonomy Comes to Court: *ABC v ST George's Healthcare NHS Trust* [2017] EWCA 336' (2018) 26 Medical Law Review 125–33.

Newson, Ainsley J, 'Whole genome sequencing in children: ethics, choice and deliberation' (2017) 43 Journal of Medical Ethics 540–2.

Nuffield Council on Bioethics, *The Forensic Use of Bioinformation: Ethical Issues* (NCOB, 2008).

Otlowski, Margaret, 'Tackling Legal Challenges Posed By Population Biobanks: Reconceptualising Consent Requirements' (2012) 20 Medical Law Review 191–226.

Rose, Nikolas, 'Race risk and medicine in the age of your own personal genome' (2008) 3 Biosocieties 423–39.

Van Ommen, Gert-Jan B and Cornel, Martina C, 'Recreational genomics? Dreams and fears on genetic susceptibility screening' (2008) 16 European Journal of Human Genetics 403–4.

10

CLINICAL RESEARCH

CENTRAL ISSUES

1. Animal experiments usually precede trials involving human subjects. To obtain a licence from the Home Office, researchers have to establish that the use of animals is necessary, and animal suffering must be minimized.

2. International codes of research ethics, most importantly the Helsinki Declaration, have established universally applicable principles of good research practice.

3. At the time of writing, it looks unlikely that the EU Clinical Trials Regulation will come into force before the UK leaves the EU. Post-Brexit, it will be important to ensure that UK law mirrors EU-wide regulation of research, in order to ensure that the UK continues to be an attractive location for clinical trials (and their funding).

4. All clinical trials must first be approved by a research ethics committee.

5. Consent to participation in research must be informed and voluntary. It is sometimes difficult to ensure that patients enrolled in clinical trials understand that they are taking part in an experiment.

6. For participants who lack capacity, consent must be sought from their 'representative', and it must be impossible to carry out the research on adults with capacity.

7. It is increasingly recognized that conflicts of interests and selective publication raise important ethical issues in the context of clinical trials.

8. In order to develop medicines to treat diseases which are prevalent in the poorest regions of the world, it may be necessary to carry out trials in low and middle-income countries, but it is important to ensure that the interests of trial participants are protected.

1 INTRODUCTION

Without research, medical progress would be impossible. New treatments can be tested on animals, but animal experiments are an imperfect way to predict how a treatment will affect human beings. As we see later, a compound which caused multiple organ failure in the six men who took part in its 'first in man' trial at Northwick Park Hospital, had not caused any adverse effects in animals. But while we all want the medical care that we receive to have been rigorously tested on human beings, serving as a research subject may pose risks to an individual's health.

One of the most basic questions raised by the regulation of clinical trials is how to balance the competing interests of society (which wants medical treatment to have been proved safe and effective), and the individual research subject (who does not want her health endangered). Although research on human subjects is not the only time when the interests of society have to be weighed against the welfare of individuals, this balancing exercise offers a good example of the conflict between deontological (duty-based) and teleological (consequentialist) reasoning that we considered in Chapter 1.

If we adopt a strict utilitarian perspective, conducting research on a small number of people—with or without their consent—in order to benefit the rest of society might be justifiable, even if it poses a considerable risk to their health. Take the example of Edward Jenner's discovery of the smallpox vaccine, described here by Margaret Brazier:

Margaret Brazier[1]

Edward Jenner, injected an eight year old boy, James Phipps, with cowpox. Months later, he injected the boy with smallpox. The vaccination 'took' and the boy survived. Jenner's experiment has saved millions of lives and led to the virtual eradication of smallpox ... [I]t has often been said no modern ethics committee would have sanctioned such an experiment. Consider the case—the experiment used a child subject, who was too young to consent for himself, in non-therapeutic research where there was a high risk of death or disfigurement. The 'exploitation' of James Phipps undoubtedly saved the lives of some of us reading this.

In contrast, a deontological approach would condemn any course of action that disregarded the wellbeing of research subjects, regardless of the benefits to the rest of society. According to the Kantian imperative, we should never treat people solely as a means, but always as an end in themselves (see further Chapter 1). Hans Jonas has gone so far as to say research on humans involves treating subjects as 'things', and he argues that we should rule this out, even if it slows down medical progress.[2]

Both extreme utilitarianism and its opposite are unattractive and caricatured moral positions. In practice, most people adopt a mixed approach, which takes into account both individual rights and the common good. We do not want to sacrifice some human beings' lives for the benefit of others, but at the same time we do not want to stifle medical progress by banning clinical trials of new medicines.

We all benefit from living in a society in which drugs and other treatments have been properly tested. It might therefore be argued that we are under a moral obligation to incur some inconvenience or slightly increased risk to our health by participating in medical research. If we want there to be experiments on humans, but are not actually willing to take part in them ourselves, are we 'free-riding' on the sacrifices of others?

It is also important to remember that there are more interests at stake than just the individual research subject's concern for her own health, and society's interest in innovation.

---

[1] 'Exploitation and enrichment: the paradox of medical experimentation' (2008) 34 Journal of Medical Ethics 180–3.

[2] 'Philosophical reflections on experimenting with human subjects' (1969) 98 Daedalus 219–47.

Researchers will benefit personally from devising, carrying out, and publishing significant research, which may, as Paul McNeill suggests, create a powerful incentive towards 'cutting corners'.

Paul M McNeill[3]

While society, or at least some individuals within it, *may* benefit from research, there are very direct and tangible benefits for the researcher ... The researcher's interest in his or her own advancement and standing may be an added pressure to cut corners and act in ways that are unsafe ...

Instances of blatant disregard for subjects' welfare have understandably gained the most attention. However, it is likely that more harm has been caused (in total) by researchers who mean no harm but are unaware of the extent of risk to their patients. Their bias towards achieving the goals of their research may lead them to minimise, in their own thinking, the risks inherent in their research and give a disproportionate value to the research enterprise ... Scientists are as capable as any other group of pursuing their own interests to the exclusion of the interests of others.

Not only is the reputation of the researcher at stake, but, as Solomon Benatar points out, sponsors of research—most importantly pharmaceutical companies—have considerable financial interests in the outcomes of clinical trials. If a new medicine with a potentially large market-share has been proved to be safe and effective, it can be phenomenally profitable.

Solomon Benatar[4]

Clinical research has become a burgeoning activity in recent years, largely stimulated by the pharmaceutical industry's interest in new drugs with high marketing profiles ... The desire to make vast sums of money from medicinal drugs can be viewed as a modern version of the gold rush. Why make drugs for sick people who cannot afford them when one can make drugs for people with resources who seek marginal improvements or those who are well and will pay for the possibility of a healthier old age. Proliferation of clinical research, much of it promotional and of dubious scientific value, follows.

Clinical trials involving human subjects have been subject to EU-wide regulation since the Clinical Trials Directive 2001/20/EC, which was transposed into English law through the Medicines for Human Use (Clinical Trials) Regulations 2004. A new EU Clinical Trials Regulation is due to come into force throughout the EU in 2019.[5] At the time of writing, it seems likely that the UK will have left the EU before this happens. If this is the case, the Regulation will not be incorporated into UK law by the EU (Withdrawal) Act 2018. The government has nevertheless said that it intends to 'align where possible with the CTR [Clinical

---

[3] *The Ethics and Politics of Human Experimentation* (CUP: Cambridge, 1993).
[4] 'Avoiding exploitation in clinical research' (2000) 9 Cambridge Quarterly of Healthcare Ethics 562–5.
[5] Regulation (EU) No 536/2014.

Trials Regulation] without delay when it does come into force in the EU, subject to usual parliamentary approvals'.[6]

In this chapter, we begin with a brief summary of the rules governing experiments on animals, which usually precede trials involving human subjects. Next, we look at what is meant by 'research'. Not all medical research consists in the testing of new treatments or drugs. Epidemiological research, for example, may simply involve tracking the incidence of a particular condition in the population, and thus raises different, and perhaps fewer, ethical issues.

We then turn to the various international ethical codes, and the UK's regulatory system, including its reliance upon research ethics committees. The subject's voluntary and informed consent to participation is widely believed to be what justifies exposing her to the risks inherent in a research trial, and we consider what counts as sufficiently 'voluntary' and 'informed' consent. We also investigate whether, and in what circumstances, it would be legitimate to carry out research on individuals who cannot give consent.

We then examine whether the benefits and burdens of research participation are evenly distributed, drawing particular attention to the special issues raised when research is conducted in low and middle-income countries. We also look at the question of conflicts of interests and publication ethics—should there be a legal duty to disseminate the results of research findings, and does a failure to do so amount to scientific misconduct? Finally, we consider the question of compensation for injuries sustained as a result of participation in research.

2 ANIMAL EXPERIMENTS

(a) REGULATION OF EXPERIMENTS INVOLVING ANIMALS

In the UK, research involving laboratory animals is regulated by the Animals (Scientific Procedures) Act 1986, as amended. The Act defines 'protected animals' as all non-human vertebrates and cephalopods (such as squid). Insects such as fruit flies are also commonly used in research but are not protected by the Act.

Before any experiment can be carried out on a protected animal, a licence must first have been obtained from the Home Office. Under section 3 of the Act, the laboratory, the individual researcher, and the project itself must all be separately approved.

Animals (Scientific Procedures) Act 1986 section 3

3. Prohibition of unlicensed procedures

No person shall personally apply a regulated procedure to an animal unless—

(a) he holds a personal licence qualifying him to apply a regulated procedure of that description to an animal of that description;

(b) the procedure is applied as part of a programme of work specified in a project licence authorising the application, as part of that programme, of a regulated procedure of that description to an animal of that description; and

(c) the place where the procedure is carried out is a place specified in the project licence.

---

[6] Department of Health and Social Care, *Guidance: How medicines, medicinal devices and clinical trials would be regulated if there's no Brexit deal* (DHSC, 2018).

To obtain a Personal Licence, the individual researcher must have been on an approved training course covering the law and ethics of animal research, the basics of caring for animals, and ways of recognizing symptoms of illness or distress. Laboratories must meet strict Home Office criteria on staffing, veterinary care, and the quality of housing, lighting, ventilation, and temperature control. Each laboratory must have a 'Named Veterinary Surgeon' and a 'Named Animal Care and Welfare Officer', responsible for protecting the health and welfare of animals within the laboratory.

Before applying for a Project Licence, the researchers must first have received the approval of an ethics committee. Applications are then made to the Home Office. In determining whether to grant a project licence, under section 5(B)(2), the Secretary of State must verify:

(a) that carrying out the programme of work is justified from a scientific or educational point of view or is required by law;

(b) that the purposes of the programme of work justify the use of protected animals; and

(c) that the programme of work is designed so as to enable the regulated procedures applied as part of it to be applied in the most humane and environmentally sensitive manner possible.

Section 5B(3)(b) specifies that the Secretary of State must 'assess the compliance of the programme of work with the principles of replacement, reduction and refinement'. This is a reference to the 3Rs approach, first developed by Russell and Burch in 1959: Replacement (of conscious, living vertebrates by non-sentient alternatives); Reduction (in the number of animals used to obtain information); and Refinement (of procedures to reduce to suffering).[7]

A European Directive in 2010 required Member States to implement the 3Rs approach, and it has been transposed into UK law via section 2A of the Animals (Scientific Procedures) Act.

Animals (Scientific Procedures) Act 1986 section 2A

2A Principles of replacement, reduction and refinement

(1) The Secretary of State must exercise his or her functions under this Act with a view to ensuring compliance with the principles of replacement, reduction and refinement.

(2) For the purposes of this Act—

(a) the principle of replacement is the principle that, wherever possible, a scientifically satisfactory method or testing strategy not entailing the use of protected animals must be used instead of a regulated procedure;

(b) the principle of reduction is the principle that whenever a programme of work involving the use of protected animals is carried out the number of protected animals used must be reduced to a minimum without compromising the objectives of the programme;

(c) the principle of refinement is the principle that the breeding, accommodation and care of protected animals and the methods used in regulated procedures applied to such animals must be refined so as to eliminate or reduce to the minimum any possible pain, suffering, distress or lasting harm to those animals.

[7] WMS Russell and RL Burch, *The Principles of Humane Experimental Technique* (Methuen & Co: London, 1959).

Section 5B(3)(d) further provides that the Secretary of State must:

> carry out a harm-benefit analysis of the programme of work to assess whether the harm that would be caused to protected animals in terms of suffering, pain and distress is justified by the expected outcome, taking into account ethical considerations and the expected benefit to human beings, animals or the environment.

Almost all animals used in experiments are bred especially for the purposes of research in order to ensure that they are free from infection or disease. Increasingly, research on animals involves genetic modification: in 2017, half of the 3.79 million animal procedures related to the creation or breeding of genetically altered animals that were not used in further experiments.[8]

For complex licence applications, such as those involving primates, the Home Office may refer the project to the Animals in Science Committee. The Animals in Science Committee also offers guidance on more general ethical issues, such as appropriate methods for humane euthanasia.

The Home Office issues detailed statistics each year on the use of animals in scientific research.[9] In 2017, mice (58 per cent), fish (16 per cent), and rats (12 per cent) were used in the largest numbers of experimental procedures, while dogs, cats, and non-human primates were used in 1 per cent of all experimental procedures (18,000 in total).[10]

(b) THE ACCEPTABILITY OF RESEARCH ON ANIMALS

In what circumstances, if any, is it acceptable to use animals in research? Opinion on this question is, as Lyle Munro explains, deeply divided.

Lyle Munro[11]

> Experimentalists claim that as there is no satisfactory alternative, the use of animals is essential to human health. The antivivisectionists maintain that the researcher's case is deeply flawed and that the availability of cruelty free alternatives renders animal experimentation morally reprehensible. Neither side is willing to compromise since each perceives the other's position as evil. That it is no exaggeration to use the term 'evil' is borne out by the language of vilification that continues to be used by some of the protagonists in the controversy.

The Nuffield Council on Bioethics has suggested that instead of thinking in terms of two diametrically opposed positions on whether animal experiments are justifiable, it would be more accurate to divide opinion into four camps.

---

[8] *Statistics of Scientific Procedures on Living Animals Great Britain 2017* (Home Office, 2018).
[9] Ibid.   [10] Ibid.
[11] 'From vilification to accommodation: making a common cause movement' (1999) 8 Cambridge Quarterly of Healthcare Ethics 46–57.

Nuffield Council on Bioethics[12]

- *The 'anything goes' view*—if humans see value in research involving animals, then it requires no further ethical justification.
- *The 'on balance justification' view*—although research involving animals has costs to animals, which must be taken seriously in moral reasoning, the benefits to human beings very often outweigh those costs in moral terms.
- *The 'moral dilemma' view*—however one decides to act, one acts wrongly, either by neglecting human health or by harming animals.
- *The 'abolitionist' view*—since any research that causes pain, suffering and distress is wrong, there is no moral justification for harmful research on sentient animals that is not to the benefit of the animal concerned.

In the next extract, Richard Ryder suggests that few scientists in fact hold the 'anything goes' view of animal research.

Richard D Ryder[13]

As scientists we acknowledge that the human species is but one of many species. We know that other animals often behave as we do when in pain and that their nervous systems and their biochemistry are similar to our own. We know that nonhumans are related to us through evolution and that, therefore, it is inconsistent to put our own species on a moral pedestal entirely separate from all the others. How can it be moral to cause pain or misery to monkeys, dogs, or rats, if it is immoral to do this to humans? There are no *rational* grounds for asserting this. If it is wrong to experiment painfully upon unconsenting humans, it must, logically speaking, be wrong to do likewise to nonhumans. We cannot, with consistency argue that nonhumans are so like us that they produce valid experimental results and then claim that they are morally different. We should remember simply this: pain is pain regardless of species.

The critical issue is whether humans are entitled to use animals for their own ends, and one obvious point of comparison is the food industry. If killing animals for food is morally acceptable (and obviously not everyone agrees that it is), then it would seem odd to rule out the use of animals in potentially valuable scientific experiments. It would be difficult to argue that laboratory animals suffer more than those bred for food, given the nature of intensive factory farming and the strict controls that govern the treatment of animals used in experiments. It is also no longer lawful to use animals for 'trivial' research, such as the testing of cosmetics or tobacco products.

In the next extract, David Thomas argues that, because animals can feel pain and cannot give consent, a better analogy would be research involving people who lack capacity.

[12] *The Ethics of Research Involving Animals* (NCOB, 2005).
[13] 'Painism: some moral rules for the civilized experimenter' (1999) 8 Cambridge Quarterly of Healthcare Ethics 35–42.

David Thomas[14]

Let us accept for the sake of argument that it was provable that the human species was more important than other species—whether because people generally (though not always) have greater capacity for rational thought, may have greater self awareness, are better able to empathise, or have more sophisticated culture. It is not explained why those attributes mean that we can cause pain to those we relegate further down the hierarchy of value. And, if cruel exploitation of *other* species is justified on a relative value basis, then, logically, so must cruel exploitation *within* our species. Some people, indisputably, have greater capacity for rational thought, have greater self awareness, are better able to empathise, or have a deeper cultural appreciation than other people. However, most people do not conclude that the more endowed are for that reason entitled to cause pain to the less endowed for their own benefit ...

With non-consensual experiments on people, a *deontological* approach is taken. The prevailing view is that such experiments are *inherently* wrong, whatever the potential benefits to others ... With animals, by contrast, the approach is a kind of *utilitarianism*. The law allows scientists to cause pain to animals if *others* might benefit.

Indeed, RG Frey has suggested that it may be preferable to carry out experiments on non-sentient human subjects than on sentient rodents.

RG Frey[15]

The truth is, I think, that some human lives have fallen so far in value, quality, richness, and scope for enrichment that some animal lives exceed in value those human lives. Anencephalic infants and people in permanently vegetative states are cases in point. It was comforting in the past to think that all human lives were more valuable than any animal life, but the quality of life of a perfectly healthy dog or cat must vastly exceed the quality of any human life that has ceased to have experiences of any sort, that has ceased to have in essence any sort of content ...

If we have to experiment ... , then which life do we use? We use that life of lower quality, and we have a non-speciesist way of determining which life that is ... How can we justify an experiment on a perfectly healthy rodent with an experiential life as opposed to an anencephalic infant with, so far as we know, no experiential life at all?

3 WHAT IS RESEARCH?

(a) USE OF ANONYMOUS DATA OR SAMPLES

A great deal of medical research is carried out without any direct contact with patients. Epidemiology, for example, is 'the study of the occurrence and distribution of diseases and other health-related conditions in populations'. Originally the study of epidemics, it now

---

[14] 'Laboratory animals and the art of empathy' (2005) 31 Journal of Medical Ethics 197–202.
[15] 'Pain, vivisection, and the value of life' (2005) 31 Journal of Medical Ethics 202–4.

involves analysis of the prevalence and distribution of medical conditions, in order to test hypotheses about causes of disease and risk factors.

Major difficulties would be posed if patients always had to give informed consent to the use of information from their medical notes. The process of tracking down every patient and asking their permission would be incredibly time-consuming, and it also might cause unnecessary alarm. Ideally, the patient's agreement to the use of information gathered during treatment should be sought, but if it would be impossible to obtain consent, then there are times, as we saw in Chapter 8, when pseudonymized patient records can be used for research purposes.

(b) INNOVATIVE THERAPY

Ordinary medical treatment must satisfy the *Bolam* test, as modified by *Bolitho*:[16] that is, it must reach a standard of care which is (a) accepted as proper by a responsible body of medical opinion, and (b) capable of withstanding logical analysis. Usually this means that doctors should only provide treatments that have been properly tested and are known to be effective. If all orthodox treatments have been exhausted, however, and the patient's condition is extremely serious, it might be acceptable to try a treatment which has not yet been licensed for use in humans. This is consistent with the Helsinki Declaration, which sanctions the use of unproven treatment where no other options exist.

Helsinki Declaration[17]

> 37. In the treatment of an individual patient, where proven interventions do not exist or other known interventions have been ineffective, the physician, after seeking expert advice, with informed consent from the patient or a legally authorised representative, may use an unproven intervention if in the physician's judgement it offers hope of saving life, re-establishing health or alleviating suffering. This intervention should subsequently be made the object of research, designed to evaluate its safety and efficacy. In all cases, new information must be recorded and, where appropriate, made publicly available.

There have been two cases in which the courts have been asked to consider whether it might be in the best interests of patients who lacked capacity to be given untested medical treatment. In a case which predated the Mental Capacity Act, *Simms v Simms*,[18] the court issued a declaration that it would be in their best interests, and hence lawful to give an untested treatment to an18-year-old boy and a 16-year-old girl, who were in the advanced stages of vCJD (variant Creutzfeldt-Jakob disease—a rare, fatal, and incurable neurodegenerative disorder). Dame Elizabeth Butler-Sloss P explained that,

> Where there is no alternative treatment available and the disease is progressive and fatal, it seems to me to be reasonable to consider experimental treatment with unknown benefits and

---

[16] See further Chapter 3.

[17] World Medical Association, *Declaration of Helsinki: Ethical Principles for Medical Research Involving Human Subjects* (version adopted at the 64th WMA General Assembly, Fortaleza, Brazil, October 2013).

[18] [2002] EWHC 2734 (Fam).

risks, but without significant risks of increased suffering to the patient, in cases where there is some chance of benefit to the patient.

More recently, in *University College London Hospitals NHS Foundation Trust v KG*, Cohen J declared that treatment with PRN100, an untested monoclonal antibody, would be in the best interests of a man who lacked capacity with sporadic CJD, a fatal neurodegenerative condition that usually causes death within about six weeks of diagnosis. Although PRN100 had been under development for many years, and met Good Manufacturing Practice standards, the rarity of sporadic CJD had meant that it had not been possible to raise the funding needed for a clinical trial.

University College London Hospitals NHS Foundation Trust v KG[19]

Cohen J

The factors against treatment are as follows: (1) there is no evidence as to whether it is safe or effective in humans because there have been no clinical trials; (2) there may be negative side effects or adverse reactions which may be serious or even life-threatening; (3) it is possible that KG's death will be accelerated or that he will be maintained in a poor state for a longer period than otherwise would have been the case; (4) it is impossible to quantify the chances of a significant or material benefit to KG. They may be small or even non-existent.

The factors in favour of treatment are (1) that he wishes to have the treatment; (2) that his wife and family wish him to have the treatment; (3) that his quality of life, though diminishing, is still one that is clearly worth preserving; (4) that there is some evidence from the animal studies that PRN100 could have a positive effect on the progression of sporadic CJD in humans; (5) that there is ... 'a sufficient possibility of unquantifiable benefit to justify the risks involved' when, without treatment, KG will certainly deteriorate further and die within a short period; and (6) that there is a clear and thorough plan for protective monitoring and oversight ...

This is not a trial; this is not an experiment; it is the provision of a treatment or procedure to an individual patient who is in need ...

It is clear that he wants the treatment. Although he is no longer able to be anything like the active man that he was before, he still has a quality of life ... The wishes of the patient and his family are an important factor in a case such as this ... It seems to me plainly in his best interests that KG should have the treatment and accordingly I approve it.

The desire of a desperately sick patient (or, in the case of a sick child, her parents) to 'try anything' is understandable, but at the same time patients (or their parents) may overestimate the likelihood of success and underestimate the risks of untested treatments. As Jonathan Darrow et al explain, 'expanded access' to unapproved medications may promote patient autonomy, but there might also be a need to protect patients against false hope.

---

[19] [2018] EWCOP 29.

Jonathan J Darrow et al[20]

The primary ethical argument for expanded access is that patients should have a right to mitigate extreme suffering and to enhance self-preservation. This logic holds that as rational actors, patients are presumed to be capable of making well-informed treatment decisions in consultation with their physicians. According to this argument, not only can patients with serious or life-threatening conditions accurately identify promising experimental drugs, but they should also be entitled to utilize their own risk–benefit thresholds in deciding whether to consume such products. Advocates of expanded access argue that deference to the assumed capacity of patients to thereby make appropriate treatment decisions should be greatest when the stakes are highest (i.e., when death is likely or certain).

By contrast, those who seek to limit access to unapproved medications argue that the odds of an experimental therapy working in many expanded-access settings are extremely small—the probability of clinically meaningful benefit from early-stage experimental trials may be less than 10%—and informational asymmetries can lead to patient vulnerability ... Risk comprehension among the general public is low, is not strongly correlated with self-perceived ability to understand risk, and may be more impaired in sicker patients. Skeptics of expanded access caution that the risk of treatment-selection decisions that could exacerbate suffering or hasten death justifies greater—not reduced—paternalism for patients with serious or life-threatening conditions.

(c) NON-THERAPEUTIC AND THERAPEUTIC RESEARCH: PHASES I, II, AND III

After satisfactory evidence from animal trials has been gathered, there are usually three phases of trials on humans. Phase I trials involve a small number of healthy volunteers, who are given the drug so that researchers can study its toxicity, and the way in which it is absorbed. Next, in a phase II trial, the drug is given to a group of people suffering from the condition it is intended to treat, in order to evaluate its effectiveness and identify common side effects. Finally, phase III trials involve testing the drug on a larger group of patients who take it under supervision for a longer period of time.

After licensing, the drug will continue to be monitored before it can be categorized as an 'established' medicine. Although no longer purely research, because the intention is now to treat patients rather than to generate knowledge, this is sometimes referred to as a phase IV or a 'pragmatic' trial. Such trials involve looking at how drugs work 'in the real world', and will therefore include patients who are routinely excluded from clinical trials, such as pregnant women and people suffering from multiple comorbidities.

Normally, phase I trials are non-therapeutic, whereas the subjects recruited for phase II and III trials will usually be patients who may hope to receive some health benefit from participation. For certain new medicines, such as highly toxic chemotherapy drugs, it would be unethical to begin trials in healthy volunteers. The benefits associated with these drugs may outweigh the risks for patients with cancer, but there could be no justification for imposing them upon healthy volunteers. Hence, some trials will involve patients from the outset.

---

[20] 'Practical, legal, and ethical issues in expanded access to investigational drugs' (2015) 372 New England Journal of Medicine 279–86.

The potential dangers of non-therapeutic phase I trials became front-page news in 2006, following a catastrophic incident at Northwick Park Hospital. Eight healthy male volunteers had been enrolled in a phase I trial of monoclonal antibody TGN1412 (thought to have potential uses in the treatment of arthritis, leukaemia, and multiple sclerosis). Primate toxicology studies had not shown any adverse effects, and it was anticipated that, at the proposed doses, TGN1412 would be well tolerated in humans. In fact, six of the men immediately suffered life-threatening multiple organ failure; the other two had been given a placebo. None of the six men died, but in August 2006, it was reported that the most seriously affected volunteer had been diagnosed with the early stages of an aggressive lymphoma, and all of them face an increased risk of ill health in the future.

An expert scientific group was appointed to investigate what had gone wrong, and its report made a number of recommendations about the proper conduct of 'first in man' studies.[21] When deciding on the dose to be given, investigators should always err on the side of caution. Careful consideration should also be given to the route and rate of administration: the Expert Group recommended slow infusion, which can be stopped immediately at the first sign of any adverse effects. The report was also critical of the decision to give all six men the active dose within minutes of each other. Instead, it recommended that 'New agents in first-in-man trials should be administered sequentially to subjects with an appropriate period of observation between dosing of individual subjects.'[22]

While the therapeutic/non-therapeutic distinction may seem straightforward, as a way of classifying clinical trials, it can be problematic.

Robert J Levine[23]

Every clinical trial has some components that are non-therapeutic. When we evaluate entire protocols as either therapeutic or non-therapeutic … we end up with what I call the 'fallacy of the package deal'. Those who use this distinction typically classify as 'therapeutic research' any protocol that includes one or more components that are intended to be therapeutic; therefore, the non-therapeutic components of the protocol are justified improperly according to the more permissive standards developed for therapeutic research.

The absence of a sharp distinction between therapeutic and non-therapeutic trials is important because the principal consequence of labelling research 'therapeutic' is to make it easier to enrol patients who lack capacity. There is then a danger that researchers might exaggerate the likelihood of a direct benefit to research subjects, in what Lars Noah refers to as 'benefit creep'.[24] It is therefore important that any claim that an experiment is 'therapeutic' is rigorously scrutinized.

A further problem with the therapeutic/non-therapeutic distinction is that the whole point of doing the trial in the first place is that we do not yet know whether the treatment is effective. To say that a trial is therapeutic implies that it is known in advance that subjects will benefit from participation.

---

[21] *The Expert Group on Phase One Clinical Trials: Final Report* (DH: London, 2006).   [22] Ibid.

[23] 'International Codes of Research Ethics: Current Controversies and the Future' (2002) 35 Indiana Law Review 557.

[24] 'Informed Consent and the Elusive Dichotomy between Standard and Experimental Therapy' (2002) 28 American Journal of Law and Medicine 361.

Randomized controlled trials (RCTs), discussed in the next section, give rise to another difficulty. In a placebo-controlled RCT, there might be a 50 per cent chance that the patient will receive no treatment at all. Is such a trial 'therapeutic'? On the one hand, there is a chance that the patient will be in the active arm of the study, and will receive a treatment that has some chance of working; but it is equally likely that the patient will receive no treatment at all.

(d) RANDOMIZED CONTROLLED TRIALS?

Although it is true that some of the most important medical breakthroughs—such as the discovery of penicillin—were the result of luck, RCTs are generally regarded as the 'gold standard' in medical research.

The purpose of research is to discover whether a new treatment works, and while this might sound straightforward, researchers have to ensure that their results are not distorted by positive results caused by factors other than the treatment itself. Some patients would have been likely to get better anyway, for example, regardless of whether they received effective treatment.

In an RCT, the research participants are randomly allocated to the control or the active arm of the study. Those in the active arm are given the new treatment, while those in the control group receive either an inert placebo or, as we see later, the best available treatment. In both groups, it can be anticipated that some patients' conditions will improve regardless of whether they have received any treatment, so researchers are interested in whether the extent of improvement in the active arm is greater than in the control group.

An RCT is also intended to eliminate the distortions that result from the 'placebo effect'. Many people will report feeling better after receiving a new 'treatment', even if they have in fact been given a sugar pill. If, say, 1,000 patients are allocated to each arm of the study, and 600 in the active arm experience some improvement, while 300 in the control group also report feeling better, this suggests that the new treatment has actually worked in 300 subjects.

Two ethical dilemmas are posed by RCTs. First, while they offer the best way to establish whether a new treatment works, randomly allocating a patient to the active or control arm of the study is in conflict with the doctor's normal duty to decide what treatment would be best for her patient. If a doctor believes that drug X is the optimum treatment for a patient's condition, enrolling that patient in an RCT—in which she may be given a placebo instead—appears to breach the doctor's duty to place the interests of the research subject above the interests of science. As a result, it has been said that RCTs are ethical only if there is 'equipoise': that is, there should be genuine uncertainty about which treatment is best.

As Alex John London explains, that does not mean that the individual researcher has to be uncertain—'individual equipoise [would prohibit] all research in which different clinicians have definite but conflicting preferences for particular interventions'[25]—rather there must be uncertainty among experts in the field.

Alex John London[26]

The principle of equipoise states that if there is uncertainty or conflicting expert opinion about the relative therapeutic, prophylactic, or diagnostic merits of a set of interventions, then it

---

[25] Alex John London, 'Learning health systems, clinical equipoise and the ethics of response adaptive randomisation' (2018) 44 Journal of Medical Ethics 409–15.

[26] 'Equipoise in Research: Integrating Ethics and Science in Human Research' (2017) 317 JAMA 525–6.

is permissible to allocate a participant to receive an intervention from this set, so long as there is not consensus that an alternative intervention would better advance that participant's interests.

If it is ethically permissible for patients to receive care from expert clinicians in good professional standing with differing medical opinions about what constitutes optimal treatment, then it ordinarily cannot be wrong to permit participants to be randomized to those same treatment alternatives. Although randomization removes the link between what a participant receives and the recommendation of a particular clinician, the presence of equipoise ensures that each participant receives an intervention that would be recommended or utilized by at least a reasonable minority of informed expert clinicians. Equipoise thus ensures that randomization is consistent with respect for participant interests because it guarantees that no participant receives care known to be inferior to any available alternative ...

An interpretation of equipoise that requires uncertainty on the part of the individual clinician is not ethically justified because it prevents studies that are likely to improve the quality of patient care without the credible expectation that this restriction will improve patient outcomes.

The conflict between the duty to protect participants' wellbeing and the need to obtain scientifically valuable results is thrown into particularly sharp focus when deciding whether a trial should be stopped. Preliminary results may indicate that subjects receiving the new treatment are doing better than those in the control group. At this point, there are two good reasons to stop the trial. First, it might be in the best interests of the individual subjects for the trial to be halted so that all patients can receive the new treatment. Secondly, the state of equipoise that justified carrying out the trial might have been lost, because there is now some evidence that the new treatment works.

On the other hand, stopping the trial in its early stages will reduce the scientific validity of the results. The patients' initial improvement might turn out to be short-lived, and treatment that has been inadequately tested may endanger the health of future patients. The interests of science and society are therefore served by continuing the research until statistically significant results have been obtained.

The dilemma here, as Franklin Miller and David Wendler explain, is that the point at which interim results become relevant to the individual's decision to continue to participate may be sooner than when they become sufficiently compelling to justify stopping the trial:

The point of becoming relevant to individual treatment decisions is reached when findings provide evidence indicating the comparative superiority of one treatment; the point necessary for stopping a trial is not reached until this evidence becomes sufficiently compelling to support a change in treatment guidelines, including evidence that will convince clinicians to adopt the preferred treatment.[27]

The second ethical dilemma raised by RCTs is whether it is ever possible to give informed consent to participation. Patients cannot be told whether they have been allocated to the active or the control arm of the test, because an RCT is dependent upon the patients not knowing which treatment they have received. As a result, it is impossible for their consent to be fully informed.

---

[27] 'Is it ethical to keep interim findings of randomised controlled trials confidential?' (2008) 34 Journal of Medical Ethics 198–201.

Against this, it could be argued that the patient gives informed consent to random allocation, and to participating in a trial in which they will be told whether they were in the active arm only after the trial has ended. As we see later, however, there is evidence that patients find the concept of randomization difficult to understand, because it is radically at odds with the way in which they expect doctors to behave.

(e) THE USE OF PLACEBOS

Giving the control group a placebo is relatively uncontroversial where there is no known treatment for the condition that the new medicine is supposed to treat. In such cases, it is probably not strictly true to say that the researcher is in complete equipoise between the new treatment and doing nothing, since animal experiments are likely to have shown that there is a fairly good chance that this treatment might work. A better way to understand the justification for using a placebo control where no treatment exists is that the participant who receives a sugar pill is not left any worse off by taking part in the trial, because if they had not taken part they would have received no treatment at all.

But if participating in a placebo-controlled trial would deprive research subjects of appropriate treatment, it would appear to offend one of the most basic principles of the Helsinki Declaration, incorporated into UK law by the Medicines for Human Use (Clinical Trials) Regulations 2004 and reproduced in the EU Clinical Trials Regulation 2014: 'While the primary purpose of medical research is to generate new knowledge, this goal can never take precedence over the rights and interests of individual research subjects.'[28]

The Helsinki Declaration's solution to this problem is, in most cases, to ensure that patients in the control group are given the 'best proven intervention' for the particular condition. Not only does this protect the wellbeing of research subjects, but it has also been suggested that it may lead to more useful results: researchers will be able to establish whether or not the new treatment is better than existing treatments, rather than proving only that it is marginally better than nothing.

Helsinki Declaration[29]

33. The benefits, risks, burdens and effectiveness of a new intervention must be tested against those of the best proven intervention(s), except in the following circumstances:

- Where no proven intervention exists, the use of placebo, or no intervention, is acceptable; or
- Where for compelling and scientifically sound methodological reasons the use of any intervention less effective than the best proven one, the use of placebo, or no intervention is necessary to determine the efficacy or safety of an intervention and the patients who receive any intervention less effective than the best proven one, placebo, or no intervention will not be subject to additional risks of serious or irreversible harm as a result of not receiving the best proven intervention.

Extreme care must be taken to avoid abuse of this option.

[28] Helsinki Declaration (WMA, 2013), para 8.   [29] (WMA, 2013).

The second bullet point captures the idea that a blanket prohibition on placebo-controlled trials where treatment exists may be inappropriate. When testing new treatments for relatively minor conditions, such as headaches or hay fever, it might seem unduly paternalistic to insist that the control group should receive 'the best proven intervention'.

Particularly for conditions where the placebo effect is especially marked, such as pain relief, statistically significant proof of efficacy can be obtained more quickly, using fewer research participants, when a placebo is used. The Helsinki Declaration therefore suggests that placebo-controlled trials where effective treatment exists are acceptable if (a) there are compelling scientific reasons, and (b) the subjects would not be exposed to a risk of serious harm. In practice, however, placebo controlled trials where there is an effective therapy appear to be 'extremely rare'.[30]

(f) PLACEBO SURGERY

So far we have assumed that the most invasive experiments involving human subjects are trials of new medicines. In a placebo-controlled drugs trial, patients in the control arm may not receive effective treatment, but the placebo itself will not harm them. Where a treatment, such as surgery, is more invasive, conducting an RCT would involve carrying out a sham procedure on patients in the control group which does expose them to additional risks. Could this ever be ethical?

The issue first arose in the context of trials of fetal tissue grafting for patients suffering from Parkinson's disease. Experiments in animals, and preliminary trials on humans, appeared to indicate that transplanting fetal tissue into patients' brains could be effective in the treatment of Parkinson's disease. Because these preliminary trials had not been RCTs, it was impossible to tell how much of this improvement was due to the placebo effect.

The placebo effect can be particularly marked in Parkinson's disease research, because one of the sources of the placebo response is that the expectation of relief triggers the release of chemicals in the brain. Invasive procedures and decisive treatment, as well as the trust engendered by personal contact with a surgeon, are also associated with a strong placebo effect. The only way to eliminate the multiple distortions caused by the placebo effect would be to carry out 'sham' or placebo surgery on a control group.

Patients receiving this placebo surgery have a hole drilled in their skull, and would therefore be exposed to the risks inherent in any surgical procedure, without receiving any effective treatment. As a result, some commentators have condemned these trials for putting the interests of science above the welfare of individual research subjects.

It could, however, be argued that unless surgical procedures are properly tested, future patients may be exposed to potentially ineffective and/or unsafe treatment. Carrying out placebo surgery on a small number of patients might then benefit thousands of people in the future, and prevent the NHS from wasting resources on useless or dangerous procedures. While this argument makes sense from a utilitarian perspective, does it involve sacrificing the interests of a few individuals in order to benefit society as a whole?

The preferred solution to this problem has not been a blanket prohibition on placebo surgery. Rather, as RL Albin explains in the next extract, its use has to be rigorously justified, and the risks to subjects must be minimized. In particular, extra care should be taken when obtaining informed consent to ensure that the research subjects understand what is meant by

---

[30] Sadhvi Batra and Jeremy Howick, 'Empirical evidence against placebo controls' (2017) 43 Journal of Medical Ethics 707–13.

randomization, and are aware that they may be about to undergo a surgical procedure which carries some risks, but which may have no chance of improving their condition.

RL Albin[31]

[I]t is common for surgical techniques to be introduced into clinical practice without rigorous evaluation. The result can be exposure of substantial numbers of patients to procedures that incur significant risks and have no benefit. In addition to becoming a public health hazard, inadequately evaluated surgical methods can consume valuable societal resources ... This is not a theoretical concern. There are abundant examples of widely adopted surgeries that were abandoned subsequently for lack of efficacy ...

Use of sham surgery is unattractive because the increased risk to control subjects is not accompanied by any possibility of benefit. In some cases, however, sham surgery controls are strongly preferred on scientific grounds and may be necessary to answer the key questions. Sham surgery controls cannot be prohibited absolutely but their use must be balanced carefully against the safety of research subjects.

In their systematic review of all 53 published trials involving placebo-controlled trials of surgery, Karolina Wartolowska et al found that such trials were an invaluable way of telling whether an intervention is worthwhile and cost-effective. They also found that it was generally possible to take steps to ensure that the placebo arm posed minimal risk to participants, for example by making the placebo surgery itself less invasive.

Karolina Wartolowska et al[32]

Surgical randomised clinical trials incorporating a placebo arm are rare but this review shows that the results of many of the trials provide clear evidence against continued use of the investigated surgical procedures and in well designed studies the risks of adverse effects are small and the placebo arm is safer than surgery ... In the reviewed trials, the placebo arm was usually designed to pose as little risk to the participants as possible and to be significantly less risky than the active surgical procedure ...

Placebo controlled trials in surgery are as important as they are in medicine, and they are justified in the same way. They are powerful, feasible way of showing the efficacy of surgical procedures. They are necessary to protect the welfare of present and future patients as well as to conduct proper cost effectiveness analyses. Only then may publicly funded surgical interventions be distributed fairly and justly. Without such studies ineffective treatment may continue unchallenged.

Remy Brim and Franklin Miller challenge the prevailing assumption that subjects who receive placebo surgery are harmed without receiving any benefit. Instead they argue that for

---

[31] 'Sham surgery controls: intercerebral grafting of fetal tissue for Parkinson's disease and proposed criteria for use of sham surgery controls' (2002) 28 Journal of Medical Ethics 322–5.

[32] 'Use of placebo controls in the evaluation of surgery: systematic review' (2014) 348 British Medical Journal g3253.

conditions where the placebo response is well understood, such as pain and Parkinson's disease (PD), the placebo effect should be treated as a possible benefit of participation in research.

Remy L Brim and Franklin G Miller[33]

Placebos can elicit strong physiological effects and produce meaningful symptomatic relief. Indeed, there is often more sound evidence on the benefits of placebos than there is for experimental treatments under investigation ...

The placebo effect should be regarded by RECs and IRBs [Institutional Review Boards] as a potential benefit to patients receiving sham invasive interventions in trials of treatments for conditions that have sound medical evidence demonstrating placebo benefit to patients. Currently, pain and PD fall into this category, and the list will likely grow. Finally, considering potential benefit from the placebo effect would ease ethical concerns about sham-controlled trials insofar as there is evidence to support a prospect of benefit from sham procedures, which can at least partially offset the risks of these procedures.

4 INTERNATIONAL ETHICAL CODES

The first national code of research ethics was promulgated in Germany in 1900, when the Prussian Minister of Religious, Educational and Medical Affairs issued a directive which provided that research should only be carried out on competent adults, who had given consent after a proper explanation of the possible adverse consequences. Ironically, it was the grotesque corruption of some German scientists and doctors under the Nazis that led to the first international code of research ethics.

(a) THE NUREMBERG TRIALS

The discovery of what had been done in the name of medical research during the Second World War resulted in the prosecution of 20 doctors and three scientists at Nuremberg.[34] Some of the defendants were eminent and internationally renowned physicians. Others, according to the prosecutor Telford Taylor, were 'the dregs of the German medical profession'.[35] The trials were conducted by the Allied Forces, and the judges were American lawyers appointed by the Military Governor of the American zone. Sixteen defendants were found guilty; seven, including Hitler's physician Karl Brandt, were hanged.

Many of the experiments carried out in the concentration camps were, as Telford Taylor and Arthur Caplan explain in the next extracts, directed towards the 'war effort'. In Dachau, victims were forced to remain outdoors without clothing for 9–14 hours, or were kept in tanks of iced water for three hours at a time, in order to find out the best way to re-warm German

---

[33] 'The potential benefit of the placebo effect in sham-controlled trials: implications for risk–benefit assessments and informed consent' (2013) 39 Journal of Medical Ethics 703–7.

[34] *Trials of War Criminals before the Nuremberg Military Tribunals, United States v Karl Brandt* (US Government Printing Office: Washington DC, 1949).

[35] Telford Taylor, *Opening Statement of the Prosecution*, 9 December 1946 (US Government Printing Office: Washington DC, 1949).

pilots who had parachuted into the North Sea. Also at Dachau, inmates were deliberately in-fected with malaria in order to test immunization and treatment options. At Ravensbrück, battle conditions were simulated by making incisions that were contaminated with glass, woodshavings, and bacteria. Vaccines for diseases such as typhus, smallpox, and cholera were tested by deliberately infecting a group of prisoners who had been given the vaccine, and members of a control group who had not been immunized, and who were obviously likely to develop life-threatening diseases as a result. Because mass surgical sterilization would be costly and time-consuming, the Nazis were keen to develop techniques which could sterilize large numbers of people, ideally without them noticing. Several thousand women were steril-ized by injection, and men were castrated using X-rays.

Telford Taylor[36]

Experiments concerning high altitude, the effect of cold, and potability of processed sea water have an obvious relation to aeronautical and naval combat and rescue problems. The mustard gas and phosphorus burn experiments, as well as those relating to the healing value of sulfanilamide for wounds, can be related to air-raid and battlefield medical problems. It is well known that malaria, epidemic jaundice and typhus were among the principal diseases which had to be combated by the German Armed Forces and by German authorities in occu-pied territories. To some degree, the therapeutic pattern outlined above is undoubtedly a valid one, and explains why the Wehrmacht, and especially the German Air Force, participated in these experiments. Fanatically bent upon conquest, utterly ruthless as to the means or in-struments to be used in achieving victory, and callous to the sufferings of people whom they regarded as inferior, the German militarists were willing to gather whatever scientific fruit these experiments might yield.

   But our proof will show that a quite different and even more sinister objective runs like a red thread through these hideous researches. We will show that in some instances, the true object of these experiments was not how to rescue or to cure, but how to destroy and kill. The sterilization experiments were, it is clear, purely destructive in purpose. The prisoners at Buchenwald who were shot with poisoned bullets were not guinea pigs to test an antidote for the poison; their murderers really wanted to know how quickly the poison would kill ...

   The thanatological knowledge, derived in part from these experiments, supplied the tech-niques for genocide, a policy of the Third Reich, exemplified in the 'euthanasia' program, and in the widespread slaughter of Jews, Gypsies, Poles, and Russians. This policy of mass ex-termination could not have been so effectively carried out without the active participation of German medical scientists.

Arthur L Caplan[37]

The most distinguished of the scientists who was put on trial, Gerhard Rose, the head of the Koch Institute of Tropical Medicine in Berlin, said that he initially opposed performing po-tentially lethal experiments to create a vaccine for typhus on camp inmates. But he came to

---

[36] Ibid.

[37] 'How did Medicine Go so Wrong?' in Arthur L Caplan (ed), *When Medicine Went Mad: Bioethics and the Holocaust* (Human Press: Totowa, NJ, 1992) 53–92.

believe that it made no sense not to risk the lives of 100 or 200 men in pursuit of a vaccine when 1000 men a day were dying of typhus on the Eastern front. What, he asked, were the deaths of 100 men compared to the possible benefit of getting a prophylactic vaccine capable of saving tens of thousands? Rose, because he admitted that he had anguished about his own moral duty when asked by the Wehrmacht to perform the typhus experiments in a concentration camp, raises the most difficult and most plausible moral argument in defense of lethal experimentation.

The prosecution encountered some difficulty with Rose's argument. The defense team for Rose noted that the Allies themselves justified the compulsory drafting of men for military service throughout the war, knowing many would certainly die, on the grounds that the sacrifice of the few to save the many was morally just.

It is worth noting that the United States' interest in prosecuting German doctors and scientists who had carried out inhuman experiments on concentration camp inmates did not extend to abuses by Japanese researchers in the 1930s and 1940s. Between 1930 and 1945, at a site in China known as Unit 731, over 3,000 people died through deliberate exposure to germs such as anthrax, cholera, and typhoid, and as a result of experiments involving being dehydrated, frozen, or given transfusions of horse blood.[38] At the end of the war, the US gave Japanese experimenters immunity from prosecution in return for information about biological warfare.

In addition to judging the conduct of the defendants, the court at Nuremberg set out a Code to govern the future conduct of medical research, the first principle of which is that 'The voluntary consent of the human subject is absolutely essential.'[39] Although the publication of the Nuremberg Code had tremendous symbolic resonance, its impact upon medical practice was limited. In part, this is because many assumed that it was specifically addressing the horrific crimes carried out by the Nazis, and that it therefore had limited relevance for medical research more generally.

Although there have not been research abuses on this scale since the Nuremberg trials, exploitative medical research did not start and stop with the Nazis. There were plenty of examples of unethical research prior to the Second World War: in the eighteenth and nineteenth centuries, for example, experiments would often be carried out on orphans, prostitutes, and other 'expendable' social groups.

There have also been incidences of exploitation since the end of the Second World War. In the 1960s, Henry Beecher's seminal article 'Ethics and Clinical Research',[40] and Maurice Pappworth's book *Human Guinea Pigs*,[41] gave details of extensive violations of the principles encapsulated in the Nuremberg Code. For example, in the US, between 1932 and 1972 the United States Public Health Services carried out the now infamous Tuskegee study, in which effective treatment for syphilis was withheld from 400 poor and uneducated black men without their knowledge or consent, so that the disease's progression could be observed.

In 2011, it was revealed that one of the doctors involved in the Tuskegee study had also carried out syphilis research in Guatemala, in which prostitutes known to be infected with syphilis were sent into prisons to have sex with prisoners, who were then given prophylactic

---

[38] See further Sheldon H Harris, *Factories of Death: Japanese Biological Warfare 1932–45 and the American Cover-Up* (Routledge: London, 1994).
[39] *Trials of War Criminals before the Nuremberg Military Tribunals under Control Council Law No. 10*, vol 2 (US Government Printing Office: Washington DC, 1949) 181–2.
[40] 'Ethics and clinical research' (1966) 274 New England Journal of Medicine 1354–60.
[41] *Human Guinea Pigs: Experimentation on Man* (Beacon Press: Boston, 1967).

treatment in order to find out if it was capable of preventing infection.[42] Indeed, as recently as the mid-1970s, approximately 85 per cent of all US phase I studies were conducted on prisoners.[43]

(b) THE HELSINKI DECLARATION

In 1954, the Eighth General Assembly of the World Medical Association drafted a set of principles to be followed in research involving human subjects. This document was redrafted in the early 1960s and adopted at the Eighteenth World Medical Association Assembly in Helsinki in 1964. The Helsinki Declaration has since been revised nine times, most recently in Brazil in 2013.

The Helsinki Declaration goes into much greater detail than the Nuremberg Code as to the circumstances in which research on human subjects is legitimate. It also now specifically states that its provisions must not be diluted by national legislation. Through regular updating, the Declaration has been able to respond to new concerns: for example, it specifies that 'Medical research should be conducted in a manner that minimises possible harm to the environment'.[44]

Helsinki Declaration[45]

9. It is the duty of physicians who are involved in medical research to protect the life, health, dignity, integrity, right to self-determination, privacy, and confidentiality of personal information of research subjects. The responsibility for the protection of research subjects must always rest with the physician or other health care professionals and never with the research subjects, even though they have given consent.

10. Physicians must consider the ethical, legal and regulatory norms and standards for research involving human subjects in their own countries as well as applicable international norms and standards. No national or international ethical, legal or regulatory requirement should reduce or eliminate any of the protections for research subjects set forth in this Declaration.

(c) THE CIOMS GUIDELINES

In 1982, in response to the concern that research was being carried out in poorer countries in order to save money and to avoid restrictive regulations, the Council for International Organizations of Medical Sciences (CIOMS) drew up international ethical guidelines for research on human subjects. Most recently updated in 2016, the purpose of the *International Ethical Guidelines for Health-related Research Involving Humans* is to address the practical

---

[42] Susan M Reverby, '"Normal exposure" and inoculation syphilis: a PHS "Tuskegee" doctor in Guatemala 1946–48' (2011) 23 Journal of Policy History 6–28.

[43] Anna Charles et al, 'Prisoners as research participants: current practice and attitudes in the UK' (2016) 42 Journal of Medical Ethics 246–52.

[44] Para 11.

[45] World Medical Association, *Declaration of Helsinki: Ethical Principles for Medical Research Involving Human Subjects* (WMA, 2013).

difficulties in implementing universally applicable ethical standards in countries with vastly different standards of health care provision.

Council for International Organizations of Medical Sciences[46]

Guideline 2

Before instituting a plan to undertake research in a population or community in low-resource settings, the sponsor, researchers, and relevant public health authority must ensure that the research is responsive to the health needs or priorities of the communities or populations where the research will be conducted.

As part of their obligation, sponsors, and researchers must also:

- make every effort, in cooperation with government and other relevant stakeholders, to make available as soon as possible any intervention or product developed, and knowledge generated, for the population or community in which the research is carried out, and to assist in building local research capacity. In some cases, in order to ensure an overall fair distribution of the benefits and burdens of the research, additional benefits such as investments in the local health infrastructure should be provided to the population or community; and

- consult with and engage communities in making plans for any intervention or product developed available, including the responsibilities of all relevant stakeholders.

(d) THE INTERNATIONAL CONFERENCE ON HARMONISATION OF TECHNICAL REQUIREMENTS FOR REGISTRATION OF PHARMACEUTICALS FOR HUMAN USE

The International Conference on Harmonisation of Technical Requirements for Registration of Pharmaceuticals for Human Use (ICH) brings together the regulatory authorities of Europe, Japan, and the US, as well as experts from the pharmaceutical industry. Its purpose is to make recommendations on ways to achieve greater harmonization of regulations, in order to reduce the need to duplicate trials of new medicines. To facilitate the mutual acceptance of data by regulatory authorities worldwide, the ICH has published a number of guidelines on the conduct of clinical trials, including the general ICH *Good Clinical Practices: Consolidated Practices Guideline* (GCP).

The ICH GCP states that: 'Compliance with this standard provides public assurance that the rights, safety and well-being of trial subjects are protected; consistent with the principles that have their origin in the Declaration of Helsinki, and that the clinical trial data are credible.' It requires there to have been ethical review, but most of its guidance in fact relates to technical, administrative matters, such as record-keeping. As a result, Sharon Kaur and Choong Yeow Choy question how far ICH guidelines are able to protect individual research subjects.

---

[46] CIOMS in collaboration with the World Health Organization (WHO) *International Ethical Guidelines for Biomedical Research Involving Human Subjects* (CIOMS, 2016).

Sharon Kaur and Choong Yeow Choy[47]

[The ICH process] is concerned with two things: first, ensuring that regardless of where drug development and manufacturing takes place, drugs are developed, tested, registered and monitored in a manner that ensures their quality and safety; and second, making the process of developing new drugs more efficient and less expensive. It does these things by prescribing harmonized standards for what are mostly scientific and quantitative processes, which mainly involve close observation and documentation . . .

Admittedly, these administrative processes lend themselves well in the scientific arena as a manner of demonstrating compliance to standards . . . To ensure that a drug is safe for use, information needs to be compiled regarding how many people have had bad reactions during the trial; the type of reactions; the severity of the events; the possible causal links between the reactions and the drugs; and so on. The accurate and careful compilation of relevant data is essential to any meaningful analysis . . . The question is whether or not this same approach is appropriate in situations that involve non-science based activities such as the activity of ethics review?

(e) IMPACT OF INTERNATIONAL CODES

Certain principles are common to all of these international documents, and the practical requirements that emerge from them could, perhaps, be summarized as follows:

(a) Before the research starts:
  - it must be established that the research is scientifically valid;
  - the risks must be proportionate to the benefits;
  - the research protocol should have been approved by an ethics committee;
  - if the subject has capacity, she must give informed consent;
  - if the subject lacks capacity, other protections must be in place.

(b) During the research:
  - the experiment must be stopped if there is a risk of injury or death;
  - the experiment must be stopped once equipoise has been lost;
  - the subject must be free to withdraw from the trial at any time.

(c) After the research has finished:
  - the subject should have access to information about the trial, and to treatment which has been proved to be effective as a result of the trial;
  - research findings should be disseminated;
  - subjects who have been injured as a result of the trial should be compensated.

While it seems obvious that risks to participants must be reasonable in relation to the trial's anticipated benefits, for several reasons, this is rather imprecise. First, it does not tell us how much risk it is reasonable to impose on subjects if the benefits might be very great indeed.

---

[47] 'Ethical considerations in clinical trials: a critique of the ICH-GCP Guideline' (2014) 14 Developing World Bioethics 20–8.

Secondly, because the outcome of the research is necessarily unknown, the researcher cannot know exactly what risks and benefits will flow from the research. If this information was known, carrying out further experiments on humans would be scientifically pointless, and hence unethical. Judging whether the risks are proportionate to the anticipated benefits will inevitably involve informed guesswork.

Invoking a risk/benefit calculation in order to justify research on human subjects might also be misleading. If told that the risks of participation in a research trial are outweighed by its benefits, not only might subjects not realize that this assessment is speculative, but also they might assume that they will be the ones to benefit. We know that most people volunteer to participate in research as a result of perceived self-interest, so unwittingly exaggerating the probability that the subject will benefit from participation may mean that her consent is based upon a misunderstanding, and hence is not fully informed. Even if participation in research might benefit the individual subject, it is important to remember that this will never be a trial's principal purpose. On the contrary, any anticipated benefit to individual research subjects will be incidental to its primary aim, which is to produce generalizable knowledge.

5 REGULATION OF RESEARCH IN THE UK

(a) THE IMPACT OF THE CLINICAL TRIALS REGULATION 2014

The new EU Clinical Trials Regulation (CTR) which applies to medicinal products for human use[48] is due to come into force in 2019. If, as seems likely at the time of writing, this happens after the UK has the EU, it will not be incorporated automatically into UK law through the EU (Withdrawal) Act 2018. The government has said that it will 'align where possible with the CTR without delay when it does come into force in the EU, subject to usual parliamentary approvals'. Extracts from the CTR are therefore included here.

At the time of writing, there is some uncertainty over exactly what rules will govern UK clinical trials post-Brexit. Because harmonization of regulation promotes free trade, it seems likely that the UK's regulation of clinical trials will continue to mirror that of the EU. Readers should check the Health Research Authority's website for the latest news about the UK's post-Brexit regulatory landscape.[49]

It is, however, hard to imagine that the UK would depart from the most basic principles of the Clinical Trials Regulation.

Clinical Trials Regulation 2014

3 A clinical trial may be conducted only if:

(a) the rights, safety dignity and well-being of subjects are protected and prevail over all other interests; and

(b) it is designed to generate reliable and robust data.

---

[48] Regulation (EU) No 536/2014 on clinical trials on medicinal products for human use, and repealing Directive 2001/20/EC (16 April 2014).
[49] <www.hra.nhs.uk>

Clinical trials must have been subject to scientific and ethics approval, carried out by a properly constituted research ethics committee. Within the EU, the CTR will introduce a single, electronic EU portal for all applications to carry out clinical trials, which will be maintained by the European Medicines Agency. Post-Brexit, clinical trial authorizations will be issued in the UK by the Medicines and Healthcare products Regulatory Agency (MHRA; we consider the work of the MHRA in Chapter 11, when we look at the licensing of medicines).

One of the main reasons for replacing the 2001 Directive (transposed into English law as the Medicines for Human Use (Clinical Trials) Regulations 2004) was that the applications process was cumbersome and bureaucratic, and especially so in the case of multi-country trials. Where trials are carried out in several European countries at once, differences in the processes for ethical approval was leading to unnecessary duplication and delay, and offered a disincentive for carrying out trials within Europe.

The CTR provides for notification, within strict time limits, of actual and suspected serious adverse events. Sponsors are required to provide an annual list of all serious adverse events, and a report on the safety of the trial's subjects. As we see below, the CTR also contains detailed provisions on obtaining informed consent from participants, and the circumstances in which trials can recruit people who lack capacity.

(b) GUIDELINES

In the UK, a variety of bodies—including the Department of Health, the Royal College of Physicians, the Royal College of Psychiatrists, the Royal College of Paediatrics and Child Health, and the Medical Research Council—have issued guidance on good practice in research. All reproduce the fundamental principle that the subject's health and wellbeing must take priority over all other considerations. For example, the General Medical Council's (GMC) guidance, *Good Practice in Research and Consent to Research*, states that:

8 You must make sure that the safety, dignity and wellbeing of participants take precedence over the development of treatments and the furthering of knowledge.

9 You must make sure that foreseeable risks to participants are kept as low as possible. In addition, you must be satisfied that:

- the anticipated benefits to participants outweigh the foreseeable risks, or
- the foreseeable risks to participants are minimal if the research only has the potential to benefit others more generally.[50]

(c) RESEARCH ETHICS COMMITTEES

Research ethics committee (REC) approval is a necessary precondition for all clinical trials. Applications are submitted centrally to the Health Research Authority, and those that raise no material ethical issues can be fast-tracked by a virtual sub-committee of two experienced research ethics advisers. Only applications which raise material ethical issues will receive full REC review.

[50] Good Practice in Research and Consent to Research (GMC, 2013).

Of course, this system depends upon a clear and consistent definition of what counts as a 'material ethical issue'. All invasive studies raise material ethical issues, and so only research which does not involve any physical interventions could plausibly bypass full REC review. An example might be gathering data using a survey or questionnaire. Some survey-based research will nevertheless raise material ethical issues, especially if it covers sensitive issues, such as exposure to sexually transmitted diseases. Poorly designed questionnaires could cause distress, and breaches of confidentiality could have serious adverse consequences.

The Clinical Trials Regulation sets a time limit of 60 days between receipt of a valid application and the issuing of the REC's opinion, unless the trial involves gene therapy, somatic cell therapy, or a medicinal product containing a genetically modified organism, in which case longer time limits (up to 180 days) apply.

RECs—of which there are about 80 in the UK—commonly have between 12 and 18 members, about one-third of whom should be 'lay' members. RECs are charged with deciding whether research proposals are ethical. There has been some debate over whether they should also judge the scientific validity of research. On the one hand, RECs may not have sufficient expertise to evaluate a project's scientific merit, and the question of whether research is ethical may be different from whether it is good science. On the other hand, if research is scientifically invalid and, as a result, will not generate any useful data, then this is also an ethical issue, because the 'anticipated benefits' to society do not justify the risks to the research subjects.

Certainly there is evidence that a considerable proportion of REC letters to applicants, which raise issues which must be addressed before approval is given, are concerned with scientific matters: in one study of REC decisions in relation to proposed oncology trials, 71 per cent raised scientific design issues.[51]

It is important to remember that the role of RECs is to determine whether what the researchers are *planning* to do is ethical. RECs exercise little ongoing scrutiny of research after the protocol has been approved. While progress reports must be submitted, the REC's role is largely confined to collecting information volunteered by the researchers, rather than investigating compliance for itself.

Standard Operating Procedures for RECs make clear that monitoring compliance is the job of the trial sponsor (which may be the pharmaceutical company whose drugs are being tested), rather than the REC:

> 10.2 The general policy from RES [Research Ethics Service] is that the REC should keep under review the favourable ethical opinion given to any research study in the light of regular progress reports and significant developments in the research ...
>
> 10.4 Other than by means of the reports that the sponsor and investigators are required to submit, the REC has no responsibility for proactive monitoring of research studies. The accountability for this lies with the sponsor and the employing organisation.[52]

The MHRA does have a role in ensuring that trials comply with good clinical practice (GCP), and it carries out inspections of trial sites when companies apply for marketing authorizations, or if the researchers have notified it of a serious breach of GCP, or under its 'risk-based compliance programme' of inspections.[53] If it does not amount to a serious breach of GCP,

---

[51] Mary Dixon-Woods et al, 'What do research ethics committees say about applications to do cancer trials?' (2008) 9 Lancet Oncology 700–1.

[52] *Standard Operating Procedures for Research Ethics Committees* Version 7.2 (HRA, 2017).

[53] MHRA, *Good clinical practice for clinical trials* (MHRA, 2017).

the MHRA will not necessarily know if there has been a deviation from the original protocol. Evidence from the US, however, suggests that such deviations are common: one study of the reasons for 'warning letters' issued by the Food and Drug Administration found that 95 per cent had involved 'deviation from the investigational plan'.[54]

6 CONSENT TO PARTICIPATION IN RESEARCH

(a) THE COMPETENT SUBJECT

(1) Voluntariness

Because the research subject will commonly be exposing herself to some increased risk, without necessarily gaining any benefit in return, her consent must have been given voluntarily, and she must not have been pressurized into taking part.

We begin by looking at whether payments to research subjects might unduly influence their decisions. Next we consider the special vulnerability of patients. Finally, we look at other 'vulnerable' groups, such as prisoners and medical students.

(a) Payments

Paying people to participate in research has been criticized for several reasons. First, it has been argued that the offer of money may prove irresistible, especially for the poorest members of society.

Paul McNeill[55]

> The reason that inducement is particularly of concern is that those most susceptible to inducement may be the least able to assess the aims and technical information relating to the research and to decide on whether or not the risk is worth taking. It is already the poor and socially disadvantaged who volunteer for most research yet it is typically the better off members of society who benefit from research . . .
>
> There is something repugnant about offering money to relatively poor people, impecunious students, travellers and others, to take part in research, which, by its nature, exposes them to risks of harm. The poor in our societies already have higher risks of poor health and other adverse life events. Inducement to take part in experimentation should not be allowed when it adds to those risks.

Not only could money persuade poor people to volunteer for research, but it might also offer an incentive to misrepresent characteristics—such as depression or drug use—which would otherwise disqualify someone from participation. This may increase the health risks to participants, as well as potentially invalidating the trial's results. In the next extract, JP Bentley and PG Thacker draw on empirical research which suggests that payments increase

---

[54] Yashashri C Shetty and Aafreen A Saiyed, 'Analysis of warning letters issued by the US Food and Drug Administration to clinical investigators, institutional review boards and sponsors: a retrospective study' (2015) 41 Journal of Medical Ethics 398–403.

[55] 'Paying people to participate in research: why not?' (1997) 11 Bioethics 391–6.

subjects' willingness both to participate in research, and to conceal information about 're-stricted activities'.

JP Bentley and PG Thacker[56]

> This study suggests that monetary payment increases respondents' willingness to partici-pate in research regardless of the level of risk; higher levels of payment make respondents more willing to participate, even if the study is relatively risky ...
>
> Monetary payments appeared to influence respondents' propensity to neglect to tell re-searchers about restricted activities they have engaged in either before or during a study, with higher payment levels leading to a higher propensity to neglect to tell.
>
> This study also showed that higher levels of monetary payment may influence subjects' behaviours regarding concealing information about restricted activities. If such activities were actually engaged in, the results of the hypothetical studies may have been distorted (that is, alcohol, caffeine, medications, herbal products may all affect the pharmacokinetics of a study drug).

Secondly, some commentators believe that the 'taint' of money contaminates the ethical virtue of altruism. Tod Chambers, for example, argues that 'the gift of one's own health should not be thought of as a commodity'.[57]

Thirdly, because payments may skew subject selection, they might also undermine the ro-bustness of trials' results. Testing medicines on students in their early twenties, for example, does not establish that they are safe for middle-aged or elderly patients. In an empirical study of phase I participants in Tayside, Pamela Ferguson found that they 'conform[ed] to the stereotype of the typical Phase I volunteer; ... they were predominantly male (74 per cent), aged between 18 and 45 (73 per cent), with a minority (23 per cent) in full-time employment'; 25 per cent were students, and half of these were medical students.[58]

The advertisement for recruitment to the TGN1412 trial, described previously, was de-signed to appeal to young adults: 'You'll be paid for your time ... Free food ... digital TV, pool table, video games, DVD player and now FREE internet access!' Volunteers were paid around £2,000. Following media coverage of the terrible side effects experienced by the six men who had received TGN1412, agencies that recruit volunteers for trials reported an increase in in-quiries from the public. As Pamela Ferguson explains: 'Paradoxically, the case helped to ad-vertise the high fees that could be earned by taking part, and the rarity of adverse events'.[59]

In favour of payments, it could be argued, first, that since participation in medical research will often be time-consuming, inconvenient, and uncomfortable, without payments it might be difficult to recruit enough participants. Secondly, it is not clear why being paid to assume the burdens of research participation is necessarily more problematic than paying wages to people whose jobs pose a risk to their health, such as cycle couriers, firefighters, and soldiers. In the next extract, Martin Wilkinson and Andrew Moore argue that inducements are not necessarily coercive.

---

[56] 'The influence of risk and monetary payment on the research participation decision making process' (2004) 30 Journal of Medical Ethics 293–8.

[57] 'Participation as commodity, participation as gift' (2001) 1 American Journal of Bioethics 48.

[58] Pamela R Ferguson, 'Clinical Trials and Healthy Volunteers' (2008) 16 Medical Law Review 23–51.

[59] Ibid.

Martin Wilkinson and Andrew Moore[60]

Many people would not work if they were not paid; in that sense wages are inducements. Few people think that, as a result, it is wrong to offer wages. Those that do have concerns about the existing wage system usually object that wages are too *low*, not that they are too high, or that they are offered at all . . .

If badly off people were in some way coerced into participating as subjects, then their autonomy would be infringed upon and their consent invalidated. Coercion is paradigmatically a case of the denial of autonomy, since it consists in the deliberate imposition of one person's will on another. However, coercion usually takes the form of threats, which restrict people's options. Inducements are offers, not threats, and they expand people's options.

Thirdly, the offer of experimental treatment to desperately ill patients, and the 'therapeutic misconception' (considered in the next section), will often offer a more powerful incentive than money for agreeing to participate in research, and for misrepresenting disqualifying characteristics. A research subject who has been paid is probably more likely to have given fully informed consent to participation in a trial than a patient who is mistakenly under the assumption that her doctor is treating her in her best interests.

The assumption behind the guidance that exists on payments is that payments are acceptable provided that they are not so large that they might prompt someone to act against her better judgement.

General Medical Council[61]

17 You should make sure that participants are not encouraged to volunteer more frequently than is advisable or against their best interests. You should make sure that nobody takes part repeatedly in research projects if it might lead to a risk of significant harm to them.

In the next extract, Christine Grady defends modest payments to research subjects.

Christine Grady[62]

Commentators and common wisdom have argued that limiting the amount of payment offered for research participation minimizes the possibility that money will distort judgment and push people towards deception. Payment as recognition of the research participant's contribution and calculated according to some regularly applied and locally acceptable standard (per day, visit, or procedure) is likely to be more modest and less likely to distort judgement than amounts designed solely to attract subjects and outperform the competition in terms of recruitment.

---

[60] 'Inducement in research' (1997) 11 Bioethics 373–89.
[61] *Good Practice in Research and Consent to Research* (GMC: London, 2009) 13.
[62] 'Money for research participation: does it jeopardize informed consent?' (2001) 1 American Journal of Bioethics 40–4.

In contrast, writing from a Canadian perspective, Trudo Lemmens and Carl Elliott suggest that the compromise position in which subjects are paid, but not much, is disingenuous. They argue that it would be better straightforwardly to admit that the researcher is employing the research subject. This would enable these 'employees' to benefit from health and safety rules that would prevent them from being exposed to unreasonable risks.

Trudo Lemmens and Carl Elliott[63]

In the world that regulatory bodies have created, healthy subjects take part in studies because of the money, yet researchers have to pretend that the subjects are motivated by something other than money. Research subjects cannot negotiate payment, since payment is not supposed to be the focus of the transaction ...

It is time to stop pretending that the relationship between for-profit, multibillion-dollar corporate entities and healthy volunteers is the same as the relationship between an academic physician-investigator and sick patients. We have argued that research studies on healthy subjects—unlike research on sick patients—are best characterized as a kind of labor relation. If regulatory bodies realized this, they would be in a far better position to protect these subjects from exploitation. Labor-type legislation could give research agencies the clout of occupational health and safety agencies by giving them the power to conduct inspections and ensure that 'working' conditions are safe. Collective negotiations and unionization could give research participants a stronger voice in arguing for good working conditions. Research participants could negotiate standards of payment based on the level of discomfort they are asked to undergo, the number and types of procedures, the duration of the studies and other factors ...

Ethical guidelines and regulations ought to protect healthy research subjects from exploitation. But instead, the current regulatory scheme prohibits subjects from receiving a fair wage and denies them the legal resources available to other high-risk workers.

There is certainly evidence that some people are effectively professional trial participants. Roberto Abadie carried out an ethnographic study of self-identified 'professional guinea pigs' in Philadelphia and found that some volunteers had taken part in more than 80 phase I trials.

Roberto Abadie[64]

Most clinical trial volunteers are in their twenties and thirties, single and childless, with flexible schedules and no permanent attachments. Trial income offers them the opportunity to have fun and travel ... In their spending habits, guinea pigs show a clear understanding that their bodies are commodities, almost using their bodies as ATMs to fund their lifestyles.

Volunteers understand their participation as trial subjects as a particular type of work not based on physical labor ... Professional guinea pigs have the sense that while volunteering for a trial they do not do much except just lie there ... Most guinea pigs would agree with Spam, who was quoted in the introduction as describing the trials as 'a weird type of work' in a 'mild torture economy' in which one is paid not to produce something, but to 'endure something'.

---

[63] 'Justice for the professional guinea pig' (2001) 1 American Journal of Bioethics 51–3.
[64] Roberto Abadie, *The Professional Guinea Pig: Big Pharma and the Risky World of Human Subjects* (Duke UP: Durham, NC, 2010).

Since 2013, the Health Research Authority has maintained The Over-Volunteering Prevention System (TOPS), and it is a standard condition of ethical approval that all phase I studies using healthy volunteers register participants onto TOPS, and record whether each volunteer received a dose of the study medicine. The HRA explains its function as follows, while admitting that it is not likely to be able to detect 'professional over-volunteering'.

Health Research Authority[65]

Why do we need TOPS?

Healthy volunteers must not take part too often in trials of new medicines, for scientific, medical and ethical reasons:

- if the gap between two trials is too short, or the trials overlap, the medicines might interact
- taking too many blood samples could cause anaemia
- it's unethical to expose healthy people too often to medicines they don't need.

How does TOPS help?

TOPS allows volunteers to be identified and for it to be determined when they were last registered to take part in a study.

The database is designed to detect most cases of accidental or deliberate over-volunteering, but it is not designed to detect professional over-volunteering or fraud.

In the next extract, Rebecca Dresser points out that 'subversive subjects', who might lie about their compliance with a trial's requirements, are not limited to those who are paid. Patients too have powerful self-interests which may prompt them to act subversively.

Rebecca Dresser[66]

Clinical trial subjects are not passive followers of researchers' orders, they are active agents living their own lives and promoting what they see as their own interests. In rejecting the constraints research imposes, however, subversive subjects diminish the value of research results ... Volunteers focused on earning money through research participation adopt a variety of deceptive practices to gain admission to studies ... Patients who see trial participation as a means to obtain better treatment commit a variety of subversive acts. Some enter trials with the specific intent to drop out early if their symptoms do not improve within a certain time. Subjects have also been known to share drugs to ensure that each person receives at least some of the preferred one ...

Thus, the best way to proceed is to replace practices that devalue subjects' contributions with practices that demonstrate appreciation for what they do ... Simple quality-of-life upgrades could go a long way toward improving the situation ... The research staff also plays a major role in subjects' commitment to play by the rules. Subjects have high praise for studies

---

[65] The Over-Volunteering Prevention System (HRA, 2018).
[66] 'Subversive subjects: rule-breaking and deception in clinical trials' (2013) 41 Journal of Law, Medicine and Ethics 829–40.

conducted by personable and efficient teams. Subjects are grateful when staff members pay attention and respond to their concerns. Subjects appreciate sincere expressions of thanks for the pain, discomfort, and disruption they endure.

(b) Patients

There is a danger that patients who volunteer for clinical trials may not understand that they are taking part in research, where the purpose is to generate generalizable knowledge, rather than to improve their health. This is known as the 'therapeutic misconception', and for obvious reasons it is only a problem in phase II and III trials, when the participants are patients suffering from the condition the new drug is intended to treat.

Standard consent forms may exacerbate this problem by setting out what the study hopes to achieve for future patients. Nancy King advocates a much blunter approach: 'When benefit cannot reasonably be expected, the consent form should say, "You will not benefit"'.[67]

The doctor–patient relationship is based upon trust, and, as A Charuvastra and SR Marder explain, it is often difficult for patients to understand that their doctor might be suggesting a course of action which may not be in their best interests.

A Charuvastra and SR Marder[68]

[W]hen a patient is reading an informed consent document, he is also seeing a person in a white coat and appreciating that he is in a hospital or medical centre, and his evaluation of the intention of the researcher and the benefits and risks of his relationship with this researcher will reflect to some degree all his prior social encounters with similar people in similar white coats in similar settings. A therapeutic misconception is even more likely to take place if the person proposing the research is someone the patient already knows, and especially if it is someone the patient already receives care from.

Certainly, there is evidence that some subjects do not realize that they have taken part in research, even when they have apparently given informed consent. It also seems clear that patients find it especially difficult to understand the concept of randomization. In their study of cancer patients who had signed informed consent forms for RCTs, Virginia Sanchini et al found that nearly 40 per cent of participants were unaware that they had taken part in a trial, and only 11 per cent understood that the trial had involved randomization.[69] In the next extract, Katie Featherstone and Jenny L Donovan describe interviews with trial participants who clearly found it hard to believe that the treatment they received had been randomly allocated.

---

[67] 'Defining and describing benefit appropriately in clinical trials' (2000) 28 Journal of Law, Medicine and Ethics 332–43.

[68] 'Unconscious emotional reasoning and the therapeutic misconception' (2008) 34 Journal of Medical Ethics 193–7.

[69] Virginia Sanchini et al, 'Informed consent as an ethical requirement in clinical trials: an old, but still unresolved issue. An observational study to evaluate patient's informed consent comprehension' (2014) 40 Journal of Medical Ethics 269–75.

Katie Featherstone and Jenny L Donovan[70]

Allocation according to randomisation appeared to some to be very haphazard. It was difficult for these men to believe that such a haphazard procedure was reasonable, particularly when they had completed so many questionnaires about their symptoms and undergone clinical tests, some of which were very invasive. The men reasoned that the data from the questionnaires and clinical tests must be useful, not just for research purposes, but also for clinicians to make individualised treatment decisions—hence the unacceptability of randomisation ...

[E]ven when trials adhere to strict informed consent procedures and ensure that 'simple language' is used, this does not guarantee that subjects will fully understand the implications of participation and that they may still have unrealistic treatment expectations.

Terminally ill patients may be an especially vulnerable group, particularly if none of the standard treatments have worked, and they have been told that no more can be done for them. In such circumstances, enrolling in a trial of an experimental new drug may offer the best hope of a cure. As Frances Miller has put it, 'these desperate souls want to believe in the omnipotence of medicine'.[71] Of course, someone's desperation to try anything does not vitiate their consent, but it does suggest that researchers should be careful not to overstate the likelihood that the patient will receive a direct health benefit.

What is described as 'HIV cure research' offers a compelling example of some of the ethical challenges that may result from the therapeutic misconception. With effective antiretroviral therapy, patients who are diagnosed as HIV positive can now expect to have a normal life expectancy, and to have virtually no risk of passing on the virus to their sexual partners. Being on antiretroviral drugs for the rest of one's life is not without costs, however. In addition to the expense (generic antiretroviral drugs cost the NHS over £1 billion per year[72]), lifelong medication regimes are inconvenient, and some users experience unpleasant side-effects. As a result, there is considerable interest in finding a one-off cure for HIV, which would be either functional (ie achieving long-term remission) or sterilizing (ie eliminating the virus completely). At the same time, because HIV cure research will require participants to stop taking antiretroviral drugs, it is important that they understand that this poses a serious risk to their health, and to that of their sexual partners.

Nir Eyal[73]

[T]he challenge in HIV cure studies is special. Many patients who consider joining risky early-phase studies for cancer, for instance, are doing poorly, arguably with sound reason to try just about anything. HIV patients tend nowadays to have good alternatives to study participation, namely, remaining on ART ...

---

[70] ' "Why don't they just tell me straight, why allocate it?" The struggle to make sense of participating in a randomized controlled trial' (2002) 55 Social Science and Medicine 709–19.

[71] FH Miller, 'Trusting Doctors: Tricky Business When it Comes to Clinical Trials' (2001) 81 Boston University Law Review 423.

[72] Andrew Hill et al, 'Predicted savings to the UK National Health Service from switching to generic antiretrovirals, 2014–2018' (2014) 17 Journal of the International AIDS Society 19497.

[73] 'The benefit/risk ratio challenge in clinical research, and the case of HIV cure: an introduction' (2017) 43 Journal of Medical Ethics 65–6.

[A] small chance of a slight improvement, accompanied by a greater chance of gaining nothing or being severely burdened or harmed, seems on the face of it like a bad 'gamble' for patients. It fails to maximise their medical prospects. A decision to join some early-phase HIV cure and remission trials may appear irrational for patients who are doing well on ART.

Hence, an ethical challenge. We want to identify and hone cure and remission strategies for HIV—we owe as much to patients. But to do so we need study participants, and we must treat these particular patients right too.

In order not to exacerbate the therapeutic misconception in these trials, George Annas has suggested that researchers should not use the word 'cure'.

George J Annas[74]

[T]he words we use in the informed consent process (and in our politics) matter—and that there are words, arguably including 'cure', that are illegitimate to use in recruiting research subjects, and obtaining their consent to be a research subject ... So my conclusion is that 'cure' is simply too strong a word—promising so much more than it is likely to deliver, that it is misleading per se and so should not be used either in the name of the study, or in the informed consent form or discussion ...

Of course, cures are desirable, and many, if not most, patients with HIV/AIDS would prefer not to have to take their ARVs. In this context, it is predictable that they will see research designed to identify a cure for HIV as therapy, and as promising much more than it is likely to be able to deliver. To the extent this is true, the word cure should never be used in the consent process (or in the consent form).

Rebecca Dresser further explains that, while there may be good ethical reasons to recruit to only patients who are not doing well on existing antiretroviral drugs, such patients may have unrealistic expectations of benefit.

Rebecca Dresser[75]

Individuals whose health status and quality of life are good with existing therapies would face high relative risk in FIH [first in human] HIV-remission studies. In contrast, individuals who cannot be successfully treated with existing therapies would face lower relative risk in FIH trials. If HIV-remission researchers can obtain the information they need from FIH studies involving patients who fail to benefit from existing therapies, enrolling such subjects would be a risk-reduction measure. But patients with HIV lacking good therapeutic options could be susceptible to unrealistic optimism about the health improvements available through FIH trial participation.

---

[74] 'Cure research and consent: the Mississippi Baby, Barney Clark, Baby Fae and Martin Delaney' (2017) 43 Journal of Medical Ethics 104–7.

[75] 'First-in-human HIV-remission studies: reducing and justifying risk' (2017) 43 Journal of Medical Ethics 78–81.

Even when patients understand that they have taken part in a trial which is not intended to benefit them, they may have decided to participate in order to secure what they perceive to be incidental benefits from taking part, such as additional monitoring. Rosalind McDougall et al describe this as 'therapeutic appropriation', and, once again, clear and unambiguous information is necessary to ensure that participants understand that excessive monitoring may carry risks to their health.

Rosalind McDougall et al[76]

Some patients thoroughly understood the research protocol, including the fact that it was not intended to benefit them individually. At the same time patients actively sought to use their participation in research to obtain or create opportunities for individual therapeutic benefit, such as additional monitoring, increased access to their GP, opportunities for discussions with additional health professionals and new pathways to services. We call this phenomenon 'therapeutic appropriation' of research …

The first ethical risk is that the incidental effect that the patient believes will be beneficial may in fact be harmful, or its therapeutic value may be overestimated. For example, an increased frequency of investigations may be perceived by patients as beneficial, but in some circumstances may cause greater harm than good.

(c) Other vulnerable groups

It is worth noting that the category of people who are considered vulnerable in the context of consent to research extends beyond those who lack capacity. Medical students or junior employees, for example, may feel pressure to agree to participate in their teachers' or employers' research projects. The Helsinki Declaration requires researchers to be particularly cautious if the subject is in a dependent relationship, and to ensure that consent is taken by an independent physician.

Helsinki Declaration[77]

27. When seeking informed consent for participation in a research study the physician must be particularly cautious if the potential subject is in a dependent relationship with the physician or may consent under duress. In such situations the informed consent must be sought by an appropriately qualified individual who is completely independent of this relationship.

In the past, prisoners were often used as research subjects. Not only did their lowly social status make them expendable, but also using captive research subjects is particularly convenient: follow-up studies are much more straightforward when research subjects can be guaranteed to stay in the same place for many years. Now, however, for several reasons prisoners are categorized as a vulnerable group for the purposes of consent to research.

---

[76] 'Therapeutic appropriation: a new concept in the ethics of clinical research' (2016) 42 Journal of Medical Ethics 805–8.
[77] (WMA, 2013).

Small financial rewards may be disproportionately attractive in prison, where the opportunities for earning money are limited. Boredom too might encourage prisoners to enrol in scientific studies. Of course, a prisoner who wants to take part in research in order to relieve the monotony of prison life, or to earn a small amount of money, has not been coerced. But more worryingly, prisoners may wrongly believe that agreeing to take part in research might lead to early parole or other privileges, and as a result may not feel that refusal is an option. It has been argued that, because of their special vulnerability, prisoners should only be recruited when their incarceration is directly relevant: an example might be a psychological study investigating whether imprisonment increases the incidence or severity of depression. For example, the Royal College of Physicians' guidelines state that:

> Research that can be conducted on patients or healthy volunteers who are not in prison should not be conducted on prisoners. Incarceration in prison creates a constraint which could affect the ability of prisoners to make truly voluntary decisions without coercion to participate in research.[78]

Others, like Anna Charles et al, have argued that this degree of paternalism is unwarranted, and that prisoners should have an equal right to participate in research.

Anna Charles et al[79]

> While the pattern of excluding prisoners may stem from well-intentioned efforts to protect them, this raises a number of issues. First, there has been a shift in attitudes towards the risks and benefits of research participation with the prevailing protectionist attitude of previous decades being replaced by an emphasis on equality and access, and the inclusion of vulnerable groups as a matter of equity ...
>
> Second, it is arguable that participation in clinical research may benefit participants directly by affording them access to cutting-edge interventions that are otherwise unavailable ... This possibility is particularly significant where individuals have a life-threatening condition and no remaining treatment options, leaving research participation as the only meaningful opportunity for treatment ...
>
> Third, in addition to health benefits of research participation, participants may benefit through the moral satisfaction of contributing to society. Research contribution can be regarded as a public good. As such, excluding prisoners denies them the opportunity to make the same moral contribution as free members of society, disengaging them from the wider moral community.

(2) Information

As we saw in Chapter 4, for consent to be valid, the patient must have been informed 'in broad terms' about the nature of the procedure she is about to undergo.[80] If someone was not told

---

[78] Royal College of Physicians, *Guidelines on the Practice of Ethics Committees in Medical Research with Human Participants*, 4th edn (RCP: London, 2007) para 8.47.
[79] 'Prisoners as research participants: current practice and attitudes in the UK' (2016) 42 Journal of Medical Ethics 246–52.
[80] *Chatterton v Gerson* [1981] QB 432.

that she was participating in a trial, her apparent consent might not be real and a charge of battery is possible.

The rule that subjects must give fully informed consent to participation in research is common to all of the various guidelines and codes governing experiments on human subjects from Nuremberg onwards. The Clinical Trials Regulation spells out what 'informed consent' entails.

Clinical Trials Regulation 2014

Chapter V Article 29

2. Information given to the subject or, where the subject is not able to give informed consent, his or her legally designated representative for the purposes of obtaining his or her informed consent shall:

  (a) enable the subject or his or her legally designated representative to understand:

    (i) the nature, objectives, benefits, implications, risks and inconveniences of the clinical trial;

    (ii) the subject's rights and guarantees regarding his or her protection, in particular his or her right to refuse to participate and the right to withdraw from the clinical trial at any time without any resulting detriment and without having to provide any justification;

    (iii) the conditions under which the clinical trial is to be conducted, including the expected duration of the subject's participation in the clinical trial; and

    (iv) the possible treatment alternatives, including the follow-up measures if the participation of the subject in the clinical trial is discontinued;

  (b) be kept comprehensive, concise, clear, relevant, and understandable to a layperson;

  (c) be provided in a prior interview with a member of the investigating team who is appropriately qualified . . .

  (d) include information about the applicable damage compensation system . . .

  (e) include the EU trial number and information about the availability of the clinical trial results . . .

3. The information referred to in paragraph 2 shall be prepared in writing and be available to the subject or, where the subject is not able to give informed consent, his or her legally designated representative.

4. In the interview referred to in point (c) of paragraph 2, special attention shall be paid to the information needs of specific patient populations and of individual subjects, as well as to the methods used to give the information.

5. In the interview referred to in point (c) of paragraph 2, it shall be verified that the subject has understood the information.

6. The subject shall be informed that the summary of the results of the clinical trial and a summary presented in terms understandable to a layperson will be made available in the EU database.

GMC guidance fleshes out what doctors should do in order to ensure that participants give informed consent.

General Medical Council[81]

> 7. You must make sure that people are given information in a way that they can understand. You should check that people understand the terms that you use and any explanation given about the proposed research method. If necessary, you should support your discussions with simple and accurate written material or visual or other aids.

Participants must obviously be told about any risks involved, but there are also grey areas, where it is less clear whether disclosure is essential. Do participants need to know about any personal or financial benefit that the researcher may receive as a result of the trial, for example? Should they be told if the researcher has been paid to recruit subjects?

As with consent to medical treatment, there is a danger that the provision of information happens only once, when a consent form is signed before the trial begins. But researchers should also be under a duty to ensure that subjects are provided with information that emerges after the trial has begun, so that their decision to continue to participate is also properly informed. As we saw earlier, however, this raises an obvious problem—if researchers must disclose their preliminary findings, participants might exercise their right to withdraw from the trial before statistically significant data has been gathered.

The subject's informed consent should normally be formally recorded on a signed, written consent form. It is, however, important to remember that a signed consent form is not the same thing as a binding contract. The existence of a signature on a consent form does not mean that a participant is under any obligation to keep her side of the 'bargain': on the contrary, she is free to withdraw from the trial, at any time, and without being subject to any penalty at all.

It is also worth noting that there is an important difference between providing information and ensuring that patients actually understand what they have been told. Evidence that patients are sometimes unaware that they have taken part in research, despite having signed an unambiguous consent form, suggests that simply providing information will not always be sufficient to ensure that the subject's consent is informed.

As Jay Katz explains in the following extract, obtaining fully informed consent to research participation takes time.

Jay Katz[82]

> Patients come to hospitals with the trusting expectation that their doctors will care for them. They will view an invitation to participate in research as a professional recommendation that is intended to serve their individual treatment interests. It is that belief, that trust, which physician-investigators must vigorously challenge so that patient-subjects appreciate that in research, unlike therapy, the research question comes first. This takes time and is difficult to convey. It can be conveyed to patient-subjects only if physician-investigators are willing to challenge the misperceptions that many patients bring to the invitation. Thus, recruitment of subjects will prove to be more time consuming.

---

[81] Good Practice in Research and Consent to Research (GMC: London, 2009).
[82] 'Human Experimentation and Human Rights' (1993) 38 Saint Louis University Law Journal 7.

In the next extract, Franklin Miller and Alan Wertheimer query the priority given to informed consent, and draw an interesting comparison with consumer contracts, where informed consent is not regarded as the solution for poor understanding.

Franklin G Miller and Alan Wertheimer[83]

The lengths to which investigators should be expected to go in assessing the quality of informed consent should be reasonable in view of the risk–benefit profiles of different studies ... [R]igorous testing of informed consent is costly in time and energy for both investigators and subjects, which seems neither reasonable nor fair in the case of many low-risk studies that offer subjects a personally favorable risk–benefit ratio ...

Consider, for example, ordinary consent in the case of employment or purchase of goods and services ... When people rent automobiles or take out mortgages, they are asked to sign lengthy boilerplate contracts, which few people bother to read. Consumers who sign such contracts should be adequately protected by regulatory guidelines ... , despite their uncomprehending consent, and, therefore, we don't deem such consent to be invalid. As the recent crisis over subprime mortgages suggests, when those institutional protections are not in place, we do not think that the remedy is to assure that people adequately understand the terms of their agreements. Rather, the remedy is to institute regulations to protect consumers from predatory lenders.

In the case of research, prior review and approval and ongoing monitoring by research ethics committees in accordance with detailed regulations (should) provide comparable safeguards.

(b) PARTICIPANTS WHO LACK CAPACITY

In Chapter 6, we saw that parents usually give consent to their children's treatment, subject to the courts' power to overrule their decisions in order to protect the child's best interests. Under the Mental Capacity Act 2005, unless the adult who lacks capacity has made a valid and applicable advance decision, she should be treated in her best interests.

These rules would not appear to facilitate participation in research. Since taking part in a trial involves being exposed to uncertain risks, it may not be in a patient's best interests. But a blanket ban on research involving those who lack capacity might also be inappropriate. If no trials can ever take place involving children and mentally incapacitated adults, members of these groups will have access only to inadequately tested treatments.

In the next extract, Paul Miller and Nuala Kenny explain that shielding children from the dangers of research might itself cause children significant harm.

Paul B Miller and Nuala P Kenny[84]

Ironically, the protective impulse to shield children entirely from the harms of research participation has the potential to cause them significant harm. History tells of the dangerous

---

[83] 'The fair transaction model of informed consent: an alternative to autonomous authorization' (2011) 21 Kennedy Institute of Ethics Journal 201–18.

[84] 'Walking the moral tightrope: respecting and protecting children in health-related research' (2002) 11 Cambridge Quarterly of Healthcare Ethics 217–29.

consequences of presuming treatments tested on adults to be safe and efficacious for children ... For scientific and ethical reasons, children should receive wherever possible only those treatments that have been adequately evaluated on children ... Reliance on the results of research involving adults as the knowledge base from which to develop the care of children may make the provision of such care unnecessarily dangerous.

As Lainie Friedman Ross points out, we allow parents to subject their children to activities which present greater risks than research participation, such as 'contact sports and traveling as a passenger in the family car'.[85] In addition, as we can see from the following two extracts, there is evidence that taking part in research is often a positive experience for children.

Malou Luchtenberg et al[86]

Young people's reasons for taking part included both personal benefit and helping others ... Regarding personal benefit, young people's experiences covered a wide range of interwoven motivations, which include much more than just health benefit. Participation also contributed to enrichment of their personal life and dealing with their disease. The young people felt special and acquired more confidence ... Our participants wanted to help future patients, parents, and their doctors. In addition, they experienced a feeling of moral duty and acknowledged the contribution made by past generations.

Mira S Staphorst, Joke A M Hunfeld, and Suzanne van de Vathorst[87]

All children mentioned positive experiences, and we categorised these into seven different types. Most frequently mentioned were 'helping other children' and the gratification that comes with it, having fun, (future) health benefits and gaining new knowledge. Other, less frequently mentioned positive experiences were receiving a present, not having to go to school and getting attention from healthcare staff and researchers ...

Our study shows that children (6–18 years) participating in non-therapeutic research have various kinds of positive experiences. Exclusive focus on the potential risk and burden of participation tends to ignore the positive effects of participation, which our study shows is an important aspect for children. In general, researchers can sometimes be overly cautious when including vulnerable populations in their research because they think it will only burden them, while in fact these patients positively value the opportunity to contribute to society.

In recent years, the dangers of routinely excluding children from research have been recognized. The EU's Regulation on Medicinal Products for Paediatric Use[88] has created a system

---

[85] 'Children as Research Subjects: A Proposal to Review the Current Federal Regulations Using a Moral Framework' (1997) 8 Stanford Law and Policy Review 159.

[86] 'Young People's Experiences of Participation in Clinical Trials: Reasons for Taking Part' (2015) 15 The American Journal of Bioethics 3–13.

[87] 'Are positive experiences of children in non-therapeutic research justifiable research benefits?' (2017) 43 Journal of Medical Ethics 530–4.

[88] Regulation (EC) No 1901/2006.

of incentives, including an additional six months of patent protection, for carrying out high-quality paediatric trials. It has also set up a European database of paediatric trials, including a requirement to publish both favourable and unfavourable results, in order to ensure that trials in children are not unnecessarily duplicated. The government is committed to ensuring that 'incentives remain to encourage such medicines onto the UK market' after Brexit.[89]

Since some mental illnesses impede decision-making capacity, drugs that might improve the lives of people with these conditions will have to be tested upon patients who cannot give consent. Emergency medicine may involve treating patients who have lost consciousness, and will improve only if new treatments can be tested on unconscious subjects.

If a blanket ban on the participation in research of people who lack capacity is not justified, when should it be permissible? As Neal Dickert et al explain, consent serves a number of functions in relation to research. For subjects who are unable to give consent, alternative mechanisms must be in place.

Neal W Dickert et al[90]

We argue that consent processes can serve one or more of four participant-centered ethical functions: (1) providing transparency; (2) allowing control and authorization; (3) promoting concordance with participants' values; and (4) protecting participants' welfare interests. In addition, we describe three systemic or procedural functions that are more policy focused: (5) promoting trust; (6) satisfying regulatory requirements; and (7) promoting the integrity of research and researchers ...

Recognition of the role that consent processes play in promoting trust highlights the need for additional steps to achieve this goal when consent is impossible ... Although patients with dementia may be unable to understand extensive information regarding risks and benefits, and therefore not in a position to provide authorization, they may retain a sense of their values and preferences and may be able to engage in more general discussions about the goals of research or a particular project. Adopting this approach may allow involvement of the patient by focusing more on overall goals and values.

Although the Clinical Trials Regulation contains different rules for children and adults who lack capacity, some common principles can be detected:

- It should be impossible to do the research on individuals who are able to consent to participation.
- The research should be likely to benefit either the individual subject, or other members of the group to which the subject belongs.
- Efforts should be made to gain the subject's assent to participation.

(1) Seeking a Representative's Consent

Where a research subject cannot consent to participation, consent must be obtained from her 'legally designated representative'. Usually, it is envisaged that someone will act as a subject's legal representative by virtue of their relationship with her. For a child, the personal legal

---

[89] Department of Health and Social Care, *Guidance: How medicines, medicinal devices and clinical trials would be regulated if there's no Brexit deal* (DHSC, 2018).
[90] 'Reframing Consent for Clinical Research: A Function-Based Approach' (2017) 17 American Journal of Bioethics 3–11.

representative should be someone with parental responsibility. An adult's personal legal representative should have a close relationship with her.

There will, however, be times when it is impossible to find a suitable personal legal representative, either because there is no one who is sufficiently close to the patient willing to take on this role; or in an emergency, identifying and contacting a close relative may not be feasible. In such circumstances, the patient's doctor can give consent as the subject's 'professional legal representative', unless she is involved in the trial. This disqualifies not only the principal researcher and her team, but also anyone who provides care under the direction or control of members of the investigating team. If the patient's doctor has any connection with the trial, someone else must be nominated.

Once a legal representative has been identified, her consent to the subject's participation in the clinical trial should be sought. She is expected to base her decision on the subject's 'presumed will', hence the desirability of finding a personal legal representative who knows the subject's values and preferences. The legal representative should be given an opportunity to understand the objectives, risks, and inconveniences of the trial, and the conditions under which it is to be conducted. She should be informed that her decision should be based on what the potential subject would have wanted, and that she can withdraw consent to the subject's participation at any time. Independent advice about the role should be made available. Where a professional legal representative has been appointed, subject to the duty to respect patient confidentiality, she may consult anyone who is able to advise her on the potential subject's wishes.

The legal representative is also responsible for ensuring that the subject's continued participation remains appropriate. This will be comparatively straightforward where the personal legal representative is a close friend or relative. Where a professional legal representative has been appointed, specific arrangements should be in place to ensure that the legal representative regularly re-evaluates the subject's continued participation.

(2) Children

If a child is seriously ill, and there is no standard treatment available for her condition, enrolling her in a research trial, in which she might receive an experimental new drug, could be consistent with her doctor's duty of care. But what if the research is non-therapeutic and, by definition, not in the child's best interests? The Clinical Trials Regulation permits non-therapeutic trials on minors, provided that the trial could not be carried out on adults and imposes no more than minimal risk on the child subject.

Clinical Trials Regulation 2014

Article 32 Clinical trials on minors

1. A clinical trial on minors may be conducted only where, in addition to the conditions set out in Article 28, all of the following conditions are met:

   (a) the informed consent of their legally designated representative has been obtained;

   (b) the minors have received the information referred to in Article 29(2) in a way adapted to their age and mental maturity and from investigators or members of the investigating team who are trained or experienced in working with children;

   (c) the explicit wish of a minor who is capable of forming an opinion and assessing the information referred to in Article 29(2) to refuse participation in, or to withdraw from, the clinical trial at any time, is respected by the investigator;

(d) no incentives or financial inducements are given to the subject or his or her legally designated representative except for compensation for expenses and loss of earnings directly related to the participation in the clinical trial;

(e) the clinical trial is intended to investigate treatments for a medical condition that only occurs in minors or the clinical trial is essential with respect to minors to validate data obtained in clinical trials on persons able to give informed consent or by other research methods;

(f) the clinical trial either relates directly to a medical condition from which the minor concerned suffers or is of such a nature that it can only be carried out on minors;

(g) there are scientific grounds for expecting that participation in the clinical trial will produce:

  (i) a direct benefit for the minor concerned outweighing the risks and burdens involved; or

  (ii) some benefit for the population represented by the minor concerned and such a clinical trial will pose only minimal risk to, and will impose minimal burden on, the minor concerned in comparison with the standard treatment of the minor's condition.

2. The minor shall take part in the informed consent procedure in a way adapted to his or her age and mental maturity.

3. If during a clinical trial the minor reaches the age of legal competence to give informed consent as defined in the law of the Member State concerned, his or her express informed consent shall be obtained before that subject can continue to participate in the clinical trial.

The CTR corrected an unsatisfactory aspect of the 2004 Regulations, which provided that the wishes of the minor simply had to be 'considered' by the investigator. Now, if the child is capable of forming an opinion, and assessing the information, her refusal to participate should be respected by the investigator. The Regulation also provides that researchers must adapt the informed consent process to accommodate the minor's age and maturity.

Anna Eva Westra has suggested that the wording of Article 1(g)(ii) is potentially problematic, in that it permits research which will not benefit the minor provided that it poses minimal risk 'in comparison with the standard treatment of the minor's condition'. As Westra points out, 'some standard treatments are quite risky and burdensome', and hence this provision might appear to permit research that imposes substantial risks upon seriously ill minors.[91]

(3) Adults

In addition to the consent of their legally designated representative, a number of additional conditions and principles are set out in the Clinical Trials Regulation.

Clinical Trials Regulation 2014

Article 31 Clinical trials on incapacitated subjects

1. In the case of incapacitated subjects who have not given, or have not refused to give, informed consent before the onset of their incapacity, a clinical trial may be conducted only

---

[91] Anna Eva Westra, 'Ambiguous articles in new EU Regulation may lead to exploitation of vulnerable research subjects' (2016) 42 Journal of Medical Ethics 189–91.

where, in addition to the conditions set out in Article 28, all of the following conditions are met:

(a) the informed consent of their legally designated representative has been obtained;

(b) the incapacitated subjects have received the information referred to in Article 29(2) in a way that is adequate in view of their capacity to understand it;

(c) the explicit wish of an incapacitated subject who is capable of forming an opinion and assessing the information referred to in Article 29(2) to refuse participation in, or to withdraw from, the clinical trial at any time, is respected by the investigator;

(d) no incentives or financial inducements are given to the subjects or their legally designated representatives, except for compensation for expenses and loss of earnings directly related to the participation in the clinical trial;

(e) the clinical trial is essential with respect to incapacitated subjects and data of comparable validity cannot be obtained in clinical trials on persons able to give informed consent, or by other research methods;

(f) the clinical trial relates directly to a medical condition from which the subject suffers;

(g) there are scientific grounds for expecting that participation in the clinical trial will produce:

(i) a direct benefit to the incapacitated subject outweighing the risks and burdens involved; or

(ii) some benefit for the population represented by the incapacitated subject concerned when the clinical trial relates directly to the life-threatening or debilitating medical condition from which the subject suffers and such trial will pose only minimal risk to, and will impose minimal burden on, the incapacitated subject concerned in comparison with the standard treatment of the incapacitated subject's condition ...

3. The subject shall as far as possible take part in the informed consent procedure.

It is worth noting that there might be cases—such as longitudinal dementia research—where participants have capacity when the research begins, but lose it during the course of the trial. As a result, there may be participants who were able to give a valid consent to participate, but whose interests are subsequently protected by Article 31.

Adults who lack capacity exist on a spectrum from those who are in permanently comatose to those with borderline capacity, who might have capacity in relation to some decisions, but not others. Some individuals who are unable to give a valid consent to participation might nevertheless be able to express their unwillingness to take part. Just as with minors, the CTR gives incapacitated adults more say over their participation than the 2004 Regulations. The explicit wish of an incapacitated adult who can express an opinion and understand the relevant information should be respected, and, as far as is possible, the subject must take part in the informed consent procedure. This is consistent with GMC guidance, which has long been clear that if someone who lacks capacity does not want to participate, this should be the end of the matter.

General Medical Council[92]

30. You must make sure that a participant's right to withdraw from research is respected. You should consider any sign of objection, distress or indication of refusal, whether or not it is spoken, as implied refusal.

[92] Good Practice in Research and Consent to Research (GMC: London, 2009).

It is, however, important to remember that if a person is used to being treated without consent, she may have no reason to believe that her reluctance to take part in research will be respected. As we saw earlier, it is difficult for all patients to understand the difference between treatment and research, and this problem may be even more acute for mentally incapacitated individuals. Simply stating that research should not be carried out against the wishes of an adult who lacks capacity presupposes that such patients will understand that they have more robust rights to refuse to participate in research than they do for treatment, and that they will feel able to make their feelings known.

The Mental Capacity Act 2005 (MCA) applies to 'intrusive' research, other than clinical trials. Research is 'intrusive' if it would be unlawful if carried out on a capacitious adult without consent. As well as research ethics committee approval, such research must satisfy the conditions in sections 31 to 33 of the MCA. These include that it must not be possible to carry out the research on people who could give consent, and that:

> 31(5) The research must—
>
> (a) have the potential to benefit P without imposing on P a burden that is disproportionate to the potential benefit to P, or
>
> (b) be intended to provide knowledge of the causes or treatment of, or of the care of persons affected by, the same or a similar condition.

If the research does not have the potential to benefit P, the risk to P must be likely to be negligible: ie it must not significantly interfere with P's freedom of action or be unduly invasive or restrictive. Under section 32, the researcher must identify someone who is caring for or interested in the welfare of P (other than in a professional capacity), in order to ask for advice on how P would feel about taking part, if P had capacity. If this person advises that P would not want to take part, or would want to withdraw, P must not participate. Section 33 further bolsters the need to take account of P's views.

Mental Capacity Act 2005 section 33

> 33(2) Nothing may be done to, or in relation to, him in the course of the research—
>
> (a) to which he appears to object (whether by showing signs of resistance or otherwise) except where what is being done is intended to protect him from harm or to reduce or prevent pain or discomfort, or
>
> (b) which would be contrary to—
>
>   (i) an advance decision of his which has effect, or
>
>   (ii) any other form of statement made by him and not subsequently withdrawn ...
>
> (4) If he indicates (in any way) that he wishes to be withdrawn from the project he must be withdrawn without delay.

(4) Emergencies

In an emergency, it may not be possible to identify and appoint a representative before the trial starts. The CTR provides for a mechanism to enrol subjects in trials of emergency medicine, with safeguards in place to ensure that the view of their representative, and their own view, is sought as soon as practicable.

Clinical Trials Regulation 2014

Article 35 Clinical trials in emergency situations

1. By way of derogation from ... Article 28(1), ... Article 31(1) and ... Article 32(1), informed consent to participate in a clinical trial may be obtained, and information on the clinical trial may be given, after the decision to include the subject in the clinical trial, provided that this decision is taken at the time of the first intervention on the subject, in accordance with the protocol for that clinical trial and that all of the following conditions are fulfilled:

    (a) due to the urgency of the situation, caused by a sudden life-threatening or other sudden serious medical condition, the subject is unable to provide prior informed consent and to receive prior information on the clinical trial;

    (b) there are scientific grounds to expect that participation of the subject in the clinical trial will have the potential to produce a direct clinically relevant benefit for the subject resulting in a measurable health-related improvement alleviating the suffering and/or improving the health of the subject, or in the diagnosis of its condition;

    (c) it is not possible within the therapeutic window to supply all prior information to and obtain prior informed consent from his or her legally designated representative;

    (d) the investigator certifies that he or she is not aware of any objections to participate in the clinical trial previously expressed by the subject;

    (e) the clinical trial relates directly to the subject's medical condition because of which it is not possible within the therapeutic window to obtain prior informed consent from the subject or from his or her legally designated representative and to supply prior information, and the clinical trial is of such a nature that it may be conducted exclusively in emergency situations;

    (f) the clinical trial poses a minimal risk to, and imposes a minimal burden on, the subject in comparison with the standard treatment of the subject's condition.

Where a professional legal representative has been appointed in an emergency, review of the person's continued participation is especially important. The role of legal representative should also be transferred subsequently to an individual who is closely connected with the subject.

Where a patient has been temporarily incapacitated in an emergency, and is likely to regain capacity, under section 4(3)(a) of the Mental Capacity Act, the decision-maker should consider 'whether it is likely that the person will at some time have capacity in relation to the matter in question'. If the decision to participate could wait until the patient regains capacity, she should not be enrolled in a trial without her consent.

7 FACILITATING PARTICIPATION IN RESEARCH

(a) THE BENEFITS OF PARTICIPATION

So far, our focus has been on the special vulnerability of research subjects. Because the outcome of research is, by definition, uncertain, our assumption has been that participants are exposed to risks, without necessarily receiving any benefits in return. But this view of participation in clinical trials as a burden has been challenged in recent years as a result of the recognition that being a research subject might sometimes hold out the possibility of very great benefits.

The catalyst for this was the HIV/AIDS pandemic. Before the first antiretroviral drugs were licensed for use in humans, most people who were diagnosed as HIV-positive could expect to die from an AIDS-related illness within a comparatively short space of time. People living with HIV knew that research into drugs that might be capable of prolonging their lives was ongoing. Unsurprisingly, there was no shortage of volunteers for these trials. For some cancer patients too, the very latest treatments may only be available to participants in clinical trials.

Different ethical issues arise if the issue is access to the benefits of taking part in research, rather than protection from its dangers. As Jecker et al explain, the need to ensure fair and equitable access to trials is particularly striking where there has been early and dramatic evidence of efficacy.

Nancy S Jecker et al[93]

We use the term 'breakthrough therapy' to refer to drugs used alone or in combination to treat a disease or condition in which there is preliminary clinical evidence, usually during phase I or II trials, that the drug may represent substantial improvement over existing treatments.

We submit that likelihood of benefit comprises a continuum, from the complete uncertainty (equipoise) associated with standard research, to an intermediate stage where evidence of benefit mounts and reaches a peak, to a final stage of clearly demonstrated benefit that is sufficient to gain approval for clinical applications. With breakthrough therapies, evidence of benefit emerges rapidly and in an especially striking way, because an experimental therapy shows dramatic benefit early on. Somewhere along this continuum, ethical issues of fair allocation emerge, becoming more apparent and weighty as evidence of benefit accumulates.

(b)   EXCLUSION FROM RESEARCH

Several different groups within society have traditionally been under-represented among research participants. It used to be suggested that, because women's physiology is different, female participants might complicate a trial's results, and lead to less 'clean' data. Of course, women's monthly hormonal fluctuations are only a complicating factor if the male body is regarded as the norm.

There is also a central paradox in this justification for women's exclusion. If the female body reacts differently, and hence might distort a study's results, then dosages of a treatment that have only been tested on men are likely to be either ineffective or unsafe for female patients. Despite having been historically under-tested in women, most drugs are prescribed to both sexes, and it is therefore unsurprising that women are more likely than men to report adverse drug reactions.

A second reason for excluding women is the possibility that they might become pregnant, and thus expose their fetuses to the new drug's unknown teratogenic effects, and researchers

---

[93] 'From protection to entitlement: selecting research subjects for early phase clinical trials involving breakthrough therapies' (2017) 43 Journal of Medical Ethics 391–400.

to potential liability for prenatal injury. Of course, there might be good reasons for not re-cruiting pregnant women, or women who are trying to conceive, onto 'first in man' toxicity trials, but a blanket ban on all women's participation is unwarranted. Not all women of repro-ductive age are heterosexually active and fertile, and a less paternalistic approach would be to ask women whether there is a chance that they might become pregnant during the trial.

In addition, while the exclusion of pregnant women might seem sensible, if drugs are never tested on pregnant women it will be impossible to know whether they can be taken safely during pregnancy. This is why so many medicinal products contain a warning that they should not be used by pregnant women. Most of these warnings are not designed to protect women and fetuses from drugs that are known to be harmful; rather, they simply indicate that the product has not been proved to be safe, because no studies have been carried out.

For many women, abstaining from taking medicines during pregnancy is relatively un-problematic, but this is not true for everyone. A woman who suffers from severe depression, and who might be likely to harm herself if she stops taking her medication, is faced with an invidious dilemma. She must either take a medicine that has not been proved safe during pregnancy, or risk the potentially serious consequences of stopping her medication.

In the next extract, Carleigh Krubiner and Ruth Faden criticize the routine exclusion of pregnant women from clinical trials.

Carleigh B Krubiner and Ruth R Faden[94]

There is nothing about the state of pregnancy that renders pregnant women incapable of offering valid research consents or refusals. Moreover, rather than protecting the health inter-ests of pregnant women and their offspring, this designation has had the opposite effect. It has contributed to the widespread exclusion of pregnant women from research activities, which is itself pernicious to the health of pregnant women.

We know that pregnant women encounter a range of health needs across their pregnan-cies … Yet because pregnant women have largely been excluded from the clinical research enterprise, in part due to being considered a 'vulnerable population' in need of protection from research, we often lack the necessary evidence to inform what medications can be safely and effectively used in pregnancy and at what dose …

To make matters worse, the lack of previous inclusion of pregnant women in research fur-ther stifles new research studies from including them. This is because without much existing data to draw upon, it is difficult to assess potential risks to pregnant women or their offspring in clinical trials of new medical interventions. In our work exploring barriers to appropriately including pregnant women in HIV research, one clinical investigator identified this as a 'Catch-22 dilemma: limited safety data on HIV-related drugs in pregnancy sparks concerns about unknown potential maternal-fetal exposure risks; this leads to reluctance to study pregnant women, in turn perpetuating the lack of safety data that could inform next steps for research.'

Other groups have also tended to be under-represented in research, with obvious implica-tions for their access to safe and effective medical treatment. Elderly people, for example, have been excluded in part as a result of concerns that long-term follow-up might be impeded by the subjects' deaths, and in part because they might suffer from comorbidities that could

---

[94] 'Pregnant women should not be categorised as a 'vulnerable population' in biomedical research studies: ending a vicious cycle of "vulnerability"' (2017) 43 Journal of Medical Ethics 664–5.

distort the trial's results. But not only is research on older people essential in order to improve the quality of care available to the elderly, it is also a mistake to assume that all old people are infirm and close to death. On the contrary, many elderly people are healthier and more independent than younger adults.

As Catherine Spong and Diana Bianchi point out, excluding certain populations from research means that the promise of 'personalised medicine', considered in Chapter 9, might be better described as 'exclusive medicine'.

Catherine Y Spong and Diana W Bianchi[95]

Advances in genomics have ushered in promising therapies tailored to the individual . . . Despite these advances, for many sectors of the population—children, older adults, pregnant and lactating women, and individuals with physical and intellectual disabilities—limited evidence-based therapies optimized to their specific medical needs exist . . .

Although personalized medicine offers the opportunity to tailor therapies to the individual, given the large gaps in data for certain populations, in actuality it is 'exclusive medicine'. Now, more than ever, it is imperative not to lose sight of the critical need to obtain evidence for medical therapies for major underrepresented populations.

Excluding whole categories of people from clinical trials is increasingly regarded as illegitimate. And according to the UK's Governance Arrangements for Research Ethics Committees, researchers must now justify any recruitment restrictions in their protocols.

Health Research Scotland, Health and Care Research Wales and Health Research Authority[96]

3.2.3 The benefits and risks of taking part in research, and the benefits of research evidence for improved health and social care, should be distributed fairly among all social groups and classes. Selection criteria in research protocols should not unjustifiably exclude potential participants, for instance on the basis of economic status, culture, age, disability, gender reassignment, marriage and civil partnership, pregnancy and maternity, race, religion or belief, sex or sexual orientation. RECs should take these considerations into account in reviewing the ethics of research proposals, particularly those involving under-researched groups.

(c) A DUTY TO PARTICIPATE?

A further issue missed by the emphasis upon protecting research subjects from harm is the question of whether users of health care services should be under a duty to share the burdens of research participation. It is undoubtedly true that these burdens are not distributed evenly across society. Most experiments are carried out on people who are ill. Among

---

[95] 'Improving Public Health Requires Inclusion of Underrepresented Populations in Research' (2018) 319 JAMA 337–8.
[96] Governance Arrangements for Research Ethics Committees (DHSC, 2018).

healthy volunteers, certain groups—in particular students and the unemployed—are over-represented, while wealthy individuals in full-time employment seldom participate.

Uneven recruitment of research subjects gives rise to two problems. First, if medicines are not tested on certain groups, we cannot be sure that they will be safe or effective when prescribed to members of those groups. Secondly, it could be argued that the risks associated with participation in research should be distributed fairly across society, and that it is unjust for some sections of society to bear a disproportionate burden. Should all NHS users therefore be under a duty to participate in research? We could, for example, view serving as a research subject as one of the obligations we assume under the 'social contract', in which we accept some restrictions upon our freedom in return for the benefits of living in a safe and cohesive community.

In the UK, there is no legal duty to participate in research, but it could be argued that anyone who expects to have access to NHS services is under a moral duty to agree to take part in research, if asked. Indeed, under the NHS Constitution for England, the NHS pledges 'to inform you of research studies in which you may be eligible to participate'.[97] Arthur Caplan would go further, arguing that, in certain circumstances, it might be appropriate to refuse to treat 'free-riders'.

Arthur L Caplan[98]

Modern medicine is a vast social enterprise in which certain benefits are produced at the cost of various burdens, which include the need to conduct medical research. If individuals consciously, knowingly, and continuously accept the benefits of medical care by seeking out physicians and hospital personnel when they are ill, then they would seem to meet the conditions for being bound by the principle of fair play. If the only way the knowledge and skills utilized in modern medicine can be generated is through research involving human subjects, then those who accept the fruits of such research would appear to be under a duty to bear the burdens of research when called upon by the group to do so . . .

Medical institutions which clearly and forthrightly identify themselves to patients as research institutions would be within their rights to exclude persons who refuse to participate in any form of research.

John Harris also believes that we have an obligation to participate in research, because we all benefit from living in a society in which medical research takes place.

John Harris[99]

We all benefit from the existence of the social practice of medical research. Many of us would not be here if infant mortality had not been brought under control, or antibiotics had not been invented. Most of us will continue to benefit from these and other medical advances . . . Since we accept these benefits, we have an obligation in justice to contribute to the social practice which produces them . . .

---

[97] The NHS Constitution for England (DHSC, 2015).
[98] 'Is There an Obligation to Participate in Biomedical Research?' in Stuart F Spicker et al (eds), *The Use of Human Beings in Research* (Kluwer: Dordrecht, 1988) 229–48.
[99] 'Scientific research is a moral duty' (2005) 31 Journal of Medical Ethics 242–8.

We all also benefit from the knowledge that research is ongoing into diseases or conditions from which we do not currently suffer but to which we may succumb. It makes us feel more secure and gives us hope for the future, for ourselves and our descendants, and for others for whom we care. If this is right, then I have a strong general interest that there be research, and in all well founded research; not excluding but not exclusively, research on me and on my condition or on conditions which are likely to affect me and mine. All such research is also of clear benefit to me. A narrow interpretation of the requirement that research be of benefit to the subject of the research is therefore perverse ...

If it is right to claim that there is a general obligation to act in the public interest, then there is less reason to challenge consent and little reason to regard participation as actually or potentially exploitative. We do not usually say: 'are you quite sure you want to' when people fulfil their moral and civic obligations.

Indeed, Baris Ozdemir et al found that patient mortality rates are lower in research-active hospitals. It is therefore also in a patient's individual best interests to be treated by research-active healthcare professionals.

Baris A Ozdemir et al[100]

Furthermore it has been suggested that patients in research-active hospitals may have better outcomes than patients in poorly research-active hospitals because greater research participation leads to accumulated knowledge, develops infrastructure and, brings in resources that can be used to improve clinical care ... The suggestion was that hospitals within research networks implement research findings more easily and more quickly, and that clinicians were more likely to adopt evidence-based practice and, follow up-to-date clinical guidelines.

(d) THE IMPACT OF SOCIAL MEDIA

The internet has the potential to make it much easier to reach potential research participants, and for research participants to make contact with each other. This can facilitate 'participant led research' (PLR), described in the next extract by Effy Vayena et al.

Effy Vayena et al[101]

Perhaps the most well known case [of PLR] is the amyotrophic lateral sclerosis (ALS) lithium study carried out on the online platform PatientsLikeMe. It was initiated by two patients with advanced-stage ALS from Brazil and the USA, both of whom died prior to the completion of the study. One hundred and forty-nine patients with ALS on the platform took lithium in

---

[100] 'Research Activity and the Association with Mortality' (2015) 10 PLoS ONE e0118253.
[101] 'Research led by participants: a new social contract for a new kind of research' (2016) 42 Journal of Medical Ethics 216–19.

order to test the findings of a small earlier study into its effects on disease progression and symptom alleviation. The PatientsLikeMe ALS study, which was completed over 8 months, was eventually published in *Nature Biotechnology*. Its finding that lithium had no effect was subsequently confirmed by standard clinical trials.

Among the various ways in which PLR tends to contrast with standard research are the following: PLR is usually pursued outside of institutional frameworks and without official endorsement or support; it is often a less formally structured peer-to-peer activity, but not one in which power relations among participants are absent; participants often have a direct health interest in the outcome of research; the research conducted may address issues outside of the scientific mainstream, or may challenge mainstream approaches; the research is often not motivated by commercial profit or career advancement; it is more likely to involve forms of self-experimentation; it may be conducted in a more 'open' or 'transparent' manner, especially when enabled by online media.

Less positively, research participants' use of social media can also result in the 'unblinding' of RCTs and the spread of misinformation.

Luke Gelinas et al[102]

First, participants who post detailed online descriptions of their experience may jeopardize the scientific integrity of the trial by including information that threatens to unblind themselves, other participants, or the research team. This may occur, for example, when different participants describe in detail the interventions they are receiving or how they feel or react to investigational agents, and speculate online about what arm of the trial they are in. Second, participants posting explicitly incorrect information about the trial can undermine the understanding of other participants (and potential participants). Similarly, participants portraying their experiences in an unduly negative light may harm study recruitment and retention and thereby introduce selection bias into the trial. Finally, participants reporting their experiences with certain drugs or devices may unjustifiably influence the public perception and worth of these products.

8 CONFLICTS OF INTEREST AND RESEARCH MISCONDUCT

The legacy of the research abuses of the twentieth century was a system of ethical review which emphasizes the importance of voluntary and informed consent. More recently, it has been acknowledged that unethical research practices are not confined to putting pressure on people to consent, or failing to tell them that they are taking part in research. There is, for example, increasing interest in unethical practices that happen during and after the research has taken place, such as the failure to publish results.

---

[102] 'Using Social Media as a Research Recruitment Tool: Ethical Issues and Recommendations' (2017) 17 American Journal of Bioethics 3–14

(a) SELECTIVE PUBLICATION

If information gathered during a trial is not disseminated, participants will have been exposed to the trial's risks without any benefit to society. A failure to publish a trial's results also undermines the subjects' informed consent: if the participants had known that the trial would serve no useful purpose, they are less likely to have agreed to take part.

It is important that both negative and positive results are published. While positive results (which prove that a new treatment works) may be more interesting and newsworthy than negative results (which show that the treatment is ineffective or harmful), unless negative results are also published, there is a danger that other researchers may conduct identical and futile trials, thus exposing more research participants to wholly avoidable risks. Researchers should therefore be under a duty to ensure that a trial's results are properly disseminated, regardless of whether they are positive or negative. The Helsinki Declaration is clear that 'negative and inconclusive as well as positive results should be published or otherwise made publicly available'.[103]

In addition to the dangers of under-reporting of negative results, if positive results are published multiple times,[104] the published data will not be representative of the total body of evidence. On the contrary, it will overemphasize positive results (which are thereby double-counted) and underemphasize negative results (which may not be counted at all). Meta-analyses which consolidate all publicly available data will then magnify and exaggerate this publication bias.[105]

If both prescribing and funding decisions are made on the basis of distorted meta-analyses, the over-publication of positive results and the under-publication of negative data may have negative consequences for patient care, and result in the wasteful use of healthcare resources.

As Richard Smith, former editor of the British Medical Journal explains, it is difficult for the editors of medical journals to know whether articles submitted to them duplicate data that is already in the public domain.

Richard Smith[106]

A large trial published in a major journal has the journal's stamp of approval ... will be distributed around the world, and may well receive global media coverage, particularly if promoted simultaneously by press releases from both the journal and the expensive public-relations firm hired by the pharmaceutical company that sponsored the trial ... Fortunately from the point of view of the companies funding these trials—but unfortunately for the credibility of the journals who publish them—these trials rarely produce results that are unfavourable to the companies' product ...

Journal editors are becoming increasingly aware of how they are being manipulated ... Editors work by considering the studies submitted to them. They ask the authors to send them any related studies, but editors have no other mechanism to know what other unpublished studies exist. It's hard even to know about related studies that are published, and it

---

[103] Para 36.

[104] Martin R Tramèr et al, 'Impact of covert duplicate publication on meta-analysis: a case study' (1997) 315 British Medical Journal 635.

[105] Hans Melander et al, 'Evidence b(i)ased medicine—selective reporting from studies sponsored by pharmaceutical industry: review of studies in new drug applications' (2003) 326 British Medical Journal 1171–3.

[106] 'Medical journals are an extension of the marketing arm of pharmaceutical companies' (2005) 2 PLoS Medicine 138.

may be impossible to tell that studies are describing results from some of the same patients. Editors may thus be peer reviewing one piece of a gigantic and clever marketing jigsaw—and the piece they have is likely to be of high technical quality. It will probably pass peer review, a process that research has anyway shown to be an ineffective lottery prone to bias and abuse.

There have been several attempts to solve this problem. One of the first was mandatory pre-trial registration of all clinical trials, so that unfortunate results cannot be buried. The Helsinki Declaration now states that 'Every research study involving human subjects must be registered in a publicly accessible database before recruitment of the first subject'.[107] And the International Committee of Medical Journal Editors (ICMJE) has published *Recommendations for the Conduct, Reporting, Editing, and Publication of Scholarly Work in Medical Journals* which unequivocally requires pre-trial registration as a condition of publication.

The International Committee of Medical Journal Editors[108]

[T]he ICMJE requires, and recommends that all medical journal editors require, registration of clinical trials in a public trials registry at or before the time of first patient enrollment as a condition of consideration for publication ...

The purpose of clinical trial registration is to prevent selective publication and selective reporting of research outcomes, to prevent unnecessary duplication of research effort, to help patients and the public know what trials are planned or ongoing into which they might want to enroll, and to help give ethics review boards considering approval of new studies a view of similar work and data relevant to the research they are considering. Retrospective registration, for example at the time of manuscript submission, meets none of these purposes.

Pre-trial registration is now the norm. Within the EU, the European Clinical Trials Database (EudraCT) is a searchable, publicly available registry of all clinical trials taking place in the EU.[109] At the time of writing, it contains detailed information about 33,523 trials.

Pre-trial registration may not be sufficient, however, if other information—most importantly the trial's outcomes—are not also reported. Ross et al analysed a random sample of trials that had been registered on the US trials registry, ClinicalTrials.gov, and found that only 40 per cent of industry-sponsored registered trials had published their results and, of those, only one-third had the citation recorded on ClinicalTrials.gov.[110]

It has therefore been recognized that mandatory reporting needs to go beyond the initial registration of a trial, and extend to the mandatory reporting of results in trial registries. Within the EU, a requirement to publish trial results was introduced in 2012.[111] Results should be posted in EudraCT within a year of the end of the trial (or six months in the case of

---

[107] Para 35.

[108] International Committee of Medical Journal Editors, *Recommendations for the Conduct, Reporting, Editing, and Publication of Scholarly Work in Medical Journals* (2017).

[109] www.clinicaltrialsregister.eu/.

[110] Joseph S Ross et al, 'Trial publication after registration in ClinicalTrials. Gov: a cross-sectional analysis' (2009) 6 PLoS medicine e1000144.

[111] European Commission, Guidance on posting and publication of result-related information on clinical trials in relation to the implementation of Article 57(2) of Regulation (EC) No 726/2004 and Article 41 of Regulation (EC) No 1901/2006, Official Journal of the European Union 2012/C 302/03.

paediatric trials). Result-related data should be posted earlier if it becomes available, for example if the results are published in a scientific journal. Since 2015, the European Medicines Agency has also published proactively the clinical reports submitted with applications for marketing authorizations (see Chapter 11).

Section 110 of the Care Act 2014 gives the Health Research Authority a statutory duty to promote transparency in research.

Care Act 2014 section 110

... (2) The main objective of the HRA in exercising its functions is—

    (a) to protect participants and potential participants in health or social care research and the general public by encouraging research that is safe and ethical, and

    (b) to promote the interests of those participants and potential participants and the general public by facilitating the conduct of research that is safe and ethical (including by promoting transparency in research) ...

(7) Promoting transparency in research includes promoting—

    (a) the registration of research;

    (b) the publication and dissemination of research findings and conclusions;

    (c) the provision of access to data on which research findings or conclusions are based;

    (d) the provision of information at the end of research to participants in the research.

In 2018, as well as recommending that the UK implements the Clinical Trial Regulations' transparency requirements (which require Member States to set out penalties for non-compliance with the duty to publish results within a year), the House of Commons Science and Technology Committee was critical of the HRA's track record on promoting transparency.

House of Commons Science and Technology Committee[112]

14. A range of UK and EU rules and guidelines are in force to improve clinical trials transparency, in terms of tackling non-registration, non-reporting and mis-reporting. Despite these rules, around half of clinical trials are left unreported, clinical trial registration is not yet universal in the UK and reported outcomes do not always align with the original study proposal. Further action is needed to improve reporting and registration of clinical trials ...

15. The Government should explicitly commit to introducing the clinical trials transparency requirements in the EU Clinical Trials Regulation that are expected to be applied in the EU shortly after Brexit ...

45. The Health Research Authority has been explicitly responsible for 'promoting research transparency' as part of its statutory objectives since 2014, but this does not appear to have brought about significant change in this area over the last four years. We recommend that the Government ask the HRA to publish, by December 2019, a detailed strategy for achieving full clinical trials transparency, with a clear deadline and milestones for achieving

---

[112] *Research integrity: clinical trials transparency*, Tenth Report of Session 2017–19.

> this. We also recommend that the Government write to the HRA to clarify that it should interpret the Care Act 2014 to mean that it is responsible for driving improvements in clinical trials transparency—as opposed to 'promoting' transparency as a virtue ... If further financial resource for the HRA is required to tackle clinical trials transparency then the Government should consider favourably such requests.
>
> 46. We recommend that the Government consult further with the HRA on whether it is capable of delivering the improvements to clinical trials transparency needed within its current remit. If necessary its remit should be extended through introducing legislation which amends the provisions of the Care Act 2014.

(b) OUTSOURCING

In relation to clinical trials, it is increasingly common for drug companies to pay commercial organizations to design trials, recruit subjects, and disseminate results.

(1) Contract Research Organizations (CROs)

Outsourcing the running of trials to CROs is now the norm.[113] CROs recruit healthy volunteers themselves, and they pay doctors to find willing patients for phase II and III trials. While outsourcing to CROs is efficient, these organizations are employed by drugs manufacturers in order to speed up approval times, rather than to investigate how best to treat a particular condition. Satisfying their commercial clients means ensuring that drugs are approved as quickly as possible. CROs therefore have a clear financial interest in the outcomes of trials.

David Hunter draws attention to CROs' 'pre-recruitment' of potential volunteers, who only later are allocated to a particular research project. Because pre-recruitment is not constrained by the strict rules which govern direct recruitment to a particular trial, CROs are able to make extravagant claims about how much money volunteers can make, and how much good they can do.

David Hunter[114]

> These adverts appear to violate the three well-established general requirements of the recruitment of research participants ... They emphasise in emotive language the likely benefits for others of participating, they focus on the financial recompense and portray the research as likely to succeed ... Since the advert was for *general* recruitment rather than to a specific trial, there is no formal regulation of this activity. You do not currently need research ethics committee approval to approach people to pre-recruit them, nor is there any formal guidance for this sort of recruitment either from the Health Research Authority (HRA) or from the ABPI ...
>
> The present disparity in practices of the pre-recruitment and recruitment of research participants seems problematic—to put it starkly, if you are recruited onto a list of potential

---

[113] Carl Elliott, 'The mild torture economy' (2010) 32 London Review of Books 26–7.
[114] 'We could be heroes: ethical issues with the pre-recruitment of research participants' (2015) 41 Journal of Medical Ethics 557–8.

participants on the promise of riches and heroism via clinical trials and are then recruited from that list into a specific trial in a much more neutral fashion, your beliefs about the actual trial will be informed by what you were told during pre-recruitment—in other words, you will think you are being heroic and earning lots of money, precisely the views that the current regulations are trying to prevent participants from having. As such, unregulated pre-recruitment runs the risk of making a mockery of the careful standards which have evolved to try and protect people from exploitation and harm in clinical trials.

The Health Research Authority (HRA) recognized this problem in 2013, when it set up the Phase 1 Generic Advert Review Group. Admitting that it is not a requirement that pre-recruitment materials have REC approval, the HRA has nevertheless said that its 'expectation [is] that ethical advice regarding any proposed generic advertising is sought from the HRA, prior to its being used, as a matter of best practice'. The Phase 1 Generic Advert Review Group is made up of three experienced members of Research Ethics Committees that review Phase 1 studies, and it has so far considered posters, website adverts, scripts for radio broadcasts, and television adverts.

(2) Medical Writing Agencies

A second type of outsourcing involves the writing up of results, both for publication and for submission to regulators. There are now several companies that write medical manuscripts, liaise with the formally identified 'authors', and submit articles to prestigious medical journals.

In 2009, the *New York Times* published 'A case study in medical writing', using documents released in a personal injury action against Wyeth.[115] Wyeth had paid DesignWrite $25,000 to draft an article about the treatment of vasomotor symptoms (hot flushes and sweating) in menopausal and pre-menopausal women. According to the documentation, the author was 'to be determined' later. An outline was sent to an eminent professor who agreed to be its author. After being sent a first draft, this time with her name attached, she made one correction. The article was then published in her name in the Journal of Reproductive Medicine.

Ghost authorship of articles is a significant ethical issue. Students who put their name to papers they have not written are guilty of plagiarism, for which the penalties are serious. Carl Elliott has suggested that similar penalties should apply to academics who agree to be ghost authors: 'Department heads could treat faculty who sign onto paid editorials the same way they treat students who sign their names to papers they buy on the Internet'.[116] Ghost authorship is also not uncommon: David Resnik reports the results of one study which found that '7.9% of articles published in medical journals have ghost authors', and another that found that '75% of papers reporting the results of industry-initiated clinical trials had ghost authors'.[117]

In 2012, the *British Medical Journal* and the Committee on Publication Ethics issued *A Consensus Statement on Research Misconduct in the UK* which specified that ghost-writing, and other practices, amount to research misconduct.

---

[115] See further Natasha Singer, 'Medical papers by ghostwriters pushed therapy', *New York Times*, 4 August 2009.

[116] Carl Elliott, 'The mild torture economy' (2010) 32 London Review of Books 26–7.

[117] 'Authorship policies of scientific journals' (2016) 42 Journal of Medical Ethics 199–202.

British Medical Journal and the Committee on Publication Ethics[118]

Research misconduct is defined as behaviour by a researcher, intentional or not, that falls short of good ethical and scientific standards. Research misconduct includes fabrication, falsification, suppression, or inappropriate manipulation of data; inappropriate image manipulation; plagiarism; misleading reporting; redundant publication; authorship malpractice such as guest or ghost authorship; failure to disclose funding sources or competing interests; misreporting of funder involvement; and unethical research (for example, failure to obtain adequate patient consent). Research misconduct is important as it wastes resources, damages the credibility of science, and can cause harm (for example, to patients and the public).

9 RESEARCH IN LOW AND MIDDLE-INCOME COUNTRIES

People living in low and middle-income countries need access to affordable medical treatments. Clinical trials of low-cost medicines are desperately needed but, at the same time, the populations of low and middle-income countries should not be exposed to unacceptable risks. In the next extract, Benjamin Mason Meier explains how governments are sometimes complicit in ensuring that researchers face comparatively few obstacles when planning clinical trials in low-income countries.

Benjamin Mason Meier[119]

National regulation of human experimentation differs dramatically between developed and developing, particularly African, nations. Many African nations lack any legislative protections for subjects of medical research. To a large degree, this legislative vacuum is intentional. While governments of these nations are desperate to bring medical research to their dying populations, their nations cannot afford such research without subsidies from multinational pharmaceutical corporations. To court these pharmaceutical corporations, African nations vie to minimize regulation on the conduct of medical research. They fear that legislation, and resulting lawsuits, could have a chilling effect on beneficial research efforts. As a result, African nations have shown great reluctance to impose any restrictions on human research, thereby creating a medical 'race to the bottom' at the expense of human rights and human life.

India has become a particularly attractive site for trials. Most Indian doctors speak English, and many have been trained in the UK or the US. India's system for robust ethical review has, however, been subject to criticism.[120] The principal task for regulation must therefore be to ensure that high-quality research capable of improving the lives of people in low and

---

[118] (2012) 344 British Medical Journal 1111.

[119] 'International Protection of Persons Undergoing Medical Experimentation: Protecting the Right of Informed Consent' (2001) 20 Berkeley Journal of International Law 513.

[120] Priya Satalkar and David Shaw, 'Not fit for purpose: the ethical guidelines of the Indian Council of Medical Research' (2015) 15 Developing World Bioethics 40–7.

middle-income countries is encouraged, while also ensuring that these countries do not become the pharmaceutical industry's 'sweat shop'.

What Danielle Wenner describes as the 'responsiveness requirement' is an attempt to address this concern.

Danielle M Wenner[121]

When critics complain about exploitation in clinical research, they are typically not claiming that trial agreements were not entered into voluntarily. Even when all parties consent to research, critics can claim that host communities are exploited. Moreover, the charge of exploitation need not imply that host communities aren't benefiting from research; often they are. Rather, the charge of exploitation is a complaint about the resulting distribution of the social surplus generated by the interaction: it is somehow unjust or unfair. Typically, the claim is that the exploited party receives a benefit that is disproportionately small compared with the benefit to the exploiting party or the needs of the exploited party. Insofar as proponents of a responsiveness requirement are seeking to reduce exploitation, then, the claim must be that responsiveness serves to ensure that research transactions result in greater benefits for host communities, or that some research transactions that don't provide sufficient benefits to host communities are thereby prevented.

The Helsinki Declaration is clear that research should be carried out in vulnerable populations only where it is responsive to their health needs.

Helsinki Declaration[122]

20. Medical research with a vulnerable group is only justified if the research is responsive to the health needs or priorities of this group and the research cannot be carried out in a non-vulnerable group. In addition, this group should stand to benefit from the knowledge, practices or interventions that result from the research.

As Bege Dauda and Kris Dierickx explain, it is now widely accepted that sponsors of trials in low and middle-income countries should make some provision for 'benefit sharing'.

Bege Dauda and Kris Dierickx[123]

There is a consensus within the ethics community that individuals and communities that participate in a research study ought to have some benefits from it, especially when the study is on commercial products that generate profits for the sponsors and is conducted in resource-limited countries where there are many healthcare challenges . . .

---

[121] 'The Social Value of Knowledge and the Responsiveness Requirement for International Research' (2017) 31 Bioethics 97–104.

[122] (WMA, 2013).

[123] 'Viewing benefit sharing in global health research through the lens of Aristotelian justice' (2017) 43 Journal of Medical Ethics 417–21.

> [I]f benefits are not allocated, we would presuppose a case of exploitation and the sponsor would be regarded as having taken undue advantage of the participants and communities.

But what exactly does benefit sharing demand? It would be difficult to compel drug companies to assume responsibility for all of the future health needs of a low-income country, but providing post-trial access to the participants themselves is a different matter.

Helsinki Declaration[124]

> 34. In advance of a clinical trial, sponsors, researchers and host country governments should make provisions for post-trial access for all participants who still need an intervention identified as beneficial in the trial. This information must also be disclosed to participants during the informed consent process.

Notice that the Helsinki Declaration highlights the obligations of host country governments, as well as trial sponsors. In the context of a study of HIV trials, Bridget Haire and Christopher Jordens point out that governments of low and middle-income countries have a vital role to play in facilitating post-trial access.

Bridget Haire and Christopher Jordens[125]

> Securing the reasonable availability of a successful intervention post-trial is intended to ensure that research conducted in lower income countries is responsive to needs, and does not exploit vulnerable population to test interventions for the consumption of those in high income countries. A major problem with this requirement, however, is the determining who is responsible for this form of access. It is clearly beyond the control of principal investigators, and is a matter for governments and their regulatory bodies—though sponsors certainly have a responsibility to actually apply for regulatory approval ... Careful alignment of national HIV strategies with approval criteria for ethical review committees might be a mechanism for ensuring that the research that goes ahead tests interventions that the national government will be prepared, later down the line, to fund, should the intervention prove successful. Even with such safeguards, however, political expediency may hamper funding, promotion and uptake of proven interventions.

A range of other ethical issues arise in trials in low and middle-income countries. For example, incentives to participation in research may work differently in poorer countries. Not only might comparatively small sums of money be disproportionately attractive, but also simply taking part in a trial may involve access to medical care that is otherwise unavailable. Regular contact with a team of healthcare professionals may mean that an unrelated medical condition is diagnosed and treated more speedily than normal. The offer of any medical care at all can represent a considerable incentive to participation.

---

[124] (WMA, 2013).
[125] 'Mind the gap: an empirical study of post-trial access in HIV biomedical prevention trials' (2015) 15 Developing World Bioethics 85–97.

In addition, levels of trust in the medical profession may be especially high in some low and middle-income countries. In northern India, DeCosta et al found that one of the most important reasons for people's willingness to take part in research 'was an implicit faith in doctors and the medical system'.[126] This confidence in the medical profession led a significant minority (17.5 per cent) of their interviewees to report that they would not want any information before deciding whether to participate. One subject explained that 'doctors are in a way godly. Who would know better than them?'[127]

In some poorer countries, it may be usual practice for decisions—such as whether to participate in research—to be taken by the leader of the community, or a senior family member, rather than by the individual herself. Does respect for cultural difference demand that consent should be sought from this authority figure, or is the duty to obtain the individual subject's free and informed consent a universal moral requirement?

The CIOMS Guidelines recommend that seeking consent from someone other than the research subject may sometimes be advisable in order to show appropriate respect for a community's cultural traditions, but that it could never replace the additional need to obtain the subject's own consent.

Council for International Organizations of Medical Sciences[128]

Commentary on Guideline 9

In some circumstances, a researcher may enter a community or institution to conduct research or approach potential participants for their individual consent only after obtaining permission from an institution such as a school or a prison, or from a community leader, a council of elders, or another designated authority. Such institutional procedures or cultural customs should be respected.

In no case, however, may the permission of a community leader or other authority substitute for individual informed consent.

The Nuffield Council on Bioethics further recommends that where an individual does not wish to participate in research, despite the community leader's agreement, researchers have a duty to facilitate their non-participation.

Nuffield Council on Bioethics[129]

6.22 ... In some cultural contexts it may be appropriate to obtain agreement from the community or assent from a senior family member before a prospective participant is approached. If a prospective participant does not wish to take part in research this must be respected. Researchers must not enrol such individuals and have a duty to facilitate their non-participation.

---

[126] A DeCosta et al, 'Community based trials and informed consent in rural north India' (2004) 30 Journal of Medical Ethics 318–23.

[127] Ibid.

[128] CIOMS in collaboration with the World Health Organization (WHO) *International Ethical Guidelines for Biomedical Research Involving Human Subjects* (CIOMS, 2016).

[129] *The Ethics of Research Related to Healthcare in Developing Countries* (NCOB, 2002).

One of the most controversial questions raised by trials in low and middle-income countries is the use of placebo or no-intervention controls when their use would be impermissible in high-income countries. In 1997, Peter Lurie and Sidney Wolfe published an article in the New England Journal of Medicine in which they criticized 15 placebo-controlled clinical trials, involving 12,000 HIV-positive women in nine countries, which were designed to test whether low-cost treatments might be effective in reducing perinatal (mother-to-baby) transmission of the HIV virus.[130]

Standard treatment for HIV-positive pregnant women in high-income countries at that time was known as the 076 protocol, and it involved oral and intravenous doses of an antiretroviral drug (brand name AZT) to pregnant women throughout pregnancy, and during childbirth; abstaining from breastfeeding; and the provision of AZT to babies for six weeks after birth. On its own, the 076 protocol reduced transmission rates from 25 per cent to 8 per cent, and delivery by caesarean section could further reduce the risk to approximately 1 per cent.

The 076 protocol was unavailable in low-income countries, however. Not only was it prohibitively expensive, but it also required the provision of health services—such as early pregnancy testing and intravenous drug delivery during childbirth—that were often unavailable. In addition, in countries without reliable clean water supplies, abstaining from breastfeeding may represent a greater threat to infant health than HIV transmission.

The trials criticized by Lurie and Wolfe had involved a simpler and cheaper course of treatment. They were RCTs, in which one group of HIV-positive pregnant women received a short course of AZT during the last four weeks of pregnancy, and a control group received a placebo. Following positive preliminary results from a trial in Thailand, in which perinatal transmission rates were halved (19 per cent of babies in the control group were infected, compared with nine per cent of the babies whose mothers had received the short course of AZT), the research was halted. Controversy continues, however, over whether these trials should ever have taken place.

In short, the problem was that the control group was given a placebo despite the existence of effective treatment (the 076 protocol). It has been estimated that before the trials were stopped, over 1,000 babies in the control group became infected with the HIV virus. This would appear to conflict with two basic ethical principles. First, using a placebo control in these HIV trials deprived the patients in the control group of the 'best proven' treatment to prevent the perinatal transmission of the HIV virus. Secondly, could it really be said that a state of equipoise existed over which treatment was best for the patients? Because the 076 protocol had been proved to be effective, the uncertainty which justifies imposing risks on research subjects may have been absent.

Lurie and Wolfe accused researchers of a double standard in research, whereby subjects in rich countries receive a higher level of care than those from poorer nations. Not only is this unfair, it also offers an incentive for sponsors of trials to locate them in countries where subjects can legitimately be offered a lower standard of care.

Peter Lurie and Sidney M Wolfe[131]

What are the potential implications of accepting such a double standard? Researchers might inject live malaria parasites into HIV-positive subjects in China in order to study the effect on

---

[130] 'Unethical trials of interventions to reduce perinatal transmission of the human immunodeficiency virus in developing countries' (1997) 337 New England Journal of Medicine 853–6.
[131] Ibid.

the progression of HIV infection, even though the study protocol had been rejected in the United States and Mexico ...

Residents of impoverished, postcolonial countries, the majority of whom are people of color, must be protected from potential exploitation in research. Otherwise, the abominable state of health care in these countries can be used to justify studies that could never pass ethical muster in the sponsoring country ... It is time to develop standards of research that preclude the kinds of double standards evident in these trials ... Tragically, for the hundreds of infants who have needlessly contracted HIV infection in the perinatal-transmission studies that have already been completed, any such protection will have come too late.

In contrast, supporters of the trials argued that local solutions to the burden of disease should be sought, and that research capable of having practical application in poor countries should not be stopped in order to ease Western consciences. No woman in the control group was any worse off than she would have been if she had not enrolled in the trial, and using a placebo control meant that statistically significant results could be, and indeed were, obtained quickly.

In the debates over the ethical legitimacy of these trials, the prohibitive cost of treatment was often taken for granted. It is, however, important to remember that, while it may have cost a lot to develop, AZT is not expensive to manufacture. The 076 protocol was unaffordable in part because the TRIPS Agreement enabled one company to hold the global patent on AZT for 20 years, during which time no generic equivalent could be produced. Permitting poor countries to manufacture generic versions of expensive patented drugs within this 20-year period might offer a more ethically defensible solution to the problem of unaffordable medicines than permitting a double standard in research ethics.

The TRIPS Agreement has always allowed for the compulsory licensing of medicines in an emergency. In the 2001 Doha Declaration, the World Trade Organization reaffirmed that this could be used in response to public health crises, like the HIV/AIDS pandemic.

World Trade Organization[132]

4. We agree that the TRIPS Agreement does not and should not prevent members from taking measures to protect public health. Accordingly, while reiterating our commitment to the TRIPS Agreement, we affirm that the Agreement can and should be interpreted and implemented in a manner supportive of WTO members' right to protect public health and, in particular, to promote access to medicines for all.

In this connection, we reaffirm the right of WTO members to use, to the full, the provisions in the TRIPS Agreement, which provide flexibility for this purpose.

5. Accordingly and in the light of paragraph 4 above, while maintaining our commitments in the TRIPS Agreement, we recognize that these flexibilities include: ...

b. Each member has the right to grant compulsory licences and the freedom to determine the grounds upon which such licences are granted.

c. Each member has the right to determine what constitutes a national emergency or other circumstances of extreme urgency, it being understood that public health crises, including those relating to HIV/AIDS, tuberculosis, malaria and other epidemics, can represent a national emergency or other circumstances of extreme urgency.

---

[132] *Declaration on the TRIPS Agreement and public health* (WTO, 2001).

Consistent with TRIPS, public health concerns can therefore override intellectual property rights by allowing a country to compulsorily license generic drugs without the consent of the original manufacturer. This looks like a good solution to the problem of unaffordable medicines, so at first sight it might seem surprising that the Doha Declaration has not made much difference in practice.

The problem is that governments in low and middle-income countries are concerned about the impact compulsory licensing might have upon their country's reputation as a trading partner.[133] This problem is exacerbated by the negotiation of regional and bilateral free trade agreements (FTAs)—described as TRIPS-plus measures—between richer and poorer countries. Most commonly, these involve the US or the EU negotiating FTAs with low or middle-income countries, in which the poorer countries agree to waive some of their rights under TRIPS in return for import/export agreements.[134] TRIPS is, after all, a minimum standards agreement and countries which are concerned about finding markets for their goods are free to negotiate away the rights they would normally have under TRIPS.[135]

10 COMPENSATION FOR INJURIES

If a subject did not consent to participate in a research trial, an action in battery is possible (see further Chapter 4). In practice, because a person who takes part in a research project will invariably have signed a consent form, it will be difficult for her to establish that she was not informed 'in broad terms' about the nature of the trial.

If a subject suffers injury during a trial, she might be able to claim that the researcher, who undoubtedly owes her a duty of care, was in breach of that duty. This could happen in two ways. First, a person might be injured as a result of negligence in the design or execution of the trial. Secondly, the information provided to the subject, although sufficient to avoid a charge of battery, may have been inadequate, and amount to a breach of the researcher's duty of care. As we saw in Chapter 4, there can only be liability for a breach of the duty to provide sufficient information where the claimant has been injured as a result. The research subject would therefore have to establish that she would not have participated in the trial if she had been properly informed about the risk of an injury which has now materialized.

Where it is the design of the research project that caused the subject's injuries, could the members of the REC also be liable for failing to notice that the protocol itself was defective? It could be argued that it is foreseeable that negligent approval of a dangerous research project will cause injury, and that there is a relationship of proximity between members of the REC and research participants. But would it be fair, just, and reasonable to impose liability on the members of the REC? There have been no cases in which injured research subjects have sued REC members, and such actions are improbable, given the much deeper pockets of other potential defendants, such as the pharmaceutical company.

As we saw in Chapter 3, victims of medical mishaps face numerous obstacles when bringing actions in negligence, and, as Joanna Manning explains, the obstacles are even greater for individuals who have been injured during research.

---

[133] Vanessa Bradford Kerry and Kelley Lee, 'TRIPS, the Doha Declaration and paragraph 6 decision: what are the remaining steps for protecting access to medicines?' (2007) 3 Globalization and Health 1–12.

[134] Oxfam, *Trading Away Access to Medicines: How the European Union's Trade Agenda has Taken a Wrong Turn* (Oxfam: Brussels, 2009).

[135] Carlos Maria Correa, 'Implications of bilateral free trade agreements on access to medicines' (2006) 84 Bulletin of the World Health Organization 399–404.

Joanna M Manning[136]

The most serious obstacle lies in proving fault by researchers or sponsors. Some risks in research are unpredictable and unforeseen, even if the research is carried out carefully. Discovering what the risks are and their extent is often the very purpose of undertaking the research in the first place. When injury occurs, it is more often because an unforeseeable risk occurred, rather than any negligence or deviation from the research protocol by researcher or sponsor. Participants are therefore likely to experience major difficulty in proving that harm was reasonably foreseeable ...

Because all clinical research, even therapeutic research, requires participants to assume a position of risk for the benefit of society, the beneficiaries of research (researchers, sponsors and society) have a moral responsibility to compensate for research-related injury. Tort law is an unfair system of compensation for research-related injury, because, despite undertaking the risks of the research in the interests of others for no or uncertain individual benefit, injured participants are almost always left to bear the full financial burden of their injuries alone.

In 1978, the Pearson Commission advocated a 'no fault' compensation scheme for people injured during medical research, drawing an analogy with the statutory compensation offered to people injured by vaccination programmes. The community as a whole benefits from both vaccination and research, and should therefore be prepared to compensate the small proportion of the population who suffer injuries as a result. This proposal was never implemented. While not having to prove fault might make it easier to obtain compensation, it should be remembered that the subject would still have to establish causation, which can be a significant obstacle, particularly where the subject was ill when she took part in the trial.

Principle 15 of the Helsinki Declaration provides that: 'Appropriate compensation and treatment for subjects who are harmed as a result of participating in research must be ensured', and the Clinical Trials Regulation requires Member States to have compensation mechanisms in place.

Clinical Trials Regulation 2014

Article 76

1. Member States shall ensure that systems for compensation for any damage suffered by a subject resulting from participation in a clinical trial conducted on their territory are in place in the form of insurance, a guarantee, or a similar arrangement that is equivalent as regards its purpose and which is appropriate to the nature and the extent of the risk.

It might be thought that the adverse publicity which would result from litigation against a pharmaceutical company for injuries to a research subject would represent a powerful incentive towards the making of *ex gratia* payments. Certainly, the Association of the British Pharmaceutical Industry's guidelines recommend that compensation should be paid, even if the victim cannot establish negligence.

---

[136] 'Does the Law on Compensation for Research-Related Injury in the UK, Australia, and New Zealand Meet Ethical Requirements?' (2017) 25 Medical Law Review 397–427.

The assumption that the pharmaceutical industry would move quickly to compensate anyone injured in a drugs trial, in order to avoid negative press coverage, was undermined in the UK in the immediate aftermath of the TGN1412 trial at Northwick Park Hospital. Although the case has now been settled, initially the injured men were offered an interim payment of just £5,000 in return for an agreement not to sue, and it was revealed that TGN1412's manufacturer, TeGenero, which was subsequently declared insolvent, only had insurance coverage of £2 million.

Joanna Manning suggests that information sheets should be clearer about the lack of a legally binding right to compensation in the event of injury, and that the government should consider setting up a fund to cover the costs of compensation.

Joanna M Manning[137]

As a first step, ethics committees must demand that sponsors and researchers spell out unequivocally the lack of legally enforceable no-fault compensation in information sheets and take reasonable steps to ensure that subjects understand its implications, so that they give a properly informed consent . . .

If reliance on non-legislative guidelines is to continue, these need to be re-drafted, so as to be made legally enforceable, fairer and more balanced, a role for which key ethics bodies are ideally suited. Governments need to make it clear to industry that legally enforceable, no-fault compensation is the price of continued self-regulation. But, it is suggested that the most ethically defensible and efficient reform option for compensating for research-related injury is to establish an aggregate no-fault compensation fund. The ethical corollary of the fact that society is the ultimate beneficiary of its members' participation in clinical research, is that the fund be financed and administered by the state.

11 CONCLUSION

Throughout this chapter, we have seen that there is generally assumed to be a sharp distinction between research and ordinary medical treatment. In particular, in relation to research, there has long been a duty to obtain 'informed consent', whereas, as we saw in Chapter 4, the judiciary was slower to introduce the 'doctrine of informed consent' for routine medical treatment. People who volunteer to take part in research are regarded as more vulnerable, and in greater need of clear and frank information than patients. But is this special concern for research subjects justified?

On the one hand, the long history of the abuse of research subjects should undoubtedly alert us to the need to have protective mechanisms in place to ensure that vulnerable individuals do not end up taking part in research without knowing that this is what they are doing, or without being given the option of refusal. Yet, on the other hand, it is worth remembering that the decision to consent to treatment will also sometimes be difficult, requiring an individual to balance uncertain risks and benefits. Rather than viewing research subjects as uniquely vulnerable and in need of sensitively provided information, perhaps we should acknowledge

---

[137] 'Does the Law on Compensation for Research-Related Injury in the UK, Australia, and New Zealand Meet Ethical Requirements?' (2017) 25 Medical Law Review 397–427.

that patients too are often faced with complex decisions, and with information which may be difficult for them to understand and evaluate.

A final interesting distinction between patients and research subjects is the insistence, in the Helsinki Declaration, that any control group should be assured of the 'best proven treatment'. Again, this draws a distinction between participants in research and patients. Within the NHS at least, patients are clearly not assured of the best proven treatment. Rather, it is generally accepted that limited resources mean that sometimes less than optimal treatment may have to be provided in order to ensure that the NHS can continue to run a comprehensive health service. As we saw in Chapter 2, the reality of rationed health care is that patients are deprived of beneficial treatment. If it is absolutely clear that patients do not have the right to demand the 'best proven treatment', is it anomalous that participating in research, in theory at least, gives subjects precisely this right?

FURTHER READING

Brim, Remy L and Miller, Franklin G, 'The potential benefit of the placebo effect in sham-controlled trials: implications for risk–benefit assessments and informed consent' (2013) 39 Journal of Medical Ethics 703–7.

Dresser, Rebecca, 'Subversive subjects: rule-breaking and deception in clinical trials' (2013) 41 Journal of Law, Medicine and Ethics 829–40.

Elliott, Carl, 'The mild torture economy' (2010) 32 London Review of Books 26–7.

Eyal, Nir, 'The benefit/risk ratio challenge in clinical research, and the case of HIV cure: an introduction' (2017) 43 Journal of Medical Ethics 65–6.

Gelinas, Luke et al, 'Using Social Media as a Research Recruitment Tool: Ethical Issues and Recommendations' (2017) 17 American Journal of Bioethics 3–14

London, Alex John, 'Learning health systems, clinical equipoise and the ethics of response adaptive randomisation' (2018) 44 Journal of Medical Ethics 409–15.

Miller, Franklin G and Wertheimer, Alan, 'The fair transaction model of informed consent: an alternative to autonomous authorization' (2011) 21 Kennedy Institute of Ethics Journal 201–18.

Smith, Richard, 'Medical journals are an extension of the marketing arm of pharmaceutical companies' (2005) 2 PLoS Medicine 138.

Wenner, Danielle M, 'The Social Value of Knowledge and the Responsiveness Requirement for International Research' (2017) 31 Bioethics 97–104.

11

THE REGULATION OF MEDICINES

CENTRAL ISSUES

1. Before any new medicine can be put into circulation, it must have a marketing authorization.

2. Safety and efficacy must be established before a medicine can be licensed for use, but it is also important that safety continues to be monitored after a drug is put into circulation.

3. There has been European harmonization of the rules covering the licensing

and marketing of medicines, in order to protect consumers and facilitate free trade. It seems likely that the UK will continue to mirror European medicines regulations after Brexit.

4. The Consumer Protection Act 1987 implemented a European Directive and introduced strict liability for injuries caused by defective products. There have been hardly any cases involving medicines.

---

1 INTRODUCTION

In this chapter, we consider the regulation of medicines. Although the availability of safe and effective pharmaceutical drugs is not the only reason why average life expectancy nearly doubled over the course of the twentieth century—better sanitation and nutrition were at least as important—there is no doubt that the availability of effective medicines has significantly improved public health.[1] It is now comparatively rare for people living in the world's richest countries to die from infectious diseases, and it is the degenerative diseases of old age, such as cancer and heart disease, which have become the most common causes of death.

In high-income countries, huge profits can be made from successful drugs. Blockbuster drugs are defined as medicines that generate over $1 billion per year. In the year before Pfizer's statin Lipitor came out of patent protection, it made $10.7 billion. For obvious reasons, an effective treatment for depression or obesity is likely to generate much higher profits than a cure for a 'neglected disease', like malaria or sleeping sickness. A British Medical Journal editorial spelled out the problem.

---

[1] Jasper Woodcock, 'Medicines—The Interested Parties' in R Blum et al (eds), *Pharmaceuticals and Health Policy: International Perspectives on Provision and Control of Medicines* (Croom Helm: London, 1981) 27–35.

British Medical Journal[2]

When it comes to the world's most neglected diseases ... these present absolutely no market opportunities. Without such opportunities, there is no incentive for the pharmaceutical industry to invest in drug research and development. The patients have no purchasing power, no vocal advocacy group is pleading for their needs, and no strategic interests—military or security—are driving concern about these conditions.

For example, sleeping sickness, which claims thousands of lives annually in Africa, can be considered as a most neglected disease. Current drug treatments are in scarce supply, difficult to administer, and often toxic. Melarsoprol, which was developed over 50 years ago, kills up to 10% of people who are given the drug, and in some regions drug resistance means it is ineffective in a third of patients. An effective, less toxic drug, has been developed—eflornithine—but the company that developed it stopped its production in 1995, citing commercial failure. African patients could not afford to buy the drug. Eflornithine became available again five years later in the United States, when it was found to reduce unwanted facial hair in women.

The drive to provide a pharmacological solution to an ever-increasing range of conditions is referred to as 'medicalization'. The menopause can be treated with hormone replacement therapy; medication exists for behavioural difficulties in children; and drugs can be used to combat some of the normal consequences of ageing.

The research and development of new drugs involves enormous financial investment. On average it takes between 10 and 12 years to develop a new medicine.[3] Of every 10,000 compounds that are synthesized and tested, only one or two will reach the market,[4] and 90 per cent of compounds which get as far as the preclinical development stage will fail before launch.[5] The money invested in these failures inevitably increases the price of successful drugs.

In order to recoup their investment, pharmaceutical companies can hold the patent on a new drug for 20 years, during which time they have the right to prevent others from making or selling an identical product.[6] Some of this patent term will expire while the drug is being tested, and so in reality there may be less than ten years of 'on the market' patent protection. Once the patent expires, other companies can produce generic and much cheaper versions of the same drug. For example, in 2000, treatment for HIV/AIDS in low-income countries was prohibitively expensive, costing an average of $10,000 per person per year; when the patent on AZT expired in 2010, the cost dropped to $67.[7]

There is some evidence that pharmaceutical companies attempt to delay or block competition from generic manufacturers. One strategy, described by the House of Commons Health Select Committee, is to make minor modifications to the patented drug. For example, when Prozac, an antidepressant, was about to lose its patent protection, its manufacturer, Eli Lilly, rebranded the active ingredient—fluoxetine—by producing pink and lavender pills (Prozac was green and white), naming it Sarafem, and marketing it for the treatment of premenstrual dysphoric disorder.

---

[2] 'The world's most neglected diseases' (2002) 325 British Medical Journal 176–7.

[3] Zosia Kmietowicz, 'Regulations are stifling development of new drugs' (2004) 328 British Medical Journal 600.

[4] Richard Sykes, New Medicines, The Practice of Medicine, and Public Policy (Nuffield Trust: London, 2000) 65.

[5] Ibid.

[6] Patent Act 1977, s 25(1). World Trade Organization (WTO) Agreement on Trade-Related Intellectual Property Rights (TRIPS), Art 33.

[7] United Nations Development Programme, Good Practice Guide: Improving Access to Treatment by Utilizing Public Health Flexibilities in the WTO TRIPS Agreement (UNDP: New York, 2010).

House of Commons Health Select Committee[8]

Evergreening involves extending the patented life of a branded product, typically by reformulating the drug, for instance by using a different drug delivery system, changing a dosage form, or presentation (e.g. from tablet to capsule) ...

The significance of evergreening is underlined by the increased range of drug attributes eligible for patent protection ... In the 1990s, the list extended protection in relation to range of use, methods of treatment, mechanism of action, packaging, delivery profiles, dosing route, regimen and range, drug combinations, screening and analytical methods, biological targets and field of use.

The British Generic Manufacturers Association (BGMA) listed five examples in which the originating company had employed evergreening methods, resulting in little or no therapeutic gain, but at a cost to the NHS estimated between £164 and £369 million.

Although intellectual property rights undoubtedly raise the price of medicines, and hence might not appear to be in the interests of consumers, the counter-argument is that, without them, investing in research and development would be so risky that the development of innovative medicines would be stifled, and public health would suffer. This claim is disputed in the next extract by Graham Dukes, who argues that the pharmaceutical industry's commercial accountability to shareholders takes priority over its duty to the community.

MN Graham Dukes[9]

Two definitions of industry accountability predominate: commercial duty to shareholders; and duty to the community.

In the commercial sense, a pharmaceutical company is obliged to deliver a sound return on investment for shareholders. That return must be adequate to reward investors but also be sufficient to attract new capital when needed. From this point of view, the pharmaceutical industry has done very well. Throughout periods of economic stagnation and even recession over the past 30 years, it has remained highly and increasingly profitable ...

The much-repeated argument from pharmaceutical companies, that high drug prices are mainly attributable to research costs, merits cautious scrutiny. With publicly available data, we can ascertain that costs of advertising and promotion generally much exceed research expenditure. Furthermore, industrial research usually benefits from public support, either in the form of tax breaks or as direct scientific input.

A good example of this last point comes from so-called 'orphan' drugs, which are defined by the European Medicines Agency (EMA) as:

- intended for the diagnosis, prevention or treatment of a life-threatening or chronically debilitating condition affecting no more than five in 10,000 persons in the European Union, or

---

[8] *The Influence of the Pharmaceutical Industry*, Fourth Report of Session 2004–05.
[9] 'Accountability of the pharmaceutical industry' (2002) 260 The Lancet 1682–4.

• intended for the diagnosis, prevention or treatment of a life-threatening, seriously debilitating or serious and chronic condition and without incentives it is unlikely that expected sales of the medicinal product would cover the investment in its development.[10]

Although each rare disease will, by definition, affect very few people (most affect fewer than
one person in every 100,000), there are so many rare diseases that the total affected population is, in fact, substantial. It has been estimated that there are 8,000 diseases which qualify
as 'rare', and that these affect 8 per cent of the population. Developing drugs to treat rare diseases is nevertheless unlikely to be profitable, and hence will be a low priority for companies
whose duty is to maintain shareholder value. As a result, a system of tax breaks and incentives
is in place to ensure that people with rare diseases are not abandoned by the pharmaceutical
industry.

For several reasons, medicines are unlike other products. First, in the case of prescribed
drugs, the decision to purchase a medicine is not taken by its consumer, but by her doctor.
Moreover, neither the consumer of the drug, nor its prescriber, will actually pay the full cost
of the medicine.

Secondly, any medicine that is powerful enough to cure disease or alleviate symptoms will
also be strong enough to cause adverse side effects, in at least some users. If complete safety is
unattainable, deciding when a medicine is safe *enough* involves a complex risk/benefit calculation. Chemotherapy, for example, has a long list of extremely unpleasant side effects, which
would rule it out as a treatment for a comparatively trivial condition, like hay fever. Where the
benefit might be the successful treatment of cancer, the risk/benefit calculation is different.

Thirdly, the cultural and symbolic significance of medicines is demonstrated by the placebo
effect, which we considered in Chapter 10. The placebo effect is also at work, as Jacky Law explains, when the same active ingredient is marketed, often under different names, for a range
of different purposes.

Jacky Law[11]

The drugs work according to what the label says, what the doctor says, and what we believe.
Our minds and bodies respond, in other words, to what the label says, to what we are told
the drug will do. GlaxoSmithKline's Zyban for smoking cessation, for example, is a long-acting
form of Wellbutin for depression, by another name. And Organon's antidepressant, Zispin is
also marketed for sleeping disorders ... Different studies are done to get different licensing
data to get them known as different drugs so they can operate in different markets.

The active ingredient, however, remains the same. As such, the various effects the drugs
have can be put down to the response elicited from expectation. What makes a smoker more
likely to kick their habit on Zyban than on the identical drug posing as an antidepressant is
the fact that this is what the doctor says, what the label says, and what the data from clinical
studies corroborate. Such drugs are a triumph of branding.

We begin this chapter by considering what counts as a medicine. Next we examine the licensing process which is supposed to prevent unsafe and ineffective drugs reaching the
market. We then consider the standardization of the regulation of medicines within the EU,

---

[10] *Orphan Drugs and Rare Diseases at a Glance* (EMA: London, 2007).
[11] *Big Pharma: Exposing the Global Healthcare Agenda* (Carroll and Graf: New York, 2006) 63–4.

and the dangers of regulatory divergence post-Brexit.[12] Finally, we consider the law's response to defective medicines, examining in turn the roles of contract, negligence, and statute.

At the outset it is worth noting that government policy in this area will be influenced by several competing factors, which may pull in different directions. On the one hand, the government has an interest in containing costs within the NHS, perhaps by restricting access to new and expensive drugs. On the other hand, in order to improve health outcomes, the government may want to make new medicines widely available. In addition, the pharmaceutical industry is phenomenally profitable, and a major employer: in the UK, it has a turnover of £41.8 billion, supplies 8.2 per cent of goods exports and generates employment for more than 113,000 people.[13] As a result, the government also has an interest in ensuring that the UK is an attractive location for the industry, by, for example, making sure that its licensing processes are not overly cumbersome and that its product liability regime does not stifle innovation. At the same time, however, in order to promote patient safety, the government might want to ensure that the licensing process is rigorous and that there is strict liability for drug-related injuries.

2 WHAT IS A MEDICINE?

(a) DEFINING MEDICINAL PRODUCTS

In practice, it will sometimes be difficult to determine whether a product, like a food supplement or a herbal remedy, is a medicine. Because the Human Medicines Regulations apply only to medicinal products, it is obviously important to be able to tell whether a particular product needs a marketing authorization. This is a decision for the Medicines and Healthcare products Regulatory Agency (MHRA; previously the Medicines Control Agency (MCA)).

As we can see from *R v Medicines Control Agency, ex parte Pharma Nord*, the courts will be slow to interfere with the Agency's determination of whether or not something is a medicinal product. The applicants marketed melatonin tablets in the UK, and they applied for judicial review of the MCA's classification of it as a medicinal product. Recognizing that they were unlikely to succeed in proving *Wednesbury*[14] unreasonableness, they sought a full trial on the merits of whether melatonin should be considered a medicinal product. Collins J refused to exercise his discretion to transfer the case to the civil courts, and in *R v Medicines Control Agency, ex parte Pharma Nord*, the Court of Appeal dismissed the applicant's appeal.

R v Medicines Control Agency, ex parte Pharma Nord[15]

Lord Woolf MR

Under European and domestic law it is the MCA which has the initial heavy responsibility of protecting the public against the dangers to health which can result from the unlicensed marketing of medicinal products. It is also the MCA's equally important initial responsibility to

---

[12] House of Commons Business, Energy and Industrial Strategy Committee, *The impact of Brexit on the pharmaceutical sector* Ninth Report of Session 2017–19.

[13] Ibid.

[14] Ie that the decision was so unreasonable that no reasonable regulator could have taken it: *Associated Provincial Picture Houses v Wednesbury Corporation* [1948] 1 KB 223.

[15] (1998) 44 BMLR 41.

decide what is or is not a medicinal product. Unless it determines that a substance is a medicinal product there is no action which it can lawfully take to control its use ...

The determination of the facts and the application of the policy in a case such as this are not ideally suited to the adversarial processes of the courts ... [T]he MCA is in a better position to evaluate the evidence than a judge. It has accumulated experience in relation to other products which a court lacks. It is an expert body. The MCA has to develop a consistent policy between similar products. The issues are ... ones in relation to which the court should be wary of becoming involved.

So how does the MHRA decide whether a product is a medicine? 'Medicinal products' are defined in the Human Medicines Regulations 2012, regulation 2(1) as follows:

(a) any substance or combination of substances presented as having properties of preventing or treating disease in human beings; or

(b) any substance or combination of substances that may be used by or administered to human beings with a view to—

   (i) restoring, correcting or modifying a physiological function by exerting a pharmacological, immunological or metabolic action, or

   (ii) making a medical diagnosis.

There are therefore two tests for whether something is a medicinal product: is it *presented* as a medicine, or does it *function* as one? If a product is either marketed for the treatment or prevention of disease, or used to modify physiological function, it is a medicinal product, and needs a marketing authorization.

When determining whether a product has been *presented* for the treatment of disease, the MHRA will consider any claims—both explicit and implicit—made for it, and will look at the presentation of the product as a whole, including its packaging and advertising.[16] Also relevant will be the form the product takes and the way it is to be used: in effect, does it look like a medicine? Claims that a product relieves symptoms, such as stress or anxiety, will be regarded as medicinal claims.[17] The reference to 'prevention' means that pills that claim to 'protect against' disease will be treated as medicinal products.[18] Just saying that a product 'helps to maintain a healthy lifestyle', in contrast, has not been regarded by the MHRA as a medicinal claim.[19]

The second limb of the test refers to the medicinal *purpose* of the product. The MHRA must consider whether products are medicines on a case-by-case basis, rather than applying a general rule to all similar products. In *R (on the application of Blue Bio Pharmaceuticals Ltd) v Secretary of State for Health*,[20] the claimants held marketing authorizations permitting them to sell Dolenio, a glucosamine-containing product (GCP) as a medicine for the treatment of osteoarthritis (OA) of the knee. Other GCPs—usually supplied to 'maintain healthy joints'—with exactly the same quantity of active ingredient (1500mg), were sold as food supplements, and subject to a much lighter regulatory regime. The MHRA argued that non-licensed GCPs 'were sold simply as food supplements', and hence the manner of their

---

[16] MHRA, 'A guide to what is a medicinal product' (MHRA Guidance Note 8, revised 2016).
[17] Ibid.   [18] Ibid.   [19] Ibid.   [20] [2016] EWCA Civ 554.

use was different. In fact, there was 'substantial evidence' that patients with OA commonly took GCPs in order to relieve their symptoms. As a result, the Court of Appeal agreed with the claimants that drawing a distinction between medicinal and non-medicinal GCPs was contrary to EU law.

R (on the application of Blue Bio Pharmaceuticals Ltd) v Secretary of State for Health[21]

Lewison LJ

First, the question is not whether 'many' GCPs have been sold as food supplements. The question is whether a significant proportion (and if so what proportion) have been sold as medicinal products. Second, the question is not whether they have been 'sold as' food supplements, but how (and why) they have been used. The mere fact that they have been sold as food supplements does not exclude the possibility (for which there is substantial evidence) that they have in fact been used to relieve the symptoms of OA . . .

In short, orally ingested GCPs whose active ingredient is glucosamine sulphate and which carry a recommended daily dose of 1500 mg share several significant characteristics with a product classified in the UK as a medicinal product; and in accordance with article 2.2 of the Medicinal Products Directive must be classified in the same way unless they have another significant characteristic which takes them outside the definition of 'medicinal product'. That characteristic may well be the manner in which they are used, but it has not so far been demonstrated.

(b) LIFESTYLE DRUGS AND ENHANCEMENTS

We generally assume that people take medicines when they are unwell, in order to alleviate their symptoms and/or make them better. In recent years, however, there has been increasing interest in the use of medicines not to restore normal functioning, but to improve upon it. It is by no means easy to draw a line between enhancements and ordinary medical treatment. Many modern medicines are intended to reverse some of the symptoms of ageing, such as forgetfulness, baldness, and sexual dysfunction. Are these treatments for age-related conditions, or enhancements?

Treatments for medical disorders may also be taken by people who have nothing wrong with them, but who want to feel 'better than well'.[22] Sildenafil citrate (brand name Viagra) is licensed for the treatment of erectile dysfunction, but it is also taken recreationally. An effective treatment for memory loss might be regarded as treatment for patients with Alzheimer's disease, but it could be used as an enhancement by students or professional chess players.[23] In the next extract, Peter Conrad and Deborah Potter consider whether there is anything wrong with using medicines as a 'quick fix'.

---

[21] [2016] EWCA Civ 554.
[22] Carl Elliott, *Better than Well: American Medicine meets the American Dream* (Norton: New York, 2003); Peter Kramer, *Listening to Prozac* (Penguin: New York, 1994).
[23] Peter Conrad and Deborah Potter, 'Human growth hormone and the temptations of biomedical enhancement' (2004) 26 Sociology of Health and Illness 184–215.

Peter Conrad and Deborah Potter[24]

In a sense, we can see biomedical enhancement as a double temptation: the object itself is tempting (e.g. several inches of height, younger features or improved performance) *and* the biomedical route to the enhancement is a temptation as well (e.g. a rapid road to improvement, a technological strategy, a medical solution) . . .

Biomedical enhancements do not involve hard work, in fact they are something of a technological fix. It seems likely most people do not . . . consider runners who raise their aerobic ability and run marathons in under three hours unnatural. Indeed we admire such individuals for their fortitude. They have achieved their enhancement through diligence and hard work, exemplary characteristics in our culture. If women could enhance their breasts at the gym or children increase their height by working out, would unnaturalness be an issue at all? . . .

[W]e might note that our society has adopted a sort of 'pharmaceutical Calvinism' when it comes to taking medications. This entails a belief that it is better to achieve an objective naturally than with drugs or medications; this includes pleasure, sexual satisfaction, mental stability and bodily fitness. Using drugs is an inferior and even suspect way of reaching a goal.

How should doctors respond to patients' requests for so-called 'lifestyle' drugs? Improving a person's quality of life can be a legitimate use of NHS resources: the contraceptive pill, for example, does not treat a disease, but rather enhances women's quality of life by enabling them to control their fertility.[25] It is nevertheless regarded as such a public health good that it has never been subject to the prescription charge. Other 'life enhancing' medications may be less deserving of NHS funding. In the next extract, the British Medical Association advises that patients do not have the right to be provided with any drug that they believe will improve their quality of life.

British Medical Association[26]

It is generally accepted that doctors should prescribe medication only if they consider it necessary for the patient, but views of what is 'necessary' differ. More frequent request from patients for what have been termed 'lifestyle drugs', such as anti-obesity drugs, antidepressants, and hair loss treatments, illustrate the way in which perceptions of 'clinical need' have changed. Although there are certainly those for whom antidepressants and appetite suppressants are clinically indicated and cannot be considered as lifestyle drugs, for many others they are seen as a quick and easy solution . . .

There are inherent risks with virtually all medication and part of the doctor's role is to balance those risks against the anticipated benefits for the patient. When the drug is not clinically indicated, the benefits the patient will, or believes he or she will, derive need to be weighed against the risks. Doctors must be willing to justify their decisions to prescribe in these circumstances and should not prescribe based on patient demand or preference alone.

---

[24] Ibid.

[25] See further, Silvia Pezzini, 'The effect of women's rights on women's welfare: evidence from a natural experiment' (2005) 115 The Economic Journal C208.

[26] *Medical Ethics Today: The BMA's Handbook of Ethics and Law*, 3rd edn (BMA: London, 2012) 547–8.

It is not always easy to tell whether a medicine is being used therapeutically or as an enhancement. For example, Shakespeare et al examined GP prescribing practices of Norethisterone, a drug which used to treat menorrhagia (abnormally heavy periods) and the menopause, but which can also be used to delay menstruation.[27] They found peaks of Norethisterone prescribing during the summer holidays, and concluded that it was being used by women in order to stop their periods when they were on holiday. Is this 'lifestyle' prescribing? In responding to Shakespeare et al's study, Bryant et al argue that it is not.[28] Women suffering from menorrhagia often decide to put up with their problem periods—thus saving the NHS £100 per year per woman. Using Norethisterone to delay menstruation once a year costs about £5. Bryant et al therefore conclude that 'women who tolerate their symptoms for most of the year but who take a period holiday make efficient use of NHS resources'.[29]

(c) MEDICALIZATION

Medicalization, or 'pharmaceuticalization', refers to the increasing tendency for there to be a 'pill for every ill'.[30] Common experiences like heartburn and shyness are renamed as gastro-oesophageal reflux disease and social phobia, for which medication becomes appropriate. This process is also sometimes referred to as 'disease mongering', defined by Ray Moynihan et al as:

> the selling of sickness that widens the boundaries of illness in order to grow markets for those who sell and deliver treatments. It is a process that turns healthy people into patients, causes iatrogenic harm, and wastes precious resources.[31]

The tobacco industry is increasingly diversifying away from cigarettes towards 'pharmaceuticalized tobacco products'.[32] Even for serious medical conditions, like advanced terminal cancer, there is evidence of over-use of chemotherapeutic drugs, when they are no longer capable of doing any good, but may do very considerable harm.[33]

As Carl Elliott explains, the pharmaceutical industry has learned that to sell new drugs successfully, it is sometimes first necessary to 'sell' the existence of the disease that they are intended to treat.

Carl Elliott[34]

> The pharmaceutical industry ... has learned that the key to selling psychiatric drugs is to sell the illnesses they treat. Antidepressants are a case in point. Before the 1960s, clinical

---

[27] Judy Shakespeare, Elizabeth Neve, and Karen Hodder, 'Is Norethisterone a lifestyle drug? Results of database analysis' (2000) 320 British Medical Journal 291.

[28] Gerry Bryant, Ian Scott, and Anne Worrall, 'Is Norethisterone a lifestyle drug? Health is not merely the absence of disease' (2000) 320 British Medical Journal 1605.

[29] Ibid.

[30] Joan Busfield, ' "A pill for every ill": Explaining the expansion in medicine use' (2010) 70 Social Science & Medicine 934–41.

[31] Ray Moynihan, Evan Doran, and David Henry, 'Disease mongering is now part of the global health debate' (2008) 5 PLoS medicine e106.

[32] Yogi Hale Hendlin, Jesse Elias, and Pamela M Ling, 'The pharmaceuticalization of the tobacco industry' (2017) 167 Annals of Internal Medicine 278–80.

[33] Courtney Davis, 'Drugs, cancer and end-of-life care: a case study of pharmaceuticalization?' (2015) 131 Social Science & Medicine 207–14.

[34] Better than Well: American Medicine meets the American Dream (Norton: New York, 2003) 123–4.

depression was thought to be an extremely rare problem. Drug companies stayed away from depression because there was no money to be made in antidepressants. So when Merck started to produce amytriptaline, a tricyclic antidepressant, in the early 1960s, it realised that in order to sell the antidepressant it needed to sell depression.

Forty years later, of course, it is now clear to everyone that the market for antidepressants was not a shallow one at all: that it was, in fact, a tremendously lucrative market, as the remarkable success of Prozac and its sister drugs have demonstrated. The notion of 'clinical depression' has expanded tremendously to include many people who might once have been called melancholic, anxious, or alienated ...

This does not mean that drug companies are simply making up diseases out of thin air, or that psychiatrists are being gulled into diagnosing well people as sick. No one doubts that some people genuinely suffer from, say, depression, or attention-deficit/hyperactivity disorder, or that the right medications make these disorders better. But surrounding the core of many of these disorders is a wide zone of ambiguity that can be chiseled out and expanded.

The phenomenal profitability of Viagra has led to interest in whether it might be possible to market an equivalent pill to women. Of course, this would be possible only if women suffer from a medical condition which such a pill would be treating. Hypoactive sexual desire disorder (HSDD) has therefore been marketed as an underdiagnosed, serious, and widespread medical condition, for which current treatments are inadequate. As Weronika Chańska and Katarzyna Grunt-Mejer explain, this was preceded by an industry-sponsored marketing campaign, masquerading as a feminist cause.

Weronika Chańska and Katarzyna Grunt-Mejer[35]

The Even The Score campaign was launched in June 2014. Its website does not provide much information concerning who initiated the campaign, nor who is running it. However, Susan Scanlan, the woman chairing the campaign, admitted ... that Sprout Pharmaceuticals played a significant role at its outset ...

The campaign presents three main lines of argumentation: (1) sexual dysfunctions in women are serious medical disorders; (2) women's health is treated less seriously than men's and (3) government agencies do not treat women as fully autonomous persons capable of making their own decisions ...

The campaign provides information about the existing imbalance in the number of drugs available for men and women with sexual problems. This alleged chasm is portrayed by one of the main faces of the campaign as an effect of long-term 'institutionalised sexism', manifesting in the disregard of women's health problems ...

Although presenting itself as an advocacy group, Even the Score is in fact a classic type of marketing campaign that aims at raising the awareness of an alleged disorder ... The marketing campaign started by the launch of Even The Score is based on much deceitful and inaccurate information... Cleverly disguised as a campaign to empower women and give them the possibility to make autonomous decisions, it does in fact diminish women's autonomy and push them back within the narrow confines of the feminine role.

---

[35] 'The unethical use of ethical rhetoric: the case of flibanserin and pharmacologisation of female sexual desire' (2016) 42 Journal of Medical Ethics 701–4.

Another way in which HSDD is marketed is through industry-sponsored continuing medical education (CME) training modules. Antoine Meixel et al studied CME modules and found that they often contained direct marketing messages around HSDD, including encouraging doctors 'to bring up the subject, because "the topic of sexual dysfunction may never come to light if the responsibility for initiating a discussion is left to the patient"'.[36]

3 LICENSING

Thalidomide was marketed in the late 1950s as a remedy for morning sickness in pregnancy. Clinical trials gave no indication of its propensity to cause birth defects, and its manufacturer claimed that it could 'be given with complete safety to pregnant women and nursing mothers without adverse effect on mother or child'.[37] This claim turned out to be untrue, and between 1956 and 1961 12,000 children were born in over 30 countries with very severe limb defects. A third of these 'thalidomide' babies died within a month.

Before the 1960s, pharmaceutical companies were not under a legal obligation to establish the safety and efficacy of new medicines before putting them into circulation. Unsurprisingly, the thalidomide tragedy prompted interest in regulating the safety of medicines, and the result was the Medicines Act 1968, and the setting up of the MCA, which was merged subsequently with the Medical Devices Agency to form the MHRA.

In 2012, the Medicines Act and the bewildering set of amendment regulations which had implemented a series of EU Directives were repealed and consolidated in the Human Medicines Regulations 2012. These will continue to apply after Brexit, and it would undoubtedly be sensible for the UK to amend them in line with future changes to EU medicines regulation, in order to facilitate the movement of pharmaceutical products between the UK and the EU.[38]

(a) MARKETING AUTHORIZATION

Only when clinical trials (considered in Chapter 10) have indicated that a drug is reasonably safe and effective can a drug company apply for what used to be called a product licence, and is now known as a marketing authorization. Before any medicinal product (including generic equivalents of established drugs) can be sold or supplied, under regulation 46(2) of the Human Medicines Regulations, it must have a marketing authorization.

Human Medicines Regulations 2012 regulation 46

46. … (2) A person may not sell or supply, or offer to sell or supply, a medicinal product otherwise than in accordance with the terms of—

(a) a marketing authorisation;

(b) a certificate of registration [this applies to homeopathic 'medicines'];

---

[36] Antoine Meixel, Elena Yanchar, and Adriane Fugh-Berman, 'Hypoactive sexual desire disorder: inventing a disease to sell low libido' (2015) 41 Journal of Medical Ethics 859–62.

[37] Pamela Ferguson, *Drug Injuries and the Pursuit of Compensation* (Sweet & Maxwell: London, 1996) 5.

[38] House of Commons Business, Energy and Industrial Strategy Committee, *The impact of Brexit on the pharmaceutical sector* Ninth Report of Session 2017–19.

(c) a traditional herbal registration; or

(d) an Article 126a authorisation [this applies to vitamins that are known to be safe].

Although the Secretary of State for Health and Social Care is responsible for the licensing of medicines, in practice this role is undertaken by the MHRA, with advice from the Commission on Human Medicines (formerly the Committee on the Safety of Medicines (CSM)). Regulation 58(4) specifies a number of factors that the MHRA should take into account when deciding whether to grant a marketing authorization.

Human Medicines Regulations 2012 regulation 58

58(4) The licensing authority may grant the application only if, having considered the application and the accompanying material, the authority thinks that—

(a) the applicant has established the therapeutic efficacy of the product to which the application relates;

(b) the positive therapeutic effects of the product outweigh the risks to the health of patients or of the public associated with the product;

(c) the application and the accompanying material complies with regulations 49 to 55; and

(d) the product's qualitative and quantitative composition is as described in the application and the accompanying material.

Notice that one factor which is not relevant is the price of the medicinal product. The fact that a medicine is prohibitively expensive is not a good reason to deny it a marketing authorization. Of course, the National Institute for Health and Care Excellence (see Chapter 2) might subsequently decide that an expensive medicine should not be prescribed within the NHS, but provided that it meets the threshold levels of safety, effectiveness, and quality, it should be granted a marketing authorization.

Also irrelevant to the MHRA's assessment of a drug's efficacy is the comparative question of whether other medicines are equally or more effective. This is important because it facilitates the licensing of what are known as 'me too' drugs: that is, drugs that are new versions of medicines which are already on the market. As Huseyin Naci et al explain, this means that most new drugs do not offer patients significant benefit over existing ones.

Huseyin Naci, Alexander W Carter, and Elias Mossialos[39]

According to Luijn, approximately 10% of 122 new medicines that entered the European market between 1999 and 2005 were deemed superior to drugs already on offer. Among the set of drugs reviewed by German authorities between 2012 and 2013, approximately 20% were concluded to offer significant benefit compared to existing alternatives and none were deemed to offer major benefit. Between 1990 and 2003, only 6% of 1147 drugs approved in

---

[39] 'Why the drug development pipeline is not delivering better medicines' (2015) 351 British Medical Journal h5542.

Canada provided a substantial improvement over existing drug products. Canadian authorities considered 10% of new drugs approved between 2004 and 2009 as highly innovative ...

More than one drug alternative may be warranted in some therapeutic areas to allow for
patient-centred, individualised treatment options; however the industry's overreliance on me-
too drugs (there are >5 statins; >15 beta-blockers; and >30 anti-diabetics) cannot always be
justified – particularly when they do not offer demonstrable quality of life, convenience, or
therapeutic benefits in different patient sub-groups ...

[P]ricing and reimbursement policies should reward clinically superior medicines and not
me-too drugs.

When applying for a marketing authorization, the pharmaceutical company must submit full
details of the clinical trials that have been carried out and their results, including any adverse
reactions. It must also provide information about the manufacturing process and quality control mechanisms, and must indicate how the drug will be marketed, and submit any leaflets to
be supplied with the product. The Commission on Human Medicines' recommendation that
a medicine should or should not be licensed for use will be based upon all of this industry-
submitted data. Once granted, a marketing authorization lasts for five years, after which a
manufacturer must apply for renewal.

If a manufacturer is applying for a marketing authorization for a generic medicine, then
provided it is 'essentially similar' to a product which has been in circulation for at least ten
years, it is not necessary to provide the MHRA with such full information.[40] In *R (on the
application of Merck Sharp & Dohme Ltd) v Licensing Authority*, Merck Sharp and Dohme
Limited (MSD) held marketing authorizations for Fosamax 5mg, 10mg (product A) and
Fosamax Once Weekly, 70mg (product B), both of which were used to treat osteoporosis.
A generics company wished to rely on its data in order to obtain a marketing authorization for
a drug (product C) which was identical to product B. Product B (which was essentially seven
times the dose of the daily version, to be taken weekly) had not yet been in circulation for the
requisite ten years. MSD therefore claimed that the generics company was not entitled to rely
on the data for product A, which had been in circulation for more than ten years, because
product C's dosage was not 'essentially similar' to product A, only to product B.

Moses J gave this argument short shrift. There were no new safety or efficacy questions in
relation to product C, and so requiring the generics company to submit new data would result
in unnecessary additional testing, with no benefit to public health. The only purpose of this
exercise would be to grant additional protection to innovators' ten-year right to keep their
data confidential, and this was not within the spirit of the Directive.

R (on the application of Merck Sharp & Dohme Ltd) v Licensing Authority[41]

Moses J

The right to cross-refer stems from the notion of one medicinal product being 'essentially
similar' to another. Public health is safeguarded by ensuring that ... a medicinal product is only
authorised without reliance on further data if it is essentially similar to a product which has
already been authorised ...

---

[40] Article 10 of Directive 2001/83/EC, as amended by Directive 2004/27/EC.
[41] [2005] EWHC 710 (Admin).

[T]he suggestion that the generic companies should be compelled to produce their own data, from their own tests, in relation to a product which is identical to Fosamax Once Weekly 70mg has nothing whatever to do with safety or efficacy ... Since it is agreed that the product generic companies wish to develop is identical to Fosamax Once Weekly, any further data the generic companies were required to produce would involve unnecessary testing ...

Product C is no less safe or efficacious because it is essentially similar to B rather than A. The only purpose to be achieved is to give a further period of protection to innovators.

A similar issue arose more recently in *R (on the application of Napp Pharmaceuticals Ltd) v Secretary of State for Health*, in which Whipple J confirmed that a company seeking a marketing authorization for a generic product could rely upon appropriate 'bridging data', which had already been provided by the patent holder.

R (on the application of Napp Pharmaceuticals Ltd) v Secretary of State for Health [42]

Whipple J

Where bridging data has already been provided to support the application for Product B, there is no obvious reason why it should be repeated to support an application for Product C, if Product C is the same as or materially identical to Product B. The issue of paramount importance under the Medicinal Code is to show that Product C is safe and effective; and that can be done by showing that it is the same as or equivalent in effect to Product B, knowing that Product B has already been demonstrated as safe and effective by reference to Product A ...

To read the word 'appropriate' as being limited to data derived from pre-clinical tests or clinical trials undertaken by or on behalf of the party making the application, would be to go far beyond any exercise of construction, even strict construction, of a derogating provision in EU law. Instead, it would impose a significant limitation on the provision itself by reading in a separate and free-standing condition. The result would be at odds with the stated purposes of the Medicinal Code, because it would lead to unnecessary repeat testing which is contrary to the public interest; it would also act as a disincentive to the development of generic alternatives which are in the public interest.

Another recent case in which the pharmaceutical industry has sought to use the marketing authorization requirement in order to protect its commercial interests was *Bayer and Novartis v NHS Darlington CCG and others*. The claimant pharmaceutical companies had challenged a policy adopted by 12 Clinical Commissioning Groups that Avastin should be the preferred treatment for wet macular degeneration (AMD).

Avastin was licensed for use in the treatment of cancer, but it did not have a marketing authorization for ophthalmic use. It had, however, been known for some time that when split into much smaller doses, Avastin was an effective treatment for AMD, at a fraction of the price of similar medicines which were licensed for ophthalmic use. Per injection, Avastin cost around £28 (compared with £816 per injection for Eylea and £551 for Lucentis). In 2018, the National Institute for Health and Care Excellence (NICE) issued a guideline on the treatment of age-related macular degeneration, in which it stated that 'there is equivalent clinical

---

[42] [2016] EWHC 1982 (Admin).

effectiveness and safety of different anti-VEGF agents (aflibercept [Eylea], bevacizumab [Avastin] and ranibizumab [Lucentis])'.[43]

The prescription of Avastin for AMD would therefore be off-label, and before prescribing a drug outside the terms of its licence, doctors must be satisfied that there is sufficient evidence to demonstrate its safety and efficacy for the unlicensed use. The manufacturers of Lucentis (Novartis) and Eylea (Bayer) argued that the CCG's policy was unlawful, in part because the repackaging of Avastin in order to make it suitable for ophthalmic use should require a new marketing authorization. Whipple J rejected their arguments. The marketing authorization process was not the only way through which safety and efficacy could be established, rather NICE and CCGs were also capable of doing this; and its principal purpose was not to protect commercial interests.

Bayer and Novartis v NHS Darlington CCG and others[44]

Whipple J

It is perfectly clear that domestic authorities, specifically (in this case) NICE and the CCGs, have competence to assess whether Avastin is an effective drug in treating wet AMD, to assess its overall clinical effectiveness for that purpose taking account of safety and cost, and to conduct that assessment by comparing it to the other medicines available to treat wet AMD ...

The Claimants argue that the policy will undermine the coherence of the EU regime overall in two ways: (i) patient safety will be jeopardised; and (ii) the coherence of the system, including the protection afforded to pharmaceutical companies in relation to their products, will be damaged ...

I cannot accept that the scheme and purpose of the Directive should extend to protecting the commercial interests of the pharmaceutical companies in a case such as this, where the facts are unusual and the jeopardy to the public purse is enormous.

In *Organon v Department of Health and Social Security*, the Court of Appeal had to consider whether it was appropriate to take into account not only a drug's safety when taken in the recommended dose for its intended purpose, but also its toxicity following overdose. Organon wanted to submit evidence that Mianserin was less toxic than other antidepressants, and hence less likely to be fatal if a patient took an overdose. The CSM considered that it was only entitled to take account of the drug's safety when taken for the purposes indicated in the licence, and hence evidence of toxicity following misuse was not relevant. The Divisional Court disagreed and held that the risks a drug posed if it was misused could be relevant to an assessment of its safety, and this decision was upheld by the Court of Appeal.

Organon v Department of Health and Social Security[45]

Mustill LJ

It strikes me as plain, and this much was virtually conceded, that however sympathetically paragraph (g) is read, administering the drug for the purposes of alleviating the symptoms of depression cannot be stretched to include the taking of the drug for the purpose of suicide ...

[43] Age-related macular degeneration (NICE, 2018).   [44] [2018] EWHC 2465 (Admin).
[45] The Times, 6 February 1990.

I do not, however, believe that this is the right approach to the Medicines Act, the object of which is to promote public health and safety, and which should, if at all possible, be construed in a way favourable to the attainment of that object. To read paragraph (g) in the narrow sense for which the Authority contends, and which the words at first sight themselves seem to indicate, would work in the opposite direction. This would entail that if the Authority discovered, after the grant of a licence, that although in the intended dosage the drug remained acceptably safe, nevertheless if taken in even moderate excess it was potentially lethal, it would be beyond the Authority's jurisdiction even to consider whether the original risk/benefit analysis should be reconsidered, with a view to variation, suspension or cancellation of the licence. This result strikes me as so absurd that it cannot have been within the contemplation of Parliament. It must therefore be taken that the references to 'administered' and 'purposes' extend beyond circumstances which involve strict compliance with the intended use of the drug, and that the risks attaching to misuse can properly be brought into account.

(b) COMPLEMENTARY AND ALTERNATIVE MEDICINE

Under regulation 3(6) of the Human Medicines Regulations 2012, an exception from the need to obtain a marketing authorization exists for herbal remedies, which are made up on the premises from which they are supplied, after a one-to-one consultation. Although over-the-counter herbal remedies which make therapeutic claims must have a marketing authorization, the Traditional Herbal Medicines Registration Scheme allows for the marketing of traditional herbal remedies, which do not meet the criteria for a marketing authorization. The scheme requires manufacturers to demonstrate safety and quality, but not efficacy.

Evidence of efficacy is often unavailable for herbal medicines because there are usually no randomized controlled trials, which as we saw in Chapter 10 are the 'gold standard' in clinical research. Applicants must submit a review of safety data and an expert report on quality, in addition to evidence of at least 30 years of traditional use, 15 of which should have been in the EU. In exceptional circumstances, registration will be possible even if the product has not been in use in the EU for 15 years, but it will still be necessary to prove that it has been used elsewhere for at least 30 years. The product label must inform the consumer that the basis for registration is traditional use, rather than clinical trial data.

In order to avoid the submission of duplicate evidence, the Committee for Herbal Medicinal Products (CHMP), which is part of the European Medicines Agency (EMA), has developed a European 'positive list' of ingredients. Establishing that a product contains an ingredient that is on the indicative list does not necessarily mean that an application for registration will be successful, but it will mean that applicants do not need to submit detailed evidence of safety or traditional use. Evidence of quality will still be necessary.

The assumption behind the 'traditional use' requirement is that there must be some level of efficacy if the remedy has been used for this length of time. This is problematic, to say the least. People have been reading horoscopes and having their palms read for many years, but this does not amount to evidence that astrologers and palm readers can predict the future.

There is also a special scheme for homeopathic 'medicines'. Homeopathy involves taking highly diluted substances, usually in tablet form. It is, however, scientifically improbable. In evidence to the House of Commons Science and Technology Committee, David Colquhoun stated bluntly: 'If homeopathy worked the whole of chemistry and physics would have to be overturned.'[46]

There are two ways in which a new homeopathic product can be registered. First, under the simplified registration scheme, data must be submitted to demonstrate the quality of the product and to show that it is dilute enough to guarantee safety. No therapeutic claims can be made. Secondly, under the national rules scheme, homeopathic medicinal products can be marketed for the relief or treatment of minor symptoms and conditions, defined as those that can be relieved or treated without the supervision or intervention of a doctor. Applications must establish quality, safety, *and efficacy*; that is, they must provide study reports in relation to the product or published scientific literature or what are referred to as 'homoeopathic provings'. The MHRA has suggested that, 'whatever data is provided, it should be sufficient to demonstrate that UK homeopathic practitioners would accept the efficacy of the product for the indications sought.'[47] This, once again, is problematic insofar as it amounts to the claim that a homeopathic medicine works if other people, who believe in homeopathy, believe that it works.

In addition to the questionable assumption that proof of traditional use, or proof that other homeopaths believe it works, amounts to proof of efficacy, two further problematic assumptions underpin the common view that complementary and alternative medicines—while not necessarily very effective—are essentially harmless. First, it is often assumed that anything that is herbal or natural is necessarily safe. This is simply wrong. Many plants—an example would be digoxin from foxgloves—can be highly toxic.

Secondly, it is also often assumed that complementary and alternative medicines are used by the worried well, who may be wasting their money on ineffective 'natural' remedies, but who are not likely to suffer any serious ill effects as a result. Again, this is mistaken. It is common for people with, or at risk of, extremely serious illnesses, like cancer and malaria, to consult alternative medical practitioners.[48] Choosing to rely on alternative medicine may mean that access to effective treatment is delayed or foregone altogether, which may have serious consequences for the person's health,[49] and perhaps for NHS resources as well.

In the next extract, Arianne Shahvisi suggests that because it is impossible to explain how alternative medicines work, informed consent may be impossible.

Arianne Shahvisi[50]

What these 'therapies' have in common is that they do not draw on plausible physical causes, and may suggest implausible physical causes (as in homeopathy), or supernatural causes (as in faith healing). Where causes that cohere with our conception of cause and effect in other contexts are not forthcoming, explanations cannot be given. Without explanations, there can be no understanding . . .

It would seem responsible for those working within the medical establishment to visibly distance themselves from treatments which cannot be understood, so that AM [alternative medicine] does not obtain vicarious legitimacy through some presumed resemblance or

---

[46] House of Commons Science and Technology Committee, *Evidence Check 2: Homeopathy*, Fourth Report of Session 2009–10, para 59.
[47] 'The Homeopathic National Rules Scheme: Brief Guidance for Manufacturers and Suppliers' (MHRA, 2006).
[48] Eric H Liu et al, 'Use of alternative medicine by patients undergoing cardiac surgery' (2000) 120 Journal of Thoracic and Cardiovascular Surgery 335–41.
[49] Ben Goldacre, 'Benefits and risks of homoeopathy' (2007) 370 The Lancet 1672–3.
[50] 'No Understanding, No Consent: The Case Against Alternative Medicine' (2016) 30 Bioethics 69–76.

connection to medicine. This would have the positive effect of stemming the new wave of commercialized AM which exploits the good faith and finances of desperate patients. Further, since AM practitioners are ethically bound by the same IC [informed consent] obligations as orthodox medicine, the arguments just made would seem to compromise their ability to practise at all, or at the very least, to undermine any claims to efficacy regarding AM treatments (which may amount to the same thing).

(c) CLASSIFICATION OF MEDICINES

In addition to deciding whether to grant a marketing authorization, the MHRA also classifies medicines into one of three categories:

(a) prescription-only medicines (POM);

(b) suppliable by a pharmacist without prescription (P);

(c) general sale list medicines, which can be sold over the counter and do not need to be dispensed by a pharmacist (GSL).

Regulation 62(3) of the Human Medicines Regulations specifies the factors relevant to this classification. When deciding whether a medicine should be prescription-only, the MHRA must consider whether it:

(a) is likely to present a direct or indirect danger to human health, even when used correctly, if used without the supervision of a doctor or dentist; or

(b) is frequently and to a very wide extent used incorrectly, and as a result is likely to present a direct or indirect danger to human health; or

(c) contains substances or preparations of substances of which the activity requires, or the side effects require, further investigation;

(d) is normally prescribed by a doctor or dentist for parenteral administration [i.e. intravenously or by injection].

Regulation 62(4)(c) also specifies that the Secretary of State should take into account whether a medicine is likely, if incorrectly used, to present a substantial risk of medicinal abuse, lead to addiction, or be used for illegal purposes.

Medicines can be reclassified and, in recent years, an increasing number of prescription-only medicines have been reclassified so that they can be bought in pharmacies. In 2000, for example, the MCA and the CSM agreed that the risks posed by post-coital contraception (the 'morning-after pill') did not justify its prescription-only status, so it was reclassified as a pharmacy-available medicine.

More recently, in 2017, the MHRA reclassified Viagra, allowing its manufacturer Pfizer to sell Viagra Connect in pharmacies. Pfizer has supplied pharmacists with an optional checklist of questions for customers, about their cardio-vascular health, other conditions and drug use (for example: 'Have you had a heart attack or stroke within the last 6 months?' and 'Are you using drugs called "poppers" for recreational purposes?'), with the instruction 'if the patient answers YES to any of the following: do not supply the product and refer to the doctor'.

Where self-medication is safe, as is the case in relation to treatments for colds or hay fever, for example, there are obvious advantages in enabling individuals to buy medicines over the counter. This will often be more convenient, and it will save the NHS money. Not only will the patient pay for the drug themselves (Viagra Connect costs £34.99 for eight pills; in the first 12 weeks after reclassification, sales of £4.3 million were reported), but also there will be no need for a GP appointment in order to obtain a prescription.

Of course, one consequence of reclassification is that the leaflets supplied with medicines become more important, since they may represent the only information the patient receives about how to take the medicine safely. In the next extract, David Prayle and Margaret Brazier evaluate this trend towards the reclassification of medicines.

David Prayle and Margaret Brazier[51]

[T]he pharmaceutical industry has an obvious and powerful interest in reclassification. Increased sales of P and GSL medicines can be expected, particularly as such medicines, unlike POM medicines, can be advertised to the general public. As a number of previously profitable POM medicines reach the stage when patent protection expires, the manufacturer must seek means of combating competition from generic copies. Altering the medicine's status to P and enthusiastically advertising the product under its tried and tested brand name is a useful strategy to maintain, if not increase sales figures.

A brave new world of more open access to medicines beckons. Should it be applauded? A restrictive approach to access to medicines restricts individual autonomy. The longer the list of POM medicines, the less able individuals are to control their own health status via self-diagnosis and self-medication ... Reducing the list of POM medicines might be seen as enhancing autonomy. The flaw in this approach derives from the anomalous P category of medicines. They can be purchased, but only from a pharmacy under the supervision and control of a pharmacist. Persons seeking a P medicine must in theory submit to an interrogation from the pharmacist (or his assistant) about their familiarity with the drug, their medical history and their potential use of the product. This 'consultation' may well take place before an audience of other customers.

(d) ONLINE PHARMACIES

The system for the classification of medicines rests upon the assumption that doctors can control access to prescription-only medicines. Online pharmacies pose a significant challenge to this. Some websites offer virtual 'consultations', which may amount to no more than filling in a questionnaire. Doctors employed by the owners of these websites then prescribe and dispense medicines to patients without a face-to-face encounter. It is hard to see how this is compatible with a doctor's duty of care. The General Medical Council (GMC)'s good practice guidance instructs doctors that:

In providing clinical care you must ... prescribe drugs or treatment, including repeat prescriptions, only when you have adequate knowledge of the patient's health, and are satisfied that the drugs or treatment serve the patient's needs.[52]

---

[51] 'Supply of medicines: paternalism, autonomy and reality' (1998) 24 Journal of Medical Ethics 93–8.
[52] Good Medical Practice (GMC, 2013) para 16(a).

Even more worryingly, there are websites, based offshore, which advertise that there is 'no need for a prescription', and in these cases control over access to prescription-only medicines, or counterfeit products, is non-existent.

For many reasons, it is unwise to buy medicines online. If drugs are purchased from an unregistered online pharmacy, they are more likely than not to be counterfeit medicines.[53] Fake drugs pose a serious risk to consumers' health, both because the substance ingested may be dangerous, or in a dangerous dosage, and because access to effective treatment may be delayed.

Even if the drugs are real, in the absence of a professional gatekeeper, there is no way to ensure that the purchaser's self-diagnosis is accurate. Online pharmacies may be willing to supply medicines to patients in whom they are clearly contraindicated.[54] Buying antibiotics online contributes to the rise of drug resistant infections, and thus poses a risk to public health.[55]

Despite these risks, it is increasingly common for people to buy prescription drugs online. Currently, the group of people most likely to be taking many different medicines, namely the very elderly, is also the section of society which is least likely to use the internet to self-diagnose and manage their health problems. As people who spend much of their life online grow older, use of online pharmacies is likely to become much more common.

The sanctions that exist in relation to online drug supply are focused on the supplier rather than the purchaser. Unless the medicine is a controlled substance—when importing into the UK is subject to particular restrictions—it is not an offence to buy prescription drugs online from an overseas website. It is, however, a criminal offence for someone who is not properly qualified and registered to prescribe and supply a prescription-only medicine. The MHRA monitors online pharmacies, and if websites are based in the UK, and not registered, their owners can be prosecuted. If the MHRA is concerned about a site that is registered abroad, it will inform the relevant regulatory authority in that country, but it is clearly impossible for the MHRA to control the activities of overseas internet pharmacies.

In the next extract, Nicola Glover-Thomas and John Fanning draw attention to a further consequence of the rise of e-pharmacies, namely a blurring of the line between illegal recreational drugs and prescription medicines.

Nicola Glover-Thomas and John Fanning[56]

In some countries, the scale of the abuse of pharmaceutical products is second only to that of cannabis, surpassing all other illicitly produced substances combined ... e-Pharmacies are beginning to define a generation. The *Wall Street Journal* revealed in March 2008 that some teenagers and young people had begun throwing 'pharm parties', to which they 'bring whatever pharmaceuticals they can find, mix the drugs up in a big bowl and eat them like candy'... Sandhill notes that the increased availability of prescription drugs illustrates 'how hazy the line is that separates the gear you buy from a dealer on the street and the stuff prescribed by the guy in a white coat'.

---

[53] Susan Mayor, 'More than half of drugs sold online are fake or substandard' (2008) 337 British Medical Journal 618.

[54] Gunther Eysenbach, 'Online prescribing of sildanefil (Viagra) on the world wide web' (1999) 1 Journal of Medical Internet Research e10.

[55] Sara Elizabeth Boyd et al, 'Obtaining antibiotics online from within the UK: a cross-sectional study' (2017) 72 Journal of Antimicrobial Chemotherapy 1521–8.

[56] 'Medicalisation: The Role of E-Pharmacies in Iatrogenic Harm' (2010) 18 Medical Law Review 28–55.

Laura Orsolini et al found that customers using online pharmacies for recreational purposes were, most commonly, 'Caucasian, men, in their 20s, highly educated, and using the web to impact as minimally as possible on their existing work/professional status', whereas people seeking access to affordable prescription medicines online were more likely to be from disadvantaged backgrounds.[57]

(e) POST-LICENSING REGULATION

(1) Pharmacovigilance

Because clinical trials are, by necessity, carried out on a relatively small number of patients, compared with the number of eventual users, they will detect only common and immediate adverse reactions. It is therefore important to monitor adverse reactions that may be identified when the drug is taken for longer, and by larger groups of patients, including people who are usually excluded from clinical trials, such as pregnant women and people with multiple comorbidities. As a result, manufacturers are under a duty to keep a record of all reported adverse drug reactions (ADRs), and to report them to the European Medicines Agency's Eudravigilance web-system for the management of safety reports.[58] At the time of writing, it is unclear whether the UK will continue to be part of this scheme after Brexit.

The 'yellow card scheme' enables GPs, nurses, midwives, health visitors, and patients to report ADRs electronically to the MHRA.[59] Drugs are divided into two groups for the purposes of the yellow card scheme: new drugs (denoted by a black triangle) are monitored closely for a minimum of two years, during which time all suspected ADRs should be reported. For established drugs, only serious suspected ADRs must be reported. Other areas of special interest have been identified, for which all suspected ADRs should be reported, such as reactions in children and the elderly. In 1996, following the identification of liver toxicity associated with a traditional Chinese medicine, the yellow card scheme was extended to include unlicensed herbal products. Monitoring ADRs from herbal remedies has proved particularly difficult, however, because patients seem to be less willing to report their adverse reactions.

In 2017, 44,168 ADRs were reported.[60] This number, while high, is a massive underestimate: most ADRs are not reported. The purpose of the yellow card scheme is not, however, to provide accurate data on the extent of ADRs, but rather to indicate the existence of safety signals that warrant further investigation.

Very few medicines are withdrawn as a result of safety concerns. The existence of an adverse reaction does not necessarily mean that a medicine has become unacceptably unsafe. Aspirin is unsafe for use in children, for example, but that does not mean that it should not be available to other patients, who benefit enormously from it. It is therefore necessary to balance the risks to a minority of patients against the benefits the drug may have for the majority, and so, rather than withdrawing a product which causes adverse reactions in some users, it might be more appropriate to give a warning about contraindications for its use.

---

[57] 'Profiling online recreational/prescription drugs' customers and overview of drug vending virtual marketplaces' (2015) 30 Human Psychopharmacology: Clinical and Experimental 302–18.

[58] Directive 2010/84/EU amending, as regards pharmacovigilance, Directive 2001/83/EC on the Community code relating to medicinal products for human use.

[59] <www.yellowcard.mhra.gov.uk>.

[60] *Human Medicines Regulations 2012 Advisory Bodies Annual Report 2017* (MHRA, 2018).

As Trudo Lemmens and Shannon Gibson point out, one defect of the drug licensing system is that it provides an incentive for drug companies to produce pre-approval information, rather than to monitor a drug's post-marketing safety.

Trudo Lemmens and Shannon Gibson[61]

The pharmaceutical industry has little inherent interest in evaluating or questioning whether the production of pre-approval data is sufficient or provides the most meaningful information; this is not what the industry is asked to do, and there is no incentive for industry to do so once a drug receives market approval. In fact, the contrary is true: drug producers often benefit from the deficit of data on drug safety and efficacy caused by, first, a lack of transparency and of rigorous control during the pre-market phase, and subsequently, a lack of post-market surveillance ...

In recent decades, the nature of post-market risk has shifted due to the rise of 'blockbuster' drugs that are so widely prescribed—and often for the long-term treatment of chronic conditions—that even a minor change in relative risk can result in thousands of adverse reactions.

(2) Marketing

Schedule 27 of the Regulations specifies the information that must be provided with a medicine, such as instructions for use, contraindications, and warnings about side effects. Leaflets supplied with medicines must contain information about its active ingredients; indications for its use; warnings about the product's interaction with other substances, such as alcohol; and about any effect it might have on the user's capacity to drive or operate machinery. Dosage instructions, such as how the medicine should be taken, and how frequently, must also be included, and if appropriate, what should be done in the event of an overdose.

The advertising of medicines is also controlled. Prescription-only medicines cannot be marketed directly to the public (unlike in the US), but they can be advertised to healthcare professionals. It is, however, illegal to advertise 'off-label' uses of medicines. This is important because off-label prescription—that is, when a doctor prescribes a medicine for a condition outside of its marketing authorization—is lawful. If doctors can be persuaded to prescribe more medicines off-label, pharmaceutical companies are able to expand a product's market without the expense of conducting trials and obtaining a marketing authorization.

There may be times when off-label prescription is reasonable, most frequently in paediatrics or oncology, when a doctor may have run out of 'on-label' options. Earlier, we considered the unusual case of Avastin, in which NICE had evaluated the safety and efficacy of its off-label usage for the treatment of AMD. More usually, when there has not been any assessment of the safety or efficacy of a drug's off-label use, it poses an unknown risk of harm to patients.

In the US, some of the largest financial penalties imposed upon drugs companies have been for encouraging off-label prescription. In 2012, GlaxoSmithKline (GSK) agreed to pay $1.043 billion after it was found to have made false claims in the off-label promotion of several of its medicines. In the UK, the Prescription Medicines Code of Practice Authority (PMCPA) is able to impose fines upon companies who engage in off-label promotion, and it can report them to the MHRA for possible prosecution. In practice, Andreas Vilhelmsson et al found that in a ten-year

[61] 'Decreasing the Data Deficit: Improving Post-Market Surveillance in Pharmaceutical Regulation' (2014) 59 McGill Law Journal 943–88.

period the total amount of fines paid for 72 breaches in the UK was a meagre £260,000, and no companies had been reported to the MHRA.[62] Given the vast profits that can be made from off-label prescription, this could hardly be described as an effective deterrent. Vilhelmsson et al also found that most of these cases were reported to the PMCPC by competitor companies, and they therefore consisted in highly visible breaches, such as adverts in medical journals. In the US, reports of off-label promotion have more commonly come from whistleblowers, who may be able to uncover 'complex marketing campaigns that remain concealed to company outsiders'.[63]

As well as marketing their products to doctors, the pharmaceutical industry sponsors 'disease awareness' campaigns. These can be effective ways of drawing the public's attention to the possibility that they might have a condition, and to the existence of effective drugs. The aim of these initiatives is to persuade people to visit their GP and ask for treatment. Where there is only one medicine to treat a condition, promoting that condition to the public comes very close to direct promotion of that product.

The House of Commons Health Select Committee found that the ban on direct advertising to consumers does not stop the pharmaceutical industry from thinking creatively about how to persuade more people to make an appointment to discuss their symptoms with their GP, in the hope that this will increase prescription rates.

House of Commons Health Select Committee[64]

There is clear evidence that the industry is concerned with identifying populations who are not currently presenting for diagnosis. In one document relating to the 'strategic planning process,' these patients, who, 'do not currently present to their GP or take prescription medications,' are referred to as 'the missing millions' and are estimated to comprise almost 2 million people in the UK. This population is viewed as providing a 'significant opportunity' for the company.

Research is then conducted on behalf of the company that aims to understand what barriers exist to prevent these people from presenting and to identify factors, both rational and emotional, that will overcome these barriers and encourage patients to seek professional advice.

The pharmaceutical industry also attempts to influence prescribing practices by funding and supporting patient groups, as explained by psychiatrist Tim Kendall in his evidence to the Health Select Committee:

I am aware that there are some … like Depression Alliance, which have very substantial funding at times from drug companies. They do lobby for an increased accessibility to drugs which the drug companies are selling to these patient organisations. They are persuading them that these are the drugs they must have, with very little evidence to support it.[65]

---

[62] Andreas Vilhelmsson, Courtney Davis, and Shai Mulinari, 'Pharmaceutical Industry Off-label Promotion and Self-regulation: A Document Analysis of Off-label Promotion Rulings by the United Kingdom Prescription Medicines Code of Practice Authority 2003–2012' (2016) 13 PLoS Med e1001945.

[63] Ibid.

[64] House of Commons Health Select Committee, *The Influence of the Pharmaceutical Industry*, Fourth Report of Session 2004–05, paras 253–4.

[65] Ibid, para 265.

As Barbara von Tigerstrom points out, industry funding of patient groups is especially signifi-cant given the trend towards patient representation in the drug approvals process.

Barbara von Tigerstrom[66]

Direct input and participation by patients in the regulation of drugs and medical devices is believed to enhance the quality, legitimacy, and transparency of regulatory decisions. There is particular emphasis on the value of patients' and caregivers' experiential know-ledge, which can complement scientific expertise in the agencies' decision-making processes ...

[F]unding of patient groups is a major concern that is particularly relevant to patient rep-resentatives' participation in medical product regulation ... Various studies have estimated that between 30% and 71% of patient organizations accept industry funding ... Patient organizations' approaches vary widely, with some accepting no industry or corporate funding, others accepting some (in varying amounts), and a few seeming to be almost entirely co-opted or even created by pharmaceutical companies. Industry funding tends to be in areas relevant to companies' products, suggesting that their sponsorship of patient organ-izations is motivated by business interests as well as altruism. There are concerns that industry funding may influence patient groups to focus more on advocating for reimburse-ment and faster approval of drugs, and some evidence suggests that patient advocacy has influenced drug approvals.

(f) THE IMPACT OF REGULATION

Obviously, the stricter the licensing requirements, the more difficult it is to introduce new medicines to the market. A stringent regulatory framework might increase patient safety, but at the cost of stifling innovation, which in turn may mean that patients are denied access to beneficial medicines. Lighter-touch regulation may facilitate speedier access to new medi-cines, but as Huseyin Naci et al explain, the consequence may be an increase in adverse side effects.

Huseyin Naci, Alexander W Carter, and Elias Mossialos[67]

Regulators in recent years have in fact progressively lowered their evidence requirements for market entry of new drugs by requiring smaller trials, surrogate endpoints, and placebo com-parisons, and increasingly adopted expedited approvals. Such rushed approvals had signifi-cant implications for drug safety. Several regulatory designations are aimed at shortening the timeline for regulatory review with the ultimate goal of making drugs available as rapidly as possible. A significant unintended consequence of this regulatory enthusiasm for fast market access of new drugs has been an estimated 35% increase in safety warnings and market

---

[66] 'The patient's voice: Patient involvement in medical product regulation' (2016) 16 Medical Law International 27–57.

[67] 'Why the drug development pipeline is not delivering better medicines' (2015) 351 British Medical Journal h5542.

withdrawals, with over one fourth of drugs approved since 1992 receiving black-box warnings or being withdrawn from the market.

In the next two extracts, Courtney Davis et al and Deborah Cohen describe and comment upon the alarming results of a systematic evaluation of cancer drugs which had received marketing authorizations over a four-year period.

Courtney Davis et al[68]

This systematic evaluation of oncology drug approvals by the EMA [European Medicines Agency] in 2009-13 shows that most of the drugs (39/68, 57%) entered the market without evidence of improved survival or quality of life ... Among 68 cancer drug indications approved by the EMA in the period 2009-13, and with a median of 5.4 years' follow-up, only 35 (51%) were associated with significant improvement in survival or quality of life over alternative treatment options, placebo, or as add on treatment.

Most new oncology drugs authorised by the EMA in 2009-13 came onto the market without clear evidence that they improved the quality or quantity of patients' lives, and, when survival gains over available treatment alternatives were shown, they were not always clinically meaningful. Little new information to guide patients, their treating clinicians, or decisions about whether or not to pay for treatments was generated in the postmarketing period. This situation has negative implications for patients and public health. When expensive drugs that lack clinically meaningful benefits are approved and paid for within publicly funded healthcare systems, individual patients can be harmed, important societal resources wasted, and the delivery of equitable and affordable care undermined.

Deborah Cohen[69]

The findings raise serious questions about why the current regulatory environment supports the approval of cancer drugs that may leave patients at risk of experiencing toxicity and reduced quality of life without deriving meaningful benefit ...

Perhaps most importantly, however, the fact the drugs have been given the imprimatur of regulatory approval may cause patients and doctors to have unrealistic expectations about their benefits and harms ... For patients, approval of such drugs may lead to unrealistic expectations, fuelled by patient organisations ... In the words of one EMA adviser who spoke to *The BMJ*, however, 'no one wants to say no to a cancer drug'.

There have also been concerns that the pharmaceutical industry has too much influence over the licensing authority, leading to what John Abraham describes as 'regulatory capture'.

---

[68] 'Availability of evidence of benefits on overall survival and quality of life of cancer drugs approved by European Medicines Agency: retrospective cohort study of drug approvals 2009-13' (2017) 359 British Medical Journal j4530.

[69] 'Cancer drugs: high price, uncertain value' (2017) 359 British Medical Journal j4543.

John Abraham[70]

Pharmaceutical firms have well-oiled lobbying strategies to capture regulatory agencies: more subtly, industry can penetrate into the heart of regulatory political subculture via the so-called revolving door ... In the UK, a large proportion of scientists in the British drug regulatory authority started their careers in industry, and many move back there ...

Regulatory capture is especially important because the risk–benefit assessment of drugs has a high degree of technical uncertainty, which is inherent in toxicology, clinical trials, and epidemiology. Therefore, it is crucial to know how far regulators are willing to give the manufacturer the benefit of scientific doubt about safety and efficacy of their product. Indeed, regulators too often consistently award industry the benefit of scientific doubt when reviewing products.

For the past 50 years, industry has been quick to ward off regulation it perceives to be contrary to its interests by threatening that such regulation will have damaging results for the nation's export trade, balance of payments, or employment. Too often, regulatory agencies have accepted these threats uncritically.

The MHRA is funded entirely by the pharmaceutical industry, through licensing and other fees. Some years ago, the House of Commons Health Select Committee was concerned that this may put pressure on the MHRA to provide a speedy licensing service.

House of Commons Health Select Committee[71]

In return for the licensing and service fees paid by the industry, companies expect an efficient and rapid service ... The speed at which the UK regulatory authority has historically processed licence applications has been one of the fastest in the world, which means that its services are much in demand from EU applications. In 2003, time from application to the granting of a licence of a new chemical entity, if no further information was needed, was approximately 70 working days, whereas a response may now usually be expected in approximately 30 working days.

A particularly striking example of failures in the system of pharmacovigilance emerged in March 2008, when the MHRA announced that there would be no prosecution of GSK, for withholding trial data and meta-analyses, which demonstrated conclusively that paroxetine should not be prescribed to under-18s.

GSK had carried out two trials, Studies 329 and 377, which tested the efficacy of paroxetine (known as Seroxat in the UK and Paxil in the US) in children and adolescents in the mid-1990s in 11 countries. The trials were concluded by October 1998. The data, and a meta-analysis carried out on the data in 2002, were not submitted to the MHRA until May 2003, as part of an application to extend Seroxat's licensed indications for use. As soon as it was received, this information was analysed by the Committee on the Safety of Medicines, which found that (a) 'there is no good evidence of efficacy in major depressive disorder in the population studied', and (b) there was 'a clear increase in suicidal behaviour versus placebo'.[72]

---

[70] 'The pharmaceutical industry as a political player' (2002) 360 The Lancet 1498–502.
[71] Paras 99, 100.   [72] MHRA Assessment Report: Paroxetine (Seroxat) 4 June 2003.

The MHRA immediately published a 'Dear Doctor' letter, informing doctors that Seroxat should not be prescribed to under-18s. A few months later, a criminal investigation into GSK's failure to submit this data was launched.

In early 2004, a leaked internal GSK document suggested that the decision to withhold Studies 329 and 377 had been intentional. The document, dated October 1998, stated that it would be 'commercially unacceptable to include a statement that efficacy had not been demonstrated, as this would undermine the profile of paroxetine'.[73]

Following a four-and-a-half year criminal investigation, the conclusion was reached that GSK could not be prosecuted for withholding this data, not because GSK had acted properly, but because the law was insufficiently clear to give a reasonable prospect of conviction. This was because the duty placed upon manufacturers to provide '*any* information relevant to the evaluation of benefits and risks' (my emphasis), could be read as applying only to information which emerged during 'normal conditions of use'.

Seroxat had not been specifically licensed for use in children, because at the time carrying out paediatric clinical trials was not encouraged, and so its widespread use by under-18s was effectively 'off-label'. Perhaps ironically, GSK had carried out paediatric trials, but again because these adverse reactions had emerged during trials, and not during 'normal conditions of use', they were not captured by the relevant provisions. The duty to report adverse reactions in clinical trials, at the relevant time only applied to UK trials, and so again did not bite on this withheld data.

Linsey McGoey and Emily Jackson[74]

The existence of so many qualifications to what initially looks like a clear and comprehensive duty to submit '*any* other information relevant to the evaluation of the benefits and risks afforded by a medicinal product' is perhaps surprising. Certainly, two ordinary rules of statutory interpretation would militate against this conclusion. First, the words used in legislation are normally assumed to have their 'ordinary language meaning', unless otherwise specified. Use of the word 'any', according to the Oxford English Dictionary, captures the idea of 'indifference as to the particular one or ones that may be selected', which would suggest that 'any relevant information' should not, without a clear indication to the contrary, be qualified to mean 'only information gathered in a particular setting'.

The second rule of statutory interpretation which is at odds with the existence of these legal loopholes is that, in the event of statutory ambiguity, it is legitimate to ask what the legislator's intention was in drafting the provision in question. Here the intention was evidently to create a duty to report all relevant data, and in particular, to disclose suspected adverse reactions and other information relevant to the regulator's evaluation of risks and benefits.

The interpretation of the law which has led to the decision not to prosecute would seem to subvert the intention of the creators of the regulatory regime, which was indubitably not to provide a series of 'get-out' clauses for drugs companies who withhold, deliberately, evidence of lack of efficacy and serious side effects for a group of patients who are routinely being prescribed the drug in question.

---

[73] 'GSK Seroxat/Paxil Adolescent Depression: Position Piece on the Phase III Clinical Studies', available at <https://www.justice.gov/sites/default/files/opa/legacy/2012/07/02/complaint-ex1.pdf>.

[74] 'Seroxat and the suppression of clinical trial data: regulatory failure and the uses of legal ambiguity' (2009) 35 Journal of Medical Ethics 107–12.

Following the collapse of this criminal investigation, the MHRA pressed for a change in the law, in order to provide for a comprehensive duty of candour. This is now contained in regulation 75.

Human Medicines Regulations 2012 regulation 75

75.—(1) The holder of a UK marketing authorisation must provide the licensing authority with any new information that might entail the variation of the authorisation.

(2) The holder must, in particular, provide the licensing authority with the following information—

(a) information about any prohibition or restriction imposed in relation to the product to which the authorisation relates by the competent authority of any country in which the product is on the market;

(b) positive and negative results of clinical trials or other studies in all indications and populations, whether or not included in the marketing authorisation;

(c) data on the use of the medicinal product where such use is outside the terms of the marketing authorisation; and

(d) any other information that the holder considers might influence the evaluation of the benefits and risks of the product.

4 EUROPEAN REGULATION

Within Europe there has been progressive harmonization of rules on labelling and package leaflets,[75] advertising,[76] and the reporting of adverse side effects.[77] These Directives amended the UK's regulations and are now consolidated in the Human Medicines Regulations 2012. The European Medicines Agency (EMA) was established in 1993, and a European system for the authorization of medicinal products was set up in January 1995.

Most new, innovative medicines are licensed through the centralized procedure, where applications are made directly to EMA, and assessments are carried out by a sub-committee, the Committee for Medicinal Products for Human Use (CHMP). Within the EU, the centralized procedure is compulsory for products derived from biotechnology and other high-technology processes, and for medicines intended for the treatment of HIV/AIDS, cancer, diabetes, neurodegenerative diseases, autoimmune and other immune dysfunctions, and viral diseases, as well as so-called 'orphan medicines' for the treatment of rare diseases. It is also possible, where the centralized procedure is not compulsory, for medicines to be licensed through the mutual recognition procedure, whereby one EU Member State's marketing authorization is recognised by other Member States.

The House of Commons Business, Energy and Industrial Strategy Committee explains what is likely to happen if the UK leaves the EU without having been able to negotiate continued membership of the EMA.

---

[75] Directive 92/27/EEC.   [76] Directive 92/28/EEC.   [77] Directive 75/319/EEC.

House of Commons Business, Energy and Industrial Strategy Committee[78]

32. Should the UK leave the EU without an agreement to continue as part of a regulatory system with the EMA or recognising its decisions, applications for marketing authorization for new medicines would need to be submitted both to the EU following one of the approval routes, and separately to the MHRA for authorisation for use in the UK. As a result, the MHRA, which currently benefits from the shared expertise and workloads of the distributed model of the EMA's approvals process, would require increased resources to manage a significantly higher workload ... On this basis, the MHRA could expect to see a reduction in the number of authorisations that it is capable of granting or would require additional funding, either through the existing health budget or new public funding.

Efforts to harmonize the regulation of medicines also exist outside the EU, and these will undoubtedly apply post-Brexit. Mutual recognition arrangements exist between the EU and Switzerland, Canada, Australia, and New Zealand, and are intended to facilitate trade by eliminating the need to undergo duplicate testing and scrutiny of new products. It is, however, necessary to go through more than one marketing authorization process, and this is where the additional costs post-Brexit will be unavoidable, unless it is possible to secure continued membership of the EMA.

The International Conference on Harmonisation (ICH), launched in 1990, attempts to harmonize regulatory requirements in the US, Europe, and Japan, so that a company can prepare the same data set in order to obtain approval worldwide.[79] The first ICH steering committee reaffirmed its:

commitment to increased international harmonisation, aimed at ensuring that good quality, safe and effective medicines are developed and registered in the most efficient and cost-effective manner. These activities are pursued in the interest of the consumer and public health, to prevent unnecessary duplication of clinical trials in humans and to minimise the use of animal testing without compromising the regulatory obligations of safety and effectiveness.

If international harmonization has the twin goals of speeding up the licensing of medicines and improving safety standards, it is important to recognize that these may be in tension with each other. John Abraham and Tim Reed's study suggests that industry interests often take priority.

John Abraham and Tim Reed[80]

[W]e conclude that, in the field of carcinogenicity testing, the ICH management of international harmonisation of medicines regulation is not achieving the simultaneous improvements in safety standards and acceleration of drug development ... Rather, our research supports the more sceptical view that the latter is being achieved *at the expense of* the former... Reductions in drug testing requirements and increased flexibility in interpretations

---

[78] *The impact of Brexit on the pharmaceutical sector* Ninth Report of Session 2017–19.
[79] See further www.ich.org.
[80] 'Reshaping the carcinogenic risk assessment of medicines: international harmonisation for drug safety, industry/regulator efficiency or both?' (2003) 57 Social Science & Medicine 195–204.

of what counts as evidence of carcinogenic risk make it easier for regulators to approve drugs—and approve them more quickly.

5 PRODUCT LIABILITY

No drug is 100 per cent safe; most will produce ADRs in some users. A patient who suffers an ADR will only have a remedy if she can establish that the medicine was unacceptably unsafe, such that it should not have been marketed at all; or that it was unsafe for her, and so either it should not have been prescribed to her, or it should have been marketed with an appropriate warning. In the following sections, we briefly consider the options open to a patient who wishes to seek compensation for a drug-related injury.

(a) CONTRACT

Contractual remedies are of limited relevance. When a drug is prescribed under an NHS prescription, there will be no contract with either the pharmacist or the doctor who wrote the prescription.[81] It is only when drugs are supplied privately, or when medicines are bought over the counter, that a contractual remedy for a defective medicine is possible.

If the consumer does have a contract, either with the pharmacist or with a doctor dispensing a private prescription, then the ordinary rules of contract law apply. If the product does not correspond with its description, or is not of satisfactory quality, there might be a breach of the Sale of Goods Act 1979.[82] Liability does not require proof of fault. It would be relatively straightforward to establish liability for what are known as manufacturing defects, such as the contamination of a particular batch of medicines. But since almost all drugs cause side effects, it will be difficult to establish that an adverse reaction to a medicine breaches the implied condition of satisfactory quality.

One complicated question raised by the application of contract law to the sale of medicines relates to section 14(2B) and 14(3) of the Sale of Goods Act, under which goods must be fit for the purpose for which they are commonly supplied, or if the buyer makes known the particular purpose for which they are being bought, that they are reasonably fit for that purpose. How much information about the consumer's condition must the pharmacist obtain in order to assess whether the medicine is fit for the purpose for which it is being bought? If a consumer has a contraindication, such as high blood pressure or diabetes, for taking an over-the-counter medicine, then arguably that medicine is not fit for the purpose for which she has bought it. Pharmacists who fail to inquire whether a medicine is fit for the purpose for which the particular consumer has purchased it might then find themselves strictly liable for any consequent injuries.

(b) NEGLIGENCE

The manufacturer of a medicine could be liable in negligence if the consumer can prove that she was owed a duty of care, and the manufacturer's breach of that duty caused her injury.

---

[81] *Pfizer Corporation v Minister of Health* [1965] 2 WLR 387.
[82] Sections 14(2) and 14(3), as amended.

Since *Donoghue v Stevenson*,[83] it is uncontroversial that manufacturers owe the ultimate consumers of their products a duty to take reasonable care to ensure that the product is safe.

In order to determine whether the manufacturer has breached its duty, it is necessary to work out what standard of care a pharmaceutical manufacturer owes to the consumers of its products. The duty is to exercise such care as is reasonable in all the circumstances. Factors relevant to this assessment include the magnitude of any risk; the probability of harm; the burden of taking precautions to prevent the risk materializing; and the utility of the defendant's conduct. Manufacturers are certainly not under a duty to ensure that every drug is completely safe for every consumer. All medicines present some risks: penicillin, for example, is generally considered safe and effective, even though it causes very serious allergic reactions in some people.

Three different types of product defect might be identified: manufacturing defects, design defects, and the failure to give adequate warnings. It will be relatively straightforward to prove that there has been a breach of duty when the patient's injury was caused by a manufacturing defect: an example might be where an error during the manufacturing process massively increased the quantity of the active ingredient in each pill. If a manufacturer does not take reasonable care to ensure that medicines leave its premises in a fit state for human ingestion, it is clearly in breach of its duty to consumers.

Design defects are more complicated. Plainly, manufacturers have a duty to design medicines safely, but what if the medicine turns out to have an unforeseen adverse side effect, as happened with thalidomide. The claimants would have to prove that the risk of injury was foreseeable, and that supplying the product in the light of this risk was unreasonable. Not only will it be difficult for claimants to gain access to the information necessary to prove this, but also clinical trials cannot be expected to discover every possible side effect in every possible consumer. The benefits of new medicines mean that it will generally be reasonable to put them into circulation once clinical trials indicate that they meet an acceptable level of safety.

Requiring manufacturers to identify all possible ADRs before a new drug is marketed would stifle innovation, delay access to medicines, and require vastly increased rates of participation in clinical trials. If the company that manufactured thalidomide could not reasonably have been expected to have found out that it would cause devastating birth defects, if taken at a particular time in pregnancy, it would not have been in breach of its duty of care.

Manufacturers might also be liable for defective warnings. No drug is completely safe for all users, and a manufacturer will generally have acted reasonably if it took steps to alert consumers to the risk of a side effect, or to contraindications for use. Prescription drugs are a rather special case in that it is not necessary for them to be made safe for everyone. Unlike products that can be bought over the counter, it should be possible to ensure that a drug is not prescribed to individuals in whom it would be unsafe. For example, if the information supplied to doctors categorically states that medicine X should never be taken by anyone with high blood pressure, the manufacturer would be able to avoid liability if someone with high blood pressure subsequently suffers injuries after being wrongly prescribed medicine X.

In the US, this is known as the 'learned intermediary' rule: that is, it is for the doctor to determine whether to prescribe a particular drug to her patient, and to give appropriate warnings. Patients generally rely upon their doctors' advice, and a manufacturer's package insert is unlikely to override a doctor's assurance that it is safe to take a prescribed medicine. Of course, doctors might make prescribing errors or fail to explain how to take the medicine

---

[83] [1932] AC 562.

safely. If a patient then wanted to sue her GP, this would be a straightforward clinical negligence action (see Chapter 3).

If the patient's claim is that a manufacturer's failure to warn her of possible side effects caused her injury, then, even if she succeeds in establishing that it breached its duty of care, she will come up against the vexed problem of proving causation in 'failure to warn' cases (considered in Chapter 4). In short, the problem is that she must prove that she would not have been injured if she had been properly informed and, in this context, this means that she must establish that she would not have taken the drug in question if she had been warned of the particular side effect.

Let us imagine that a patient was not warned about a 0.1 per cent risk of hair loss associated with taking an antidepressant. Even if she had been warned, she might have judged that the benefits of alleviating her depression outweighed this very small risk of losing her hair. But after this risk has materialized, and with the benefit of hindsight, she now knows for certain that she is the one of the unfortunate minority who will suffer hair loss. How reliable is her evidence that, if she had known about this tiny risk, she would have chosen not to take the drug?

Pharmacists also owe the consumers of medicines a duty of care. If a pharmacist negligently dispenses the wrong drug, or the wrong dosage, she could be liable for the resulting injury. In *Prendergast v Sam and Dee Ltd*,[84] a doctor had written a prescription for Mr Prendergast, an asthmatic suffering from a chest infection, which included Amoxil tablets. The pharmacist misread the doctor's unclear handwriting, and dispensed Daonil instead, a drug used in the treatment of diabetes. As a result of taking an excessive dose of Daonil, Mr Prendergast suffered permanent brain damage. He sued both the doctor and the pharmacist, and both were found to have been negligent. Despite the unclear handwriting, the pharmacist should have realized that it was extremely unlikely that the doctor had meant to write Daonil on the prescription. The prescription was for a short course of Amoxil, to be taken three times a day. Diabetics would usually be on continuous courses of Daonil, which is taken once a day. The dosage would also have been unusually high for Daonil. Since Mr Prendergast paid for his prescription, the pharmacist should have realized that he was not diabetic (people with diabetes do not pay the prescription charge). The Court of Appeal refused to overturn the judge's apportionment of liability: the pharmacist was liable to pay 75 per cent of Mr Prendergast's damages, and the doctor 25 per cent.

Might it also be possible for an injured patient to bring an action against the regulator for its failure to ensure that a drug was safe enough? Liability for breach of statutory duty is extremely unlikely, since it seems implausible that parliament intended to create a private law action for damages for breach of the Human Medicines Regulations, which were passed in order to protect public health, rather than to provide redress to individuals.

In a negligence action, it would be necessary for the claimant to establish that there was a relationship of proximity between the regulatory agency and the injured patient, and that it would be fair, just, and reasonable to impose a duty in these circumstances. This will be difficult to establish. In *Smith v Secretary of State for Health (on behalf of the Committee on Safety of Medicines)*,[85] Morland J found that neither the Secretary of State for Health, nor the CSM, owed a common law duty of care to a six-year-old girl, who suffered Reye's syndrome as a result of taking aspirin, just before they were due to publish a warning that aspirin should not be given to children under the age of 12, except on medical advice.

Even if a claimant were to succeed in establishing that a regulatory authority owed her a duty of care, proving that it had breached its duty would not be straightforward. If the CSM's

---

[84] The Times, 14 March 1989.   [85] [2002] EWHC 200 (QB).

duty is to act in accordance with a responsible body of medical opinion, given that it is composed of medical experts, proving that their collective judgement represented a breach of their duty of care would be exceptionally difficult.

(c) CONSUMER PROTECTION ACT 1987

In 1985, the EU adopted a Directive which was intended to harmonize European product liability regimes,[86] both in order to remove the distorting impact differing standards of legal liability within the EU were having upon competition, and to ensure that consumers throughout Europe enjoyed equal protection against dangerous products through the introduction of a strict liability regime. Rather than the costs of injuries falling on individual consumers, strict liability imposes them instead upon manufacturers, who are better able to absorb and spread the costs by purchasing insurance and raising prices, so the costs are ultimately borne by all consumers.

The Directive was given effect in the UK by the Consumer Protection Act 1987 (CPA). There are some differences in wording between the Directive and the CPA, but in *Commission v United Kingdom*,[87] the European Court of Justice (ECJ) found that there was no evidence that the UK courts were interpreting the Act in a way that was inconsistent with the Directive, though this may have been because there had been virtually no cases. In any case, section 1 of the CPA specifically states that the provisions in the relevant part of the Act were passed in order to comply with the Directive, and should be construed accordingly.

The Act imposes strict liability on manufacturers and, in certain circumstances, suppliers for defective products which cause physical injury, or property damage. Pure economic loss is not covered. Any claim must be brought within three years of the discovery of the damage or injury, with a longstop of ten years from when the product was first put into circulation. This ten-year time limit is intended to make it easier for manufacturers to insure against liability, because no claims are possible more than ten years after a product reaches the marketplace. Some adverse reactions take many years to manifest themselves, and if this happens more than ten years after the product was first marketed, the consumer's only option will be an action in negligence.

Because the Act only applies to products put into circulation after it came into force in 1988, it could have been anticipated that there would be relatively little litigation immediately after its introduction. The paucity of cases in the past decades has, however, been surprising—certainly the evidence does not bear out Lord Griffiths (writing extra-judicially) et al's prediction in 1988: 'We have little doubt that, once it is no longer necessary to prove negligence, there will be a significant increase in product liability litigation in England.'[88]

In fact, there have been hardly any reported cases involving medicines. *XYZ and Others v Schering Health Care Ltd* involved a group action by claimants who had taken different brands of the Combined Oral Contraceptive pill (COC), and who claimed to have suffered various cardio-vascular injuries (which come under the collective description of venous-thromboembolism (VTE)). The women argued that the pills they had taken were defective under the CPA and/or the Product Liability Directive. Their claims followed a 'pill scare' in 1995, when the CSM had written to doctors stating that three unpublished studies into the

---

[86] Products Liability 85/374/EEC.   [87] [1997] All ER (EC) 481.
[88] Lord Griffiths, Peter De Val, and RJ Dormer, 'Developments in English Product Liability Law: A Comparison with the American System' (1988) 62 Tulane Law Review 353–91.

safety of COCs had indicated 'around a twofold increase in the risk' of VTE. The defendants claimed that there is, in fact, no increased risk and that the CSM's warning was misjudged.

Both the defendants and the claimants agreed that the action under the CPA could proceed only if there was a twofold increase in the risk of VTE associated with oral contraceptive pills. After an extraordinarily lengthy analysis of the evidence, Mackay J concluded that:

> [T]here is not as a matter of probability any increased relative risk of VTE carried by any of the third generation oral contraceptives supplied to these Claimants by the Defendants as compared with second generation products containing Levonorgesterel.[89]

Because the claimants' case had failed on this preliminary issue, it was not necessary for Mackay J to consider the application of the CPA.

In a more recent medicines case, and another one involving a class action, *Multiple Claimants v Sanifo-Synthelabo*,[90] Andrew Smith J was asked to resolve a number of questions, including whether Epilim, an anti-epileptic drug, was defective within the meaning of the Act. The claimants in this case were children whose mothers had taken Epilim during pregnancy. Their claim was that Epilim is a known teratogen (ie that it damages the fetus *in utero*), but for some women it is the only effective treatment for epilepsy. This clearly places pregnant women with epilepsy in an impossible dilemma, but does it mean that the product is 'defective' under the CPA? Andrew Smith J declined to make preliminary findings on this point. Following a number of preliminary hearings and having already provided around £3 million in legal aid, the Legal Services Commission (LSC) withdrew any further funding 'at the door of the courtroom', and the case had to be dropped.

The problem for claimants is that, in the absence of legal aid, this sort of litigation is prohibitively expensive. Because the factual issues are complex, trials involving injuries caused by medicinal products are likely to be lengthy, and so the decision not to grant legal aid, or to withdraw it, will almost inevitably mean that the action cannot continue. This happened in relation to a class action against the manufacturer of the MMR vaccine after the LSC decided that there was insufficient chance of success to justify continued funding. Andrew Wakefield's claim, in 1998, that there was a link between the MMR vaccine and autism has subsequently been discredited, and his paper retracted, and so there would almost certainly be no chance of succeeding on the question of causation.

Legal aid was also refused, more surprisingly, to claimants who wished to sue Merck, the manufacturer of Vioxx, which was withdrawn after evidence emerged that it caused strokes and heart attacks. In the US, actions against Merck had been successful, and Merck had set aside $4.85 billion with which to settle further legal claims. After legal aid was refused in the UK, the UK victims attempted to bring actions in the US courts, but these were rejected on the grounds that US juries could not be expected to understand another country's system of drug regulation.[91] Following this decision, one of the lawyers responsible for bringing the claims, Martyn Day, commented: 'We are in a total quandary. I am totally stumped as to how we can get these cases into the courts anywhere ... [The Vioxx case was] the strongest drug-related case we've seen in the UK for a long time.'[92]

---

[89] *XYZ and Others v Schering Health Care Ltd* [2002] EWHC 1420 (QB).
[90] [2007] EWHC 1860 (QB).
[91] Clare Dyer and Sarah Boseley, 'US court ruling shuts door on drug claimants' compensation hopes', *The Guardian*, 7 October 2006.
[92] Ibid.

There is a connection between the challenges of regulating the pharmaceutical industry considered in the first half of this chapter and the inadequacies of the mechanisms for seeking compensation for drug-related injuries. In a country like the US, where litigation against drug companies is much more likely to be successful, the information gathered during court proceedings can be fed back to the regulator, and may prompt it to take action, such as insisting on a new warning. Where the chances of a successful claim against a drug company are almost non-existent, this 'feedback loop' is absent.

(1) Who Can be Liable?

Under section 2, a number of actors may be jointly and severally liable under the Act. This means that an injured consumer can choose to sue any of the various possible defendants, each of whom may be liable for the total loss. It would then be up to the losing defendant to recoup its losses from the other defendant(s). Those who can be strictly liable for defective products include producers, importers into the EU, and 'own-brand' suppliers (for example, Boots could be liable for defects in their own-brand cold remedies). Under section 2(3) suppliers will be liable if they are unable to identify the producer.

It is clear that a pharmacist is a supplier. Doctors might also be suppliers if they actually provided the medicine, as opposed to simply writing a prescription. To absolve themselves of responsibility, both supplying doctors and pharmacists should therefore keep detailed records of the manufacturers of the drugs which they supply for at least ten years.

(2) What is a Product?

Medicines and medical devices are unquestionably 'products', for the purposes of the Act. In *A v National Blood Authority*,[93] it was accepted by both parties that blood was a product under the Act. While calling them 'products' seems counter-intuitive, it is also possible that gametes (ie sperm and eggs) might be subject to the Act's provisions.

(3) What is a Defect?

In order to have a remedy, the consumer must establish that the product was 'defective'. The definition of defect under section 3 of the Act is, to say the least, rather confusing.

Consumer Protection Act 1987 section 3

3(1) Subject to the following provisions of this subsection, there is a defect in a product for the purposes of this Part if the safety of the product is not such as persons generally are entitled to expect; and for those purposes 'safety', in relation to a product, shall include safety with respect to products comprised in that product and safety in the context of risks of damage to property, as well as in the context of risks of death or personal injury.

(2) In determining for the purposes of subsection (1) above what persons generally are entitled to expect in relation to a product all the circumstances shall be taken into account, including—

(a) the manner in which, and purposes for which, the product has been marketed, its get-up, the use of any mark in relation to the product and any instructions for, or

[93] [2001] 3 All ER 289.

> warnings with respect to, doing or refraining from doing anything with or in relation to the product;
>
> (b) what might reasonably be expected to be done with or in relation to the product; and
>
> (c) the time when the product was supplied by its producer to another; and nothing in this section shall require a defect to be inferred from the fact alone that the safety of a product which is supplied after that time is greater than the safety of the product in question.

The Act does not distinguish between manufacturing, design, or failure to warn defects. It simply states that a product is defective if its safety is not such as persons generally are entitled to expect. This definition of defect will apply easily and straightforwardly to manufacturing defects, caused by a mistake in the production process.

Because manufacturers must have rigorous quality management systems in place, manufacturing defects in medicines are unusual, however. Instead, patients who have been injured by a medicine will generally want to allege either that its design was defective, or that they were inadequately warned about a particular risk, and in both cases, working out what level of safety 'persons generally' are entitled to expect is more difficult. Indeed, Jane Stapleton has argued that a consumer expectation test is inherently unhelpful: 'The core theoretical problem with the definition, however, is that it is circular. This is because what a person is entitled to expect is the very question a definition of defect should be answering.'[94]

In relation to new or complex products, such as medicines, consumers may have no clear expectations about the level of safety they are entitled to expect. Of course, it could be argued that consumers never actually expect to be injured by a medicine, so that any drug which causes injury is defective. The test is an objective one, however; it is what consumers are entitled to expect, and people are not entitled to expect that medicines will never cause unwanted side effects. On the contrary, it is to be expected that medicines which are powerful enough to alter physiological function will sometimes cause adverse reactions.

Section 3(2) sets out a number of factors which are relevant to what consumers generally are entitled to expect, such as, under section 3(2)(a), any warnings provided with the product. Of course, the existence of a warning does not rule out a finding that a product is defective. If it did, then given the relatively low cost of warnings, manufacturers would simply warn of every conceivable risk in order to avoid liability. This would be undesirable, however, because the danger signal imparted by warnings is diluted if they are ubiquitous and over-inclusive. Moreover, it should not be possible for manufacturers of manifestly unsafe products, which could have been made safer, to avoid liability by warning of the risk. Rather, warnings should only absolve a manufacturer of liability if avoiding the risk altogether was not feasible.

Also relevant under section 3(2)(b) is what might reasonably be expected to be done with the product. Plainly, this means that injuries caused by taking an overdose are not covered by the Act. A more difficult question is the extent to which it is reasonable to expect consumers to take medicines exactly according to the manufacturer's instructions. Because it is common for patients to make mistakes,[95] and it can reasonably be expected that a patient might take two pills instead of one, or leave too short a time between doses, a medicine should be safe enough even if there is a minor deviation from the product's instructions.

---

[94] *Product Liability* (Butterworths: London, 1994) 234.

[95] Richard Sykes, *New Medicines, The Practice of Medicine, and Public Policy* (Nuffield Trust: London, 2000).

Section 3(2)(c) specifies that a product is not to be considered defective simply because a better product is subsequently put into circulation. A product's defectiveness must be judged according to prevailing safety standards at the time when it was supplied, rather than at the time when the claim is brought.

A different sort of approach to the question of whether a product is defective would be to adopt a straightforward risk/benefit calculation: are the risks which the product presents justified by its benefits? So, for example, aspirin and penicillin cause adverse side effects in a minority of users, but given their overwhelming benefits for other patients, persons generally are not entitled to expect that aspirin or penicillin can safely be taken by everyone.

In contrast, thalidomide might have alleviated morning sickness, but the risks of premature death and severe disability are far too grave to justify its use in relieving nausea in early pregnancy, and adopting a risk/benefit approach, it is clearly a defective product. Interestingly, there has been some interest in using thalidomide in the treatment of leprosy, and to slow the growth of brain tumours. Gravely ill patients, suffering from advanced brain cancer, are very unlikely to object to the condition that they do not become pregnant while taking thalidomide, and hence for them the benefits may outweigh its risks.

A risk/benefit safety assessment would also enable us to take account of the availability of alternative products. Let us imagine that a new contraceptive pill will cause a very undesirable side effect, such as blindness, in 0.01 per cent of consumers. Not only might we want to weigh the risk of blindness against the benefit of effective contraceptive protection, but it would also be relevant that other contraceptive pills exist which do not have this undesirable side effect. If, however, a drug with this risk profile was capable of curing people with stage 4 liver cancer, a 0.01 per cent risk of blindness might be judged acceptable.

So how has the consumer expectation test worked in practice? Before Burton J's judgment in *A v National Blood Authority*, in a handful of cases the courts appeared to suggest that what consumers were entitled to expect depended upon the reasonableness of the defendant's conduct. In practice, this looked very like an assessment of whether the defendant had been negligent.

In *Richardson v LRC*,[96] for example, a condom had failed inexplicably. Ian Kennedy J held that although users did not expect condoms to fail, persons generally were not entitled to expect any contraceptive to be 100 per cent effective. He reached this conclusion after extensive discussion of the reasonableness of the testing procedures adopted by the defendants. But if what the defendant could have done differently is relevant to what consumers generally are entitled to expect, 'strict liability' may be indistinguishable from negligence.[97]

This trend towards a negligence-based interpretation of 'defectiveness' was interrupted by the decision of Burton J in *A v National Blood Authority*. The claimants had become infected with Hepatitis C from blood transfusions at a time when it was known that there was a strain of Hepatitis known only as non-A non-B Hepatitis, with which a small percentage of blood was infected. While the risk was known, reliable tests to identify this new strain of Hepatitis had not yet been devised. In deciding whether the infected blood was defective, Burton J asked himself what consumers were entitled to expect, and explicitly declined to take into account whether the defendants had acted reasonably.

---

[96] [2000] PIQR P164.
[97] See also *Worsley v Tambrands* [2000] PIQR P95 and *Foster v Biosil* (2000) 59 BMLR 178.

A v National Blood Authority[98]

Burton J

It is quite plain to me that the directive was intended to eliminate proof of fault or negligence. I am satisfied that this was not simply a legal consequence, but that it was also intended to make it easier for claimants to prove their case, such that not only would a consumer not have to prove that the producer did not take reasonable steps, or all reasonable steps, to comply with his duty of care, but also that the producer did not take all legitimately expectable steps either ...

I conclude therefore that avoidability is not one of the circumstances to be taken into account ... I am satisfied that it is not a relevant circumstance, because it is outwith the purpose of the directive, and indeed that, had it been intended that it would be included as a derogation from, or at any rate a palliation of, its purpose, then it would certainly have been mentioned; for it would have been an important circumstance.

Consumers were therefore entitled to expect blood products to be 100 per cent safe, even if this is an unreasonable and impractical expectation Also irrelevant was the practicability of taking precautionary measures, and the utility of the product.

In the next extract, Richard Goldberg argues that adopting a risk/benefit approach to the question of whether a product is defective would have made more sense in *A v National Blood Authority*, because it would have allowed the utility of blood to be weighed against the unavoidable risk of infection.

Richard Goldberg[99]

It is arguable that all medicinal products carry a risk of adverse reactions, even in a minority of consumers, and that these consumers are not necessarily entitled to expect that the products will be risk free. Despite the emphasis on consumer expectation in Burton J's judgment, there is an inherent logic in addressing the problems of defective medicinal products by weighing the risks against the anticipated benefits and against the 'costs' of not using the product, such as the risk of disease.

More recently, in two cases involving patients injured by prosthetic hip replacements, Hickinbottom J and Andrews J have cast doubt on whether Burton J was right to say that avoidability and a risk/benefit calculation were irrelevant to what consumers are entitled to expect.

In the first case, *Wilkes v DePuy International Ltd*,[100] the claimant's artificial hip joint had been manufactured by the defendant. It contained a fine groove in the neck of one of its components, which fractured after three years. The claimant argued that the groove was a design defect, because it caused an excessive concentration of stress at its neck. Hickinbottom J held that the hip was not defective, and both a risk/benefit calculation and avoidability were relevant to this conclusion.

---

[98] [2001] 3 All ER 289.
[99] 'Paying for Bad Blood: Strict Product Liability after the Hepatitis C Litigation' (2002) 10 Medical Law Review 165–200, 174.
[100] [2016] EWHC 3096 (QB).

Wilkes v DePuy International Ltd [101]

Hickinbottom J

[S]afety is inherently and necessarily a relative concept. Certainly, as I have indicated, no medicinal product, if effective, can be absolutely safe ...

Given that such a product will inevitably have some risks attached, ... any assessment of its safety will necessarily require the risks involved in use of that product to be balanced against its potential benefits including its potential utility. As such a product will almost always involve design compromises, the effect of eliminating or reducing a particular risk can only be seen in the context of any adverse consequences of doing so, in the form of increased risks of a different sort or reduced benefit and utility. Consequently, the practicability of producing a product of risk-benefit equivalence must therefore potentially be a relevant circumstance in the assessment of a product's safety. It is inherent in the relative nature of 'safety' ...

[I]n my view, in an appropriate case ..., the ease and extent to which a risk can be eliminated or mitigated may be a circumstance that bears upon the issue of the level of safety that the public generally is entitled to expect.

Two years later, in a group action case against the same prosthetic hip manufacturer, Andrews J held that a different hip was not defective within the terms of the Act. In *Gee v Depuy International Limited*, 312 claimants claimed to have suffered an adverse reaction to metal wear debris from their replacement hips. Because all artificial hips shed metal debris through ordinary wear and tear, once again Andrews J held that this was not a defect.

Gee v Depuy International Limited [102]

Andrews J

All hip prostheses will eventually wear out and fail, if the patient survives long enough, and some will fail within 10 years: the natural propensity of a hip implant to fail therefore cannot be a 'defect', any more than the inevitable wear and tear that causes minute particles of debris to enter the patient's body. Otherwise all hip implants would be 'defective' ...

If Burton J's analysis had gone no further than stating that avoidability and benefit were irrelevant considerations in assessing whether the blood products with which he was concerned met the requisite standard of safety, it would have been unobjectionable. The problems with *A v NBA* lie in the passages that appear to lay down rigid rules of more general application pertaining to the circumstances that fall to be legally excluded from consideration when evaluating safety (at least in a non- standard product) because they are somehow deemed to undermine, or run counter to, the no-fault basis of liability ...

I respectfully beg to differ. Dictating that certain circumstances can *never* be considered relevant in law or taken into consideration (however relevant they may be in fact), undermines the flexibility of the Act and the Directive, which caters for the fact that the suitable approach for one product may be inapposite for another.

---

[101] [2016] EWHC 3096 (QB).   [102] [2018] EWHC 1208 (QB).

(4) Causation

Even if a claimant does succeed in establishing that a product is defective, the problem of establishing causation remains. The 'but for' test applies, which means that the claimant must prove that 'but for' the defendant's negligence, she would not have suffered her injuries.

There are several reasons why causation causes particular difficulties in product liability cases. People who take medicines are generally ill, which means that their symptoms might be caused by their underlying condition, rather than by a reaction to a medicine. Many adverse drug reactions are indistinguishable from conditions that occur spontaneously, and so it may be difficult to prove that the patient's symptoms were caused by a particular medicine.

In addition, patients will often take many different medicines, either simultaneously or over a period of time. Pinpointing which drug was responsible for the adverse reaction is therefore difficult, and exacerbated by the fact that the reaction might have been triggered by a combination of drugs. If each taken singly would be safe, could any manufacturer be said to be responsible for a reaction caused by several drugs' interaction with each other?

In the next extract, Pamela Ferguson discusses some of the practical difficulties which claimants face in trying to prove causation.

Pamela Ferguson[103]

Studies have shown that many people who are neither ill nor taking any medication perceive that they are suffering from 'symptoms'. Had such people been receiving drug therapy, they might have attributed their symptoms to the treatment.

A person who is injured by a car which has faulty brakes or by an exploding kettle is at least aware that the car or the kettle was 'involved' in causing the injury ... This is in contrast to the position with pharmaceutical drugs which may leave little or no trace once consumed ... [W]hile some people do suffer from immediate allergic reactions to drugs, in the majority of cases ... , the injuries which are alleged to have been caused by these drugs took several months, or in some cases years, to become manifest.

Even if it is clear that the patient's injuries were caused by taking a particular drug, a further problem is that it might be difficult to prove which manufacturer produced the drug in question. Once a drug can be produced generically, many different manufacturers will be producing an identical product, and by the time the patient's injury materializes, it may be impossible to establish which company manufactured the drug that was taken by this patient. Additionally, patients may have taken the same drug, manufactured by a number of different companies, for several years, in which case it will be virtually impossible to identify which manufacturer's medicine actually caused the patient's injury.

In the US, the courts have adopted a variety of strategies in order to assist claimants who cannot identify the correct defendant. Probably the most well-known is 'market share liability',[104] described in the next extract.

---

[103] *Drug Injuries and the Pursuit of Compensation* (Sweet & Maxwell: London, 1996).
[104] See further *Sindell v Abbott Laboratories* 607 P 2d 924 (1980).

Pamela Ferguson[105]

> The market share theory requires a plaintiff to demonstrate that the defendants were responsible for a substantial share of the drug market. Each defendant must then show that it did not produce the particular drug which was responsible for the plaintiff's injury … Each manufacturer which fails to demonstrate this is liable to pay a percentage of the compensation awarded to the plaintiff, and this percentage is dependent on the share of the market for which the company was responsible at the relevant time (that is, at the time when the plaintiff's injury or loss occurred). A defendant may bring other producers of the drug into the action as co-defendants.

In essence, market share liability means that the defendants are held liable for creating a risk of harm. In *Fairchild v Glenhaven Funeral Services*,[106] in which the House of Lords adopted a flexible approach to the causation of mesothelioma (because the claimants had been exposed to asbestos in several different workplaces), Lord Hoffmann distinguished the market share approach adopted in *Sindell*:

> The case bears some resemblance to the present but the problem is not the same. For one thing, the existence of the additional manufacturers did not materially increase the risk of injury. The risk from consuming a drug bought in one shop is not increased by the fact that it can also be bought in another shop.

Nevertheless, he described the market share approach adopted in *Sindell* as 'imaginative', and suggested that such cases should 'be left for consideration when they arise'.

Although holding defendants liable in the absence of proof that their product actually caused the claimant's injuries might initially appear to be a measure which protects consumers' interests, it is important to remember that pharmaceutical companies would have to insure against the possibility of market share liability. Inevitably, premiums would rise and the costs of medicines would increase.

(5) Defences

If an injured consumer is able to establish that the product was defective and that it caused her injury, the manufacturer might nevertheless be able to take advantage of one of the defences in section 4 of the Consumer Protection Act. First, it is a defence if the defect is attributable to compliance with a statutory obligation. This does not amount to a 'regulatory compliance' defence, which would offer a defence simply because the defective product had obtained a marketing authorization; rather, it offers a defence only if the defect itself could be attributed to compliance with a regulatory requirement.

But while regulatory compliance is not a defence, in *Wilkes v DePuy International Ltd*, Hickinbottom J suggested that the rigour of the regulatory process may make it difficult for a claimant to establish that the product was defective.

---

[105] *Drug Injuries and the Pursuit of Compensation* (Sweet & Maxwell: London, 1996) 140–1.
[106] [2002] UKHL 22.

Wilkes v DePuy International Ltd [107]

Hickinbottom J

Certainly, where every aspect of the product's design, manufacture and marketing has been the subject of the substantial scrutiny, by a regulatory body comprised of individuals selected for their experience and expertise in the product including its safety, on the basis of full information, and that body has assessed that the level of safety is acceptable, then it may be challenging for a claimant to prove that the level of safety that persons generally are entitled to expect is at a higher level . . .

Of course, the simple fact of regulatory approval is not an automatic defence under the Act – nor even a prima facie defence, as in the United States. However, in my view, such approval may be evidence (and, in an appropriate case, powerful evidence) that the level of safety of the product was that which persons generally were entitled to expect.

Secondly, a defence exists if the defendant can prove that the product was never supplied to another, or was not supplied in the course of a business.

Thirdly, there is a defence if the defect was not present when the product was supplied. This was the case in *Piper v JRI Ltd*. The claimant, Terence Piper, had undergone a hip replacement operation, which involved the insertion of a prosthetic hip, manufactured by the defendant company. Eighteen months later, the hip fractured. Mr Piper had to undergo a further operation, and was left with significantly impaired movement and mobility. He brought an action against the defendants, claiming that the hip had been defective within the meaning of section 3 of the Act.

By the time of the trial, expert examination had established that the prosthesis fractured as a result of a defect in the titanium alloy from which it was made. The question then was whether the defect was present when the hip was supplied to the hospital, in which case the defendant would be liable, or whether it occurred subsequently, perhaps during implantation, in which case the defendant could avoid liability.

At first instance, the judge found that the defendant had subjected this product to a 'vigorous and meticulous process of work and inspection of the highest quality'. As a result, it would have spotted the defect, if it had existed before it left the factory, and the judge was 'not prepared to accept that such a mistake was made with the product.' The Court of Appeal dismissed Mr Piper's appeal.

Piper v JRI Ltd [108]

Thomas LJ

As the system was capable of detecting the only type of surface point defect capable of initiating the fatigue failure, given the view taken of those operating the system, it could be inferred that any such defect would have been detected had it been present prior to delivery to the hospital and that in the case of the prosthesis implanted into the claimant that the inspection system had not failed.

---

[107] [2016] EWHC 3096 (QB).   [108] [2006] EWCA Civ 1344.

> It seems to me that on an analysis of the evidence before the judge and on the way the case was presented to him, the judge was therefore correct in making the finding of fact made by him that the prosthesis was not defective at the time it was supplied to the hospital.

In essence, the Court of Appeal rejected the claimant's case because he had been unable to prove that the manufacturer had made a mistake. This appears to re-introduce a negligence-type enquiry—did the manufacturer take reasonable care?—into the question of whether the product was defective when it left its premises.

Fourthly, contributory negligence applies, and so a patient who takes the wrong dose of a drug which subsequently causes injury may be responsible in whole or in part for her injuries. The application of contributory negligence to a strict liability regime is rather complicated. If damages are apportioned according to the parties' degree of fault, how might this work when the defendant was not necessarily at fault at all? In practice, the application of contributory negligence just means that the claimant's damages will be reduced according to the extent to which their injury was caused by their own blameworthy conduct.

The most important and controversial defence is known as the development risks defence and is contained in section 4(1)(e).

Consumer Protection Act 1987 section 4

> 4(1)(e) [I]t shall be a defence ... that the state of scientific and technical knowledge at the relevant time was not such that a producer of products of the same description as the product in question might be expected to have discovered the defect if it had existed in his products while they were under his control.

This defence was included because it was feared that liability for undiscoverable defects would impede innovation. In particular, it was thought that strict liability for undiscoverable risks would make it impossible to obtain liability insurance.

In relation to design defects and failures to warn, a manufacturer might try to avoid liability by claiming that the risk in question was not discoverable when the product was put into circulation. The question of discoverability is, as Charles Pugh and Marcus Pilgerstorfer point out, of critical importance.

Charles Pugh and Marcus Pilgerstorfer[109]

> There is an additional limit on what knowledge is relevant for the purposes of Article 7(e). Knowledge must be accessible in what has become known as the 'Manchurian' sense. [In *Commission v United Kingdom*] the ECJ held that it was 'implicit in the wording of article 7(e) that the relevant scientific and technical knowledge must have been accessible at the time when the product in question was put into circulation'. The much debated example given by the Advocate General is of an academic in Manchuria publishing in a local scientific journal in

---

[109] 'The Development Risk Defence: Knowledge, Discoverability and Creative Leaps' (2004) 4 Journal of Personal Injury Law 258–69.

Chinese which does not go outside the boundaries of the region. In such cases the defence will remain available notwithstanding that the total world body of scientific and technical knowledge might have enabled the defect to be discovered. The relevant body of knowledge on which to focus is 'accessible knowledge' ...

Once the relevant knowledge has been ascertained, the next stage in the Court's enquiry into the availability of the Article 7(e) defence is to consider the discoverability of the defect. The presence of this second criterion puts it beyond doubt that it is insufficient for the producer to show simply that the defect was not 'known' at the time the product was put into circulation. A producer must go further and show that the relevant knowledge was not such as to 'enable the existence of the defect to be discovered'.

The development risks defence has been controversial. Jane Stapleton has questioned why we should treat unforeseeable design errors more leniently than equally blameless manufacturing errors:

We still have no principled explanation of why, for example, it is fair to hold a manufacturer strictly liable for some product flaws he could not discover (for example, some manufacturing errors), but not fair to do so in relation to a different set of product flaws he could not discover (namely, unforeseeable design dangers).[110]

Christopher Newdick further explains that unforeseen risks are precisely the sort of defects that are most likely to occur in medicines. If manufacturers have a defence for such risks, the impact of strict liability on the pharmaceutical industry will be minimal.

Christopher Newdick[111]

It will be recalled that it was the tragedy of thalidomide that gave rise to the debate concerning strict liability in this country. Ironically, however, it is the future victims of an accident of precisely this form that would most seriously be prejudiced by a state of the art defence. The pharmaceutical industry in this country has not generally been accused of irresponsible or unreasonable behaviour. By its very nature it works in an area in which unforeseeable accidents are inevitable, where fault is usually absent and known risks frequently judged acceptable as regards the few, in the interests of the many. In addition, their actions have the approval of an official licensing body. These factors would effectively be sufficient to guarantee that, unless a special exception were made to such a defence, the pharmaceutical industry would be its principal beneficiary.

The development risks defence does have its supporters, however. Christopher Hodges, for example, points out that the defence's positive impact upon innovative practices is, in the long run, likely to serve the interests of patients as well as manufacturers.

---

[110] 'Bugs in Anglo-American Products Liability' (2002) 53 South Carolina Law Review 1225.
[111] 'Strict Liability for Defective Drugs in the Pharmaceutical Industry' (1985) 101 Law Quarterly Review 405–31.

Christopher Hodges[112]

It is the essence of innovation that the risks which may be encountered in the use of a product cannot reasonably be identified or quantified at the time at which it is marketed—either fully or, in some cases, at all. Of course, one approach might be to require producers to test products fully before marketing them. But that would be unrealistic. First, testing usually includes testing in use by real humans in real life situations ... there must be a limit to the duration and cost of such an exercise. With medicines, the limit is effectively prescribed by regulation, taking into account ethical constraints on repetitive or excessive testing. If testing were required to continue until all possible risks which might occur with use of a product had now been identified, few producers could afford to innovate and consumers would not benefit from advances in science and technology. Research would stagnate if denied practical application and commercial advantage ...

The basic problem with the defence is that a literal concept of *undiscoverability* is an unworkable test. The truth is that *any* defect can be discovered prior to marketing given sufficient testing. Such testing simply requires time and money ... The issue, however, is how much testing it is reasonable to expect the producer of an innovative product to undertake pre-marketing.

Until Burton J's judgment in *A v National Blood Authority*, most people had assumed that the development risks defence meant that liability under the Act would in practice be indistinguishable from negligence, in that manufacturers which had acted reasonably in attempting to discover possible risks would be able to avoid liability for defective products. In *A v National Blood Authority*, the defendants knew about the risk of infection from non-A non-B Hepatitis, but they did not yet know how to detect it in individual bags of blood. The only way in which it would have been possible to ensure that no recipients of blood transfusions became infected with what became known as the Hepatitis C virus would have been to stop carrying out blood transfusions altogether, which would have breached the National Blood Authority's obligation to supply blood.

Nevertheless, in *A v National Blood Authority*, Burton J held that once the manufacturer knew of the existence of a defect, it was a known risk and the development risks defence could not apply, even if there was no way of avoiding the risk in question.

A v National Blood Authority[113]

Burton J

[T]he risk ceases to be a development risk and becomes a known risk not if and when the producer in question ... had the requisite knowledge, but if and when such knowledge were accessible anywhere in the world outside Manchuria. Hence it protects the producer in respect of the unknown ...

In the light of my construction of art 7(e), and the conclusion that the risk of Hepatitis C infection was known, the art 7(e) defence does not arise.

---

[112] 'Development Risks: Unanswered Questions' (1998) 61 Modern Law Review 560–70.
[113] [2001] 3 All ER 289.

Geraint Howells and Mark Mildred point out that Burton J:

> certainly did not fit the stereotype of a judge intoxicated by a negligence-based world view. Rather, he displayed a reformist zeal to show that he appreciated that the Directive was intended to make a break with the past and introduce a new form of civil liability.[114]

In the next extract, Jane Stapleton argues that this 'reformist zeal' was misplaced.

Jane Stapleton[115]

> In short, the court in the Hepatitis C case was determined to give the Directive 'work to do' in the United Kingdom; that is to give it a wider ambit of entitlement than existed elsewhere in the English law of obligations. It was eager to avoid a construction that would 'not only be toothless but pointless'. The trial judge seems to have thought this required an adoption of the construction urged by the claimants. In my view, this was mistaken ... In my view, the 'reformist zeal' of the trial judge in the Hepatitis C case simply preferred the heroic rhetoric of the claimants' cause.

A v National Blood Authority is a difficult case. On the one hand, it is hard not to feel sympathy for the claimants, who had already had the misfortune to be in need of blood transfusions, from which they were then unlucky enough to contract a potentially life-threatening illness. On the other hand, the National Blood Authority is unlike a manufacturer of a defective product, and so an Act which was designed to apply to manufacturers which have deliberately chosen to put defective products into circulation may apply somewhat awkwardly to this sort of public body.

First, the manufacturer of a medicine is not under a legal duty to supply that medicine. If the manufacturer has any doubts about a product's safety, on the contrary, its duty would be to ensure that it is not put into circulation. The National Blood Authority, in contrast, is under a duty to supply blood. It was not open to it to stop all blood transfusions in the UK.

Secondly, as we saw earlier, a principal purpose of the CPA was to facilitate loss spreading. Rather than the loss falling on the unlucky victim, it would be transferred to the manufacturer, and the assumption was that the manufacturer would be able to spread the loss among all consumers by raising the price of its products. This is not an option for the National Blood Authority, which does not charge recipients for blood and so cannot spread its losses in the same way as a drug manufacturer.

Even if, on balance, it is thought fair for the National Blood Authority to bear the costs of the claimants' injuries, it is perhaps ironic that, in the field of medical law, the first successful action under the CPA was not against the deep pockets of the pharmaceutical industry, but rather against a part of the financially overstretched NHS.

---

[114] 'Infected Blood: Defect and Discoverability. A First Exposition of the EC Product Liability Directive' (2002) 65 Modern Law Review 95–106.
[115] 'Bugs in Anglo-American Products Liability' (2002) 53 South Carolina Law Review 1225.

(6) Vaccine Damage

A special compensation scheme exists for patients who are disabled as a result of population-wide vaccination programmes. Vaccines are different from ordinary medicines in that the intention is not just to benefit the individual child who is immunized, but also to contribute towards the public health goal of eliminating certain diseases through population-wide immunization. Peter Cane explains the problem.

Peter Cane[116]

> [V]accination is a classic case of the 'free-rider' problem much discussed by economists. The benefit to each individual child of being vaccinated may not be very great in view of the fact that most other children are likely to be vaccinated, and that the risk of infection has been thus greatly reduced; yet if the parents of all children reasoned in this way, vaccination would decline and the diseases in question would spread more widely again, with greater risk to all. Further, the main beneficiary from vaccination is often not the vaccinated child but other younger children with whom he or she comes into contact: whooping cough is most dangerous for very young babies, prior to the normal age for vaccination; by the time a child is vaccinated it is normally past the age at which the disease could prove fatal. There is thus a case for arguing that young children who are vaccinated before they are old enough to understand the issues are being used for the benefit of others.

Because vaccination involves the injection of small quantities of active, infectious agents in order to trigger the body's immune response, the existence of rare but serious adverse reactions is unsurprising. There is evidence of a causal link between some vaccinations and adverse reactions, but not others. Most notably, there is no evidence of any link between the MMR vaccine and autism.

It would be difficult for an individual who suffers an adverse reaction following routine vaccination to establish negligence on the part of either the health care professional who performed the vaccination or the vaccine's manufacturer. Since responsible medical opinion strongly supports all of the recommended vaccinations, it will be impossible to establish that vaccinating a child was negligent, unless the child has some special characteristics which make vaccination unwise. Similar difficulties would be present in an action against the vaccine's manufacturer, given that it is impossible to ensure that vaccines will never cause adverse effects.

Yet if vaccination programmes pose a small risk of injury, which is outweighed by the enormous public health benefits of universal immunization, it would seem fair to offer some compensation to those individuals whose health is compromised for the greater good.

In the next extract, Gareth Millward explains that the government in the 1970s accepted the need for a no-fault compensation scheme in order to address a specific imminent public health emergency from declining vaccination rates.

---

[116] *Atiyah's Accidents, Compensation and the Law*, 6th edn (Butterworths: London, 1999) 89–90.

Gareth Millward[117]

A series of coinciding factors forced the government into action in the summer of 1977. The entire vaccination programme was in crisis. Vaccination rates for whooping cough had declined 59 per cent between 1971 and 1975 …

The Cabinet resolved to accept the general principle of compensation for victims of vaccine damage in order to restore faith in the vaccination programme … The belief was that by accepting the compensation principle, it would allay the fears of parents by showing that if something went wrong the state would protect them. It was also seen as a sign of strength and confidence. The government was explicitly stating that it was sure that there were so few cases that it was willing to compensate parents even if they could not definitively prove that vaccines were the sole cause of their child's disability …

The provisions contained within the Act were relatively cheap, a welcome relief in the economic circumstances. Initial estimates predicted only around 300 to 500 initial claims, followed by 14 to 70 claims per year thereafter … The Act, and pronouncements leading to it, were part of a specific political response to a particular public threat

As amended, the Vaccine Damage Payments Act 1979 continues to apply today. Under section 1, a person who has been severely disabled as a result of vaccination against a number of specified diseases, including diphtheria, tetanus, whooping cough, poliomyelitis, measles, rubella, tuberculosis, mumps, Haemophilus type b infection (hib), and meningitis C, is entitled to a sum of £120,000.

Applicants must have been vaccinated in the UK since 1948. Under section 3(1), claims must usually be made before the claimant's 21st birthday (this was increased from a six-year time limit in 2000), unless the vaccine is one given to adults, such as those for pandemic flu and meningitis C. 'Severe disability' is defined in section 1(4) as 60 per cent disablement (this was reduced in 2000 from 80 per cent). And under section 3(5), the causal link between the vaccine and the disability has to be proved, on the balance of probabilities.

The scheme is funded from the welfare budget, and claims are made initially to the Department for Work and Pensions. If the claim is rejected, under section 4 the claimant can appeal to an independent tribunal. There is no further appeal to a court, although the Secretary of State is empowered to reverse the tribunal's decision.[118] Successful claims are rare. From 2007–2017, there were 759 claims under the scheme, but only 11 awards were made.[119]

Although the disability threshold was reduced in 2000, it could plausibly be argued that setting any threshold level of disablement is unfair. Leaving aside the question of whether it is, in fact, possible to evaluate the extent of a child's disablement with this sort of precision, why should a child who suffers 59 per cent disablement receive nothing, while a child with 60 per cent disablement might be entitled to £120,000? A sliding scale that compensated a child according to the extent of her disabilities might be fairer.

Moreover, the sum of £120,000, while undoubtedly substantial, will not necessarily be sufficient to meet all of the child's needs throughout her life, especially if the vaccine caused severe brain damage. It is certainly much less than an award in tort, where full compensatory damages are the norm, and brain-damaged children can receive many millions of pounds.

---

[117] 'A Disability Act? The Vaccine Damage Payments Act 1979 and the British Government's Response to the Pertussis Vaccine Scare' (2017) 30 Social History of Medicine 429–447.

[118] SI 1999/2677.

[119] Freedom of Information Request to the Department of Health (<https://www.whatdotheyknow.com/request/statistics_vaccine_damage_paymen>).

Unsurprisingly, given the existence of a no-fault compensation scheme, there has been hardly any litigation involving vaccines in the UK. Laura Smillie et al draw attention to a rather alarming European Court of Justice (ECJ) case in which a man claimed that the Hepatitis B vaccine had caused his multiple sclerosis (MS). What is worrying about this case is that anecdotal reports of a link appeared to be given as much weight as scientific evidence that there is no link.

Laura R Smillie, Mark R Eccleston-Turner, and Sarah L Cooper[120]

The court stated that 'medical research neither confirms nor rules out a link between' the administration of the Hepatitis B vaccine and the on-set of MS ... The court's language suggests it views the research as being equally weighted about whether there is a link between the Hepatitis B vaccine and the onset of MS ...

The studies which demonstrate no link between the administration of a Hepatitis B vaccine and the onset of MS have several thousand study participants. By contrast, the claim that the administration of the vaccine did cause Mr W's MS is informed largely by a temporal correlation between administration and onset of the disease in the case study of Mr W, as well as 'significant number of reported cases of the disease occurring following such vaccines being administered'.

In the case study of Mr W, as well as the 'significant number of reported cases', the individual sample size for each of these studies is likely to be one. It is improper to reach a conclusion regarding the causal link between the administration of a drug and an adverse event occurring on the basis of such small sample sizes ...

Our final point is that the CJEU's overall approach in C-621/15 generally feeds the growing vaccine scepticism in the developed world, particularly in France.

6 CONCLUSION

In this chapter, one of the recurring themes has been the existence of a tension between the pharmaceutical industry's drive to increase shareholder value, and the needs of patients and the NHS. Regulating the pharmaceutical industry is difficult, not least because a series of take-overs means that there are now a handful of hugely profitable companies supplying medicines within a global market. These companies wield considerable economic and political power, and time-limited patent protection means that they are under continual pressure to bring new and profitable medicines to the marketplace. The consequences of this pressure are, as we have seen, not necessarily always in the best interests of patients.

The regulation of medicines, once they are ready to be marketed, cannot be viewed in isolation from the rules that govern the stages before medicines can be licensed for general use. It is worth noting that when we considered the regulation of clinical trials in Chapter 10, it was also apparent that European law has played an increasingly dominant role. This is interesting, because in many of the other areas of medical law that we consider in this book, European law has been of comparatively little importance. In relation to issues

---

[120] 'C-621/15 - *W And Others v Sanofi Pasteur*: An Example of Judicial Distortion and Indifference to Science' (2017) 26 Medical Law Review 134–45.

such as abortion, euthanasia, organ transplantation, and stem cell research, for example, there are significant differences between the laws in different European countries. The European Convention on Human Rights has Europe-wide application, but Member States often have a wide margin of appreciation in its interpretation.

When regulating the pharmaceutical industry and access to medicines, however, there has been almost complete European harmonization. Why is this? One obvious answer is that it involves the regulation of a market, rather than sensitive ethical issues. Protecting consumers and promoting economic growth are familiar aims for European regulation, whereas balancing the rights and wrongs of complex ethical dilemmas has usually been left to individual nation states.

As a result of European harmonization of medicines regulations, it is very clearly in the UK's best interests to continue to align its regulations with those of the EU after Brexit, and, if possible, to maintain some sort of associate membership of the EMA. The House of Commons Health and Social Care Select Committee and the Business, Energy and Industrial Strategy Committee have set out the reasons why this is desirable. The Government clearly agrees, but whether this will be achievable is another matter.

House of Commons Health and Social Care Committee[121]

The overriding message from almost all of the evidence received in this inquiry is that the UK should continue to align with the EU regulatory regimes for medicines, medical devices and substances of human origin both during any transition period and afterwards. Evidence submitted from large pharmaceutical companies, SMEs, academics, healthcare and workforce charities was all almost unanimous in the view that regulatory alignment with the EU would be the best post-Brexit option for the NHS, for patients, and for the UK life sciences industry.

If the UK diverges from the EU regimes in a manner that adds to the cost and timeliness of existing supply chains, then the UK will become a less attractive market for businesses. In this scenario, patients in the UK would not only experience delays in access to new treatments, but could also stand to wait longer to access generic drugs coming off patent ...

As a third country, the UK could align with the EU through either a regulatory cooperation agreement or a mutual recognition agreement. However, according to the Medical Research Council, Switzerland gains access to new medicines 157 days later on average than the EU, despite bilateral trade agreements. Similarly, Canada and Australia have mutual recognition agreements with the EMA, but wait on average 6–12 months longer than the EU or US for new drugs to come to market ...

The UK must look to secure, as a priority in the next round of negotiations, the closest possible regulatory alignment with the EU. The continued supply of safe and effective medical devices, medicines and substances of human origin currently on the UK market will depend on continued alignment with European regulations ...

We welcome the Government's announcement that it will seek associate membership of the European Medicines Agency (EMA). We call on negotiators from both sides to put the needs of patients first and foremost as negotiations on this matter progress. However, the EU's draft negotiating position appears to suggest that continued UK EMA membership may be rejected. We therefore recommend that the Government publish any contingency planning it has undertaken for a situation in which associate membership of the EMA is not achieved ...

Evidence presented to us made the point that failure to gain access to EU pharmacovigilance systems would have serious consequences for UK medicine and drug safety. It would not

---

[121] *Brexit: Medicines, Medical Devices and Substances of Human Origin*, Fourth Report of Session 2017–19.

be possible, let alone desirable, to draw up a UK standalone system by the time the UK exits the UK.

House of Commons Business, Energy and Industrial Strategy Committee[122]

As a highly-regulated industry, the prospect of regulatory divergence from the European Medicines Agency is the deepest concern for the industry. Any divergence could lead the need for the duplication of facilities and roles across the UK and EU to enable access to products, costing companies tens of millions to establish and millions each year to run. Some large companies have already begun to implement contingency plans to ensure continued access to the market, but much of the sector has not …

35. If the UK leaves the EMA at the same time it leaves the EU, there is a significant risk that we will become a less attractive destination for innovative medicines, and cannot expect to be an early recipient of new medicines through our approvals process. At an estimated extra cost of £45,000 for marketing authorisation for each new medicine, the UK's comparatively small market compared to the EU risks us losing out entirely on access to new specialised medicines …

44. Pharmaceutical trade bodies have been clear in their support for a continued relationship with the EMA, which delivers a regulatory cooperation agreement between the UK and EU, continued alignment of current and future regulations; and continued UK participation in EU regulatory processes and supervision of medicines, including the sharing of data… We believe that the Government should work towards the closest possible arrangement, up to and including some form of membership of the EMA …

The best potential approach we found for the UK to grow as a world leader in the development, manufacture and regulation of pharmaceuticals is to maintain as close a relationship with the EU as possible.

HM Government[123]

We are committed to working together on medicines regulation, given its crucial and mutually beneficial role in improving patient outcomes, driving innovation in new medicines and supporting growth. We know the exact relationship with the EU may not be the same but are open to finding innovative solutions as we move forward.

We want to retain a close working partnership with the EU to ensure patients continue to have timely access to safe medicines and medical innovations, and, as part of that, are committed to continuing a close working relationship with the EMA …

The UK wants to explore with the EU the terms on which we could remain part of EU agencies, including the EMA. The Government recognises the importance of a close and cooperative relationship between the UK and EU in the field of medicines, medical devices and substances of human origin regulation.

---

[122] *The impact of Brexit on the pharmaceutical sector* Ninth Report of Session 2017–19.
[123] *Brexit: medicines, medical devices and substances of human origin: Government response to the Health and Social Care Committee's Fourth Report of Session 2017–19* (2018).

FURTHER READING

Chańska, Weronika and Grunt-Mejer, Katarzyna, 'The unethical use of ethical rhetoric: the case of flibanserin and pharmacologisation of female sexual desire' (2016) 42 Journal of Medical Ethics 701–4.

House of Commons Business, Energy and Industrial Strategy Committee, *The impact of Brexit on the pharmaceutical sector* Ninth Report of Session 2017–19.

Jackson, Emily, *Law and the Regulation of Medicines* (Hart Publishing: Oxford, 2012).

Millward, Gareth, 'A Disability Act? The Vaccine Damage Payments Act 1979 and the British Government's Response to the Pertussis Vaccine Scare' (2017) 30 Social History of Medicine 429–47.

Naci, Huseyin, Carter, Alexander W, and Mossialos, Elias, 'Why the drug development pipeline is not delivering better medicines' (2015) 351 British Medical Journal h5542.

Shahvisi, Arianne, 'No Understanding, No Consent: The Case Against Alternative Medicine' (2016) 30 Bioethics 69–76.

von Tigerstrom, Barbara, 'The patient's voice: Patient involvement in medical product regulation' (2016) 16 Medical Law International 27–57.

12

ORGAN TRANSPLANTATION

CENTRAL ISSUES

1. Organ transplantation is a successful and cost-effective treatment for organ failure. Not everyone who could benefit from a transplant is able to do so, however, because there is a shortage of organs.

2. Under the Human Tissue Act 2004, consent to cadaveric donation is necessary, either from the deceased person, her nominee, or from the highest-ranking qualified relative. A system of 'deemed consent' has been in place in Wales since 2015, and a similar system will be introduced in England by 2020. More extreme legal reforms might include offering financial or non-financial incentives to donation, or treating the organs of the dead as a public resource.

3. Most transplantation involves solid organs, like kidneys and lungs. Other types of transplant—for example, of hands, faces, and wombs—are more unusual, and they will not be included in the new 'deemed consent' system.

4. Regulation of living organ donation is directed towards ensuring that the donor has given informed consent, and that she has not been paid.

5. Xenotransplantation (animal-to-human transplantation) raises ethical and practical issues. Currently, the most compelling objection to xenotransplantation is the unknown, and possibly unknowable risk of cross-species infection.

1 INTRODUCTION

For two reasons, initial attempts to transplant an organ from one person's body into another were unsuccessful. First, before it became possible to suppress the recipient's immune system, foreign tissue would automatically be rejected. Secondly, because organs deteriorate rapidly as soon as a person's cardiorespiratory system stops working, it was also difficult to ensure that organs taken from cadavers 'survived' the transplant process.

The first successful organ transplant was a live kidney transplant, between identical twins, which took place in Boston in 1954. Six years later, a similar operation was performed successfully in the UK. Since the 1960s, techniques for maintaining the quality of organs before and during transplantation have improved, and immunosuppressant therapy can minimize the problem of rejection.

The prognosis for transplant patients is now extremely good. After one year, 84 per cent of heart transplants, 94 per cent of liver transplants, 98 per cent of living donor kidney transplants, and 95 per cent of cadaveric kidney transplants will still be functioning well (after five years, the percentages are 68, 84, 92, and 87 respectively).[1] Of course, transplant surgery sometimes fails, and there are risks—an increase in the lifetime risk of developing certain cancers, for example—associated with taking immunosuppressant drugs. But transplantation is usually the optimum treatment for organ failure. Heart and liver transplants are life-saving. Kidney failure is not necessarily fatal, but a transplant will enable someone who would otherwise be dependent upon dialysis to lead a relatively normal life.

A successful transplant may also save the NHS money. Kidney transplantation is much cheaper than providing dialysis to a patient with renal failure. In 2011, the National Institute for Health and Care Excellence estimated that a 25 per cent increase in the number of kidney donors would save the NHS £9.2 million per year.[2]

In short, transplantation surgery is a successful and often cost-effective medical procedure. The chief difficulty, as is well known, is that there are insufficient organs to meet demand. NHS Blood and Transplant issues detailed statistics on transplant activity in the UK each year.[3]

Year	Cadaveric donors	Cadaveric transplants	Waiting list	Living donors
2013/14	780 DBD[4] 540 DCD	4,655	7,026	1,146
2017/18	955 DBD 619 DCD	4,473	6,044	1,051

The organ shortage is exacerbated by improvements in transplant technology which expand the pool of potential recipients to include older patients, and those who might previously have been judged too ill to undergo such a major operation.

Given average waiting times of well over a year, it is not surprising that mortality rates on the organ donor waiting list are high: in 2017–18, 411 patients on the transplant waiting list died, while a further 755 were removed from the list because they had become too sick to receive a transplant. This understates the scale of the problem, however, because many potential recipients are never put on the waiting list because their doctors recognize that it is unlikely that they would become eligible for a transplant in time.

The most important issue raised by organ transplantation is therefore how to increase the number of available organs. There is, it seems, widespread public support for organ transplantation. Opinion polls consistently indicate that 70–90 per cent of the population would want their organs to be used to save others in the event of their death, while only 36 per cent of the population is registered on the organ donor register. The paradox of this situation is pointed out by Sheila McLean:

[1] NHS Blood and Transplant, *Annual Activity Report 2017–18: Survival Rates Following Transplantation* (NHSBT, 2018).

[2] *Organ Donation for Transplantation Costing Report: Implementing NICE Guidance* (NICE, 2011).

[3] NHS Blood and Transplant, *Annual Activity Report 2017–17: Summary of Transplant Activity* (NHSBT, 2018).

[4] DBD is donation after brain death, and DCD is donation after cardiac death; what this means is discussed in more detail below.

> We have the doctors ready, willing and able to undertake the surgery, we have people dying with usable organs and we apparently have a compliant public. Why then is the programme so strapped?[5]

Some people believe that organ donation is incompatible with their religious beliefs, but scholars from all the major religions have endorsed transplantation, on the grounds that the imperatives of healing and saving life trump other considerations, such as a proscription of the mutilation of corpses. A 1995 Fatwa, for example, stated that giving and receiving organs is compatible with Islam.[6]

It is, however, important to recognize that approval of organ transplantation is not necessarily the same thing as endorsing a brain stem definition of death (see further below). So the statement that organ donation is compatible with Judaism and Islam may miss the point that some Jewish and Islamic scholars are not convinced that the soul leaves the body when the brain stem is dead,[7] but rather that that happens only after the heart stops beating. This does not rule out donation, but it does suggest that donation following cardiorespiratory diagnosis of death (as opposed to brain death) may be more acceptable for some religious groups.

In the UK, relatives from minority ethnic groups are more likely to refuse to agree to transplantation. In 2017–18, for potential donors after brain-stem death, the consent rates were 78.2 per cent for white donors and 43.8 per cent for donors from minority ethnic groups (for donors after cardiac death, the rates were 62.3 and 37.5 per cent, respectively). In addition, renal failure is more common in non-white populations, in part as a result of increased rates of type 2 diabetes.

Given a greater need for organs, and fewer tissue-matched donors, the organ shortage has a disproportionate impact upon minority ethnic groups. Thirty-five per cent of the people on the kidney waiting list people are from Black, Asian, and minority ethnic (BAME) groups, while only 7 per cent of donors are from these groups. The median time on the waiting list for a white patient is 723 days; while for Asian and Black patients, it is 891 and 985 days, meaning these patients are more likely to die before a suitable organ becomes available.

The law relating to organ donation is contained in the Human Tissue Act 2004, which came into force in 2006. The Act's remit is much broader than transplantation—it covers research, post-mortems, anatomy, and public display. It was not passed in order to improve the law relating to organ transplantation. The catalyst for reform was instead the retained organs scandals at Bristol Royal Infirmary and Alder Hey Children's Hospital, and as a result, the Act's central organizing principle is the need for specific consent to the storage and use of tissue and organs.

The Human Tissue Authority (HTA), set up by the 2004 Act, issues licences for the storage and use of tissues. Most organs that are used in transplantation cannot be stored for any length of time, and so licensing is only relevant to the transplantation of tissue, such as bone marrow, which is routinely banked for future use. Because our focus in this chapter is on solid organ donation, of more importance are the HTA Codes of Practices covering consent, solid organ donation and the Human Transplantation (Wales) Act.

---

[5] 'Transplantation and the "Nearly Dead"; The Case of Elective Ventilation' in Sheila McLean (ed), *Contemporary Issues in Law, Medicine and Ethics* (Dartmouth: Aldershot, 1996) 143–61.

[6] See further Clare Hayward and Anna Madill, 'The meaning of organ donation: Muslims of Pakistani origin and white English nationals living in north England' (2003) 57 Social Science and Medicine 389–401; Mohammed Ghaly, 'Religio-ethical discussions on organ donation among Muslims in Europe: an example of transnational Islamic bioethics' (2012) 15 Medicine, Health Care and Philosophy 207–20.

[7] Ahmet Bedir and Şahin Aksoy, 'Brain death revisited: it is not "complete death" according to Islamic sources' (2011) 37 Journal of Medical Ethics 290–4.

In Wales, the Human Tissue Act 2004 was amended by the Human Transplantation (Wales) Act 2013. An 'opt-out' system for donation came into force in Wales in 2015, and the government has recently announced that a similar system will be in place in England by 2020. At the time of writing, the Organ Donation (Deemed Consent) Bill is before parliament, and it appears to have almost unanimous cross-party support. Scotland is also planning to move towards an opt-out system.[8]

In this chapter, we begin with cadaveric donation, looking first at who may become a donor, and which organs can be taken. The system of organ retrieval in the UK is then summarized, and we look at the consent-based model adopted in the Human Tissue Act 2004, and the move to an opt-out system. We also consider other ways in which the number of cadaveric organs might be increased.

Next we look at living organ donation. We consider the legitimacy of performing such a serious operation in order to benefit a third party. We look at the restrictions placed on living organ donation in the Human Tissue Act, and the controversial question of whether it would be acceptable to pay people to 'donate' their organs. Finally, we consider the ethical, practical, and legal obstacles to animal-to-human transplantation.

2 DEAD DONORS

(a) THE 'DEAD DONOR' RULE AND BRAIN DEATH

Cadaveric organ transplantation depends upon dead donors whose organs are still capable of functioning in live recipients. This means (a) that organs can be removed only after someone has died, and (b) that they must be taken immediately after the diagnosis of death. Accurately pinpointing the moment of death is therefore vitally important. The problem is that death is a process: a person's organs do not all stop functioning at the same moment, rather they fail progressively once the brain has irreversibly died. Brain death itself involves two distinct changes. One is the permanent loss of consciousness (caused by death of the upper brain), and the other is the loss of the brain's ability to regulate other bodily functions, such as breathing (caused by death of the lower brain).

Centuries ago, a body could not conclusively be considered dead until putrefaction had begun. In the nineteenth century, death started to be diagnosed after a person had stopped breathing and their heart had stopped beating. During the twentieth century, it became possible sometimes to resuscitate a person whose heart had stopped. If someone can be resuscitated successfully, then she was not dead, despite her temporary loss of heart function.

The invention of the artificial ventilator made it necessary to decide whether a diagnosis of death could be made while a person's heart was being maintained artificially. Continuing to ventilate a person who has been diagnosed as brain dead enables doctors to remove their organs while their heart function is being maintained artificially. It is, of course, essential that these 'heart beating donors' must have been satisfactorily diagnosed as dead before their organs are taken: in Hans Jonas's words, 'the patient must be absolutely sure that his doctor does not become his executioner'.[9]

---

[8] Scottish Government, *Opt out organ donation: a rapid evidence review* (Scottish Government, 2018).

[9] *Philosophical Essays: From Ancient Creed to Technological Man* (Prentice Hall: Englewood Cliffs, NJ, 1974) 131.

Brain death was formally defined in 1968 by an Ad Hoc Committee of the Harvard Medical School.[10] The concept of brain death has now been adopted by most countries, including, since 2010, Japan. As a result of cultural attitudes towards death and traditional Japanese death rituals, opposition to the concept of brain death had been particularly strong in Japan, and indeed the Japanese surgeon who performed the first heart transplant in 1968 was charged with murder. Even now, in Japan the dead person's family is entitled to refuse to accept brain death, in addition to being able to veto organ donation.

In the UK there is no statutory definition of death. Rather, the diagnosis of death is regarded as a matter of clinical judgement. Since the late 1970s, brain-stem death, or the irreversible loss of brain-stem function, has been treated as the definitive criterion for diagnosing death, defined by a Code of Practice issued by the Academy of Medical Royal Colleges.

Academy of Medical Royal Colleges[11]

Death entails the irreversible loss of those essential characteristics which are necessary to the existence of a living human person and, thus, the definition of death should be regarded as the irreversible loss of the capacity for consciousness, combined with irreversible loss of the capacity to breathe. This may be secondary to a wide range of underlying problems in the body, for example, cardiac arrest.

The irreversible cessation of brain-stem function whether induced by intracranial events or the result of extracranial phenomena, such as hypoxia, will produce this clinical state and therefore irreversible cessation of the integrative function of the brain-stem equates with the death of the individual and allows the medical practitioner to diagnose death . . .

[T]here are some ways in which parts of the body may continue to show signs of biological activity after a diagnosis of irreversible cessation of brain-stem function; these have no moral relevance to the declaration of death for the purpose of the immediate withdrawal of all forms of supportive therapy.

The diagnosis of brain-stem death must be made by at least two senior registered medical practitioners, and to avoid conflict of interests, neither of these should be a member of the transplant team.[12] Although death is pronounced following two sets of brain-stem tests, the legal time of death is when the first test indicated brain-stem death.[13]

Because organ transplantation depends so heavily upon public goodwill, it is important that the public accepts that brain-stem death is not an especially 'early' diagnosis of death. In 1980, a *Panorama* TV programme questioned the validity of brain-death criteria, leading to an immediate and sharp reduction in the number of organs becoming available for transplant. It took 15 months for organ donation rates to recover.

It has been difficult for the public to accept that a person whose heart is still beating, and who appears to be breathing, albeit with mechanical assistance, is really dead. A warm, breathing body certainly does not look dead, and relatives often find it difficult to contemplate organ retrieval before the cessation of heart and lung function. Seema Shah et al found that it was not

---

[10] Ad Hoc Committee of the Harvard Medical School to examine the definition of death, 'A Definition of Irreversible Coma' (1968) 205 Journal of the American Medical Association 85–8.

[11] Academy of Medical Royal Colleges, *A Code of Practice for the Diagnosis and Confirmation of Death* (AoMRC, 2008).

[12] Ibid, para 3.3.   [13] Ibid. See also *Re A* [1992] 3 Med LR 303.

uncommon for people to believe that, following a diagnosis of brain death, doctors would, in fact, wait until the person's heart stopped beating before removing their organs.[14]

In the next extract, Robert Truog points to a further possible reason for confusion. If brain-dead 'patients' are anaesthetized before organ retrieval, does this imply that we are not sure whether they are really dead?

Robert D Truog[15]

Most interesting is a debate that has occurred in the European anesthesia literature regarding the question of whether brain dead patients should receive an anesthetic during organ procurement. Some argue that the brain death criterion is insufficient to be absolutely sure that patients are incapable of experiencing pain, even if only at a rudimentary level, and so should receive 'the benefit of the doubt' and be given an anesthetic. Others respond, not by defending the criterion itself, but by arguing that administration of anesthesia to these patients will send a message to society that we are uncertain whether brain death is truly a state of permanent unconsciousness. As such, they argue, administration of an anesthetic to these patients will undermine the trust of the public and jeopardize the organ transplantation enterprise.

Peter Singer argues that the concept of brain death is a 'convenient fiction', which has nevertheless proved to be relatively uncontroversial.

Peter Singer[16]

Human beings are not the only living things in the world. All living things eventually die, and we can generally tell when they are alive and when they are dead. Isn't the distinction between life and death so basic that what counts as dead for a human being also counts as dead for a dog, a parrot, a prawn, an oyster, an oak, or a cabbage? . . . 'Brain death' is only for humans. Isn't it odd that for a human being to die requires a different concept of death from that which we apply to other living beings? . . .

When warm, breathing, pulsating human beings are declared to be dead, they lose their basic human rights. They are not given life support. If their relatives consent . . . , their hearts and other organs can be cut out of their bodies and given to strangers. The change in our conception of death that excluded these human beings from the moral community was one of the first in a series of dramatic changes in our view of life and death. Yet, in sharp contrast to other changes in this area, it met with virtually no opposition? How did this happen? . . .

In summary, the redefinition of death in terms of brain death went through so smoothly because it did not harm the brain-dead patients and it benefited everyone else: the families of brain-dead patients, the hospitals, the transplant surgeons, people needing transplants, people who worried that they might one day need a transplant, people who feared that they might one day be kept on a respirator after their brain had died, taxpayers and the government.

[14] Seema K Shah, Kenneth Kasper, and Franklin G Miller, 'A narrative review of the empirical evidence on public attitudes on brain death and vital organ transplantation: the need for better data to inform policy' (2015) 41 Journal of Medical Ethics 291–6.
[15] 'Brain death—too flawed to endure, too ingrained to abandon' (2007) Journal of Law, Medicine and Ethics 273–81.
[16] *Rethinking Life and Death: The Collapse of our Traditional Ethics* (OUP: Oxford, 1994).

Indeed, Robert Truog has predicted that if xenotransplantation were perfected, and the need for cadaveric donors disappeared, 'the raison d'être of brain death will disappear'.[17] If we no longer need to obtain human organs, 'the concept [of brain death] and the philosophical debate that has surrounded it, will become historical footnotes'.[18]

Michael Nair-Collins makes the controversial claim that discussions of the nature of death have been hindered by the need to treat organ transplantation as 'nearly sacrosanct'.

Michael Nair-Collins[19]

Academic inquiry into the nature of death, or positions on the ethics of killing and vital organ procurement, must accommodate the inviolate practice of organ transplantation—but not the other way around. For example, James DuBois writes that scholarly articles which challenge prevailing medical and legal criteria for death should be published only if they are accompanied by an editorial rejoinder, so as not to disturb organ donation rates. James Bernat argues that those who challenge 'brain death' must provide alternative policies that will maintain the public's confidence in the organ transplantation enterprise ...

It is high time that we took a more nuanced gaze at organ transplantation, and not assume that all other concerns must yield before its practical requirements ...

[T]he organ transplantation enterprise impacts only a small proportion of the population, yet at great financial cost; the goods it has to offer are not allocated justly; and the outcomes vary for those individuals who do receive transplants ... This is not to say we should eliminate organ transplantation; it does indeed save or improve many people's lives. But it is not deserving of the vaunted status it has been granted either. We should not accept the assumption that the practical requirements of organ procurement set the boundaries of reasonable views in the dialogue on death and the dead donor rule.

It has also been suggested that new medical techniques, which might enable brain-stem function to be maintained artificially, cast doubt upon the continued validity of brain-stem death. Ian Kerridge et al point out that people who have been diagnosed as brain dead can have some bodily functions maintained artificially for increasingly long periods of time. If brain-dead patients can 'survive' on a ventilator for several months, are they really dead?

Ian H Kerridge et al[20]

When the concept of brain death was first introduced it was argued that death of the brain stem inevitably implied the imminent death of the whole body . . . This argument is no longer tenable as medical therapy and intensive care have become increasingly sophisticated at replacing brain stem function, and we now know that bodies with a dead brain stem may be kept alive for prolonged periods of time. Brain dead pregnant women have been maintained

---

[17] 'Brain death—too flawed to endure, too ingrained to abandon' (2007) Journal of Law, Medicine and Ethics 273–81.

[18] Ibid.

[19] 'An unquestioned assumption in the debate on the dead donor rule' (2018) 44 Journal of Medical Ethics 872–3.

[20] 'Death, dying and donation: organ transplantation and the diagnosis of death' (2002) 28 Journal of Medical Ethics 89–94.

for months and later given birth to healthy infants and brain dead children have been reported to survive for up to 14 years with ventilatory and nutritional support . . .

Suggestions that the brain stem is the supreme regulator of the body seem both biologically and philosophically simplistic . . . Furthermore the heart, the liver, the kidneys, and other organs are all required to maintain bodily integrity, and loss of the functions of any of these organs will result in eventual disintegration of the organism without artificial support. Many individuals who are clearly alive depend upon technology such as pacemakers, dialysis machines or even ventilators to live. Whether there is a 'supreme regulator' therefore seems open to question. This argument may also be confused by the fact that the functions of the kidneys, heart, and lungs can be replaced by technological means, whereas that of the brain stem cannot. This is, however, very dependent upon technology; indeed aspects of brain stem function can now be replaced and it seems likely that more progress might be made in this area.

Perhaps it should be admitted that it is impossible to define the moment of death with complete certainty and precision, and that the important task therefore is to determine at what point *in the process of dying* organ retrieval becomes legitimate. The rule that organs may only be taken once a person is dead, fosters public trust in the transplantation system. It is, however, at least arguable that the certainty implied by this 'dead donor' rule misrepresents the ambiguity of death.[21]

Robert Truog has argued that the dead donor rule (DDR) is a distraction from what makes organ procurement ethical, namely that 'unequivocally dying' patients are free from suffering and that their wishes are respected.

Robert Truog[22]

In sum, the DDR is built upon the illusion that there can be a bright line drawn between the dying process and organ procurement. This illusion has led to the myth that organ procurement is unethical if it does not comply with the DDR. In reality, organ procurement is ethical if it assures that the patient is free of unwanted pain and suffering and if it respects the patient's altruistic wishes by procuring organs in ways that maximise the value of the donor's gift. This approach is ethical and would dramatically increase the number of lives that could be saved by organ transplantation. It is time we recognised the DDR for what it is, an impediment to good ethics for donors and recipients alike.

Julian Savulescu suggests that we should straightforwardly admit that it is legitimate to retrieve organs from the 'imminently dying', with their consent.

Julian Savulescu[23]

Since I believe we die when our meaningful mental life ceases, organs should be available from that point, which may significantly predate brain death. At the very least, people should

---

[21] Elyssa R Koppelman, 'The dead donor rule and the concept of death: severing the ties that bind them' (2003) 3 American Journal of Bioethics 1–9.

[22] 'The price of our illusions and myths about the dead donor rule' (2016) 42 Journal of Medical Ethics 318–19.

[23] 'Death, us and our bodies: personal reflections' (2003) 29 Journal of Medical Ethics 127–30.

be allowed to complete advance directives that direct that their organs be removed when their brain is severely damaged or they are permanently unconscious.

In the next extract, M Potts and DW Evans criticize these sorts of argument on the grounds that taking organs from living patients, even if they have given consent and are close to death, would involve doctors killing their patients.

M Potts and DW Evans[24]

One difficulty with this is that once utilitarian considerations are used to justify killing ventilator/dependent patients who are dying, those same considerations could also be used to justify killing non-ventilator/dependent patients or patients who are not dying . . . Currently, the statement on organ donor cards asserts that organs may be taken 'after my death'. We believe that such wording should be changed to reflect the fact that 'brain dead' individuals are not dead in the usual understanding of what death is. Explanatory literature accompanying organ donor cards should be frank that a 'brain dead' donor's heart is beating during part of the organ removal surgery.

In an attempt to sidestep debates over whether brain-stem death is really death, Torbjörn Tännsjö suggests that the search for one definition of death is futile. The circulatory and respiratory criteria make sense in some circumstances: we would only bury or cremate someone after their heart has stopped beating. In contrast, the brain-stem criterion makes practical sense in relation to organ donation.

Torbjörn Tännsjö[25]

We can now define death of a person as the point at which the person in question ceases to exist. This happens when there is too little psychological continuity and connectedness left over. If there is no consciousness at all, then there is no person at all. And we can define the death of the body as the point at which the body ceases to function as a unified organism. This means that bodies, in contradistinction to persons, often continue to exist after their death . . .

But could it not be objected that to have a beating heart is to be a person? I do not think that this is a plausible move. First of all, it could simply be rejected on linguistic grounds. Most of us would not call someone without a working brain, someone whose brain had irreversibly ceased to exist, a 'person'.

Secondly, and more importantly, even if some would do so, they would still have to admit that something of importance was gone once someone's brain had ceased to exist.

Patients in a permanent vegetative state, or anencephalic infants (see below), have permanently lost the capacity for consciousness: that is, their upper brain is dead, but their lower brain

[24] 'Does it matter that organ donors are not dead? Ethical and policy implications' (2005) 31 Journal of Medical Ethics 406–9.
[25] 'Two concepts of death reconciled' (1999) 2 Medicine, Health Care and Philosophy 41–6.

continues to function. Because a person can be categorized as brain dead only after the whole brain has stopped functioning, such patients are undoubtedly still alive. There are, however, those who would argue that the current definition of death is too restrictive, and that categories of patients whom we now treat as alive—such as patients in a permanent vegetative state, or anencephalic infants—should instead be regarded as potential organ donors.

Anencephalic babies are born without a cerebral cortex. Most will be stillborn, and those that are born alive will die shortly after birth. Anencephalic babies will never achieve consciousness, but they do have a functioning brain stem. Because there is no chance that an anencephalic baby will recover, it will not be in her best interests to be connected to an artificial ventilator. If ventilation is started in order to ensure that she can become an organ donor, does this involve using the baby as a means to an end? There may be some emotional value to her parents from the knowledge that their baby was able to save another child's life, but again, the benefit is to a third party, and not to the anencephalic infant herself.

The solution advocated by John Robertson is to suggest that when the capacity for sentience is irrevocably absent, an anencephalic baby or a patient in an irreversible coma cannot be harmed by organ retrieval.

John Robertson[26]

A major reason for the requirement that the organ donor be dead is to protect the donor from being harmed by organ removal. If the donor is dead, taking his organs will not harm him. In contrast, if he or she is alive, it is assumed that removing organs will kill or otherwise injure the donor.

This view of the dead donor rule, however, assumes that the live donor has interests in continued living and in not being physically injured. Whereas this assumption is true in most instances and thus should be strictly followed, it may not apply to situations of irreversible coma, near-dead pediatric patients and anencephalics . . . Such patients, though legally still alive, may no longer have interests in living or in avoiding physical harm that should be respected.

Treating the destruction or absence of the cerebral cortex as evidence of death would increase the pool of potential organ donors, but not everyone would agree that this is a good reason to redefine death. William May, for example, warns of the dangers of the slippery slope (see further Chapter 1).

William F May[27]

To invoke the need for organs as a reason for declaring a specific class of people dead creates a runaway, imperial argument, difficult to limit. Under the press of one kind of exigency or another, one could redefine death to include anencephalics, and then perhaps the next time, hydrocephalics, microcephalics, and so on, denying any independent and firm boundaries to mark off the dead from the dying or the vegetative . . .

---

[26] 'Relaxing the Death Standard for Organ Donation in Pediatric Situations' in Deborah Mathieu (ed), *Organ Substitution Technology: Ethical, Legal and Public Policy Issues* (Westview Press: Boulder, CO, 1988) 69–76.
[27] *The Patient's Ordeal* (Indiana UP: Bloomington, IN, 1991).

An opportunistic redefinition of death would eventually produce other unfortunate results. It would lead patients to distrust doctors and hospitals, and would weaken the readiness of families to donate the organs of truly dead patients. Convenience and utility should not justify enlarging the kingdom of the dead. While, historically the need for organs and the development of the technology for perfusing and successfully transplanting them supplied the *occasion* for reflection on the criteria for determining death, the need for healthy organs should not influence the standards for determining that a patient or a class of patient is dead. That decision should rest solely on the patient's condition.

(b) CIRCULATORY DEATH

Until relatively recently, deceased donors were almost exclusively people who had been diagnosed as brain dead, while their heart-lung function was being artificially maintained on a mechanical ventilator. Now, however, there are two sorts of deceased donation: donation after brain death (DBD) and donation after circulatory death (DCD). DBD donors are those for whom death has been confirmed using neurological criteria. Most DCD donors were patients in whom imminent death was anticipated, and treatment was withdrawn. This is known as 'controlled DCD'. 'Uncontrolled DCD' would involve donation after sudden and unexpected death, and, according to NHS Blood and Transplant, 'although a number of transplant units have in the past supported uncontrolled DCD organ retrieval from nearby Emergency Departments, these programmes are currently inactive'.[28]

DCD donors are used most frequently for kidney transplantation; in 2017–18, 39 per cent of all deceased donor kidney transplants were DCD donors. Lung, liver, and pancreas donation is also possible, and in the future, it may possible to retrieve hearts as well. As Anne Laure Dalle Ave et al explain, for obvious reasons, heart transplantation from DCD donors is especially controversial: how could a diagnosis of death based upon cessation of heart function be accurate if the heart is able subsequently to function normally in someone else?

Anne Laure Dalle Ave, David Shaw, and James L Bernat[29]

[A] deceased organ donor who has been previously determined dead by irreversible cessation of heart function cannot donate her/his heart for transplantation because the heart will have lost any possibility of functional restoration, and thus cannot be used for successful transplantation. If heart transplantation were to succeed in such a case, the donor 'cannot have been previously declared dead'. The criterion of irreversible cessation of heart function is thus incompatible with heart DCDD programmes.

James Bernat notes an interesting difference between families' and doctors' concerns about the definition of death in DBD and DCD donors. Families are more likely to worry that DBD donors are not really dead, while being untroubled about the diagnosis of death in someone whose heart has stopped beating. Conversely, doctors may be concerned that someone whose

---

[28] See further NHS Blood and Transplant, Organ Donation and Transplantation website <https://www.odt.nhs.uk/>
[29] 'An analysis of heart donation after circulatory determination of death' (2016) 42 Journal of Medical Ethics 312–17.

heart has stopped beating could be resuscitated, while being confident in the diagnosis of brain-stem death.

James L Bernat[30]

Family members of DCDD donors usually consider the patient to be dead immediately once breathing and heartbeat cease. Physicians, by contrast, do not consider the donor dead at that moment because they worry that breathing or heartbeat might restart spontaneously within a few minutes and that if cardiopulmonary resuscitation (CPR), extracorporeal membrane oxygenation (ECMO), or other resuscitative technologies were employed, they might be able to restore circulation, even though these interventions will not be initiated because of a DNR [Do Not Resuscitate] order. They therefore mandate a 5-minute 'hands off' period after circulation and respiration cease before declaring death . . . I have observed the opposite pattern of attitudes in organ donation after brain determination of death (DBDD). Physicians generally accept brain death as equivalent to human death but families often question its validity because they are unfamiliar with the concept of brain death, they erroneously equate brain death with coma, which they know may be reversible, or they intuit that the patient does not appear dead. The discordance of family versus physician attitudes toward death determination between DCDD and DBDD usually follows this recurring theme: Physicians seem more concerned about DCDD while family members seem more concerned about DBDD.

When death is diagnosed using cardiac criteria, rather than brain-stem tests, the organs will be cooled by in situ perfusion, in order to preserve their viability. The Human Tissue Act 2004 confirms the legality of cold perfusion techniques: under section 43, if part of a body is or may be suitable for use for transplantation, it is lawful to take the minimum necessary steps for the purpose of preserving the part for use for transplantation, until it has been established that consent for transplantation has not been, and will not be, given.

More complex is the question of whether steps to ensure that organs are suitable for transplantation may be taken before the patient has died, such as giving her anti-coagulant drugs. On the one hand, treatment which is not intended to benefit the dying patient would not appear to be in her best interests. On the other hand, if donation is her clear wish, then facilitating this might be compatible with the Mental Capacity Act 2005. This was the view of the now disbanded UK Donation Ethics Committee.

UK Donation Ethics Committee[31]

1.6.2 . . . [I]f the patient is known to have wanted to be a donor, or to have values and beliefs compatible with being a donor, the possibility of facilitating donation provides a reason to continue treatments which may have no direct medical benefit to the patient; rather the benefit accrues to the potentially donatable organs and thereby ultimately to the recipients. This concept can leave some clinicians feeling conflicted, concerned that they are no longer acting for the overall benefit of the patient, but rather for the overall benefit of the potential recipients.

1.6.3 This is a narrow interpretation of 'overall benefit' . . . The Mental Capacity Act Code of Practice emphasises the importance of considering a person's social, emotional, cultural and

---

[30] 'Harmonizing standards for death determination in DCDD' (2015) 15 American Journal of Bioethics 10–12.
[31] *An Ethical Framework for Controlled Donation after Circulatory Death* (AoMRC, 2011).

religious interests in determining what course of action may be in their best interests, and the clinician is legally obliged to take this wider view. When planning end of life care for a patient for whom life-sustaining treatment is no longer appropriate, if the patient wished to become an organ donor, then care that facilitates successful donation is likely to be highly compatible with their best interests (or to be of overall benefit to them).

Joe Brierley and David Shaw suggest that, with parental consent, it should also be possible to carry out premortem interventions to improve organ viability in children.

Joe Brierley and David Shaw[32]

Arguably with children the ability to explain interventions explicitly to those with PR [parental responsibility], to ensure complete understanding and therefore ability to provide fully informed consent confers greater authority than is the case in the non-competent adult. Overall, the use of such premortem interventions in children may, therefore, be more justified than in adult registered organ donors, given that those with decisional authority (the parents) can have the procedures specifically explained to them and give informed consent, unlike with an unconscious adult donor who might have wanted to donate organs, but was unaware that particular interventions might be used ...

Many children die with ongoing futile invasive therapies due to cultural differences in end-of-life practice, or at parental insistence despite contrary medical advice. If cultural differences are sufficient to justify futile invasive therapy, facilitating life-saving donation in a way that is compatible with the wishes of the child as expressed through his/her parents would appear easier to justify.

(c) TYPES OF TRANSPLANT

The organ donation register allows people to specify which organs they are prepared to donate for use: it is preferable to allow people to opt out of donating certain parts of their body (commonly hearts and corneas), if this will increase the chance that they will donate their kidneys, lungs, and pancreas.

In recent years, it has become possible to transplant other body parts, such as limbs, faces, tongues, and wombs, and these transplants raise new ethical and practical issues. First, while the side effects and health risks of immunosuppressant drugs will often be worth taking when the alternative is death, or very severely impaired existence, the risk/benefit calculation may be less clear when the alternative is an otherwise normal and healthy life without the use of a hand, or with a disfigured face. Indeed, it has been argued that hand or face transplants convert a healthy person with an amputated hand or facial disfigurement 'into a morbidly ill individual who must endure a toxic regime of drugs for the remainder of their life'.[33]

On the other hand, restoring hand function can improve someone's quality of life significantly. Living with facial disfigurement can be difficult: the recipient of one of the first full face

---

[32] 'Premortem interventions in dying children to optimise organ donation: an ethical analysis' (2016) 42 Journal of Medical Ethics 424–8.

[33] Richard Huxtable and Julie Woodley, 'Gaining face or losing face? Framing the debate on face transplants' (2005) 19 Bioethics 505–22.

transplants had been a recluse for 15 years.[34] Without a functioning tongue, it is impossible to speak, swallow, and eat normally, leading one commentator to claim that while 'the tongue is not a vital organ in sustaining life, it may be a vital organ in sustaining the will to live in many people'.[35] There is even some evidence that people might be willing to incur more risk in order to have a new face than a new kidney.[36]

Secondly, the long-term impact, both physiological and psychological, of receiving another person's hand, limb, or face remain unknown. People may feel less comfortable about the transplant of a visible part of another person's body than they do about an internal organ. For the same reason, it is also likely that fewer people would be willing to donate their face or their limbs after death, and there is the further concern that people might be less likely to agree to donate their internal organs because of some vague, albeit unfounded, fear that their face might be used as well. As a result, the government has made it clear that the planned opt-out system will only apply to internal solid organs, and not to 'novel transplants'.[37]

(1) Limbs and Hands

The first human hand transplant took place in 1998. The recipient regretted the operation and could not cope with his new hand. He failed to comply with the drug regime, and, following chronic rejection, the transplanted hand had to be amputated. Since then, many hand and limb transplants have been successful, and have dramatically improved the quality of life of amputees or people born without functioning hands or limbs. The first successful hand transplant in the UK took place in 2012, and the recipient was soon able to wash and dress himself, and pick up his grandchildren.

Charles Hedges and Philip Rosoff argue that while adults may be able to give informed consent to the 'narrow risk-benefit ratio' of hand transplantation, this is not the case for children, for whom they argue the operation should be delayed 'until meaningful consent can be acquired'.

Charles E Hedges and Philip M Rosoff[38]

Subjecting a child to a life of intensive physical therapy, risk of acute and chronic rejection, and, most worrisome, substantially higher risks of cancer, infection and cardiovascular disease would require the promise of extensive medical benefits. With our current understanding of hand transplantation, the benefits that can be hoped for are some improvement in function over prosthetics and an improvement in body image. Since the functional benefits are modest at best, it is possible that this operation fulfils more of a cosmetic role and should be evaluated as such. This is not to say that further advances in the field as more experience is gained with adult subjects would not alter the current risk–benefit profile at some point in the future. But at the present time, our analysis of the current state of affairs suggests that children should not undergo hand transplantation at this time.

---

[34] See further <www.umm.edu/programs/face-transplant>.

[35] TA Day, quoted in Martin Birchall, 'Tongue transplantation' (2004) 363 The Lancet 1663.

[36] Michael Cunningham et al, 'Risk acceptance in composite tissue allotransplantation reconstructive procedures—instrument design and validation' (2004) 30 European Journal of Trauma 12–16.

[37] Department of Health and Social Care, *The New Approach to Organ and Tissue Donation in England: Government Response to Consultation* (DHSC, 2018).

[38] 'Transplants for non-lethal conditions: a case against hand transplantation in minors' (2018) 44 Journal of Medical Ethics 661–5.

(2) Faces

The first face transplant took place in France in 2005. The recipient, Isabelle Dinoire, had been attacked by her dog and had suffered very severe facial injuries. The operation was a success, and improved both appearance and function. Since then, there have been more than 35 face transplants worldwide. Someone with a transplanted face will not look exactly the same as the donor, because the shape of her skull will alter the face's appearance.

Face transplants raise a particularly difficult issue in the event of transplant failure. Removal of a face is not as straightforward as the amputation of a failed hand transplant. On the contrary, the failure of a face transplant might leave the recipient in a worse position than they were before the operation. In their 2014 review of all of the face transplants performed to date, Saami Khalifian et al reported that none had failed spontaneously.[39] There was only one case in which the graft did not succeed, and this was because the patient had stopped taking immuno-suppressant medication.

While facial disfigurement can have an effect on function, disfigured people suffer principally as a result of others' reactions to them, which can include 'visual and verbal assaults, and a level of familiarity from strangers, naked stares, startled reactions, double takes, whispering, remarks, furtive looks, curiosity, personal questions, advice, manifestations of pity or aversion, laughter, ridicule and outright avoidance'.[40]

Richard Huxtable and Julie Woodley have argued that the need for face transplant surgery arises from society's intolerance of disfigured people.

Richard Huxtable and Julie Woodley[41]

In an important sense, one must query whether the 'patient' is actually society, and in particular image-conscious Western society . . . This apparent obsession with beauty is probably one of the strongest reasons for permitting this procedure and also ironically one of the main reasons why it gives cause for concern. Ideally, of course, society would celebrate, rather than alienate, such diversity. There nevertheless lingers the suspicion that the influence of societal norms amounts to a form of coercion, which might again threaten the validity of any consent. Furthermore, we wonder whether alternative responses to disfigurement, such as counselling, would suffer once the transplantation doors are opened. As Strauss has pointed out, 'when something is correctable, our willingness to accept it as untouched is reduced'.

Of course, disfigured people should not have to endure discrimination and hostility, but if a person finds her disfigurement disabling and distressing, and gives voluntary and informed consent to facial transplantation, the operation may be justified, even if we might wish that society was a more tolerant place.

In the UK, the Royal College of Surgeons has adopted a permissive but cautious approach to facial transplantation, concluding that 'there is no a priori reason why prospective patients who have been shown to be sufficiently autonomous cannot be accurately informed about both known and unknown risks of transplantation—assuming that the REC has agreed the

---

[39] Saami Khalifian et al, 'Facial transplantation: the first 9 years' (2014) 384 The Lancet 2153–63.
[40] A Clarke, 'Psychosocial aspects of facial disfigurement' (1999) 4 Psychology, Health and Medicine 127–42.
[41] 'Gaining face or losing face? Framing the debate on face transplants' (2005) 19 Bioethics 505–22.

risk benefit ratio to be acceptable'.[42] Its Working Party emphasized the psychological challenges facing not only recipients, but also their families and the families of donors.

Royal College of Surgeons[43]

All stages of the face transplantation process will present psychological challenges for recipients, their families and donor families . . .

The prospective patient should be sufficiently resilient to cope with the considerable stress associated with the transplant, including the 'unknowns' associated with a new procedure of this nature, the complex immunological and behavioural post-operative regimen, the risks of rejection and intrusive media interest . . .

Teams should be vigilant for signs of psychological rejection of the donor face, for example, lack of interest in looking at the face in a mirror, or indications that the patient feels the new face is 'not the real me' . . . The recipient may need assistance to resolve complex feelings about the donor (for example, curiosity about the sort of person, guilt about the donor's death, gratitude to the family) . . .

Post-operatively, family members should be monitored for signs of excessive stress and anxiety . . . Strategies may be needed to encourage acceptance of the new face.

Saami Khalifian et al's review of the first 28 face transplants bears out these concerns, reporting that the most important predictor of success was rigorous pre-transplant screening of recipients.

Saami Khalifian et al[44]

Initial concerns about feelings of depersonalisation towards the new face and donor identity transfer or split have not been substantiated, and recipients do not resemble donors according to donor families, recipients, and transplant teams. A review of psychological outcomes after face transplantation showed a decreased prevalence of depression and verbal abuse and significantly improved body image, sense of self, and social reintegration. Patients have accepted their new face and describe improved quality of life, with several patients returning to work.

The overwhelmingly positive psychological outcome is probably a result of rigorous pre-operative psychiatric and psychological selection of patients deemed to be stable, motivated, and compliant by a multidisciplinary team. The most notable exception is the patient who—displeased with the side-effects of immunosuppressive treatment—came to rely instead on traditional remedies on several occasions, leading to multiple rejection episodes and death. This outcome might have been prevented by more careful preoperative assessment and education, and postoperative psychiatric follow-up . . .

The best candidate is one who: fully understands the implications of potentially lifelong immunosuppression and its serious morbidities, including infections, cancer, graft loss, and death; is motivated, committed, and compliant with intense post-operative rehabilitation, psychological treatment, and immunosuppression protocols; and has a strong social support system that will help them to address the many challenges, including media exposure, body image adaptation, and societal reintegration.

---

[42] Royal College of Surgeons of England, *Facial Transplantation. Working Party Report* (2003; 2nd edn 2006).
[43] Ibid.   [44] 'Facial transplantation: the first 9 years' (2014) 384 The Lancet 2153–63.

(3) Wombs

The first birth to a woman who had received a uterus transplant took place in Sweden in 2014, and there have since been more than 42 transplants and 11 babies born. At the time of writing, the first operations in the UK are due take place before the end of 2018.

Wombs can be transplanted from living or dead donors.[45] A more complete transplant might be possible if a deceased donor is used, because it would be possible to extract more arteries and veins.[46] Using a deceased donor might also be preferable in order not to impose the risks of such a serious operation on living donors. On the other hand, if a relative donates her womb, there is a better chance that she will be a good tissue match. In the first Swedish cases, all the transplanted wombs came from living donors; in two cases, mothers donated their uteruses to their daughters. Following the transplant, the woman will be monitored for a year before embryos created by *in vitro* fertilization are implanted into the transplanted womb.

Some of the same considerations apply to womb transplants as to other novel transplants, but there are also differences. Just like face or limb transplants, uterine transplantation is not life-saving, but, as Ruby Catsanos et al point out, the lack of a functioning uterus is not as disabling as the lack of a hand or face; nor does it prevent women from becoming mothers through surrogacy or adoption. The point of a womb transplant is to enable a woman without a uterus to become pregnant and give birth, although it should be noted that her experience of pregnancy will be closely monitored and highly medicalized, and a lack of nerve endings will affect the sensations of fetal movement and contractions.

Ruby Catsanos, Wendy Rogers, and Mianna Lotz[47]

Women who lack a functioning uterus do not have compromised health in terms of impaired day-to-day physiological function; nor is their lack of a uterus visible or socially inhibiting in the way that prosthetic upper limbs or facial deformities typically are. Furthermore, access to adoption and surrogacy would allow such women to become mothers; their children may even be genetically related to them. However, it would seem that a key motivating factor for UTx [uterine transplantation] is the desire to actually *bear* genetically-related children.

The strength of this desire may stem from a number of factors. For many women, experiencing pregnancy is a central aspect of their identity as women. The uterus represents a symbol of femininity, of women's biological difference from men. Pregnancy and childbirth is a unique physical and emotional experience shared only by women. Many women facing the removal of their uterus through hysterectomy undergo feelings of loss and damage to their gender identity; like the heart, the uterus is an organ with symbolic significance.

Given that uterine transplantation is not necessary in order to become a mother, should it be publicly funded, in the same way as other transplants? Mianna Lotz has argued that public funding for uterus transplantation might communicate the message that gestating your own biologically related child is superior to adoption.

---

[45] In 2018, it was reported that the first baby had been born after a deceased womb transplant in Brazil in 2016, see further Dani Ejzenberg et al, 'Livebirth after uterus transplantation from a deceased donor in a recipient with uterine infertility' (2018) 392 The Lancet 2697–704.

[46] Giuseppe Del Priore et al, 'Uterine transplantation—a real possibility? The Indianapolis consensus' (2013) 28 Human Reproduction 288–91.

[47] 'The ethics of uterus transplantation' (2013) 27 Bioethics 65–73.

Mianna Lotz[48]

> UTx provision may potentially communicate the message that the importance and value of having biologically related offspring is sufficient to warrant the use of substantial resources and expertise, the undertaking of extremely complicated medical procedures and the assumption of very significant physiological risks, in pursuit of the goal of gestating offspring that are biologically and/or genetically 'one's own'. A further concern is that this message will receive additional validation and force if UTx is *publicly* funded ...
>
> What exactly is the potential *harm* of the validation I am referring to? To answer this involves acknowledging that adoption is still significantly stigmatized and devalued within contemporary culture. Fisher draws on findings from a significant 1997 national survey to conclude that adoption is still widely regarded as 'not quite as good as having your own child'.

In contrast, Stephen Wilkinson and Nicola Jane Williams argue that public funding for uterus transplantation could be justifiable.

Stephen Wilkinson and Nicola Jane Williams[49]

> [S]hould we view surrogacy as a sufficiently good alternative, given the costs associated with UTx? As we have conceded, it may well be the case at present that the extra benefits delivered by UTx are insufficient to justify the considerable extra expense that it entails. However, if UTx became cheaper, the case ... could become sufficiently strong to justify funding. For, while the primary purpose of ARTs is to provide a child, the experience of pregnancy—although *less* important than social parenthood—is not *unimportant*, at least for those who desire it. In addition, we must keep in mind the far from ideal social and legal position of surrogacy in many countries ...
>
> We conclude therefore that the case for ruling out state funding for UTx is weak. This does not mean that funding should actually be provided in the circumstances that obtain at present. For, just as with all other medical treatments, it must first be shown to be effective, safe and cost-effective. Also, surrogacy law reform could go a long way towards making surrogacy a 'sufficiently good' alternative and, if such reform occurred, the case for funding UTx would be significantly weakened.

Three further special issues are raised by womb transplants. First, the woman will have to take immunosuppressant drugs while she is trying to conceive and during pregnancy. Evidence from women who have had children after receiving other organs indicates that immunosuppressive drugs are associated with a small increased risk of miscarriage, prematurity, growth retardation, and low birthweight, although not with any increased risk of fetal anomaly.[50] These are risks which are judged to be worth taking in women who wish to have children after having undergone solid organ transplantation, and so it is hard to see why they should rule out uterus transplantation.

---

[48] 'Uterus transplantation as radical reproduction: Taking the adoption alternative more seriously' (2018) 32 Bioethics 499–508.

[49] 'Should uterus transplants be publicly funded?' (2016) 42 Journal of Medical Ethics 559–65.

[50] Giuseppe Del Priore et al, 'Uterine transplantation—a real possibility? The Indianapolis consensus' (2013) 28 Human Reproduction 288–91.

Secondly, if the transplant were to fail after the woman had become pregnant, but before the baby could be delivered safely, the removal of the uterus would cause the death of the fetus. This risk is minimized by the requirement that a year should elapse between the transplant and the first embryo transfer, but it cannot be eliminated.

Thirdly, the woman only needs the transplanted womb for the purposes of pregnancy. The risks associated with immunosuppressant drugs are such that the transplanted womb will be removed once the woman no longer needs it. A full hysterectomy would then be carried out soon after the birth of the woman's first or second child. Uniquely, then, uterine transplants are *temporary* organ transplants.

(d) AUTHORIZATION OF REMOVAL

(1) The Human Tissue Act 2004

Until the law is changed to introduce an opt-out system, under section 1 of the Human Tissue Act 2004, no organ can be taken without 'appropriate consent'.[51]

(a) Adults

Under section 3, for adults 'appropriate consent' means either the consent of the person who has died; the consent of someone she appointed to consent on her behalf, or the consent of a person 'who stood in a qualifying relationship' to her immediately before her death.

If the deceased has consented to organ transplantation by being registered on the organ donor register, the doctors would act lawfully in retrieving her organs. Of course, some would argue that the process of signing up to the register is very far removed from what we normally understand by informed consent. People can fill in a brief registration form online, or they can sign up by ticking the relevant box on an application form for a driving licence. Registration rates have also been boosted by the inclusion of a tick box on applications for a Boots Advantage Card.[52] But ticking a box online gives no opportunity to assess the person's capacity to make the decision, and there is no formal information-giving process.

Of course, agreeing to become a donor after death is different from giving informed consent to medical treatment. But because 'consent' has such a specific meaning in medical law, might it be preferable to use a different term? For example, the Human Tissue (Scotland) Act 2004 refers to 'authorization', rather than consent.

David Shaw argues for more than just a change of terminology. As a result of the lack of information given to potential donors, he maintains that there is considerable vagueness about what they had consented to, which makes it harder for families—in both an opt-in and an opt-out system—to be certain what the deceased would have wanted.

David M Shaw[53]

In the case of deceased donors, we are willing to give them much less information and allow them to consent broadly to organ donation without actually informing them about what could

---

[51] Taking organs without appropriate consent is a criminal offence under section 5 of the Human Tissue Act 2004.

[52] A loyalty card from one of the UK's largest chain of pharmacists.

[53] 'The Consequences of Vagueness in Consent to Organ Donation' (2017) 31 Bioethics 424–31.

> be involved. It is unsurprising that so much vagueness surrounds their intentions when what they actually agreed to was so very vague ...
>
> Current attempts to reduce the incidence of family objections to and refusals of organ dona-tion are based upon counselling them to respect the wishes of their deceased relatives. But the donor's wishes are often extremely vague. Vagueness about the validity of the patient's consent leads to much of the other vagueness surrounding donation; all of the attempts to reduce family objection rates involve some degree of guesswork about what a patient would have wanted ...
>
> Most importantly, preventing vagueness at the point of registration is better than attempting to cure it at the point of donation when the family is upset. Creating a new consent system and providing more detailed information might discourage some people from donating, but it would increase the chances that the wishes of someone who does want to donate will be respected, substantially increase health professionals' and families' confidence in the consent of donors, and consequently reduce the distress currently caused to both families and staff.

The deceased's consent does not have to be in writing, and if the deceased is not on the organ donor register, other efforts should be made to find out whether she wished to donate her organs after death. Although unusual in practice, it is possible to appoint someone to deal with consent to donation after one's death. Someone might do this if members of her family disagree about transplantation, in order to ensure that the decision is taken by someone who shares her views. An appointment can be made orally, if witnessed by two people, or in writing, with one witness.

Where the deceased person had not given consent and had not nominated someone to give proxy consent, or under section 3(7) and (8) their nominee is unable to consent, or 'it is not reasonably practicable to communicate with [him or her] within the time available', then con-sent can be sought from someone in a qualifying relationship.

Qualifying relationships are defined in section 27(4) and are ranked, so that the consent of a spouse, civil partner, or partner should be sought first, and that of a parent or child only if no spouse, civil partner, or partner is available to consent; and that of a brother or sister only if no spouse, civil partner, partner, parent, or child can give consent, and so on. The full hier-archy is as follows:

(a) spouse, civil partner, or partner;[54]

(b) parent or child;

(c) brother or sister;

(d) grandparent or grandchild;

(e) child of a brother or sister;

(f) stepfather or stepmother;

(g) half-brother or half-sister;

(h) friend of long standing.

Because organs must be retrieved as quickly as possible after death, it may not be feasible to contact the person at the top of this hierarchy of qualifying relatives, or they may not wish to make the decision, or may lack the capacity to do so. In such circumstances, the HTA's Code

---

[54] Partner is defined in s 54(9): 'For the purposes of this Act, ... a person is another's partner if the two of them (whether of different sexes or the same sex) live as partners in an enduring family relationship.'

of Practice provides that 'A person may be omitted from the hierarchy' and 'the next person in the hierarchy would become the appropriate person to give consent'.[55]

Section 27(5) of the Act states that 'Relationships in the same paragraph of subsection (4) should be accorded equal ranking', so where there is both a parent and a child, either is able to give consent. And under section 27(7): 'If the relationship of each of two or more persons to the person concerned is accorded equal highest ranking . . . it is sufficient to obtain the consent of any of them.' This means that if the deceased has both an estranged husband and a new partner, the consent of the estranged husband would be sufficient, even if her current partner objects. Similarly, if the deceased is single but has several children, any one of them can give consent, even if all of the other children are opposed to organ retrieval.

It is important to remember that under the Human Tissue Act 2004, it is lawful to take organs where an appropriate consent exists, but not obligatory. In practice, relatives' views will be taken into account even if the deceased has made her wishes known. Although the deceased's family do not have a legal right of veto, doctors may be reluctant to retrieve organs where relatives object, both for compassionate reasons and from the more pragmatic desire to avoid the bad publicity that might result from ignoring the wishes of recently bereaved relatives. The Code of Practice suggests that health professionals should try to encourage the family to respect the deceased's wishes.

HTA Code of Practice[56]

120. Where valid consent has been given by the donor, but relatives object to organ or tissue donation proceeding, then they should be sensitively supported to respect the prospective donor's consent to ensure his or her wishes are fulfilled. A relative's objection does not nullify appropriate, valid consent from the prospective donor.

121. The existence of appropriate, valid consent permits an activity to proceed, but does not mandate that it must. The final decision about whether to proceed with the activity rests with the medical practitioner.

Adnan Sharif and Greg Moorlock have argued that it would be a good idea to use nudge theory (discussed in Chapter 2) in order to prompt families to respect the donor's wishes.

Adnan Sharif and Greg Moorlock[57]

We already have insight into some of the factors that influence family consent for donation. For example, when the formal request for organ donation is made, and by whom it is made, can make families more or less likely to give consent for donation. We also know that emotional or affective factors are stronger predictors of people's intentions to register for organ donation than rational, cognitive components. If we assume similar cognitive obstacles with family consent, there may be benefit to collaborating with behavioral science experts to explore psychological strategies to improve family consent by altering behaviour.

One such behavioral intervention strategy is based on nudge theory ... By challenging inherent cognitive biases, a carefully designed nudge may support families to make decisions they would

[55] Code A: Guiding principles and the fundamental principle of consent (HTA, 2017) para 39.
[56] Code F: Donation of solid organs and tissue for transplantation (HTA, 2017).
[57] 'Influencing relatives to respect donor autonomy: Should we nudge families to consent to organ donation?' (2018) 32 Bioethics 155–63.

> normally have made (absent the stress of the situation), reduce the risk of decision instability, and result in fewer cases of long-term regret. Nudges can therefore provide benefit to relatives in terms of helping them to make decisions that they are satisfied with over the longer term ...
>
> The challenge is to develop an intervention that fulfils the multiple roles—championing organ donation, promoting respect for the wishes of the deceased patient, while concomitantly supporting families during their bereavement process.

What sort of intervention might work as a nudge in this context? David Shaw and Dale Gardiner propose giving families more information about the patients who benefit from organ donation.

David Shaw and Dale Gardiner[58]

> Making faceless patients in need of an organ transplant more real to families may make decisions easier—and donation may also be more likely as a result ...
>
> The first ethical objection that we anticipate is that it would amount to coercion to give details of recipients to families of potential donors. Even if a picture is not used, saying that a 20 year-old is likely to die unless donation goes ahead would still apply considerable pressure to the family in question—and this at a time when they are already grieving because of the death of a relative ...
>
> An alternative strategy, and one we recommend should be piloted, is giving families more detailed information not of the actual proposed recipients, but rather of a representative sample of true and typical recipients ... A leaflet explaining donation and transplantation which includes photographs and quotes from those who have benefited from organ transplantation and/or a representative sample of those on the waiting list could be the mechanism by which this information is given to families when consent or confirmation of consent is sought from families ... It might even be possible to use photographs of real patients on the waiting list, while not implying they are likely to be the actual recipient of any organs from a particular donor.

Rather than trying to persuade relatives to consent, it could be argued that giving relatives any say over what happens to a person's body after death is inconsistent with the dominant principle of patient autonomy. Why should one of my relatives who has absolutely no say over my medical treatment during my life be permitted, in practice, to overrule my decision to donate my organs after my death?

Against this, Margaret Lock suggests that it is families, rather than donors, who make the greatest sacrifice when organs are taken from a dead body.

Margaret Lock[59]

> [W]e encourage the idea that donation is a selfless act, but it can also be thought of as the giving away of something no longer of any use: it takes virtually no effort to sign a donor card. But donor

[58] 'Increasing organ donation rates by revealing recipient details to families of potential donors' (2018) 44 Journal of Medical Ethics 101–3.

[59] *Twice Dead: Organ Transplants and the Reinvention of Death* (University of California Press: Berkeley, 2002) 373.

families make a much greater emotional sacrifice. They must usually come to terms with the fact that someone dear to them has been transformed, in the space of a few hours, and often through a violent encounter, from a healthy individual into an irrevocably damaged entity, suspended between life and death. To give selflessly under these circumstances requires courage, as well as faith in the ICU [intensive care unit] staff and in the truth of their assessments.

Each year NHS Blood and Transplant carries out an audit of all potential donors. In 2017–18, there were 1,954 people on mechanical ventilation where all of the criteria for neurological testing of death were satisfied.[60] Neurological tests to confirm death were performed on 1,676 potential donors, and in 1,641 cases, death was confirmed using neurological criteria. Fifty-nine potential DBD donors were ruled out because of medical contraindications for donation, and the families were then approached in 1,471 cases. Of these, 1,066 families agreed to donation, and solid organ donation took place in 955 cases.

A similar audit for DCD patients revealed that there were 17,721 deceased people on mechanical ventilation in whom death was not confirmed using neurological criteria. Imminent death was anticipated in 6,821 cases, and treatment was withdrawn in 5,640 cases. In 1,184 cases there were contraindications to donation, but of the 4,456 in whom there were no contraindications, the family was asked about donation in 1,858 cases. Of these, 1,115 families agreed to donation, and donation occurred in 613 cases.

It is therefore clear that although it is normal practice to ask the family about donation in the cases of DBD donors, practice is more variable in relation to DCD donors. In both cases, however, there is considerable scope to increase the number of donors, at almost every stage. Given that an average of 3.7 organs are taken from each DBD donor and 2.8 from each DCD donor, obtaining organs from all of the unused but suitable potential donors undoubtedly has the potential massively to increase the number of transplants.

In practice, when a patient is known to have expressed a wish to donate, 92 per cent of families give consent. This means that 8 per cent of families refuse to agree to donation, despite the individual having consented to donation during his or her lifetime. NHS Blood and Transplant records the reasons for relatives' refusal. Other than either knowing that the person did not want to be a donor (22 per cent), or not knowing their wishes (15 per cent), common reasons given were not wanting surgery to the body (11 per cent), a feeling that the deceased has suffered enough (6 per cent), and religious beliefs (6 per cent).[61]

In 2011, the National Institution for Health and Care Excellence issued a clinical guideline on improving donor identification and consent rates which stressed the importance of presenting donation in a positive light.

National Institute for Health and Care Excellence[62]

1.1.17 Approach those close to the patient in a setting suitable for private and compassionate discussion . . .

---

[60] NHS Blood and Transplant, *Annual Activity Report 2017–18: National Potential Donor Audit* (NHSBT, 2018).
[61] NHS Blood and Transplant, *Delivering a Revolution in Public Behaviour in Relation to Organ Donation: A Summary of the Evidence* (NHSBT, 2014).
[62] *Organ Donation for Transplantation: Improving Donor Identification and Consent Rates for Deceased Organ Donation* (NICE: London, 2011).

1.1.20 Discussions about organ donation with those close to the patient should only take place when it has been clearly established that they understand that death is inevitable or has occurred.

1.1.21 When approaching those close to the patient:

- discuss with them that donation is a usual part of the end-of-life care
- use open-ended questions—for example 'how do you think your relative would feel about organ donation?'
- use positive ways to describe organ donation, especially when patients are on the NHS organ donor register or they have expressed a wish to donate during their lifetime—for example 'by becoming a donor your relative has a chance to save and transform the lives of many others'
- avoid the use of apologetic or negative language (for example 'I am asking you because it is policy' or 'I am sorry to have to ask you').

(b) Children

Where the deceased is a child, organ retrieval will be lawful if there is appropriate consent under section 2(7). This can be the consent of the child herself, or of a person with parental responsibility, or, failing that, consent can come from someone in a qualifying relationship.

A *Gillick*-competent minor's consent will be sufficient for organ retrieval to be lawful.[63] The problem is that the child is now dead, and so establishing that they were, in fact, *Gillick*-competent when they consented to donation may be difficult. As the Code of Practice makes clear, even where the child's wishes are known, retrieval should not go ahead without discussion with someone with parental responsibility.

HTA Code of Practice[64]

91. In some cases it may be advisable to establish with the person who had parental responsibility for the deceased child whether the child was competent to make the decision ... In any case where a child has consented to the use of their body or tissue, it is essential to discuss this with the child's relatives.

(e) SYSTEM FOR REMOVAL AND ALLOCATION

NHS Blood and Transplant oversees transplantation arrangements in the UK. Its responsibilities include maintaining the national transplant waiting list; matching and allocating organs; transporting organs to recipient centres; and maintaining the organ donor register. It also promotes organ donation and transplantation, and maintains transplant coordination services.

Once a patient is identified as a potential organ donor, the local specialist nurse for organ donation (SN-OD) should be contacted. SN-ODs are responsible for ascertaining the views of the potential donor's family, and they will also contact NHS Blood and Transplant in order to find out

---

[63] See Chapter 6 for a description of *Gillick*-competence.

[64] Code A: Guiding principles and the fundamental principle of consent (HTA, 2017).

whether the donor is on the organ donor register. Once agreement to organ donation has been obtained, the SN-OD will notify NHS Blood and Transplant, which maintains a national database of all potential organ recipients. When the appropriate recipient has been identified, the SN-OD liaises between the surgical teams responsible for both the donor and the recipient's care.

Cadaveric organ donation is usually anonymous. It is, however, possible for the donor's family to be given some information, such as the age and sex of the people who have benefited from the donation. Patients who receive organs can obtain similar information about their donors.

Obviously, efforts must be made to ensure that the potential donor does not have a serious condition that could jeopardize the recipient's health. Contraindications for donation include severe or untreated infections, cancers that have spread within the last 12 months, and Creutzfeldt–Jakob disease (CJD).

Given advances in treatments for people who are HIV-positive, it is interesting to consider whether it could be in the best interests of an HIV-negative individual to receive an organ from an HIV-positive donor. Clearly this is not ideal, especially in the light of the immunosuppressant drugs which must be taken post-transplantation, but if the potential recipient is likely to die before an HIV-negative organ becomes available, Bram Wispelwey et al argue that the risk of HIV infection and the need to take more medication after transplantation might be risks an individual would consider worth taking.

Bram P Wispelwey, Ari Z Zivotofsky, and Alan B Jotkowitz[65]

If the potential recipient demonstrates full awareness of the risks of receiving an organ from an HIV-positive donor, he or she has the right via the principle of autonomy to accept those risks along with the potential life-saving benefits … It is true that informed consent … may be more difficult to achieve given the complexities of living with HIV, and significant patient counselling and education over multiple sessions would likely be necessary. But there is no reason to believe that a robust informed consent could never be given …

When the consequence of doing nothing is uniformly fatal, as in the case of liver transplantation, the ethical obligation of beneficence—offering the possibility of survival—in the absence of non-infected donation surely outweighs the potential harm of risking transmission of a controllable if lifelong viral infection.

(f) LAW REFORM

In 2008, the Organ Donation Taskforce did not advocate any changes to the law relating to organ donation, but instead recommended improving the donation system in the UK by making the preparatory steps for donation routine; removing bureaucratic obstacles to donation, and facilitating greater recognition of donors. All of their recommendations were implemented.

Each hospital now has a clinical lead for transplantation, who is responsible for ensuring that processes are in place to optimize potential donor identification and management. There has also been success in establishing regional multi-organ retrieval teams, which are available

---

[65] 'The transplantation of solid organs from HIV-positive donors to HIV-negative recipients: ethical implications' (2015) 41 Journal of Medical Ethics 367–70.

24 hours a day, seven days a week, in order to advise on donor management prior to donation, and increase the quality and effectiveness of organ retrievals. Throughout the UK, steps have also been taken to recognize and thank organ donors. An online book of remembrance has been set up,[66] and many hospitals now have public commemorative plaques to organ donors.

While there is no doubt that the Taskforce's proposals have increased the number of deceased donors, most of this increase has been attributable to an 87 per cent increase in the numbers of DCD donors. The number of DBD donors increased by only 4 per cent.

Ten years later, the government is in the process of changing the law in England so that a system based upon 'deemed consent' will operate in England by 2020. Below we consider the pros and cons of such a move, before looking at how it works in Wales and what is proposed for England.

(1) Why Should We Move to an 'Opt-Out' System?

In an 'opt-out' system, sometimes also referred to as 'presumed consent', it is assumed that all potential donors are willing to donate their organs, but people can opt out by formally registering their unwillingness to donate. An opt-out system therefore requires the maintenance of an accurate and rapidly searchable database on which objections can be recorded and amended.

The assumption that most people want to be organ donors does seem to be warranted: public opinion surveys consistently find that 70–90 per cent of the population would be willing to donate their organs after death. Of course, people may respond to opinion polls by giving the answer that they think will show themselves in a good light. Nevertheless, even if 90 per cent is an overestimate, it seems clear that donation is supported by a majority of the population.

The main reason for moving towards an opt-out system is the possibility of increasing the supply of organs for transplantation. Alberto Abadie and Sebastien Gay studied the impact of presumed consent laws in 22 countries over a ten-year period, and concluded that, while it is not a 'silver bullet', there were more deceased donors in countries which had implemented presumed consent.

Alberto Abadie and Sebastien Gay[67]

[O]ur empirical results suggest that presumed consent laws may greatly increase the supply of cadaveric organs for transplantation. However, it would be erroneous to interpret our results as evidence that presumed consent is the sometimes-portrayed silver-bullet for organ shortage. First, it is unlikely that a 25–30% increase in cadaveric donation would eliminate completely the organ shortage problem in some countries ... Moreover, it seems likely that an increase in the supply of cadaveric organs would be followed by a reduction in the supply of organs from living donors ... Although recent studies have reported successful transitions to a presumed consent default, it seems likely that, in some countries, imposing a presumed consent law without first building sufficient social support could generate an adverse response to organ procurement efforts.

---

[66] <www.donorfamilynetwork.co.uk/book-of-remembrance/>.

[67] 'The Impact of Presumed Consent Legislation on Cadaveric Organ Donation: A Cross-Country Study' (2006) 25 Journal of Health Economics 599–620.

In its Impact Assessment for the new law in England, the Department of Health and Social Care reviewed the evidence on the impact of opt-out systems on donation rates.

Department of Health and Social Care[68]

Would opt-out change the organ donation consent rate?

The evidence is inconclusive. While it seems that moving to an opt-out system is unlikely to decrease the consent rate, there is no unambiguous evidence that opt-out by itself increases consent rates. There is evidence that in some cases, when opt-out is implemented alongside other pro-organ donation policies, such as communications campaigns, consent rates increase. However, the available evidence does not allow the individual contribution of changing the system of organ and tissue donation to opt-out to be identified. There is currently insufficient evidence from the experience of opt-out in Wales to conclude whether it has had a statistically significant positive impact on consent rates ...

[T]he Chief Scientific Adviser advised that it is possible to say, with moderate certainty, that when introduced as part of a wider communication and logistical package, opt-out systems can be associated with higher donation rates. He has drawn three conclusions from the data:

- Opt-out systems do not reduce organ donation (high certainty), which is relevant as some have expressed concerns that such systems could anger people and cause them to withdraw consent which may have been given otherwise.

- There is reasonable evidence from before-and-after studies that, when introduced as part of a wider package, opt-out systems are associated in some cases with higher organ donation. What fraction of this increase is attributable to the opt-out is difficult to say as they are not introduced in isolation.

- There is an association between opt-out and higher rates in geographical studies, but they should be interpreted with caution as this may be reverse causation – societies where donation is more acceptable may be more likely to accept opt-out.

One of the main concerns about presumed or 'deemed' consent is whether it is, in fact, any sort of consent at all. Can we be sure that the public is sufficiently well informed that any failure to register an objection reflects a person's willingness to donate, rather than their lethargy or ignorance? It has been predicted that fewer people would register an objection than actually have reservations about donation, and that less educated or minority groups will be both less likely to consent to donation, and less likely to understand how to opt out. Consent in medical law is generally assumed to be active and positive, rather than something which can be assumed from inaction. The reality, in an opt-out system, is that organs could be taken without consent.[69]

A number of countries have adopted opt-out systems, but in most of these relatives continue to be consulted about organ transplantation. Taking organs in the face of a relative's objection would generally be counterproductive because of the adverse publicity it would be likely to generate. It would be possible to implement a 'hard' opt-out system, where the failure to register an opt-out would be decisive, and organs would be taken even if relatives object. This happens in Singapore (where kidney donation rates increased from from 4.7 to 31.3 per

[68] *An opt-out system of organ and tissue donation: Impact Assessment* (DHSC, 2018)
[69] Charles A Erin and John Harris, 'Presumed consent or contracting out' (1999) 25 Journal of Medical Ethics 365–6.

million population in the three years after the law was changed), and in Austria (where donation rates increased from 4.6 to 10.1 donors per million population in the four years after the introduction of presumed consent).[70] Austria's donation rates increased further to 27.2 donors per million after infrastructure changes, including the introduction of full-time transplant coordinators.[71]

(2) Wales

The Human Transplantation (Wales) Act 2013 introduced a soft opt-out system which came into force in 2015. It was preceded by a major public awareness campaign so that those who wished to opt out understood how to do so. The Welsh opt-out system applies only to adults who have been ordinarily resident in Wales for at least 12 months (so that it can be assumed that they had had a chance to find out about the opt-out system), who also die in Wales.

Children's consent cannot be deemed, but it is possible for children to express their wish to donate before their death: that is, an 'opt-in' system continues to apply to those under the age of 18. The same is true for adults who lacked the capacity to understand the notion of deemed consent for a significant period (ie for a year or more) before their deaths, whose consent to donation cannot be deemed.

Human Tissue Authority[72]

68. The exact duration that a person lacked capacity is not specified in the Human Transplantation (Wales) Act, but the period must be significant and this means a sufficiently long period as to lead a reasonable person to conclude that it would be inappropriate for consent to be deemed to be given. The significant period test is, therefore, an objective test in the sense that it must be based on the circumstances of each case and the facts presented. The significant period only negates deemed consent; if the person had made a decision to consent, or not to consent, then that express consent remains in force regardless of a subsequent loss of capacity.

69. In practice, a significant period should mean that the person did not have capacity to understand the notion of deemed consent for a period of at least twelve months before their death. The person's family, friends or carers should consider the significant period to be a period, which is long enough that the person's decision not to register a decision in regard to organ donation could not be said to be a conscious decision.

The Welsh system gives people four options: to opt in to donation; to opt out of donation; to nominate someone to make the decision; or to do nothing and be 'deemed' to consent. When the new system came into force on 1 December 2015, three per cent of the population had opted out, and 34 per cent had opted in. Organs donated in Wales will be available in the normal way throughout the UK. It is therefore possible that people living in other parts of the UK might benefit from the Welsh opt-out system.

If a Welsh resident has not opted out, clinicians will nevertheless approach family members in order to find out if the deceased had an unregistered objection. According to the

---

[70] Scottish Government, *Opt out organ donation: a rapid evidence review* (Scottish Government, 2018).
[71] Ibid.   [72] Code of Practice on the Human Transplantation (Wales) Act 2013 (HTA, 2017).

HTA's Code of Practice, in order to avoid consent being deemed, there must be evidence that would convince the reasonable person that the deceased did not want to be an organ donor.

Human Tissue Authority[73]

126. If the SNOD is informed by relatives or friends that the person did not want to be an organ donor, they should make reasonable enquiries as to why the relatives or friend thought that to be the case. In terms of who can provide the information that the person would have objected, the Human Transplantation (Wales) Act provides for a relative or a friend of long standing to be able to do so.

127. When information is provided by a relative or friend of long standing that the person did not want to be an organ donor, this must satisfy a reasonable person that the person would not have given consent ...

133. In order to assess the weight of the evidence presented, the following questions may be considered to aid the SNOD in reaching a decision:

a) Is the evidence presented as reflecting the views of the person, or the views of the family/friends presenting it? The test requires that evidence must be presented of the person's view. Therefore, more weight should be given to evidence which is presented as being a reflection of the person's view.

b) Is the evidence in writing, signed and dated by the person and witnessed? If this is the case, then this is likely to form an express decision of the person.

c) Is the evidence oral? If so, is it corroborated by more than one person? It is more likely to pass the reasonable person test if more than one person is able to confirm that the person orally stated that they would not have given their consent to donation.

d) How recent is the evidence? The Human Transplantation (Wales) Act requires the most recent evidence to be relied on, therefore the SNOD should establish when the record was made or the conversation took place and note this in the person's medical record or other appropriate document.

e) How well does the person providing the evidence know the person? It is not necessarily always the case that a person knows someone well simply because they are related. For example, a person may have had a carer who is not related to them, but spends every day with them.

134. Stating that the person was not aware that deemed consent affected them is not sufficient evidence, on its own, that a person did not want to be an organ donor.

While the Code suggests that relatives will be able to veto deemed consent only where there is convincing evidence of an unregistered objection, James Douglas and Antonia Cronin suggest that, in practice, donation is unlikely to take place in the face of relatives' opposition.

James F Douglas and Antonia J Cronin[74]

The central ethical question of whether it is justifiable, even with the support of the law, to ignore family opposition to donation is not resolved under the Act, nor is the corollary of

[73] Code of Practice on the Human Transplantation (Wales) Act 2013 (HTA, 2017).
[74] 'The Human Transplantation (Wales) Act 2013: an Act of Encouragement, not Enforcement' (2015) 78 Modern Law Review 324–48.

whether it is ethical to give in to such opposition in the presence of donor consent, either deemed or expressed. These issues already arise under the 2004 Act, but are accentuated under the HTWA [Human Transplantation (Wales) Act]. The absence of any statutory obligation to retrieve lawfully donated organs leaves a great deal to the discretion of the retrieval teams and, since the living speak more effectively than the dead, very few, if any, cases of successful retrieval in the face of unyielding opposition have been recorded.

What impact has deemed consent had on donation rates in Wales? There has been an increase in the number of deceased donors: from 60 in 2014/5 to 74 in 2017/8, and in the number of cadaveric transplants, from 128 to 149,[75] but because the numbers are small, it is hard to tell how much of this increase is due to the new deemed consent system, and how much might be the result of the publicity campaign associated with the change in the law, or an increase in the size of the Welsh population, or whether this is just annual fluctuation. At the time of writing, 40 per cent of the Welsh population have opted in to the organ donor register, and 6 per cent have opted out, leaving 54 per cent whose consent would be likely to be deemed.

(3) The opt-out scheme for England

Following a public consultation, the government announced in 2018 its support for a system based on deemed consent, to be put in place by Spring 2020. This will be accompanied by changes to the Organ Donor Register in order to give people more options to record their preferences. During the lifetime of this book, therefore, the law is likely to change and readers should be advised to check for updates on the Department of Health and Social Care website.

At the time of writing, the Organ Donation (Deemed Consent) Bill is before parliament. If passed in its current form, it will amend the Human Tissue Act in order to provide that, in the absence of a registered objection, consent to donation will be deemed, 'unless a person who stood in a qualifying relationship to the person concerned immediately before death provides information that would lead a reasonable person to conclude that the person concerned would not have consented'. There is no change in the law for people who have registered their willingness to donate, or for those who have nominated someone to make the decision on their behalf.

Deemed consent will also not apply (a) to adults who have not been ordinarily resident in England for a period of at least 12 months immediately before dying (it will therefore not cover temporary residents, such as international students), or (b) to an adult who has died and who for a significant period before dying lacked capacity to understand the effect of deemed consent. Just like in Wales, a 'significant period' is defined as 'a sufficiently long period as to lead a reasonable person to conclude that it would be inappropriate for consent to be deemed'.

Novel transplants, such as faces, limbs, wombs and hands, are not included. The list of novel transplants will be set out in regulations made by the Secretary of State, and an opt-in system will continue to apply to them, and to cadaveric donation from children and adults who lack capacity.

The Bill places a duty on the Human Tissue Authority to issue Codes of Practice to provide practical guidance about how deemed consent will work in practice, including what information a person in a qualifying relationship would need to provide in order to establish that the deceased person would not have agreed to donation. In addition to the wide-ranging public

---

[75] NHS Blood and Transplant, *Organ Donation and Transplantation Activity Data: Wales* (NHSBT, 2018).

education campaign which will take place in the 12 month transition period before the new legislation comes into effect, the government is also intending to make the register more flexible.

Department of Health and Social Care[76]

- Those who do wish to donate will still be able to express their wish on the Register and select the organs they are willing to donate. People will continue to be able to change or amend their decision at any time.

- From December 2018, there will be a more inclusive Register with the option to state that your faith is important to your organ donation decision and that your family and/or faith leader should be consulted if organ donation is a possibility on your death to ensure that any religious considerations are observed.

- There will also be greater accessibility to the Register through the new NHS app due to launch in England at the end of the year.

- As before, people will still be able to appoint somebody else to make the final decision for them after death. Children will still be able to sign up on the Register.

- There will be a year-long communication campaign to give people time to familiarise themselves with the changes. And we will be working to integrate the new NHS app and the Register to allow users more flexibility to add and check their registration details.

(g) ALTERNATIVE STRATEGIES

While many have welcomed the move to an opt-out system, it is not the only possible way to increase the number of available cadaveric organs.

(1) Elective Ventilation

Elective ventilation involves transferring imminently dying patients to an intensive care unit (ICU) and maintaining them on a ventilator, in order to ensure that their organs are suitable for transplant. These patients are likely to lack capacity, and therefore should be treated in their best interests. Could placing them on a ventilator in order to benefit someone else ever be in their best interests? A trial of elective ventilation took place in Exeter in the early 1990s, and was halted because the Department of Health declared it to be unlawful (on the grounds that it was not in the dying patients' best interests).

Now when judging what treatment is in an incapacitated patient's best interests, much more emphasis is placed upon her wishes and values, so it could be argued that fulfilling a patient's wish to donate her organs after death would be in her best interests.[77] If, however, there is a risk that once placed on a ventilator, the dying patient might lapse into a permanent vegetative state, this would be contrary to her best interests.[78]

---

[76] *The New Approach to Organ and Tissue Donation in England: Government Response to Consultation* (DHSC, 2018).

[77] John Coggon, 'Elective ventilation for organ donation: law, policy and public ethics' (2013) 39 Journal of Medical Ethics 130–4.

[78] JK Mason, 'Contemporary Issues in Organ Transplantation' in Sheila McLean (ed), *Contemporary Issues in Law, Medicine and Ethics* (Dartmouth: Aldershot, 1996) 117–41.

A further consideration is that beds in ICUs are scarce and expensive. There are often not enough beds for every patient who might need one, and it would be unreasonable to give priority access to people who have no chance of recovery. Of course, this would not rule out placing a dying patient in a bed that would otherwise be unused, in order to ensure that her organs could be used to save others after her death.

Nevertheless, the Academy of Medical Royal Colleges' Code of Practice is clear that ventilation should only be initiated and maintained if it is in the patient's best interests: 'Endotracheal intubation and artificial ventilation of the patient should only be initiated and maintained to further the patient's benefit and not as a means of preserving organ function'.[79]

(3) Allowing Conditional Donation

In July 1998, a man who was unconscious and in a critical condition was admitted to an ICU in the north of England. His relatives agreed to organ donation, but on condition that the organs went to white recipients. In this instance, the person on the waiting list who was most urgently in need of a liver transplant was white, and without the organ he would have died within 24 hours. The people who would have received his kidneys also happened to be white. Because the condition made no difference in practice, the organs were accepted and two kidneys and a liver were successfully transplanted into three individuals.

The Department of Health set up a panel to investigate, and its conclusion was that organs should not be accepted if the family wishes to impose conditions upon their use. Ruling out conditional donation is made more complicated by the existence of identifiable individuals on the waiting list who will die if a suitable organ is turned down. Drawing on their interviews with potential donors, recipients and transplant staff, Greg Moorlock et al found that many donors and recipients regarded the avoidance of waste as more important than the preference for unconditional donation.

Greg Moorlock et al[80]

[M]any participants felt uneasy about the cost of turning down potential donations. For these participants, saving lives carried more weight than strict adherence to medical criteria ... For many participants (mostly in the recipient and donor groups), the consequence of saving additional lives could justify the acceptance of conditions that would otherwise be considered unacceptable, including the racist conditions in the 1998 case ...

Many participants thought that accepting conditions should be a last resort, justified only if the alternative was to turn down a donation, because refusing a donation is a waste of a potentially life-saving resource ...

In contrast to some of the non-staff participants, many (although not all) of the staff participants viewed turning down conditional donations as unfortunate but necessary in order to maintain the integrity of the transplantation system ...

[I]n relation to conditional and directed donations, it has been argued that a convincing justification for allocating organs primarily according to medically relevant criteria – the avoidance of waste – also provides a reason to consider other criteria when the alternative is to turn down an offer of organs.

---

[79] Academy of Medical Royal Colleges, *A Code of Practice for the Diagnosis and Confirmation of Death* (AoMRC, 2008), para 7.3.

[80] 'Should We Reject Donated Organs on Moral Grounds or Permit Allocation Using Non-Medical Criteria?: A Qualitative Study' (2016) 30 Bioethics 282–92.

It might further be argued that there is an inconsistency with living organ donation, where donation is almost always to a specified individual. As TM Wilkinson points out in the next extract, it is hard to see what would be wrong with allowing directed donation to a close friend or relative after death.

TM Wilkinson[81]

Is it really so bad to attach a condition to an organ donation? Of course it was bad in the case of the racist. The motive there was some mix of hatred and contempt and there is nothing to be said for it. But what about the condition that an organ go to a relative? There seems nothing morally wrong about agreeing to donate a kidney, say, on condition that it go to a sibling, whether the donation is to be from a living person or a dead one . . .

Setting aside a special concern for one's nearest and dearest, let us consider the panel's explanation of what is wrong with attaching a condition to a donation. The panel claims that conditional donation 'offends against the fundamental principle that organs are donated altruistically and should go to patients in the greatest need'. Altruism in its normal sense refers roughly to a non-self-interested concern for the interests of others. Importantly, a wide variety of other-regarding motives can be regarded as altruistic, such as a special concern for children, or the deaf, or the poor . . . Wanting organs to go to a child—although also apparently opposed by the panel—is not a violation of altruism any more than donating to a children's charity is.

Of course, it is seldom possible for cadaveric donation to be directed to a specific individual because organ donors will often be unaware of their impending sudden death. But in rare cases, a person might die after expressing a preference that one of her organs should be used to treat a close relative.

This happened in 2008, when the HTA was criticized for not permitting conditional donation in the case of Laura Ashworth, who had expressed an interest in becoming a living kidney donor for her mother. Laura then died from an acute attack of asthma, before having taken any formal steps towards becoming a living donor. Because she was registered on the organ donor register, her organs were retrieved for transplantation, and her kidneys went to the two strangers at the top of the waiting list. Of course, if Laura Ashworth had been a living, rather than a deceased donor, there would have been no question of her donated kidney being given to a stranger in preference to her mother.

This case led the Department of Health to issue new guidance which allows for 'requested allocation' in exceptional circumstances, 'where the deceased had indicated a wish to donate to a specific named relative or friend of long standing in need of an organ; or, in the absence of that indication, the deceased's family expresses such a wish',[82] provided that there is no one on the waiting list in desperately urgent clinical need for the organ; if there is, her need for an organ must trump the requested allocation.

(6) Mandated Choice

A mandated choice system would allow people to opt in or opt out; what it would not allow them to do is not to make a decision. Mandated choice would be analogous to other

---

[81] 'What's not wrong with conditional organ donation?' (2003) 29 Journal of Medical Ethics 163–4.
[82] *Requested Allocation of a Deceased Donor Organ* (DH: London, 2010).

non-optional public duties, such as filling in the electoral register or paying taxes. Like an opt-out system, it would require the maintenance and updating of an easily accessible database. A number of practical difficulties would have to be resolved, however. What penalty would there be for failing to make a decision, for example? There would also be questions about what to do in the case of children or adults who lack the capacity to make a choice.

(7) Incentives

(a) Financial incentives

Financial incentives to cadaveric donation could not operate as a straightforward sale, in the same way as payments to living donors (considered later). When the organs are retrieved, the donor is dead and is therefore unable to receive money. Instead, there are several other ways in which payments might be used to incentivize cadaveric donation.

First, people could receive a payment in return for their agreement to donate their organs after death. However, since few of us are likely to be suitable organ donors after death, money would generally be paid to non-donors. More plausibly, money could be paid to a third party after death; an example might be meeting the funeral expenses of someone who has registered on the organ donor register, and whose organs are suitable for donation.

A few years ago, the Nuffield Council on Bioethics suggested that there should be a pilot study in order to determine whether a system of payment of funeral expenses would increase donation rates. Families would not be offered money in return for their agreement to donation. Rather, an offer to pay for funeral expenses would be triggered only if someone had agreed in advance to donate their organs, and families would be free to decline the payment if they found it offensive.[83]

Nuffield Council on Bioethics[84]

6.46 . . . [P]ayment of funeral expenses in these circumstances could be ethically justified. Donors cannot be physically harmed—and are highly unlikely to have signified their willingness to donate in these circumstances if they had strong objections. Those close to the donor may benefit directly, and also would clearly have the option of declining the offer of burial costs being met by the NHS. While there is no direct evidence as to how effective or popular such a system would be, the fact that a very similar system exists for covering cremation costs of those who donate their bodies to medical science (which appears to be regarded by both professionals and families as an appropriate acknowledgment of the person's gift), suggests that the extension of such a scheme to organ donors would not be detrimental either to professional values or the common good.

Of course, it would be important to ensure that people were not under the mistaken impression that signing up for the organ donor register would mean that their funeral expenses would be covered. Most of us do not die in circumstances in which it is possible for us to donate our organs.

---

[83] Gill Haddow, ' "Because you're worth it?" The taking and selling of transplantable organs' (2006) 32 Journal of Medical Ethics 324–8.
[84] *Human Bodies: Donation for Medicine and Research* (NCOB, 2011).

(b) Non-financial incentives

A different sort of incentive would be to give priority to those who have indicated their willingness to donate, if they ever need an organ themselves. While it would almost certainly be unethical and impracticable to make willingness to donate the only relevant factor when allocating organs to potential transplant recipients,[85] the points system for allocation, which takes into account a range of factors such as immediacy of clinical need and time spent on the waiting list, could be adjusted so that willing donors receive a higher ranking than similarly situated individuals who would not be prepared to donate their own organs.

This sort of system was introduced in Israel, in response to concerns that some groups in society were willing to receive organs, but were not willing to donate. The new law gives priority to organ donors and their first-degree relatives, and to people who have been registered on the organ donor register for at least three years (this is to stop someone who finds that they need an organ from signing up solely in order to jump the queue).[86]

Priority under the Israeli system is also weighted, so that a transplant candidate with a first-degree relative who has signed a donor card is given half the allocation priority of a candidate who has signed his or her own donor card. A transplant candidate with a first-degree relative who has actually donated their organs after death is given allocation priority 1.5 times greater than that of candidates who have just signed an organ donor card.

In the US, the United Network for Organ Sharing (UNOS) guidelines specify that living donors should have priority for organs in the future. This may be better described not as an incentive, however, but as the removal of a disincentive to donation. Insofar as someone might be reluctant to donate a kidney out of fear that her remaining kidney might fail in the future, this provision offers reassurance that, in such circumstances, she would be given priority for a new organ.

Incorporating priority for donors as part of a move to an opt-out system would involve warning someone who was about to opt out that doing so might reduce her likelihood of receiving an organ, if she ever needed one. The hope is, as Stephanie Eaton explains, 'that the unease that will be felt when opting-out is acknowledged as being a form of free riding will have the consequence that few people will choose to opt out'.[87]

(8) A Duty to Donate? Organs as a Public Resource?

If it were possible to take organs from dead bodies without the need for anyone's agreement, more lives could be saved. In the next extract, HE Emson argues that, once dead, a person's organs should be treated as a public resource, to be distributed to those in need of them.

HE Emson[88]

The body should be regarded morally as on loan to the individual from the biomass, to which the cadaver will inevitably return . . .

I am deeply concerned with the right of the person to govern disposal of their body after death, when separation of body and soul is irrevocably complete and the individual is incapable

---

[85] 'On giving preference to prior volunteers when allocating organs for transplantation' (1995) 21 Journal of Medical Ethics 195–6.

[86] Jacob Lavee, Tamar Ashkenazi, Gabriel Gurman, and David Steinberg, 'A new law for allocation of donor organs in Israel' (2010) 375 The Lancet 1131–3.

[87] 'The subtle politics of organ donation: a proposal' (1998) 24 Journal of Medical Ethics 166–70.

[88] 'It is immoral to require consent for cadaver organ donation' (2003) 29 Journal of Medical Ethics 125–7.

of reconstitution. The person no longer exists, the soul has departed, and the individual who was but is no longer has no further use for the body which has been part of him or her during life. The concept of the right of a person to determine before death, the disposal of their body after death, made sense only when there was no continuing use for that body. It makes neither practical nor moral sense now, when the body for which the dead person no longer has any use, is quite literally a vital resource, a potential source of life for others . . .

If this argument is correct, then it is even more morally unacceptable for the relatives of the deceased to deny utilisation of the cadaver as a source of transplantable organs. Their only claim upon it is as a temporary memorial of a loved one, inevitably destined to decay or be burned in a very short time. To me, any such claim cannot morally be sustained in the face of what I regard as the overwhelming and pre-emptive need of the potential recipient.

Alternatively, could it be argued that we are under a moral duty to donate our organs after death, equivalent to the duty of easy rescue?

James Lindemann Nelson[89]

[T]here is a strong presumption that refusing to save another person's life when doing so is virtually costless to the person in a position to act, is seriously wrong . . .

I think that people typically have duties to provide organs to others, should the opportunity arise, and indeed, duties to reconsider and possibly refigure their attitudes about themselves and others insofar as those attitudes threaten their inclinations to be organ providers. Or, to put it a bit more carefully, since it seems a bit strained to think of dead people having duties, I think that removing organs from the dead typically neither harms nor wrongs them, and that therefore we the living have a prima facie duty to support the retrieval of useful organs, both from our own dead bodies, and from those of others. If we find ourselves repulsed or otherwise distressed by this prospect, we have a derivative duty: to seek to revamp our attitudes.

John Harris further points out that since the human body never remains intact for very long after death, objections to organ donation are intrinsically irrational, and, in any event, must be of less importance than the interests of potential recipients, who might otherwise die.

John Harris[90]

My point is that it is surely implausible to think that having one's body remain whole after their death is an objective anyone is entitled to pursue at the cost of other people's lives! It is implausible to the point of wickedness, not least because the objective is irrational and impossible of achievement . . . No dead body remains intact; the worms . . . or the fire and eventually dust claim it . . . The alternatives are not burial intact or disintegration. There is no

---

[89] *Hippocrates' Maze: Ethical Explorations of the Medical Labyrinth* (Rowman & Littlefield: New York, 2003) 119.

[90] 'Organ procurement: dead interests, living needs' (2003) 29 Journal of Medical Ethics 130–4.

alternative which does not involve disintegration. Given the irrationality of the aim, it is difficult to defend a right to pursue such an aim when it is clear that doing so costs lives.

In the next extract, Sheelagh McGuinness and Margaret Brazier are critical of Harris's brisk dismissal of the views of those who find organ donation difficult.

Sheelagh McGuinness and Margaret Brazier[91]

Death is not akin to a switch that once 'off' means that the dead person ceases to matter at all. Death is described by some as, and can traditionally be seen to be, a socially constructed event. Death rituals have formed an important part of the grieving process. Throughout history there has been an expectation that in death the body will be respected as a symbol of the living person. Death of someone close to you is difficult to accept. We struggle to adjust to an understanding that the person is gone. Identifying with the dead is so hard that we think of the dead body as a symbol of the pre-mortem person.

The dead infant, the wife succumbing to breast cancer at 35, the elderly father dying suddenly of a heart attack, do not change their nature for their mother, husband or daughter. They remain Susannah, Lucy and Dad. They are not simply things.

Walter Glannon goes further and contends that our interest in what is done to our bodies after our death outweighs the interests of those in need of organs.

Walter Glannon[92]

Because the body is so closely associated with who we are, we can have an interest in what is done to it even after we cease to exist. The fact that my body is mine and is essential to my life plan means that I have a deep interest in what is done to it. If it is treated in a way that does not accord with my wishes or interests, then in an important respect this can be bad for me and I can be harmed. The special relation between humans and their bodies can make it wrong for others to ignore the expressed wish that one's organs not be harvested at death, despite their viability for transplantation . . .

Given the special relation between humans and their bodies, the moral importance of individual autonomy in having a life plan, and that what happens to one's body after death is part of such a plan, the negative right to bodily integrity after death outweighs any presumed positive right of the sick to receive organs from those who did not consent to cadaver donation.

It is, however, worth noting that we do not allow relatives to object to forensic post-mortems. This is not because they are less invasive than transplantation. Rather, the public interest in the detection of serious crime trumps concern about the family's feelings about what happens during a post-mortem. It is perhaps interesting that the death of identifiable people on the transplant waiting list is not regarded as of comparable public importance.

---

[91] 'Respecting the Living Means Respecting the Dead Too' (2008) 28 Oxford Journal of Legal Studies 297–316.
[92] 'Do the sick have a right to cadaveric organs?' (2003) 29 Journal of Medical Ethics 153–6.

3 LIVE DONORS

(a) THE ETHICAL ACCEPTABILITY OF LIVING ORGAN DONATION

As we saw at the beginning of this chapter, survival rates for recipients of kidneys from living donors are slightly higher than those for recipients of cadaveric organs. In part, this may be because the organ is taken from a healthy, living person, rather than from someone who has died. But perhaps more importantly, the timing of the transplant can be controlled. When a cadaveric organ becomes available, the operation has to take place as soon as possible after the donor's (usually sudden) death, with no time for the recipient to prepare herself for major surgery.

Despite the obvious advantages in increasing the pool of potential organ donors to include living people, the practice remains controversial. Unlike cadaveric donation, living organ donation does pose real, albeit small, health risks to the donor. For a living kidney donor, the risk of death from the operation itself is 1 in 3,000, which is about the same as the risk of death from appendix removal. Large cohort studies of the longer term health risks faced by living kidney donors are, according to the British Transplantation Society, 'reassuring, indicating that the lifetime risk of ESRD (end stage renal disease) after kidney donation is low, occurring in less than 1:200 donors (0.5%)'.[93]

Holscher et al found that 2.1 per cent of living kidney donors in their study regretted their decision to donate, a finding that was 'within the range of reported prevalence of regret, ranging from 0 to 7 per cent'.[94] Of course, this means that the vast majority of donors do not regret their decision. On the contrary, there is evidence that donors more commonly experience increased self-esteem and feelings of wellbeing.[95] Watching someone one loves suffer is itself a miserable experience, and being able to alleviate her suffering, or save her life, is likely to have substantial non-clinical benefits for the donor.

Interestingly, there appears to be a gender imbalance both among living organ donors, who are more likely to be female, and among recipients, more of whom are male.[96] A German study found that mothers were the most frequent donors (27 per cent), followed by wives (19 per cent), fathers (13 per cent), sisters (12 per cent), and husbands (11 per cent).[97] The reasons for this are unclear, although suggested explanations have included men's greater capacity to resist family pressure, and their higher wage-earning capacity, which may mean that sparing time for donation and recuperation is perceived to be easier for women.

While the altruistic act of the donor might be laudable, Carl Elliott argues that both recipients of live organs, and doctors who perform living organ retrieval, are encouraging the donor's self-sacrifice, and that this is more problematic.

---

[93] *Guidelines for Living Donor Kidney Transplantation* 4th edition (BTS, 2018).

[94] Courtenay M Holscher et al, 'Anxiety, depression, and regret of donation in living kidney donors' (2018) 19 BMC Nephrology 218.

[95] Roberta G Simmons, Susan D Klein, and Richard L Simmons, *Gift of Life: the Social and Psychological Impact of Organ Transplantation* (Wiley: New York, 1977).

[96] Nikola Biller-Andorno, 'Gender imbalance in living organ donation' (2002) 5 Medicine, Health Care and Philosophy 199–204.

[97] Ibid.

Carl Elliott[98]

> [W]hile it is admirable to risk harm to oneself, it is not admirable to encourage another person to risk harm to himself for one's own benefit . . .
>
> Accepting a sacrifice of great magnitude is not mere passive acquiescence, devoid of any moral import. If I allow someone else to risk his life or health for my sake, I am endorsing his self-sacrifice and agreeing to profit by it . . . If an ailing patient were to take advantage of a healthy donor's self-sacrifice, it might well be understandable, but it would not be morally admirable. It would not be the sort of behaviour that we would aspire to and want to encourage.
>
> [T]he doctor is also a moral agent who should be held accountable for his actions . . . This shifts the moral balance of the problem in an important way, because while we admire the person who *undergoes* harm to himself for the sake of another, we do not necessarily admire the person who *inflicts* harm on one person for the sake of another. And the latter is what the doctor must do.

Concern about the possibility of harm to living donors should perhaps lead us to be reluctant to encourage living donation until we have exhausted all possible means of increasing the number of cadaveric organs. Increased rates of cadaveric donation have health benefits not only for the recipients of those organs, but also for potential living donors, whose services might no longer be needed.

(b) TYPE OF TRANSPLANT

Obviously, it is only possible for living organ donors to donate non-vital organs, such as kidneys and lobes of the lung or liver. Most living organ donation involves kidneys: in 2017–18, there were 1,020 living donor kidney transplants, 29 living donor liver lobe transplants, and no living lung transplants.[99]

A difficult ethical question about the limits of autonomous decision-making arose in the US in 1998 when a father wanted to donate his second kidney to his daughter, after her first transplant failed.[100] The operation would not have killed Mr Patterson, but it would have left him dependent upon dialysis for the rest of his life, unless he himself received a kidney transplant. Unlike his first kidney donation, the donation of his second kidney would result in a dramatic and substantial deterioration in his own health, and his request was turned down.

Drawing upon on a fictitious example of a father who wishes to donate both of his kidneys to his identical twin sons with end stage renal disease, on the grounds that 'his main priority in life is to ensure that his children are happy and healthy, and . . . he values their well-being above his own', Philippa Bailey and Richard Huxtable suggest that there could be times when dual kidney donation should be permitted. In contrast, Lainie F Ross and Richard J Thistlethwaite argue that doctors are moral agents, rather than mere instruments of their patients' wishes, and that there are limits upon how much harm transplant professionals should be willing to inflict upon living donors.

---

[98] 'Doing harm: living organ donors, clinical research and the tenth man' (1995) 21 Journal of Medical Ethics 91–6.

[99] NHS Blood and Transplant, *Annual Activity Report 2017–18: Summary of Transplant Activity* (NHSBT, 2018).

[100] Ryan Sauder and Lisa S Parker, 'Autonomy's limits: living donation and health-related harm' (2001) 10 Cambridge Quarterly of Healthcare Ethics 399–401.

Phillippa Bailey and Richard Huxtable[101]

> Requests for dual living kidney donation are likely to be rare, and are most likely to be associated with familial conditions, in which multiple members of one family develop renal failure, while others are disease free. We have argued that there may be a *prima facie* case for allowing such donations to occur, provided that both the donor and the recipients are willing and that due attention is paid to such considerations as the autonomy and welfare of all parties, as well as to the wider ramifications of acting on such a request . . .
>
> [W]e have argued for broader interpretations of the concepts of autonomy and welfare, which recognize the importance of relationships and the relevance of more than merely physical well-being. We suspect that, with such a holistic assessment, a case can be made for allowing dual living kidney donation.

Lainie F Ross and Richard J Thistlethwaite[102]

> [T]he reason to reject the parent's offer to donate his second kidney is not that his calculation is wrong, but rather, because there are limits to how much harm that transplant professionals, as moral agents, should be willing to voluntarily cause a potential living donor... That is, the members of the transplant team are moral agents who must concur that the risks and benefit:risk to both parties individually and jointly is reasonable or they should refuse to proceed with performing the living donor surgery.

(c) LIVE TRANSPLANTATION IN THE UK

While Human Tissue Act 2004 covers consent to the use and storage of tissue taken from the living, its removal from the living donor's body continues to be dealt with at common law and under the Mental Capacity Act 2005.

The law covering living organ donation will be unchanged by the move to an opt-out system.

(1) Consent to the Removal of Tissue

The criminal law places limits upon the extent to which an adult can consent to the infliction of harm. Nephrectomy (kidney removal) is a serious operation which would undoubtedly qualify as grievous bodily harm, for which consent is no defence. As we saw in Chapter 5, 'proper medical treatment' has been said to stand outside the criminal law, and, according to the Law Commission: 'there is no doubt that once a valid consent has been forthcoming, English law now treats as lawful donation of ... non-regenerative tissue that is not essential to life'.[103]

---

[101] 'When Opportunity Knocks Twice: Dual Living Kidney Donation, Autonomy and the Public Interest' (2016) 30 Bioethics 119–28.

[102] 'Developing an ethics framework for living donor transplantation' (2018) 44 Journal of Medical Ethics 843–50.

[103] Law Commission Consultation Paper No 139, *Consent in the Criminal Law* (HMSO: London, 1995) para 8.32.

This assumption of legality has been questioned, however. Govert den Hartogh, for example, has suggested that in other contexts, we would not allow someone to incur this level of risk in order to help others. He asks us to imagine that we are 'a member of a medical ethics committee that has to assess a medical experiment that involves a similar set of invasive procedures, risks, and burdens for its participants':

> Even if the therapy to be tested could save people's lives, would you approve the experiment? I have put that question to some members of such committees, and their answer is that their committee would almost certainly reject it.[104]

Because the living organ donor is undergoing non-therapeutic surgery, it is especially important that her consent is fully informed and voluntary. In practice, however, as Ryan Sauder and Lisa Parker point out, many living donors feel that donating an organ to a desperately sick relative is effectively 'non-optional'.

Ryan Sauder and Lisa S Parker[105]

> Frequently, a prospective donor, particularly a parent or sibling of the prospective recipient, will experience the decision to donate as automatic. They frequently report feeling that they had no choice but to donate, and proceed to offer their organs willingly and without hesitation, sometimes even before hearing of the risks involved in such a donation. Disclosure of risks frequently has no effect on the decision to donate. These decisions hardly seem to meet the traditional requirements of informed consent. Failing to take risks of an intervention into account when deciding whether to consent to it, and feeling compelled to consent, are typically hallmarks of a failure of the informed consent process. Yet we are reluctant to suggest that these prospective donors are not making autonomous decisions to donate and, consequently, that their decisions (and organs) should not be accepted.

Most of us can put ourselves in the shoes of someone who has the chance to donate an organ to someone we love, and we would not consider that our eagerness to donate made us unable to make an autonomous choice. Indeed, in their interviews with parents who had donated organs to their children, Philippa Burnell et al found not only that they were making a choice to donate, but also that they felt lucky to have that option.

Philippa Burnell, Sally-Anne Hulton, and Heather Draper[106]

> The majority of participants made reference to choice: they felt that they were making a decision where not donating was a genuine alternative, just not one they personally could countenance ...

---

[104] 'Is consent of the donor enough to justify the removal of living organs?' (2013) 22 Cambridge Quarterly of Healthcare Ethics 45–54.
[105] 'Autonomy's limits: living donation and health-related harm' (2001) 10 Cambridge Quarterly of Healthcare Ethics 399–401.
[106] 'Coercion and choice in parent–child live kidney donation' (2015) 41 Journal of Medical Ethics 304–9.

> When they described the first discussion with health professionals about live donation, this was not reported as a situation where they felt pressure to donate. Instead, parents *wanted* to donate ... Parents were typically pleased that live donation was a possibility: 'I never resented being put in that position' ...
>
> Commonly, participants felt 'lucky' when they discovered they *could* donate and the only circumstance in which they envisaged themselves not donating was if they were tissue incompatible. Some parents described the upset this would have caused for them. Indeed, it was being *incompatible* that one participant described as being a situation of 'no choice' ...
>
> They reported donating because improving the well-being of their child was important for that child *and* therefore for themselves. For our participants, donation also served their own interests because they tended not to separate their child's interests from their own.

Of course, not all potential donors will want to donate to relatives or friends, and in practice, clinicians will commonly provide a 'medical alibi' if someone does not want to donate, but is fearful of their family's reaction.[107] This does not necessarily involve deception: after all, if a potential donor is not happy to consent to donation, it would be true to say that she is not a suitable donor. A potential donor is not simply a supplier of tissue, but a patient in her own right, to whom transplant professionals owe a duty of care.

In addition to full disclosure of the risks to their own health, potential living organ donors should also be given frank information about the possibility that the transplant might not work, and the emotional impact of an unsuccessful donation. If the recipient's need for a transplant results from a genetic condition, more than one family member may require the same transplant, and donors need to understand that they may be able to act as a donor only once.

Given the need for informed consent, could organs ever be taken from those who lack the capacity to consent?

(a) Children

In the case of children, in sibling-to-sibling organ donation, parents have a responsibility for the wellbeing of both the recipient and the donor. As with other especially controversial procedures, court approval should be sought.

There have, as yet, been no cases but there were *obiter* comments in *Re W (A Minor)*,[108] that the Family Law Reform Act 1969, which gives 16- and 17-year-olds the right to consent to medical treatment, would not apply to organ donation because, 'so far as the donor is concerned, these do not constitute either treatment or diagnosis'.[109] Instead, until the age of 18, 'the jurisdiction of the court should always be invoked'.[110] Until such a case arises, it is not clear whether the courts would ever be prepared to authorize such an operation.

There have been instances of child organ donation in the US. In *Hart v Brown*,[111] for example, the court was satisfied that the psychological benefit to the donor from her identical twin sister's survival and continued companionship, justified the risks of donation. And Kristof Van Assche et al have argued that disregarding a mature minor's 'genuine willingness to donate' could itself be unfair: 'an absolute prohibition is difficult to reconcile with the

---

[107] Mary Simmerling et al, 'When duties collide: beneficence and veracity in the evaluation of living organ donors' (2007) 12 Current Opinions in Organ Transplantation 188–92.

[108] [1993] Fam 64.   [109] Per Lord Donaldson.   [110] Per Nolan LJ.

[111] 289 A 2d 386 (Conn Sup Ct 1972).

tendency to grant minors who can demonstrate maturity a high degree of self-determination in medical decision-making'.[112]

(b) Adults who lack capacity

Paragraph 8.20 of the Mental Capacity Act Code of Practice makes it clear that cases 'involving organ or bone marrow donation by a person who lacks capacity to consent should ... be referred to the Court of Protection'. The court would then have to decide whether organ donation was in the person's best interests, and it would be guided by the checklist of factors in section 4 which, as we saw in Chapter 5, places particular emphasis upon the values and wishes of the patient who lacks capacity.

In *Re Y (Mental Patient: Bone Marrow Donation)*[113]—a pre-Mental Capacity Act case— bone marrow donation from a woman who lacked capacity was authorized, on the grounds that it would be in her social or emotional interests, but Connell J doubted whether similar reasoning could be used to justify organ donation. As yet, no cases have arisen and so, as with children, it is unclear whether a court would ever be satisfied that solid organ donation was in the best interests of an adult who lacked capacity. Again, this has happened in the US. In *Strunk v Strunk*,[114] the court approved kidney donation on the grounds that the death of his brother would have caused the potential donor psychological and emotional injury greater than the risks associated with the removal of one of his kidneys.

(2) The Human Tissue Act 2004

Under section 33(1) and (2), taking an organ from a living person for the purposes of transplantation is an offence, unless the requirements in section 33(3) and (5) are satisfied. These are, under section 33(3), that no payment or reward has been given in contravention of section 32, and that such other conditions and requirements as may be specified in regulations are satisfied. Section 33(5) offers a defence if the person who takes an organ reasonably believes that the transplant satisfies the section 33(3) requirements.

(a) Consent to use in transplantation

Under section 1 of the Act, there must be 'appropriate consent' to the use of human tissue for transplantation. For competent adults, under section 3(2) 'appropriate consent' means 'his consent'. The HTA Code of Practice contains detailed guidance on the information that should be provided as part of the consent process.

HTA Code of Practice[115]

70. To ensure that the informed consent of the donor is secured, the transplant team must make sure the following areas are discussed with the donor:

   a) the nature of the surgical/medical procedure and medical treatments involved for the donor, and any material short and long term risks (this should be explained by a medical

---

[112] Kristof Van Assche et al , 'Living tissue and organ donation by minors: Suggestions to improve the regulatory framework in Europe' (2016) 16 Medical Law International 58–93.
[113] [1997] Fam 110.   [114] 445 SW 2d 145 (1969).
[115] Code F: Donation of solid organs and tissue for transplantation (HTA, 2017).

practitioner with appropriate qualifications to give this information) ... This information should include the risk of death to the donor;

b) the chances of the transplant being successful, and any significant side effects or complications for the recipient, and in particular the donor should be made aware of the possibility of graft failure in the recipient;

c) the right to withdraw consent at any time before the removal of the transplantable material;

d) that the decision to donate must be free of duress or coercion;

e) that it is an offence to give or receive a reward for the supply of, or for an offer to supply, any organ. It is also an offence to seek to find a person willing to supply any organ for reward. If found guilty of this offence a person may face up to three years in prison, a fine, or both.

71. The donor must have a clear understanding of the benefits and disadvantages of living donor transplantation in their particular case, as well as the general risks and benefits.

As with the common law on organ retrieval, the Act does not rule out the possibility of using organs taken from adults who lack capacity, but any such transplants would have to be approved by a panel of at least three members of the HTA and comply with the Human Tissue Act 2004 (Persons who Lack Capacity to Consent and Transplants) Regulations 2006. These effectively duplicate the assessment that the court would carry out in deciding whether the retrieval would be lawful, namely that the use of tissue in transplantation must be in the best interests of the child or adult who lacks capacity.

Human Tissue Act 2004 (Persons who Lack Capacity to Consent and Transplants) Regulations 2006 regulation 3(2)

(2) An adult ('P') who lacks capacity to consent . . . is deemed to have consented to the activity where—

(a) the activity is done for a purpose specified in paragraph 4 or 7 [7 is transplantation] by a person who is acting in what he reasonably believes to be P's best interests.

Under section 2(3) of the Human Tissue Act, children who have sufficient maturity to consent to such a serious operation (see Chapter 6) might be able to consent to the use of their organ in transplantation.

Human Tissue Act 2004 section 2

2(3) Where—

(a) the child concerned is alive,

(b) neither a decision of his to consent to the activity, nor a decision of his not to consent to it, is in force, and

(c) either he is not competent to deal with the issue of consent in relation to the activity or, though he is competent to deal with that issue, he fails to do so,

'appropriate consent' means the consent of a person who has parental responsibility for him.

Where the child lacks capacity or does not wish to make a decision, anyone with parental responsibility could give consent, but this alone would not be sufficient for the donation to go ahead, and court approval should also be sought.

HTA Code of Practice[116]

44. Children can be considered as living organ donors only in extremely rare circumstances. The HT Act defines a child as being under 18 years old. If a clinician intends to consider a child as a living organ donor, they are advised to discuss the case with the HTA at the earliest opportunity.

45. In accordance with common law and the Children Act 1989 (which established the legal basis for who has parental responsibility), court approval should be obtained before the removal of a solid organ or part organ from a child for donation. Transplant Units should obtain their own legal advice regarding seeking court approval.

46. Living donation by a child under the HT Act can only go ahead with the approval of an HTA panel. Such cases must only be referred to the HTA for decision after court approval for the removal has been obtained.

(b) Restrictions on live donation

Independent Assessors (IAs) should be NHS consultants, or of equivalent standing, should not be working in the field of organ transplantation, and should have been trained and accredited by the HTA. They interview donors and recipient and certify that all statutory and other requirements are satisfied. Their reports to the HTA are valid for six months, after which a further report will become necessary, in case the circumstances have changed. The HTA will then decide whether the donation can go ahead.

In directed donations, the donor's organs are to be donated to a specified individual, usually a partner or family member. In non-directed donation, the recipient's identity is not known to the donor. Paired donation takes place when a person volunteers to donate to someone she knows, but she turns out to be a poor tissue match. In such circumstances, the would-be donor and donee might be paired with a similar couple so that each recipient can receive a compatible organ. Pooled donation works in the same way, but involves a larger pool of willing but unmatched known donors.

Non-directed donations include 'domino' transplants, where the primary purpose of the donation is the medical treatment of the donor. Because it is more straightforward to carry out a heart and lung transplant than to transplant lungs alone, someone who is in need of a lung transplant might receive the heart and lungs from a cadaveric donor. The recipient's heart is then available for transplant into another person. While this would be a living unrelated transplant, the donor would be undergoing the operation for her own benefit.

In 2017–18, there were 89 non-directed altruistic living kidney transplants. These are cases where the living donor does not know the recipient. The HTA takes extra care to ensure that consent has been given voluntarily, and requires there to have been a psychiatric assessment of the would-be donor. Walter Glannon and Lainie Friedman Ross argue that suspicion of the motives of non-directed altruistic donors is not necessarily justified, since a potential organ

[116] Ibid.

donor who has no emotional ties to the recipient may in fact be better able to make a free and unpressurized decision to donate.

Walter Glannon and Lainie Friedman Ross[117]

An altruistic donor has no obligation to donate. The decision to donate goes beyond the obligatory and permissible to the supererogatory, and a decision not to donate does not invite or warrant moral criticism because there is no moral basis on which to criticize not performing an act that would have been beyond the call of duty. In contrast, the family member who is a potential donor has a prima facie obligation to donate because of the nature of relationships within the family.

In contrast, in their interviews with healthcare professionals involved in living liver donation, Elin Thomas et al found that many believed it was too risky in the case of strangers, but that where the donor was very close to the recipient (especially if the donor was a parent), the emotional benefits to the donor tipped the risk/benefit calculation in favour of allowing donation.

Elin H Thomas et al[118]

[A]lthough HCPs [healthcare professionals] claim that their assessments are more objective (less clouded by emotion) than those of the donor and recipient, their assessment of risk often reflects their own values regarding the nature of familial relationships. For example, a greater level of risk was judged to be acceptable in the case of an LLD [living liver donation] from a parent to his or her adult child than an LLD from an adult child to his or her parent (despite the similar medical risk associated with both cases). Here, the participants seemed to be factoring into their judgement, a view that it is more acceptable for parents to take risks for their children than vice versa. Likewise ... altruistic (stranger) donation was regarded as too risky, even though the risks are similar to those between relatives or family friends.

In recent years, people in need of a kidney, or their relatives, have searched for potential living donors online, by setting up Facebook pages, or advertising on donor matching websites. Greg Moorlock and Heather Draper set out some of the risks of what they call publicly solicited donation (PSD).

Greg Moorlock and Heather Draper[119]

For patients in need of a transplant, PSD is an opportunity to actively improve their own situation, something they are arguably entitled to do, given the costs and burdens of not

---

[117] 'Do genetic relationships create moral obligations in organ transplantation?' (2002) 11 Cambridge Quarterly of Healthcare Ethics 153–9.
[118] 'Live liver donation, ethics and practitioners: "I am between the two and if I do not feel comfortable about this situation, I cannot proceed"' (2014) 40 Journal of Medical Ethics 157–62.
[119] 'Empathy, social media, and directed altruistic living organ donation' (2018) 32 Bioethics 289–97.

gaining an organ ... Although everyone waiting for a kidney may be free to advertise, some patients are better placed and able to promote themselves more effectively than others ...

PSD disrupts the usual criteria that balance clinical need, benefit, and waiting time. Instead kidneys may be 'allocated' according to distinctly non-medical factors, such as religion, social value, and how photogenic the patients are. There are related issues stemming from unequal access to social media, varying social media savviness, and ability or otherwise to fund impressive and engaging campaigns ...

Faced with the choice of allocating a kidney according to potentially arbitrary criteria, or not having the kidney available for transplantation at all, it is arguably wasteful to take the latter option ... Its potential to evoke empathy may result in more living donations, but there is a significant risk that this will come at a cost to the fairness of the allocation system, which, in turn, may undermine trust in the transplantation system.

Greg Moorlock has further questioned the behaviour of potential recipients in what EM Neidich et al have described as 'the beauty contest' model of directed altruistic living donation (DALD).[120]

Greg Moorlock[121]

Instead of patiently waiting to move to the top of a waiting list due to being the best match for an organ, patients can increase their chances of being offered a transplant by creating the most compelling back-story, creating the best viral video or by directly contacting the greatest number of potential donors ...

The behaviour of recipients in impartial allocation systems who cooperatively wait their turn is aligned with the altruistic basis of the system because the waiting list is ordered to provide the best overall balance for everyone waiting for organs. By accepting that organs are allocated according to the waiting list order, patients allow for their needs and interests to be considered against the needs and interests of other patients to ensure that overall need is effectively met. The behaviour of many recipients in DALD, however, can work against the role of altruism because those taking an 'every person for him/herself' approach would likely be much more self-serving. Rather than embracing a communal and collective approach to meeting the needs of those who require transplants, DALD allows recipients to actively further their own interests by leveraging their personal appeal to place their needs above those of others, potentially at a significant cost to those with more urgent need.

The Human Tissue Authority has issued guidance on living organ donation matching websites and social media, which explains that advertising for a donor is not illegal, 'providing there is no offer of a reward, payment or material advantage to the potential donor'. It also recommends that anyone contemplating advertising in this way should be wary of paying a fee to a matching website, and should first contact their local transplant unit.

[120] EM Neidich et al, 'The ethical complexities of online organ solicitation via donor–patient websites: avoiding the "beauty contest"' (2012) 12 American Journal of Transplantation 43–7.
[121] 'Directed altruistic living donation: what is wrong with the beauty contest?' (2015) 41 Journal of Medical Ethics 875–9.

Human Tissue Authority[122]

Transplant units are not obliged to consider all potential living donors and this approach may raise logistical difficulties. For example, a transplant unit may not have the capacity or resources to test all of those who may come forward as potential donors as a result of the advert ...

Transplant units will take a wide variety of factors into account in deciding whether to take on a donor and recipient pair. Your wish to proceed with your particular donor is only one factor. You should be aware that you may not be a suitable recipient for the person who has offered you an organ ...

The British Transplantation Society (BTS) has recently issued guidance that transplant units should not accept cases for living donor assessment that arise from websites where potential transplant recipients pay a fee to register their need for an organ transplant. People considering using these websites should be aware therefore, that even if a donor were to be found via this route, the transplant community has been advised not to proceed with such cases.

(c) Payment

In 2015, the Council of Europe adopted a Convention against Trafficking in Human Organs, Article 4 of which requires each of the following acts to be a criminal offence:

(a) where the removal is performed without the free, informed and specific consent of the living or deceased donor, or, in the case of the deceased donor, without the removal being authorised under its domestic law;

(b) where, in exchange for the removal of organs, the living donor, or a third party, has been offered or has received a financial gain or comparable advantage;

(c) where in exchange for the removal of organs from a deceased donor, a third party has been offered or has received a financial gain or comparable advantage.

Under section 32 of the Human Tissue Act, payment for human organs is a criminal offence.

Human Tissue Act 2004 section 32

32 Prohibition of commercial dealings in human material for transplantation

(1) A person commits an offence if he—

(a) gives or receives a reward for the supply of, or for an offer to supply, any controlled material;

(b) seeks to find a person willing to supply any controlled material for reward;

(c) offers to supply any controlled material for reward;

(d) initiates or negotiates any arrangement involving the giving of a reward for the supply of, or for an offer to supply, any controlled material;

(e) takes part in the management or control of a body of persons corporate or unincorporate whose activities consist of or include the initiation or negotiation of such arrangements.

---

[122] Living organ donation matching websites and social media (HTA, 2018).

Under section 32(8) and (10), the prohibition covers both cadaveric and living organ donation. It is not just organ traffickers who would commit an offence under section 32; recipients of organs could also face prosecution, as could anyone involved in arranging an organ sale. The maximum penalty is three years' imprisonment. Under section 32(2), it is also an offence to publish or distribute an advertisement for the sale of an organ, with a maximum penalty of 51 weeks' imprisonment.

Under section 32(6)(a) payment to the holder of a licence (ie the hospital) in money or money's worth is not to be considered a reward if it 'is in consideration for transporting, removing, preparing, preserving, or storing controlled material'. This means that covering the costs associated with the transplantation process is not to be treated in the same way as a payment for an organ. Similarly, section 32(7)(a) provides that 'any expenses incurred in, or in connection with, transporting, removing, preparing, preserving or storing the material' are not to be treated as a reward.

Section 32(7)(c) permits payments to living organ donors to cover 'any expenses or loss of earnings incurred by the person from whose body the material comes so far as reasonably and directly attributable to his supplying the material from his body'. A living organ donor could therefore expect to receive compensation for time that she has to take off work during the organ donation process, and for associated expenses, such as travel costs. The reference to expenses or loss of earnings makes it clear that any such payments are not to be seen as payment for the organ itself, or even compensation for the inconvenience of donation, but rather must simply cover financial costs that are directly attributable to the donation.

(d) WHAT, IF ANYTHING, WOULD BE WRONG WITH A MARKET IN ORGANS?

Several reasons are commonly put forward for prohibiting the sale of organs. First, it is argued that there is something intrinsically wrong with commodifying the human body, and that it would be either impossible or degrading to put a value on human body parts. Secondly, commercialization of organ transplantation is believed to undermine the principle that donation should be altruistic.

Thirdly, a black market in organs already exists in some parts of the world. Wealthy patients travel for transplant surgery which depends upon the (illegal) payment of relatively modest sums to 'donors'. It is, as Simon Rippon has pointed out, 'a matter of empirical fact' that 'people who are not financially desperate generally do not want to become living organ vendors'.[123] The next extracts highlight the consequences of markets in organs for the poor and vulnerable.

Giovanni Berlinguer[124]

The truth of the matter is that, as far as human organs are concerned, the traffic always takes place between the South and the North of the world, or between the poor who sell and the rich who buy . . . [I]n the twenty-first century, the North could attempt to treat its more seriously ill by importing and using organs from members of the poorer classes, in particular from the underdeveloped countries. Supplies would be more than sufficient, as bodies are the only goods that these countries produce in abundance.

[123] Simon Rippon, 'Organ markets and harms: a reply to Dworkin, Radcliffe Richards and Walsh' (2014) 40 Journal of Medical Ethics 155–6.
[124] *Everyday Bioethics: Reflections on Bioethical Choices in Daily Life* (Baywood Publishing: New York, 2003) 101.

M Goyal, RL Mehta, LJ Schneiderman, and AR Seghal[125]

[S]elling a kidney did not help poor donors overcome poverty. Family income actually declined by one third, and most participants were still in debt and living below the poverty line at the time of the survey ... [M]ost participants would not recommend that others sell a kidney, which suggests that potential donors would be unlikely to sell a kidney if they were better informed of the likely outcomes ... [N]ephrectomy was associated with a decline in health status. Previous qualitative reports suggest that a diminished ability to perform physical labor may explain the observed worsening of economic status . . . A majority of donors were women. Given the often weak position of women in Indian society, the voluntary nature of some donations is questionable. In fact, two participants said that their husbands forced them to donate.

Fourthly, it has been argued that financial incentives may overbear a person's will, and thus cast doubt upon the voluntariness of their consent.

Eugene B Brody[126]

In countries without legal prohibition of organ selling, recruitment campaigns have used selling techniques which effectively negate informed consent among the poorest citizens for whom the possibility of a one-time financial gain of previously unimaginable proportions is so irresistible as to obviate rational judgement. Financial incentives in these circumstances are tantamount to coercion.

Kate Greasley objects to organ markets not because vendors cannot consent, but because we know that they would not have consented but for their poverty.

Kate Greasley[127]

[T]he real concern does not turn on consent as such, but rather, on the claim that consensual or not, the kind of trading entailed by a living donor market in organs will almost always play on the natural disadvantages of the poor. The situation of the kidney-seller in the imaginary example continues to be deeply disconcerting, not because we are unsure of whether he consented, but because we are certain that he never *would* have consented but for his poverty.

Fifthly, donation involves pain, discomfort, and risk, and there are those who are troubled by the prospect of people assuming risks to their health in return for financial reward. Indeed, as Julian Koplin points out, the evidence appears to indicate that the outcomes for organ vendors are, on average, worse than for organ donors, perhaps because of their pre-existing poverty.

---

[125] 'Economic and health consequences of selling a kidney in India' (2002) 288 Journal of the American Medical Association 1589–93.

[126] *Biomedical Technology and Human Rights* (UNESCO: Paris, 1993) 100.

[127] 'A legal market in organs: the problem of exploitation' (2014) 40 Journal of Medical Ethics 51–6.

Julian Koplin[128]

Almost every study that has asked the question has found that the majority of vendors regret selling a kidney and/or would not recommend doing so to others. Moreover, a study of 100 Iranian donors (97 of whom were vendors) found that 76% were in favor of banning kidney sales. According to vendors' own accounts, selling a kidney left them worse off physically, psychologically, socially, and financially. In the face of this body of research, and in the absence of compelling reasons to believe that such outcomes are entirely attributable to black-market abuses, the ubiquitous claim that regulated systems of kidney selling would improve vendors' well-being lacks evidential warrant. The available research, despite its limitations, suggests the opposite: that vendors will usually experience a range of significant harms that ultimately leave them worse off than before the sale.

Against this, Luke Semrau has argued that those who claim that selling organs is harmful do not judge it against the other options that are available to vendors, which might be likely to be even more harmful.

Luke Semrau[129]

What happens to those who would vend if that option is closed? ... Perhaps desperation makes prostitution more appealing. Perhaps it leads one to see one's children as economic resources, or to think criminal activity choiceworthy. Perhaps one is drawn to take up dangerous labor. And, perhaps those who take these options do not escape from debt, later regret their choices, and would not recommend them to others. That is to say, all of the consideration thought to suggest that vending is non-optimific may arise with equal or greater force when the nonvending option is taken ... It is a sad fact about the world that some people's lives may be improved by acts that are not on balance beneficial. Before substituting our own judgment for that of those who bear the consequences of our choices, we ought to think more carefully about the limited options of the desperately poor.

It is not just the risks of donation that worry some commentators. Simon Rippon has argued that, if organ sale were permitted, a poor person facing debts or bankruptcy might be harmed by their refusal to sell their kidney.

Simon Rippon[130]

Selling your organs would become something that is simply expected of you as and when financial need arises. Our new 'option' can thus easily be transformed into a social or legal demand, and it can drastically change the attitudes that others adopt towards you ... My

---

[128] 'Assessing the likely harms to kidney vendors in regulated organ markets' (2014) 14 American Journal of Bioethics 7–18.

[129] 'Reassessing the likely harms to kidney vendors in regulated organ markets' (2017) 42 The Journal of Medicine and Philosophy 634–52.

[130] 'Imposing options on people in poverty: the harm of a live donor organ market' (2014) 40 Journal of Medical Ethics 145–50.

contention, then, is that because people in poverty often find themselves either indebted or in need of cash to meet their own basic needs and those of their families, they would predictably find themselves faced with social or legal pressure to pay the bills by selling their organs, if selling organs were permitted ... Once we have come to conceptualise our 'excess' organs and organ parts as pieces of unnecessary property by commodifying them, there would naturally follow genuine social and legal costs to pay for failing to sell them when economically necessary, just as there are social and legal costs to pay for failing to take employment when you are able to do so. We should ask questions such as the following: Would those in poverty be eligible for bankruptcy protection, or for public assistance, if they have an organ that they choose not to sell? Could they be legally forced to sell an organ to pay taxes, paternity bills or rent?

Finally, a free market in organs would mean that only rich people would be able to afford to buy them, thus disrupting the principle that scarce health care resources should be distributed according to need rather than ability to pay.

There are those who would dispute some of these claims. For example, it is not strictly true that it is impossible to put a value on a human organ, nor that doing so is inevitably degrading. Tort law routinely quantifies the loss of various body parts. Victims of criminal injuries are paid damages, without any assumption that such damages undermine the intrinsic value of the human body.

Secondly, even if poor people do find the offer of money in return for a kidney especially attractive, this may also be true of other sources of income that may pose a risk to a person's health (often much greater than the small risk of living with one kidney). Against this, Kate Greasley argues that the exploitation involved in organ selling is more 'extreme' than in most dangerous jobs.

Kate Greasley[131]

[O]rgan selling is quite simply one of the more extreme cases, so that it falls more clearly within the bracket of exploitative behaviour which is serious enough to invoke the coercive power of the law (slavery and child labour being clear examples of other practices in that category). The permanency of losing one's organ, the invasiveness of surgery, the particular health repercussions and psychological impact on the vendor may lead one to the conclusion *this* form of exploitation is especially objectionable ...

Clearly though, serious poverty is often an inducement for people to accept risks in employment which they otherwise would not. It might be argued that there is yet a morally significant difference, in that although there may be a risk involved, there is every chance that the risk will not materialise. In contrast, poor people who sell their organs do not just take a risk—they incur a *certain* loss, a loss which they only deem justified on the pretext that it will do something that in reality it does not: help alleviate their poverty.

Thirdly, it is clear that a black market in human organs already exists, and Janet Radcliffe-Richards et al argue that it is this, rather than a regulated market, which poses the greatest risk to organ donors.

---

[131] 'A legal market in organs: the problem of exploitation' (2014) 40 Journal of Medical Ethics 51–6.

Janet Radcliffe-Richards et al[132]

> If our ground for concern is that the range of choices is too small, we cannot improve matters by removing the best option that poverty has left, and making the range smaller still . . . The only way to improve matters is to lessen the poverty until organ selling no longer seems the best option; and if that could be achieved, prohibition would be irrelevant because nobody would want to sell . . .
>
> [A]ll the evidence we have shows that there is much more scope for exploitation and abuse when a supply of desperately wanted goods is made illegal. It is, furthermore, not clear why it should be thought harder to police a legal trade than the present complete ban.

Only one country has a legal market in organs. The Iranian government provides each kidney vendor approximately US $1,200 plus a year's health insurance.[133] The recipient or, if the recipient is poor, a charitable organization will give the vendor an additional sum of between US $2,300 and US $4,500. Recipients must be Iranian, so Iran is not a destination for transplant tourism. Vendors must be aged between 20 and 35 years of age and their next of kin must have given consent. While there is no shortage of kidney vendors, and hence no shortage of kidneys, vendors commonly find themselves stigmatized and ostracized.[134]

Fourthly, as we saw in Chapter 5, the principle of patient autonomy means that we let people assume considerable risks to their own health by refusing life-sustaining treatment, and they are entitled to do this for irrational reasons or even for no reason at all. Is it then unduly paternalistic to prevent someone from incurring a less serious risk to her health in order to save another person's life?

Fifthly, it is not clear that paid organ donation is necessarily incompatible with altruism. We would permit a mother to donate a kidney to her son if he had kidney failure, but what if her son is instead suffering from a rare form of cancer, and optimum treatment is expensive and only available abroad? We would forbid this mother from selling a kidney in order to pay for her son's life-saving treatment, even though her motivation could be said to be as altruistic as the mother whose son has renal failure.

Sixthly, as Stephen Wilkinson points out, there is something wrong with the argument that we should not allow paid organ donation because it is risky. If this is true, then unpaid organ donation is equally risky, and presumably should also be prohibited.

Stephen Wilkinson[135]

> No matter how dangerous paid donation is, it needn't . . . be any more risky than unpaid donation, since the mere fact of payment doesn't *add* any danger. So if paid donation is wrong because of the danger to which the donor is subjected, then free donation must also be wrong on the very same grounds. Free donation, though, is not wrong; on the contrary, we tend to regard it as commendable, heroic even. Therefore paid donation isn't wrong either—or, if it is wrong, it's wrong because of something other than the danger to which the donor is subjected.

---

[132] 'The case for allowing kidney sales' (1998) 351 The Lancet 1950–2.

[133] Benjamin E Hippen, 'Organ sales and moral travails: lessons from the living kidney vendor program in Iran' (2008) Cato Institute Policy Analysis No 614.

[134] Mohammad Mehdi Nayebpour and Naoru Koizumi, 'The Social Stigma of Selling Kidneys in Iran as a Barrier to Entry: A Social Determinant of Health' (2018) 10 World Medical & Health Policy 55–64.

[135] *Bodies for Sale: Ethics and Exploitation in the Human Body Trade* (Routledge: London, 2003) 108.

Seventhly, allowing payments for organs does not necessarily mean embracing a completely free market. Instead, it would be possible for payments to be made by the NHS rather than individual recipients, and for the organs to be distributed according to need. Because the cost savings of kidney transplantation are significant, NHS-funded payments to kidney donors could be cost-effective. In the next extract, Charles Erin and John Harris suggest that it is possible to contemplate an 'ethical market' in organs.

Charles A Erin and John Harris[136]

There is a lot of hypocrisy about the ethics of buying and selling organs and indeed other body products and services . . . What it usually means is that everyone is paid but the donor. The surgeons and medical team are paid, the transplant coordinator does not go unremunerated, and the recipient receives an important benefit in kind. Only the unfortunate and heroic donor is supposed to put up with the insult of no reward, to add to the insult of the operation . . .

The bare bones of an ethical market would look like this: the market would be confined to a self-governing geopolitical area such as a nation state or indeed the European Union. Only citizens resident within the union or state could sell into the system and they and their families would be equally eligible to receive organs. Thus organ vendors would know they were contributing to a system which would benefit them and their families and friends since their chances of receiving an organ in case of need would be increased by the existence of the market . . . There would be only one purchaser, an agency like the National Health Service (NHS), which would buy all organs and distribute according to some fair conception of medical priority. There would be no direct sales or purchases, no exploitation of low income countries and their populations (no buying in Turkey or India to sell in Harley Street). The organs would be tested for HIV etc, their provenance known, and there would be strict controls and penalties to prevent abuse.

Sellers of organs would know they had saved a life and would be reasonably compensated for their risk, time, and altruism, which would be undiminished by sale. We do not after all regard medicine as any the less a caring profession because doctors are paid.

Of course, while Erin and Harris's ethical market would eliminate one unsatisfactory aspect of a completely free market in organs—in that organs would not be distributed according to ability to pay—it would not, as Kate Greasley points out, eliminate the other:

the organ vendors themselves would still be self-selecting, and quite naturally, will self select on the basis of poverty and desperation. Hence, it will remain the case, whoever benefits from the organs, that it will be largely (if not wholly) poor people selling them.[137]

Finally, insofar as the offer of money might persuade someone to volunteer to be a live organ donor, should we perhaps be equally or even more concerned about non-financial pressure, such as that exerted within families?

[136] 'An ethical market in human organs' (2003) 29 Journal of Medical Ethics 137–8.
[137] 'A legal market in organs: the problem of exploitation' (2014) 40 Journal of Medical Ethics 51–6.

J Harvey[138]

> Now I think there is financial pressure when the potential donor is in poverty. And perhaps it may be argued that this alone is sufficient for banning all paid-for donations. But then, in consistency, the same reasoning should be applied to related donors: since *some* of them are open to heavy psychological and emotional pressure (for example, perhaps by being the submissive and 'guilt'-ridden offspring of an extremely domineering and now ailing parent), then all donations from relatives should be forbidden.

4 XENOTRANSPLANTATION

Although whole organ transplants from animals to humans are still at the experimental stage, other sorts of animal tissues have been used in human medicine for many years. Pig heart valves, for example, can be processed so that they act like inert material rather than living tissue, and their safe and effective use in human patients is well established.

There have been examples of animal-to-human whole organ transplants, but none has been successful. In the most infamous case, a baboon heart was transplanted into a 14-day-old baby, known as 'Baby Fae', and she died within three weeks. Her parents were poor and uneducated, and the consent form they signed appeared to overstate the likely benefits from the transplant. It suggested that: 'Long-term survival with appropriate growth and development may be possible following heart transplantation . . . this research is an effort to provide your baby with some hope of immediate and long term survival.'[139]

In the next extract, Jeffrey Barker and Lauren Polcrack explain that the history of experimentation in xenotransplantation is not 'ethically promising'.

Jeffrey H Barker and Lauren Polcrack[140]

> Many early xenotransplant recipients were unconscious and therefore never consented to the procedure; many were poor and uneducated. Some were prisoners, some were children. The first cardiac xenotransplantation subject (in 1964) was a deaf-mute who never consented to the procedure, and the consent form signed by his step-sister did not mention a non-human organ. Throughout the history of xenotransplantation, the medically, ethically and socially vulnerable have been used as experimental subjects.
>
> The first documented xenotransplantation involving a human host occurred in 1902, when a pig kidney was used in the case of a young woman suffering from end-stage renal failure. Early in the twentieth century, kidneys were transplanted into humans from rabbits, pigs, lambs, goats, macaques, chimpanzees, marmosets and baboons. In each case, however, the transplant failed, and in most cases the patient died as a result.

The principal reason for pursuing research into xenotransplantation is that it would enable many more patients to receive potentially life-saving organ transplants. If we could breed

---

[138] 'Paying organ donors' (1990) 16 Journal of Medical Ethics 117–19.
[139] Jeffrey H Barker and Lauren Polcrack, 'Respect for persons, informed consent and the assessment of infectious disease risks in xenotransplantation' (2001) 4 Medicine, Health Care and Philosophy 53–70, 59.
[140] Ibid.

animals for their organs, in the same way as we breed them for food, the organ shortage might disappear. Not only would this benefit the thousands of patients currently on the organ waiting list, but it could also eliminate the risks incurred by living organ donors.

Pigs, rather than primates, are regarded as the most promising source animal, for a number of reasons. First, chimpanzees and other primates, such as orangutans, are endangered species. Secondly, primates are much 'closer' to humans: they look like us and we do not eat them. Although Marie Fox suggests that such reasoning is morally arbitrary.

Marie Fox[141]

Certainly, given that pigs and primates are alike in the morally relevant respects, since both species are sentient, intelligent and sociable, the real reason to distinguish them seems not to rest on mental ability or capacity for suffering but on practical or emotional grounds . . . [B]y permitting use of certain animals, but not others, as research tools and potential organ donors, law reflects the moral arbitrariness in our response to them.

Thirdly, the risk of zoonosis, that is, cross-species disease transmission, is greater when transplants take place between more closely related species. Fourthly, pigs breed more quickly than primates, and the organ supply could therefore be replenished more quickly. Finally, pig organs are about the same size as human organs.

Despite the obvious advantages in locating a potentially unlimited supply of transplantable organs, xenotransplantation is controversial, in part as a result of practical problems, such as the risk of rejection and disease transmission, and in part because of ethical concerns, such as animal welfare considerations. We consider these in turn, before looking at the regulation of xenotransplantation in the UK.

(a) PRACTICAL PROBLEMS

(1) Rejection

The first major obstacle to successful xenotransplantation is the likelihood of a hyper-acute rejection reaction within minutes or hours of the transplant. Although immunosuppressant therapy can largely eliminate the risk of rejection in human-to-human transplants, much larger doses might be necessary in animal-to-human transplants, and if given in sufficient quantities these drugs will destroy a person's immune system, and themselves cause death.

A more promising solution is to introduce human genes into the animal's genome. There has been some success in creating transgenic pigs, and experiments involving primates appear to indicate that the rejection of organs from transgenic pigs can be controlled using drugs.[142]

More promising still are recent successes involving the creation of hybrid animals, known as chimeras. Scientists have bred mice embryos with genetic mutations which mean that they develop without a specific organ, such as a pancreas. If rat stem cells are injected into these embryos, the rat cells effectively take over, and a rat pancreas develops inside the rat/mouse

---

[141] 'Re-Thinking Kinship: Law's Construction of the Animal Body' (2004) 57 Current Legal Problems 469–93.
[142] Matthias Längin et al, 'Consistent success in life-supporting porcine cardiac xenotransplantation' (2018) Nature December 5; Christopher GA McGregor et al, 'Cardiac xenotransplantation: early success in the orthotopic position' (2005) 24 Journal of Heart and Lung Transplantation S95.

chimera. If this technique could be applied to humans and pigs, it might therefore be possible to grow human organs inside the bodies of pigs. As David Shaw et al explain:

> Anyone in need of a new organ could provide iPSCs [induced pluripotent stem cells] which would be inserted in a pig embryo prior to implantation and gestation. After around 6 months, the resulting pig would be sacrificed and the human organ removed and implanted in the original donor.[143]

(2) Risk of Cross-Species Infection

Variant Creutzfeldt-Jakob disease (vCJD), the human form of bovine spongiform encephalitis (BSE) or 'mad cow disease', is a dramatic example of cross-species disease transmission. The risk of infection from transplantation would be particularly acute since placing an animal organ inside a human body provides a perfect 'platform' for cross-species infection.

It is thought that some viruses, such as the porcine endogenous retrovirus (PERV), which is harmless to pigs, and incorporated into the pig genome, would be impossible to eliminate from transgenic pigs. If it then crossed the species barrier, it might be likely to cause cancer, or irreversible damage to the human immune system. The risk of cross-species infection would be exacerbated if the recipient is taking immunosuppressive drugs.

It is also important to remember that if a disease crosses the species barrier, the risk of infection is faced not only by the recipient herself, but also by her close contacts and the rest of society.

(a) Impact upon the recipient and her close contacts

First, could someone's consent to receiving an animal's organ in the light of the risk of cross-species infection ever be adequately informed? Insofar as the risks of cross-species infection cannot be known with any certainty before trials in humans have begun, and perhaps for some time afterwards, it will be impossible to give a potential recipient full disclosure of the risks associated with xenotransplantation.

Nuffield Council on Bioethics[144]

> It is not possible to predict or quantify the risk that xenotransplantation will result in the emergence of new human diseases. But in the worst case, the consequences could be far-reaching and difficult to control . . . Put bluntly, it may be possible to identify any infectious organism transmitted by xenografting only if it causes disease in human beings, and after it has started to do so.

A second problem comes from the fact that allografts (human-to-human transplants) will continue to be the best treatment for individuals with acute organ failure. It might be argued

---

[143] 'Creating human organs in chimaera pigs: an ethical source of immunocompatible organs?' (2015) 41 Journal of Medical Ethics 970–4.
[144] Nuffield Council on Bioethics, *Animal-to-Human Transplants: The Ethics of Xenotransplantation* (NCOB, 1996) paras 10.25, 6.14.

that xenotransplantation should therefore only be tried in patients who would not be eligible for a human organ transplant. Patients who are not on the organ donor waiting list might be offered a xenograft on the grounds that this could have a greater chance of success than the treatment—that is, nothing—that would otherwise be available to them.

Related to this, if the first recipients are asked to choose between immediate death or the unknown risks of xenotransplantation, it is of course understandable that they might opt for the latter. But being faced with such an invidious choice leads Sheila McLean and Laura Williamson to suggest that 'there must be questions about whether or not the vulnerability of the patients likely to be involved in early trials would cast doubt upon their competence or capacity to consent'.[145]

A further issue is the restrictions that would have to be placed on xenograft recipients. It would be necessary to monitor their health for the rest of their lives. If infection occurred, very serious restrictions might have to be placed upon their liberty. It is also possible that their present and future sexual partners would have to be monitored, and that, at least at first, their freedom to have children and unprotected sex might be restricted. Recipients could be asked to consent in advance to these limitations, and might be likely to do so if the alternative is death. In the next extract, however, Jeffrey Barker and Lauren Polcrack question whether it would, in fact, be possible to give fully informed consent to such a serious curtailment of one's future liberty.

Jeffrey H Barker and Lauren Polcrack[146]

> The recipient must understand as completely as possible the risks to him or herself, to his or [her] contacts, and the risks to society at large, and must be willing to move forward despite those risks. The immediate contacts of the potential recipient must also consent to the probable risks. Any clinical trials of xenotransplantation would require long-term—and probably lifetime—monitoring and surveillance of recipients and their contacts, with the possibility of lifetime quarantine should serious xenosis occur. All recipients would need to be registered and monitored in order to protect public health. Truly informed consent to these types of radical changes in personal freedom would be difficult to obtain.

If third parties, such as recipients' sexual partners, might be subject to surveillance and restrictions upon their liberty, should their informed consent also be necessary? Informing them about the recipient's medical treatment would not only represent a breach of confidentiality, but also, as Sheila McLean and Laura Williamson point out, it would be most unusual to give a third party a right of veto over another's medical treatment.

Sheila McLean and Laura Williamson[147]

> If the consent of third parties is an essential prerequisite to a xenograft, then they are placed in the unusual position of being able, by refusal, to prevent the potential recipient

---

[145] Sheila AM McLean and Laura Willliamson, 'Xenotransplantation: A Pig in a Poke?' (2004) 57 Current Legal Problems 443–68.

[146] 'Respect for persons, informed consent and the assessment of infectious disease risks in xenotransplantation' (2001) 4 Medicine, Health Care and Philosophy 53–70.

[147] 'Xenotransplantation: A Pig in a Poke?' (2004) 57 Current Legal Problems 443–68.

from accepting a therapy which may be of benefit. Secondly, it is unclear just how such agreements [to restrict liberty] could be policed; agreement pre-transplant does not guarantee compliance post-transplant, yet compliance is presumably of the highest order of significance otherwise it would not be required in the first place. What, for example, would be done if a recipient decided not to use barrier contraception? It must be doubted whether or not the state could effectively enter the bedroom and prevent this from happening . . .

To continue with this example, it must be asked what would be the state's authority should an individual xenotransplant recipient or the partner of one become pregnant. Could the state compel a pregnancy termination, and if so on what grounds—ethical or legal? In other words, if the surveillance regime is necessary—as seems to be generally agreed—then there are serious concerns about its enforceability. Indeed the . . . working party which drafted the surveillance document noted that any attempt to require rather than invite patients to agree to the limitations to be imposed on their future life would be likely to run contrary to the terms of the Human Rights legislation, in particular Article 8.

(b) Impact upon society

Interestingly, xenotransplantation reverses the usual risk/benefit calculation in clinical trials. Generally, as we saw in Chapter 10, the research subject assumes some risk to her own health and wellbeing for the benefit of medical progress. Although the subject may hope to obtain a health benefit from participation, this is not its principal purpose, which is instead to benefit society through the furthering of scientific knowledge and the development of new treatments.

In xenotransplantation, the benefit may be to the individual recipient, since it is likely that she would die soon without a transplant. The risk instead may be to society as a whole through the introduction of animal viruses into the human population. It would, however, be impossible to obtain the public's informed consent before a clinical trial began. Instead, Jeffrey Barker and Lauren Polcrack advocate greater public participation in the decision to go ahead with clinical trials.

Jeffrey H Barker and Lauren Polcrack[148]

Xenografts put at risk not only the recipient but those directly associated with the recipient, including caregivers and family members. They also put at risk the public at large by creating the distinct possibility of introducing new or modified pathogens into the human species, pathogens whose virulence, infectivity and mode of retransmission, and potential for treatment are all highly uncertain . . .

Where there is a significant risk to the public, as we believe there is in xenotransplantation, there must be a public process for informing and educating the public, and for ascertaining the willingness of the public to encounter, to consent to these risks. This process of 'collective informed consent' requires not merely public education but active public participation in the decision-making process.

---

[148] 'Respect for persons, informed consent and the assessment of infectious disease risks in xenotransplantation' (2001) 4 Medicine, Health Care and Philosophy 53–70.

Sara Fovargue and Suzanne Ost reject the idea that public consultation is a sufficient response to the unknown risks xenotransplantation might pose to society. They claim that the risks are so great that, even if it could solve the organ shortage, xenotransplantation should be banned.

Sara Fovargue and Suzanne Ost[149]

Even if xenotransplantation could solve the organ shortage, the potential public health benefits would need to outweigh the risks to justify going ahead with it—the condition of proportionality. This is hard to satisfy. Societal public health is likely to suffer more of a detriment from the severity of the potential risk of an infectious disease pandemic than the benefit potentially achieved through increased organs available for transplantation. Everyone in society is placed at risk of a pandemic by allowing xenotransplantation to proceed. As a consequence, society's infrastructure might collapse ...

In the light of the limited pre-clinical survival times, uncertainty as to the ability of genetically engineered pig organs to support human life, the potentially catastrophic risks, and the difficulties in identifying, managing, and controlling those risks, it is unclear why some still view xenotransplantation as a viable solution to the shortage of organs. In this environment, the public interest in health and state obligations to protect public health *require* the state to prohibit clinical xenotransplantation.

Of course, even if we were to ban xenotransplantation in the UK, then, in the absence of an enforceable global prohibition, 'xenotourism' is likely to make it difficult for a country to eliminate the risks posed by xenotransplantation.

Megan Sykes, Anthony d'Apice, and Mauro Sandrin[150]

The potential risks of xenotransplantation will not be confined to the country in which the transplant is performed. Even the most assiduous safety efforts of any nation or group of nations may be ineffective in the absence of internationally agreed regulations and monitoring procedures for xenotransplantation. This problem arises because patients are mobile and could receive a xenograft in one country, which may or may not have appropriate regulatory and monitoring processes, and later leave that country and enter another without ever having to state that they are the recipient of a xenograft ...

The scale of such 'casual' xenotourism is likely to be small. However, there is a risk that entrepreneurial xenotransplanters may deliberately set up business in countries with minimal or no regulation and set about attracting foreigners with organ failure to come to be transplanted and then return home. The absence of questioning about xenotransplantation upon re-entry, and the absence of a mechanism for bringing such patients into surveillance programs in their home countries almost guarantee that such patients will avoid surveillance when they return home.

---

[149] 'When Should Precaution Prevail? Interests in (Public) Health, the Risk of Harm and Xenotransplantation' (2010) 18 Medical Law Review 203–329.

[150] 'Position paper of the Ethics Committee of the International Xenotransplantation Association' (2003) 10 Xenotransplantation 194–203.

(b) ETHICAL CONCERNS

(1) Revulsion

Many people are repelled by the idea of transplanting animal organs into human beings. For some, this will be prompted by their religious beliefs. If a person's faith means that they do not eat pork, it is possible that they might also object to receiving a pig's organ. In any future regulation of xenotransplantation there would undoubtedly have to be a conscientious objection clause, similar to that in the Abortion Act, so that doctors did not have to participate in xenotransplantation; and patients too would be reassured that their refusal to accept an animal organ would not mean that they would be removed from the transplant waiting list. Provided that no one is compelled to take part in xenotransplantation against their wishes, some people's instinctive revulsion should not be allowed to determine whether xenotransplantation goes ahead, especially since potential recipients' lives may be at stake.

There have also been suggestions that introducing human genes into pigs, and animal organs into humans, threatens to blur the barriers between the species.

Jason Scott Robert and Françoise Baylis[151]

[S]cientifically, there might be no such thing as fixed species identities or boundaries. Morally, however, we rely on the notion of fixed species identities and boundaries in the way we live our lives and treat other creatures . . .

All things considered, the engineering of creatures that are part human and part nonhuman animal is objectionable because the existence of such beings would introduce inexorable moral confusion in our existing relationships with nonhuman animals and in our future relationships with part-human hybrids.

Of course, barriers between the species are constantly evolving, albeit slowly. We share about 96 per cent of our DNA with chimpanzees, and so basing moral status upon biology is fraught with difficulty. Moreover, there would seem to be no doubt that patients who have received inert pig heart valves continue to be members of the human species. Perhaps, as Henry Greely suggests, it is a question of degree.

Henry T Greely[152]

[A]fter a few early reports of patient qualms, the use of pig heart valves for medical procedures now raises little concern. Apart from pragmatic fear of the passage of disease and some animal rights concerns that are quite distinct from issues of chimerism . . . other plausible single organ xenotransplants into human beings seem unlikely to be heavily controversial. On the other hand, if it were feasible to transplant a chimpanzee brain into a human, or if a human were given a large number of organs from nonhuman sources, people might worry whether the resulting organism was really human . . .

---

[151] 'Crossing species boundaries' (2003) 3 American Journal of Bioethics 1–13.
[152] 'Defining chimeras . . . and chimeric concerns' (2003) 3 American Journal of Bioethics 17–20.

Chimeras made by moving human parts into nonhuman beings would raise concerns when they are significant enough to raise the question of the possible humanity of the recipient. In both cases the 'importance' of the parts—brains and gametes are more important than heart valves or skin—and the number of parts moved—transplanting five visceral organs would be more troubling than transplanting one—seems significant.

(2) Animal Rights

It is often said that if we are prepared to breed and kill animals for food, we should logically also accept xenotransplantation, especially since the purpose of breeding animals for their organs—ie saving lives—would seem to be more valuable and of more immediate benefit than the production of meat. This simple analogy between eating meat and xenotransplantation has, however, been challenged.

Robin Downie[153]

[W]hereas the eating of animal flesh may or may not be ethically right, it is 'natural' in the sense that many other animal species in fact do it and (as has been claimed by some) human beings are biologically carnivorous or at least omnivorous. On the other hand, the transplant of animal tissue into human beings is 'unnatural'.

Of course, as Downie goes on to admit, all medical interventions, including human-to-human transplants, are also 'unnatural'. But Downie further claims that the insertion of human genes into animals, and the transplant of their organs into humans is 'profoundly different from previous medical interventions'. This is, of course, a subjective judgement, and it is not clear why xenotransplantation is necessarily any more 'profoundly unnatural' than, say, *in vitro* fertilization.

Secondly, donor animals would have to be bred and raised in isolation, in completely barren and sterile surroundings, and their genetic modification might further impair their quality of life. Would this represent a more substantial interference with their welfare than happens when they are bred for meat? Possibly, although animal welfare is hardly maximized in battery farms, or in the production of veal and foie gras. Of course, the inhumane treatment of animals by the food industry does not justify their inhumane treatment in xenotransplantation. But it would be odd to more squeamish about animal welfare in xenotransplantation—where the goal is to save the lives of people who would otherwise die—than where the animal's suffering results in cheap chicken or expensive duck and goose liver.

A better analogy might be with the use of animals in research, when it is common for animals to be specially bred to take part in experiments, after which they are killed. In animal experiments, we are using animals in order to further scientific knowledge and to improve the treatments that are available to humans. The benefits to individuals may be less direct and immediate than they would be if xenotransplantation were successful, but the ethical issues are similar.

---

[153] 'Xenotransplantation' (1997) 23 Journal of Medical Ethics 205–6.

Just like experiments on animals and eating meat, xenotransplantation rests upon the assumption that it is ethically acceptable to kill other species in order to benefit human lives. According to Peter Singer, this is an example of speciesism (ie favouring one's own species and devaluing other species), which he argues is as morally objectionable as racism or sexism.

Peter Singer[154]

What kind of ethic can tell us that it is all right to rear sentient animals in barren cages that give them no decent life at all, and then kill them to take their organs, while refusing to permit us to take the organ of a human being who is not, and never can be, even minimally conscious? Obviously a speciesist ethic . . .

In a world that needlessly rears several billion animals in factory farms each year and then kills them to satisfy a mere preference of taste, it is difficult to argue persuasively against the rearing and slaughter of a few thousand animals so that their organs can be used to save people's lives. That, however, is not a reason for using animals: it is, rather, a reason for changing our views about animals. In a better world, a world that cared properly for the interests of animals, we would do our utmost to avoid choices that pit the essential interests of animals against our own . . . This might involve more effective ways of obtaining organs from humans who are brain dead, or cortically dead. It might involve the development of artificial organs. Or it might involve using our limited medical resources to educate people in looking after the organs with which they were born.

Why do we think that human beings' lives are more valuable and important than animals' lives? Often some appeal is made to distinctively human qualities, such as sentience, consciousness, and the capacity for reason. But, as Singer explains, not all human beings possess these characteristics—patients in a permanent vegetative state or anencephalic infants, for example, do not—whereas they are possessed to some degree by animals such as chimpanzees and dolphins. If it is these qualities, and not species membership per se, that count morally, then as Jonathan Hughes points out, two possible consequences follow. Either we should refuse to contemplate using animals that possess the relevant characteristics as xenograft sources. Or we should also be prepared to take organs from human beings who have irrevocably lost those capacities.[155]

Jonathan Hughes[156]

Imposing harms on animals in order to benefit humans is acceptable, it is argued, because the harms and benefits that humans are capable of experiencing are greater than those that can be experienced by other animals . . .

[T]his kind of argument is vulnerable to a well-known objection. The problem is that capacities for pleasure and pain, fulfilment and suffering vary not only between but within species, including humans. So while it is true that the capacities of a normal adult exceed those of a pig,

---

[154] 'Xenotransplantation and speciesism' (1992) 24 Transplantation Proceedings 728–32.

[155] See also, RG Frey, 'Medicine, animal experimentation, and the moral problem of unfortunate humans' (1996) 12 Social Philosophy and Policy 181–211.

[156] 'Xenografting: ethical issues' (1998) 24 Journal of Medical Ethics 18–24, 23.

the same cannot be said for all humans. There are many whose mental capacities are severely and tragically impaired, and it follows that if we are prepared to take organs from animals on the grounds of their limited capacities we should also be prepared to take the organs of those humans whose capacities are similarly restricted. Or conversely, if we insist that we should *not* take organs from such humans, then consistency demands that we refrain also from taking the organs of animals with similar or greater capacities.

Against this, Arthur Caplan argues that humans matter more morally because of their relationships with others.

Arthur L Caplan[157]

Severely retarded children and those born with devastating conditions such as anencephaly have never had the capacities and abilities that confer a greater moral standing on humans as compared with animals. Should they be used as the first donors and recipients in xenografting research instead of primates?

The reason they should not has nothing to do with the properties, capacities and abilities of children or infants who lack and have always lacked significant degrees of intellectual and cognitive function. The reason they should not be used is because of the impact using them would have upon other human beings, especially their parents and relatives. A severely retarded child can still be the object of much love, attention, and devotion from his or her parents. These feelings and the abilities and capacities that generate them are deserving of moral respect. Animals do not appear to be capable of such feelings.

If a human mother were to learn that her severely retarded son had been used in lethal xenografting research, she would mourn this fact for the rest of her days. A baboon, monkey, dog or pig would not.

Of course, this argument might lead to the unedifying conclusion that where a profoundly incapacitated individual has no family or friends, there is no one to be harmed by treating her as a means to an end. If we want to argue that friendless people's membership of our species determines that we should treat them differently from animals, is this differential treatment simple speciesism?

It might also be argued that we should not address the question of xenotransplantation's ethical legitimacy in isolation from other possible solutions to the shortage of organs, especially since human-to-human transplants are, for the foreseeable future, likely to be more successful than animal-to-human transplants. We could increase the availability of organs if we moved away from a consent model for cadaveric donation, and instead treated the organs of the recently dead as a public resource. This would, admittedly, offend some people's desire to control what happens to their bodies after death, and it could cause distress to their relatives. But animal rights advocates might argue that these harms are relatively trivial when compared with the harm endured by a sentient animal, bred in an entirely sterile environment and then killed for its organs.

---

[157] *Am I my Brother's Keeper? The Ethical Frontiers of Biomedicine* (Indiana UP: Bloomington, IN 1997) 111.

(c) XENOTRANSPLANTATION IN THE UK

In 1997, the UK Xenotransplantation Interim Regulatory Authority (UKXIRA) was set up, in order to add an additional layer of review to applications to carry out clinical trials involving xenotransplantation. UKXIRA was disbanded nine years later, partly because no trials were taking place, and partly because the system of research ethics governance, considered in Chapter 10, was assumed to offer sufficient safeguards. Laura Williamson et al are critical of the decision to disband UKXIRA. They are also concerned that the first uses of xenografts may not come through organized trials, with REC approval, but through clinicians' freedom to use innovative therapies, which have not been properly tested, when the person's condition is extremely grave and there are no other available treatments.

Laura Williamson, Marie Fox, and Sheila McLean[158]

While, as we have stressed, updating governance arrangements is to be welcomed in the face of developments in medicine and science, it is important that the drive for modernization does not result in a relaxation of safeguards necessary to protect the individual and the public. Elsewhere in healthcare law the normalization of certain biotechnologies, such as embryo research and IVF, has prompted calls for less state intervention, and a drive toward liberalization may well be a factor in the current review of the law in this area. However, the history of xenotransplantation to date, particularly difficulties in calculating the safety risks that it poses and its potential to transcend regulatory and national borders, should make us wary of acceding to attempts to normalize this technology as simply another form of research.

5 CONCLUSION

The move to an opt-out system in England may increase the supply of organs, but it could also plausibly be argued that it is extraordinary that we routinely burn or bury organs that could save lives. Of course, taking organs without the consent of the deceased person, or in the face of their relatives' objections, might cause offence and distress, but it is worth remembering that the cost of avoiding this offence and distress is the certain death of identifiable individuals with acute organ failure.

It is, perhaps, interesting that the emphasis medical law places upon patient autonomy and the need for consent has spilled over into the treatment of our bodies after death. I do not mean to suggest that there is no value in respecting an individual's wishes after her death. For many people, exercising some control over what happens to their resources and their bodies after they have died is of critical importance. But, in relation to testamentary freedom, the deceased's wishes are not always decisive. If I choose to leave all of my assets to a donkey sanctuary, when this will leave my family destitute, my choice can be overridden. In relation to organ donation, could it be argued that the decision to have one's organs cremated or buried, when they could be used to save lives, should be similarly open to challenge?

---

[158] 'The regulation of xenotransplantation in the United Kingdom after UKXIRA: legal and ethical issues' (2007) 34 Journal of Law and Society 441–64.

Here we may have another interesting example of the difference between legal and moral duties. It would be difficult (though perhaps not impossible) to argue that I have a legal duty to donate my organs after death, but the moral duty of easy rescue—that is, the duty to save a life when to do so would be virtually costless—might be said to be unarguable. Julian Savulescu is more forceful, arguing that the organ 'shortage' represents a failure of practical ethics.

Julian Savulescu[159]

Organ transplantation is another example of the lethal effects of bad ethics. Organ transplantation is a lifesaving intervention. Millions of people die around the world because of a shortage of organs. But there is no shortage in reality—we just don't use all the organs that could be used because of bad ethical reasons ...

[T]his is not just an easy rescue, it is a *zero cost* rescue. Organs are of no use to us when we are dead, but they are literally lifesaving to others. Nonetheless, most people choose to bury or burn these lifesaving resources, and are allowed to. Yet the state extracts death duties and inheritance taxes, but not the most important of their previous assets—their organs. The failure to meet even our most minimal moral obligations is damning. It represents the failure of modern practical ethics.

FURTHER READING

Burnell, Philippa, Hulton, Sally-Anne, and Draper, Heather, 'Coercion and choice in parent–child live kidney donation' (2015) 41 Journal of Medical Ethics 304–9.

Erin, Charles A and Harris, John, 'An ethical market in human organs' (2003) 29 Journal of Medical Ethics 137–8.

Fovargue, Sara and Ost, Suzanne, 'When Should Precaution Prevail? Interests in (Public) Health, the Risk of Harm and Xenotransplantation' (2010) 18 Medical Law Review 203–329.

Greasley, Kate, 'A legal market in organs: the problem of exploitation' (2014) 40 Journal of Medical Ethics 51–6.

McGuinness, Sheelagh and Brazier, Margaret, 'Respecting the Living Means Respecting the Dead Too' (2008) 28 Oxford Journal of Legal Studies 297–316.

Moorlock, Greg and Draper, Heather, 'Empathy, social media, and directed altruistic living organ donation' (2018) 32 Bioethics 289–97.

Shaw, David M, 'The Consequences of Vagueness in Consent to Organ Donation' (2017) 31 Bioethics 424–31.

Thomas, Elin H et al, 'Live liver donation, ethics and practitioners: "I am between the two and if I do not feel comfortable about this situation, I cannot proceed"' (2014) 40 Journal of Medical Ethics 157–62.

Wilkinson, Stephen and Williams, Nicola Jane, 'Should uterus transplants be publicly funded?' (2016) 42 Journal of Medical Ethics 559–65.

---

[159] 'Bioethics: why philosophy is essential for progress' (2015) 41 Journal of Medical Ethics 28–33.

13

EMBRYO RESEARCH, STEM CELLS, AND EMERGING BIOTECHNOLOGIES

CENTRAL ISSUES

1. Embryo research is strictly regulated by the Human Fertilisation and Embryology Act 1990, as amended, and by the Human Fertilisation and Embryology Authority (HFEA). No research can be carried out on an embryo after 14 days; the research must be necessary or desirable for one of the statutory purposes; and the use of embryos must be necessary.

2. Stem cells are pluripotent cells which are capable of differentiating into different body parts and tissues. Stem cell therapies are new and many are still experimental, but in the future it is thought that they might deliver a new sort of regenerative medicine.

3. There is considerable interest in the combination of artificial intelligence (AI) and neurotechnologies, which enable third parties to observe and modify our brain activity.

4. It is possible that some emerging biotechnologies could radically enhance human capabilities, leading to the creation of posthuman beings. For bioconservatives, this is something to fear; whereas bioliberals celebrate the prospect of transcending human frailties.

1 INTRODUCTION

Two decades ago, there were fierce debates over whether it could ever be ethical to carry out research on human embryos. There are still those who oppose such research on principle, but as human embryonic stem cell therapies start to have clinical application, it is important to move beyond debates over whether basic research is acceptable in order to consider their implications. And while stem cell therapy is an 'emerging biotechnology'—that is, a new and potentially transformative technology—it is not the only one. This chapter therefore also looks briefly at some other emerging biotechnologies and the questions they pose for medical law and ethics.

For reasons of space, this chapter can provide only a short and incomplete taste of this vast and complex field. Whole journals are devoted to some of the issues we touch on here, such as neuroethics and transhumanism. There are also some obvious omissions. Readers might want to investigate synthetic biology and nanotechnology on their own, and there are plenty of resources online to enable them to do this.[1]

This chapter begins with embryo research, and a brief survey of debates over the embryo's moral status, before turning to how embryo research is regulated in the UK. It then looks at stem cell therapies, considering whether they might lead to a new sort of regenerative medicine. We also look at the alarming global market in unregulated stem cell therapies, and the question of whether stem cells derived from human embryos are patentable. Next we consider how neurotechnologies and artificial intelligence open up for scrutiny and manipulation what was previously the 'black box' of our brains and minds. Finally we turn to consider whether the cumulative impact of new biotechnologies might be the creation of beings so radically different from us that they have become posthuman.

At the outset, it is worth considering what is distinctive about the regulation of emerging biotechnologies.

Nuffield Council on Bioethics[2]

[W]e identify three distinctive characteristics that make governance of emerging biotechnologies especially problematic. The three characteristics are uncertainty, ambiguity and transformative potential.

- By 'uncertainty' we mean an inescapable lack of knowledge about the range of possible outcomes or about the likelihood that any particular outcome will in fact occur. This seriously limits the possibility of accurately forecasting the consequences of decisions with regard to biotechnologies (positive or negative) and similarly limits the effectiveness of prospective efforts to control these outcomes.

- By 'ambiguity' we mean a lack of agreement about the implications, meanings or relative importance of a given range of possible outcomes, irrespective of the likelihood of their occurrence. Ambiguity reveals the association of different and possibly incompatible meanings and values within the practices, products and consequences of biotechnologies.

- By 'transformative potential' we mean the capacity that some emerging biotechnologies may have to transform or displace existing social relations, practices and modes of production, or create new capabilities and opportunities that did not previously exist, or may not even have been imagined. These outcomes might be entirely unexpected or unsought.

As long ago as 1980, David Collingridge set out a fundamental dilemma in the regulation of new technologies (known as the Collingridge dilemma):

---

[1] The Nuffield Council on Bioethics report on Emerging Biotechnologies is a good place to start. It is available at <http://nuffieldbioethics.org/project/emerging-biotechnologies>.

[2] *Emerging Biotechnologies: Technology, Choice and the Public Good* (NCOB, 2012).

attempting to control a technology is difficult ... because during its early stages, when it can be controlled, not enough can be known about its harmful social consequences to warrant controlling its development; but by the time these consequences are apparent, control has become costly and slow.[3]

In short, the full consequences of a new technology can only be known when it may be too late to introduce effective controls. This leads some to advocate adopting the precautionary principle, whereby regulation errs on the side of caution and protects against potential harms, even when it is unclear whether they will, in fact, materialize.

According to the precautionary principle, a new technology should be introduced only when there is evidence of safety, rather than an absence of evidence of harm. In practice, this would paralyse innovation. To take some simple examples, if our predecessors had adopted the precautionary principle, we would have no organ transplantation, no *in vitro* fertilization (IVF) and very few medicines. The precautionary principle also overlooks the costs associated with *not* introducing a new technology. If we never conduct 'first in man' trials of new medicines, we eliminate the risks such trials pose for participants, but millions of people might die from untreatable diseases.

Cass Sunstein has instead advocated the 'anti-catastrophe' principle, that is, when 'regulators are operating under conditions of uncertainty, they might well do best to follow maximin, identifying the worst-case scenarios and choosing the approach that eliminates the worst of these'.[4]

2 EMBRYO RESEARCH

When an egg (oocyte) is fertilized by a sperm, a single cell zygote is formed. This then begins the process of cell division. After approximately four to five days, a blastocyst is formed, which will contain 50 to 150 cells. At the blastocyst stage it is possible to distinguish between the outer shell or trophoblast and the inner cell mass. The trophoblast will become the placenta. The inner cell mass contains stem cells. These are undifferentiated cells that will subsequently differentiate in order to become skin, bones, blood, solid organs, etc. The goal of stem cell therapy is to use stem cells, derived either from embryos or from reprogrammed adult cells (see below), and then control the process of differentiation in order to produce specialized tissue. Although stem cell therapy is in its infancy, in the future it may lead to a new sort of regenerative medicine, in which defective tissues and organs can simply be replaced.

(a) WHAT IS THE MORAL STATUS OF THE EMBRYO?

Deciding upon the embryo's moral status is not just an abstract question of philosophy, theology, or morality. As Maureen Junker-Kenny explains, because the embryo's status determines how we should treat it, this is also a question of enormous practical importance.

---

[3] David Collingridge, *The Social Control of Technology* (Pinter, London, 1980) 19.
[4] *Laws of Fear: Beyond the Precautionary Principle* (CUP: Cambridge, 2005) 109.

Maureen Junker-Kenny[5]

Any definition of the beginning and end of human personhood is caught up in a hermeneutical circle. We define its starting point because we want to act in a certain way, and we act according to how we have defined it. If we consider the moment of implantation in the uterus, or the presence of brain activity, or the ability to communicate, as the starting-point for ascribing personhood, we are free to use the embryo prior to this stage in any way we consider useful.

Each definition has a practical intent. Once we ascribe human life and personhood to an entity, we want to protect it. If one wants to give maximum protection, one has to use a minimal definition, such as the new genetic unity created by egg and sperm. A maximal definition of human life, such as the ability to communicate, or to act independently, offers minimal protection to the stages prior to these competencies and after they have been lost.

At the risk of drastic simplification, it is possible to identify four positions on the moral status of the embryo.

(i) Embryonic Personhood

If an embryo is a person, then because embryos that are used in research are destroyed or allowed to perish, all embryo research would be unacceptable. While the law is clear that a legal person exists only after a child has been born alive, according to some religions, most notably Roman Catholicism, a person exists from the moment of conception. In 2008, an updated Papal *Encyclical on Bioethics* was issued, which restated the Catholic Church's opposition to all research on embryos.

Congregation for the Doctrine of the Faith[6]

The obtaining of stem cells from a living human embryo . . . invariably causes the death of the embryo and is consequently gravely illicit: 'research, in such cases, irrespective of efficacious therapeutic results, is not truly at the service of humanity. In fact, this research advances through the suppression of human lives that are equal in dignity to the lives of other human individuals and to the lives of the researchers themselves. History itself has condemned such a science in the past and will condemn it in the future, not only because it lacks the light of God but also because it lacks humanity' (Benedict XVI).

Interestingly, this Catholic position is relatively new. Until the nineteenth century, ensoulment was believed to be the point at which the developing fetus achieved humanity, and this took place sometime after fertilization. Male fetuses were ensouled at 40 days, and female fetuses at 80 days.

In the next extract, Margaret Foley offers a different Catholic perspective.

---

[5] 'The Moral Status of the Embryo' in Neil Messer (ed), *Theological Issues in Bioethics: An Introduction with Readings* (Darton, Longman and Todd: London, 2002) 8–75.
[6] 'Instruction *Dignitas Personae* on Certain Bioethical Questions' (Vatican, 2008).

Margaret Foley[7]

[A] case for human embryo stem cell research can be made on the basis of positions developed within the Roman Catholic tradition. Growing numbers of Catholic moral theologians, for example, do not consider the human embryo in its earliest stages (before development of the primitive streak or implantation) to constitute an individualized human entity with the settled inherent potential to become a human being. In this view the moral status of the embryo is therefore not that of a person, and its use for certain kinds of research can be justified. Since it is, however, a form of life, some respect is due to it; for example, it should not be bought and sold. Those who make this case prefer a return to the centuries-old Catholic position that a certain amount of development is necessary in order for a conceptus to warrant personal status. Embryologic studies now show that fertilization (conception) is itself a process (not a moment), and provide warrant for the opinion that in its earliest stages (including the blastocyst stage, when the inner cell mass is isolated to derive stem cells for purposes of research) the embryo is not sufficiently individualized to bear the moral weight of personhood.

Fertilization is a gradual process rather than an 'existential pop'.[8] In normal sexual reproduction, fertilization can take more than 24 hours, and implantation takes longer still. Nor is an embryo guaranteed to become a baby. On the contrary, most fertilized eggs fail to implant, and this natural wastage is imperceptible. Even if a fertilized egg does implant in the woman's uterus, some of its cells will divide to form the placenta and umbilical cord. These are tissues that are discarded at birth, and are obviously not a 'person'. Up to about 14 days after fertilization begins, an embryo may split and become two embryos (which will, if born, be identical twins), so the early human embryo is not necessarily one human being, but may become two different ones.

Adherents of some religions—perhaps most notably Anglicanism and Judaism—believe that, while it is important to treat the human embryo with respect, this does not necessarily rule out embryo research. According to the then Chief Rabbi's evidence to the House of Lords Select Committee on Stem Cell Research, in certain circumstances Judaism would allow the respect due to the early human embryo to be 'trumped' by the benefits that might flow from research:

In Jewish law neither the foetus nor the pre-implanted embryo is a person; it is, however, human life and must be accorded the respect due to human life. Personhood, with its attendant rights and responsibilities begins at birth. Prior to birth, we have duties to both the embryo and the foetus, but these may, in certain circumstances, be overridden by other duties, namely those we owe to persons.[9]

Judaism's emphasis upon healing weighs strongly in the balance when considering the morality of embryonic stem cell research. As Laurie Zoloth puts it, 'if stem cells can save a life, then not only can they be used, they must be used'.[10]

---

[7] 'Roman Catholic Views on hES Cell Research' in Suzanne Holland, Karen Lebacqz, and Laurie Zoloth (eds), *The Human Embryonic Stem Cell Debate: Science, Ethics and Public Policy* (MIT Press: Cambridge, MA, 2001) 113–18.

[8] Kate Greasley, *Arguments about Abortion: Personhood, Morality and Law* (Oxford UP, 2017), 105.

[9] *Stem Cell Research Report* (February 2002) para 4.19.

[10] 'The Ethics of the Eighth Day: Jewish Bioethics and Research on Human Embryonic Stem Cells' in Suzanne Holland, Karen Lebacqz, and Laurie Zoloth (eds), *The Human Embryonic Stem Cell Debate: Science, Ethics and Public Policy* (MIT Press: Cambridge, MA, 2001) 95–111.

(ii) The Argument From Potential

Even if the early human embryo is not a person, does its potential to become a person give it a special moral status? According to John Marshall, 'because the entity has the potential to become a person, one affirms that it should *not* be interfered with, that *nothing* should be done that prevents it realizing that potential, and things *can* be done which will help it to attain that potential. Therefore one opposes experimentation'.[11] In contrast, Dan Brock argues that while an entity's potential is relevant to how it should be treated when it realizes that potential, it does not confer a right to be treated as if the potential were already realized.

Dan W Brock[12]

> Sam has the potential to run faster than all the other competitors in the race, then he has the potential to claim the prize, but he has no actual claim or right to the prize until this potential becomes actuality and he has in fact run faster than all the other competitors. Moral rights in general have this character—they are grounded in the actual, not just potential, properties of a being. So the embryo's potential to become a person is relevant to the moral status it will have if and when it does become a person, but it does not confer the moral status on it when still an embryo that it will have later when it has become a person.

In practice, not all embryos have the potential to become persons. In IVF, as with natural conception, it is not uncommon for embryos to be chromosomally or morphologically so abnormal that they have no chance of implanting in a woman's womb and developing to term. Does the potentiality argument then mean that a particular embryo's moral status will depend upon whether it is viable or not?

In the next extract, John Harris explains another difficulty with the argument from potential. If the embryo is special because it has the potential to become a human being, then since gametes (eggs and sperm) have the potential to become an embryo, logically they must also have the potential to become a human being.

John Harris[13]

> There are two sorts of objections to the 'potentiality argument' for the moral significance of the embryo. The first is simply that the fact that an entity can undergo changes that will make it significantly different does not constitute a reason for treating it as though it had already undergone those changes. We are all potentially dead, but no-one supposes that this fact constitutes a reason for treating us as if we were already dead.
>
> The second objection is simply that if the potentiality argument suggests that we have to regard as morally significant anything which has the potential to become a fully fledged human being and hence have some moral duty to protect and actualize all human potential, then we are in for a very exhausting time of it. For it is not only the fertilized egg, the embryo that is

---

[11] 'The Case Against Experimentation' in Anthony Dyson and John Harris (eds), *Experiments on Embryos* (Routledge: London, 1990) 55–64.

[12] 'Is a consensus possible on stem cell research? Moral and political obstacles' (2006) 32 Journal of Medical Ethics 36–42.

[13] Peter Singer and Karen Dawson, 'On the Moral Status of the Embryo' in Anthony Dyson and John Harris (eds), *Experiments on Embryos* (Routledge: London, 1990) 65–81.

potentially a fully fledged adult. The egg and the sperm taken together but as yet ununited have the same potential as the fertilized egg.

Of course, the embryo is clearly a significant step further on in the process of becoming a person than a spermatozoa or an unfertilized egg. The mixing of the DNA from the sperm and the egg give it an entirely new genome. It is also true that most human gametes have the potential to be a person only in a rather remote sense. But for the sperm and eggs in a petri dish immediately before fertilization occurs, there is little difference between their potential and that of the newly fertilized egg.[14]

A different sort of problem with the argument from potential is that if the early human embryo's potential to become a human being rules out its destruction, this would cast doubt on the legitimacy of certain types of contraception, such as the intrauterine device (IUD) and the morning-after pill, both of which may prevent the implantation of a newly fertilized egg. Indeed, the ordinary oral contraceptive pill sometimes works by preventing implantation. If interfering with a fertilized egg's progress towards personhood is always illegitimate, the only acceptable contraceptive would be the condom.

In addition to the creation of embryos that are unsuitable for implantation, IVF also commonly results in more embryos than will be used in treatment. The destruction of embryos is therefore an inevitable feature of IVF. If we accept post-coital contraception and IVF—on the grounds that the benefits of enabling women to control their fertility and have babies may justify the destruction of embryos—does this give us a good reason also to accept research on embryos?

In the next extract, John Harris goes further and argues that anyone who believes that normal sexual reproduction, which inevitably involves the creation and destruction of embryos, is acceptable should, as a matter of consistency, also accept research on human embryos.

John Harris[15]

We now know that for every successful pregnancy that results in a live birth many, perhaps as many as five, early embryos will be lost or will 'miscarry' (although these are not perhaps 'miscarriages' as the term is normally used because this sort of very early embryo loss is almost always entirely unnoticed) ...

How are we to think of the decision to attempt to have a child in the light of these facts? One obvious and inescapable conclusion is that God and/or nature has ordained that 'spare' embryos be produced for almost every pregnancy and that most of these will have to die in order that a sibling embryo can come to birth. Thus, the sacrifice of embryos seems to be an inescapable and inevitable part of the process of procreation. It may not be intentional sacrifice, and it may not attend every pregnancy, but the loss of many embryos is the inevitable consequence of the vast majority (perhaps all) pregnancies.

Given that decisions to attempt to have children using sexual reproduction as the method (or even decisions to have unprotected intercourse) inevitably create embryos that must die, those who believe having children or even running the risk of conception is legitimate cannot consistently object to the creation of embryos for comparably important moral reasons ...

[14] 'IVF Technology and the Argument from Potential' in Peter Singer et al (eds), *Embryo Experimentation* (CUP: Cambridge, 1990) 76–89.
[15] 'Stem cells, sex, and procreation' (2003) 12 Cambridge Quarterly of Healthcare Ethics 353–71.

> [A]lthough we might rather not have to sacrifice embryos to achieve a live healthy birth, we judge it to be defensible to continue natural reproduction in the light of the balance between the moral costs and the benefits. And if we make this calculation in the case of normal sexual reproduction we should, for the same reasons, make a similar judgment in the case of the sacrifice of embryos in stem cell research.

Finally, new scientific developments add interesting twists to the potentiality argument. If human reproductive cloning (using the technique which created Dolly the sheep) is possible, then, in theory at least, any cell could become a new human being. If, on the other hand, cloned human embryos are not viable, they would not be entitled to special protection, if that protection derives from the potential to become a human being. Parthenotes are entities created from unfertilized eggs. At the moment, they cannot develop beyond the earliest embryonic stages, but if it becomes possible for them to develop into human beings, would unfertilized eggs also require protection, on the grounds of their potential?

(iii) The Compromise Position

An embryo is a member of our species, but most people do not think we are required to treat a four-cell embryo as if it had the same rights as a person. The 1984 Warnock Report (see below), which formed the basis of the Human Fertilisation and Embryology Act 1990, embodied this compromise position.[16] It admitted that the instrumental use of the early human embryo will offend those who believe that a person comes into being at fertilization, but that that offence has to be put into the balance with the benefits which may flow from embryo research. The Warnock Committee recommended that embryo research should be permitted, provided that the embryo is not simply treated as a resource for scientists but is instead accorded proper 'respect'.

Interestingly, Baroness Warnock has since suggested that the report's use of the word 'respect' to describe the treatment of embryos used in research was 'foolish'.

Baroness Warnock[17]

> I regret that in the original report that led up to the 1990 legislation we used words such as 'respect for the embryo'. That seems to me to lead to certain absurdities. You cannot respectfully pour something down the sink—which is the fate of the embryo after it has been used for research, or if it is not going to be used for research or for anything else.
>
> I think that what we meant by the rather foolish expression 'respect' was that the early embryo should never be used frivolously for research purposes. That is perfectly exemplified by the regulations that are brought in and the licensing provisions that are looked after by the HFEA [Human Fertilisation and Embryology Authority]. It is the non-frivolity of the research which is conveyed by such expressions as 'respect for' or 'protection for' the embryo.

In contrast, Karen Lebacqz argues that it is possible to treat an embryo that will be used in research with respect.

---

[16] *Report of the Committee of Enquiry into Human Fertilisation and Embryology* (HMSO: London, 1984).
[17] Hansard 5 December 2002, col 1327.

Karen Lebacqz[18]

> I believe that one can indeed speak meaningfully of respecting embryos or embryonic tissue . . . Specifically, the tissue must not be treated cavalierly, but as an entity with value . . . To approach something with awe or reverence means that we never become hardened to its intrinsic value, its value apart from us . . .
>
> An entity is treated cavalierly if it is demolished without any sense of violation or loss; if it is treated as only one of many and easily replaceable; if its existence is made the butt of jokes or disrespectful stereotyping. Thus, to require that a blastocyst not be treated cavalierly is to require that it be treated as an entity with incredible value; as something precious which cannot be replaced by any other blastocyst, whose existence is to be celebrated and whose loss is to be grieved.

Regardless of whether the word 'respect' is useful in the context of embryo research, it is clear—as John Robertson explains—that the compromise position is not concerned to protect individual human embryos, but is instead directing towards protecting the symbolic value of early human life.

John A Robertson[19]

> Many people, for example, reject the view that the embryo is a person but believe that the embryo is different from ordinary human tissue because of the unique potential it has to develop into a new human being. Sometimes described as 'special respect', this attitude towards human embryos shows or symbolizes our respect for human life generally . . .
>
> In the context of *in vitro* fertilization treatment, for example, the generation of more embryos than can be safely transferred to the uterus is widely accepted as not being unduly disrespectful of human life, because it enables children to be born to infertile couples. Similarly, destroying embryos that are left over from IVF procedures to develop cell-replacement therapies should also be ethically acceptable, for the goal of treating disease and saving life justifies the symbolic loss that arises from destroying embryos in the process. By contrast, selling human embryos or using them in cosmetic-toxicology testing seems to be disrespectful of the symbolic meaning that many people attach to embryos because those uses fulfil no life-affirming or other important purpose.

An analogy might be drawn with research on non-human primates. Aside from the great apes, it is possible to use non-human primates in medical research, provided that the research serves an important scientific purpose and could not be done on creatures with lower neurophysiological sensitivity. Dan Brock has suggested that primates, like embryos, have an intermediate moral status: they need not be treated in the same way as a human person, but at the same time it would be unacceptable to use and destroy them for trivial purposes.[20]

---

[18] 'On the Elusive Nature of Respect' in Suzanne Holland, Karen Lebacqz, and Laurie Zoloth (eds), *The Human Embryonic Stem Cell Debate: Science, Ethics and Public Policy* (MIT Press: Cambridge, MA, 2001) 149–62.

[19] 'Human embryonic stem cell research: ethical and legal issues' (2001) 2 Nature Reviews Genetics 74–8.

[20] 'Is a consensus possible on stem cell research? Moral and political obstacles' (2006) 32 Journal of Medical Ethics 36–42.

One important dimension of the compromise position is that alternatives should always be pursued in preference to embryo research. The destruction of human embryos is therefore permissible only if there are no other ways of carrying out the research. As we see later, this limiting criterion became especially significant once scientists reported that they had induced pluripotency in adult cells.[21]

(iv) More Robust Arguments in Favour of Embryo Research

The compromise position involves a utilitarian calculation: do the good consequences from permitting research outweigh the symbolic harm of disposing of early human life? There are, however, those who believe that embryos do not possess the qualities which ground our respect for persons—such as consciousness and sentience—and that it would therefore be legitimate to use them as a resource for experimentation up to the point at which they can feel pain, which would be several months later than the current 14-day limit.

Helga Kuhse and Peter Singer[22]

We believe the minimal characteristic needed to give the embryo a claim to consideration is sentience, or the capacity to feel pleasure or pain. Until that point is reached, the embryo does not have any interests and, like other non-sentient organisms (a human egg, for example), cannot be harmed—in a morally relevant way—by anything we do . . .

Finally, we point to a curious consequence of restrictive legislation on embryo research. In sharp contrast to the human embryo at this early stage of its existence, non-human animals such as primates, dogs, rabbits, guinea pigs, rats and mice clearly can feel pain, and thus often are harmed by what is done to them in the course of scientific research . . . Why, then, is it considered acceptable to poison conscious rabbits in order to test the safety of drugs and household chemicals, but not considered acceptable to carry out tests on totally non-sentient human embryos?

In the next extract, Julian Savulescu defends embryonic stem (ES) cell research from a utilitarian perspective, arguing that it is likely to be of such overwhelming benefit that it is justified, even if embryos are considered persons.

Julian Savulescu[23]

To employ the Rawlsian veil of ignorance again, I would prefer a world in which I have some chance of being snuffed out as an embryo but a much higher chance of having my fatal diseases successfully treated as an embryo, foetus, child or adult . . .

---

[21] Kazutoshi Takahashi et al, 'Induction of pluripotent stem cells from adult human fibroblasts by defined factors' (2007) 31 Cell 861–72; Gretchen Vogel and Constance Holden, 'Developmental biology: Field leaps forward with new stem cell advances' (2007) 318 Science 1224–5; Junying Yu et al, 'Induced pluripotent stem cell lines derived from human somatic cells' (2007) 318 Science 1917–20; In-Hyun Park et al, 'Reprogramming of human somatic cells to pluripotency with defined factors' (2008) 451 Nature 141.

[22] 'Individuals, Humans and Persons: The Issue of Moral Status' in Peter Singer et al (eds), *Embryo Experimentation* (CUP: Cambridge, 1990) 65–75.

[23] 'The embryonic stem cell lottery and the cannibalization of human beings' (2002) 16 Bioethics 508–29.

We are all at risk of death and serious disability. ES cell technology stands to benefit everyone: embryos, children and adults. It is this property which makes it reasonable to kill some embryos to conduct ES cell research even if the embryo is a person . . . Opponents of ES cell research will likely remain unconvinced. They will argue that whatever the benefits, intentionally killing embryos is failing to 'respect human dignity' . . .

Is it respecting of human dignity to allow people to wither in nursing homes, unable to swallow, speak or move while all the time embryos are destroyed? What more twisted version of respect for human dignity could there be? It is ES cell research, like organ transplantation, that is respectful of human dignity in its reverence for the lives of the living.

(b) REGULATION IN THE UK

Research into the possibility of *in vitro* fertilization started in the first half of the twentieth century. In 1969, Bob Edwards, Barry Bavister, and Patrick Steptoe published a ground-breaking paper in Nature, in which they reported that they had successfully fertilized human oocytes *in vitro*.[24] With the benefit of hindsight, the tentativeness of the paper's conclusion is striking: 'There may be certain clinical and scientific uses for human eggs fertilized by this procedure'.

Four years after the birth of Louise Brown, the first IVF baby, in July 1978, the government appointed an academic philosopher, Mary Warnock, to chair a committee to consider how both embryo research and fertility treatment should be regulated. By a majority, its 1984 report recommended a compromise position, which would permit embryo research within strict limits. Legislation based upon this recommendation was not introduced to parliament until 1989. In the meantime, a number of Private Members Bills which would have banned all embryo research secured considerable majorities in the House of Commons, but failed for lack of parliamentary time.[25] The Human Fertilisation and Embryology Act 1990 came into force in 1991, and was updated by an amending statute in 2008.

(i) The UK's Restrictions on Embryo Research

Responsibility for ensuring that research on embryos takes place only within strict limits lies with the Human Fertilisation and Embryology Authority (HFEA). The HFEA's Licence Committee is charged with deciding, on a case-by-case basis, whether an application for a research licence satisfies the statutory criteria. The committee receives legal advice, reports from peer reviewers, and information gathered by the HFEA's inspectors. Licences are normally granted for three years, although for novel projects, 12-month licences can be issued in order to facilitate closer monitoring.

(1) The 14-Day Limit

Under the Act, no research can be carried out on an embryo after 14 days. After this point, as Jonathan Montgomery explains, the question of whether it is acceptable to experiment

---

[24] 'Early stages of fertilization in vitro in human oocytes matured in vitro' (1969) 221 Nature 632–5.
[25] In both 1985 and 1986, there were significant majorities in the House of Commons in favour of the Unborn Children (Protection) Bill.

on embryos ceases to involve a balancing exercise, in which the benefits of the research are weighed against the special status of the embryo.

Jonathan Montgomery[26]

The 14-day rule serves to distinguish those cases where the law has determined that the moral value of the embryo will always preclude the pursuit of knowledge through research from those in which a 'balancing exercise' needs to be separately undertaken into each research proposal. Under the current framework, human embryo research cannot be lawful in pursuit of the recognised objectives after 14 days, no matter how important the results might be. However, in the period before this, the Human Fertilisation and Embryology Authority is empowered to license projects provided that the statutory purposes that Parliament laid down are being pursued. In effect, it distinguishes ethical questions that are to be regarded as closed from those which are to be treated as open to further reflection.

As Mary Warnock explains, 14 days was chosen in part because this is when the 'primitive streak' first appears. The primitive streak is the heaping up of cells that will eventually become the spinal column. Fourteen days is also the last point at which twinning can occur, so before this time it is not clear whether the embryo will become one individual or two.

Mary Warnock[27]

Fourteen days was decided on as the limit because of the great change in the development of the embryo heralded by the development of the primitive streak. It is only after that that an individual exists with its own now quickly developing central nervous system, its own limbs, its own brain. Even though before that an embryo has a genetic individuality, it has no pattern of human identity, any more than human tissue has. The history of each person who is born can be traced back to the development of the primitive streak and not before. Before that there could have been two or three people formed of the same material. It is because of the enormous change that comes at this stage of development that scientists generally prefer to think of the embryos as actually beginning to exist at this stage. Before that there is the egg and the sperm, and the *conceptus*, that which comes from their conjunction. All these, egg sperm and *conceptus* are human (that is, they differ from the eggs, sperm and *conceptus* of other animals) and are of course alive, but are not yet distinct embryos.

Others would contest the idea that something special happens to the embryo at 14 days. Bernard Williams, for example, suggests that the 14-day limit does not reflect a relevant characteristic in the embryo itself, but is instead simply a reasonable regulatory response to fears of a slippery slope. The limit could equally well, Williams implies, have been drawn a bit earlier or later, but that does not undermine the value of choosing to draw a line somewhere.

---

[26] Introduction to Nuffield Council on Bioethics, *Human Embryo Culture: Discussions concerning the statutory time limit for maintaining human embryos in culture in the light of some recent scientific developments* (NCOB, 2017).

[27] 'Experimentation on Human Embryos and Fetuses' in Helga Kuhse and Peter Singer (eds), *A Companion to Bioethics* (Blackwell: Oxford, 1998) 390–6.

Bernard Williams[28]

Is drawing a line in this way reasonable? Can it be effective? The answer to both these questions seems to me to be 'yes, sometimes' . . . It may be said that a line of this kind cannot possibly be reasonable since it has to be drawn between two adjacent cases in the range, that is to say, between two cases that are not different enough to distinguish. The answer is that they are indeed not different enough to distinguish if that means that their characteristics, unsupported by anything else, would have led one to draw a line there. But though the line is not, in this sense, uniquely reasonable, it is nevertheless reasonable to draw a line there. This follows from the conjunction of three things. First, it is reasonable to distinguish in some way unacceptable cases from acceptable cases; second, the only way of doing that in these circumstances is to draw a sharp line; third, it cannot be an objection to drawing the line just here that it would have been no worse to draw it somewhere else—if that were an objection, then one could conclude that one had no reason to draw it anywhere.

Dan Brock makes a similar point, drawing an analogy between the 14-day limit and setting the voting age at 18.[29] Both limits are inherently arbitrary. Just as the moral status of the embryo is not transformed on its 14th day, so a person does not miraculously acquire the capacity to exercise sound political judgement on her 18th birthday. In both cases, however, it is desirable to draw a line somewhere, and, in the context of embryo research, 14 days has been judged a reasonable time limit, not only in the UK but in many other countries, including Australia, Japan, and Singapore.

Until recently, there was little pressure on this time limit because it was not possible to keep a developing embryo alive *in vitro* for more than about nine days. In 2016, it was reported that scientists in the UK and the US had succeeded in sustaining embryos *in vitro* for 13 days after fertilization (the embryos had to be destroyed at this point, in order not to breach the 14-day rule).[30] Unsurprisingly, these announcements were followed by calls for the 14-day limit to be extended, on the grounds that it is now impeding potentially beneficial scientific research, particularly into the causes of pregnancy loss and fetal abnormalities.

Magdalena Zernicka-Goetz[31]

[T]here is a growing feeling that the current restriction of 14 days for in vitro culture might be limiting, as many extraordinary developmental events take place during the following week and these will set up the architecture of all the major tissues.

Why might society want to follow these events? Largely because these are the developmental stages at which many defects in early human development occur. The failure to establish a pregnancy or its termination through natural miscarriage resulting in the spontaneous

---

[28] 'Types of Moral Argument Against Embryo Research' in The Ciba Foundation, *Human Embryo Research: Yes or No?* (Tavistock: London, 1986) 184–94.

[29] 'Is a consensus possible on stem cell research? Moral and political obstacles' (2006) 32 Journal of Medical Ethics 36–42.

[30] Alessia Deglincerti et al, 'Self-organization of the in vitro attached human embryo' (2016) 533 Nature 251 and Marta N Shahbazi et al, 'Self-organization of the human embryo in the absence of maternal tissues' (2016) 18 Nature cell biology 700.

[31] 'A need to expand our knowledge of early development' in Nuffield Council on Bioethics, *Human Embryo Culture: Discussions concerning the statutory time limit for maintaining human embryos in culture in the light of some recent scientific developments* (NCOB, 2017).

death and loss of a baby is a misery for many would-be mothers. It is believed that almost half of all fertilised eggs die spontaneously before a woman knows she is pregnant. Thereafter, it is believed that as many as 25 per cent of pregnancies fail within the first seven weeks (before a heartbeat can be detected). These huge numbers of spontaneous deaths are largely due to defects in development. Even when pregnancies develop to term, many new-borns die within weeks of birth every year due to congenital anomalies (mainly abnormalities in heart and neural tube development). These place great strain on families, the healthcare system and society. Understanding early post-implantation development will enable us to predict when developmental defects are likely to arise and, with time, to establish treatments. This will help to address the causes of spontaneous abortion; congenital defects in the heart and central nervous system; as well as childhood cancers of the germ line.

Others, such as Giulia Cavaliere, have recommended proceeding with caution.

Giulia Cavaliere[32]

[I]t is important to note that extending the limit beyond the 14th day of development will provide support to those who rely on the slippery slope argument to oppose embryo research. This might have non-negligible social consequences. For example, extension of the limit for embryo research would show that what is feared by 'slippery slopers' (i.e. that once a practice becomes legal it is difficult to prevent the permission of its future developments) can eventually become a reality . . .

   [T]he 14-day limit for embryo research is not valuable *in spite of* being a solution of compromise, but rather *because of* it. The idea of a democratic society is that even those who do not accord intrinsic value to the human embryo should respect value pluralism and accord moral worth to opposing views. For this reason, any proposal to change the 14-day rule needs careful evaluation of the scientific feasibility and effective benefits of embryo research; it needs an extensive inquiry into public attitudes concerning embryos; and it needs a deliberative process that takes these elements into account.

John Harris disagrees that extending the 14-day limit would provide evidence of a slippery slope. On the contrary, he suggests that scientists' adherence to this rule for nearly three decades demonstrates that it is possible to draw a line and stick to it.

John Harris[33]

So far in the UK we have not seen any good reason to redraw the 14-day line, and so there has been no slipping at all. Now, thanks to scientific advances, we do have a reason. Despite its somewhat bizarre origins, the 14-day rule has proved its worth, not because it was drawn for the best of reasons or in the best place, but because it has shown that we are capable of sticking to a rule that was needed to inspire public confidence in the regulation of science. Now that the time has come to consider redrawing the line, we can do so in the knowledge

---

[32] 'A 14-day limit for bioethics: the debate over human embryo research' (2017) 18 BMC Medical Ethics 38.
[33] 'It's time to extend the 14-day limit for embryo research' The Guardian, 6 May 2016.

that any change will not lead to slippery chaos. If we do not change the rules to enable research that is fully consistent with our values and proven regulatory capacity, we risk forgoing valuable therapeutic and humanitarian benefit to future generations.

(2) The Sources of Embryos

There are two possible sources of embryos for use in research. First, research might use the embryos that are commonly left over after a couple has had fertility treatment, either because they have completed their family and no longer wish to store their frozen embryos, or because the embryos were of poor quality and are unsuitable for use in treatment. The vast majority of embryos used in research in the UK are donated by people who have undergone fertility treatment. Because IVF would have been impossible without embryo research, many ex-patients are happy to donate their leftover embryos to research in order to 'give something back'.[34]

It is, however, clear that IVF patients commonly object to use of the word 'spare' to describe embryos that could have become a member of their family. It can be difficult to come to terms with an embryo's transition from a potential future sibling for one's children to research material. Bobbie Farsides and Rosamund Scott's interviews with embryologists suggest that they too found the use of the word 'spare' challenging, and that they had a preference for using embryos that could never have been used in treatment, because they were known to affected by a serious genetic disorder.

Bobbie Farsides and Rosamund Scott[35]

We were greatly struck by the fact that participants were typically very cautious about describing any embryo created for treatment purposes as *spare*, and thus potentially available for research. For instance, Embryologist 2 emphasised that the embryos that are given to research by a couple are only 'spare' for them 'after the patient's use, yes they're spare at that point technically. So when you've got enough heads on pillows or you've decided you don't want any more out of your treatment, then they're spare embryos.' In this way, s/he might be thought to be concerned to protect the reproductive interests of parents so that, only if such parents decide not to have further treatment, should remaining embryos be seen as ones which can legitimately pass from the treatment to the research context. At the same time, caution around the definition of an embryo as 'spare' could be seen to reflect the importance of the origins of the embryo within a treatment context aimed at the creation of a child . . .

We were also struck by what one might call an 'ethical hierarchy' of the ethical suitability of embryos for research. A number of participants commented that fresh affected PGD [preimplantation genetic diagnosis] embryos were those in relation to which they felt most comfortable seeking consent for research . . . An ethical hierarchy of embryos, in which the first choice for research embryos is affected PGD ones and the next are frozen embryos that will never be used in treatment, could be seen as protecting the embryo's chance of life as a born person as much as possible.

---

[34] See further Sarah Franklin, 'Embryonic economies: the double reproductive value of stem cells' (2006) 1 BioSocieties 71–90.

[35] 'No Small Matter For Some: Practitioners' Views on the Moral Status and Treatment of Human Embryos' (2012) 20 Medical Law Review 90–107.

Secondly, embryos can be specifically created for use in research, perhaps because scientists wish to create embryos with particular characteristics, such as a particular genetic disease. It is not generally possible to control the characteristics of embryos which are left over from IVF treatment, but if embryos are deliberately created from the genetic material of people who suffer from particular conditions, disease-specific research can be carried out on stem cell lines extracted from these embryos. In addition, if scientists wish to create cloned embryos using cell nuclear replacement (CNR), there will obviously not be any embryos left over after fertility treatment, since reproductive cloning is a criminal offence. CNR research therefore requires embryos to be created specifically for research.

Is there a moral difference between conducting research on spare IVF embryos and creating embryos with the express purpose of carrying out experiments upon them? Many people believe so, but why? The House of Lords Stem Cell Research Committee suggested that where the initial intention is to create a baby, the embryo is less instrumentalized than where the intention is to create an embryo for use in research.

House of Lords Stem Cell Research Committee[36]

4.27 ... Some argue that, if an embryo is destined for destruction, it is more honest to create it specifically for the purpose of research than to use one created for reproductive purposes. But most of those who commented on this issue regarded it as preferable to use surplus embryos than to create them specifically for research. They took the view that an embryo created for research was quite clearly being used as a means to an end, with no prospect of implantation, whereas at the time of creation the surplus embryo had a prospect of implantation, even if, once not selected for implantation (or freezing), it would have to be destroyed. We agree that for this reason it is preferable to use surplus embryos for research purposes if the same results can be achieved with them.

In contrast, Erik Parens argues that it is unusual to base an entity's moral status upon the intention of its creator.

Erik Parens[37]

One ethical intuition that seems to motivate the discarded-created distinction is that whereas the act of creating an embryo for reproduction is respectful in a way that is commensurate with the moral status of embryos, the act of creating an embryo for research is not ... In this view, the moral status of the embryo (and thus the moral status of research on it) is a function of the intention of its maker. The problem with this intuition is that it is difficult to see what the intention of the maker of something has to do with the moral status of that thing once it has come into being. We do not think, for example, that the moral status of children is a function of their parents' intentions at the time of conception. If what something is obliges us to treat it some ways and not others, how it came to being is usually thought to be morally irrelevant.

---

[36] *Stem Cell Research Report* (February 2002).
[37] 'On the Ethics and Politics of Embryonic Stem Cell Research' in Suzanne Holland, Karen Lebacqz, and Laurie Zoloth (eds), *The Human Embryonic Stem Cell Debate: Science, Ethics and Public Policy* (MIT Press: Cambridge, MA, 2001) 37–50.

In the UK, it is permissible to create embryos for research purposes. Under Schedule 2 para (3)(1) (a) to the 1990 Act, as amended, a research licence may authorize 'bringing about the creation of embryos in vitro . . . for the purposes of a project of research'. But this does not mean that scientists in the UK are free to create as many research embryos as they like. There is no statutory limit upon the number of embryos which can be created for research purposes in the Act, but in deciding whether to grant a licence, the HFEA's Licence Committee must be satisfied that the creation of the proposed number of embryos is *necessary*.

(3) The Purposes of Research

(a) *The statutory purposes*

A further restriction on the use of embryos in research is that they can only be used for certain purposes. The restrictions are contained in Schedule 2 to the Act, as amended:

The Human Fertilisation and Embryology Act 1990 Schedule 2

2(3A)(1) A licence under paragraph 3 cannot authorise any activity unless the activity appears to the Authority—

    (a) to be necessary or desirable for any of the purposes specified in sub-paragraph (2) ('the principal purposes')

    (b) to be necessary or desirable for the purpose of providing knowledge that, in the view of the Authority, may be capable of being applied for the purposes specified in sub-paragraph (2)(a) or (b), or

    (c) to be necessary or desirable for such other purposes as may be specified in regulations.

  (2) The principal purposes are—

    (a) increasing knowledge about serious disease or other serious medical conditions,

    (b) developing treatments for serious disease or other serious medical conditions,

    (c) increasing knowledge about the causes of any congenital disease or congenital medical condition that does not fall within paragraph (a),

    (d) promoting advances in the treatment of infertility,

    (e) increasing knowledge about the causes of miscarriage,

    (f) developing more effective techniques of contraception,

    (g) developing methods for detecting the presence of gene, chromosome or mitochondrion abnormalities in embryos before implantation, or

    (h) increasing knowledge about the development of embryos.

Notice that the Schedule builds in the possibility of the statute's revision by Regulations that can extend the purposes for which embryo research may be carried out. This is an attempt to 'future-proof' the legislation, in case unanticipated research purposes subsequently emerge.

The provision was used in 2001 to extend the statutory research purposes to include increasing knowledge about, and developing treatments for serious disease in order to accommodate human embryonic stem cell (hESC) research. As we saw earlier, the inner cell mass of the early human embryo contains stem cells of remarkable plasticity, capable of differentiating into every cell in the human body. Stem cells are also immortal: they can

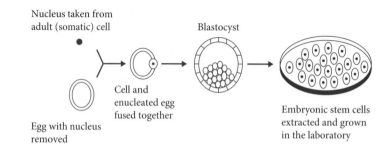

Figure 13.1

continue to divide indefinitely without losing their genetic structure. In 1998, researchers at the University of Wisconsin published a paper explaining how they had, for the first time, derived and cultured a human embryonic stem cell line.[38] If these pluripotent embryonic stem cell lines could be directed into differentiating into different types of tissue, this could be used to repair damaged tissues or organs.

CNR—that is, cloning—and the development of induced pluripotent stem (iPS) cells add a further dimension to stem cell research. Therapeutic cloning would involve the extraction of embryonic stem cells from cloned embryos, as illustrated in Figure 13.1.

If the embryo from which embryonic stem cells are removed had been cloned from the person with a damaged organ, the replacement tissue would be a perfect genetic match, and there would be no possibility of rejection. Similarly, following the discovery that it was possible to induce adult cells to act in the same way as embryonic stem cells,[39] these iPS cells could be created from the patient's own tissue, and, if they could be used to create replacement tissue, it would again be a perfect match.

For example, imagine that I need some replacement tissue—perhaps because I have a degenerative neurological condition such as Parkinson's disease. If stem cells could be created from my cells (either through cloning or via iPS cells), and they could be differentiated into becoming new brain tissue, it will be genetically identical to me. This removes the problem of rejection, and the need to suppress my immune system with immunosuppressant drugs. If this process were to become relatively straightforward, it potentially offers a solution to the organ shortage we considered in Chapter 12: anyone whose organs had failed could simply generate genetically compatible replacement tissue.

Complete organ replacement is not yet possible, but there have been successes in trials involving hESC-derived tissue transplantation, particularly for the treatment of macular degeneration. In 2018, it was reported that two severely visually impaired individuals had had their sight restored after a patch of cells made from ES cells was injected into their damaged retinas.[40] It is thought that 'the next big clinical breakthrough' may come from trials in which

---

[38] James A Thomson et al, 'Embryonic stem cell lines derived from human blastocysts' (1998) 282 Science 1145–7.

[39] Kazutoshi Takahashi and Shinya Yamanaka, 'Induction of pluripotent stem cells from mouse embryonic and adult fibroblast cultures by defined factors' (2006) 126 Cell 663–76.

[40] Lyndon da Cruz et al, 'Phase 1 clinical study of an embryonic stem cell–derived retinal pigment epithelium patch in age-related macular degeneration' (2018) 36 Nature Biotechnology 328–37.

ES and iPS cells are used to replace dopamine-producing neurons for patients suffering from Parkinson's disease.[41]

(b) The 'necessity principle'

It is important to remember that scientists are not entitled to a licence from the HFEA just because they want to do research that is desirable for one of the specified purposes. The Licence Committee must also be satisfied that the proposed use of embryos is necessary (sometimes referred to as the 'necessity principle'), that is, that the research could not be done *without* using human embryos. If it were possible to conduct the research on animals or on tissue taken from adults, the Licence Committee could not be satisfied that the use of embryos was necessary, and no licence could be granted.

The 'necessity principle' is fairly easily satisfied where the research is directed towards improving IVF techniques. Research into new embryo freezing methods, or new techniques for preimplantation genetic diagnosis, can only discover their impact upon the human embryo if human embryos are used in the research.

But if a stem cell research project could use iPS cells, rather than embryonic stem cells, then the use of embryos is not necessary, and no licence could be granted. So far, pluripotency can only be induced in adult cells with the help of viral factors, and, because of the risk of carcinogenicity, such cells would not be suitable for clinical use.

Most scientists believe that hES research and research on iPS cells should continue in parallel. Opponents of embryo research, on the other hand, have invoked iPS cell research in order to argue that using embryos in research is not only unethical, but also unnecessary. This, as Mark Brown explains in the next extract, misses the point that it will only be possible to do the research necessary to understand how far iPS cells can be reprogrammed to behave in the same way as hES cells if hES are used as controls.

Mark Brown[42]

In order to know the degree to which iPS cells can function as substitutes for ES cells in science and in medicine it will be necessary to understand in much greater detail the differences and similarities between reprogramming induced in the laboratory and the natural processes of reprogramming in fertilization and embryological development ... At some point iPS derived tissues may enable mainstream medicine to avoid institutionalized production of human embryonic stem cells for drug development, disease modeling and cell replacement therapy, but that day has not yet come ... Embryo protection advocates who hail iPS as an ethically uncompromised source of pluripotent cell should recognize that as a matter of fact they are promoting a research program that depends upon embryo sacrifice. The science that might make iPS substitutes available almost certainly will require comparative pluripotency studies in which embryonic stem cells function as models for the molecular mechanisms of reprogramming.

An interesting twist to the claims made for iPS cells by opponents of embryo research is described in the next extract. With appropriate reprogramming, iPS cells might themselves be able to become embryos. Far from resolving debates over the instrumental use of human embryos, this might create a new dilemma.

---

[41] David Cyranoski, 'How human embryonic stem cells sparked a revolution' (2018) 555 Nature 428–30.
[42] 'No ethical bypass of moral status in stem cell research' (2013) 27 Bioethics 12–19.

RM Green[43]

Nor is it clear that this technology really solves the ethical problem of embryo destruction that has generated the opposition to hES cell research. iPS cell technology brings an adult cell back to its pluripotent embryonic state. As the work of Nagy and others has shown, with appropriate technical manipulations and sufficient support, such a cell might have the potential to develop into a human being. Since opponents of stem cell research and therapeutic cloning research usually base their arguments for the sanctity of fertilised or nuclear transfer embryos on precisely this kind of developmental capacity, it is not clear why they have not voiced similar concerns about iPS cell technology . . .

The opponents of hES cell research—now enthusiasts for iPS cell research—appear less concerned about the lives of the entities that could become people than with declaring victory in a cultural war.

(c) In-vitro derived gametes

Of course, if it is possible to create any human cell type from a stem cell line, it will also be possible to create reproductive cells, or gametes.[44] In 2011, researchers in Japan created fully functioning sperm from mouse embryonic stem cells. These sperm cells were used to fertilize mouse eggs *in vitro*. The resulting embryos were implanted in female mice, leading to the birth of healthy offspring.[45]

It is possible, and perhaps even likely, that human eggs and sperm will be generated from stem cell lines during the lifetime of the amended 1990 Act.[46] The 2008 amendments specifically allow stem-cell derived gametes to be created for research purposes, but forbid their use in treatment. This is achieved by allowing only 'permitted embryos' and 'permitted eggs and sperm' to be used in treatment services.

Human Fertilisation and Embryology Act 1990 sections 3 and 3ZA

3(2)   No person shall place in a woman—

    (a) an embryo other than a permitted embryo (as defined by section 3ZA), or

    (b) any gametes other than permitted eggs or permitted sperm (as so defined) . . .

3ZA(2) A permitted egg is one—

    (a) which has been produced by or extracted from the ovaries of a woman, and

    (b) whose nuclear or mitochondrial DNA has not been altered.

(3)   Permitted sperm are sperm—

    (a) which have been produced by or extracted from the testes of a man, and

    (b) whose nuclear or mitochondrial DNA has not been altered.

---

[43] 'Embryo as epiphenomenon: some cultural, social and economic forces driving the stem cell debate' (2008) 34 Journal of Medical Ethics 840–4.

[44] See further Giuseppe Testa and John Harris, 'Ethics and synthetic gametes' (2005) 19 Bioethics 146.

[45] Katsuhiko Hayashi et al, 'Reconstitution of the mouse germ cell specification pathway in culture by pluripotent stem cells' (2011) 146 Cell 519–32.

[46] Hannah Devlin, 'Scientists a step closer to mimicking way human body creates sperm' The Guardian 1 January 2018.

(4) An embryo is a permitted embryo if—

    (a) it has been created by the fertilisation of a permitted egg by permitted sperm,

    (b) no nuclear or mitochondrial DNA of any cell of the embryo has been altered, and

    (c) no cell has been added to it other than by division of the embryo's own cells.

Stem-cell derived gametes will be useful for research purposes, because it would be possible to simply create eggs for use in stem cell research (rather than needing to obtain them from women). Stem-cell derived gametes might also be very useful for treatment purposes. If people who cannot use their own gametes in treatment could make them instead, gamete donation would become unnecessary. All of the issues that arise in relation to gamete donation—such as whether donors should be paid; whether the child has a right to information about her donor, and how donors feel about being contacted by their genetic offspring many years later—would simply disappear.

Given the benefits of eliminating the need for gamete donation, it is interesting that the government chose not to future-proof the statute through the inclusion of a power to make Regulations to permit the use of stem-cell derived gametes in treatment services, once it becomes safe to do so. Instead, new primary legislation will be necessary in order to repeal the ban on the use of stem-cell derived gametes in treatment.

The reason for the government's caution was the fact that stem-cell derived gametes might fundamentally change the way in which people have children. If it is possible to create sperm from stem cells derived from a woman, and eggs from stem cells derived from a man, it would be possible for a same-sex couple to produce a child that is genetically related to both of them.

While this would indeed be novel, Timothy Murphy does not see any reason to be suspicious about facilitating genetic parenthood in a same-sex couple.

Timothy F Murphy[47]

Interpretations like these treat same-sex couples as a novelty act in bioethics, primarily by suggesting that their moral standing as parents requires levels of moral scrutiny not required of other parents. At the very least, discussions like these still suppose that someone—moral and social authorities—have to function as gatekeepers for homosexual men and women wanting to be parents, as against assuming in advance that any safe and effective treatment for infertility should be presumptively available to any adult.

In theory, it would also be possible for someone to reproduce with herself. The child would not be a clone of her parent, because of the shuffling of genes that takes place at fertilization. It would, however, be inadvisable to try this, given that we know that reproducing with close (but not identical) genetic relatives increases the chance of genetic abnormalities.

A further mind-boggling possibility is what César Palacios-González et al refer to as 'multiplex parenting'.

---

[47] 'The meaning of synthetic gametes for gay and lesbian people and bioethics too' (2014) 40 Journal of Medical Ethics 762–5.

César Palacios-González, John Harris, and Giuseppe Testa[48]

IVG [*in vitro*-derived gametes] could permit instead a much more substantive sharing of genetic kinship, through what is in essence a generational shortcut. Imagine that four people in a relationship want to parent a child while being all genetically related to her. IVG would enable the following scenario: first, two embryos would be generated from either couple through IVF with either naturally or in vitro generated gametes. hESC lines would be then established from both embryos and differentiated into IVG to be used in a second round of IVF. The resulting embryo would be genetically related to all four prospective parents, who would technically be the child's genetic grandparents.

It would also be possible to skip more than one generation. Instead of implanting the new embryo, it could be used to derive more embryonic stem cells, from which new eggs and sperm could be created, and used to fertilize other *in vitro*-derived gametes. This process could continue indefinitely, or it could be interrupted at any stage so that an embryo could be implanted into a woman. In this scenario, all of the child's immediate ancestors would have been embryos that had been allowed to perish *in vitro*. At first sight, it is hard to see why anyone would want to do this, but, as Robert Sparrow explains, it could be used to study hereditary diseases, or to engage in the sort of selective breeding that would otherwise be impracticable in humans.

Robert Sparrow[49]

Repeated iterations of this process would allow scientists to proceed through multiple human generations 'in the lab'. *In vitro* eugenics might be used to study the heredity of genetic disorders and to produce cell lines of a desired character for medical applications. More controversially, it might also function as a powerful technology of 'human enhancement' by allowing researchers to use all the techniques of selective breeding to produce human individuals with a desired genotype.

If a child is born as a result of skipping one or more generations, the child's genetic 'parents' would be embryos that had never 'lived' outside the Petri dish in which she was created. Robert Sparrow has argued that embryos cannot be parents within any normal understanding of what it means to be a parent. Instead such children would have no genetic parents, although when only one generation is skipped, it might make sense to say that they had genetic grandparents.

Robert Sparrow[50]

Individuals cannot interpret their lives and experiences in the light of 'biographies' of embryos. Institutions cannot assign responsibility for the care of children to embryos or consult embryos about the fate of embryos created with their gametes. More fundamentally, it is internal to the concept of parenthood that parents are *persons*, living or dead, who stand in the

---

[48] 'Multiplex parenting: IVG and the generations to come' (2014) 40 Journal of Medical Ethics 752–8.
[49] '*In vitro* eugenics' (2014) 40 Journal of Medical Ethics 725–31.
[50] 'Orphaned at conception: the uncanny offspring of embryos' (2012) 26 Bioethics 173–81.

appropriate (social, gestational, causal, genetic, etc) relationship to the child. Thus, I would suggest that to have embryos as genetic 'parents' is to have no genetic parents at all. Instead, the children born of such matings might be said to be 'orphaned at conception'.

It is also true that, while such children would not have genetic parents, they would have genetic *grandparents*. The couple who conceived the embryos from which the stem cell lines were derived would be the genetic grandparents of children conceived using gametes derived from these stem cells. However, once it becomes possible to create gametes from stem cell lines it will also be possible to create new embryos via the fusion of these gametes and then to derive gametes from these embryos. Repeated iterations of this process would lead to the creation of embryos that had no meaningful genetic relation to any living individual.

(d) The need for eggs

CNR is impossible without a supply of eggs, from which the nucleus can be removed in order to insert a cell, commonly a skin cell, taken from an adult. As a result, some feminists have drawn attention to the emphasis placed upon the scientific and therapeutic potential of stem cell lines extracted from CNR embryos, and the lack of attention paid to the need for a plentiful supply of eggs. Renate Klein, for example, is concerned about 'the biotech industry's voracious appetite for eggs', and has argued that 'women's lives and bodies should not be invaded for the so-called public good'.[51]

It is, of course, true that there are risks associated with ovarian stimulation, but proper monitoring should be able to minimize the chance of a woman suffering from ovarian hyperstimulation syndrome (OHSS). In clinical trials, subjects not uncommonly expose themselves to unknowable risks.[52] In relation to egg donation, the risks are at least well known, usually controllable, and the donor can be properly informed in advance.

There is also the possibility that women may volunteer to donate eggs because they are under the mistaken impression that the research project will lead to a cure for someone they love. This is a variation of the 'therapeutic misconception' that we considered in relation to clinical trials in Chapter 10, whereby patients misunderstand the benefits that are likely to flow from their participation in research. The solution normally adopted to this problem is not, however, to prevent patients from participating in research at all, but rather to ensure that information sheets and consent forms are as frank and comprehensive as possible.

In 2005, it was revealed that Professor Woo Suk Hwang—a Korean scientist who claimed to have cloned the first human embryo and extracted the first patient-specific stem cell line[53]— had falsified research results and obtained eggs, in large quantities, by paying donors and recruiting them from his junior technicians and PhD students. Because Hwang himself was deeply involved in the consent process, this almost certainly amounted to a breach of para 27 of the Helsinki Declaration, which provides that 'the physician must be particularly cautious if the potential subject is in a dependent relationship with the physician', and that, in such cases, 'the informed consent must be sought by an appropriately qualified individual who is completely independent of this relationship'.[54]

---

[51] 'Rhetoric of Choice Clouds Dangers of Harvesting Women's Eggs for Cloning', available at <www.onlineopinion.com.au/view.asp?article=5229>.

[52] See, eg, the TGN1412 trial discussed in Chapter 10.

[53] See further Emily Jackson, 'Fraudulent stem cell research and respect for the embryo' (2006) 1 BioSocieties 349–56.

[54] World Medical Association, *Declaration of Helsinki: Ethical Principles for Medical Research Involving Human Subjects* (version adopted at the 64th WMA General Assembly, Fortaleza, Brazil, October 2013).

In the UK, women might donate eggs to research, either as a one-off donation or through an egg-sharing scheme. Egg-sharing involves women who need IVF being offered cheap or free treatment in return for donating some of their eggs. The HFEA's Code of Practice sets out that where women donate via an egg-sharing arrangement, the eggs must be divided by someone independent of the research project, and that there should be no difference in the benefits provided to women sharing their eggs for research, compared with those sharing their eggs for the treatment of others.

HFEA 9th Code of Practice

12.32 If gametes are being donated to research through a benefits in kind agreement, the centre must ensure that the eggs are divided between the donor and the recipient (the research project) by someone not directly involved in the research project.

12.33 If a centre offers benefits in kind in exchange for donating gametes to fertility treatment, mitochondrial donation and to research, equal benefits in kind should be available. This ensures there is no advantage in donating to one recipient rather than the other.

Women who are not sharing their eggs can receive up to £750 per cycle of donation, to cover all of their out-of-pocket expenses, such as taking time off work, travel costs, and childcare expenses.

(e) Consent

One important prerequisite to the use of embryos in research is that, with three strictly limited exceptions, gamete or tissue providers must have specifically donated them to research. Under Schedule 3 para (2) to the 1990 Act, consent to an embryo's use in any project of research must be in writing. Consent can be withdrawn under Schedule 3 para (4) at any time until the embryo has been used in the project of research. Schedule 3 para (3) specifies that the person giving consent must have been given a suitable opportunity to receive counselling, and must be provided 'with such relevant information as is proper'. Guidance on the information which should be provided is contained in the HFEA's Code of Practice.

HFEA 9th Code of Practice

22.7 For any research project, the centre should ensure that before donors give their consent to their gametes or embryos, or cells used to create embryos, being used in research, they are given oral information (supported by relevant written material) that confirms:

    (a) the specific research project and its aims

    (b) details of the research project, including likely outcomes and how any individual donation will impact on the overall project

    (c) whether the embryos will be reversibly or irreversibly anonymised, and the implications of this

    (d) whether donors will be given any information that is obtained during the research and is relevant to their health and welfare

(e) that donors are expected to have an opportunity to ask questions and discuss the research project

(f) that donating gametes or embryos to research in the course of treatment services will not affect the patient's treatment in any way

(g) that patients are under no obligation to donate gametes and embryos for research and that their decision whether to do so will have no repercussions for any treatment they may receive

(h) that only fresh or frozen gametes and embryos not required for treatment can be used for research

(i) that research is experimental, and so any gametes and embryos used and created for any research project must not be used in treatment

(j) that donors may specify conditions for the use of the gametes or embryos

(k) that after the research has been completed, all donated gametes and embryos will be allowed to perish, and

(l) that, for any individual who donates cells for creating embryos for research, consent to use these cells includes consent to do so after the individual's death, unless stated otherwise.

Important consent issues are raised by the fact that stem cell lines are potentially immortal and might be useful to scientists (and pharmaceutical companies) for many years to come. Again, the HFEA's Code of Practice specifies that it must be made clear to potential donors 'that any stem cell lines created may continue indefinitely and be used in many different research projects'.[55]

The HFEA and the Medical Research Council have jointly contributed towards a standard consent form for the use of embryos for stem cell research. This stresses, among other things, that the donors will not benefit, medically or financially, from any discoveries made during research on their cells. The HFEA will not grant licences for stem cell research unless the researchers have made a commitment to deposit each stem cell line with the UK stem cell bank; and donors must be informed of the intention to bank any stem cell lines derived from their embryos.

Centralized banking of stem cell lines is important because their immortality means that they can continue to be made freely available to scientists throughout the world. It is possible that there will come a time when the worldwide stem cell banks contain sufficient high-quality embryonic stem cell lines to meet researchers' needs, and it will no longer be necessary to create more.

Two issues arise from this. First, the open sharing of stem cell lines with researchers throughout the world means that it would be highly desirable, albeit perhaps impractical, to have greater regulatory harmonization. If scientists in California, say, are only permitted to carry out research on stem cell lines where the gamete/embryo donors received no direct or indirect compensation, a high-quality stem cell line deposited in the UK bank, derived from eggs provided by a woman who received £750 in return, may be unavailable to them. While cross-national regulation of embryonic stem cell research would have many practical advantages, it is unlikely ever to become a reality. There is no global consensus on the moral status of the embryo, and, in the future, countries may effectively be in competition with each other as attractive locations for pharmaceutical companies producing lucrative stem cell therapies.

[55] Para 22.8(f).

Secondly, in an application to carry out human embryonic stem cell research, the Licence Committee must now ask itself a further question, namely whether it would be possible to carry out the research project using stem cell lines which can be obtained from a stem cell bank. Only if the answer to this question is 'no'—perhaps because the researchers wish to create a disease-specific cell line for a disease which is not among those represented in the bank—could a licence be issued. This issue arose in a case in which the Licence Committee had refused an application for a licence on the grounds that it could not be satisfied that it would be impossible to use existing stem cell lines in the particular drug toxicology research project. A preference to create a new line, free from third party entanglements, did not amount to a necessity to do so, and the application was refused.[56]

(f) Creating Embryos without Consent

The 2008 reforms to the 1990 Act create three exceptions to the need to obtain consent to the use of an embryo in a research project. Two are intended to cover research into conditions which only affect people who cannot give consent. An obvious example is Tay-Sachs disease, which will lead to a child's death, normally by the age of five. Schedule 3 provides that, provided the 'parental consent conditions' are met and it would not be possible to do research using cells taken from someone else who can give consent,[57] someone with parental responsibility can give consent to the use of their child's cells to create an embryo for research purposes.

A similar provision applies to adults who lack capacity. Again, provided it would not be possible to carry out the research on cells taken from people who can give consent, it may be possible to use cells from an adult who lacks capacity.[58] The licence holder must also consult someone close to the person who lacks capacity (P) in order to find out what 'P's wishes and feelings about the use of P's human cells for that purpose would be likely to be if P had capacity in relation to the matter'.[59]

The final way in which the need for consent can be dispensed with is if the person's cells were stored before the Act came into force, and they have since died. This is so that cells stored in an existing tissue bank could be used for stem cell research, where it is not possible to obtain similar cells from someone who could give consent. There must be no evidence that the person would have objected to the use of their cells in this sort of research, and there must be agreement from someone who stands in a qualifying relationship to them (this is from the Human Tissue Act 2004, and refers to a list of relatives, described in Chapter 12).

It will be difficult to establish that it is necessary to use cells from deceased people, because there must be 'reasonable grounds for believing that scientific research will be adversely affected to a significant extent' if the only human cells that can be used are ones for which there is effective consent (or ones covered by the first two exceptions).[60]

3 STEM CELL THERAPIES

Some cell therapies, including blood transfusions, bone marrow transplantation, and skin grafts, have been around for many years. As we have seen, newer stem cell therapies, using cells derived from hESCs and iSCs, are currently moving from 'bench to bedside'.

---

[56] Minutes available at <www.hfea.gov.uk>. [57] Schedule 3, para 15. [58] Schedule 3, para 17.
[59] Schedule 3, para 18(4). [60] Schedule 3, para 21.

Kalina Kamenova and Timothy Caulfield studied media reports of stem cell (SC) therapies and found that they were overwhelmingly optimistic, both about the promise of stem cell therapies and about how soon they might be available to patients.

Kalina Kamenova and Timothy Caulfield[61]

Overall, the news reporting on the clinical translation of SC therapies between 2009 and 2013 has remained optimistic and very much in tune with the predominantly optimistic slant in media reporting of emerging technologies in biomedicine and heightened public expectations established by previous studies. Remarkably, 69% of all news reports that indicated timelines predicted that SC therapies will be available within 5 to 10 years or sooner, just around the corner, or in the near future ...

Another key finding was the shift from ethical, legal, and social issues, which were central to media framing and public debates in the past, to stories about clinical translation (37.1%) and new discoveries (22.8%). Previous research on the evolution of the SC controversy has established that questions concerning the moral status of the human embryo and reproductive cloning no longer dominate public, policy, or scholarly debates; rather, clinical translation and new ethical issues arising from it have become increasingly important.

Giulio Cossu et al point out that stem cell therapies, even if successful, may not be sufficiently cost-effective. In addition, drawing on the case of Henrietta Lacks—a poor black woman whose cancer biopsy was used without her knowledge or consent to derive the lucrative HeLa cell line[62]—they point out that stem cell therapies may lead to complex questions of ownership.

Giulio Cossu et al[63]

In view of the personalised nature of regenerative medicine and high manufacturing costs, these therapies will probably need to be highly beneficial to patients (compared with current therapies) to be cost-effective. Alternatively, they might seek to target diseases for which treatment options are limited or unavailable, for which value for money might be easier to show ...

Several questions about the ownership and control of cell lines also arise: for example, is a cell line derived from me still my property? ... [T]he HeLa cell lines used to this day by many researchers were derived from cell samples from Henrietta Lacks in 1951. No consent was received at the time from Henrietta Lacks, and it was only 20 years later that family members became aware of the global usage of the cell line derived from her. The nature of their subsequent struggle for recognition revealed a wide gap between the regulatory concerns and the perceptions of her family about what should come back to them.

---

[61] 'Stem cell hype: Media portrayal of therapy translation' (2015) 7 Science Translational Medicine 278ps4.
[62] See further Rebecca Skloot, *The Immortal Life of Henrietta Lacks* (New York, Random House, 2010).
[63] 'Lancet Commission: Stem Cells and Regenerative medicine' (2018) 391 The Lancet 883–910.

(a) REGENERATIVE MEDICINE

If stem cell therapies become routine, they could lead to a new sort of regenerative medicine. Most people in the west now die as a result of degenerative diseases, such as heart disease and cancer. If it is possible to generate new replacement tissue whenever it is required, the human body's natural degeneration is no longer inevitable. In the next extracts, John Harris and John K Davis consider the implications of significantly extending our life expectancy.

John Harris[64]

There are people who regard the prospect of immortality with distaste or even horror; there are others who desire it above all else. In that most people fear death and want to postpone it as long as possible, there is some reason to suppose that the prospect of personal immortality would be widely welcomed. But it is one thing to contemplate our own personal immortality, quite another to contemplate a world in which increasing numbers of people were immortal, and in which we and all or any future children would have to compete indefinitely with previous generations for jobs, space and everything else . . .

To come down to earth, there is no doubt that immortality would be a mixed blessing, but we should be slow to reject cures for terrible diseases even if the price we have to pay for those cures is increasing life expectancy and even creating immortals. Better surely to accompany the scientific race to achieve immortality with commensurate work in ethics and social policy to ensure that we know how to cope with the transition to parallel populations of mortals and immortals.

John K Davis[65]

First, if you cease to age, or age very slowly, death will seem less imminent, and it may therefore be harder to accept death. If you don't feel that death is inevitable and predictable within a few decades, you won't be forced to learn to transcend death by becoming involved in things beyond yourself, such as children, future generations, a suitable cause, or something else that will last beyond the time you die. Second, when we age and expect to die within a century, we are forced to focus on accomplishing something and use our time well. This is less likely if you halt or dramatically slow your aging. Third, some virtues may be harder to get; facing death forces us to cultivate the virtue of courage, for example – something we will not do if we do not fear death . . . Finally, extended life may be characterized by ennui, boredom, and the sense that you've seen it all and done it all a hundred times before. Extended life is a drag.

On the one hand, an endless supply of replacement tissue for people whose bodies are degenerating might appear to give rise to some complex ethical issues. For example, these techniques are likely to be expensive, at least at first, and so significantly increased life expectancy might be available only to a small minority of very rich people, raising important questions

---

[64] 'The Ethics and Justice of Life-Extending Therapies' (2002) 55 Current Legal Problems 65–95.
[65] 'Four Ways Life Extension will Change Our Relationship with Death' (2016) 30 Bioethics 165–72.

of distributive justice. If, in time, regenerative medicine became more widely available, would significantly increased lifespans put pressure on the world's resources?

On the other hand, it could be argued that finding cures for diseases such as cancer and heart disease is self-evidently desirable. Just as the discovery of cures for infectious diseases increased lifespans dramatically during the twentieth century, we should not be surprised if average lifespans continue to increase during the 21st century.

It could also be argued that there is already a difference between the average lifespans of rich and poor people. In the UK, average life expectancy is just over 80 years, but for homeless women it is 43 years. In Japan, the average lifespan is 84; in the Central African Republic it is 52 years. Regenerative medicine would not then pose uniquely difficult questions about distributive justice.

Moreover, it could be argued that there is something peculiar about our attitudes to life extension. Saving someone's life is normally regarded as a very good thing, whereas people are suspicious and fearful of extreme life extension. As ADNJ de Grey explains:

> Humanity has long demonstrated a paradoxical ambivalence concerning the extension of a healthy human lifespan. Modest health extension has been universally sought, whereas extreme (even indefinite) health extension has been regarded as a snare and delusion—a dream beyond all others at first blush, but actually something we are better off without.[66]

But if we welcome modest life extension and want to rule out extreme life extension, we will need to decide upon the cut-off point. At what age does saving someone's life stop being laudable? Setting an age after which we should refuse to treat old people will not be straightforward, and even more difficult questions will arise if we seek to enforce this cut-off age upon someone who wants to go on living.

(b) STEM CELL TOURISM

Most stem cell therapies are still at the experimental stage. This has not stopped clinics based in comparatively unregulated countries from aggressively marketing unproven stem cell therapies to desperate patients, or as a miraculous 'cure' for ageing. In the next extract, Dave Archard sets out the problem.

Dave Archard[67]

> In animal studies, stem-cell therapies have shown promise in arresting ageing – by repairing age-related damage to organs, including the brain – and increasing life span. The effects of stem cell therapy on age-related conditions such as Alzheimer's disease are being explored in early-stage clinical trials in the United States. While these research avenues seem promising, we are still some way away from having good evidence for any specific intervention in humans. Yet, at the very same time, unproven and potentially harmful stem cell therapies that

---

[66] ADNJ de Grey, 'Life extension, human rights, and the rational refinement of repugnance' (2005) 31 Journal of Medical Ethics 659–63.

[67] 'Ethics of regenerative medicine and innovative treatments' Nuffield Council of Bioethics blog, 13 October 2017. Available at <http://nuffieldbioethics.org/blog/ethics-regenerative-medicine-innovative-stem-cell-treatment>.

promise anti-ageing and rejuvenating effects are already offered by clinics around the world at enormous cost to the patient.

This highlights the key problem: people desperate for cures for awful conditions can access information about apparently miraculous treatments. There is also interest in treatments for other reasons too, including the desire simply to look younger. At the same time, some private clinics are prepared to provide them ahead of adequate tests of their safety and efficacy. Yet patients may, in seeking such treatments, be unaware of their status and be prepared to pay exorbitant amounts of money to secure them. Unscrupulous clinics and clinicians can also escape regulation by exporting the treatment to other countries. Medical tourism is an increasing reality and as long as patients are prepared to travel across borders, any demand for better national regulation must acknowledge how it can be escaped.

The danger in all of this is not just that of the exploitation of those desperate for a cure and unaware of the high costs of opting for unapproved, unproven, and unlicensed treatments... Bad therapies will erode trust in those that may well work – indeed secure remarkable results – and that are properly regulated... Privately provided experimental interventions may actually make 'proper' clinical research more difficult – for example, by making it more difficult to recruit people into a trial that will provide statistically significant data.

Tsung-Ling Lee et al agree that unregulated stem cell therapies have costs beyond those suffered by the individual patient/consumer.

Tsung-Ling Lee et al[68]

[I]n some countries, the costs of adverse health effects caused by stem cell interventions are borne by public health-care systems, not by stem cell clinics or patients ... [R]egulatory failure not only enables unscrupulous providers to operate with little oversight, but also means that adverse effects are likely to be under-reported, as patients who are harmed by failed stem cell interventions rarely seek legal redress. Because of this lack of oversight, patients harmed by these interventions – and their families – may also be affected financially; as well, objective data on the impact of this industry on patients and on public health systems may be incomplete.

It might be thought that the answer to the problem of patients being sold 'false hope' by rogue providers is to provide them with accurate, evidence-based information. As Alan Petersen et al point out, however, patients increasingly seek information and support from online communities, where 'discourses of hope' may 'trump expert constructions of risk'.

Alan Petersen, Casimir MacGregor, and Megan Munsie[69]

Discourses of hope circulate widely on the Internet, increasingly via the numerous online patient forums and social media platforms that have emerged in recent years, and coexist

---

[68] 'Regulating the stem cell industry: needs and responsibilities' (2017) 95 Bulletin of the World Health Organisation 663–4.

[69] 'Stem cell miracles or Russian roulette?: patients' use of digital media to campaign for access to clinically unproven treatments' (2016) 17 Health, Risk and Society 592–604.

and compete with contending discourses of risk and risk-benefit, created and disseminated largely by scientists, clinicians, bioethicists and regulatory authorities . . .

Web 2.0 user-generated-content social media provides a significant means for citizens to build and lead biosocial 'communities of hope' that create optimistic 'framings' of particular treatments and conceptions of risk . . . [D]igitalisation enables patient stories, such as those of technological optimism, to be stored and circulated long after events have played out off screen or offline, giving them potential impact over time. This makes these stories a key element in the reconfiguring of risk and sustaining a political economy of hope; in countering alternative claims about the benefits and risks of treatments and the trustworthiness of providers. Stories may be framed in ways that enable prosumers [producers and consumers of digital content] to construct discourses of risk that may differ from expert discourses . . .

As noted, Facebook is a place where users may share criticisms of doctors and of what they see as uncaring authorities. It is in such communities, we contend, that hope tends to trump expert constructions of risk and risk-benefit and that undertaking treatment is seen to be, as some of our patients reasoned, 'worth the risk', or to involve risks that were deemed to be 'small'.

It is also worth noting, as Fadhila Mazanderani et al point out, that for patients suffering from devastating incurable disorders, hope may be of some value to them, even if it is not grounded in robust clinical evidence.

Fadhila Mazanderani, Jenny Kelly, and Ariel Duce[70]

For the most part these patients were well informed and carefully weighed up various medical, personal and financial factors before deciding to have [the liberation procedure, a controversial endovascular intervention proposed as a treatment for Multiple Sclerosis (MS)]. We have discussed how they negotiated and rationalised this decision around different kinds of risks associated with the intervention and conflicting forms of evidence for its efficacy. Furthermore, we described how hope was (a) seen as a value in its own right in the experiential rationality of patients; (b) deployed as an important factor in the decision-making processes that led them to pursue an unproven therapy; and (c) actively cultivated and embodied through therapeutic experimentation and online experiential information sharing.

The critical (hope-generating) 'benefits' of the liberation procedure lay in the very process of learning about it and researching it online, in exchanging information and experiences pre- and post-procedure, in becoming an activist or online debater on the issue, in being inspired to take part in formal studies or informal self-monitoring campaigns. Critical was also the performative turning of 'the neurologists', 'the pharmaceutical industry' and 'mainstream MS medicine' into external obstacles that needed to be overcome or sidestepped. What is more, the very unpredictability of the experimental procedure in which the patients decided to become actively involved inspired more hope than the tentative results of evidence-based clinical trials about new drugs or other therapies.

---

[70] 'From embodied risk to embodying hope: Therapeutic experimentation and experiential information sharing in a contested intervention for Multiple Sclerosis' (2018) 13 BioSocieties 232–54.

(c) PATENTING STEM CELLS

As stem cell research moves from the laboratory to the clinic, the question of whether it is possible to patent a stem cell line arises. On the one hand, stem cell therapies are costly to develop, and without patent protection to enable researchers to recoup their investment, research might grind to a halt. On the other hand, would patenting a stem cell line amount to taking out a patent on life itself?

Article 6(1) of the EU Biotechnology Directive[71] provides that inventions must be considered unpatentable where their commercial exploitation would be contrary to *ordre public* or morality. In order to provide national courts and patent offices with guidance on what this means, there is, in Article 6(2), an illustrative list of examples, which includes, in Article 6(2) (c), 'uses of human embryos for industrial or commercial purposes'.

In *Brüstle v Greenpeace*,[72] the Grand Chamber of the European Court of Justice (ECJ) held that 'human embryo' should be uniformly interpreted to include any entity that is 'capable of commencing the process of development of a human being'. Three years later, in *International Stem Cell Corp v Comptroller General of Patents, Designs and Trade Marks*,[73] the question for the Grand Chamber was whether 'unfertilised human ova whose division and further development have been stimulated by parthenogenesis and which, in contrast to fertilised ova, contain only pluripotent cells and are incapable of developing into human beings' are human embryos within the meaning of Article 6(2) of the Directive. Parthenogenesis involves asexual reproduction, in which the egg is not fertilized. It happens in some other species, but in humans, while eggs have been 'tricked' into starting the process of cell division, parthenotes cannot develop beyond the blastocyst state.

In *Brüstle v Greenpeace*,[74] the ECJ had appeared to include parthenotes within the definition of 'human embryo' because they are 'capable of *commencing* the process of development of a human being'. In *International Stem Cell Corp*, however, the court found that because a parthenote does not have the capacity to develop into a human being, it was not a human embryo, and therefore could be patented.

It has been argued that the ECJ was too interventionist in both of these judgments, insisting on an EU-wide definition of human embryo, rather than leaving individual Member States to decide for themselves when commercial exploitation would be contrary to morality.[75] In the next extract, Julian Hitchcock and Clara Sattler de Sousa e Brito go further and suggest that, given the steps taken by the EU to regulate and license stem cell research and stem cell therapies, it is 'ludicrous' to ban on patents on the grounds of morality.

Julian Hitchcock and Clara Sattler de Sousa e Brito[76]

Any claim that it is 'necessary' to ban hESC patents in order to uphold *ordre public* or morality is immediately punctured by the EU Directives on Human Tissue and Cells (EUTCD), which since 2004 have provided a clear legislative framework for the clinical use of human embryo derived products in the EU. The claim that a clinical use sanctioned by Europe's highest legislature is immoral is, therefore, ludicrous ...

---

[71] Directive on the Legal Protection of Biotechnological Inventions (98/44/EC).
[72] [2012] 1 CMLR 41.   [73] Case C-364/13, 18 December 2014.   [74] [2012] 1 CMLR 41.
[75] Andrea Faeh, 'Judicial activism, the Biotech Directive and its institutional implications: is the court acting as a legislator or a court when defining the "human embryo"?' (2015) 40 European Law Review 613–27.
[76] 'Should patents determine when life begins?' (2014) 36 European Intellectual Property Review 390–8.

> Given that the Council of Ministers and European Parliament have passed laws to facilitate and encourage the development and commercial exploitation of human embryo-derived inventions in Europe, it is plainly impossible to maintain that it is 'necessary' for the European Union and its Member States to *prevent* it, whether the supposed purpose is that of protecting *ordre public*, morality or satisfying religious or environmental pressure groups.

Hannah Schikl et al are critical of the *International Stem Cell Corp* decision from another direction, pointing out that morphologically abnormal embryos produced through fertilization do not have the potential to become human beings, but this does not mean that they are not embryos.

Hannah Schickl, Matthias Braun, and Peter Dabrock[77]

> [I]n light of the fact that certain (sub)classes of embryos also do not typically reach the stage of birth (for example embryos with chromosome aberrations like monosomies, trisomies etc, that lead to an early abortion) and are nevertheless referred to as human embryos (and protected in the same way), this conclusion regarding the designation of human parthenotes is wrong. Thus, there is no reason why parthenotes should not also form a subclass of human embryos that typically do not reach the stage of birth …
>
>   Within the ethical and legal debates on the handling of human parthenotes, the descriptive question of whether human parthenotes fall into the extension of the term 'human embryo' and the normative question of whether human parthenotes should be protected in the same way as human embryos are often imprecisely treated as one question: whether parthenotes are human embryos or not.

If stem cell therapies which involve the destruction of embryos are unpatentable throughout the EU, some commentators, like Andrea Faeh, have been concerned that Europe may be left behind.

Andrea Faeh[78]

> [I]n the current economic climate it was not wise to deprive a whole innovative sector of future investment by denying the patentability of their inventions. Investments in such a promising area are now more important than ever, since they not only promise growth for the economy and employment of highly skilled workers but also contribute to the advancement of health treatment and care. These aims should equally have been taken into account in the Court's judgments instead of allowing extreme moral and religious views to decide the future of human embryonic stem cell research and the economic value it could have given the Union. Now the US will lead developments and the Union will lose out economically, scientifically and at the health and ethical levels by the Court not foreseeing the consequences of its judgments.

---

[77] 'Ways Out of the Patenting Prohibition? Human Parthenogenetic and Induced Pluripotent Stem Cells' (2017) 31 Bioethics 409–17.

[78] 'Judicial activism, the Biotech Directive and its institutional implications: is the court acting as a legislator or a court when defining the "human embryo"?' (2015) 40 European Law Review 613–27.

It is, however, worth noting that it may be possible to patent other aspects of a proposed new therapy, such as a diagnostic tool, so that the unpatentability of the stem cell line may not have the chilling effect on research that some have feared.

4 NEUROTECHNOLOGIES AND AI

Brain-computer interface (BCI) technologies involve a neuro-prosthesis which is able to detect and process brain activity in order to direct the use of an external electrical device. Although BCIs are currently at a fairly rudimentary stage, research is progressing rapidly. BCI devices can already enable users to perform simple tasks, such as moving the cursor on a computer, or controlling a robotic limb. It has been reported that BCI devices have been able to restore some motor function in the fingers of a quadriplegic patient.[79] Elon Musk's company Neurolink is developing a device to enable people with severe brain injuries to communicate by 'consensual telepathy', and Facebook is working on a brain-scanning system capable of understanding words that users are silently speaking to themselves, so that they can type 100 words a minute directly from their brains.

Functional magnetic resonance imaging (fMRI) scans can map basic neural activity, and are being used in order to better understand conditions such as chronic pain. More controversially, they may enable a third party to gain some insight into a person's attitudes and intentions. In the US, for example, fMRI scans have been able to identify differences in the brains of Democrats and Republicans.[80]

We all now leave extensive data trails, through our use of smartphones, computers and fitness tracking devices, which in combination with machine learning, can be used in order to diagnose the earliest signs of conditions like Parkinson's disease and Alzheimer's. Unlike other health data, this information is generally in the hands of private tech companies, rather than the NHS.

So what regulatory issues are raised by novel neurotechnologies? In the next extract, Rafael Yuste et al set out some of them, and advocate the introduction of ethics training in the tech industry.

Rafael Yuste et al[81]

Privacy and consent

For all neural data, the ability to opt out of sharing should be the default choice, and assiduously protected. People readily give up their privacy rights to commercial providers of services, such as Internet browsing, social media or entertainment, without fully understanding what they are surrendering ... Even with this approach, neural data from many willing sharers, combined with massive amounts of non-neural data — from Internet searches, fitness monitors and so on — could be used to draw 'good enough' conclusions about individuals who choose not to share. To limit this problem, we propose that the sale, commercial transfer and use of neural data be strictly regulated ...

---

[79] Chad E Bouton et al, 'Restoring cortical control of functional movement in a human with quadriplegia' (2016) 533 Nature 247–50.

[80] Darren Schreiber et al, 'Red brain, blue brain: Evaluative processes differ in Democrats and Republicans' (2013) 8 PLoS One e52970.

[81] 'Four ethical priorities for neurotechnologies and AI' (2017) 551 Nature 159–63.

Agency and identity

Some people receiving deep-brain stimulation through electrodes implanted in their brains have reported feeling an altered sense of agency and identity ... As neurotechnologies develop and corporations, governments and others start striving to endow people with new capabilities, individual identity (our bodily and mental integrity) and agency (our ability to choose our actions) must be protected as basic human rights.

Augmentation

People frequently experience prejudice if their bodies or brains function differently from most. The pressure to adopt enhancing neurotechnologies, such as those that allow people to radically expand their endurance or sensory or mental capacities, is likely to change societal norms, raise issues of equitable access and generate new forms of discrimination ... In particular, we recommend that the use of neural technology for military purposes be stringently regulated ...

A first step towards [responsible neuroengineering] would be to expose engineers, other tech developers and academic-research trainees to ethics as part of their standard training on joining a company or laboratory. Employees could be taught to think more deeply about how to pursue advances and deploy strategies that are likely to contribute constructively to society, rather than to fracture it.

(a) CONSENT

Some interesting new consent issues arise as a result of BCI technologies. If a BCI device enables a person with locked-in syndrome to communicate for the first time, obviously it can only be implanted in the absence of her consent. Implantation would therefore need to be in her best interests. But because the device will enable her to communicate her wishes, it will also be important to ensure that the patient has the option of its removal, as soon as she is able to express an opinion.

If an invasive neurotechnological device could 'cure' psychopathy, could it ever be ethical to make such treatment mandatory as part of an offender's sentence? Or could offenders be offered a choice between neurotechnological treatment and incarceration?

Farah Focquaert[82]

Imagine that effective neurotechnological treatments for psychopathy are developed that have no side effects; would it be ethically permissible to mandate such treatment as part of an offender's sentence? One could argue that the benefits substantially outweigh the costs because we are not harming the individuals in question, or at the very least, because any potential harm that is inflicted is equal to or less than other forms of sentencing (i.e., incarceration) that we typically regard as ethically permissible ...

It can be ethical to *offer* effective, non-invasive neurotechnological treatments to offenders as a condition of probation, parole, or (early) prison release provided certain general conditions are

---

[82] 'Mandatory neurotechnological treatment: ethical issues' (2014) 35 Theoretical Medicine and Bioethics 59–72

met. The following general conditions need to be investigated and met in every *offer* in question: (1) the status quo is in no way cruel, inhuman, degrading, or in some other way *wrong*, (2) the treatment option is in no way cruel, inhuman, degrading, or in some other way *wrong*, (3) the treatment is in the best interests of the offender, and (4) the offender gives his/her informed consent. If the offender subsequently fails to comply with the treatment or chooses to withdraw from treatment, the remainder of the prison sentence needs to be served. An offender may thus be given the choice between effective, non-invasive neurotechnological treatment and (further) incarceration if the treatment in question is in line with these conditions.

(b) AGENCY AND IDENTITY

As Sven Nyholm explains, concerns about changes to a person's identity have emerged especially strongly in relation to deep brain stimulation (DBS). DBS is already in clinical use for patients suffering from Parkinson's disease, and trials are underway for other neurological conditions.[83]

Sven Nyholm[84]

DBS is a technology whereby surgically implanted electrodes directly stimulate specifically targeted brain areas. This targeted stimulation can modulate certain functions and behaviors. For this reason, DBS is used as a treatment for several medical conditions, including Parkinson's disease. There are also more experimental trials underway, for example for anorexia nervosa ...

However, the very idea of 'merging' with a piece of medical technology in this way, and in effect getting an 'on/off' switch between different modes of functioning, raises the question of what impact DBS might be thought to have on the self. Indeed, when interviewed about their experiences with DBS, patients and their families have voiced thoughts and concerns about apparent effects on the patient's self. Some speak of the impact as being positive – e.g. as 'a second birth' – and some as negative – e.g. 'I no longer feel like myself'.

An extreme, and extremely rare example of personality change resulting from DBS is described in the next extract.

Felicitas Kraemer[85]

The patient who had a brain pacemaker implant and was under treatment with DBS, developed, along with other psychological and social problems, a permanent manic state that could not be controlled via medication ...

---

[83] See also Frederic Gilbert, 'Deep Brain Stimulation: Inducing Self-Estrangement' (2018) 11 Neuroethics 157–65.

[84] 'Is the Personal Identity Debate a "Threat" to Neurosurgical Patients? A Reply to Müller et al' (2018) 11 Neuroethics 229–35.

[85] 'Authenticity or autonomy? When deep brain stimulation causes a dilemma' (2013) 39 Journal of Medical Ethics 757–60.

When the patient's mania became so severe that he ran up excessive debts, had an altercation with the police and eventually faced hospitalisation in a psychiatric clinic, his physicians decided to ask the patient whether they should deactivate his implant. When the device was in the switched-on mode, the patient was in a manic state. In this mode, ... he was considered to be mentally incompetent and not legally accountable, that is, he was *not an autonomous agent* ... By contrast, when the device was in the switched-off mode, the patient was believed to be 'normal', meaning, he possessed a rational and accountable state of mind in which he was able to autonomously make rational decisions. At the same time, however, in this state, he was physically disabled, bedridden and dependent on others; he was severely depressed and suffered physically and mentally from the burden of his disease.

Eventually, the physicians agreed to ask the patient while he was in the *switched-off mode* ... whether the device should be deactivated. Additionally, he was asked to fill out an advance directive about the future, stating that he agreed to be kept under psychiatric care for the rest of his life if he kept the device activated.

The patient decided to have his implant permanently left switched on, and to spend the rest of his life in a psychiatric clinic—in a decent bodily condition, but in a permanent manic state.

(c) ENHANCEMENT?

Combining artificial intelligence and neurotechnologies to manipulate brain activity could lead to dramatic new treatments for brain injury and paralysis. Enhancing people's mental and physical capabilities might also have less edifying uses in wartime, for example by boosting soldiers' capacity to fight and inflict damage on others, and by reading the brains of prisoners of war.

Not all brain stimulation involves surgically implanted devices. Transcranial direct current stimulation (tDCS) is instead a simple and non-invasive brain stimulation method, which involves delivering a low electrical current to the brain through electrodes placed on the head. While there is some evidence from laboratory studies that non-invasive brain stimulation (NIBS) can improve performance in healthy subjects, its effects are variable and it is not clear that they are of sufficient magnitude to make any difference to daily life. Nevertheless, there has been considerable interest in their deployment in military training. For example, if NIBS can improve motor response time by 32 milliseconds, that would make no difference at all to me, but 'an improvement of 32 ms may make a vital difference in the context of a one-on-one gunfight or during aircraft combat'.[86] As Bernhard Sehm and Patrick Ragert point out, altering the brain processes of people who are responsible for making life and death decisions is rather different from monitoring patients in a clinical setting.

Bernhard Sehm and Patrick Ragert[87]

First, the use of NIBS in military or security services is problematic with respect to the autonomy of individuals receiving NIBS: In the military context, the risk of coercion is much

---

[86] Jean Levasseur-Moreau, Jerome Brunelin, and Shirley Fecteau, 'Non-invasive brain stimulation can induce paradoxical facilitation. Are these neuroenhancements transferable and meaningful to security services?' (2013) 7 Frontiers in Human Neuroscience 449.

[87] 'Why non-invasive brain stimulation should not be used in military and security services' (2013) 7 Frontiers in Human Neuroscience 553.

more pronounced and autonomous decisions cannot always be warranted. Second, safety issues might be aggravated in this context and might not only apply to the person receiving NIBS but also to third persons …

In a clinical setting, patients are under close medical supervision and individually elected for specific treatments, based on a careful assessment of individual risks and benefits. In addition, due to longitudinal medical monitoring, potential long-term changes may possibly be identified. This, however, does not hold true in military/security context … Even though hypothetical, the question that comes up is: Do we want to take the risk of changing the brain processing in people who (i) potentially cannot make autonomous decisions concerning the application of NIBS and (ii) are responsible for their own lives as well as the lives of others …

In this context it might be important to consider questions related to the responsibility of individuals undergoing NIBS whose actions harmed themselves or others. Is a soldier that is receiving NIBS responsible for erroneous decisions? Can 'wrong' brain stimulation parameters be blamed? These questions still remain unanswered but have tremendous moral and legal implications.

Low-tech NIBS devices are cheap and readily available online. People buy them because the websites selling them make claims like this:

Scientific studies have shown that tDCS has the ability to enhance language and mathematical ability, attention span, problem solving, memory, and coordination. In addition, tDCS has also been documented as having impressive potential to treat depression, anxiety, PTSD, as well as chronic pain.[88]

In fact, the evidence is not this clearcut. Even if there is evidence that occasional tDCS use is safe, home use devices may be used outside of the recommended limits. In addition to the known risks of burns and headaches, stimulating the brain might also have unintended and unwanted consequences. Rachel Wurzman et al point out that 'it is important to know that: (1) the tissue stimulated and effects induced are less deterministic than a user may think, (2) significant tradeoffs may be part of the bargain for functional gains, and (3) whatever brain changes occur may be long-lasting—for better or worse.'[89]

(d) IMPLICATIONS FOR LAW

In the next extract, Marcella Ienca and Roberto Andorno highlight how neurotechnologies might be used within the legal system.

Marcella Ienca and Roberto Andorno[90]

While the body can easily be subject to domination and control by others, our mind, along with our thoughts, beliefs and convictions, are to a large extent beyond external constraint.

---

[88] <https://thebrainstimulator.net/what-is-tdcs/> (last accessed 12 November 2018).

[89] 'An open letter concerning do-it-yourself users of transcranial direct current stimulation' (2016) 80 Annals of neurology 1–4.

[90] 'Towards new human rights in the age of neuroscience and neurotechnology' (2017) 13 Life Sciences, Society and Policy 5.

Yet, with advances in neural engineering, brain imaging and pervasive neurotechnology, the mind might no longer be such unassailable fortress …

Examples of potentially legally relevant applications of neurotechnology are numerous. Brain imaging techniques, for instance, might possibly contribute to more evidence-based decisions in criminal justice, from investigation and the assessment of criminal responsibility, to punishment, rehabilitation of offenders, and the evaluation of their risk of recidivism. The tools offered by neuroscience could potentially play also a role in civil law procedures, for example, in the assessment of an individual's capacity to contract, or of the severity of the plaintiff's pain in compensation claims. New and more reliable lie detection technologies based on our knowledge of the brain functioning might help to assess the reliability of witnesses. Memory erasure of recidivist violent criminals and of victims of especially traumatic offences (e.g. sexual abuse) is also mentioned as another possibility opened by our new knowledge of the brain.

As John Meixner points out, neuroscience might appear to be most helpful to criminal law, but being able to offer insight into a defendant's mental state sometime after a crime was committed does not tell us whether he had the requisite *mens rea* at the time of the offence.

John B Meixner[91]

Neuroscience is likely to be especially helpful to *criminal* law because neuroscience is, in many ways, a study of the mind, and mental states are of central importance in criminal law. In most areas of criminal law, an individual cannot be held responsible for an offense unless the prosecution demonstrates that the suspected offender (1) committed some voluntary act or omission that is unlawful (*actus reus*) and (2) committed that voluntary act with the requisite intent or mental state (*mens rea*) … Thus, in addition to determining what physical acts occurred, jurors in criminal cases must become amateur mind readers, deciding, based on the limited evidence available to them, whether the defendant had a sufficiently guilty mind.

Can neuroscience be of some help in making determinations of *actus reus* and *mens rea*? I think the answer is yes, though currently only in limited ways …

[W]hile neuroscience may be able to offer insight as to individuals' mental capacities and mental states, the relevant mental state for legal purposes is often one that occurred in the past, at the time of the relevant conduct (i.e., at the time a crime was committed). For example, if neuroscience was, at some point in the future, able to assess whether an individual was acting with intent to harm another individual when committing a certain action, that ability would be most useful if we could test the individual *during* his crime—not a likely possibility in the relatively near future.

5 POSTHUMAN ENHANCEMENTS

Many emerging biotechnologies have the potential not only to treat ill health, but to improve upon normal human functioning. This has led some to contemplate a future in which enhanced individuals are no longer properly described as human, but rather have become

---

[91] 'Applications of neuroscience in criminal law: legal and methodological issues' (2015) 15 Current Neurology and Neuroscience 513.

posthuman beings. As Nick Bostrom has explained, the difference in intelligence between a posthuman and a human being will not be comparable to the difference between a genius and someone of average intelligence. Rather a better comparison might be the difference in intelligence between a human and a beetle or worm.[92]

Of course, as a preliminary matter, there may not be agreement on what counts as an enhancement. While we might be able to agree that we would be enhanced by resistance to disease and improved cognitive capacity, in other cases, what counts as an enhancement might be a matter of opinion. Earlier we saw that not everyone would welcome immortality, while some people undoubtedly would. Radically improved memory might seem like an enhancement, but in fact most of us have experiences in our past that we are happy to forget about, and remembering everything that has ever happened to us in excruciating detail might be quite hard to live with. To take a much more trivial example, what if it were possible to read a book in 20 seconds?[93] There are certainly times when this would be useful (such as when I am updating this text for the next edition), but would this always be an enhancement?

It is also important to acknowledge that enhancement technologies may simply result from improvements in 'assistive technologies', which help disabled people with their daily lives. As Francesca Minerva and Alberto Giubilini explain, in the near future, these might enable disabled people to function at a higher level than the 'able-bodied'.

Francesca Minerva and Alberto Giubilini[94]

[I]t is not unreasonable to claim that, at least in the case of running, prosthetics can make disabled athletes faster than the fastest able-bodied ones. If technologies keep developing at this pace, we can easily imagine a not-so-distant future wherein disabled athletes consistently outcompete their non-disabled counterparts . . .

Now, it is possible that disabled people who opt for enhancement will gain an undeserved advantage over both able-bodied people and disabled ones who choose not to or cannot be enhanced. In turn, this could bring about a society wherein some people have more and better opportunities in virtue of their enhanced capacities. However, we already live in a world where the 'genetic lottery' has randomly distributed physical and cognitive capacities, resulting in some people being more gifted than others in activities such as singing, running, painting, processing complex information, etc. It is therefore already the case that certain people have more opportunities. Suppose we could create a society wherein disabled people—those who have access to technologies like the bionic eye—develop capacities that go well beyond the level of those currently in the normal range. There is no reason to believe that such a society would necessarily be worse and less fair than the one in which we currently live, where human capabilities are already distributed unequally . . .

For those who perceive their impairments as a burden without which they would be happier, future technology might offer the option of fixing the impairment, and of enhancing certain traits. If it is their desire to have the impairment fixed, or to be enhanced, they should be given the option to do so. Those who perceive their disability as a valuable and defining feature of themselves, meanwhile, should be supported in their decision to forgo therapeutic or enhancing options.

---

[92] *Superintelligence: Paths, Dangers, Strategies* (Oxford University Press, 2014) 112.

[93] Inmaculada de Melo-Martín, 'Defending human enhancement technologies: unveiling normativity' (2010) 36 Journal of Medical Ethics 483–7.

[94] 'From assistive to enhancing technology: should the treatment-enhancement distinction apply to future assistive and augmenting technologies?' (2018) 44 Journal of Medical Ethics 244–7.

Obviously, posthumans are not going to emerge overnight, and instead the transhumanist movement is committed to the development of technologies to overcome human limitations, thus eventually producing super-enhanced beings, or posthumans. Would there be anything wrong with this?

'Bioconservatives' argue that there would. While debates about transhumanism are complex and multifaceted, two particular concerns might be highlighted. First, it has been argued that in the process of transcending the human condition we would lose something inherently valuable about human nature. Francis Fukuyama, for example, has suggested that 'nature itself, and in particular human nature, has a special role in defining for us what is right and wrong, just and unjust, important and unimportant'.[95] Similarly, Michael Sandel has advocated appreciating the 'giftedness' of human nature.

Michael Sandel[96]

In order to grapple with the ethics of enhancement, we need to confront questions largely lost from view—questions about the moral status of nature, and about the proper stance of human beings toward the given world ...

The problem is not the drift to mechanism but the drive to mastery. And what the drive to mastery misses and may even destroy is an appreciation of the gifted character of human powers and achievements.

To acknowledge the giftedness of life is to recognize that our talents and powers are not wholly our own doing, despite the effort we expend to develop and to exercise them. It is also to recognize that not everything in the world is open to whatever use we may desire or devise ...

It is more plausible to view genetic engineering as the ultimate expression of our resolve to see ourselves astride the world, the masters of our nature. But that promise of mastery is flawed. It threatens to banish our appreciation of life as a gift, and to leave us with nothing to affirm or behold outside our own will.

Interestingly, although the title of Sandel's article (and subsequent book) was *The Case Against Perfection*, it could be argued that he regards the status quo as embodying a sort of perfection, with which we should be slow to interfere.

Against this, 'bioliberals' and transhumanists question the idea that there is something inherently good about human nature now, and instead celebrate the possibility of improving upon our human frailties. As Nick Bostrom puts it: 'Our own species-specified natures are a rich source of much of the thoroughly unrespectable and unacceptable—susceptibility for disease, murder, rape, genocide, cheating, torture, racism'.[97]

A second more utilitarian concern about radical enhancement technologies are their implications for distributive justice and social cohesion. Because they are likely to be expensive, only some people would be able to afford to become posthuman. If posthumans coexist with mere mortals, would ordinary humans be likely to be discriminated against, or worse still, might we find ourselves in a narrative familiar from science-fiction movies,

---

[95] Our Posthuman Future: *Consequences of the Biotechnology Revolution* (Picador, 2003).

[96] Michael Sandel, 'The Case Against Perfection: Ethics in the Age of Genetic Engineering' (2004) 293 *The Atlantic Monthly* 51–62.

[97] 'In defense of posthuman dignity' (2005) 19 Bioethics 202–14.

in which the posthumans seek to eradicate the human race? George Annas, for example, has warned that '"improved" posthumans would inevitably come to view the "naturals" as inferior, as a subspecies of humans suitable for exploitation, slavery, and even extermination'.[98]

An obvious response to these concerns is to point out that radical differences between human beings already exist. In the next extract, Nick Bostrom points out that existing differences in human capacities do not necessarily cause genocide, and that we are already super-enhanced compared to our hunter-gatherer ancestors.

Nick Bostrom[99]

Modern, peaceful societies can have large numbers of people with diminished physical or mental capacities along with many other people who may be exceptionally physically strong or healthy or intellectually talented in various ways. Adding people with technologically enhanced capacities to this already broad distribution of ability would not need to rip society apart or trigger genocide or enslavement . . .

Our current extended phenotypes (and the lives that we lead) are markedly different from those of our hunter-gatherer ancestors. We read and write, we wear clothes, we live in cities, we earn money and buy food from the supermarket, we call people on the telephone, watch television, read newspapers, drive cars, file taxes, vote in national elections, women give birth in hospitals, life-expectancy is three times longer than in the Pleistocene, we know that the Earth is round and that stars are large gas clouds lit from inside by nuclear fusion, and that the universe is approximately 13.7 billion years old and enormously big. In the eyes of a hunter-gatherer, we might already appear 'posthuman'. Yet these radical extensions of human capabilities – some of them biological, others external – have not divested us of moral status or dehumanized us in the sense of making us generally unworthy and base.

6 CONCLUSION

The concept of Responsible Research and Innovation (RRI) was first developed by the European Commission in the context of its funding programmes for research, such as Horizon 2020. It is intended to ensure that scientific inquiry and the development of novel technologies are not divorced from their wider social context. That means paying attention to the social and other implications of innovation and research, and ensuring that inclusive public engagement takes place at all stages. It has particular significance in the context of emerging biotechnologies, because it assumes that public support for the aims of research, and for its outcomes, is a necessary prerequisite for responsible research and innovation.

Within the UK, calls for more public consultation are a common response to a new biotechnology. In Chapter 15, we consider the possibilities raised by genome editing for human reproduction. When the Nuffield Council on Bioethics published its report on genome editing

---

[98] George Annas, 'Cell Division' Boston Globe, April 21, 2005.
[99] 'In defense of posthuman dignity' (2005) 19 Bioethics 202–14.

in 2018, one of its key recommendations was that there should be 'sufficient opportunity for a broad and inclusive societal debate', and that:

> Consideration should be given to the establishment of a separate body or commission in the UK, independent of Government and independent of existing regulatory agencies, which would have the function of helping to identify and produce an understanding of public interest(s) through promotion of public debate, engagement with publics and monitoring the effects of relevant technological developments on the interests of potentially marginalised subjects and on social norms.[100]

In the context of embryo research and novel reproductive technologies, the HFEA has considerable experience of effective and thorough public engagement, which has in turn engendered public trust in regulation. If consideration were to be given to extending the 14-day time limit for embryo research, there is no doubt that the HFEA would take the lead in producing accessible materials to inform a broad public debate on the matter, and would set up a wide range of engagement activities, such as focus groups and public debates. For other innovative biotechnologies, it is less clear which body bears responsibility for public engagement. The Nuffield Council on Bioethics itself produces valuable reports on innovative technologies, including short, accessible versions, but it does not have the resources to engage in hands-on public engagement throughout the country.

While it could be argued that we already have a body which carries out effective public engagement in the context of human reproduction, it might be sensible to ensure that other innovative technologies are subject to the same level of public engagement. As yet, for example, has been no systematic attempt to engage the public on the ethics of enhancement technologies. In the next extract, Jane Calvert suggests that focussing only on risks, misses some of these 'bigger picture' questions.

Jane Calvert[101]

> If we merely focus on measurable risks, we cannot ask bigger questions like, is this research field one in which we want to invest society's limited resources? This question demonstrates that technology choice is an ethical issue. This next step, away from analysis of the risks and harms of an already-existing technology and toward a focus on 'what kind of future do we want innovation to bring into the world?', is challenging but, I think, potentially liberating. Unlike the technical details of the research, these broader goals can (and arguably should) be opened up to wider public discussion ...
>
> This leads to questions about when public engagement should take place. The discussion of social goals clearly comes at the early stages of technology development, and may even occur at the stage of science policy-making. Such 'upstream' engagement provides an opportunity for broader goals to be 'consciously incorporated into technological development before particular trajectories and attitudes become set.' This can allow new types of conversation to happen ... Finally, and most familiarly, engagement can take place 'downstream,' at the level of applications and products ...
>
> There are not only different stages at which public engagement can take place but also different reasons for doing it in the first place ... The first rationale is instrumental: public

---

[100] Nuffield Council on Bioethics, *Genome Editing and Human Reproduction* (NCOB, 2018).
[101] 'Governing in the Context of Uncertainty' (2014) 44 Hastings Center Report S31–S33.

engagement is conducted in the services of a predefined end such as the restoration of legitimacy or trust. The second is normative. Here, public engagement is undertaken because it is considered 'the right thing to do.' This might, for example, be based on a commitment to the idea of democracy. The third rationale is substantive, and it is grounded in the idea that public engagement will lead to better decision-making and more socially robust science.

FURTHER READING

Bostrom, Nick, 'In defense of posthuman dignity' (2005) 19 Bioethics 202–14.

Cossu, Giulio et al, 'Lancet Commission: Stem Cells and Regenerative medicine' (2018) 391 The Lancet 883–910.

Minerva, Francesca and Giubilini, Alberto, 'From assistive to enhancing technology: should the treatment-enhancement distinction apply to future assistive and augmenting technologies?' (2018) 44 Journal of Medical Ethics 244–7.

Nuffield Council on Bioethics, *Emerging Biotechnologies: Technology, Choice and the Public Good* (NCOB, 2012).

Nuffield Council on Bioethics, *Human Embryo Culture: Discussions concerning the statutory time limit for maintaining human embryos in culture in the light of some recent scientific developments* (NCOB, 2017).

Petersen, Alan, MacGregor, Casimir, and Munsie, Megan, 'Stem cell miracles or Russian roulette?: patients' use of digital media to campaign for access to clinically unproven treatments' (2016) 17 Health, Risk and Society 592–604.

14

ABORTION

CENTRAL ISSUES

1. Abortion may be common and routine, but there is bitter disagreement over its legitimacy. On one side, the 'pro-life' lobby think that it is incompatible with the fetus's moral status, while on the other, 'pro-choice' advocates argue that pregnant women should have the right to terminate their unwanted pregnancies.

2. When the Abortion Act was passed in 1967, its principal purpose was to enable doctors to carry out safe, lawful abortions, rather than to give women rights.

3. Access to abortion under the Act depends upon whether two doctors believe that the woman's circumstances fit within one of the statutory grounds. The most commonly used ground for abortion is that continuing the pregnancy poses a greater risk to the woman's physical or mental health than termination. Abortions carried out for this reason are subject to a 24-week time limit.

4. Abortion on the grounds of serious fetal abnormality is lawful until birth. Doctors have considerable discretion in determining what counts as a sufficiently serious condition.

1 INTRODUCTION

In this chapter we consider a contentious but common medical procedure: the termination of pregnancy. In 1969—the first full year in which the Abortion Act was in operation—49,829 abortions were notified to the Department of Health. In 2017, 189,859 abortions were performed on women resident in England and Wales, and 4,809 on non-residents.[1] Twenty years ago, access to abortion within the NHS was patchy, and approximately half of all abortions took place in the private sector.[2] In 2017, 98 per cent of abortions were funded by the NHS, 70 per cent of which took place in the independent sector, under NHS contract.

---

[1] *Abortion Statistics, England and Wales: 2017* (DHSC: London, 2018).
[2] Emily Jackson, *Regulating Reproduction* (Hart Publishing: Oxford, 2001).

We begin this chapter with a necessarily brief survey of the acrimonious debate over abortion's moral legitimacy. Should pregnant women have the right to terminate their unwanted pregnancies, or do fetuses have a right to life that 'trumps' women's reproductive freedom? As will be obvious, there is never likely to be agreement on the morality of abortion.

Abortion has been legal in England, Scotland, and Wales for half a century. We then examine the current legal position, and consider how the Abortion Act 1967, as amended, works in practice. The conflict between the interests of the fetus and those of the pregnant woman could also be framed in terms of 'rights', and so we briefly consider the impact of the Human Rights Act 1998.

Next we look at some questions that have proved especially controversial, such as sex selection and the impact of non-invasive prenatal testing. We highlight some differences between the regulation of abortion in England, Scotland, and Wales and other jurisdictions, including Northern Ireland, before considering the prospects for law reform in the UK.

2 THE ETHICS OF ABORTION

In what circumstances, if any, is it legitimate for a woman to terminate an unwanted pregnancy? Instinctive responses to this question will lie somewhere upon a spectrum which has 'never' at one end, and 'whenever she likes' at the other, with many people falling somewhere in between, believing that abortion is sometimes, but not always, justifiable. Towards the restrictive end of the spectrum, it might be argued that abortion is legitimate where the woman's life is in danger, or when she is pregnant as a result of rape. At the more permissive end, it might be contended that abortion should be available upon request, at least during the first few months of pregnancy.

But while an instinctive response to the legitimacy of abortion may be a useful starting point, as we saw in Chapter 1, the requirement to give reasons, or to justify one's moral views, is an important feature of ethical reasoning. Fortunately, in relation to abortion, there is a rich philosophical literature from which to draw. At the risk of drastic oversimplification, three different perspectives are worth identifying:

- an emphasis on the moral status of the fetus, and in particular upon its personhood, or potential personhood;
- an emphasis upon the physical invasiveness of pregnancy, and upon the degree of self-sacrifice which would be forced upon a woman who is compelled to continue an unwanted pregnancy;
- a compromise position in which abortion is permitted, but subject to restrictions which are designed to offer the fetus some protection.

(a) THE MORAL STATUS OF THE FETUS

A central concern of opponents of abortion is the moral status of the fetus. In the next extract, John Finnis argues that conception is the moment at which a new individual comes into being, and that this should be the point at which it acquires all the rights of personhood.

John Finnis[3]

I have been assuming that the unborn child is, from conception, a person and hence is not to be discriminated against on account of age, appearance or other such factors insofar as such factors are reasonably considered irrelevant where respect for basic human values is in question ...

[At conception] two sex cells, each with only twenty-three chromosomes, unite and more or less immediately fuse to become a new cell with forty-six chromosomes providing a unique genetic constitution ... which thenceforth throughout its life, however long, will substantially determine the new individual's makeup. This new cell is the first stage in a dynamic integrated system that has nothing much in common with the individual male and female sex cells, save that it sprang from a pair of them and will in time produce new sets of them. To say that *this* is when a person's life began is not to work backwards from maturity, sophistically asking at each point 'How can one draw the line *here*?' Rather it is to point to a perfectly clear-cut beginning to which each one of us can look back.

Against this, Mary Ann Warren contends that while the fetus may be human, it is not yet a person, and so its interests cannot take priority over the rights of an actual person, namely the pregnant woman.

Mary Ann Warren[4]

What characteristics entitle an entity to be considered a person? ... I suggest that the traits which are most central to the concept of personhood ... , are, very roughly, the following:

(1) Consciousness ..., and in particular the capacity to feel pain.

(2) Reasoning (the *developed* capacity to solve new and relatively complex problems);

(3) Self-motivated activity ...

(4) The capacity to communicate ...

(5) The presence of self-concepts, and self-awareness ...

We needn't suppose that an entity must have *all* these attributes to be properly considered a person ... Neither do we need to insist that any one of these criteria is necessary for personhood ...

All we need to claim, to demonstrate that a fetus is not a person, is that any being which satisfies *none* of (1)–(5) is certainly not a person. I consider this claim to be so obvious that I think anyone who denied it, and claimed that a being which satisfied none of (1)–(5) was a person all the same, would thereby demonstrate that he had no notion at all of what a person is—perhaps because he had confused the concept of personhood with that of genetic humanity ...

[A] fetus is a human being which is not yet a person, and which therefore cannot coherently be said to have full moral rights ... But even if a potential person does have some prima facie

[3] 'The rights and wrongs of abortion: a reply to Judith Thomson' (1973) 2 Philosophy and Public Affairs 117–45.
[4] 'On the moral and legal status of abortion' (1973) 1 The Monist 43–61.

> right to life, such a right could not possibly outweigh the right of a woman to obtain an abortion, since the rights of any actual person invariably outweigh those of any potential person, whenever the two conflict.

Warren's criteria for personhood are themselves controversial. Philip Abbott, for example, points out that this test for personhood would exclude not only fetuses, but also some seriously disabled children and adults.

Philip Abbott[5]

> What makes one a person (or human in the moral sense)? Warren suggests five 'traits' . . . Note how deftly Warren plies her trade. A fetus *might* be able to feel pain, but surely he or she is unable to reason, especially with *developed* capacity. What is shocking about this criterion (2) is that a two-year old may fail to meet it. What this means . . . , and let us be direct about this, is that we must restrain our emotions and come to regard an infant as not a person at all but a mere clump of genetic humanity. Are not then the comatose patient, the schizophrenic, the catatonic, the unaided mute, the paraplegic in danger of slipping into that awful category 'genetic human'.

While, in legal terms at least, it is clear that a person with rights exists after birth but not before, Raanan Gillon claims that a newborn baby is not a morally different entity to a fetus immediately prior to birth.

Raanan Gillon[6]

> While in practical terms the simple criterion of birth is generally easy to apply and corresponds to a stage when what was previously hidden and private inside another human being is now a revealed, public, and clearly separate social entity, as a criterion for moral differentiation of a human being's intrinsic moral status it seems highly implausible. Essentially it is a criterion of what might be dubbed biological geography, asserting that a human being does not have a right to life if it lies north of a vaginal introitus but has a right to life once it has passed south and has (entirely) emerged from the vagina. What morally relevant changes can there have been in the fetus in its passage from inside to outside its mother's body to underpin such a momentous change in its intrinsic moral status?

Of course, it could be argued that being inside another person is rather more significant than a simple matter of 'geography'. In addition, as Kate Greasley explains, birth 'is a dramatic biological event'.

---

[5] 'Philosophers and the abortion question' (1978) 6 Political Theory 313–35.
[6] 'Is there a "new ethics of abortion"?' (2001) 26 suppl II Journal of Medical Ethics ii5–ii9, ii8.

Kate Greasley[7]

[M]any significant biological and behavioural state changes are triggered at birth. These in-clude a number of biological adaptations which need to take place to enable a newborn to breathe in air for the first time. One such adaptation is the clearing of fluid from the lungs to allow them to inflate and draw in breath. Other significant adaptations include changes in the circulatory system, the activation of new enzyme systems, the digestive system, and the re-lease of hormones to regulate temperature outside of the womb—to name just a few. In an explanation of the transition from intrauterine to extrauterine life, Noah Hillman *et al* describe that transition as 'the most complex adaptation that occurs in human experience' ...

Upon emergence into the world, a new baby also exhibits radical behavioural state tran-sitions, most notably: crying for the first time; heightened wakefulness and reactivity, and increased responsiveness to environmental stimuli like noise, light, and touch. Some experi-ments have documented the capacity for neonates to imitate other people's facial expres-sions as early as forty-two minutes after birth, which is taken to indicate a primitive form of self-consciousness.

Don Marquis attempts to avoid the person/not a person question, and instead claims that abortion is wrong because, like killing an adult human being, it deprives the fetus of every-thing it might value in the future.

Don Marquis[8]

[W]hen I die, I am deprived of all of the value of my future. Inflicting this loss on me is ul-timately what makes killing me wrong. This being the case, it would seem that what makes killing *any* adult human being prima facie seriously wrong is the loss of his or her future ...

The claim that the primary wrong-making feature of a killing is the loss to the victim of the value of its future has obvious consequences for the ethics of abortion. The future of a standard fetus includes a set of experiences, projects, activities, and such which are identical with the futures of adult human beings and are identical with the futures of young children. Since the reason that is sufficient to explain why it is wrong to kill human beings after the time of birth is a reason that also applies to fetuses, it follows that abortion is prima facie seriously morally wrong.

Of course, using contraception or even deciding not to have sexual intercourse on a particular day may also deprive a potential person of a future that they would value, but that does not necessarily mean that either is the wrong thing to do.[9]

A different criticism of Marquis comes from Mark T Brown, who argues that people are de-prived of futures they might value whenever they die prematurely. Someone who needs a heart transplant, but does not get one in time, has been deprived of a future of value, but that does not mean that they had a right to that future, nor that they had any rights over someone else's heart. To give fetuses the right not to be killed would, according to Brown, be to give them:

[7] *Arguments about Abortion: Personhood, Morality and Law* (Oxford: OUP, 2017) 191.
[8] 'Why abortion is immoral' (1989) 86 Journal of Philosophy 183–202, 192.
[9] Julian Savulescu, 'Abortion, embryo destruction and the future of value argument' (2002) 28 Journal of Medical Ethics 133–5.

[A] right to satisfy their needs at the expense of the autonomy, bodily integrity and wellbeing of another person. If I need a bone marrow transplant in order to realise my potential future of value, I do not thereby gain a right to your bone marrow.[10]

(b) THE PREGNANT WOMAN'S RIGHT TO SELF-DETERMINATION

This approach to abortion emphasizes the physical invasiveness of carrying a pregnancy to term, and argues that restrictions on women's access to abortion compel them to exercise a wholly unprecedented degree of self-sacrifice. As Margaret Olivia Little explains:

To be pregnant is to be *inhabited*. It is to be *occupied*. It is to be in a state of physical intimacy of a particularly thorough-going nature. The fetus intrudes on the body massively; whatever medical risks one faces or avoids, the brute fact remains that the fetus shifts and alters the very physical boundaries of the woman's self.[11]

The woman's right to an abortion is not, on this view, necessarily dependent upon proving that the fetus is not a person. Rather, as Judith Jarvis Thomson argues in the next extract, even if the fetus is a person, pregnant women might have the right to defend themselves from the physical invasion of an unwanted pregnancy.

Judith Jarvis Thomson[12]

[S]urely a person's right to life is stronger and more stringent than the mother's right to decide what happens in and to her body, and so outweighs it ... It sounds plausible. But now let me ask you to imagine this. You wake up in the morning and find yourself back to back in bed with an unconscious violinist. A famous unconscious violinist. He has been found to have a fatal kidney ailment, and the Society of Music Lovers has canvassed all the available medical records and found that you alone have the right blood type to help. They have therefore kidnapped you, and last night the violinist's circulatory system was plugged into yours, so that your kidneys can be used to extract poisons from his blood as well as your own. The director of the hospital now tells you, 'Look, we're sorry the Society of Music Lovers did this to you—we would never have permitted it if we had known. But still, they did it, and the violinist is now plugged into you. To unplug you would be to kill him. But never mind, it's only for nine months. By then he will have recovered from his ailment, and can safely be unplugged from you.' Is it morally incumbent on you to accede to this situation? No doubt it would be very nice of you if you did, a great kindness. But do you *have* to accede to it? ... What if the director of the hospital says, 'Tough luck, I agree, but you've now got to stay in bed, with the violinist plugged into you, for the rest of your life. Because remember this. All persons have a right to life, and violinists are persons. Granted you have a right to decide what happens in and to your body, but a person's right to life outweighs your right to decide what happens in and to your body. So you cannot ever be unplugged from him.' I imagine you would regard this as outrageous, which suggests that something really is wrong with that plausible-sounding argument I mentioned a moment ago.

---

[10] 'The morality of abortion and the deprivation of futures' (2000) 26 Journal of Medical Ethics 103–7.
[11] 'Abortion, intimacy, and the duty to gestate' (1999) 2 Ethical Theory and Moral Practice 295–312.
[12] 'A defence of abortion' (1971) 1 Philosophy and Public Affairs 47–66.

There is, however, one rather obvious difference between unplugging a violinist and abortion. Abortion involves killing the fetus, not simply detaching it, and however burdensome pregnancy and unwanted motherhood might be, as Kate Greasley has pointed out, they are generally not sufficient to justify killing in self-defence.

Kate Greasley[13]

The main burdens of unwanted pregnancy, serious though they are, are simply not of the sort that ever justify killing in self-defence. This is brought out even more sharply when considering the fact that born children can pose exactly the same kinds of threats to their parents. But a parent is not taken to act in legitimate self-defence if she kills her children to live a less encumbered and better life, or because the alternative of having her children adopted entails too much emotional distress.

It is often assumed that deciding to have an abortion is a more difficult and serious moral choice than deciding to carry a pregnancy to term, even though motherhood involves an extraordinarily demanding and long-lasting commitment. Through the presumptions that women seeking abortion need counselling, and conversely, that women who are about to become mothers do not, motherhood is assumed to be an easy and natural choice for women, whereas, as Reva Siegel explains, rejecting motherhood is perceived to be unnatural and selfish.

Reva Siegel[14]

Legislators may condemn abortion because they assume that any pregnant woman who does not wish to be pregnant has committed some sexual indiscretion properly punishable by compelling pregnancy itself. Popular support for excusing women who are victims of rape or incest from the proscriptions of criminal abortion laws demonstrates that attitudes about abortion do indeed rest on normative judgments about women's sexual conduct . . .

If legislators assume that women are 'child-rearers', they will take for granted the work women give to motherhood and ignore what it takes from them, and so will view women's efforts to avoid some two decades of life-consuming work as an act of casual expedience or unseemly egoism. Thus, they will condemn women for seeking abortion 'on demand', or as a mere 'convenience', judging women to be unnaturally egocentric because they do not give their lives over to the work of bearing and nurturing children—that is, because they fail to act like mothers, like normal women should.

The idea that women should have the right to decide for themselves whether they want to become mothers is disputed by Rosalind Hursthouse, who analyses abortion from the perspective of virtue ethics (considered in Chapter 1). According to Hursthouse, because motherhood is intrinsically good, a woman who rejects it without a compelling or 'virtuous' reason, is acting wrongly.

---

[13] *Arguments about Abortion: Personhood, Morality and Law* (Oxford: OUP, 2017) 61.
[14] 'Reasoning from the Body: A Historical Perspective on Abortion Regulation and Questions of Equal Protection' (1992) Stanford Law Review 261–381.

Rosalind Hursthouse[15]

The familiar facts support the view that parenthood in general, and motherhood and child-bearing in particular, are intrinsically worthwhile, are among the things that can be correctly thought to be partially constitutive of a flourishing human life. If this is right, then a woman who opts for not being a mother (at all, or again, or now) by opting for abortion may thereby be manifesting a flawed grasp of what her life should be, and be about—a grasp that is childish, or grossly materialistic, or shortsighted, or shallow.

I say '*may* thereby': this *need* not be so. Consider, for instance, a woman who has already had several children and fears that to have another will seriously affect her capacity to be a good mother to the ones she has—she does not show a lack of appreciation of the intrinsic value of being a parent by opting for abortion. Nor does a woman who has been a good mother and is approaching the age at which she may be looking forward to being a good grandmother. Nor does a woman who discovers that her pregnancy may well kill her, and opts for abortion and adoption. Nor, necessarily, does a woman who has decided to lead a life centred around some other worthwhile activity or activities with which motherhood would compete ...

But some women who choose abortion rather than have their first child, and some men who encourage their partners to choose abortion, are not avoiding parenthood for the sake of other worthwhile pursuits, but for the worthless one of 'having a good time', or for the pursuit of some false vision of the ideals of freedom or self-realisation.

(c)   A COMPROMISE POSITION?

The compromise position occupies the middle ground between the pro-fetus and pro-women approaches discussed so far. It acknowledges that the fetus's potential personhood is a good reason to afford it some protection, while at the same time recognizing that the pregnant woman has a legitimate interest in self-determination. This 'third way' would protect the woman's right to terminate her pregnancy, but only in certain circumstances. This is consistent with most countries' regulation of abortion: abortion is permitted within parameters—such as time limits—which are supposed to indicate the seriousness of fetal destruction.

Ronald Dworkin has argued that pro-life and pro-choice activists have more in common than is often assumed. Both share a deep belief in the sanctity of human life, and therefore regard abortion as a morally serious matter, but they also do not believe that the fetus has exactly the same status as a person, otherwise it would be impossible to justify abortion if the pregnant woman's life is in danger, or if she is pregnant as a result of rape.

Ronald Dworkin[16]

[D]iscussions of abortion almost all presume that people disagree about abortion because they disagree about whether a fetus is a person with a right to life from the moment of its conception, or becomes a person at some point in pregnancy, or does not become one until birth. And about whether, if a fetus is a person, its right to life must yield in the face of some stronger right held by pregnant women ...

---

[15] 'Virtue Theory and Abortion' in Daniel Statman (ed), *Virtue Ethics* (Edinburgh: Edinburgh UP, 1997) 227–44.

[16] *Life's Dominion* (HarperCollins: London, 1993).

[T]his account of the abortion debate, in spite of its great popularity, is fatally misleading...
[E]ven those conservatives who believe that the law should prohibit abortion recognize exceptions. It is a very common view, for example, that abortion should be permitted when necessary to save the mother's life. Yet this exception is ... inconsistent with any belief that a fetus is
a person with a right to live. Some people say that in this case a mother is justified in aborting
a fetus as a matter of self-defense; but any safe abortion is carried out by someone else—a
doctor—and very few people believe that it is morally justifiable for a third party, even a doctor,
to kill one innocent person to save another.

Abortion conservatives often allow further exceptions. Some of them believe that abortion
is morally permissible ... when pregnancy is the result of rape or incest. The more such exceptions are allowed, the clearer it becomes that conservative opposition to abortion does not
presume that the fetus is a person with a right to life. It would be contradictory to insist that
a fetus has a right to life ... that ceases to exist when the pregnancy is the result of a sexual
crime of which the fetus is, of course, wholly innocent.

Kate Greasley has suggested a different explanation for these apparent inconsistencies.

Kate Greasley[17]

Strategic necessity in particular strikes me as a very plausible reason why some political
opponents and supporters of abortion rights might make concessions which *look like* inconsistencies. Ideological opponents of abortion may support exceptions in cases of rape,
incest, or grave risk to the pregnant woman's life for a number of pragmatic reasons: to
avoid ostracizing moderates, to focus firepower on the more winnable battles, and so on. If
this explanation were correct, we might well expect to see those opponents withdrawing
the traditional concessions as and when political climates change and platforms can be
radicalized without risking too much of the overall objective: to preserve as much fetal life
as possible.

Certain 'inconsistencies' embraced by defenders of abortion rights could equally be driven
by a political need to make concessions. Abortion rights campaigners often admit that abortion is always sad or a shame, even when justified. Although this admission does not chime
well with the extremely low moral status they accord to the fetus, it can placate moderate
sensibilities.

3 THE LAW

(a) THE CRIMINAL LAW

Until 1803, abortion was governed by the common law, which drew a distinction between fetal destruction before and after 'quickening' (the moment when the woman can
first feel the fetus moving inside her), which is normally about 16–18 weeks into the
pregnancy.

---

[17] *Arguments about Abortion: Personhood, Morality and Law* (Oxford: OUP, 2017) 19.

William Blackstone[18]

Life ... begins in contemplation of law as soon as an infant is able to stir in the mother's womb. For if a woman is quick with child, and by a potion, or otherwise, killeth it in her womb; or if any one beat her, whereby the child dieth in her body, and she is delivered of a dead child; this, though not murder, was by the ancient law homicide or manslaughter. But at present it is not looked upon in quite so atrocious a light, though it remains a very heinous misdemeanor.

Since Lord Ellenborough's Act of 1803, abortion has been regulated by statute, and a 19th-century statute continues to apply to abortion today. Statutory defences do now exist, but under sections 58 and 59 of the Offences Against the Person Act 1861, the maximum sentence for a woman who intentionally procures her own miscarriage is life imprisonment, and anyone who assists her could be imprisoned for up to five years.

Offences Against the Person Act 1861 sections 58 and 59

8. Every woman, being with child, who, with intent to procure her own miscarriage, shall unlawfully administer to herself any poison or other noxious thing, or shall unlawfully use any instrument or other means whatsoever with the like intent, and whosoever, with intent to procure the miscarriage of any woman, whether she be or not with child, shall unlawfully administer to her or cause to be taken by her any poison or other noxious thing, or shall unlawfully use any instrument or other means whatsoever with the like intent, shall be guilty of felony.

9. Whosoever shall unlawfully supply or procure any poison or other noxious thing, or any instrument or thing whatsoever knowing that the same is intended to be unlawfully used or employed with intent to procure the miscarriage of any woman, whether she be or not be with child, shall be guilty of a misdemeanor.

The critical ingredients of the offences under sections 58 and 59 are, first, that someone must *do* something with a poison or instrument or other noxious thing, and, secondly, that they must *intend* to procure a miscarriage. Notice also that the first limb of section 58 applies only to women who are in fact 'with child'. A woman could not be convicted of the full offence under section 58 unless she was actually pregnant. A woman who mistakenly believed that she was pregnant could instead be guilty of conspiring to procure an abortion.[19] Other people can be guilty 'whether she be or not with child', provided that they believe her to be pregnant, and intend to cause her to miscarry.

It is also important to note that sections 58 and 59 refer to poison or instruments being used *unlawfully*. If the offence is committed only if the abortion is carried out unlawfully, this suggests that it might be possible to procure an abortion lawfully. Because it has never been doubted that doctors are entitled to carry out life-saving surgery, even if its consequence would be to end a woman's pregnancy, the word 'unlawfully' creates an exception—akin to the one contained in the Infant Life Preservation Act 1929 (mentioned below)—for terminations performed to preserve the pregnant woman's life.

---

[18] *Commentaries on the Laws of England*, vol 1 (1765).   [19] *R v Whitchurch* (1890) LR 24 QBD 420.

This was the interpretation preferred by Macnaghten J in his summing up to the jury in *R v Bourne*, a case in which a distinguished obstetric surgeon, Aleck Bourne, had carried out an abortion on a 14-year-old girl, who was pregnant following a violent rape. Bourne's defence had been that the operation was not unlawful, because, in his opinion, the continuance of the pregnancy posed a serious risk to the girl's mental health. In his direction to the jury, Macnaghten J said that it would be possible for an abortion to be carried out lawfully not only where the pregnant woman was in imminent danger of death, but also where the effect of carrying the pregnancy to term might be to 'make the woman a physical or mental wreck'.

R v Bourne [20]

Macnaghten J

A man of the highest skill, openly, in one of our great hospitals, performs the operation. Whether it was legal or illegal you will have to determine, but he performs the operation as an act of charity, without fee or reward, and unquestionably believing that he was doing the right thing, and that he ought, in the performance of his duty as a member of a profession devoted to the alleviation of human suffering, to do it ...

[T]he words of that section are that any person who 'unlawfully' uses an instrument with intent to procure miscarriage shall be guilty of felony. In my opinion the word 'unlawfully' is not, in that section, a meaningless word. I think it imports the meaning expressed by the proviso in s. 1, sub-s. 1, of the Infant Life (Preservation) Act, 1929 [that 'no person shall be found guilty of an offence under this section unless it is proved that the act which caused the death of the child was not done in good faith for the purpose only of preserving the life of the mother'] and that s. 58 of the Offences Against the Person Act, 1861, must be read as if the words making it an offence to use an instrument with intent to procure a miscarriage were qualified by a similar proviso.

[I]f the doctor is of opinion, on reasonable grounds and with adequate knowledge, that the probable consequence of the continuance of the pregnancy will be to make the woman a physical or mental wreck, the jury are quite entitled to take the view that the doctor who, under those circumstances and in that honest belief, operates, is operating for the purpose of preserving the life of the mother ...

[N]o doubt you will think it is only common sense that a girl who for nine months has to carry in her body the reminder of the dreadful scene and then go through the pangs of childbirth must suffer great mental anguish, unless indeed she be feeble-minded or belongs to the class described as 'the prostitute class' ... But in the case of a normal, decent girl brought up in a normal, decent way you may well think that Dr Rees [a clinical psychologist] was not overstating the effect of the continuance of the pregnancy when he said that it would be likely to make her a mental wreck, with all the disastrous consequences that would follow from that.

Following Aleck Bourne's acquittal, it was apparent that an abortion could be performed lawfully if the pregnant woman's mental health was endangered by her pregnancy. Some doctors were prepared to interpret this 'mental wreck' exception quite broadly, and terminate the pregnancies of women who were distressed, rather than mentally ill. Because such doctors

[20] [1939] 1 KB 697.

were risking prosecution, their fees tended to be high, and these safe 'legal' abortions were therefore inaccessible to the majority of women, who relied instead on the services of illegal abortionists. It is thought that there were probably at least 100,000 illegal abortions each year prior to abortion's partial decriminalization in 1967. Some of these 'backstreet' abortionists' practices were extremely dangerous, and mortality rates were high.

Although it is now of minimal practical relevance, brief mention should be made of the Infant Life (Preservation) Act 1929, under which it is an offence to destroy the life of a child capable of being born alive, unless the act is done in good faith for the purpose only of preserving the life of the mother. The purpose of this Act was to close a legal loophole. In 1929, it was unlawful to kill a fetus *in utero*, and it was murder to kill a child after birth. However, no protection was afforded to the child during the process of birth, before it had been completely separated from its mother. In order to fill this gap, the Infant Life (Preservation) Act provided that killing the child during childbirth would also be an offence.

Although not intended to apply to abortion, which was, of course, unlawful in 1929, once the Abortion Act 1967 came into force, the 1929 Act had the effect of setting a time limit for lawful abortion, since it provided that it is an offence to destroy the life of a fetus which is 'capable of being born alive'. In 1929, this was the case at around 28 weeks. By the time a statutory time limit was added to the Abortion Act in 1990, the age at which a fetus was capable of being born alive had dropped to around 24 weeks.

The 1929 Act is no longer relevant in determining whether a proposed abortion is lawful. The Abortion Act 1967 was amended in 1990 to provide that no offence under the Infant Life (Preservation) Act is committed provided that the pregnancy is terminated in accordance with the provisions in the 1967 Act. The 1990 amendments also set a 24-week time limit for the most common ground for abortion.

(b) THE ABORTION ACT 1967

(1) The Background to Legalization

In order to understand the form that abortion's legalization took in 1967, it is important to realize that the Abortion Act 1967 was not enacted in order to give women the right to an abortion. Rather, the principal factor behind public and parliamentary support for legalization was concern about high mortality rates resulting from illegal abortions, especially among the poor. By the mid-1960s, it was clear that the law was not preventing women from terminating their unwanted pregnancies; instead it was ensuring that abortions were performed by amateurs, often using dangerous techniques in unhygienic surroundings. Successful prosecutions were rare; women who had had abortions would seldom be prepared to give evidence and the police were reluctant to prosecute. The law was, in short, completely ineffective.

It had, however, become common for doctors to encounter the consequences of botched illegal abortions, which included large numbers of avoidable deaths. Unsurprisingly, the medical profession resented the criminal law's interference with their freedom to act in the best interests of their patients. Abortion, then, was not legalized in order to enhance women's reproductive autonomy; rather, the Abortion Act's principal purpose was to enable doctors to act lawfully in assisting desperate women to end their pregnancies.

In the next extract, Sally Sheldon argues that supporters of David Steel's Abortion Bill in fact shared their opponents' belief that women were incapable of making rational decisions about their unwanted pregnancies.

Sally Sheldon[21]

[In] the parliamentary debates preceding the introduction of the Abortion Act ... [t]he doctor is talked of as a 'highly skilled and dedicated', 'sensitive, sympathetic' member of a 'high and proud profession' which acts 'with its own ethical and medical standards' displaying 'skill, judgement and knowledge'. The woman who experiences an unwanted pregnancy, on the other hand, is portrayed as someone who is fundamentally incapable of taking such an important decision for herself—either because she is downtrodden and driven to desperation (in the language of the reformers) or, for the opponents of reform, because she is selfish and morally immature. The first of these two images is summed up in the following quotation taken from the parliamentary debates:

> There is the woman who already has a large family, perhaps six or seven children ... There is the question of the woman who loses her husband during pregnancy and has to go out to work, and obviously cannot bear the strain of doing a full day's work, and looking after a child. There is the woman whose husband is a drunkard or a ne'er-do-well, or is in prison serving a long term, and she has to go to work.

On the other side of the debate, the opponents of reform portrayed the woman as selfish, feckless and irresponsible. Jill Knight, a Conservative MP, was one of the leading opponents of reform ... She reveals an image of women seeking abortion as selfish, treating babies 'like bad teeth to be jerked out just because they cause suffering ... simply because it may be inconvenient for a year or so to its mother'. She later adds that a 'mother might want an abortion so that a planned holiday is not postponed or other arrangements interfered with'. The ability and willingness of the woman to make a serious decision regarding abortion, considering all factors and all parties, is dismissed. Rather, she will make a snap decision for her own convenience. The task of the law is thus perceived essentially as one of responsibilization: if the woman seeks to evade the consequences of her carelessness, the law should stand as a barrier.

Given this background, the form that legalization took is not surprising. Abortion is not available upon request. Rather, abortion continues to be proscribed by the Offences Against the Person Act 1861 (and in Scotland by the common law), but the Abortion Act 1967 provides that abortion will be lawful (in England, Scotland, and Wales—the Act does not apply in Northern Ireland), and no offence will have been committed, if the criteria laid out in the Act are met. These are, in short, that two doctors must agree that the woman's circumstances satisfy one of the four statutory 'grounds' for abortion; the abortion must be carried out by a registered medical practitioner in an approved place, and it must be notified to the relevant Chief Medical Officer.

In 2016, as a result of the Scotland Act 2016, abortion became a devolved matter in Scotland, although the Scottish government has said that it has no plans to change the law on abortion. In late 2018, a Private Members Bill which would decriminalize abortions under 24 weeks in England, Wales, and Northern Ireland was introduced to parliament.[22] There is little chance that it will secure sufficient parliamentary time to become law, but debates in parliament have revealed that there is some cross-party support for a degree of liberalization, and in particular for giving Northern Irish women access to abortion services.

---

[21] 'The Abortion Act 1967: A Critical Perspective' in Ellie Lee (ed), *Abortion Law and Politics Today* (Macmillan: London, 1998) 43–58.

[22] Its progress can be followed at <https://services.parliament.uk/bills/2017-19/abortion.html>.

It is important to stress that if a woman's abortion does not satisfy the criteria in the Abortion Act, she has committed a criminal offence. In 2012, Sarah Catt bought abortion pills from an internet site which she took in order to terminate her own pregnancy, shortly before she was due to give birth. She was convicted under section 58 of the Offences Against the Person Act and initially sentenced to eight years in prison.[23] In *R v Sarah Catt*, the Court of Appeal reduced her sentence to three-and-a-half years.

R v Sarah Catt[24]

Rafferty LJ

There are the following aggravating features: the termination was at full term; the body has never been recovered; there was careful planning and acquisition of the abortifacient; the criminal acts were done despite considerable experience of pregnancy and its range of consequences. There are these mitigating features: the plea of guilty, the views of Dr Frazer, a man of significant experience, that Mrs Catt appeared very remorseful, and of Ms Lowe that her emotional attachment to a child in utero is difficult; Mrs Catt has two young children to whom it is accepted she is a good mother and whose development will be adversely affected by her absence from the family home ...

[T]his woman from, at the latest, her undergraduate years had a history of struggle. Her obstetric history we suggest would, without more, prompt attention to her emotional state ... Of one thing we are confident: a wise disposition of this case should remember two young children and a notably forbearing husband ...

In our view, however, a starting point of 12 years was manifestly excessive and, after reduction for plea, eight years similarly so. The appropriate starting point was in the region of five years and, loyal to the judge's assessment of credit for the plea, the end result should be a term of imprisonment of three-and-a-half years.

(2) The Grounds for Abortion

The statutory defences to the criminal offences in the Offences Against the Person Act are contained in section 1 of the Abortion Act 1967, as amended.

Abortion Act 1967 section 1

1(1) Subject to the provisions of this section a person shall not be guilty of an offence under the law relating to abortion when a pregnancy is terminated by a registered medical practitioner if two registered medical practitioners are of the opinion, formed in good faith:

(a) that the pregnancy has not exceeded its twenty fourth week and that the continuation of the pregnancy would involve risk, greater than if the pregnancy were terminated, of injury to the physical or mental health of the pregnant woman or any existing children of her family; or

---

[23] *R v Sarah Louise Catt*, 17 September 2012. Sentencing remarks available at <www.judiciary.gov.uk/>.
[24] [2013] EWCA Crim 1187.

> (b) that the termination is necessary to prevent grave permanent injury to the physical or mental health of the pregnant woman; or
>
> (c) that the continuance of the pregnancy would involve risk to the life of the pregnant woman, greater than if the pregnancy were terminated; or
>
> (d) that there is a substantial risk that if the child were born it would suffer from physical or mental abnormalities as to be seriously handicapped.
>
> (2) In determining whether the continuance of a pregnancy would involve such risk of injury to health as is mentioned in paragraph (a) or (b) of subsection (1) of this section, account may be taken of the woman's actual or reasonably foreseeable environment.

In what follows, we investigate the meaning of this section, and how it works in practice.

(a) Unsuccessful terminations

There is an unfortunate ambiguity in the first sentence of section 1. It appears to suggest that the defence only exists 'when a pregnancy is terminated'. Does this mean that the defence does not exist where the pregnancy is *not* terminated? Because the 1861 Act criminalizes anything done with the intention to procure a miscarriage, a literal interpretation of section 1 might leave unsuccessful terminations in an awkward lacuna: a person can be guilty of an offence under the 1861 Act even if the woman's pregnancy is not terminated, but the defence only exists if the pregnancy *is* terminated.

A similar problem arises if the woman having the abortion turns out not to have been pregnant. The doctor could still be charged under the 1861 Act for attempting to procure a miscarriage, but no defence would exist if there had not in fact been a pregnancy to terminate.

The issue was considered by the House of Lords in *Royal College of Nursing v Department of Health and Social Security* (discussed in more detail later).[25] A majority held that it would be 'absurd' and 'cannot have been the intention of Parliament' that anyone taking part in an unsuccessful termination would be unable to rely upon the defences contained in the Abortion Act and would therefore be guilty of an offence under the Offences Against the Person Act 1861.

Hence, a doctor who attempted unsuccessfully to terminate a pregnancy within the terms of the Abortion Act 1967 would nevertheless have a defence to the criminal offence contained in section 59 of the Offences Against the Person Act.

(b) The need for medical approval

Notice that the Act does not entitle a woman to decide to terminate an unwanted pregnancy, even if her circumstances fit within the statutory grounds. Instead, what matters are two doctors' opinions that one or more of the grounds is satisfied. It is also worth noting that the statute does not specify that the section 1(1) criteria have to actually be satisfied. The legality of an abortion rests wholly upon whether two doctors have formed the opinion, in good faith, that the woman's case fits within the statutory grounds, not upon whether those grounds in fact exist. An abortion would be legal even if the woman's circumstances did not satisfy the statutory grounds, provided that the two doctors who authorized her termination had acted in good faith. Doctors performing abortions will therefore only fail to be protected by the defence in section 1(1) if there is evidence that they did not act in good faith.

[25] [1981] AC 800.

There has been one successful prosecution of a doctor since the Act came into force. In *R v Smith*,[26] the evidence indicated that the doctor had failed to carry out an internal examination, had made no inquiries into the pregnant woman's personal situation, and had not sought a second doctor's opinion. He was convicted on the grounds that he had not, in good faith, attempted to balance the risks of pregnancy and termination. The Court of Appeal appeared to indicate that a doctor will have acted in good faith if he complies with accepted medical practice: 'good faith' thus seems to be synonymous with the *Bolam* test (discussed in Chapter 3).

Further evidence that the statute's purpose is to protect medical discretion comes from the inherent vagueness of the statutory grounds. The Act does not, for example, specify that abortion is legal where the pregnancy has resulted from an act of rape or incest. This ambiguity was deliberate. David Steel's Abortion Bill did initially contain more specific clauses, such as one which permitted abortion where the woman was pregnant as a result of rape, but these were opposed by both the British Medical Association (BMA) and the Royal College of Obstetricians and Gynaecologists (RCOG). While doctors will invariably allow rape victims to terminate their pregnancies, a definitive list of situations in which abortion is lawful was rejected, in part because it would erode medical discretion, and might give women the impression that in certain circumstances they would have the right to an abortion.

In *Paton v British Pregnancy Advisory Service Trustees*, a case in which a man wanted to stop his wife from terminating her pregnancy, Sir George Baker P explained that, under the 1967 Act, it is doctors rather than pregnant women who bear principal responsibility for deciding whether a pregnancy should be terminated:

> not only would it be a bold and brave judge ... who would seek to interfere with the discretion of doctors acting under the Abortion Act 1967, but I think he would really be a foolish judge who would try to do any such thing, unless, possibly, where there is clear bad faith and an obvious attempt to perpetrate a criminal offence.

In the next extract, Sally Sheldon criticizes the Abortion Act's delegation of abortion decision-making to doctors, arguing that the decision to terminate a pregnancy is not necessarily one that requires clinical expertise.

Sally Sheldon[27]

> The granting of such power to doctors in the field of abortion is often justified by the argument that abortion is essentially a medical matter. However, the actual decision whether or not a given pregnancy should be terminated is not normally one that requires expert medical advice, or the balancing of medical criteria. Further, the doctors' decision-making power is not, according to the terms of the Abortion Act, contained within a narrow, limited medical field. In judging whether or not abortion could be detrimental to the mental or physical health of the pregnant woman, under s. 1(2) of the Act, 'account may be taken of the pregnant woman's actual or reasonably foreseeable environment'. The woman's whole lifestyle, her home, finances and relationships are opened up to the doctor's scrutiny, so that he may judge whether or not the patient is a deserving case for relief. The power given to doctors here far exceeds that which would accrue merely on the basis of a technical expertise.

---

[26] [1974] 1 All ER 376.
[27] *Beyond Control: Medical Power and Abortion Law* (Pluto: London, 1997).

Doctors themselves increasingly regard the power they have under the Abortion Act as incompatible with good medical practice, as Ellie Lee et al found out when they interviewed individuals involved in abortion provision.

Ellie Lee, Sally Sheldon, and Jan Macvarish[28]

Those we interviewed communicated a strong perception that the law undermines their medical professionalism … In general, we found the requirement for two signatures was strongly resented. Most talked about the 'two doctors' requirement in markedly critical terms, as 'crap', 'bizarre', 'unnecessary', 'valueless', 'irrelevant', 'superfluous', 'completely outdated', 'silly', 'stupid', 'pointless' and 'ridiculous' …

The first objection drew a 'bright line' between the professional responsibility to obtain consent to treatment and the 'authorisation' requirement: 'It's something that you discuss with someone and informed consent is the basis of all medical interventions and that is all there should be' …

Accessing abortion, we were told, becomes harder than it should be for women, partly because the 'two signatures' requirement creates delays and partly because it can make it seem to women as though their access to abortion is in question. Interviewees commented: 'It does hold things up enormously, the second signature'; 'The biggest problem is time. Sometimes scrapping around finding somebody to sign a form' …

The problem of having to do this duplicate form-signing when a woman was attending a clinic was also presented as having negative effects for women in another way, because it 'stigmatises abortion', which, we were told impacts negatively on women's experience of abortion services …

We found evidence of an almost uniform refutation of a claim to authority in abortion-decision making. It was, most doctors indicated, their responsibility to provide healthcare in the form of abortion services, and this meant *upholding* decision-making by women.

We now turn to look at the statutory grounds for abortion in more detail.

(c) The 'social' ground

Abortion Act 1967 section 1

1(1)(a) that the pregnancy has not exceeded its twenty fourth week and that the continuation of the pregnancy would involve risk, greater than if the pregnancy were terminated, of injury to the physical or mental health of the pregnant woman or any existing children of her family[.];

(i) The time limit

Section 1(1)(a), often referred to as the 'social ground', is the only one with a time limit. The other three grounds for abortion are—in theory at least—available until birth.

---

[28] 'The 1967 Abortion Act fifty years on: Abortion, medical authority and the law revisited' (2018) 212 Social Science and Medicine 26–32.

Obviously, the existence of a time limit means that it is important to know the moment at which a pregnancy begins. When calculating the length of a pregnancy that is being carried to term, the convention is to treat the first day of the pregnant woman's previous period as the relevant start date, even though conception would usually have occurred about two weeks later. The reason for this is that it is impossible to tell when the fertilized egg attaches itself to the wall of the uterus, a process that can itself take several days.

For the purposes of the Abortion Act, however, using this convenient fictional start date is more problematic. Insofar as section 1(1)(a) contains a defence to a criminal offence, any ambiguity must be construed in favour of the defendants: that is, the pregnant woman and her doctor. It would seem unfair to deny a woman an abortion when she was, as a matter of fact, 22 weeks pregnant, but the date of her previous period fell outside the 24-week limit. Rather, the better interpretation is that the pregnancy began when, according to medical judgement, implantation is likely to have occurred. This undoubtedly introduces a margin of uncertainty, but again, if a borderline case were to arise, the ambiguity would have to be construed in favour of the pregnant woman and her doctors.

In practice, 77 per cent of abortions take place during the first ten weeks of pregnancy, and 90 per cent take place within the first 12 weeks.[29] Only a tiny minority (fewer than 2 per cent) take place after the 19th week of pregnancy, most of which are carried out as a result of the late detection of a serious fetal abnormality, and which would therefore be justifiable under section 1(1)(d).[30] The introduction of a 24-week time limit has therefore had almost no practical impact, especially since the Infant Life Preservation Act had already been interpreted as imposing a 24-week time limit upon abortion.

It is, however, important to remember that women do not have the right to an abortion up to 24 weeks: rather, doctors are permitted to carry out terminations if they believe the grounds in the Act are satisfied. In practice, there are relatively few providers willing to carry out abortions for 'social' reasons late into the second trimester. Medical discretion, therefore, may lead to an earlier time limit than that specified in the statute.

Advances in neonatal medicine, which have lowered the age at which premature babies are capable of survival, coupled with developments in visualization techniques, such as 4D ultrasound, which can now show fetal movements in extraordinary detail, have led some to call for a reduction in the 24-week time limit. In the next extract, D Kirklin discusses the role of medical imaging in the abortion debate.

D Kirklin[31]

What interests me here is the powerful role that biomedical imaging, and the human artifice it involves, can play in influencing the nature, timing, and tone of this debate. The ultrasound technology involved is without doubt impressive. A computer is used to simulate the 3D appearance of the fetus in the womb by combining a series of 2D images and then filling in any gaps; the 4D images are generated by using the simulated 3D images to produce a rapidly changing sequence of images, an illusion of fetal movement is thereby created ... What is not immediately apparent when viewing the video clips is that these video clips are in fact video loops, with the same movement shown again and again. Thus the waving fetus is an illusion created by showing the movement of the fetus' arm, from left to right across its body, over and over again. The smiling fetus, who appears to coyly smile then relax its mouth before

[29] *Abortion Statistics, England and Wales: 2017* (DHSC: London, 2018). [30] Ibid.
[31] 'The role of medical imaging in the abortion debate' (2004) 30 Journal of Medical Ethics 426.

coyly smiling again, is also an illusion. We do indeed see the fetus draw back its lips but instead of seeing what happens next, the illusion of smiling is created by the loop presentation of the images.

John Wyatt argues that developments in neonatal medicine since 1967 have also affected attitudes towards late abortion.

John Wyatt[32]

Medical practice in modern perinatal centres can have a paradoxical element. In one part of the hospital a huge concentration of resources, human expertise, parental concern and professional dedication is devoted to ensuring the survival of babies born as early as twenty-three to twenty-four weeks. In an adjacent part of the hospital agonised discussions about the possibility of feticide in a much more mature fetus are taking place. Hospital staff may feel deeply uneasy about raising the option of feticide when a major abnormality is detected in the third trimester ... Although late feticide is performed relatively rarely, the juxtaposition of this practice with neonatal intensive care units inevitably poses ethical conflicts for health professionals.

The development of neonatal intensive care is predicated on the belief that even tiny, immature and uniquely vulnerable babies deserve the very best care and that professionals have an ethical duty to act in each baby's own interests even at considerable cost to society. If there is no responsibility to consider fetal interests until delivery, then it must be explained why the moment of birth in itself leads to a transformation of our ethical responsibilities.

It is not self-evident that fetal viability should determine the time limit for abortion. Viability is not necessarily an intrinsic property of the fetus, but may depend upon the availability of sophisticated medical facilities. A baby born next door to a neonatal intensive care unit (NICU) will be 'viable' at an earlier stage than a baby delivered without medical assistance in a croft in the Outer Hebrides.

Furthermore, deciding that 23 or 24 weeks marks the point at which a baby is 'viable', and abortion thereby impermissible, assumes that we can accurately date the duration of a pregnancy, whereas most doctors would say that there is a margin of error of a week or more in their capacity to diagnose gestational age.

It is also important to be clear about what we mean by viability. Is a fetus viable if it is born alive but dies in the delivery room, or in the NICU? Or should we only consider a fetus to be viable if it has a reasonable chance of surviving, without a life-threatening condition?

Some countries, such as France, have chosen a lower cut-off point for the legality of abortion. The time limit for abortion is not a biologically determined fact, but a political decision. Indeed, in the UK it is possible to terminate a fetus until birth where the pregnant woman's life is at risk, or where abortion would prevent grave permanent injury, or where the fetus is likely to be seriously disabled. In these cases, the fact that the fetus might be viable is outweighed by other factors, such as the need to protect the woman's life.

In the next extract, Sally Sheldon argues that reliance on viability as the cut-off point for lawful abortion might have negative consequences for women's access to abortion services.

---

[32] 'Medical paternalism and the fetus' (2001) 27 Journal of Medical Ethics ii15–ii20.

Sally Sheldon[33]

The adoption of viability as the cut-off point for abortions was heralded as a victory for pro-choice campaigners, as it currently ensures an upper limit which is high in comparison to other Western abortion laws. However, the effect of the 1990 debates has been to entrench in the public—and parliamentary—consciousness that abortion is permissible prior to viability, but should be forbidden after this point. This is a notion which future campaigns may find hard to dislodge... While the present state of medical science makes it impossible to sustain neo-natal life at much less than twenty-four weeks of gestational development for reasons of lung development, it is surely not inconceivable that this limit will be gradually pushed downwards. If this happens, pro-choice groups will face a particularly bitter struggle to try and separate out the legitimacy of abortion from the notion of viability.

Pro-choice campaigners have argued that it is important that abortion continues to be available in the second trimester. Roger Ingham et al investigated the reasons why women have second trimester abortions, and found a combination of 'women-related' reasons—such as not realizing one is pregnant or finding the decision difficult—and 'service-related' reasons, such as encountering delays in referral for termination.

Roger Ingham et al[34]

A lack of early awareness of pregnancy is a significant factor in second-trimester abortions. Half of the respondents were more than seven and a half weeks' gestation when they first suspected they were pregnant, while one quarter were over 11 weeks 2 days' gestation. For women who were more than seven and a half week's gestation, the key factors for a delay in suspecting pregnancy included:

- irregular periods (49 percent)
- continuing periods (42 percent)
- they were using contraception (29 percent) ...

Around half of the respondents took one week or less between taking their test and then making the decision to have an abortion. For those who took more than one week to make the decision, the most commonly cited reason (by 65 percent of respondents) was: 'I was not sure about having the abortion, and it took a while to make up my mind and ask for one.' Reasons for this indecision included:

- concerns about what was involved in having an abortion
- difficulties in agreeing a decision with their partner.

A relatively large proportion of the sample (60 percent) reported a delay between requesting an abortion and having the procedure. Forty-two percent of the respondents waited more than two weeks between requesting and having an abortion, and 23 percent waited more than three weeks—beyond the minimum standard recommended by the Royal College of

[33] 'The Law of Abortion and the Politics of Medicalisation' in Jo Bridgeman and Susan Millns (eds), *Law and Body Politics: Regulating the Female Body* (Dartmouth: Aldershot, 1995) 105–24.
[34] Centre for Sexual Health Research University of Southampton, *Second Trimester Abortions in England and Wales* (University of Southampton, 2007).

Obstetricians and Gynaecologists (RCOG). Some of the reasons for delay at this stage were clearly service related, and included:

- the person I first asked for an abortion took a long time to sort out further appointments for me (30 percent)
- there were confusions about where I should go to have the abortion (24 percent).

It is common for campaigners who wish to lower the time limit for abortion to argue that the abortion decision is a difficult one, for which women need counselling and time for reflection. If the time limit were to be lowered, those women who need time to reflect upon a difficult choice might feel pressured into making a decision quickly.

(ii) The risk to health

For an abortion to be lawful under section 1(1)(a), continuing the pregnancy must pose a risk, greater than if the pregnancy were terminated, of injury to the physical or mental health of the pregnant woman or her children. Under section 1(2) the doctor is specifically directed to take account of the woman's actual or reasonably foreseeable environment. In 2017, 98 per cent of all abortions were authorized on the grounds that the pregnancy posed a risk to the pregnant woman's own health, and 99.5 per cent of these were authorized solely because of the risk to her mental health. One per cent were authorized because of a risk to her children's health.[35] Usually, of course, having another brother or sister does not pose a direct risk to a child's health. Rather, by overstretching the family's resources and diverting the mother's attention away from her existing children, the arrival of a new baby may have an adverse effect upon their health.

For two reasons, section 1(1)(a) is very easily satisfied. First, if the World Health Organization's definition of 'health', as 'a state of physical and mental wellbeing, not merely an absence of disease or infirmity' is used, the abortion only needs to be necessary in order to promote the woman's mental wellbeing, rather than to prevent her from suffering physical or psychiatric harm. The mental wellbeing of a woman who does not want to be pregnant is, almost by definition, promoted by allowing her to end her pregnancy. Secondly, in practice, pregnancy and childbirth are almost always more risky to the woman's physical health than termination. As a result, it could be argued (through what is sometimes called the 'statistical argument') that section 1(1)(a) is satisfied in *every* pregnancy.

(d) Prevent grave permanent injury

Abortion Act 1967 section 1

1(1)(b) that the termination is necessary to prevent grave permanent injury to the physical or mental health of the pregnant woman.

An abortion may be lawful under section 1(1)(b) if it is necessary to prevent grave permanent injury to the pregnant woman's physical or mental health, or to prevent a risk to her life. The

---

[35] *Abortion Statistics, England and Wales: 2017* (DHSC: London, 2018).

ground is very seldom used: in 2017, 176 abortions took place under grounds (b) and (c) together. 'Grave permanent injury' is not defined in the statute, but it seems clear that it applies only to very serious conditions, and an abortion must also be 'necessary' to prevent this injury materializing. If the injury could be prevented without aborting the fetus, then an abortion would not be justifiable under this section.

(e) Risk to the pregnant woman's life

Abortion Act 1967 section 1

1(1)(c) that the continuance of the pregnancy would involve risk to the life of the pregnant woman, greater than if the pregnancy were terminated.

Under section 1(1)(c), doctors must judge that continuing the pregnancy poses a greater risk to the pregnant woman's life than abortion. It is not necessary that abortion should remove the risk to the pregnant woman's life: rather, abortion merely has to reduce the risk. An abortion may not save a terminally ill woman's life, but it might pose less risk to her than carrying a pregnancy to term. Recall that in *R v Bourne*, 'risk to life' was broadly interpreted to encompass situations in which the pregnancy would 'make the woman a physical or mental wreck'. For the purposes of section 1(1)(c), a wide interpretation of 'risk to life' would not be appropriate because it would make this section synonymous with section 1(1)(a), and therefore redundant as a separate ground.[36]

(f) The fetal abnormality ground

Abortion Act 1967 section 1

1(1)(d) that there is a substantial risk that if the child were born it would suffer from physical or mental abnormalities as to be seriously handicapped.

Approximately 2 per cent of all abortions in England and Wales are carried out under section 1(1)(d), which permits abortion until birth where there is a 'substantial risk' that the resulting child would be born 'seriously handicapped'.[37] Access to abortion under this ground depends upon two doctors agreeing that a particular abnormality is 'serious', and that the risk of it materializing is 'substantial'. Again, notice the doctors' wide discretion to decide whether a fetal abnormality meets the threshold level of seriousness, and whether the risk of it materializing is substantial. This flexibility means that doctors might refuse to perform a very late abortion unless the fetus would be likely to die shortly after birth. There is no definitive list of conditions which justify abortion, or of conditions which do not, rather the test is whether the two doctors consider, in good faith, that the child would be 'seriously handicapped'.

---

[36] Ibid.   [37] Ibid.

The question of what might count as a 'serious handicap' was raised in an application for judicial review by Joanna Jepson in 2003, following her discovery that an abortion had been carried out on a fetus with a cleft palate after 24 weeks. Her argument was that when parliament debated the 1990 amendments to the Abortion Act, which enabled abortion until birth for serious abnormalities, its intention had been that third-trimester abortions would be justifiable only for extremely serious conditions. West Mercia police launched an investigation following her complaint, but no prosecution was instigated. After she was granted to leave to apply for judicial review of this decision not to prosecute,[38] West Mercia police conceded that their initial investigation may not have been sufficiently thorough, and the case was re-opened under a different team of officers, who referred it to the Crown Prosecution Service (CPS). In 2005, the CPS determined that the doctors who authorized the abortion had acted in good faith.

Chief Crown Prosecutor[39]

This complaint has been investigated most thoroughly by the police and the CPS has considered a great deal of evidence before reaching its decision ... I consider that both doctors concluded that there was a substantial risk of abnormalities that would amount to the child being seriously handicapped. The evidence shows that these two doctors did form this opinion and formed it in good faith. In these circumstances I decided there was insufficient evidence for a realistic prospect of conviction and that there should be no charges against either of the doctors.

Under section 1(1)(d) there only needs to be a substantial *risk* of handicap, so an abortion could be justified under this section even if the fetus turns out not to suffer from any disability, provided that the doctors were of the opinion that there was a substantial risk of serious disability.

How might section 1(1)(d) apply to genetic tests which can identify future susceptibility to disease? Is a fetus with the genetic mutation that causes Huntington's disease (a degenerative adult-onset condition), at substantial risk of suffering from such abnormalities as to be 'seriously handicapped'? If the child must be seriously handicapped from birth, many genetic diagnoses will not satisfy section 1(1)(d), and abortion would instead be lawful only within the first 24 weeks of pregnancy under section 1(1)(a). Where, as with Huntington's, possessing the genetic mutation will mean that, in adulthood, the child will develop an incurable degenerative disease, resulting in premature death, arguing that the child is at risk of 'serious handicap' would seem fairly straightforward. More difficult questions arise in relation to tests for genes that increase the susceptibility to adult-onset diseases.

Some commentators are troubled by the existence of the fetal abnormality ground. In the next extract, Simo Vehmas argues that once a woman has decided to have a baby, it is not legitimate for her to reject a particular fetus because it does not have the characteristics she requires.

---

[38] *Jepson v Chief Constable of West Mercia Police Constabulary* [2003] EWHC 3318 (Admin).
[39] CPS Press Release, 'CPS decides not to prosecute doctors following complaint by Rev Joanna Jepson' (16 March 2005).

Simo Vehmas[40]

> When considering the parenting of a child with a cognitive impairment, people seem to forget the fact that *every* child is more or less a burden to her parents. Children without impairments may cause stress to their parents due to problems (e.g., drug and alcohol abuse and eating disorders) which children with cognitive impairments usually do not get involved in. Families of children with cognitive impairments do not necessarily experience any more difficulties than families with so-called normal children—their problems are just different . . .
>
> Often . . . social and cultural factors contribute more to the well-being or ill-being of families than the child's impairment in itself. Families which receive support from their societies and communities are, despite a child's impairment, likely to cope better than families which are emotionally and financially on their own . . .
>
> It is true that parents generally wish their future child to conform more or less to some culturally formed ideal. This means that parents characteristically prefer having a good-looking, healthy and intellectually average (or, preferably, above average) child instead of an ugly, sickly and intellectually subaverage child. But to perform parental tasks well, the parents' commitment to care for their child has to be unconditional, which means that the commitment holds even if the child turns out to be ugly, sickly and intellectually subaverage.

Sally Sheldon and Stephen Wilkinson have criticized the fetal abnormality ground from a different perspective, arguing that it is difficult to find a defensible reason for treating abortion on the grounds of fetal abnormality differently from other sorts of abortion. They consider three possible justifications for maintaining section (1)(1)(d) as a separate ground: first, the interests of the child-to-be; secondly, allowing the pregnant woman to conceive a non-disabled child instead; and, thirdly, protecting the pregnant woman's interests. The only logical justification for allowing women to terminate pregnancies where the fetus is disabled is—they suggest—to protect the woman's own interests, in which case this ground for abortion would be indistinguishable from section (1)(1)(a).[41]

Even if section (1)(1)(a) more accurately describes the reason for aborting an abnormal fetus, a time limit is attached to it. Maintaining fetal abnormality as a separate ground might therefore be necessary in order to accommodate the tiny number of abortions carried out in the third trimester of pregnancy following the late discovery of a grave fetal abnormality, like anencephaly (a fatal condition in which much of the fetus's brain and skull is missing).

If, however, the reason for retaining section 1(1)(d) as a separate ground is to permit post-24-week terminations for conditions which are either incompatible with life, or so grave that they would justify withholding or withdrawing life-prolonging treatment from a neonate, Sheelagh McGuinness suggests that it should be worded differently.

Sheelagh McGuinness[42]

> It would be illogical to refuse a termination for a condition that, if realised at birth, would justify a 'best interests' decision of non-treatment of a neonate . . . Where the best interests

---

[40] 'Parental responsibility and the morality of selective abortion' (2002) 5 Ethical Theory and Moral Practice 463–84.

[41] Sally Sheldon and Stephen Wilkinson, 'Termination of Pregnancy for Reason of Foetal Disability: Are There Grounds for a Special Exception in Law?' (2001) 9 Medical Law Review 85–109.

[42] 'Law, Reproduction and Disability: Fatally "Handicapped"' (2013) 21 Medical Law Review 213–42.

standard allows medical decisions that will end the life of neonate to be informed by parental values, the baby's condition must be severe. So, even if the law were applied using this standard of foetal interests, it would rule out as impermissible all abortions after 24 weeks, save in those few instances where the analogous threshold for non-treatment of a neonate is reached ...

If a foetus-centred approach is the justification for some abortions, it may be better to frame the wording of s.1(1)(d) as permitting abortion when the presence of a 'severe abnormality incompatible with any significant period of survival' or any quality of life is identified.

(3) Other Restrictions upon Access to Abortion

(a) Places

Under section 1(3) of the 1967 Act, except in an emergency, 'any treatment for the termination of pregnancy' must be carried out in an NHS hospital, or in a place approved for the purposes of the Act by the Secretary of State. As we saw earlier, the majority of NHS-funded terminations now take place in independent clinics, such as those run by charities like Marie Stopes and the British Pregnancy Advisory Service (BPAS). Regulations provide that special approval is necessary to perform an abortion after 20 weeks in an abortion clinic, and that pregnancies of 24 weeks or more can only be terminated in NHS hospitals.

Until recently, this rule raised particular difficulties in the 66 per cent of abortions which are now terminated using pills rather than surgery.[43] Early medical abortion involves a woman taking two different pills (mifepristone and misoprostol) over a 48-hour time period. The need to take both pills in an approved place meant that women had to make two clinically unnecessary trips to the abortion clinic.[44]

Taking the second pill, misoprostol, at home would undoubtedly be more convenient, especially for women with young children or those who live a long way from their nearest clinic. More importantly, the need to take misoprostol in the abortion clinic meant that there was a risk that the woman might miscarry on her way home. Indeed, it was ironic that a provision in the statute which was supposed to protect women's safety—by ensuring that surgical abortions could only be carried out in properly equipped and staffed premises—in the case of early medical abortions, made them *less* safe.

Section 1(3A) of the 1967 Act was added in 1990 to allow the Secretary of State for Health to approve classes of places where the treatment consists 'primarily in the use of such medicines as may be specified'. In 2018, this provision was finally invoked in order to change the law to allow women to take misoprostol at home in England and Wales.

The Scottish government had announced its intention to do this first, and was challenged unsuccessfully by the Society for the Protection of the Unborn Child (SPUC). In *SPUC Pro-Life Scotland Limited v Scottish Ministers*,[45] Lady Wise had held that:

The requirement that the medical practitioner be in charge or in control throughout the treatment is met by there being knowledge of where the woman will be when she takes the misoprostol coupled with the ability to make contact with the medical practitioner, should that be required.

[43] *Abortion Statistics, England and Wales: 2017* (DHSC: London, 2018).
[44] This was challenged unsuccessfully by BPAS in *British Pregnancy Advisory Service (BPAS) v Secretary of State for Health* [2012] 1 WLR 580.
[45] [2018] CSOH 85.

At the time of writing, the Department of Health and Social Care is working with professional bodies to develop clinical guidance on the home use of misoprostol.

(b) Personnel

Section 1 of the Abortion Act specifies that abortion will be lawful only if it is carried out by a doctor. There is, however, no reason why doctors should have to carry out early medical abortions, and nurse-led abortion services would have obvious cost advantages.

Nurses' involvement in medical abortions was approved nearly 40 years ago in *Royal College of Nursing v Department of Health and Social Security*. A majority in the House of Lords held that nurses could actively participate in terminating pregnancies, provided that a registered medical practitioner is supervising the procedure.

Royal College of Nursing v Department of Health and Social Security [46]

Lord Diplock

What limitation ... is imposed by the qualifying phrase: 'when a pregnancy is terminated by a registered medical practitioner'? In my opinion in the context of the Act, what it requires is that a registered medical practitioner, whom I will refer to as a doctor, should accept responsibility for all stages of the treatment for the termination of the pregnancy. The particular method to be used should be decided by the doctor in charge of the treatment for termination of the pregnancy, he should carry out any physical acts, forming part of the treatment, that in accordance with accepted medical practice are done only by qualified medical practitioners, and should give specific instructions as to the carrying out of such parts of the treatment as in accordance with accepted medical practice are carried out by nurses or other members of the hospital staff without medical qualifications. To each of them, the doctor, or his substitute, should be available to be consulted or called on for assistance from beginning to end of the treatment. In other words, the doctor need not do everything with his own hands; the requirements of the subsection are satisfied when the treatment for termination of a pregnancy is one prescribed by a registered medical practitioner carried out in accordance with his directions and of which a registered medical practitioner remains in charge throughout.

(c) Conscientious objection

Under section 4 of the Act, medical staff have a right of conscientious objection to participation in the provision of abortion services, unless the abortion is necessary to prevent grave permanent injury to the physical or mental health of a pregnant woman, or to save her life.

Abortion Act section 4

4(1) ... no person shall be under any duty, whether by contract or by any statutory or other legal requirement, to participate in any treatment authorised by this Act to which he has a conscientious objection.

---

[46] [1981] AC 800.

Section 4 not only protects doctors who believe abortion is always wrong, but could also be used by doctors who are willing to perform abortions in the early stages of pregnancy, but who 'conscientiously object' to later abortions.

While the right is not limited to doctors, it is limited to a right not to 'participate'. What does 'participation' mean? In *Janaway v Salford Health Authority* the House of Lords rejected a medical receptionist's claim that she had been unlawfully dismissed for refusing to type a letter of referral for an abortion.[47] Lord Keith held that participation 'in its ordinary and natural meaning referred to actually taking part in treatment administered in a hospital or other approved place in accordance with section 1(3), for the purpose of terminating a pregnancy'.

More recently, in the Scottish case of *Doogan v Greater Glasgow and Clyde Health Board*, two Catholic midwives had initially failed to persuade the Court of Session that section 4(1) entitled them to refuse to supervise and support staff who were directly involved with the provision of abortion services.[48] The midwives appealed successfully to an Extra Division of the Inner House,[49] which gave the right to conscientious objection a 'wide interpretation', on the grounds that this was 'in keeping with the reason for the exemption'. In 2014, in *Doogan v Greater Glasgow and Clyde Health Board*, that decision was overturned unanimously by the UK Supreme Court.

Lady Hale (with whom the other Lords Justices agreed) explained that section 4 is concerned with a conscientious objection to those acts which were made lawful by section 1, that is, to the termination of pregnancy itself, rather than to various administrative, managerial, and ancillary tasks associated with the provision of an abortion service.

Doogan v Greater Glasgow and Clyde Health Board[50]

Lady Hale

The more difficult question is what is meant by 'to participate in' the course of treatment in question. The employers accept that it could have a broad or a narrow meaning. On any view, it would not cover things done before the course of treatment began, such as making the booking before the first drug is administered. But a broad meaning might cover things done in connection with that treatment after it had begun, such as assigning staff to work with the patient, supervising and supporting such staff, and keeping a managerial eye on all the patients in the ward, including any undergoing a termination. A narrow meaning would restrict it to 'actually taking part', that is actually performing the tasks involved in the course of treatment.

In my view, the narrow meaning is more likely to have been in the contemplation of Parliament when the Act was passed. The focus of section 4 is on the acts made lawful by section 1. It is unlikely that, in enacting the conscience clause, Parliament had in mind the host of ancillary, administrative and managerial tasks that might be associated with those acts. Parliament will not have had in mind the hospital managers who decide to offer an abortion service, the administrators who decide how best that service can be organised within the hospital (for example, by assigning some terminations to the Labour Ward, some to the Fetal Medicine Unit and some to the Gynaecology Ward), the caterers who provide the patients with food, and the cleaners who provide them with a safe and hygienic environment. Yet all may be said in some way to be facilitating the carrying out of the treatment involved. The managerial and supervisory tasks carried out by the Labour Ward Co-ordinators are closer to these roles than they are to the role of providing the treatment which brings about the termination of the pregnancy. 'Participate' in my view means taking part in a 'hands-on' capacity.

[47] [1989] AC 537.   [48] [2012] CSOH 32.   [49] [2013] CSIH 36.   [50] [2014] UKSC 68.

Mary Neal is critical of this decision, arguing that the point of the conscience clause is to protect healthcare professionals from being forced to be morally complicit in an act they consider wrongful.

Mary Neal[51]

Conscience clauses exist primarily to protect people from moral responsibility for what they regard as wrongdoing; this, it seems to me, has little if anything to do with whether activity was previously criminal.

Rather than asking whether the provision should be interpreted broadly or narrowly, then, the appropriate question is whether the action from which the individual seeks to be exempt would render her *morally responsible* for the outcome she perceives as immoral. In considering the scope of section 4(1) specifically, the appropriate question to ask is whether a midwife doing what these midwives seek *not* to do shares in any moral responsibility (blame or credit, depending on one's view) for the abortion. If the task renders the practitioner morally complicit in the outcome, it must be covered, regardless of whether it is 'hands-off' or was lawful prior to 1967; if it does *not* render her morally responsible, she can be expected to undertake it, even if it involves direct, one-to-one contact with patients undergoing terminations . . .

[W]hen the issue is viewed through the lens of moral responsibility, it is immediately apparent that someone who *authorises* a process (for example, the general practitioner who signs the form) has moral responsibility for it, as do those who support the process by arranging practicalities, allocating tasks, and supervising those directly involved. Viewed through this lens, the phrase 'delegation, supervision and support' (which came to sum up the role of Labour Ward Co-ordinator in this case) clearly describes a role that is not morally neutral, but rather involves *actively supporting* the abortion process.

It seems clear, however, that a doctor cannot claim that referring a pregnant woman to another doctor is 'participating' in her treatment. In *Barr v Matthews*, Alliott J suggested that 'once a termination of pregnancy is recognized as an option the doctor invoking the conscientious objection clause should refer the patient to a colleague at once'.[52] The RCOG guidelines advise doctors with a conscientious objection to abortion that they should, at the very least, inform women of their right to see another doctor, but more usually they should refer the woman themselves:

Doctors who have a conscientious objection to abortion must tell women of their right to see another doctor. NHS GPs who have contracted to provide contraceptive services and who have a conscientious objection to the abortion must, where appropriate, refer women promptly to another doctor.[53]

Of course, as Christopher Cowley has pointed out, a 'conscience absolutist' might believe that a duty to refer 'involves complicity with wrong', but, as Cowley goes on to explain, a doctor is also a representative of the state's health services, from whom a 'patient is legitimately entitled

---

[51] 'When conscience isn't clear: Greater Glasgow Health Board v Doogan and another' [2014] UKSC 68 (2015) 23 Medical Law Review 668–82.

[52] (2000) 52 BMLR 217.

[53] *The Care of Women Requesting Induced Abortion: Evidence-Based Clinical Guideline Number 7* (RCOG, 2011).

to expect . . . *at the very least* information about how the health system works, and about where certain services are provided'.[54]

Doctors are not legally obliged to publicize their conscientious objections to abortion, so a woman may not know that her GP is a conscientious objector. However, the General Medical Council's latest guidance on doctors' personal beliefs instructs doctors that they must tell women that they have a right to see another doctor, and that they should also take steps prospectively to inform their patients about their unwillingness to refer for abortion. If the woman cannot easily make her own arrangements to see another doctor, the doctor is under a duty to assist her.

General Medical Council[55]

10. If, having taken account of your legal and ethical obligations, you wish to exercise a conscientious objection to particular services or procedures, you must do your best to make sure that patients who may consult you about it are aware of your objection in advance. You can do this by making sure that any printed material about your practice and the services you provide explains if there are any services you will not normally provide because of a conscientious objection . . .

12. Patients have a right to information about their condition and the options open to them. If you have a conscientious objection to a treatment or procedure that may be clinically appropriate for the patient, you must do the following.

   (a) Tell the patient that you do not provide the particular treatment or procedure, being careful not to cause distress. You may wish to mention the reason for your objection, but you must be careful not to imply any judgement of the patient.

   (b) Tell the patient that they have a right to discuss their condition and the options for treatment (including the option that you object to) with another practitioner who does not hold the same objection as you and can advise them about the treatment or procedure you object to.

   (c) Make sure that the patient has enough information to arrange to see another doctor who does not hold the same objection as you.

13. If it's not practical for a patient to arrange to see another doctor, you must make sure that arrangements are made – without delay – for another suitably qualified colleague to advise, treat or refer the patient . . .

16. Whatever your personal beliefs about the procedure in question, you must be respectful of the patient's dignity and views.

While a woman whose GP has a conscientious objection to abortion clearly has the right to seek another doctor's assistance, if she lives in a rural or remote part of the country, her need to find another doctor may delay her abortion.

Because conscientious objections to abortion are not formally recorded, it is impossible to tell exactly how many doctors conscientiously object, though it has been estimated to be between 18 and 24 per cent.[56] Significantly, there seems to be some evidence that conscientious

---

[54] Christopher Cowley, 'Conscientious objection in healthcare and the duty to refer' (2017) 43 Journal of Medical Ethics 207–12.
[55] *Personal Beliefs and Medical Practice* (GMC, 2013).
[56] *General Practitioners: Attitudes to Abortion* (Marie Stopes International, 1999).

objection is becoming more common among medical students, who are also less likely to specialize in obstetrics and gynaecology. This may have implications for abortion provision in the future.

R Gleeson et al[57]

One of the most striking results was that only half of all students thought they would sign paperwork and only 36% would perform an abortion in cases where the child was unwanted ... If there were a risk to the mother's health or life, 80% and 84% of students, respectively, would sign paperwork, and even most pro-life students would sign in these circumstances. Therefore, even though the students in our study would be willing to provide abortion services in these more extreme situations, their views might well prevent them from providing services in the vast majority of cases where abortion is requested.

Whether or not doctors *should* be able to conscientiously object to participation in abortion services has been the subject of considerable debate in recent years. Julian Savulescu and Udo Schuklenk have argued that doctors have an obligation to provide lawful medical services.

Julian Savulescu and Udo Schuklenk[58]

Doctors must put patients' interests ahead of their own integrity. They must ensure that legal, beneficial, desired services are provided, if not by them, then by others. If this leads to feelings of guilty remorse or them dropping out of the profession, so be it. As professionals, doctors have to take responsibility for their feelings. There is an oversupply of people wishing to be doctors. The place to debate issues of contraception, abortion and euthanasia is at the societal level, not the bedside, once these procedures are legal and a part of medical practice ...

In any case, if society thinks contraception, abortion and assistance in dying are important, it should select people prepared to do them, not people whose values preclude them from participating. Equally, people not prepared to participate in such expected courses of action should not join professions tasked by society with the provision of such services ...

If a service a doctor is requested to perform is a medical practice, is legal, consistent with distributive justice, requested by the patient or their appointed surrogate, and is plausibly in their interests, the doctor must ensure the patient has access to it ...

It is important to understand that when doctors have a monopoly over a procedure like surgery, it is not a luxury that they can choose to give or withhold on personal grounds.

In contrast, Daniel Sulmasy argues that the 'get another job' argument misunderstands the nature of medicine as a profession.

---

[57] 'Medical students' attitudes towards abortion: a UK study' (2008) 34 Journal of Medical Ethics 783–7.
[58] 'Doctors Have no Right to Refuse Medical Assistance in Dying, Abortion or Contraception' (2017) 31 Bioethics 162–70.

Daniel P Sulmasy[59]

The 'get another job' argument contends that although wide tolerance for conscientious action might generally be appropriate regarding action in the public sphere, physicians have a moral and legal duty to perform, upon patient request, any service that is legally permitted and within the scope of practice of their specialty . . .

Professionals are held to a higher standard of ethics than ordinary citizens. A shoe salesperson, for example, has no moral obligation to tell you that your shoes are ugly if you are willing to pay for them. By contrast, a physician has a moral obligation not to provide unnecessary medical services, such as a CT scan for a muscle tension headache, even if the patient requests it and the physician could make money providing it . . .

Because these professional judgments are both technical and moral in all cases, it seems even more important to respect and protect a wide discretionary space for physicians regarding ethically controversial interventions. Precisely because there can be no a priori legislation of each and every medical decision, society has a deep interest in cultivating practitioners of conscience. This is in the interest of patients. Just as it is important to allow general surgeons the discretionary space to decide, conscientiously, which operations they will train themselves to perform and to decide when they think an operation is indicated in a particular case, so too, gynecologists should be permitted to decide, conscientiously, whether to be trained to perform abortions and whether (for those who have been trained) an abortion is indicated for sex selection or other controversial reasons . . .

Those who hold that professionals must supply upon request any and every service for which they are licensed by the state hold a distorted view of what a profession is, what a professional does, and the role of professions in a pluralistic, liberal democratic society.

(d) Emergencies

Abortion Act 1967 section 1

1(4) Subsection (3) of this section, and so much of subsection (1) as relates to the opinion of two registered medical practitioners, shall not apply to the termination of pregnancy by a registered medical practitioner in a case where he is of the opinion formed in good faith that the termination is immediately necessary to save the life or to prevent grave permanent injury to the physical or mental health of the pregnant woman.

Under this provision, emergency abortions do not have to be performed in an NHS hospital or other approved place, and may be carried out without a second doctor's opinion. A similarly worded provision in section 4 means that doctors cannot invoke the conscientious objection clause where the abortion is necessary to save the woman's life or prevent grave permanent injury.

[59] 'Tolerance, professional judgment, and the discretionary space of the physician' (2017) 26 Cambridge Quarterly of Healthcare Ethics 18–31.

(e) Patients who lack capacity

(i) Adults

Unlike sterilization or organ donation, abortion is not a 'special case' for which court approval is necessary.[60] The Social Care Institute for Excellence's *Good Practice Guidance on Accessing the Court of Protection* sets out when cases involving termination of pregnancy should be taken to the Court of Protection:

> This includes situations where:
>
> - there is a dispute about capacity
> - the patient may regain capacity during or shortly after pregnancy
> - the decision of the medical team is not unanimous
> - the patient, the potential father or the patient's close family disagree with the decision
> - the procedures under section 1 of the Abortion Act have not been followed or
> - there are other exceptional circumstances, for example the pregnancy is the patient's last chance to conceive.[61]

For cases that do not need to be taken to the Court of Protection, it will generally be up to the woman's doctor to determine that she lacks capacity, and to decide whether abortion is in her best interests, bearing in mind the emphasis the Mental Capacity Act 2005 places on the woman's own values, beliefs, and feelings. Of course, that is not the end of the matter and before the abortion can take place, two doctors must additionally certify that the woman's circumstances fit within one of the grounds in section 1(1) of the Abortion Act 1967.

(ii) Children

As we saw in Chapter 6, 16- and 17-year-old girls' consent to medical treatment, which would clearly include abortion, is as valid as it would be if they were adults. Where a girl is under 16, but *Gillick*-competent, as in *R (on the application of Axon) v Secretary of State for Health*,[62] it is clear that she can give a valid consent to abortion, and that the termination can take place without her parents' consent or knowledge.

What about girls who are not yet *Gillick*-competent? Decisions about their medical treatment would normally be taken by their parents, subject to the possibility of being overridden by the courts if their decision is not in the child's best interests. It is, however, hard to imagine circumstances in which it could be in the best interests of a girl who lacks capacity to terminate her pregnancy, or force her to carry a pregnancy to term, against her wishes. Certainly this was the view of Sir James Munby P in *Re X (A Child) (Capacity to Consent to Termination)*, a case involving a pregnant 13-year-old.

Re X (A Child) (Capacity to Consent to Termination)[63]

Sir James Munby P

I find it hard to conceive of any case where such a drastic form of order—such an immensely invasive procedure—could be appropriate in the case of a mother [sic] who does not want

---

[60] Mental Capacity Act 2005 Code of Practice. This was also the case at common law, *Re SG (Adult Mental Patient: Abortion)* [1991] 2 FLR 329.
[61] *Good Practice Guidance on Accessing the Court of Protection* (SCIE, 2011).
[62] [2006] EWHC 37 (Admin).   [63] [2014] EWHC 1871 (Fam).

a termination, unless there was powerful evidence that allowing the pregnancy to continue would put the mother's life or long-term health at very grave risk. Conversely, it would be a very strong thing indeed, if the mother wants a termination, to require her to continue with an unwanted pregnancy ...

A child or incapacitated adult may, in strict law, lack autonomy. But the court must surely attach very considerable weight indeed to the albeit qualified autonomy of a mother who in relation to a matter as personal, intimate and sensitive as pregnancy is expressing clear wishes and feelings, whichever way, as to whether or not she wants a termination.

(e) Selective reduction

Fetal reduction, or the selective termination of one or more fetuses, is a more complex procedure than complete termination, made possible by advances in ultrasonography. Initially it was unclear how the Offences Against the Person Act 1861 and the Abortion Act 1967 would apply to a procedure in which one or more fetuses are destroyed, but the woman continues to be pregnant. This confusion was addressed by an amendment to the Abortion Act in 1990, which spells out that the ordinary Abortion Act grounds apply equally to selective reduction.

Abortion Act 1967 section 5

5(2) For the purposes of the law relating to abortion, anything done with intent to procure a woman's miscarriage (or, in the case of a woman carrying more than one foetus, her miscarriage of any foetus) is unlawfully done unless authorised by section 1 of this Act and, in the case of a woman carrying more than one foetus, anything done with intent to procure her miscarriage of any foetus is authorised by that section if—

(a) the ground for termination of the pregnancy specified in subsection (1)(d) of that section applies in relation to any foetus and the thing is done for the purpose of procuring the miscarriage of that foetus, or

(b) any of the other grounds for termination of the pregnancy specified in that section applies.

In 2017, there were 108 abortions which involved selective terminations: in 71 cases, two fetuses were reduced to one fetus; in 24 cases, three fetuses were reduced to two; and in 11 cases three fetuses were reduced to one. Eighty-three per cent of all selective terminations were justified under section (1)(d); that is, there was a substantial risk that if the child were born it would suffer from such physical or mental abnormalities as to be seriously handicapped.

(f) Third parties' rights (or lack of them)

Given that the Abortion Act treats the decision to authorize abortion as a medical one, to be taken by two doctors, it is unsurprising that the pregnant woman's sexual partner has no right to obstruct medical discretion and prevent her from obtaining an abortion. In a handful of cases, men have made unsuccessful attempts to stop their partners from terminating their pregnancies, and in *Paton v Trustees of the British Pregnancy Advisory Service*,[64] the husband's claim for an injunction was described as 'completely misconceived'.

---

[64] [1979] QB 276. See also *Paton v United Kingdom* (1980) 3 EHRR 408 and *C v S (Foetus: Unmarried Father)* [1988] QB 135.

It would be possible for the woman's sexual partner to notify the police if he believed that there had not been compliance with the Abortion Act 1967. But given that the statute gives doctors very broad discretion to determine the legality of abortion, this strategy would be unlikely to succeed.

Aside from the putative father, other third parties might be interested in trying to prevent a woman from having an abortion, an obvious example being anti-abortion campaigners. On one occasion, an anti-abortion pressure group sought a court injunction in order to try to prevent an abortion from taking place. The case was withdrawn after it was revealed that the abortion had already taken place. SPUC's claim had been that the hospital was under a duty to inform the pregnant woman about their offer of financial assistance. Once again, this would have been unlikely to succeed, given the breadth of discretion doctors have in deciding whether the grounds for abortion are satisfied.[65]

(g) Reporting

All terminations must be notified to the Chief Medical Officer (CMO) of the relevant jurisdiction within 14 days. In addition to notifying the CMO of the grounds on which the abortion has been authorized, and the length of gestation, the notification form also records information such as the woman's age and marital status, her place of usual residence, and the outcome of any previous pregnancies. This data allows detailed abortion statistics to be produced each year.

(5) The Human Rights Act 1998

It would, of course, be possible to frame the abortion issue in terms of rights, and in the context of the Human Rights Act, to pit the woman's right to respect for her private and family life under Article 8 against any right to life which the fetus might have under Article 2. In *Vo v France*,[66] a case that did not involve abortion, but negligence which led to a fetus's death, the European Court of Human Rights (ECtHR) decided that, at the European level, there was no consensus on the moral status of the fetus. The only common ground was that the fetus was a member of the human race. Its capacity to become a person meant that it should be protected as a matter of human dignity, but did not make it a person with a right to life.

More recently, the Council of Europe has suggested that Member States' 'margin of appreciation' on the moral status of the fetus should not be sufficiently wide to permit some states to make abortion unlawful. Rather, while Member States have the right to restrict access to abortion beyond a 'reasonable gestational limit', they should ensure that all women have access to safe and legal abortion. A number of countries, including Northern Ireland, do not satisfy this requirement.

Council of Europe[67]

> 7. The Assembly invites the member states of the Council of Europe to:
>
>   7.1. decriminalise abortion within reasonable gestational limits, if they have not already done so;

---

[65] Sally Sheldon, 'Multiple pregnancy and reproductive choice' (1997) 5 Feminist Legal Studies 99–106.
[66] (2005) 40 EHRR 12.
[67] Resolution 1607 (2008) on access to safe and legal abortion in Europe.

7.2. guarantee women's effective exercise of their right of access to a safe and legal abortion;

7.3. allow women freedom of choice and offer the conditions for a free and enlightened choice without specifically promoting abortion;

7.4. lift restrictions which hinder, *de jure* or de facto, access to safe abortion, and, in particular, take the necessary steps to create the appropriate conditions for health, medical and psychological care and offer suitable financial cover.

A further human rights dimension to the abortion issue is the freedom of expression of those who are opposed to abortion. This was an issue in *Connolly v Director of Public Prosecutions,*[68] in which the defendant, Mrs Connolly, had sent photographs of dead 21-week-old fetuses to pharmacists who stocked the morning-after pill. Dyson J held that Article 10 (which protects freedom of expression) was engaged, but that the interference was justifiable under Article 10(2), in order to protect the rights of others, namely the pharmacists' employees' right to be protected from offensive material.

It is more common for opponents of abortion to hold vigils and protests outside abortion clinics, often trying to talk to, or harass, women entering and leaving the clinic. In *Dulgheriu v Ealing LBC*, Turner J had to determine whether Ealing Council's decision to make a Public Spaces Protection Order (PSPO) to prevent protests outside of an abortion clinic breached pro-life activists' right to freedom of religion and freedom of expression. Given that the Article 8 rights (to respect for private and family life) of women entering and leaving the clinic were engaged, Turner J found that the interference with the protesters' rights to thought, conscience and religion (Article 9); freedom of expression (Article 10), and freedom of assembly and association (Article 11) was justified.

Dulgheriu v Ealing LBC[69]

Turner J

I am satisfied that their rights to a private life were engaged ... In particular, women of reproductive age who are entering the Centre are quite likely to be going there in order to have an abortion. Those leaving may well have undergone an abortion. They thereby become objects of attention not as ordinary members of the public but as women in the early stages of pregnancy who are considering the prospect of an abortion or who have just had an abortion ... To be the focus of open public attention, often at the very moment when sensitivities are at their highest, is an invasion of privacy even when it occurs in a public place ...

In the circumstances of this case, I do not doubt that there has been a significant interference with the rights of activists under Article 9, 10 and 11. I do not underestimate the seriousness of taking steps which are bound to conflict with that special degree of protection afforded to expressions of opinion which are made in the course of a debate on matters of public interest. Nevertheless I am satisfied that the defendant was entitled to conclude on the entirety of the evidence and information available to it that the making of this PSPO was a necessary step in a democratic society. There was substantial evidence that a very considerable number of users of the clinic reasonably felt that their privacy was being very seriously invaded at a time and place when they were most vulnerable and sensitive to uninvited attention.

---

[68] [2007] EWHC 237 (Admin).   [69] [2018] EWHC 1667 (Admin).

4 CONTROVERSIAL QUESTIONS

(a) THE BOUNDARY BETWEEN CONTRACEPTION AND ABORTION

Post-coital contraception, such as the morning-after pill, works by preventing the implant-ation of a fertilized egg. If a woman is considered to be pregnant as soon as fertilization occurs, then preventing a fertilized egg from implanting would trigger an extremely early abortion, and this could be lawful only if the conditions set out in the Abortion Act were satisfied. Two doctors would have to certify that, in their opinion, one of the statutory grounds exists, which would make the use of post-coital contraception time-consuming, expensive, and inconvenient.

As we saw earlier, the Offences Against the Person Act 1861 defines abortion as 'procuring a miscarriage', so an offence would be committed only if the morning-after pill causes a woman to 'miscarry'. Miscarriage is the antonym of 'carriage', a word that seems to imply that the fertil-ized egg must have attached itself to the pregnant woman's body. The legislation itself is silent on the meaning of miscarriage, leading Glanville Williams to suggest that 'there is, therefore, nothing to prevent the courts interpreting the word "miscarriage" in a way that takes account of customary and approved birth control practices'.[70] In a written answer to parliament when the morning-after pill was first licensed for use in 1983, the Attorney General explained that the words in the 1861 statute should be presumed to have been used 'in their popular, or-dinary or natural sense', and that 'in its ordinary sense, the word 'miscarriage' is not apt to describe a failure to implant ... Likewise, the phrase "procure a miscarriage" cannot be con-strued to include the prevention of implantation'.[71]

It seems to be settled medical opinion that pregnancy occurs when the fertilized egg im-plants in the woman's uterus (which will normally be around six or seven days after fertiliza-tion). Pregnancy tests reveal the presence of the hormone human chorionic gonadotropin (hCG), which is released only once implantation has begun. It is therefore impossible to tell whether or not an egg has been fertilized unless and until it implants itself. The majority of naturally fertilized eggs will be lost before the woman's next period, and it would be counter-intuitive to describe these losses as miscarriages.

Despite the widespread belief that post-coital contraception does not involve the termin-ation of pregnancy, Regulations which allowed the morning-after pill to be dispensed by pharmacists were challenged by SPUC on the grounds that the morning-after pill is an abor-tifacient. In *R (on the application of Smeaton) v Secretary of State for Health*, Munby J held that there were multiple reasons for dismissing SPUC's claim. First, because miscarriage is not defined in the 1861 Act, it should be used in its ordinary sense, which is the termination of an established pregnancy. Secondly, complying with the conditions set out in the Abortion Act would delay the use of the morning-after pill. Because this would make it less effective, it would be likely to lead to an increase in the number of unwanted pregnancies and abortions. Thirdly, because other contraceptives, such as the pill and intra-uterine devices (IUDs) may also work by inhibiting the implantation of a fertilized egg, if SPUC's arguments were to be accepted, *every* method of contraception, except the condom, might involve the commission of a criminal offence. Munby J spells out the implications of this below.

---

[70] *Textbook on Criminal Law* (Stevens and Son: London, 1983) 294.
[71] Hansard Written Answers for 10 May 1983.

R (on the application of Smeaton) v Secretary of State for Health [72]

Munby J

Finally, it is not irrelevant to note that my decision accords with social realities. I am declaring licit—not criminal—that which has in fact been the daily practice of countless people in this country for many, many years.

There would in my judgment be something very seriously wrong, indeed grievously wrong with our system—by which I mean not just our legal system but the entire system by which our polity is governed—if a judge in 2002 were to be compelled by a statute 141 years old to hold that what thousands, hundreds of thousands, indeed millions, of ordinary honest, decent, law abiding citizens have been doing day in day out for so many years is and always has been criminal. I am glad to be spared so unattractive a duty ...

Government's responsibility is to ensure the medical and pharmaceutical safety of products offered in the market place and the appropriate provision of suitable guidance and advice. Beyond that, as it seems to me, in this as in other areas of medical ethics, respect for the personal autonomy which our law has now come to recognise demands that the choice be left to the individual.

In the next extract, John Keown criticizes the *Smeaton* decision on two grounds. First, he disputes whether there is in fact a medical consensus as to when pregnancy begins, and when a 'miscarriage' could therefore be procured, and, secondly, he suggests that Munby J placed too much emphasis upon the social consequences of a finding that the morning-after pill is an abortifacient.

John Keown [73]

[T]o assert that 'carriage' requires implantation seems the merest invention. The judge cited not a single dictionary of English to ground his assertions about the popular meaning of the word or that there cannot be 'carriage' without 'attachment'. The dictionary meaning of 'carry' is simply 'To transport ...' There is no requirement here of physical attachment ...

There can surely be little doubt that ... the 'great object' of s 58 was the protection of the unborn child from fertilisation ... Any suggestion that the legislature which enacted s 58 intended its prohibition on attempted abortion to apply only after implantation is unsustainable.

Early in his judgment Munby J correctly observed that the issue for his decision was whether the use of the MAP [morning-after pill] may constitute an offence under the 1861 Act. It was not whether the MAP was either morally right or socially desirable ... In view of this it may be thought surprising that significant portions of the judgment in *Smeaton* were devoted to the social implications of the case and disclosed the judge's opinion that the social consequences of finding for the claimant would have been highly undesirable.

Even if it is clear that the morning-after pill (which must be taken within 72 hours of sexual intercourse) does not 'procure a miscarriage' within the terms of the Offences Against the Person Act, newer types of contragestive contraceptives might do so. A 'contraceptive' which a women could take once a month, or only if her period was late, might be more convenient

[72] [2002] Crim LR 664.
[73] '"Morning after" pills, "miscarriage" and muddle' (2005) 25 Legal Studies 296–319.

than the daily pill, and it could have considerable public health benefits, if it reduced unwanted pregnancy rates. If it were to act after implantation, it would amount to 'procuring a miscarriage', however, and both the person prescribing the medicine and the woman taking it would commit a criminal offence, unless the terms of the Abortion Act 1967 were satisfied.

In the next extract, Sally Sheldon is critical of the fact that the wording of a Victorian statute could prevent women in the twenty-first century from benefiting from new contragestive methods of birth control.

Sally Sheldon[74]

The regulatory cliff edge between 'contraception' and 'abortion' in English law results not from careful consideration but from historical accident ... That archaic legislation, which has remained largely unconsidered for one and a half centuries, is drafted so as to block the development and use of safe, effective forms of fertility control that operate so soon after intercourse provides a compelling argument for a fundamental review of, at least, this aspect of its operation ... The fact that life exists as a seamless continuum means that the attempt to identify markers that allow us to make moral and legal distinctions between different stages of biological development is a fraught enterprise, with any purported bright lines liable to be criticised as misplaced or arbitrary ... While such lines will be inevitably (and appropriately) subject to contestation, it is important to ensure that the process by which they are drawn is capable of robust defence: that they are grounded in careful consideration, informed by clear moral reasoning and a solid medical evidence base. The modest claim defended in this paper is that the current basis for distinguishing between contraception and abortion falls woefully short of meeting this test. Rather, it is determined by a statutory phrase that is a product of a world, which 'in matters sexual was almost unimaginably different from ours' having been passed by a Victorian Parliament within which women had no voice. This is an indefensible basis for the regulation of health services that matter so intimately to modern women.

(b) THE LIVING ABORTUS

The vast majority of abortions are performed when the fetus is not capable of surviving outside the pregnant woman's body, so removing the fetus from the woman's uterus inevitably leads to its death. Although abortion and fetal destruction are normally indistinguishable, they are not necessarily so. If the fetus is born alive after an abortion, it will have an existence separate from its mother, and she could not insist upon its destruction. Where the fetus might be viable, abortion normally involves killing the fetus first, while it is still inside the woman's body. In practice, a tiny number of abortions involve feticide, and in most of these, the fetus has an abnormality—like anencephaly—so serious that it would be likely to die shortly after birth. Performing feticide in such circumstances has not been especially controversial because the baby will in any event die during or very soon after birth.

More complicated ethical dilemmas will be raised if 'artificial wombs' are developed which enable babies to live outside their mothers' bodies much earlier in pregnancy. During the second half of the twentieth century, progress in neonatal medicine has reduced the age at

---

[74] 'The regulatory cliff edge between contraception and abortion: the legal and moral significance of implantation' (2015) Journal of Medical Ethics 762–5.

which a fetus became viable, so that now survival at 22 or 23 weeks, while unusual, is not un-precedented.[75] Before about 21 weeks, however, the fetus's lungs are solid and hence breathing would be impossible. A fetus that could not breathe could only survive outside the pregnant woman's body if scientists were able to develop some sort of 'artificial womb' that could simu-late the uterine environment until the baby became capable of independent life.

If a fetus at 12 weeks' gestation could be transferred to an artificial womb to continue its development, could we say that a woman has the right to the fetus's removal from her body, but not the right to its death? Artificial wombs might enable the partners of pregnant women both to respect their partner's decision not to continue with the pregnancy and to bring up the child, after its artificial gestation.

Given that the conflict between fetal life and women's self-determination has proved so in-tractable, the prospect of artificial wombs might seem to offer an attractive solution. Because a woman could end her unwanted pregnancy without also ending the fetus's life, it might be possible simultaneously to protect both the woman's reproductive autonomy *and* fetal life.[76]

In practice, however, it is unlikely that ectogenesis (gestation outside the woman's body) would satisfy either pro-choice or anti-abortion advocates. According to Leslie Cannold's em-pirical research, those who are against abortion would also reject ectogenesis on the grounds that it represents an abdication of the woman's duty to gestate and raise every fetus she con-ceives.[77] Cannold also encountered opposition among women who are pro-choice, who pointed out that women want abortions not just to avoid pregnancy and childbirth, but be-cause they do not want to be responsible for bringing an unwanted child into the world.[78] It is unwanted motherhood and its responsibilities which lie behind the overwhelming majority of abortion decisions.

In addition, carrying out a fetal extraction rather than a termination would impose an add-itional physical burden on the woman. Medical abortions would not be possible, and a woman would have to undergo a caesarean section in order to remove the living fetus from her body. This would be a more serious, risky, and expensive operation, to which she would be entitled to refuse to consent.

(c) SEX SELECTION

In 2012, undercover reporters from the *Daily Telegraph* filmed abortion providers allegedly agreeing to carry out terminations on the grounds of fetal sex. The reaction from the then Secretary of State for Health, Andrew Lansley, and the Chief Medical Officer, Sally Davies, was to declare that such abortions are unlawful.

The Act does not specify that abortion on the grounds of fetal sex is unlawful, however. Under section 1(1)(a) a termination's legality depends solely upon two doctors, in good faith, deciding that the woman's health would be more at risk if she continued the pregnancy than it would if her pregnancy was terminated. If a woman's mental health would be at risk if she feared rejection by her family on the grounds of the sex of her new baby, termination would not necessarily be unlawful.

---

[75] MA Rysavy et al, 'Between-Hospital Variation in Treatment and Outcomes in Extremely Preterm Infants' (2015) 372 New England Journal of Medicine 1801–11.

[76] Peter Singer and Deane Wells, *The Reproduction Revolution: New Ways of Making Babies* (OUP: Oxford, 1984) 135.

[77] 'Women, ectogenesis and ethical theory' (1995) 12 Journal of Applied Philosophy 55–64.

[78] Ibid.

Nevertheless, it has become common for politicians and others to claim that abortion on the grounds of fetal sex is unlawful. In 2014, for example, the Department of Health issued *Guidance in Relation to Requirements of the Abortion Act*, in order 'to provide support for doctors by setting out how the law is interpreted by the Department of Health'. According to this guidance: 'Abortion on the grounds of gender alone is illegal. Gender is not itself a lawful ground under the Abortion Act.'[79]

This sort of claim often relies upon the fact that 'fetal sex' does not appear as one of the grounds for abortion in section 1(1) of the Abortion Act. But, as Kate Greasley explains, this is to misunderstand how the Abortion Act works. It does not contain a list of legitimate reasons for abortion: rape, for example, does not appear as a ground for abortion in section 1(1), but this does not mean that abortion on the grounds of rape is unlawful. Instead, the Act gives two doctors considerable discretion to determine whether a woman's health would be better served by termination or by carrying the pregnancy to term.

Kate Greasley[80]

[W]e can see that those who infer the illegality of sex selection from the Abortion Act's silence about it have conflated two distinct things: the statutory grounds for abortion, and the background circumstances giving rise to those grounds – what we might term the 'explanations' for abortion. The Abortion Act makes demands only about the grounds, not about the explanations behind them. Every lawful abortion must be supported by good faith medical belief in a specified ground, but there are no specifications as to explanations, either in terms of those which are required or those which are excluded …

[T]he ordinary protocol of the Abortion Act is to isolate the grounds for abortion from the explanations and only to make demands in respect of the former. Abortions in which pregnancy was brought about through rape, or where a woman faces severe financial hardship, are never, legally speaking, abortions on those grounds, but only ever on grounds of risk to physical or mental health which those circumstances generate.

An attempt was made in 2015 to put the supposed illegality of sex-selective abortions beyond doubt through a backbench amendment to the Serious Crime Bill, which would have read: 'Nothing in section 1 of the Abortion Act 1967 is to be interpreted as allowing a pregnancy to be terminated on the grounds of the sex of the unborn child'. This amendment was defeated following concerns that it might prevent women from terminating pregnancies where the fetus has a serious sex-linked disorder. Anxieties were also expressed about the use of the term 'unborn child' in legislation. Instead, an alternative amendment was passed which required research to be carried out into the incidence of sex-selective abortion in the UK.

The Department of Health duly carried out this research and published its findings in August 2015.[81] It had investigated sex ratios at birth in the UK, according to the mothers' country of birth and her ethnic group. Out of 171 different countries of birth, and 13 ethnic groups, there was only one case—that of women born in Nepal, giving birth to their third child—where the sex ratio at birth was not within the normal range. Given how small this group is, the most

---

[79] (DH, 2014).

[80] 'Is Sex-Selective Abortion against the Law?' (2015) 36 Oxford Journal of Legal Studies 535–64.

[81] Department of Health, *Assessment of termination of pregnancy on grounds of the sex of the foetus: Response to Serious Crime Act 2015* (DH: London, 2015).

likely explanation for this abnormal result was random variation. When a further statistical test was carried out, comparing the birth ratios for third born (or more) across all countries of birth, including Nepal, the result was instead normal. Although the Department of Health said that it would continue to monitor the issue, its conclusion was: 'we have found no substantiated concerns of gender abortions occurring in England, Wales and Scotland'.[82]

As Ellie Lee points out in the second extract below, concern about sex-selective abortion is noteworthy, in part because it often involves feminist *opposition* to liberal abortion provision, set out in the first extract by Clare Chambers.

Clare Chambers[83]

Sex-selective abortions are, by definition, chosen in response to a cultural norm that girls and women are inferior. Allowing such abortions both legitimates and strengthens the norm, and thus undermines sex equality more generally. The norm is legitimated because, by allowing the practice, the state refrains from insisting upon sex equality and implies that the inferiority of women is a reasonable ground on which to abort a female foetus ... Sex-selective abortion aggressively emphasizes that girls and women are viewed as inferior within their culture – and, of course, that boys and men are seen as superior. As a result, the equality of women and girls not directly involved in sex-selective abortion is further undermined.

Sex-selective abortions may also reduce the autonomy of other women. If sex-selective abortions are available to all and chosen by some, there will be increased pressure on a woman who becomes pregnant to find out the sex of her foetus and, if it is a girl, to abort it. If sex selection is not permitted and is not generally available, a pregnant woman has an 'excuse' for failing to abort a girl – an excuse that is unavailable to her if the practice is lawful and relatively common. In other words, women who autonomously choose sex-selective abortions in response to cultural norms of female inferiority make it more difficult for other women autonomously to refuse an abortion in response to the same norms.

Ellie Lee[84]

Public feminism, in the form of commentary in the media and in the political sphere, allied itself most strongly with claims that 'something must be done' about sex selection abortion. This meant, first, that for the first time in Britain, those who oppose abortion gained a significant degree of endorsement of their feminised claims. Second, it highlighted that some feminists were also prepared to racialize the abortion problem. As we noted previously, one aspect to claims made about sex selection abortion in the USA has been about 'Asian problems' taking root 'over here', and part of the feminist contribution to the British debate was to make claims along these lines. Some high-profile feminists saw the furore surrounding *The Telegraph*'s undercover operation as an opportunity to link abortion in Britain to 'gendercide' ...

The main focus of commentary [on the Abortion Act 1967] from a feminist perspective has been that women are, as a result, detrimentally affected because women are denied the right

[82] Ibid.
[83] 'Autonomy and Equality in Cultural Perspective: Response to Sawitri Saharso' (2004) 5 Feminist Theory 329–32.
[84] 'Constructing abortion as a social problem: "Sex selection" and the British abortion debate' (2017) 27 Feminism and Psychology 15–33.

to make a choice about their pregnancies (decision-making instead rests ultimately with doctors) and may be denied access to abortion. One overriding feature of the debate discussed here, in stark contrast, was that some abortion doctors specifically, and abortion providers in general, were claimed on 'feminised' grounds to have acted to the detriment of women not by *denying* women abortion, *but by providing it too easily*. (emphasis in original)

(d) PRE-SIGNED FORMS

Following the *Daily Telegraph*'s allegations about sex-selective abortions, the Care Quality Commission (CQC) was ordered to cancel 600 planned inspections of hospitals and care homes, and to instead carry out unannounced inspections at 300 abortion providers. At these inspections, the CQC found evidence that abortion forms had been pre-signed, which once again the Secretary of State for Health declared to be unlawful.

Of course, it is true that a pre-signed form may raise a suspicion that the doctor does not plan to evaluate the woman's case in order to judge whether her circumstances fit within the statutory grounds, but it does not prove that he will not do so. The Department of Health's own advice had been that the second doctor does not actually have to see the pregnant woman himself, so a doctor might plan to have a telephone consultation with her, before authorizing a pre-signed form to be used.

In 2014, the Department of Health issued new guidance which sets out Required Standard Operating Procedures for independent providers of abortion services,[85] and states that: 'DH considers pre-signing of forms (without subsequent consideration of any information relating to the woman) to be incompatible with the requirements of the Abortion Act'. In the next extract, Sally Sheldon questions this assumption.

Sally Sheldon[86]

The legality of 'pre-signing' is moot. The Abortion Act requires doctors to provide notification that an abortion has been authorised but makes no specific provision for when certification should take place, beyond the requirement that doctors must form an opinion in 'good faith' . . .

[W]hile the concept of 'good faith' clearly place limits on how a doctor's judgment may be reached, it is not self-evident that either a literal or purposive interpretation of the Act requires an individualised assessment. Here, it is noteworthy that the legislation specifically allowed broad scope for clinical discretion, leaving the question of how a decision should be reached to the doctors involved. It is arguable that a 'good faith' opinion that abortion is justifiable in all cases could be reached on the basis of the relative risks to a woman's mental or physical health (. . . relying on the 'statistical argument') . . .

Neither is it clear why a face to face assessment should be thought 'good practice' in this context while, in others, doctors are encouraged to work collaboratively as part of a multi-disciplinary team and to rely on information gathered and assessments made by their colleagues.

---

[85] *Procedures for the Approval of Independent Sector Places for the Termination of Pregnancy* (DH: London, 2014).

[86] 'British Abortion Law: Speaking from the Past to Govern the Future' (2016) 79 Modern Law Review 283–316.

Taken together, a common theme in recent media and political interest in abortion provision seems to be to build suspicion about the legitimacy of abortion providers and their practices. In the next extract, Sheelagh McGuinness and Michael Thomson point out that the tendency for abortion services to be provided in the independent sector enables abortion providers to be kept at arm's length from the mainstream medical profession, thus making it easier to impugn their professional integrity.

Sheelagh McGuinness and Michael Thomson[87]

The independent sector has clear benefits; in particular, the women-focused ethos that organisations such as BPAS advocate. However, there are also some negative effects, specifically a reduction in the perceived legitimacy of abortion care when compared with general health services. Noting the situation in the US, Joffe states that 'heavy reliance on clinics has further isolated abortion from the dominant medical institutions'. Both the service and its providers are corralled on the periphery of proper medical practice. This allows medicine to provide abortion but to not fully engage with it ... This corralling of abortion provision on the periphery of proper medical practice has also meant that abortion providers often lack the support of the medical establishment and the full support of the RCOG. This was graphically evidenced in 2012 with the RCOG silence in the face of the *Telegraph* stings on abortion clinics and providers. The RCOG was silent even as the integrity of providers (their members) was impugned, notwithstanding the central place that professional integrity has to the professional project. Their response can be contrasted with the vociferous response of BPAS when the practice of their clinicians was called into question.

(e) NON-INVASIVE PRE-NATAL TESTING

Pregnant women are routinely offered a combined blood test for Down's syndrome, followed by invasive testing (amniocentesis or chorionic villus sampling) for women who are identified to be at increased risk. The combined test has a false positive rate of around five per cent, which means that a significant number of pregnant women unnecessarily undergo invasive testing, which carries a 0.5–1 per cent risk of miscarriage. The identification of fetal DNA in maternal plasma has led to the development of non-invasive prenatal testing (NIPT), which involves a simple test on the pregnant woman's blood sample. This can be carried out earlier in pregnancy (at around nine weeks), with no risk at all to the fetus. It can be used to diagnose chromosomal abnormalities and genetic conditions, as well as identify the fetus's sex. Initially, NIPT was only available privately, but it is now part of the NHS fetal anomaly screening programme, for women for whom the combined test gives a risk greater than 1:150.

While no-risk, early, and accurate prenatal diagnosis has obvious advantages over riskier, later diagnostic techniques, as Adriana Kater-Kuipers et al explain, there are anxieties over its implications.

---

[87] 'Medicine and Abortion Law: Complicating the Reforming Profession' (2015) 23 Medical Law Review 177–99.

Adriana Kater-Kuipers et al[88]

It is feared that the test is 'too easy' and influences the way the test is perceived and presented, namely as a routine offer, which a pregnant woman will accept as a matter of course. This might impede the informed choice of women, or lead to pressure to test. In the literature, this concern is often referred to as *routinisation* of prenatal testing ...

Routinisation also refers to normalisation of the termination of affected pregnancies. When prenatal screening becomes unquestioned, it is suggested, more people will opt for termination of affected pregnancies, not as a result of well-considered choices, but, likewise, as a matter of course, or because of social pressure ...

[S]ome authors have used routinisation to refer to the consequences of the offer of first-trimester prenatal screening for people with a chromosomal abnormality or other disability. The total number of people with a disability might decrease over time, and this might provoke discrimination and stigmatisation of people with a disability ... If women are blamed for bringing children with chromosomal abnormalities into this world or if children are discriminated against or lacking in appropriate healthcare and social support, it will no longer be an (equally) valuable or realistic option to continue a pregnancy following the detection of an abnormality.

There is some evidence that a significant proportion of women who currently decline testing for Down's syndrome, and who would not terminate an affected pregnancy, would opt for NIPT in order to prepare for the birth of an affected child.[89] Indeed, in one recent study, 31 per cent of women who received a positive NIPT result for Down's syndrome chose not to confirm the result through invasive testing and to continue the pregnancy.[90] Nevertheless, Rachèl van Schendel et al describe how parents of children with Down's syndrome, while welcoming more accurate and less risky testing, also worry about its consequences.

Rachèl V van Schendel et al[91]

Parents of children with Down syndrome considered the accuracy, safety and possibility to test earlier as advantages of using NIPT in prenatal screening. However, they thought that prenatal screening in general, and the use of NIPT in particular, put too much focus on Down syndrome, making it seem like Down syndrome is the worst thing that can happen to one's child. They expected that NIPT would lower the barrier for participation in screening, which has both advantages and disadvantages. Participants argued that NIPT gives people a more accurate option to test for Down syndrome without having to risk a miscarriage; but because of that, testing for Down syndrome and terminating the pregnancy could also become more normal. They feared the latter could erode the acceptance, facilities and research for Down syndrome, which in turn leaves women with little room to decline testing. Participants stated that, when implementing NIPT, the counseling should be improved by giving more balanced, accurate information, including more information about living with Down syndrome.

---

[88] 'Ethics of routine: a critical analysis of the concept of "routinisation" in prenatal screening' (2018) Journal of Medical Ethics 626–31.

[89] Celine Lewis et al, 'Non-invasive prenatal testing for trisomy 21: a cross-sectional survey of service users' views and likely uptake' (2014) 121 BJOG: An International Journal of Obstetrics & Gynaecology 582–94.

[90] Lyn Chitty et al, 'Uptake, outcomes and costs of implementing non-invasive prenatal testing for Down syndrome into NHS maternity care: a prospective cohort study in eight diverse maternity units' (2016) 354 British Medical Journal i3426.

[91] 'What Do Parents of Children with Down Syndrome Think about Non-Invasive Prenatal Testing (NIPT)?' (2017) 26 Journal of Genetic Counseling 522–31.

There have also been concerns that NIPT will make sex-selective abortions easier. In their interviews with women who had had personal experience of NIPT, Meredith Vanstone et al found that women valued early prenatal testing for themselves, but were concerned about *other* women using the information to terminate for 'irresponsible reasons'.

Meredith Vanstone[92]

Positively, they described how receiving NIPT results early could facilitate self-determination by providing more time to deliberate about the course of the pregnancy in the event of a finding of aneuploidy or other condition. If a woman chooses to terminate the pregnancy, our participants described several reasons why this choice is easier earlier in pregnancy . . .

[O]ur participants were concerned that other women may use the information from NIPT to terminate for 'what some of us consider irresponsible reasons'. Many women talked about sex selection as an unethical application of NIPT. As our conversations broadened to the potential expansion of the conditions tested for by NIPT, the concern that women may use NIPT to terminate for reasons the participant deemed 'frivolous' deepened.

Using NIPT 'for information only' could simply mean that a couple wishes to be able to prepare themselves for their child's special needs. It could also mean acquiring information about whether the child will suffer from an adult-onset condition in the future. As we saw in Chapter 9, genetic testing in childhood is possible only where there would be a health benefit to the child, in order to protect the child's future autonomy, and her right 'not to know'. If pregnant women could use NIPT to test for *anything*, might this interfere with children's privacy? Zuzana Deans et al argue that the rules that apply to genetic testing in childhood should apply to prenatal testing of a continuing pregnancy.

Zuzana Deans, Angus J Clarke, and Ainsley J Newson[93]

Parents who access personal information relevant to the adult their child will become are arguably invading her future privacy. Similarly, healthcare professionals who divulge information to parents about their future adult child are breaching confidentiality. Therefore there needs to be good justification for accessing and revealing personal facts about another (future) adult . . .

[I]n cases in which a decision has been made to continue pregnancy, it is likely (all being well) to be on the same path to adulthood as an existing child. Thus, any argument for not testing a child in order to protect the privacy of the future adult also applies to not testing a foetus in a continuing pregnancy . . .

If our claim that predictive genetic testing in children is usually inappropriate can be supported, and our claim that a foetus in utero in a continuing pregnancy will be subject to the same considerations, then it would appear that testing a foetus 'purely for information' will not always be appropriate.

---

[92] 'Women's perspectives on the ethical implications of non-invasive prenatal testing: a qualitative analysis to inform health policy decisions' (2018) 19 BMC Medical Ethics 27.

[93] 'For Your Interest? The Ethical Acceptability of Using Non-Invasive Prenatal Testing to Test "Purely for Information"' (2015) 29 Bioethics 19–25.

(f) ABORTION AND WOMEN'S MENTAL HEALTH

It is noteworthy that, in recent years, anti-abortion campaigners have sought to mobilise what might be called 'pro-women' arguments against abortion. In particular, they have claimed that abortion has a negative impact upon women's mental health. As Reva Siegel explains, this tactic is regarded as more likely to persuade a larger section of the population that access to abortion should be restricted.

Reva B Siegel[94]

Growing numbers of movement leaders came to appreciate that woman-focused antiabortion discourse might have strategic utility in persuading segments of the electorate the movement had heretofore been unable to reach: it might reassure those who hesitated to prohibit abortion because they were concerned about women's welfare that legal restrictions on abortion might instead be in women's interest. And so in the early 1990s, leaders of the antiabortion movement began to use PAS [post-abortion syndrome] for new purposes and for a new audience ...

In Making Abortion Rare, [David] Reardon is quite clear that empirical research on the psychological consequences of abortion is a useful way of talking about the moral evil of abortion in terms that have authority for audiences not moved by direct appeals to divine authority ... [O]f course to make this claim about women's interest persuasive, Reardon needed some explanation for the large numbers of women seeking abortions ... Reardon's response was to insist that women who have abortions do not in fact want them; they are coerced into the procedure or do not grasp its implications ...

In Making Abortion Rare, Reardon urged antiabortion politicians to 'take back the terms "freedom of choice" and "reproductive freedom"' and 'emphasize the fact that we are the ones who are really defending the right of women to make an informed choice; we are the ones who are defending the freedom of women to reproduce without fear of being coerced into unwanted abortions'.

In practice, the evidence does not bear out the claim that women's mental health suffers as a result of having had abortions. The Academy of Medical Royal Colleges' systematic review of the evidence of the impact of abortion upon women's mental health, found that the most important predictor of emotional and mental wellbeing in women who have terminated unwanted pregnancies is their wellbeing before the abortion took place.[95] According to the Royal College of Obstetricians and Gynaecologists (RCOG)'s evidence-based guideline, women who have previous mental health problems may experience further problems as a result of an unwanted pregnancy, whether they terminate it or continue it to term:

Women with an unintended pregnancy should be informed that the evidence suggests that they are no more or less likely to suffer adverse psychological sequelae whether they have an abortion or continue with the pregnancy and have the baby.[96]

---

[94] 'Dignity and the Politics of Protection: Abortion Restrictions under *Casey/Carhart*' (2008) 117 Yale Law Journal 1694.

[95] Academy of Medical Royal Colleges, *Induced Abortion and Mental Health: A Systematic Review of the Evidence* (AoMRC, 2011).

[96] *The Care of Women Requesting Induced Abortion: Evidence-Based Clinical Guideline Number 7* (RCOG, 2011), para 5.13.

5 ABORTION IN OTHER JURISDICTIONS

There is insufficient space to provide a detailed survey of abortion laws throughout the world. Instead, we briefly consider the law in Northern Ireland, Ireland, and the US. It is, however, worth noting that there is enormous cross-national variation in the regulation of abortion. Moreover, within different countries, abortion laws have changed dramatically in order to reflect shifts in political and religious affiliations. For example, the liberal abortion regime that existed in Poland prior to the break-up of the Soviet bloc was replaced by a much more restrictive system, in part as a result of the power the Catholic Church acquired through its role in the anti-Soviet Solidarity movement.

Global reviews of abortion provision consistently find that the abortion rate is, in fact, higher in countries with restrictive abortion laws than it is where the law is more liberal.[97] In 2016, for example, Gilda Sedgh et al reported that the abortion rate was '37 abortions per 1000 women where abortion is prohibited altogether or allowed only to save a woman's life, and 34 where it is available on request'.[98]

Bela Ganatra et al[99]

> During 2010–14, 55.7 million abortions occurred annually worldwide, of which 30.6 million (54·9%) were safe ... 25.1 million (45·1%) abortions were done in unsafe circumstances each year ...
>
> The subregions with the highest proportions of safe abortions (northern Europe and northern America) also showed the lowest incidence of abortion. Most countries in these two subregions have less restrictive laws on abortion, high contraceptive use, high economic development, high levels of gender equality, and well developed health infrastructures, suggesting that achievement of both low incidence of abortion and high safety in such contexts is possible.

There is now a weight of evidence that the illegality of abortion poses a serious risk to women's health. In Brazil, for example, there is a ban on abortion in most circumstances, but it is estimated that 500,000 illegal abortions take place each year, of which 200,000 end in complications and 500 in death.

The United Nations' Committee on the Elimination of Discrimination Against Women (CEDAW) has consistently found that the criminalization of abortion violates women's rights. In 2018, it held that the criminal prohibition of abortion in Northern Ireland (NI) (discussed below) was a breach of the UK's obligations under the Convention on the Elimination of All Forms of Discrimination against Women.

---

[97] Gilda Sedgh et al, 'Induced abortion: incidence and trends worldwide from 1995 to 2008' (2012) 379 The Lancet 625–32.

[98] Gilda Sedgh et al, 'Abortion incidence between 1990 and 2014: global, regional, and subregional levels and trends' (2016) 388 The Lancet 258–67.

[99] 'Global, regional, and subregional classification of abortions by safety, 2010–14: estimates from a Bayesian hierarchical model' (2017) 390 The Lancet 2372–81.

CEDAW[100]

> Criminal regulation of abortion serves no known deterrent value. When faced with restricted access women often engage in clandestine abortions including self-administering abortifacients, at risk to their life and health. Additionally, criminalisation has a stigmatising impact on women, and deprives women of their privacy, self-determination and autonomy of decision, offending women's equal status, constituting discrimination . . .
>
> The Committee finds that the State party [the UK] is responsible for:
>
> (a) Grave violations of rights under the Convention considering that the State party's criminal law compels women in cases of severe foetal impairment, including FFA [fatal fetal abnormality], and victims of rape or incest to carry pregnancies to full term, thereby subjecting them to severe physical and mental anguish, constituting gender-based violence against women; and
>
> (b) Systematic violations of rights under the Convention considering that the State party deliberately criminalises abortion and pursues a highly restrictive policy on accessing abortion, thereby compelling women to:
>
> (i) Carry pregnancies to full term;
>
> (ii) Travel outside NI to undergo legal abortion; or
>
> (iii) Self-administer abortifacients . . .
>
> The Committee recommends that the State party urgently:
>
> (a) Repeal sections 58 and 59 of the Offences against the Person Act, 1861 so that no criminal charges can be brought against women and girls who undergo abortion or against qualified health care professionals and all others who provide and assist in the abortion.

(a) NORTHERN IRELAND

The Abortion Act 1967 does not apply in Northern Ireland, and so there are no statutory defences to sections 58 and 59 of the Offences Against the Person Act 1861. *R v Bourne* applies, so a defence would exist if the pregnancy is endangering the pregnant woman's life. Thus individual doctors must decide, on a case-by-case basis, and with the potential threat of criminal prosecution, whether a woman's circumstances are such that continuing with the pregnancy would leave her a 'physical or mental wreck'.

Court rulings in Northern Ireland have confirmed that there are circumstances in which abortion will not be a criminal offence, but because there is no statutory defence, the parameters within which abortion may be lawful remain unclear.[101] Guidance produced by the Department of Health, Social Services, and Public Safety has stated that abortion is lawful only where it is necessary to preserve the life of the pregnant woman, or 'there is a risk of real and serious adverse effect on a pregnant woman's physical or mental health if she continues

---

[100] Report of the inquiry concerning the United Kingdom of Great Britain and Northern Ireland under article 8 of the Optional Protocol to the Convention on the Elimination of All Forms of Discrimination against Women (CEDAW, 2018).

[101] *Northern Health and Social Services Board v F & G* [1993] NILR 268; *Northern Health and Social Services Board v A* [1994] NIJB 1; *Western Health and Social Services Board v CMB*, 29 September 1995, unreported; *Down Lisburn Health and Social Services Board v CH & LAH*, 18 October 1995, unreported.

with the pregnancy, which is either long term or permanent'.[102] Given inevitable uncertainty over whether any risk to the mother's mental health is sufficiently grave to justify abortion in Northern Ireland, and the serious consequences for doctors who break the law, it is not surprising that abortion is largely unavailable in Northern Ireland.

Northern Irish women who wish to terminate unwanted pregnancies commonly travel to England, Scotland, or Wales. Officially, 917 women did so in 2017,[103] though because this figure only includes women who gave a Northern Irish address to the clinic, it is undoubtedly an underestimate. In addition to being inconvenient, the need to travel often delays Northern Irish women's abortions.

Until recently, Northern Irish women were not entitled to NHS abortions, and so in addition to covering the costs of travel, they had to pay for private terminations. Although a challenge to the English Secretary of State for Health's failure to exercise his power to require free abortion services to be provided to women from Northern Ireland failed in the UK Supreme Court, pressure on the government from within parliament led to an announcement in 2018 that not only would Northern Irish women be given access to free NHS abortion services, but also that women on low incomes would be entitled to help with their travel costs. The then Minister for Women and Equalities also announced the introduction of a central booking service through which women from Northern Ireland could access abortion providers in England.

It is also not uncommon for women from Northern Ireland to purchase abortion pills online, and there have been a handful of cases in which women, or their mothers, have been prosecuted for unlawfully procuring a miscarriage.

In 2018, the UK Supreme Court handed down its judgment in a case in which the Northern Ireland Human Rights Commission had applied for judicial review of Northern Ireland's failure to provide for the option of termination in cases of lethal fetal abnormality and sexual crime. In *Re (Northern Ireland Human Rights Commission's Application for Judicial Review)*, a majority (Lords Mance, Kerr, Wilson, and Lady Hale) found that the prohibition of abortion in cases of rape, incest, and fatal fetal abnormality was incompatible with the right to respect for private and family life, under Article 8. Lords Kerr and Wilson additionally held that it was incompatible with the right not to be subjected to inhuman or degrading treatment under Article 3. However, a majority (Lords Mance, Reed, Lloyd-Jones, and Lady Black) also held that the Northern Ireland Human Rights Commission (NIHRC) did not have standing to bring these proceedings and hence the court had no jurisdiction to make a declaration of incompatibility.

Re (Northern Ireland Human Rights Commission's Application for Judicial Review) [104]

Lord Mance

[T]he fact that the present Northern Ireland law does not achieve its identifiable aims, in most cases, but merely outsources the issue, by imposing on the great majority of women within the categories in issue on this appeal the considerable stress and the cost of travelling abroad, away from their familiar home environment and local care, to undergo the humiliating

---

[102] Department of Health, Social Services and Public Safety, *Guidance for health and social care professionals on termination of pregnancy in Northern Ireland* (DHSSPSNI, 2016).
[103] *Abortion Statistics, England and Wales: 2017* (DHSC: London, 2018).
[104] [2018] UKSC 27.

'conveyor belt' experience described in evidence, is a potent indication that the present law is disproportionate. In so far as it does achieve such aims, it in effect victimises unfortunates who miss this humiliating opportunity, because of stress, confusion or lack of funding or organisation in the situation in which they find themselves. I cannot therefore regard the present law as striking a proportionate balance between the interests of women and girls in the cases of fatal foetal abnormality, when it fails to achieve its objective in the case of those who are well-informed and well-supported, merely imposing on them harrowing stress and inconvenience as well as expense, while it imposes severe and sometimes life-time suffering on the most vulnerable, who, commonly because of lack of information or support, are forced to carry their pregnancy to term . . .

I am in short satisfied that the present legislative position in Northern Ireland is untenable and intrinsically disproportionate in excluding from any possibility of abortion pregnancies involving fatal foetal abnormality or due to rape or incest. My conclusions about the Commission's lack of competence to bring these proceedings means that there is however no question of making any declaration of incompatibility. But the present law clearly needs radical reconsideration. Those responsible for ensuring the compatibility of Northern Ireland law with the Convention rights will no doubt recognise and take account of these conclusions, at as early a time as possible, by considering whether and how to amend the law, in the light of the ongoing suffering being caused by it as well as the likelihood that a victim of the existing law would have standing to pursue similar proceedings to reach similar conclusions and to obtain a declaration of incompatibility in relation to the 1861 Act.

Lord Kerr (with whom Lord Wilson agreed)

We need to be clear about what the current law requires of women in this context. It is not less than that they cede control of their bodies to the edict of legislation passed (in the case of the 1861 Act) more than 150 years ago and (in the case of the 1945 Act) almost 75 years ago. Binding the girls and women of Northern Ireland to that edict means that they may not assert their autonomy in their own country. They are forbidden to do to their own bodies that which they wish to do; they are prevented from arranging their lives in the way that they want; they are denied the chance to shape their future as they desire. If, as well as the curtailment on their autonomy which this involves, they are carrying a foetus with a fatal abnormality or have been the victims of rape or incest, they are condemned, because legislation enacted in another era has decreed it, to endure untold suffering and desolation. What is that, if it is not humiliation and debasement?

Lord Reed

[T]he difficulty in the form of the present appeal is that it does not invite the court to investigate the facts of individual cases where Northern Irish women undergoing particular categories of pregnancy have been unable to obtain an abortion, and to decide whether they justify the conclusion that the legislation itself is incompatible with article 8 . Instead, the court is invited, as an abstract exercise, to define categories of pregnancy in respect of which a termination must be legally available if the legislation is to be compatible with article 8...

These are highly sensitive and contentious questions of moral judgement, on which views will vary from person to person, and from judge to judge, as is illustrated by the different views expressed in the present case. They are pre-eminently matters to be settled by democratically elected and accountable institutions, albeit, in the case of the devolved institutions, within limits which are set by the Convention rights as given effect in our domestic law.

A process of democratic consideration of these issues has begun in Northern Ireland and has not yet been completed, as a result of the breakdown of devolved government in January

2017. It is important that a review of these issues should be completed. It appears from the accounts of individual cases put forward in these proceedings that there is every reason to fear that violations of the Convention rights will occur, if the arrangements in place in Northern Ireland remain as they are. In those circumstances, these issues need to be discussed and determined in a democratic forum, which is where they pre-eminently belong.

Although this case did not result in a declaration of incompatibility, this was for procedural reasons, rather than because the Supreme Court considered that the law in Northern Ireland was compatible with women's Article 8 rights. While abortion is a devolved matter, the plight of Northern Irish women has become a focus for particular concern among parliamentarians, and has been made even more stark by the result of the 2018 referendum in the Republic of Ireland.

(b) IRELAND

Until 2018, the Irish Constitution provided that the 'unborn' and the pregnant woman had an equal right to life. Hence, unless the pregnant woman's life was in danger, the fetus's right to life had to take priority. As in Northern Ireland, women from the Republic of Ireland commonly travelled to England, Wales, or Scotland in order to terminate their unwanted pregnancies and, in 2017, 3077 women gave Irish addresses to UK abortion clinics.[105]

Despite the fact that it had always been lawful to terminate a pregnancy when the woman's life is at risk, in 2012 Savita Halappanavar died in a hospital in Galway after being denied a termination of pregnancy on the grounds that the doctors could still detect a fetal heartbeat. Mrs Halappanavar was 17 weeks pregnant when she started to miscarry. She was admitted to hospital and told that her baby would not survive. In extreme pain, Mrs Halappanavar begged for a termination of pregnancy, but was told that this was not allowed because Ireland was a Catholic country, and the fetus could not be removed until its heartbeat had stopped. This was done several days later and Mrs Halappanavar died from blood poisoning.

Public outcry following Mrs Halappanavar's death resulted in the Protection of Life During Pregnancy Act (PLDPA) 2013, which provided that termination will be lawful where there is a real and substantial risk of loss of the woman's life which could only be averted by carrying out a termination. This was superseded in 2018 by a referendum in which the Irish public voted by 66.4 per cent to 33.6 per cent to repeal the 8th Amendment. At the time of writing, the Health (Regulation of Termination of Pregnancy) Bill is before the Irish parliament. It will allow abortion up to 12 weeks of pregnancy without any specific indication. Beyond 12 weeks, there must be a risk to health of the pregnant woman, a medical emergency or a fatal fetal abnormality.

Interestingly, therefore, Ireland will move from prohibiting abortion in almost all circumstances to allowing abortion on request in the first trimester, leaving Northern Ireland's almost complete ban looking even more anomalous.

(c) THE UNITED STATES

In *Roe v Wade*,[106] the US Supreme Court recognized for the first time that a woman's freedom to choose whether to bear a child was a constitutionally protected liberty, which the state could restrict only in order to promote a compelling state interest. The right to privacy, the

---

[105] *Abortion Statistics, England and Wales: 2017* (DHSC: London, 2018).   [106] 410 US 113 (1973).

Supreme Court held, 'is broad enough to encompass a woman's decision whether or not to terminate her pregnancy'. Prior to viability, the state did not have a compelling interest in fetal life, and hence restrictions on a woman's right to decide to terminate her pregnancy would be unconstitutional.

The decision in *Roe v Wade* has not (yet) been explicitly overturned, but its scope has been significantly narrowed over the years, both by subsequent decisions of the Supreme Court and by the passing of restrictive state legislation. In *Webster v Reproductive Health Services*,[107] the Supreme Court weakened the notion of a constitutionally protected right to abortion, holding that restrictions on this right would be unconstitutional only if they imposed an 'undue burden', and even then, they might be justified by important state interests.

Three years later, in *Planned Parenthood v Casey*,[108] the Supreme Court upheld all but one of the restrictions that a Pennsylvania statute had imposed upon women's access to abortion. A mandatory 24-hour waiting period and a parental consent requirement for minors were held to be constitutional; only the spousal notification requirement was rejected on the grounds that, given the proportion of women who may fear assault at the hands of their sexual partner, it did represent an 'undue burden' on women's right to choose abortion.

More recently, in around half of all US states, women seeking abortion must be offered an ultrasound scan, so that they have an opportunity to 'see' the fetus they wish to abort,[109] the assumption being that this will prompt some women to change their minds. In three states—Louisiana, Texas, and Wisconsin—abortion providers must perform an ultrasound on every woman seeking an abortion and must show or describe the image to her.

In the following extract, Sylvia Law argues that by permitting states to place obstacles in the path of women choosing abortion, the Supreme Court in *Casey* effectively overturned *Roe v Wade*.

Sylvia A Law[110]

Many times over the past few months I have been puzzled when sophisticated people . . . ask me whether the Supreme Court will overrule *Roe v Wade*. This surprises me because, like Justices Blackmun and Scalia, I believe that the Supreme Court effectively overruled *Roe* in 1989 . . .

From a pro-choice point of view, one plausible assessment of the *Casey* decision is that it represents the worst of all possible worlds. The joint opinion affirmed a woman's 'fundamental constitutional right' to abortion, but simultaneously allowed the state to adopt measures that effectively curtail many women's exercise of the abortion right. This curtailment hits hardest those women who are most vulnerable, i.e. the poor, the unsophisticated, the young, and women who live in rural areas.

The twenty-four-hour waiting requirement sends a powerful message that is degrading, condescending, and paternalistic to all women. It assumes that women make rash decisions, and reinforces negative stereotypes about women. It imputes women's competence as moral and practical decision-makers. Just as seriously, the impact of the twenty-four-hour waiting requirement will be sharply differentiated on lines of class, age, sophistication, and geography . . .

A compromise that says the rich and sophisticated can have abortions but the poor and naïve cannot should be rejected as hostile to our most fundamental commitments to equal treatment.

---

[107] 492 US 490 (1989).   [108] 112 S Ct 2791 (1992).
[109] Guttmacher Institute, *State Policies in Brief: Requirements for Ultrasound* (Guttmacher Institute, 2015).
[110] 'Abortion Compromise: Inevitable and Impossible' (1992) 25 University of Illinois Law Review 921.

States have further sought to restrict access to abortion by banning certain abortion procedures, such as those used in abortions carried out later in pregnancy. While not a medical term, late abortions have been emotively described as 'partial birth' abortions. In *Gonzales v Carhart*,[111] by a 5:4 majority, the Supreme Court decided that a state law which banned a certain type of abortion procedure, used late in pregnancy, called intact D&X, did not impose an 'undue burden' on women's access to abortion, and hence was constitutional. The majority opinion, written by Justice Kennedy, claimed that women would be protected by a rule which prevents them from consenting to a particular sort of abortion. Because intact D&X is, in Kennedy's words, 'gruesome', the majority thought it likely that many doctors would not tell their patients precisely what it involves. This would therefore compromise the woman's ability to give informed consent and, as a result, the state was justified in banning the procedure.

There have also been attempts to close the majority of abortion clinics. In Texas, a law known as House Bill 2 (HB2) required abortion providers to have admitting privileges with a local hospital and to 'comply with hospital-like "ambulatory surgical center" standards'. Given that most abortions involve taking pills, and can be safely provided in an office, these standards are clinically unnecessary. They are also difficult for abortion providers to satisfy: admitting privileges are conditional on there being a certain number of admissions per year, but because abortions are safe, providers do not have any patients to admit. HB2's practical effect was to shut down the majority of abortion providers in Texas, and dramatically increase the number of women living hundreds of miles from their nearest provider. Similar laws were passed in Alabama, Kansas, Louisiana, Mississippi, Oklahoma, Tennessee, and Wisconsin.

In *Whole Women's Health v Hellerstedt*, by a 5:3 majority, the US Supreme Court held that because it would lead to the closure of more than half of all of Texas's abortion providers, HB2 placed a substantial burden in the path of a woman seeking an abortion, while not advancing the state's interest in protecting women's health. As pointed out by Justice Breyer in his majority opinion, and Justice Ginsburg, in her concurring opinion, the Texas law subjected abortion to more onerous regulation than much riskier procedures, including childbirth, and served to make abortion, if anything, less safe.

Whole Women's Health v Hellerstedt [112]

Justice Breyer

[I]n the face of no threat to women's health, Texas seeks to force women to travel long distances to get abortions in crammed-to-capacity superfacilities. Patients seeking these services are less likely to get the kind of individualized attention, serious conversation, and emotional support that doctors at less taxed facilities may have offered. Healthcare facilities and medical professionals are not fungible commodities. Surgical centers attempting to accommodate sudden, vastly increased demand may find that quality of care declines. Another commonsense inference that the District Court made is that these effects would be harmful to, not supportive of, women's health.

---

[111] 550 US 124 (2007).   [112] 136 S Ct 2292 (2016).

Since 2018, with the appointment of a second conservative Justice nominated by President Trump, there has been a shift in the political balance of the Supreme Court and the impact that this will have on access to abortion is as yet unknown.

In the next extract, Carol Sanger argues that the restrictions placed upon women's access to abortion in the US help to construct abortion as a suspect and shameful practice, rather than an exceptionally common and straightforward medical procedure.

Carol Sanger[113]

I suggest that women, along with everyone else in the United States, cannot help but be aware of the public reputation of abortion. There must be something suspect about a medical procedure excluded from public funding, denied to military personnel and dependents except in cases of rape, unavailable in 87% of counties across the country, and subject to unprecedented levels and modes of regulation. *Roe* may have cleared away abortion's basic criminality, but even noncriminal requirements can create something like sanctions. The law can provide unpleasant options that fall short of formal retribution but still register as punishment ... To borrow an old sociolegal concept, the process is the punishment.

Hyper-regulation may not in every instance be intended punitively. It is, however, based on a particular conception of women which takes as its starting point that women do not quite understand what they are doing when they decide to end a pregnancy. That is why they must be told when human life starts, that this is their own fetus, that they could place it for adoption, and so on.

6 LAW REFORM IN THE UK AND DECRIMINALIZATION

It is often claimed that the medicalization of abortion in England, Wales, and Scotland has effectively depoliticized the issue. If the decision to terminate a pregnancy is taken by a woman's doctor, on the grounds that pregnancy poses a risk to health, it becomes very difficult to challenge both individual abortion decisions, and the rules governing access to abortion. In recent years, however, there has been increasing political and media interest in the question of access to abortion.

In 2008, several amendments to the Human Fertilisation and Embryology Act were tabled, both from those seeking to restrict access and those seeking to liberalize it. First, the House of Commons voted on a series of amendments designed to reduce the 24-week time limit. None succeeded, although the vote on changing the time limit to 22 weeks was much closer (304 against, 233 in favour) than the vote to reduce the time limit to 12 weeks (393 against, 71 in favour).

Secondly, a set of what might be described as pro-choice amendments were tabled. The need for two doctors' signatures; the prohibition of nurse-led treatment, and abortion's continued illegality in Northern Ireland were the subject of liberalizing amendments supported by, among others, the RCOG. For reasons which are hard to understand, the government ensured that these amendments were effectively 'guillotined', and lack of parliamentary time meant that there was no chance of them being voted upon, let alone becoming law.[114]

---

[113] 'Talking About Abortion' (2016) 25 Social & Legal Studies 651–66.
[114] Sally Sheldon, 'A missed opportunity to reform an outdated law' (2009) 4 Clinical Ethics 3–5.

More recently, there has been a campaign to decriminalize abortion law in the UK, supported by a coalition of women's rights groups, reproductive rights campaigners, and professional bodies. In 2017, A ten-minute rule bill introduced by Diana Johnson, the Labour MP for Hull North, seeking permission to introduce legislation to decriminalize abortion in England, Wales, and Northern Ireland succeeded by 172 votes to 142. The Abortion Bill was then introduced to parliament in late 2018, and at the time of writing, it is awaiting its second reading. Lack of parliamentary time means that it is unlikely to become law.

The Bill would repeal section 59 of the Offences Against the Person Act and amend section 58. It would decriminalize only pre-24 week abortions. The Abortion Act would continue to apply to post-24 week abortions, but a defence would exist if the defendant 'believed, in good faith, that the pregnancy had not exceeded its twenty-fourth week'. Doctors would continue to have the right conscientiously to object to participation in abortion services, and the Bill would also create a new offence of non-consensual termination of pregnancy.

The Irish referendum result, and the UK Supreme Court decision in *Re (Northern Ireland Human Rights Commission's Application for Judicial Review* have undoubtedly led to increased parliamentary interest in abortion law reform, and it is notable that in an emergency debate in June 2018, on the question of reforming the law in Northern Ireland and decriminalizing abortion throughout the UK, women MPs spoke publicly and passionately about having had abortions themselves. On the other side of the argument, there were impassioned speeches from 'pro-life' MPs, who claimed that there are 100,000 people alive in Northern Ireland today as a result of the prohibition of abortion.

In the next extract, Sally Sheldon argues in favour of decriminalization.

Sally Sheldon[115]

One powerful justification advanced in the 1960s in favour of entrenching the doctor as 'gatekeeper' was precisely that doctors might somehow take control of a woman's situation and offer the kind of persuasion and support that would convince her to continue with her pregnancy. Yet whatever force this idea had in the 1960s, to modern eyes it appears troublingly coercive to suggest that the doctor's role should be one of active discouragement of abortion. Such conduct would constitute as clear a breach of the professional obligation to provide accurate information and non-directive counselling as would an attempt to persuade a woman to end a pregnancy ...

Writing some 30 years ago, the veteran pro-choice campaigner, Madeleine Simms, argued that 'the 1967 Abortion Act was a half-way house. It handed the abortion decision to the medical profession. The next stage is to hand this very personal decision to the woman herself.' In practice, this second step has already been taken: doctors have used the broad discretion accorded to them under the AA to respect patient autonomy in this as in other contexts. What remains is to update the law to bring it into line with modern medical practice, leaving abortion services subject to the same complex web of regulation that governs other aspects of healthcare provision. Such a change would not remove social contestation around abortion. It would, however, recognise that a law is overdue reform when there is no appetite for enforcing it in the context for which it was intended, where it has no impact on abortion rates, where it imposes clinically unnecessary impediments that restrict the provision of a high quality, safe and compassionate service, and where it stigmatises one third of British women and the healthcare professionals who care for them.

---

[115] 'The Decriminalisation of Abortion: An Argument for Modernisation' (2016) 36 Oxford Journal of Legal Studies 334–65.

Decriminalization is now almost universally supported by doctors' and nurses' professional bodies. The President of the Royal College of Obstetricians, Lesley Regan, has explained that:

> the Royal College of Obstetricians and Gynaecologists Council's support for the removal of criminal sanctions associated with abortion is part of a wider shift of attitude across both Parliament and wider society, supporting the premise that abortion care is an integral part of women's health care and should be treated and regulated accordingly.[116]

7 CONCLUSION

Students studying abortion law for the first time are often surprised to learn both that women do not have the right to terminate their unwanted pregnancies, and that abortion is still, prima facie, a criminal offence. This surprise is understandable, given that, in practice, abortion is available upon request in England, Scotland, and Wales within at least the first 13 weeks of pregnancy, and perhaps up to about 16 weeks. Regardless of the letter of the law, the reality is that women do make their own abortion decisions, and that the medical profession will seldom interfere with their 'right' to do so.

Nevertheless, it is still peculiar for the regulation of what is now a straightforward and common medical procedure to consist in a set of defences to the criminal offence of terminating pregnancy. For women seeking an abortion to have to persuade two doctors that their health is at risk if they continue their pregnancies is radically out of step with the principle of patient autonomy. Rather than making a decision for herself about whether she wants to become a mother (again), the law suggests that abortion-seeking women should instead adopt the role of a supplicant, portraying themselves as mentally fragile and unable to cope. One-third of all women in the UK will have at least one abortion during their lives, and the vast majority regard the question of whether this is the right thing to do as a decision for them, generally in consultation with their partners, rather than a choice which is best made by two registered medical practitioners.

FURTHER READING

Kater-Kuipers, Adriana et al, 'Ethics of routine: a critical analysis of the concept of "routinisation" in prenatal screening' (2018) 44 Journal of Medical Ethics 626–31.

Lee, Ellie, Sheldon, Sally, and Macvarish, Jan, 'The 1967 Abortion Act fifty years on: Abortion, medical authority and the law revisited' (2018) 212 Social Science and Medicine 26–32.

McGuinness, Sheelagh and Thomson, Michael, 'Medicine and Abortion Law: Complicating the Reforming Profession' (2015) 23 Medical Law Review 177–99.

Neal, Mary, ' "When conscience isn't clear" *Greater Glasgow Health Board v Doogan and another* [2014] UKSC 68' (2015) 23 Medical Law Review 668–82.

Sanger, Carol, 'Talking About Abortion' (2016) 25 Social & Legal Studies 651–66.

---

[116] 'Abortion: View from Westminster' (2018) International Journal of Gynecology & Obstetrics (2018).

Savulescu, Julian and Schuklenk, Udo, 'Doctors Have no Right to Refuse Medical Assistance in Dying, Abortion or Contraception' (2017) 31 Bioethics 162–70.

Sheldon, Sally, 'British Abortion Law: Speaking from the Past to Govern the Future' (2016) 79 Modern Law Review 283–316.

Sulmasy, Daniel P, 'Tolerance, professional judgment, and the discretionary space of the physician' (2017) 26 Cambridge Quarterly of Healthcare Ethics 18–31.

15

ASSISTED CONCEPTION

CENTRAL ISSUES

1. Assisted conception services are regulated by the Human Fertilisation and Embryology Act 1990, as amended, and clinics must be licensed by the Human Fertilisation and Embryology Authority (HFEA). The HFEA inspects against more detailed guidance in its Code of Practice and in the Directions that it issues to clinics.

2. In theory, there are few restrictions upon access to fertility treatment in the UK. In practice, treatment is expensive and NHS funding is patchy.

3. It is increasingly common for people to travel overseas in order to receive fertility treatment.

4. Anonymity used to be the norm when donated gametes (sperm and eggs) were used in treatment, but since 2005, donors have had to be identifiable. Donors receive a fixed sum to compensate them for their expenses and inconvenience. Egg-sharing schemes involve women receiving free or cheaper treatment in return for donating half of their eggs.

5. Preimplantation genetic diagnosis (PGD) is used to screen embryos for genetic conditions, so that only unaffected embryos can be transferred to the woman's uterus. PGD can also be used to find out if the child would be a compatible tissue donor for a sick older sibling. Mitochondrial replacement is a new technique used to prevent children inheriting mitochondrial disease from their mothers. In the future, it may be possible to 'edit' an embryo's genome before implantation.

1 INTRODUCTION

The birth of Louise Brown, the first baby created by *in vitro* fertilization (IVF) in Oldham on 25 July 1978, undoubtedly represented one of the most important scientific breakthroughs of the twentieth century. It came nine years after Robert Edwards et al reported the first successful *in vitro* fertilization of human eggs in 1969,[1] and after 457 unsuccessful IVF cycles in 282 patients.[2]

---

[1] RG Edwards, BD Bavister, and PC Steptoe, 'Early stages of fertilisation in vitro of human oocytes matured in vitro' (1969) 221 Nature 632–5.

[2] Sarah Franklin, '*Louise Brown: my life as the world's first test-tube baby* by Louise Brown and Martin Powell, Bristol Books (2015)' (2016) 3 Reproductive Biomedicine and Society Online 142–4.

Initially, the creation of 'test-tube' babies, as they were then described, was greeted with scepticism, and even hostility. Although there are still those who oppose assisted conception on principle,[3] there is now widespread acceptance of techniques that can help people to have children. Infertility affects around one in seven couples, and approximately 2 per cent of children born in the UK are conceived *in vitro*.

It is important to remember that fertility treatment is not always successful, and IVF has certainly not ended involuntary childlessness. In particular, and contrary to popular belief, IVF does not provide a solution to the problem of women's age-related fertility loss. The live birth rate per fresh treatment cycle for women under the age of 35 is 32 per cent, falling to 27 per cent for women aged 38–39, 15 per cent for women aged 40–42, and 11 per cent for women aged 43–44.[4] As Irenee Daly and Susan Bewley point out, changes in society are responsible for a widening gap between the age at which women feel ready to become mothers and the age at which they are most likely to get pregnant, and IVF is not the solution.

Irenee Daly and Susan Bewley[5]

There is a public perception that fertility can be restored via IVF. For example, a participant in [a] study of childless women over thirty said: 'Women are having babies later because of technology. Fertility technology that allows us to kind of extend our fertility period, where before we couldn't you know?' ...

Although IVF has brought joy to millions of people, it was not developed with the intention to encourage older motherhood. Assisted reproduction treatment may be able to assist a man with a low sperm count or overcome the problem of a woman with blocked Fallopian tubes, but unfortunately it is not designed to overcome egg degeneration ...

It takes the current younger generation longer to reach adult milestones which were more easily attainable for previous generations. These include moving away from home, financial independence, getting married and starting a family ... Passing through adult milestones at a later age has itself now become normalized. Given this, it is no wonder that many women no longer think in terms of a normative age to have children. Instead they focus on feeling psychologically ready to have children, a status attained by moving through these milestones.

In this chapter, we begin by looking at the regulation of assisted conception in the UK, which involves looking at both the legislation—the Human Fertilisation and Embryology Act 1990, as amended in 2008—and the work of the Human Fertilisation and Embryology Authority (HFEA). We consider the licensing procedures through which clinics are inspected and authorized to perform certain procedures; access to treatment; consent to the use of gametes (sperm and eggs); gamete donation; rules governing the parentage of children; preimplantation genetic diagnosis; and mitochondrial replacement. We also consider the implications of genome editing for human reproduction. In Chapter 16 we consider the regulation of surrogacy.

---

[3] In 2008, a Papal Encyclical reaffirmed the Catholic Church's opposition to IVF, on the grounds that the only licit way to reproduce is through the 'conjugal act'. See further *Instruction Dignitas Personae on Certain Bioethical Questions* (Vatican, 2008).

[4] *Fertility treatment 2014–2016: Trends and figures* (HFEA, 2018).

[5] 'Reproductive ageing and conflicting clocks: King Midas' touch' (2013) 27 Reproductive BioMedicine Online 722–32.

2 REGULATION OF ASSISTED CONCEPTION

In 1982, four years after Louise Brown's birth, the Committee of Inquiry into Human Fertilisation and Embryology, chaired by Mary Warnock, was commissioned to make recommendations on the regulation of fertility treatment and embryo research. The Warnock Committee's report was published in 1984,[6] and although it was debated in the House of Commons shortly afterwards, a Human Fertilisation and Embryology Bill, based upon its recommendations, was not introduced to parliament until 1989. This time-lag was in practice helpful, because during the 1980s there was considerable support for Private Members Bills which would have prohibited embryo disposal, and hence IVF treatment. By the time the Human Fertilisation and Embryology Bill finally came before parliament, hostility towards embryo destruction appeared to have softened, and there was greater acceptance of both fertility treatment and embryo research. The Human Fertilisation and Embryology Act 1990 came into force in 1991, and was amended in 2008, in part in order to accommodate scientific developments since 1991.

(a) THE HUMAN FERTILISATION AND EMBRYOLOGY AUTHORITY

Section 5 of the Human Fertilisation and Embryology Act set up the Human Fertilisation and Embryology Authority (HFEA). The HFEA currently has 14 members, of which a majority must be 'lay', that is, they must not be clinicians or scientists.[7]

The HFEA has a number of different functions. It regulates fertility treatment and embryo research (see further Chapter 13) by inspecting clinics and issuing licences, and by maintaining a register of information about the provision of treatment and its outcomes. The HFEA is under a duty to maintain a Code of Practice which gives guidance to clinics about the proper conduct of licensable activities,[8] and it is under a duty to promote compliance with the Code.[9] In addition to the Code, the HFEA also has the power to issue Directions on specific issues, with which clinics must comply.

There are obvious advantages in using a Code of Practice and Directions, rather than primary legislation, to regulate such a fast-moving area of clinical practice and scientific research. A good example of the flexibility offered by this model is the HFEA's multiple birth reduction policy.

The health risks associated with multiple pregnancies are serious for babies and for women. Twins and triplets are much more likely to be born prematurely, and the risk of death around the time of birth is 3–6 times higher for twins and nine times higher for triplets. As a result, HFEA policy—set out in the Code and via Directions—has been directed towards ensuring that those women who are most likely to have a multiple pregnancy have only one embryo put back per cycle. All clinics must now have a 'multiple birth reduction strategy', and should not exceed the HFEA's maximum multiple birth rate (this has come down from 24 to 10 per cent).

---

[6] *Report of the Committee of Enquiry into Human Fertilisation and Embryology* (HMSO: London, 1984).
[7] See further <www.hfea.gov.uk>.   [8] Section 25.   [9] Section 8(cb).

HFEA 9th Code of Practice

Interpretation of mandatory requirements 7A

General Directions require centres to have a documented strategy to minimise multiple births. Its purpose is to reduce the annual rate of multiple births resulting from treatments at the centre.

The strategy must set out:

(a) how the centre aims to reduce the annual multiple birth rate following treatment at that centre, and to ensure the rate does not exceed the maximum rate specified by the Authority as set out in Directions,

(b) the circumstances in which the person responsible would consider it appropriate to recommend single embryo transfer (SET) to a patient (in setting out such circumstances, the centre should give proper consideration to relevant professional guidance).

A breach of the Code of Practice is not a criminal offence, unlike many breaches of the Act itself. Nevertheless, breaches of the Code can be taken into account by a licence committee when deciding whether to vary or revoke a licence.

The HFEA is also responsible for advising the Secretary of State for Health on, among other things, the need for new primary legislation. Under section 7 of the Act, it must produce an Annual Report to the Secretary of State for Health and Social Care, describing the activities it has undertaken in the previous 12 months, and setting out its work programme for the following year.

(b) LICENSING

One of the HFEA's most important purposes is to control the activities of licensed clinics and research centres. Sections 3 and 4 of the Human Fertilisation and Embryology Act 1990 provide that the creation, use, and storage of embryos, and the storage and use of gametes, can only be carried out under a licence granted by the HFEA. Carrying out any of these activities without a licence is a criminal offence.[10] It is also a criminal offence to procure, test, process, or distribute gametes without a licence.

Given that fertility treatment is both routine and safe, what is the justification for subjecting it to a special regulatory regime? One possible explanation is the special moral concern for embryos created outside the female body. But this would not explain the HFEA's powers over treatments, like donor insemination, which do not involve *in vitro* fertilization. Alternatively, it could be argued that the creation of children through artificial means raises ethical dilemmas, such as who should be permitted to have access to treatment, but this is undermined by the comparatively lax regulation of surrogacy, discussed in Chapter 16.

The most persuasive explanation is that the form regulation takes in the UK reflects the historical context in 1989, when the original Bill was drafted. Professional bodies, such as the Royal College of Obstetricians and Gynaecologists, had not yet produced their own good practice guidance. Given the novelty and ethical controversy of IVF in 1989, it seemed sensible to consolidate the rules on best practice within a licensing regime.

---

[10] Section 41.

Under section 11 of the Act, the HFEA can grant four different types of licence: for treatment services; non-medical fertility services;[11] storage of gametes and embryos; and research on embryos (see Chapter 13). Once an application for a licence has been received by the HFEA, an inspection team will visit the premises and prepare a report. Licences are issued and renewed by the Executive Licensing Panel of HFEA staff, or in more complex or controversial cases, by the Licence Committee of HFEA members. Licences for treatment and storage can be granted for a maximum of five years;[12] shorter licences can be used to ensure more regular oversight. In addition to its planned programme of renewal and interim inspections, the HFEA also carries out unannounced inspections.

Centres are under a duty to report incidents and 'near misses' to the HFEA. In 2016, 502 incidents were reported, only one of which was classified as Grade A, that is involving severe harm to an individual (in this case, the birth of a child with cystic fibrosis after the parents were mistakenly identified as not being carriers). Centres are not penalized for reporting incidents; on the contrary, the HFEA encourages them to do so as part of the trend towards learning from mistakes, which we explored in Chapter 3.

Sections 12–15 of the Act specify a number of standard licensing conditions, which are automatically attached to each licence. We look at some of these in detail later, but they include that the consent provisions contained in Schedule 3 are complied with; that account has been taken of the welfare of any child that might be born; and that the statutory storage periods for gametes and embryos are not exceeded.

Under section 16(2) each licence application must designate a Person Responsible (PR), whom the licence committee must consider a suitable person to supervise the activities authorized by the licence, and, under section 17, to ensure that suitable practices are used. Until the *Attorney General's Reference (No 2 of 2003)*,[13] it was not clear whether the PR might be vicariously criminally liable for offences committed by his staff. In this case, a rogue embryologist had been guilty of extremely serious misconduct, but the Court of Appeal decided that the PR had not vicariously committed an offence.

Under section 18, a licence can be revoked or varied for a number of reasons, including if misleading information was provided for the purpose of the licence application; or if the premises are no longer suitable; or if the PR has failed to discharge her responsibilities or comply with Directions; or if there has been any other material change in circumstances. Revocation and variation are also possible if the licence committee is not satisfied that the PR is a suitable person to discharge her duties, or if the PR dies or is convicted of an offence under the Act. Section 19 sets out the procedure for refusing, varying, or revoking a licence. Notice must be given to the PR, who then has an opportunity to make representations to the Licence Committee within 28 days, with a further appeal possible to the Authority's separate Appeal Committee, made up of non-members.

As a public body, decisions of the Authority and its licence committees must comply with the Human Rights Act, and are judicially reviewable. Licensing decisions must therefore be proportionate, lawful (ie licence committees must act within their statutory powers), and rational (ie decisions must not be *Wednesbury*[14] unreasonable). Committees must take into account relevant factors, and disregard irrelevant considerations. There have been several

---

[11] Defined in section 2 as any services that are provided, in the course of a business, for the purpose of assisting women to carry children, but are not medical, surgical, or obstetric services.
[12] Schedule 2, paras 1(5) and 2(3).   [13] [2004] EWCA Crim 785.
[14] The test is whether no reasonable body could have come to the same decision: *Associated Provincial Picture Houses v Wednesbury Corporation* [1948] 1 KB 223.

applications for judicial review of decisions of the HFEA. In the most recent, a clinic's application for judicial review of the way in which the HFEA presents 'success rate' data was unsuccessful.

R (on the application of Assisted Reproduction and Gynaecology Centre) v Human Fertilisation and Embryology Authority [15]

O'Farrell J

The minutes of the HFEA board meeting identify the consideration given to the arguments and record the reasons for the decision. The decisive factors identified by the HFEA were that the 'live births per embryo transferred' metric promotes good practice around embryo transfer, reinforces the HFEA's policy to reduce multiple births, is understandable if explained well, and is supported by the majority of professionals, the advisory group and the BFS [British Fertility Society]. The decision is supported logically by the reasons given and constitutes one out of the available rational responses to the arguments.

It is not for this court to decide whether either metric, neither or both should be used as headline figures. This court must consider whether the HFEA's decision was within the range of reasonable decisions open to it in all the circumstances. In my judgment, the decision was not irrational or outside the range of reasonable decisions available.

(c) LIMITS ON THE HFEA'S POWERS

It is worth noting that the HFEA's ability to regulate fertility services is not comprehensive. Somewhat prophetically, in 1999 Margaret Brazier pointed out that the HFEA exercises little control over the market in fertility services, and that it has no power at all when people travel abroad for treatment.

Margaret Brazier[16]

The most profound change in regulating reproductive medicine since Warnock is, I would argue, the dramatically increased role of commerce. Warnock based its recommendations in relation both to fertility treatment and research on the supposition that fertility services would be integrated into the NHS . . . The enormous commercial potential of developments in reproductive medicine was hardly foreseen . . .

The reproduction business, even in the United Kingdom, is set to spawn two rather different sorts of market. The first, which effectively exists today, is the market in fertility services. The private sector, involving both private licensed fertility clinics and the companies who will seek to develop both new fertility treatments and therapeutic cloning, necessarily operates on a profit-making basis. They have a vested interest in the expansion of their business. The more treatment cycles a woman undergoes, the more people who seek treatment, the greater the profit to a clinic . . .

---

[15] [2017] EWHC 659 (Admin).
[16] 'Regulating the Reproduction Business?' (1999) 7 Medical Law Review 166–93.

Another nightmare awaits the HFEA and its counterparts in continental Europe. Each national jurisdiction has sought to fashion a scheme of regulation acceptable to its own culture and community. However those wealthy enough to participate in reproduction markets can readily evade their domestic constraints. If I can order sperm on the internet, or hire a surrogate mother from Bolivia, are British regulators wasting their time? The international ramifications of the reproductive business may prove to be a more stringent test of the strength of British law than all of the difficult ethical dilemmas that have gone before.

There are several reasons why people might seek assisted conception services overseas: cost (IVF is cheaper in India); avoiding long waiting lists (egg donors are more readily available in Spain); avoiding legal restrictions (such as the bans on sex selection and anonymous sperm donation); and a perception that care abroad will be better or more likely to succeed. In their interviews with UK couples who had travelled abroad for fertility treatment, Lorraine Culley et al found that many had done so after years of unsuccessful treatment in the UK.

Lorraine Culley et al[17]

We found that 78% of cases had received some form of treatment in the UK before going overseas. In our sample, a substantial proportion of those needing donor oocytes were seeking treatment abroad at the end of a long history of other forms of treatment. In some cases they had been unsuccessful in treatment with their own gametes, and had now reached an age where donor oocytes were the only realistic option. In other cases, patients using their own gametes had experienced repeated treatment failures in the UK, but reported that they were not being offered any alternative treatments by UK clinics and felt that they needed to 'try something different'. In a small number of cases (17%), patients were motivated to go overseas by a dissatisfaction with the level of care they received in their UK clinic and several mentioned better success rates abroad (29%).

Cross-border reproductive care has been called 'reproductive tourism', but many patients object to this label, with its implication that travelling for treatment is fun and pleasurable. In their interviews, Culley et al found that:

All our participants . . . actively resisted the 'fertility tourist' label and felt that the connotations of pleasure and leisure in no way represented the process of organizing and undertaking fertility treatment. They felt strongly that this was an unfair and inaccurate representation of their experiences.[18]

In some countries there are no restrictions upon the number of embryos transferred in any one cycle. In 2009, for example, it was reported that a woman in the US had given birth to octuplets after a doctor put six embryos back into her womb. While this is an extreme example, British women have returned from having IVF treatment in India pregnant with triplets and quads. In addition to the health risks for pregnant women and their children, higher

---

[17] L Culley et al, 'Crossing borders for fertility treatment: motivations, destinations and outcomes of UK fertility travellers' (2011) 26 Human Reproduction 2373–81.
[18] Ibid.

order multiple births impose significant costs on NHS neonatal services: a triplet pregnancy costs the NHS ten times as much as a singleton. In Alastair McKelvey et al's study of UCLH's specialist multiple pregnancy unit, a quarter of patients had had fertility treatment overseas.[19]

In the next extract, Debora Spar suggests that part of the problem of cross-border reproductive care is that it is only available to the wealthy.

Debora Spar[20]

One might argue that this market for reproductive services is not so remarkable. We trade all kinds of services internationally—why not babies, or the components thereof? One might also argue that the current regulatory patchwork makes political and commercial sense: if Germany wants to ban egg transfer, it should. And if German couples want to avoid this regulation, they should procure their eggs abroad. The problem with this approach, however, is that it turns assisted reproduction into a for-profit business, a lucrative marketplace in which rich couples scour the world in pursuit of high-tech offspring, while poorer would-be parents are consigned to fate. A cross-border market for reproduction also means that societies that oppose assisted reproduction may nevertheless pay its costs. For who can prove that premature quintuplets born in Bremen were conceived in Istanbul?

RF Storrow further suggests that the 'safety valve' function of citizens' freedom to travel abroad may have 'emboldened' some countries—such as Germany, Austria, and Italy—to enact more restrictive provisions.[21]

RF Storrow[22]

[T]he availability of cross-border reproductive travel emboldens legislatures to enact stricter and more symbolic prohibitions than they might otherwise have the political wherewithal to do. The result is the export of claimed harms into other jurisdictions that are inadequately equipped to address the complications and burdens that arise when foreigners enter their borders in search of solutions to reproductive problems. The exploitation of young gamete providers and the distortion in the delivery of medical care to the local population are the likely results of the cross-border reproductive phenomenon.

In *SH v Austria*,[23] for example, the Grand Chamber of the European Court of Human Rights (ECtHR) relied in part upon the availability of cross-border reproductive treatment in order to uphold Austria's restrictive rules on gamete donation:

the Court also observes that there is no prohibition under Austrian law on going abroad to seek treatment of infertility that uses artificial procreation techniques not allowed in Austria and that

---

[19] Alastair McKelvey et al, 'The impact of cross-border reproductive care or "fertility tourism" on NHS maternity services' (2009) 116 British Journal of Obstetrics & Gynaecology 1520–3.

[20] 'Reproductive tourism and the regulatory map' (2005) 352 New England Journal of Medicine 531–3.

[21] See also Guido Pennings, 'Legal harmonization and reproductive tourism in Europe' (2004) 19 Human Reproduction 2689.

[22] 'The pluralism problem in cross-border reproductive care' (2010) 25 Human Reproduction 2939–43.

[23] (2011) Application no 57813/00.

in the event of a successful treatment the Civil Code contains clear rules on paternity and maternity that respect the wishes of the parents.

(d) RECORDING AND DISCLOSING INFORMATION

Section 31 of the Human Fertilisation and Embryology Act requires the HFEA to keep
a register of information collected from licensed centres. Through Directions, the
HFEA requires licence holders to collect information about donors, recipients, treatment services, and the children born as a result, and, under section 33A, to maintain its
confidentiality.

Since 2009, it has been possible to use the HFEA's register for research purposes. Section
33D(1) provides that regulations can require 'the processing of protected information for the
purposes of medical research' where this is 'necessary or expedient in the public interest or
in the interests of improving patient care'. This enables researchers, with ethics committee approval and the approval of the HFEA's Research Register Panel, to use HFEA data and link it
with other health databases, such as cancer registries, in order to carry out epidemiological
research into the safety of IVF.

(e) THE CONSCIENCE CLAUSE

As with the Abortion Act 1967, section 38(1) of the Human Fertilisation and Embryology
Act 1990 gives healthcare professionals the right to refuse to participate in activities to
which they have a conscientious objection: 'No person who has a conscientious objection to participating in any activity governed by this Act shall be under any duty, however
arising, to do so.'

The burden of proof of conscientious objection lies with the person claiming to rely upon
it.[24] A person can invoke section 38 to exclude themselves from any activity governed by the
Act, but they cannot use it to refuse to treat particular sorts of patients, such as single women
or lesbians. Not only is this not an 'activity governed by the Act', but also such a refusal would
be incompatible with equality legislation, and unlawful on human rights grounds. Certainly,
the HFEA's Code of Practice stresses that Persons Responsible are under a duty to familiarize
themselves with relevant equality legislation, and to ensure that their staff members do not
discriminate against patients.

HFEA 9th Code of Practice

29.4 Equality legislation prohibits service providers (such as clinics) from discriminating
against service users (patients and donors) by treating them less favourably because of a
protected characteristic or particular status . . .

29.17 The person responsible should satisfy themselves that the staff member has a conscientious objection to providing a particular licensed activity, and is not unlawfully discriminating against a patient on the basis of a protected characteristic.

---

[24] Section 38(2).

(f) REGULATING ACCESS TO TREATMENT

In the UK there are two ways in which access to fertility treatment is restricted. First, the Act provides that treatment services must not be provided unless account has first been taken of the welfare of any child who may be born as a result. Secondly, there are restrictions on NHS funding for fertility treatment, and private treatment is expensive. As a result, access to treatment often depends upon a patient's ability to pay for it.

(1) Section 13(5)

The Human Fertilisation and Embryology Act contains no formal restrictions upon access to treatment, so any individual, regardless of their age, sexual orientation, or marital status, can legally receive fertility treatment in the UK. When the Bill was debated in 1990, an amendment that would have confined access to married couples was defeated by one vote. As a result, in order to shore up support for the Bill, an amendment was introduced to specify that treatment services should not be provided to a woman 'unless account has been taken of the welfare of any child who may be born as a result of the treatment (*including the need of that child for a father*) ...' (my emphasis).

In 2008, the then government had assumed that deleting the 'need for a father' clause in section 13(5) would straightforwardly bring the 1990 Act into line with post-1990 family law reform and with equality legislation. Given that single women and same-sex couples could adopt, and that sexual orientation and marital status are protected characteristics, it seemed anomalous for the statute governing fertility treatment to contain a statutory provision that, on the face of it, looks like an invitation to discriminate against women without male partners.

A presumption against treating single women and lesbian couples, on child welfare grounds, was also not supported by the evidence, which has established that children conceived through donor insemination by women without male partners are doing as least as well, if not better, than similarly conceived children who are being brought up by heterosexual couples.[25]

Deleting the 'need for a father' clause nevertheless proved to be hugely controversial, because it appeared to imply that fathers had become unimportant. As a result, the 'need for a father' was instead replaced by 'the need for supportive parenting', and section 13(5) now provides that:

> A woman shall not be provided with treatment services unless account has been taken of the welfare of any child who may be born as a result of the treatment (including the need of that child for supportive parenting), and of any other child who may be affected by the birth.

Interestingly, while section 13(5) no longer discriminates against women without male partners, Ellie Lee et al's study of its application in fertility clinics found that it has led to a more direct focus upon child welfare.

---

[25] C Murray and S Golombok, 'Solo mothers and their donor insemination infants: follow-up at age 2 years' (2005) 20 Human Reproduction 1655–60.

Ellie Lee, Sally Sheldon, and Jan Macvarish[26]

However, it seems that one effect of this move against 'discrimination' has been to encourage a more direct focus on 'child welfare' ...

Notably, the perception of what should be discussed seemed to go in some instances well beyond that considered necessary by the regulations, in particular as set out in the HFEA's COP [Code of Practice]. Our research thus detected, first, no real rejection of the idea that it should be part of the work of staff to 'gatekeep' and concern themselves with the welfare of future children. Indeed, many respondents were unexpectedly forthright in their comments about the importance of their responsibility to 'the child' and to 'society', not only (and occasionally in opposition to) the prospective parent's interest in being treated ...

This is not to diminish the importance of the more permissive approach to service provision taken, and the effects this has for same-sex couples particularly. It is, however, to indicate that this permissiveness can pertain in a way consistent with the continued and even deeper opening up of private aspects of people's lives to scrutiny by professionals.

(a) Theoretical difficulties with section 13(5)

Section 13(5) has been the subject of considerable academic debate. If interpreted literally, it appears to instruct a clinician to base his decision as to whether to bring a child into the world upon a consideration of that child's welfare. It is difficult to see how a clinician could decide that a child would be benefited by not being conceived, unless its life would be likely to be so terrible that non-existence would be preferable. In practice, the section has not been interpreted literally, and is instead used to check whether prospective patients are likely to be inadequate parents. But this interpretation too is not without difficulty.

First, clinicians will not have access to all of the information which might be necessary in order to judge prospective patients' parenting abilities. Unlike adoption agencies, infertility clinicians do not make home visits, and nor do they undergo any specialist training in the evaluation of parenting capacity.

Secondly, policing section 13(5) is difficult. It is a standard licensing condition that account must be taken of the welfare of any child that might be born, and in practice clinics must have a protocol in place that sets out how this is done. It would, however, be difficult to prove that the clinic had erred in its assessment. If account was not properly taken of the welfare of any child, and a future child's welfare suffered as a result, it is not clear that anyone would be able to sue the clinic for non-compliance with section 13(5). If the child were to bring an action, this would amount to a 'wrongful life' claim: the child would have to argue that her birth should have been prevented. As we saw in Chapter 3, the courts have given short shrift to the idea that life itself, however difficult, could amount to compensatable damage.

Thirdly, section 13(5) has also been criticized for placing an unfair burden upon infertile individuals, who are no more likely to pose a risk to their children than fertile people, who can reproduce without anyone scrutinizing their parenting ability.[27] Indeed, the evidence suggests that outcomes for children born following fertility treatment are at least as good or better

---

[26] 'After the "need for ... a father": "the welfare of the child" and "supportive parenting" in assisted conception clinics in the UK' (2017) 6 Families, Relationships and Societies 71–87.

[27] See, for example, Emily Jackson, 'Conception and the Irrelevance of the Welfare Principle' (2002) 65 Modern Law Review 176–203.

than those of children conceived naturally.[28] This should not be surprising since, as Susan Golombok et al point out in the next extract in the contact of reproductive donation, these are planned pregnancies and wanted children.

Susan Golombok et al[29]

Despite the concern that children born through reproductive donation would be at risk for psychological difficulties at adolescence, the findings of the present phase of this longitudinal study of families formed through egg donation, donor insemination, and surrogacy showed that these families did not differ from natural conception families when the children reached age 14 … Children born through reproductive donation are, by necessity, planned and there is evidence to show that planned pregnancies are associated with more positive psychological outcomes for mothers and children.

Although it has been suggested that the additional challenges of adolescence may result in greater difficulties in parenting for families created by reproductive donation than for natural conception families, no differences were found between family types in negative parenting from middle childhood to adolescence.

Of course, there is a difference between refraining from interfering with a fertile couple's decision to conceive a child naturally and an infertile couple's need for positive assistance. But if we think that pre-conception assessment of parenting ability is necessary whenever positive steps are taken to help a couple to conceive, we may need to draw a line between procedures that do require pre-conception parental assessment, and procedures that do not. Should there also be a duty to assess a woman's parenting ability before repairing her fallopian tubes or selling her an ovulation predictor kit, for example?

In 2005, House of Commons Science and Technology Committee criticized section 13(5) and recommended its abolition in future legislation, but when it reformed the Act in 2008, the government did not take up this suggestion.

House of Commons Science and Technology Committee[30]

The welfare of the child provision discriminates against the infertile and some sections of society, is impossible to implement and is of questionable practical value in protecting the interests of children born as a result of assisted reproduction. We recognise that there will be difficult cases but these should be resolved by recourse to local clinical ethics committees. The welfare of the child provision has enabled the HFEA and clinics to make judgements that are more properly made by patients in consultation with their doctor.

---

[28] See, for example, S Golombok, R Cook, A Bish, and C Murray, 'Families created by the new reproductive technologies: quality of parenting and social and emotional development of the children' (1995) 66 Child Development 285–98; S Golombok, A Brewaeys, MT Giavazzi, D Guerra, F MacCallum, and J Rust, 'The European study of assisted reproduction families: the transition to adolescence' (2002) 17 Human Reproduction 830–40; C Murray and S Golombok, 'Solo mothers and their donor insemination infants: follow-up at age 2 years' (2005) 20 Human Reproduction 1655–60.

[29] 'A Longitudinal Study of Families Formed Through Reproductive Donation: Parent-Adolescent Relationships and Adolescent Adjustment at Age 14' (2017) 53 Developmental Psychology 1966–1977.

[30] *Human Reproductive Technologies and the Law*, Fifth Report of Session 2004–05, paras 101, 107.

(b) Section 13(5) in practice

Since 2005, the HFEA's Code of Practice has framed the welfare of the child assessment as a welfare of the child *risk* assessment. Rather than trying to ensure that prospective patients would be good or ideal parents, clinicians are instead instructed to consider whether there are any specific risk factors which might give cause for concern. The Code of Practice fleshes out the relevant considerations.

HFEA 9th Code of Practice

8.14 The centre should consider factors that are likely to cause a risk of significant harm or neglect to any child who may be born or to any existing child of the family. These factors include any aspects of the patient's or (if they have one) their partner's:

(a) past or current circumstances that may lead to any child mentioned above experiencing serious physical or psychological harm or neglect, for example:
  (i) previous convictions relating to harming children
  (ii) child protection measures taken regarding existing children, or
  (iii) violence or serious discord in the family environment

(b) past or current circumstances that are likely to lead to an inability to care throughout childhood for any child who may be born, or that are already seriously impairing the care of any existing child of the family, for example:
  (i) mental or physical conditions
  (ii) drug or alcohol abuse
  (iii) medical history, where the medical history indicates that any child who may be born is likely to suffer from a serious medical condition, or
  (iv) circumstances that the centre considers likely to cause serious harm to any child mentioned above.

The Code of Practice also specifies that, in the absence of specific risk factors, all parents should be assumed to be supportive.

HFEA 9th Code of Practice

8.15 When considering a child's need for supportive parenting, centres should consider the following definition:

Supportive parenting is a commitment to the health, wellbeing and development of the child. It is presumed that all prospective parents will be supportive parents, in the absence of any reasonable cause for concern that either the child to be born, or any other child, may be at risk of significant harm or neglect. Where centres have concern as to whether this commitment exists, they may wish to take account of wider family and social networks within which the child will be raised.

In their empirical study of how welfare of the child assessments work in practice, Ellie Lee et al found that refusals of treatment were rare, but that the 'spectre' of the child abuser meant that staff believed that it was important to be vigilant. They also found an interesting distinction between lesbian patients, often portrayed by clinic staff as 'ideal', and single women, whose motives for seeking treatment were sometimes regarded with suspicion.

Ellie Lee, Jan Macvarish, and Sally Sheldon[31]

In all cases, set against the size of the clinics, numbers of cases of concern are low. The clinics reported that the cases that would trigger further investigation typically related to mental illness (including depression), transmissible or inherited illness, physical illness or disability and drugs and alcohol. Only 10 clinics reported dealing with cases involving violence in the family environment and 11 had encountered convictions for harming children ...

The study detected, in particular, a view that vigilance was necessary because 'you can never really know': the spectre of the child abuser as a person hardly ever encountered but whose threat nevertheless creates a powerful rationale for pre-emptive action influenced staff perceptions. As one nurse put it:

'... you wouldn't want to bring a child into a relationship where the child was at any danger of child abuse or sexual abuse ... [A]nything ... that sets those alarm bells going would be something that we wouldn't want to risk'.

In general, treating lesbians was seen as straightforward, with some respondents keen to point out how good lesbian patients could be as parents because they were seen as well-prepared for parenthood: fully aware of the facts and consequences, equipped with strong support networks and open and honest in discussions with clinic staff ...

The discussion of single women patients had a rather different tone ... A minority of interviewees worried about other issues: the costs of childcare, the level of support needed from family or friends, or the demands a child might place on the mother, sometimes also expressing vaguer concerns that a particular single woman was rather odd and her personal circumstances were not conducive to raising a child.

If refused treatment in an NHS clinic, a patient could apply for judicial review, on the grounds that the decision breached Articles 8, 12, or 14 of the European Convention of Human Rights. In practice, however, if a patient is turned down by one clinic, they are likely to seek treatment somewhere else, rather than pursue expensive and time-consuming litigation. There have, however, been two cases in which male prisoners have challenged refusals to grant them access to artificial insemination facilities while still in prison.

In the first case, *R v Secretary of State for the Home Department, ex parte Mellor*,[32] the Court of Appeal found that the restrictions on prisoners' right to found a family and their right to family life were justifiable and proportionate under Article 8(2). The Mellors' case was not exceptional, because Mrs Mellor would be 31 years old at the time of Mr Mellor's release.

In contrast, in *Dickson v United Kingdom*, Mrs Dickson would be 51 years old at her husband's earliest possible release date. Without access to AI, they would be unable to have a child together. The Court of Appeal decided that, despite this, the Secretary of State had acted lawfully by deciding that their need for AI was trumped by other factors, such as legitimate public concern that the punitive and deterrent elements of Kirk Dickson's sentence would be being circumvented.

---

[31] 'Assessing child welfare under the Human Fertilisation and Embryology Act 2008: a case study in medicalisation?' (2014) 36 Sociology of Health & Illness 500–15.
[32] [2001] EWCA Civ 472.

The Dicksons appealed successfully to the Grand Chamber of the ECtHR. By a majority, in *Dickson v United Kingdom*, the Grand Chamber held that prisoners retained their human rights on incarceration, and so any interference with a prisoner's Article 8 rights had to be justified. It was not sufficient justification that providing AI facilities to prisoners would offend public opinion. Because the Secretary of State's policy set an 'inordinately high exceptionality burden', it amounted to a disproportionate interference with the Dicksons' Article 8 rights.

Dickson v United Kingdom[33]

Decision of the Grand Chamber

[T]he court considers that the policy as structured effectively excluded any real weighing of the competing individual and public interests, and prevented the required assessment of the proportionality of a restriction, in any individual case.

In particular, . . . the policy placed an inordinately high 'exceptionality' burden on the applicants when requesting artificial insemination facilities. They had to demonstrate, in the first place, as a condition precedent to the application of the policy, that the deprivation of artificial insemination facilities might prevent conception altogether (the starting point). Secondly, and of even greater significance, they had to go on to demonstrate that the circumstances of their case were 'exceptional' within the meaning of the remaining criteria of the policy (the finishing point).

(2) Financial Restrictions on Access

Infertility treatment is expensive—one cycle of IVF can cost more than £5,000—and its availability within the NHS is patchy. The National Institute for Health and Care Excellence (NICE)'s 2013 clinical guideline recommended that the NHS should fund three full cycles of IVF (ie a fresh cycle followed by further cycles using the frozen embryos) for women under 40 years old, and one full cycle for women aged 40–42, who must additionally not have received IVF treatment before and not have low ovarian reserve. The NICE guideline confines NHS access to those who have failed to conceive through sexual intercourse or artificial insemination. For single and lesbian women, this may mean that they will be able to access NHS treatment only after they have self-funded six unsuccessful cycles of intrauterine insemination.[34]

National Institute for Health and Care Excellence[35]

1.11.1 Criteria for referral for IVF

1.11.1.3 In women aged under 40 years who have not conceived after 2 years of regular unprotected intercourse or 12 cycles of artificial insemination (where 6 or more are by intrauterine insemination), offer 3 full cycles of IVF, with or without ICSI [intracytoplasmic sperm injection]. If the woman reaches the age of 40 during treatment, complete the current full cycle but do not offer further full cycles.

---

[33] Application no 44362/04 (2007).

[34] See further, Atina Krajewska, 'Access of single women to fertility treatment: a case of incidental discrimination' (2015) 23 Medical Law Review 620–45.

[35] *Fertility: Assessment and treatment for people with fertility problems* (NICE, 2013).

1.11.1.4 In women aged 40–42 years who have not conceived after 2 years of regular unprotected intercourse or 12 cycles of artificial insemination (where 6 or more are by intrauterine insemination), offer 1 full cycle of IVF, with or without ICSI, provided the following 3 criteria are fulfilled:

- they have never previously had IVF treatment
- there is no evidence of low ovarian reserve
- there has been a discussion of the additional implications of IVF and pregnancy at this age.

Unlike NICE's technology appraisals (considered in Chapter 2), implementation of this sort of NICE guideline is not mandatory. In 2017 it was reported that only 12 per cent of Clinical Commissioning Groups (CCGs) provide three full cycles of IVF to eligible women; 61 per cent offer one NHS-funded cycle, and 3 per cent provide no NHS services at all.[36] Access to NHS-funded fertility treatment is therefore subject to a postcode lottery.

In the next extracts, Emily McTernan argues that there should be no privileged state funding for fertility treatment, as compared with other 'goods', like education or foreign holidays, that might make our lives go well, while Rebecca Brown et al suggest that the losses associated with involuntary childlessness are comparable to other serious threats to our wellbeing.

Emily McTernan[37]

[F]ertility treatment is one among many goods that states could provide to enable citizens to pursue their diverse valuable life projects or have access to activities that make their life go well or seem meaningful . . .

Yet, at present, many countries are disproportionately generous in their funding of fertility treatment, as compared to the other goods that might make one's life go well or enable valuable life projects. To illustrate, consider the following UK-based examples. IVF is not means-tested in its distribution as are other similar goods, like grants for higher education. So too, is it justifiable that a 40-year-old woman is funded to have a chance at having a child, but housing benefit is limited such that those under 35 cannot live in a flat of their own and unemployment benefit restricted so those on it are not permitted to holiday abroad? Alternatively, why is fertility treatment funded but not undergraduate or master's degrees that might provide a better choice of careers? Indeed, the cost of a master's degree is fairly similar to the cost of a couple of IVF cycles. Or, why fund a chance at having a child of one's own, but not the goods that might enable the formation of other kinds of valuable intimate relationships, such as dating websites?

Rebecca CH Brown et al[38]

The practical disadvantages and social stigma of childlessness can be acute. . . At the individual level, thwarted attempts to establish parental relationships may damage a person's social identity and sense of self . . .

---

[36] See further www.fertilityfairness.co.uk.

[37] 'Should fertility treatment be state funded?' (2015) 32 Journal of Applied Philosophy 227–40.

[38] 'Reframing the Debate Around State Responses to Infertility: Considering the Harms of Subfertility and Involuntary Childlessness' (2016) 9 Public Health Ethics 290–300.

The language people use to describe their sense of failure and disappointment in the context of involuntary childlessness can be powerful: bereavement, guilt, loss and grief feature frequently amongst the expressions used to explain how it feels to be missing the desired child/children. Affected individuals describe struggling to maintain good relationships with others or even to venture out from home because the sight of families with children is so painful. There are also many accounts of people spending vast sums of money and years of their lives trying to conceive, indicating the depth and strength of their desire ...

Essentially, our contention is that different causes of suffering and life project disruption should be treated symmetrically in terms of state support, according to their magnitude. While there are no agreed metrics for measuring suffering or incommensurate forms of harm, it is plausible to postulate that involuntary childlessness may cause harm of a similar nature and/or degree as other threats to valued life projects, such as homelessness, lack of education, unemployment, ill health, loss of loved ones and relationship breakdown.

(3) Counselling

A further standard licensing condition, under section 13(6) of the Act, is that all patients, and where relevant their partners, should not be provided with certain treatments—involving the use of donated gametes or of embryos created outside the body—unless they have been given 'a suitable opportunity to receive proper counselling'. Counselling is not mandatory, however, and nor is there any duty upon clinics to make it available free of charge. The Code of Practice specifies that counselling must be clearly separated from other forms of 'information giving' and from the welfare of the child assessment,[39] and it must be confidential.[40]

(g) REGULATING THE USE OF GAMETES AND EMBRYOS

(1) Consent to the Use of Gametes

Consent to the storage and use of one's gametes must be voluntary and informed. Under Schedule 3 to the 1990 Act, unlike other more invasive medical procedures, consent to the creation of an embryo, or to the use of one's gametes in the treatment of others, *must* be in writing.

Consent must state what is to be done with the stored gametes in the event of the donor's death or incapacity, and must specify the maximum period of storage, if this is to be less than the statutory storage period of ten years. This ten-year limit can be extended for individuals if their fertility has been, or is likely to become, significantly impaired, perhaps because they are about to undergo treatment for cancer which will leave them infertile.[41]

(a) *Consent to the posthumous use of gametes*

In the UK, gametes and embryos can be used posthumously, but only if the gamete provider has explicitly consented to posthumous use. The HFEA has a wide discretion to permit the export of sperm samples, however, and a person who is unable lawfully to use their deceased

---

[39] Para 3.7.   [40] Para 3.12.
[41] The Human Fertilisation and Embryology (Statutory Storage Period for Embryos and Gametes) Regulations 2009, section 4.

partner's gametes in the UK can seek permission to export them to a country where their use in treatment would be lawful.

This issue arose for the first time in *R v Human Fertilisation and Embryology Authority, ex parte Blood.*[42] Sperm samples had been extracted, at Mrs Blood's request, while her husband was in a coma. Although Mrs Blood said that she and her husband had discussed the post-humous use of his sperm, Mr Blood had not given written consent, and hence the samples could not be used lawfully in the UK. Mrs Blood therefore applied for permission to export them to Belgium. When the HFEA refused, she sought judicial review of this decision.

On appeal, Mrs Blood succeeded. The Court of Appeal took the view that despite the un-lawfulness of the sperm retrieval, in exercising its discretion the HFEA had not taken ad-equate account first, of Mrs Blood's right under European law to receive treatment in another Member State,[43] and, secondly, of the fact that there should be 'no further cases where sperm is preserved without consent'.

In 2008, this prediction that there would be no further cases in which sperm was stored without consent was proved wrong. L's husband, H, had died suddenly following routine sur-gery. L and H already had one child and were keen to have a second. An out-of-hours applica-tion was made to the court, and Macur J declared that it would be lawful to remove and store sperm from H's body. This declaration was made on the basis of misinformation provided to Macur J about the scope of the Human Tissue Act 2004. She had been told that the Human Tissue Act permitted posthumous sperm retrieval, with the consent of a qualifying relative. In fact, the Human Tissue Act does not apply to gametes.

Because there was no written consent, H's sperm could not be used in the UK. An applica-tion to the HFEA for the sperm to be exported to a country where it could be used without H's consent was postponed pending L's application to the court to determine the lawfulness of the storage, use, and export of the sperm.

In *L v Human Fertilisation and Embryology Authority*,[44] Charles J found that the evidence that H would have wanted his sperm used posthumously by L was 'at least as compelling as that advanced by Mrs Blood': L and H already had a child together and six days before H's death they had made inquiries about access to IVF, as a result of L's age. Charles J also found that the law was clear, and that both the storage and use of H's sperm in the UK would be un-lawful, but that the HFEA had a wide discretion to permit export. Following this judgment, and taking into account the decision in the *Blood* case, and the fact that L could rely not only on European Treaty rights but also on Articles 8 and 12 of the European Convention on Human Rights, the HFEA permitted export to a clinic in the US.

R (on the application of M) v Human Fertilisation and Embryology Authority was the first case involving a request to export eggs, in order that they could be used in the absence of written consent. A, who had been being treated for cancer, had had her eggs frozen in 2008, and had signed a form permitting their posthumous storage. In January 2010, she had said this to her mother:

> They are never going to let me leave this hospital, Mum; the only way I will get out of here will be in a body bag. I want you to carry my babies. I didn't go through the IVF to save my eggs for nothing. I want you and Dad to bring them up. They will be safe with you. I couldn't have wanted for better parents, I couldn't have done without you.

---

[42] [1997] 2 WLR 806 (CA). [43] At that time, protected by Art 59 of the EC Treaty.
[44] [2008] EWHC 2149 (Fam).

According to A's parents, it was A's wish strong wish that one or more of her eggs should be fertilized with donor sperm and implanted in her mother, who would then bring up the baby, along with A's father. But in the absence of A's written consent to the use of her eggs in her mother's treatment, this would be unlawful. The HFEA's Statutory Approvals Committee refused to permit A's parents to export her eggs to the US. A's parents applied for judicial review, and although this was rejected at first instance, the Court of Appeal found that the Committee had not taken adequate account of evidence of A's wishes.

R (on the application of M) v Human Fertilisation and Embryology Authority[45]

Arden LJ

[T]he Committee wrongly stated that it had no evidence that A had explicitly expressed a wish for her mother to carry her child after her death 'with the possible exception of the comments made in January 2010'. Disregarding for a moment the Committee's description of the January 2010 conversation as a 'possible exception', the statement that there was no evidence on this point is, as I have said, a most surprising conclusion which flies in the face of A's mother's evidence, none of which was rejected. The January 2010 conversation did provide the Committee with evidence that A wanted her mother to be the surrogate mother of her child if she had died ...

The Committee also stated that there was no evidence to support the view that A would have consented to the use of anonymous donor sperm. As already stated, it would be perverse to conclude that A did not realise that there would have to be donor sperm ...

I agree that the Committee should not make inferences which are not fairly capable of being made, but there is nothing in law to prevent it from making appropriate inferences from the evidence or on the basis of the inherent probabilities of the case.

A different solution to the problem that someone who dies suddenly may not have given written consent to the posthumous use of his gametes was adopted recently in *Y v A Healthcare NHS Trust*. Z and his wife Y had one child, and wanted a second. The couple had been undergoing fertility investigations, and they had discussed what would happen if either of them died, when they filled in forms before their appointment at a fertility clinic. Eleven days before they were due to begin a cycle of IVF treatment, Z suffered a catastrophic brain injury in a motorcycle crash. He was not going to recover, and Y wanted sperm samples to be retrieved.

Before he died, the matter came before Knowles J. He was satisfied that Z and Y had a settled intention to have a brother or sister for their son, and that Z had discussed with Y the posthumous use of his sperm, and had agreed to it. As a result, she declared that that the retrieval, storage and use of Z's sperm would be in lawful in his best interests, under the Mental Capacity Act 2005, and directed that a relative (other than Y) should be able to sign the written consent to use on his behalf.

---

[45] [2016] EWCA Civ 611.

Y v A Healthcare NHS Trust[46]

Knowles J

I have also taken account of what Z would choose to do about this issue if he knew that he was catastrophically injured, was being kept alive by means of life-support and was on the point of that medical treatment being withdrawn resulting in his death. It seems to me that Z would have chosen to allow clinicians to retrieve his sperm so that it might be stored and then used after his death so that his little boy might be able to have a brother or sister. That choice was entirely consistent with the evidence before me and consistent with what I had learned about Z's hopes and dreams for a family life with Y and children of their own. I was also satisfied that Z had contemplated what might happen if he died and that family life might not include him in person but might, however, include a child conceived by Y after his death using his sperm. Standing back and applying the law to the facts of this case, I am in no doubt that the decisions I have taken on Z's behalf were in his best interests even though his death was imminent . . .

My order declared that, by reason of his traumatic brain injury, Z lacked capacity to provide his written consent for fertility treatment for the purposes of the HFE Act, such written consent being required for the storage and use (but not for the retrieval) of his gametes. Notwithstanding that Z lacked capacity, I declared that it was lawful for a doctor to retrieve his gametes and lawful for those gametes to be stored both before and after his death on the signing of the relevant consents storage and use and that it was lawful for his gametes and any embryos formed from his gametes to be used after his death. I also declared that the court was satisfied that the requirements of Schedule 3 to the HFE Act in relation to consent were met in those circumstances. My order provided for a relative to sign the relevant consents in accordance with the provisions of sub-paragraph 1(2) of Schedule 3 to the HFE Act.

Under section 39 of the Human Fertilisation and Embryology Act 2008, it is possible for a man to consent to be treated as the father of a child conceived after his death, but only for the purposes of birth registration. It is also possible for a man who was married, or a woman who was in a civil partnership or married to a woman, at the time of an embryo's creation with donated gametes to be treated as the father, or the second legal parent, if that embryo is subsequently used after his or her death. Again, this is solely for the purposes of birth registration, and is possible only if the deceased consented to the embryo's posthumous use and to the posthumous attribution of parenthood.

In the next extract, Kelton Tremellen and Julian Savulescu question the need for explicit consent to the posthumous use of sperm.

Kelton Tremellen and Julian Savulescu[47]

At the moment, we have the situation where the majority of men do not make their views on posthumous conception known to their partner and family, primarily because they have never given it any consideration. This is understandable since most men of reproductive age do not seriously contemplate the possibility of their untimely death. However, when men of reproductive age are asked to give serious consideration to posthumous conception, the evidence

---

[46] [2018] EWCOP 18.
[47] 'Posthumous conception by presumed consent. A pragmatic position for a rare but ethically challenging dilemma' (2016) 3 Reproductive Biomedicine & Society Online 26–9.

to date suggests that the majority are happy to support their partners' use of their sperm posthumously. Therefore, the current default position requiring explicit consent is preventing the majority of women from having the opportunity to use their partner's sperm posthumously, even though it is more likely that he would have supported such an action . . .

We therefore mount an argument that moving to a default position of presumed consent protects the reproductive rights of the majority, where the current standard of explicit consent only protects the rights of the minority (non-consenting men who have not expressed their views to others).

(2) Consent to the Use of Embryos

When embryos are created *in vitro* they will be graded by an embryologist in order to determine which embryos are suitable for use in treatment. Unsuitable embryos can be disposed of, or donated to research. Of the remaining embryos, one or two fresh embryos may be transferred to the woman's uterus, and the rest may be frozen for future use. These embryos can be stored for up to ten years, or for longer if either partner is, or is likely to become prematurely infertile.[48]

Of course, it is possible that the gamete contributors will subsequently disagree about the use of their frozen embryos. The Human Fertilisation and Embryology Act 1990 allows for the variation or withdrawal of consent to the use or storage of an embryo.[49] In practice, this gives whichever partner does not want their embryos to be used in treatment a right of veto over their use.

This provision was challenged in *Evans v United Kingdom*. After Natallie Evans was diagnosed with ovarian cancer, she and her partner Howard Johnston underwent a cycle of IVF treatment resulting in the storage of six embryos. When the couple subsequently split up, Mr Johnston withdrew his consent to the storage and use of the embryos. Ms Evans sought a declaration that the relevant provisions of the 1990 Act were incompatible with her rights under Article 8 of the European Convention on Human Rights. She failed at first instance, and before the Court of Appeal, and her appeals to the ECtHR and to the Grand Chamber were also unsuccessful.

Evans v United Kingdom[50]

Decision of the Grand Chamber

While the applicant contends that her greater physical and emotional expenditure during the IVF process, and her subsequent infertility, entail that her art 8 rights should take precedence over J's, it does not appear to the court that there is any clear consensus on this point . . .

As regards the balance struck between the conflicting art 8 rights of the parties to the IVF treatment, the Grand Chamber, in common with every other court which has examined this case, has great sympathy for the applicant, who clearly desires a genetically related child above all else. However, given the above considerations, including the lack of any European consensus on this point, it does not consider that the applicant's right to respect for the decision to become a parent in the genetic sense should be accorded greater weight than J's right to respect for his decision not to have a genetically-related child with her.

---

[48] Human Fertilisation and Embryology (Statutory Storage Period for Embryos and Gametes) Regulations 2009 section 4.

[49] Schedule 3, para 4.   [50] Application no 6339/05 (2007).

The ECtHR thus affirmed that there were strong public policy justifications—namely the promotion of certainty and the avoidance of arbitrariness and inconsistency—for the inflexibility of the 'bright line' rule in the 1990 Act that requires both partners' consent to an embryo's use and storage.

The dissenting judges in both courts took a different view, and argued that this 'bright line' rule had a disproportionate impact upon Natallie Evans's Article 8 rights. Rosy Thornton agrees, and argues that the Courts were wrong to treat Ms Evans and Mr Johnston as though they were similarly situated.

Rosy Thornton[51]

> To treat as like two such unlike situations does not produce true equality in terms of the law's effects … The bright-line rule itself, though rooted in formal equality, in fact operates inconsistently and arbitrarily in terms of its real, differential impact on the female and male gamete providers in cases such as *Evans*. Second, if a bright-line rule is desirable at all, then why should it be fixed, as it is under the 1990 Act, at the time of implantation rather than allowing male consent to be withdrawn only up to the point of fertilization (as, for instance, in Austria and Estonia)? The latter threshold would both recognize the greater impact of the decision on the female partner and mirror more closely the situation of natural conception.

When it reformed the 1990 Act in 2008, the government chose to retain these consent provisions, so each partner continues to have the right to veto the use of embryos. But under Schedule 3 para 4A, if one party withdraws his or her consent to the use of embryos, the Act now provides for a 12-month 'cooling off period', during which the embryos cannot be used or disposed of without both parties' consent. The hope is that this will enable couples to come to an agreement about the embryos' use or disposal. In practice, however, this scenario is unlikely to arise in the future. Improvements in egg freezing (discussed below) mean that women are no longer likely to freeze embryos before cancer treatment, and their frozen eggs will be available for their future use, without the need for anyone else's consent.

(3) Status of Gametes

In *Yearworth v North Bristol NHS Trust*,[52] the court was faced with the question of whether or not stored gametes, in this case sperm, were property for the purposes of a claim in negligence. Following a reduction in nitrogen levels in the containers that are used to store 'straws' of sperm, the claimants' sperm samples had been thawed, and were no longer suitable for use in treatment.

The claimants sought damages for the loss of their sperm samples, and for the psychiatric disorders that they had suffered as a result. The Court of Appeal invoked the 1990 Act's consent provisions in order to justify its conclusion that 'for the purposes of their claims in negligence, the men had ownership of the sperm which they ejaculated'. Given the emphasis put upon consent, and the freedom people have under the Act to determine what should happen to their gametes, the Court of Appeal found that the rights the men had had in relation to

---

[51] 'European Court of Human Rights: Consent to IVF Treatment' (2008) 6 International Journal of Constitutional Law 317–30.
[52] [2009] EWCA Civ 37.

their stored sperm samples were equivalent to property rights: 'the Act recognises in the men a fundamental feature of ownership, namely that at any time they can require the destruction of the sperm'.

Taschi Keren-Paz argues that the gist of the claim in *Yearworth* is, however, better understood as an interference with the claimants' reproductive autonomy, rather than the destruction of their property.

Tsachi Keren-Paz[53]

[T]he nub of the claimants' complaint was not about the destruction of property, commonly understood ... While the 'peg' for the award of damages was the distress (or the psychiatric injury) stemming from the destruction of property, it is clear that the *raison d'être* of the award is protecting the claimants' reproductive autonomy. The real injury was the loss of the option to become a father and the consequential distress, rather than the destruction of the sperm as property *per se*.

(4) Storage Time Limits

Sections 14(3) and 14(4) of the Human Fertilisation and Embryology Act 1990 provide for a ten year storage time limit for gametes and embryos. This is not because extended storage might damage gametes and embryos, but because indefinite storage would create practical difficulties for clinics, who might never be able to dispose of any unused gametes and embryos. Ex-patients often find it difficult to make the decision to dispose of their genetic material, and the existence of a time limit means that, after ten years, the decision will be taken for them.

Of course, if someone is storing gametes or embryos because they are about to undergo treatment for cancer that will leave them infertile, ten years' storage might be insufficient. As a result, under the Human Fertilisation and Embryology (Statutory Storage Period for Embryos and Gametes) Regulations 2009, ten-year extensions, up to a total maximum of 55 years, are possible, provided that the person has consented to extended storage, and a registered medical practitioner has given a written opinion that the person 'is prematurely infertile or is likely to become prematurely infertile'.[54]

If a child's gametes are retrieved before he is old enough to provide a valid consent, the consent of someone with parental responsibility is treated as the child's own 'effective consent',[55] until he is old enough to make his own decision about continued storage. It will be easy to justify the retrieval itself as a procedure which is in his best interests, unless he is unlikely to live to adulthood.

While the storage time limit and the option for extension is largely unproblematic for sperm and embryos, it creates difficulties for what is known as 'social egg freezing', discussed further below. If a woman freezes her eggs at the age of 25, she is unlikely to be prematurely infertile at the age of 35, and hence her eggs would have to be disposed of before she is likely to want to use them in treatment. The poor fit between the storage time limit and social egg freezing is

---

[53] 'Compensating Injury to Autonomy in English Negligence Law: Inconsistent Recognition' (2018) 26 Medical Law Review 585–609.

[54] Human Fertilisation and Embryology (Statutory Storage Period for Embryos and Gametes) Regulations 2009, regulations 3(3) and 4(3).

[55] Schedule 3, para 8(2ZA).

not deliberate: social egg freezers were simply not within the contemplation of the drafters of the 2009 Regulations. It is therefore to be hoped that it will be remedied by an amendment to the Regulations, to allow for extensions to the ten-year limit if a woman has not yet completed her family or decided whether she wants to use her eggs in treatment.

(5) Egg Freezing

Until recently, while sperm and embryos could be used successfully after being frozen, success rates using frozen eggs were very poor. This has changed following the development of a new fast-freezing technique, known as vitrification, which means that success rates for IVF using frozen eggs are now comparable to success rates with fresh eggs. As a result, 'social' egg freezing has emerged as an option for women concerned about their age-related fertility decline. Some employers have even started to offer egg freezing as a workplace benefit.[56]

Some commentators are concerned that social egg freezing involves the 'medicalization' of a social problem: that is, if women are delaying having children until an age at which it is difficult to conceive, would making it easier for working women to have babies be preferable to encouraging women to undergo expensive and invasive egg retrieval? Against this, it could be argued that the decision about when to have children is a deeply personal one, and that for many women, the biologically optimum time is not the right time in terms of their personal circumstances and life plans.

In reality, interview studies with women who have chosen to freeze their eggs have found that very few do so because it was difficult to combine motherhood and a career in their twenties. Rather, as Kylie Baldwin and Marcia Inhorn explain in the next extracts, women generally freeze their eggs because they have not yet found a male partner who is willing and able to commit to fatherhood.

Kylie Baldwin[57]

All the research participants had achieved some success and security in their professional lives. Many were financially stable, had travelled and become emotionally ready to commit to motherhood. However, what the participants reported as 'absent' from their lives was a suitable partner with whom they could pursue parenthood. The importance of pursuing parenthood with the right partner was reflected across all the participant accounts . . .

As several women noted, the possibility of pursuing parenthood with either the wrong partner or without the male partner's 'buy-in' was seen as foolish and unlikely to produce the family unit the women desired . . .

Whilst all the research participants had been in relationships with male partners in the past, a few of which were serious and spanned several years, they reported that they had found it difficult to find a male partner as equally committed to parenthood as they were. Instead, several reported that they had encountered negative attitudes from men with regards to settling down and pursuing parenthood. For many women it was the difficulties they had experienced in finding the right partner whilst aware of their declining fertility which led them to pursue social egg freezing.

[56] Mark Tran, 'Apple and Facebook offer to freeze eggs for female employees' The Guardian, 15 October 2014.
[57] ' "I suppose I think to myself, that's the best way to be a mother": how ideologies of parenthood shape women's reproductive intentions and their use of social egg freezing' (2017) 22 Sociological Research Online.

Marcia C Inhorn[58]

> Women seem to see egg freezing as a kind of 'stop-gap' measure to stop the 'ticking' of the biological clock while still holding out for the possibility of a future happy marital relationship ... [O]nline dating seems to create a limitless marketplace of options, but one that actually works in favor of college-educated men, who, instead of committing to one woman, 'keep their options open' and 'play the field'. Unfortunately, egg freezing may increase women's illusions about their ability to eventually find a 'perfect' partner while putting their fertility on hold ...
>
> Beyond the high costs of egg freezing, the procedure itself involves a significant degree of bodily discomfort and lifestyle disruption ... As 'half an IVF cycle,' egg freezing is time consuming (i.e. several weeks of medication and multiple IVF clinic visits) and potentially risky (i.e., involving rare but serious reactions to hormonal medications) ...
>
> Egg freezing, furthermore, involves difficult decisions about egg disposition, either through prolonged storage, eventual disposal, donation to other women, or donation to research ...
>
> Among older women who have frozen their eggs for elective reasons, there are additional considerations about age and the limits of motherhood. Egg freezing effectively allows women to postpone their childbearing well into their postmenopausal years. Indeed, egg freezing gives women in their 40s and 50s—and potentially 60s, 70s, or 80s—the chance to bear children, because 'egg age' rather than 'womb age' appears to be the crucial variable in a women's ability to carry a pregnancy to term.

In practice, the average age at women freeze their eggs is around 37. This is not the optimum clinical age at which to freeze, because women's fertility is already in decline, so more cycles of egg retrieval may be necessary in order to retrieve sufficient eggs to give a reasonable chance of pregnancy in the future. Freezing in one's late 30s is, however, be sensible in relation to the ten-year storage time limit, since it will give a women until her late forties to use her eggs.

It is also important that clinics do not misrepresent egg freezing as a guaranteed way to preserve one's fertility. A woman will only be able to conceive using her previously frozen eggs if she undergoes IVF, and, as we have seen, most IVF cycles do not result in a live birth.

(6) Gamete Donation

Around 10 per cent of treatment cycles in the UK involve the use of donor gametes. A number of distinctive questions are raised by gamete donation, such as whether donors should be anonymous, and whether they should be paid.

(a) Informal donation

All egg donation in the UK necessarily takes place in licensed and regulated clinics. In contrast, it is possible for men to donate sperm informally, without being subject to any regulation at all. In recent years, informal donation arrangements between strangers are becoming more common as a result of introduction websites—akin to dating websites—through which potential donors and recipients make contact with each other. These websites are subject to regulation only if they involve the 'procurement' of sperm, for which a licence from the HFEA

---

[58] See also Marcia C Inhorn, 'The Egg Freezing Revolution? Gender, Technology, and Fertility Preservation in the Twenty-First Century' in *Emerging Trends in the Social and Behavioral Sciences: An Interdisciplinary, Searchable, and Linkable Resource*, Robert Scott and Marlis Buchmann (eds) (John Wiley & Sons, 2017).

is necessary. If sperm is 'procured' without a licence, a criminal offence is committed: in 2010, two men who had run a website which arranged couriers to deliver sperm were convicted of procuring sperm without a licence, and given suspended jail sentences.[59] Introduction websites, in which would-be donors and recipients get in touch with each other and make their own arrangements, do not involve procurement, and are therefore unregulated.

There are risks associated with informal sperm donation arrangements. There is no vetting of would-be donors, some of whom advertise themselves as offering 'NI [natural intercourse] only'. Sperm is not routinely tested for HIV and common genetic disorders. There is no limit on how many families can be produced from one donor, and there is no register of information for donor-conceived individuals. As we can see from the case of *M v F (Legal Paternity)*, a case discussed later in relation to the attribution of legal fatherhood, these arrangements can also go badly wrong.

M v F (Legal Paternity)[60]

Peter Jackson J

[R]egulation is broadly successful in protecting participants from exploitation and from health risks, while providing some certainty about legal relationships. Codes of Practice limit the number of times a person can donate sperm: in this country a donor can normally donate to a maximum of 10 families. In comparison, participants in informal arrangements have to judge all risks for themselves. They may not be in a good position to do so. Those seeking to conceive may be in a vulnerable state and not all donors are motivated by altruism.

This informal trade is not unlawful, but it is not regulated in any meaningful way. The website in this case ... is a case in point. It charges not inconsiderable fees to those looking for donors while projecting a rose-tinted account of successful, problem-free conception. It supplies a document entitled 'Donor Agreement' that purports to record agreement that the donor will have no rights in relation to the child and that the mother *and the child* will have no rights against the donor in any circumstances. The concern is that documents of this kind create the false impression that these informal arrangements are somehow regulated ...

In reality, on the evidence I have heard, there is no effective control whatever of the activities resulting from websites of this kind: for example, although it is said to be a cardinal rule of the website that it is 'AI only', Mr F's own public profile on the site openly advertised him as offering 'AI and NI'.

The present case amply demonstrates the risks involved for all participants in this process. It has taken a high toll on the well-being of each of the adults and has threatened Mr F's career. The costs are enormous. The parties have spent almost £300,000 in legal fees.

One obvious source of conflict is if the parties have different expectations of the arrangement. In *Re X (No 2: Application for Contact by the Biological Father)*,[61] the child's parents, HS and KS, who were civil partners and X's legal parents, claimed that they had wanted a known donor. The sperm donor, JK, thought that they had been looking for a co-parent. Relations between the parents and JK had broken down catastrophically, and the Children's Guardian told the court: 'it is unfortunate that the parties did not fully discuss matters before conception.

---

[59] BBC News, 'Suspended jail term for illegal sperm website pair' 12 October 2010.
[60] [2013] EWHC 1901 (Fam).   [61] [2015] EWFC 84.

It appears that the differing expectations caused great difficulty during the early weeks in X's life.' HS had lost her job, and was scared to leave the house, and the couple had been forced to sell their home. Theis J made an order for JK to have indirect contact with X once a year (not to include photographs for at least three years, after JK had posted pictures of X on Facebook immediately after being warned in court not to do so).

Informal sperm donation may be cheaper than treatment in a licensed clinic, but cost is not the only reason why people seek informal donors. Vasanti Jadva et al's survey of members of an introduction website found that many of them were looking for someone with whom to raise a child.

Vasanti Jadva et al[62]

Overall, the motivations for seeking a co-parenting arrangement that were ranked as most important were 'Wanting the child to know both biological parents' and 'Wanting to know the person who provides the sperm/egg to create the child' ...

A particular concern arising from these findings is the length of time prospective co-parents planned to be in contact with each other prior to attempting conception. Most expected to be in contact for a few months which raises the question of whether this allows sufficient time to establish a sustainable co-parenting relationship ... The open-ended responses revealed that participants' expectations of co-parenting were idealised in that they wanted a friendship with the co-parent and a happy loving family in which all parents were accepted and the child was loved.

In *JB v KS (Contact: Parental Responsibility)*, a case in which the agreement had broken down, Hayden J explained why the mother had chosen to find a sperm donor via an introduction website, rather than seeking treatment in a licensed centre.

JB v KS (Contact: Parental Responsibility)[63]

Hayden J

In her evidence she told me that she was very aware that there were less personal options for acquiring semen donation in organisations regulated by the HFEA in which she would not have to run the gauntlet of potential future disagreements. She told me that she wanted to identify a father who would be a 'real' and 'physical presence' at stages throughout the child's life rather than 'just a name' that her son would be entitled to know when he reached his majority.

Tabitha Freeman et al found that online sperm donors were not an homogenous group, and that heterosexual men had a preference for anonymous donation, while gay and bisexual donors more commonly wanted to have contact with the child.

---

[62] '"Friendly allies in raising a child": a survey of men and women seeking elective co-parenting arrangements via an online connection website' (2015) 30 Human Reproduction 1896–906.
[63] [2015] EWHC 180 (Fam).

Tabitha Freeman et al[64]

> This study indicates that online sperm donors form a demographically diverse group with primarily altruistic motivations for donating. These donors varied in their attitudes towards donation, with marked differences arising according to sexual orientation. Gay and bisexual men expressed a preference for open-identity donation and were more likely to be in contact with children conceived with their donated sperm, whilst heterosexual men more frequently sought anonymous donation. The website was perceived as facilitating these different goals by allowing greater choice and control over the donation process than clinics. Heterosexual men were also more likely to favour natural insemination compared with the gay and bisexual group who preferred donation at a clinic, although the vast majority of men who conceived children had used artificial insemination in practice.
>
> Most strikingly, a sizeable minority pursued online donation to facilitate their anonymity and minimal contact with recipient families. The meaning of anonymity in this context requires further investigation: as well as referring to anonymity from the child, donors and recipients may make practical arrangements to conceal the donor's identity from the recipient as well ...
>
> An overall finding is that, despite the concerns raised, online sperm donation is being utilized in large numbers: within this sample, 70 men had successfully donated and helped create over 150 children. Furthermore, a small proportion of these donations had occurred in clinics and an even greater number of donors wished for clinic donation, particularly gay and bisexual men. This demonstrates that the distinction between 'clinic' and 'online' sperm donation is being blurred in practice and highlights the importance of considering ways that online donors may be further incorporated into clinic treatments.

(b) Anonymity

Until 2005, most gamete donation was anonymous. Children born following anonymous donation can be given access to non-identifying information, such as the donor's ethnicity and occupation, and, once they reach the age of 16, they can ask the HFEA whether they were born following fertility treatment, and if they are related to a prospective spouse, civil partner, or 'person with whom the applicant is in an intimate physical relationship or with whom the applicant proposes to enter into an intimate physical relationship'.[65]

In the past, anonymity was believed to be in the interests of donors, recipients, and children. It shielded donors from unwanted contact with their offspring, and protected the privacy and security of the recipient family. It also helped to persuade young men, often medical students, to donate sperm.

Attitudes have changed, however, and donor-conceived people's interest in access to information about their genetic origins is widely believed to trump other considerations. In *R (on the application of Rose) v Secretary of State for Health*,[66] the court was faced with the question of whether a child's right to information about her genetic parentage might be protected by Article 8 of the Human Rights Act 1998. Scott Baker J accepted that Article 8 was engaged, but the full hearing to determine whether the failure to supply such information amounted to a breach of Article 8 was superseded by the government's decision to abolish anonymity.

Since 2005, all gamete donors must be identifiable. As a result, the profile of sperm donors has changed: it is less common for students to donate, and more common for donors to have

---

[64] 'Online sperm donation: a survey of the demographic characteristics, motivations, preferences and experiences of sperm donors on a connection website' (2016) 31 Human Reproduction 2082–9.
[65] Section 31ZB(2).   [66] [2002] EWHC 1593 (Admin).

children of their own. In order to meet demand, clinics also import sperm from foreign sperm banks.

Children born following non-anonymous donation will have access to identifying information about their donor once they reach the age of 18. Anonymity was not removed retrospectively, but pre-2005 donors can register their willingness to be identified. This means that some children will be able to access identifying information before 2023, when the first children conceived after anonymity was abolished reach the age of 18.

Of course, a child will only be able to apply to the HFEA for identifying information if she knows, or suspects, that she was conceived using donated gametes. While children born to lesbian couples or to single women, will be 'put on notice' that a third party played a role in their conception,[67] unless a child born to heterosexual parents is told about the circumstances of her conception, she will assume that she was conceived naturally.

Although there has undoubtedly been a trend towards openness, many parents of children conceived using donated gametes do not tell their children. In one study of 36 donor insemination families and 32 egg donation families, 'about half of the children conceived by egg donation and nearly three-quarters of those conceived by donor insemination remained unaware that the person they know as their mother or father is not, in fact, their genetic parent'.[68] Even among parents who intend to tell their children, many do not, in fact, do so, perhaps because 'parents who wait for "the right moment" are unlikely to ever find such a time'.[69]

Given widespread non-disclosure, the right to identifying information may make little difference to a significant proportion of children conceived using donated gametes. All possible solutions to this problem are problematic, however. The use of donated gametes could be recorded on the child's birth certificate, or the child could be informed by letter when she reaches the age of 18. During the 2008 debates, there was some support in parliament for the first option, but it is hard to see how this could be in a child's best interests. Not only would endorsing birth certificates unnecessarily stigmatize children, it might lead to them finding out that they were donor-conceived in a shocking and unhelpful way. Many people only see their birth certificate when they need it to obtain a passport, to get married, or because a new employer asks to see it. Sometimes people come across their birth certificates for the first time when going through their parents' personal effects after their deaths.

Instead, the hope is that the removal of anonymity will help to promote a culture of openness. Section 13(6C) of the 1990 Act specifies that counselling given to couples having treatment with donated gametes 'must include such information as is proper about the importance of informing any resulting child at an early age that the child results from the gametes of a person who is not a parent of the child, and suitable methods of informing such a child of that fact'. And the Code of Practice makes it clear that patients should be strongly advised of the merits of being frank with their offspring from early childhood.

---

[67] Andrew Bainham, 'Arguments about Parentage' (2008) 67 Cambridge Law Journal 322–51.

[68] Jennifer Readings et al, 'Secrecy, disclosure and everything in-between: decisions of parents of children conceived by donor insemination, egg donation and surrogacy' (2011) 22 Reproductive BioMedicine Online 485–95.

[69] Maria Anna Tallandini et al, 'Parental disclosure of assisted reproductive technology (ART) conception to their children: a systematic and meta-analytic review' (2016) 31 Human Reproduction 1275–87.

HFEA 9th Code of Practice

20.7 The centre should tell people who seek treatment with donated gametes or embryos that it is best for any resulting child to be told about their origin early in childhood. There is evidence that finding out suddenly, later in life, about donor origins can be emotionally damaging to children and to family relations.

20.8 The centre should encourage and prepare patients to be open with their children from an early age about how they were conceived. The centre should give patients information about how counselling may allow them to explore the implications of treatment, in particular how information may be shared with any resultant children.

Elena Ilioi et al's research confirms the Code of Practice's claim that later disclosure is worse for children than early disclosure.

Elena Ilioi et al[70]

The findings showed that adolescents who were unaware of their biological origins did not differ from adolescents who had been told about the circumstances of their birth (at any age), or from naturally conceived adolescents, in terms of psychological wellbeing or the quality of family relationships. However, there appears to be variation within families formed through reproductive donation. When the age at which adolescents had learned of their biological origins was examined, more positive family relationships and higher levels of psychological wellbeing were found for adolescents who had been told at a younger age. Specifically, families in which parents had started the process of disclosure before age 7 showed more positive parenting in terms of maternal warmth and sensitivity, and less negative parenting in terms of conflict, as assessed by a standardised interview designed to assess quality of parenting . . .

From a practical perspective, the findings suggest that parents' concerns about telling their young children about the circumstances of their birth are unfounded. Indeed, it appears that the earlier that disclosure takes place, the more positive the outcomes for children and their parents. Thus, just as adoptive parents are encouraged be open with their children about their adoption from the start, it seems that parents of children born through reproductive donation should similarly be advised to begin to talk to their children about their origins in their preschool years.

In contrast, Guido Pennings points out that evidence that later disclosure is harmful does not establish that not disclosing at all is harmful, and hence he questions the received wisdom that that disclosure is always in the child's best interests.

[70] 'The role of age of disclosure of biological origins in the psychological wellbeing of adolescents conceived by reproductive donation: a longitudinal study from age 1 to age 14' (2017) 58 Journal of Child Psychology and Psychiatry 315–24.

Guido Pennings[71]

It has been argued that secrecy will have an adverse effect on family relationships and, consequently, on the child. However, as far as the present evidence goes, this belief has proven to be false in the case of donor conception. The studies that compared disclosing and nondisclosing families showed no differences, neither in child well-being, nor in parent-child relationships. So the claim made by counselors and psychologists that secrecy interferes with relationship dynamics and child adjustment has been shown to be wrong, at least in the early and middle childhood years . . .

The question 'are there any measurable, stable differences in psychological well-being of donor offspring who are informed of the mode of their conception compared to those who are not?' should be answered in the negative.

Given the lack of evidence, the current directive position on disclosure is in essence a moral conviction, based on mainly deontological arguments. The absence of evidence of harm to children should in a pluralistic society be a reason for restraint. For counselors and practitioners, this restraint is moreover strongly supported by the general principle of non-directiveness. For the government, restraint is appropriate out of respect for the moral convictions of others, in this case the parents. There might be good reasons to argue for disclosure but the best interest of the child is not one of them.

It could, however, be argued that there is always a risk that children who are not told about their donor conception will find out anyway, especially since most parents who do not tell their children have told *someone else*. In addition, as Joyce Harper et al point out, direct-to-consumer genetic testing may increase the likelihood of inadvertent disclosure.

Joyce C Harper, Debbie Kennett, and Dan Reisel[72]

One such case has already come to light as a result of a family testing at 23andMe and receiving unexpected DNA results. Pam and John Branum's daughter, Annie, had been conceived by artificial insemination, supposedly using John's sperm, at Reproductive Medical Technologies, a fertility clinic in Salt Lake City, Utah. However, the 23andMe test results showed that Annie was not John's biological daughter . . . This led to the discovery that John's semen had been substituted with the semen of Thomas Lippert, an employee at the fertility clinic.

Parents using donor conception need to be fully informed that their children's DNA will identify that they are not the biological parents. Furthermore, they should be encouraged to disclose the use of donor gametes to their children . . .

The same is also true for the donors themselves. Whether they are donating in a country that uses anonymous donation or not, donors should be informed that their anonymity is not guaranteed. They may be traced if their DNA, or that of a relative, is added to a database. There will also need to be consideration of any children that a donor might have, as they might find out their parent was a donor from such publicly available information.

---

[71] 'Disclosure of donor conception, age of disclosure and the well-being of donor offspring' (2017) 32 Human Reproduction 969–73.
[72] 'The end of donor anonymity: how genetic testing is likely to drive anonymous gamete donation out of business' (2016) 31 Human Reproduction 1135–40.

A comparison is often made between gamete donation and adoption, where openness about adoption is widely accepted to be in the child's best interests. But, as I Glenn Cohen has pointed out, a comparison could instead be made with sexual reproduction, through which it is estimated that between two and five per cent of children are mistaken about the true identity of their genetic fathers. If we are serious about children's right to know their origins, should we therefore set up what Cohen calls a 'one night stand' registry: 'why not require every individual who engages in coital sex with a fixed probability of conception to put his or her name and contact information in a registry?'[73]

(c) Opening the register

The HFEA's register of information can be 'opened' in order to provide information to donor-conceived people and to donors, and in 2017–18, there were 238 requests for information from the register.[74]. Requests for information under the 1990 Act became possible in 2007 when the first children born since the Act came into force in 1991 reached the age of 16, and could ask if they were related to a potential spouse. In 2009, the first children became 18, and could ask for further non-identifying information. In practice, donor-conceived individuals are more likely to seek information about the circumstances of their conception when they are contemplating marriage or starting a family themselves, rather than when they turn 18.

More requests for information are also likely when children conceived using identifiable donors become old enough to access information. When this happens, offspring will be told of the donor's:

(a) full name (and any previous name);

(b) date of birth, and town or district where born;

(c) last known postal address.

Section 31ZA(3) of the Act provides that, before information about donor conception is given, the recipient of the information must have had an opportunity to receive counselling.

It is also now possible for donor-conceived offspring to find out non-identifying information about the number, age, and sex of any half-siblings, and, if they and the other siblings consent, to find out identifying information about each other. Despite having the same genetic connection, the donor's own children do not have the same right to information about their half-siblings.

Donors can be told the number, age, and sex of children born following their donation, but not their identity. It is also possible to forewarn donors that a person conceived using their gametes has made a request for identifying information, though in practice this may be difficult, if the donor's contact details have changed in the intervening decades.

(d) Payment

Since 2011, sperm donors have been entitled to a fixed sum of £35 per clinic visit to cover all of their expenses, and egg donors to a fixed sum of £750 per cycle of donation, again including all expenses. This 'one size fits all' payment reduces the paperwork associated with processing expense claims, but it inevitably means that women who have few or no expenses will receive

---

[73] I Glenn Cohen, 'Response: Rethinking Sperm-Donor Anonymity: Of Changed Selves, Non-Identity, and One-Night Stands' (2012) 100 Georgetown Law Journal 431.

[74] *Annual report and accounts 2017-18* (HFEA, 2018).

more 'compensation' than women who have to pay for expensive train journeys or childcare, or whose income will be affected by taking time off work.

Modest compensation is believed to be fair to donors, who undergo a series of medical tests and who will have to make several visits to the clinic, and, in the case of egg donors, undergo an invasive surgical procedure, while not offering an incentive capable of 'overbearing their will'. An Ravelingien et al's study of Belgian recipients of sperm found that most recipients believed that donors should be compensated, provided that they did not receive 'too much'.

An Ravelingien et al[75]

Although the participants claimed that the donor should receive some payment, at the same time, it seemed essential that donors are not paid too much … [T]he amount must be modest enough to avoid attracting donors who were motivated only by the money. In the end, their donor should be driven by principles and intentions to help, 'an altruistic donor with a good heart' …

Our results suggest that sperm donors … are considered legitimate only when they have a central desire to help families. The participants assumed that a mere focus on financial gain would attract the 'wrong kind of donor': lazy opportunists, people who are only interested in the money and don't realize what is important in life. Underlying these fears is apparently the wish to foster a favourable image of the 'genetic father' of their (future) child. They wanted to view their donor as someone with high moral standards, someone who is helpful and caring rather than egotistic and materialistic. It is possible that such a positive image is emotionally desirable when talking and thinking about one's family. It may also have to do with genetic deterministic assumptions about the heritability of certain traits … [I]t was clear the participants wanted to envisage their donor as a distant, albeit good person.

Egg-sharing schemes involve a woman who needs IVF treatment agreeing to donate half of the eggs retrieved during one cycle in return for free or much cheaper treatment for herself. Given inadequate NHS funding, these schemes are attractive to women who need treatment, but cannot afford it. Nevertheless, it is clear that egg-sharing schemes involve substantial, albeit indirect, payment for egg donation. In the next extract, Stephen Wilkinson argues that it does not make sense to effectively pay egg-sharers £5,000 for their eggs, while limiting non-patient egg donors to £750.

Stephen Wilkinson[76]

The consistency problem is most simply expressed in a question. If £2,500 or £5,000 in money is an inducement for egg donors, then how can £2,500 or £5,000 in benefits-in-kind *not* be an inducement for egg sharers? Similarly, the Threshold Problem is perhaps best understood as a question: if £750 is not an inducement to donate eggs, then what makes £2,500 or £5,000 an inducement? What we need (or what the HFEA needs) is a threshold (and, what is more, a non-arbitrary and justified threshold) such that sums of money below it do not constitute an undue inducement to donate eggs, while sums above it do.

---

[75] 'Recipients' views on payment of sperm donors' (2015) 31 Reproductive BioMedicine Online 225–31.
[76] 'Is the HFEA's Policy on Compensating Egg Donors and Egg Sharers Defensible?' (2013) 21 Medical Law Review 173–212.

It has been suggested that, although egg sharing does not pose any additional clinical risks to women, it might be difficult for a woman whose own treatment failed to come to terms with another woman's successful treatment with her eggs. This is not supported by the evidence, however, which indicates that egg sharers feel considerable empathy for other infertile women.

Zeynep B Gürtin, Kamal K Ahuja, and Susan Golombok[77]

Contrary to expectations, however, none of these women [donors whose own treatment had failed while the recipient had conceived] expressed negative feelings regarding their recipient's conception, and three explicitly reported positive feelings (although one noted that she was 'upset at first'). Although the number of women in this category is very small, the data are nevertheless important. Considered in conjunction with the open-ended messages donors would write to their recipients if they could, which were 'well-wishing' in nature (as reported earlier), and findings from this study on egg-sharers' retrospective assessments and the very low levels of regret even among unsuccessful donors we can begin to paint a picture of participants in egg-sharing schemes as more robust, less fragile and much more positive about their experiences than some critics had feared.

In the US, egg donors are paid substantial sums of money, typically between $5,000 and $10,000 per donation, with higher sums reported for Ivy League graduates. Men receive much less, typically around $100 per donation. Drawing upon her research with US sperm banks and egg agencies, Rene Almeling argues that differences in the market between eggs and sperm are not simply the result of biological differences between men and women.

Rene Almeling[78]

When a woman calls her donation 'just an egg', she is removing herself from any suspicion of being a bad mother, the kind who would sell her baby, and underscoring her contribution to the recipient's motherhood project, a contribution she defines as a 'huge gift' . . .

Clocking in at the bank on a regular basis, men must produce high-count samples, and they hear little about recipients. As a result, sperm donors conceptualize donation as a job, and the fact that payment is based on bodily performance leaves them feeling like 'assets' or 'resources' for the sperm bank. Drawing on broader cultural understandings of paternity, they offer straightforward definitions of themselves as fathers to offspring . . .

In this market, gendered cultural norms of maternal femininity and paternal masculinity operate in complicated ways, some of which seem almost contradictory. Relying on such norms, egg agencies recruit women who express altruistic motivations that are consistent with nurturing caregiving, but staffers expect donors to stop short of actually seeing themselves as mothers. Sperm banks frame donation as a job, reflecting cultural expectations that men be productive breadwinners, but they, too, do not want sperm donors defining themselves as fathers who will be responsible for offspring. These organizational practices result from the *selective* mobilization of gendered ideals, with egg agencies and sperm banks drawing on some

---

[77] 'Emotional and relational aspects of egg-sharing: egg-share donors' and recipients' feelings about each other, each others' treatment outcome, and any resulting children' (2012) 27 Human Reproduction 1690–701.
[78] *Sex Cells: The Medical Market for Eggs and Sperm* (University of California Press, 2011) 167–8.

elements of maternal femininity and paternal masculinity to manage donors. And it is the confluence of those organizational practices with the broader cultural norms that lead sperm donors to simultaneously see themselves as fathers and feel like 'assets', while egg donors can simultaneously consider their donation to be 'just an egg' and a 'huge gift'.

(e) Screening and number of offspring

The Code of Practice refers centres to professional guidelines on age limits, which currently state that eggs should not be taken from donors aged 36 or over, and sperm should not be taken from donors aged 41 or over.[79] Older male donors can be used, provided that reasons are recorded,[80] while older female donors should be used only in exceptional circumstances.[81] All donors must be negative for HIV and hepatitis.[82] Recruiting centres should take a medical and family history from each prospective donor, and consider whether to accept a donor who cannot give a full and accurate family history.[83]

The gametes from one donor can be used to create up to ten families, though in practice, this upper limit is seldom reached. Donors are entitled to choose to set a lower limit, and this would be the norm for known donors, who donate their gametes only in order to create one (named) family. The British Fertility Society has suggested—in the light of the shortage of donated sperm in the UK—that it would make sense to set a higher limit than ten families, drawing attention to the fact that in the Netherlands, which has a smaller and less geographically dispersed population, the upper limit is 25.[84] Against this, others argue that it may be challenging for children to come to terms with the prospect of having a very large number of half-siblings.

In the next extract, Jenni Millbank suggests that the evidence does not support the claim that the limit should be based upon a 'manageable' number of future relationships between donor and children.

Jenni Millbank[85]

[A] a new rationale for family limits has arisen in anticipation of future contact following donor identity disclosure, both between donor and offspring and between offspring. This new rationale posits containing the number of genetic relatives so that the number of available contacts is manageable, in particular to protect the psychological well-being of offspring. Some versions of this rationale have slipped over from anticipation of possible contact to embedded assumptions about the kinds of relationships that will ensue, with some proposing lower family numbers so that 'meaningful relationships' can be created and maintained or traditional families resembled. The limited available research on the experiences of donor conceived individuals and families in seeking contact through voluntary registers to date does not bear out these latter assumptions. Not all offspring desire contact with donors or other offspring. Of those who did pursue contact, and whose parents pursued it early on their behalf, in existing studies most contact was limited or periodic and made through email rather than

---

[79] Para 11.2   [80] Para 11.4   [81] Para 11.3   [82] Licence Condition T50.
[83] Code of Practice, para 11.10.
[84] British Fertility Society, 'Working party on sperm donation services in the UK' (2008) 11 Human Fertility 147–58.
[85] 'Numerical Limits in Donor Conception Regimes: Genetic Links and "Extended Family" in the Era of Identity Disclosure' (2014) 22 Medical Law Review 325–36.

face-to-face meetings. Seeking information and a sense of understanding the connection or link appears to be the dominant motivation for those initiating contact in previous studies, rather than the desire for an intimate or on-going relationship.

(h) PARENTAGE

A further special feature of treatment with donated gametes is the separation of genetic and social parenthood, thus necessitating a mechanism through which the child's legal parents can be identified. While the test for legal motherhood is clear and unambiguous, for fathers and 'second legal parents' (in the case of same-sex couples), the rules are more complicated.

An added complexity is the way in which the 2008 Act's changes to the rules on parenthood were brought into force. Sections 27 and 28 of the 1990 Act remain on the face of the statute, because these provisions describe the ascription of parenthood for children born before April 2009. The new parenthood provisions apply only to children whose mothers were treated with donated sperm after April 2009, and they have not been incorporated into the 1990 Act like the other 2008 amendments. Instead, they are to be found in the free-standing Human Fertilisation and Embryology Act 2008.

(1) Maternity

At common law,[86] and under both the 1990 Act (section 27) and the 2008 Act, the woman who gives birth to a child is her mother.

Human Fertilisation and Embryology Act 2008 section 33

33(1) The woman who is carrying or has carried a child as a result of the placing in her of an embryo or of sperm and eggs, and no other woman, is to be treated as the mother of the child.

Section 47 of the 2008 Act further spells out that a woman cannot be treated as a child's parent merely because of egg donation. In some ways, this is redundant. Given the clarity of the rule that the woman who gives birth is the child's mother, an egg donor could never be treated as the mother of any child born following egg donation. The reason for this provision is so that lesbian couples are clear that, for both of them to acquire parenthood, they will need to fulfil the agreed parenthood conditions, or be spouses or civil partners. A lesbian couple might assume that if one woman gives birth to a child created using the other woman's egg, then they would both be the child's legal parents, but the non-gestational genetic 'mother' could acquire parenthood only via marriage, civil partnership, or the agreed parenthood conditions.

It is also irrelevant that the egg donation took place in a country with different rules about parenthood. If a woman gives birth to a child in the UK, she is the child's mother.

---

[86] *The Ampthill Peerage Case* [1977] AC 547.

(2) Paternity

The special rules governing paternity only apply where the mother has conceived through artificial insemination or IVF.

Human Fertilisation and Embryology Act 2008 section 34[87]

> (1) Sections 35 to 47 apply, in the case of a child who is being or has been carried by a woman (referred to in those sections as 'W') as a result of the placing in her of an embryo or of sperm and eggs or her artificial insemination, to determine who is to be treated as the other parent of the child.

The artificial insemination does not need to have taken place in a licensed clinic. Hence, these provisions can apply to children conceived as a result of informal sperm donation, provided that conception was not the result of sexual intercourse. In *M v F (Legal Paternity)*,[88] a case we encountered earlier in the context of internet introduction websites, the question for the court was whether the child's legal father was the sperm donor (if conception had been through sexual intercourse), or the mother's husband (if conception had been the result of artificial insemination). Although this was a simple question of fact, it was one on which the accounts of the mother and the donor differed.

Resolving this question was problematic not only because of the absence of witnesses, but also because the judge found that both parties had 'over long periods of time been untruthful, devious and manipulative'. The mother alleged that she had sex with the donor on multiple occasions and that, on some occasions, this had been non-consensual. The donor claimed that the child's conception had been through artificial insemination, although he admitted to having had sexual intercourse with the mother while she was pregnant by him for the second time, her first pregnancy having been terminated after her husband reacted violently to the news of her pregnancy. Peter Jackson J found that 'sexual intercourse took place between Ms M and Mr F on all occasions bar the first meeting', and he therefore declared 'that the child was conceived by ordinary sexual intercourse and that in consequence Mr F is not only his biological father but also his legal parent'.

(a) Married couples

If the woman receiving treatment is married to a man, the presumption in section 35 of the 2008 Act (section 28(2) of the 1990 Act) applies, and the mother's husband will be the child's father unless he did not consent to her treatment.

Human Fertilisation and Embryology Act 2008 section 35

> 35(1) If—
>
> (a) at the time of the placing in her of the embryo or of the sperm and eggs or of her artificial insemination, W was a party to a marriage, and

---

[87] For children conceived before April 2009, section 28 of the Human Fertilisation and Embryology Act 1990 contains the same wording.

[88] [2013] EWHC 1901 (Fam).

(b) the creation of the embryo carried by her was not brought about with the sperm of the other party to the marriage, then, subject to section 38(2) to (4), the other party to the marriage is to be treated as the father of the child unless it is shown that he did not consent to the placing in her of the embryo or the sperm and eggs or to her artificial insemination (as the case may be).

(b) Unmarried fathers before April 2009

Where a child's mother was treated with donated sperm before April 2009, and the mother is not married, under section 28(3) of the 1990 Act, her male partner will be the child's father if they were provided with treatment services 'together'. At first sight, this wording is puzzling because the partner of a woman who receives treatment with donor sperm is not provided with any treatment himself. In practice, a man will acquire fatherhood under this section if he and his partner had jointly requested treatment 'as a couple'.[89]

(c) Agreed fatherhood conditions after April 2009

Where the woman having treatment is not married or in a civil partnership, and wishes a man to be the father of a child conceived using donated sperm, the agreed fatherhood conditions apply:

Human Fertilisation and Embryology Act 2008 section 37

37 The agreed fatherhood conditions

(1) The agreed fatherhood conditions referred to in section 36(b) are met in relation to a man ('M') in relation to treatment provided to W under a licence if, but only if,—

(a) M has given the person responsible a notice stating that he consents to being treated as the father of any child resulting from treatment provided to W under the licence,

(b) W has given the person responsible a notice stating that she consents to M being so treated,

(c) neither M nor W has, since giving notice under paragraph (a) or (b), given the person responsible notice of the withdrawal of M's or W's consent to M being so treated,

(d) W has not, since the giving of the notice under paragraph (b), given the person responsible—

(i) a further notice under that paragraph stating that she consents to another man being treated as the father of any resulting child, or

(ii) a notice under section 44(1)(b) stating that she consents to a woman being treated as a parent of any resulting child, and

(e) W and M are not within prohibited degrees of relationship in relation to each other.

---

[89] *U v W (Attorney General Intervening)* [1997] 2 FLR 282.

Thus under the 2008 Act, fatherhood can be acquired through the mother's and father's consent. It is interesting that the government did not limit access to agreed fatherhood to the mother's unmarried partner (for example, by adopting the Human Tissue Act 2004's definition: 'living together in an enduring family relationship'). The only limit upon who may become a father under these provisions is that he cannot be within the prohibited degrees of relationship (for the purposes of incest) with the mother. This means that, with his consent, a woman could agree to a male friend being her child's father, but not her brother.

(d) Same-sex couples

Under the 1990 Act, unlike male partners, the female partner of a woman undergoing treatment with donated sperm could not acquire parenthood from birth. The woman's female partner would be a legal stranger to the child at birth, even if she was the child's genetic mother. She could subsequently apply for a parental responsibility order, or could become the child's second parent via adoption. The 2008 Act changes this, and, with the exception of a difference in terminology, equalizes the position of civil partners/same-sex married couples with that of opposite sex married couples, and treats unmarried same-sex and opposite sex partners in the same way.

The terminological difference is that while a mother's male partner can become a child's father from birth, her same-sex partner cannot become a child's second mother. If a child has two female parents, the one who gives birth will be the mother, and the other one is legally simply a 'parent'. In the next extract, Alan Brown draws upon a case involving lesbian parents and a known donor, referred to throughout as the biological father, to suggest that this terminological difference is in practice significant.

Alan Brown[90]

[I]t is suggested that 'parent' is not being conceptualised as an equivalent to either mother or father in judicial discourse and this is combined with the paucity of specific consideration of the role itself within the decisions. Consequently, the precise role of 'the parent' remains unclear and it is still the case that, in the courts, 'the parent' is not being constructed as a replacement for either the mother or the father, but rather is viewed as providing an additional, somewhat ill-defined, parenting presence ...

The constraints that ordinary language places on our ability fully to express the nature and extent of this parenting role, on its own terms, prevents the courts from being able to conceptualise this role as deserving to be on the same level as either 'mother' or 'father'... [T]he 'parent' continues to be viewed as additional to rather than as a substitute for 'father' and therefore ... the 'father' is still deemed to be serving a crucial parental role.

(i) Civil partners and married same-sex couples

Same-sex civil partners and married same-sex couples are in the same position as husbands in relation to the acquisition of parenthood.

---

[90] 'Re G; Re Z (Children: Sperm Donors: Leave to Apply for Children Act Orders): Essential Biological Fathers and Invisible Legal Parents' (2014) 26 Child and Family Law Quarterly 237–51.

Human Fertilisation and Embryology Act 2008 section 42

42 Woman in civil partnership or marriage to a woman at time of treatment

(1) If at the time of the placing in her of the embryo or the sperm and eggs or of her artificial insemination, W was a party to a civil partnership or a marriage with another woman, then subject to section 45(2) to (4), the other party to the civil partnership or marriage is to be treated as a parent of the child unless it is shown that she did not consent to the placing in W of the embryo or the sperm and eggs or to her artificial insemination (as the case may be).

(ii) Agreed female parenthood conditions

For same-sex couples who are neither married nor in a civil partnership, the agreed female parenthood conditions mirror the agreed fatherhood conditions for unmarried heterosexual couples. The only limit on who may become a second legal parent in this way is that she must not be within the prohibited degrees of relationship, so a woman could nominate a friend to be her child's second legal parent, but not her sister.

Human Fertilisation and Embryology Act 2008 section 44

44 The agreed female parenthood conditions

(1) The agreed female parenthood conditions referred to in section 43(b) are met in relation to another woman ('P') in relation to treatment provided to W under a licence if, but only if,—

(a) P has given the person responsible a notice stating that P consents to P being treated as a parent of any child resulting from treatment provided to W under the licence,

(b) W has given the person responsible a notice stating that W agrees to P being so treated,

(c) neither W nor P has, since giving notice under paragraph (a) or (b), given the person responsible notice of the withdrawal of P's or W's consent to P being so treated,

(d) W has not, since the giving of the notice under paragraph (b), given the person responsible—

(i) a further notice under that paragraph stating that W consents to a woman other than P being treated as a parent of any resulting child, or

(ii) a notice under section 37(1)(b) stating that W consents to a man being treated as the father of any resulting child, and

(e) W and P are not within prohibited degrees of relationship in relation to each other.

It is noteworthy that the outcry in parliament and in the press over the move to delete the largely symbolic reference to the child's 'need for a father' in 2008 was not mirrored by similar outrage over these, in practice, much more radical changes to the parenthood provisions, which permit a child to have, in law and from birth, two female parents.

In the next extract, Andrew Bainham criticizes the parenthood provisions on the grounds that parentage should denote only a biological relationship.

Andrew Bainham[91]

The argument, therefore, is that while it may be appropriate to give to the lesbian partner and other social parents parental responsibility (depending on the extent to which the individual actually performs parenting functions), it is *inappropriate* to make that person the legal parent because this is to distort and misrepresent kinship. The lesbian partner's mother and father, for example, would become the child's grandparents and her brothers and sisters the child's uncles and aunts . . .

The concept of parentage should rather be confined, to reflect as far as possible the unique position of biological parents and, through the child's filiation with them, the wider kinship links to the extended maternal and paternal families.

Not everyone would agree that we should privilege genetic ties in this way, however. Many people believe that we should recognize as a child's parents the individuals who do the exhausting and often thankless work of parenting, rather than someone who simply shares some of her DNA.

(e) The importance of record-keeping

Because the agreed fatherhood and parenthood provisions depend upon a record of the parties' consents, it is obviously important that clinics have robust record-keeping systems in place. Consent to being treated as the child's parent must be recorded in writing before the treatment takes place, in order that that consent has been properly informed, and that there has been the opportunity for counselling.

In *AB v CD and the Z Fertility Clinic*, CD had undergone donor insemination treatment, unsuccessfully and then successfully, with her female partner AB, both before and after the law changed in April 2009 (to enable the mother's female partner to be the child's legal parent from birth). The clinic had not given either AB or CD adequate information about the change in the law, and the right forms had not been signed before their third treatment cycle, in May 2009, when CD finally conceived. CD had downloaded the forms from the internet and handed them to clinic staff after treatment had taken place, but Cobb J found that this was insufficient to attribute legal parenthood to AB.

AB v CD and the Z Fertility Clinic[92]

Cobb J

There is a proper basis for requiring the WP and PP forms—in accordance with the principles of good practice—to be completed and submitted no less than one day before treatment; the treatment is almost always at some level a stressful one. It would be quite wrong to require the parties to consider for the first time important legal issues on the day of treatment.

[91] 'Arguments about Parentage' (2008) 67 Cambridge Law Journal 322–51.
[92] [2013] EWHC 1418 (Fam).

This case brought the failings at Z Fertility Clinic to the attention of the HFEA. It immediately required all 109 licensed clinics to carry out an audit of their records. Alarmingly, this revealed that there were anomalies in the records at 51 clinics, including forms being absent, incomplete, unsigned, or completed after treatment had begun. The HFEA required clinics to contact affected patients, causing huge distress to parents who were alarmed to discover that they might not, in fact, be their children's legal parents.

In *Re A (Human Fertilisation and Embryology Act 2008)*, Sir James Munby P was asked to make declarations of parenthood in eight cases in which the forms had not been properly completed. He did so in all of them, finding in some cases that the court could rectify mistakes on the face of the forms. He was scathing about the evidence of incompetence that these cases had brought to light.

Re A (Human Fertilisation and Embryology Act 2008)[93]

Sir James Munby P

The picture thus revealed, and I am referring not just to Barts, is alarming and shocking. This is, for very good reason, a medical sector which is subject to detailed statutory regulation and the oversight of a statutory regulator—the HFEA ... The picture revealed is one of what I do not shrink from describing as widespread incompetence across the sector on a scale which must raise questions as to the adequacy if not of the HFEA's regulation then of the extent of its regulatory powers. That the incompetence to which I refer is, as I have already indicated, administrative rather than medical is only slight consolation, given the profound implications of the parenthood which in far too many cases has been thrown into doubt.

This case was followed by several more, and by the time he decided the following case towards the end of 2017, Sir James Munby P had made declarations of parentage in 37 cases in which forms had been wrongly filled in.

Human Fertilisation and Embryology Act 2008 (Cases AI and AJ)[94]

Sir James Munby P

From the outset of that treatment, it was the intention of both X and Y that X would be a legal parent of C. Each was aware that this was a matter which, legally, required the signing by each of them of consent forms. Each of them believed that they had signed the relevant forms as legally required and, more generally, had done whatever was needed to ensure that they would both be parents ...

X and Y, believing that they were entitled to, and acting in complete good faith, registered the birth of their child, as they believed C to be, showing both of them on the birth certificate as C's parents, as they believed themselves to be.

The first they knew that anything was or might be 'wrong' was when they were contacted by the clinic.

---

[93] [2015] EWHC 2602 (Fam).   [94] [2017] EWHC 3351 (Fam).

(f) Single women

If a woman receives treatment on her own, and does not wish anyone to be her child's second parent, or if her spouse or civil partner does not consent to her treatment, the child's mother will be the only legal parent.

(g) Transgender parents

The statutory scheme does not specifically address the possibility of transgender parenthood. While normally couples who use their own gametes in treatment are self-evidently the child's parents, and not subject to any special rules, this may not be true for parents who have changed their gender. It is possible that people who store gametes, or embryos created using their gametes, before their gender is reassigned may find that their stored gametes or embryos have to be treated as those of a third party donor, rather than as their own.

For example, if a male-to-female trans person wants her female partner to be inseminated with sperm she stored before she became a woman, she could become the child's second legal parent, via the 'agreed parenthood conditions'. It would be irrelevant that her own gametes were used in treatment.

Or, if a female-to-male trans person had eggs, or embryos created with her eggs, stored before gender reassignment, these could be used in the treatment of his female partner, but the trans man could again only acquire fatherhood through the agreed parenthood conditions, rather than because he is the child's genetic 'mother'.

Not only are the statutory provisions silent about the possibility of trans parenthood, but also, as Sheelagh McGuinness and Amel Alghrani point out, it is interesting that the preservation of fertility was not always a routine aspect of preparation for gender reassignment surgery.

Sheelagh McGuinness and Amel Alghrani[95]

There is some evidence which suggests that transsexuals are not being counselled about their reproductive options pre-operatively. This may be due to the fact that in the past, infertility was seen as a 'price to pay' for transitioning—being a transsexual and being a parent were seen as mutually exclusive. We reject the notion that transsexuals have in some way chosen to be infertile and that this negates their rights to access artificial reproductive technologies. It is, correctly we believe, no longer accepted that same sex couples have somehow waived any options to parent by the mere fact they have elected to be in a relationship where natural reproduction is not possible. Nor do patients who elect treatment that may affect their fertility waive their reproductive interests; it is recognised that patients undergoing cancer treatment should be counselled about fertility preservation techniques. Transsexuals should not be deemed to have chosen to be infertile by opting for a treatment that results in infertility.

The most recent edition of the HFEA's Code of Practice for the first time includes guidance on treating trans patients.

---

[95] 'Gender and Parenthood: The Case for Realignment' (2008) 16 Medical Law Review 261–83.

HFEA 9ᵗʰ Code of Practice

> 4.14 Before treatment or storage is offered to a trans person, the centre should (as with all patients) consider the treatment and storage options that are available to the patient, depending on their individual circumstances. For example, if a trans person is visiting the clinic prior to gender reassignment they may be seeking options for fertility preservation (i.e., storage of either testicular or ovarian tissue, or eggs or sperm depending on whether they have undergone puberty); or if a trans person is visiting the clinic after gender reassignment they may be seeking ways to use their preserved tissue, eggs or sperm in treatment with a partner and/or a surrogate, or extend their storage periods due to premature infertility.

In addition to freezing sperm or eggs before gender reassignment, a more dramatic way to become a trans parent first arose in the US when a man who had previously been a woman gave birth to a baby girl. Thomas Beatie had not had his female reproductive organs removed, but had relied upon testosterone therapy and reconstructive surgery to change gender, so when he and his wife, a woman who had had a hysterectomy, wanted to start a family, he stopped taking testosterone in order to become pregnant. There have since been other trans men who have given birth, including several in the UK.

(i) PREIMPLANTATION GENETIC DIAGNOSIS (PGD)

(1) What is PGD?

PGD is used by couples who are at risk of passing on a genetic disorder, and who will often have previously had affected children or pregnancies. When a newly fertilized egg has started the process of cell division, it is possible to remove one or two cells without compromising its capacity for normal development. The removed cell is then subject to genetic testing, and affected embryos will be discarded, or donated for research, and only unaffected embryos will be transferred to the woman's uterus, or frozen for use in future treatment. PGD therefore enables couples to start a pregnancy in the knowledge that the resulting child will not have a particular abnormality. It is also possible to discover the embryo's sex, and hence avoid the transmission of X-linked conditions.[96]

Removing one cell from an early human embryo and testing it is a complex and time-consuming process, requiring considerable technical expertise. Because it is used to prevent the birth of children who will suffer from serious diseases, which may be very expensive to treat, NHS funding is available to couples who are at risk of passing on a serious genetic condition, and who do not already have an unaffected child (in addition, the woman must be under 40 and both partners must be non-smokers).[97] It is by no means a common procedure: in 2016, of the 68,090 IVF cycles started, only 702 involved PGD.[98]

---

[96] Because females have two X chromosomes, they will invariably have a 'normal' gene that can correct a defective gene on the other X chromosome. Males, on the other hand, have only one X chromosome, so if they inherit a defective gene on the X chromosome, they will develop the disease in question.

[97] See further, *Clinical Commissioning Policy: Pre-implantation Genetic Diagnosis* (NHS England, 2014).

[98] *Fertility treatment 2014–2016: Trends and figures* (HFEA, 2018).

(2) How is PGD Regulated?

The original legislation did not mention PGD and instead guidance was developed by the HFEA in its Code of Practice. Since 2008, however, the circumstances in which it is lawful to carry out PGD have been set out on the face of the statute.

Human Fertilisation and Embryology Act 1990 Schedule 2

Activities For Which Licences May Be Granted

Licences for treatment: embryo testing

1ZA(1) A licence . . . cannot authorise the testing of an embryo, except for one or more of the following purposes—

  (a) establishing whether the embryo has a gene, chromosome or mitochondrial abnormality that may affect its capacity to result in a live birth,

  (b) in a case where there is a particular risk that the embryo may have any gene, chromosome or mitochondrion abnormality, establishing whether it has that abnormality or any other gene, chromosome or mitochondrion abnormality,

  (c) in a case where there is a particular risk that any resulting child will have or develop—

   (i) a gender-related serious physical or mental disability,

   (ii) a gender-related serious illness, or

   (iii) any other gender-related serious medical condition, establishing the sex of the embryo,

(2) A licence . . . cannot authorise the testing of embryos for the purpose mentioned in sub-paragraph (1)(b) unless the Authority is satisfied—

  (a) in relation to the abnormality of which there is a particular risk, and

  (b) in relation to any other abnormality for which testing is to be authorised under sub-paragraph (1)(b),

  that there is a significant risk that a person with the abnormality will have or develop a serious physical or mental disability, a serious illness or any other serious medical condition.

(3) For the purposes of sub-paragraph (1)(c), a physical or mental disability, illness or other medical condition is gender-related if the Authority is satisfied that—

  (a) it affects only one sex, or

  (b) it affects one sex significantly more than the other.

Schedule 2(1ZA) reproduces the rules that the HFEA had developed before 2008, which permitted PGD only where there is a significant risk that the child to be born will have or develop a serious illness, disability, or other condition. This wording clearly mirrors that of the Abortion Act 1967, but why? What are the reasons for confining PGD to serious conditions? As Melisa Soto-Lafontaine et al point out the reasons 'are not always spelled out', but might include the costs of treatment; the 'moral sensitivity of embryo selection'; concerns about 'adverse long-term health effects', and 'the fear that allowing PGD for less serious conditions would be a step on a slippery slope towards the dreaded "designer child"'.[99]

---

[99] 'Dealing with treatment and transfer requests: how PGD-professionals discuss ethical challenges arising in everyday practice' (2017) Medicine, Health Care and Philosophy 1–12.

It is possible to use PGD to establish the sex of a child, but only if there is a risk that the child would have a serious 'gender-related condition'. In practice, sex selection for medical reasons is becoming less common because tests are usually able to identify affected embryos, rather than employing the cruder technique of excluding all male embryos.

Jeanne Snelling and Colin Gavaghan are critical of the HFEA's 2014 decision to refuse an application to carry out sex selection in order to avoid the inheritance of autism spectrum disorder (ASD) in a family with two 'severely affected' male children. In turning down the application, the HFEA cited its peer reviewers' evidence that PGD could not guarantee that a female child would be free from ASD. Snelling and Gavaghan point out that the Act does not confine lawful sex selection to X-linked disorders, but instead refers to conditions that affect one sex 'significantly more' than another, which is the case for ASD.

Jeanne Snelling and Colin Gavaghan[100]

The reasoning underpinning the Committee's decision is not clear. It is possible that the HFEA were wary that sex selection for ASD was moving closer to 'social' sex selection or parental 'preference', and sought to avoid public criticism. Alternatively, it is possible that the Authority may not have wanted to be involved with facilitating the conception and birth of a child that might, because of the inherent uncertainty, nevertheless be born with ASD. Clearly a line was being drawn, but in the absence of further explanation, it is unclear on what basis . . .

[T]he Licensing Committee's refusal to license sex selection in the case of a family with two sons affected by Autism Spectrum Disorder appears, at least *prima facie*, to be inconsistent with the statutory parameters governing permissible sex selection.

(a) What is a serious disease?

Some genetic conditions are self-evidently serious. If a child is born with Tay-Sachs disease, for example, her nervous system will start to degenerate during her first year of life, and she will die within three or four years. For other conditions, it may be less clear. The statute appears to assume that an objective assessment of seriousness is possible, whereas many have argued that different people judge seriousness differently, often as a result of their personal experience of a particular condition. The Code of Practice acknowledges this, and suggests that when deciding whether to offer PGD, the family's particular circumstances and their subjective views of the condition are relevant.

HFEA 9th Code of Practice

10.5 When deciding if it is appropriate to provide PGD in particular cases, the centre should consider the circumstances of those seeking treatment rather than the particular heritable condition.

10.6 . . . The perception of the level of risk for those seeking treatment will also be an important factor for the centre to consider . . .

---

[100] 'PGD past, present and future: Is the HFE Act 1990 now "fit for purpose"?' in Kirsty Horsey (ed), *Revisiting the Regulation of Human Fertilisation and Embryology* (Routledge: Abingdon, 2015) 80–97.

10.9 The centre should consider the following factors when deciding if PGD is appropriate in particular cases:

(a) the views of the people seeking treatment in relation to the condition to be avoided, including their previous reproductive experience

(b) the likely degree of suffering associated with the condition

(c) the availability of effective therapy, now and in the future

(d) the speed of degeneration in progressive disorders

(e) the extent of any intellectual impairment

(f) the social support available, and

(g) the family circumstances of the people seeking treatment.

In Rosamund Scott et al's empirical research into the views of scientists and healthcare professionals, it was clear that the couple's previous experience—commonly of having an existing child with the condition—meant that their perception of the condition's seriousness carried considerable weight. In addition, they found that some couples with an existing child had a further reason to prefer PGD to termination of pregnancy.

Rosamund Scott et al[101]

Doctor 20 recalls an interesting couple:

I saw a couple last week who came for Cystic Fibrosis, a fertile, intelligent couple, who have a Cystic Fibrosis child. And I said, 'What are you doing this for? Why don't you just have another pregnancy?' And they couldn't consider terminating a Cystic child because, firstly they said, 'we do not want to have another child that we have to watch die or be very ill. But on the other hand, if we kind of [terminate the] pregnancy it's like terminating [our existing child] . . . And we feel we can't do that. And we want some other way of approaching this.'

In this case, the testing seems very much in the interests of the parents: although PGD is not 100% accurate, these parents clearly saw the possibility of a pregnancy achieved through PGD as a way of avoiding the potentially very painful issues they might face if a foetus tested positive for Cystic Fibrosis. The question of trying to avoid the dilemmas around termination is extremely important in PGD . . .

[W]hen people approach a clinic about the possibility of PGD for something they have experienced in some way, they must think that it is important enough to try to 'do something about it'. As one member of staff put this, 'of course it must be serious for them to come here'.

This latter point also emerged from Melisa Soto-Lafontaine et al's focus group study with European PGD professionals.

---

[101] 'The Appropriate Extent of Preimplantation Genetic Diagnosis: Health Professionals' and Scientists' View on the Requirement for a Significant Risk of a Serious Genetic Condition' (2007) 15 Medical Law Review 320–56.

Melisa Soto-Lafontaine et al[102]

In both focus groups, there was much support for the view that the seriousness of the disorder for which PGD is requested cannot be determined in isolation from the psychosocial impact as experienced by the applicants. Repeatedly, it was said that the mere fact that people are willing to accept the burdens (and costs) of PGD treatment to avoid the transmission of a specific condition, indicates that for them that condition is serious, even if this seriousness would not seem obvious either in terms of the severity of the disorder per se, or in view of co-determinants such as a lower penetrance and/or variable expression. To illustrate this for severity per se, a participant in the Dutch focus group came up with the following case.

> Only last week we had a discussion concerning a patient suffering from congenital hair loss. You may say that is nothing, but for the patient this was unbelievably burdensome. She was almost suicidal because of having no hair on her entire body and she absolutely didn't want to transmit this. This is a serious disorder, of which the hospital's PGD-committee said: well, hair loss, what's the fuss? And that in my view is the main problem, that the patient has a completely different perception than the professional. (FG-1).

More fundamental than the difficulty in drawing a line between serious and non-serious conditions is the idea that some disabilities are social rather than medical. It is increasingly recognized that some people whom we think of as disabled are, in fact, disabled more by society's attitude towards them, and its failure to adapt to their needs, than they are by their condition. In the next extract, Jonathan Glover argues that only disabilities that limit functioning and human flourishing should properly be described as disabilities.

Jonathan Glover[103]

Belonging to a minority that suffers discrimination is not a disability. One consequence may be the need to reclassify some conditions now thought of as disabilities. For instance, achondroplasia, severely restricted height resulting from a genetic mutation, is normally classified as a disability. But the purely functional impairments are trivial, such as needing a stool to boost height when speaking in public. Provided that there are no associated medical complications, the only serious disadvantages result from the reactions of other people. This makes it the same as being Jewish in an anti-Semitic society or gay in a homophobic society. This could push us towards saying that sometimes ethnic or religious membership, or sexual orientation, can count as a disability. Or, with less offence to our linguistic and moral intuitions, we can say that achondroplasia is not a disability.

(b) Adult-onset conditions

It is possible to carry out PGD for adult-onset genetic conditions, such as Huntington's disease, and for an increased susceptibility to late-onset diseases, such as breast cancer. In such cases, the child would be born healthy, but would be at risk of developing a serious disease in adulthood. Someone with a faulty BRCA1 or BRCA2 gene has an 80 per cent chance of

---

[102] 'Dealing with treatment and transfer requests: how PGD-professionals discuss ethical challenges arising in everyday practice' (2017) Medicine, Health Care and Philosophy 1–12.
[103] Choosing Children: Genes, Disability and Design (Clarendon Press: Oxford, 2006) 10.

developing breast cancer and a 60 per cent chance of developing ovarian cancer, often at a relatively young age. The HFEA has decided that, in principle, it is acceptable to use PGD to detect these lower penetrance late-onset conditions, and it has licensed PGD for a number of different cancer susceptibility genes, including the BRCA1 mutation.

Of course, unless PGD is permitted for all susceptibility genes, it may become necessary to draw a line between penetrance which does justify PGD and penetrance which does not. Locating the tipping point on the scale between an 85 per cent risk—which clearly is substantial—and a 0.01 per cent risk, which is not, is going to be difficult, not least because a range of other factors, such as the risk of mortality, age of onset, and availability of treatment options, may be relevant.

(c) Carrier embryos

It is possible to detect whether embryos are carriers of recessive disorders. These are diseases, like cystic fibrosis, where the defective gene must be inherited from both parents for the disease to manifest itself. Someone who has only one copy of the defective gene will be a carrier of the disease, but will not develop it herself. If she reproduces with another carrier, her offspring will have a 1 in 4 chance of receiving a double dose and inheriting the disease, and a 1 in 2 chance of inheriting one gene, and again being a carrier.

If a carrier embryo implants and is carried to term, the resulting child will be free from the condition, but might have an affected child or face difficult reproductive choices in the future. Testing for carrier status alone would not fit within the statutory criteria. In practice, however, carrier embryos may be identified during PGD cycles carried out where both parents are carriers, and are undergoing PGD in order to avoid the birth of a child with the recessive condition. In such circumstances, if there are embryos available for transfer that are neither affected nor carriers, it may make sense to transfer those embryos to the woman's womb.

(d) PGD with non-disclosure

As we saw in Chapter 9, most people who are at risk of inheriting the Huntington's mutation choose not to undergo pre-symptomatic genetic testing, preferring 'not to know' that they will develop an incurable, degenerative disease in middle age. It is, however, understandable that these people might wish to undergo PGD to ensure that their children do not have the Huntington's mutation.

The difficulty is that once the embryos are tested, it is likely that the clinicians will be able to tell whether the at-risk patient has the condition: if any of the embryos are affected, then the clinician knows that the patient has the genetic mutation and will develop the disease. Conversely, if the couple produces, say, ten embryos, and none are affected, it is unlikely that the at-risk patient is affected. There is therefore a risk of inadvertent disclosure: we all know how hard it is to ensure that our expressions and body language do not unwittingly communicate whether news is good or bad.

Moreover, it has been argued that practices which are intended to preserve parental ignorance might themselves be unethical: if no embryos are suitable for transfer because all are affected, should the doctors try to fabricate an alternative reason why none are suitable (ie should they lie to the patients?), or should they carry out a sham transfer (which would be clinically inappropriate)? Neither option is good medical practice. If the couple were to seek a second cycle of PGD, when the treating clinicians are sure that the at-risk patient is unaffected, and that there is no risk that the child would inherit a serious condition, would it be unethical and perhaps also unlawful to carry out PGD?

Some of these difficulties can be resolved by employing what is known as exclusion testing, which involves excluding embryos which have inherited the relevant chromosome from the affected grandparent. This means excluding embryos which are statistically at the same risk of inheriting the disease as the parent—that is, there is a 50/50 chance that an embryo which has inherited this chromosome from the affected parent will have the condition, and a 50/50 chance that it will not. The advantage to exclusion testing is that the clinic staff will not find out the status of the patient, but it is likely to result in normal embryos being discarded. Exclusion testing is also dependent upon being able to test the grandparent who has Huntington's disease, so it is possible only if he or she has not yet died from the disease.

The HFEA Code of Practice specifies that exclusion testing should be carried out where possible, and that PGD with non-disclosure should be offered only in exceptional circumstances.

HFEA 9th Code of Practice

10.10 Where patients seek PGD, but do not wish to discover their own genetic status, centres should, where possible, only offer PGD with exclusion testing . . .

10.11 In exceptional circumstances the centre may offer PGD, but withhold the patient's test results (PGD with non-disclosure). However, this should only be offered under the following conditions:

(a) that patients are given the opportunity to receive genetic counselling on the implications prior to giving consent,

(b) that protocols are established to limit, as far as possible, the risk of unwanted disclosure to the patients. Centres should consider using a different embryology laboratory from their own, in order to minimise the number of centre staff who know the patient's genetic status, and

(c) that no dummy embryo transfers are to be performed.

10.12 The centre should document its reasons for offering PGD with non-disclosure to a patient. This record should include:

(a) written informed consent from the patient to perform PGD with non-disclosure,

(b) a statement from the people seeking treatment confirming that they have been given the opportunity to receive genetic counselling and that they have, prior to giving consent, received information:

(i) on the risks of inadvertent disclosure,

(ii) that where all embryos are suitable for transfer this is not evidence of the patient's genetic status,

(iii) that where no embryos are suitable for transfer this is not evidence of the patient's genetic status,

(iv) that therefore dummy embryo transfers are not necessary or permissible, and

(v) that treatment may go ahead which is not medically necessary in cases where the patient (or partner) does not have the genetic condition. This includes information about the potential costs and risks of any medically unnecessary treatments.

As E Asscher and B-J Koops point out, even with exclusion testing, the ethical issue remains that potentially unnecessary PGD is carried out because the at-risk patient does not wish to know his or her status, but that this must be put in the balance with the 'harms' to parents forced to choose between finding out their status or having children who will themselves be at risk, or not having children at all.

E Asscher and B-J Koops[104]

The objections against honouring the right not to know in the Huntington PGD context all relate to the same issue: in half of the cases, PGD is strictly speaking unnecessary because the parents are unaffected. In these cases, we face the costs of the small but real IVF risks to the child ultimately to be born, the financial costs of the procedure, and the strain this puts on the solidarity of a publicly funded health system. The question is then whether these costs outweigh the costs of overriding the right not to know and disallowing the exclusion test. These costs consist, first, of psychological harm of those parents who want to have disease-free children and choose to undergo the procedure and thus have to relinquish their right not to know. Second, other parents will decide to forego genetic diagnosis at all and will conceive unselected children; these children will have to face exactly the same dilemmas as their parents. In addition, 50% of these children will carry the gene for Huntington's disease and thus become seriously ill and die in their third or fourth decade of life. Third, some of the prospective parents may decide against having genetically related children in order to preserve their right not to know.

(e) Testing for disability

The 2008 Act amendments prohibit a further possible use of PGD, namely the positive selection of embryos affected by a particular condition. There had not been any such cases, and it had been anticipated that clinicians might be likely to invoke section 13(5)—the need to take the future child's welfare into account—in order to refuse to provide PGD to someone who wanted to screen in a genetic condition. Now the selection of embryos or donors known to have a particular abnormality is specifically prohibited.

Human Fertilisation and Embryology Act 1990 section 13

13(9) Persons or embryos that are known to have a gene, chromosome or mitochondrion abnormality involving a significant risk that a person with the abnormality will have or develop—

    (a) a serious physical or mental disability,

    (b) a serious illness, or

    (c) any other serious medical condition,

must not be preferred to those that are not known to have such an abnormality.

The Act does not ban the transfer of affected embryos: rather, it does not allow them to be 'preferred'. This means that it is not possible to select embryos known to suffer from a condition such as congenital deafness, where unaffected embryos are available. If, however, the only embryos suitable for transfer happen to be affected, then they would not be being 'preferred' to unaffected embryos, and it would be acceptable to transfer them to the woman's uterus.

---

[104] 'Law, ethics and medicine: the right not to know and preimplantation genetic diagnosis for Huntington's disease' (2010) 36 Journal of Medical Ethics 30–3.

Aside from the fact that it is not clear that anyone actually wants to use PGD in order to select embryos affected by a disability, this scenario is unlikely to arise because to be in a position to choose embryos known to be affected by a genetic abnormality, the couple must have first undergone PGD in order to *avoid* the birth of an affected child. If a couple wanted to have affected children, they are more likely to reproduce naturally, when there is a one in four chance of having an affected child.

Section 13(9) also provides that a couple must not 'prefer' a gamete donor who suffers from a condition like congenital deafness. However, if a couple prefer to use a relative—say, the infertile man's brother—as a donor, and he happens to be deaf, it could be argued that they would not be preferring him because of his deafness, but rather because of his genetic related-ness. Of course, it is almost impossible to legislate for people's preferences, and so a couple might prefer to use a deaf donor, but as long as they have other grounds for preferring him, it would be hard to establish that his deafness was the principal reason.

During the legislative process, this provision was heavily criticized by disability groups, and most vociferously by the deaf community, which argued that it sent a negative message about living with disability. A deaf couple, who already had a deaf child but were contem-plating using IVF in order to have a second child, became a focus of media attention. They did not want positively to select a deaf embryo, and would have been equally happy to have a hearing child, but they did not want to be compelled to reject an embryo on the grounds of its deafness.[105] It is not clear that this would, in fact, have happened to them: there is no requirement for congenitally deaf IVF patients to undergo PGD. Nevertheless, they argued powerfully that it was offensive for legislation to insist that embryos that had inherited their deafness must be discarded in favour of embryos that had not.

In the next extract, Julian Savulescu criticizes the prohibition on selecting for deafness from another direction, sometimes described as the non-identity problem. He argues that, unless the child's life would be so impaired as to be not worth living, it will always be better to be born rather than not born, and hence positively selecting for disability should be allowed.

Julian Savulescu[106]

What if a couple has in vitro fertilisation and preimplantation genetic diagnosis and they select a deaf embryo? Have they harmed that child? Is that child worse off than it would otherwise have been (that is, if they had selected a different embryo)? No—another (different) child would have existed. The deaf child is harmed by being selected to exist only if his or her life is so bad it is not worth living. Deafness is not that bad. Because reproductive choices to have a disabled child do not harm the child, couples who select disabled rather than non-disabled offspring should be al-lowed to make those choices, even though they may be having a child with worse life prospects.

(3) Is PGD Acceptable?

It is not uncommon for critics of PGD to make the slippery slope claim that allowing people to test for serious and often fatal diseases makes it more likely that one day parents will select embryos on the basis of trivial traits, like sporting ability or IQ.[107] In practice, however, there

---

[105] Robin McKie and Gaby Hinsliff, 'This couple want a deaf child. Should we try to stop them?', The Observer, 9 March 2008.

[106] 'Deaf lesbians, "designer disability", and the future of medicine' (2002) 325 British Medical Journal 771–3.

[107] David King, 'Preimplantation genetic diagnosis and the "new" eugenics' (1999) 25 Journal of Medical Ethics 176–82.

is no gene 'for' athleticism or intelligence, and it would be impossible to use PGD in order to have sporty or clever children.

A further problem with this sort of slippery slope claim is its assumption that PGD is straightforward and that it always works. Nothing could be further from the truth, as demonstrated by Sarah Franklin and Celia Roberts' ethnographic study of couples who had undergone PGD.

Sarah Franklin and Celia Roberts[108]

The question of how patients had 'arrived' at PGD was the first thing couples were asked during interviews—and was always met with lengthy and upsetting replies. These 'how we got to PGD' stories could begin far back in time, with an initial miscarriage, an affected birth, or a chance occurrence, such as reading a newspaper article about PGD. In discussing their 'route' to PGD, couples often provided epic tales of hardship and struggle, in which a characteristic determination featured prominently. 'Getting to PGD' had often involved going through numerous painful experiences—not only of tragic events such as the deaths of children or repeated miscarriages—but also of previous failed forms of treatment, complicated family situations, and challenges to the couple's relationship . . .

In casual conversations, and also formal interviews with clinicians, nurses, PGD coordinators and genetic counsellors, a constant and consistent theme is that although PGD is a valid and necessary choice, it is not for everyone, is very difficult and often fails.

Others are worried that PGD sends a message to disabled people that it would be better if they did not exist. Colin Gavaghan turns this 'expressivist' objection to PGD on its head, arguing that one way to ensure that PGD does not send any offensive messages to disabled people would be to make it freely available, for any reason at all.

Colin Gavaghan[109]

When law and policy restrict the use of PGD to the avoidance of children with genetic defects, . . . , it becomes at least arguable that our approach to this technology, far from being driven by an agenda of promoting individual choice and respecting diversity, is underpinned by judgments about the value of those lives that are avoided. It is scarcely surprising if those affected by genetic illnesses or disabilities, or those who care about or for such people, look with some offense and suspicion at those laws and policies.

It is my contention, though, that their concerns could better be addressed by loosening the regulations applicable to PGD, thereby allowing . . . any other prospective parents to utilize this technology to implement their own values and preferences. In so doing, we might avoid the imposition by the state of a single, simplistic view of what constitutes 'normality' and 'disability,' a view that is clearly not universally shared. The appropriate response—from the state, from the public, and from the Authority itself—to the HFEA's question about the desirability of testing for cancer genes should be: 'We hold no view on this, other than that prospective

---

[108] *Born and Made: An Ethnography of Preimplantation Genetic Diagnosis* (Princeton UP: Princeton, 2006).
[109] 'Right problem wrong solution: a pro-choice response to "expressivist" concerns about preimplantation genetic diagnosis' (2007) 16 Cambridge Quarterly of Healthcare Ethics 20–34.

parents should be permitted to make informed choices for themselves, free from coercion, and safe in the knowledge that whatever choice they make will be respected and supported.' Nothing, I submit, could be further removed from the pernicious taint of eugenics.

As we saw in Chapter 9, there has been rapid progress in identifying genes that increase susceptibility to a wide range of common diseases. At present, PGD is used by people who know that their family is at risk of passing on a serious genetic condition, and this is comparatively rare. In contrast, all of us possess genes which increase our susceptibility to a range of conditions. If this sort of testing becomes available *in vitro*, anyone potentially becomes a candidate for PGD. While few people are likely to want to undergo stressful IVF treatment, costing thousands of pounds, in order to screen their embryos in this way, the cost and burden of additional screening might be less off-putting for couples who are already undergoing IVF.[110] Such screening would not currently be lawful, however, since there could not be said to be a significant risk of the child inheriting a serious disability.

(4) Tissue Typing

A new use for PGD emerged at the start of the 20th century. Tissue or HLA (Human Leukocyte Antigen) typing involves taking a cell from an early embryo, in the same way as for PGD, and testing it to see if the resulting child would be a good tissue match for a sick sibling in need of a bone marrow transplant. If the selected embryo is a good tissue match, when the baby is born, blood taken from her umbilical cord can be used to treat her brother or sister. Once again, the 2008 reforms put the HFEA's criteria for tissue typing on a statutory basis.

Human Fertilisation and Embryology Act 1990 Schedule 2

Activities For Which Licences May Be Granted

Embryo testing

1ZA(1) A licence . . . cannot authorise the testing of an embryo, except for one or more of the following purposes— . . .

  (d) in a case where a person ('the sibling') who is the child of the persons whose gametes are used to bring about the creation of the embryo (or of either of those persons) suffers from a serious medical condition which could be treated by umbilical cord blood stem cells, bone marrow or other tissue of any resulting child, establishing whether the tissue of any resulting child would be compatible with that of the sibling . . .

(4) In sub-paragraph (1)(d) the reference to 'other tissue' of the resulting child does not include a reference to any whole organ of the child.

Tissue typing is lawful only to select a tissue donor for an older sibling, and not for any other family member. A mother who needed a bone marrow transplant could not use

---

[110] See also ZO Merhi and L Pal, 'Gender "tailored" conceptions: should the option of embryo gender selection be available to infertile couples undergoing assisted reproductive technology?' (2008) 34 Journal of Medical Ethics 590–3.

tissue typing in order to give birth to a child who would be a good match for her. Why not? At first sight, it might seem that the mother would be seeking tissue typing for self-interested reasons, though, of course, a woman who does not want to leave her existing children without a mother would also be acting out of concern for their welfare. This restriction is not, however, directed at the intention behind the request for tissue typing; it simply reflects the practical reality that while the chance of producing an embryo that is a good tissue match for an existing sibling is 1 in 4, for parents or more distant relatives, the chance of producing a tissue match is much more remote. For siblings, there is a realistic chance that one IVF cycle will produce at least one compatible embryo, but this is not the case for other relatives.

The Act also provides that it is legitimate to use tissue typing where the intention is to take bone marrow or other tissue, as long as there is no intention to take a solid organ. This means that it would be possible for parents who have a child with leukaemia, which is currently in remission, to undergo tissue typing so that she would have a tissue-matched sibling, should her leukaemia return, making a bone marrow transplant immediately necessary.

The restriction upon taking a solid organ was inserted during the 2008 parliamentary debates. It undoubtedly means that a clinic could not carry out preimplantation tissue typing in order to select a child to be an organ donor in the future, but it could not operate as a lifetime ban on the child ever becoming an organ donor. As we saw in Chapter 12, the Human Tissue Act 2004 does not rule out childhood organ donation, although court approval would be necessary. And, of course, if a child born as a result of tissue typing were to choose, when she reaches adulthood, to become a live organ donor for her sick sibling, the Human Fertilisation and Embryology Act could not prevent this happening.

When the Act was reformed, the creation of 'saviour siblings' sparked considerable controversy and debate, largely as a result of concern about the welfare of the child who is born in order to be a tissue donor.

Susan M Wolf, Jeffrey P Kahn, and John E Wagner[111]

[W]e know almost nothing about the psychological impact of being conceived to serve as an HLA-matched donor and save a sibling's life. The effects on the donor child are potentially profound. Indeed, if the cord blood transplant fails or the donor child is otherwise repeatedly considered for harvest over a prolonged period of time, there may be a potential for serious effects. The potential may be all the greater if the donor child comes to resist or refuse further procedures . . .

Moreover, even if one debates whether using PGD solely to conceive an HLA-matched donor may be said to harm the donor child, this use of PGD exclusively to create an opportunity for later harvesting may be wrong on other grounds, such as violating the ethical injunction to respect each individual and avoid using persons as mere means . . .

The donor child is at lifelong risk of exploitation, of being told that he or she exists as an insurance policy and tissue source for the sibling, of being repeatedly subjected to testing and harvesting procedures, of being used this way no matter how severe the psychological and physical burden, and of being pressured, manipulated, or even forced over protest.

---

[111] 'Using preimplantation genetic diagnosis to create a stem cell donor: issues, guidelines and limits' (2003) 31 Journal of Law, Medicine and Ethics 327.

The argument that the child conceived in order to save an older sibling's life is being used solely as a means, and not as an end in herself,[112] would be equally true if a couple with a sick child decided to conceive another child naturally, in the hope that she might be a good tissue match. It is unthinkable that the law would prevent parents from having another child in such circumstances. In any event, a child born following HLA typing is not used solely as a means, since she is not abandoned after the donation, but rather is overwhelmingly likely to be loved in her own right as a new and welcome member of the family.

People have children for a wide range of instrumental, and sometimes unedifying reasons, such as trying to save a failing relationship or producing an heir to take over the family business. It is common to have a second child in order to provide an only child with a companion. In addition, it could be argued that although the psychological risks associated with being conceived in order to be a donor are speculative, we know that the impact of bereavement in childhood is overwhelmingly negative. Children conceived naturally in an unsuccessful attempt to create a good tissue match are likely to be born into families that either have or will soon experience the death of a child. As a result, Sally Sheldon and Stephen Wilkinson argue that child welfare arguments might be mobilized to support the use of HLA typing. The child born following tissue typing is benefited by being a good tissue match for an older sibling, since this enables her to be born into a family which is not wracked by bereavement, and to benefit from a relationship with her older sibling.

Sally Sheldon and Stephen Wilkinson[113]

But even if we concede for the sake of argument that it would be hurtful or upsetting for a selected sibling (A) to discover that she had been conceived for the primary purpose of saving the life of an existing child (B), is it really plausible to suppose that A would be less happy than another, randomly selected sibling (C) who was unable to act as a tissue donor? For it could surely be argued that A would benefit from B's company and may well derive pleasure from knowing that she has saved B's life. In contrast, imagine the psychological impact on C, born into a bereaved family, later to discover that she was a huge disappointment to her parents because of her inability to save B's life . . . [W]e can at least say that it is far from obvious that child welfare considerations should count against, rather than for, the practice of saviour sibling selection.

Michelle Taylor-Sands has further argued that the child's interests are inseparable from those of the family into which she is born, and that it therefore makes sense to adopt a 'relational approach' to the welfare of the child.

Michelle Taylor-Sands[114]

I propose a relational approach to the welfare of the child to be born based on the notion of human flourishing, which situates the interests of the child within the context of his/her

---

[112] Thus offending the Kantian imperative, which we considered in Chapter 1.
[113] 'Hashmi and Whitaker, "An Unjustifiable and Misguided Distinction"' (2004) 12 Medical Law Review 137–63.
[114] 'Summary of *Saviour Siblings*' (2015) 41 Journal of Medical Ethics 926.

family. Given that a child living in an intimate family is both an individual and the member of an intimate collective, I argue that the child's interests should be considered *in connection with* rather than in opposition to the interests of other family members. I examine familial duty as a justification for compromising some individual interests of family members for the welfare of the family as a whole, but conclude there should be limits on what parents can ask of a child in order to protect the child from exploitation, abuse or neglect.

(5) Non-Medical Sex Selection

The legitimacy of sex selection for social reasons was considered by the HFEA following a public consultation in 2003. As is clear from the following extract, the HFEA was heavily influenced by the weight of public opinion against sex selection.

Human Fertilisation and Embryology Authority[115]

147. In reaching a decision we have been particularly influenced by the considerations set out above relating to the possible effects of sex selection for non-medical reasons on the welfare of children born as a result, and by the quantitative strength of views from the representative sample polled by MORI and the force of opinions expressed by respondents to our consultation. These show that there is very widespread hostility to the use of sex-selection for non-medical reasons. By itself this finding is not decisive; the fact that a proposed policy is widely held to be unacceptable does not show that it is wrong. But there would need to be substantial demonstrable benefits of such a policy if the state were to challenge the public consensus on this issue. In our view the likely benefits of permitting sex-selection for non-medical reasons in the UK are at best debatable and certainly not great enough to sustain a policy to which the great majority of the public are strongly opposed.

Again, the 2008 reforms simply place previous HFEA policy on sex selection on a statutory footing.

Human Fertilisation and Embryology Act 1990 Schedule 2 para 1ZB

(1) A licence . . . cannot authorise any practice designed to secure that any resulting child will be of one sex rather than the other . . .

(3) Sub-paragraph (1) does not prevent the authorisation of any other practices designed to secure that any resulting child will be of one sex rather than the other in a case where there is a particular risk that a woman will give birth to a child who will have or develop—

(a) a gender-related serious physical or mental disability,

(b) a gender-related serious illness, or

(c) any other gender-related serious medical condition.

What are the arguments against allowing sex selection for social reasons? First, some people have argued that sex selection reflects a consumerist attitude towards children, in which

---

[115] *Sex Selection: Options for Regulation* (HFEA, 2003).

parents try to ensure that a new child meets their specifications. Secondly, some claim that sex selection for social reasons is inherently sexist and discriminatory. Thirdly, it is argued that allowing people to select the sex of their offspring might have devastating demographic consequences.

Jodi Danis[116]

Some predict that a population in which males significantly predominate, known as a 'high sex ratio society', would have devastating results for women. A high sex ratio society might value women for their reproductive capacities, but would also be likely to force women to return to traditional roles centered around the home and family. Demographic imbalances would exacerbate existing sex discrimination because women would not have the political power or economic resources to change the status quo. The underrepresentation of women in positions of power would be even more significant. Oppression and violence against women might increase in male-dominated societies, especially if men felt the need to possess a limited resource and to ensure fidelity . . .

Males, through their greater numbers, would also know that they were selected more often and were thus more desired, increasing their sense of self-worth and self-importance while diminishing the self-esteem of their younger sisters or other girls. . .

[B]ecause only those in the middle or upper class can afford sex selection technology, and only those in the upper class can afford the more accurate in vitro technology, a higher proportion of boys would be born to the wealthy. This trend might result in the future masculinization of wealth.

Of course, a couple with three sons are not necessarily guilty of discriminating against boys when they hope that their fourth child will be a girl. But it is further argued that even this sort of preference depends upon sexist preconceptions about a child's gendered characteristics. A couple with three boys only want a girl, some would argue, because they think that she will be different from their sons.

Jonathan Berkowitz and Jack Snyder[117]

[T]o choose a boy or a girl, parents must have preconceived notions, however vague, about the ramifications of having a certain sexed child: notions which are fundamentally sexist as they are predicated upon anticipated gender based behaviour. Preconceptive sex selection is disturbing because it can be used as a vehicle for parents to express spoken or unspoken sexual prejudice . . .

Furthermore, by making a choice, parents must essentially prefer one sex over another. This emphasis upon sex is in direct conflict with larger societal goals directed against sexism and which urge individuals to be sex-blind. Pre-conceptive sex-selection represents sexism in its purest most blatant form as prior to conception, before parents can possibly know anything about their child, a child's worth is based in large part upon its sex.

---

[116] 'Sexism and "the superfluous female": arguments for regulating pre-implantation sex selection' (1995) 18 Harvard Women's Law Journal 219.
[117] 'Racism and sexism in medically assisted conception' (1998) 12 Bioethics 25–44.

Even if we accept that gender stereotyping is undesirable, it is not PGD that causes this sort of behaviour. Rather, parents with sexist attitudes are likely to inflict them upon any child that they might have naturally.

The principal argument in favour of allowing sex selection for social reasons derives from John Stuart Mill's harm principle. Liberty, according to Mill, should be restricted only when its exercise might cause harm to others. If, and of course this is a contentious question, sex selection does not harm anyone, then there is insufficient justification for restricting people's reproductive freedom. Critics of sex selection would argue that it does harm others, such as the child herself (see Jonathan Berkowitz and Jack Snyder), or society in general (see Jodi Danis). Others, such as David McCarthy, contend that these harms are too speculative to justify a restriction on freedom.

David McCarthy[118]

In a pluralistic democratic society built upon the ideals of free and equal citizenry, there is always a presumption in favour of liberty. The burden of proof is always on those who want to restrict the liberty of others. Defenders of the legality of sex selection are not seeking to restrict anyone's liberty, whereas opponents are. So the burden of proof is on the opponents to show that those whose liberties they propose to restrict cannot reasonably reject this restriction. It is never sufficient grounds for one group to restrict the liberty of others that it is clear, as they see it, that the behaviour they are trying to restrict is morally objectionable. What must be established is that the behaviour they are trying to restrict itself results in something like significant harm to others or infringement of their basic liberties or significant social costs. In the case of sex selection, I have argued that no such grounds have been established.

In addition, Sara Fovargue and Rebecca Bennett are critical of the role played by public opinion in the criminalizastion of non-medical sex selection.

Sara Fovargue and Rebecca Bennett[119]

Although it is admitted that there is no evidence that children born for these reasons will suffer serious harm, this practice is not only prohibited but is also criminalised on the basis that there is not enough evidence of the benefits in order to outweigh the supposed public distaste for sex selection for these reasons ...

The 2008 Act's amendments to the 1990 Act, in general, introduced a clear moral stance on the regulation of assisted reproduction, with an explicit foundation in the harm principle and a commitment to reproductive autonomy. Yet, non-medical sex selection was singled out for different treatment. As a result, we have a general approach to regulation which is based on reason, evidence and critical thinking about the issues in hand, with one issue treated differently without good reason. Here, the cry of 'it's what the public wants' has been used to endorse the prohibition on using PGD to select an embryo on the basis of its sex for non-medical reasons only. The singling out of non-medical sex selection is both curious and indefensible. We hope that the use of public opinion as the basis for regulation is carefully considered and that it remains the exception rather than the rule.

The so-called non-identity problem poses a difficulty for those who argue against sex selection for social reasons: any harm caused by choosing a child's sex is unlikely to be so bad that it would be better for a sex-selected child not to exist. If I found out that my parents had selected me because I am female, I might think that they were a bit weird, but I cannot imagine thinking that it would have been preferable if I had never been born.

In the next extract, Rosalind McDougall sidesteps this intractable debate between those who believe sex selection should be prevented because it harms the child to be born, and those who believe that either it does not cause harm, or, even if it does, that harm is unlikely to be so great that it would be preferable for the child not to exist. Instead she advocates looking at sex selection from the point of view of virtue ethics (see Chapter 1). Because a virtuous parent accepts their children, regardless of their characteristics, a sex-selecting parent does not act virtuously, even if the child herself is not harmed.

Rosalind McDougall[120]

Because a child's characteristics are unpredictable, acceptance is a parental virtue . . . Accepting one's child, regardless of his or her particular current characteristics, is already perceived as a necessary characteristic of the good parent . . .

In acting on a preference to parent only a child of a particular sex, the sex selecting agent fails to act in accordance with the parental virtue of acceptance. . . The wrong is the sex selecting agent's failure to act in accordance with a parental character trait, acceptance, which is intrinsically linked on a general conceptual level to the flourishing of children. Sex selection is wrong because it is not in accordance with the parental virtue of acceptance, regardless of the outcome for a specific child.

Some people have argued in favour of limited access to sex selection in order to facilitate 'family balancing'. The American Society for Reproductive Medicine, for example, has argued that it is ethical to help couples to choose the sex of their babies for reasons of 'gender variety'. In 2005, the House of Commons Science and Technology Committee concluded that there was 'no adequate justification for prohibiting the use of sex selection for family balancing'.[121] In Israel, sex selection for social reasons may be permissible for couples with at least four children of one sex and none of the other.[122]

Why do some people regard sex selection for 'family balancing' as more innocuous than other sorts of social sex selection? One possible argument is that the family balancer is not preferring one sex to another; rather, they value both sexes equally and would like to see both represented among their children. A second argument might be that family balancing would be unlikely to

---

[120] 'Acting parentally: an argument against sex selection' (2005) 31 Journal of Medical Ethics 601–5.
[121] *Human Reproductive Technologies and the Law*, Fifth Report of Session 2004–05 (TSO: London, 2005) para 142.
[122] Ruth Landau, 'Sex selection for social purposes in Israel: quest for the "perfect child" of a particular gender or centuries old prejudice against women?' (2008) 34 Journal of Medical Ethics e10.

skew the sex ratio, because it might be predicted that the number of parents with daughters who would also like a son is likely to be roughly the same as the number with sons who would also like to have a daughter. In the next extract, however, Stephen Wilkinson disputes the suggestion that family balancing is necessarily less 'sexist' than 'regular' social sex selection.

Stephen Wilkinson[123]

[W]hile 'regular' sex selection is not *necessarily* supremacist, 'family balancing' *can* be supremacist. For example, a father who believes females to be second-rate might suffer (what he sees as) the misfortune of numerous daughters and want to even things up, not because he desires balance, but because he believes that boys are better . . .

As with 'regular' sex selection, whether 'family balancing' involves stereotyping depends on what exactly it is that the parents are aiming at.

(6) Mitochondrial Replacement

Mitochondria have been described as the cell's battery: they produce energy to enable each cell in the human body to function normally. Mutations in the 13 genes contained in the mitochondria can cause serious disease. Because we inherit our mitochondrial genes from our mother's egg cell, replacing the defective mitochondria can prevent a woman from passing mitochondrial disease on to her offspring.

Replacing the mother's defective mitochondrial genes with mitochondria from a healthy donor means that the child will inherit genetic material from two women (about 25,000 genes from her mother and 13 genes from the mitochondria donor). Does this child then have three parents (as the predictable tabloid headlines claimed), or is this more akin to other kinds of transplant such as a blood transfusion or bone marrow transplant, when we would certainly not say that a blood or tissue donor was a third parent? One important difference between bone marrow transplantation and mitochondrial transfer is that by altering the embryo's genetic make-up, the germline of the resulting child will be altered—that is, it alters her DNA—and this will be passed on to her descendants.

In 2008, research into mitochondrial transfer had not yet established that it would be safe in treatment, and so the amending legislation did not include it as a licensable activity, but—sensibly—it enabled this to be changed by regulation-making powers. In 2011, the HFEA was asked by the Secretary of State to seek expert views on the effectiveness and safety of mitochondrial transfer, and a year later, it was invited to seek public views on techniques designed to prevent the transmission of mitochondrial disease. Following this public consultation, in 2013 the HFEA advised the government that 'there is general support for permitting mitochondria replacement in the UK, so long as it is safe enough to offer in a treatment setting and is done so within a regulatory framework'.[124] Regulations permitting mitochondrial replacement came into force in October 2015.

Part 2 of the Human Fertilisation and Embryology (Mitochondrial Donation) Regulations 2015 enable eggs and embryos created using two different techniques known as maternal spindle transfer (MST) and pro-nuclear transfer (PNT) to be 'permitted' for use in treatment.

---

[123] 'Sexism, Sex Selection and "Family Balancing"' (2008) 16 Medical Law Review 369–89.
[124] *Mitochondria Replacement Consultation: Advice to Government* (HFEA, 2013).

Certain conditions must be satisfied, such as that the HFEA has determined (a) that there is a particular risk that the eggs or embryos of the woman seeking treatment may have mitochondrial abnormalities caused by mitochondrial DNA, and (b) that there is a significant risk that a person with those abnormalities will have or develop serious mitochondrial disease.[125]

The government had accepted the HFEA's recommendation that children born following mitochondrial donation should not have access to identifying information about the mitochondrial donor. Also following the HFEA's recommendation, the Regulations modify sections 31ZA–31ZE of the 1990 Act to give children access to limited, non-identifying, information. Likewise, the mitochondrial donor will be able to access limited, non-identifying, information about children born from their donation.

In the next extracts, Françoise Baylis argues that the money spent on mitochondrial replacement could be better spent elsewhere, while Martin Johnson disagrees, and points out that similar arguments were used against IVF.

Françoise Baylis[126]

While it is possible to argue that the numbers do not matter, and more specifically that the exceedingly low number of potential beneficiaries should not deter us from pursuing human nuclear genome transfer, it seems reasonable to assert that a maximum potential direct benefit of less than 15–22 births per year in the UK and less than 77–113 births per year in the US is inconsequential against the backdrop of a combined total current population in these two countries of close to 400 million ...

Some of these resources could be better spent responding to the needs of those living with mitochondrial disease. In the alternative, some of these resources could perhaps be directed to other health priorities.

There are billions and billions of us on this planet and our numbers are growing at a staggering rate. As our population grows, so too does the demand for resources including food, air and water quality and energy. And yet, we continue to invest in the development of increasingly esoteric reproductive technologies largely for the benefit of a very small number of persons in high-income countries.

Martin H Johnson[127]

Had Edwards and Steptoe accepted these arguments, then would the infertile still have just adoption as the only route to 'parenthood'? ...

It first appears to diminish the pain of those confronted with transmitting mitochondrial disease by their categorization as a 'very small minority'... It is a conclusion which I find unsympathetic to the plight of those faced with mitochondrial disease and disempowering of them in its paternalism. I am reminded of those referees that dismissed Edwards and Steptoe's bid for research funding on the grounds that infertility affected only a small group and that the real

---

[125] Human Fertilisation and Embryology (Mitochondrial Donation) Regulations 2015, regulations 5 and 8.

[126] 'Human Nuclear Genome Transfer (So-Called Mitochondrial Replacement): Clearing the Underbrush' (2017) 31 Bioethics 7–19.

[127] 'Tri-parenthood—a simply misleading term or an ethically misguided approach?' (2013) 26 Reproductive BioMedicine Online 516–19.

problem was overpopulation ... Even the economic argument does not add up. Thus, whilst disease due to mutant mtDNA may be relatively rare, it costs a lot to treat the health problems of the affected children and the psycho-sociological impact on the parents.

In the next extract, Cathy Herbrand points out that the debates over mitochondrial replacement techniques were in some important respects misleading and incomplete.

Cathy Herbrand[128]

MRTs [mitochondrial replacement techniques] only concern mitochondrial disorders that are maternally inherited. Although this was not mentioned in the public and parliamentary debates, it is important to highlight that most maternally inherited mitochondrial disorders only develop in adulthood (e.g. Melas or MERRF syndromes), whereas mitochondrial disorders which severely affect babies and children are caused in about 80% of cases by nuclear defects which are inherited from both parents. This means that these techniques will not be accessible to most families who have already lost a child from mitochondrial disorders and who wish to have another one ...

Amongst the women who had maternally inherited disorders in my study, a number had already developed significant symptoms that would prevent them from carrying a child (e.g. using a wheelchair) or that made them feel too weak to raise one. Some participants were also afraid that their condition would worsen and did not know if they would still be able to take care of a child later on in life. Interestingly, these crucial elements have never been mentioned in the public debates surrounding MRTs. Not only were the implications of mitochondrial disorders on the future mother's health condition not mentioned, but it was rarely pointed out that the future mother could herself be ill or was likely to become ill ...

[T]here is an important gap between the ways these techniques have been presented in the media and in the public domain, i.e. often as a kind of 'miracle solution' that will eradicate the disorders, and the social and medical constraints surrounding their use.

(7) Gene Editing

Currently, the only way in which genetic knowledge can be used before implantation is by discarding embryos discovered to have some genetic abnormality, or by replacing defective mitochondria. There has recently been considerable interest in a ground-breaking new technique which enables the genome to be edited, potentially allowing for the deletion of harmful genes and the insertion of beneficial ones.

In 2014, researchers from the Broad Institute and Massachusetts Institute of Technology reported that they had created a new mouse model (known as CRISPR-Cas9) to simplify *in vivo* genome editing. Four years later, in a 'proof of concept' study, it was reported that scientists in the US had successfully used CRISPR-Cas9 in order to eliminate inherited liver disease in mice embryos.[129] At the time of writing, one centre in the UK has a licence to carry out genome editing research on human embryos. As with mitochondrial replacement, genetically

---

[128] 'Mitochondrial Replacement Techniques: Who are the Potential Users and will they Benefit?' (2017) 31 Bioethics 46–54.

[129] Avery C Rossidis et al, 'In utero CRISPR-mediated therapeutic editing of metabolic genes' (2018) 24 Nature Medicine 1513–18.

edited embryos could not be used in treatment unless Regulations are passed to enabled the use of modified embryos in treatment.

It might be thought that genome editing could be used to prevent parents from passing on serious monogenic disorders, such as Huntington's disease or cystic fibrosis. But, of course, before attempting to edit an affected embryo's genome, it would first be necessary to identify that it was affected, using PGD. At that point, it would be easier, cheaper, and less risky to simply discard the affected embryo, rather than attempt to modify its genome. Genome editing might therefore be useful only in rare cases in which it is impossible for parents to produce unaffected embryos.

A further possibility would be to insert a gene known to be protective against a common and debilitating disease, such as malaria. This is not straightforward, however, because genetic variants that decrease risk for some conditions may elevate the risk for others; for example, there are mutations that appear to protect against HIV, but which increase the risk of developing West Nile virus. In mice, the genetic modification of a gene that protected against cancer unexpectedly caused premature ageing. It would be difficult to predict every possible 'off target' effect, and hence many advocate taking a precautionary approach.

Eric S Lander[130]

Genetic modification of human embryos is not a new idea. At least among Western governments, there has been a long-standing consensus that manipulating the human germline is a line that should not be crossed ... The discussions that will begin in the fall may solidify a broad international consensus that germline editing should be banned—with the possible exception of correcting severe monogenic disease genes, in the few cases in which there is no alternative ... A ban could always be reversed if we become technically proficient, scientifically knowledgeable, and morally wise enough and if we can make a compelling case. But authorizing scientists to make permanent changes to the DNA of our species is a decision that should require broad societal understanding and consent. It has been only about a decade since we first read the human genome. We should exercise great caution before we begin to rewrite it.

In 2015, the Organizing Committee for the International Summit on Human Gene Editing reached the following conclusions on germline gene editing.

Organizing Committee for the International Summit on Human Gene Editing[131]

Germline editing poses many important issues, including: (i) the risks of inaccurate editing ... ; (ii) the difficulty of predicting harmful effects that genetic changes may have under the wide range of circumstances experienced by the human population, including interactions with other genetic variants and with the environment; (iii) the obligation to consider implications for both the individual and the future generations who will carry the genetic alterations; (iv) the fact that, once introduced into the human population, genetic alterations would be difficult

---

[130] 'Brave new genome' (2015) 373 New England Journal of Medicine 5–8.
[131] *International Summit on Human Gene Editing: A Global Discussion* (National Academies Press (US), 2016). Available from https://www.ncbi.nlm.nih.gov/books/NBK343651/.

to remove and would not remain within any single community or country; (v) the possibility that permanent genetic 'enhancements' to subsets of the population could exacerbate social inequities or be used coercively; and (vi) the moral and ethical considerations in purposefully altering human evolution using this technology.

It would be irresponsible to proceed with any clinical use of germline editing unless and until (i) the relevant safety and efficacy issues have been resolved, based on appropriate understanding and balancing of risks, potential benefits, and alternatives, and (ii) there is broad societal consensus about the appropriateness of the proposed application. Moreover, any clinical use should proceed only under appropriate regulatory oversight. At present, these criteria have not been met for any proposed clinical use ... However, as scientific knowledge advances and societal views evolve, the clinical use of germline editing should be revisited on a regular basis.

Christopher Gyngell et al are more positive about the potential advantages of germline gene editing, and they point out that fears about enhancement are not sufficient in other contexts to restrict a new technology's therapeutic use.

Christopher Gyngell, Thomas Douglas, and Julian Savulescu[132]

Using GGE [germline gene editing] to remove all disease-causing genes from an embryo will lower the total frequency of disease-causing genes in the gene pool, and therefore the incidence of such diseases in future generations ...

Most common diseases are not the result of single gene mutations. They are the result of a polygenic disposition together with environmental influences ... GGE allows multiple changes to be made to a single embryo, and could therefore target many different genes simultaneously ... Three out of every ten deaths in those under 70 are caused by chronic diseases, like cancer, diabetes and heart disease. GGE could be a powerful tool in the fight against these diseases and could ensure that those treated with gene editing have the best chance to live healthily into old age.

One common concern about GGE is that it will be used a tool of human enhancement and not merely to prevent disease. GGE has much greater capacity to be used as a means of enhancement than conventional selection methods. This is because it can target a large number of genes simultaneously and could be used to insert genes that would not occur naturally. While genetic selection allows selection within the normal human range, gene editing would allow the enhancement of human capacities to supranormal levels ...

Many medical technologies currently being used or developed for the treatment of disease could also be used as enhancements. Many of those who are against the use of these technologies for enhancement purposes are still in favour of pursuing their development and therapeutic uses. Lasik eye surgery, pre-implantation genetic diagnosis, and plastic surgery can be used non-therapeutically, but this fact is not considered to provide reasons to prohibit or restrict funding for their therapeutic uses.

In contrast, others have argued that consideration should be given to the opportunity cost of developing a new technology which is likely to benefit relatively few people. Erika Check Hayden, for example, has said that people living with disabilities argue that, 'at a minimum ... the investment in developing CRISPR should be matched by investments in innovations to help people who are already living with conditions that cause

---

[132] 'The Ethics of Germline Gene Editing' (2017) 34 Journal of Applied Philosophy 498–513.

disability'.[133] And Giulia Cavaliere has pointed out that there may be other less costly options for the small number of people that might benefit from gene editing.

Giulia Cavaliere[134]

> Two of the criteria that are often employed to assess whether to invest resources in certain clinical research and whether it will bring about significant improvements to health and well-being are the severity of the condition and the number of individuals that it affects. If we consider these two criteria, the benefits of the introduction of genome editing as a new reproductive option are arguably minor and thus may not warrant the investment of public resources. The number of cases for which PGD is not an option ... is limited ...
>
> [I]t is important to consider that improvements in the health and well-being of future children can also be achieved by looking at alternative solutions, for instance third party reproduction or adoption. For those limited number of parents for whom PGD is not an option, the choice is not between genome editing and a sick child. The choice is much wider than that ...
>
> Perfecting existing technologies such as PGD, and possibly widening the criteria of access to adoption or third party reproduction, would be a less costly and possibly quicker strategy to grant future children's welfare while at the same time respecting prospective parents' wishes.

In 2018, the Nuffield Council on Bioethics distilled two necessary conditions for the moral permissibility of genome editing. First, it must secure the welfare of the future child, and, second, it must be consistent with social justice and solidarity, and should not increase disadvantage, discrimination, or division. The Nuffield report also recommended more research; broad and inclusive public debate and the establishment of an independent body to promote dialogue on genomic technologies.

Nuffield Council on Bioethics[135]

> 5.15 Among the potential collateral effects of heritable genome editing interventions are increased marginalisation or stigmatisation of those who have or do not avoid certain heritable conditions. It is therefore particularly important that the voices of people who may be collaterally affected are attended to and that they are not obscured by a focus on the goals of prospective parents ... We conclude, therefore, that efforts are needed to engage in open and inclusive consultation with those whose vulnerability to adverse impacts might be increased by the introduction or extension of heritable genome editing interventions.

(8) Human Reproductive Cloning

The first cloned mammal was born in the UK in 1996. The birth of Dolly the sheep (named after Dolly Parton because she had been cloned from an adult mammary cell) was announced

---

[133] 'Should you edit your children's genes?' (2016) 530 Nature News 402.

[134] 'Genome editing and assisted reproduction: curing embryos, society or prospective parents?' (2017) Medicine, Health Care and Philosophy 1–11.

[135] *Genome Editing and Human Reproduction* (NCOB, 2018).

the following year, and was immediately followed by demands for the complete prohibition of human reproductive cloning.

There was initially some confusion over whether cloning by cell nuclear replacement (CNR) was covered by the Human Fertilisation and Embryology Act 1990.[136] In response to Crane J's (subsequently reversed) decision that in the *Quintavalle* case that it was not,[137] emergency legislation created a new criminal offence—of placing 'in a woman a human embryo which has been created otherwise than by fertilisation'. This was superseded by the 2008 reforms, which introduce the concept of the 'permitted embryo' (ie an embryo created using eggs produced or extracted from the ovaries of a woman and sperm from the testes of a man). Since section 3(2)(a) specifies that only a 'permitted embryo' may lawfully be transferred to a woman's body, reproductive cloning is against the law.

Human reproductive cloning would present an unacceptable risk to the health of the pregnant woman and any child that might be born. Dolly was the sole survivor following the successful transplantation of nuclei to 277 enucleated ewe's eggs.[138] Cloning in animals appears to cause high rates of spontaneous late abortion and early postnatal death.[139] Dolly herself developed arthritis at an abnormally young age, and died prematurely of an unrelated condition. When an adult cell is cloned, it is possible that its advanced age will create an increased risk of cancer and other degenerative diseases. Given these risks, it would clearly be unethical to clone human beings for reproductive purposes. If scientific progress means that at some point in the future the safety objection to cloning is removed, would human reproductive cloning be ethically acceptable?

First, it is sometimes argued that cloning would violate the individual's right to her own unique identity. This claim is, however, undermined by the existence of identical twins, who have identical DNA but separate identities. A clone and her DNA source would be less alike than monozygotic twins because their uterine environments, childhood experiences, and upbringing will be completely different.

But even if we acknowledge that a clone and her DNA source would not be identical, it has secondly been argued that clones would be burdened by the anticipation of similarity. Thirdly, because a cloned child would be produced by replicating one parent's DNA, some people are concerned about the impact this might have upon family relationships. Would it be disturbing to raise a child who was genetically identical to one's spouse?

Not only is cloning unsafe, but very few people are interested in engaging in it. John Harris's defence of human reproductive cloning is essentially that we need a good reason to interfere with people's freedoms, and that the arguments against human reproductive cloning, which tend to be grounded in intuitive feelings of revulsion or uneasiness, offer insufficient justification for a ban.

John Harris[140]

In a long discussion entitled 'The Wisdom of Repugnance' [Leon] Kass tries hard and thoughtfully to make plausible the thesis that thoughtlessness is a virtue. 'We are repelled by the

---

[136] See Chapter 13 for a description of what CNR involves.
[137] *R v Secretary of State for Health ex parte Quintavalle* [2001] EWHC Admin 918; *R v Secretary of State for Health ex parte Quintavalle* [2003] UKHL 13.
[138] I Wilmut et al, 'Viable offspring derived from fetal and adult mammalian cells' (1997) 385 Nature 810–13.
[139] Y Kato et al, 'Eight calves cloned from somatic cells of a single adult' (1998) 282 Science 2095–8.
[140] 'Clones, Genes and Human Rights' in Justine Burley (ed), *The Genetic Revolution and Human Rights* (OUP: Oxford, 1999) 61–94.

prospect of cloning human beings not because of the strangeness or novelty of the undertaking, but because we intuit and feel, immediately and without argument, the violation of things that we rightfully hold dear'. The difficulty is, of course, to know when one's sense of outrage is evidence of something morally disturbing and when it is simply an expression of bare prejudice or something even more shameful.

3 CONCLUSION

The UK's regulatory system was the first of its kind in the world. It is widely admired, and has been the model for regulation in many other countries. It is not without its critics, however. Pro-life groups are concerned about the routine destruction of embryos in techniques. Disability rights groups have expressed anxiety about increasing recourse to embryo testing. Criticism has also come from a completely different direction, namely from those, like Sheila McLean, who believe that any regulation in this area unnecessarily restricts reproductive liberty.

Sheila McLean[141]

The state's interventionist role in assisted reproduction is based not in principle but on a general presumption of legitimacy: a presumption which can—and in my view should—be challenged. Most importantly it allows the imposition of the values of one group on others. Our relatively recent history—if nothing else—should teach us how potentially dangerous it is to cede authority over reproduction and reproductive practices to the state. Even if regulation is relatively benign, its very existence attacks freedom of choice; if it did not do so, it would have no reason to exist . . .

Certainly we will want to ensure that choices are taken in full knowledge of the risks, benefits and possible consequences of the decision, but this is a matter for the law on consent. It is not an argument against reproductive liberty . . .

De-regulating the provision of assisted reproductive services is the only option that adequately respects the liberties of citizens in this area, and the only one which reflects an appropriate role for the state in our intimate, private lives.

FURTHER READING

Baldwin, Kylie et al, 'Oocyte cryopreservation for social reasons: demographic profile and disposal intentions of UK users' (2015) 31 Reproductive BioMedicine Online 239–45.

Fovargue, Sara and Bennett, Rebecca, 'What role should public opinion play in ethico-legal decision making? The example of selecting sex for non-medical reasons' (2016) 24 Medical Law Review 34–58.

---

[141] *Modern Dilemmas: Choosing Children* (Capercaillie Books: Edinburgh, 2006).

Freeman, Tabitha et al, 'Online sperm donation: a survey of the demographic characteristics, motivations, preferences and experiences of sperm donors on a connection website' (2016) 31 Human Reproduction 2082–9.

Gyngell, Christopher and Douglas, Thomas, and Savulescu, Julian, 'The Ethics of Germline Gene Editing' (2017) 34 Journal of Applied Philosophy 498–513.

Horsey, Kirsty (ed), *Revisiting the Regulation of Human Fertilisation and Embryology* (Routledge: Abingdon, 2015).

Lee, Ellie, Sheldon, Sally and Macvarish, Jan, 'After the "need for ... a father": "the welfare of the child" and "supportive parenting" in assisted conception clinics in the UK' (2017) 6 Families, Relationships and Societies 71–87.

Pennings, Guido, 'Disclosure of donor conception, age of disclosure and the well-being of donor offspring' (2017) 32 Human Reproduction 969–73.

Soto-Lafontaine, Melisa et al, 'Dealing with treatment and transfer requests: how PGD-professionals discuss ethical challenges arising in everyday practice' (2017) Medicine, Health Care and Philosophy 1–12.

Tremellen, Kelton and Savulescu, Julian, 'Posthumous conception by presumed consent. A pragmatic position for a rare but ethically challenging dilemma' (2016) 3 Reproductive Biomedicine & Society Online 26–9.

16

SURROGACY

CENTRAL ISSUES

1. Surrogacy agreements are not unlawful in the UK, but they are unenforceable.

2. In theory, surrogates cannot be paid but, in practice, payments to surrogates can be authorized retrospectively by the courts.

3. In the UK, the surrogate is always the legal mother of the child from birth.

4. There are two ways in which legal parenthood can be formally transferred to the intended parents: through a parental order or adoption. Not all intended parents acquire legal parenthood, and some of the criteria for parental orders have come under pressure in recent years.

5. Cross-border surrogacy arrangements are becoming more common. As well as concerns about the exploitation of foreign surrogates, these can raise complicated questions about the child's citizenship.

6. The law relating to surrogacy is widely agreed to be unsatisfactory, and in 2018, the Law Commission started work on a comprehensive review.

1 WHAT IS SURROGACY?

Surrogacy is the practice whereby a woman (the surrogate) becomes pregnant with the intention that the child should be handed over to the intended parent(s) after birth. A surrogate could simply inseminate herself with the intended father's sperm. This is known as 'partial' or 'genetic' surrogacy, and because pregnancy can be achieved without professional assistance, it is difficult to exercise any control over these arrangements.

Alternatively, in 'gestational' or 'full' surrogacy an embryo is created *in vitro*, usually using the intended parent(s)' gametes, and is transferred to the surrogate's uterus. Because IVF is involved, gestational surrogacy arrangements in the UK will involve treatment in a centre licensed under the Human Fertilisation and Embryology Act 1990, and regulated by the Human Fertilisation and Embryology Authority (HFEA).

Although the numbers are increasing, in part as a result of the growth in cross-border surrogacy arrangements and in part because more gay men are having children through surrogacy, surrogacy is still not a common way to have children. In 2007–8, there were 56 applications for parental orders; by 2017 this figure had risen to 332. This is not the total number of surrogacy arrangements, however, because not all surrogacy arrangements result in applications for parental orders.

In this chapter, we begin with a brief summary of debates first over the ethics of surrogacy in general and, secondly, over the particular issues raised by cross-border surrogacy arrangements. We then turn to look at how surrogacy is, and is not, regulated and we focus on the increasingly important role of the family courts in resolving questions of parenthood and residence for children born through agreements 'in which the statutory requirements have not only not been met, but in some cases flagrantly breached'.[1] Finally, we consider how the law relating to surrogacy might be reformed.

2 THE ETHICS OF SURROGACY

At the outset, it is worth noting that attitudes towards surrogacy have changed dramatically in both the general public and among academic commentators. Thirty years ago, this sort of condemnation of surrogacy was not uncommon.

Elizabeth Anderson[2]

Commercial surrogacy substitutes market norms for some of the norms of parental love ... For in this practice the natural mother deliberately conceives a child with the intention of giving it up for material advantage. Her renunciation of parental responsibilities is not done for the child's sake, nor for the sake of fulfilling an interest she shares with the child, but typically for her own sake (and possibly, if 'altruism' is a motive, for the intended parents' sakes). She and the couple who pay her to give up her parental rights over her child thus treat her rights as a kind of property right. They thereby treat the child itself as a kind of commodity, which may be properly bought and sold ...

The unsold children of surrogate mothers are also harmed by commercial surrogacy ... Furthermore, the widespread acceptance of commercial surrogacy would psychologically threaten all children. For it would change the way children are valued by people (parents and surrogate brokers)—from being loved by their parents and respected by others, to being sometimes used as objects of commercial profit-making.

As well as harming children, some feminist commentators argued that surrogacy was demeaning for women.

Janice Raymond[3]

Surrogacy, situated within the larger context of women's inequality, is not simply about the commercialization of women and children. On a political level, it reinforces the perception and

---

[1] Claire Fenton-Glynn, 'The Difficulty of Enforcing Surrogacy Regulations' (2015) 74 Cambridge Law Journal 34.

[2] 'Is women's labor a commodity?' (1990) 19 Philosophy and Public Affairs 71–92.

[3] *Women as Wombs: Reproductive Technologies and the Battle over Women's Freedom* (HarperCollins: New York, 1993).

use of women as a breeder class and the gender inequality of women as a group. The practice of surrogacy strikes at the core of what a society allows women to be and become. Taking the commerce out of surrogacy but leaving the practice intact on a non-commercial and contractual basis glosses over the essential violation—the social definition of women as breeders.

Of course, not everyone believed that there was something inherently wrong with surrogacy. Richard Arneson, for example, argued that 'the thought that commercial surrogacy should be banned because the poor working women who mostly choose it are too incompetent to be entrusted to make their own decisions in this sphere has an ugly, elitist sound'.[4] And Lori Andrews pointed out that while money may influence a woman's decision to become a surrogate, it was seldom her only reason.

Lori Andrews[5]

Studies have found that some surrogates have been affected by the plight of infertile family members and friends. Others enjoyed parenting and wanted to help infertile couples become parents. Many of the women I interviewed described the tremendous psychic benefits they received from the feeling that they were helping someone meet a joyous life goal. Many viewed themselves as feminists who were exercising reproductive choice and demonstrating an ethic of care. It seems crass not to try to understand the arrangement from the surrogate's vantage point, in which this type of employment is viewed as a higher calling, like being a health care professional or educator, and may consequently be preferable to working as a check-out clerk in a grocery store or at some other minimum wage job.

Although there are still those who believe that surrogacy is always ethically problematic, it is now more commonly argued that surrogacy has the potential to be exploitative. Rather than banning the practice altogether, commentators focus instead upon ensuring that the interests of the parties to an arrangement, and of course the interests of the child herself, are protected.

Concerns over the potential for exploitation have often crystallized around cross-border surrogacy arrangements in which intended parents from high-income countries seek out surrogates from middle or low-income countries.

3 CROSS-BORDER SURROGACY

Until it decided to ban foreign, commercial surrogacy, India was one of the most popular destinations for cross-border surrogacy, but it was by no means the only one. Intended parents have also travelled to the US, Russia, Ukraine, Georgia, Greece, Canada, Mexico, Thailand, Laos, Nepal, and Kenya. The US continues to be a popular destination for those that can afford it (one birth can cost as much as $130,000). Cheaper options include Ukraine and Georgia, where a typical surrogacy arrangement costs between £30,000 and £50,000. As Helen Prosser

---

[4] 'Commodification and commercial surrogacy' (1992) 21 Philosophy and Public Affairs 132–64.
[5] 'Beyond Doctrinal Boundaries: A Legal Framework for Surrogate Motherhood' (1995) 81 Virginia Law Review 2343–75.

and Natalie Gamble explain, bans on foreign surrogacy arrangements in Thailand and India have led to the emergence of other destinations, like Cambodia and Vietnam.

Helen Prosser and Natalie Gamble[6]

[H]istory suggests that other destinations will keep emerging as destinations close, in response to demand. These are perhaps the most risky international surrogacy arrangements of all because they operate entirely in an absence of law and regulation. The pattern is that surrogacy blossoms among inexperienced providers, before being shut down virtually overnight, leaving parents and surrogates mid-process in a difficult and uncertain position. Overall, international surrogacy is a very varied, fast-changing landscape and the choices are not easy to navigate or assess.

Although cost was undoubtedly a principal reason for India's popularity as a destination for cross-border surrogacy arrangements, intended parents were also attracted by the certainty offered by Indian surrogacy brokers.

Sheela Saravana[7]

One intended mother found the financial deal with this particular clinic convenient because it did not charge any upfront payment until the baby is handed over. In her words,

'One of the things that made me come to this clinic was the way the payment scheme works. Only a nominal payment is made to the surrogate mother, but you don't actually pay until the very end ... it's a good incentive for her (the SM) to keep the baby and not do much work so she doesn't miscarry. She (the SM) doesn't really get compensated until she hands over the baby'.

The procedure in India was perceived as comparatively simple. One intended mother explained, 'Although it is legal in my country, the process is very complex and much more expensive than [in] India. The law expects surrogate mothers in India to sign over all rights to the baby even before the surrogacy begins, which is a big relief'.

Two aspects of Indian surrogacy arrangements were perhaps especially troubling. The first was the contracts themselves, over which the surrogates had little or no control and which were additionally usually in English. In *AB v CT*, for example, a case in which a same-sex couple had had twins as a result of a surrogacy arrangement in India, Theis J shared the Australian judge's concern (the couple had been living in Australia at the time) about the contractual terms, to which the surrogate had agreed with her thumbprint.

---

[6] 'Modern surrogacy practice and the need for reform' (2016) 4 Journal of Medical Law and Ethics 257–74.
[7] 'An ethnomethodological approach to examine exploitation in the context of capacity, trust and experience of commercial surrogacy in India' (2013) 8 Philosophy, Ethics, and Humanities in Medicine 10.

AB v CT [8]

Theis J

The surrogacy agreement was 'signed' by CT by way of a thumb print. It is 29 pages long and contains numerous clauses, including some which limit CT's ability to manage her health during the pregnancy and make decisions about the delivery of the babies. I agree with the observations of Justice Ryan in her judgment in June 2013 in proceedings issued by the applicants in Australia that these provisions are '*troubling*'. There is some evidence that some documents were explained to CT although I share the concerns expressed by Justice Ryan in her judgment that '*there is nothing in the document which suggests that before the birth mother signed it that it was read and translated to her*' at the time she signed it.

Secondly, Indian surrogates often lived away from their families in surrogacy hostels. While this may have protected women from the stigma that they might have faced at home, separation from their families was difficult for many surrogates.[9]

Sharvari Karandikar et al [10]

More often than not, surrogates chose to live in the hostel to avoid stigma at home. Because the agency only allowed women who had previously successfully given birth to become surrogates, all the participants had biological children who were forced to remain at home while the surrogates lived in the surrogacy hostel. Typically, the surrogate's family home was located far from the surrogacy hostel, which resulted in limited contact with family members ...

While family members' reactions to the surrogacy varied from negative to relatively supportive, community members' reactions were always negative. Surrogate mothers were typically stigmatized if community members became aware of the surrogacy ...

While the major incentive cited for the creation of the surrogate hostel was the maintenance of the surrogate's health, the information mentioned above points to an additional reason: To maintain seclusion of the pregnant surrogate, thus shielding her from the eyes of a disapproving community. By providing a means of isolation, the surrogacy clinic is both meeting their own need for supervision of the pregnancy and meeting the need of the women to keep the surrogacy private. A third stakeholder in this arrangement is the community itself. By quarantining the practice of gestational surrogacy out of public view, it is a way to maintain the social norms of traditional reproduction, even as surrogacy becomes more and more common.

But is a ban the best solution to concerns about the outsourcing of reproductive labour to women in low and middle-income countries? Given that the Indian surrogacy industry was estimated to be worth around $2.3 billion per annum, as Amrita Pande explains, 'a blanket ban on surrogacy in India will as likely just shift it to another country in the global South'.[11]

---

[8] [2015] EWFC 12.

[9] N Lamba et al, 'The psychological well-being and prenatal bonding of gestational surrogates' (2018) 33 Human Reproduction 646–53.

[10] 'Economic necessity or noble cause? A qualitative study exploring motivations for gestational surrogacy in Gujarat, India' (2014) 29 Affilia 224–36.

[11] Amrita Pande 'Global reproductive inequalities, neo-eugenics and commercial surrogacy in India' (2016) 64 Current Sociology 244–58.

When India banned surrogacy for gay couples in 2012, fertility specialists found ways to 'work around' the ban. One Mumbai-based fertility specialist 'revealed that he was recruiting surrogate mothers from Kenya to come to Mumbai'.[12] The Kenyan women would undergo IVF in Mumbai, using embryos created with the clients' sperm. They would stay in Mumbai for the first 24 weeks of pregnancy, before being flown back to Kenya for the births. Clients would pick up their babies from Kenya. As Sharmila Rudrappa explains:

> The Mumbai doctor maintained that he had not broken the law, because technically, he had not interacted with gay clients within Indian territory, and all he had provided was in vitro fertilization for Kenyan 'health-care' seekers.

Indeed, Sharmila Rudrappa suggests that the new Indian law may lead to more rather than less exploitation of Indian women.[13]

Sharmila Rudrappa[14]

> With this current ban, if the past offers any lessons, surrogacy brokers will in all probability map out global routes to continue their brisk trade in reproduction, moving working-class pregnant women from one country to the other to take advantage of the uneven juridical-legal terrain of country-specific laws that govern surrogacy. Sending Indian women to Nepal and bringing Kenyan women to India: in these sorts of developments surrogate mothers become analogous to shipping containers. Working-class women of the global South become cargo carriers of life—life that *a priori* belong to clients—across borders to facilitate family-making in the global North ...
>
> There is nothing to stop indigent women from providing surrogacy services to wealthy intended parents. National Boards and authorization committees of the sort meant to monitor altruistic surrogacy, as in the case of kidney donation, tend toward loose interpretations of who constitutes a 'close' relative. 'Altruistic' surrogate mothers might be in deeply dependent, long-standing relationships with intended parents and unable to refuse when asked to provide their biological reproductive services for free ...
>
> The reality, however, is that for a large number of women around the world and not just India, the family is the site for the materialization of substantial inequalities and domestic violence. Families are never quite safe havens from the corrupting forces of the market; instead, they are sites that engender gender subordination ...
>
> The state endorsement of altruistic surrogacy is premised on the notion that women are expected to provide free biological and social reproductive labor, but only within kin networks. But by moving gestation back into the folds of the family the state has effectively deregulated surrogacy ...
>
> If the Indian state is genuinely interested in protecting surrogate mothers' rights, then it has to recognize surrogacy as a legitimate form of work and extend the kinds of protections

[12] Sharmila Rudrappa, 'India outlawed commercial surrogacy – clinics are finding loopholes' (2017) The Conversation 24.

[13] See also Melanie G Fellowes, 'Commercial surrogacy in India: the presumption of adaptive preference formation, the possibility of autonomy and the persistence of exploitation' (2017) 17 Medical Law International 249–72.

[14] 'Reproducing Dystopia: The Politics of Transnational Surrogacy in India, 2002–2015' (2018) 44 Critical Sociology 1087–101.

democratic societies extend to their working citizens. This would mean health insurance schemes, the right to unionize and form collectives and cooperatives, and protecting the mothers' collective bargaining rights on wages and work conditions.

If transnational surrogacy is inevitable, and a ban likely to be ineffective, the most pressing concern should be to ensure that surrogates give properly informed consent and are not subject to oppressive and exploitative contractual terms. For example, a future international convention on transnational surrogacy (see below) might introduce some minimum requirements, such as that women should never be expected to sign contracts that they cannot understand, and that they must retain decision-making authority over their bodies during pregnancy.

4 REGULATION OF SURROGACY IN THE UK

In contrast to the regulation of assisted conception, considered in Chapter 15, surrogacy has never been the subject of a comprehensive regulatory regime. Such regulation as exists consists in piecemeal and often unsatisfactory amendments to the law and, increasingly importantly, the compassionate exercise of judicial discretion. Indeed, the judiciary has had to find ways to safeguard the interests of children *despite* the rules governing surrogacy.

(a) NON-ENFORCEABILITY

The Surrogacy Arrangements Act 1985 was passed hastily in response to the baby Cotton case (in which a British woman had been employed to act as a surrogate for a Swedish couple by a US agency). It was intended to discourage the practice of surrogacy. Section 1B of the Act specifies that 'No surrogacy arrangement is enforceable by or against any of the persons making it.' It is not an offence to enter into a surrogacy arrangement, but the agreement itself is not enforceable.

Hence, the intended parents cannot sue the surrogate if she refuses to hand over the baby, and nor can she sue them if she does not receive any of the agreed payments, or if they refuse to take the baby after birth. So while it is lawful to enter into a surrogacy contract, none of the parties are bound by it.

(b) COMMERCIALIZATION

Section 2 of the Surrogacy Arrangements Act 1985 prohibits commercial involvement in the initiation and negotiation of surrogacy arrangements. Under section 3, the commercial publication or distribution of advertisements indicating a willingness to take part in surrogacy arrangements is also a criminal offence. The Act was amended by the Human Fertilisation and Embryology Act 2008 to permit non-profit-making bodies to charge a reasonable fee in order to recoup their costs.

Organizations which help to put potential surrogates in touch with intended parents—including Childlessness Overcome Through Surrogacy (COTS), Surrogacy UK, and Brilliant Beginnings—must therefore operate on a non-commercial basis. Solicitors can offer clear and accurate information about the legal consequences of surrogacy, but the law undoubtedly places obstacles in the way of the professionalization of the practice of surrogacy, and this has resulted in some people entering into decidedly ill-advised arrangements.

(c) REGULATED AND UNREGULATED SURROGACY

When a surrogacy arrangement involves IVF treatment carried out in the UK, it must take place in a clinic which has a licence from the HFEA, and which is under a duty to comply with the Human Fertilisation and Embryology Act 1990, as amended (see further Chapter 15). Under section 13(5) of the Act, before providing a woman with treatment services, the clinician must take account of the welfare of any child who may be born, and any other children who may be affected by the birth. Hence, before providing treatment, a clinician should not only evaluate the impact of the surrogacy arrangement upon the resulting child, but must also take into account the welfare of the surrogate's existing children.

Although people seeking surrogacy in licensed clinics must find their own surrogates, the HFEA's Code of Practice requires all parties to receive separate implications counselling,[15] and information about legal parenthood. It also suggests that clinics should look out for signs of coercion, and protect people from entering into unsuitable or unethical arrangements.

HFEA 9th Code of Practice

14.2 The centre should ensure that those involved in surrogacy arrangements have received information about legal parenthood under the HFE Act 2008 and other relevant legislation. This information should cover who may be the legal parent(s) when the child is born . . .

14.3 The centre should ensure that those involved in surrogacy arrangements have received information about the effect of the parenthood provisions in the HFE Act 2008 and in particular the Parental Orders provisions in the Act . . .

14.4 The centre should advise patients that surrogacy arrangements are unenforceable and that they are encouraged to seek legal advice about this and any other legal aspect of surrogacy.

14.5 The centre should satisfy itself that those involved in surrogacy arrangements have received enough information and understand the legal implications of these arrangements well enough to be able to give informed consent to treatment . . .

14.13 The centre should encourage those involved in a surrogacy arrangement to reflect on their decisions before it obtains their consent. The centre should provide detailed information, advice and guidance and encourage questions. The centre should be satisfied that all parties fully understand all aspects of the surrogacy arrangement and are entering into the arrangement freely and voluntarily, before obtaining their consent. This should include testing the understanding of both the intended surrogate and intended parents and ensuring that information is provided clearly and at an appropriate level of complexity tailored to an individual's capacity to understand it.

14.14 The centre should exercise particular caution and sensitivity when discussing and taking consents for surrogacy arrangements and be aware of the vulnerable positions of both

---

[15] HFEA 9th Code of Practice (HFEA, 2019), paras 14.7–14.10.

the intended surrogate and intended parents and serious implications for all concerned of a surrogacy arrangement breaking down. The centre should be alert to any sign of coercion. The centre's role should be to protect both parties from entering into a surrogacy arrangement which it suspects may be unsuitable or unethical for any reason.

In contrast, if people enter into a partial or genetic surrogacy arrangement, involving home insemination, they may have no idea about the legal implications of what they are doing, and there will be no screening of surrogates and intended parents.

The HFEA's Code of Practice requires centres to advise patients planning to travel abroad for surrogacy to obtain legal advice, but of course many people make contact directly with surrogacy agencies and clinics in other countries, and will not therefore discuss their plans with staff in a licensed clinic in the UK.

HFEA 9th Code of Practice

14.6 The centre should advise patients intending to travel to another country for the purpose of entering into a surrogacy arrangement that they are encouraged not to do so until they have sought legal advice about:

(a) legal parenthood of the prospective child

(b) immigration status and passport arrangements

(c) the adoption or parental orders procedures for that country, and

(d) the degree to which those procedures would be recognised under the law of the part of the United Kingdom in which the patients live.

In practice, it is simply impossible for UK law to regulate prospectively the agreements that people enter into overseas. UK law becomes relevant only when the intended parent(s) try to bring the child back to the UK, and acquire legal parenthood.

(d) STATUS

When a child is born as a result of a surrogacy arrangement, who are her legal parents?

(1) Maternity

As we saw in Chapter 15, the legal definition of 'mother' in the UK is clear and unequivocal: the woman who gives birth to a baby is its mother.

Human Fertilisation and Embryology Act 2008 section 33

33 The woman who is carrying or has carried a child as a result of the placing in her of an embryo or of sperm and eggs, and no other woman, is to be treated as the mother of the child.

The law does not distinguish between different types of surrogacy and so the surrogate will always be the child's legal mother from birth, regardless of whether she is also the child's genetic mother. This means that, from birth, the surrogate has prima facie legal responsibility for a child that she did not want, while the intended parents have no legal responsibility for a child whose creation they brought about.

It used to be thought that the fact that the surrogate is the child's mother from birth protected her right to change her mind. However, as we see below, the best interests of the child are the court's paramount consideration, so the surrogate does not have the right to keep the baby. If the court decides that it is in the child's best interests to live with the intended parents, the surrogate does not have the right to prevent this from happening.

In addition, given that in the vast majority of cases the surrogate is happy to hand over the child after birth, UK law means that unless or until the intended parents obtain a parental order or adoption (and not all do so), the surrogate will continue to be the legal parent of a child who is being brought up in another family.

(2) Paternity

Because the provisions governing the ascription of legal fatherhood in the Human Fertilisation and Embryology Acts 1990 and 2008 were designed to apply to sperm donation, they lead to some rather odd results when applied to surrogacy (for a full description, see Chapter 15).

Section 28 of the 1990 Act and section 38 of the 2008 Act treat the surrogate's husband (if she has one) as the father of the child, unless it can be shown that he did not consent to her treatment. If the surrogate is married to another woman or in a civil partnership, there will be a presumption that her spouse or civil partner is the child's second legal parent. Where a married surrogate's husband (or spouse/civil partner) knows of her decision to become a surrogate and does not object, he (or she) may be assumed to consent, and will, as a result, be the child's father (or second legal parent).

If the surrogate is not married or in a civil partnership, provided that the intended father's sperm was used in the surrogacy arrangement, he will be the child's father at common law. He can be registered as the father on the child's birth certificate, and thereby acquire parental responsibility. An intended parent whose gametes were not used in the child's conception could become the child's father or second legal parent, along with the surrogate, through the agreed parenthood conditions (see further Chapter 15), provided he or she and the surrogate consent to this.

(e) TRANSFERRING LEGAL PARENTHOOD

At birth, then, the surrogate will be the child's legal mother, and the intended father might or might not be the child's legal father. For the intended parents to become the child's only legal parents, they must either adopt the child or apply for a parental order under the Human Fertilisation and Embryology Act 2008.

There are many reasons why parental orders are preferable to adoption. They are a better 'fit' for surrogacy in that they attribute legal parenthood to people with whom the child has usually lived from birth and who are also the child's genetic parent(s). The process is also less time-consuming and burdensome. If a parental order is an option, it is, as Sir James Munby P explained in *Re X (A Child) (Surrogacy: Time limit)*, very clearly preferable to adoption.

Re X (A Child) (Surrogacy: Time limit)[16]

Sir James Munby P

Adoption is not an attractive solution given the commissioning father's existing biological relationship with X. As X's guardian puts it, a parental order presents the optimum legal and psychological solution for X and is preferable to an adoption order because it confirms the important legal, practical and psychological reality of X's identity: the commissioning father is his biological father and all parties intended from the outset that the commissioning parents should be his legal parents.

Similarly in *Re A (A Child)*, Russell J pointed out that while both parental orders and adoption would protect the children's lifelong welfare, parental orders were the only way to fully recognize the children's identity and protect their Article 8 rights.

Re A (A Child)[17]

Russell J

However in terms of their identity only parental orders will fully recognise the children's identity as the Applicants' natural children, rather than giving them the wholly artificial and, in their case, inappropriate status of adopted children ...

To make adoption orders would effectively deny adequate recognition of the Applicants' and children's identity and their right to family life under Article 8 ECHR, particularly their established identity, their biological and social ties. There is no doubt in this case that as far as these children are concerned their identity has already been formed as the biological children of their father and the commissioning of their conception and birth involving their mother.

Furthermore this court is mindful of the fact that parental orders are the only orders which will enable the registration of A and B's births in the UK, as opposed to the issue of adoption certificates.

And in *AB v CT*, Theis J agreed that parental orders better reflected the reality of the children's relationship with their parents.

AB v CT[18]

Theis J

I agree a parental order and the consequences that flow from it are, from a welfare perspective, far more suited to surrogacy situations. They were specifically created to deal with these situations. Put simply, they are a more honest order which reflects the reality of what was intended, the lineage connection that already exists and more accurately reflects the child's identity. An adoption order in these situations leaves open the risk of a fiction regarding identity that may need to be resolved by the child later in life. The effect of an adoption order ... of

---

[16] [2014] EWHC 3135 (Fam).   [17] [2015] EWHC 911 (Fam).   [18] [2015] EWFC 12.

> treating the child 'as if' the child is born as a child of the adopter or adopters is not the reality; the child is born with a biological connection to one of the applicants.

As we shall see, when deciding whether to make a parental order, the child's welfare throughout her life is now the court's paramount consideration.[19] The paramountcy principle has shaped the courts' interpretation of the statutory requirements for parental orders, but it is also worth noting that it operates to make adoption now very much a last resort in surrogacy cases.

(1) Parental Orders

When a court makes a parental order, the Registrar General will re-register the child's birth. As with adoption, it will not be possible for the public to make a link between entries in the register of births and the parental order register, but once a child reaches adulthood, she can, after being offered counselling, have access to her original birth certificate. Section 54 of the 2008 Act contains the rules governing access to parental orders for children born after April 2010 (section 30 of the 1990 Act applied to children born before then).

Human Fertilisation and Embryology Act 2008 section 54

54 Parental orders

(1) On an application made by two people ('the applicants'), the court may make an order providing for a child to be treated in law as the child of the applicants if—

    (a) the child has been carried by a woman who is not one of the applicants, as a result of the placing in her of an embryo or sperm and eggs or her artificial insemination,

    (b) the gametes of at least one of the applicants were used to bring about the creation of the embryo, and

    (c) the conditions in subsections (2) to (8) are satisfied.

(2) The applicants must be—

    (a) husband and wife,

    (b) civil partners of each other, or

    (c) two persons who are living as partners in an enduring family relationship and are not within prohibited degrees of relationship in relation to each other.

(3) Except in a case falling within subsection (11), the applicants must apply for the order during the period of 6 months beginning with the day on which the child is born.

(4) At the time of the application and the making of the order—

    (a) the child's home must be with the applicants, and

    (b) either or both of the applicants must be domiciled in the United Kingdom or in the Channel Islands or the Isle of Man.

(5) At the time of the making of the order both the applicants must have attained the age of 18.

(6) The court must be satisfied that both—

    (a) the woman who carried the child, and

---

[19] The Human Fertilisation and Embryology (Parental Orders) Regulations 2010 applied s 1 of the Adoption and Children Act 2002 to applications for parental orders.

(b) any other person who is a parent of the child but is not one of the applicants (including any man who is the father by virtue of section 35 or 36 or any woman who is a parent by virtue of section 42 or 43),

have freely, and with full understanding of what is involved, agreed unconditionally to the making of the order.

(7) Subsection (6) does not require the agreement of a person who cannot be found or is incapable of giving agreement; and the agreement of the woman who carried the child is ineffective for the purpose of that subsection if given by her less than six weeks after the child's birth.

(8) The court must be satisfied that no money or other benefit (other than for expenses reasonably incurred) has been given or received by either of the applicants for or in consideration of—

(a) the making of the order,

(b) any agreement required by subsection (6),

(c) the handing over of the child to the applicants, or

(d) the making of arrangements with a view to the making of the order,

unless authorised by the court.

Section 54 sets out several conditions that must be satisfied before a parental order can be made: for example, at least one of the applicants must be genetically related to the child (thus ruling out parental orders for couples who need to use a sperm and an egg donor, as well as a surrogate); the applicants must be domiciled in the UK,[20] and conception must not have been by sexual intercourse.

In the following sections, we consider five of the section 54 requirements which have caused particular difficulties in recent years: the need for the surrogate's free and unconditional agreement; the six-month time limit; the need for there to be two applicants; the requirement that the child must be living with the applicants at the time of the application, and the requirement that no money or benefit, other than for expenses reasonably incurred, has been paid, unless authorized by the court.

It should be noted that because the Human Fertilisation and Embryology (Parental Orders) Regulations 2010 require the child's welfare throughout its life to be the court's paramount consideration, it is almost impossible for the court to carry out any sort of balancing exercise between public policy considerations and the interests of the child. Instead, when making decisions about parental orders, the welfare of the child from birth to death must take priority over any other considerations.

(a) Consent (section 54(6))

Under section 54(6) a parental order can only be made if both the surrogate and any other person who is the child's parent, such as her husband, have given their free and informed consent. Unlike adoption, it is not possible to dispense with their consent on the ground that it is being unreasonably withheld. As a result, if the surrogate refuses to consent, the courts simply do not have the option of making a parental order.

This was the case in the unusual case of *Re AB (Surrogacy: Consent)*.[21] Twins who had been born as a result of a surrogacy arrangement were living happily with their intended

---

[20] See, for example, *Y v W* [2017] EWFC 60.   [21] [2016] EWHC 2643 (Fam).

parents (the applicants). The surrogate (E) and her husband (the respondents) had made it clear that they did not want to have any active involvement in the twins' lives, but they refused to agree to the making of a parental order, because of 'their own feelings of injustice'. As Theis J explained, they believed that the intended parents 'did not show sufficient concern for [E's] wellbeing' after a consultant had raised concerns about her health at the 12-week scan.

Re AB (Surrogacy: Consent)[22]

Theis J

Without the respondent's consent the application for a parental order comes to a juddering halt, to the very great distress of the applicants. The result is that these children are left in a legal limbo, where, contrary to what was agreed by the parties at the time of the arrangement, the respondents will remain their legal parents even though they are not biologically related to them and they expressly wish to play no part in the children's lives ...

Even though the children's lifelong welfare needs require a parental order to be made, which would secure their legal relationship with the applicants in a lifelong way and extinguish the respondents' legal status with the children, under the provisions of s 54 (6) HFEA 2008 if the respondents' consent is not forthcoming the court cannot make a parental order ...

The respondents have each filed a statement where they set out their account of the background and their reasons for not agreeing to the court making a parental order. Their reasons include highlighting how E felt so unsupported when the relationship between the parties broke down, to increase awareness and emphasise the need for intended parents and surrogates to work co-operatively and to support and show compassion to the surrogate ...

E powerfully describes in her statement what drew her to becoming a surrogate mother. The court can only express the hope that she will be able to rediscover what led her to undertake such a selfless role and see the situation from the view point of these young children. From the perspective of these children's lifelong emotional and psychological welfare parental orders are the only orders that accurately and properly reflect the children's identity as surrogate born children.

The only exception to the consent requirement is, under section 54(7), where a person cannot be found or is incapable of giving consent. This provision was invoked for the first time in *Re D (Minors) (Surrogacy)*, in which twins had been born to an Indian surrogate, as a result of an arrangement entered into by a British same-sex couple. They had taken specialist legal advice before entering into the agreement and were aware of the need for the surrogate to give consent six weeks after the children's birth. The clinic proved to be unhelpful, however, and the couple sought to rely upon this exception in section 54.

Baker J accepted that, in this case, all reasonable steps had been taken to find the surrogate. There was evidence that the surrogate had agreed to give consent, shortly after the birth, and it was clearly in the twins' best interests that a parental order should be made.

---

[22] [2016] EWHC 2643 (Fam).

Re D (Minors) (Surrogacy)[23]

Baker J

First, when it is said that the woman who gave birth to the child cannot be found, the court must carefully scrutinise the evidence as to the efforts which have been taken to find her. It is only when all reasonable steps have been taken to locate her without success that a court is likely to dispense with the need for valid consent. Half-hearted or token attempts to find the surrogate will not be enough. Furthermore, it will normally be prudent for the Applicants to lay the ground for satisfying these requirements at an early stage. Even where, as in this case, the Applicants do not meet the surrogate, they should establish clear lines of communication with her, preferably not simply through one person or agency, and should ensure that the surrogate is made aware during the pregnancy that she will be required to give consent six weeks after the birth.

Secondly, although a consent given before the expiry of six weeks after birth is not valid for the purposes of section 54, the court is entitled to take into account evidence that the woman did give consent at earlier times to giving up the baby. The weight attached to such earlier consent is, however, likely to be limited. The courts must be careful not to use such evidence to undermine the legal requirement that a consent is only valid if given after six weeks.

Thirdly, in the light of the changes affected by the 2010 regulations, the child's welfare is now the paramount consideration when the court is 'coming to a decision' in relation to the making of a parental order. [Counsel] submits, and I accept, that this includes decisions about whether to make an order without the consent of the woman who gave birth in circumstances in which she cannot be found or is incapable of giving consent. It would, however, be wrong to utilise this provision as a means of avoiding the need to take all reasonable steps to attain the woman's consent.

Applying these principles to this case, I accept that these Applicants have taken all reasonable steps to obtain the woman's consent.

In *R v T*, a different issue arose. It was impossible for the court to be satisfied that the surrogate had freely and with full understanding agreed unconditionally to the making of the order. Although the mother had signed consent documents more than six weeks after the child's birth, the court had limited information about what information she had received. The clinic was uncooperative and the political situation in Ukraine ruled out a media appeal to find the mother. As a result, the question for Theis J was whether the surrogate 'could not be found'.

R v T[24]

Theis J

On an issue as fundamental as consent, in the context of circumstances where what is being sought is to change the status of a child the court, in my judgment, should be very cautious about drawing inferences in circumstances such as this ... In my judgment, the court cannot be satisfied that the surrogate mother has 'freely, and with full understanding of what is involved, agreed unconditionally to the making of a parental order' as required by s 54(6).

In those circumstances the court needs to consider whether the surrogate mother 'cannot be found' (s54(7)) and whether the applicants have taken all reasonable steps to find her. In my

---

[23] [2012] EWHC 2631 (Fam).   [24] [2015] EWFC 22.

> judgment they have. The only avenue not explored has been notification through the media. In circumstances such as this where the arrangement concerns a very sensitive subject, it is not known what country the surrogate mother is in and there is continued civil unrest in Ukraine this is not a step, in the circumstances of this case that is reasonable to take.

(b) The six-month time limit (section 54(3))

Until the judgment of the President of the Family Division, Sir James Munby P, in *Re X (A Child) (Surrogacy: Time limit)*,[25] it was thought, with good reason, that section 54(3)—which states that 'the applicants must apply for the order during the period of six months beginning with the day on which the child is born'—meant applications for parental orders had be made within six months of the child's birth.[26] For example, in in *JP v LP (Surrogacy Arrangement: Wardship)*,[27] Eleanor King J was clear that her hands were tied in relation to a child who was 33 weeks old:

> There is no provision within the Act to provide for a discretionary extension to the statutory time limit and no one sought to argue that the court could, or should, whether by means of the use of its inherent jurisdiction or otherwise, seek to circumnavigate the mandatory provisions of the statute.

Then, in *Re X (A Child) (Surrogacy: Time limit)*, Sir James Munby P decided that this cannot have been parliament's intention.

Re X (A Child) (Surrogacy: Time limit) [28]

Sir James Munby P

Can Parliament really have intended that the gate should be barred forever if the application for a parental order is lodged even one day late? I cannot think so. Parliament has not explained its thinking, but given the transcendental importance of a parental order, with its consequences stretching many, many decades into the future, can it sensibly be thought that Parliament intended the difference between six months and six months and one day to be determinative and one day's delay to be fatal? I assume that Parliament intended a sensible result. Given the subject matter, given the consequences for the commissioning parents, never mind those for the child, to construe section 54(3) as barring forever an application made just one day late is not, in my judgment, sensible. It is the very antithesis of sensible; it is almost nonsensical . . .

I have considered whether the result at which I have arrived is somehow precluded by the linguistic structure of section 54, which provides that 'the court may make an order . . . if . . . the [relevant] conditions are satisfied'. I do not think so. Slavish submission to such a narrow and pedantic reading would simply not give effect to any result that Parliament can sensibly be taken to have intended.

I conclude, therefore, that section 54(3) does not have the effect of preventing the court making an order merely because the application is made after the expiration of the six-month period.

---

[25] [2014] EWHC 3135 (Fam).
[27] [2014] EWHC 595 (Fam).
[26] See also, for example, *J v G (Parental Orders)* [2014] 1 FLR 297.
[28] [2014] EWHC 3135 (Fam).

As Claire Fenton-Glynn points out, it would be hard to confine *Re X (A Child) (Surrogacy: Time limit)* to its facts, and, as a result, Sir James Munby P's judgment created a potentially far-reaching precedent.

Claire Fenton-Glynn[29]

This decision will almost certainly have significant repercussions for the wider regulation of international surrogacy, and particularly for other surrogate mothers and commissioning parents who will know that the legal requirements carry little weight, despite being expressed in a mandatory manner. Although Munby P emphasised that this judgment did not create a general rule, and instead relied on the particular facts of the case, there was nothing unique about this case that would make it distinguishable from the many hundreds of other surrogacy cases that go through the courts each year.

The decision strikes another blow to statutory regime in England, and throws into sharp relief the difficulty, indeed near impossibility, of trying to regulate surrogacy through reassigning parenthood after the fact. For this reason, there is an urgent need to review the regulation of surrogacy, both in this country, and internationally. Until this occurs, the courts will continue to have little choice but to stretch, manipulate, or even disregard the statutory wording in order to achieve justice for the child.

Unsurprisingly, *Re X* has been followed by other cases that would have otherwise been out of time. Although Sir James Munby P used the example of applications made a day late in order to illustrate his claim that this could not be what parliament had intended, parental orders have now been granted several years later,[30] and in *A v C*, Theis J made parental orders in respect of a 13-year-old and 12-year-old twins.

A v C[31]

It was not until a chance reading of an article by one of the applicants in a Sunday newspaper in February this year, that she realised the need to make such an application to secure her and her husband's legal relationship with their children in this jurisdiction. They had obtained pre-birth orders in the State where the children were born in the US, which secured their legal relationship there and until reading the article earlier this year had no idea of the need to take any legal steps here ...

I have no doubt in this case each child's lifelong welfare needs require a parental order to be made. Parental orders will confer joint and legal parenthood and parental responsibility upon the applicants in relation to each of the children, and will fully extinguish the residual parental status and parental responsibility of the respondent surrogate mother and her husband in this jurisdiction. This is not a case where there has been any wilful delay in making the application and having considered the public policy considerations set out above, in my judgment the balance comes down firmly in favour of the court making parental orders, to secure the lifelong legal relationship between each of the children and the applicants.

In *LB v SP*,[32] the parents had known in 2010 that they could apply for a parental order, but chose not to do so because of 'the uncertainty and the risk of publicity'. Nevertheless, in 2017

---

[29] 'The Difficulty of Enforcing Surrogacy Regulations' (2015) 74 Cambridge Law Journal 34–37.
[30] *Re A (A Child)* [2015] EWHC 911 (Fam).   [31] [2016] EWFC 42.   [32] [2016] EWFC 77.

Theis J once again, had 'no hesitation in concluding that B's lifelong welfare needs require this court to make a Parental Order' in order to 'ensure that B's security and identity as a lifelong member of the applicants' family is secured in the best way possible'.

(c) Couples only (section 54(2))?

Under section 30 of the 1990 Act, applicants for parental orders had to be married to each other. Section 54 of the 2008 Act extended access to parental orders to civil partners and unmarried partners, and in the six months after it came into force (in April 2010), this operated retrospectively so that people who were previously ineligible could have their parental status recognized.

Although the 2008 Act broadened eligibility for parental orders, it continued to require the application to be made by a couple. Single people were ineligible, and the only way to transfer legal parenthood from the surrogate to a single intended parent was adoption.

In *A v P*, an unusual issue arose in that, although the application for a parental order for B, who had been born to a surrogate in India, had been made by Mr and Mrs A together, Mr A had died before the hearing. The question for the court was whether the word 'applicants' could be construed so as to require two people to make the application, but not to require there to be two living applicants at the time of the making of the order. Theis J held that it could, and in making this decision, she took into account that a failure to make an order in these circumstances would interfere with the family's Article 8 rights, and that that interference could not be justified.

A v P[33]

Theis J

Article 8 is engaged and any interference with those rights must be proportionate and justified. In the particular circumstances of this case the interference cannot be justified as no other order can give recognition to B's status with both Mr and Mrs A in the same transformative way as a parental order can. To interpret [the Act] in the way submitted will not offend against the clear purpose or policy behind the requirements listed in section 54. It will not pave the way for single commissioning parents to apply for a parental order.

In *Re Z (A Child) (Human Fertilisation and Embryology Act: Parental Order)*,[34] Sir James Munby P was invited to 'read down' section 54, in the same way as he had in relation to the six-month time limit, so that one person, rather than two, could apply for a parental order. He declined to do so, quoting from the parliamentary debates in 2008. An amendment to extend parental orders to single applicants had been rejected by the government, on the grounds, as the then health minister, Dawn Primarolo MP explained, that there is an important difference between surrogacy and adoption:

The difference is this: adoption involves a child who already exists and whose parents are not able to keep the child, for whom new parents are sought. That is different, which is why there is no parallel ... Surrogacy, however, involves agreeing to hand over a child even before

---

[33] [2011] EWHC 1738 (Fam).   [34] [2015] EWFC 73.

conception. The Government are still of the view that the magnitude of that means that it is best dealt with by a couple. That is why we have made the arrangements that we have.[35]

Sir James Munby P found that the law was clear, and that he did not have the discretion to grant a parental order to a single applicant, whose child, Z, had been born to a surrogate in the US.[36]

Before Z's father applied for a declaration of incompatibility, some commentators were puzzled by the apparent inconsistency between Sir James Munby P's decision in this case and his decision in *Re X*, where the six-month time limit was 'read down', or, in effect, trumped by child welfare considerations. Certainly, the minister's claim that surrogacy is of a different 'magnitude' to, say, single parent adoption seems rather obviously weak. Alan Brown has suggested that the difference between the cases lies in the enduring significance of the 'two-parent nuclear family' for the regulation of surrogacy, which would be threatened by the single applicant in *Re Z*, but which remained intact following the time-limit extension in *Re X*.[37]

Z's father then applied for a declaration that section 54(1) and (2) of the Human Embryology and Fertilisation Act 2008 were incompatible with his and Z's human rights under Articles 8 and/or Article 14 taken in conjunction with Article 8.

Before the court could hear this application, the Secretary of State conceded that the ban on single applicants was incompatible with Article 14, taken in conjunction with Article 8. As a result, in *Re Z (A Child) (No 2)*, Sir James Munby made a declaration that:

sections 54(1) and (2) of the Human Fertilisation and Embryology Act 2008 are incompatible with the rights of the Applicant and the Second Respondent under Article 14 ECHR taken in conjunction with Article 8 insofar as they prevent the Applicant from obtaining a parental order on the sole ground of his status as a single person as opposed to being part of a couple.

Re Z (A Child) (No 2)[38]

Sir James Munby P

It will be seen that the Secretary of State's concession was very precisely formulated and narrowly drawn. The Secretary of State does *not* accept that there is any incompatibility with article 8 taken alone. The concession is that the relevant provisions are incompatible with article 14, taken in conjunction with article 8 . As it was put in the letter: 'This is in reality, a discrimination case. That is the basis of the concession.'

The reason for drawing this concession narrowly was in order not to suggest that Article 8 gave anyone a right to engage in surrogacy, or to any particular sort of order in a surrogacy case.

In 2017, the government laid a draft remedial order before Parliament which would have enabled single people to obtain parental orders, but only if they could establish that they were not in a relationship with anyone. This removed one source of discrimination, but potentially

[35] Hansard 12 June 2008, col 249.
[36] *Re Z (A Child) (Human Fertilisation and Embryology Act: Parental Order)* [2015] EWFC 73.
[37] 'Two means two, but must does not mean must: an analysis of recent decisions on the conditions for parental orders in surrogacy' (2018) Child and Family Law Quarterly 23.
[38] [2016] EWHC 1191 (Fam).

created another based upon relationship status. Following criticism by the Joint Committee on Human Rights, this restriction was dropped and a new remedial order was laid before Parliament in 2018. This adds a new section 54A to the 2008 Act.

Human Fertilisation and Embryology Act section 54A

Parental orders: one applicant

(1) On an application made by one person ('the applicant'), the court may make an order providing for a child to be treated in law as the child of the applicant if—

    (a) the child has been carried by a woman who is not the applicant, as a result of the placing in her of an embryo or sperm and eggs or her artificial insemination,

    (b) the gametes of the applicant were used to bring about the creation of the embryo, and

    (c) the conditions in subsections (2) to (8) are satisfied [these reproduce section 54(2) to (8)] ...

(11) An application which relates to a child born before the coming into force of this section may be made within the period of six months beginning with the day on which this section comes into force.

The remedial order has retrospective effect for the first six months, in order that parental orders can be made in respect of children whose single parents were previously ineligible. In *M v F*,[39] for example, the intended parents' relationship had broken down during the surrogate's pregnancy, and the intended (and genetic) father had played no role in the child (A)'s life. While continuing 'the wardship and the grant of care and control in respect of him to the applicant', which enabled A to live with his intended mother, Keehan J noted that:

> The applicant earnestly hopes that that the terms of the remedial order will be such that she will be able to apply for a parental order. This 'transformative' order would enable her to be a legal parent of A.

In *AB v CD*, a parental order was also not an option for the genetic and intended mother of twins born through surrogacy, who was divorced from their intended father. The twins were living with her and her new partner, but their legal parents continued to be the Indian surrogate and her husband. Keehan J made the twins wards of court, with a child arrangements order in favour of the child's 'mother' and 'step-father', while also expressing frustration with the law.

AB v CD[40]

> The absurdity of the law not recognising the first and second respondent as the mother and the father of these children is plain. The losers are predominantly the children who do not have their biological parentage recognised in law.
>
> I find myself extremely frustrated, as no doubt are the first and second respondents, that I am prevented, without any obvious good, legal or policy reason from making orders which explicitly recognise them as the legal mother and the legal father of these children. Instead,

---

[39] [2017] EWHC 2176 (Fam).   [40] [2018] EWHC 1590 (Fam).

> I am forced, as have other judges before me, to construct a set of orders to secure the welfare of the children which fall very far short of the transformative effect of a parental order.

(d) No payments, other than expenses reasonably incurred, unless authorized by the court (section 54(8))

The court has the power to authorize payments other than expenses reasonably incurred, and there has, as yet, been no case in which an application for a parental order has been refused on the grounds that an unacceptably large sum of money had changed hands.

Within the UK, the Surrogacy UK Working Group on Surrogacy Law Reform's survey of 100 UK surrogates found that payments to surrogates are most commonly between £12,000–£15,000.

Surrogacy UK Working Group on Surrogacy Law Reform[41]

> 89 of 100 respondents to a question about payments received some money to cover expenses for their most recent surrogacy journey. None said that they received more than £20,000, with the majority receiving between £12,001 and £15,000, and the next highest group receiving between £10,001 and £12,000. In total these sums were reported by 58.4% of the respondents. In the 2015 survey, 68.2% of surrogates reported receiving between £10,000 and £15,000 for their expenses. There has been an increase in surrogates reporting receiving between £15,001 and £20,000, from 4.7% in 2015 to 14.6% in 2018. The proportion of those reporting receiving less than £10,000 was very similar: 27.1% in 2015 and 27% in 2018. This suggests that the levels of payments to UK surrogates is remaining relatively static, with small increases in higher payments being attributable to rising costs of living, reflected in surrogates' expenses.

In one of the first foreign surrogacy cases to reach the courts, *Re X & Y (Foreign Surrogacy)*, a case in which a British couple had employed a Ukrainian surrogate, it had to be conceded that the payments of €235 per month to the surrogate during pregnancy and a lump sum of €25,000 on the live birth of the twins, to enable her to put down a deposit for the purchase of a flat, significantly exceeded 'expenses reasonably incurred'. Taking the twins' welfare into account, Hedley J agreed to authorize these payments in order to enable a parental order to be made, but he expressed considerable unease about doing so.

Re X & Y (Foreign Surrogacy)[42]

Hedley J

> I feel bound to observe that I find this process of authorisation most uncomfortable. What the court is required to do is to balance two competing and potentially irreconcilably conflicting concepts. Parliament is clearly entitled to legislate against commercial surrogacy and is clearly entitled to expect that the courts should implement that policy consideration in its decisions. Yet it is also recognised that as the full rigour of that policy consideration will bear

---

[41] *Surrogacy in the UK: further evidence for reform* (Surrogacy UK, 2018).
[42] [2008] EWHC 3030 (Fam).

on one wholly unequipped to comprehend it let alone deal with its consequences (i.e. the child concerned) that rigour must be mitigated by the application of a consideration of that child's welfare. That approach is both humane and intellectually coherent. The difficulty is that it is almost impossible to imagine a set of circumstances in which by the time the case comes to court, the welfare of any child (particularly a foreign child) would not be gravely compromised (at the very least) by a refusal to make an order.

In *Re L (A Minor)*, a case involving a British couple who had made a commercial surrogacy arrangement in Illinois, Hedley J explained that the application of the paramountcy principle made it almost impossible to refuse a parental order.

Re L (A Minor)[43]

Hedley J

What has changed, however, is that welfare is no longer merely the court's first consideration but becomes its paramount consideration. The effect of that must be to weight the balance between public policy considerations and welfare decisively in favour of welfare. It must follow that it will only be in the clearest case of the abuse of public policy that the court will be able to withhold an order if otherwise welfare considerations supports its making. It underlines the court's earlier observation that, if it is desired to control commercial surrogacy arrangements, those controls need to operate before the court process is initiated i.e. at the border or even before.

There is effectively now a checklist for judges to consider when deciding whether to authorize retrospectively payments other than expenses reasonably incurred. Indeed, the judgments on payments are now almost formulaic. In *Re P-M*, for example, when deciding whether to exercise her discretion under section 54(8), Theis J turned once again to what she described as a 'well-trodden path'.

Re P-M[44]

Theis J

Turning now to the well-trodden path laid out by Hedley J as to the relevant considerations in considering whether the court can authorise any payments under section 54(8), the questions the court has to ask are as follows:

i. Was the sum paid disproportionate to reasonable expenses?

ii. Were the applicants acting in good faith and without moral taint in their dealings with the surrogate?

iii. Were the applicants' party to any attempt to de-fraud the authorities?

---

[43] [2010] EWHC 3146 (Fam). [44] [2013] EWHC 2328 (Fam).

In addition to these questions, the incorporation of the paramountcy principle means that, as Theis J put it, 'where the welfare considerations demand that an order should be made, the court will only in the clearest case of abuse of public policy consider not making an order'.[45]

In practice, then, the prohibition on payments in the 2008 Act is a prohibition on grossly disproportionate payments, but with no payment ever having been found to be grossly disproportionate. Is there a sum of money so huge that the courts would be likely to refuse to make a parental order? Given the need to put the child's welfare first, it is impossible to imagine the circumstances in which a court would decide that a child's legal parentage should be left unresolved, with all of the potentially disastrous consequences this might have for the child, because the surrogate had been paid too much money. The UK's prohibition on commercial surrogacy is therefore completely ineffective.

(e) At the time of the application and the making of the order the child's home must be with the applicants (section 54(4))

What if the applicants are living apart at the time of the application and/or the making of the order? Could it nevertheless be argued that the child's home is 'with' both of them? In addition to the application being made after six months, this was also an issue in *Re X (A Child) (Surrogacy: Time limit)*. The applicants had separated at the time of the application, but were living together again when the case came before the court. Sir James Munby P found that X's home was with both of the commissioning parents at the time of the application, albeit that they were not living in the same place.

Re X (A Child) (Surrogacy: Time limit)[46]

Sir James Munby P

The real question arises in relation to section 54(4)(a) can it be said that X's 'home' was 'with' them at the time of the application (it plainly is now)? There are, in my judgment, two reasons why this question should be answered in the affirmative. In the circumstances as I have described them ... , X had his 'home' with the commissioning parents, with both of them, albeit that they lived in separate houses. He plainly did not have his home with anyone else. His living arrangements were split between the commissioning father and the commissioning mother. It can fairly be said that he lived with them.

In the light of his reasoning in relation to the time limit, Sir James Munby P's conclusion on section 54(4) was inevitable. If parliament must have intended a sensible result, it could not have intended that children born through surrogacy arrangements should be disadvantaged if their parents separate. There is no guarantee that parents who are together on the day of the making of the order will be together six months afterwards, so it would be odd to penalize children for something as arbitrary as the date of parental separation. And, of course, if parental orders can be granted beyond the six-month time limit, as is now the case, there are likely to be more cases in which the child's parents have split up.

In *Re A and B (No 2 Parental Order)*,[47] for example, Theis J was faced with applications for parental orders in relation to three-year-old twin girls born as a result of a surrogacy arrangement in India. In addition to having to decide whether to make an order outside the

[45] Ibid. [46] [2014] EWHC 3135 (Fam). [47] [2015] EWHC 2080 (Fam).

six-month time limit, the parents had since separated from each other. Both parents were 'committed to the children and ensuring their needs are met', and Theis J had no difficultly in concluding that the children's home was with both applicants despite the fact that they lived separately.

In the matter of X (A Child),[48] a parental order was also 'manifestly in the best interests of the child' whose intended parents were in a platonic marriage (one parent was gay), and who did not live together. As Sir James Munby P explained:

> In the present case the applicants have different homes, with each of which the child is very familiar. When the child is not with both parents, the child's time is split between them and their homes. The child does not live with anyone else. I need not go into further detail. In my judgment it is clearly established on the authorities that, in the circumstances of this case, the child's 'home' was and is 'with' the applicants.

(f) The role of social workers

In order to satisfy itself that the section 54 criteria are satisfied, the court will be assisted by a report from an experienced social worker from the Child and Family Court Advisory and Support Service (Cafcass). Known as Parental Order Reporters (PORs), their duties are to investigate arrangements in order to establish whether the statutory criteria are satisfied; to find out how much money, if any, has changed hands; to assess the welfare of the child; and to advise the court as to whether an order is in the child's best interests.

Because the child must already be living with the intended parents before an application is made, her welfare will seldom be promoted by removing her from a settled home. In their interviews with PORs, Crawshaw et al found that some were frustrated by what they perceived to be a 'fait accompli'.[49] According to one of their interviewees:

> from the point of view of the child I felt it was in the best interests of the child, but it left me feeling quite uncomfortable ... [W]hat an absolutely ridiculous situation that we are put in, that we are doing all of this work after the horse has bolted, and where it's almost too late to have a significant you know, impact on it, and my feeling was that this should have been done be- forehand ... [Y]ou wouldn't do an adoption assessment you know, on carers' ability to adopt a child, after you've just placed a baby with them for six months ... [I]t just struck me as being completely bizarre and ridiculous.

(2) Adoption

If the intended parent(s) are not able to apply for a parental order, the only way in which they can both acquire legal parenthood and extinguish the surrogate's legal motherhood, is through adoption.

This was the case in *B v C,*[50] a case in which a single man (B)'s mother (C) acted as a sur- rogate for him. This meant that B and his child (A) had the same mother; legally they were

---

[48] [2018] EWFC 15.

[49] Marilyn Crawshaw, Satvinder Purewal, and Olga van den Akker, 'Working at the margins: the views and experiences of court social workers on parental orders work in surrogacy arrangements' (2012) 42 British Journal of Social Work 1–19.

[50] [2015] EWFC 17.

brothers. While at first sight one might think that this would complicate matters, in fact, it meant that when C and her husband placed the child for adoption with B, they had not committed a criminal offence because it was an intra-familial adoption. Theis J made the adoption order in order to 'provide the legal security to A's relationship with B, which will undoubtedly meet A's long term welfare needs', while also stressing the importance of seeking expert legal advice in order to navigate this 'legal minefield'.

Adoption might also become necessary if neither the surrogate nor the intended parents are able to look after the child. *Re A (A Child)* was a tragic case in which the adults had met via an internet website and quickly embarked upon a partial surrogacy arrangement. Child protection measures had been taken in relation to some of the intended mother's existing children, and she had no contact with three of them. After A's birth, the relationship between the surrogate, and the intended parents had deteriorated badly, and none were judged capable of providing for A's needs. The judge also found it hard to believe anything any of the adults said.

Re A (A Child)[51]

HHJ Matthews QC

This case represents a tragedy for all concerned but most particularly for the child at its centre. It is a cautionary tale as to what can go wrong in unregulated surrogacy. Such arrangements can no doubt work very well and there are likely to be many happy families in this country where surrogacy has been a success. However, because of the special nature of surrogacy arrangements, they demand mature, balanced and sensitive handling. Surrogacy should not be approached without very considerable and careful reflection in respect of all of the ramifications for the child and the members of the families involved. A child is not a commodity to be bought and sold. This child is an individual for whom the consequences of the arrangements will have a lifelong impact.

A was taken into care and placed with prospective adopters, and the following year, Her Honour Judge Matthews QC made a closed adoption order.[52]

(3) Disputes over Residence

Not all surrogacy cases result in parental order or adoption applications. In other cases, particularly when the arrangement has broken down, the courts have used child arrangement orders creatively in order to protect the child's best interests.

In *Re Z (A Child) (Surrogacy Agreements: Child Arrangements Orders)*, A and B appealed unsuccessfully against Russell J's decision to make a child arrangements order that the child should live with his mother (X) and her partner (P), and have contact with the intended parents, his father (A) and his partner (B). A and B had met Z through a Facebook surrogacy site. After a brief face to face meeting, A and X had travelled to Cyprus for the transfer to X of two embryos, created for a previous surrogacy arrangement which had resulted in twins. X had learning difficulties and was described as a 'vulnerable young woman'.

[51] [2014] EWFC 55.   [52] [2015] EWFC 63.

Re Z (A Child) (Surrogacy Agreements: Child Arrangements Orders)[53]

Black LJ

Russell J found A and B to be in a much more secure position socially and economically than X. The picture that emerges from the judgment is that they were by far the dominant partners in the surrogacy arrangement. The judge was heavily critical of the way in which they treated X, in relation to whom the judge considered they had failed to show consideration, concern and respect. The surrogacy agreement between the parties was entered into with little planning or preparation ...

Z needed to have both A and B and also X in his life, and it was X that the judge thought would be most able to secure this ... [I]t can be seen that she laid particular emphasis on X being the parent who is more able and more likely to treat A and B in an open and generous way and to enable Z to develop a good relationship with A, B and his siblings, and so to allow him to develop a wider and more positive sense of his own identity.

In *Re H (A Child) (Surrogacy Breakdown),* the relationship between C and D (the surrogate and her husband) and A and B (the intended parents) had broken down before H was born. C and D decided that they would not hand H over to A and B, and they registered H's birth themselves. Theis J had concluded that it would nevertheless be best for H to live with A and B, with contact every three weeks with C and D. C and D appealed on the grounds that Theis J had 'effectively made a parental order in all but name'. The Court of Appeal dismissed their appeal.

Re H (A Child) (Surrogacy Breakdown)[54]

McFarlane LJ

It is undoubtedly correct that a surrogate mother has the right to change her mind, but Ms Markham wisely withdrew from the submission that such a mother also had the right to have her own way about where the child should live. She was also forced to concede that, while the six-week 'cooling off' period protects a mother in relation to the important issue of consent to a parental order, it tells one nothing about what the best welfare arrangements for the child will be after birth ...

The Judge therefore concluded that it would be best for H to live with A and B because (1) H's identity needs as a child of gay intended parents would be best met by living with a genetic parent, (2) A and B could meet H's day-to-day needs in an attuned way, (3) A and B were best able to promote the relationship with C and D, having remained positive about their significance despite the difficulties, and (4) C and D were unlikely to significantly change their views about A and B ...

We cannot agree that the Judge's order was equivalent to the making of a parental order. A parental order is transformative. It leaves the surrogate with no rights, and no right to apply to court. It would not provide for ongoing contact ...

Even without the clear evidence of the Guardian, it would have been obvious that it was not likely to be in H's interests to have more than one secure home base, and one couple who could be clearly identified as parents. In consequence, there was inevitably going to be a radical reduction in the amount of time spent in the other home, however painful that would surely be. This was, in legal language, necessary and proportionate. In our view, the Judge could not have been criticised had she chosen a lower level of contact, but she was certainly entitled to accept the evidence of the Guardian. Nor do we accept that the level of contact could fairly be described as 'identity contact', an expression generally used to describe meetings once or twice a year that are just sufficient for a child to know who a relative is, but insufficient to allow a relationship to develop ...

[W]e note that surrogacy is a complex area, ethically and legally, and that there are no internationally agreed norms. The subject has now been taken up as part of the Law Commission's current programme, and in parting from the case, we endorse the Judge's observations:

> This case is another example of the complex consequences that can arise from entering into this type of arrangement. Even though C was an experienced surrogate, this case demonstrates the risks involved when parties reach agreement to conceive a child which, if it goes wrong, can cause huge distress to all concerned. For all the adults involved, who all clearly love H, the one thing I know they will agree is that their dispute and this contested litigation has been a harrowing experience for them all. This case is another example of the consequences of not having a properly supported and regulated framework to underpin arrangements of this kind.

(4) Conflict of Laws and Immigration Issues

Particular difficulties arise in cross-border surrogacy arrangements. If overseas intended parents make an arrangement with a British surrogate, they would be ineligible for a parental order because they are not domiciled in the UK. Adoption would also be problematic because there are restrictions upon foreigners adopting British children. This issue arose in *Re G (Surrogacy: Foreign Domicile)*, in which McFarlane J found a way to enable Mr and Mrs G to take M back to Turkey with them. His judgment is notable for the criticism he makes of the lack of effective regulation of surrogacy.

Re G (Surrogacy: Foreign Domicile)[55]

McFarlane J

I am sufficiently concerned by the information uncovered in these two cases to question whether some form of inspection or authorisation should be required in order to improve the quality of advice that is given to individuals who seek to achieve the birth of a child through surrogacy. Given the importance of the issues involved when the life of a child is created in this manner, it is questionable whether the role of facilitating surrogacy arrangements should be left to groups of well-meaning amateurs.

When UK couples travel abroad for surrogacy, because the surrogate is the child's mother, the child may not be a British citizen from birth. Regardless of what the local birth certificate says, for the purposes of British citizenship, the surrogate will always be the child's legal mother from birth. As the Foreign and Commonwealth Office's guidance explains: 'even if your names appear on the local birth certificate, a baby born to a foreign national surrogate mother who

---

[55] [2007] EWHC 2814 (Fam).

is married will not be automatically eligible for British nationality'.[56] If the child is not entitled to a British passport, she may not be entitled to come to the UK with the intended parents.

In *Re X & Y (Foreign Surrogacy)*, the clash between UK and local law left the child parentless and stateless, leading Hedley J to warn of the 'many pitfalls' involved in foreign surrogacy arrangements.

Re X & Y (Foreign Surrogacy)[57]

Hedley J

It will be readily apparent that many pitfalls confront the couple who consider commissioning a foreign surrogacy. First, the quality of the information currently available is variable and may, in what it omits, actually be misleading. Secondly, potentially difficult conflict of law issues arise which may (as in this case) have wholly unintended and unforeseen consequences as for example in payments made. Thirdly, serious immigration problems may arise ... Children born to foreign surrogate mothers, especially to married women, may have no rights of entry nor may the law confer complementary rights on the commissioning couple ...

If one googles 'find a surrogate online', it is easy to find websites making misleading claims about the ease of cross-border surrogacy arrangements. UK citizens may be lulled into a false sense of security if they are promised, and given a local birth certificate with their names on it. This was the case in *Re JB (A Child) (Surrogacy: Immigration)*,[58] in which the intended parents of a child who was still in India nearly two years after his birth had been 'wholly unaware of the immigration and nationality policies as they applied to children born as the result of surrogacy'. In her oral evidence, the intended mother had said 'it was a shock that we were not parents under English law'.

In order to respond to the increasing number of foreign surrogacy cases which raise immigration issues, the UK Border Agency issued guidance on *Inter-Country Surrogacy and the Immigration Rules*.[59] In bold and underlined typeface, paragraph 6 warns:

Even if the surrogate mother's home country sees the commissioning couple as the 'parents' and issues documentation to this effect, UK law and the Immigration Rules will not view them as 'parents'.

The Foreign and Commonwealth Office (FCO) has also issued guidance on the acquisition of British citizenship,[60] for children born as a result of overseas surrogacy. This warns prospective parents, again in bold typeface:

Please note, it can take several weeks, if not months, to process applications for children born through surrogacy overseas and you should be prepared for an extended stay overseas once your child is born.

Matters are simplest if the foreign surrogate is single when, provided that the intended father is British, has a genetic link to the child, and is able to pass on his nationality (ie he was born

---

[56] *Surrogacy Overseas* (FCO, 2014).   [57] [2008] EWHC 3030 (Fam).
[58] [2016] EWHC 760 (Fam).   [59] Available at <www.ukba.homeoffice.gov.uk/>.
[60] *Surrogacy Overseas* (FCO, 2014).

in Britain rather than qualifying for citizenship only by descent), the child has an automatic claim to British nationality, and the intended parents can apply for a British passport for her. The FCO guidance, however, stresses the importance of being able to *prove* that the surrogate is, in fact, single. In practice, this can be difficult.

The Foreign and Commonwealth Office[61]

For the application to be processed we will need to be completely satisfied that the surrogate mother is single. If there are any concerns as to surrogate mother's marital status, Her Majesty's Passport Office may need to complete additional checks and the passport application process may take longer. You should be prepared to provide documentary evidence of the surrogate mother's single status, including confirming that the surrogacy clinic or surrogate mother will be able to provide you with relevant and genuine documentation before you enter into the surrogacy arrangement. Please bear in mind that it may be difficult to prove the single status of the surrogate mother, particularly if she is claiming never to have married. Also, a divorcee or widow may have remarried, so a divorce decree or death certificate alone may not be sufficient proof.

If the foreign surrogate is married, the intended parents will need to apply to register the child as a British citizen under section 3(1) of the British Nationality Act 1981, which allows children who are not automatically entitled to British citizenship at birth to be registered as British citizens at the discretion of the Home Secretary. According to FCO guidance, the Home Office must be satisfied that:

- at least one of the commissioning parents is a British Citizen
- the surrogate parents have consented
- had the child been born to the commissioning couple legitimately, s/he would have had an automatic claim to British citizenship or would have qualified for registration under the British Nationality Act 1981.

To make matters more complicated still, if the surrogate's home country changes its laws on surrogacy, because surrogacy inevitably takes place over a period of at least nine months, it is inevitable that some people will have already embarked on surrogacy arrangements when the rules change. As we saw in *R v T*,[62] it is also possible that that unrest or political instability may complicate arrangements.

There might also be a clash between the steps that a couple are told to take in the country where the child is born and UK law For example, in *Re G (Parental Orders)*, a British couple had entered into a surrogacy arrangement in the US, and had been through a US adoption process. By doing so, they were potentially in violation of section 83 of the Adoption and Children Act 2002, which makes it a criminal offence for a person who is habitually resident in the British Isles to bring a child into the UK having adopted that child overseas, without first having obtained the approval of the Home Secretary, and complied with a series of other procedural requirements. As Theis J explained, the couple had been caught between 'a rock

---

[61] Ibid.   [62] [2015] EWFC 22.

and a hard place', and the case illustrated the importance of securing expert legal advice in both jurisdictions.

Re G (Parental Orders)[63]

Theis J

This case provides yet another timely illustration of the legal minefield in international surrogacy arrangements. It underscores the critical importance of anyone considering this type of arrangement to secure expert advice, in particular legal advice in both jurisdictions at each stage of the process.

The applicants were clearly between a rock and a hard place. It is clear that from a welfare standpoint, and because of their obligations under the surrogacy agreement, the steps they took in the US were the right steps to take and were done with the best of intentions and with the children's welfare uppermost in their minds. They had no idea that by undertaking those steps, they would potentially be in breach of s.83.

Moylan J in *Re D (A Child) (Surrogacy)* is not alone in suggesting that—in the light of increasing numbers of international surrogacy arrangements, and the clashes between jurisdictions which inevitably result—some sort of cross-national regulation would be desirable.

Re D (A Child) (Surrogacy)[64]

Moylan J

This case provides a clear example of the difficulties created as a result of surrogacy arrangements being subject to varying degrees of domestic regulation, from significant regulation to none at all, and also because of the existence of significant differences in the effect of such domestic regulation. There is, in my view, a compelling need for a uniform system of regulation to be created by an international instrument in order to make available an appropriate structure in respect of what can only be described as the surrogacy market.

Any cross-national regulation would have to happen at a relatively high level of abstraction: it is hard to imagine global agreement on acceptable levels of compensation, for example. Within Europe, states have a margin of appreciation on how to regulate surrogacy, although the first decision of the European Court of Human Rights (ECtHR) in an international surrogacy case made it clear that this does not extend to being able to deny the existence of a parent–child relationship between a child and her genetic parent(s).

In *Mennesson v France* and *Labassee v France*,[65] the ECtHR found that France's margin of appreciation did not permit it to refuse to issue birth certificates to children who had been born as a result of surrogacy arrangements in the US, and who were being brought up by their

---

[63] [2014] EWHC 1561 (Fam).   [64] [2014] EWHC 2121 (Fam).
[65] *Mennesson v France* (Application no 61592/11), judgment of 26 June 2014; *Labassee v France* (Application no 65941/11), judgment of 26 June 2014.

intended parents in France. Respect for the children's private life, under Article 8, required them to be able to establish their identity as a human being, and 'filiation'—that is, the fact of being descended from a genetic parent, in this case the father—was an essential aspect of this. Denial of filiation led to legal uncertainty for the children; they would have no automatic inheritance rights, and it also inaccurately represented their relationship with their biological father. France had therefore breached the children's Article 8 rights.

Interestingly, the court in *Mennesson* was concerned only with the importance of recognising the children's genetic link with their *father*. In a gestational surrogacy arrangement, a child will usually also have a genetic link with her intended mother. Andrea Mulligan explains why the court may not have wished to address whether this also gave rise to a child's identity right:

> For the Court to extend its analysis to genetic mothers would require the Court to stray into the complex territory of defining whether a genetic or gestational mother has the greater right to be recognised as a child's mother, a question that it might understandably not wish to address, and one which certainly engages sensitive ethical issues which generally tend towards a wide margin of appreciation.[66]

Three years later, in *Paradiso v Italy*, the Grand Chamber of the ECtHR found that there had not been a breach of the applicants' Article 8 rights when a child born as a result of a surrogacy arrangement in Russia had been taken into care. Although the Russian clinic had said that the intended father's sperm had been used to create the embryo with a donor egg, a DNA test subsequently proved that this was not the case. The court rejected the intended parents' claim that the removal of the child interfered with their Article 8 rights on three grounds: the absence of biological ties; the fact that the child had lived with the intended parents for only eight months; and the illegality of the arrangement under Italian law.

Paradiso and Campanelli v Italy [67]

Grand Chamber

Given the child's young age and the short period spent with the applicants, the court did not agree with the psychologist's report submitted by the applicants, suggesting that the separation would have devastating consequences for the child. Referring to the literature on the subject, it noted that the fact of mere separation from the care-givers, without any other factors being present, would not cause a psychopathological state in a child. It concluded that the trauma caused by the separation would not be irreparable.

The Court does not underestimate the impact which the immediate and irreversible separation from the child must have had on the applicants' private life ... However, the public interests at stake weigh heavily in the balance, while comparatively less weight is to be attached to the applicants' interest in their personal development by continuing their relationship with the child. Agreeing to let the child stay with the applicants, possibly with a view to becoming his adoptive parents, would have been tantamount to legalising the situation created by them

---

[66] 'Identity Rights and Sensitive Ethical Questions: The European Convention on Human Rights and the Regulation of Surrogacy Arrangements' (2018) 26 Medical Law Review 449–75.
[67] Ibid.

> in breach of important rules of Italian law. The Court accepts that the Italian courts, having assessed that the child would not suffer grave or irreparable harm from the separation, struck a fair balance between the different interests at stake, while remaining within the wide margin of appreciation available to them in the present case.

Paradiso is a surprising judgment, for several reasons.[68] It places considerable weight on the non-existence of biological ties, which is especially odd in this case, given that the absence of a genetic link with the father was the result of fraud or negligence on the part of the clinic. At the same time, the court seemed surprisingly unconcerned about the impact of separation on the child. Andrea Mulligan points out that it also sits oddly with the previous decision in *Mennesson*.

Andrea Mulligan[69]

> On one level, the decisions in *Mennesson* and in *Paradiso* seem to be contradictory. *Mennesson* might be framed as eroding the discretion of the member states to prohibit surrogacy, while *Paradiso* appears to restore the discretion of the Member States to legislate in this field . . .
>
> The result of these cases is that the States retain a wide discretion in the prohibition of surrogacy generally. In principle, it seems that that discretion is very broad indeed, extending even to the extreme steps taken by the Italian authorities in *Paradiso*. That discretion is radically reduced, however, in relation to legal recognition of the parent–child relationship. Where there is a genetic link between father and child, and where both parties wish that link to be recognised, then there is an obligation on the State to recognise it . . .
>
> The strong implication of these decisions is that the Member States are only required to recognise a parental relationship arising from surrogacy where a genetic link exists. In the absence of a genetic link, it would appear that Member States are fully entitled to refuse to recognise any legal relationship between parent and child.

The Hague Conference on Private International Law, which has been responsible for drafting conventions on, for example, inter-country adoption and child abduction, has taken up the issue of international surrogacy arrangements, and in 2015, an Expert Group was set up in order to explore further the feasibility of drawing up a similar private international law instrument to cover surrogacy.[70] There have been several meetings of the Expert Group, which at the time of writing continues to grapple with the tension between the need for certainty of a child's legal parentage, and differences between states' approaches both to the attribution of parentage, and to the recognition of foreign public documents, such as birth certificates.

---

[68] See further Marianna Iliadou, 'Surrogacy and the ECtHR: Reflections on *Paradiso and Campanelli v Italy*' (2019) 27 Medical Law Review 144–54.

[69] 'Identity Rights and Sensitive Ethical Questions: The European Convention on Human Rights and the Regulation of Surrogacy Arrangements' (2018) 26 Medical Law Review 449–75.

[70] *Council on General Affairs and Policy of the Conference: Conclusions and Recommendations* (HCCH, 2015).

Hague Conference on Private International Law[71]

5. The Group recognised the importance of legal parentage as a status from which children derive many important rights. The Group generally agreed with the following overarching aims of its work, which should be reflected in a possible future international instrument:

- provide predictability, certainty and continuity of legal parentage in international situations for all persons involved;

- resolve conflicts between legal systems in respect of the establishment and contestation of legal parentage; and

- take into account in the context of legal parentage, the fundamental rights of all persons involved, and in particular the best interests of children as a primary consideration . . .

34. The Group noted the significant diversity in types of birth certificates and other public documents that record legal parentage. The Group acknowledged the reality that the majority of States give domestic and foreign public documents, birth certificates in particular, only evidential weight. The Group noted that parentage usually arises by operation of law. Therefore, further consideration needs to be given as to whether, and if so how, a parent-child status could be recognised where there is no judicial decision on parentage . . .

45. The Group acknowledged the different approaches of States to ISAs [international surrogacy arrangements]. The Group recognised the continued concerns at international level and the public policy considerations relating to ISAs, including, for example, limping parentage and the potential for exploitation. The Group identified that public policy and the best interests of the child are key issues which warrant further discussion.

(5) Informal Transfers

While parental orders and adoption are the only ways in which the intended parents can become the legal parents of a child born following a surrogacy arrangement, this does not mean that every surrogate birth is followed by a formal transfer of legal parenthood. A child may be handed over by the surrogate, and live with the intended parents without any legal formalities. For obvious reasons, it is impossible to tell how many unofficial transfers of children take place each year.

It is indubitably not in a child's best interests for her 'parents' to have no legal relationship with her, while someone else, perhaps on another continent, retains legal parenthood. In *A v B*, Theis J spelled out the importance of seeking a parental order.

A v B[72]

Theis J

If such an order is not sought, one or both of them are not the legal parents of the child, which can have long term detrimental consequences. An obvious example is that testamentary provision for the child may be open to challenge . . . Those who may maintain that a parental order is not required are not considering the best interests of the child who they care for and

---

[71] Hague Conference on Private International Law, *Report of the February 2018 meeting of the Experts' Group on Parentage/Surrogacy* (HCCH, 2018).

[72] [2015] EWHC 1059 (Fam).

> risk sleepwalking into future legal difficulties for the child, which can readily be avoided by a parental order being made.

It is impossible to tell how many children are in this sort of legal limbo, but specialist solicitors Helen Prosser and Natalie Gamble suggest that it is not uncommon for parents to choose not to apply for parental orders.

Helen Prosser and Natalie Gamble[73]

> Many perceive the UK's legal process to be inappropriate and resent having to justify themselves as parents of a child they already consider theirs ... The process of applying for a parental order is also often perceived as being complex, lengthy and expensive, and without a tangible practical benefit. We are commonly asked by parents whether any issues could really arise in practice if they do not apply, and who will ever question their child's foreign birth certificate. Quite apart from the legal difficulties being created for children left in permanent limbo, this gives rise to concerns about whether such parents are indirectly being encouraged to be secretive about the fact their children have been born through surrogacy, which may create significant issues for their children long term.

(f) LAW REFORM

In 2018, the Scottish and English Law Commissions embarked upon a joint review of the law relating to surrogacy. Expected to last three years, the Law Commissions intend to carry out 'extensive public consultation' in 2019, after which they will develop recommendations for law reform. The Law Commissions have identified three potential areas of concern:

> • difficulties with parental orders – a parental order transfers parentage from the surrogate mother to the intended parents. But that process can only happen after the baby is born and is subject to conditions which may require reform.
>
> • international surrogacy – the uncertainty in the current law may encourage use of international arrangements, where there are concerns about exploitation of surrogates.
>
> • how surrogacy is regulated – the rules governing how surrogacy is undertaken should be brought up to date and further improved.[74]

The recognition that the law relating to surrogacy is in dire need of reform is welcome, and perhaps also overdue. As long ago as 1997, the then Labour government appeared to accept the need for reform when it appointed a committee, chaired by Margaret Brazier, to review aspects of the regulation of surrogacy in the UK. Published in 1998,[75] none of the Brazier Committee Report's recommendations were ever implemented.

Two decades later, it is clear that there are multiple problems with the law governing surrogacy in the UK. First, as we have seen, the ban on commercialization is completely ineffective. If

---

[73] 'Modern surrogacy practice and the need for reform' (2016) 4 Journal of Medical Law and Ethics 257–74.

[74] Surrogacy laws set for reform as Law Commissions get Government backing (Law Commission, 2018).

[75] *Surrogacy: Review for Health Ministers of Current Arrangements for Payments and Regulation* (Cm 4068, 1998).

payments are to be permitted, it would be preferable for them to prospectively regulated (as happens with egg donation, for example), rather than retrospectively authorized. As Helen Prosser and Natalie Gamble explain, this creates confusion and anxiety.

Helen Prosser and Natalie Gamble[76]

We see no evidence that the payment of some reasonable compensation detracts from [surrogates'] altruism, taints their relationship with their intended parents, or creates a risk of exploitation. The problem is the lack of transparency. The current law encourages dishonesty, the making (and demanding) of undeclared gifts and payments, and it creates confusion, anxiety and scope for either side to renege on what was agreed. Honest parents go through the whole surrogacy process anxious about whether their payments will be accepted at the end. Less honest parents do not tell the truth – we are frequently asked by clients what sum the court would 'like to hear'... The way payments are dealt with in UK surrogacy feels confused, murky and unhealthy.

Secondly, the Human Fertilisation and Embryology Act's legal fatherhood provisions are intended to cover cases in which donated sperm is used, and they apply awkwardly and inappropriately to surrogacy arrangements. Thirdly, even if the number of intended parent(s) who do not acquire a formal relationship with 'their' child is low, this is very clearly not in a child's best interests. Fourthly, surrogacy agreements are often made without expert legal advice, with potentially disastrous consequences for all concerned.

Cross-national surrogacy arrangements can result in especially tricky legal problems. Although there are clearly difficulties in trying to regulate an international market in surrogacy, there is surely no excuse for leaving surrogacy in a regulatory vacuum within the UK.

It is rare for academic commentary to speak with one voice on any matter, but there is now a consensus that the law on surrogacy is a mess.[77]

Margaret Brazier and Sacha Waxman[78]

UK law is muddled and contradictory . . . The difficulty in the law as it stands – the 1985 Act outlawing contracts, the conditions for the grant of a parental order banning payments and the rules defining parental status at birth – make it near to impossible for judges hearing applications for parental orders to prioritise welfare without flagrantly flouting other provisions of the law. Judicial creativity has so far found a way to avoid disastrous outcomes for children at the cost of making the law look like an ass.

---

[76] 'Modern surrogacy practice and the need for reform' (2016) 4 Journal of Medical Law and Ethics 257–74.
[77] See also Kirsty Horsey and Sally Sheldon, 'Still Hazy After All These Years: The Law Regulating Surrogacy' (2012) 20 Medical Law Review 67–89; Kirsty Horsey and Katia Neofytou, 'The Fertility Treatment Time Forgot: What Should be Done About Surrogacy in the UK' in Kirsty Horsey (ed), *Revisiting the Regulation of Human Fertilisation and Embryology* (Routledge: Abingdon, 2015) 117–35.
[78] 'Reforming the law regulating surrogacy: extending the family' (2016) 4 Journal of Medical Law and Ethics 159–80.

Kirsty Horsey[79]

What the law singularly fails to reflect is lived experience: the view of surrogates that they are *not* mothers, the fact that IPs (who may have already expended a great deal of time, energy and money on unsuccessful IVF treatments and/or suffered from repeated miscarriages) are vulnerable too, frightened about the 'risk'—foregrounded by the law—that the surrogate will change her mind. They are also worried about achieving legal parenthood. It is no wonder that some turn to overseas surrogacy, particularly when marketed as the 'safer' and more certain option. Our legal provisions and an accessible overseas surrogacy marketplace lead to a lack of understanding of the legal intricacies involved in surrogacy among many prospective parents, which unfortunately drives some abroad.

Claire Fenton-Glynn[80]

The high proportion of intended parents using overseas instead of domestic surrogacy arrangements shows that English public policy in this area is failing. The shortage of donors and surrogates resulting from restrictions on payments and opaque laws has meant that couples are flowing abroad to avoid English statutory provisions, often to places where market laws of supply and demand drive arrangements between commissioning parents, surrogacy agencies, and potential surrogates. As such, prohibitive practices in England are leading to the expansion of foreign markets, and opening up exploitation dynamics in other countries.

It is also increasingly common for people to argue that the altruistic/commercial distinction is unhelpful. While there are those who believe that surrogacy should not be commercialised, including one of the UK's non-profit surrogacy agencies Surrogacy UK, many people now argue that it is unhelpful to characterise commercial surrogacy as always bad, and altruistic surrogacy as universally good. Rather, it is more important to ensure that surrogacy agreements are fair and entered into voluntarily, with full understanding of their consequences.

Julie Shapiro[81]

[C]ompensation is not the critical issue with regard to surrogacy. If surrogacy is properly constructed and properly regulated, then some women will choose to be surrogates. Indeed, some will find it a uniquely satisfying experience. While their motives may not be purely altruistic – compensation is also important – they are not unwilling participants in the enterprise . . .

---

[79] 'Fraying at the Edges: UK Surrogacy Law in 2015: *H v S (Surrogacy Agreement)* [2015] EWFC 36, *Re B v C (Surrogacy: Adoption)* [2015] EWFC 17, *Re Z (A Child: Human Fertilisation and Embryology Act: Parental Order)* [2015] EWFC 73, *A & B (Children) (Surrogacy: Parental Orders: Time Limits)* [2015] EWHC 911 (Fam)' (2016) 24 Medical Law Review 608–21.

[80] 'Outsourcing Ethical Dilemmas: Regulating International Surrogacy Arrangements' (2016) 24 Medical Law Review 59–75.

[81] 'For a feminist considering surrogacy, is compensation really the key question?' (2014) 89 Washington Law Review 1345–73.

Whether or not surrogates should receive compensation is, to me, a secondary question. The acceptability of surrogacy does not turn on this point. If the conditions of surrogacy are exploitative (as they sometimes are, particularly in some of the overseas surrogacy destinations), the question of whether surrogates should be compensated seems to me to be irrelevant. However, assuming that the conditions of surrogacy are favorable, women should be compensated. Too often in our history the labor of women has gone unpaid or undervalued. We should not repeat that pattern here.

Jenni Millbank[82]

Why is ethical debate so often focused on whether surrogates are paid too much and so rarely on whether they are paid too little? Women who undertake pregnancies for others in surrogacy arrangements are performing labour (in both senses) and they are undertaking significant risks. It is not self-evident that paying them nothing is the best or only way to protect and value their unique role . . .

The principal ethical precondition for surrogacy is informed and continuing consent of the surrogate . . . In the context of surrogacy laws, informed and continuing consent requires that the surrogate has full control of pregnancy care and relinquishment of the baby with consensual transfer of parentage *after* birth. These elements are not incompatible with compensated surrogacy or the involvement of intermediaries. Indeed, high-quality and truly independent professional intermediaries have an important role to play in ensuring that choices are freely made and fully understood.

An Australian study of cross-border reproduction found that many intended parents rejected the assumption that altruistic surrogacy is 'morally superior' to commercial surrogacy. On the contrary, the prohibition of payments to the surrogate was regarded as 'unfair to her, as she was then, effectively, the only volunteer surrounded by a number of professional participants—including doctors, counsellors and lawyers—all of whom were acting for profit'.[83]

So what form might law reform take? Perhaps the simplest change would be to enable people to apply for something akin to a parental order before the child is conceived. At the moment, as we have seen, the central problem with parental order applications is that, by the time the case comes to court, the child has been born and has welfare needs that trump other considerations. By having a mechanism through which a couple could be pre-authorized for a parental order, it might be possible to exercise some oversight and control over surrogacy agreements before a child is conceived. It would also mean that the child's parentage could be resolved before she is born, rather than leaving the child in an unsatisfactory legal limbo until parenthood is formally transferred.

Once again, there is near consensus that some sort of pre-conception parental order authorization process would be the most sensible approach.[84]

---

[82] 'Surrogacy in Australia' (2015) 12 Journal of Bioethical Inquiry 477–90.
[83] Emily Jackson et al, 'Learning from Cross-Border Reproduction' (2017) 25 Medical Law Review 23–46.
[84] 'Are contracts and pre-birth orders the way forward for UK surrogacy?' (2015) 2 International Family Law 101–96.

Margaret Brazier and Sacha Waxman[85]

Given societal interests in child welfare, to take legal effect the agreement would require prospective scrutiny by a court or a regulatory authority. The parties to the agreement would need to demonstrate that they have addressed the matters of concern to each of them, including the relationship between the surrogate and the child and her family after birth, payments and expenses, health care provision and what might ensue in certain contingencies, for example if intended parents separate or one partner dies. The agreement must be one entered into wholly voluntarily, fully informed, with all parties having had time to reflect. The approving authority must be satisfied that the agreement meets the needs of the child.

Such an agreement would be scrutinised before conception and the intended parents granted a provisional parental order with the caveat that the surrogate has a set time, normally expiring before the birth, to register an objection relating to changed circumstances and/or risks to the child triggering a full re-hearing.

In the absence of objection from the surrogate or other concerns being expressed about the welfare of the child once born, the provisional order could be simply confirmed, rather as a decree nisi becomes a decree absolute.

Kirsty Horsey[86]

Overall, many of the problems being highlighted in recent surrogacy cases could be avoided if there was sensible law reform. If IPs were recognised as legal parents of children born to a surrogate from the outset, fewer people would travel overseas for surrogacy. Parenthood is what these people desperately desire. For those who did travel, for whatever reason (perhaps cultural connections), immigration problems would be more easily resolved. POs would be rendered unnecessary (this would also better align surrogacy with other assisted reproductive practices and disassociate it from adoption) or, if retained, could be made to become effective at birth, as happens in some other jurisdictions.

Claire Fenton-Glynn[87]

A reconsideration of the regulation of surrogacy in England does not mean that we must descend into a surrogacy market driven by supply and demand, but instead requires that the optimal conditions for autonomous decision-making are developed, and adequately enforced. Most importantly, this requires a shift away from the current model of ex-post facto regulation, to one in which authorities are able to exercise control over the agreement before it takes place. This could involve a requirement that the details of the arrangement—either domestic or international—are put before the court, or an independent specialised body,

---

[85] 'Reforming the law regulating surrogacy: extending the family' (2016) 4 Journal of Medical Law and Ethics 159–80.

[86] 'Fraying at the Edges: UK Surrogacy Law in 2015: *H v S (Surrogacy Agreement)* [2015] EWFC 36, *Re B v C (Surrogacy: Adoption)* [2015] EWFC 17, *Re Z (A Child: Human Fertilisation and Embryology Act: Parental Order)* [2015] EWFC 73, *A & B (Children) (Surrogacy: Parental Orders: Time Limits)* [2015] EWHC 911 (Fam)' (2016) 24 Medical Law Review 608–21.

[87] 'Outsourcing Ethical Dilemmas: Regulating International Surrogacy Arrangements' (2016) 24 Medical Law Review 59–75.

and their details approved *before* the impregnation of the surrogate takes place. The English courts have proved over the last 6 years that attempting to do it on an ex-post facto basis is futile, whereas requiring the registration and examination of arrangements before they are implemented gives a level of control over the transaction not currently exercised.

Of course, one of the issues which would have to be resolved is whether pre-birth orders would leave the current parentage rules intact, and would simply enable speedier transfer of parenthood once the child is born, or whether parentage would vest in the intended parents from birth. The latter is obviously more radical, since it could involve recognizing someone other than the child's birth mother as her mother from birth. It is advocated in the next extract by Amel Alghrani and Danielle Griffiths.

Amel Alghrani and Danielle Griffiths[88]

We suggest that the present requirements for a parental order that mandate the surrogate consents to any parental order be removed from the legislation. This would resolve the inherent uncertainty that permeates the current law, which stems from the fact that surrogacy arrangements are not legally enforceable and it is the woman who gives birth to the baby who is regarded as the legal 'mother' . . .

A change in the regulation of surrogacy to make surrogacy contracts enforceable would offer more security to commissioning couples and might incentivise individuals to find surrogates located within the UK . . .

Disputes that do arise between surrogate and commissioning parents after the birth could be litigated and the court can assess which party can best meet the best interests of the child, as is the situation at present when a dispute occurs and a child arrangements order is sought.

If surrogacy contracts were enforceable, surrogates would no longer have the right to change their mind. In practice, however, while a surrogate can refuse to consent to the making of a parental order, she no longer could be said to have a right to keep the child. Rather, as we saw earlier in *Re H (A Child) (Surrogacy Breakdown),*[89] the courts' paramount consideration is the best interests of the child, so if it is in the child's best interests to live with the intended parents, the surrogate's 'right to change her mind' works only to rule out the making of a parental order, even if this would be in the child's best interests.

In *Re X (A Child)(No 2)(Private Surrogacy Arrangement: Contact with Birth Family),*[90] for example, the birth mother had changed her mind during the pregnancy and wanted to bring up the child herself, but Holman J was at pains to 'state in the clearest and strongest possible terms that it is now firmly settled that this child will live with, and be brought up by, the father and the mother as their own child'. He was also clear that contact with the birth mother should not be allowed to threaten 'the stability and permanence of that placement'.

In Israel, one of the only countries to have introduced a regulatory regime to approve surrogacy arrangements, the surrogate is can renege on her agreement only if there has been a

---

[88] 'The regulation of surrogacy in the United Kingdom: the case for reform' (2017) 29 Child and Family Law Quarterly 165.
[89] [2017] EWCA Civ 1798   [90] [2016] EWFC 55.

change of circumstances, and the welfare of the child would not be harmed. In the next extract, Rhona Schuz points out that the rigorous approval process that precedes any surrogacy arrangement in Israel minimizes the chance that the surrogate will in fact change her mind.

Rhona Schuz[91]

The Approvals Committee's guidelines for drawing up the surrogate motherhood agreement start with a clear statement that it is necessary to ensure, so far as is possible, that the birth mother understands the nature of the commitments involved in the agreement and agrees thereto voluntarily and without coercion. A number of the Approvals Committee's requirements are designed to further this end.

First, the physician who examines the birth mother has to declare that s/he has explained to the birth mother the consequences and significance of acting as a surrogate ... Secondly, the Approvals Committee will not consider any application until it is satisfied that the birth mother has obtained independent legal advice from a lawyer who is an expert in surrogate motherhood agreements ... Thirdly, the birth mother is interviewed separately by the Approvals Committee and will be asked questions designed to test whether her consent is voluntary and informed. Finally, the Approvals Committee's practice is only to approve birth mothers who have previously given birth ...

We are not aware of any cases where the birth mother has requested to keep the child. One reason for this may be the screening by the Approvals Committee.

As we have seen, surrogacy arrangements most commonly go wrong when the relationship between the surrogate and the intended parents has broken down. While pre-conception screening would not be able to eliminate all disputes, it might help to ensure that surrogates and intended parents understand what is involved in advance.

Julie Shapiro[92]

The need for screening and counseling is readily apparent. Both serving as a surrogate and using surrogacy are difficult undertakings. For the surrogate there are substantial physical consequences, including some risk of permanent harm. Clearly not every woman can be a surrogate. The fact that a woman believes she can be a surrogate may not be sufficient guarantee. Best practices suggest that trained counselors can successfully help people determine whether surrogacy is the right choice for them. It is not only the surrogate's role that is difficult, however. Surrogacy is taxing – emotionally and psychologically – for all parties. The intended mother must accept that another woman will be pregnant with and give birth to the child she will raise. Given the cultural centrality of childbearing to the construction of women's experience in our culture, this can be a difficult task.

---

[91] 'Surrogacy in Israel: An Analysis of the Law in Practice' in Rachel Cook, Shelley Day Sclater, with Felicity Kaganas (eds), *Surrogate Motherhood: International Perspectives* (Hart Publishing: Oxford, 2003) 35–53.

[92] 'For a feminist considering surrogacy, is compensation really the key question?' (2014) 89 Washington Law Review 1345–73.

5 CONCLUSION

Although surrogacy arrangements can go disastrously wrong, this is the exception. Susan Imrie and Vasanti Jadva carried out interviews with surrogates and found that the vast majority of surrogacy arrangements had been a positive experience (89 per cent; eight per cent had had 'neutral' experiences and five per cent had had negative experiences, though most of these had also had positive experiences in other surrogacy arrangements). Almost all surrogates were happy with the ongoing contact they had with the child and their parents.

Susan Imrie and Vasanti Jadva[93]

Overall, in the majority of surrogacy arrangements surrogates remained in contact with surrogacy families, and viewed most of the relationships formed through surrogacy as positive. The variety of contact arrangements maintained, and surrogates' high levels of satisfaction with the amount of contact they had with surrogacy families, suggests that, in most cases, the parties involved in UK surrogacy arrangements managed to negotiate this potentially problematic relationship with a high degree of success and create relationships that were sustained over time and enjoyed.

The latest report of the Surrogacy UK Working Group on Surrogacy Law Reform confirms this finding.

Surrogacy UK Working Group on Surrogacy Law Reform[94]

Our up-to-date research continues to show that the majority of surrogacy arrangements undertaken in the UK are relationships and not transactions. Many of these relationships end up resulting in long-term, close friendships. Most arrangements raise no problems and do not trouble the courts when the parental order application is considered: most will be heard in the Magistrates' Court in domestic cases. Surrogates do not regularly 'change their minds': there have been only a handful of disputed surrogacy cases in the last 30 years. As in 2015, our data again showed high levels of long-term contact maintained by surrogates and the families they helped to create. It also continues to show that there are high levels of openness and honesty with children about the means of their creation, and a great deal of pride and positivity about the surrogacy experience.

Drawing upon their anthropological studies with US and Israeli surrogates, Elly Teman and Zsuzsa Berend explain that surrogates believe that they are looking after the intended parents' child, rather than giving away their own child.

---

[93] 'The long-term experiences of surrogates: relationships and contact with surrogacy families in genetic and gestational surrogacy arrangements' (2014) 29 Reproductive BioMedicine Online 424–35.
[94] *Surrogacy in the UK: further evidence for reform* (Surrogacy UK, 2018).

Elly Teman and Zsuzsa Berend[95]

Surrogates did not see themselves as the mother of this baby, and most were vocal about never having the emotions that they felt toward their 'own' child ...

Both Israeli and US surrogates often compare surrogacy to 'babysitting' – it is a nurturing relationship that entails responsibilities but does not make the child yours ... Both Israeli and US surrogates firmly believe that the goal of surrogacy is to create families; they see their role as helping the baby's parents to realize their 'dream' and maintain that the child always *belongs* to the IPs ...

One way of designating parenthood in both contexts was to 'share' the pregnancy and the birth as much as possible with the IPs, insisting it was 'their' pregnancy rather than the surrogates' ... Israeli surrogates also worked out the designation of the pregnancy and of the baby by enabling the IM [intended mother] to participate in all medical appointments and by making sure she 'carried' the responsibility for all the scheduling, filing, and having the necessary documents, and speaking to the doctor ... When IPs lived farther or were unable to attend doctors' appointments, US surrogates often sent ultrasound images and the fetus' tape-recorded heartbeat ...

After enabling their couple 'to be as pregnant as possible,' both Israeli and US surrogates wanted to give the IPs privileged access to the birth because it is 'their birth' and 'their baby.' In both samples, surrogates spoke of rituals of participation, and IPs sometimes cut the umbilical cord.

There is also evidence that the children born through surrogacy and their intended parents are doing well.[96] Data from the most recent phase of the UK's Longitudinal Study of Assisted Reproduction Families found that the majority of children conceived through surrogacy 'feel indifferent or unconcerned about being born in this way'.[97] According to one of their 14-year-old interviewees: 'Mum would always say "Oh Auntie [surrogate's name] helped us give birth to you" and I'd be like "Oh okay, that's nice, fine, normal, whatever".[98]

As compared with donor conception, and for obvious reasons (the arrival of a child without a pregnancy will have to be explained), openness tends to be the norm in families which have had children as a result of surrogacy.

Vasanti Jadva et al[99]

[M]ost children who are aware of their surrogacy conception are able to show some understanding of surrogacy by age 7 years ... For those who were in contact with their surrogate

---

[95] 'Surrogate non-motherhood: Israeli and US surrogates speak about kinship and parenthood' (2018) Anthropology & Medicine 1–15.

[96] L Van Rijn-van Gelderen et al, 'Wellbeing of gay fathers with children born through surrogacy: a comparison with lesbian-mother families and heterosexual IVF parent families' (2018) 33 Human Reproduction 101–108; L Blake et al, 'Gay fathers' motivations for and feelings about surrogacy as a path to parenthood' (2017) 32 Human Reproduction 860–7.

[97] Sophie Zadeh et al, 'The perspectives of adolescents conceived using surrogacy, egg or sperm donation' (2018) 33 Human Reproduction 1099–106.

[98] Vasanti Jadva, 'Surrogates and intended parents in the UK' (2016) 4 Journal of Medical Law and Ethics 215–27.

[99] 'Surrogacy families 10 years on: relationship with the surrogate, decisions over disclosure and children's understanding of their surrogacy origins' (2012) 27 Human Reproduction 3008–14.

mother, the majority said that they liked her and most children were positive about their surrogacy birth at age 10 years ... In contrast to families who use gamete donation to have a
child, this study shows that families who use surrogacy are more open with their child about
their use of assisted reproduction, with over 90% of families having explained surrogacy to
their child.

But while surrogacy arrangements usually work well, in the UK this is in spite of, rather than
because of, the law on surrogacy. In the absence of clear prospective regulation, it is left to
family judges to resolve *ex post facto* how to protect the best interests of the child born through
surrogacy.

Kirsty Horsey and Sally Sheldon[100]

[T]he existence of cross-border provision should greatly heighten concerns regarding exploitation where surrogacy services are provided in countries where women may not have
access to the same health services and legal protections as in the UK. Further, concerns
regarding the possible harms suffered by intending parents are greater still where such individuals feel left with no alternative but to travel to other countries and navigate their way
through foreign legal and health care systems and domestic immigration rules. Most crucially, if the central concern of a good law is to protect the welfare of the child, this is surely
not best achieved by exporting surrogacy, yet this is the almost inevitable consequence
of our current regime. While any changes to the UK law are unlikely to yield any means of
overseeing surrogacy arrangements that occur oversees, it is at least possible that making
surrogacy services more readily available in the UK would reduce the incidence of cross-
border arrangements.

FURTHER READING

Crawshaw, Marilyn, Purewal, Satvinder, and van den Akker, Olga, 'Working at the margins: the views and experiences of court social workers on parental orders work in surrogacy arrangements' (2012) 42 British Journal of Social Work 1–19.

Fenton-Glynn, Claire, 'Outsourcing Ethical Dilemmas: Regulating International
Surrogacy Arrangements' (2016) 24 Medical Law Review 59–75.

Imrie, Susan and Jadva, Vasanti, 'The long-term experiences of surrogates: relationships
and contact with surrogacy families in genetic and gestational surrogacy arrangements'
(2014) 29 Reproductive BioMedicine Online 424–35.

Jadva, Vasanti et al, 'Surrogacy families 10 years on: relationship with the surrogate, decisions over disclosure and children's understanding of their surrogacy origins' (2012) 27
Human Reproduction 3008–14.

---

[100] 'Still Hazy After All These Years: The Law Regulating Surrogacy' (2012) 20 Medical Law Review 67–89.

Mulligan, Andrea, 'Identity Rights and Sensitive Ethical Questions: The European Convention on Human Rights and the Regulation of Surrogacy Arrangements' (2018) 26 Medical Law Review 449–75.

Prosser, Helen and Gamble, Natalie, 'Modern surrogacy practice and the need for reform' (2016) 4 Journal of Medical Law and Ethics 257–74.

Surrogacy UK Working Group on Surrogacy Law Reform, *Surrogacy in the UK: further evidence for reform* (Surrogacy UK, 2018).

17

ASSISTED DYING

CENTRAL ISSUES

1. Euthanasia involves a doctor deliberately killing a patient. In the UK, this would be murder, for which the only sentence is life imprisonment.

2. Assisted suicide is also a criminal offence, but the Director of Public Prosecutions (DPP) must give consent to prosecution. In response to the House of Lords' judgment in the *Purdy* case, the DPP has published the factors that are taken into account when making this decision.

3. The principal arguments in favour of legalizing assisted dying are respect for patient autonomy; compassion; offering reassurance to patients; the inconsistency and incoherence of the status quo (whereby some life-shortening practices are lawful, and UK citizens can access assisted suicide in Switzerland); and the benefits of open regulation.

4. The arguments against legalization include respect for the sanctity of human life; the view that high-quality palliative care ought to make assisted dying unnecessary; the difficulty of ensuring that requests are genuine; the negative impact legalization might have on the doctor–patient relationship; and the dangers of the slippery slope.

5. As a result of the increasing number of jurisdictions which have legalized euthanasia and/or assisted suicide, there is now considerable evidence of how legalization works in practice.

---

1 INTRODUCTION

Although it will happen to all of us, no one knows what it is like to die. We may have watched life slip away from another person, and some people's religious faith leads to expectations about what happens after death. But when judging whether death could ever be preferable to life, we are all inevitably behind a 'veil of ignorance'.[1]

---

[1] John Rawls, *A Theory of Justice* (Harvard UP: Cambridge, MA, 1971).

Interest in the legitimacy of taking steps to speed up the process of dying is not new. Some Greek and Roman philosophers, among them Seneca, believed that suicide was a rational response to extreme physical and mental deterioration:

> I shall not abandon old age, if old age preserves me intact as regards the better part of myself; but if old age begins to shatter my mind, and to pull its various faculties to pieces, if it leaves me, not life, but only the breath of life, I shall rush out of a house that is crumbing and tottering.[2]

For several reasons, the question of whether it could ever be legitimate for the medical profession to help patients to die has become more prominent in recent years. First, although life expectancy increased dramatically over the course of the 20th century, medical progress has not been as successful in extending the period during which we are able to lead healthy, independent lives. As a result, many of us fear becoming increasingly dependent upon others.

Secondly, as we have seen in previous chapters, the principle of patient autonomy is now dominant within medical law, raising the question of whether a patient's right to make decisions about her medical treatment should extend to being able to decide to end her life. Thirdly, when we looked at religious bioethics in Chapter 1, one common theme was the idea that life is not ours to dispose of as we please. In a secular society, less weight may be given to the proscription of suicide and euthanasia within religious teachings.

Fourthly, a number of high-profile legal cases, such as those brought by Debbie Purdy, Tony Nicklinson, and Noel Conway, have received intense media attention. There has also been considerable interest in the hundreds of UK citizens who have made the journey to Switzerland to access assisted suicide through Dignitas.

In this chapter, we begin by looking at the UK's legal prohibitions of euthanasia and assisted suicide. In euthanasia, it is the doctor's action that causes the patient's death. In assisted suicide, the patient causes her own death, but someone else (often, but not necessarily, a doctor) has helped her, for example by prescribing a lethal dose of drugs. Assisted dying is a non-specific umbrella term that refers to euthanasia and assisted suicide. Both are against the law in the UK, but other life-shortening practices are lawful. We then consider the arguments for and against a change in the law, and examine other jurisdictions' experience with legalization.

2 THE CURRENT LAW

(a) EUTHANASIA

The word 'euthanasia' comes from the Greek words *eu* (good) and *thanatos* (death). In modern usage, it has a more specific meaning. The Oxford English Dictionary's definition is 'a gentle and easy death, the bringing about of this, especially in the case of incurable and painful disease'. We would also usually confine the term 'euthanasia' to cases in which a doctor kills a patient at her request: if someone kills a relative in order to relieve her suffering, we would tend to say that this was a 'mercy killing', rather than euthanasia.

---

[2] Seneca, *58th Letter to Lucilius* in TE Page et al (eds), *Seneca: Ad Lucilium Epistulae Morales*, vol I (trans Richard M Gummere) (Heinemann: London, 1961) 409.

(1) Mercy Killing

If someone who is suffering unbearably is killed by a friend or family member, it may be possible to reduce the charge to one of manslaughter on the grounds of diminished responsibility, thus allowing for some discretion, and hence leniency in sentencing. Under section 2 of the Homicide Act 1957, as amended by the Coroners and Justice Act 2009, the partial defence of diminished responsibility is available where someone is 'suffering from an abnormality of mental functioning' which—

> (a) arose from a recognised medical condition,
>
> (b) substantially impaired D's ability to do one or more of the things mentioned in subsection (1A), and
>
> (c) provides an explanation for D's acts and omissions in doing or being a party to the killing.
>
> (1A) Those things are—
>
> (a) to understand the nature of D's conduct;
>
> (b) to form a rational judgment;
>
> (c) to exercise self-control.

There is some evidence that, in order to avoid the charge of murder, an inference is commonly drawn that the defendant in a mercy killing case must have been suffering from a mental abnormality at the time of the offence, even though there is no sign of mental abnormality when the defendant is examined by a psychiatrist. Indeed, Susanne Dell goes so far as to say that mercy killers, in general, display a 'total lack of mental disorder'.[3] Nevertheless, there seems to be what has been described as a 'benevolent conspiracy' to use the partial defence of diminished responsibility in order to mitigate the harshness of applying the ordinary law of murder to mercy killers.[4]

In theory, this should be more difficult as a result of the 2009 reforms which introduced the requirement that the defendant must have 'a recognised medical condition'. In practice, however, because so much depends upon juries' evaluation of the totality of the evidence, the 'benevolent conspiracy' is unlikely to disappear, even though, as Matthew Gibson points out, it will require an even more artificial interpretation of the defence:

> Sympathy for [mercy killers] by benign medical experts, lawyers, judges and juries therefore risks undermining the narrower conceptual framework of the revamped s 2(1). The continuation of the benevolent conspiracy requires them to expand the borders of the defence *more* artificially than under the former plea.[5]

There have been cases where 'mercy killers' have chosen not to invoke their own mental disorder in order to explain their actions. In 2008, Kay Gilderdale had injected her adult daughter, Lynn Gilderdale, who was paralysed and unable to swallow, with morphine. Lynn had attempted to commit suicide, had a 'Do Not Resuscitate' order in place, and had been considering going to Dignitas in Switzerland to end her life. She had told her mother that she did not want to continue living. Mrs Gilderdale wished to plead guilty to a charge of assisting

---

[3] Susanne Dell, 'The mandatory sentence and section 2' (1986) 12 Journal of Medical Ethics 28–31.

[4] The Law Commission, *Partial Defences to Murder* (Report No 290, 2004) para 2.34.

[5] Matthew Gibson, 'Pragmatism preserved? The challenges of accommodating mercy killers in the reformed diminished responsibility plea' (2017) Journal of Criminal Law 177.

her daughter's suicide, but she was charged with attempted murder instead. The jury refused to convict her, and the trial judge was critical of the decision to pursue a murder charge.

In contrast, at around the same time, another mother who had purchased enough heroin to kill her severely brain-damaged son was convicted of the full crime of murder. Frances Inglis did not plead the defence of diminished responsibility, even though she had been diagnosed with a depressive illness and post-traumatic stress disorder. She wanted to plead not guilty instead, but given the clear evidence that she had taken her son's life, she was convicted of murder. In *R v Inglis*, her appeal against conviction was dismissed by the Court of Appeal.

R v Inglis[6]

Lord Judge CJ

[W]e must underline that the law of murder does not distinguish between murder committed for malevolent reasons and murder motivated by familial love. Subject to well established partial defences, like provocation or diminished responsibility, mercy killing is murder. The offences of which the appellant was convicted, and for which she fell to be sentenced, were attempted murder and murder. The sentence on conviction for murder is mandatory.

(2) Medical Killing

A doctor (or other healthcare professional) who deliberately ends the life of her patient is subject to the ordinary criminal law, and would often satisfy both the *actus reus* (proof of conduct, and proof that the conduct caused death), and the *mens rea* (the intention to kill or to cause grievous bodily harm) for the crime of murder. The doctor's motive and the consent of the victim are irrelevant, as is the fact that the patient would have died soon anyway. Because murder carries a mandatory life sentence, the fact that the doctor acted for compassionate reasons cannot be taken into account in sentencing.

A healthcare professional who ends a patient's life will seldom be able to claim that she was suffering from an 'abnormality of mental functioning'.[7] Of course, when a doctor gives a fatal dose of drugs to a patient who is terminally ill, there may be some evidential difficulty in establishing that it was what the doctor did, rather than the pre-existing illness, that caused the patient's death. To be guilty of murder, the defendant's conduct must have 'contributed significantly' or been 'a substantial cause' of death; it need not, therefore, be the sole reason for the patient's death. If causation cannot be established, the doctor who administered a potentially lethal injection might be charged with attempted murder (as happened to Dr Cox, below).

While there have been prosecutions, no doctor who has complied with a patient's request to end her life has ever been convicted of the full offence of murder. As we can see in the following cases, both juries and the judiciary have tended to be lenient towards doctors whom they judge to have acted for compassionate reasons.

Dr Moor was arrested after taking part in a media debate about voluntary euthanasia, during which he admitted to having helped a number of his patients to die painlessly. In *R v*

---

[6] [2010] EWCA Crim 2637.   [7] Homicide Act 1957, section 2(1).

Moor he was prosecuted for the murder of George Liddell, an 85-year-old man who had been suffering from bowel cancer. Given the tone of Hooper J's direction to the jury, it is not surprising that the jury acquitted Dr Moor, reaching a unanimous verdict in less than an hour.

R v Moor[8]

Hooper J

You have heard that this defendant is a man of excellent character, not just in the sense that he has no previous convictions but how witnesses have spoken of his many admirable qualities. You may consider it a great irony that a doctor who goes out of his way to care for George Liddell ends up facing the charge that he does. You may also consider it another great irony that the doctor who takes time on his day off to tend to a dying patient ends up on this charge.

R v Cox is the only case to have resulted in a doctor's conviction, this time for attempted murder. It was impossible to establish exactly what had killed Mrs Boyes because her body had been cremated, so only the lesser charge of attempted murder was possible. Dr Cox had given Mrs Boyes a dose of potassium chloride that was guaranteed to kill her, so it was difficult to avoid the conclusion that he had intended to end her life, especially since potassium chloride is not a painkiller.

Mrs Boyes was 70 years old and terminally ill; she had rheumatoid arthritis and had developed gastric ulcers, gangrene, and body sores. She suffered extreme pain, which could not be controlled by pain-killing drugs. There was evidence that she had repeatedly asked Dr Cox, a consultant rheumatologist who had been treating her for the last 13 years, and others, to kill her.

R v Cox[9]

Ognall J

There can be no doubt that the use of drugs to reduce pain and suffering will often be fully justified notwithstanding that it will, in fact hasten the moment of death, but please understand this, ladies and gentleman, what can never be lawful is the use of drugs with the primary purpose of hastening the moment of death ... [I]n the context of this case potassium chloride has no curative properties ... it is not an analgesic. It is not used by the medical profession to relieve pain ..., injected into a vein it is a lethal substance. One ampoule would certainly kill ... the injection here was therefore twice that necessary to cause certain death.

Dr Cox was convicted of attempted murder, and was given a 12-month suspended prison sentence. It is noteworthy that in a separate General Medical Council (GMC) hearing, he was not struck off the medical register, and, after a formal reprimand, he returned to practise within a year of his conviction.

---

[8] [1999] Crim LR 2000 Jul 568–90.   [9] (1992) 12 BMLR 38.

In 2012, Tony Nicklinson applied for a number of declarations which, if granted, would have a dramatic effect upon the prohibition of euthanasia in the UK. In his statement to the court, he explained his predicament.

Tony Nicklinson[10]

[The stroke] left me paralysed below the neck and unable to speak. I need help in almost every aspect of my life. I cannot scratch if I itch, I cannot pick my nose if it is blocked and I can only eat if I am fed like a baby—only I won't grow out of it, unlike the baby. I have no privacy or dignity left. I am washed, dressed and put to bed by carers who are, after all, still strangers. You try defecating to order whilst suspended in a sling over a commode and see how you get on.

I am fed up with my life and don't want to spend the next 20 years or so like this … I'm not depressed so do not need counselling. I have had over six years to think about my future and it does not look good. I have locked in syndrome and I can expect no cure or improvement in my condition as my muscles and joints seize up through lack of use. Indeed, I can expect to dribble my way into old age. If I am lucky I will acquire a life-threatening illness such as cancer so that I can refuse treatment and say no to those who would keep me alive against my will.

By all means protect the vulnerable. By vulnerable I mean those who cannot make decisions for themselves just don't include me. I am not vulnerable, I don't need help or protection from death or those who would help me. If the legal consequences were not so huge i.e. life imprisonment, perhaps I could get someone to help me. As things stand, I can't get help.

Tony Nicklinson sought a declaration that it would not be unlawful, on the grounds of necessity, for his GP or another doctor to terminate or assist the termination of his life. He also sought a declaration that by criminalizing euthanasia and assisted suicide, and by imposing a mandatory life sentence for cases of genuinely compassionate voluntary euthanasia, the law was incompatible with his right to respect for his private life.

The *Nicklinson* case is complicated for several reasons. First, after the Divisional Court rejected his application for judicial review, Tony Nicklinson stopped eating and drinking and he died six days later. His widow Jane was given permission to pursue an appeal in the Court of Appeal, and then in the UK Supreme Court and the European Court of Human Rights (ECtHR). Secondly, Tony Nicklinson's case was joined with those of two other men. First, and while Tony Nicklinson was still alive, it was joined with that of a man with locked-in syndrome, referred to only as 'Martin', whose claim was different and is considered later. After his death, his case was joined with that of Paul Lamb, whose predicament was similar. Thirdly, the arguments pursued differed substantially at different stages of the appeal. The Court of Appeal was the highest court to consider the question of whether there could be a common law defence to murder if Tony Nicklinson's or Paul Lamb's life was ended deliberately at their request. For four reasons, they rejected this part of their claim.

Nicklinson v Ministry of Justice[11]

Lord Dyson MR

In our view, this submission that the common law should recognise a defence of necessity to apply to certain cases of euthanasia is wholly unsustainable for a variety of reasons …

---

[10] Quoted by Charles J in *Nicklinson v Ministry of Justice* [2012] EWHC 304 (QB).
[11] [2013] EWCA Civ 961.

> There is no self-evident reason why [the sanctity of life] should give way to the values of autonomy or dignity and there are cogent reasons why sensible people might properly think that it should not. So the mere fact that there may be rights to autonomy and to be treated with dignity does no more than raise the question whether they should be given priority in circumstances like this; it does not of itself carry the day.
>
> Second ... it is wrong to say that there is a right to commit suicide; section 1 of the 1961 Act can more accurately be described as conferring an immunity from the criminal process for those who actually commit suicide. A fortiori, if there is no right to kill yourself, there can be no right, fundamental or otherwise, to require the State to allow others to assist you to die or to kill you ...
>
> The third reason is that it is simply not appropriate for the court to fashion a defence of necessity in such a complex and controversial field; this is a matter for Parliament ... Parliament as the conscience of the nation is the appropriate constitutional forum, not judges who might be influenced by their own particular moral perspectives; the judicial process which has to focus on the particular facts and circumstances before the court is not one which is suited to enabling the judges to deal competently with the range of conflicting considerations and procedural requirements which a proper regulation of the field may require; and there is a danger that any particular judicial decision, influenced perhaps by particular sympathy for an individual claimant, may have unforeseen consequences, creating an unfortunate precedent binding in other contexts ...
>
> Fourth, as we have already said, any defence provided to those who assist someone to die would have to apply not merely to euthanasia but also to assisted suicide. That immediately raises the question: how can the courts develop a defence to assisted suicide when Parliament has stated in unequivocal terms that it is a serious criminal offence carrying a maximum sentence of 14 years' imprisonment... If a defence of necessity cannot be fashioned for assisted suicide, it certainly cannot for euthanasia.

In the Supreme Court, the applicants chose not to pursue their argument that the offence of murder, in the absence of a defence of necessity, was incompatible with their Article 8 rights. Their appeal to the Supreme Court focused exclusively on whether the prohibition on assisted suicide, discussed below, was compatible with Article 8 of the Convention. Paul Lamb sought to resurrect his complaint about the illegality of euthanasia before the ECtHR, but having not pursued this before the Supreme Court, the ECtHR rejected his claim as inadmissible.

(b) ASSISTED SUICIDE

At common law, suicide was regarded as self-murder, and was a criminal offence. According to Blackstone's *Commentaries*:

> The suicide is guilty of a double offence; one spiritual, in invading the prerogative of the Almighty, and rushing into his immediate presence uncalled for; the other temporal, against the King, who hath an interest in the preservation of all his subjects.[12]

Obviously, it was only those who had tried unsuccessfully to commit suicide who could actually be prosecuted for their attempted suicide. If the suicide had been successful, it was the

---

[12] *Commentaries on the Laws of England*, vol IV (1775).

relatives of the deceased who would suffer, through the confiscation of property and restrictions upon burial rites.

In 1961, suicide and attempted suicide were decriminalized, for compassionate reasons, by section 1 of the Suicide Act which states that: 'The rule of law whereby it is a crime for a person to commit suicide is hereby abrogated'. The fact that it is not now unlawful to commit, or attempt to commit, suicide does not, however, mean that there is a right to do so. The criminal offences of suicide and attempted suicide were not abolished in order to facilitate ending one's life, but rather to ensure that people who had attempted suicide unsuccessfully could seek medical help, without fearing prosecution, and to protect already distressed relatives from additional hardship.

Despite suicide's decriminalization, under section 2(1) of the Suicide Act 1961, assisting another person to commit suicide is a criminal offence, punishable by up to 14 years' imprisonment.

Suicide Act 1961 (as amended) section 2

2(1)   A person ('D') commits an offence if—

   (a) D does an act capable of encouraging or assisting the suicide or attempted suicide of another person, and

   (b) D's act was intended to encourage or assist suicide or an attempt at suicide....

(1C) An offence under this section is triable on indictment and a person convicted of such an offence is liable to imprisonment for a term not exceeding 14 years ...

(4)   No proceedings shall be instituted for an offence under this section except by or with the consent of the Director of Public Prosecutions.

While it is unusual for assisting a non-crime to itself be a criminal offence, there are undoubtedly sound public policy reasons for proscribing phony suicide pacts (when one person persuades another to take their own life first, in order to inherit their property), and for criminalizing the disgraceful 'egging on' of people with suicidal thoughts on social media. As long ago as 1961, it was recognized that cases of assistance with suicide will vary, and that prosecution will not always be in the public interest; hence, section 2(4) provides that no prosecution can go ahead without the consent of the Director of Public Prosecutions.

Given that a person can commit suicide without committing a criminal offence, what reason could there be for implicating someone else in one's suicide attempt, potentially exposing her to criminal charges? There are two principal reasons why people might need assistance in committing suicide. First, they may be physically incapable of arranging their own suicide. Secondly, patients need expert advice on the combination and quantity of drugs needed to achieve a quick and painless death. Simply overdosing on painkillers can lead to a prolonged and agonizing death, or can leave someone alive but profoundly incapacitated.

Since the case of Dianne Pretty in 2002,[13] there has been increasing pressure on the prohibition of assisted suicide in the courts. In the following sections we examine four key cases and their implications.

---

[13] *R (on the application of Pretty) v Director of Public Prosecutions* [2001] UKHL 61; *Pretty v United Kingdom* (2002) 35 EHRR 1.

(1) Dianne Pretty

Mrs Pretty had been diagnosed with motor neurone disease, a progressive and degenerative terminal illness, during which the sufferer's mental faculties remain sharp while their body fails. Mrs Pretty's husband was willing to help her to commit suicide, but the couple were anxious that he might be prosecuted under section 2(1) of the Suicide Act 1961.

Because section 2(4) of the Suicide Act specifies that no proceedings can be brought without the consent of the Director of Public Prosecutions (DPP), Mrs Pretty asked the DPP to give an undertaking that he would not consent to Mr Pretty's prosecution. She then sought judicial review of his refusal, on the grounds that it violated her human rights.

In *R (on the application of Pretty) v Director of Public Prosecutions*, the House of Lords found that there had been no prima facie violations of any of Mrs Pretty's Convention rights.

R (on the application of Pretty) v Director of Public Prosecutions [14]

Lord Steyn

The Director of Public Prosecutions may not under section 2(4) exercise his discretion to stop all prosecutions under section 2(1). It follows that he may only exercise his discretion, for or against a prosecution, in relation to the circumstances of a specific prosecution. His discretion can therefore only be exercised in respect of past events giving rise to a suspicion that a crime under section 2(1) has been committed. And then the exercise of this discretion will take into account whether there is a realistic prospect of securing a conviction and whether a prosecution would be in the public interest.

Mrs Pretty then appealed to the European Court of Human Rights (ECtHR). In *Pretty v United Kingdom*, the ECtHR was prepared to admit that Article 8 was engaged, but it nevertheless rejected her claim on the grounds that a complete prohibition of assisted suicide was not a disproportionate response to the state's concern to protect vulnerable members of society. Mrs Pretty died 12 days later.

Pretty v United Kingdom [15]

Judgment of the ECtHR

The applicant in this case is prevented by law from exercising her choice to avoid what she considers will be an undignified and distressing end to her life. The Court is not prepared to exclude that this constitutes an interference with her right to respect for private life as guaranteed under Article 8(1) of the Convention.

The law in issue in this case, section 2 of the 1961 Act, was designed to safeguard life by protecting the weak and vulnerable and especially those who are not in a condition to take informed decisions against acts intended to end life or to assist in ending life. Doubtless the condition of terminally ill individuals will vary. But many will be vulnerable and it is the vulnerability of the class which provides the rationale for the law in question. It is primarily for States to assess the risk and the likely incidence of abuse if the general prohibition on assisted

---

[14] [2001] UKHL 61.   [15] (2002) 35 EHRR 1.

suicides were relaxed or if exceptions were to be created. Clear risks of abuse do exist, notwithstanding arguments as to the possibility of safeguards and protective procedures. The Court does not consider therefore that the blanket nature of the ban on assisted suicide is disproportionate.

It was probably inevitable that Mrs Pretty's request for the DPP to issue a 'blank cheque', giving her husband future immunity from prosecution, would fail. If circumstances changed, for example, and Mrs Pretty had a change of heart, it would clearly be unacceptable for her husband to be immune from any future prosecution.

(2) Debbie Purdy and the DPP's Policy

(a) Debbie Purdy's legal claim

A few years later Debbie Purdy, who suffered from primary progressive multiple sclerosis, mounted the more modest claim that she and her husband, Omar Puente, should be entitled to know what factors the DPP would take into account when deciding whether to prosecute him.

Almost all of the UK citizens who have accessed assisted suicide at Dignitas in Switzerland have been helped by another person. Booking someone's flight; driving her to the airport, or taking her on her final journey could all be instances of assisting suicide. There have been police investigations when family members have returned from Switzerland—adding, inevitably, to the family's grief—but no one has yet faced prosecution.

Debbie Purdy's argument was that the DPP is plainly exercising his discretion not to prosecute in such cases, and that the criteria that are being used to make these decisions should be open and transparent. If the factors relevant to the DPP's decisions about prosecution were to be made public, Ms Purdy and Mr Puente could consider them before deciding whether he would accompany her to Switzerland, if her condition became unbearable. Ms Purdy said that unless she was able to weigh up the likelihood of prosecution in advance, she might have to go to Switzerland earlier than she would like, when she could still make the trip unaided.

At first instance, the court held that it was bound by the decision in *Pretty*, and that Ms Purdy's Article 8 rights were not engaged. Before her case was heard by the Court of Appeal, the then DPP, Keir Starmer QC, published a detailed explanation of his decision not to prosecute the parents of Daniel James, a 23-year-old man who had been left paralysed after a rugby accident. Daniel James died at Dignitas in September 2008, accompanied by his parents. Although there was sufficient evidence to prosecute his parents, and a family friend who had booked his air ticket (and who had, in fact, booked a return flight for Daniel in the hope that he might be persuaded to change his mind), the DPP decided that prosecution was not in the public interest.[16]

When it handed down its judgment in the *Purdy* case, the Court of Appeal agreed that it was bound by the House of Lords' decision that Dianne Pretty's Article 8 rights were not engaged.[17] At the same time, the Court of Appeal implied that there was ample evidence, not

---

[16] 'DPP Decision On Prosecution—The Death by Suicide of Daniel James' (CPS, 2008).
[17] *R (on the application of Purdy) v Director of Public Prosecutions* [2009] EWCA Civ 92.

least from the DPP's decision in relation to Daniel James's parents, upon which Debbie Purdy's legal advisers might base advice to her about the likelihood of her husband's prosecution. Without spelling it out explicitly, it was clear that the Court of Appeal believed that Mr Puente would be unlikely to face prosecution if he accompanied his wife to Switzerland.

Debbie Purdy then appealed successfully to the House of Lords. In *R (on the application of Purdy) v Director of Public Prosecutions*, its last judgment before it was replaced by the UK Supreme Court, the House of Lords found that Ms Purdy's Article 8 rights were engaged by the DPP's refusal to give more specific guidance on how he exercised his discretion under section 2(4). The interference with her Article 8 rights could be justifiable under Article 8(2) only if the manner in which the DPP exercised his discretion was accessible and sufficiently precise to enable a person to regulate her conduct accordingly. In order to be compliant with Article 8, the Lords agreed that there should be an offence-specific policy identifying the facts and circumstances that the DPP would take into account when deciding whether a prosecution was in the public interest.

R (on the application of Purdy) v Director of Public Prosecutions[18]

Lord Brown

Obviously no advance undertaking can be sought from the Director of Public Prosecutions that he will refuse consent to a prosecution in a particular case ... Surely, however, there can be no similar objection to the Director indicating in advance what will be his general approach towards the exercise of his discretion regarding the prosecution of this most sensitive and distressing class of case ...

What to my mind is needed is a custom-built policy statement indicating the various factors for and against prosecution, many but not all of which are touched on in the *James* case, factors designed to distinguish between those situations in which, however tempted to assist, the prospective aider and abettor should refrain from doing so, and those situations in which he or she may fairly hope to be, if not commended, at the very least forgiven, rather than condemned, for giving assistance.

(b) *The DPP's policy for prosecutors*

Following the publication of an interim policy and a consultation process, the DPP's final policy was published in 2010.

DPP Policy for Prosecutors in Respect of Cases of Encouraging or Assisting Suicide[19]

43. Public interest factors tending in favour of prosecution

A prosecution is more likely to be required if:

- The victim was under 18 years of age.

---

[18] [2009] UKHL 45. [19] (CPS, 2010).

- The victim did not have the capacity (as defined by the Mental Capacity Act 2005) to reach an informed decision to commit suicide.

- The victim had not reached a voluntary, clear, settled and informed decision to commit suicide.

- The victim had not clearly and unequivocally communicated his or her decision to commit suicide to the suspect.

- The victim did not seek the encouragement or assistance of the suspect personally or on his or her own initiative.

- The suspect was not wholly motivated by compassion; for example, the suspect was motivated by the prospect that he or she or a person closely connected to him or her stood to gain in some way from the death of the victim.

- The suspect pressured the victim to commit suicide.

- The suspect did not take reasonable steps to ensure that any other person had not pressured the victim to commit suicide.

- The suspect had a history of violence or abuse against the victim.

- The victim was physically able to undertake the act that constituted the assistance himself or herself.

- The suspect was unknown to the victim and encouraged or assisted the victim to commit or attempt to commit suicide by providing specific information via, for example, a website or publication.

- The suspect gave encouragement or assistance to more than one victim who were not known to each other.

- The suspect was paid by the victim or those close to the victim for his or her encouragement or assistance.

- The suspect was acting in his or her capacity as a medical doctor, nurse, other healthcare professional, a professional carer (whether for payment or not), or as a person in authority, such as a prison officer, and the victim was in his or her care. [NB this factor was revised in 2014, see below.]

- The suspect was aware that the victim intended to commit suicide in a public place where it was reasonable to think that members of the public may be present.

- The suspect was acting in his or her capacity as a person involved in the management or as an employee (whether for payment or not) of an organisation or group, a purpose of which is to provide a physical environment (whether for payment or not) in which to allow another to commit suicide.

45. Public interest factors tending against prosecution

A prosecution is less likely to be required if:

- The victim had reached a voluntary, clear, settled and informed decision to commit suicide.

- The suspect was wholly motivated by compassion.

- The actions of the suspect, although sufficient to come within the definition of the crime, were of only minor encouragement or assistance.

- The suspect had sought to dissuade the victim from taking the course of action which resulted in his or her suicide.

- The actions of the suspect may be characterised as reluctant encouragement or assistance in the face of a determined wish on the part of the victim to commit suicide.
- The suspect reported the victim's suicide to the police and fully assisted them in their enquiries into the circumstances of the suicide or the attempt and his or her part in providing encouragement or assistance.

The first thing to note is the number of factors that must be considered. Andrew Sanders suggests that this makes police investigations unnecessarily complicated.

Andrew Sanders[20]

The DPP could have formulated a policy that simply said he would not prosecute if the 'victim' had a voluntary, informed, clear and settled wish to die. Instead, the focus on the motivation and role of the perpetrator restricts assisted suicide more than *Purdy* required.

[T]he number of factors in the policy requires extensive police investigation to enable CPS to make a decision in accordance with it. Every assisted suicide that is reported to the police is investigated by them, who then send a file to the CPS. Suspects are interviewed under caution and frequently following arrest. Yet hardly any are prosecuted.

As Sanders points out, the policy focuses principally on the motive of the suspect, rather than on the condition of the victim(s). The DPP's interim policy did originally contain, as a factor against prosecution, that the victim had a terminal illness; a severe and incurable physical illness; or a severe degenerative physical condition, but this was removed following pressure from disability activists. They claimed that including disability as a reason not to prosecute sent a message that their lives were less likely to be worth living.

The condition of the victim is not completely irrelevant, however. Being motivated by compassion will generally mean that relief of the victim's suffering is the suspect's principal reason for helping her to commit suicide. It is also a factor against prosecution that the victim had reached a settled and definite decision to die. If a person's decision to die is settled and definite, it is more likely to be a response to her bleak condition and prognosis.

(c) Professional vs amateur assisters?

It is noteworthy that several of the factors in favour of prosecution are essentially that the suspect was acting in a professional capacity, especially as a healthcare professional. This is significant for several reasons. First, there is a tension between this aspect of the policy and its focus on the suspect's motive. Professional assisters are less likely than relatives to have mixed or non-compassionate motives for acting. Professional assisters are unlikely to profit from the person's death, for example, and nor will they wish to escape from the burdens of caring for her. In practice, most professional assisters are likely to be motivated solely by compassion.

Secondly, this aspect of the policy has made some healthcare professionals nervous about how to respond if a patient tells them that she is planning to travel to Dignitas. Might providing a patient with a copy of her medical records to take to Dignitas count as 'assistance',

---

[20] 'The CPS, policy-making and assisted dying: towards a "freedom" approach' (2017) Journal of Criminal Law, available at <http://sro.sussex.ac.uk/id/eprint/71867/>.

for example? Given that patients have a statutory right of access to their medical records, this is improbable, especially since we know that others who have played a far more active role in assisting relatives' suicides have escaped prosecution. Certainly, the GMC has taken the view that simply providing a patient who wished to have an assisted death with her records would not be sufficient to challenge a doctor's fitness to practise.

General Medical Council[21]

Allegations that will not normally give rise to a question of impaired fitness to practise

22 Some actions related to a person's decision to, or ability to, commit suicide are lawful, or will be too distant from the encouragement or assistance to raise a question about a doctor's fitness to practise. These include but are not limited to:

   a. providing advice or information limited to the doctor's understanding of the law relating to encouraging or assisting suicide

   b. providing access to a patient's records where a subject access request has been made ...

   c. providing information or evidence in the context of legal proceedings relating to encouraging or assisting suicide.

Some commentators have argued that it is odd that the policy explicitly favours amateur assisters. As Penney Lewis explains, the consequence could be more distressing assisted deaths, and Andrew Sanders points out that amateur assisters might be *more* likely than professional assisters to pressure someone to end her life.

Penney Lewis[22]

Unlike all of the other jurisdictions which permit assisted suicide (and in the Netherlands and Belgium, euthanasia as well), where the activity is carried out in whole or in part by physicians, the inclusion of these factors will discourage the involvement of healthcare professionals ... The advantages of open medical involvement are manifold, and include a lower risk of botched suicides and suffering during the suicide or attempted suicide ... and the possibility of screening for possibly hitherto unknown mental disorders including depression ... By strongly discouraging medical involvement, the policy places a heavy burden on supportive friends and family ...

Whether intentionally or not, these factors may keep the number of assisted suicides which take place entirely within the UK relatively low. Travel to a jurisdiction which does permit medical involvement will remain attractive to some, and this may have to be done earlier than the victim would otherwise wish. If travelling to a permissive jurisdiction is not possible, for financial or health reasons, then the burden of assisting the suicide will fall on someone with no experience and no access to relevant information ... Without this knowledge, and without access to appropriate medications, the policy is likely to result in assisted suicides which are more difficult, less successful and more stressful for the victim and his or her friends and

---

[21] *Guidance for the Investigation Committee and Case Examiners When Considering Allegations About a Doctor's Involvement in Encouraging or Assisting Suicide* (GMC, 2013).

[22] 'Informal Legal Change on Assisted Suicide: The Policy for Prosecutors' (2011) 31 Legal Studies 119–34.

family (including the suspect) than would be the case if medical expertise were permitted in some form.

Andrew Sanders[23]

The policy rightly seeks to protect victims from those who might pressure them into suicide. But ... those most likely to exert such pressure are those with most to gain from a person's suicide (such as family and close friends), and those least likely to exert such pressure are those with little or nothing to gain (such as professionals). Yet the policy facilitates AS by family and friends, and discourages AS by professionals.

A further problem with the preference for amateur assisters is that some people will not have friends or family who are willing to help. In 2012, a man identified as 'Martin' applied for judicial review of the DPP's policy on the grounds that it did not provide sufficient clarity to someone like him, who did not know anyone who was willing to help him organize his assisted suicide. Martin had suffered a massive stroke in 2008, at the age of 43. As a result, he could not speak and could hardly move, communicating only through tiny movements of his head and eyes, and with the help of a computer that could detect where on the screen he was looking. His wife, who cared for him at home with the help of professional carers, did not agree with his decision to travel to Dignitas and was not prepared to assist him, although she had said that she would want to be there to provide comfort and to say goodbye.

Martin did not have any other family members he could ask, and he was concerned that someone else would be reluctant to help, on the grounds that they might be more likely to face prosecution. Although it raised different issues, Martin's case was joined with that of Tony Nicklinson, discussed earlier.

In the Court of Appeal, Lord Judge LCJ dissented on Martin's appeal because he thought that a professional assister would only be more likely to face prosecution if she had abused a position of trust. Lord Dyson MR and Elias LJ did not think it was possible to read this qualification into the statement that acting in a professional capacity is a factor in favour of prosecution. Because the new DPP, Alison Saunders, agreed with Lord Judge LCJ's interpretation, by the time Martin's case reached the Supreme Court, there was a discrepancy between what the policy said and what the DPP thought it should say. The Supreme Court therefore left it to her to resolve this.[24]

In 2014, the DPP amended the relevant factor in favour of prosecution (paragraph 14), so that it now reads:

14. the suspect was acting in his or her capacity as a medical doctor, nurse, other healthcare professional, a professional carer [whether for payment or not], or as a person in authority, such as a prison officer, and the victim was in his or her care.[1]

[1] This factor does not apply merely because someone was acting in a capacity described within it: it applies only where there was, in addition, a relationship of care between the suspect and the victims such that it will be necessary to consider whether the suspect may have exerted some influence on the victim.

[23] 'The CPS, policy-making and assisted dying: towards a 'freedom' approach' (2017) Journal of Criminal Law, available at <http://sro.sussex.ac.uk/id/eprint/71867/>.
[24] R (on the application of AM) v Director of Public Prosecutions [2014] UKSC 38.

(3) R (Nicklinson and Another) v Ministry of Justice and the Compatibility of Section 2(1) with Article 8

As we saw earlier, once Tony Nicklinson and Paul Lamb's cases reached the Supreme Court, they were concerned with one question only: is section 2(1) of the Suicide Act compatible with Article 8 of the Convention? Nine Supreme Court Justices heard the appeal and, because each of them chose to deliver their own judgment, unpicking the decision is complicated.

To summarize briefly: the Supreme Court was unanimous that the question of whether the current law on assisted suicide was incompatible with Article 8 lay within the UK's margin of appreciation, and was therefore for the UK to decide. On the case before them, five Justices (Lords Neuberger, Mance, Kerr, and Wilson, and Lady Hale) held that the Supreme Court had the constitutional authority to make a declaration that the prohibition on assisted suicide in section 2(1) was incompatible with Article 8. Of those five, Lords Neuberger, Mance, and Wilson declined to grant a declaration of incompatibility in these proceedings, whereas Lady Hale and Lord Kerr would have been prepared to do so.

Four Justices (Lords Clarke, Sumption, Reed, and Hughes) concluded that this case involved the consideration of matters that parliament was better qualified to assess. Of those four, Lords Clarke and Sumption were prepared to countenance the future possibility of a declaration, but only if parliament abdicated its responsibility to consider the issue; whereas Lords Reed and Hughes were of the view that this was purely a matter for parliament.

In short, then, although their reasoning differed, a majority of the Supreme Court was not prepared to grant a declaration of incompatibility at this time.

R (Nicklinson and Another) v Ministry of Justice [25]

Lord Neuberger

The interference with Applicants' article 8 rights is grave, the arguments in favour of the current law are by no means overwhelming, the present official attitude to assisted suicide seems in practice to come close to tolerating it in certain situations, the appeal raises issues similar to those which the courts have determined under the common law, the rational connection between the aim and effect of section 2 is fairly weak, and no compelling reason has been made out for the court simply ceding any jurisdiction to Parliament.

Accordingly . . . I am of the view that, provided that the evidence and the arguments justified such a conclusion, we could properly hold that section 2 infringed article 8 . . .

However, I consider that . . . it would not be appropriate to grant a declaration of incompatibility at this time. In my opinion, before making such a declaration, we should accord Parliament the opportunity of considering whether to amend section 2 so as to enable Applicants, and, quite possibly others, to be assisted in ending their lives, subject of course to such regulations and other protective features as Parliament thinks appropriate . . .

There is a number of reasons which, when taken together, persuade me that it would be institutionally inappropriate at this juncture for a court to declare that section 2 is incompatible with article 8, as opposed to giving Parliament the opportunity to consider the position without a declaration. First, the question whether the provisions of section 2 should be modified

---

[25] [2014] UKSC 38.

raises a difficult, controversial and sensitive issue, with moral and religious dimensions, which undoubtedly justifies a relatively cautious approach from the courts. Secondly, this is not a case ... where the incompatibility is simple to identify and simple to cure: whether, and if so how, to amend section 2 would require much anxious consideration from the legislature; this also suggests that the courts should, as it were, take matters relatively slowly. Thirdly, section 2 has, as mentioned above, been considered on a number of occasions in Parliament, and it is currently due to be debated in the House of Lords in the near future; so this is a case where the legislature is and has been actively considering the issue. Fourthly, less than 13 years ago, the House of Lords in *R (Pretty) v Director of Public Prosecutions* gave Parliament to understand that a declaration of incompatibility in relation to section 2 would be inappropriate ... : a declaration of incompatibility on this appeal would represent an unheralded volte-face ...

Parliament now has the opportunity to address the issue of whether section 2 should be relaxed or modified, and if so how, in the knowledge that, if it is not satisfactorily addressed, there is a real prospect that a further, and successful, application for a declaration of incompatibility may be made ...

Before we could uphold the contention that section 2 infringed the article 8 rights of Applicants, we would in my view have to have been satisfied that there was a physically and administratively feasible and robust system whereby Applicants could be assisted to kill themselves, and that the reasonable concerns expressed by the Secretary of State (particularly the concern to protect the weak and vulnerable) were sufficiently met so as to render the absolute ban on suicide disproportionate.

Lord Sumption

The question whether relaxing or qualifying the current absolute prohibition on assisted suicide would involve unacceptable risks to vulnerable people is in my view a classic example of the kind of issue which should be decided by Parliament. There are, I think, three main reasons. The first is that, as I have suggested, the issue involves a choice between two fundamental but mutually inconsistent moral values, upon which there is at present no consensus in our society. Such choices are inherently legislative in nature. The decision cannot fail to be strongly influenced by the decision-makers' personal opinions about the moral case for assisted suicide. This is entirely appropriate if the decision-makers are those who represent the community at large. It is not appropriate for professional judges. The imposition of their personal opinions on matters of this kind would lack all constitutional legitimacy.

Secondly, Parliament has made the relevant choice. It passed the Suicide Act in 1961, and as recently as 2009 amended section 2 without altering the principle. In recent years there have been a number of bills to decriminalise assistance to suicide, at least in part, but none has been passed into law ... Sometimes, parliamentary inaction amounts to a decision not to act. But this is not even an issue on which Parliament has been inactive. So far, there has simply not been enough parliamentary support for a change in the law. The reasons why this is so are irrelevant. That is the current position of the representative body in our constitution ...

Third, the parliamentary process is a better way of resolving issues involving controversial and complex questions of fact arising out of moral and social dilemmas. The legislature has access to a fuller range of expert judgment and experience than forensic litigation can possibly provide. It is better able to take account of the interests of groups not represented or not sufficiently represented before the court in resolving what is surely a classic 'polycentric problem'.

Lady Hale

Why then is the present law incompatible? Not because it contains a general prohibition on assisting or encouraging suicide, but because it fails to admit of any exceptions ...

The only legitimate aim which has been advanced for this interference [with Article 8] is the protection of vulnerable people, those who feel that their lives are worthless or that they are a burden to others and therefore that they ought to end their own lives even though they do not really want to ...

Is it then reasonably necessary to prohibit helping *everyone* who might want to end their own lives in order to protect those whom we regard as *vulnerable* to undue pressures to do so? ...

It would not be beyond the wit of a legal system to devise a process for identifying those people, those few people, who should be allowed help to end their own lives. There would be four essential requirements. They would firstly have to have the capacity to make the decision for themselves. They would secondly have to have reached the decision freely without undue influence from any quarter. They would thirdly have had to reach it with full knowledge of their situation, the options available to them, and the consequences of their decision ... And they would fourthly have to be unable, because of physical incapacity or frailty, to put that decision into effect without some help from others. I do not pretend that such cases would always be easy to decide, but the nature of the judgments involved would be no more difficult than those regularly required in the Court of Protection or the Family Division ...

To the extent that the current universal prohibition prevents those who would qualify under such a procedure from securing the help they need, I consider that it is a disproportionate interference with their right to choose the time and manner of their deaths. It goes much further than is necessary to fulfil its stated aim of protecting the vulnerable. It fails to strike a fair balance between the rights of those who have freely chosen to commit suicide but are unable to do so without some assistance and the interests of the community as a whole.

Several aspects of the judgments in *Nicklinson* are worth noting. First, the tone of almost all of the judgments is considerably more sympathetic towards the legalization of assisted suicide than any of the judgments in the cases that preceded it. Only 12 years earlier, the House of Lords was of the view that Article 8 was not even engaged in Dianne Pretty's case. Now a majority in the Supreme Court not only believed it to be engaged, but appeared to be seriously concerned about whether section 2 of the Suicide Act is compatible with it.

Secondly, there is something curious about declining to make a declaration of incompatibility now, but being prepared to do so should parliament fail to act. All a declaration of incompatibility would do, as Lady Hale and Lord Kerr both pointed out, is invite parliament to consider whether to act. In the next extract, Elizabeth Wicks explains that a declaration of incompatibility certainly does not take the decision away from parliament.

Elizabeth Wicks[26]

[T]he majority approach seems to overlook, misconceive, or misrepresent the consequence of a declaration of incompatibility. The declaration has two elements that would be particularly useful in the context of this case: it is of declaratory effect only and it refers the matter back to Parliament ... It is this fact that renders so much of the judicial agonising about whether assisted dying is an issue for the courts or Parliament misguided and unnecessary. The declaration of incompatibility does not take the issue away from Parliament; it relinquishes the issue to it ...

[26] 'The Supreme Court Judgment in *Nicklinson*: One Step Forward on Assisted Dying; Two Steps Back on Human Rights' (2015) 23 Medical Law Review 144–56.

Thus, the view of the majority of the Supreme Court judges that a declaration of incompatibility should not be made in relation to the statutory universal offence of assisted suicide, even if it is in the view of the court incompatible with Article 8, undermines the very nature of the HRA [Human Rights Act] scheme of protection for individual rights in domestic law. It ignores the fact that the declaratory power is one expressly granted by Parliament for the very purpose of the courts highlighting to Parliament laws that are incompatible with the Convention rights, and that a declaration does not have any legal effect, refers the issue back to Parliament, and leaves Parliament entirely free to retain the existing law.

Stevie Martin further argues that once it was admitted that Tony Nicklinson's Article 8 rights were engaged, the burden of proof should have been on the state to prove that a blanket ban was necessary in order to protect the vulnerable.

Stevie Martin[27]

In circumstances where it was accepted by the court that the blanket ban constituted an interference with the applicant's art. 8 rights, *the state* bore the burden of proving that the interference was justified by reference to art. 8(2). The approaches taken by the majority in *Nicklinson*, both in refusing to even consider the compatibility of the blanket ban (per Lords Clarke, Sumption, Reed and Hughes) and in deciding not to issue a declaration because Parliament was the better forum given the complexity of the matter (per Lords Neuberger, Mance and Wilson), were based on the untested assumption that the state's justifications for the ban were valid. By failing to properly examine the evidential merits of these justifications (and, indeed, by additionally requiring the applicants to meet those untested assertions), the majority erroneously shifted the burden of justifying the interference on to the applicants ...

The second error underpinning the reasoning of Lords Neuberger, Mance and Wilson stems from the suggestion that before the court can issue a declaration pursuant to s. 4, it must be 'satisfied that there [is] a physically and administratively feasible and robust [alternative]'... To require that a court formulate a means of addressing that compatibility before it can declare a particular provision incompatible not only runs the risk of erroneously shifting the burden of justifying the interference on to the applicants (as occurred in *Nicklinson* and ... in *Conway*), it also puts the court at risk of usurping the role of Parliament and offending the separation of powers.

(4) Noel Conway and Omid T

Noel Conway's case was similar to that of Tony Nicklinson, in that his argument was that the blanket ban in section 2 of the Suicide Act is incompatible with his Article 8 rights. It differed in two respects, however. First, Noel Conway had motor neurone disease and was terminally ill, and his claim was that an exception should be made only for cases of terminal illness. Secondly, Noel Conway proposed 'an alternative statutory scheme', which he claimed would 'sufficiently protect the weak and vulnerable' and, as a result, 'demonstrate that the blanket prohibition in section 2(1) is an unnecessary and disproportionate interference with his Article 8(1) rights'.

The Divisional Court rejected his claim, citing 'a rational connection between the prohibition in section 2 and the protection of the weak and vulnerable'. In addition, it held that the

---

[27] 'Declaratory misgivings: assisted suicide in a post-Nicklinson context' (2018) Public Law 209–23.

prohibition 'serves to reinforce a moral view regarding the sanctity of life, ... [and] promote relations of full trust and confidence between doctors and their patients'. Noel Conway's appeal was dismissed by the Court of Appeal.

R (on the application of Conway) v Secretary of State for Justice [28]

Sir Terence Etherton MR, Sir Brian Leveson P, and King LJ

We were referred to evidence of arrangements for assisted suicide in Oregon, Canada, the Netherlands and Belgium. The arrangements in each of them are different. Some are statutory and some are not. No doubt they reflect the priorities in values and the compromises which are deemed appropriate in those particular countries. They are of interest and no doubt of varying degrees of relevance to the debate about assisted suicide in this jurisdiction but they can hardly carry any decisive weight in a court here, and certainly not on the limited state of the evidence before us ...

There can be no doubt that Parliament is a far better body for determining the difficult policy issue in relation to assisted suicide in view of the conflicting, and highly contested, views within our society on the ethical and moral issues and the risks and potential consequences of a change in the law and the implementation of a scheme such as that proposed by Mr Conway. The contentious nature of the proposal is reflected in the fact that assisted suicide is unlawful in the great majority of Convention countries. It is particularly of note that Mr Conway's proposed scheme is broadly equivalent to the Falconer Bill, which never became law, and the Marris Bill, which was rejected by the House of Commons ...

Furthermore, the evidence available to the court is necessarily limited to that which the parties wish to adduce. Unlike Parliament, or indeed the Law Commission of England and Wales, the court cannot conduct consultations with the public or any sector of it and cannot engage experts and advisers on its own account ...

[W]e consider that it is impossible to say that the Divisional Court did not have material on which properly to come to their conclusions on the inadequacy of the proposed scheme to protect the weak and vulnerable, on the scheme's failure to give proper weight to the moral significance of the sanctity of life and on the scheme's potential to undermine relations of trust and confidence between doctors and their patients.

In November 2018, the Supreme Court refused permission to appeal, on the grounds that Mr Conway's prospects of success were insufficient to justify giving permission.

Lady Hale, Lord Reed, and Lord Kerr [29]

Under the United Kingdom's constitutional arrangements, only Parliament could change this law. But the Supreme Court could, if it thought right, make a declaration that the law was incompatible with the Convention rights, leaving it to Parliament to decide what, if anything, to do about it. The questions for the court would therefore be twofold: (1) Is the hard and fast rule banning all assistance to commit suicide a justified interference with the Convention rights of those who wish for such assistance? (2) If it is not, should this court make a declaration

---

[28] [2018] EWCA Civ 1431.
[29] Available at <www.supremecourt.uk/docs/r-on-the-application-of-conway-v-secretary-of-state-for-justice-court-order.pdf>.

to that effect? In particular, is it appropriate to make such a declaration in this case? These are questions upon which the considered opinions of conscientious judges may legitimately differ. Indeed, they differ amongst the members of this panel.

Ultimately, the question for the panel is whether the prospects of Mr Conway's succeeding in his claim before this court are sufficient to justify our giving him permission to pursue it, with all that that would entail for him, for his family, for those on all sides of this multi-faceted debate, for the general public and for this court. Not without some reluctance, it has been concluded that in this case those prospects are not sufficient to justify giving permission to appeal.

Writing after the Court of Appeal granted Noel Conway permission to appeal against the Divisional Court judgment, Clark Hobson argues that the lower courts were too quick to accept that parliament had satisfactorily addressed the issue after the Supreme Court's judgment in *Nicklinson*.

Clark Hobson[30]

Nicklinson is a radical case; the Supreme Court is open to the argument that an exception to the blanket ban on assisted suicide would be advantageous. Certainly, a number of judges believe at some point it will be institutionally appropriate to entertain another application for a declaration that section 2(1) Suicide Act is incompatible, even if Parliament is the preferable forum for addressing the issue. Both decisions in the *Conway* litigation are important for their interpretation of *Nicklinson*. Unfortunately, the High Court and Court of Appeal settle on an unjustifiably deferential approach regarding what it means for Parliament to have 'satisfactorily addressed' assisted suicide legislation, post-*Nicklinson*.

At the same time, Omid T, a 54-year-old man suffering from multiple system atrophy, mounted a similar claim that the blanket ban on assisted dying breached his Article 8 rights. Given the Court of Appeal's decision in *Conway*, Omid T's case was bound to fail in the lower courts. His legal team sought permission to cross-examine a particular witness, Baroness Ilora Finlay, and to 'leapfrog' his appeal to the Supreme Court. Omid T travelled to Switzerland for an assisted suicide days before the High Court dismissed his application.[31] It held that his application to 'leapfrog' the case to the Supreme Court was 'premature', and Irwin LJ said:

I do not see that there is a need for oral evidence or cross-examination. It appears to me that the factual foundations for the views of the various experts are either already clear, or can be clarified in submissions from counsel based on the written material.

At the time of writing, given that the cases of Noel Conway and Omid T did not result in full hearings in the UK Supreme Court, a declaration of incompatibility looks less likely than it did immediately after *Nicklinson*.

---

[30] 'Is It Now Institutionally Appropriate for the Courts to Consider Whether the Assisted Dying Ban is Human Rights Compatible? *Conway v Secretary of State for Justice*' (2018) 26 Medical Law Review 514–30.
[31] *R (on the application of T) v Ministry of Justice* [2018] EWHC 2615 (Admin).

(5) Pressure on the Status Quo

In addition to the applications for judicial review outlined above, there are several sources of pressure on the status quo in the UK. First, it could be said that the option of assisted suicide at Dignitas acts as a 'safety valve' for UK citizens, who can access lawful assisted suicide provided that they are able and willing to travel to Switzerland in order to do so. If Switzerland were to close this safety valve, citizens who might think that they had a reasonable expectation of being able to access an assisted death would no longer be able to do so.

Secondly, the Swiss option is only available to patients with considerable financial and social resources. An assisted death at Dignitas can cost more than £8000. For older people who may be unfamiliar with the internet, finding out how to join Dignitas may be difficult. Profoundly incapacitated people, like Martin, who do not have willing family or friends, may also find it difficult to travel to Switzerland unaided.

Thirdly, people seeking an assisted death in Switzerland must be physically fit enough to travel. In the final stages of a disease like cancer, this will often be impossible. As a result, it is not uncommon for people who are scared of what lies ahead of them to seek an assisted death at Dignitas sooner than they would like, while they are still capable of making the journey. If assisted suicide had been available in the UK, they could have waited until their condition became unbearable, and in practice, many of them might never have accessed an assisted death. It is therefore possible that some people who have died at Dignitas would have had longer lives, and experienced natural deaths, if assisted dying was lawful in the UK.

Fourthly, best practice in end-of-life care is to try to facilitate what most patients want, which is often to die in the comfort of their own home. For patients travelling to Dignitas in Switzerland, not only can they not die at home, but they must die in a foreign country, far away from family, friends, and other sources of support and comfort such as their family doctor or spiritual adviser.

Fifthly, as we see later, there are comparatively few legal safeguards in Switzerland. Not only is the UK exporting assisted suicide, but it is doing so to a country in which the only legal restriction is that the assister's motive must not be selfish. Finally, as Charles Foster has pointed out, there is something uncomfortable about outsourcing the 'dirty work' of assisted dying to another country.

Charles Foster[32]

If Switzerland is happy to continue providing the facility then, however intellectually dishonest it may be to allow her to siphon off all our own English pain, fear, angst and debate, it is likely to do less harm overall than introducing any conceivable assisted suicide law into England.

There are two possible connections between suicide tourism and English policy. The first is the liberalisation of public opinion that comes naturally, if irrationally, with familiarity. And the second is the slowly growing public acknowledgement that there is something intellectually, if not morally, uncomfortable, about getting another country to do your dirty work.

---

[32] 'Suicide tourism may change attitudes to assisted suicide, but not through the courts' (2015) 41 Journal of Medical Ethics 8.

(6) The Assisted Dying Bill

(a) *Legislative history*

There have been several unsuccessful attempts to introduce legislation to legalize assisted dying in the UK. The legislatures' hostility (so far) to assisted dying contrasts with the stable and clear majority of the public, who say that they would support legalization, in strictly limited circumstances. In addition to its finding that levels of support for euthanasia had not changed much over the past 30 years, according to the 2017 British Social Attitudes survey, 78 per cent of the British public are in favour of allowing voluntary euthanasia where it is carried out by a doctor for a person with an incurable disease (there was less support for euthanasia carried out where the person is not suffering from a terminal illness (51 per cent) or is completely dependent but not in pain or danger of death (50 per cent)).[33]

While not disputing the existence of a majority of public opinion in favour of assisted dying, Peter Saunders argues that this may be due to the successful media strategy of pro-legalization campaigners and the result of inherent bias in some parts of the media.

Peter Saunders[34]

Why is public opinion so much out of step with parliament and the institutions? One answer might be that whilst both parliament and the institutions tend to hear both sides of the argument most of the public do not. Exposure solely to hard cases and emotive testimonies understandably induces support; and those trying to change the law will always attract more media interest than those working to preserve the status quo. [Dignity in Dying] has therefore built its media strategy around high-profile legal cases, personal interest stories and celebrity endorsement. Finding itself frustratingly blocked by parliament and the institutions it has turned to the courts and to the media in order to build pressure for change.

In 2012, the Commission on Assisted Dying, chaired by Lord Falconer, published a report that concluded that the current legal status of assisted suicide was inadequate and incoherent.[35] The Commission's report led directly to the drafting of the first iteration of the Assisted Dying Bill, introduced into the House of Lords by Lord Falconer in 2014. The Bill's progress was halted by the 2015 general election, and was reintroduced into the Commons by Rob Marris MP, where it was defeated by 330 votes to 118 (the Bill has subsequently been introduced in the House of Lords, but without time for debate).

Elizabeth Wicks suggests that when it was debated in the House of Commons, most MPs failed to grasp the significance of the *Nicklinson* judgment.

---

[33] British Social Attitudes Survey 35 (NatCen Social Research, 2018).

[34] 'The Role of the Media in Shaping the UK Debate on "Assisted Dying" ' (2011) 11 Medical Law International 239–56.

[35] Commission on Assisted Dying, '*The Current Legal Status of Assisted Dying is Inadequate and Incoherent...*' (Demos: London, 2011). Because it had received funding and support from people and organizations known to be in favour of legalization, the Commission's report was dismissed by some commentators, who questioned its claim to be independent.

Elizabeth Wicks[36]

> Marris introduced the Bill by explaining that the Supreme Court had 'recognised that there is a problem that needs to be addressed by Parliament'... The significance of the Supreme Court's message to Parliament was later recognised by Keir Starmer (former DPP and now an MP) who noted that in *Nicklinson* 'the majority held that there was an incompatibility between our current position and fundamental human rights, but because of the margin of appreciation [sic] they should not themselves make a declaration to that effect but leave it to Parliament to further consider the issue, and today is that opportunity'. The message did not stick, however, and in a brief and somewhat self-congratulatory debate peppered with personal stories of dying relatives, the bandying of conflicting statistics and declarations of religious principle, the House overlooked the disproportionate infringement of Article 8 by the current law.

(b) THE LATEST ASSISTED DYING BILL AND ITS RESTRICTIONS

Assisted Dying Bill 2016-17

> 1(1) Subject to the consent of the High Court (Family Division) pursuant to subsection (2), a person who is terminally ill may request and lawfully be provided with assistance to end his or her own life.
>
> (2) Subsection (1) applies only if the High Court (Family Division), by order, confirms that it is satisfied that the person—
>
> (a) has a voluntary, clear, settled and informed wish to end his or her own life;
>
> (b) has made a declaration to that effect in accordance with section 3; and
>
> (c) on the day the declaration is made—
>
>   (i) is aged 18 or over;
>
>   (ii) has the capacity to make the decision to end his or her own life; and
>
>   (iii) has been ordinarily resident in England and Wales for not less than one year.

Two doctors, who must be completely independent of each other, would have to separately examine the patient and her medical records, and each of them would have to be satisfied independently that the person is terminally ill; that she has the capacity to make the decision to end her own life; and that she 'has a clear and settled intention to end their own life which has been reached voluntarily, on an informed basis and without coercion or duress'. They would also have to be satisfied that the person seeking an assisted suicide 'has been fully informed of the palliative, hospice and other care which is available to that person'.

Terminal illness is defined in section 2 as 'an inevitably progressive condition which cannot be reversed by treatment', and 'as a consequence of that terminal illness, [the person] is reasonably expected to die within six months'. The 'terminal illness' requirement illustrates neatly

---

[36] 'Nicklinson and Lamb v United Kingdom: Strasbourg Fails to Assist on Assisted Dying in the UK' (2016) 24 Medical Law Review 633–40.

that there may be a tension between what is politically feasible, in terms of a change in the law, and what is intellectually defensible. On the one hand, because public opinion surveys suggest that there is considerable support for legalized assisted dying for the terminally ill, confining access to the terminally ill might seem pragmatically sensible. On the other hand, we know that doctors' predictions of life expectancy are insufficiently accurate for 'having less than six months to live' to operate as a clear and precise boundary between those who should, and those who should not have access to assisted dying.

In addition, unbearable suffering is not confined to those who are imminently dying, and it might even be argued that someone with longer to live will experience more suffering, in quantitative terms, than someone whose death is expected within days. Certainly three of the most vocal campaigners for assisted dying in recent years—Debbie Purdy, Tony Nicklinson, and author Terry Pratchett[37]—would not have been eligible for assistance under the Assisted Dying Bill. As Samantha Halliday has explained, the 'terminal illness' restriction fails to capture the reason why people might seek assisted dying, which is not because they expect to die within six months, but because they are 'suffering unbearably without prospect of improvement'.[38]

There are those who defend restricting assisted dying to the terminally ill, however. Trudo Lemmens argues that those who are not imminently dying might, in the future, change their mind, and that without a terminal illness requirement, it becomes 'difficult to contain a change in practice'.

Trudo Lemmens[39]

If the person is not at the end of life, physician-assisted death will foreclose over a long period the possibility of the person changing their mind... We do not know, in the end, whom of these people may not regain the desire and energy to live after being offered adequate support and the time to adjust ...

Even though we may have much sympathy in individual cases for the argument that a person is fully aware of the consequences, has not given up quickly, and wants to have control over the ending of her life if and when she so wishes, expanding MAiD [Medical Assistance in Dying] to individuals outside the end-of-life context can have a cascading effect on others. Once end-of-life is abandoned as an access criterion, setting limits becomes very difficult if not impossible.

The competency requirement might appear less problematic: at first sight it seems obvious that anyone making such a profoundly important and final decision should have the capacity to do so. In practice, however, it might have unintended consequences. If mental capacity is a prerequisite, someone with a progressive, degenerative condition, who knows that she is likely to lose capacity at some point in the future, might opt for an assisted death earlier than she would like, fearing that if she leaves it too long, she might lose capacity and become ineligible. Moreover, if the justification for allowing assisted suicide is relief of unbearable suffering, is it cruel to confine this relief to a subset of suffering patients? As Jukka Varelius puts it: 'the

[37] Terry Pratchett, 'My case for a euthanasia tribunal' The Guardian, 2 February 2010.
[38] 'Comparative reflections upon the Assisted Dying Bill 2013: a plea for a more European approach' (2013) 13 Medical Law International 135–67.
[39] 'Charter Scrutiny of Canada's Medical Assistance in Dying Law and the Shifting Landscape of Belgian and Dutch Euthanasia Practice' (2018) 85 Supreme Court Law Review (2nd Series) 459–544.

suffering experienced by psychiatric patients who lack autonomy can be as bad as the distress that autonomous, or rational, psychiatric patients undergo, if not worse'.[40]

The proposal to legalize only assisted suicide (and not euthanasia) would also rule out access to assisted dying for patients who are incapable of completing the final act themselves. It might also create difficulties where the patient fails to ingest the whole lethal dose. If the patient is unable to swallow it all, or vomits, unless a doctor can take steps to end her life, she might be left in a worse state than she was before.

In the next extract, Elizabeth Peel and Rosie Harding argue that the Bill would create more problems than it would solve.

Elizabeth Peel and Rosie Harding[41]

It appears that the bill has been drafted in such a way as to head off many of the usual arguments against assisted suicide. For instance, first, the limitation to those with a terminal illness diagnosis with less than six months to live is designed to avoid any charge that those with chronic health problems or long-term disabilities that require long-term care (on average £32,250 per person with dementia in the UK for example) would feel pressurised into assisted suicide to avoid being a burden on either their families or on the state. Second, the requirement that a prescribed lethal dose must be approved by two healthcare professionals, and that the administering doctor needs to remain with the patient until they have self-administered the drug is intended to prevent familial misuse of the provisions. Third, the bill contains not one, but two, capacity-related 'safeguards': first that the patient must have a settled wish to die, which implies that they must have the capacity to make that decision ... Second, the patient must have the physical capacity to self-administer the lethal prescription provided by the prescribing doctor. Arguably then, the Assisted Dying Bill as it is currently configured may create more injustice and inequity in death than it would solve, given the significant limitations on its applicability. Instead of providing a solution to all those who wish to end their lives early, it would help only a minority. And many of those who find their lives intolerable would be excluded from its provision of a peaceful and dignified death.

(c) PALLIATIVE CARE THAT MAY HASTEN DEATH: THE DOCTRINE OF DOUBLE EFFECT

We turn now to potentially life-shortening practices that are lawful in the UK. Recall that in his summing up to the jury in *R v Cox*,[42] Ognall J said that there 'can be no doubt' that doctors are entitled to administer painkilling drugs, notwithstanding the fact that they may simultaneously hasten the moment of death. And it does appear to be an accepted and well-established principle of law that it can be lawful to administer painkilling or sedative drugs which might also 'hasten death' or 'shorten life'. In *Airedale NHS Trust v Bland*,[43] for example, Lord Goff referred to 'the established rule that a doctor may, when caring for a patient who is, for example,

---

[40] Jukka Varelius, 'On the Moral Acceptability of Physician-Assisted Dying for Non-Autonomous Psychiatric Patients' (2015) 30 Bioethics 227–33.

[41] 'A right to "dying well" with dementia? Capacity, Choice and Relationality' (2015) 25 Feminism & Psychology 137–42.

[42] (1992) 12 BMLR 38.   [43] [1993] AC 789.

dying of cancer, lawfully administer painkilling drugs despite the fact that he knows that an incidental effect of that application will be to abbreviate the patient's life'.

This principle is the doctrine of double effect, which has its origins in Roman Catholic moral theology, and distinguishes between results that are intended and results that are foreseen as likely, but unintended, consequences of one's actions. So a doctor might give a patient a very large dose of an opioid drug, like diamorphine, in order to relieve her pain, even if this might shorten the patient's life.

Many palliative care specialists would challenge the idea that proper pain management could ever result in a patient's death. Nevertheless, according to the doctrine of double effect, a doctor who intends a good consequence (relieving pain) would not be guilty of murder just because she foresees, but does not intend, a bad consequence (death). But, while the doctrine of double effect may make sense when a procedure, such as surgery, carries a small risk to the patient's life, which is nevertheless worth taking in order to attempt to improve the patient's condition, in the context of palliative care, it has been invoked to excuse conduct where death is very likely indeed.

Despite its widespread acceptance, the doctrine of double effect may be at odds with ordinary principles of criminal law. To be guilty of murder, the patient's death does not have to be the sole purpose of the defendant's action. Instead, the criminal law is clear that the jury may infer that a person has the requisite *mens rea* for murder if they engage in conduct which is virtually certain to cause death, even if this is not their primary purpose. As Lord Steyn explained in *R v Woollin*:

> Where a man realises that it is for all practical purposes inevitable that his actions will result in death or serious harm, the inference may be irresistible that he intended that result, however little he may have desired or wished it to happen.[44]

It is, however, worth noting that Lord Steyn does not go so far as to say that where death is inevitable, the inference must be irresistible that he intended that result; rather, he merely says that the inference *may* be irresistible. Plainly, although Lord Steyn envisages that there will be times when intention may be inferred from the inevitability of death, by implication there could also be times when this may not be the case, and an example might plausibly be the provision of proper palliative care.

Regardless of the precise meaning of intention within the criminal law, when a doctor foresees that the dose of analgesics or sedatives that she is about to give to a patient may cause her death, she must have reached the conclusion that death has become an acceptable outcome. If a doctor were to give a healthy patient with a mild headache a life-threatening injection of diamorphine, her conduct would not be excused by the doctrine of double effect. She could not claim that her intention was merely to relieve pain, and that the patient's death was a foreseen but unintended side effect. Instead, while death may not be the principal purpose of a doctor who administers a potentially lethal dose of opioids, she must have decided that the patient's interest in pain relief now outweighs her interest in continued life.

In the next extract, Glanville Williams suggests that it is artificial for doctors to think only about one consequence of their action (relieving pain), while ignoring another (causing death).

---

[44] [1999] 1 AC 82 (HL).

Glanville Williams[45]

It is altogether too artificial to say that a doctor who gives an overdose of a narcotic having in the forefront of his mind the aim of ending his patient's existence is guilty of sin, while a doctor who gives the same overdose in the same circumstances in order to relieve pain is not guilty of sin, provided that he keeps his mind steadily off the consequence which his professional training teaches him is inevitable, namely the death of his patient. When you know that your conduct will have two consequences, one in itself good and one in itself evil, you are compelled as a moral agent to choose between acting and not acting by making a judgement of value, that is to say by deciding whether the good is more to be desired than the evil is to be avoided.

On the other hand, in the next extract, Charles Douglas et al draw upon their interviews with clinicians to suggest that a degree of ambiguity in relation to what is intended may be helpful for doctors.

Charles Douglas, Ian Kerridge, and Rachel Ankeny[46]

The most striking feature of these interviews is a sense of uncertainty and ambiguity with regard to intention ... As almost all the respondents stated in one way or another, there is a 'grey area', where the intention is not explicitly to hasten death, but is no longer merely to palliate ... Instead of always expressing discomfort or even displaying equanimity about the dual effects of AS [analgesics and sedatives], there was often a sense that the possibility of a double effect was a good thing, that both outcomes (an expedited death and relief of suffering) were desirable, but that only one needed to be the apparent intention.

Provided the drugs that caused a patient's death could be used as painkillers or sedatives, it would in practice be difficult to disprove a doctor's assertion that her principal aim was the relief of suffering. Hence, in *R v Adams*,[47] it was possible for Dr Adams to argue that he had intended to relieve Mrs Morrell's pain by administering massive doses of morphine and diamorphine. In his summing up to the jury, Devlin J explained the doctrine of double effect:

If the first purpose of medicine, the restoration of health, can no longer be achieved, there is still much for a doctor to do, and he is entitled to do all that is proper and necessary to relieve pain and suffering, even if the measures he takes may incidentally shorten life.

It is, as Richard Huxtable has pointed out, perhaps 'somewhat ironic' that Dr Adams' conduct in this case 'imported a doctrine concerned with "pure" intentions into the criminal law', given

---

[45] *Sanctity of Life and the Criminal Law* (Faber: London, 1957) 286.
[46] 'Managing intentions: the end-of-life administration of analgesics and sedatives, and the possibility of slow euthanasia' (2008) 22 Bioethics 388–96.
[47] Unreported, 8 April 1957.

that, as the Detective who investigated Adams later revealed, Adams had inherited under 132 wills, and may have murdered a prosecution witness.[48]

In contrast, in *R v Cox*,[49] Dr Cox's use of potassium chloride (which has no analgesic properties) effectively ruled out the application of the doctrine of double effect. If Dr Cox had used morphine rather than potassium chloride to kill Lillian Boyes, he might have been able to argue that his primary intention was to relieve her suffering.

In addition to the administration of large doses of analgesic drugs, palliative care can also involve the use of sedation. The distress caused by being unable to breathe or swallow may be relieved by sedatives, which can usually be titrated until a dosage is found that makes the patient comfortable. It has, however, been said that it could be lawful to sedate someone into unconsciousness, at which point—if she is not going to recover—the clinically assisted nutrition and hydration which is keeping her alive might be removed, leading inevitably to her death. It is not clear that this happens in practice in the UK—indeed many palliative care specialists are adamant that it does not—but, provided the principal purpose of giving the sedatives is to relieve pain and suffering, this might be lawful palliative care, justified by the doctrine of double effect.

From the patient's perspective, as Margaret Pabst Battin explains, 'terminal sedation' may be indistinguishable from being given a lethal injection.

Margaret Pabst Battin[50]

Some kinds of conditions, such as difficulty in swallowing, are still difficult to relieve without introducing other discomforting limitations... Severe respiratory insufficiency may mean... 'a singularly terrifying and agonizing final few hours'...

[O]f course, the patient can be sedated into unconsciousness; this does indeed end the pain. But in respect of the patient's experience, this is tantamount to causing death: the patient has no further conscious experience and thus can achieve no goods, experience no significant communication, satisfy no goals. Furthermore, adequate sedation, by depressing respiratory function, may hasten death. Thus, although it is always technically possible to achieve relief from pain, at least when the appropriate resources are available, the price may be functionally and practically equivalent, at least from the patient's point of view, to death.

In France, since 2016, terminally ill patients who refuse life-prolonging treatment have the right to ask for continuous deep sedation.[51] Does this effectively allow patients to choose to bring their lives to an end, but without the need to legalize euthanasia?

A scenario that tests the limits of the doctrine of double effect to, or even perhaps beyond, breaking point is the use of muscle relaxants to stop the distressing gasping noise, sometimes referred to as 'agonal gasping', that is not uncommon immediately before death, and which can be upsetting for relatives. A muscle relaxant will prevent the gasping noise, but only because it stops the patient's breathing. The dying person has by this stage lost consciousness and will be unaware that their life has been shortened by seconds or minutes. The muscle relaxant is not given to reduce pain or suffering, because—despite the gasping sounds—by this stage

---

[48] 'Get out of jail free? The doctrine of double effect in English law' (2004) 18 Palliative Medicine 62.
[49] (1992) 12 BMLR 38.
[50] *The Least Worst Death: Essays in Bioethics on the End of Life* (OUP: Oxford, 1994).
[51] Ruth Horn, 'The "French exception": the right to continuous deep sedation at the end of life' (2018) 44 Journal of Medical Ethics 204–5.

there is none. Instead, as Govert den Hartogh explains, the muscle relaxant is given for the benefit of relatives, so that their loved one's death is as peaceful as possible.

Govert den Hartogh[52]

> Gasping is a normal phenomenon in all dying patients ... [A]t the stage of profound hypoxaemia which is also indicated to exist by the very phenomenon of gasping, it is unlikely that the dying person has any remnants of consciousness ... The standard view therefore is that gasping by itself is not a proper indication for the use of muscle relaxants. And from the descriptions we have of the practice it seems clear that the actual aim of this use ... is not to alleviate any supposed suffering of the dying person, but to relieve or prevent the distress of her relatives.

Where a newborn baby is close to death, it is easy to see why a doctor might want to make her death as peaceful as possible for the benefit of her parents. In 2005, Michael Munro, a neonatologist, who had given a muscle relaxant (in this case, pancuronium) to two dying babies had had his fitness to practise challenged by the GMC. Dr Munro told the fitness to practise panel that the parents 'were utterly distraught':

> If you put yourself in their shoes, they have already said their last goodbyes to their baby, then suddenly there are these massive, racking agonal gasps that appeared to build up—they were utterly, utterly distraught. The parents were in tears, saying things like 'I can't take any more.' I took the decision then to administer pancuronium. I explained to the parents that this drug was to be used to ease the suffering but that one of the consequences of its use may be to hasten death. They were happy with that.[53]

Despite the GMC describing what he did as 'tantamount to euthanasia', Michael Munro was cleared of malpractice by the fitness to practise panel.

(d) WITHDRAWING AND WITHHOLDING LIFE-PROLONGING TREATMENT

(1) Refusal of life-sustaining treatment

As we saw in Chapter 5, capacitous adult patients have the right to refuse medical treatment, even if this will result in their death. Although this right is not absolute, there are very few exceptions.[54] For our purposes, the important point, as Lord Mustill explained in *Airedale NHS Trust v Bland*, is that doctors must comply with a competent adult's refusal of life-sustaining medical treatment.

---

[52] 'Comforting the parents by administering neuromuscular blockers to the dying child: a conflict between ethics and law?' (2014) 31 Journal of Applied Philosophy 91–103.
[53] Owen Dyer, 'Doctor cleared of act "tantamount to euthanasia"' (2007) 335 British Medical Journal 67.
[54] An example would be s 63 of the Mental Health Act 1983, see further Chapter 7.

Airedale NHS Trust v Bland[55]

Lord Mustill

If the patient is capable of making a decision on whether to permit treatment and decides not to permit it his choice must be obeyed, even if on any objective view it is contrary to his best interests. A doctor has no right to proceed in the face of objection, even if it is plain to all, including the patient, that adverse consequences and even death will or may ensue.

One of the clearest illustrations of the robustness of the law's protection of a patient's right to insist on the withdrawal of life-prolonging medical treatment is a case decided around the same time as the Dianne Pretty case. In *Re B (Adult: Refusal of Treatment)*, Ms B was completely paralysed from the neck down. She had respiratory problems, and was connected to a ventilator. Ms B had repeatedly requested that she be removed from the ventilator, but the clinicians treating her were reluctant to comply with her wishes. Ms B sought, and was granted, a declaration that she had mental capacity and that, as a result, her doctors had been treating her unlawfully.

Re B (Adult: Refusal of Treatment)[56]

Dame Elizabeth Butler-Sloss P

There is a serious danger, exemplified in this case, of a benevolent paternalism which does not embrace recognition of the personal autonomy of the severely disabled patient. I do not consider that either the lack of experience in a spinal rehabilitation unit and thereafter in the community or the unusual situation of being in an ICU for a year has had the effect of eroding Ms B's mental capacity to any degree whatsoever.

I am therefore entirely satisfied that Ms B is competent to make all relevant decisions about her medical treatment including the decision whether to seek to withdraw from artificial ventilation . . .

In the light of my decision that the Claimant has mental capacity and has had such capacity since August 2001 I shall be prepared to grant the appropriate declarations. I also find that the Claimant has been treated unlawfully by the Trust since August.

It is worth noting that, despite the finding that they had been treating her unlawfully, the clinicians who had been caring for Ms B were not forced to participate in bringing about her death. Ms B was transferred to another hospital where she was removed from the artificial ventilator and died. We return to the significance of this later.

As we saw in Chapter 5, if a patient has capacity, her reasons for refusing treatment are irrelevant. As Lord Donaldson MR explained in *Re T (Adult: Refusal of Treatment)*:[57] 'the patient's right of choice exists whether the reasons for making that choice are rational, irrational, unknown or even non-existent'. So, even if a patient refuses medical treatment *because* she wants to die, the doctor is still bound to comply with her wishes.

---

[55] [1993] AC 789.   [56] [2002] EWHC 429 (Fam).   [57] [1993] Fam 95.

(2) The Acts/Omissions Distinction

If a doctor removes a feeding tube or a mechanical ventilator from a patient knowing that this will lead to the patient's death, could she satisfy both the *actus reus* and the *mens rea* of murder? If the withdrawal of medical treatment is an act done with the knowledge that it will cause the patient's death, then the patient's consent to the doctor's action is irrelevant. In order to avoid this conclusion, the law regards the withdrawal of life-prolonging medical treatment in such circumstances as an omission rather than an action.

It is possible to commit murder by omission, but only if the defendant was under a duty to act: an obvious example being a mother whose failure to feed her baby causes his death. Doctors are, of course, under a duty to care for their patients. Does this mean that doctors who respect their patients' refusals of life-sustaining treatment are potentially subject to prosecution for murder?

Almost certainly not. Because the doctor must comply with the patient's refusal, the doctor no longer has a duty to provide the rejected treatment, and hence the omission can no longer constitute the *actus reus* of murder. A doctor who maliciously unplugs the ventilator from a patient who is temporarily unconscious, but expected to make a full recovery, might be guilty of murder because she had a duty to provide life-prolonging treatment. In contrast, a doctor who respects a patient's capacitous refusal of life-sustaining treatment no longer has a duty to provide that treatment—on the contrary, her duty is to comply with the patient's wishes—and she therefore acts lawfully by removing life support from the patient.

A further reason for treating the withdrawal of life support as an omission is that not starting life-sustaining treatment in the first place is plainly an omission, rather than an action. If doctors could be guilty of murder if they withdraw life-support, but not if they fail to initiate it, there would be a powerful incentive to withhold such treatment from patients altogether, which would clearly be undesirable.

In *Airedale NHS Trust v Bland* the House of Lords decided, for the first time, that clinically assisted nutrition and hydration (CANH) could be withdrawn from a patient in a permanent vegetative state. Although the decision in *Bland* depended upon characterizing the withdrawal of treatment as an omission, some members of the House of Lords were less than enthusiastic about the acts/omissions distinction.

Airedale NHS Trust v Bland[58]

Lord Goff

I must however stress, at this point, that the law draws a crucial distinction between cases in which a doctor decides not to provide, or to continue to provide, for his patient treatment or care which could or might prolong his life, and those in which he decides, for example by administering a lethal drug, actively to bring his patient's life to an end. As I have already indicated, the former may be lawful ... But it is not lawful for a doctor to administer a drug to his patient to bring about his death, even though that course is prompted by a humanitarian desire to end his suffering, however great that suffering may be ... So to act is to cross the Rubicon which runs between on the one hand the care of the living patient and on the other hand euthanasia—actively causing his death to avoid or to end his suffering.

---

[58] [1993] AC 789 (HL).

Lord Browne-Wilkinson

Finally, the conclusion I have reached will appear to some to be almost irrational. How can it be lawful to allow a patient to die slowly, though painlessly, over a period of weeks from lack of food but unlawful to produce his immediate death by a lethal injection, thereby saving his family from yet another ordeal to add to the tragedy that has already struck them? I find it difficult to find a moral answer to that question. But it is undoubtedly the law.

Lord Mustill

The conclusion that the declarations can be upheld depends crucially on a distinction drawn by the criminal law between acts and omissions ... The acute unease which I feel about adopting this way through the legal and ethical maze is I believe due in an important part to the sensation that however much the terminologies may differ the ethical status of the two courses of action is for all relevant purposes indistinguishable. By dismissing this appeal I fear that your Lordships' House may only emphasise the distortions of a legal structure which is already both morally and intellectually misshapen. Still, the law is there and we must take it as it stands ...

The whole matter cries out for exploration in depth by Parliament and then for the establishment by legislation not only of a new set of ethically and intellectually consistent rules, distinct from the general criminal law, but also of a sound procedural framework within which the rules can be applied to individual cases. The rapid advance of medical technology makes this an ever more urgent task, and I venture to hope that Parliament will soon take it in hand.

In the next extract, Andrew McGee argues that there is an important causal difference between euthanasia and treatment withdrawal.

Andrew McGee[59]

[I]n the case of withdrawal, the principle of the inviolability of life remains undisturbed. In withdrawal, we are not taking control of death in the way we do in the practice of euthanasia, because the issue in withdrawal is when we should stop artificially prolonging life and allow nature to take its course—to stop deferring what, at some point, is inevitable. In euthanasia, by contrast, we anticipate nature and override it by bringing about the patient's death before its time.

As we can see from the following extracts, the description of the removal of mechanical ventilation or an artificial feeding tube as an omission is, nevertheless, controversial.

Ian Kennedy[60]

[T]o describe turning off the machine as an omission does some considerable violence to the ordinary English usage. It represents an attempt to solve the problem by logic chopping. Such

---

[59] Finding a Way through the Ethic and Legal Maze: Withdrawal of Medical Treatment and Euthanasia' (2005) 13 Medical Law Review 357–85.

[60] *Treat Me Right: Essays in Medical Law and Ethics* (Clarendon Press: Oxford, 1998) 351.

an approach may demonstrate to the satisfaction of some that no crime is involved, but it is surely most unsatisfactory to rest the response of the law to what is seen as a testing moral and philosophical issue on some semantic sleight of hand.

Dan W Brock[61]

Consider the case of a patient terminally ill with ALS [Amyotrophic Lateral Sclerosis] disease. She is completely respirator dependent with no hope of ever being weaned. She is unquestionably competent and persistently requests to be removed from the respirator and allowed to die. Most people and physicians would agree that the patient's physician should respect the patient's wishes and remove her from the respirator, though this will certainly cause the patient's death ...

Suppose the patient has a greedy and hostile son ... Afraid that his inheritance will be dissipated by a long and expensive hospitalization, he enters his mother's room while she is sedated, extubates her, and she dies. Shortly thereafter the medical staff discovers what he has done and confronts the son. He replies, 'I didn't kill her. I merely allowed her to die. It was her ALS disease that caused her death.' I think this would rightly be dismissed as transparent sophistry—the son went into his mother's room and deliberately killed her. But, of course, the son performed just the same physical actions, did just the same thing, that the physician would have done. If that is so, then doesn't the physician also kill the patient when he extubates her?

I underline immediately that there are important ethical differences between what the physician and the greedy son do. First, the physician acts with the patient's consent whereas the son does not. Second, the physician acts with a good motive—to respect the patient's wishes and self-determination—whereas the son acts with a bad motive—to protect his own inheritance. Third, the physician acts in a social role through which he is legally authorized to carry out the patient's wishes regarding treatment whereas the son has no such authorization. These and perhaps other ethically important differences show that what the physician did was morally justified whereas what the son did was morally wrong. What they do not show, however, is that the son killed while the physician allowed to die... Both the physician and the greedy son act in a manner intended to cause death, do cause death, and so both kill.

Further evidence that it may be inappropriate, albeit convenient, to describe the withdrawal of life-prolonging treatment as an omission comes from the suggestion that doctors' conscientious objections to treatment withdrawal should be respected. As we saw earlier, the doctors who had been caring for Ms B were permitted to refuse to participate in the removal of the ventilator that was keeping her alive. Since it is hard to see how doctors could object to refraining from assaulting their patients, it is surely more plausible to admit that doctors who wish to refuse to participate in the withdrawal of life-prolonging treatment are unwilling to act deliberately to cause their patients' deaths. This was certainly the perspective of the treating clinicians in *Re B (Adult: Refusal of Medical Treatment)*:

[Dr C] had studied and spent her professional life trying to do her best to improve and preserve life. She did not feel able to agree with simply switching off Ms B's ventilation. She would not be able to do it. She felt she was being asked to kill Ms B.[62]

[61] 'Voluntary active euthanasia' (1992) Hastings Center Report 10–22.   [62] [2002] 1 FLR 1090.

(3) Do Not Attempt Cardio-Pulmonary Resuscitation Orders

What if the doctor recommends that life-prolonging treatment (such as cardiopulmonary resuscitation (CPR)) should not be attempted if the patient suffers a respiratory or cardiac arrest? Guidance issued by the BMA, the Resuscitation Council, and the Royal College of Nursing refers to 'Do Not *Attempt* Cardio-Pulmonary Resuscitation' (DNACPR) in order to make clear that resuscitation is not always successful. The guidance emphasizes that it is good practice to discuss DNACPR orders with patients, but stresses the need for sensitivity.

British Medical Association, Resuscitation Council, and the Royal College of Nursing[63]

6.3 Communication and discussion with patients with capacity

When a person with capacity is at foreseeable risk of cardiac or respiratory arrest, they should be offered information about CPR, about the local resuscitation policy and services, and about their role in decision-making in relation to CPR. In order to determine whether the benefits of CPR would be likely to outweigh the harms and burdens, or whether the level of recovery expected would be acceptable to the patient, there should be sensitive exploration of the patient's wishes, feelings, beliefs and values.

In practice, it is difficult to find a sensitive way to ask a patient who has just been admitted to hospital if she would want to be resuscitated if she has a heart attack. An added difficulty is that representations of CPR in TV hospital dramas convey an unrealistic impression of CPR's success in reviving people whose hearts have stopped. In fact, CPR may just prolong the dying process; it works in only 10–15 per cent of patients, and it is not uncommon for patients to be left with serious brain damage.

The practice of not discussing DNACPR orders with patients was challenged in *R (on the application of Tracey) v Cambridge NHS Foundation Trust*. Janet Tracey had been diagnosed with terminal lung cancer and was admitted to hospital after being seriously injured in a road traffic accident. Her condition deteriorated, and on two occasions DNACPR notices were issued, cancelled, and then reinstated before her death. She had expressed a wish to receive full active treatment and was not told about the first decision to include a DNACPR notice in her notes. The Court of Appeal found that this had breached her Article 8 rights.

R (on the application of Tracey) v Cambridge NHS Foundation Trust[64]

Lord Dyson MR

I think it is right to say that, since a DNACPR decision is one which will potentially deprive the patient of life-saving treatment, there should be a presumption in favour of patient involvement. There need to be convincing reasons not to involve the patient.

Lord Pannick submits that it is … inappropriate to involve the patient if the clinician forms the view that CPR would be futile even if he considers that involvement is unlikely to cause the

---

[63] *Decisions Relating to Cardiopulmonary Resuscitation: Guidance from the British Medical Association, the Resuscitation Council (UK) and the Royal College of Nursing* (Resuscitation Council, 2014).

[64] [2014] EWCA Civ 822.

patient harm. I would reject this submission for two reasons. First, a decision to deprive the patient of potentially life-saving treatment is of a different order of significance for the patient from a decision to deprive him or her of other kinds of treatment. It calls for particularly convincing justification. Prima facie, the patient is entitled to know that such an important clinical decision has been taken. The fact that the clinician considers that CPR will not work means that the patient cannot require him to provide it. It does not, however, mean that the patient is not entitled to know that the clinical decision has been taken. Secondly, if the patient is not told that the clinician has made a DNACPR decision, he will be deprived of the opportunity of seeking a second opinion.

Patients cannot compel doctors to offer CPR where it would be futile, and the Court of Appeal decision in *Tracey* does not interfere with clinical judgement about CPR's appropriateness. While there is some logic to saying that patients have the right to know that a decision as significant as this has been taken, it might be confusing and disturbing for patients to be informed about an option that is not, in fact, going to be available to them.

3 SHOULD EUTHANASIA AND/OR ASSISTED SUICIDE BE LEGALIZED?

Thus far, we have seen that the law draws a bright line between lawful practices that result in a patient's death (withholding/withdrawing life-prolonging medical treatment and providing palliative care which may, incidentally, shorten life), and unlawful practices which have the same effect (euthanasia and assisted suicide). This means that doctors are allowed to help their patients to die provided that they happen to be connected to a ventilator or nasogastric feeding tube. They can also potentially shorten the lives of those who happen to require life-threatening doses of painkillers or sedatives. Some commentators argue that access to medical assistance in dying should not depend upon a patient's fortuitous need for life support or substantial doses of diamorphine. Others believe that there is a fundamental difference between doctors letting their patients die and killing them, and that the integrity of the medical profession depends upon the absolute prohibition of doctors acting deliberately to end their patients' lives. Who is right?

Before we review arguments for and against legalizing euthanasia and assisted suicide, it is worth pointing out that those who are for and against assisted dying are often talking past each other, by focusing their attention on different groups of people. Advocates of assisted dying are often concerned with the situation of individuals who might benefit from assisted dying, either because their suffering is unbearable or because they would find it reassuring to know that there would be a way out, if their suffering were to become intolerable. In contrast, opponents of assisted dying tend to focus upon vulnerable individuals whose interests, they argue, would be positively harmed by legalization.

(a) ARGUMENTS FOR

(1) Autonomy

It is often assumed that one of the strongest arguments in favour of legalizing euthanasia and assisted suicide is respect for patient autonomy; that is, that a patient's right to make decisions about her medical treatment should extend to deciding to end her life. As Sylvia Law suggests, giving patients some control over how they die might then appear to be an especially important aspect of respect for autonomous decision-making.

Sylvia A Law[65]

> The dying patient has lost control of most significant aspects of his or her life. The assurance that assisted death is an option provides a measure of autonomy and control, however that autonomy is exercised … [I]t is not easy to hasten death in a private, non-violent way. Bans on physician assistance, therefore, aggravate … suffering. It is, of course, possible to jump off a tall building or to leap in front of an oncoming train. But most terminally ill patients seek a death that is both more private and less violent.

In contrast, John Keown argues that a 'right to choose' is essentially meaningless and that an emphasis upon individualistic values such as autonomy marginalizes the impact our actions have upon others.

John Keown[66]

> The 'right to choose x' often serves as a slogan with powerful emotional appeal. But crude slogans are no substitute for rational reflection, and one can hardly sensibly assert a right to choose 'x' until one has considered whether it is right to choose 'x'; to do otherwise is simply to beg the question. Is there a 'right to choose … paedophilia'? Or a 'right to choose … cruelty to animals'? Does the mere fact that someone *wants* to blind ponies or to have sex with children carry any moral weight? The 'right to choose' only arguably makes any moral sense in the context of a moral framework which enables us to discern what it is *right* to choose and what choices will in fact promote human flourishing. And not only *our* flourishing, but that of others. For we do not live as atomised individuals, as much loose talk about absolute respect for personal autonomy appears to assume, but in community, where our choices can have profound effects not only on ourselves but on others.

For two reasons, autonomy could not be the only justification for the legalization of assisted dying. First, few advocates of legalization would allow unrestricted access to medical assistance in dying. On the contrary, most would accept that a doctor should only be allowed to help a patient end her life in certain, limited circumstances. The fact that a person wants to die is not, on its own, a sufficient reason for a doctor to kill her. Although opinion differs over whether terminal illness should be a prerequisite, most people would agree that a doctor should only act to bring about a patient's death in order to relieve her suffering.

Secondly, as we saw in Chapter 5, a patient's right to make decisions about her medical treatment is usually confined to a right to refuse treatment. A patient does not have the right to demand access to whatever treatment she wants. So while the principle of autonomy requires

---

[65] 'Physician-Assisted Death: An Essay on Constitutional Rights and Remedies' (1996) 55 Maryland Law Review 292.
[66] *Euthanasia, Ethics and Public Policy: An Argument against Legalisation* (CUP: Cambridge, 2002) 54.

doctors to respect an adult patient's capacitous refusal of life-prolonging medical treatment, it could not require doctors to comply with a request for euthanasia or assisted suicide.

In response, advocates of legalization accept that patients would not be entitled to demand that their doctors kill them. Rather, their right would be to ask for assistance in dying, a request which a doctor could legitimately turn down, either because she has a conscientious objection or because it would be incompatible with her duty of care. As the authors of the next extracts suggest, the purpose of legalization would simply be to allow doctors to act lawfully when they comply with a patient's request for assistance.

Ronald Dworkin, Thomas Nagel, Robert Nozick, John Rawls, Thomas Scanlon, and Judith Jarvis Thomson[67]

Most of us see death—whatever we think will follow it—as the final act of life's drama, and we want that last act to reflect our own convictions, those we have tried to live by, not the convictions of others forced on us in our most vulnerable moment . . .

Since patients have a right not to have life-support machinery attached to their bodies, they have, in principle, a right to compel its removal. But that is not true in the case of assisted suicide: patients in certain circumstances have a right that the state not forbid doctors to assist in their deaths, but they have no right to compel a doctor to assist them. The right in question, that is, is only a right to the help of a willing doctor.

David Orentlicher[68]

Some commentators distinguish the withdrawal of treatment from euthanasia/assisted suicide on the ground that a right to refuse treatment is a negative right to be left alone while a right to euthanasia or assisted suicide would be a positive right to command aid. This argument mischaracterizes the nature of a right to euthanasia or assisted suicide. Such a right would not mean that patients could require physicians to assist suicides or perform euthanasia. Rather, the right would prevent the state from interfering when a patient and physician voluntarily agree on a course of euthanasia/assisted suicide. Physicians would participate in euthanasia/assisted suicide only if they were willing to do so.

(2) Compassion and Reassurance

A different sort of argument for legalization could be framed in terms of the principle of beneficence (see further Chapter 1). If a cure is no longer possible, the doctor's duty to 'do good' involves trying to relieve the patient's suffering. If the patient's suffering has become both unbearable and untreatable, might it be possible to argue that relieving suffering by ending the patient's life could be compatible with a doctor's duty to act beneficently?

---

[67] In two cases heard by the US Supreme Court at the same time (*Washington et al v Glucksberg* 117 S Ct 2258 (1997) and *Vacco v Quill* 117 S Ct 2293 (1997)), six distinguished philosophers presented an Amici Curiae Brief for Respondents—referred to as The Philosophers' Brief—to the Supreme Court.

[68] 'The Alleged Distinction between Euthanasia and the Withdrawal of Life-Sustaining Treatment: Conceptually Incoherent and Impossible to Maintain' (1998) University of Illinois Law Review 837.

In addition to helping patients whose suffering has become unbearable, the legalization of euthanasia might also benefit a wider group of patients by reassuring them that a doctor would be allowed to help them to die if their condition were to become intolerable. Some patients are so fearful of a protracted and distressing death that they take their own lives prematurely, while they are still able to do so. For such patients, the availability of legalized euthanasia might, in fact, prolong their lives.

In the next extract Rinat Nissim et al draw on their interviews with patients with advanced cancer to suggest that for many of them, the benefit of legalization would come from having the option of a 'hypothetical exit plan'.

Rinat Nissim, Lucia Gagliese, and Gary Rodin[69]

DHD [desire for hastened death] as a hypothetical exit plan

This was the most common and persistent experience, expressed by 24 (89%) participants. It involved the contemplation of hastening death, not as a present option, but as a future exit plan when all other means of controlling the illness had failed ... This hypothetical exit plan was generated as a reaction to the multiple fears participants reported regarding the final active dying phase, including that it would be an undignified and painful process, which would inflict suffering on both patient and family. The thought of such a dying process was terrifying and was more difficult to accept with equanimity than was death itself. In this context, hastening death as a hypothetical exit plan was contemplated as a reassuring safety net that would be available when this dying process becomes a reality ...

Contemplating the hypothetical exit plan of hastening death provided reassurance and enhanced the ability to tolerate the hurdles of the present and the uncertainty of the future. It allowed participants to imagine maintaining a sense of control and autonomy until the very end... In this regard, the thought that they could enact an exit plan of hastening death often allowed participants to maintain a strong commitment to continue with life-prolonging medical treatment. Indeed, the experience of contemplating a hastened death paradoxically often coexisted with the wish to undergo medical treatment.

Using compassion or beneficence, rather than autonomy, as the justification for legalizing assisted dying explains the restrictions that most people believe should be placed upon its use. A doctor would only be acting beneficently in helping a patient to die if she has reasonable grounds for believing that the patient's life has ceased to be a benefit to her.

Philippa Foot considers euthanasia from the perspective of virtue ethics (considered in Chapter 1). She does not rule out the possibility that euthanasia might, in certain circumstances, be 'compatible with both justice and charity', but this would be the case only where its 'purpose is to benefit the one who dies'.

Philippa Foot[70]

Disease too can so take over a man's life that the normal human goods disappear. When a patient is so overwhelmed by pain or nausea that he cannot eat with pleasure, if he can eat at

[69] 'The desire for hastened death in individuals with advanced cancer: a longitudinal qualitative study' (2009) 69 Social Science & Medicine 165–71.
[70] 'Euthanasia' (1977) 6 Philosophy & Public Affairs 85–112.

all, and is out of the reach of even the most loving voice, he no longer has ordinary human life in the sense in which the words are used here ... crippling depression can destroy the enjoyment of ordinary goods as effectively as external circumstances can remove them.

(3) Inconsistency of the Status Quo

Another reason commonly given for legalizing assisted dying is that the line the law currently draws between lawful and unlawful life-shortening practices is incoherent and morally irrelevant.[71] On this view, if we are prepared to allow doctors to engage in some practices that will end their patients' lives (like treatment withdrawal and giving life-threatening doses of painkillers), there is no logical reason why we should not also allow doctors to give their patients lethal injections, particularly since dying from starvation or suffocation may be more protracted and distressing (both for the patient and her family) than the quick and painless death that would be induced by a single fatal injection. Paradoxically then, as James Rachels points out, the lawful means of hastening a patient's death may result in a more prolonged and less peaceful death than the unlawful means.

James Rachels[72]

Part of my point is that the process of being 'allowed to die' can be relatively slow and painful, whereas being given a lethal injection is relatively quick and painless ... The doctrine that says that a baby may be allowed to dehydrate and wither, but may not be given an injection that would end its life without suffering, seems so patiently cruel as to require no further refutation.

As RG Frey argues in the next extract, making the lawfulness of medical assistance in dying contingent upon whether a patient happens to be connected to a ventilator or a morphine drip could be said to discriminate against patients whose suffering may be equally unbearable, but whose illnesses deprive them of access to a lawful means of ending their life.

RG Frey[73]

It seems little short of incredible that the fact that a terminally ill patient is on a life-support system could so transform cases, morally, when both cases show quite clearly that patient and doctor are acting together to bring about the patient's death at the instigation of the patient ... Withdrawing feeding tubes and starving the patient to death is permissible, supplying the patient with a pill that produces death is not. Yet both sorts of assistance assuredly produce death, and both sorts involve the patient and doctor acting together to produce that death.

To be prepared to see the patient dead; to take the step that will assuredly produce death; to know as a certainty that death will ensue or be hastened: is this not morally equivalent to

---

[71] See, for example, Emily Jackson, 'Whose Death is it Anyway? Euthanasia and the Medical Profession' (2004) 57 Current Legal Problems 415–42.

[72] 'Active and passive euthanasia' (1975) 292 New England Journal of Medicine 79–80.

[73] 'Distinctions in Death' in Gerald Dworkin, RG Frey, and Sissela Bok, *Euthanasia and Physician-Assisted Suicide: For and Against* (CUP: Cambridge, 1998) 36, 38.

intending the patient's death? If so, there is little difference here between the supply of pills and the withdrawal of feeding tubes, so far as intending the patient's death is concerned.

Sheila McLean agrees. In discussing the Ms B case, she says 'on all logic, Ms B's death was assisted', people who happen to need artificial ventilation can therefore 'orchestrate their deaths even when they need assistance in doing so'.[74]

The sort of death which most of us would prefer—quick, painless, at home, and holding the hand of someone we love—is not facilitated by any of the lawful means of hastening patients' deaths. On the contrary, the withdrawal of life-sustaining treatment will generally take place in hospital, and death can take about two weeks, meaning the patient's family may not be present.

Euthanasia or assisted suicide, on the other hand, can take place in a patient's home, in the presence of the people she loves. In Oregon, for example, 90.2 per cent of assisted deaths take place in the patient's home;[75] in the Netherlands, the figure is 80.6 per cent.[76] Evidence from the Netherlands appears to indicate that the bereaved relatives of patients who die as a result of euthanasia cope better with bereavement, and suffer fewer post-traumatic stress reactions than the bereaved of comparable patients who die naturally.[77] The opportunity to say goodbye; being prepared for the time and manner of the death; and having talked openly about dying all appear to have a positive impact upon a family's ability to come to terms with a person's death.

A further argument from inconsistency is that, despite the illegality of assisted dying, prosecutions are rare, and convictions are rarer still. Cases of compassionate killing, whether by doctors or relatives, are not prosecuted or sentenced in the same way as other homicides. Sheila McLean asks 'what purpose is served by a law which technically criminalizes behaviour which it then effectively ignores and forgives?', and she further points out that this gap between the prohibition of assisted dying and its lenient treatment by prosecutors and the courts is 'an interesting indication of the law's actual rather than its theoretical approach to assisted dying'.[78]

The non-prosecution of relatives who have helped people to die in Dignitas offers a compelling illustration of the gulf between the law on the books—in which assisted suicide is a serious crime, punishable by 14 years in prison—and the reality, in which patients can access assisted suicide in Switzerland, and their relatives are unlikely to be prosecuted.

(4) Benefits of Regulation

If, despite its illegality, doctors do help their patients to die,[79] might there be advantages to openly regulating the practice? Currently, the threat of criminal charges means that doctors do not report these deaths, and there are no safeguards, such as seeking a second opinion or psychiatric assessment. In the next extract, Margaret Pabst Battin argues that the purpose of legalization in the Netherlands was precisely to enable control to be exercised over an otherwise secretive practice.

---

[74] *Assisted Dying: Reflections on the Need for Law Reform* (Routledge-Cavendish: Abingdon, 2007) 84.
[75] Oregon Health Authority, *Oregon's Death with Dignity Act: 2017 Data Summary* (2018).
[76] Regional Review Committees *Annual Report 2017* (RTE, 2018).
[77] Nikkie B Swarte et al, 'Effects of euthanasia on the bereaved family and friends: a cross sectional study' (2003) 327 British Medical Journal 189.
[78] *Assisted Dying: Reflections on the Need for Law Reform* (Routledge-Cavendish: Abingdon, 2007) 144.
[79] Sarah-Kate Templeton, 'Thousands of doctors helping people die' The Sunday Times, 12 June 2016.

Margaret Pabst Battin[80]

[For] the Dutch ... bringing euthanasia and related practices out into the open is a way of gaining control. For the Dutch, this is a way of identifying a practice that, in the Netherlands as in every other country, has been going on undercover and entirely at the discretion of the physician. It brings the practice into public view, where it can be regulated by guidelines, judicial scrutiny, and the collection of objective data. It is not that the Dutch or anyone else have only recently begun to practise euthanasia for the dying patient, nor is this a new phenomenon in the last decade or so; rather, the Dutch are the first to try to assert formal public control over a previously hidden practice and, hence, to regulate it effectively.

In the next extract, Roger Magnusson draws upon his interviews with healthcare professionals to argue that we do not have a choice between legalized physician-assisted dying, where doctors help their patients to die, and illegal assisted dying, where it never happens. Rather, euthanasia's illegality instead means that it will instead be practised 'underground', which may be much more dangerous for patients.

Roger S Magnusson[81]

In *Angels of Death: Exploring the Euthanasia Underground*, I reported on 49 detailed, yet pseudonymous interviews with doctors, nurses, and therapists working in HIV/AIDS health care, principally in Sydney, Melbourne, and San Francisco ... Despite their mostly good intentions, interviewees painted a troubling picture of covert PAS/AE [physician-assisted suicide/ active euthanasia] ...

For me, the most striking feature of these accounts was the way they betrayed the absence of norms or principles for deciding when it was appropriate to proceed. One doctor injected a young man on the first occasion they met, despite concerns from close friends that the patient was depressed ... In another case, a patient brought his death forward by a week so as not to interfere with the doctor's holiday plans ...

It is important to remember that our ability to castigate the Dutch about their rates of non-compliance comes courtesy of the relative transparency created by the Dutch policy of legalisation. If we wish to make ambit claims about slippery slopes, it is only fair to point out that the reporting rate for Britain, Australia, and most other countries, is zero. Nevertheless, even partial compliance with statutory safeguards may represent an improvement on the kinds of clinical decisions that currently occur in secret.

(b) ARGUMENTS AGAINST

(1) Sanctity of Life

The legalization of euthanasia and assisted suicide would necessarily involve accepting that death can rationally be preferred to life. According to Luke Gormally, this is inconsistent with the principle that all human life is intrinsically valuable.

---

[80] *The Least Worst Death: Essays in Bioethics on the End of Life* (OUP: Oxford, 1994) 141.
[81] 'Euthanasia: above ground, below ground' (2004) 30 Journal of Medical Ethics 441–6.

Luke Gormally[82]

Euthanasiast killing, even when it is voluntary, involves denial of the ongoing worth of the lives of those reckoned to be candidates for euthanasia. It is a type of killing, therefore, which cannot be accommodated in a legal system for which belief in the worth and dignity of every human being is foundational ... If the claim that a person lacks a worthwhile life is held to make killing lawful, then the state has ceased to recognize the innocent as having binding claims to protection ...

Those who attempt suicide are clearly moved by the (at least transient) belief that their lives are no longer worthwhile. Since just legal arrangements rest on a belief in the ineliminable worth of every human life, the law must reject the reasonableness of a choice which is so motivated.

Hence the law must also refuse to accommodate the behaviour of those who effectively endorse the choice of the suicide: for they too are acting on the view that the person they are helping no longer has a worthwhile life.

Of course, it could be argued that it is up to the person whose life it is to determine whether their life is 'sacred', rather than having this view imposed upon them by others. Certainly, in the context of treatment refusal, it is clear that the principle of self-determination trumps the sanctity of human life.

(2) Legalization is Unnecessary

Opponents of assisted dying often claim that if all patients were to given access to high quality palliative and hospice care, none would request assisted dying, and legalization would be un-necessary. This is, to some extent, an empirical claim that might be substantiated by evidence that all suffering at the end of life can be adequately relieved by palliative care.

It is probably true that relatively few patients now endure unbearable levels of pain, but pain is seldom the principal reason for patients' requests for euthanasia. In both Oregon and Washington State in 2017, the most common reasons for requesting physician-assisted suicide were loss of autonomy (87.4 and 90 per cent respectively); decreasing ability to participate in activities that made life enjoyable (88.1 and 87 per cent), and loss of dignity (67.1 and 73 per cent); inadequate pain control was less commonly mentioned (30 and 38 per cent). [83]

Optimum palliative care may be able to minimize physical pain, but it is less clear that it can eradicate the helplessness and mental anguish that many people experience as a result of their bodies' progressive deterioration. In their interviews with 31 people in the Netherlands who had requested euthanasia, Marianne Dees et al found that it was the hopelessness of their condition which patients found unbearable.

---

[82] 'Euthanasia and Assisted Suicide: 7 Reasons Why They Should Not be Legalized' in Donna Dickenson, Malcolm Johnson, and Jeanne Samson Katz (eds), *Death, Dying and Bereavement*, 2nd edn (Sage: London, 2000) 286–90.

[83] Oregon Health Authority, *Oregon's Death with Dignity Act: 2017 Data Summary* (2018); Washington State Department of Health, *2017 Death with Dignity Act Report* (2018).

Marianne K Dees et al[84]

All patients experienced existential suffering. There were four categories within this theme: loss of important and pleasurable activities, hopelessness, pointlessness and being tired of life . . .

As an 80-year-old man, a former mathematics teacher and musician put it: 'I can't do anything anymore, I used to play music, participated in various clubs, all so very companionable, I had to say farewell to all of it. It feels so awful just waiting to become bedridden and then waiting to die'. All patients considered hopelessness to be a main factor in the perception of unbearableness. This is illustrated by a 55-year-old woman with nasopharyngeal cancer: 'You lie on a bed and none of the normal functions come back. They will never come back and it will only get worse' . . .

In addition, patients placed unbearable suffering in the broader context of their personality characteristics. They explained how the irreversible consequences of disease or ageing resulted in loss of self, loss of autonomy and mental exhaustion until they felt themselves no longer the persons they used to be. This is exemplified by a 53-year-old woman with lung cancer: 'I lost my dignity, lying in bed in diapers, I am no longer the independent person I used to be'.

As Hadi Karsoho et al explain, evidence presented in the *Carter* case in Canada suggested that, while palliative care was important, it could not offer a solution to the desire for assisted dying.

Hadi Karsoho et al[85]

Elayne Shapray, a woman with Multiple Sclerosis (MS), writes:

'The suffering I and others with progressive, degenerative illnesses such as MS endure, is both psychological and social, involving a loss of autonomy, independence, privacy and ability to do the things that give joy to one's life. These losses cannot be meaningfully addressed by any form of palliative care'. (Affidavit, Shapray.)

In arguing that there are certain losses that cannot be addressed by palliative care, Shapray thus construes palliative care as irrelevant and unhelpful to her situation. Proponents use existential suffering as a discursive sign to denote a space of lived experience that lies outside of the reach of palliative care.

In contrast, Daniel Sulmasy et al argue that doctors should not be involved in assisted dying in such cases, because it is impossible for them to judge whether a patient's existential suffering justifies the prescription of lethal drugs.

---

[84] '"Unbearable suffering": a qualitative study on the perspectives of patients who request assistance in dying' (2011) 37 Journal of Medical Ethics 727–34.

[85] 'Suffering and medicalization at the end of life: The case of physician-assisted dying' (2016) 170 Social Science & Medicine 188–96.

Daniel P Sulmasy et al[86]

Some suffering is amenable to direct medical intervention, but many experiences of suffering, such as loneliness and existential distress, are not. It is beyond the ken and expertise of the physician to judge whether such suffering is adequate to fulfill the criteria for the provision of lethal drugs. Among the legal requirements is that a request for PAS must be voluntary and free of undue pressures. Yet most doctors have limited knowledge of their patients' lives beyond the examination room—for example, what family dynamics are at work or what internal pressures may exist. This problem is particularly acute because the majority of doctors refuse to participate so that requests are often considered by doctors who have no prior relationship with the patient ...

Medicine's central task is to heal. Although healing is a much broader concept than curing, it makes no sense to claim that patients have been healed by having assisted them in ending their lives. Symptom relief heals, and forgoing treatment acknowledges the limits of healing, but PAS undermines the very meaning of medicine ...

The public sometimes falsely believes that, if terminally ill, they face a stark dilemma—either a gruesome death, strapped to machines, sickened by drugs, and stabbed with needles, or a peaceful death via a lethal prescription. Progress in symptom control, hospice, and palliative care belies this depiction of care at the end of life... There should be no need for PAS for uncontrolled symptoms; the response of medicine should be to ensure that physicians become skilled in providing good care at the end of life and assuring that all patients have access to that care.

(3) Difficulties in Ensuring that a Request has been made Voluntarily

Obviously, if it were to be legalized, it would be important to ensure that patients' requests for euthanasia had been made voluntarily. For three reasons, some argue that this represents an insuperable obstacle to legalization. First, as Susan M Wolf explains, it is possible that the judgement of some patients who request euthanasia might be distorted by depression.

Susan M Wolf[87]

First, patients actually exercise little control over end-of-life care ... In reality, patients are profoundly dependent on health professionals, with many patients reporting that they want their physician to make treatment decisions for them ... The research shows ... that depression is even more strongly correlated with requests for assisted suicide than pain is. Yet patients routinely face inadequate diagnosis and treatment of depression. Given these data, a patient requesting assisted suicide may actually be seeking relief from depression or pain ...

Terminal patients are quite unlike independent rights-bearers freely negotiating in business transactions. Instead, they are profoundly dependent, often at the mercy of health professionals for everything from toileting to life-saving care, and may be experiencing too much pain, discomfort, or depression to make independent and truly voluntary decisions.

---

[86] 'Physician-Assisted Suicide: Why Neutrality by Organized Medicine Is Neither Neutral Nor Appropriate' (2018) 33 Journal of General Internal Medicine 1394–9.
[87] 'Pragmatism in the Face of Death: The Role of Facts in the Assisted Suicide Debate' (1998) 82 Minnesota Law Review 1063.

Diagnosis of depression in terminally ill patients is difficult because many of the symptoms of depression—such as weight loss, insomnia, loss of energy, and an inability to concentrate—may also be symptoms of conditions like cancer or the side effects of medication. Nevertheless, there have been attempts to use standardized diagnostic tests to work out the frequency of depression among those requesting assistance in dying. A study in Oregon suggests that the overwhelming majority of people who have died as a result of assisted suicide did not suffer from any sort of depressive disorder.[88] Ilana Levene and Michael Parker's systematic review found that in the Netherlands there was a high incidence of depression in patients requesting euthanasia, but that almost of these requests were turned down.[89]

Secondly, because the consequence of euthanasia will be the patient's death, there is no scope for correcting mistaken decisions if it subsequently emerges that the patient had in fact lacked capacity when she made the decision to die. Nor is there room for the correction of decisions made following a mistaken diagnosis of terminal illness. Given the finality of euthanasia and the inevitable risk of error, opponents of legalization have suggested that we could never be sufficiently certain that a person's request for euthanasia was voluntarily made and properly informed.

Thirdly, as we saw in Chapter 8, consultations between patients and their doctors are confidential. So while supporters of legalization often suggest that regulation would enable euthanasia to be scrutinized and monitored, in practice, it might be difficult to exercise much control over doctors' oral discussions with their patients.

Daniel Callahan and Margot White[90]

If it is true, as it indubitably is, that 'decisions about medical treatment are normally made in the privacy of the doctor–patient relationship', then an obvious question must be asked: how is it possible, or could it ever be possible, to monitor and regulate those decisions regarding physician-assisted suicide that occur within the ambit of that privacy? . . .

There are two possible ways to proceed here: either we can station a policeman in every doctor's office and next to every sickbed to monitor all conversations, or we can depend upon the individual physician to voluntarily reveal that he or she has been part of an agreement to pursue physician-assisted suicide. Since the former course would both violate doctor–patient confidentiality and be utterly impractical, only the latter option is available. But that course means, in effect, that any physician-assisted suicide regulation must, in the end, be physician self-regulated.

One response to these arguments against legalization might be that we already allow patients to make decisions that result in their deaths when we respect their refusals of life-prolonging medical treatment. Patients who are connected to mechanical ventilators may be depressed, and we may wrongly judge them to have capacity, yet this risk of error, coupled with the finality of the outcome, does not persuade us that patients should be prevented from taking

---

[88] Linda Ganzini et al, 'Prevalence of depression and anxiety in patients requesting physicians' aid in dying: cross sectional survey' (2008) 337 British Medical Journal 1682.

[89] 'Prevalence of depression in granted and refused requests for euthanasia and assisted suicide: a systematic review' (2011) 37 Journal of Medical Ethics 205–11.

[90] 'The Legalization of Physician-Assisted Suicide: Creating a Regulatory Potemkin Village' (1996) 30 University of Richmond Law Review 1.

life-or-death decisions. Nor do we think that patient confidentiality represents an insurmountable obstacle to our ability to protect vulnerable patients from being pressured into agreeing to the withdrawal of life-prolonging treatment.

Moreover, we should also be concerned about vulnerable patients who are physically capable of taking their own lives, and who may be temporarily depressed. While protecting the vulnerable is often cited as the main reason for a blanket ban on assisted dying, it offers rather haphazard protection in that only those who are too physically incapacitated to commit suicide will be prevented from ending their lives.

(4) Risk of Abuse and Protection of the Vulnerable

In a related argument, some commentators are concerned that if assisted dying were readily available, elderly patients would be pressured into choosing a premature death against their wishes. In extreme cases, pressure might come from greedy relatives, but it is also common for elderly people to worry about being a burden to others, and if death were an option, is there a danger that they might feel under an obligation to request euthanasia, despite their desire to go on living?

It has been suggested that some groups in society might be particularly at risk. Because women live longer than men, on average, elderly women are less likely to have a partner to care for them, and may worry more about being a burden to their children.[91] Older lesbian women and gay men might also be particularly vulnerable, because they are less likely to have children and grandchildren to look after them.[92]

In countries that have legalized assisted dying, in practice, men receive assistance in dying more frequently than women. In Oregon, between 1998 and 2016, 51.7 per cent of those who had died assisted deaths were men.[93] In the Netherlands and Belgium too, men represent the majority of those accessing assisted deaths.[94]

Sheila McLean would also question the assumption that there is something wrong with requesting euthanasia because one would prefer not to be a burden. Instead, she suggests that 'being a burden—rather than simply perceiving oneself to be one—is arguably a morally acceptable and perfectly reasonable factor to take into account when planning for the future'.[95] McLean argues that an elderly parent, contemplating a future in which the costs of her care will eat away the inheritance she hopes to leave to her children, or in which her children's lives will be taken over with caring duties, might reasonably take these factors into account.

Could there also be institutional pressure to request euthanasia? Luke Gormally and Christopher Kazcor are concerned about the implications of regarding euthanasia as a cost-effective 'treatment' for the terminally ill.

[91] Hazel Biggs, 'I Don't Want to be a Burden! A Feminist Reflects on Women's Experiences of Death and Dying' in Sally Sheldon and Michael Thomson (eds), *Feminist Perspectives on Health Care Law* (Cavendish: London, 1998) 279–95.

[92] Sue Westwood, 'Older lesbians, gay men and the "right to die" debate: "I always keep a lethal dose of something, because I don't want to become an elderly isolated person"' (2017) 25 Social and Legal Studies 606–28.

[93] Oregon Health Authority, *Oregon's Death with Dignity Act: 2017 Data Summary* (2018).

[94] Regional Review Committees *Annual Report 2017* (RTE, 2018); ML Rurup et al, 'The first five years of euthanasia legislation in Belgium and the Netherlands: Description and comparison of cases' (2012) 26 Palliative Medicine 43–9.

[95] *Assisted Dying: Reflections on the Need for Law Reform* (Routledge-Cavendish: Abingdon, 2007) 54.

Luke Gormally[96]

It is very important to bear in mind that a key element in the context of contemporary debates about legalizing euthanasia is the drive to reduce health care costs. One of the conspicuous dangers of legalization is that, before long, euthanasia would be seen as a convenient 'solution' to the heavy demands on care made by certain types of patient. Medicine would thereby be robbed of the incentive to find genuinely compassionate solutions to the difficulties presented by such patients. The kind of humane impulses which have sustained the development of hospice medicine and care would be undermined because too many would think euthanasia a cheaper and less personally demanding solution.

Christopher Kaczor[97]

Doctors who kill their patients rather than relieving their pain have less incentive to learn about and less practice in administering palliative care. This relative lack of expertise adversely affects the majority of dying patients who do not choose euthanasia. The legalisation and use of euthanasia also deflates the incentives for investing money and effort into increasing the quality of palliative care. The more people who choose euthanasia instead of palliative care, the smaller is the market for palliative care. Once there is a legal option for ending pain other than palliative care, the pressure from patients, families and doctors to improve palliative care is lessened. Finally, legalised euthanasia may dampen sympathy for many patients suffering at the end of life. Some people may think, 'She had a way out of this suffering, but she refused euthanasia. Her suffering is self-inflicted. Why should I feel sorry for her? Why should I make efforts to alleviate her suffering when she refuses to end her own suffering?'

The argument that euthanasia will effectively crowd out investment in palliative care is not, in fact, borne out by the evidence from countries which have legalized assisted dying; instead there seems to be evidence that investment in palliative care has increased since legalization.[98]

In recent years, there has been particular lobbying against legalization by and on behalf of people with disabilities. In the next extract, John Keown argues that voluntary euthanasia (VE) and physician assisted suicide (PAS) pose a particular threat to people with disabilities, whereas Christopher Riddle suggests that the way in which opponents of assisted dying portray people with disabilities is itself patronising and unfair.

---

[96] 'Euthanasia and Assisted Suicide: 7 Reasons Why They Should Not Be Legalized' in Donna Dickenson, Malcolm Johnson, and Jeanne Samson Katz (eds), *Death, Dying and Bereavement*, 2nd edn (Sage: London, 2000) 285, 287.

[97] 'Against euthanasia for children: a response to Bovens' (2016) 42 Journal of Medical Ethics 57–8.

[98] Kenneth Chambaere and Jan L Bernheim. 'Does legal physician-assisted dying impede development of palliative care? The Belgian and Benelux experience' (2015) 41 Journal of Medical Ethics 657–60; S Moreels et al, 'Trends in palliative care at the end of life in Belgium, 2005-2014' (2016) 26 European Journal of Public Health Issue supplement ckw174.011; Ezekiel J Emanuel et al, 'Attitudes and practices of euthanasia and physician-assisted suicide in the United States, Canada, and Europe' (2016) 316 JAMA 79–90.

John Keown[99]

[L]aws which permit VE/PAS trade on the notion that there are two categories of patient: those with lives 'worth living' and those who would be 'better off dead'... The superficially attractive argument that VE/PAS are justified by respect for patient choice fails. Laws and proposed laws to allow VE/PAS ... do not allow them for any patient who autonomously wants them. They allow them only for some patients who want them, such as those at the 'end of life' or those 'suffering unbearably'. So, VE/PAS are not fundamentally about patient choice at all but about the judgment that the choices of some patients should be accommodated because it is thought by others in society that death would benefit them, that they would be 'better off dead'. (It is small wonder that many disability groups, who see this more clearly than many others, are strongly opposed to legalization).

Christopher A Riddle[100]

[T]he disability advocacy group *Not Dead Yet* is perhaps one of the loudest and most influential disability rights groups internationally. Their position is clear when they state that 'if we oppose assisted dying on the grounds put forth by many disability rights activists, we risk subjugating people with disabilities to negative stereotypical attitudes' ...

Anita Silvers has made the point forcefully that 'characterizing people with disabilities as incompetent, easily coerced, and inclined to end their lives places them in the roles to which they have been confined by disability discrimination'. LW Sumner emphasizes this point when he insists that 'many people in the disability community find this stereotyping to be itself demeaning and patronizing, complaining that it feeds rather than starves social prejudices' ...

By denying individuals with disabilities the right to seek assistance in dying, we are perpetuating harmful attitudes towards the disabled while simultaneously creating a doubly disadvantaged group: not only do people with disabilities suffer from social injustices or harms associated with impairment, but they are forced to endure tremendous pain at the end of life from a misguided effort to provide protection ... Denying people with disabilities the right to seek assistance in dying denies basic autonomy rights and further marginalizes and segregates people with disabilities from other populations.

(5) Effect on the Doctor–Patient Relationship

A further argument against legalization is that it would damage the doctor–patient relationship, and threaten the integrity of the medical profession. There are two interrelated aspects to this argument. First, from the point of view of the patient, it might be argued that knowing your doctor could legally kill you would reduce patient trust.

Whether or not patients share this assumption is unclear. According to a 2015 Populus opinion poll, 50 per cent of respondents said that the legalization of assisted suicide would not affect their trust in their doctors, while 37 per cent would trust their doctors more, and 12 per cent would trust their doctors less.[101]

---

[99] '"Voluntary Assisted Dying" in Australia: The Victorian Parliamentary Committee's Tenuous Case for Legalization' (2018) 33 Issues in Law & Medicine 55–81.
[100] 'Assisted Dying and Disability' (2017) 13 Bioethics 484–9.   [101] See further populus.co.uk.

Secondly, from the point of view of the doctor, if killing were to become a treatment option, might this undermine the ethical foundations of the medical profession? According to the British Medical Association, for example, legalization would be 'contrary to the ethics of clinical practice'.[102]

Of course, individual doctors would not be forced to participate in assisted dying: any statute legalizing the practice would inevitably include a 'conscientious objection' clause, in the same way as the Abortion Act 1967. But as the authors of the next extracts explain, the right not to participate in assisted dying may be insufficient to protect the views of doctors who believe that assisted dying is incompatible with good medical practice.

Søren Holm[103]

Conscientious objection to PAD [physician-assisted death] is often assumed as 'the solution' to assuage the concerns of doctors and other healthcare professionals who do not want to participate in PAD or do not want PAD to be part of medical practice ... The concerns doctors have may not only be personal or fully captured by 'I do not want to perform PAD'; they are often about a wider set of actions than direct performance, and often about changes in healthcare that will inevitably follow the introduction of PAD, and can perhaps be more accurately expressed as 'introducing PAD will inevitably make it part of the context of my professional life, and that worries me because it will change that life'.

Benny Chan and Margaret Somerville[104]

Physicians already have unique opportunities to inflict death in the course of discharging their usual functions, and, as such, it is not prudent to augment the power that physicians have over life and death.

There is also a less immediately obvious, though equally compelling, reason why physicians should not be involved in assisted death. Physician-assisted suicide and euthanasia are not medical treatment as evidenced by the medical profession's nearly two and a half thousand years rejection of those interventions and present reluctance to accept them. This rejection and reluctance has much to do with physicians' conception of the medical mandate, especially as it relates to healing ...

Making euthanasia and assisted suicide part of medical practice is not, as pro-assisted death advocates claim ... a small incremental change consistent with accepted interventions such as honoring patients' refusals of life-sustaining treatment. Allowing physicians to inflict death on their patients is different in kind—and not just different in degree—from other interventions we accept as ethical and legal.

---

[102] BMA Policy, *Physician-assisted dying* (BMA, 2018).

[103] 'The debate about physician assistance in dying: 40 years of unrivalled progress in medical ethics?' (2015) 41 Journal of Medical Ethics 40–3.

[104] 'Converting the "right to life" to the "right to physician assisted suicide and euthanasia": An analysis of *Carter v Canada (Attorney General), Supreme Court of* Canada' (2016) 24 Medical Law Review 143–75.

Of course, one way to neutralize this sort of objection to legalization would be to allow assisted dying to be provided by non-doctors. In the next extract, Ronald Kipke advocates commercial assistance in suicide.

Roland Kipke[105]

If not physicians but laypersons assist people in their suicides, no breach of medical ethos may be present and medicine cannot be corrupted. This would deprive the opponents of two main arguments against assisted suicide: a deontological argument (medical ethos) and a consequentialist argument (corruption of medicine, loss of confidence) ...

Another problem that is specific to PAS would also fall away. According to the prevailing view of the proponents, doctors ... would not be obliged to provide assistance to suicide ... Although this practice seems to be well justified by the principle of autonomy it could be very problematic for persons who seek assistance for their suicide. Whether their wish is fulfilled or not does not depend on clear, generally applicable criteria, but on the personal attitude of the physician ... Obviously, this problem would not occur with commercial assistants ...

[T]he necessary knowledge about the correct dosage is limited and can easily be acquired by non-physicians ... [I]it must be remembered that commercial suicide assistants are likely to have a great self-interest in carefully assessing the voluntariness of the decision of their customers and not curtailing the autonomous nature of that decision in any way. For the impunity of their actions would depend on these conditions.

(6) Slippery Slope

When someone invokes a slippery slope argument (see further Chapter 1), they are not arguing that there is something intrinsically wrong with doctors helping their patients to die. Of course, they may also believe this to be true, but this would not be a slippery slope claim. Rather, the slippery slope claim is that allowing some compassionate acts of killing would make it difficult to prevent those with less benevolent motives from ending patients' lives.

It might, for example, be argued that it would be virtually impossible to police the boundary between acceptable and unacceptable medical killings. Carl Schneider has argued that there is also 'a psychological aspect of slippery slopes', namely that 'they work partly by domesticating one idea and thus making its nearest neighbor down the slope seem less extreme and unthinkable'.[106] It is this latter type of slippery slope argument that is invoked in the next extract by Dieter Giesen, who argues that allowing doctors to kill their patients would weaken the absolute prohibition upon the taking of innocent life, and that we would all therefore become progressively desensitized to the horror of murder.

Dieter Giesen[107]

Recent history shows us that once firm constraints against killing are removed, a general moral decline will result. The German experience of the Nazi euthanasia programme, during

---

[105] 'Why not Commercial Assistance for Suicide? On the Question of Argumentative Coherence of Endorsing Assisted Suicide' (2014) 29 Bioethics 516–22.

[106] 'Rights Discourse and Neonatal Euthanasia' (1988) 76 California Law Review 151.

[107] 'Dilemmas at Life's End: A Comparative Legal Perspective' in John Keown (ed), *Euthanasia Examined* (CUP: Cambridge, 1995) 200–24.

which 100,000 disabled persons were killed because they were classified as living 'lives not worth living', demonstrates the potential for perverse thinking and inhuman deeds once the first step upon the slippery slope is taken.

In some ways, as Dan Brock points out, a slippery slope argument is a straightforward empirical claim: does legalizing euthanasia make involuntary killing more likely?

Dan W Brock[108]

Slippery slope arguments ... are the last refuge of conservative defenders of the status quo. When all the opponent's objections to the wrongness of euthanasia itself have been met, the opponent then shifts ground and acknowledges both that it is not in itself wrong and that a legal policy which resulted only in its being performed would not be bad. Nevertheless, the opponent maintains, it should still not be permitted because doing so would result in its being performed in other cases in which it is not voluntary and would be wrong. In this argument's most extreme form, permitting euthanasia is the first and fateful step down the slippery slope to Nazism. Once on the slope we will be unable to get off ...

It must be relevant how likely it is that we will end with horrendous consequences and an unjustified practice of euthanasia ... Opponents of voluntary euthanasia on slippery slope grounds have not provided the data or evidence necessary to turn their speculative concerns into well-grounded likelihoods.

Given their empirical nature, we might evaluate slippery slope claims by examining data from countries which have legalized assisted dying. But as we will see in the next section, the problem is that there are different (and often flatly contradictory) interpretations of the available data. John Keown, for example, is convinced that the Dutch have already slid some way down the slope:

[T]he Dutch experience lends weighty support to the slippery slope argument ... Within a decade, the so-called strict safeguards against the slide have proved signally ineffectual; non-voluntary euthanasia is now widely practised and increasingly condoned in the Netherlands.[109]

In contrast, Helga Kuhse et al's confidential survey of 3,000 Australian doctors found that non-voluntary euthanasia was five times more common in Australia, where euthanasia is illegal, than in the Netherlands.[110] Australian doctors were less likely than their Dutch counterparts to discuss the decision to hasten a patient's death with the patient herself, or to seek her consent. In their study of six European countries, Agnes van der Heide et al found that non-voluntary euthanasia was more than twice as common in Denmark, where euthanasia is unlawful, than it was in the Netherlands.[111]

---

[108] 'Voluntary active euthanasia' (1992) Hastings Centre Report 10–22.

[109] 'Euthanasia in the Netherlands: Sliding Down the Slippery Slope?' in John Keown (ed), *Euthanasia Examined* (CUP: Cambridge, 1995) 261–96.

[110] Helga Kuhse et al, 'End-of-life decisions in Australian medical practice' (1997) 166 Medical Journal of Australia 191–6.

[111] Agnes van der Heide et al, 'End-of-life decision-making in six European countries: descriptive study' (2003) 362 The Lancet 345–50.

If patients' lives are ended in the absence of an explicit request with similar (or greater) frequency in countries that have not legalized euthanasia, it is not clear that the legalization of euthanasia in the Netherlands has caused non-voluntary euthanasia. Moreover, all of the Dutch data cited by those who claim that it proves the existence of a slippery slope was gathered after legalization. In order to have compelling evidence of a slippery slope, we would need to compare data from before and after legalization. Otherwise, evidence (if there is such evidence) that poor practices coexist with legalization could simply mean that poor practices existed previously, and legalization made no difference.

Indeed, as Stephen Smith explains, even if it could be proved that non-voluntary euthanasia has increased in the years following legalization, this does not necessarily establish a causal connection.

Stephen Smith[112]

The simple fact that something occurs after something else does not indicate, in any meaningful way, that the first action logically required the second to happen. Even if one can find a connection such that the first tends to precede the second, this will not provide evidence of a logical connection. Especially in the realm of human actions (as opposed to say the actions of physical laws), the preceding of an action by a first action does not indicate they must be connected in any logical way.

Let us consider a different claim in order to see what Smith means. There appears to be some evidence that palliative care provision in Oregon improved after the legalization of assisted suicide. This is not sufficient to prove that legalization *caused* palliative care to improve. We could use this evidence to show that legalization has not resulted in a decline in the provision of palliative care, but we could not use it to establish a causal relationship between legalization and better palliative care.

Even if we could establish that the slope is slippery and that it would be difficult to draw or police the line between acceptable and unacceptable instances of euthanasia, it is not obvious that an absolute prohibition is the best regulatory response.

Emily Jackson[113]

Let us apply slippery slope reasoning to a more mundane regulatory problem. Should I maintain an absolute prohibition on the late submission of essays on the grounds that giving an extension to student A who has a very compelling reason—say, the death of a close family member—might make it difficult for me to draw a line between her case and those of students B, C, D, and E who have progressively less persuasive grounds for late submission? An absolute prohibition would relieve me of the difficulty of drawing distinctions between borderline cases: perhaps student C's computer has stopped working, and student D left her essay on the bus. But I do a grave injustice to student A by preferring the simplicity of

[112] 'Fallacies of the Logical Slippery Slope in the Debate on Physician-Assisted Suicide and Euthanasia' (2005) 13 Medical Law Review 224.
[113] 'Whose Death is it Anyway? Euthanasia and the Medical Profession' (2004) 57 Current Legal Problems 415–42.

an absolute ban over the admittedly more time-consuming and complex task of drawing fine distinctions between serious and trivial excuses for late submission ...

Nor is it obvious that a blanket ban is the optimum response to concerns about a practice's potential misapplication. If we can imagine circumstances in which euthanasia might be legitimate, prohibiting it completely in order to prevent it being employed in other less compelling situations is a peculiarly blunt approach to regulation ... It would be more logical to advocate regulations which confine access to euthanasia to patients whose circumstances lie at the top of the moral slope (whatever those might be), and prohibit it in all other cases.

(c) A THIRD WAY?

It would be a mistake to assume that there are only two options: legalization or criminalization. Rather, a different solution would be to treat euthanasia as a particular *type of killing*; less grave than murder, but still a criminal offence. In the next extract, Richard Huxtable explains that this sort of compromise would be more transparent than the status quo, in which the harsh consequences of euthanasia's illegality are mitigated by the leniency of judges, juries, and prosecutors.

Richard Huxtable[114]

As the law in operation in England demonstrates, stern pronouncements that assistance in dying is unlawful rarely translate into convictions for murder. Instead, ways are found to divert defendants from court, bring lesser charges, or impose mild non-custodial sentences. Such manoeuvres do, at least, signal that the law-in-action is capable of achieving a compromise. Yet this model of compromise seems to require subterfuge and to rely upon legal fictions, such as that the assistant must have acted with 'diminished responsibility'. The interests of clarity, consistency and fair labelling are surely better served by the creation of an explicit category of compassionate killing, which translates a shadowy, unpredictable and *ad hoc* compromise wrought in the law-in-action into an appropriately scrutinized, articulated and open component of the law-as-stated.

Heather Keating and Jo Bridgeman also advocate a middle-ground between criminalization and legalization. They argue that, in certain circumstances, the fact that a killing was compassionate should offer a partial defence to murder. This would not mean that someone who killed for compassionate reasons had done nothing wrong, but, like the partial defence of diminished responsibility, it would permit discretion in sentencing.

Heather Keating and Jo Bridgeman[115]

[W]e regard compassion as providing a (partial) excuse for killings which would otherwise be categorised as murder. The fact that the DPP's guidelines on assisting suicide suggest that

---

[114] 'Splitting the difference? Principled compromise and assisted dying' (2014) 28 Bioethics 472–80.
[115] 'Compassionate Killings: The Case for a Partial Defence' (2012) 75 Modern Law Review 697–721.

it is inappropriate to prosecute someone who has been wholly motivated by compassion also supports the conclusion that an excusatory partial defence is the most appropriate way forward . . .

[W]e stress that there would need to be evidence that the deceased was experiencing extreme and unbearable suffering prior to death. It would not be enough for the accused to have an honest belief about the level of the suffering being experienced; it would need to be one based on reasonable grounds and thus a reasoned and caring response to the suffering of their loved one. In sum, the partial defence of compassionate killing we propose would be available to a relative or family member who had been fulfilling intensive caring responsibilities for the deceased and who, in response to an honest and reasonable belief that he or she had been experiencing extreme and unbearable suffering, ended the deceased's life in order to end his or her suffering.

4 EXPERIENCE IN OTHER JURISDICTIONS

It would be a mistake to ignore evidence from jurisdictions where euthanasia and/or assisted suicide is lawful, but it is important to remember that what happens in a country with a different legal and health care system, and different cultural, religious, and social attitudes towards death, does not necessarily translate into evidence of how legalized assisted dying would work, or not work, in the UK.

For reasons of space, we confine our discussion here to (1) the Benelux countries, that is, the Netherlands, Belgium, and Luxembourg; (2) the US model, which began in Oregon and has now been extended to six more states (Washington, Vermont, Hawaii, California, Colorado, and Washington DC); (3) Switzerland, and (4) Canada. It is worth noting, however, that Victoria in Australia passed the Voluntary Assisted Dying Act in 2017, and at the time of writing, New Zealand is debating an End of Life Choice Bill.

(a) THE NETHERLANDS, BELGIUM, AND LUXEMBOURG

(1) The Netherlands

Since the *Postma* case in 1973,[116] the Dutch courts had gradually been developing exceptions to the express prohibitions on euthanasia and assisted suicide in the Dutch Penal Code (Articles 293 and 294). Through a series of court decisions, a set of guidelines had emerged which—if followed—protected doctors from criminal liability. To some extent, the 2001 statute simply formalized existing practice in the Netherlands.

The Termination of Life on Request and Assisted Suicide (Review Procedures) Act 2001 amended the Criminal Code, and came into force on 1 April 2002. Euthanasia and assisted suicide continue to be criminal offences under Articles 293(1) and 294(1), but exceptions are introduced in Article 293(2) and 294(2), which now read:

The act referred to in the first subsection shall not be an offence if it is committed by a physician who fulfils the due care criteria set out in Section 2 of the Termination of Life on Request and Assisted Suicide (Review Procedures) Act, and if the physician notifies the municipal

---

[116] *Nederlandse Jurisprudentie* 1973 No 183, District Court of Leeuwarden, 21 February 1973.

pathologist of this act in accordance with the provisions of section 7, subsection 2 of the Burial and Cremation Act.

Under section 2, the requirements of due care are that the physician:

(a) holds the conviction that the request by the patient was voluntary and well considered;

(b) holds the conviction that the patient's suffering was lasting and unbearable;

(c) has informed the patient about the situation he was in and about his prospects;

(d) and the patient holds the conviction that there was no other reasonable solution for the situation he was in;

(e) has consulted at least one other independent physician who has seen the patient and has given his written opinion on the requirements of due care referred to in parts (a)–(d); and

(f) has terminated a life or assisted in a suicide with due care.

The Act allows children over the age of 12 to request euthanasia or assisted suicide. A doctor is only allowed to comply with a request from a minor between the ages of 12 and 15 with parental consent. For children aged 16 and 17, parents should be consulted, but they do not have a right of veto. There have been very few cases of euthanasia in children, and no cases of assisted suicide.[117]

In practice, it is important to remember that Dutch citizens do not have the right to access assisted death, rather, as Ton Vink explains, the decision is one for doctors.

Ton Vink[118]

It is of vital importance to realize that in the Netherlands under the LRTS [Law on the Review of the Termination of life on request and assistance with Suicide] the requirements of due care are requirements that have to be met *by the physician*, not by the patient. Although the patient must indeed make his well-considered request, the decisive voice is the physician's, that is to say: the physician has to decide whether he or she is *in principle* prepared to put an end to a/the patient's life. If 'no', the request fails and the physician is expected (but not formally obliged) to refer the patient to a colleague. If 'yes', the physician has next to determine whether or not he (the physician) is able answer the requirements of due care. Again, if 'no', the request fails; if 'yes', the request succeeds.

Each case of euthanasia or assisted suicide is considered retrospectively by a regional review committee, usually consisting of a lawyer, a doctor, and an ethicist. If the committee is satisfied that the criteria have been fulfilled, the case is closed without informing the public prosecutor, who is notified only if the committee finds that the doctor did not fulfil the due care criteria. In about one per cent of cases each year,[119] the regional review committee asks for

---

[117] Margaret P Battin et al, 'Legal physician-assisted dying in Oregon and the Netherlands: evidence concerning the impact on patients in "vulnerable" groups' (2007) 33 Journal of Medical Ethics 591–7.

[118] 'Self-Euthanasia, the Dutch Experience: In Search for the Meaning of a Good Death or Eu Thanatos' (2016) 30 Bioethics 681–8,

[119] Regional Review Committees *Annual Report 2017* (RTE, 2018).

more information. Findings of non-compliance are rarer still: in 2017, there were 12 cases out of 6,585 (0.18 per cent) in which the regional review committee found that not all of the due care criteria had been complied with.[120]

Every five years, the Dutch national statistics authority produces statistics which set out how many deaths are preceded by a medical decision. As is evident, euthanasia and assisted suicide are much less common than deaths preceded by decisions to withhold treatment or to use 'intensifying' palliative care measures.

Deaths by medical end-of-life decision 2015[121]

	Total deaths	Percentage of deaths
Total deaths in 2015	147,134	100
Deaths without an end-of-life decision	61,607	42
Deaths with an end-of-life decision	85,522	58
Deaths preceded by withholding treatment while taking into account the possible hastening of death	7,437	5
Deaths preceded by withholding treatment with the explicit intention of hastening death	18,213	12
Deaths preceded by intensifying measures to alleviate pain or other symptoms while taking into account the possible hastening of death	50,911	35
Deaths preceded by intensifying measures to alleviate pain or other symptoms while partly intending the possible hastening of death	1,712	1
Euthanasia	6,672	4.5
Assisted suicide	150	0.1
Ending life without explicit request	431	0.2

There is a consistent pattern of euthanasia being more common than assisted suicide. It is also worth noting that a minority of patients who request euthanasia actually die assisted deaths. This is usually because the patient dies first from her underlying condition.

(a) DIFFICULT CASES: ADVANCE DECISIONS, DEMENTIA, PSYCHIATRIC ILLNESS, AND BEING 'TIRED OF LIFE'

In the Netherlands, the standard case of euthanasia performed in the last days of someone dying from cancer is now widely accepted. There is much less support, especially among the medical profession, for what Timothy Quill describes as 'edgy' cases—where the patient's suffering is existential or psychiatric.[122]

---

[120] Ibid.

[121] *Deaths by medical end-of-life decision; age, cause of death* (Statistics Netherlands, 2017).

[122] See also Marianne C Snijdewind et al, 'Developments in the practice of physician-assisted dying: perceptions of physicians who had experience with complex cases' (2018) 44 Journal of Medical Ethics 292–6.

Timothy Quill[123]

[A]t least sometimes the criteria are being stretched and adapted to meet the perceived needs of patients, and some participating physicians are relatively uncomfortable with some of the requests with which they are faced . . .

Three main themes were identified from these interviews:

1. The physicians' role as an active participant who should carefully evaluate the patient and make sure all criteria had been met and all alternatives explored was perceived by some to be changing to a more passive role as 'mere provider' of EAS [euthanasia and assisted suicide] on request. There was discomfort from some respondents that EAS was becoming routine rather than reserved for exceptional cases where suffering was severe and intractable.

2. Some physicians reported moral discomfort about their role when the underlying reasons for the EAS request were mainly non-medical. They wondered if directly assisting patients in this way was appropriate when the patient's suffering was 'mostly existential' in large measure, because these dimensions of suffering were outside of their realm of expertise. If such cases were to be condoned by society, perhaps physicians should not be the ones providing the assistance.

3. Finally, some responding physicians expressed concern that both of the major criteria for EAS were being at times compromised. This included allowing EAS for patients with dementia or limited decision-making capacity from other diseases, as well as allowing EAS for capacitated patients whose primary suffering was non-physical including some whose motivating distress was from 'old age' without any substantial physical suffering.

The Dutch legislation specifically allows for advance euthanasia decisions (AEDs): section 2(2) provides that doctors may comply with a request in a written declaration provided that the person was capable of making a reasonable appraisal of his own interests when the request was made. In practice, however, advance euthanasia directives are almost never implemented.[124]

Eva Elizabeth Bolt et al[125]

[I]n case of advanced dementia, many physicians point out that it is impossible to determine whether a patient is suffering unbearably, due to a lack of meaningful communication . . . Many elderly care physicians state that it is impossible to determine at what moment an advance euthanasia directive is to be carried out if the patient can no longer specify this. Also, it is probable that physicians cannot conceive of performing euthanasia in a patient with dementia who might not fully comprehend what is happening. Our study suggests that, in actual practice, physicians would rarely act upon an advance euthanasia directive in case of advanced dementia. People who write such directives are often unaware of this.

---

[123] 'Dutch practice of euthanasia and assisted suicide: a glimpse at the edges of the practice' (2018) 44 Journal of Medical Ethics 297–8.

[124] Mette L Rurup et al, 'Physicians' experiences with demented patients with advance euthanasia directives in the Netherlands' (2005) 53 Journal of the American Geriatric Society 1138–44; CMPM Hertogh, 'The role of advance euthanasia directives as an aid to communication and shared decision-making in dementia' (2009) 35 Journal of Medical Ethics 100–3.

[125] 'Can physicians conceive of performing euthanasia in case of psychiatric disease, dementia or being tired of living?' (2015) 41 Journal of Medical Ethics 592–8.

Dementia undoubtedly raises difficult issues in relation to euthanasia. While a majority of the public and the nursing profession support euthanasia in cases of advanced dementia, this is true for a minority of physicians.[126] Ending the life of a patient who is unable to say unambiguously that this is what she wants is challenging in itself,[127] and the passage of time between the writing of an advance decision and its implementation creates room for doubt as to whether the patient might have changed her mind.[128]

At the same time, there is significant demand for AEDs in the context of dementia, and there is evidence that those with experience of Alzheimer's disease are 'less likely to want to live as long as possible with Alzheimer disease' than those who do not have that experience.[129]

In 2017, there was considerable media interest in the Netherlands in a euthanasia case involving Mrs A, a woman suffering from Alzheimer's disease. The Regional Review Committee found that the due care criteria had not been followed, and a criminal investigation was triggered.[130] In the next extracts, David Gibbes Miller et al explain that this case raises a question we considered in Chapter 5—namely, whether a person with dementia should be bound by her previous self—while Henk Blanken suggests that Dutch patients with dementia are caught in a Catch-22 situation.

David Gibbes Miller, Rebecca Dresser, and Scott YH Kim[131]

Mrs A's case also highlights a more fundamental challenge to applying AEDs: the 'then-self versus now-self' problem. As cognitive abilities of patients with dementia decline, they typically forget about their AEDs and the requests the documents contain. What matters to them as patients with later-stage dementia will ordinarily be different than what mattered to them when they prepared their AEDs. As a result, the decision to perform euthanasia can be contrary to their interests and preferences as patients with dementia ...

Determining the relative weight of a patient's advance directive request and that patient's current welfare interests and preferences is a complex task, one that we believe should not be left to an individual physician's judgement.

The geriatrician in Mrs A's case prioritised Mrs A's advance euthanasia directive over her later assertions that she was not ready to die. The geriatrician also regarded the patient's previous euthanasia request as an adequate basis for using deception and coercion in carrying out the AED request ...

Mrs A's case reflects weaknesses of the Dutch EAS retrospective review system. The retrospective nature of the review system allows physicians to act on personal judgements about philosophically controversial dilemmas, rather than requiring a more formal and thorough

[126] Pauline SC Kouwenhoven et al, 'Opinions of health care professionals and the public after eight years of euthanasia legislation in the Netherlands: A mixed methods approach' (2012) 27 Palliative Medicine 273–80.

[127] Kathy Davis, 'Dying, self-determination, and the (im)possibilities of a "good death"' (2015) 25 Feminism & Psychology 143–7.

[128] Government of the Netherlands, *Guide to Written Euthanasia Requests* (2015) <https://www.rijksoverheid.nl/documenten/brochures/2015/12/17/handreiking-schriftelijk-euthanasieverzoek-publieksversie>; Regional Review Committees *Annual Report 2017* (RTE, 2018).

[129] Kara B Dassel et al 'The Influence of Hypothetical Death Scenarios on Multidimensional End-of-Life Care Preferences' (2018) 35 American Journal of Hospice and Palliative Medicine 52–9.

[130] Daniel Boffey, 'Dutch prosecutors to investigate euthanasia cases after sharp rise' The Guardian, 12 March 2018.

[131] 'Advance euthanasia directives: a controversial case and its ethical implications' (2019) 45 Journal of Medical Ethics 84–9.

evaluation ... Furthermore, any abuses or errors will come to light only if physicians fully report their actions. Improper actions by physicians who are not as forthcoming as Mrs A's physician will not be detected.

Henk Blanken[132]

Of the 10,000 Dutch patients with dementia who die each year, roughly half of them will have had an advance euthanasia directive. They believed a doctor would 'help' them. After all, this was permitted by law, and it was their express wish. Their naive confidence is shared by four out of 10 Dutch adults, who are convinced that a doctor is bound by an advance directive. In fact, doctors are not obliged to do anything ...

[E]ven though the law says it's legal, almost no doctors *are* willing to perform euthanasia on patients with severe dementia, since such patients are no longer mentally capable of making a 'well-considered request' to die.

This is the catch-22. If your dementia is at such an early stage that you are mentally fit enough to decide that you want to die, then it is probably 'too early' to want to die. You still have good years left. And yet, by the time your dementia has deteriorated to the point at which you wished (when your mind was intact) to die, you will no longer be allowed to die, as you are not mentally fit to make that decision. It is now 'too late' to die.

Euthanasia for psychiatric suffering is also in theory permitted in the Netherlands, but in practice rare. One of the issues, on which the authors of the next two extracts disagree, is whether it is ever possible to be certain that there is no hope of a change in the future.

Franklin G Miller[133]

Despite the fact that a patient with depression has been resistant to a succession of standard treatments, it is doubtful that a clinician can know that the patient has no possibility of significant therapeutic help. Might a change in therapist or therapeutic strategy, the intervention of friend or loved one, or some environmental change such as a residential treatment programme make the difference between unremitting suffering driving the urge to die and finding life worth living? ...

Finally, another consideration should give us pause about extending physician-assisted death to patients with treatment-resistant depression. In making a request of a physician for aid in dying, these patients may be seeking 'permission' or endorsement by an authority figure for the decision to end their lives. Physicians should be reluctant to play this role for patients with depression, who need help in coping with, rather than ending, their lives.

---

[132] ' "My death is not my own": the limits of legal euthanasia' The Guardian, 10 August 2018.
[133] 'Treatment-resistant depression and physician-assisted death' (2015) 41 Journal of Medical Ethics 885–6.

Udo Schuklenk and Suzanne VD Vathorst[134]

Denying patients who meet the due care criteria the right to make this end-of-life choice, in the hope of preserving their lives until a successful treatment is developed, ignores unjustifiably the high burden that is paid by patients who happen to wait unsuccessfully for a successful treatment that may not come about at all or that may come about too late for many patients to enjoy its fruits. This argument seems to assume without further justification that refusing treatment-resistant patients with major depressive disorder access to assisted dying is cost-neutral or that the cost is sufficiently minor that it ought to be borne by the patients in question. Our view would be that this is exactly an evaluation that competent patients ought to be permitted to make based on their life reality ... Patients with TRD [treatment resistant depression] suffer in ways that may be hard to comprehend by those of healthy mind, but that should not prevent us from recognising their suffering, and it should not prevent us from making assisted dying available to this group.

Also especially controversial is the prospect of euthanasia for people who are simply 'tired of life'. In the *Sutorius/Brongersma* case in 2002, the Dutch Supreme Court decided that that 'a doctor who assists in suicide in a case in which the patient's suffering is not predominantly due to a "medically classified disease or disorder", but stems from the fact that life has become meaningless for him, acts outside the scope of his professional competence'.[135] In its advice to doctors, the Royal Dutch Medical Association (KNMG) is clear that unbearable suffering without a medical basis 'falls outside the scope of current Dutch legislation and is always a criminal offence'.[136]

If a Dutch patient's request is turned down by her own physician, she can turn to the End of Life Clinic, where doctors may be more comfortable with non-standard requests for euthanasia.[137] Even so, the End of Life Clinic turns down almost all requests grounded in psychiatric suffering (95 per cent), and the majority of those grounded in being 'tired of life' (72.5 per cent).

In the next extract, Lynn Jansen et al argue against physician assisted dying (PAD) for patients who are tired of life.

Lynn A Jansen, Steven Wall, and Franklin G Miller[138]

Tired of life patients frequently express concerns that their lives are no longer valuable, that they have become a burden to others, that their bodies are deformed or that they have no significant contribution to make to their societies. We do not say that such concerns could not be valid. We do contend that they reflect, and are influenced by, wider societal perceptions about the aged.

There is a tendency, at least among those who press to extend the legal option to PAD to more and more populations, to view the decisions of patients to engage in PAD as reflecting

---

[134] 'Treatment-resistant major depressive disorder and assisted dying' (2015) 41 Journal of Medical Ethics 577–83.

[135] *Nederlandse Jurisprudentie* 2003, no 167.

[136] Dutch Medical Association (KNMG), *Position Paper: The Role of the Physician in the Voluntary Termination of Life* (Utrecht, Netherlands: 2011).

[137] Marianne C Snijdewind et al, 'A study of the first year of the end-of-life clinic for physician-assisted dying in the Netherlands' (2015) 175 JAMA Int Med 1633–40.

[138] 'Drawing the line on physician-assisted death' (2019) 45 Journal of Medical Ethics 190–7.

nothing more than isolated assessments of the personal value of their own lives… This kind of individualism is not plausible. No one should dispute that people's attitudes and decisions are deeply influenced by their social environment. Responsible consideration of policies on PAD must consider all the risks involved—direct and indirect, long term and short term. And one risk of extending PAD to tired of life patients is that doing so will contribute to the social devaluation of the elderly …

Rather than making it easier for elderly patients to end their lives when they feel they no longer have anything to live for, a humane society, and the medical practice that is a constituent part of it, might do better to combat the social attitudes and social conditions that lead to the self-devaluing attitudes in the first place. True, this course of action might not comfort those tired of life patients who are denied the legal option to PAD. They might feel as if their interests were being sacrificed for the sake of the larger social good.

(2) Belgium and Luxembourg

Belgium decriminalized euthanasia and assisted suicide in 2002.[139] To be eligible, the patient must have a serious and incurable mental or physical disorder, and must be suffering from persistent and unbearable pain or distress that cannot be alleviated. The physician must give the patient full information about her condition and about palliative care. A second doctor must examine the patient and confirm both that her suffering is unbearable, and that it cannot be alleviated.

If the patient is not terminally ill, two additional requirements are imposed. First, the physician must consult two colleagues, one of whom must assess whether the request is voluntary, considered, and repeated and, secondly, at least a month must elapse between the request and the performance of euthanasia. As in the Netherlands, it is possible to make an advance decision requesting euthanasia: this must be in writing, signed by the patient, and witnessed by two adults, at least one of whom must have no material interest in the patient's death.

In 2014, access to euthanasia was extended to minors, provided that the minor's condition is terminal and incurable, her death imminent, and her unbearable suffering physical (rather than mental). The minor must be judged capable of making the decision, and have the agreement of her parents. In practice, however, euthanasia involving minors is extremely rare; in 2017, there was one case.[140]

Doctors are not under a duty to comply with a patient's request for euthanasia; on the contrary, they are entitled to refuse on grounds of conscience or for medical reasons. There is, however, a duty to give reasons for the refusal.

The physician who has performed euthanasia or assisted a suicide must fill in a registration form and deliver it within four days of the death to a national commission, whose members are doctors, lawyers, and palliative care experts. If the commission is satisfied that any of the criteria were not satisfied, the file will be sent to the public prosecutor. The commission reports to parliament on the implementation of the legislation. Since the law came into force, the number of cases of euthanasia has increased each year. In its first full year of operation, there were 349 cases, rising to 2028 cases in 2016 and 2309 cases in 2017.[141] Of these, 78 per cent involved individuals from Dutch-speaking Flanders, amongst whom euthanasia—perhaps as a result of cultural affinities with the Dutch—is more common than in French-speaking Wallonia.

[139] *Loi relative l'euthanasie* (Act Concerning Euthanasia), 28 May 2002, in force 23 September 2002.
[140] Commission Fédérale de Contrôle et D'Évaluation de L'Euthanasie, Huitième Rapport Aux Chambres Législative Années 2016–2017 (2018).
[141] Ibid.

It is important to bear in mind, as C Gastmans et al explain, that the legalization of euthanasia in Belgium took place within a context in which there is a strong emphasis upon the provision of palliative care, and where the first response to a request for euthanasia is extensive investigation of other palliative options.

C Gastmans, F Van Neste, and P Schotsmans[142]

The starting point of this clinical practice guideline is the principle that everything possible should be done to provide support and assistance to the competent, terminally ill person who asks for euthanasia, and his or her relatives. The aim is that such an active and integral palliative care approach can in many cases displace the request and allow the patient to die in a dignified manner without euthanasia ... In Belgium, the development of palliative care preceded the euthanasia debate. As a result, Belgian palliative care (for example, the Flemish Palliative Care Federation) played a very active role in the Belgian euthanasia debate. The Belgian euthanasia debate itself functioned as a lever that facilitated the further development of palliative care, as is illustrated by the new law on palliative care that was approved at the same time as the euthanasia law.

The decision-making process in Belgium does not just involve the patient and her doctor. Nurses and the patient's family also play an important role. Following a request for euthanasia, a palliative care nurse will spend time with the patient in order identify the reasons for her request.[143] Finding out why a patient wants to end her life helps the nurse to work out what palliative response might be able to alleviate her underlying suffering. The legalization of euthanasia in Belgium rests upon the assumption that high-quality palliative care may be able to obviate most, but not all requests for euthanasia. Euthanasia is a last resort and should be available only when other options have been exhausted.

As Sigrid Dierickx et al explain, most patients who request euthanasia in Belgium do so while receiving palliative care.

Sigrid Dierickx et al[144]

Palliative care services were involved in the end-of-life care of 70.9% of those who requested euthanasia compared with 42.5% of those who died non-suddenly without having expressed a euthanasia request ... For people who were not referred to a palliative care service, the most frequently indicated reason for nonreferral was that existing care already sufficiently addressed the palliative and supportive care needs.

Considering the prevailing idea that palliative care and euthanasia are incompatible, it is striking that our study found that requests for euthanasia were associated with higher rates of palliative care involvement ... Moreover, our study found that, at least in Flanders, the involvement of palliative care does not reduce the likelihood that a euthanasia request is granted and people retain their right to end their lives despite being enrolled in palliative care. This finding

[142] 'Facing requests for euthanasia: a clinical practice guideline' (2004) 30 Journal of Medical Ethics 212–17.

[143] B Dierckx de Casterlé et al, 'Nurses' views on their involvement in euthanasia: a qualitative study in Flanders (Belgium)' (2006) 32 Journal of Medical Ethics 187–92.

[144] 'Involvement of palliative care in euthanasia practice in a context of legalized euthanasia: A population-based mortality follow-back study' (2018) 32 Palliative Medicine 114–22.

> is at odds with the widely held belief that palliative care will alter most requests for euthanasia ... In Flanders, in the context of legalized euthanasia, euthanasia and palliative care do not seem to be contradictory practices.

Luxembourg passed similar legislation in 2009. Doctors in Luxembourg will not face penal sanctions for carrying out either euthanasia or assisted suicide provided that they consult a colleague to ensure that the adult patient with capacity has an incurable terminal illness, and is suffering unbearably—either physically or mentally—without any prospect of improvement. The patient's request must be made voluntarily, after reflection, and must not result from external pressure. As in Belgium, legislation to improve palliative care provision was passed at the same time. Because Luxembourg's population is so small, it is hard to draw conclusions from its National Commission's reports.[145] From 2009 to 2016, there were a total of 52 cases of euthanasia, 43 of which involved patients with cancer.

(b) THE US (OREGON, WASHINGTON, VERMONT, HAWAII, CALIFORNIA, COLORADO, WASHINGTON DC, AND MONTANA)

In the US, a distinction has been drawn between euthanasia—which is illegal throughout the US—and physician-assisted suicide, the legality of which is a matter for individual states. Oregon was the first state to vote in favour of the legalization of assisted suicide. The introduction of the Death with Dignity Act 1994 was delayed as a result of a series of legal challenges.[146] It came into force in 1998, and in its first year there were 15 assisted suicides. Since then, the number of assisted suicides in Oregon has increased, though the numbers remain fairly small: in 2017, 218 prescriptions were written under the Death with Dignity Act, and 143 people died as a result of ingesting medications prescribed under the Act.[147]

Section 2(1) of the Death with Dignity Act provides that:

> An adult who is capable, is a resident of Oregon, and has been determined by the attending physician and consulting physician to be suffering from a terminal disease, and who has voluntarily expressed his or her wish to die, may make a written request for medication for the purpose of ending his or her life in a humane and dignified manner.

The patient must make an initial oral request, followed by a formal written request. At least 15 days after the written request, the patient must repeat their request orally, and a further 48 hours must elapse before the prescription can be filled. The patient's request must be witnessed by two people other than the doctor, at least one of whom must not be a relative, an heir, or an employee of the institution in which the patient is receiving care. The patient must be asked to notify her family. A second doctor must confirm the patient's diagnosis and that the patient has capacity and is acting voluntarily.

The patient must have received complete information about her diagnosis, prognosis, and alternatives, such as hospice care and pain control. If there is any suggestion that the patient is depressed or has a psychiatric disorder, she must be referred to a psychiatrist or psychologist.

---

[145] Commission Nationale de Contrôle et d'Évaluation de la loi du 16 mars 2009 sur l'euthanasie et l'assistance au suicide, *Quatrième rapport à l'attention de la Chambre des Députés* (Années 2015 et 2016).

[146] *Gonzales v Oregon* 546 US 243 (2006).

[147] Oregon Health Authority, *Oregon's Death with Dignity Act: 2017 Data Summary* (2018).

In Oregon there were fears that PAS would be chosen by patients who did not have health insurance and could not afford high-quality palliative care, but the evidence does not bear this out.[148] The majority of patients who have sought PAS have been middle class and well educated.[149] In 2017, 49 per cent had been educated to degree level;[150] 90.9 per cent of the patients who died were enrolled in hospice care; and 99.1 per cent had some form of healthcare insurance, though a minority had private health insurance.[151]

There is also evidence that access to palliative care has improved.[152] In a study of all the physicians eligible to prescribe drugs under the Act, 30 per cent had increased their referrals to hospice care and 76 per cent reported that they made efforts to improve their knowledge of pain medication for the terminally ill. Sixty-nine per cent reported that they had sought to improve their recognition of psychiatric disorders, such as depression.[153]

Sandy Macleod[154]

The Oregonian data suggest that patients do not request PAS because of unrelieved physical symptoms, or inadequacy of palliative care services (most are simultaneously enrolled in hospice programmes), and neither are they depressed or socially vulnerable. They request assisted suicide for psychological and existential reasons: they value control, dread dependence on others, are ready to die, and assess current quality of life as poor. The most important reasons for their requests concerned loss of control, wishing to die at home, loss of dignity and independence, concerns about future pain, poor quality of life and self-care ability. Significantly the requests did not relate to distressing physical symptoms, financial concerns or poor social support. The concerns were about future worries of declining welfare. The majority who request PAS are in their seventh decade, well educated, middle-class, white, married, with cancer diagnoses, and complaining of loss of enjoyment and quality of life. The poor, the ill-educated, the uninsured and those without access to palliative care are not those who request PAS.

In Kathryn Smith et al's study of people in Oregon who had requested PAS, they found low levels of spirituality and 'dismissive styles of attachment', that is people prioritized self-reliance, autonomy, and independence. They concluded that PAS 'may be a way for individuals to maintain an ultimate sense of control and autonomy within a process that allows very little opportunity for either'.[155]

In the next extract, IG Finlay and R George argue that evidence that people who ask for PAS are comparatively well educated and middle class may, in fact, establish that this

[148] Lois L Miller et al, 'Attitudes and experiences of Oregon hospice nurses and social workers regarding assisted suicide' (2004) 18 Palliative Medicine 685–91.

[149] E Dahl and N Levy, 'The case for physician assisted suicide: how can it possibly be proven?' (2006) 32 Journal of Medical Ethics 335–8.

[150] Oregon Health Authority, *Oregon's Death with Dignity Act: 2017 Data Summary* (2018).

[151] Ibid.

[152] E Dahl and N Levy, 'The case for physician assisted suicide: how can it possibly be proven?' (2006) 32 Journal of Medical Ethics 335–8.

[153] Linda Ganzini et al, 'Oregon physician attitudes about and experiences with end of life care since the passage of the Death with Dignity Act' (2001) 285 Journal of the American Medical Association 2363–9.

[154] 'Assisted dying in liberalised jurisdictions and the role of psychiatry: A clinician's view' (2012) 46 Australian & New Zealand Journal of Psychiatry 936–45.

[155] Kathryn Smith et al, 'Predictors of pursuit of physician-assisted death' (2015) 49 Journal of Pain and Symptom Management 555–61.

socioeconomic group are more vulnerable in relation to assisted dying, since they may find dependency especially hard to bear.

IG Finlay and R George[156]

First, are people who are better educated more vulnerable, in the context of PAS, because illness and potential dependence are more frightening to them or because they have fewer psychosocial supports? Second, perhaps more interestingly, why did the finding that college graduates were 7.6 times more likely resort to PAS than others not lead Battin and her associates to question whether, if the less well educated are not especially vulnerable to PAS, perhaps the better educated are? There is a need to dig somewhat deeper in order to try and establish whether, for example, educated patients may resort more frequently to PAS because they are people who are familiar with the intricacies of the law and can argue more persuasively with their physicians ...

We are told that 'death under the ODDA [Oregon Death with Dignity Act] was associated with having health insurance and with high educational status, both indirect indicators of affluence' ... Yet Battin et al do not reflect on the vulnerabilities that wealth may bring, for example, perceptions of suffering, dignity, control, or the stigmatisation of illness and disability.

In 2008, following a referendum, a similar statute was introduced in Washington State. Since 2009, the Death with Dignity Act has allowed Washington State residents with less than six months to live to request a prescription for lethal medication. In 2017, medication was dispensed under the Act to 212 individuals.[157] Once again, most were well educated and 97 per cent had health insurance.[158] Vermont passed the Patient Choice and Control at End of Life Act in 2013 and became the third US state to legalize assisted suicide for terminally ill, competent adults, resident in Vermont. Since then, Hawaii, California, Colorado, and Washington DC have followed suit.

The state of Montana has not introduced specific legislation legalizing assisted suicide; rather, in *Montana v Baxter*,[159] its Supreme Court decided that 'physician aid in dying' was not contrary to public policy. Robert Baxter was 75 and had been suffering from lymphocytic leukaemia. He posthumously won his claim against the State of Montana that the right to die 'with dignity' should have extended to offering protection from liability under the state's homicide laws to a physician who prescribed him lethal medication. Without prospective authorization of assisted suicide, however, this decision leaves the medical profession in Montana in limbo. Although it was decided *ex post facto* in Robert Baxter's case that there could have been no liability, doctors who help their patients to die still run the risk of prosecution.

(c) SWITZERLAND

Assisting suicide is a criminal offence under Article 115 of the Swiss Penal Code, but only if the defendant's motive is 'selfish'. Article 115 does not specify that the suicide must be assisted

---

[156] 'Legal physician-assisted suicide in Oregon and the Netherlands: evidence concerning the impact on patients in vulnerable groups—another perspective on Oregon's data' (2011) 37 Journal of Medical Ethics 171–4.
[157] Washington State Department of Health, *Death with Dignity Act Report* (2018).   [158] Ibid.
[159] 224 P 3d 1211 (Mont Sup Ct 2009).

by a doctor, nor does the patient have to be terminally ill or suffering unbearably. Provided that the person's motive for assisting the suicide is compassionate, no offence is committed.

According to the Swiss Academy of Medical Sciences, physicians whose consciences allow them to offer assistance in suicide are responsible for ensuring that additional criteria are met.

Swiss Academy of Medical Sciences[160]

[I]n the final phase of life, when the situation becomes intolerable for the patient he or she may ask for help in committing suicide and may persist in this wish.

In this borderline situation a very difficult conflict of interests can arise for the doctor. On the one hand assisted suicide is not part of a doctor's task, because this contradicts the aims of medicine. On the other hand, consideration of the patient's wishes is fundamental for the doctor–patient relationship. This dilemma requires a personal decision of conscience on the part of the doctor. The decision to provide assistance in suicide must be respected as such. In any case, the doctor has the right to refuse help in committing suicide. If he decides to assist a person to commit suicide, it is his responsibility to check the following preconditions:

- The patient's disease justifies the assumption that he is approaching the end of life.
- Alternative possibilities for providing assistance have been discussed and, if desired, have been implemented.
- The patient is capable of making the decision, his wish has been well thought out, without external pressure, and he persists in this wish. This has been checked by a third person, who is not necessarily a physician.
- The final action in the process leading to death must always be taken by the patient himself.

In Switzerland, assistance with suicide is generally provided by one of the 'right to die' societies, and these impose additional requirements. EXIT (Deutsche Schweiz) has over 105,000 members, and its affiliated francophone organization, EXIT (Romandie), has over 20,000 members. To be eligible for an assisted suicide with EXIT, a patient must be over the age of 18, mentally competent, and must have a 'hopeless' prognosis and/or be suffering unbearably/unacceptably. EXIT members must be either Swiss citizens or permanent residents.

Dignitas, a smaller organization set up in 1998, will assist non-Swiss residents to die. From 1998 to 2018, 415 UK citizens ended their lives with Dignitas's help. Dignitas will provide assisted suicides for members who are of sound judgement and possess a minimum level of physical mobility (sufficient to self-administer the drug). The person must also have a disease that will lead to death and/or an unendurable incapacitating disability and/or unbearable and uncontrollable pain.

Some in Switzerland are alarmed by its reputation as the destination for 'suicide tourism', and there have been attempts to prohibit foreigners from joining Swiss right to die societies, but none has been successful. In March 2011, 78 per cent of voters in a referendum in the canton of Zurich were in favour of continuing to allow foreigners to access assisted suicide.

---

[160] *Care of Patients in the End of Life* (SAMS, 2013).

(d) CANADA

The Supreme Court of Canada's decision in *Carter v Canada (Attorney General)*[161] required the Canadian government to legalize assisted suicide within a year. The Supreme Court endorsed the finding of the trial judge that the prohibition of assisted suicide engaged the right to life under the Canadian Charter of Rights and Freedom, because it forced people to take their own lives prematurely, while they were still physically capable of doing so.

Both euthanasia and assisted suicide are now lawful, and are collectively described as Medical Assistance in Dying (MAiD). In 2017, there were 1961 medically assisted deaths in Canada, representing around 1.07 per cent of all deaths. All but one of the MAiD deaths was clinically assisted (ie euthanasia) rather than self-administered (assisted suicide). Sixty-four per cent involved patients with cancer.

Eligibility is confined to adults who are mentally capable and eligible for health services in Canada (this means visitors are not eligible). Requests must be voluntary and not the result of outside pressure or influence, and the person must have a 'grievous and irremediable medical condition', defined in the Criminal Code as follows:

Criminal Code 241.2(2)

A person has a grievous and irremediable medical condition only if they meet all of the following criteria:

(a) they have a serious and incurable illness, disease or disability;

(b) they are in an advanced state of irreversible decline in capability;

(c) that illness, disease or disability or that state of decline causes them enduring physical or psychological suffering that is intolerable to them and that cannot be relieved under conditions that they consider acceptable; and

(d) their natural death has become reasonably foreseeable, taking into account all of their medical circumstances, without a prognosis necessarily having been made as to the specific length of time that they have remaining.

As Jocelyn Downie and Jennifer Chandler explain, these criteria leave some room for uncertainty and inconsistency.

Jocelyn Downie and Jennifer A Chandler[162]

[Q]uestions were immediately raised about the meaning of 'incurable illness, disease, or disability', 'advanced state of irreversible decline in capability', 'enduring physical or psychological suffering that is intolerable to them' and 'natural death has become reasonably foreseeable'... Too narrow an interpretation could mean people who should have access may be denied MAiD; too broad an interpretation could mean some people may be given access who should not. Two persons in the same circumstances may be treated differently (one allowed

---

[161] [2015] 1 SCR 331.
[162] *Interpreting Canada's Medical Assistance in Dying Legislation* (IRPP Report, 2018).

access and one denied it) simply because their providers or their counsel interpret the legislation differently . . . Finally, the uncertainty about the meaning of key terms and phrases may raise concerns about potential criminal liability, producing a chilling effect on medical and nurse practitioners' willingness to provide MAiD.

Lori Seller et al analysed all of the MAiD requests in Quebec over 18 months after the law came into force. The majority of requests came from patients with cancer. More surprisingly, they found that, for a significant number of patients, their first palliative care consultation took place less than a week before their MAiD request.

Lori Seller, Marie-Ève Bouthillier, and Veronique Fraser[163]

The average age of a patient requesting MAiD was 70 years (range 32–92) and almost half of requests (49%) came from patients over 70. Cancer was the primary diagnosis in the majority of cases (81%), followed by neurological disease. Men were slightly more likely to request MAiD (54%) than women (46%.) Of those who requested MAID, 54% received it. For those who did not receive MAiD, the primary reasons were that patients lost capacity during the process (35%), did not meet eligibility criteria (22%) or died from natural causes before the intervention could be provided (19%). In 14% of cases, MAiD was not performed because patients changed their minds . . .

Palliative care was consulted in the majority of MAiD requests (85%) captured by our study. However, in 50% of these cases, the palliative care consultation was initiated less than 5 days before or after MAiD was requested. Although 80% of our MAiD requests came from patients with cancer, for the majority, palliative care consultation came 'late' in relation to the request for hastened death as per definitions used in the literature.

The late involvement of palliative care in the context of patients who requested MAiD raises questions as to whether timing could have an impact on requests for hastened death by ensuring that benefits such as improved quality of life, reduced depression and so on have an opportunity to be fully realised.

One issue which has been discussed in Canada in the context of the question whether MAiD should be extended to competent minors is whether it is ever ethical for doctors to introduce the idea of MAiD, or whether discussions must always be initiated by patients.

Carey DeMichelis, Randi Zlotnik Shaul, and Adam Rapoport[164]

Scholarly and applied literatures are united in their presumption that conversations about MAID will begin with a patient request. This is diametrically opposed to the way virtually all other medical communication is structured, in which the onus is on healthcare providers to inform patients of the full range of medical options that are available to treat a particular condition. The positive ethical and legal obligation for clinicians to inform patients is important

---

[163] 'Situating requests for medical aid in dying within the broader context of end-of-life care: ethical considerations' (2019) 45 Journal of Medical Ethics 106–11.

[164] 'Medical Assistance in Dying at a paediatric hospital' (2019) 45 Journal of Medical Ethics 60–7.

because it is a foundational building block of informed consent and autonomous decision-making. In order for patients to make autonomous choices about their medical care, they must know the full range of options that are available to them. Healthcare providers are expected to be the medical experts, not patients …

[Mara] Buchbinder points out that public knowledge may lag behind legislative developments and, therefore, some patients may not know enough about assistance in dying to request it. She adds that the people who are most likely to be uninformed about the existence of MAID are those who are already socially marginalised in other ways (linguistically, educationally, etc), and that this may potentially lead to an untenable situation in which patients who are already socially vulnerable receive a different range of care options at the end of life than those who are otherwise socially located. A positive obligation on clinicians to discuss MAID with their patients is a mechanism that levels the playing field, ensuring that all capable patients have access to information that will allow them to make autonomous medical decisions about how their life will end.

5 EUTHANASIA OR ASSISTED SUICIDE OR BOTH?

As we have seen, the Benelux countries and Canada have legalized both euthanasia and assisted suicide, but euthanasia is more common, whereas the US jurisdictions have legalized only assisted suicide. What reasons might there be for preferring one practice rather than the other, or for legalizing both?

Doctors can end patients' lives more effectively than patients themselves, who might be unable to swallow the whole dose and be left both alive and severely injured by partially ingesting a lethal substance. If assisted suicide is more likely to go wrong, preferring it to euthanasia is justifiable only in order to provide an additional safeguard, or 'firewall'. As Dr Nick Gideonse, a general practitioner in Oregon, explained to the House of Lords Select Committee in 2005: 'The fact that the patient self-administers in a way that is not easy to do, drinking ounces of a bitter liquid, provides a final piece of clear evidence that this is completely volitional and self-administered.'[165] Against this, it might be argued that it is unfair to impose an unpleasant burden upon a dying patient, when the priority should be making her as comfortable as possible.

It could also be argued that allowing only euthanasia provides a different sort of control over the practice. If the doctor has to inject the medication, as opposed to simply writing a prescription for it, there is less chance that it will fall into the hands of a third party. In Oregon, between 1997 and 2017, 1,967 people had prescriptions written under the DWDA, and 1,275 patients died as a result.[166] This statistic could be read in two ways. First, it might suggest that terminally ill patients do not, in practice, feel under pressure to complete their assisted suicide, and that changing one's mind is not uncommon. Secondly, although most of the prescriptions which were issued were probably never filled, it is possible that the patient obtained the medication but either chose not to use it or died first. The dangers of unused drugs falling into the hands of others are obvious.

---

[165] House of Lords, Assisted Dying for the Terminally Ill Committee (2005) 146.
[166] Oregon Health Authority, *Oregon's Death with Dignity Act: 2017 Data Summary* (2018).

6   CONCLUSION

If anything, it is likely that the debate over the legalization of assisted dying will become more intense in the coming years. With an ageing population, more people will experience extended periods of dependency. A further demographic change is that the generation often described as baby boomers, that is, people who were born between 1946 and 1964, are now entering old age. As Udo Schuklenk points out, this generation has been used to being able to exercise much more choice and control over their lives than their parents' generation.

Udo Schuklenk[167]

With baby boomers being anywhere between 52 and 70 years of age, invariably the end of life is coming into focus for an increasing number of people belonging to this generation. They would have seen parents and relatives suffering, often terribly, at the hands of a medical system that ignored their end-of-life choices in favour of life support at nearly all cost . . .

It is not terribly surprising, with baby boomer finding themselves – perhaps to their greatest surprise – at the levers of power of the system that they rebelled against in the 1960s and 1970s, that the number of jurisdictions that have decriminalised assisted dying is steadily increasing. Many legislators and judges are baby boomers. Just as baby boomers fought hard for the right to live their life by their own lights, they were bound not to hand control over to others when it came to their own dying. Their own foreseeable demise has clearly focused minds in many a jurisdiction and highest court room.

But while it can be predicted that there will be increased interest in the legalization of assisted dying, there will continue to be those who are implacably opposed to it, believing, like Justin Welby, that it 'would be to cross a fundamental legal and ethical rubicon'.

Justin Welby[168]

[W]e need to reflect on what sort of society we might become if we were to permit assisted suicide. At present, we can show love, care and compassion to those who at all ages and stages of life are contemplating suicide. We can try to intervene, to support them to embrace life once more. We can do all in our power to surround those who are terminally ill with the best possible palliative care, including physical, emotional and spiritual support. We can redouble our efforts to alleviate suffering. We can show that we love even when people have given up on caring for themselves. We can support our doctors and nurses as they act consistently in the best interests of their patients, affirming life and caring for the vulnerable.

We risk all this for what? Becoming a society where each life is no longer seen as worth protecting, worth honouring, worth fighting for? The current law and the guidelines for practice work; compassion is shown, the vulnerable are protected. In spite of individual celebrity opinions and the 'findings' of snap opinion polls (that cannot hope to do justice to the intricacies of the issue) the current law is not 'broken'. There is no need to fix it.

---

[167] 'Is Assisted Dying the Baby Boomers' Last Frontier?' (2016) 31 Bioethics 470.
[168] 'Why I believe assisting people to die would dehumanise our society for ever' The Guardian, 5 September 2015.

Finally, it is important not to lose sight of Jonathan Herring's impassioned plea that we should pay as much attention to the routine and banal neglect of the old and the ill as we do to the rights and wrongs of assisted dying.

Jonathan Herring[169]

While we debate the rights and wrongs of assisted dying, older people are dying in poverty, freezing temperatures, and desperate hunger. So many are neglected by their communities, abandoned by their families, living isolated, socially excluded lives. For many, their last months or, if they unlucky, years are spent in care homes marked by abuse, neglect, and over-medication. Recently, it seems barely a month goes by without stories of horrific abuse in our institutional settings for the old. But far more common than physical abuse is a setting of utter boredom, with minimal personal interaction. No love. No tenderness. No hope.

With this background, we dare to discuss the right to die? Are those supporting a right to die not concerned at the misery facing so many of our older people which will lead them to request death? Are those opposing a right to die aware of what we are otherwise leaving older people to face?

Of course we cannot avoid the debate over assisted dying, but I saddened at the amount of time, intellectual energy, and political pressure taken up over it, when the far more important issues of trying to improve the lot of older people; improving the quality of palliative care; combating the prevalent ageist attitudes in society are left aside. These are the issues the books need to be written on; the marches organised for and the Internet petitions signed. Given the way we treated older people, those with mental health issues and the disabled those who trumpet either sanctity of life or a right to die should be blushing.

FURTHER READING

Bolt, Eva Elizabeth et al, 'Can physicians conceive of performing euthanasia in case of psychiatric disease, dementia or being tired of living?' (2015) 41 Journal of Medical Ethics 592–8.

Hobson, Clark, 'Is It Now Institutionally Appropriate for the Courts to Consider Whether the Assisted Dying Ban is Human Rights Compatible? *Conway v Secretary of State for Justice*' (2018) 26 Medical Law Review 514–30.

Huxtable, Richard, 'Splitting the difference? Principled compromise and assisted dying' (2014) 28 Bioethics 472–80.

Jackson, Emily and Keown, John, *Debating Euthanasia* (Hart Publishing: Oxford, 2011).

Jackson, Emily (2018) 'Legalising assisted dying: cross purposes and unintended consequences' 41 Dalhousie Law Journal 60–91.

Jansen, Lynn A, Wall, Steven, and Miller, Franklin G, 'Drawing the line on physician-assisted death' (2019) 45 Journal of Medical Ethics 190–7.

---

[169] 'Escaping the Shackles of Law at the End of Life: *R (Nicklinson) v Ministry of Justice*' (2013) 21 Medical Law Review 487–98.

Keown, John, '"Voluntary Assisted Dying" in Australia: The Victorian Parliamentary Committee's Tenuous Case for Legalization' (2018) 33 Issues in Law & Medicine 55–81.

Kipke, Ronald, 'Why not Commercial Assistance for Suicide? On the Question of Argumentative Coherence of Endorsing Assisted Suicide' (2014) 29 Bioethics 516–22.

Lemmens, Trudo, 'Charter Scrutiny of Canada's Medical Assistance in Dying Law and the Shifting Landscape of Belgian and Dutch Euthanasia Practice' (2018) 85 Supreme Court Law Review (2nd Series) 459–544.

Mullock, Alexandra, 'The Supreme Court decision in *Nicklinson*: human rights, criminal wrongs and the dilemma of death' (2015) 31 Journal of Professional Negligence 18–28.

Quill, Timothy, 'Dutch practice of euthanasia and assisted suicide: a glimpse at the edges of the practice' (2018) 44 Journal of Medical Ethics 297–8.

Riddle, Christopher A, 'Assisted Dying and Disability' (2017) 13 Bioethics 484–9.

Sulmasy, Daniel P et al, 'Physician-Assisted Suicide: Why Neutrality by Organized Medicine Is Neither Neutral Nor Appropriate' (2018) 33 Journal of General Internal Medicine 1394–9.

Wicks, Elizabeth, 'The Supreme Court Judgment in *Nicklinson*: One Step Forward on Assisted Dying; Two Steps Back on Human Rights' (2015) 23 Medical Law Review 144–56.

INDEX